EXECUTIVE DECISION-MAKING AND THE COURTS

ı this book, leading experts from across the common law world assess the npact of four seminal House of Lords judgments decided in the 1960s: *Ridge v aldwin*, *Padfield v Minister of Agriculture*, *Conway v Rimmer*, *and Anisminic Foreign Compensation Commission*. The 'Quartet' is generally acknowledged ɔ have marked a turning point in the development of court centred administra-ive law, and can be understood as a 'formative moment' in the emergence of nodern judicial review.

These cases are examined not only in terms of the points each case decided, and their contribution to administrative law doctrine, but also in terms of the underlying conception of the tasks of administrative law implicit in the Quartet. By doing so, the book sheds new light on both the complex processes through which the modern system of judicial review emerged and the constitutional choices that are implicit in its jurisprudence. It further reflects on the implications of these historical processes for how the achievements, failings and limitations of the common law in reviewing the actions of the executive can be evaluated.

Executive Decision-Making and the Courts

Revisiting the Origins of Modern Judicial Review

Edited by
TT Arvind
Richard Kirkham
Daithí Mac Síthigh
and
Lindsay Stirton

•HART•
OXFORD • LONDON • NEW YORK • NEW DELHI • SYDNEY

HART PUBLISHING

Bloomsbury Publishing Plc

Kemp House, Chawley Park, Cumnor Hill, Oxford, OX2 9PH, UK

1385 Broadway, New York, NY 10018, USA

29 Earlsfort Terrace, Dublin 2, Ireland

HART PUBLISHING, the Hart/Stag logo, BLOOMSBURY and the Diana logo are trademarks of Bloomsbury Publishing Plc

First published in Great Britain 2021

A catalogue record for this book is available from the British Library.

Library of Congress Cataloging-in-Publication data

Names: Arvind, TT (Thiruvallore Thattai), editor. | Kirkham, Richard, editor. | Mac Síthigh, Daithí, editor. | Stirton, Lindsay, editor.

Title: Executive decision-making and the courts : revisiting the origins of modern judicial review / edited by TT Arvind, Richard Kirkham, Daithí Mac Síthigh, and Lindsay Stirton.

Description: Gorodnsville : Hart Publishing, an imprint of Bloomsbury Publishing, 2021. | Includes bibliographical references and index.

Identifiers: LCCN 2020048490 (print) | LCCN 2020048491 (ebook) | ISBN 9781509930333 (hardback) | ISBN 9781509944774 (paperback) | ISBN 9781509930357 (pdf) | ISBN 9781509930340 (Epub)

Subjects: LCSH: Judicial review—Great Britain. | Judicial review of administrative acts—Great Britain. | Administrative courts—Great Britain. | Administrative law—Great Britain. | Executive power—Great Britain.

Classification: LCC KD4902 .E94 2021 (print) | LCC KD4902 (ebook) | DDC 347.41/012—dc23

LC record available at https://lccn.loc.gov/2020048490

LC ebook record available at https://lccn.loc.gov/2020048491

ISBN: HB: 978-1-50993-033-3
ePDF: 978-1-50993-035-7
ePub: 978-1-50993-034-0

Typeset by Compuscript Ltd, Shannon

Acknowledgements

THE PAPERS IN this book were initially presented at the 2018 Annual Seminar of the Society of Legal Scholars, held at the University of Sussex in May 2018. We are grateful to the Society of Legal Scholars for their generous financial support, and to Sussex Law School for providing additional financial and administrative support for the event. In particular, we could not have managed the event without the expertise and assistance of Dr Hannah Lynch at Newcastle University and Laura Arnold at the University of Sussex.

Thanks are also due to Dr Jack Simson Caird, Dr Lucy Finchett-Maddock, Ms Antonia Murillo, Dr Charlotte Skeet and Dr Hélène Tyrrell for kindly chairing sessions at the event; to Robert Craig for presenting a paper at the event and contributing to discussions; to the contributors to this volume for their overwhelming support for the venture; and to Kelly-Marie Blundell for her assistance with producing the index of authorities. We have also, as ever, relied heavily on the excellent support and patience provided throughout the process by Sinead Moloney and all of the team at Hart Publishing, in particular Vicki Hillyard, Rosamund Jubber, Rosemarie Mearns, Linda Staniford and Kate Whetter.

Contents

List of Contributors

Gordon Anthony, Professor of Public Law at Queen's University Belfast.

TT Arvind, Professor of Law at the University of York.

Stephen Bailey, Professor of Public Law at the University of Nottingham.

Daphne Barak-Erez, Justice of the Supreme Court of Israel and formerly Dean and Professor of Law at the Faculty of Law of Tel Aviv University.

Paul Bowen, Barrister at Brick Court Chambers, London, and Honorary Professor at the University of Sussex.

Peter Cane, Distinguished Senior Research Fellow at Christ's College, Cambridge and Emeritus Professor at Australian National University.

David Feldman, Emeritus Rouse Ball Professor of English Law, University of Cambridge; Emeritus Fellow, Downing College, Cambridge.

David C Gardner, Barrister at No5 Barristers' Chambers, Bristol.

Richard Kirkham, Senior Lecturer in Law at the University of Sheffield.

Dean R Knight, Associate Professor at the Faculty of Law and New Zealand Centre for Public Law, Victoria University of Wellington.

Alexander Latham-Gambi, Lecturer in Law at Swansea University.

Daithí Mac Síthigh, Professor of Law and Innovation at Queen's University Belfast.

Sarah Nason, Senior Lecturer in Administrative Law and Jurisprudence at Prifysgol Bangor University.

Robert Reed, Lord Reed of Allermuir, President of the Supreme Court of the United Kingdom.

Paul F Scott, Senior Lecturer in Public Law at the University of Glasgow.

Lindsay Stirton, Professor of Public Law at the University of Sussex and Adjunct Researcher, Faculty of Law, University of Tasmania.

Maurice Sunkin, Professor of Public Law and Socio-Legal Studies at the University of Essex.

Robert Thomas, Professor of Public Law at the University of Manchester Law School.

Joe Tomlinson, Senior Lecturer in Public Law at the University of York and Research Director, Public Law Project.

Dimitrios Tsarapatsanis, Lecturer in Law at the University of York.

Table of Statutes

Hong Kong

Israel (and British Mandate in Palestine)

New Zealand

United Kingdom

Table of Secondary Legislation

Table of Cases

Australia

Bahamas

Canada

European Court of Human Rights

Hong Kong

Ireland

Israel (and British Mandate in Palestine)

Malaysia

New Zealand

Pakistan

Sri Lanka

Trinidad and Tobago

United Kingdom

United States

Part I

Setting the Scene

1

Introduction: Judicial Review and the Quartet

TT ARVIND, RICHARD KIRKHAM, DAITHÍ MAC SÍTHIGH AND LINDSAY STIRTON*

I. INTRODUCTION

A. The Quartet as a Formative Movement

THE ESSAYS IN this volume arose out of the 2018 Annual Seminar of the Society of Legal Scholars, held to mark the fiftieth anniversary of three seminal cases on administrative law decided by the House of Lords in 1968: *Padfield v Minister of Agriculture*,[1] *Conway v Rimmer*,[2] and *Anisminic v Foreign Compensation Commission*.[3] These three decisions, taken together with the slightly earlier case of *Ridge v Baldwin*[4] decided in 1963, are often described as the 'Quartet' of cases which played a key role in the emergence of modern judicial review. By demonstrating that judges could take on a broader role in policing executive decision-making, they not only created a base upon which subsequent cases could build, but also provided implicit support for the proposition that it was constitutionally appropriate for judges to take on a more assertive role in policing the executive than in the immediately preceding decades.[5]

Against the backdrop of that anniversary, this volume uses the Quartet as the organising theme for a collection of essays which, cumulatively, seek to subject the modern system of judicial review to critical scrutiny. The structure of the

* We are grateful to David Feldman for his comments on an earlier draft of this chapter.

[1] *Padfield v Minister of Agriculture* [1968] AC 997 (HL).

[2] *Conway v Rimmer* [1968] AC 910 (HL).

[3] *Anisminic v Foreign Compensation Commission* [1969] 2 AC 147 (HL).

[4] *Ridge v Baldwin* [1964] AC 40 (HL).

[5] Other cases are sometimes considered alongside the Quartet, in particular *Burmah Oil v Lord Advocate* [1965] AC 75 (HL) which, like the Quartet, also featured a lead judgment by Lord Reid, and *Wiseman v Borneman* [1971] AC 297.

volume and the position the Quartet occupies within it were influenced by the editors' view that the Quartet was a formative moment in the development of judicial review.[6] In the social sciences, formative moments are periods of time in which the institutional structures of a polity are reconfigured or reshaped in response to social or political pressures with which they do not deal satisfactorily (or, at least, are perceived as not dealing satisfactorily). Formative moments occur when these transient pressures result in lasting institutional shifts which become the new normal for that polity. Studying a period of change as a formative moment looks beyond existing institutional structures to consider the context in which they emerged, why those shifts came to be accepted as the new normal, and the complex legacies the specificities of that moment have left on modern institutions.[7]

Although our editorial approach was influenced by the theory of formative moments, this is not a volume of essays applying that theory, nor is it primarily focused on historically studying the institutional changes that produced judicial review (although history plays an important role in several chapters). Our purpose was not to produce a volume where all chapters adopted a single approach, and the essays in this volume adopt a broad range of perspectives. Peter Cane has recently suggested that modern public law scholarship contains three broad families of approaches.[8] The first, a development of the traditional common law method, focuses on locating individual decisions in wider contexts which, depending on the scholar, may be doctrinal, social, or oriented towards making the law 'as internally consistent and coherent as reasonably possible'.[9] The second, the 'philosophical', evaluates law with reference to its contribution to a larger project, such as deciding how one ought to behave. The third, the 'social-scientific' or empirical, 'treats legal processes as social phenomena to be described and explained'.[10] Each of these families of approaches is represented in this volume.

Nevertheless, the idea that the Quartet was a formative moment has exercised a significant influence over the selection of topics and themes in this volume. There are a number of issues, such as the political legitimacy of judicial review, with which this volume does not engage. Debates about political legitimacy of their nature tend to be articulated in timeless terms. The focus of this volume, in contrast, is on the temporal and the contextual. Rather than asking whether modern judicial review is legitimate according to an externally determined

[6] The origin of the term 'judicial review' is open to debate but, as Bailey notes in this collection, its usage was well known by the sixties, see SA de Smith's *Judicial Review of Administrative Action*, 1st edn (London, Stevens, 1959).

[7] The classic theoretical account of formative moments is B Rothstein, 'Explaining Swedish Corporatism: The Formative Moment' (1992) 15 *Scandinavian Political Studies* 173. We discuss the theory further in the concluding chapter.

[8] P Cane, 'Dean R Knight: Vigilance and Restraint in the Common Law of Judicial Review' (2019) 82 *MLR* 200.

[9] ibid, 206.

[10] ibid.

standard, it asks what made it appear legitimate and acceptable during the 1960s, and whether the system that emerged out of that period remains fit for purpose in dealing with the challenges that face judicial review today. The volume, to put it differently, seeks to shed new light on the circumstances and problems which led to the emergence of the modern system of judicial review in the formative period of the 1960s, and their relationship to the factors that drive the use of judicial review today. The chapters in this volume are, accordingly, united by their focus on three sets of issues: the manner in which the law set out in the Quartet was shaped by the context in which the cases arose; the influence the Quartet subsequently exercised over judicial review; and the adequacy of the law that emerged from the Quartet in dealing with the issues and concerns that face judicial review today.

B. The Structure of this Volume

The chapters in this volume are divided into six parts. The first, introductory, part consists of two chapters looking at the broader picture. In this first chapter, we set out the volume's ambition, the issues it considers, and the broader themes that emerge from the chapters taken as a whole. In chapter two, Lord Reed, President of the Supreme Court, reflects on the judge-made and judge-led nature of the Quartet's development of judicial review through a discussion of the judicial career and juristic views of Lord Reid. Lord Reid not only delivered an expertly reasoned and influential judgment in each of the four cases that constitute the Quartet, but also played a leading role in moving away from the declaratory theory of the law. Drawing on this background, Lord Reed presents a nuanced and persuasive account of the necessity for judges to take on the task of developing the law, but also the challenges judges face when they go beyond the incremental.

Part II of this volume puts the focus on the four cases that make up the Quartet. There are four chapters in this part, each examining one of the cases in the Quartet in detail. The chapters follow the chronological order of the cases. Robert Thomas opens the Part with a discussion of *Ridge v Baldwin* (chapter three), followed by a chapter by Maurice Sunkin on *Padfield* (chapter four), a chapter by TT Arvind and Lindsay Stirton on *Conway v Rimmer* (chapter five), and a chapter by David Feldman on *Anisminic* (chapter six). All four cases have been the subject of extensive commentary. Nevertheless, these chapters break new ground in their study of the cases. The chapters set the four cases in the context of the law, politics and society of their time. They look not just at the law as it stood in the 1960s, but also to debates, issues and controversies that were salient at the time and formed part of the contextual background to the cases. In doing so, some of the papers draw on sources, such as archival records, which have not previously been examined or analysed in this context.

Parts III and IV build on this analysis. A key theme running through the chapters in these two parts is the distinction between the doctrinal impact of the cases and their symbolic value. In symbolic terms, the influence of the Quartet has been dramatic. Over time, they came to jointly stand for the proposition that all administrative discretion was limited by law, and that there was no administrative decision upon the legality of which the courts could not rule. The influence of these cases on actual legal rules, and their usefulness in answering the type of legal issues that come before courts today, however, is both harder to assess and more controversial. Questions have been asked about whether subsequent cases remained true, or even could have remained true, to the principles the Quartet sought to embed within the law. Concerns have also been raised about whether the Quartet's approach to disaggregating the legal and political dimensions of executive action is defensible, and whether it deals adequately with the complex mesh of needs generated by the modern administrative state.

The three chapters in Part III take their starting point in the legal needs and juridical approaches underlying present-day judicial review across the UK. As they show, judicial review has taken on a range of additional tasks since the Quartet. At the same time the context in which it operates has changed, in some ways becoming more controversial and in others more socially and politically embedded. These shifts have altered and reshaped the practical effect and evaluative significance of the positions taken in the Quartet. This reshaping makes it necessary to ask whether the law should move beyond the legacy of the Quartet, or whether the balance between the structure the Quartet provides and the flexibility it leaves is adequate to deal with the challenges that arise in the present day. The chapters present a complex and nuanced set of answers to these questions, but they cumulatively strongly suggest that judicial review will need to move beyond the confines of the Quartet if it is to respond effectively to modern legal needs.

Sarah Nason (chapter seven) uses empirical data to highlight the implicit tension between the constitutional role of judicial review, and the everyday legal needs that underpin the actual use of the action of judicial review. As she shows, reactions against the former have had a disproportionate impact on the latter, to the extent that there is now a real need to investigate whether expanding other remedies such as tribunals is a more efficacious way of providing access to justice in the individual case than judicial review. Paul Bowen (chapter eight) analyses the relationship between the Quartet's principles and approach, the approach that underlay the development of common law rights in the 1990s, and the more recent changes that have been brought about by the Human Rights Act 1998. He argues that they reflect very different, and frequently contrasting, impulses, and that the modern system depends on the co-existence and simultaneous operation of the common law and the HRA. Joe Tomlinson (chapter nine) examines the jurisprudence of ouster clauses and argues that notwithstanding the symbolic value of the case law from *Anisminic* to *Privacy International*, in reality the cases only make a marginal contribution to limiting the ability to exclude persons from judicial review. Other mechanisms of exclusion are now far more potent than ouster clauses, and public law jurisprudence must move beyond a focus on ouster clauses if it is to address this problem.

If Part III focuses on the need for a deeper reconceptualisation, Part IV looks at how devolution has already begun to lead to such a reconceptualisation, at least in the local context of Scotland, Wales and Northern Ireland. Each of these devolved jurisdictions has faced issues that are specific to them. Scotland and Northern Ireland have also had the opportunity to develop distinctive approaches to judicial review due to their partially distinct judicial systems. As the chapters in this Part show, although the Quartet has played and continues to play an important framing role, other factors have led the local courts to move beyond them and look to other sources of principles and remedies.

David Gardner (chapter ten) opens the Part by looking at the experience of Wales, arguably the youngest of the jurisdictions within the United Kingdom in that it until relatively recently formed part of a composite jurisdictional entity with England. Gardner highlights the challenges in balancing the ostensible universality of judicial review doctrine, stemming from its foundations in the Quartet, with the growing prominence of Wales-specific issues, and argues for the creation of a distinct system of administrative law in Wales. Paul Scott (chapter eleven) considers the position of Scotland which, unlike Wales, has long been recognised to have its own body of principles of administrative law. Scott argues that the distinctively Scottish conception of the 'supervisory jurisdiction', which unlike judicial review elsewhere in the UK makes no distinction between public and private, has the potential to support a far richer conception of the rule of law than the standard reading of the Quartet, one capable of responding to the presence of arbitrary power in private relations as much as public relations. Gordon Anthony (chapter twelve) argues that the peculiarities of administration in Northern Ireland, including extended periods with neither devolved government nor direct rule, have accentuated the constitutionalising function of judicial review and raised difficult questions about the functions of courts when the executive and legislature are unable to discharge their constitutional functions. Whilst the Quartet forms the underpinnings of the system of law within which these issues have been argued and decided, the cases also develop the law in ways that represent a distinctive conception that responds to the specific context of Northern Ireland.

Part V of the volume adopts a more comparative perspective, by examining how the judge-led creation of judicial review in the UK maps onto patterns of judicial decision-making in other jurisdictions. A detailed set of comparisons is, of course, impossible in a volume of this type, but the chapters in this Part take three illustrative examples, looking at developments in jurisdictions whose administrative law is either strongly influenced by that of the UK (New Zealand and the New Commonwealth) or based on similar principles (Israel). These form useful comparators in a volume whose purpose is reflecting both on the creation of modern judicial review, and the course it has taken over its subsequent life.

In her discussion of administrative law in Israel (chapter thirteen), Justice Barak-Erez describes how the judiciary in Israel developed a system of administrative law that closely parallels the system created by the Quartet, but did so well before the Quartet. The similarities between the developments she highlights and the subsequent development of the Quartet raise interesting questions about the extent to which the Quartet was truly the novel break that it is often represented as being. Dean Knight's contribution on New Zealand (chapter fourteen), in contrast, highlights the challenges of developing a transplanted law. As he shows, although New Zealand began with an adoption of the Quartet, the subsequent development of the law has seen those imported principles applied in an indigenous judicial style, even if the principles themselves remain largely English. Peter Cane's chapter on the new Commonwealth (chapter fifteen) uses an examination of a range of common law jurisdictions to highlight the diversity of local solutions that have been reached through common law methods. As he shows, the relevant areas of law have now evolved so much that, in some instances, the 'horizontal diffusion' of the law across common law countries is becoming evident. At the same time, there are examples of both more expansive and weaker bodies of administrative law, reflecting the common law method's ability to use a shared body of principles to develop solutions responsive to local conditions.

Part VI looks at the relevance of the Quartet to ongoing debates about judicial review and the character and proper role of judicial decision-making. The three chapters in this Part draw together themes from across past and present that were central to the historical development of judicial review since the Quartet, and are likely to remain central to the future development of judicial review. Stephen Bailey (chapter sixteen) considers the legal context in which the Quartet were decided, and sets out six bases or yardsticks by which to evaluate them and judge their successes. He includes not just what the cases decided but also the arguments they rejected, the broader messages they conveyed, and the extent to which each case can be seen as a misstep. He argues that when seen from this perspective, and in the light of what came before, there is much to celebrate in the Quartet. Alex Latham-Gambi (chapter seventeen) evaluates the Quartet from the perspective of a common criticism that is made of them, namely, that they represent an increase in judicial power at the expense of the power of political institutions. As he shows, judicial power can – and in the case of the Quartet actually did – operate to enhance rather than diminish the power of the political branches of government. Richard Kirkham and Dimitrios Tsarapatsanis (chapter eighteen) ask how one might characterise the shift in judicial decision-making seen in the Quartet (which they term the 'the Reid shift', because of its close association with Lord Reid). Through a systematic content analysis, they show that its doctrinal dimensions were limited, and that the courts were aware of the dangers and limits of a project to restructure administrative law. The shift represented, rather, a loosening of legal norms to permit future evolution in a way that remained firmly within the orthodox common law method.

In a concluding essay (chapter nineteen), we consider the broader implications of these chapters and, in doing so, return to the idea of the Quartet as a formative moment. Does a better understanding of the history, context and purposes that underpinned the development of judicial review give us a better understanding of its strengths and limits? Does it shed deeper light on hidden faultlines, and uncover possibilities for how judicial review's task might be better discharged in the present day? As the concluding chapter discusses, the essays in this volume strongly suggest that these questions should be answered in the affirmative.

C. Key Themes and Concerns

As the above summary has shown, there are significant points of contact between the arguments and findings of the individual chapters, and a number of common themes and concerns emerge from them. The remaining sections of this chapter discuss these themes and concerns in more detail. We focus, in particular, on three sets of concerns which recur consistently across the chapters, and which speak to issues of broader relevance to current debates in public law.

The first relates to the issue of continuity and discontinuity in the law of judicial review. There is a rich body of literature discussing whether, and if so in what way, the Quartet represented a break with the past as opposed to continuity with the past.[11] As we discuss in section II below, the essays in this volume suggest a complex mix of continuity and discontinuity, in which the shift was not simply a matter of doctrine but also concerned the ends of doctrine, and where immediate discontinuities were at the time widely viewed as manifesting a deeper constitutional continuity.

Section III takes up a second concern, relating to the doctrinal legacy of the Quartet, and the structure and direction it gave the subsequent development of judicial review. The Quartet did not mark the end of the development of judicial review. As the chapters in this volume show, post-Quartet developments also exercised a (re)shaping influence over judicial review, as did the shifting political, intellectual and social context in which judicial review has operated in the five decades since the Quartet were decided. These suggest that there is a need to reconceptualise the basic principles underlying judicial review and rethink the manner in which we describe its tasks and purposes.

The third and final concern relates to issues that the Quartet left unaddressed, and the impact that unresolved legacy had on the subsequent development of judicial review. As Section IV discusses, this legacy lies at the heart of many of the features of judicial review that make it so contested today. A better understanding of their aetiology and relationship to circumstances specific to the

[11] eg L Blom-Cooper and G Drewry, 'Towards a System of Administrative Law: The Reid and Wilberforce Era, 1945–82' in L Blom-Cooper, B Dickson and G Drewry (eds), *The Judicial House of Lords: 1876–2009* (Oxford, OUP, 2009); S Sterett, *Creating Constitutionalism? The Politics of Legal Expertise and Administrative Law in England and Wales* (Michigan, University of Michigan Press, 1997) 31–42; S Sedley, 'The Sound of Silence: Constitutional Law Without a Constitution' (1994) 110 *Law Quarterly Review* 271; A Paterson, *The Law Lords* (London, MacMillan, 1982).

context in which the Quartet was decided puts us in a better position to begin understanding how they might be resolved.

II. CONTINUITY OR DISCONTINUITY? THE QUARTET AND THE LEGACY OF THE PAST

A striking feature of the aftermath of the Quartet, on which several chapters in this volume comment, is the relative lack of resistance to House of Lords decisions. Even where the initial political reaction to the outcome of particular cases was unfavourable, it was swiftly countered by a broader groundswell of support for the position taken by the Court.[12] The essays in this volume suggest that this was a consequence of the Quartet's complex intertwining of continuity and change. This combination of change and continuity is fundamental to understanding the nature and character of the shift the Quartet represented, and the chapters in this volume suggest that it had two dimensions. The first, discussed in subsection A, was that the Quartet was in sympathy with a political consensus that emerged in the 1950s and early 1960s, and leaned towards a greater degree of legal control of the executive. The Quartet responded to the same underlying discontents as did that consensus, and had close parallels with developments elsewhere. Simultaneously, as subsection B discusses, the Quartet also exhibited a second dimension of continuity with the past. What was novel about the Quartet lay not so much in the actual doctrine as in the willingness to apply those doctrines in new contexts and situations. This meant there were strong resonances between the Quartet and aspects of the common law's past, which made it possible for the cases to rapidly entrench themselves as part of the settled legal understanding.

A. Building on Consensus: Putting the Quartet in Context

All four cases in the Quartet were heavily influenced by the conditions that prevailed in mid-twentieth-century Britain. In the years preceding the Quartet, the growth of the post-war state had begun to make itself felt across multiple branches of the state, producing not just expansion but also a succession of innovations in government. This growth, however, also gave rise to anxiety about the implications of increasing the power of executive government. The functioning of central government now had a significant direct impact on private persons, and government power was starting to be seen across the political spectrum as having the potential to adversely affect the liberty of the individual. By the 1950s,

[12] See eg the political aftermath of *Anisminic*, which two of us have described elsewhere. See TT Arvind and L Stirton, 'Why the Judicial Power Project Is Wrong about *Anisminic*', UK Constitutional Law Blog (20 May 2016), available at ukconstitutionallaw.org/2016/05/20/tt-arvind-and-lindsay-stirton-why-the-judicial-power-project-is-wrong-about-anisminic.

a social and political consensus had emerged in favour of fundamental reforming administrative remedies to control the growing power of government.[13] This included a greater degree of legal control over public administration, which Parliament took steps to facilitate at the end of the decade through the Tribunals and Inquiries Act 1958. Arvind and Stirton show that the need for reform was recognised even within administrative departments. The civil service did not favour judicial oversight, but they constituted a succession of official committees which attempted to formulate internal solutions to ameliorate the problems and combat the increasingly negative views about the conduct of public administration coming from lawyers, politicians and the media.[14]

Despite the political consensus in favour of reform, however, administrative law was quiescent in the years before the Quartet, a phase described as its 'long sleep'.[15] The law practised in the courts followed an approach that is today sometimes called 'substantive formalism'.[16] Substantive formalism sought to check the judicial tendency to intervene in executive decision-making by setting strict limits on what could be reviewed. It did this through the creation of tightly defined analytical categories delineated through bright line rules. In *Ridge*, Lord Reid attributed this approach to the courts' reluctance to accept the need for a system of administrative law – a reluctance which, in his view, they were belatedly beginning to overcome.[17] In historical terms, however, this quiescence was far from the norm. As Cane discusses in his contribution, the judiciary had asserted a more expansive role several times before the nineteenth century, often controversially.[18] Nevertheless, the dominance of substantive formalism in the years before the Quartet meant that scholarly[19] and judicial[20] commentary was pessimistic in relation to judicial review's ability to play any significant supervisory role in relation to the executive.

The juxtaposition of legal rules providing limited and tightly circumscribed redress with a social consensus supporting more expansive redress is an

[13] New ideas on administrative justice reform included the Franks Committee (1957) and the Whyatt Report (1961). See *Administrative Tribunals and Enquiries*, Cm.218 and J Whyatt, *The Citizen and the Administration: The Redress of Grievances* (London, Justice, 1961). Other proposals from this period include Law Commission, Exploratory Working Paper on Administrative Law (Law Com WP No 13, 1967) and SA de Smith, *Judicial Review of Administrative Action* (London, Stevens, 1959). For a general discussion of the era, see TT Arvind and L Stirton, 'The curious origins of judicial review' (2017) 133 *LQR* 91.

[14] Ch 5 in this volume.

[15] Eg S Sedley, 'The Long Sleep' in M Andenas and D Fairgrieve (eds), *Tom Bingham and the Transformation of the Law: A Liber Amicorum* (Oxford, OUP, 2009).

[16] See A Paterson, *The Law Lords* (London, MacMillan, 1982) 132.

[17] *Ridge v Baldwin* [1964] AC 40, 72.

[18] Ch 15 in this volume.

[19] Thus, for example, HWR Wade and B Schwartz initially argued that the creation of the unified action of judicial review was a blind alley, because the emergence of a new form of action would not solve the problem of administrative redress. B Schwartz and HWR Wade, *Legal Control of Government: Administrative Law in Britain and the United States* (Oxford, Clarendon Press, 1972) 327 fn 59.

[20] Eg P Devlin, 'The Common Law, Public Policy and the Executive' (1956) 9 *Current Legal Problems* 1; AT Denning, *Freedom under the Law* (London, Stevens, 1949) 126.

important part of the background to the Quartet. As Thomas's chapter shows, it is simplistic to treat the 1960s as the sole defining moment in administrative law.[21] The consensus in favour of administrative justice reform and critical scrutiny of administration that emerged a decade earlier was equally important. The 'Franks spirit', as he terms it, meant that governments of both political parties wanted more legal control of the administration. The Quartet was decided at a time when this spirit was in the ascendant. As Thomas points out, 'By the time the courts decided the Quartet in the 1960s, they were not so much leading the way, but playing catch-up with both public opinion and legislative policy'.[22] The effect was to make the direction in which they took the law considerably more acceptable that it otherwise might have been.

These contextual pressures were not unique to the UK. As other chapters in this volume show, jurisdictions elsewhere also faced similar issues. Barak-Erez discusses the situation in Israel which, as a newly independent country, could draw on the common law tradition without being constrained by substantive formalism.[23] As she shows, its greater freedom to develop administrative law standards meant that it adopted positions similar to the Quartet well before the House of Lords. New Zealand, in contrast, only developed judicial review following the Quartet, and borrowed most of its law from the Quartet. But, as Knight shows, this was largely due to the similarity of its institutions to the UK's, as well as the relative shortage of administrative law cases and administrative law specialists.[24] Its adoption of the Quartet was a response to actual pressures facing its legal system, and not simply a case of following trends in the UK. Countries which faced different pressures could take different routes. Cane uses case studies from Africa and Asia to show how the decolonialisation of the mid-twentieth century 'involved fundamental changes in political, governmental and legal norms and practices in the newly-independent nations'. This created the space for developments in administrative law leading in very different directions, which sometimes led to weaker checks on the executive, but could also lead to the reverse.[25] In each case the context of the local legal system, including not just its constitution but also its politics, played a key role in framing the pace and direction of the development of judicial review.

B. The Spirit of *Soixante-Huit*: Continuity, Discontinuity, or Both?

The previous section has shown that the Quartet were part of a more general shift in perceptions of the role of law in relation to administration, and were

[21] Ch 3 in this volume, section VI.
[22] ibid.
[23] Ch 13 in this volume.
[24] Ch 14 in this volume.
[25] Ch 15 in this volume.

embedded within a broader process that was already under way outside the courtroom before the Quartet. Yet, although the Quartet displayed continuity with political views on the need to subject the administration to legal control, the position in relation to the legal rules they articulated is more complex. The case studies in Part II of this collection show that the Quartet broke down a number of legal doctrines that had previously sustained substantive formalism. On one level, therefore, this collection could be read to support the 'break with the past' reading of the Quartet that is shared both by those who view it as a wrong turn which muddied the separation of powers in the UK, and those who view it as reviving a judicial tradition of restraining arbitrary executive power.

Despite this, however, the chapters in this volume also demonstrate that the Quartet showed a significant amount of continuity with the past. As Kirkham and Tsarapatsanis discuss, there is little evidence of new grounds being created or deployed during the period, as a truly radical break with the past would have done.[26] Thomas's chapter on *Ridge* notes that Bradley, in his contemporaneous comment on the case, read it as establishing no new principle.[27] Bailey concurs with this view, and suggests that the case represented 'more like the (entirely proper) restoration of the *status quo ante* rather than a giant leap forward'.[28] He similarly suggests that *Padfield* was a cautious decision based on well-understood principles. If it had import it was the identity of the respondent, a government Minister with wide discretionary power, a view which receives support from the analysis Sunkin presents in his chapter.[29]

Anisminic and *Conway* are often taken to have been more radical but, as the chapters devoted to them in this volume show, they were also in many ways impeccably orthodox. *Anisminic* took a less cautious approach to ouster clauses than the House of Lords had done 12 years earlier in *Smith v East Elloe RDC*,[30] which (with a powerful dissent from Lord Reid) faithfully applied a privative clause and was once described as the 'high water mark of judicial timidity'.[31] But as Feldman demonstrates, the *Anisminic* principle itself was not seen as being particularly revolutionary at the time, even if its application to the facts of the case was politically controversial.[32] The major shift came in how *Anisminic* was later interpreted rather than in the judgment itself. Similarly, although *Conway* was on its face a clear break with the past, involving the invocation of the then new 1966 Practice Statement[33] to overrule the prior decision in *Duncan v Cammell Laird*,[34] Arvind and Stirton show that it did so by following

[26] Ch 18 in this volume.
[27] AW Bradley, 'A Failure of Justice and A Defect of Police' [1964] *CLJ* 83.
[28] Ch 16 in this volume, section II.B.
[29] Ch 4 in this volume.
[30] *Smith v East Elloe RDC* [1956] AC 736 (HL).
[31] Blom-Cooper and Drewry, 'Towards a System of Administrative Law' (2009) 260.
[32] Ch 6 in this volume.
[33] Practice Statement (Judicial Precedent) [1966] 1 WLR 1234.
[34] *Duncan v Cammell Laird* [1942] AC 624 (HL).

long-established Scottish authority rather than through an innovation, and it did so to uphold an understanding of the courts' constitutional role that had strong defenders in Parliament.[35]

At a functional level, too, the scale of the break that the Quartet achieved is less powerful than is sometimes assumed. As Nason demonstrates,[36] the modest impact it had on the actual number of grievances against the administration resolved by the courts challenges the oft-cited idea that it heralded an avalanche in administrative law claims. Tomlinson similarly highlights the failure of the Quartet to devise doctrines addressing the lack of access to justice for the vast majority with grievances against the administration.[37] Latham-Gambi likewise shows that the Quartet did not represent the vast accretion of judicial power and diminution of executive and legislative power that it is sometimes taken to – indeed, he argues at least one of the cases actually operated to diminish rather than increase judicial power.[38] *Padfield*'s import was famously undermined by the Government's immediate reversal of the farmer's victory in its fresh decision,[39] an outcome which paralleled that in *Conway* where, as Arvind and Stirton show, Michael Conway was defeated when the case went back to trial, due to Rimmer's use of a clever legal strategy.

How, then, can we characterise the spirit of the Quartet, and the nature of the shift it brought about? The essays in this volume suggest that the Quartet's most significant effect lay in altering the lens through which the judiciary viewed disputes. It signalled, in Thomas's words, 'the collapsing of formalist analytical distinctions; and a move away from precedent toward a focus on underlying principles'.[40] The main impact of the Quartet lay in its departure from the analytical categories and technical distinctions built up by substantive formalism, substituting for them a more context-dependent approach that sought to match administrative practice against the backdrop of the growing complexity and expanding functions of the state. As Bailey's chapter[41] makes clear, a key feature of the new lens offered by the Quartet was its nullification of various lines of legal reasoning that had hitherto been deployed to restrict the reach of judicial review. *Ridge*, for example, breathed new life into the concept of natural justice in administrative law by effectively nullifying the 'administrative-judicial' analytical dichotomy that had restricted the reach of administrative law in the preceding years. The Quartet also signalled a move away from the distinction between decisions taken by the central Government and those taken by other levels of government. As the chapters by Bailey and Cane show,[42] the power of the courts to review the decisions of local authorities and unelected boards was

[35] Ch 5 of this volume.
[36] Ch 7 in this volume.
[37] Ch 9 in this volume.
[38] Ch 17 in this volume.
[39] Ch 4 in this volume.
[40] Ch 3 in this volume, section I.
[41] Ch 16 in this volume, section II.D.
[42] Ch 16 in this volume, section I.

well established by the nineteenth century, as were many of the principles on which that review would be conducted. Challenging central government actions through judicial review, in contrast, only became the subject of serious consideration in the mid-twentieth century, and the Quartet did much to establish these challenges as a routine feature of judicial review.

The spirit of the Quartet, in other words, was to bring a new focus to the wealth of ideas contained within the common law as well as the need to look across that entire set of ideas when deciding how to deal with the challenges posed by the rise of administrative government. In this, the Quartet reflected an approach that assigned greater weight to general principles of law than to the analytical categories that dominated case law in the preceding decades. But here, too, the break with the past was less sharp than it might seem. The appropriateness of the shift away from substantive formalism and towards a more contextual approach is much disputed today,[43] but at the time the technical distinctions on which it was based were viewed by many as unhelpful and even legally dysfunctional,[44] and they stood in opposition to the social and political consensus which, as discussed in the previous section, favoured greater legal control of central government. Nor was there anything inherently unusual about the idea of legal challenges against central government actions and decisions. Tort actions had long lain against government officers who acted in excess of their powers or in contravention of rights, and several iconic constitutional cases of the past, including *Entick v Carrington*,[45] originated as tort actions brought to challenge the legality of a Secretary of State's acts. *Padfield* laid bare the full extent to which ministerial acts could now be challenged on the basis of the underlying objects of the legislation, but it did not invent the idea that ministerial discretion was controlled by law and, as Sunkin shows in his chapter, it explicitly sought to support Parliamentary scrutiny by creating a judicial mechanism through which an ordinary individual could trigger that scrutiny.[46] The ability of the ordinary individual – 'the little farmer with four acres and a cow'[47] – to use the legal process to hold officials to account occupied a powerful place in the constitutional imagination, and if tort had proven itself unequal to the task in the context of the modern state,[48] then it was only logical to let other legal remedies grow to fill that gap.

[43] See, eg, CF Forsyth, 'Showing the Fly Out of the Flybottle: The Value of Formalism and Conceptual Reasoning in Administrative Law' [1997] *CLJ* 325 and '"Blasphemy Against Basics": Doctrine, Conceptual Reasoning and Certain Decisions of the UK Supreme Court' in J Bell, M Elliott and J Varuhas (eds), *Public Law Adjudication in Common Law Systems: Process and Substance* (Oxford, Hart Publishing, 2016).

[44] See eg the discussion in the chapters by Thomas (ch 3) and Arvind and Stirton (ch 5).

[45] *Entick v Carrington* (1765) 19 ST 1030.

[46] Ch 4 in this volume.

[47] Whyatt, *The Citizen and the Administration* (1961) xiii.

[48] In the first half of the 20th century reformers sought to revive tort law as a way of dealing with the growing powers of the state. See TT Arvind, 'Restraining the state through tort? The Crown Proceedings Act 1947 in retrospect' in TT Arvind and J Steele (eds), *Tort Law and the Legislature: Common Law, Statute, and the Dynamics of Legal Change* (Oxford, Hart Publishing, 2012).

This gives us a better insight into how we might characterise the intertwining of continuity and change in the Quartet. In his study of radical movements in the early nineteenth century, Calhoun made the point that many movements do not fit the usual dichotomies of revolutionary change and continuity, because they seek to preserve remembered ways of life in the face of changes that threaten them.[49] This also holds true of the Quartet. As the summary in this section has shown, the cases did not seek to reshape constitutional values as much as they sought to find ways of continuing to uphold what they believed those values to be, in the face of challenges posed by the rise of administrative government. The 'Reid shift', to use Kirkham and Tsarapatsanis' terminology, was a response to problems that were widely perceived as being real and pressing, and the form it took built on principles that were widely perceived as being impeccably orthodox. It moved away from a recent present, but did so in a way that was seen as maintaining continuity with the constitutive essence of an older past. The immediate practical consequences of the shift may well have been radical, but their radicalism was the radicalism of tradition.

This is not, of course, to suggest that the process by which this development unfolded or the solutions it reached were perfect. As we discuss in Section IV below, the Quartet left several issues unresolved which continue to trouble judicial review to the present day. Nevertheless, the chapters in this volume demonstrate unambiguously that the problems cannot simply be attributed to the Quartet having muddied the waters of the separation of powers or trespassing on the executive's domain. They represent, rather, challenges that are intrinsic to the task of adapting an existing institution to deal with a radically altered operational context with which neither it nor any other institution was designed to deal.

III. THE QUARTET'S LEGAL AND SYMBOLIC LEGACY

Once we factor in the prevailing context within which the House of Lords was operating in the 1960s, some of the question marks surrounding their doctrinal legacy become easier to understand. The purpose of the Quartet was as much about signalling a change in judicial attitude as detailing new legal solutions. Messages were being given to claimants, and the legal community, about the possibilities for future litigation. This was a subtle approach which freed up space for the future evolution of the law. The judges deciding the Quartet were careful to operate within the standard parameters of the common law, and to deploy older case law in opposition to more recent developments in the law. For instance, the logic of the decision in *Ridge* was explicitly rooted in an earlier era 'replete with cases applying natural justice beyond the strict confines of judicial

[49] C Calhoun, *The Roots of Radicalism: Tradition, the Public Sphere, and Early Nineteenth Century Social Movements* (Chicago, University of Chicago Press, 2012) ix–x, 82–120.

decision-making'.[50] Lord Reid's decision was based not on the invention of new techniques, but on holding that recent dicta suggesting that older methods were no longer applicable 'should not be followed'.[51]

The underlying technique may have been subtle, but its results were impressive. For instance, Feldman concludes that *Anisminic*, was 'by any standards … one of the most significant decisions of the House of Lords on a public-law matter'.[52] As the chapters in Part II discuss, even when not directly cited, the Quartet underpinned legal arguments made in subsequent cases involving further judicial development of areas including natural justice, procedural fairness, ouster clauses, jurisdictional errors of law, improper purpose and relevant considerations. Indeed, to cite Knight, such is the uncontentious nature of the principles they stand for 'Their citation is almost a signal to say, "there's nothing to see here"'.[53]

An important legacy of the Quartet, therefore, was symbolic. The shift in the law which it brought about, even if not as radical as sometimes assumed, demonstrated that judges could significantly alter the path of the law, while also maintaining fidelity to the past and working incrementally rather than through radical restructuring. As Barak-Erez shows with her analysis of equivalent developments in Israel, this innovatory potential inheres in the common law method: the common law of Israel anticipated the direction taken by the Quartet before the Quartet itself.[54] Indeed, each of the comparative studies demonstrates the variety of interpretive routes that sophisticated judges can travel. Knight, for example, shows how judges in New Zealand could engage in 'a fledging fight for indigeneity' while maintaining an overall fidelity to the principles set out in the Quartet.[55] Cane, similarly, shows how the common law facilitated a diversity of solutions in the countries in the new Commonwealth, even at a time when the states in question were still subject to the common appellate jurisdiction of the Privy Council.

That a formative moment's impact is predominantly symbolic is not surprising. Formative moments do not resolve all future questions themselves. Instead, they create a potential for change, and it is a matter for subsequent cases – and the context in which those cases are decided – whether and in what direction that potential is taken up.[56] Nevertheless, in evaluating the Quartet's legacy, it is important to note that the symbolic nature of its impact meant that the cases, although creating the space for new solutions to be devised, did not provide

[50] Ch 3 in this volume, section IV.

[51] *Ridge* (n 4) 72–73.

[52] Ch 6 in this volume, section IV.

[53] Ch 14 in this volume, section III.D.

[54] Ch 13 in this volume.

[55] Ch 14 in this volume, section I.

[56] cf Feldman's analysis of the shifts in judicial attitudes to intervening in prisons during the 1970s: D Feldman, 'Changing boundaries: crime, punishment and public law' in JNE Varuhas and SW Stark (eds), *The Frontiers of Public Law* (Oxford, Hart, 2019).

clear answers to doctrinal questions. At one level, a legacy that 'only' lays the foundations for the evolution of new solutions is still a strong one. But it also means that the Quartet's actual doctrinal legacy was less powerful and looser, as the case studies in Part II highlight. Feldman, for example, critiques *Anisminic* for the long-term doctrinal uncertainty it created,[57] which would ultimately lead to the distinction between questions of law and questions of jurisdiction being erased – an outcome that was arguably contrary to what *Anisminic* actually intended. Thomas concludes that the House of Lords in *Ridge* provided no convincing theoretical rationale for the right to a hearing being applied or much by way of assistance for the future judge in understanding how this principle might be applied in other circumstances.[58] Arvind and Stirton point out that *Conway* set in motion a chain of development that led to not just its doctrine but its entire conceptual framework being superseded.[59] As Sunkin discusses, even *Padfield*, despite probably having had the most sustained mention in subsequent case law, appears to a modern eye to be formalistic and out of step with the more recent focus on rights.[60]

Secondly, the Quartet gave little guidance to future courts on how they could or should respond to new questions and issues thrown up by the new external pressures that continued to crop up in the decades after the Quartet. Whilst the Quartet undoubtedly facilitated the development of the law which took place in this later case law and which significantly extended the Quartet's move away from tightly defined analytical categories, the actual principles articulated had to be considerably tempered and reworked to address the new circumstances.[61] This did not, of course, entail repudiating the Quartet, but it did require moving beyond its confines.[62] Bowen, for example, shows that the extensive use made by the judiciary of the Human Rights Act 1998 reflects the challenges of using the Quartet, or even a common law rights jurisprudence built on principles similar to the Quartet, to protect individual interests against encroachment, in no small part due to the thinness of the Quartet's contribution to actual doctrine.[63] Yet, as the chapters by Nason and Tomlinson show, where it is neither possible to rework the Quartet to address new circumstances, nor is Parliament minded to erect a new legislative framework, the consequence can be that problems go unaddressed. Nason and Tomlinson focus on the difficulty in providing broad access to administrative justice to individuals aggrieved by governmental action. Despite their role in enabling common law creativity, in these areas the Quartet's choice of a particular constitutional framing has both constrained the range of responses which a later court can make to the problems of the day and left

[57] Ch 13 in this volume.
[58] Ch 3 in this volume, section VIII.
[59] Ch 5 in this volume.
[60] Ch 4 in this volume.
[61] Ch 16 in this volume, section II.C.
[62] Ch 14 in this volume, section III.C.
[63] Ch 8 in this volume.

it without obvious doctrinal tools which it can use to respond to these issues. Other chapters similarly allude to the extent to which expanding the range of possibilities offered by administrative law will require future shift in the foundations or 'meta-structure' of administrative law.

IV. THE UNFINISHED LEGACY OF THE QUARTET: QUESTIONS LEFT UNRESOLVED

The Quartet may have represented a particularly well-designed nudge to the legal community of the day, but it left unanswered many bigger questions about the true purpose of public law. A focus on these questions, and the consequences of leaving them unresolved, is a final theme of this volume. We identify three debates about administrative law which remain relevant today, and – as the chapters in this collection point out – arise out of issues which the Quartet did not resolve. These relate, respectively, to the nature of the rule of law, the tasks of judicial review, and the role of judges vis-à-vis other branches of the state.

A. The Idea of the Rule of Law

The Quartet did not resolve the question of what the rule of law means in public law terms and left considerable scope for the legal academy to debate thereafter. This dilemma is referred to at various points in the collection, most notably by Scott,[64] who analyses the flaws in the rule of law conception relied upon Dicey, and the British legal failure ever since to establish a clear settlement as to what should replace Dicey's conception. As Feldman shows, the ruling in *Anisminic* was not determinative of the issue, but it nevertheless created space for subsequent judges to build up a jurisprudence founded on a fidelity to the *idea* of the rule of law without actually deciding what the rule of law is or how it fits with other constitutional principles. This is most evident in *Anisminic's* successor case, *Privacy International*. Judicial loyalty to a principle of the 'rule of law' whose nature is never fully defined has been matched by an entrenched academic disagreement on the subject. As Tomlinson identifies with regard to the scholarly analysis of ouster clauses, the responses to recent judgments have become 'to a large extent, predictable',[65] as evidenced, for instance, in the academic response to the *Miller* cases.[66] For the time being, the outlook of different scholars' views on role of legal doctrine and administrative law has become framed by predetermined theoretical perspectives on the respective power of the rule of law, Parliamentary sovereignty and the separation of powers.

[64] Ch 11 in this volume, section II.B.

[65] Ch 9 in this volume, section II.

[66] *R (Miller) v Secretary of State for Exiting the EU* (SC(E)) [2017] UKSC 5 ('*Miller No 1*'); *R (Miller) v Prime Minister (SC(E))* [2019] UKSC 41 ('*Miller No 2*').

Nason's chapter further details this debate. She takes into account what happened after the Quartet, the gradual reform of the process applying for judicial review, culminating in the Supreme Court Act 1981, section 31 (later renamed the Senior Courts Act) and the Civil Procedure Rules, Part 54. This renovation of the incoherent procedural mess through which judicial review was formerly delivered was as much a formative moment for modern judicial review as the Quartet. Commenting on these reforms, she raises questions about their consequences, hinting that, alongside the doctrinal reforms of the Quartet, they enabled the creation of a near-monist uniformity in administrative law, without addressing what that uniformity is built upon. Is it built around a judicial role of protecting the public interest *against* private claims? Does it deliver a set of general administrative law standards? Or is the practice of administrative law one of defining the public interest through a heavily rationed selection of claims, and working towards a body of bespoke good administration guidance dependent on the statutory context of the administrative function under scrutiny?

Implicit in the critique advanced by Nason, and by other contributors, is that the symbolic importance of the Quartet, combined with its vagueness on the idea of the rule of law, diverts attention away from the importance of developing a richer account of its implications for practical administrative law doctrine and the ends which judicial review could serve. Along these lines, two other chapters offer contrasting suggestions as to the roles and purposes towards which the rule of law could be applied, were scholarship to engage more directly with its function. Arvind and Stirton highlight a dormant 'hortatory' potential in the judicial role that could be deployed to create and advance standards of good administration through a process of institutional dialogue with the administration, in a manner not too dissimilar to private law.[67] In a similar vein, Bowen's chapter considers how far the common law can be stretched to protect civil liberties, whether that would require a development 'to rival that of the sixties'[68] and, indeed, the extent to which a respect for civil liberties is part of the rule of law.

B. The Tasks of Judicial Review

A second unresolved debate that recurs throughout the volume, and which follows on from the debates on the nature of the rule of law, relates to the task of judicial review. As the discussion of context in section II of this chapter has shown, the position of the courts in judicial review and the role that it is able to perform, is dependent on features which are liable to change over time including, not least, the politics of the day, the relationships the judiciary shares with the political branches of the state, and the extent of mutual trust and parity of esteem in that relationship. The importance of this relationship,

[67] Ch 5 in this volume, section IV.
[68] Ch 8 in this volume, section I.

and the tensions implicit in it, are discussed in a number of chapters in this book, including Kirkham and Tsarapatsanis, Arvind and Stirton, Thomas, as well as Cane. Cane reminds as that this tension is fluid and a permanent part of the constitutional order, and uses his chapter to reprise his earlier work[69] which argues that 'there is a significant relationship between the way public power is allocated and distributed in a system of government and the way public power – particularly administrative power – is controlled'. To understand the role of judicial review requires a better understanding of the nature of these relationships. This applies not just to the relationship between the judiciary and the legislature, but also to the relationship between the executive and the legislature. As Cane argues, the seventeenth century saw what could be described as 'a revolutionary power-grab', during which the courts in England successfully adapted the 'prerogative writs' to enhance the control both they and Parliament exercised over the King.[70] Against this background, it is perhaps significant that both *Padfield* and *Anisminic*, in shifting the law, argued that the courts were upholding and protecting the position of Parliament and its legislative intention, a move which we see repeated more recently in the *Miller* cases.[71]

The nature of the UK Constitution, however, means that this is not always the case. The party system and the control which the Government frequently exercises over Parliament mean that the political branch can claw back the ground claimed by the courts, if judicial intervention in administration ceases to be exercised cautiously. As Nason discusses in her chapter,[72] this means that the acquiescence of public administration to the work of the courts is essential for its continued success. As the growth of restrictive regulations which she outlines demonstrates, this acquiescence cannot be assumed. At the same time, the complexity of this institutional dialogue resists simplistic bright line formulations of rules as to what a judge should and should not deliver through administrative law.

Both Nason and Tomlinson highlight the danger of an excessive focus on legal doctrine derived from leading case law in defining the tasks of judicial review. This, they suggest, leads to loss of perspective, drawing attention away from issues that are of critical importance to judicial review, including the issue of the lack of access to securing administrative justice, or redress against administrative grievances, through judicial review. Both chapters detail the real barriers to that access, such as cost, process and the availability of legal advice. The rising importance of online decision-making is also a matter that was, for obvious reasons, completely absent from the original discussions around the Quartet. Indeed, on access to justice, Tomlinson details the various reasons to conclude that the contribution of *Anisminic* was at best a heavily qualified, and marginal,

[69] P Cane, *Controlling Administrative Power: An Historical Comparison* (Cambridge, Cambridge University Press, 2016).

[70] Ch 15 in this volume, section II.

[71] *Miller (No 1)* (n 66); *Miller (No 2)* (n 66).

[72] Ch 7 in this volume.

victory for the promotion of access to justice, leading him to argue for a greater focus on creating 'a wider public law jurisprudence on legal exclusion'.[73]

Arvind and Stirton put the focus on a different question, namely, the extent to which judicial review meets the needs of the administration, including the need for certainty. They point out that despite the frequently asserted idea that public law seeks to enforce standards of good administration, there is in fact little engagement in public law with the challenges and choices that face administrators, and with which any set of principles of good administration would need to deal. There is, in particular, little engagement with the 'administrative constitutionalism' of the civil service, despite the role this constitutionalism plays in the actual conduct of administration.[74] Against this background, it is somewhat easier to understand the civil service's resistance to administrative law reform and their attempt to manage and confine the impact of judicially imposed solutions, a point to which Thomas's chapter also speaks.[75]

A second focus of the chapters in this volume is on the question of how much uniformity administrative law requires, and how much fragmentation can be tolerated in the interests of making the law more socially responsive. To some extent, fragmentation is already present within the legal system. Bowen, for example, argues that the common law ultimately lacks key powers and abilities when compared to the jurisprudence of the ECHR and the Human Rights Act, and it is only the express recognition of diversity, and the absence of any sustained pursuit of uniformity of approach between the two, that has enabled both to thrive. Yet, as numerous chapters also point out, the Quartet has exercised a powerful harmonising function over public law doctrine, which makes achieving a balance between uniformity and responsiveness to local needs anything but straightforward. This difficulty extends beyond the UK. Whilst Cane highlights the extent to which the common law facilitates diversity, as seen in the different routes taken in the 'offsprings' of 'parent legal systems', Knight in contrast highlights the challenges New Zealand as a small jurisdiction has faced in achieving an acceptable measure of indigeneity within its system of administrative law, and queries whether the rights revolution that has already occurred in the UK has been mirrored in New Zealand.[76]

Devolution within the UK and diverging legal needs across its four jurisdictions give this question a particularly strong contemporary importance. The territorial dimension of judicial review was weak in the 1960s and, despite the separate jurisdictions in Northern Ireland and Scotland, was not directly addressed in the Quartet. Indeed, as Scott details, in Scotland, the Quartet was treated as indistinguishable from Scots law.[77] Even though Scottish nationalism

[73] Ch 9 in this volume, section I.
[74] Ch 5 in this volume, section I.
[75] Ch 3 in this volume.
[76] Ch 14 in this volume, section III.D.
[77] Ch 11 in this volume.

was becoming a factor during the period of the Quartet, administrative law barely featured in debates on legal nationalism at the time. However, as he discusses, the Scottish conception of the supervisory jurisdiction, and the lack of differentiation between public and private entities in relation to this jurisdiction gives Scotland the potential to achieve something very different. This difference could be based on a richer and more nuanced conception of the rule of law, if there is a greater willingness to embrace divergence instead of the uniformity that is implicit in the Quartet.

In relation to Wales and Northern Ireland, the need to respond to local pressures has created a set of factors which weigh more strongly in favour of divergence. As Anthony discusses in his chapter on Northern Ireland, the peculiar interregnum in Northern Ireland during the latter years of the last decade, when its political situation meant it had neither functioning devolved institutions nor direct rule, required the courts to consider issues that courts elsewhere in the UK are unlikely ever to have to consider. The result was the accentuation of judicial review's constitutionalising functions, whose long-term impact on Northern Irish public law remains unclear.[78] Gardner's chapter on Wales, in contrast, is more focused on the possibilities that devolution offers for Wales to tread a new road in judicial review.[79] Although a fledgling new administrative law jurisdiction is developing in Wales, which might over time include a different slant on legal doctrine, the scope of these variations will be restricted by the oversight of the senior courts which Wales shares with England, and its position as part of what in theory remains a unified Anglo-Welsh legal system. As Gardner discusses, the impact of discrete obligations imposed by Welsh-only legislation[80] and the influence of a Welsh Administrative Court on the interpretation of such legislation, raise interesting questions about the future of this fusion. So, too, do the connections between alternative dispute resolution and the courts which the development of codes of good administration in Wales might highlight.[81] The positive merits of codification identified by Gardner, in terms of greater clarity and organisation, could conceivably acquire much more immediate relevance on a UK-wide basis in the event of a future codification initiative under the Conservative Government.[82] Such a development would, needless to say, also raise head on the extent to which judicial review can and should be based on unified, as opposed to differentiated principles, and the conceptions of the rule of law and the judicial/executive relationship that should be embedded in them.

[78] Ch 12 in this volume.

[79] Ch 10 in this volume.

[80] Eg Welsh Language Act 1993, Housing (Wales) Act 2014, Social Services and Well-being (Wales) Act 2014, Well-being of Future Generations (Wales) Act 2015, Public Health (Wales) Act 2017.

[81] Ch 10 in this volume.

[82] ibid.

C. The Role of the Judge

The final, and perhaps most controversial, unresolved tension which the volume highlights relates to the role of the individual judge. On one vision, the judge is a mere agent within the legal process, whose role is primarily one of giving effect to any constraints Parliament may impose on executive decision-making. The development and enforcement of common law constraints on the political branches is a task that is at the very most secondary, and which must only be exercised in a cautious and heavily circumscribed way. Arguably, a clear preference for this position is shown by those who advocate the pursuit of narrow and restrained administrative law principles which are as directed towards confining the role of the judge as they are to restraining the administration. On another perspective, however, the judge is an active actor within the state who works with the other branches to move administration in a more constitutionally appropriate manner. The chapters in this volume, taken as a whole, suggest that the Quartet is implicitly – but only implicitly – built on a constitutional tradition that viewed the judiciary in the latter light. A key theme that emerges from the chapters is the extent to which the Quartet, and subsequent cases building on it, envisages a genuine collaboration between the judiciary and the other branches of government. Latham-Gambi[83] and Sunkin[84] in their individual contributions demonstrate that the cases in the Quartet sought to create judicial remedies that strengthened Parliamentary scrutiny and Parliamentary control of public administration, rather than supplanting it. Similarly, both Thomas[85] and Bowen[86] show that judicial boldness in the 1960s and the 2000s was brought about by signs of Parliamentary support for a more assertive judicial role. Several chapters, in particular those by Scott and Lord Reed, see the Quartet as a demonstration of the power of the individual judge, but also highlight the extent to which the exercise of that power is shaped by existing institutional arrangements.

Seeing judges as actors, however, also entails seeing them as exhibiting a kind of leadership and a consciously choice-driven approach to adjudication. The chapter by Kirkham and Tsarapatsanis, for example, draws upon the judicial strategy literature to highlight the extent to which the House of Lords during the period of Lord Reid set in motion a chain of reasoning that would leave judges with a wider domain of active choice.[87] They also detail the various 'moves' that the Quartet opened, and which remain open, to individual judges to make use of the inherent indeterminacy in the law to shift the parameters of administrative law. Cane observes that uncodified constitutions encourage such creativity by

[83] Ch 17 in this volume.
[84] Ch 4 in this volume.
[85] Ch 3 in this volume.
[86] Ch 8 in this volume.
[87] Ch 18 in this volume.

not establishing clear boundaries around judicial action.[88] The chapters by Lord Reed and Nason in their references to the evolution of a 'constitutional strand' within the work of the courts, particularly the UK Supreme Court, provide further evidence of this tendency.

Viewing judges in this light puts the focus on the judges' personal background and on judicial choices in a manner that is not without precedent in public law scholarship in the UK – for example, the work of JAG Griffiths, Alan Paterson, David Robertson and Robert B Stevens – but that sits uneasily with the dominant current trend in public law scholarship. From this perspective, the Quartet may never have been decided had the judicial committee of the House of Lords been differentially constituted between 1963 and 1968. The context of the 1950s and 1960s may have been such that there was an opportunity available for a shift in the nature of judicial reasoning, but that moment still needed someone to do the grasping.[89] Much about the timing of Lord Reid's tenure was important, but so was his character. To understand the Quartet you need to understand Lord Reid's political background and career as a Solicitor-General for Scotland,[90] his Scottishness[91] and his brilliance as a lawyer,[92] which gave him an array of characteristics fit to identify what was 'both politically and administratively possible' for a senior court judge to achieve at that moment.[93]

Legal historians are, of course, familiar with the idea that the law is the product of human thought and action, and of human responses to specific circumstances and problems.[94] Not all readers of this volume will, however, be comfortable with this view of the making of public law or of the judiciary. Indeed, the emphasis that many more recent decisions have placed on the fact that the judiciary, in making a decision in an area of political controversy, is doing no more than giving effect to Parliament's will suggests that many judges themselves are likely to take an unfavourable view of the idea that judges are actors in their own right. Nevertheless, a serious consideration of the Quartet requires us to grapple with the possibility that it does, in fact, implicitly depend on this view of the judiciary.

In all these unresolved debates, the story of the Quartet remains relevant and instructive. As Thomas tells us: 'Despite all the changes of time, the world we inhabit is fundamentally the same world as existed in the past. It is governed by the same timeless features of human nature'.[95] The context of the Quartet may have been very different, but the questions around the role of the judge in

[88] Ch 15 in this volume, section IV(C).
[89] Ch 18 in this volume.
[90] Ch 3 in this volume, section IV.
[91] Ch 11 in this volume.
[92] Ch 2 in this volume.
[93] Ch 3 in this volume, section IV.
[94] As SFC Milsom put it, in typically vivid language, in an early essay: 'It is not the nature of plaster that determines the shape of the cast.' SFC Milsom, '*The Action on the Case* by A.K. Kiralfy' (1953) 11 *Cambridge Law Journal* 463, 466.
[95] Ch 3 in this volume, section I.

resolving the tensions between the citizen and the state remain the same, and involve identifying the extent to which it is appropriate to juridify the political process.[96] In the words of Feldman:

> It is quite possible that, after another 50 years, lawyers will still be arguing about the same issues, and perhaps coming up with yet more ways of trying to resolve them. Judgments come and go, but problems do not disappear.[97]

[96] On this point, see Ch 3 in this volume, sections II–III.
[97] Ch 6 in this volume, section IV.

2

Lord Reid: The Judge as Law Maker?

ROBERT REED, LORD REED OF ALLERMUIR*

LORD REID OF Drem was held, and continues to be held, in the highest regard by judges both in the United Kingdom and overseas. Very few judges have had as much influence as he had on the development of the common law throughout the world. None, in modern times, seems to me to have had a greater influence.

It was particularly appropriate to remember Lord Reid in 2018, when the conference was held which formed the springboard for this collection of essays. That year was the fiftieth anniversary of three of the four great cases, in all of which he gave the leading speech, which established the fundamental principles of modern administrative law. The first of the four cases, *Ridge v Baldwin*[1] in 1963, in which a chief constable challenged his dismissal from office, established the modern approach to the right to a fair hearing. On reading the report, the first point to strike a modern judge is that the hearing lasted eight days. A comparable case today would be allowed two days at most. The length of the report – 103 pages of the Appeal Cases – is also a reminder that long reports are not a recent development.

Lord Reid's speech is very characteristic of his style, and it is said that he himself regarded it as the case of which he was proudest.[2] It exhibits great confidence, in describing the law at a high level of generality, but also with precision and accuracy, and in disapproving earlier decisions by prestigious judges.[3] Previous authorities are cited to illustrate how the law has developed, and the principles involved, but are not analysed in detail. His vocabulary is simple and his syntax is lucid. The paragraphs are for the most part relatively brief, and follow each other in logical order. In short, his style of writing is a model of how a judgment should be written.

* I am grateful to my Judicial Assistants, Alexandra Littlewood, Michal Hain and Ailsa McKeon, for their assistance in the preparation of this paper.

[1] [1964] AC 40.

[2] M Berlins, 'The One Judge We Will Really Miss' *The Times* (14 January 1975) 14.

[3] For example, the opinion of Viscount Radcliffe in *Nakkuda Ali v Jayaratne* [1951] AC 66. Viscount Radcliffe was still serving on the Appellate Committee when *Ridge v Baldwin* was decided.

What strikes me most about the judgment is Reid's clarity in explaining how the law had developed in the past, and his vision of how it should develop in the future. The former was reflected in his use of the nineteenth-century (and earlier) case law,[4] which enabled him to distinguish a twentieth-century line of more narrowly decided cases, and to establish a contextual approach to the requirements of procedural fairness in administrative decision-making, which could then be developed in subsequent cases. In a recent article on the case,[5] Professor Stephen Bailey has observed that Lord Reid's speech stands out among decisions of the House of Lords on administrative law as the first to involve extended analysis of a broad sweep of cases and to recognise that there was a need to develop a systematic approach to administrative law, while emphasising the importance of context. I agree with that assessment.

Then in 1968 came the other three cases. The first was *Conway v Rimmer*,[6] where the House was invited to reconsider its previous decisions in *Duncan v Cammell Laird & Co.*[7] Interestingly, in the light of the current expectation that such cases should be decided by an enlarged panel, it was decided by an ordinary panel of five Law Lords. The hearing lasted 13 days, and the report takes up 88 pages of the Appeal Cases. The decision disapproved what were said to be dicta in *Duncan* and held that courts should inspect documents which ministers had certified should be withheld from disclosure in legal proceedings, and decide for themselves whether the public interest required non-disclosure. If disclosure was not prejudicial to the public interest, or if the possibility of damage to the public interest was not enough to outweigh the prejudice caused by not disclosing the documents (in that case, reports about a police officer who had brought proceedings for malicious prosecution), it would be ordered. Having examined the documents, the House of Lords ordered disclosure. Lord Reid's speech exhibited all the characteristics earlier displayed in *Ridge*, and was again based on a careful analysis of nineteenth-century case law. It was more nuanced in its approach than some later cases concerned with similar subject matter, probably reflecting his practical experience of government, for example in his comments on Cabinet papers.

The next case, *Padfield v Minister of Agriculture, Fisheries and Food*,[8] was decided by an identical constitution of the Appellate Committee.[9] The case

[4] If I remember correctly, Desmond Ackner QC, who appeared for the appellant, received considerable assistance from HWR Wade.

[5] SH Bailey, '*Ridge v Baldwin* [1964]: "Nuff Said"' in S Juss and M Sunkin (eds), *Landmark Cases in Public Law* (London, Bloomsbury, 2017).

[6] [1968] AC 910.

[7] [1942] AC 624.

[8] [1968] AC 997.

[9] As in *Ridge*, the selection was not based simply on seniority: Lord Guest would then have been included in the panels for *Conway* and *Padfield*, rather than Lord Upjohn. If the panel for *Ridge v Baldwin* had been based on seniority, it would have looked very different: Lords Radcliffe, Jenkins and Guest would have sat instead of Lords Evershed, Hodson and Devlin. The panel in *Anisminic* would also have had a different look if seniority had prevailed: Lords Hodson and Guest would

concerned a refusal by the Minister to exercise a discretionary power conferred on him by statute. It established that a statutory power must be exercised in accordance with purpose of the statutory provision under which it was granted. Lord Reid's speech is again characteristic, based on general principle and citing only one authority, from the nineteenth century. *Padfield* is arguably the single most important case in administrative law, important above all for the way in which it demonstrates that the courts provide a vital element of Parliamentary democracy by keeping the executive within the limits of the powers conferred on it by legislation.

The last of these cases, *Anisminic v Foreign Compensation Commission*,[10] concerned the effect of a statutory provision which stated that the determination by the commission of any application made to them was not to be called in question in any court of law. The House of Lords held that it could nevertheless quash a decision based on a misconstruction by the commission of the provision defining its jurisdiction, since a decision taken without jurisdiction was not a determination within the meaning of the legislation, but merely a purported determination. This is the most problematical of these decisions, particularly because the way it has been interpreted in later cases is more far-reaching than anything the case itself decided.[11] Lord Reid, for example, explicitly reaffirmed the continuing existence of errors of law within jurisdiction.[12] It was speeches in later cases, particularly that of Lord Diplock in *O'Reilly v Mackman*,[13] which held that all errors of law rendered a decision void. The other aspect of the decision in *Anisminic* – that the ouster clause in question did not protect a decision made without jurisdiction – is equally controversial, but, as Lord Reid explained, it fits into a long line of authorities placing a narrow construction on ouster clauses which have the aim of preventing any judicial scrutiny of administrative action.

These four cases, especially *Ridge* and *Padfield*, have become so absorbed into legal thinking that the principles they established have become second nature even for lawyers who could not tell you the names of the authorities which established them. But administrative law is only one example of an area of the law which Lord Reid greatly influenced. One could say the same about a number of others.

Lord Reid's speeches seem to me to be especially notable for the clarity and simplicity of their language: a simplicity which he managed to combine with

have sat instead of Lords Wilberforce and Pearson. But the panels as actually constituted contained a diversity of views. In *Ridge*, Lord Evershed dissented, and Lord Devlin also adopted a different position from Lords Reid, Morris of Borth-y-Gest and Hodson on an aspect of the case. In *Padfield*, Lord Morris dissented. In *Anisminic*, Lords Morris and Pearson dissented.

10 [1969] 2 AC 147.

11 See *R (Privacy International) v Investigatory Powers Tribunal* [2019] UKSC 22 [43], [51]–[57], [128] and [181].

12 *Anisminic* (n 10) 171.

13 [1983] 2 AC 237.

a highly sophisticated analysis of the problems before him. Lord Kilbrandon wrote, after Lord Reid's death, that the last thing he would tolerate was attention to irrelevant detail.[14] That was perhaps what enabled him, in so few words,[15] to review principle, authority and policy. This he did in a tone of voice which is notable for its lucidity and absence of either intellectual overbearing or an ostentatious display of learning. I know him only from his speeches and from the recollections of others, but he is one of the judges from whom I feel that I have learned most about how an appellate judge should behave and write.

In the remainder of this chapter, I would like to begin by saying something about Lord Reid himself, as I think his experience of life, particularly before he became a judge, is relevant to his judicial philosophy. Then I would like to make some observations about his approach to developing the law: an approach which he set out most clearly in a lecture which he gave in Edinburgh in 1971, from which I have borrowed my title, although I have added a question mark for reasons which will become apparent.[16] Finally, I would like to consider the idea of the judge as lawmaker in relation to the present day.

Not long after I was appointed to the Supreme Court, I was invited to give a lecture at a university which I shall leave unnamed. Introducing me to the audience, the president of the law students' society said that it was a great honour for them to welcome me. They had studied so many of my judgments: *Hedley Byrne*,[17] *Dorset Yacht*,[18] *Conway*[19] ...

As the student introducing me failed to realise – unless, of course, I looked to him as though I might be over 120 years old – Lord Reid was born in 1890. He took a double first at Cambridge in Natural Sciences and Law. After taking a further degree in Scots law at Edinburgh University, he was admitted to the Faculty of Advocates a few weeks after the outbreak of the First World War. He is said to have been the first person to be called to the Bar wearing uniform. He served from 1914 until 1919, and saw action in several theatres, initially in an infantry regiment, the Royal Scots, and later in the Machine Gun Corps. That formative experience seems likely to be part of the explanation for Lord Reid's later involvement in public life, and his emphasis, for example in his lecture on 'The Judge as Law Maker', on respect for the views of what he called the common ordinary reasonable man.

After being demobbed, Reid began practice at the Bar. In time, he came to be recognised as an exceptionally competent counsel in handling complex cases, but he never developed a large practice, and his priority became the pursuit of

[14] (1975) *Scots Law Times* (News) 81.

[15] By modern standards, his judgments are notably short: even his leading judgments typically occupy no more than 20 pages of the law reports.

[16] Lord Reid, 'The Judge as Law Maker' (1972) 12 *Journal of the Society of Public Teachers of Law (New Series)* 22.

[17] *Hedley Byrne & Co Ltd v Heller & Partners Ltd* [1964] AC 465.

[18] *Home Office v Dorset Yacht Co Ltd* [1970] AC 1004.

[19] [1968] AC 910.

a career in politics. In 1931 he was elected to Parliament as a Unionist (in effect, a Scottish Conservative). He was to remain an MP, mostly for what was then the safe Unionist seat of Glasgow Hillhead, almost without interruption for 17 years. He served as Solicitor General for Scotland from 1936 to 1941, and as Lord Advocate from 1941 until 1945. So he had long experience as a government Law Officer, including in times of crisis. From 1945, he was a front-bench Opposition spokesman in the House of Commons, a position he combined with that of the leader of the Scottish Bar, the Dean of Faculty.

When Lord Thankerton died in 1948, the Prime Minister, Clement Attlee, invited Reid to take his place as a Law Lord. It was of course unusual for a Prime Minister to offer such a position to a front-bench Opposition spokesman, but he and Reid had worked together in Churchill's coalition Government during the war, and Attlee's Lord Chancellor, Lord Jowitt, had also worked alongside Reid as a Law Officer. Reid did not decide to accept the appointment until he had consulted the Conservative hierarchy about his prospects in a future Conservative Government (there was some thought that he might become Lord Chancellor),[20] but he did not receive adequate encouragement. So he became a Law Lord. In 1962 he succeeded Lord Simonds as the Senior Law Lord, and in that highly influential role, spurred on by the arrival of Lords Morris, Devlin and Pearce, he inaugurated a new era in the Appellate Committee. He went on to serve as a Law Lord until 1975: a period of over 26 years, longer than anyone before or since.

That period, between 1948 and 1975, was one during which British society underwent very significant changes, including the growth of the administrative state. Not the least of Reid's achievements was to steer the common law through those changes, with a confident sense of when it should be developed by the House of Lords in its judicial capacity, and when its development should be left to Parliament in its legislative role. A parallel achievement was to bring about an important evolution in the role of the final Court of Appeal. This was reflected in the Practice Statement of 1966, but also in a wider move away from a technical approach to the law, based on the fairly strict application of precedent, towards a more pragmatic approach which acknowledged that the judiciary, as well as Parliament, had a role in developing the law so as to maintain it in a condition which met the changing needs of society.

A few points might be made about this life story. First, it is extremely unlikely that anyone would now be appointed to an appellate judicial position who had no judicial experience whatsoever.[21] Secondly, it is even more unlikely that anyone would now be appointed to such a position who had immediately

[20] Sir J Simon, 'Review' (1965) 81 *LQR* 289, 294.

[21] Lord Reid is by no means the only example of a successful appointment of that nature. Lord Radcliffe, and earlier Lord Dunedin, are two other examples in the 20th century of excellent appellate judges who were appointed without any previous judicial experience. The same was true of Lord Chancellors, who often presided in the House of Lords.

beforehand been a prominent politician.[22] Thirdly, the experience which Reid had gained before becoming a judge, as a soldier, an MP and a government minister as well as an advocate, was richer than a newly appointed judge would be likely to possess today.

I think one can infer that that range of experience, as well as the developments in society which were occurring during his tenure of office as a Law Lord, influenced his conception of the role of the judge in a democracy, particularly his view of the importance of policy as a guide to judicial decision-making, his confidence in his assessment of public opinion, and his self-assurance in judging how far the courts should go in the development of the law. He spoke himself of the benefit of having at least some Law Lords with previous political experience: 'they know how the machinery of government works and are able to understand better issues concerning the administration'.[23] Of course, experience of government is not absent today: the present Justices of the Supreme Court include people with experience of working in government departments, of involvement in the preparation of Parliamentary legislation, of working on the Law Commissions, and of representing government departments as counsel. That experience is important and valuable, but it cannot be compared with the breadth and depth of Lord Reid's experience.

In the lecture from which I have taken my title, Lord Reid famously debunked the declaratory theory of the common law as a fairy tale,[24] and described judges as lawmakers. He also said in his lecture that, where the court has some freedom as to how to decide a case, it should 'have regard to common sense, legal principle and public policy in that order'.[25]

When Lord Reid spoke of the judge as lawmaker, he was referring to the judicial development of the common law. But describing judges as lawmakers risks conveying a misleading impression: hence the question mark in my title. Judges do not legislate, but in a common law system based on precedent, judicial decisions at the highest level not only authoritatively settle the point in dispute between the parties, but also, in doing so, set a precedent which is binding on lower courts before which the same point arises on a later occasion. And in doing so, the court may build on what has previously been decided in other cases and develop it further. It may also overrule decisions of lower courts which it considers erroneous, or, much less commonly, depart from its own previous

[22] This was not unprecedented in the 20th century. For example, Lord Dunedin was a Cabinet Minister in Balfour's Government immediately before his appointment as Lord President of the Court of Session. Lord Chancellors were, by their nature, politicians as well as judges. Lord Simon is one of only three people to have held the offices of Home Secretary, Foreign Secretary and Chancellor of the Exchequer, before he became Lord Chancellor. Both he and Lord Dunedin proved to be outstanding judges. There were also, of course, other appointments of politicians to the bench which were much less successful.

[23] Berlins, 'The One Judge' (1975).

[24] Lord Reid, 'The Judge as Law Maker' (1972) 22.

[25] ibid.

decisions. It is primarily in that limited sense that judges can be said to make law: I can leave to one side the more creative role which English judges adopted historically in relation to equity.[26] I had occasion to explain my conception of the judicial role in developing the common law more fully in the recent case of *Elgizouli v Secretary of State for the Home Department*.[27]

So, when Lord Reid described the judge as a lawmaker, it is important to understand the limited sense of that description. What he had in mind was primarily the development of the common law: a process which judges have undertaken continuously for over 800 years in order to enable the law to meet the ever-changing needs of society from medieval times to the present day. And they have done so not as a law reform agency, but by adjudicating on the disputes which are brought before them.

Lord Reid also saw limits to the role of the judge as lawmaker. He can be regarded as an advocate for judicial restraint as much as a proponent of judicial activism. Writing about him shortly after his death, Robert Stevens contrasted his 'cautious introverted common lawyerism' with the approach of Lord Denning, and commented that 'Reid had a more developed sense than the other law lords about areas where it was inappropriate for the judiciary to legislate even interstitially'.[28] His restraint is most obvious in criminal cases such as *Shaw v DPP*[29] (the case of the Ladies' Directory).

If I can digress from Lord Reid for a moment, it is also necessary to remember that the development of the law plays little part, if any, in the work of the vast majority of judges. Even in the work of a Law Lord such as Lord Reid, or today a Justice of the Supreme Court, it is far from being an everyday occurrence. I write perhaps four or five judgments a year which develop the law to a significant extent, and they mostly concern technical questions which have arisen in areas of the common (and therefore judge-made) law, for example in the law of contract, tort or unjust enrichment. While these are important to lawyers, they may be of limited if any interest to anyone else.

It is important to emphasise these points in the light of comments sometimes made about the methods by which judicial appointments are made in this country, particularly to the Supreme Court, when compared with the political methods of appointing Supreme Court Justices in the United States. How come in a democracy, the question is asked, that non-elected judges make law? Should they not in that case be selected through a democratic process, as in the United States?

This is to compare apples and pears. The US Supreme Court has acted, not without controversy, as a law-making body in a much more substantial sense. For

[26] See *Re Hallett's Estate* (1880) 13 Ch D 696, 710.
[27] [2020] UKSC 10 [170].
[28] R Stevens, 'Judicial Legislation and the Law Lords: Four Interpretations – II' (1975) 10 *Irish Jurist* 216, 222 and 237.
[29] [1962] AC 220.

example, it was not Congress that guaranteed abortion rights for all American women, but the Supreme Court.[30] It was not Congress that required same-sex marriage to be available across the 50 states, but the Supreme Court.[31] It is the Court that has the final word: its decisions cannot be reversed by Congress, other than by a constitutional amendment. And what it has granted, it can also take away.

In the United Kingdom, the Supreme Court does not have the power to change the law in that way, and the Justices would not want to have that power. It was Parliament which enacted the Abortion Act 1967 and the Marriage (Same Sex Couples) Act 2013, and the Scottish Parliament which enacted the Marriage and Civil Partnership (Scotland) Act 2014. British judges recognise that courts are not suited in any way to carry out the work of legislatures, and that the judiciary in this country cannot adopt the role given to the Supreme Court under the Constitution of the United States. They also see the way in which the politicised nature of the appointments process in the United States affects public debate about the courts, and public confidence in judicial decisions in controversial cases. They understand that, in the United Kingdom, the level of trust which is placed in the courts by the public, and by political institutions of different political stripes, is dependent on confidence in their political impartiality, and therefore on their appointment on a basis other than their alignment with a particular set of political values.

So the context of judicial appointments in this country is different from that in the United States. In this country, when in 2005 Parliament established the Supreme Court, and gave it the power to apply the Human Rights Act 1998 and to determine devolution issues, it also ended the system of appointments to our highest court on the recommendation of a politician, the Lord Chancellor. In its place, there was established a less politicised system of appointments which has at its heart the assessment of candidates on merit by an independent statutory commission, although there remain aspects of the procedure which retain a political character. That was the balance struck by the democratic legislature.

Returning to Lord Reid and considering next the three factors which he said were important in judges as lawmakers – common sense, legal principle and public policy, in that order – he considered it important to have regard to common sense in order to prevent the law from becoming static, and to counter what he called 'technically minded judges … inclined to press precedents to their logical conclusion'.[32] But he also considered that where public opinion was sharply divided on a matter, the question whether and how to develop the law should be left to Parliament.[33]

[30] *Roe v Wade*, 410 US 959 (1973).
[31] *Obergefell v Hodges*, 135 S Ct 2584 (2015).
[32] Lord Reid (n 16) 26.
[33] ibid 23.

His second factor was legal principle: an expression he used to refer to the broad framework of a legal subject, in distinction to the more detailed level of rules or precedents. He saw legal development as building on those principles, even though it might involve departing from precedent and the rules established by those decisions. The extent to which he saw himself as free to develop the law in that way depended to a great extent on the context, and especially on the importance of legal certainty in the particular context.

The third factor, public policy, was one to which he attached a level of importance which may reflect the context of his times, when society was undergoing rapid changes, and also the fact that appellate courts then included a number of judges, such as himself, with political or other experience of public life, often derived from wartime service in Whitehall or elsewhere. His view was that

> so long as the powers that be can see to it that the new race of judges are not mere technicians, but are men of the world as well, we can – indeed, we must – trust them to acquaint themselves with public policy and apply it in a reasonable way to such new problems as will arise from time to time.[34]

In that connection, he regarded it as 'so valuable for a judge to have given public service of some kind in his earlier days'.[35]

How relevant are these factors, and more generally the idea of the judge as lawmaker, to the present-day work of the Supreme Court? Different members of the Court may well have different views of this question, so I can only speak from a personal perspective. As it seems to me, it is necessary to take the declaratory theory more seriously than Lord Reid's description of it as a fairy tale might suggest. I certainly do not deny that judges develop the common law, and that this is a vital and legitimate aspect of their function. Lord Reid roundly guyed the idea that 'in some Aladdin's cave there is hidden the Common Law in all its splendour and that on a judge's appointment there descends on him knowledge of the magic words Open Sesame'.[36] But I doubt whether any judge in modern times has ever subscribed to the notion that there is an ideal form of the common law which the judges from time to time reveal in their decisions.

In modern practice, the declaratory theory reflects the fact that judicial decisions are necessarily backward-looking, since they decide what the law was at the time which is relevant to the dispute between the parties. They are in that sense declaratory. As Lord Reid himself said, 'judge-made law is always retrospective. We cannot say that the law until yesterday was one thing, from tomorrow it will be something different. That would indeed be legislating'.[37] The retrospective effect of judicial decisions means that, in order to preserve a reasonable measure of legal certainty, developments in the common law should

[34] ibid 27.
[35] ibid.
[36] ibid 22.
[37] ibid.

normally be based on existing principles, building on them incrementally rather than radically departing from them. Indeed, in addition to considerations of legal certainty, it seems to me to be important that the courts should recognise that there are constitutional and institutional limits to their role in developing the law, arising from the pre-eminent role of Parliament in making new law, and the limitations of litigation as an engine of law reform.

For this combination of reasons, it seems to me that when judges develop the common law, it should normally be by building incrementally on established principles. Development of the law on that basis permits the courts to introduce a new rule, or to reformulate or depart from an existing rule, while continuing to apply broader principles which form an established part of the law, and which it is therefore justifiable to apply to the case before the court.

When courts effect changes in the law which are not incremental, and which do not build on existing principles, they not only disrupt legal certainty, but they also risk creating serious and unforeseen problems in future cases. Lord Reid himself made this point forcefully in the case of *Myers v DPP*, concerned with the law of hearsay.[38] I do not deny that there may be circumstances in which a departure from settled principles can be justified – I can think of some decisions of my own which have been criticised as departing from a settled, but in my view mistaken, understanding of the law by lower courts[39] – but it seems to me that the courts have to think long and hard before they go down that path.

Lessons might, for example, be learned from the difficulties which arose in recent times as a consequence of the decisions in *Kleinwort Benson*[40] and *Deutsche Morgan Grenfell*[41] to allow the recovery of payments made on the basis of an understanding of the law which a later judicial decision retrospectively holds to have been erroneous, without any limitation period running until the later decision has been made: decisions which had the effect of exposing the Government to claims for many billions of pounds in respect of tax which had been paid decades earlier under an understanding of EU law which was later held to be erroneous; the decision in *Sempra Metals*[42] to allow the recovery of compound interest on awards based on unjust enrichment, which greatly aggravated the problems arising from *Kleinwort Benson* and *Deutsche Morgan Grenfell*, and from which the Supreme Court has recently departed;[43]

[38] [1965] AC 1001, 1021–22.

[39] As, for example, in *AXA General Insurance Ltd v The Lord Advocate* [2011] UKSC 46, *ICL Plastics Ltd v David T Morrison & Co Ltd* [2014] UKSC 48 and *Commissioners for Her Majesty's Revenue and Customs v Prudential Assurance Company Ltd* [2018] UKSC 39.

[40] *Kleinwort Benson Ltd v Lincoln City Council* [1999] 1 AC 153.

[41] *Her Majesty's Commissioners of Inland Revenue v Deutsche Morgan Grenfell Group plc* [2006] UKHL 49.

[42] *Her Majesty's Commissioners of Inland Revenue v Sempra Metals Limited* [2007] UKHL 34.

[43] *Commissioners for Her Majesty's Revenue and Customs v Prudential Assurance Company Ltd* [2018] UKSC 39.

the decision in *Attorney-General v Blake*[44] to order an account of profits as a remedy for breach of contract, which created confusion that the Supreme Court has recently attempted at least to diminish;[45] and the decision in *Fairchild*[46] to allow the recovery of damages in tort in cases of mesothelioma in the absence of proof of a 'but for' causal connection between the negligence of the defendant and the illness suffered by the claimant, a decision which has caused widening uncertainty as its ripples have spread. Each of these developments caused dislocations elsewhere in the legal system, illustrating that it can be very difficult for the court to carry out a systematic examination or evaluation of the wider implications of a radical development in the law.

Returning to the three factors to which Lord Reid suggested the judge should have regard as a lawmaker, the first was common sense. We are more suspicious of common sense today, as it can shade into preconceptions or unconscious bias. Nevertheless, I think Lord Reid was right in what he said about its importance. Notwithstanding its diversity, our society has some prevailing and enduring values which command general acceptance, and it is clearly right that judges should take them into account when developing the law. Problems can arise when courts have to decide difficult and novel cases in areas where there is no guidance provided by precedents and where no clearly prevailing norms can be discerned. Lord Reid said that such cases should be left to Parliament, and in principle I agree. But it is not always possible for the courts to do that, as Parliament sometimes enacts laws which require them to determine difficult and controversial issues. They cannot refuse to give a decision when cases are brought before them, no matter how difficult or controversial the issue raised by the case may be. Nevertheless, if one takes the Human Rights Act 1998 or the devolution statutes as examples, the way in which judges approach the application of those Acts has become increasingly settled, and similar to adjudication in other areas of the law, as time has passed, and a coherent body of legal principles has been established by a body of case law. What may have been difficult and controversial to decide becomes relatively easy and uncontroversial to apply as a precedent.

The second of Lord Reid's factors was legal principle. As I have made clear, I agree with him about its importance, and personally would place it in his first position in his list of factors.

His third factor was public policy. He observed that it had been said to be an unruly horse, but that that had been at a time when most judges had led cloistered lives. He commented that, in his own time, such judges were a much smaller proportion than they used to be, partly because most judges had had war service in the field, and partly because economic circumstances prevented most judges from living in a world of their own.

[44] [2001] 1 AC 268.
[45] *One Step (Support) Ltd v Morris-Garner* [2018] UKSC 20.
[46] *Fairchild v Glenhaven Funeral Services Ltd* [2002] UKHL 22.

Although judges today have not had wartime service, many of them have given public service of some other kind, and they certainly do not live in a world of their own. Nevertheless, it seems to me that public policy has only a limited role to play in judicial reasoning. As Justice Scalia once said:

> As every law student learns, one finds in a very wide range of cases indeed, that arguments – rational, persuasive, decent arguments – can be made on both sides of the question. The law thus requires real choices from both judges and lawyers, but it informs those choices, which should not be merely a matter of preference or calculation, but should rather express the result of the mind's engagement with the materials of the law.[47]

So in hard cases, although there may be some judges of a pragmatic cast of mind who decide on their preferred outcome from a policy perspective, and then reason backwards to find an acceptable legal route to that conclusion, most senior judges adopt a more principled approach. They worry and lose sleep over legal problems, and struggle to solve them. Their decision may turn on their understanding of the deep structure of a branch of the law, or of its historical development, or of the construction which will best give effect to the meaning of an obscure provision in an Act of Parliament, or on what might be described as their judicial philosophy. But the resultant decision is the product of a diligent and honest effort to apply the law.

Of course, when considering whether the common law should be developed, courts will consider what the practical implications might be. The practice has developed, particularly in the Supreme Court, of allowing interventions by bodies whose experience may help the court in making that assessment. Nevertheless, the courts are not policymakers in the same sense as a Law Commission or a government department.

In summary, if judges are to make law – and I accept that they should do, in some circumstances – it should, in my view, normally be by developing existing principles. Cases which come before the courts may demonstrate that a particular rule established by past decisions should be modified or departed from, but that should normally be done only in so far as it is consistent with the continued application of the wider principles of the relevant area of the law. By applying those principles, judges do no more and no less than fulfil their oaths, to do right to all manner of people 'after the laws and usages of this realm'.

[47] JB White and Jeanne Gaakeer, 'Interview with James Boyd White' (2007) 105 *Michigan Law Review* 1403, 1418.

Part II

The Quartet in Context

3

Ridge v Baldwin: *Executive and Judicial Approaches to Administrative Law Before and During the Quartet Years*

ROBERT THOMAS*

I. INTRODUCTION

EXAMINING CASES IS an essential part of what we lawyers do. Considering precedents and arguing about what they really decided and how they should be interpreted is part of the tangled relationship between law and history. And this is itself only part of our own complex and paradoxical relationships that we as human beings have with the past. From one perspective, 'the past is a foreign country. They do things differently there'.[1] Cases from the past show us characters and people now long gone whose lives, relationships and conduct by chance resulted in a court decision that is still cited today as authority for some legal principle. These cases give us a glimpse into a world long since overtaken by new events and changes and which now seems very different to us today. Yet, at the same time, 'the past is never dead. It's not even past'.[2] Despite all the changes of time, the world we inhabit is fundamentally the same world as existed in the past. It is governed by the same timeless features of human nature. Similarly, because law is so often path-dependent, cases from the past are still relevant and many continue to comprise part of our intellectual legal background and memory. They come to be reinterpreted and seen as part of wider trends that often only become discernible in retrospect. Memory shapes not just the past, but also potentially the present and the future.

This chapter considers the background to and importance of the first of the Quartet cases. *Ridge v Baldwin*, 'the Magna Carta of natural justice', was

[1] LP Hartley, *The Go Between* (London, Penguin, 2004).
[2] W Faulkner, *Requiem for a Nun* (London, Vintage, 1996).

immediately recognised as 'the most important case to have been decided in recent years on the general principles governing judicial review of administrative action'.[3] The case will forever be associated with the reinvigoration of natural justice in administrative law and the common law right of a person to be heard by a public authority before an important decision is to be taken. The House of Lords decided that the decision of the Watch Committee of the Brighton Police Force to dismiss its Police Constable, Mr Charles Ridge, was null and void because the committee had neither given any notification of the charges nor any opportunity for Ridge to be heard. The wider message from the case was that natural justice no longer applied solely to decisions of a judicial nature. It also applied to decisions taken by administrative bodies that affected the rights and interests of individuals. By overturning the 'administrative-judicial' analytical model, the clear signal was that natural justice applied more broadly and that its content would depend on the specific context involved.

From a wider perspective *Ridge* marked a more fundamental turning point in the general posture of the judiciary toward judicial control of administrative action. Hitherto, the approach of the higher courts had been one of legal formalism: judicial minimalism; strict adherence to precedent; and a general reluctance to review government decisions despite the expansion of administrative power. *Ridge* signalled a new approach: a more expansive method toward judicial intervention; the collapsing of formalist analytical distinctions; and a move away from precedent toward a focus on underlying principles. Precisely why and how did this change of attitude come about? Legal doctrine alone cannot provide an answer. Courts analyse, apply and develop doctrine, but are also deeply embedded within their wider political, social and economic environment which conditions and influences what they do. The argument advanced here is that the change in judicial attitudes did not emerge from nowhere and the courts were not acting unilaterally. Instead, the change in the wider mood music of *Ridge* and the three other Quartet cases should be seen as a response to the lead already largely taken by the Government and Parliament following deep public unease concerning arbitrary administration and the lack of available remedies.

II. THE BACKGROUND

Ridge v Baldwin arose from The Great Conspiracy Case, the investigation and prosecution of police officers from the Brighton Police Force, including the Chief Constable, Mr Charles Ridge in the late 1950s. This episode has long faded from public memory and was soon overshadowed by the much more salacious Profumo scandal (1963). Nonetheless, at the time, the Brighton police

[3] [1964] AC 40; CK Allen, *Laws and Orders*, 3rd edn (London, Stevens & Sons, 1965) 242; SA de Smith, 'The House of Lords on Natural Justice' (1963) 26 *MLR* 543.

conspiracy case was the most intensive and highly publicised investigation ever conducted into the conduct of a British police force.

On 2 October 1957, it was publicly announced that police officers from the Metropolitan Police had, for some months, been investigating claims of bribery and corruption in the Brighton police force. On 25 October, two police officers – Heath and Hammersley – were arrested along with two other men, Bellson and Lyons, and charged with conspiring to obstruct justice. The Chief Constable of the Brighton force, Charles Ridge, was suspended from his duties by the Watch Committee. Ridge had been an officer in the Brighton force since 1925, starting off as a constable. In 1956, Ridge had been one of five candidates to become Chief Constable and had been interviewed and appointed by the Watch Committee.

In late 1957, the committal trial of Heath, Hammersley, Bellson and Lyons was heard by Brighton Magistrates' Court. It is an indication of how seriously the issue was taken within Government that the prosecution was led by the Solicitor-General, Sir Harry Hylton-Foster QC MP.[4] The committal trial last for 10 days and generated much public and media interest.[5] The magistrates decided to commit all of the defendants for trial. Ridge was later charged with conspiring to obstruct the course of justice. The charges related to events between 1949 and 1957. The criminal trial was held before Donovan J at the Central Criminal Court in 1958. Hammersley, Heath and Bellson were convicted. Ridge was acquitted. In his sentencing remarks, the judge, Donovan J, speaking to Hammersley and Heath said: 'neither of you had that professional and moral leadership which both of you should have had and were entitled to expect from the chief constable of Brighton'. Although they had acted with 'the nod' from Ridge, the prosecution found it impossible to substantiate the charges against him.

In March 1958, Ridge pleaded not guilty to a second indictment for corruptly receiving money for showing favour to the person concerned. However, the prosecution, led by the Solicitor-General, decided not to offer any evidence. In doing so, the prosecution had taken into account of Ridge's previous acquittal and concluded that there was no realistic prospect of a conviction. Having directed the jury to give formal verdicts of not guilty, Ridge left the dock. Donovan J then directly addressed the Solicitor-General:

> It is not difficult now, however, to foresee the use to which the incidents I mentioned, and others like them to be found in the case, will or may be put for the purpose of discrediting the officers of that force when they give evidence in future prosecutions, and the results in some cases may be unfortunate. This prospect and this risk will remain until a leader is given to the force who will be a new influence, and who will set a different example from that which has lately obtained. I realise that this is a matter which is about to engage the attention of those persons whose responsibility

[4] Later Speaker of the House of Commons (1959–65).

[5] For a detailed account, see D Rowland, *Bent Cops: The Brighton Conspiracy Trial* (Peacehaven, Finsbury Publishing, 2007).

> it is, and I have no desire to trespass upon their domain, but since the matter will also affect the administration of justice in the courts, I felt it right to make these observations.[6]

Ridge had been acquitted – but it was a scathing and damning acquittal.

Events then moved quickly. The Watch Committee, the local government body then responsible for overseeing its local police force, met the next day and dismissed Ridge for being unfit to continue in office.[7] The previous night, the chairman of the Brighton Watch Committee, Councillor GB Baldwin, had said that neither Ridge nor his solicitor would be allowed to attend the meeting.[8] For Ridge, dismissal meant not just loss of salary, but also his pension.

Ridge's solicitors immediately wrote to the Home Secretary contending that the Watch Committee had acted contrary to natural justice and unlawfully. When Ridge's solicitor, a Mr Bosley, later appeared in person before the Watch Committee, he was 'received with courtesy but in silence' and was not given any further information.[9] By a majority, the Watch Committee maintained its previous decision. In October 1958, Ridge commenced his legal action for a declaration that his dismissal was ultra vires and for the payment of his salary or pension.

III. THE HIGH COURT AND THE COURT OF APPEAL

Ridge's case was dismissed by both the High Court and the Court of Appeal.[10] In the High Court, Streatfeild J dealt with the natural justice ground relatively briefly: Ridge had received natural justice because he had been able to speak in his own defence during the criminal trial; 'there was no need for the Watch Committee to do other than they in fact did'.[11] The Court of Appeal amplified this conclusion. Holroyd-Pierce LJ held that the Watch Committee was not obliged to follow natural justice. The committee was making an administrative decision and was not engaged in judicial or quasi-judicial proceedings. Both Harman LJ and Davies LJ were sympathetic to the argument that, had the rules of natural justice applied, then Ridge would have been denied fairness.[12] Nevertheless, the court held firm to the administrative–judicial divide: 'in dismissing the plaintiff, the defendants were acting in an administrative or executive capacity, just as they did when they appointed him'.[13] Both courts took a very dim view of Ridge's behaviour. Ridge had 'convicted himself of

[6] *Ridge* (n 3) 45.
[7] Municipal Corporations Act 1882, s 191.
[8] 'Police Need of "Leader"' *The Times* (7 March 1958).
[9] *Ridge* (n 3) 47.
[10] *Ridge v Baldwin* [1963] 1 QB 539.
[11] ibid 556 (Streatfeild J).
[12] ibid 577 (Harman LJ); 582 (Davies LJ).
[13] ibid 576 (Harman LJ).

unfitness before the world at the Old Bailey … Any further hearing … would have been a waste of time'.[14]

IV. NATURAL JUSTICE PRE-*RIDGE*

How had the law come to this? Long before the nineteenth century revolution in government, natural justice had been applied by the courts to both judicial decisions and non-judicial decisions. Venerable cases such as *Bagg's Case* and *Bentley's case* demonstrated clearly how natural justice applied to adjudicative decisions taken by non-judicial entities such as local boroughs and universities.[15] This approach was maintained in the 1830s, the decade in which 'administrative law', broadly defined, first came into existence.[16] Nineteenth century case law is replete with cases applying natural justice beyond the strict confines of judicial decision-making. Judges held 'a persistent assumption' that common law standards of procedural fairness applied to new forms of decision-making.[17] Natural justice was applied to local corporations, administrative decisions by Justices, and also to ecclesiastical decisions – not least by the Archbishop of Canterbury.[18]

The classic case is *Cooper v. Wandsworth Board of Works* (1863) in which the right to a hearing was said to be 'of universal application, and founded on the plainest principles of justice'.[19] *Cooper* is now a justly celebrated case – in large part because of its resurrection in *Ridge*. At the time, though, *Cooper* was an entirely unexceptional application of established principles. As Anderson notes:

> The principle's breadth and the heterogeneity of the situations to which it was being applied may explain why the decision in *Cooper* v. *Wandsworth Board of Works* in 1863, which a century later became an obligatory point of reference, caused no excitement at the time.[20]

In announcing that 'the justice of the common law will supply the omission of the legislature' Byles J had been merely paraphrasing Paley's 1814 textbook to the effect that 'even where the statutes are silent … magistrates … are

[14] ibid 570 (Holroyd-Pierce LJ).

[15] *James Bagg's Case* (1615) 11 Co Rep 93b, 77 ER 1271, 1 Str 557; *Dr Bentley's case* (1723) Fort 202, 92 ER 818; (1724) 2 Ld Raym 1334, 93 ER 698; S Anderson, 'Judicial Review' in J Baker (ed), *The Oxford History of the Laws of England Volume XI: 1820–1914: English Legal System* (Oxford, Oxford University Press, 2010) 506–10.

[16] CT Carr, *Concerning English Administrative Law* (New York, Columbia University Press, 1941) ch 1.

[17] Anderson, 'Judicial Review' (2010) 506.

[18] *R v Archbishop of Canterbury* (1859) 1 Ellis and Ellis 545; 120 ER 1014.

[19] *Cooper v Wandsworth Board of Works* (1863) 14 CBNS 180, 190.

[20] Anderson (n 15) 508.

nevertheless bound to observe the rules of natural justice'.[21] Natural justice was widely thought to apply to non-judicial decisions. In 1874 Kelly CB noted that the right to a fair hearing was 'not confined to the conduct of strictly legal tribunals, but is applicable to every tribunal or body of persons invested with authority to adjudicate upon matters involving civil consequences to individuals'.[22] The right to a fair hearing was applied with vigour to the statutory tribunals and decision-making bodies during the nineteenth century.[23]

What then happened in the twentieth century? The courts started well with Lord Loreburn's recognition that the need to proceed fairly was 'a duty lying upon everyone who decides anything'.[24] But *Arlidge* muddied the water.[25] The House of Lords seemed to pour scorn on the whole idea of natural justice. Conscious of imposing traditional judicial methods upon administrative officers – 'a usurpation' – the judges went too far the other way.[26] After the Second World War, two decisions confirmed the wrong turn: *Nakkuda Ali* and *Parker*. In the first, the Privy Council upheld the revocation of a textile dealer's licence without a hearing because the proceedings were administrative not judicial.[27] In *Parker*, the High Court held that the refusal by the Metropolitan Police Commissioner to hear a witness before revoking a taxi driver's licence was not contrary to natural justice: the Commissioner had not been exercising any judicial or quasi-judicial function, but merely making a disciplinary decision.[28]

By the 1950s, the full implications of this doctrinal rigidity in the face of expanding administrative activity were apparent. Scholars were in despair. Wade wrote about 'the twilight of natural justice'.[29] In 1955, de Smith noted that 'the salutary principle of *audi alteram partem* has lately shown disturbing signs of debility'.[30] The courts would ensure inferior courts acted in accordance with natural justice, but there had been an 'unfortunate derogation from the full rigour of this doctrine' by the High Court in its supervision of administrative bodies.[31]

Why this decline? First, the courts assumed that natural justice could only mean the panoply of full judicial court-like procedures and that it only applied

[21] *Cooper v Wandsworth Board of Works* (1863) 14 CBNS 180, 194; W Paley, *Summary Convictions*, 1st edn (London, Pheney, 1814) 16–17.

[22] *Wood v Woad* (1874) LR 9 Ex 190, 196.

[23] C Stebbings, *Legal Foundations of Tribunals in Nineteenth Century England* (Cambridge, Cambridge University Press, 2006) 263.

[24] *Board of Education v Rice* [1911] AC 179, 182.

[25] *Local Government Board v Arlidge* [1915] AC 120.

[26] ibid 138 (Lord Shaw).

[27] *Nakkuda Ali v Jayaratne* [1951] AC 66.

[28] *R v Metropolitan Police Commissioner, ex parte Parker* [1953] 1 WLR 1150.

[29] HWR Wade, 'The Twilight of Natural Justice?' (1951) 67 *LQR* 103.

[30] SA de Smith, 'The Right to a Hearing in English Administrative Law' (1955) 68 *Harvard Law Review* 569, 588.

[31] *Rule of Law: A Study by the Inns of Court Conservative and Unionist Society* (London, Conservative Political Centre, 1957) 46.

to decision-makers which had to act 'judicially', that is, to act as an adjudicator determining a *lis inter partes*, a dispute between two parties. Absent the triangular judicial model of adjudicator and two private parties, no duty to act judicially – and hence no natural justice – arose. Simply put, there was a lack of judicial imagination to envisage how the courts could require fair and flexible procedures that were less formal than those of used in adversarial trials. Combined with the highly formalistic judicial culture and rigid application of precedent, the courts had tied their own hands. The old Victorian cases applying fair procedure to administrative decisions lay 'neglected and half-forgotten, in the shadows of the past'.[32] Second, the new administrative legislation governing housing, slum clearance and town and country planning had laid down relatively detailed procedural provisions. There was distinct judicial reluctance to interfere in 'administrative' decisions taken by ministers given ministerial responsibility and the wider-ranging policy considerations involved in such decisions. Such 'policy' decisions came to be viewed as the archetypal administrative law controversies even though a good deal of administrative decision-making involved 'individualised' decisions.[33]

Of course, the decline of natural justice reflected the wider judicial malaise. In 1955, Lord Devlin noted that the common law no longer possessed 'the strength to provide any satisfactory solution to the problem of keeping the executive ... under proper control'.[34] Lord Denning was prepared to meet the challenge, but was in a minority.[35] The consensus view was that by the mid-1950s, English law was

> living in a state of decayed gentility. We maintain the façade and mouth the clichés which belong to better days which are past, while all the time we have come to tolerate an arbitrariness in governmental administration which not infrequently produces the rankest of injustices.[36]

In summary, by the 1950s, the courts were failing to supervise large tranches of the administrative process. It was not the case that only sensitive areas of government – immigration, criminal justice and prisons – were beyond judicial control. The courts were unwilling to assert any effective oversight in almost all types of administrative decision-making.

Change was required, but this needed high-calibre judicial leadership. Lord Denning had made some important steps, but others had to join in.[37] Enter Lord Reid. James Reid was in a uniquely strong position to lead the

[32] de Smith, 'The Right to a Hearing' (1955) 593.

[33] de Smith (n 30) 593.

[34] P Devlin, 'The Common Law, Public Policy and the Executive' (1956) 9 *Current Legal Problems* 1, 14.

[35] A Denning, *Freedom Under the Law* (London, Stevens & Sons, Hamlyn Lectures, 1947).

[36] FH Newark, Book review (1955) 71 *LQR* 571.

[37] *R v Northumberland Compensation Appeal Tribunal, ex parte Shaw* [1952] 1 KB 338; *R v Medical Appeal Tribunal, ex parte Gilmore* [1957] 1 QB 574.

judicial development of administrative law. He had long experience of both politics and administration. A Conservative and Unionist MP for Stirling and Falkirk (1931–35) and Glasgow Hillhead (1937–48), Reid had held office as Solicitor-General for Scotland (1936–41) and Lord Advocate (1941–45). Given his background, Reid had the experience to act as an administrative law judge in a very similar way to members of the French Conseil d'Etat.[38] Unusually, Reid had been appointed direct to the Appellate Committee of the House of Lords in 1948 despite his lack of prior judicial experience.[39] When Aneurin Bevan as Labour Health Secretary noted his fear of 'judicial sabotage of socialist legislation', Reid had been the Tory shadow spokesman.[40] All this experience gave Reid a deep awareness as a judge of what was both politically and administratively possible when developing judicial review of administrative action.[41]

V. *RIDGE* IN THE LORDS

It is therefore Lord Reid's speech in *Ridge* that deserves close analysis. While all five of the Law Lords gave separate speeches, only Reid's speech is likely to be read today.

Having briefly set out the facts, Reid noted that 'the authorities on the applicability of the principles of natural justice as in some confusion',[42] thereby identifying his task. Noting that the right to be heard 'goes back many centuries in our law and appears in a multitude of judgments of judges of the highest authority', Reid dismissed modern opinion that natural justice is so vague as to be practically meaningless, a view 'tainted by the perennial fallacy that because something cannot be cut and dried or nicely weighed or measured therefore it does not exist'.[43] The principal source of the confusion was the failure to pay sufficient attention to the differences between the kinds of cases to which natural justice had been sought to be applied; 'what a minister ought to do in considering objections to a scheme may be very different from what a watch committee ought to do in considering whether to dismiss a police constable'.[44] There were three kinds of cases: dismissal of a servant by a master; dismissal from an office held during pleasure; and dismissal from office where there must be something against a man to warrant dismissal. As regards the last category, Reid found an unbroken line of authority that dismissal could not take effect without notification of the allegations and a hearing. Ridge's case fell within

[38] CJ Hamson, *Executive Discretion and Judicial Control: An Aspect of the French Conseil d'Etat* (London, Stevens & Sons, 1954).

[39] Reid became Senior Law Lord in 1962 and retired in 1975 aged 84.

[40] *Hansard* HC (series 5) Vol 425 col 1983 (23 July 1946) (Aneurin Bevan MP).

[41] M Berlins, 'The One Judge We Will Really Miss' *The Times* (14 January 1975).

[42] *Ridge* (n 3) 64.

[43] ibid 64–65.

[44] ibid 65.

the third category: dismissal from office where there must be something against a person to warrant dismissal.

After four or five pages, Reid had said enough to dispose the case: 'Stopping there, I would think that authority was wholly in favour of the Appellant'.[45] However, further consideration was required because the Watch Committee's argument had been based on recent case law concerning the applicability of natural justice to decisions by ministers, officials and other bodies of various kinds. It was these more recent cases, such as *Nakkuda Ali*, that Reid wanted to undermine:

> It appears to me that if the present case had arisen thirty or forty years ago the Courts would have had no difficulty in deciding this issue in favour of the Appellant on the authorities which I have cited. So far as I am aware none of these authorities has ever been disapproved or even doubted. Yet the Court of Appeal have decided this issue against the Appellant on more recent authorities which apparently justify that result. How has this come about?[46]

Reid noted three factors. First, there had been many cases concerning decisions made by ministers and other bodies in which the courts had held that natural justice had limited application. Second, there were war-time cases. Third, the judgment of Atkin LJ in *Electricity Commissioners* had been misunderstood. As regards the first, Reid noted that decisions by a Board of Works dealing with a single isolated case was not, like a judge in a lawsuit, deciding the legal rights of the person; it was deciding how an individual ought to be treated. Policy factors could play some part in the decision. Nonetheless, in such an individualised adjudication context, the public body would be performing a quasi-judicial task in considering and deciding the matter. It would then be required to apply natural justice. This was to be contrasted, Reid explained, with the exercise of ministerial powers of a very different character – such as the construction of an important new road. Such decisions involved the consideration of other matters in addition to the rights of individual landowners, such as the public interest and the viability of alternative options. Natural justice did apply to individualised adjudicative decisions taken by administrative bodies, but not to the exercise of policy discretion. Lord Reid then stated:

> We do not have a developed system of administrative law – perhaps because until fairly recently we did not need it. So it is not surprising that in dealing with new types of cases the courts have had to grope for solutions, and have found that old powers, rules and procedure are largely inapplicable to cases which they were never designed or intended to deal with. But I see nothing in that to justify our thinking that our old methods are any less applicable today than ever they were to the older types of case. And if there are any dicta in modern authorities which point in that direction, then in my judgment they should not be followed.[47]

[45] ibid 67–68.
[46] ibid 71.
[47] ibid 72–73.

Reid then resolved the misunderstanding of a much-quoted passage of Atkin LJ in *Electricity Commissioners* and the gloss placed upon it by Lord Hewart CJ.[48] *Nakkuda Ali* was then comprehensively demolished; that ruling had been 'given under a serious misapprehension of the effect of the older authorities' and therefore could no longer be regarded as authoritative.[49]

Summarising his position, Reid noted that it was 'abundantly clear from the authorities I have quoted that at the time the courts would have rejected any' contention that the Watch Committee was not obliged to hear Ridge's defence before dismissing him.[50] Accordingly, Ridge could not be dismissed with being informed of the case against him and a proper opportunity to present his defence. After then mopping up the remaining issues, Ridge's dismissal was declared null and void.

The other speeches deserve briefer mention. Compared with contemporary speeches, it is striking just how rambling and unnecessarily long and discursive some of the other speeches are. Lord Reid aside, there is little sense of the Appellate Committee as a collective entity demonstrating judicial leadership on a major legal-policy issue of wider importance. There is no indication that the other judges were thinking more broadly about due process in the administrative state as a means of developing administrative law controls over government. As Lord Reid himself later noted, 'the purpose of an appeal to the House of Lords is not so much to benefit the parties to a dispute, but to clarify the law on a matter of public importance'.[51] It is not apparent that the other Law Lords were aware of this. The remaining speeches are also a salutary reminder that the case concerned issues other than natural justice – the application of the Police Discipline Regulations 1952 and the apparently vexed matter of whether a breach of natural justice rendered a decision void or voidable. Importantly, Lord Hodson drew two points from the case law. First, the absence of a *lis* or dispute between opposing parties was not a decisive feature against the applicability of natural justice, though the presence of a *lis* would require natural justice. Second, whether the decision-maker was acting judicially in an executive or administrative capacity was irrelevant; the courts had previously held that administrative decisions were subject to natural justice.[52]

Lord Reid's notebook provides some insight into what the other four Law Lords said at the conference following the hearing.[53] The handwriting can be difficult to decipher. Nevertheless, it is apparent that there are differences in

[48] *R v Electricity Commissioners, ex parte London Electricity Joint Committee Co* [1924] 1 KB 171, 205 (Atkin LJ); *R v Legislative Committee of the Church Assembly, ex parte Haynes-Smith* [1928] 1 KB 411, 415 (Lord Hewart CJ).

[49] *Ridge* (n 3) 79. See also at 77: 'nothing short of a decision of this House directly in point would induce me to accept the position that … our law is so defective that a subject cannot bring up such a decision for review however seriously he may be affected'.

[50] ibid.

[51] Berlins, 'The One Judge' (1975).

[52] Ridge (n 3) 130.

[53] Thanks to Alan Paterson for sharing.

emphasis between what the Law Lords said at the conference and the content of their speeches. First, the Watch Committee which features so strongly in the speeches is not mentioned once in the notebook. Second, three of the Law Lords (Hodson, Morris and Evershed) mention natural justice whereas four of them (Devlin, Hodson, Morris and Evershed) mention the 'exclusion of certiorari' provision in section 220 of the 1882 Act. This provision excluded *certiorari* from any matter made or done under the Act, but it did not feature prominently in the speeches. Interestingly, Lord Devlin explicitly mentioned de Smith – a clear sign that at least some of the Law Lords took seriously the views of leading academic lawyers. Evershed revealed that he did not agree with his colleagues on natural justice so his dissent was flagged up at an early stage.

VI. AFTER THE LORDS

Ridge resigned immediately following judgment by the Lords. He had started his action to secure payment of his salary (£1,990 – £41,985 in today's money) or, alternatively, his annual pension of £1,070 (£22,575 today). As it turned out, Ridge ended up with both his salary arrears and pension – and legal costs.

Ridge had taken a huge gamble on an issue – the doctrinal development of administrative law – that would otherwise have meant nothing to him.[54] He had the immense good fortune to have had his case heard by Lord Reid. There was evidence that Ridge had engaged in some very dubious activities. And, despite losing his job, it had turned out quite well for Ridge personally as he retained his pension. The wider lesson? Failing to follow fair process gives the upper hand to those whose cases otherwise lack merit.

VII. THE CHANGING CLIMATE TOWARD ADMINISTRATIVE LAW

By longstanding judicial and academic tradition, the 1960s are typically seen as the defining period in which the English courts rejuvenated judicial review. But this simplistic approach overlooks what the courts were responding to. Arguably, the real formative decade was the 1950s.

The Crichel Down affair (1954), the Franks Committee[55] (1957) and the Tribunals and Inquiries Act 1958 are now almost entirely forgotten. They no longer feature prominently, if at all, in today's administrative law courses. Yet, the debate they prompted – the so-called 'Franks spirit' – was a

[54] One wonders: did Chief Constable Charles Ridge always make policing and personnel decisions in accordance with the same standards of natural justice that he demanded from the Watch Committee?

[55] Franks Committee, *Report of the Committee on Administrative Tribunals and Enquiries* (1957) Cmd 218.

pivotal moment. There was a new emerging view toward administrative law from the public, government and both political parties. Public attitudes toward administration were changing and there was a much greater recognition of the dangers of administrative injustice and unfair procedures. This in turn prompted both the Government and Parliament to reform administrative law. Judicial review had been largely moribund, but the Government had clearly wanted an expansion of administrative law controls over the bureaucracy. The episode generated a powerful force for reform and improvement. The legacy of this would subsequently exert substantial influence over the courts. By the time the courts decided the Quartet cases in the 1960s, they were not so much leading the way, but playing catch-up with both public opinion and legislative policy.

Following its landslide victory in 1945, the Labour Government set about creating the welfare state and nationalising various industries. Given its commitment to central economic planning, nationalisation and the welfare state, Labour saw a strong powerful executive as an essential pre-condition for implementing its socialist policies. There were deep suspicions within Labour that unelected conservative elements in the constitution – the House of Lords and the judiciary – would obstruct its programme for government. Labour politicians were especially resistant to legal oversight of social welfare system. They distrusted judges and put their faith in political institutions.[56] On the other side of the debate, there had been warnings from Hayek's *The Road to Serfdom* against the risks to liberty and the rule of law presented by economic planning. However, such concerns were largely of interest only to those with fringe interests. The post-war consensus between the two parties was in favour of a mixed economy, Keynesianism and the welfare state.

By the early 1950s, neither of the political parties had much interest in providing people with remedies against the state. Yet, the growth of administrative power had generated deep public unease about the lack of sufficient safeguards for the individual against the arbitrary administration. Such concern arose from various administrative schemes, some of which directly affected property rights such as: better housing; town and country planning; and securing efficient agricultural production. Agricultural land tribunals proved to be a particularly controversial issue. Other controversies centred upon schemes concerning welfare provision, such as pension appeals, medical appeals and national insurance appeals.[57]

Debate about administrative law was nothing new. A generation earlier the Donoughmore Committee had reported on ministerial powers. However, that committee had been largely prompted by Lord Hewart's concerns over the

[56] At the same time, the Labour Government introduced the following important legal reforms: Statutory Instruments Act 1946; Crown Proceedings Act 1947; and Legal Aid and Assistance Act 1949.

[57] See contributions to the three volumes of the journal *British Journal of Administrative Law* (1954–56), edited by JAG Griffith and subsequently retitled *Public Law*.

constitutional propriety of administrative tribunals and delegated legislation. The important difference with the situation in the 1950s was that there was now much more public concern about administrative injustice. The scale of administrative decision-making had increased substantially, but without a corresponding increase in judicial control. There were also concerns over the effectiveness of tribunals.[58] They were not obliged to give reasons for decisions. Legal representation was not allowed and legal aid unavailable. Government departments saw their tribunals as mere appendages and controlled appointments and procedures. Furthermore, it was apparent that parliamentary control provided no effective safeguard for individuals aggrieved by official injustice.

Matters came to a head with the Crichel Down affair, which uncovered government ineptitude and became a beacon for many other similar grievances. As Wade put it, 'the storm over that case touched off a large accumulation of discontents connected with the more formal proceedings of tribunals and public inquiries'.[59] By 1955, the 'climate of opinion' toward administrative law had altogether changed.[60] Both the Labour and Conservative parties became acutely aware of the problems of administrative justice and the need both to do something and to be seen to be doing something. The parties might have approached the issue from quite starting points, but had arrived at essentially the same conclusion: there was a real need to reform and improve administrative law.

Following Crichel Down, the complacencies of the Conservatives was thoroughly shaken-up and abruptly replaced by a desire to stand up for the little man against the state. There were concerns that the 'Crichel Down disease' had infected other ministries. The Inns of Court Conservative and Unionist Society published an influential report, 'Rule of Law', with wide-ranging recommendations, including the establishment of an Administrative Division of the High Court. The 1955 Conservative election manifesto contained a commitment to appoint a 'strong advisory Committee ... to give practical attention to these problems of administrative law and recommend action' for improving the machinery of tribunals, of public inquiries and of departmental decisions affecting individual interests and property.[61]

Views within Labour similarly changed. Richard Crossman, a leading left-wing Labour MP, was concerned that the Conservatives would use Crichel Down to monopolise the debate and to argue against the use of executive power for socialist ends. Crossman sought to reframe the debate. He wrote that 'the growth of a vast centralised state bureaucracy constitutes a grave potential threat to social democracy. The idea that we are being disloyal to our socialist principles if we attack its excesses or defend the individual against its incipient

[58] See, eg, RSW Pollard (ed), *Administrative Tribunals at Work* (London, Stevens & Sons, 1950).

[59] HWR Wade, 'Tribunal and Inquiries Act, 1958' (1958) 16 *Cambridge Law Journal* 129, 130.

[60] WA Robson, 'Administrative Justice and Injustice: A Commentary on the Franks Report' [1958] *PL* 12.

[61] Conservative Party Election Manifesto (1955).

despotism is a fallacy'.[62] Reform of the judiciary was needed to protect individuals against the state and against any concentration of power – public or private. Pamphlets followed containing many recommendations for reform that were subsequently adopted by the Franks Committee.[63] Overall, the Franks process stimulated wide-ranging and innovative thinking concerning the values and structure of administrative law, some of which would take many years to come about. For instance, Robson's proposed general administrative appeals tribunal can be seen eventually reflected in the creation of the First-tier and Upper Tribunals in 2008.

There was then broad agreement between the political parties. The real opposition was not the official opposition, but the permanent civil service.[64] There was indeed a rearguard action from Whitehall. Sir Humphrey feared the creation of a general tribunal with a wide-ranging jurisdiction to reverse all types of government decisions and thereby weaken ministerial responsibility. As Arvind and Stirton note, 'The Permanent Secretaries' plan was ultimately successful. The Franks Committee's terms of reference were deliberately restricted to situations where an appeal or review before a final decision was taken was already provided'.[65] Nonetheless, Whitehall could not obstruct the general spirit of discontent and the need for government and Parliament to respond.

The Franks Report was published in July 1957 and the Government accepted most of its recommendations. The Tribunals and Inquiries Act 1958, arguably the major development of statutory administrative law in the post-war period, was enacted swiftly. The Act itself was relatively short, but contained important measures such as the creation of the Council on Tribunals, the introduction of reason-giving by tribunals, appeals from tribunals to the courts, and a no-ouster clause provision. As Wade put it, the 1958 Act certainly resembled Magna Carta and the Bill of Rights 1688 in one respect: it was 'a bundle of heterogeneous provisions aimed at practical problems'.[66]

But the significance of the Act was not just its technical provisions. What is more important for current purposes is that the Act embodied a wider and decisive policy choice by both the Government and Parliament to reform and improve administrative law remedies. Speaking for the Bill at second reading in July 1958, Rab Butler MP, Home Secretary, told the Commons:

> It is a long time since Parliament deliberately legislated to regulate the balance between the individual and the State. The growth, during the past quarter of a century, of great welfare services and the larger measure of equality which they have brought about have increased, rather than diminished, the need for strengthening the

[62] RHS Crossman, *Socialism and the New Despotism* (Fabian tract No 298) 6.

[63] Labour Party, *Personal Freedom: Labour's Policy for the Individual and Society* (London, Labour Party, 1956); G Borrie, *Justice and the Administration* (Fabian Research Series, No 185, 1957).

[64] *Hansard* HC (series 5) Vol 590 col 1655 (3 July 1958) (Charles Fletcher-Cooke MP) – a member of the Inns of Court Conservative and Unionist Society.

[65] TT Arvind and L Stirton, 'The Curious Origins of Judicial Review' (2017) 133 *LQR* 91, 104.

[66] Wade, 'Tribunal and Inquiries Act, 1958' (1958) 131.

> processes whereby the citizen can be satisfied that he is being fairly and considerately treated. To make these processes more judicial in kind and to ensure their subjection to the courts on matters of law is a powerful way of giving the citizen this satisfaction. De Tocqueville put it like this: 'The strength of the courts of law has ever been the greatest security which can be offered to personal independence; but this is more especially the case in democratic ages: private rights and interests are in constant danger if the judicial power does not grow more extensive and more strong to keep pace with the growing equality of conditions.' It is in that spirit that we commend the Bill to the House.[67]

Increased administrative power had limited individual freedom. Irrespective of the political rights or wrongs of that, 'what is wrong is that the judicial system – the courts of law, tribunals and inquiries – has not been adapted and extended so as to guarantee full protection to the interests of the individual'.[68] The purpose of the Act was 'to protect the individual against the arbitrary exercise of the growing powers of the State'.[69] What Butler described as the 'idea or spirit of Franks' would inform other legislation[70] and administrative action also. The general tenor of Parliamentary debates was that a highly organised society involved the growth of administrative power – and the more this trend continued, the more essential it became to create and strengthen safeguards to prevent those powers being exceeded and abused.

From a contemporary viewpoint, Butler's statement is fairly startling. We have become so accustomed to ministerial scepticism toward courts and tribunals and to Home Secretaries criticising the courts on political grounds. By contrast, in 1955, Butler was criticising the judicial system – not because it was providing too much protection of the individual, but too little. The criticism was that the wider judicial system – encompassing courts, tribunals and inquiries – had not sufficiently adapted themselves to protect the individual against the state. That the Government had swiftly introduced a Bill to Parliament to enhance judicial power spoke volumes about the marginal role of the courts.

It was widely accepted that the Franks project would be a long-term work in progress. The Act was only a modest first step in the right direction. During second reading in the Lords, Lord Salter, a former Conservative minister, noted that 'the real problem before us is much bigger than anything that has been touched upon in this Bill or has been dealt with by the Franks Committee'. The balance between individual and the state had been 'profoundly disturbed' by 'the immense extension of the sphere of government'. Looking to the future, this would 'be the great problem of our Constitution and of our system of government, now and for long to come'.[71]

[67] *Hansard* HC (series 5) Vol 590 col 1606 (3 July 1958) (Rab Butler MP, Home Secretary).
[68] ibid cols 1614–15.
[69] ibid cols 1615.
[70] The Agriculture Bill and the Land Powers (Defence) Bill 1958.
[71] *Hansard* HL (series 5) Vol 208 col 611 (1 April 1958) (Lord Salter).

The wider implications of all of this are apparent. The role of the courts in judicial review is highly conditioned by the political environment and their relationships with the political institutions. When the executive and legislature are united against the courts, the courts have far less scope to take an independent course.[72] In 1976, Lord Devlin, perhaps unwittingly anticipating public choice analysis of judicial review,[73] noted that the efficacy of judicial review 'depends upon the good will of Whitehall ... judicial interference with the executive cannot for long very greatly exceed what Whitehall will accept'.[74] Executive dominance of the legislature combined with parliamentary sovereignty raises the ever-present risk of legislative reversal of judicial rulings.[75] This naturally 'inclines the judges toward caution'.[76] Courts must apply legal doctrine, but this always operates against a wider political and administrative context in which the court makes an implicit assessment as to how legal doctrines should apply and which outcomes the court perceives are likely to be acceptable to central government. Anticipating the likely reactions of both government and Parliament is an inherent and fundamental aspect of higher-level judicial review.[77]

However, this broader constitutional–political–administrative context can, exceptionally, provide favourable conditions for the expansion of judicial review. The Franks spirit of the late 1950s was one such a moment. From 1955 onwards and particularly through the Tribunals and Inquiries Act 1958, both the Government and Parliament clearly signalled that they wanted more effective forms of judicial protection for the citizen. This arose principally in relation to tribunals and inquiries – but the courts were clearly part of the wider picture. This was a highly auspicious context for the development of judicial review. The wider mood and attitude of both government and Parliament was not merely welcoming more administrative law – they were demanding it. Given suitable judicial leadership and a willingness to innovate, the courts could develop judicial review in the knowledge that there was a broad cross-party consensus

[72] R Bill Chavez, JA Ferejohn, and BR Weingast, 'A Theory of the Politically Independent Judiciary' in G Helmke and J Rios-Figueroa (eds), *Courts in Latin America* (Cambridge, Cambridge University Press, 2011); E Ip, 'The Judicial Review of Legislation in the United Kingdom: A Public Choice Analysis' (2014) 37 *European Journal of Law and Economics* 221.

[73] MD McCubbins and DB Rodriguez, 'The Judiciary and the Role of Law' in DA Wittman and BR Weingast (eds), *The Oxford Handbook of Political Economy* (Oxford, Oxford University Press, 2008). For a 'closer-to-home' discussion of the need for good will between Whitehall and the courts, see H Woolf, *Protection of the Public* (London, Stevens, 1990).

[74] P Devlin, 'The Courts and the Abuse of Power' *The Times* (27 October 1976). For further discussion on this point, see ch 18 in this volume (Kirkham and Tsarapatsanis).

[75] As subsequently occurred: Burmah Oil War Damage Act 1965.

[76] HWR Wade & CF Forsyth, *Administrative Law*, 11th edn (Oxford, Oxford University Press, 2014) 19.

[77] cf Lord Hoffmann, 'The Separation of Powers' (2002) 7 *Judicial Review* 137, 144: 'The separation of powers raises questions of great subtlety and complexity ... It requires a degree of political awareness from judges, the ability to identify cases in which behind the formal structure of legal reasoning with which judges are so familiar, there lie questions of policy which are more appropriately decided by the democratically elected organs of the state'.

that the status quo was inadequate. Accordingly, there was little, if any, prospect of retaliation or curtailing of the expansion of judicial review from the Government or Parliament. The courts were clearly affected and influenced by this wider context and not just by formalist doctrinal logic. Lord Reid would have been all-too-well aware of the broader context. Lord Denning had spoken in the debates on the 1958 Act and supported amendments especially on tribunals being required to give reasons. Judges are influenced by a range of factors and forces – judicial and non-judicial. Successful higher-level judging requires a pragmatic approach.[78] As Lord Reid later noted, paraphrasing Holmes, 'The life blood of the law is not logic but common sense'.[79] Seeking to replace technicalities with pragmatic common sense was Reid's judicial philosophy.[80]

Ridge is often seen as the turning point in *judicial* attitudes. It was. But it is also all too often assumed that the courts alone were responsible for the revival of judicial review and this was a development of great judicial statesmanship to assert control over a wayward administrative machine. This is misleading. The analysis presented here supports a different interpretation. The judges were not leading, but playing catch-up with already changed public and political attitudes. By the 1950s, the courts were largely unable to review administrative and tribunal decisions. When Lord Denning MR ruled in 1951 that errors of law on the face of the record by a tribunal could be reviewed by the courts, tribunals then largely stopped giving reasons and the courts did nothing about this.[81] It was Parliament in the 1958 Act that required tribunals to give reasons, introduced onward appeals from tribunals to the courts and extended the courts' supervisory jurisdiction. In short, it was the Government and Parliament that had led the way and done much more than the courts to reform administrative law. By contrast, in both *Ridge* and the other Quartet cases, the courts were following in the wake of changed public and parliamentary opinion. More specifically, in *Ridge*, the court achieved a modest tribunalisation of the Watch Committee, something entirely and safely in keeping with the broader Franks spirit, while also signalling a wider and more expansionary approach to both natural justice and judicial review in the future.

VIII. ASSESSING *RIDGE V BALDWIN*

Any assessment of a leading case should focus on at least two aspects: first, the actual judgment itself; and second, its wider impact. Lord Reid later noted that of all his 600-odd speeches in the Lords, he was proudest of his speech

[78] R Posner, *How Judges Think* (Cambridge, Mass, Harvard University Press, 2008).

[79] *Cassell v Broome* [1972] AC 1027, 1087 (Lord Reid).

[80] Berlins (n 41).

[81] *R v Northumberland Compensation Appeal Tribunal, ex parte Shaw* [1950] 1 KB 711, [1952] 1 KB 338.

in *Ridge*.[82] There is clear justification for this when judged by the standards of highly restrictive substantive formalism of the time. Until 1966, the House of Lords was unable to overrule itself. Judges could not openly acknowledge their creative role. Indeed, few judges wanted to make new law. Those who did had to do so obliquely. It was Lord Reid himself dispelled the mystery.[83]

What then should we make of Reid's speech? It has many strong qualities. In terms of technique, the speech is a classic example of the common law method – reviewing and reviving the past in order to move forward in the future. This technique had been used to similar effect a decade earlier.[84] Reid's speech demonstrates clear skill in taking the law forward. By giving such an authoritative speech, Reid was clearly signalling a change of judicial mood and attitude.

By contrast, the other four speeches largely compare unfavourably. There are five full speeches. It is only really Lord Reid who seeks to clarify wider issues of law beyond the resolution of the specific dispute. Some speeches, in particular that of Lord Evershed, are too long and rambling and to the extent they make any important point it is only in an implicit or oblique way. The other four speeches indicate a distinct unwillingness or inability to deal explicitly with the key issues of law and to articulate general legal principles. Instead, discussion of the law is intermingled with consideration of the specific facts in a way which makes it difficult to extract general points of wider relevance. The other speeches are largely focused entirely upon deciding the specific dispute and any wider points are merely incidental to this. There is little or no sense of the Appellate Committee consciously acting as a supreme court that was collectively and decisively seeking to create new law or to provide clear guidance.

What then of wider impact? The principal long-lasting feature of Reid's speech was its doctrinal influence, in particular the implicit shift away from narrow analytical distinctions – judicial v administrative – toward a more wide-ranging and flexible approach to judicial control. Lord Reid does not explicitly come out and say it – Lord Hodson did[85] – but the clear implication was to sweep away rigid analytical distinctions between the 'judicial', 'quasi-judicial' and 'administrative'. Prior work had been done by academics such as Wade and Robson. As Lord Denning later noted, 'At one time it was said that the principles only apply to judicial proceedings and not to administrative proceedings.

[82] Berlins (n 41).

[83] Lord Reid, 'The Judge as Law Maker' (1972) 12 *Journal of the Society of the Public Teachers of Law* 22.

[84] *R v Northumberland Compensation Appeal Tribunal, ex parte Shaw* [1950] 1 KB 711 (see especially Goddard LJ), [1952] 1 KB 338 (Denning LJ).

[85] *Ridge* (n 3) 130: 'The answer in a given case is not provided by the statement that the giver of the decision is acting in an executive or administrative capacity as if that were the antithesis of a judicial capacity. The cases seem to me to show that persons acting in a capacity which is not on the face of it judicial but rather executive or administrative have been held by the courts to be subject to the principles of natural justice'.

That heresy was scotched in *Ridge v Baldwin*.'[86] This was recognised by commentators at the time. According to de Smith:

> From now on label-consciousness and word-worship may be less conspicuous features of administrative law in the courts ... the general tenor of the judgments delivered by Lords Reid, Morris and Hodson shows an awareness that the courts have been straying from paths of righteousness and a readiness to determine the proper scope of judicial review by reference to considerations of principle and rationality rather than formal, analytical categories. They reflect a significant change in judicial attitudes.[87]

Ridge also set the scene for a wider move away from analytical categories beyond the direct context of natural justice and a gradual shift away from legal formalism toward a more pragmatic approach. As Lord Steyn noted years later, Lord Reid's approach over time became the new orthodoxy:

> [A]cademic lawyers and judges performed their most creative work in the administrative law field. They have freed this branch of the law from its formalist shackles. Consequentialist arguments and policy factors are the very stuff of decisions in the public law field.[88]

For instance, 'void' and 'voidable' has gone.[89] *Anisminic* largely did away with errors of law inside and outside jurisdiction. 'Mandatory' and 'directory' has fallen away.[90] Such stark, mutually exclusive categories are beset with difficulties because the practical world of administrative action and law is more fluid and diverse than such classifications allow for. Rigid categories result in contortions as judges seek to fit cases into a procrustean bed. In more recent times, we have become accustomed to context being everything, variable intensity of review, spectrums, sliding scales and flexibility. Contemporary judicial law-making in administrative law has a largely pragmatic orientation in which consequential arguments and policy loom large, but may not always be openly discussed.[91] This is, of course, anathema for legal formalists.[92]

[86] *R v Gaming Board for Great Britain, ex parte Benaim and Khaida* [1970] 2 QB 417, 430 (Lord Denning MR).

[87] de Smith (n 30) 545–46.

[88] Lord Steyn, 'Does Legal Formalism Hold Sway in England?' (1996) 49 *Current Legal Problems* 43, 50–51.

[89] Wade and Forsyth, *Administrative Law* (2014) 254–25.

[90] *London & Clydeside Estates v Aberdeen District Council* [1980] 1 WLR 182, 190. Lord Hailsham: 'I do not wish to be understood in the field of administrative law and in the domain where the courts apply a supervisory jurisdiction over the acts of subordinate authority purporting to exercise statutory powers, to encourage the use of rigid legal classifications. The jurisdiction is inherently discretionary and the court is frequently in the presence of differences of degree which merge almost imperceptibly into differences of kind'. See also *R v Secretary of State for the Home Department, ex parte Jeyeanthan* [2000] 1 WLR 354.

[91] See, eg, Lord Steyn, 'Deference: A Tangled Story' [2005] *PL* 346; Lord Carnwath, 'From Judicial Outrage to Sliding Scales – Where Next for *Wednesbury*?' (ALBA Annual Lecture, 12 November 2013).

[92] See, eg, CF Forsyth, 'Showing the Fly Out of the Flybottle: The Value of Formalism and Conceptual Reasoning in Administrative Law' [1997] *CLJ* 325 and '"Blasphemy Against Basics": Doctrine,

Nonetheless, *Ridge* amounted to a relatively limited advance. The court undermined the administrative–judicial dichotomy which the judges had themselves erected. When set against the impoverished standards of the time, this was an achievement. But, there has been a tendency to over-inflate the quite limited nature of this development. The effect of *Ridge* was simply to put the law back on the path it had been prior to the highly restrictive cases of the 1950s. *Ridge* was not therefore a big advance forward by the court to expand judicial control of new administrative territory. The court was merely reclaiming previously long-held ground ceded only recently and unnecessarily by the courts themselves despite case law to the contrary.[93] 'Lost law was found, as distinct from wholly new law being made.'[94]

In theoretical terms, Reid's speech did nothing to articulate a convincing rationale for judicial intervention to require administrators to follow the principles of procedural fairness. It would be customary now to consider the various instrumental and non-instrumental rationales for procedural fairness.[95] By contrast, Reid drew not upon first principles, but upon analogy and the authority of overlooked precedent.[96] As Bradley noted, 'after his review of the authorities, Lord Reid formulates no new principle, merely asserting the requirement of a hearing'.[97] A related point is that the court was thinking solely in terms of a single-instance adjudicative decision by a minor public body such as Ridge's dismissal or a club committee expelling a member. There is no indication that the court was reluctant to impose natural justice upon individualised decision-making by central government. Reid recognised that 'sometimes the functions of a minister or department may be of that character, and then the rules of natural justice can apply in much the same way'.[98] Nonetheless, the case did not actually involve a central government minister.

Further, the focus on the single-instance administrative decision necessarily constrained the court's thinking in various ways. There was no consideration of how natural justice would apply in contexts of mass individualised decision-making, such as welfare, immigration and tax. Nor was there any recognition of the difficulties and trade-offs in deciding what degree of procedural fairness is required. Increased procedural requirements to promote better decisions and ensure dignity and enhanced process for those affected impose corresponding

Conceptual Reasoning and Certain Decisions of the UK Supreme Court' in J Bell, M Elliott, and J Varuhas (eds), *Public Law Adjudication in Common Law Systems: Process and Substance* (Oxford, Hart Publishing, 2016).

[93] As AW Bradley, 'A Failure of Justice and A Defect of Police' [1964] *CLJ* 83, 96 noted: 'it is difficult to find anything more in the speeches than a return to the older authorities and a disavowal of recent errors'.

[94] JD Heydon, 'Limits to the Powers of Ultimate Appellate Courts' (2006) 122 *LQR* 399, 416.

[95] Compare with *Osborn v Parole Board* [2013] UKSC 61.

[96] In Mashaw's analysis, Reid is applying the model of appropriateness: J Mashaw, *Due Process in the Administrative State* (New Haven, Yale University Press, 1985) ch 2.

[97] Bradley, 'A Failure of Justice' [1964] 96.

[98] *Ridge* (n 3) 72.

process costs, in particular additional costs and delays. More process requirements can involve significant organisational changes for the administrative body involved. The wider challenge of procedural review is to articulate and develop appropriate criteria to inform the application and content of fair process requirements across the entire range of administrative decision-making. This raises some complex issues of legal policy, especially in relation to the weighing-up of procedural fairness against additional administrative costs and delay and the appropriate personnel to take such decisions. None of this was recognised, let alone considered, in *Ridge*.

Reid also explicitly excluded any application of fair process to ministerial decisions involving policy discretion. The example given is of a ministerial decision concerning the building of an important new road. Such decisions will involve wider policy considerations, issues of public interest, and the consideration of alternative proposals, but could affected people seek procedural fairness over and above statutory procedures? Reid simply rejected any application of natural justice to such decisions in a conclusory way without argument. In making such decisions, it would, Reid wrote, be quite wrong

> to say that the minister should or could act in the same way as a board of works deciding whether a house should be pulled down … no individual can complain if the ordinary accepted methods of carrying on public business do not give him as good protection as would be given by the principles of natural justice in a different kind of case.[99]

While the judicial–administrative dichotomy was eroded, there is a distinct lack of judicial imagination as to how procedural fairness could apply to policy and discretionary decisions. As Shapiro has noted, the court in *Ridge* was bold against a very minor local authority body deciding a personnel rather than a policy matter.[100] The notion that UK courts might, like their US counterparts, intervene more intensively in administrative policy-making or the making of secondary legislation to ensure the participation of affected interests and parties was – and still largely is – beyond the limits of UK administrative law.[101]

Another issue to consider is the impact of *Ridge* upon both public administration and subsequent case law.[102] de Smith thought any impact on administrative procedures was unlikely to be great as procedural safeguards were increasingly

[99] ibid.

[100] M Shapiro, *Courts: A Comparative and Political Analysis* (Chicago, University of Chicago Press, 1981) 119–21.

[101] See, eg, *Bank Mellat v Her Majesty's Treasury (No. 2)* [2013] UKSC 39, [44]: 'the courts have been reluctant to impose a duty of fairness or consultation on general legislative orders which impact on the population at large or substantial parts of it' (Lord Sumption). See also *R (BAPIO Action Limited) v Secretary of State for the Home Department* [2007] EWCA Civ 1139.

[102] *Ridge* is also an important case in terms of the decline of local control over policing and the assumption of responsibility by central government. See CA Williams, 'Britain's Police Forces: Forever Removed From Democratic Control?' *History & Policy* (5 November 2003), available at www.historyandpolicy.org/policy-papers/papers/britains-police-forces-forever-removed-from-democratic-control.

being laid down by legislation. If *Ridge* did have an impact, arguably, it might have prompted central government to insert more detailed procedures into legislation so as to negate the risk of more judicial intervention. What is noticeable from some commentators, in particular Bradley, is the focus upon legislation and administrative action as the principal source of administrative procedures and indeed administrative law more widely. For instance, Bradley noted that the existence and nature of the hearing would have been 'better covered by legislation, not left to the interpretive ingenuity of the courts'.[103] He concluded that 'if the pattern of administrative law is to be redrawn, legislative and administrative action is needed. Coherent principles of public law, effective procedures and new institutions cannot be brought about by judicial decisions alone'.[104]

Ridge did, though, exert enormous influence upon the mood and attitude of subsequent judges in procedural review cases. Following *Ridge*, the courts extended procedural protection to a broader category of interests.[105] Earlier case law was soon disregarded. The 1920 decision in *Venicoff* that immigration officers could ignore natural justice as their role was administrative was overturned in *Re HK* in 1967.[106] This was accompanied by a linguistic and qualitative shift from 'natural justice' in the sense of court-like procedures to 'the duty to act fairly' and 'procedural fairness'. Subsequent cases emphasise the need for flexibility and context when determining the demands of fairness.[107] As Beatson LJ has noted, the flexible procedural fairness approach

> was a signal that, although the reach of the principles of natural justice had been expanded to new situations, the procedures required in those situations might be less onerous and less formal. Within those new areas the content of procedural protection was diluted precisely because the nature of the activity in question did not fall within the classical categories of 'judicial' or 'quasi-judicial' functions.[108]

IX. CONCLUSIONS

The first of the 1960s Quartet, *Ridge*, remains a classic case, but it also now seems very dated and is rarely cited nowadays. It is very far from the type of dispute that would now make it all the way to the Supreme Court. This is not

[103] Bradley (n 93) 106.

[104] ibid 107.

[105] Re *HK (An Infant)* [1967] 2 QB 617; *R v Liverpool Corporation ex parte Liverpool Taxi Fleet Operators' Association* [1972] 2 QB 299; *McInnes v Onslow-Fane* [1978] 1 WLR 1520.

[106] *R v Inspector of Leman Street Police Station, ex parte Venicoff* [1920] 3 KB 72; *Re HK (An Infant)* [1967] 2 QB 617.

[107] *Re HK (An Infant)* [1967] 2 QB 617, 629–30; *R v Gaming Board for Great Britain, ex parte Benaim and Khaida* [1970] 2 QB 417, 430; *Re Pergamon Press* [1971] Ch 388, 399–400, 403 and 407; *McInnes v Onslow-Fane* [1978] 1 WLR 1520, 1530; *Lloyd v McMahon* [1987] 1 AC 625, 702; *R v Secretary of State for the Home Department, ex parte Doody* [1994] 1 AC 531, 560.

[108] *R(L) v West London Mental Health NHS Trust* [2014] EWCA Civ 47, [67].

necessarily a sign of its irrelevance.[109] It is more an indication that the underlying principle – the right to be heard – is now so deeply embedded that citation is no longer necessary. *Ridge* has certainly been overtaken by more recent cases, in particular *Doody* and *Osborn*. These cases contain more explicit and clearer legal guidance and statements of principle. They embody and reflect the shift from a narrow concept of 'natural justice' to the wider notion of 'procedural fairness'. They also involved far more expansionary practical application of procedural fairness extending it far beyond an isolated one-off administrative decision to whole classes of decision-making in which procedural fairness – whether through oral hearings or reason-giving – was held to apply. Article 6 ECHR has also widened the landscape considerably by giving the scope to determine not just procedural issues, but also the institutional and structural independence and neutrality of decision-makers.[110] In this context, *Ridge* seems very much like a relic of a bygone age – both on the facts of the case itself and in terms of legal principle. Its importance today is that it remains symbolic of two key developments in post-war administrative law: the reinvigoration of natural justice; and the start of a new era in which the courts started to expand the scope of judicial review.

Having reviewed *Ridge* in detail and the wider context in which it was decided, we can put this expansion of judicial review into its wider political and legal perspectives. Contrary to the established story that the birth of modern judicial review started with the House of Lords' decision in *Ridge*, we can see that the court was largely responding to the changed climate of political opinion toward administrative law. That changed opinion arose from the recognition of both of the two main political parties that, following the expansion of public administration in the post-war world, the system of administrative law remedies was inadequate and needed to be reformed and modernised to meet the needs of individuals in that new world. Some years before *Ridge* ever came to be decided by the House of Lords, there had been significant public concern about the risks of executive injustice and the wholly inadequate machinery of administrative law by which individuals sought, often unsuccessfully, to secure effective redress against the growing administrative state. The intensity of this public concern had prompted both the Conservative and Labour parties, the Government, and Parliament to respond quickly by improving administrative law remedies through reforms such as the Tribunals and Inquiries Act 1958. In this new climate, it was the Government and Parliament that led the way in the late 1950s in reforming administrative law. This political lead enabled the court in *Ridge* to take the first of various pragmatic steps forward to reinvigorate natural justice and judicial review.

[109] For instance, *Ridge* was not cited in two important Supreme Court cases on procedural fairness. *Bank Mellat v Her Majesty's Treasury (No 2)* [2013] UKSC 39 and *Osborn v Parole Board* [2013] UKSC 61 whereas *Cooper v Wandsworth Board of Works* was cited in both.

[110] See, eg, *R (Anderson) v Secretary of State for the Home Department* [2003] 1 AC 837.

There was also the wider legal context of administrative law. This included and still includes not just judicial review, but other legal mechanisms such as tribunal and public inquiries – and nowadays ombudsmen and complaint-handling bodies. Big judicial review cases typically provide the focus for much, though not all, administrative law scholarship. But in terms of devising effective remedies against administration, the ordinary person is largely uninterested in the finer points of case law or the esoteric differences between tribunals, judicial review and public inquiries. What matters much more is whether he or she can access an effective remedy – whether by way of judicial review, an appeal to a tribunal or a hearing before a public inquiry – that provides some means or other by which he or she can have their case heard and listened to by an independent and neutral decision-maker who then makes a reasoned decision. Given the range and scale of adjudicatory bodies and decision-makers in the administrative state, the Tribunals and Inquiries Act 1958 could never have implemented the 'Franks spirit' across the entire range of these bodies. It was clearly for the courts through *Ridge* and subsequent cases to take on the more detailed work of filling in the gaps and omissions in legislation to ensure procedural fairness.

If there is a wider lesson from *Ridge* it is the intense importance of the immediate political-administrative context in which administrative courts inescapably operate. In the UK's parliamentary system, in which the Government is often, though not always, the dominant political player, the courts inevitably have to anticipate the likely reactions of both government and individual ministers to their decisions. The courts are all too conscious that extensive judicial intervention risks provoking a governmental or legislative reversal of their rulings. This typically constrains the scope for extensive judicial intervention through self-imposed judicial restraint. The specific background of *Ridge* was unusual in that both the Government and Parliament were aligned, but in favour of greater judicial control and administrative law controls over public administration. From a wider perspective, *Ridge* confirms the importance of looking beyond legal doctrine and situating the courts within the context of their structural relationship with the political institutions, the legislature and the executive.

In 1976, Lord Devlin, ruminating on the importance of the relationship between the courts and government for judicial review, openly accepted that the courts could not for long greatly exceed what central government considered to be acceptable. Nonetheless, Devlin was quite certain that Whitehall did in fact accept quite a lot of judicial intervention. Recent developments in administrative law, which included *Ridge*, owed 'as much to Whitehall as they do to the judiciary'.[111] Whether central government continues to display the same degree of willingness in the future remains to be seen.

[111] Devlin, 'Abuse of Power' (1976).

4

*Judges and Parliamentary Democracy: The Lessons of Padfield v Ministry of Agriculture, Fisheries and Food**

MAURICE SUNKIN

I. INTRODUCTION

Padfield v Ministry of Agriculture, Fisheries and Food[1] is 'a landmark in modern administrative law'[2] which provides a classic case study of the contested nature of judicial review in the UK's constitutional system. It was one of a number of judgments delivered by the Appellate Committee of the House of Lords under the leadership of Lord Reid[3] during the 1960s which are widely acclaimed as having 'inaugurated a new era of public law decision-making' and judicial creativity.[4] HWR Wade tells us that during this period: 'the judicial mood completely changed. It began to be understood how much ground had been lost and what damage had been done to the only defences against abuse of power which still remained'.[5] Even those who may not share

* This is a substantially revised version of ch 3 in S Juss and M Sunkin (eds), *Landmark Cases in Public Law* (Oxford, Hart, 2017). As well as being grateful to those who commented on the original chapter, I thank the editors of this volume for their extremely helpful suggestions and the publishers for permission to use the original chapter. I am of course responsible for any remaining errors.

1 [1968] AC 997.

2 Per Lord Denning MR *Breen v Amalgamated Engineering Union* [1971] 2 QB 175, 190. De Smith refers to *Padfield* as an 'important landmark', H Woolf, J Jowell and A Le Sueur (eds), *De Smith's Judicial Review*, 7th edn (London, Sweet & Maxwell, 2013) para 5-018.

3 L Blom-Cooper, B Dickson and G Drewry (eds), *The Judicial House of Lords 1876–2009* (Oxford, OUP, 2009) 218: 'Lord Reid was, beyond question, the pre eminent actor … of the period – an actor who was to dictate the courts role for the rest of the twentieth century'.

4 ibid. The other decisions were: *Ridge v Baldwin* [1964] AC 40; *Burmah Oil v Lord Advocate* [1965] AC 75; *Conway v Rimmer* [1968] AC 910; *Anisminic v Foreign Compensation Commission* [1968] AC 997.

5 This is reiterated in HWR Wade and CF Forsyth, *Administrative Law*, 10th edn (Oxford, OUP, 2009) 14.

Wade's enthusiasm for, and faith in, the judiciary saw these decisions as marking a significant constitutional change.[6]

In what was an exceptional decision for the period, the court held that a government minister had unlawfully exercised discretionary power conferred upon him by Parliament and in effect forced the minister to do something he had decided against doing. This was a radical outcome, especially given the deference previously shown by the courts to those exercising public powers.[7] It showed the courts willing to be involved in policy-laden matters and not content to play a purely passive role in the political and constitutional system.[8] While some may consider aspects of the court's approach, such as the focus on powers and processes rather than rights, to be somewhat formalistic when viewed against the backcloth of more recent developments,[9] such criticisms do not detract from *Padfield*'s continuing significance. As well as establishing, or perhaps re-establishing, what are now core principles relating to judicial control of executive discretion the case provides fascinating insights into how the courts of the period sought to position the role of the courts in our constitutional system and resolve tensions between the legitimate ability of the executive to make decisions based on policy on the one hand and the interests of justice on the other. As recent experience shows, such issues remain central to our administrative and constitutional law.

Unsurprisingly, the decision has attracted both praise and critical comment over the years. Certainly, there has been fierce criticism of the judges in the majority for having 'strayed outside the traditional boundaries of their constitutional function', for having 'substituted their subjective views' for those of the Minister, and for adopting an approach that 'did not … measure up to the standards of rational decision making' they sought to impose on others.[10] Such criticisms may reinforce the claim that judicial review is at best 'an ambiguous check on the arbitrary power of executives given that judges may also deliver arbitrary judgements'.[11] As we shall see later, even amongst those broadly enthusiastic about having robust legal scrutiny of executive powers there are some who regard *Padfield* and its aftermath as an example of the inherent limitations of judicial review, especially as a means of securing meaningful substantive benefits for successful claimants.

[6] Carol Harlow and Rick Rawlings say that these decisions constituted a shift 'in the constitutional tectonics': C Harlow and R Rawlings, 'Administrative Law in Context: Restoring a Lost Connection' [2014] *PL* 28, 39.

[7] The classic examples being *Liversidge v Anderson* [1942] AC 230 and *Associated Provincial Picture Houses v Wednesbury Corporation* [1948] 1 KB 223.

[8] See eg D Nicol, 'Law and politics after the Human Rights Act' [2006] *PL* 722 and T Hickman, 'The courts and politics after the Human Rights Act: a comment' [2008] *PL* 84.

[9] Thomas Poole refers to the 'ghosts' of cases such as *Padfield*, which were, he says, at core concerned with an essentially formalistic concern with the examination of powers and procedures: T Poole, 'The reformation of English administrative law' (2009) 68 *Cambridge Law Journal* 142; cf J Varuhas, 'The reformation of English administrative law? "Rights", rhetoric and reality' (2013) 72 *Cambridge Law Journal* 369.

[10] C Harlow and R Rawlings, *Law and Administration*, 3rd edn (Cambridge, CUP, 2009) 102.

[11] R Bellamy, *Political Constitutionalism* (Cambridge, CUP, 2007) 247.

There is undoubtedly room for criticism, but there can be no doubt that the decision is an important landmark in our public law. In particular it showed first, that when specific statutory provisions confer what appears to be unbridled discretion on the executive such discretion is always confined by what the judges understand to be the objects and policy of the statute. Secondly, it showed that ministers must be able to justify decisions that interfere with interests that are protected by the common law by providing legally good reasons.[12] Thirdly, the decision also showed judicial review both constraining the executive and forcing the executive to 'face the music in Parliament';[13] in other words, it illustrated how judicial review can constrain executive power and strengthen the parliamentary process. In this sense the case is a precursor of the UK Supreme Court's judgment in *Miller* and *Cherry*.[14] The overall effect of the decision was to show that government ministers are both legally and politically accountable for their decisions and that there is no inevitable conflict between legal and political constitutionalism or between judicial activism and parliamentary democracy. Before saying more about these matters we need to consider the background to *Padfield*, the judgments, and the aftermath to the litigation.

II. THE BACKGROUND

The case arose out of the operation of the milk marketing scheme, which was introduced in 1933 to ensure stability in the supply of milk for the benefit of farmers and consumers. Milk is important nutritionally but gives rise to a number of problems for farmers, largely because it has a short shelf life and therefore must be quickly transported to consumers. For this reason farmers risk losing money if their milk is not sold, while consumers could find the cost of milk varying considerably depending on factors such as their distance from farms. The milk marketing scheme was intended to remove these uncertainties and to ensure that milk was available to consumers across the country at a consistent price that did not vary according to the costs of production and transportation. At the same time, dairy farmers received a predictable sum for their milk and in this way were protected from the vagaries of the market.[15]

Under the scheme dairy farmers were required to sell their milk to the Milk Marketing Board for a price set by the Board. The Board sold the milk

[12] The recent decision of the UK Supreme Court in *R (on the application of Miller) v Prime Minister; Cherry v Advocate General for Scotland* [2019] UKSC 41 builds on this to show that when using prerogative power the executive must be able to justify action that impinges on constitutional values, in that case relating to the ability of Parliament to hold the executive to account. See further below.

[13] [1968] AC 997, 1061F (Lord Upjohn).

[14] *Miller* (n 12).

[15] For background see J Heptonstall, A dissertation upon the economic organisation of the fluid milk industry in England and wales 1900–1954 (Masters thesis, Durham University, 1955), available at http://etheses.dur.ac.uk/10454. The milk industry continues to be affected by the sort of problems with which the Milk Marketing Scheme was intended to deal.

to consumers and the sums received by the Board went into a pool of money out of which the farmers were paid. England and Wales was divided into 11 regions and the price paid to farmers varied between the regions, reflecting variations such as the costs of transporting milk to centres of consumption. Each region was represented on the Board and decisions on how much was to be paid to farmers in each region were taken by majority voting. Since payments were made out of a finite pool of money, an increase in payments to farmers in one region would leave less money for farmers in the other regions. Majority voting meant that farmers in one region would receive additional money only if the majority of the Board agreed that this was in the general interest. If a majority of the Board were not persuaded that it was in the general interest to pay more to farmers in a particular region, these farmers would normally be expected to abide by the majority decision. In this way the scheme was intended to allow the dairy industry, through the Board, to regulate the day-to-day operations of the scheme, subject to overall ministerial control in relation to broader policy issues.

Unsurprisingly, on occasion disappointed farmers were unwilling to accept majority decisions. Anticipating that there would be disputes, the legislation established machinery for dealing with complaints. How complaints were to be handled was central to the *Padfield* case.

III. THE ISSUES

Farmers in the south-east of England were close to London. In normal market conditions these farmers would have been able to charge more for their milk than dairy farmers in regions in which there were lower levels of demand; they also tended to have higher capital costs. The Milk Marketing Scheme recognised these factors by paying the south-eastern farmers an additional sum: a 'differential'. This differential had not been increased since the Second World War despite repeated complaints by the south-eastern farmers that the differential no longer reflected their costs and should be increased. Although committees which had looked into the scheme had accepted the need to increase the differential,[16] calls by the south-eastern farmers for an increase had been repeatedly rejected by the Milk Marketing Board and it was evident that a majority of the Board could not be persuaded to pay extra sums to these farmers.

The Agricultural Marketing Act 1958 (the Act) enabled the establishment of a committee of investigation to look into complaints and to make recommendations to the Minister. Section 19(3) of the Act provided that:

> A committee of investigation shall ... be charged with the duty, *if the Minister in any case so directs*, of considering, and reporting to the Minister on ... any complaint made to the Minister as to the operation of the scheme. (emphasis added)

[16] The Cutforth Committee, set up by the then Minister, reported in 1936 and the David Committee, set up by the Milk Marketing Board, reported in 1963.

Section 19(6) stated that if a committee of investigation reported to the Minister that

> any provision of a scheme or any act or omission of a board administering a scheme is contrary to the interests ... of any persons affected by the scheme and is not in the public interest, *the Minister, if he thinks fit so to do* after considering the report – (a) *may by order make such amendments in the scheme as he considers necessary or expedient ...; (b) may by order revoke the scheme ...* (emphasis added)

The south-eastern farmers asked the Minister to refer their complaint to a committee of investigation, but the Minister refused to do so. Through his officials he gave various reasons. First, he said that the complaint was not suitable for consideration by a committee because it 'raises wide issues going beyond the immediate concern of [the farmers in this region] ... It would also affect the interests of other regions and involve the regional price structure as a whole'. Second, he said that the complaint should be 'resolved through the arrangements available to producers and the board within the scheme itself' and that the Minister owed no duties to those in any particular region. Third, he said that if the complaint were referred and then upheld by the committee he 'would be expected to make a statutory Order to give effect to the committee's recommendation'. This was something he was not willing to do as a matter of policy.

Faced with this decision, representatives of the south-eastern farmers decided to challenge the Minister in the courts. They argued that the Minister's decision was unlawful and sought an order of mandamus to compel him to act in accordance with the law and refer their complaint to a committee of investigation. The Minister responded by arguing that section 19(3) of the Act gave him complete or unfettered discretion and that his decision could not be challenged. Alternatively, if his decision could be challenged, he argued the challenge could not be based on reasons he had voluntarily chosen to provide.[17]

IV. THE COURT DECISIONS

A. The Decisions

A Divisional Court (Lord Parker CJ, Sachs and Nield JJ) granted mandamus, essentially on the ground that the farmers had a bona fide complaint which, if investigated, would show the board to have acted contrary to the public interest. This decision was set aside by the Court of Appeal, which by a majority (Diplock LJ and Russell LJ) stressed that Parliament had entrusted the decision whether or not a complaint should be investigated to the Minister and that

[17] De Smith observes that the volunteering of reasons by the Minister was indicative of a trend towards greater openness within government, SA De Smith, *Judicial Review of Administrative Action*, 3rd edn (London, Stevens & Sons, 1973) 291, esp fn 85.

his decision was a matter of policy with which the courts would not interfere: 'Subject to his accountability to Parliament, it is for him and no one else to decide ... whether he will permit a complainant to set in motion the statutory [complaints] machinery'.[18] Diplock LJ also said that the Minister 'need give no reasons for his refusal to refer a complaint'[19] and that if any reasons were given as a courtesy they should not be 'meticulously examined for some mistake or omission which might lend colour to a suggestion that [the Minister] had erred in law'.[20] If the Court were to examine reasons in this way 'the High Court would only discourage such courtesy and so would stultify its own function as guardian of the rule of law'.[21]

Lord Denning MR dissented from this deferential approach taking a typically more robust position. In his view the farmers had a genuine complaint. He said that:

> [E]very genuine complaint which is worthy of investigation by the committee of investigation should be referred to the committee. The Minister is not at liberty to refuse it on grounds which are arbitrary or capricious. Nor because he has personal antipathy to the complainant or does not like his political views. Nor on any other irrelevant ground.[22]

Not only did he disagree with Diplock's view that the courts could not examine the Minister's reasons, but he went on to find that the reasons given showed the Minister to have acted unlawfully.

Pausing here, the difference between majority and minority judgments in the Court of Appeal reflects the classic distinction between a court unwilling to interfere with executive decisions on matters of policy, possibly out of deference to the Minister or respect for the broader aims of the parliamentary scheme, on the one hand, and on the other a court concerned to vigorously protect what it considers to be the interests of justice.

The farmers appealed to the House of Lords which, by a majority of four to one (Lords Reid, Hodson, Pearce and Upjohn; with Lord Morris of Borth-Y-Gest dissenting), overturned the Court of Appeal and reinstated the decision of the Divisional Court.

As in the other key decisions of the 1960s, Lord Reid delivered the leading judgment; his reasoning displays features typical of the new judicial confidence of the period and in particular the Court's ability to maximise its freedom to reconcile the competing constitutional pressures in order to achieve what the Court considers to be a just outcome. His primary motivation was to protect

[18] [1966] AC 997, 1012G.

[19] ibid 1011E–F.

[20] ibid.

[21] ibid. Lord Diplock later expressed regret for his judgment in *Padfield* saying that it was, 'another case in which a too-timid judgment of my own in the Court of Appeal was (fortunately) overruled', *O'Reilly v Mackman* [1983] 2 AC 237, 280A.

[22] [1966] AC 997, 1006E.

what he considered to be the interests of justice, that is to say, the interest of the farmers in having their complaint fully investigated. To achieve this: he worked from general principle rather from specific legal authority;[23] he took a purposive approach to statutory interpretation which enabled him to act in the name of Parliament's intentions while feeling able to depart from the actual wording of the specific statutory provisions;[24] he was not deterred from reviewing ministerial discretion by claims that the matter was one of policy with which the courts should not interfere; and he approached review of ministerial discretion on the basis that the onus was upon the Minister to justify the legality of his decision by providing lawful reasons. It is important to recognise that, while in all these respects his approach elevated the judicial role, the ultimate effect of his reasoning and that of the other judges in the majority, was to reinforce the degree to which the executive had to account to Parliament. In other words, this decision exemplifies how principle and pragmatism can combine in modern public law to maximise the ability of the court to protect common law interests (that is to say, interests which judges consider it important for the law to protect) within a constitutional system that is ultimately rooted in parliamentary democracy.

Lord Reid rejected the farmers' argument that the Minister had a duty to refer every genuine and substantial complaint and he also rejected the Minister's argument that section 19(3) of the Act gave him an unfettered and therefore unreviewable discretion. Lord Reid accepted that the Minister had discretion. However, in what has become one of the core statements of legal principle in public law, he explained that even when statute provides no express limits to discretionary power, the scope of such power is limited:

> Parliament must have conferred the discretion with the intention that it should be used to promote the policy and objects of the Act, the policy and objects of the Act must be determined by construing the Act as a whole and construction is always a matter of law for the court. ... if the Minister, by reason of his having misconstrued the Act or for any other reason, so uses his discretion as to thwart or run counter to the policy and objects of the Act, then our law would be very defective if persons aggrieved were not entitled to the protection of the court.

Lord Upjohn took this point further to suggest that the courts would impose limits on discretionary powers even in circumstances where the legislation expressly said that the discretion was 'unfettered'. In reasoning similar to that employed by the majority of the House of Lords in *Anisminic v Foreign Compensation Commission*[25] decided later in 1968, Lord Upjohn said that if

[23] The sole authority referred to by Lord Reid was the 19th-century decision *Julius v Lord Bishop of Oxford* (1880) 5 App Cas 214, which appears to have little to do with the exercise of statutory power by members of the executive in a modern industrial and policy setting.

[24] See also Lord Reid's extra-judicial writing: Lord Reid 'The Judge as Law Maker' (1972) 12 *Journal of the Society of Public Teachers of Law* 22; see also M Elliott, *The Constitutional Foundations of Judicial Review* (Oxford, Hart, 2001) 121–23.

[25] [1969] 2 AC 147.

legislation had said that discretion was unfettered that would mean that it would only be unfettered if lawfully exercised. By this he means that discretion is inevitably fettered in the sense that it can only lawfully be used within the limits that are expressly or implicitly set by the legislation that confers the discretion:

> My Lords, ... even if the section did contain ... [the adjective 'unfettered'] ... I doubt if it would make any difference in law to his powers, save to emphasise ... that acting lawfully he has a power of decision which cannot be controlled by the courts; it is unfettered. But the use of that adjective, even in an Act of Parliament can do nothing to unfetter the control which the judiciary have over the executive, namely that in exercising their powers the latter must act lawfully and that is a matter to be determined by looking at the Act and its scope and object ...[26]

B. Discovering the Objects and Policy of the Act

Having explained that the Minister would be acting unlawfully if he failed to exercise his discretion to further the objects and policy of the Act, the majority judges went on to consider what were the objects and policy of the Act. As we have seen, these were to be identified by construction of the Act as a whole rather than by focusing on the specific wording of section 19(3).

Two factors were of particular significance for the majority. One was the importance of protecting the interests of farmers who had been compelled by the scheme to sell their milk to the Board for a price fixed by a majority of the Board. The other was the ability of the majority of Board to make decisions adversely affecting minority interests. As Lord Reid put it: 'it was obvious that ... [the majority of the Board] might use their power to the detriment of consumers, distributors or a minority of the producers'. Lord Reid said that this was why Parliament had established the complaints procedure to enable an investigation into whether the Board had acted contrary to the public interest. He reasoned that if the Minister exercised his discretion so as to prevent an investigation into whether the Board has acted contrary to the public interest he would be overriding a safeguard imposed by Parliament:

> [I]f a complaint relevantly alleges that the board has [acted contrary to the public interest] ... as this complaint does, then it appears to me that the Act does impose a duty on the Minister to have it investigated. If he does not do that he is rendering nugatory a safeguard provided by the Act and depriving complainers of a remedy which I am satisfied that Parliament intended them to have.

In the view of the majority, Parliament had intended that genuine complaints that the Milk Marketing Board had acted contrary to the public interest would be fully investigated. Section 19(3) had to be read so as to give effect to this intention. And this meant that the Minister could not have complete discretion

[26] [1966] AC 997, 1060G.

to prevent an investigation. On the contrary, Lord Reid took the view that the section should be understood, not as conferring a discretion, but as imposing a duty on the Minister to refer a complaint that 'relevantly alleges that the board has … [acted contrary to the public interest]'.[27]

In his dissenting judgment Lord Morris was not convinced by Lord Reid's approach. He observed: 'If Parliament had intended to impose a duty on the Minister to refer any … complaint of a particular nature, it would have been so easy to impose a duty in plain terms'.[28]

Academic commentary has also been critical. Rodney Austin, for example, said in a close and critical assessment of the reasoning of the majority in *Padfield* that Lord Reid's 'reasoning is inconsistent. If the Minister has a *duty* to refer complaints, he cannot at the same time possess a *discretion* not to refer … Lord Reid's implication of a duty is based on no authority other than his *ipse dixit*'.[29]

There is nothing new in courts liberally interpreting legislation in order to protect interests which are important to the common law.[30] This has now been explicitly acknowledged by Parliament, albeit in the specific context of legislative compliance with Convention rights.[31] Nonetheless it is interesting that, as in *Anisminic*, Lord Reid and his colleagues felt able in effect to rewrite legislative provisions in order to ensure that complainants were not deprived of a remedy.[32] We shall return to this below.

However, Lord Reid is perhaps more circumspect than the above may suggest. While he indicates that the discretion should be treated as if it were a duty, his reasoning is not quite so emphatic. If the Minister had been under a duty to refer the complaint arguably there would have been no need to examine why that duty had not been exercised: failure to refer the complaint would be an unlawful failure to perform a duty and that would be that.[33] But, Lord Reid does not go this far. Rather, like Lord Denning in the Court of Appeal, he approaches the issue by indicating that the legislation creates a presumption that genuine complaints should be referred to a committee for investigation and that such a presumption could only be rebutted if the Minister had good reasons for not referring them.

[27] Lord Morris of Borth-y-Gest also dissented in *Anisminic*.

[28] [1968] AC 997, 1038.

[29] RC Austin, 'Judicial Review of Subjective Discretion – At the Rubicon; Whither Now?' (1975) 28 *Current Legal Problems*, 150, 169–70 (emphasis in original).

[30] After all, 100 years earlier in *Cooper v Wandsworth Board of Works* (1863) 143 ER 414, Byles J had famously said that 'the justice of the common law will supply the omission of the legislature'.

[31] Human Rights Act 1998, s 3 as explained by Lord Nicholls in *Ghaidan v Godin-Mendoza* [2004] UKHL 30.

[32] A similar approach was taken by the majority of House of Lords in *Anisminic* in relation to the wording of the Foreign Compensation Act which on its face appeared to exclude judicial review. For discussion of whether this indicates the clash of two constitutional imperatives, one being to respect Parliament's intentions and the other to ensure access to justice, see Elliott, *Constitutional Foundations* (2001) esp at 31; see also TRS Allan, *Law, Liberty and Justice,* (Oxford, Clarendon Press, 1993) esp at 65–78.

[33] Given that they were seeking mandamus, there may have been a question as to whether the duty was owed to the farmers.

In other words, the Minister had a discretion, but he could only decide not to refer the complaint for investigation if he had good reasons for doing so.[34] That the burden falls upon public bodies to justify the legality of their action is now recognised as a key principle of judicial review, and may be less radical than it was 50 years ago when the dominant judicial approach was to presume that public bodies act within their powers and to impose a heavy burden upon those who sought to challenge them.

C. Reasons

Given his approach Lord Reid, and the other judges in the majority, naturally rejected the view that the giving of reasons was purely a matter of courtesy and that the Minister could not be challenged on the basis of reasons he had volunteered. On this point, Lord Upjohn said that:

> [I]f [the Minister] does not give any reason for his decision … a court may be at liberty to come to the conclusion that he had no good reason for reaching that conclusion and order a prerogative writ to issue accordingly.[35]

Lord Reid and the other judges in the majority agreed with the Divisional Court and Lord Denning that the reasons given by the Minister for not referring the complaint were bad in law. In response to the Minister's reason that the complaint was unsuitable for investigation because it raised 'wide issues', Lord Reid said: 'Here it appears to me that the Minister has clearly misdirected himself. Section 19(6) contemplates the raising of issues so wide that it may be necessary for the Minister to amend a scheme or even to revoke it'.[36] In response to the Minister's concerns that if the complaint were upheld, he 'would be expected to make a statutory Order to give effect to the committee's recommendations.' Lord Reid said: 'If this means that he is entitled to refuse to refer a complaint because, if he did so, he might later find himself in an embarrassing situation, that would plainly be a bad reason'.[37]

D. Lord Morris's Dissent

In his dissenting judgment Lord Morris broadly agreed with the majority in the Court of Appeal. Whereas his fellow Law Lords had emphasised the need to

[34] See also TRS Allan, 'Pragmatism and theory in public law' (1988) 104 *Law Quarterly Review* 422, 434: 'Since, however, the Minister's discretion must be exercised so as to promote the policies and objects of the Act, he could only refuse to refer a complaint on limited grounds. The producers aggrieved by the operation of the marketing scheme had, therefore, the more limited rights that the Minister's discretion be properly exercised.'

[35] [1966] AC 997, 1061–62.

[36] ibid 1031E–F.

[37] ibid 1032D–E.

protect the interests of the farmers Lord Morris stressed the broader goals of the milk marketing scheme, including the Milk Marketing Board's role in government of the industry. Under the scheme the Board, he said, was intended to be the final decision-maker in relation to 'such matters as terms of sale and price fixation'.[38] Given that the Board decided pricing by majority decision-making, it was inevitable that farmers in some regions would gain while others would lose. If those who lost were always able to have their complaints examined by a committee of investigation this would undermine the role of the Board as final arbiter on matters such as pricing. He said that the farmers:

> [A]re asking that the determination of prices should be made by the committee. The committee could only recommend that the appellants should receive a higher price on the basis that other producers should receive a lower price. The position of all those others would be affected. The committee would be acting as an appellate body from the decision of the board.[39]

The Minister's discretion was therefore central to the scheme and it was a matter of policy whether the committee of investigation should become involved. This was not something the courts could decide. In short, the Minister's decision against referring the farmers' complaint for investigation furthered, rather than deviated from, the objects and policy of the legislation. Lord Morris agreed that the Minister had to exercise his discretion lawfully and could not base his decision on irrelevant or improper considerations, but he allowed the Minister much more leeway to decide what was improper than did the majority and was not prepared to place a justificatory burden upon the Minister. In these respects his approach was in accord with the dominant cautious attitude which had previously prevailed.

V. THE AFTERMATH[40]

Faced with the mandamus, the Minister had little choice but to refer the complaint to a committee of investigation. As the Minister had feared, and the judges had perhaps expected, the committee upheld the complaint and decided that the payments the south-eastern farmers had received for their milk from the Board 'were contrary to the reasonable interests of the complainants and were not in the public interest'.[41]

The farmers' success, however, was short-lived. The saga ended when the Minister announced in a written answer in the House of Commons that:

> [H]aving carefully considered the Committee's findings … [he was satisfied that the committee's recommendations] … would have a profound effect on the incomes

[38] ibid 1035G.
[39] ibid 1038B.
[40] See further SH Bailey, *Bailey, Jones & Mowbray, Cases, Materials & Commentary on Administrative law*, 4th edn (London, Sweet & Maxwell, 2005) 533–34.
[41] Report on Agricultural Marketing Schemes for 1967–68 (1968–69) HCP 445, 12.

> of milk producers in different parts of the country. Many of them … would suffer significant losses. Moreover, if the principle that … every producer should be paid according to his proximity to a … market were pursued to its logical conclusion, it would bring to an end the present system for the organised marketing of milk which has been so successful. … I have concluded that it would not be in the public interest for me to direct the Board to implement the Committee's conclusions.[42]

VI. *PADFIELD* AND THE CONSTITUTIONAL ARCHITECTURE

The core message of Lord Reid's judgment, with which his colleagues in the majority agreed, is that in order to protect what they consider the requirements of justice, the judiciary will review the exercise by the executive of discretionary power conferred by Parliament. The case illustrates AV Dicey's comment that 'powers, however extraordinary, which are conferred or sanctioned by statute, are never really unlimited, for they are confined by the words of the Act itself, *and what is more, by the interpretation put upon the statute by the judges*'.[43] *Padfield* shows the judges willing both to discern the objects and policy of the statute and then to invalidate a ministerial policy decision which they consider to be incompatible with the statute's objects and policy.

This approach contrasts with the then judicial attitude which favoured judicial restraint in relation to policy decisions with courts only willing to get involved where it could be established that decision-makers had exceeded their powers or had acted irrationally. Whether and how to regulate the milk industry and decisions about how much farmers should be paid for their milk in a regulated market are matters which might have been expected to have fallen beyond the judicial terrain.

The more activist approach evident in the majority decision in *Padfield*, along with the other decisions of the period, is of undoubted constitutional significance, not least because it laid the foundations for the expansion of judicial review since the 1960s. Of course, such developments have been contentious and have generated considerable debate around the appropriate place of the judiciary in a system such as the UK's. While enthusiasts for judicial activism draw on *Padfield* to show its value, others are more sceptical. For present purposes two forms of scepticism about judicial review can be identified; one is specific and the other general. The specific form of scepticism focuses on what the *Padfield* saga, including its aftermath, reveals about the limits of what judicial review can achieve. From this perspective judicial review tends to be seen as substantively weak and ineffectual. The broader form of scepticism argues that decisions such as *Padfield* illustrate the dangers that arise when judges trespass

[42] *Hansard* HC (series 5) Vol 780 cols 46–47 (31 March 1969) (Mr Cledwyn Hughes).

[43] AV Dicey, *An Introduction to the Study of the Law of the Constitution*, 10th edn (London, Macmillan, 1959) 413–14 (emphasis added).

into the territory of policy and politics. From this perspective, while judicial review delivers little substantive benefit for claimants, it elevates the role of the judiciary and undermines democratic and political institutions.

A. The Claim that Padfield Illustrates the Limits of what Judicial Review can Achieve

The farmers may have obtained a landmark victory in the courts and the judgment may have demonstrated the judges' willingness to assert judicial control, but the farmers appeared to achieve little of any substantive benefit, suggesting that the litigation, like much judicial review, was not worth the expense, fuss or bother. As Carol Harlow says:

> [The case] … was hailed by the judiciary and academics alike as a milestone in English administrative law and a sign of great things to come … Yet what resulted? The complaint having been duly investigated, the Minister refused to follow the advice of the committee. The remedy proved illusory; the same decision could be reached with only nominal deference to the court, and the waste of time and money entailed is a deterrent to future complainants.[44]

This being so, even at its most vigorous, judicial review may be 'seen as a tedious … detour on a previously mapped out route'.[45] John Griffith was also typically direct. For him the Minister's rejection of the committee's recommendation demonstrated the 'absurdity of the Lord's decision'[46]

The eventual outcome of the *Padfield* saga certainly warns against assuming that successful claimants in judicial review proceedings necessarily achieve tangible benefits.[47] However, there are several considerations here. It is elementary that judicial review litigation, especially as it was understood in the 1960s, tends to concentrate on matters of process rather than substance.[48] And in some ways *Padfield* provides a classic example of the process-oriented focus of

[44] C Harlow, 'Administrative reaction to judicial review' [1976] *PL* 116, 117.

[45] ibid.

[46] JAG Griffith, *The Politics of the Judiciary*, 4th edn (London, Fontana Press, 1991) 313–14. The comment does not appear in the 5th edn.

[47] See further V Bondy, L Platt and M Sunkin, 'The Value and Effects of Judicial Review' (Public Law Project, 2015), available at publiclawproject.org.uk/resources/the-value-and-effects-of-judicial-review; see also M Sunkin and V Bondy, 'The Use and Effects of Judicial Review: assumptions and the empirical evidence' in J Bell, M Elliott, JNE Varuhas and P Murray (eds), *Public Law Adjudication in Common Law Systems: Process and Substance* (Oxford, Hart Publishing, 2016).

[48] In *R v Chief Constable of the North Wales Police, ex p Evans* [1982] 1 WLR 1155, 1173–74, Lord Brightman summarised this approach by saying that 'Judicial review is concerned, not with the decision, but with the decision-making process.' Lines between process and substance, however, are often by no means clear: see generally, Bell, Elliott, Varuhas and Murray, *Public Law Adjudication in Common Law Systems* (2016). On the debates concerning process and substance in the 1950s onwards, see further: TT Arvind and L Stirton, 'The curious origins of judicial review.' (2017) 133 *LQR* 91.

traditional judicial review litigation in the UK.[49] While the farmers wanted to obtain more money, the litigation was not immediately concerned with securing this. Rather, the case concentrated on how their complaint had been handled and whether they could have their complaint fully and independently investigated. The majority judges clearly considered the complaints to be genuine and to raise serious issues; however, their task was not to decide whether the complaints should be upheld and whether the differential payments to cover transport costs should be increased. These were clearly matters of policy for the Minister and at no point did the Court seek to decide such matters. The judges knew, and one assumes the farmers also knew, that if the complaints were referred to, and upheld by, the committee of investigation the Act gave the Minister final power to decide whether or not the farmers should get any extra money.[50] The case, in other words, only focused on process, and then only on one stage of the process. So, why did the farmers expend so much energy and resource on the litigation and did the case deliver any practical benefits to the claimants?

The farmers were driven to litigate because their claim for an increase in payments had been repeatedly blocked by a majority of members of the Milk Marketing Board and had now been blocked by the Minister, from whom there was no appeal. Against this background it seems reasonable to assume that having the grievance considered by the committee of investigation was important to the farmers, perhaps because it offered a chance of success or because they wanted to get beyond the departmental or ministerial veto of their complaint. There is much literature on why issues of process matter.[51] In the context of *Padfield* two particular considerations appear relevant. First, as is often stressed, process matters because there is an intrinsic link between being able to participate in a process that is considered fair and having confidence in the system. Second, being able to participate is likely to contribute to the quality of the ultimate decision. As well as seeking what they considered to be a just process the farmers may have felt that a full investigation could lead to a favourable outcome or at least to wider, perhaps more open, reconsideration of the policy behind the Minister's decision. From this perspective their motivation may have been to force the decision out of the department and into a more public domain in order to attract attention to their cause and to keep the matter politically alive.

While this is, of course, speculation, such process aims suggest that the farmers achieved at least limited success, despite their ultimate failure to obtain a

[49] See also Poole, 'Reformation' (2009).

[50] The majority accepted that s 19(6) of the Act gave the Minister discretion to reject recommendations of the committee of investigation.

[51] See, eg, G Richardson, *Law, Process and Custody: Prisoners and Patients* (London, Weidenfield & Nicolson, 1993); TR Tyler, *Why People Obey the Law*, 2nd edn (Princeton, Princeton University Press, 2006). See also *Osborn & Others v Parole Board* [2013] UKSC 61 [67]–[71] (Lord Reed) regarding the importance of procedural justice when the parole board make decisions affecting prisoners.

substantive benefit.[52] While some may consider such process-oriented achievements to be somewhat limp, the importance of process cannot be discounted. This leads us to the broader concerns of those who are sceptical about the place of judicial review.

B. The Claim that Padfield Illustrates the Risks of Judicial Activism

The most fundamental challenge to judicial review in the UK context is that mounted by those who argue that judicial activism detracts from the political constitution and undermines parliamentary democracy, without contributing wider democratic benefits.[53] From this perspective *Padfield* may be criticised along the following lines.[54] It is fundamentally undemocratic for unelected judges to strike down a policy decision taken by an elected and politically accountable minister. This is especially so when the Minister is exercising discretion expressly conferred by Parliament to enable implementation of a scheme that is intended to correct the shortcomings of the market for the wider social good. In such situations the Minister is best equipped to make relevant decisions subject to being politically accountable to Parliament and ultimately to the electorate. An executive that is accountable to Parliament is responsible for weighing the competing public interests. Judges are not competent to decide such matters and should not trespass into the policy or parliamentary domain. This is especially so in a case like *Padfield*, that involves making what are in reality policy decisions that will affect those who are not party to the litigation at the behest of claimants with particular and self-serving interests. Most specifically it may be argued that the case illustrates how the judges can undermine parliamentary legislation intended to achieve wider social goals in order to protect the property and commercial interests of claimants who have the resources enabling them to exploit the advantages offered by litigation.[55] These are certainly telling criticisms, but to what extent are they justified in relation to the *Padfield saga*?

I will deal first with the argument regarding policy and then the broader criticism that *Padfield* shows the courts undermining the political and Parliamentary process in order to protect the interests of particular well-resourced claimants.

The concerns regarding policy can be dealt with quite briefly. It is clearly correct that judges should not seek to become policymakers in the sense that Ministers of government are policymakers. But, despite the criticisms of writers,

[52] Further research on the quality of the investigation and how the department responded may reveal more about this.

[53] See eg Bellamy, *Political Constitutionalism* (2007); see also Lord Sumption's 2019 Reith Lectures, available at www.bbc.co.uk/programmes/m00057m8.

[54] This brief summary does not claim to do justice to the fuller case against judicial review presented by writers like JAG Griffith and Bellamy, and more recently by the work of the *The Judicial Power Project*: judicialpowerproject.org.uk.

[55] JAG Griffith, *Politics of the Judiciary*, 5th edn (London, Fontana, 1997) 105, 339.

including John Griffith, it is by no means obvious that the majority in *Padfield* went too far. Indeed, as we have just seen, some have stressed that the case illustrates the limits of judicial review and its preoccupation with process rather than substance. Had the Court overturned the Minister's decision and replaced it with their own decision regarding the merits of the farmers' claim, then it could justly be said that the courts had unduly trespassed into the policy terrain. But the Court did not do this. The Court prevented the Minister from blocking further consideration of the complaint, but it did not determine the ultimate outcome. It may have slowed things down and caused inconvenience to the Minister and his department, but it did not prevent the Minister from making the final decision on the policy issues subject to his accountability to Parliament.

There is room for disagreement about where the line is to be drawn between legitimate control of, and illegitimate interference with, executive power. However, the majority in *Padfield* adopted what is now recognised to be the wholly conventional approach of policing the boundaries within which ministerial policy decisions are taken without moving into the substance. Here the Minister's power to decide was conferred by an Act of Parliament and the power was therefore to be delineated by the law, and more particularly by how the legislation was construed and applied by the courts: by what the judges identified as being the policy of the Act. Second, the Minister's decision invited judicial scrutiny because it directly affected interests that are protected by the common law. Here the Minister's decision was considered to interfere with the farmers' pursuit of justice: a matter falling within the province of the courts rather than that of the executive. On the basis of established common law principles the executive could only interfere with such interests – now, we might say rights[56] – if this was justified by positive legal authority[57] or if there were legally good reasons for the interference. Judicial intervention was justified in this case because the Minister did not establish either that he had legal authority or good reasons for preventing full investigation of the complaint. *Padfield* shows, then, that the interests of justice fall within the judicial, rather than the executive, terrain even when policy is involved.[58] As applied to the situation in *Padfield* the decision also shows that these principles can be applied by a judiciary without materially impinging on the core policy issues involved which remained firmly for the Minister.

[56] *R v Lord Chancellor ex parte Witham* [1998] QB 575 and *R (UNISON) v Lord Chancellor* [2017] UKSC 51.

[57] *Entick v Carrington* (1765) 19 St Tr 1030.

[58] See more recently, *R (Evans) v Attorney-General* [2015] UKSC 21, [2015] 2 WLR 813, discussed by M Elliott, 'A tangled constitutional web: The black-spider memos and the British constitution's relational architecture' [2015] *PL* 539. As *Anisminic* was to shortly reiterate, the courts will also protect access to justice from threats by Parliament: see now *R (Privacy International) v Investigatory Powers Tribunal* [2019] UKSC 22.

C. The Protection of Minorities

We now move to the criticism that the decision shows how judicial review skews the political and parliamentary process in the interests of certain well-resourced claimants. Those who argue that judicial review undermines democracy accept that judicial review may be justified on democratic grounds when it protects minorities from the tyranny of majorities. As we have seen, this is a factor that was also important to the judges in the majority in *Padfield*, who sought to ensure that the statutory scheme was not undermined by a majority of the Milk Marketing Board.

We earlier saw that Lord Reid stressed the importance of the complaints procedure as a safeguard to protect the minority interests of the south-eastern farmers from the majoritarian decisions of the Board. Lord Pearce paid particular attention to these aspects. His starting position was typically libertarian and rooted in concerns about the potential power of the majority. He emphasised that the scheme created a monopoly and imposed severe restrictions on the farmers' liberty of action, and noted that: 'With the aim of general betterment Parliament was interfering with the individual farmer's method of earning a livelihood and subjecting him to the mercies of the majority of the board'.[59] Like Lord Reid, Pearce stressed that the complaints procedure was intended to safeguard minority interests from the unfairness that flows from majority decision-making: 'If justice to a minority is to be imposed at the expense of a majority, it is probably more convenient that it should be imposed [by judges]'.[60]

Such statements resonate with the idea that judicial review plays a legitimate democratic role when protecting minorities from the tyranny of the majority. However, they are unlikely to persuade critics of judicial review that *Padfield* is a decision which fundamentally supports parliamentary democracy. For one thing, it was Parliament that decided that the Milk Marketing Board should use majority voting. And in any case, it is not always in the interests of democracy to protect minorities from majorities. As Bellamy puts it: 'the test of whether minority rights are being unfairly overridden cannot be that all the rights a given group … believe they should have are not yet legally acknowledged'.[61]

There are situations – and decisions of the Milk Marketing Board may be an example – when minorities simply lose out because the majority decide against them. Moreover, when the court interferes to protect some minority interests, the effect is to frustrate rather than further democracy. As Mark Tushnet observes,[62] 'we have to distinguish between *mere* losers and minorities that lose because they can't protect themselves in politics'.[63]

[59] [1966] AC 997, 1051D.
[60] ibid 1051C.
[61] Bellamy (n 11) 255.
[62] Cited by Bellamy (n 11).
[63] M Tushnet, *Taking the Constitution Away from the Courts* (Princeton, Princeton University Press, 1999) 159.

So, it is not in the interests of democracy always to protect minorities from majorities. In relation to *Padfield*, critics of judicial review are likely to argue that protection of the minority interests of the south-eastern farmers does not justify the court overturning the Minister and meddling with the scheme established by Parliament because the farmers did not need protection. On the contrary, they appeared to be a well-resourced group who chose to litigate to protect their own commercial interests. As such they were exactly the sort of claimant Bellamy seems to have in mind when he refers to litigants able to use judicial review in order to ensure that their voice is given particular weight thereby distorting the political agenda in their favour.[64]

D. Padfield and Judicial Review's Contribution to the Political Process

Critics of judicial review, then, are unlikely to be persuaded that the decision in *Padfield* can be justified on the grounds that the farmers were a minority needing judicial protection from the majority. There is, however, another aspect of the case that critics of judicial review may have more sympathy with.

As was suggested earlier, it can be plausibly argued that a key motivation for the claim was to force matters out of the Minister's office and into an arena that would allow fuller consideration of the complaints and ultimately require the Minister to justify his decision in relation to these farmers to Parliament. While *Padfield* can be presented as being about judicial interference with a minister's decision, it can also be seen as an example of the judges using judicial review to ensure that a minister is fully accountable both to the courts and to Parliament, which has the last word.

Certainly the judges in the majority were aware that their decision would increase Parliament's role. As Lord Pearce explained:

> Parliament … wished to have the published views of an independent committee of investigation … It also wished that committee to consider and weigh the public interest – a fact that makes it clear that the question of public interest was not at that stage being left to the Minister. When the report is published then the Minister may and must make up his own mind on the subject. He has power to do what he thinks best and decide whether or not to implement the report. He is then answerable only to Parliament, which will have the advantage of being able to understand the pros and cons of the matter from the published report of an independent committee.[65]

Lord Upjohn echoed this, adding that the Minister 'must be prepared to face the music in Parliament'[66] and cannot use his discretion to avoid political embarrassment or to insulate himself from parliamentary criticism.

[64] Bellamy (n 11) 245.
[65] [1966] AC 997, 1054C–E.
[66] ibid 1061F.

These observations show the judges to be very much aware of how their decision would affect the relationship between the executive and Parliament by constraining the former and enabling the latter. They knew that their judgment would force the Minister to revisit the matter in a more public and political arena, and ultimately to face Parliament. In short, the decision in *Padfield* did much of what the political constitutionalists say judicial review does not do. Far from undermining and detracting from the parliamentary process, the decision enabled Parliament to have a say when, but for the litigation, the matter is unlikely to have moved beyond the Minister's, or an official's, desk. As Lord Pearce commented, it was precisely because the complaint raised wide matters that they needed to be fully ventilated by means of a process that would ultimately lead to consideration in Parliament.[67]

That the legal process gave particular voice to the south-eastern farmers does not alter the fact that the overall result of the litigation was to enhance both the legal and political accountability of the executive. In this instance the courts forced the Minister to account to Parliament for his decision in accordance with the particular statutory scheme that applied to the case.

VII. CONCLUSIONS

The decision in *Padfield* is of enduring relevance and deserves to be revisited. As well as being of historical importance as a landmark at the dawn of the modern era of judicial review, the decision enunciated legal principles which continue to be of central relevance to our public law. In particular, *Padfield* crystallised what is arguably the single most important principle of modern judicial review, namely that when an Act of Parliament confers discretionary power on public bodies, including government ministers, however broadly expressed, the power is always circumscribed by the law and must be exercised in conformity with what the courts construe to be the objects and policy of the Act.

The judgment is an example of judicial activism in the sense that it shows the judiciary to be an active constitutional player willing to use the common law to protect what are considered to be interests in justice against encroachment by the executive. *Padfield* inevitably raises questions about the legitimacy of judicial review in a democratic age. Some see the decision as an example of the courts usurping the power of the democratic branches of government in order to further their own narrow view of the policy priorities or the interests of a well-resourced minority. This chapter, however, has argued that the majority judges in the House of Lords were well aware of the political environment in which they were working. While intent to expand their jurisdictional domain into areas of policy and legislation in order to protect what we might

[67] That the parliamentary process following the Minister's written answer may have been perfunctory was a matter for Parliament.

now call the needs of administrative justice, the judges were alive to fundamental requirements of the UK's political constitution. In particular, they knew that by increasing judicial scrutiny they would force the Minister and his officials into an arena that was likely to be more public and more political: the ultimate effect of their decision was, as Lord Upjohn put it, to compel the Minister to face the music in Parliament.[68] In this sense the decision supports, rather than detracts from, the political constitution and shows that there is no necessary contradiction between furthering common law interests or rights by means of judicial review and ensuring democratic values. In short, the saga provides an important illustration of how robust judicial review can reinforce and sustain our parliamentary democracy. In this respect it is a precursor to the decision of the UK Supreme Court in *R (on the application of Miller) v Prime Minister; Cherry v Advocate General for Scotland*[69] in which the judiciary reviewed the Prime Minister's exercise of prerogative powers in order to protect the ability of Parliament to carry out its constitutional functions.[70]

[68] [1966] AC 997, 1061F.

[69] *Miller* (n 12).

[70] This decision has attracted a substantial literature. See in particular P Craig, 'Supreme Court, Prorogation and Constitutional Principle' [2020] *PL* 248 (much of the relevant commentary is referred to in fnn 4 and 5); Martin Loughlin's response to Craig: M Loughlin, 'A Note on *Miller*, *Cherry*' [2020] *PL* 278; J Finnis, The Law of the Constitution before the Court: Supplementary Notes on the unconstitutionality of the Supreme Court's prorogation judgment (Policy Exchange, 2019), available at policyexchange.org.uk/wp-content/uploads/The-Law-of-the-Constitution-before-the-Court.pdf.

5

Legitimacy and the Courts: The Forgotten Story of Conway v Rimmer*

TT ARVIND AND LINDSAY STIRTON

I. INTRODUCTION

DESPITE GENERALLY BEING acknowledged as a landmark,[1] *Conway v Rimmer*[2] is neglected today.[3] In part, this is because it has become obsolete in a way that the other cases in the Quartet have not. Subsequent cases have built on *Conway* to move doctrine in a direction that is far more restrictive of the administration than *Conway* itself was.[4] At the same time, the Scott Report,[5] the advent of open government, and the new rights conferred by the Freedom of Information Act 2000, have so altered the functioning of government that the departmental practices which prompted *Conway* can appear to belong to a distant, almost quaint, era that has little relevance to the present day. *Conway*, from this perspective, may well have been a triumphant moment which played a key role in the historical process through which the

* We are grateful to the University of York for financially supporting our archival research in London, and to Richard Kirkham, Lord Reed and other participants at the workshop on which this volume is based for helpful comments on previous versions of this chapter. For any errors that remain, each author blames the other. Unless otherwise specified, all references to archival material in this chapter refer to materials held at the National Archives, London.

[1] It was expressly described as a 'landmark case' in *In re A (A child)* [2012] UKSC 60 [16] (Baroness Hale JSC). See also the discussion of *Conway* in T Endicott, 'Was *Entick v Carrington* a landmark?' in A Tomkins and P Scott (eds), *Entick v Carrington: 250 years of the rule of law* (Oxford, Hart Publishing, 2017) 111–12.

[2] *Conway v Rimmer* [1968] AC 910 (HL).

[3] For example, it was the only case in the Quartet to be left out of the recent volume on leading cases in public law. See SS Juss and M Sunkin (eds), *Landmark Cases in Public Law* (Oxford, Hart Publishing, 2017).

[4] *R v Chief Constable of West Midlands, ex parte Wiley* [1995] 1 AC 274.

[5] R Scott, Report of the Inquiry into the Export of Defence Equipment and Dual-Use Goods to Iraq and Related Prosecutions (1995–96, HC 115).

modern doctrine of public interest immunity emerged, but it is a moment which belongs to the past of public law, not its present.

This chapter argues, in contrast, that *Conway* belongs not to a settled past but to an unsettled present. Judicial review today is back on the political agenda in a way it has not been for the past half-century. As this chapter shows, the story of *Conway v Rimmer* sheds considerable light on why this is so. Our argument builds on a detailed examination, based on primary archival research, of the views of a group of persons whose perspective is not usually treated as central to the history of administrative law, namely, the individuals – civil servants, lawyers, and politicians – who made up the administrative branch when the leading cases of the 1960s were decided.[6] As section II discusses, *Conway* came at a time of intense and prolonged discussions within government about the disclosure of government records in litigation. These discussions began after *Duncan v Cammell Laird*,[7] and received added urgency with the enactment of the Crown Proceedings Act 1947 and the dramatic growth in the powers and functions of the post-war state. The discussions were complex and detailed, and included multiple interdepartmental committees as well as high-level Cabinet debates, culminating in a wide-ranging review of the law by the Law Reform Committee. *Conway v Rimmer* not only remade the law, but did so in a way which pre-empted the conclusion to which these internal processes were headed.

In section III, we turn to a more detailed analysis of the positions and views seen in those discussions and debates. As we show, the doctrine of Crown privilege was strongly defended not just by civil servants, but also by government lawyers in the Treasury Solicitor's Office, including some, such as Lord Bridge, who would go on to become leading members of the judiciary. Underlying this support was a clear understanding, widely held amongst those working within the administrative branch, of their constitutional role and tasks, and a conceptualisation of the public interest that differed significantly from that held by the legal community. The nature of this 'administrative constitutionalism' has received little attention in the literature but, as we show, it is fundamental to understanding departmental behaviour in relation to Crown privilege.

There is much in the history we discuss that is of interest in purely factual terms. Our aim, however, is to consider the broader lessons which the history of Conway, and of judicial and departmental attempts to get to grips with the doctrine of Crown privilege, have to offer. In section IV, we consider why the many internal efforts to reform Crown privilege failed, and use these as a basis for shedding light on why judicial review today remains so controversial. The answer, we suggest, lies in two interwoven themes: the institutional insulation

[6] Some of the archival material we discuss has been previously considered by M Spencer and J Spencer, 'Coping with *Conway v Rimmer* [1968] AC 910: How Civil Servants Control Access to Justice' (2010) 37 *Journal of Law and Society* 387. Their purpose in doing so was, however, different from ours, and as a result our conclusions differ quite significantly from theirs.

[7] *Duncan v Cammell Laird and Co Ltd* [1942] AC 624 (HL).

between the judiciary and the administration, and the legitimacy of each institution as perceived by the other. A central function of law is to discharge what Atiyah termed the 'hortatory' function, of setting standards and communicating them to those subject to law in a way that enables them to follow it.[8] This, we show, requires an active institutional dialogue between the courts and the regulated community. The reason for the failure of internal reform efforts, we argue, was that this dialogue and the mutual trust that underpins it was absent, resulting in the relationship between the courts and the administration descending into one of escalating mutual distrust. The resulting institutional tensions lie at the heart of what makes judicial review indispensable, but also controversial, 50 years after the Quartet. *Conway* is significant not only for its role as a stepping stone in the emergence of a specific modern doctrine, but because it highlights tasks, issues and concerns that were left unaddressed in the making of modern judicial review, and that remain unaddressed today.

II. THE LONG ROAD TO *CONWAY V RIMMER*

A. 'Class' Privilege and its Critics

The starting point for understanding the law in relation to Crown privilege[9] is the decision of Lord Simon in *Duncan v Cammell Laird*,[10] which *Conway* overruled. *Duncan v Cammell Laird* arose out of a disaster involving an experimental submarine, the HMS Thetis. The widow of a deceased sailor brought a civil suit against the submarine's builders, and sought disclosure of several documents from Admiralty. Admiralty claimed Crown privilege. The case was appealed to the House of Lords, which allowed the claim of Crown privilege. Lord Simon, who gave the leading speech, held that Crown privilege could be claimed either because production of the specific document would injure the public interest – for example, by harming national security or diplomatic relations – or because it fell within a class which had to be withheld from production to ensure the proper functioning of the public services.

The second of these grounds came to be known as the 'class' exception, and formed the core of the doctrine of Crown privilege until the changes brought in response to the Scott Report[11] and the decision in *Ex parte Wiley*,[12] which led to the 'class' principle being virtually abandoned. The class exception covered

[8] PS Atiyah, 'From Principles to Pragmatism: Changes in the Function of the Judicial Process and the Law' (1980) 65 *Iowa Law Review* 1249.

[9] Given the historical focus of this chapter, we refer to the doctrine as 'Crown privilege' rather than 'Public Interest Immunity', as that is the name by which it was known in the period which is the subject of this chapter.

[10] *Duncan* (n 7).

[11] Scott, Report (1995–96).

[12] *Wiley* (n 4).

situations where privilege was claimed not because the document in question contained information that should not be disclosed – indeed, in most cases where it was claimed, the content of the document was wholly unexceptionable. Privilege was claimed, rather, because the document belonged to a class or type of documents that the government for policy reasons would not disclose. Lord Simon explained the class principle with reference to candour. Candour and completeness are important for the functioning of public departments, and the Crown was entitled to use Crown privilege to refuse to disclose internal communications, if their disclosure would adversely affect the willingness of civil servants to produce candid and complete records.

Duncan v Cammell Laird was controversial almost as soon as it was decided. It was generally accepted to be correct on its facts: documents relating to the design of a submarine could not be released when the nation was at war. However, the breadth Lord Simon attached to Crown privilege was seen by many as going too far. Two points came in for particular criticism: class privilege, and the rule that it was ministers, rather than judges, who would decide whether disclosure of a document would be injurious to the public interest. These points were raised not just by the legal community,[13] but also by business groups.[14] Attempts to dismantle Crown privilege or reduce its scope began almost immediately. The Crown Proceedings Act gave these attempts impetus and created a pressure point for reformers, because the Act meant that the Crown would now have to deal with requests for discovery in civil litigation.[15]

As a result of this pressure, the Lord Chancellor gave an undertaking to Parliament during the Third Reading of the Crown Proceedings Bill, to the effect that the importance of using Crown privilege sparingly would be communicated to all ministers.[16] A memorandum was accordingly issued by the Prime Minister to all departments on how they should use the doctrine of Crown privilege.[17] The memorandum, which had been drafted by Sir Thomas Barnes, the Treasury Solicitor,[18] closely followed the language of *Duncan v Cammell Laird*.[19]

[13] See eg LCO 2/5121, Report on Crown Privilege from the General Council of the Bar, February 1956.

[14] See eg LCO 2/3363, Letter from the British Chambers of Commerce on the Crown Proceedings Bill, 30 May 1947.

[15] Before the Act, requests for evidence could only be made through subpoena in actions against a third party – either a private person, or a crown servant behind whom the department was willing to stand. Because the Crown could not be sued in most civil actions, there was little scope for discovery in actions against the Crown. See TT Arvind, 'Restraining the State through tort?: The Crown Proceedings Act in retrospect' in TT Arvind and J Steele (eds), *Tort Law and the Legislature: Common Law, Statute and the Dynamics of Legal Change* (Oxford, Hart Publishing, 2012).

[16] *Hansard*, HL Vol 146, col 925 (31 March 1947).

[17] The suggestion that the memorandum be issued by the Prime Minister was originally made by Professor AL Goodhart in correspondence with the Lord Chancellor's office. LCO 2/3363, Goodhart to Coldstream, 15 March 1947.

[18] LCO 2/3363, Owen to Mayell, 14 August 1947.

[19] The prevailing view within the Government, in contrast with the view outside it, was that *Duncan v Cammell Laird* 'had simply re-stated the law as it had been understood for a great many

Like that case, it identified two types of documents that were to be withheld from consideration: documents whose contents meant that they should not be produced, and documents which fell within a class that must be withheld from production. However, it also added further safeguards. It emphasised that documents should only be withheld from production 'after most careful consideration', and that the decision not to disclose must reflect the personal judgment of the minister, consulting with Law Officers if necessary.[20]

The controversy did not, however, die down. Whilst the judiciary accepted the existence of the doctrine of Crown immunity, there were numerous instances in which they made unfavourable remarks about the doctrine. As Sir Harold Kent put it in departmental correspondence, 'The law is settled (by Cammell Laird), but the judges do not like it'.[21] Public interest was also high. The Prime Minister received letters from members of the public 'complaining about the manner in which Crown privilege was being used to defeat the rights of the individual', and demanding a Royal Commission.[22] Newspapers, too, regularly criticised the doctrine, as did judges who encountered it in practice. In *Road Haulage Executive v Ministry of Supply*,[23] heard at Nottinghamshire Assizes, Finemore J strongly criticised a claim of Crown privilege by the Ministry of Supply in relation to a report of an accident at a depot, describing the doctrine as 'part of the stupidity we have got into these days that anything that is done in Government offices has to be kept secret',[24] and his comments were representative of the general judicial sentiment.[25]

The result was a series of attempts within the administration to refine the practice. In 1948, a meeting of the departmental solicitors and the Treasury Solicitor agreed on a common procedure to be followed before Crown privilege would be claimed.[26] This was followed by a steady stream of departmental committees which, in response to public criticism and adverse judicial comments, debated ways to refine the doctrine and make it less controversial. The work of the first of these committees – the Kent Committee, set up in 1955 in response to a series of judgments critical of crown privilege – instantiates the tensions, pressures and counter-pressures involved in this process.

years'. LCO 2/5117, Note of Meeting held on Friday, 29 May 1953 to discuss the question of disclosure of documents by the Crown.

[20] CAB 129/22/31, Crown Proceedings Act, Memorandum by the Prime Minister, 8 December 1947.

[21] TS 58/233, Kent to De Villiers, 8 March 1955.

[22] TS 58/233, Minutes of the third meeting of the Committee on Crown Privilege, 28 April 1955.

[23] 'Judge's Criticism of Secrecy' *The Times* (26 June 1956).

[24] ibid.

[25] For another example, see the remarks on class privilege in *Ellis v Home Office* [1953] 2 QB 135.

[26] No record of the meeting appears to have been kept. The outcome is discussed in a later note by Harold Kent. See TS 58/233, Crown Privilege, 18 January 1955.

B. Reforming the Law from Within: The Kent Committee and the Failure of Internal Reform

For much of the 1940s and 1950s, there were three broad strands of opinion in relation to Crown privilege. The first, strongly held by a substantial section of the legal community, was that Crown privilege was unjustifiable and should be abolished. The second, equally strongly held by a substantial section of the civil service, was that Crown privilege performed an essential function and should not be tampered with. Between the two extremes was a range of opinion within the civil service that recognised the source of the dissatisfaction with Crown privilege and sought to devise ways of ameliorating it, but ultimately failed to find a solution in which they could have confidence.

The Kent Committee was an example of this middle path. It was set up in 1955 to study departmental practice on Crown privilege and examine whether it could be reformed. The committee was formally an 'official committee of inquiry' which, in the technical terminology used by the civil service at the time, signified a committee of officials (and not politicians or independent members) set up to inquire into an aspect of the current state of affairs within departments. The chair of the committee was Sir Harold Kent, who had recently (in 1953) been appointed Treasury Solicitor after 20 years in the Parliamentary Counsel's office.

The committee was set up in the wake of growing judicial criticism of the extent to which departments claimed Crown privilege. The Treasury Solicitor's office had recently become aware that departmental practices on Crown privilege diverged substantially, and frequently failed to meet the requirements set out in the 1947 Memorandum and *Duncan v Cammell Laird*. Although this was usually for practical reasons such as the demands on ministerial time, it was feared that it would increase the criticism.[27] There was a strong sense in the civil service that some action should be taken, although it was not clear what. In 1955, Sir Edward Bridges, the head of the Home Civil Service, wrote to George Coldstream, the Permanent Secretary to the Lord Chancellor's Office, suggesting the creation of an official interdepartmental committee to

> examine the circumstances in which, and the principles on which, the Crown claims privilege in legal proceedings for documents and oral communications, and to advise whether any modification of the present practice in this matter is possible and desirable.[28]

Despite the breadth of the terms of reference, the principal aim was to have a fact-finding survey, which a more formal body could eventually take further.[29] The official was to ascertain in what circumstances departments claimed privilege, with a view to examining which of these claims were excessive, and where

[27] See TS 58/233, Crown Privilege, 18 January 1955.
[28] LCO 2/5119, Bridges to Coldstream, 8 February 1955.
[29] LCO 2/5119, Butler to Kilmuir, 14 February 1955.

the Government 'must stick in its toes'.[30] This, it was thought, would better inform ministers deciding whether to claim privilege.[31]

Kent was a consummate insider, deeply loyal to the civil service and its ways of working. JAG Griffith would later remark that Kent, like many senior civil servants of his day, believed that there was 'very little wrong within the higher reaches of the civil service'.[32] This assessment is not entirely unfair. In a memorandum written some years later in response to public demands for more effective remedies against the state, Kent lamented the fallacy of those who made such demands 'in the assumption that, contrary to all experience, life is just'.[33] Kent was also sympathetic to bureaucratic secrecy, and would defend those who argued against publication of inspectors' reports before the Franks Committee.[34]

Despite this, the Committee began with a high degree of ambition. Its early circulars to departments show a willingness not just to systematise and harmonise, but also reconsider and narrow the basis of 'class' privilege. Options it floated included waiving privilege in all commercial cases, and drawing a distinction between internal documents recording matters of opinion (over which class privilege would be claimed) and those which recorded matters of fact (over which class privilege would ordinarily be waived, subject to requirements of confidentiality).[35] Ultimately, however, the Committee decided against recommending radical change, focusing instead on harmonising practice and reducing the field in which 'class' privilege was claimed. In its final report, presented in April 1956, the Committee explained that it had decided not to pursue an approach of making practice more flexible by waiving Crown privilege 'whenever it seems reasonable to do so', because doing so threatened the entire basis of class privilege which depended on it being claimed consistently. This was, in part, because of the view that candour was foundational to existing practice. Even a file on a purely commercial contract, for example, typically contained 'frank discussions' and 'candid criticisms' about contractors, which were not always capable of factual substantiation, and involved delicate matters such as blacklisting individual contractors.[36] The prospect of waiver would remove the 'feeling of security' on which this practice depended.[37] Equally important, though, was a concern about the impact on the ability to defend claims before the judiciary:

> [I]f privilege is not claimed for a certain kind of document in one case because the requirements of justice seem particularly obvious in that case, and in a subsequent

[30] LCO 2/5119, Dobson to Coldstream, 9 February 1955.
[31] LCO 2/5119, Coldstream to Kilmuir, 15 February 1955.
[32] JAG Griffith, 'Draftsman' *The Spectator* (29 September 1979) 23.
[33] LCO 2/8439, Report by 'Justice' on 'The Citizen and the Administration', 3 November 1961.
[34] Griffith, 'Draftsman' (1979).
[35] TS 58/233, Departmental Circular on Crown Privilege, 31 March 1955.
[36] CAB 134/1314, Report of Official Committee on Crown Privilege, para 42.
[37] ibid para 8.

> case privilege is claimed for the same kind of document because the requirements of justice seem less obvious, the inconsistency may be difficult to explain and defend.[38]

This concern influenced how the committee approached the way in which classes were defined, where its aim was to help departments avoid making 'difficult decisions in individual cases' because these might risk 'weakening the principle of "class" privilege'.[39] Kent's own views are likely to have played a significant role in the committee's decision not to pursue broader changes. In correspondence with the Solicitor-General, Sir Harry Hylton-Foster, in September 1955, Kent emphasised the power which a more flexible approach to waiving Crown privilege would give the judiciary:

> I feel very nervous about waiver, because if the House of Lords suggest that the Minister can waive class privilege in cases where the interests of justice seem to require it, the judges will almost always invariably press for it.[40]

The Committee's recommendations, accordingly, focused on harmonising and refining existing practice. Its work was not perfunctory. Some departments claimed privilege for a much broader range of documents than others. The Civil Services Commission, for example, claimed class privilege over all reports, medical or otherwise, and all inter-departmental minutes,[41] whereas other departments, such as the Ministry of Labour and National Savings, were more open to disclosing medical reports in some circumstances.[42] There was also wide variation in other everyday matters such as accidents.[43] The Committee gave detailed consideration to the utility these claims had in litigation, and to whether privilege should continue to be claimed for that type of document. It ultimately made 14 recommendations, which narrowed the ambit of some classes for which claims were regularly made and refined the process for making them.

Not everybody agreed with the abandonment of the more ambitious ideas floated in the initial circular. The Central Land Board, which had only recently suffered a significant defeat in *Glasgow Corporation v Central Land Board*,[44] argued that rather than making minor modifications to practice, the Committee should be focusing on radically restricting the circumstances in which the class exception was claimed 'by contracting it to cover those classes which are already uniformly recognised by the courts, e.g. national defence, foreign relations, police reports, communications between the Lord Chancellor and Magistrates'.[45] Admiralty expressed similar misgivings, and pointed out that there was a

[38] ibid para 8.
[39] CAB 134/1314, Report of Official Committee on Crown Privilege, para 8.
[40] TS 58/233, Kent to Hylton-Foster, 30 September 1955.
[41] CSC 5/995, Note to Hayes, 7 May 1956.
[42] TS 58/234, Summary of Departmental comments (undated) 4.
[43] TS 58/233, De Villiers to Kent, 19 November 1955.
[44] *Glasgow Corporation v Central Land Board* 1956 SC (HL) 1. The case held that *Duncan* (n 7) was not good law in Scotland, and courts there were not bound by a minister's certificate.
[45] TS 58/234 (n 42) 2.

distinct possibility that by only suggesting 'minor relaxations', the report would weaken 'departments' ability to hold the new line because of the illogicalities involved' while also leaving critics unsatisfied.[46] Similar concerns were raised by officials in the Lord Chancellor's Office in their briefing note on the Report. The Report, they suggested, raised important questions of policy, because the Committee's determination to preserve the 'hard core' of the existing practice of Crown privilege meant that the concessions it made were small. The issue for Cabinet to determine was whether there was even any point making 'minor concessions' which did little to address the judicial view that the administration was 'unnecessarily reticent in withholding documents'.[47]

Kent strongly rejected these critiques of his report. Critics assumed that change to the doctrine would come sooner rather than later, but there was no reason to suppose that change would come. *Cammell Laird* was 'not in eclipse for England',[48] and 'without legislation, lawyers south of the Tweed will have to accept *Duncan v Cammell Laird*'.[49] In the light of what would eventually happen in *Conway*, this attitude now seems complacent, but at the time it was widely shared. In October 1967, the Attorney-General, Sir Elwyn Jones, confidently predicted that in his view, the Law Lords would 'confirm the existing law' when giving judgment in *Conway v Rimmer*.[50] The departmental records show that while the risk of judges embarrassing the Government by making adverse comments in individual cases was recognised, it was not thought that there was any danger of radical changes to the law. The greater concerns were public opinion, the attitudes of individual members of Parliament, and the pressures departments and ministers would come under to waive privilege in relation to specific documents in individual cases. It was towards equipping the civil service to resist the pressures of adhocism, and to put in place systems that would ensure consistency as well as fairness of practice, that internal efforts were primarily directed.

C. From Kent to *Conway*: Incrementalism and its Limits

The Kent Committee's report was an internal document, which was not intended to be for public circulation or inform public debate. It had been set up with the expectation that a differently constituted body, such as a public committee or a Royal Commission, would consider the situation from a broader point of view. As it happened, however, other circumstances intervened to force ministers to take more rapid action.

[46] ibid 4.
[47] LCO 2/5123, Note on the Report of the Official Committee on Crown Privilege, 15 May 1956, 2.
[48] TS 58/234, Kent to Johnston, 14 May 1956.
[49] TS 58/234, handwritten note (undated).
[50] TS 58/741, Note of a Meeting held on Wednesday 18 October 1967 at the Home Office.

In 1956, Jocelyn Simon, the Conservative member for Middlesbrough West, introduced an amendment to the Restrictive Trade Practices Bill. The amendment was on the subject of Crown privilege, and would have given judges the power to override a claim of Crown privilege where the basis was that the disclosure was not in the public interest, while preserving the Minister's final say on matters of national security.[51] Jocelyn Simon was no stranger to the question of Crown privilege. In 1955, he had published a well-received paper in the *Cambridge Law Journal* which was very critical of the doctrine of Crown privilege,[52] which the Kent Committee had read and considered.[53] He would also, as Baron Simon of Glaisdale, subsequently influence the development of the law on public interest immunity in leading cases such as *Rogers v Secretary of State for the Home Department*.[54]

The Government disagreed with Simon's proposed amendment. The view within Cabinet was that 'it would be wrong to allow the Court to question and, perhaps, reverse the executive decision of a Minister of the Crown in respect of the privilege of the Crown', and that making special rules in one Bill would set a bad precedent.[55] Nevertheless, because Simon's views carried weight with MPs, the Government felt that they merited a substantive response which would head off support for his amendment, and decided to do so by turning the recommendations of the Kent Committee into formal government policy. On 3 May 1956, less than a week after the Kent Committee presented its report, Cabinet decided to appoint a Cabinet Committee to consider the report and make recommendations on its implementation, with a view to heading off Simon's amendment.[56]

The Cabinet Committee considered the Kent Committee's Report on 16 May 1956. The timetable was rushed, as Simon's amendment was listed for debate on 4 June. The Cabinet Committee largely accepted the Kent Committee's Report, agreeing in particular that ministers, and not courts, were the appropriate persons to decide where the balance lay between the public interest in good public administration and the public interest in the proper dispensation of justice. Judges were in no position to assess the first of these,[57] and that the 'class' basis of privilege should be maintained to preserve candour and completeness, notwithstanding the expected pressure from the judiciary and MPs.[58] The only departure from the Kent Committee's recommendation was

[51] *Hansard*, HC (series 5) Vol 558, cols 946–57 (26 October 1956).

[52] JES Simon, 'Evidence Excluded by Consideration of State Interest' (1955) 13 *CLJ* 62.

[53] TS 58/233, Committee on Crown Privilege: Minutes of second meeting held on Friday 15th of April 1955, 4.

[54] *Rogers v Secretary of State for the Home Department* [1973] AC 388 (HL).

[55] CAB 21/3004, Restrictive Trade Practices Bill Committee Stage: Note on Amendments – Clause 18, 2.

[56] CAB 128/30/32, Conclusions of a Meeting of the Cabinet held on 3 May 1956.

[57] CAB 134/1314, Cabinet Committee on Crown Privilege: Minutes of a Meeting held on 16 May 1956, 1.

[58] ibid 2.

to disclose even fewer documents than the Committee recommended. The Kent Committee had suggested that departmental minutes about road accident cases should be disclosed. The Cabinet Committee rejected this suggestion on the basis that it 'would constitute a dangerous and significant inroad into the principle that departmental minutes should be protected'.[59] Cabinet approved the recommendations on 29 May.[60] On 6 June, the Lord Chancellor made a statement to Parliament setting out what the new practice would be, substantially in the terms of the Kent Report with the additional qualifications imposed by the Cabinet Committee.[61]

One consequence was that the broader review that had been envisaged at the time the Kent Committee was set up never took place. Instead, the following eight years mostly saw a growing systematisation of the practices and procedures recommended by the Kent Committee and publicly announced in the 1956 statement by the Lord Chancellor. Following the 1948 Memorandum issued by Attlee, the Treasury Solicitor's department had developed litigation guidance and model forms to be used in responding to discovery. These were revised to take account of the 1956 Statement. In certain cases, departments were encouraged to continue to refuse to disclose documents, but by claiming other forms of privilege (such as legal privilege) rather than Crown privilege.[62] Certificates claiming privilege were framed in generic terms, stating that the document belonged to a class whose disclosure was not in the public interest, but giving no hint of what that class might be.[63] Ministers were encouraged to use an affidavit rather than a certificate if privilege was challenged.[64]

Common types of documents received considerable amounts of time and discussion. A lot of attention was devoted to the issue of medical disclosure[65] and traffic accident reports,[66] and special committees were formed to consider the issues of disclosing addresses held by the Government (for example, to abandoned wives)[67] and disclosing police reports and documents.[68] There were occasional attempts to suggest reforms to existing practices, but most came to nothing. One of these, whose rejection seems particularly ironic given the

[59] ibid 3; see also the report of the committee: CAB 129/81/127, Crown Privilege: Report of the Committee of Ministers, pp 109–110.

[60] CAB 128/30/38, Conclusions of a Meeting of the Cabinet held on 29 May 1956, pp 4-5.

[61] HL Deb 06 June 1956, vol 197, cols 741–747.

[62] TS 27/1435, Litigation Division Circular No. 8, 1959: Discovery – claim for professional privilege, 30 October 1959.

[63] See, for example TS 27/1435, Certificate by Secretary of State for Scotland, dated 25th June 1954.

[64] TS 27/1435, Litigation Division Circular No 2, 1957, para 3(b).

[65] TS 27/1436, Crown Privilege for medical documents, 26 January 1962.

[66] TS 58/272, Claim for Crown and professional privilege in connection with traffic accidents reports.

[67] LCO 2/5124-5129, Committee on Disclosure of Addresses.

[68] LCO 2/7055-58, Official committee to consider the general policy regarding disclosure of police reports and documents.

outcome in *Conway v Rimmer*, was a suggestion by the Attorney-General made in the context of discussions around the then-ongoing litigation in *Auten v Rayner*,[69] that Crown privilege should be waived where the document pertained to malicious prosecution.

For the most part, however, there were few radical changes in departmental practice. Departments recognised, and occasionally acknowledged, that what they were doing did not in fact comply with the rule in *Duncan v Cammell Laird* or Attlee's 1948 memorandum. In particular, ministers were not personally taking decisions in the way Lord Simon, and Attlee, thought they should.[70] Yet there was little impetus for change. The courts, despite their stated dislike for Crown privilege, did little to make departments' lives harder. In principle there was much the courts could have done. Precedent gave them some leeway to, for example, reject general claims of class privilege, and to require affidavits to have clear statements as to what the class was, and why that class deserved privilege. For the most part, however, they did not do this, confining themselves instead to making adverse remarks about the practice.

In 1964, this changed as a result of two developments, one legal and one political. The first was the decision in *Merricks v Nott-Bower*,[71] in which the Court of Appeal, led by Lord Denning and Salmon LJ, ordered disclosure of documents despite a ministerial certificate that their disclosure was contrary to the public interest, holding that Lord Simon's ruling in *Duncan v Cammell Laird* was obiter as far as class documents were concerned, especially where the documents were unimportant. Although Lord Denning and Salmon LJ reiterated this in subsequent cases,[72] their approach was not taken up more broadly. Nevertheless, the possibility that disclosure might be ordered notwithstanding a ministerial certificate caused consternation in government, where the prevailing view was that courts were not equipped to make this decision. As the Treasury Solicitor, WAH Druitt, put it:

> The Courts can only be aware of one sector and not the whole field of the public interest. The Minister is responsible for this decision of policy and has to justify that policy to Parliament. For this reason it seems to me that it would be wrong for the Court to be given the power to override the Minister's decision if the Judge is of opinion that the public interest which the Minister has considered ought to give way to some other aspect of public interest. A conflict between a minister and the Court on this topic would be most regrettable.[73]

[69] *Auten v Rayner* [1958] 1 WLR 1300 and *Auten v Rayner (No 2)* [1960] 2 WLR 562. For a contemporary critical comment on the cases and the use of Crown privilege in them, see the case note by DE Nelson, 'Crown Privilege–Police Communications–Method of Claim to Privilege' (1960) 18 *CLJ* 129.

[70] TS 58/740, Crown Privilege: Meeting at the Office of the Treasury Solicitor, 21 February 1964, 3.

[71] *Merricks v Nott-Bower* [1965] 1 QB 57 (CA).

[72] See especially *In re Grosvenor Hotel, London (No 2)* [1965] 1 Ch 1210 (CA) and *Wednesbury Corporation v Minister of Housing and Local Government* [1965] 1 WLR 261 (CA).

[73] TS 58/740, Druitt to Dobson, 26 February 1964.

The second development was a speech delivered by the Prime Minister, Harold Wilson, to the Society of Labour Lawyers, one of whose themes was Crown privilege.[74] Wilson took the issue up in government, seeking to require the explicit approval of the Lord Chancellor or the Prime Minister for claims of Crown privilege.[75] Lord Gardiner, who was then the Lord Chancellor persuaded him that the issue was complex and would take time.[76] This was not a delaying tactic: Gardiner was in favour of far-reaching changes, including giving judges rather than ministers the right to have the final say.[77] After discussion, it was agreed that the Lord Chancellor would refer the matter to the Law Reform Committee.[78] The specific issue referred to the Law Reform Committee was the issue of Crown privilege, and in particular whether class privilege claimed in the interest of 'freedom and candour' should continue.[79]

The Law Reform Committee had already been asked to take up the issue of evidence under a working group led by Lord Diplock. A separate sub-committee of the working group on evidence, led by Lord Pearson, was set up to consider Crown privilege.[80] JAG Griffith was invited to join this sub-committee, and accepted. The Law Reform Committee's work remains largely unknown, because its report was never published. However, it proceeded to examine the issue very systematically, closely studying practice in other Commonwealth jurisdictions, including Australia, Canada, New Zealand and South Africa, and also in Ireland. Submissions were also invited, and received, from a large number of individuals and groups, including the Society of Public Teachers of Law (as the Society of Legal Scholars was then called), several university departments of law, and a few leading scholars, including JDB Mitchell and HWR Wade. Comments were also received from other bodies, including the Institute of Professional Public Servants, and from a small number of members of the public.[81] The Treasury Solicitor's Office made a submission on behalf of the entire administration, which was drafted on the basis of views received from other departments.[82]

The Law Reform Committee initially sought to avoid the need for legislation, seeking, like the Kent Committee had, to recommend changes in departmental practice instead. Lord Pearson met a number of times with departments to find a solution that would enable practice to be changed voluntarily. These efforts did not succeed, however, and by the final draft of its report, the Committee had reluctantly concluded that it would need to recommend legislation. This was

[74] H Wilson, *Liberty and the Law* (London, Labour Party, 1964) 4.
[75] PREM 13/1597, Prime Minister's Minute to the Lord Chancellor, 2 November 1964.
[76] PREM 13/1597, Note by the Lord Chancellor, 2 November 1964.
[77] TS 58/740, Note of meeting at Lord Chancellor's Department on 9 November 1964, para 4.
[78] PREM 13/1597, Prime Minister's Minute to the Lord Chancellor, 2 November 1964.
[79] PREM 13/1597, Cabinet Memorandum by the Prime Minister, 11 November 1964, para 3.
[80] PREM 13/1597, Note by the Lord Chancellor, 9 November 1964.
[81] LCO 65/292, Law Reform Committee Sub-committee 3, Crown Privilege: Documents circulated.
[82] TS 58/741, Crown Privilege Correspondence.

largely down to the 'class' basis of Crown privilege. The committee was faced, early on, with the problem – most cogently summarised by JAG Griffith – that if it accepted the government departments' 'candour and freedom argument' as an acceptable reason for privilege, then it would be unable to make more than 'the mildest of suggestions for reform'.[83] Lord Pearson, similarly, regarded claims 'made only on a class basis and having no other justification' as a 'very dubious category of claims for Crown privilege', which was probably an 'an illegitimate extension' of other, valid, categories of claims.[84] The doctrine, he went on to say 'is almost the opposite of "fiat justitia ruat caelum". It is justice, not the heaven, which falls down.'[85]

This did not, however, mean that the Committee simply dismissed the views of the departments. On the contrary, they accepted that the departmental concern to protect 'candour and freedom' reflected a real underlying need which must be given weight (although a better term was desirable). The difficulty, however, was that the current system gave too little room to balance it against the countervailing interest, namely, the damage withholding documents did to litigants. The solution was to empower courts to ensure that the principle was not being wrongly applied.[86] A report recommending legislation was drawn up, which would have resulted in a significant narrowing of class claims by eliminating 'general, vaguely defined' classes and requiring class claims to be clearly specified, and also be weighed against the facts of a case.[87] The report also recommended subjecting claims to a greater degree of judicial scrutiny and control, and would have given the court the power to decline to give effect to a claim of Crown privilege if 'it appeared that the interests of justice were paramount'.[88] In the meantime, however, *Conway v Rimmer* had begun making its way up the appellate hierarchy. The case was being keenly watched in the departments as well as by the legal community, and the publication of the report was put on hold while the House of Lords considered the appeal.[89] Once the decision in *Conway v Rimmer* was issued, Lord Pearson decided that the report had been rendered redundant, and it was never published.[90]

[83] LCO 65/295, Note from JAG Griffith.

[84] LCO 65/295, Memorandum from the Chairman.

[85] LCO 65/295, Note from Lord Pearson, undated.

[86] LCO 65/294, Minutes of Fifth Meeting held on Tuesday, 19th April 1966, paras 7–14. HWR Wade took a similar stance in his memorandum to the Committee, suggesting that the problem arise from the fact that the executive was in the position of 'being final judge in its own cause and of having to decide without hearing both sides of the case'. LCO 65/292, Documents circulated CP 6: Memorandum by Professor Wade.

[87] LCO 65/297, Law Reform Committee, Second Revised Draft Report of the Sub-committee on Crown Privilege, para 19.

[88] ibid paras 18, 20. Cabinet minutes, as well as documents relating to national security or containing diplomatic secrets were to be exempt from judicial scrutiny. ibid paras 5, 18.

[89] LCO 65/297, Letter from the Chairman to the Assistant Secretary, 13 June 1967; LCO 65/296, Crown Privilege: Record of vote on Lord Pearson's suggestion, June 1967.

[90] TS 58/923, Dobson to Armstrong, 2 July 1969.

D. *Conway* and its Aftermath

Conway v Rimmer related to a class of documents that had long been the subject of a claim of Crown privilege, namely, probationary reports. Michael Conway, a constable, had been dismissed from the Cheshire constabulary following an accusation of theft against him. He had been prosecuted for the alleged theft on the recommendation of his superintendent, Thomas Rimmer, but had been acquitted. Despite his acquittal, he was dismissed on the basis of a probationary report. He thereupon sued Rimmer for malicious prosecution, and sought discovery of the confidential probationary reports made about him, as well as of Rimmer's report recommending his prosecution. Class privilege was claimed, and the Home Secretary filed an affidavit to the effect that the documents sought fell within classes of documents that could not be disclosed. The District Registrar ordered the documents to be produced notwithstanding the certificate. On appeal, Browne J in the High Court set aside the Registrar's order. Even if the Court had a residual power to override a certificate (an issue which Browne J did not finally decide) it would only be appropriate to do so if the claim of privilege was 'ridiculous or wholly unreasonable or wholly unnecessary'.[91] That bar had not been crossed in this case. Conway appealed. The Court of Appeal dismissed the appeal holding, over a strong dissent from Lord Denning, that the decision of Lord Simon in *Duncan v Cammell Laird*[92] was binding, and under it the certificate of a minister was conclusive, leaving judges with no power to themselves inspect a document to decide whether it ought to be privileged.[93]

Conway appealed to the House of Lords, which allowed the appeal and ordered production of the documents. Invoking the recently issued Practice Statement,[94] the House of Lords overruled *Duncan v Cammell Laird* and held by a 4:1 majority that it no longer represented the law of England.[95] Lord Reid in his leading speech did not question ministerial certificates granted on the basis of the content of a document. 'However wide the power of the court may be,' he held, 'cases would be very rare in which it could be proper to question the view of the responsible Minister that it would be contrary to the public interest to make public the contents of a particular document.'[96] This did not, however, hold for class privilege, where the effect of the doctrine's application in individual cases was frequently 'little short of being ridiculous'.[97] As Lord Reid saw

[91] *Conway v Rimmer* (QB, 23 February 1967) 9. The High Court judgment is not reported, but a copy is available in the Law Reform Committee's papers in LCO 65/296.

[92] *Duncan* (n 7).

[93] *Conway v Rimmer*, [1967] 1 WLR 1031 (CA).

[94] Practice Statement (Judicial Precedent) [1966] 1 WLR 1234.

[95] Lord Upjohn, whilst concurring in the result, would have preferred to distinguish *Duncan v Cammell Laird* without overruling it. *Conway* (n 2) 990.

[96] *Conway* (n 2) 943.

[97] ibid 950.

it, the problem lay in the fact that 'in a doubtful case the alleged public interest in concealment should be balanced against the public interest that the administration of justice should not be frustrated'. A minister however, 'has no duty to balance these conflicting public interests'.[98] Treating a minister's decision as conclusive meant 'not only that very serious injustice may be done to the parties, but also that the due administration of justice may be gravely impaired for quite inadequate reasons', as 25 years of experience since *Duncan v Cammell Laird* had shown.[99] It was, therefore, the courts who should balance the two conflicting public interests at issue.[100]

Lord Reid also rejected the argument in relation to candour. Using Cabinet minutes as his example, he suggested that the true issue was not candour, but rather the danger that the 'premature disclosure' of documents connected with policy-making, whether in Cabinet or in departments, would 'create or fan ill-informed or captious public or political criticism' by exposing the inner workings of government 'to the gaze of those ready to criticise without adequate knowledge of the background and perhaps with some axe to grind'. This did not, however, apply to routine documents of the sort that were more typically the subject of class claims.[101] Whilst there were good reasons to adopt a cautious approach in relation to police documents, this did not apply to probationary reports. Nor, given Conway's acquittal, did it apply to Rimmer's report recommending his prosecution. The Court was not therefore bound by the Minister's certificate, but could form its own opinion.[102] Lord Reid then proceeded to examine the documents, and held that there was nothing in them to suggest that their disclosure would be 'prejudicial to the proper administration of the Cheshire Constabulary or to the general public interest', and ordered their disclosure.[103]

The victory in the House of Lords did not ultimately help Conway, who lost when the case went back to trial.[104] The impact of the House of Lord's ruling on the Government was, however, considerable. *Conway v Rimmer* had been deliberately taken further by the Government, because it was seen as 'an exceedingly good case to fight' as the documents 'could not possibly be disclosed' in proceedings.[105] The decision was, therefore, wholly unexpected. There was concern about the high degree of uncertainty which departments would face in

[98] ibid.
[99] ibid 951.
[100] ibid.
[101] ibid 952.
[102] ibid 954.
[103] *Conway v Rimmer* [1968] 2 WLR 1535 (HL).
[104] The claim was dismissed on the basis that Rimmer had not acted with malice or without probable cause in the legal sense, in part because the DPP had been consulted. Thomas Rimmer was not well liked, and his leading counsel took the view that were he to give evidence, the jury would form an unsympathetic view of him and sympathise with Conway. He therefore sought, successfully, to have the claim dismissed when the plaintiff had concluded his case, recording that it took 'some courage' for the judge to do so. See R Waterhouse, *Child of Another Century: Recollections of a High Court judge* (London, Radcliffe Press, 2013) 143–44.
[105] TS 58/741, Minute of a conference at Mr. Nigel Bridge's chambers on 19 October 1966.

their work.[106] The Treasury Solicitor's department took on the task of drafting new guidance for departments. The work was led by Charlton, who had also drafted the joint submission to the Law Reform Committee. The main thrust of the work was preserving as much as possible of the existing practice on claiming privilege on the basis of 'class'. There was considerable regret that the requirements of candour and completeness were not given weight by the House of Lords, but the overall tone of discussions was constructive. It was recognised that the decision had made it necessary to change existing practice, but there was also a clear desire to ensure that the changes went no further than absolutely necessary.[107]

For much of 1968 and the first half of 1969, discussions revolved around the class – content distinction, the utility of 'content' as a basis for refusing disclosure, and the ways if any in which class could continue to play an operative role. Although candour had been given short shrift by the House of Lords in *Conway*, the view was strongly expressed that it was candour that remained the key issue in disclosure, rather than the fear of criticism, and that it was a nettle that needed to be grasped.[108] Officials in the Lord Chancellor's Office argued that the old approach was not compatible with *Conway*. The default approach after *Conway* had to be to disclose documents unless harm (and not merely embarrassment) would result from disclosure. Whilst this would affect candour, they questioned whether candour was really such a big issue.[109] Lord Pearson, whose views on the draft memorandum of guidance were sought by the Treasury Solicitor's department, similarly recommended a more generous approach to be taken to waiving class privilege.[110] But this view was not widely shared outside the Lord Chancellor's Office. The preference was, instead, for adopting an even more inflexible approach to disclosing documents within an excepted class.[111] The reaction ensured that both class and candour would remain a fundamental part of the departments' approach to Crown privilege until they were swept away in the aftermath of the changes that followed the Scott Report[112] and *Ex parte Wiley*.[113]

III. AN ALTERNATIVE VIEW: PRINCIPLE, PRAGMATISM AND THE NEED FOR CROWN PRIVILEGE

The story thus far might seem a familiar tale of obstructive civil servants defending their privileges against the demands of justice. In reality, the picture is more

[106] CAB 165/925, Guidance to departments on Crown privilege, January 1971.
[107] See eg TS 58/921, Jones to Charlton, 24 April 1968.
[108] TS 58/922, Hall to Charlton, 26 November 1968.
[109] TS 58/922, Note from the Lord Chancellor's Office, 4 February 1969.
[110] TS 58/923, Pearson to Dobson, 2 November 1969, 7–9.
[111] TS 58/922, Note from Hankey, 17 February 1969.
[112] Scott (n 5).
[113] *Wiley* (n 4).

nuanced. Civil servants understood that Crown privilege was a controversial and unpopular doctrine, and they also understood that it had the potential to cause real injustice. Nevertheless, they felt that the doctrine was necessary, and that the potential for injustice was best ameliorated not by diluting the doctrine, but by creating procedures and processes by which pragmatic justice could be done.

In correspondence with the Law Reform Committee, officials insisted that they knew of few or no cases in which Crown privilege caused injustice. This does not appear to be a disingenuous claim. Officials genuinely believed that most issues could be avoided through appropriate practices, and the archival record shows that the administration could go to considerable lengths to ensure a just outcome where a decision was made to withhold documents from production. The actions taken by administrators in connection with the litigation brought by Barbers Removal Services Ltd against the Minister of Housing and Local Government is a typical example.

The case arose out of a compulsory acquisition order that had been made over property in Stockport, for the purpose of building a new fire station. The affected persons challenged the order and sought disclosure of the report of the Fire Inspector who had made the final decision on the site. The Fire Inspector's report revealed a serious irregularity in the decision – namely, that the Inspector had a private conversation with the local fire chief after the public inquiry had been conducted. The points emerging from this conversation influenced the final decision, but were not disclosed to the persons whose property was acquired, nor were they given a chance to respond to them. Inspectors' reports were part of a class over which privilege was customarily claimed in the interests of candour. The plaintiff was unaware of the irregularity. The decision in this case was to concede the challenge without disclosing the document, thus ensuring that the substantive dispute received a just resolution, while also protecting candour.[114]

This is not to say that the conduct of the administration was perfect or above reproach. Crown privilege did produce injustices, as we have discussed above. Nevertheless, the manner in which the administration dealt with this case was by no means exceptional, and it demonstrates that departmental pragmatism could mitigate the harm caused by Crown privilege, at least when it operated at its best. In contrast, officials did not see any way of mitigating the harm to public administration which they believed would flow if the 'class' basis for claiming Crown privilege were to be abolished or diluted. Underlying this lay a clear administrative constitutionalism – a phenomenon by which administrative actors not only apply constitutional requirements, but seek to play a part in the process by which constitutional doctrines and ideas are adapted to a changing environment.[115] Three themes, in particular, emerge from the archival record as underlying the civil servants' constitutional worldview and their resistance to radical reform: the importance they attached to candour; the difficulty they had

[114] LO 2/760, Note for the Attorney General, 30 November 1961.

[115] See GE Metzger, 'Administrative Constitutionalism' (2013) 91 *Texas Law Review* 1897.

in articulating an alternative; and their feeling that the judiciary neither understood nor cared to understand the needs of administration.

A. Candour and the 'Class' Basis of Crown Privilege

The departmental record shows an attachment to candour and completeness that was real, and not merely a convenient fig leaf to conceal a different motive. Civil servants very strongly held the view that candour would become impossible unless the 'class' rule was very strictly observed.[116] Civil servants would not be candid or make complete records if they thought there was any chance that the document might be disclosed, or if there was any possibility that the discovery process might mean that 'the Courts and Counsel could have "a field day amongst the files"'.[117] They would, in particular, be reluctant to record any views that might 'embarrass the whole administration of government'. The necessary implication was that maintaining candour and completeness required that:

> [T]he confidentiality of the document must be established for all time at the moment it comes into existence – it follows inevitably that the writer of a document of that class must know when he puts pen to paper that the document is never going to be disclosed.[118]

This was only possible through a rigid and robustly defended conception of 'class' privilege. A procedure based purely on content would not serve this purpose, because the official at the time of producing the document would not be sure whether or not the advice was being given in confidence.[119]

This view was held not only by administrators, but also by senior politicians. It underpinned both Attlee's 1947 memorandum,[120] and the Cabinet Committee's adoption of the Kent Committee Report in 1956.[121] Administrators also found confirmation of this view in the private sector. As part of the work of the Kent Committee, Kent had met with ICI and Unilever to gauge how they dealt with discovery in civil proceedings, and the impact it had on their functioning. These meetings suggested that the possibility of disclosure had indeed harmed candour in the private sector. Engineers no longer wrote reports expressing views as to the likely causes of accidents, for fear of the embarrassment caused if such reports had to be disclosed. Companies were very careful about what was written down, with confidential information only put on paper

116 TS 58/233, Departmental Circular on Crown Privilege, 31 March 1955.
117 TS 58/233, Minutes of the First Meeting of the Committee on Crown Privilege, 24 March 1955.
118 LCO 2/5122, Rankin to Bancroft, 5 June 1956.
119 CAB 134/1314, Report of Official Committee on Crown Privilege, para 49.
120 CAB/129/22, Crown Proceedings Act 1947: Memorandum by the Prime Minister.
121 CAB 134/1314, Cabinet Committee on Crown Privilege: Minutes of a Meeting held on 16 May 1956, 1–2.

where absolutely necessary.[122] The problem was likely to be even more acute for departments, whose their actions were subject to challenge on the basis of vires and subject to a higher standard of conduct than private companies, but who also had a greater need for careful recording of matters than business.[123]

In making this point, administrators were not engaging in a single-minded or unreflective defence of secret government. The practice, for example, was to waive even class privilege for documents required by individuals facing serious criminal charges.[124] The Kent Committee report (which, it should be remembered, was not written for publication, and is therefore likely to represent the true views of its authors) welcomed the fact that ministers were now more inclined 'to give full for their decisions, thus giving better opportunities for effective challenge in the courts as well as in Parliament'. This, they said, created a better balance between 'the needs of good administration and the rights of persons affected by Government decisions'.[125] But this did not apply to civil servants. Government decisions and actions should be examined in the light of the positions taken by ministers, rather than in the light of opinions expressed by civil servants.

Scholars of public administration have described the relationship between civil servants and their ministers as founded on a 'public service bargain'.[126] Under this bargain, in return for agreeing to 'anonymity, some sacrifice of political rights and proficient performance', British civil servants were assured 'prominent careers, honours and a six hour working day when the middle classes wanted just that, and neutrality was possible, credible and inexpensive'.[127] Anonymity was a key component of this bargain. At one level, anonymity represented a deferral of credit. A civil servant would no longer receive immediate credit for their contribution to policy-making or administration. Rather, the reward, if it came, would take the form of honours for their contribution over the course of their career. Equally significantly, however, anonymity also represented a shield. The ability to express views freely and frankly without fear of publicity, and to have these views weighed in any decision or giving of advice was one of the privileges of a civil service career, and part of what they had to offer in terms of proficient advice. This was not simply a matter of bureaucrats defending their interests. Rather, this 'highly complicated bargain' was the foundation of the working relationship between ministers and civil servants. Aware of the temptation on the part of Ministers to 'shuffle out' of their part of the bargain, it is perhaps not surprising that officials were highly sceptical of any attempts to interfere with the existing 'bright line' on class privilege. In the context of

[122] TS 58/233, Minute of meeting with the Secretary of Unilever Ltd, 28 October 1955.
[123] CAB 134/1314, Report of Official Committee on Crown Privilege, para 50.
[124] TS 27/1530, Newman to O'Brien, 6 August 1953.
[125] CAB 134/1314, Report of Official Committee on Crown Privilege, para 47.
[126] C Hood and M Lodge, *The Politics of Public Service Bargains: Reward, Competency, Loyalty – and Blame* (Oxford, OUP, 2006).
[127] B Schaeffer, *The Administrative Factor* (London, Cass, 1973) 252.

1956, when memory of the Crichel Down affair was still fresh (and in which, as we now know, civil servants were unfairly blamed), their concerns about the consequences of the dilution of anonymity cannot be said to be unreasonable.[128]

B. A Lack of Alternatives

A second theme that emerges from the archival record is the civil service's lack of institutional capacity to frame alternative ways of protecting candour and completeness. The civil service was not attached to Crown privilege. As we discussed above, they acknowledged its limitations, and the record displays a strong willingness to consider alternative policies. The difficulty they faced, however, was actually formulating an alternative that they could be confident would work without having unintended side-effects.

Throughout the period between the entry into force of the Crown Proceedings Act 1947 and the decision in *Conway v Rimmer*, discussions were taking place within departments about the problems created by class claims. Many suggestions were innovative and interesting. In 1965, for example, Kean, who worked within the section of the Treasury Solicitor's department that assisted the Ministry of Power, came up with a possible alternative to class privilege. With the Law Reform Committee's review in progress, he suggested that departments abandon class claims and, instead, create a new privilege expressly designed to provide candour. Instead of a certificate that a document fell within a class that was not disclosed in the public interest, he suggested that the Minister issue a certificate that the document originated in a discussion, the candour of which would have been impaired had it been known that it would be disclosed.[129] This proposal, which came to be known as the Kean Formula, attracted considerable interest and discussion and it was generally thought to be more defensible than class claims. Ultimately, however, the civil service was not able to articulate it in a way that they could be confident would be applied as intended by the judiciary.[130] Other attempts to articulate alternate bases for refusals to disclose documents – ranging from analogies with trustees or juries[131] to summarising the factual component of documents without actually disclosing any documents,[132] or simply covering up expressions of opinion in documents while letting statements of fact be disclosed[133] – faced similar problems.

This points to a deeper issue, namely, the lack of institutional capacity to resolve a problem which the civil service recognised was all too real, and to which

[128] I Nicholson, *The Mystery of Crichel Down* (Oxford, OUP, 1986).
[129] TS 49/284, Keane to Charlton, 19 March 1965, para 7.
[130] TS 49/284, Minute by Norris on Crown Privilege, 23 August 1965.
[131] TS 58/740, Johnstone to Charlton, 23 March 1965, 4–5.
[132] TS 58/741, Druitt to Bourne, 13 December 1965.
[133] LCO 2/5117, Discovery of Documents by the Crown: Note of a meeting held on 2 July 1953.

they were attempting to find workable solutions which would not create further problems. There was a genuine desire to administer well, and in the public interest; but in sharp contrast to the way in which things were seen by lawyers and judges, the issue of disclosure was seen as being relatively peripheral to this goal. As the departments saw it the question was simply one of whether existing practice should be liberalised even further, and not (as the legal profession saw it) a fundamental question of the rule of law. Against this background, it is perhaps somewhat more understandable that civil servants defaulted to supporting the status quo – a natural human response to a difficult dilemma.

C. Judges and the Public Interest

A third theme in departmental discomfort with diluting Crown immunity was the view that judges were not well placed to make a decision in relation to balancing the interests of good administration (which weighed against disclosure) against the interests of the proper administration of justice (which weighed for disclosure). Ministers, in contrast, were in a much better position to do so:

> A judge can never be in as good a position as a Minister of the Crown, responsible to Parliament, to make a true assessment of the needs of the proper functioning of the public service. To say this is certainly not to cast a slur on the Judiciary. For the Judges themselves recognise, and have always recognised, that there are some issues which they are not competent to decide, e.g. in the realm of foreign affairs, and which in the nature of things are rightly left to the Executive.[134]

As this quote suggests, two justifications were advanced in support of this view. The first was the principle of Parliamentary responsibility. A minister who happened to get the balance wrong was accountable to Parliament. A judge who misjudged the balance was accountable to no one.[135] The second was that ministers alone had the ability to judge what the interests of good public administration required. Judges did not. Ministers could explain the relevant interest in their affidavit, but it would ultimately lie outside the judge's experience. Ministers, in contrast, had the ability to consult the Law Officers for advice on where the interests of the administration of justice lay, and draw on that advice in striking a balance between the two competing interests.

As with the issue of candour, administrators's views on this were supported by ministers, including at the highest level. Attlee's 1947 Memorandum, for example, pointed out that deciding where the public interest lies frequently involved matters that were not considerations of law. This made it necessary to leave it to ministers, rather than judges, to deal with the matter, as they alone had the necessary information at their disposal.[136] Officials also felt that judges

[134] LCO 2/5122, Rankin to Bancroft, 5 June 1956.
[135] TS 58/740, Druitt to Dobson, 26 February 1964.
[136] CAB/129/22, Crown Proceedings Act 1947: Memorandum by the Prime Minister, para 5.

and lawyers were a little too ready to condemn the administration without seeking to properly understand its functioning. This view was not entirely without basis. The statements of Finemore J in *Road Haulage Executive v Ministry of Supply*, discussed in section I above, provide an excellent example. The document at issue in that case was a report of an accident. Departmental records, however, reveal that the reason the document was not produced was that it did not exist. An inquiry into the accident was conducted, but no written report was produced; and the documents for which Crown privilege was claimed were not a report, but departmental minutes and internal correspondence.[137] Incidents of this type were seen by the departments as being a frequent reminder of the distance between the worlds of the judiciary and the administration.

IV. BROADER THEMES: COURTS, ADMINISTRATORS AND THE LIMITS OF LEGITIMACY

This chapter has sought to shed light on why *Conway v Rimmer* ever came to be decided. At one level, the fact that it did is surprising in the light of the historical record. The civil service did not ignore the importance of balancing the interests of effective public administration against the interests of the administration of justice. On the contrary, they embraced it. Equally, they were not blind to the potential for injustice implicit in the doctrine of Crown privilege. On the contrary, they sought to take steps to ameliorate it. On the other side, lawyers too were not blind to the civil service's needs. Leading legal figures such as Lord Pearson expressly sought to engage with the civil service and reach a mutually acceptable compromise that could be voluntarily implemented. Why, then, did these efforts fail? In this section, we tentatively advance a diagnosis centred around two related factors, one to do with institutional insulation between the judiciary and the administration, and the other to do with the legitimacy of each institution as perceived by the other. These factors, we suggest, are not merely of historical interest: there is reason to think that they continue to affect judicial review today.

Let us begin with the first of these – the issue of institutional insulation. The failure we have just discussed is at its heart an institutional failure. There was no institution which could work out a solution that took on board both the views of civil servants on the needs of good administration, and the views of the legal profession and judiciary on the requirements of the rule of law, whilst also having an eye on the actual types of, and extent of, hardship caused by departmental practice on Crown privilege. The existence of this institutional gap is not new. Scholars in the 1960s, most notably JDB Mitchell, argued strongly that it required the creation of a new type of institution, along the lines of the French

[137] LCO 2/5122, Kent to Manningham-Buller, 26 June 1956.

Conseil d'État, which would have the ability to consider questions such as these in a trans-departmental context, examining whether a practice is justified and how it might be modified in a way that does not unduly harm the interests of good administration.[138] The nature and extent of its consequences, however, have only started to become clear with more recent empirical work into the impact of judicial review on public bodies. Two points emerge from this empirical work. The first is that judicial review does lead public bodies to alter the way in which they work, and that these changes can have beneficial effects on the quality of public administration.[139] The second is that public bodies often struggle to make sense of the outcomes of judicial review, which can very often leave them bewildered in relation to what they are expected to do.[140]

In this chapter, we have suggested that the problem is in part one of the failure of the judiciary to guide the development of – or even note or engage with – the administrative constitutionalism that underpins the administration's own view of its role, mission and priorities. Viewing the problem in terms of institutional theory, and in particular through the lens of institutional insulation, can help us make better sense of why this failure is problematic. Patrick Atiyah demonstrated that law not only performs a dispute settlement function, but also what he termed a 'hortatory' function, of setting standards which people subject to it are expected to follow, and articulating those standards so as to make them capable of being followed by those they are intended to govern.[141] In institutional theory, the hortatory function is an instance of what is termed 'isomorphism': a constraining process which induces one unit in a population to evolve so it resembles other units.[142] Isomorphism can take a number of forms: 'mimetic' where the structures or norms are imitated because they are seen as being superior or more beneficial, 'normative' where they spread through professional norms, and 'coercive' where they spread through the power of one organisation over another.

The empirical work on judicial review and the administration strongly suggests that the judiciary exerts an isomorphic effect on the administration, but that it is typically coercive rather than mimetic or normative. Much of this is down to the institutional insulation which the history of Crown privilege illustrates. Institutional insulation is, in essence, the inability of one institution to see things from another institution's perspective. The failure of the judiciary to engage with administrative constitutionalism, or even recognise its existence, highlights the extent of institutional insulation between the civil service and

[138] See TT Arvind and L Stirton, 'The curious origins of judicial review' (2017) 133 *LQR* 91.

[139] See eg L Platt, M Sunkin and K Calvo, 'The influence of judicial review on bureaucratic decision-making' (2010) 20 *Journal of Public Administration Research and Theory* 243.

[140] See eg S Halliday, 'The influence of judicial review on bureaucratic decision-making' [2000] *PL* 110.

[141] Atiyah, 'From Principles to Pragmatism' (1980).

[142] P DiMaggio and W Powell, 'The Iron Cage Revisited: Institutional Isomorphism and Collective Rationality in Organizational Fields' (1983) 48 *American Sociological Review* 147.

the judiciary. Its effects are illustrated by issue of candour. As we have seen, the potential impact of disclosure on candour and completeness was a constant source of concern to departments, and it represented a real issue as those who engaged closely with the administration eventually recognised. Yet, at the same time, the history of Crown privilege also shows that this concern was almost never taken seriously by the judiciary at any time after *Duncan v Cammell Laird*. A constant theme in legal and judicial responses from *Conway v Rimmer* to *Ex parte Wiley* is the view that the issue of candour is at best minor. The assumption that candour does not matter is, however, precisely that: an assumption which has never been tested or verified. Its validity is called into question by the literature on public interest bargains, and reinforced by the fact that candour has been constantly cited not just by administrators in Whitehall, but also by local authorities claiming public interest immunity.

Consider, for example, the 2013 divisional court decision in *Worcestershire Safeguarding Children Board v HM Coroner for the County of Worcestershire*.[143] This case arose out of an inquest into a teen in foster care, who killed herself after being temporarily removed from her foster carers. The coroner requested disclosure of the Serious Case Review and Individual Management Review reports. The board sought, unsuccessfully, to invoke public interest immunity. In evidence submitted on behalf of the board, its former independent chair used language that closely parallels the points made in the Kent Committee report in defence of class immunity:

> My concern over disclosure of the SCR overview report and the IMRs, which is a very substantial concern, related to the principle that this is intended to be a confidential process, culminating in a publicly published report. It is intended to allow all those involved to speak candidly about what happened so that lessons can be learned. That is, and has always been, a crucial aspect to the process as a whole. If that principle is not maintained the practical value of the process will be greatly reduced, if indeed any remains.[144]

The fact that candour continues to be invoked in the same language and for the same reasons by such different authorities should give some pause for thought in relation to whether it is really as irrelevant as the legal responses have assumed. The issue is not, however, merely one of candour, which is simply an illustration of a deeper issue with modern administrative law. It is an article of faith that the task of administrative law is to give effect to principles of good administration. Yet it is a peculiarity of our modern law of good administration that it has been formulated with no reference at all to the administration's own views as to what constitutes good administration, or what administrative bodies need to administer well. In this, it stands in sharp contrast with virtually every other body of law

[143] *Worcestershire Safeguarding Children Board v HM Coroner for the County of Worcestershire* [2013] EWHC 1711 (QB).

[144] ibid [76].

that discharges a hortatory function in relation to professional bodies. The law of professional negligence, which remains dominated by the profession-focused *Bolam* test, is a clear case in point.[145]

This leads us to the second broader point that emerges from the history discussed in this paper, namely, the issue of legitimacy. In contemporary debates around legitimacy in public law, legitimacy is typically treated as being a feature that flows from the *structure* of institutions. The history of Crown privilege, and the mutual distrust between the administration and the judiciary that underlay it, in contrast, points to a very different dimension of legitimacy – not as an objective fact but as a subjective perception, tied to the way in which a particular institution is perceived as functioning and the types of interests it is perceived as having a predilection to prioritise. To administrators, the judiciary lacked legitimacy when it came to balancing the public interest in good administration against litigants' interest in the administration of justice. Ministers necessarily had a broader horizon in view than the courts, and were in a better position to take all relevant considerations into account than courts were:

> [T]he public interest represented by the administration of justice is usually uncomplicated and is one upon which the Minister can obtain advice from his legal advisers whereas the Court is not in a position to take into account the consideration which the Minister must take account of when determining how the possibility of the disclosure of any particular documents in civil proceedings might operate to affect or to have affected the candour and completeness which are required in connection with such documents to the prejudice of the public interest.[146]

At the same time and coming from the opposite position, the judiciary and the legal community challenged the legitimacy of the executive when it came to balancing the public interest in good administration against the public interest in the administration of justice. Critically, the legitimacy that was challenged was not only that of civil servants, but also that of ministers. In *Conway*, as we have seen above, Lord Reid dismissed the suggestion that a minister could be trusted to balance the competing interests at stake. A minister, he held, had no duty to balance the two interests, and the Minister's view on whether a document should be disclosed could not therefore be taken to be final.[147] Nor was this confined to *Conway*. In *Padfield*,[148] the House of Lords similarly held that courts were free to disregard a minister's view as to the policy of an Act: construction of an Act's policy or purpose was always a matter for the Court. Building on this, a central feature of the development of public interest immunity in judicial review since the Quartet has been the slow loss of ministerial legitimacy in the eyes of the law. In sharp contrast with departmental discussions from Attlee's 1947 memorandum to the Law Reform Committee's review just before *Conway*,

[145] *Bolam v Friern Hospital Management Committee* [1957] 1 WLR 582.
[146] TS 58/741, Draft Memorandum from the Treasury Solicitor, July 1965.
[147] *Conway* (n 2) 950.
[148] *Padfield v Minister of Agriculture, Fisheries and Food* [1968] AC 997 (HL).

the modern approach to public interest immunity assumes that ministers have *no* role to play in balancing the interests of good administration against the interest in the administration of justice. In *Rogers*[149] and *Ex parte Wiley*[150] this is expressly so. The speech in *Rogers* of Lord Pearson, who, as we have seen, chaired the Law Reform Committee, is striking in the narrowness of the role it assigns to the minister:

> The appropriate Minister has the function of deciding, with the assistance of the Attorney-General, whether or not the public interest on the administrative or executive side requires that he should object to the disclosure of the document or information.[151]

A more recent, and even clearer, sign of this loss of ministerial legitimacy in the eyes of the judiciary is the decision of Ousley J in *AHK v Secretary of State for the Home Department*.[152] In considering the role of the Secretary of State in making public interest immunity claims in proceedings under the British Nationality Act 1981, Ousley J said:

> This means that Parliament is taken, perhaps surprisingly, to have imposed a duty on the SSHD herself to strike a balance which could mean that her statutory duty on occasions was to risk national security in the interests of justice for the applicant. If Parliament did so intend, it would also have intended the duty to operate in that way only in the most compelling circumstances.[153]

The import of this is clear. The Minister's job is to protect national security. It is the Court's job to protect the interests of justice for the applicant. The two are distinct and should not be merged, and to the extent a statute seems to give the Minister a role in the latter, that is a surprising exception which should be read narrowly.

It is, at one level, tempting to attribute this loss of legitimacy to the succession of ministerial scandals and misdeeds in the 1960s and thereafter, but the trend would be troubling even if that were true. If the civil service continued to believe that ministers played an important role in balancing public and private interests, then that perception forms part of the administration's understanding of the constitution and, by necessary implication, of their administrative constitutionalism. Seen in this light, the pessimism that underlies the judiciary's position reflects not just a failure to engage with administrative constitutionalism, but a deeper rejection of the need to engage with it, and even of the idea that it could have a productive role to play in identifying how the institutions of the state as a whole might approach the task of balancing the different interests at stake. Nor, in the light of the history discussed here, can this rejection

149 *Rogers* (n 54).
150 *Wiley* (n 4).
151 *Rogers* (n 54) 406.
152 *AHK v Secretary of State for the Home Department* [2012] EWHC 1117 (Admin).
153 ibid [27].

be attributed simply to the way in which the UK structures relations between civil servants and ministers. Although civil servants have little scope to publicly set out positions of their own, as the history of crown privilege shows they do have a range of other avenues to engage with actors in other branches of the state, including the legal and judicial branch. The insulation that characterises the modern position is very far removed from the many attempts to create an environment for constructive engagement between the judiciary and the administrative services in the years leading to *Conway* and even in the years after. However, it is a natural consequence of the approach that was set in motion in *Conway*.

V. CONCLUSION

This chapter has sought to argue that *Conway v Rimmer* remains an important case. Even if the doctrinal points to which it spoke have faded into relative obscurity, it is perhaps the most relevant case in the Quartet in terms of the light it sheds, when seen in historical perspective, on why judicial review remains so controversial in some quarters and why the judicial role in policing the conduct of administration remains so unpopular with the administration and with the executive. Isomorphism is most effective when it is mimetic or normative. Coercive isomorphism of the type that was at play in *Conway* is likely to be at worst resisted, and at best sullenly accepted, particularly when the institution producing the coercive effect lacks legitimacy in the perceptual sense we have discussed – that is to say, where it is seen as having a propensity to produce outcomes at variance with what the institution subject to the coercive power sees as being its needs – and when it is institutionally insulated from those it governs. This is seen from the history of public interest immunity itself which, until the politically driven changes following the Scott Report, was unable to put a final end to the class doctrine.

The issues we have discussed in this chapter also go some way towards pointing to how these issues with judicial review might be resolved, and the law moved closer towards embodying mimetic and normative isomorphism, if greater account is taken by judges and jurists of two dimensions that are currently for the most part ignored. The first is the existence of what we might call administrative constitutionalism – a public law counterpart to the phenomenon that is called 'rights consciousness' or 'claim consciousness' in private law. The history of Crown privilege shows that the administrative branch did, in fact, have a strong administration-internal constitutionalism. It also shows that there was little, if any, engagement with this administrative constitutionalism. It is this lack of engagement that lies at the heart of the problems we have discussed – both the institutional failure discussed in section IV, and the administration's own inability to formulate alternative ways of protecting candour that avoided the issues with class privilege, whilst also ensuring that the matters they sought to prioritise would receive adequate legal protection.

Yet there is nothing inevitable about this lack of engagement. *Conway* itself, for example, would have been less coercive and more normative if it had taken administrative constitutionalism seriously, and worked to guide and refine the manner in which ministers engaged in balancing conflicting interests to ensure that they had greater regard for the interests of justice, without banishing them wholly from the field as *Conway* did. Private law provides plenty of examples of how this may be achieved, ranging from the *Bolitho*[154] exception to *Bolam*, to the guidance provided to banks in dealing with potential cases of undue influence.[155] The failure of the courts to so engage with ministers, therefore, highlights the second dimension of which inadequate account is currently taken. Legitimacy, if seen as a perception rather than as an objective feature of an institution, fundamentally implicates institutional efficacy – the extent to which an institution is perceived as having the ability to do something – and is therefore relative rather than absolute. In administrative law scholarship, it is all too frequently assumed that if one institution is not discharging a particular task to a high degree of perfection, then the appropriate response is to assign the task to another institution. It is this that underpins the increasingly strident debates about the excessive 'power' of the judiciary, or about the need to subject the executive to 'legal control'. The history of public immunity suggests that this way of framing the problem is too simplistic. The need, rather, is to think institutionally, and investigate from first principles what the strengths and limitations of *all* institutions are when taken together, where the relative balance of abilities lies and, ultimately, what sort of institutional configuration could deal more effectively with the problem in a manner that recognises and seeks to address the full range of legal needs and legal interests implicated in the matter. Recognising the need to so broaden our scholarship is a fitting lesson to draw from the history of Crown privilege 50 years after *Conway*.

[154] *Bolitho v City and Hackney Health Authority* [1998] AC 232 (HL).
[155] *Royal Bank of Scotland plc v Etridge (No 2)* [2002] 2 AC 773 (HL).

6

Anisminic in Retrospect

DAVID FELDMAN[1]

I. PROLOGUE

On 17 December 1968 the House of Lords delivered judgment in *Anisminic Ltd v Foreign Compensation Commission*.[2] Reversing the decision of the Court of Appeal and reinstating the first-instance judgment of Browne J, the House upheld, by a 3:2 majority, a challenge to a determination of the Foreign Compensation Commission (FCC) that the company was not eligible for compensation from a fund (the Egypt Fund) because the company had a 'successor in title' which was not a 'British national', so that the company fell outside the eligibility criteria in Article 4 of the Foreign Compensation (Egypt) (Determination and Registration of Claims) Order 1962, SI 1962 No 2187.[3] In a nutshell, the majority held (i) that the FCC had misconstrued the Order, because on its correct interpretation a 'successor in title' could only exist in respect of a deceased person, so (ii) the FCC, by asking about the company's successor in title, had asked itself an irrelevant question and based its determination on its answer, and (iii) by embarking on an

[1] I am grateful to the participants at the SLS Annual Seminar in May 2018 where an early version of this paper was discussed, and to those at the Administrative Law Bar Association's conference in July 2019, where I aired some thoughts about *Privacy International*, for illuminating comments, and to Arjun Dhar, Professor Mark Elliott, Professor Stephen Bailey, Lord Leggatt, Professor Lindsay Stirton and Professor Alison Young, and to the late Lord Morris of Borth-y-Gest. Dining as a student at the Inner Temple in the early 1970s I once found myself next to 'Master Morris'. The name meant nothing to me until, discovering that I was studying administrative law, he asked what I thought of *Anisminic*. When I replied, 'It is a very good decision,' he said, 'I dissented'. With great kindness and a twinkle in his eye, he discussed it with me for a few minutes, before saying, '*De gustibus non est disputandum*', and even more kindly translating it: 'There is no need to argue about matters of taste'. We never met again, but he impressed on me the contests at the heart of the case, which has fascinated me ever since. Remaining errors and idiosyncrasies are my own.

[2] [1969] 2 AC 147. For an account of the history of the litigation and its aftermath see D Feldman, '*Anisminic Ltd v Foreign Compensation Commission* [1968]: in perspective' in S Juss and M Sunkin (eds), *Landmark Cases in Public Law* (Oxford, Hart Publishing, 2017) ch 4.

[3] This revoked and replaced the Foreign Compensation (Egypt) (Determination and Registration of Claims) Order 1959, SI 1959 No 625, as amended.

unauthorised inquiry the FCC had imposed an additional restriction on eligibility for compensation and thus acted without jurisdiction. Having done so, (iv) its determination was a nullity, and (v) therefore not protected by section 4(4) of the Foreign Compensation Act 1950, which provided: 'The determination by the commission of any application made to them under this Act shall not be called in question in any court of law'.

Fifty years later, on 3 and 4 December 2018, the United Kingdom's Supreme Court heard argument in *R (Privacy International) v Upper Tribunal*, giving judgment on 15 May 2019 (*Privacy International*).[4] Had it been planned to mark the golden jubilee of *Anisminic* the timing could not have been more appropriate. Reversing a divided Divisional Court and a unanimous Court of Appeal, a seven-Justice panel of the Supreme Court held by a 4:3 majority that a party to proceedings before the Investigatory Powers Tribunal (IPT) might, if aggrieved by the IPT's decision, in principle challenge it in the High Court by way of judicial review, notwithstanding section 67(8) of the Regulation of Investigatory Powers Act 2000 (the 2000 Act), subsequently amended but which at the relevant time provided:

> Except to such extent as the Secretary of State may by order otherwise provide, determinations, awards, orders and other decisions of the Tribunal (including decisions as to whether they have jurisdiction) shall not be subject to appeal or be liable to be questioned in any court.

In the course of deciding this preliminary issue, counsel's submissions and the four separate judgments all proceeded on the footing that the question of interpretation turned on the requirements of the rule of law, was a matter of statutory interpretation, and fell to be decided in the light of *Anisminic Ltd v Foreign Compensation Commission* and subsequent cases interpreting it.[5] Through the lens of *Privacy International*, we can reassess *Anisminic* and consider whether it still has any authority as a precedent.

The subject sits on the intersection of two complex areas of public law. The first, interpreting preclusive provisions, is difficult because rules blocking people's access to court may be at odds with fundamentally important principles of the rule of law, and access to court has itself come to be seen as a fundamental human right at common law, in international law, and under statute. The other, the concept of jurisdiction, is hard to pin down, and the range of errors which deprive a decision-maker of jurisdiction and the effect of exceeding jurisdiction are contested. This chapter examines first the relationship between the rule of law and preclusive provisions, and then the role of courts in construing statutes which confer limited jurisdiction but also restrict judicial review. These topics overlap; the separation here aims at exegetical clarity rather than conceptual robustness, and might well fail to achieve either.

[4] [2019] UKSC 22, [2020] AC 491.
[5] ibid at paras [187], [199], [201] per Lord Sumption (dissenting).

II. PRECLUSIVE PROVISIONS AND CONSTITUTIONAL PRINCIPLES: THE RULE OF LAW AND PARLIAMENTARY SOVEREIGNTY

A feature of *Privacy International* is the prominence explicitly given to the rule of law. 'Rule of law' was not mentioned in the judgments and (so far as one can tell) arguments in *Anisminic*. Nevertheless, the judges are likely to have been familiar with Dicey's view that the rule or supremacy of law had been one of the characteristic features of the English constitution since the Norman Conquest (alongside the 'undisputed supremacy throughout the whole country of the central government').[6] One meaning of the term was that 'here every man, whatever be his rank or condition, is subject to the ordinary law of the realm and amenable to the jurisdiction of the ordinary tribunals', so that 'every official … is under the same responsibility for every act done without legal justification as any other citizen'.[7] The supremacy not just of law but of ordinary tribunals makes any attempt to exclude people's access to court to test the lawfulness of their treatment by officials constitutionally suspect. From this flowed the principle that a statutory provision limiting access to court should be interpreted as still preserving access to the greatest extent possible. In particular, power-conferring legislation would not be interpreted as conferring power on an 'inferior tribunal' (a decision-maker of status lower than the High Court) to determine finally the extent of its own powers; a body could not extend its powers beyond the limits imposed by Parliament by adopting an erroneous interpretation of the empowering legislation. It had been well established since the seventeenth century,[8] and was accepted by all judges in *Anisminic*, that a decision outside the area designated by legislation would be made without jurisdiction and would be a 'nullity'; as such it would not be protected by a preclusive provision, 'because there is in truth no order or decision of the tribunal at all'.[9] In *Anisminic*, accommodating Dicey's equally fundamental feature of parliamentary sovereignty, there was a similarly tacit consensus that an Act of Parliament might, if appropriately expressed, confer power on an inferior tribunal to decide issues of law authoritatively, including decisions as to its own jurisdiction; but this had never happened. Courts had always been able to maintain supervision over jurisdictional limits

[6] AV Dicey, *Lectures Introductory to the Study of the Law of the Constitution*, 1st edn (London, Macmillan, 1885) 169; 8th edn (London, Macmillan, 1915) 169 (the final edition to be edited by Dicey himself).

[7] ibid, (1st edn) 179–80; 8th edn 189–90.

[8] *Smith, Lluellyn v Commissioners of Sewers* (1669) 1 Mod 44,86 ER 719, cited by Lord Sumption in *Privacy International* (n 4) at [174].

[9] Note: *Anisminic v Foreign Compensation Commission* (1966) [1969] 2 AC 223, Browne J at 234. His Lordship referred to *Evans v McLoughlan* (1861) 4 LT 31 at 33, 34, 35 (HL); *R v Mahony* [1910] 2 IR 695 at 738, 743, 750; *R v Nat Bell Liquors* [1922] 2 AC 128 (PC) at 152; *The State v O'Donnell* [1945] IR 126 at 161; *R v Northumberland Compensation Appeal Tribunal, ex parte Shaw* [1952] 1 KB 338 (CA) at 716 per Lord Goddard CJ; *R v Medical Appeal Tribunal, ex parte Gilmore* [1957] 1 QB 574 at 586, 588; *R v Hurst, ex parte Smith* [1960] 2 QB 133 (DC); and, on the distinction between errors of law on the face of the record and other errors of law, *ex parte Bradlaugh* (1878) 3 QBD 509, and the *Northumberland* case, above.

through a combination of interpretation of the empowering and preclusive provisions and the doctrine of jurisdictional error.

That is not to say that preclusive provisions were never effective. They might exclude review for error of law on the face of the record and for error of fact (unless it was a jurisdictional fact). Time limits, allowing recourse to a court only within a set time, were effective, perhaps because they did not entirely deprive people of access to court; in *Smith v East Elloe Rural District Council* the House of Lords had held that even a decision flawed in a way that might have deprived a decision-maker of jurisdiction, such as fraud or bad faith, was protected by a time limit,[10] an extreme example of the fact that, where a statute granted an appeal to a court (even subject to limits), courts would be less determined to maintain the High Court's supervisory jurisdiction. Nevertheless, by the time of *Privacy International* it was treated as axiomatic that there was a presumption against imputing to Parliament an intention to remove the High Court's supervisory jurisdiction, because judicial review by the High Court as an independent and impartial adjudicator on questions of law made an important contribution to combatting abuse of law and maintaining the rule of law in the UK. While parliamentary sovereignty required courts to give effect to Acts of Parliament, all their Lordships either expressly or by implication embraced the reasoning of Laws LJ in the Divisional Court in *R (Cart) v Upper Tribunal Cart (Public Law Project intervening)*,[11] where he had written of the need, if parliamentary sovereignty were to be a reality, for statutory texts to be mediated by a body 'impartial, independent both of the legislature and of the persons affected by the texts' application, and authoritative – accepted as the last word, subject only to any appeal. Only a court can fulfil the role' if its meaning is not to be 'degraded to nothing more than a matter of opinion'.[12]

Allied to this, there was an argument founded on the functional inconsistency between imposing limits on what a body could lawfully do and excluding the only independent system for policing those limits. As Farwell LJ had said in *R v Shoreditch Assessment Committee, ex parte Morgan*, 'it is a contradiction in terms to create a tribunal with limited jurisdiction and unlimited power to determine such limit at its own will and pleasure',[13] or as Lord Wilberforce

[10] [1956] AC 736 (Lord Reid and Lord Somervell dissenting). *The Spectator*, 20 April 1956, described it as 'a deplorable decision'. When the matter was raised in the Commons, the Attorney-General, Sir Reginald Manningham-Buller (later Viscount Dilhorne) saw no need for the law to be reconsidered (*Hansard*, HC (series 5) Vol 552, col 1640 (14 May 1956)): 'The Crown won.' He had been counsel for East Elloe.

[11] [2009] EWHC 3052 (Admin), [2011] QB 120 at [37]–[40], [42].

[12] In *Privacy International* (n 4), the passage was endorsed at [160] (Lord Lloyd-Jones), [190] (Lord Sumption, with whom Lord Reed agreed), [236] (Lord Wilson). The judgment of Lord Carnwath (with whom Lady Hale and Lord Kerr agreed) is at least consistent with it: at [138] he noted, in relation to the second issue, that Sir James Eadie QC had accepted the need for judicial review by a court or tribunal which was both independent and authoritative, while arguing that the IPT was such a tribunal.

[13] [1910] 2 KB 859, 880 (CA).

had said in *Anisminic*, 'What would be the purpose of defining by statute the limit of a tribunal's powers if, by means of a clause inserted in the instrument of definition, those limits could safely be passed?'[14] In *Privacy International*, Lord Lloyd-Jones considered it to be 'a necessary corollary of the sovereignty of Parliament that there should exist an authoritative and independent body which can interpret and mediate legislation made by Parliament'.[15]

What Lord Carnwath described as 'the critical importance of the common law presumption against ouster' followed from this, and it had to be taken into account when interpreting preclusive provisions. It did not follow, however, that the presumption would never be rebutted. Their Lordships all agreed that in some circumstances it might carry less weight or simply be inapplicable. Whilst they disagreed as to how to apply that insight in practice, they all thought that the nature and functions of the decision-maker, the character of the alleged error, and the drafting of both empowering and preclusive provisions were relevant in one way or another.

The possibility of making distinctions according to the nature of the decision-maker had been discussed in *Anisminic*, when Lord Wilberforce said:

> It is now well established that specialised tribunals may, depending on their nature and on the subject-matter, have the power to decide questions of law, and the position may be reached, as the result of statutory provision, that even if they make what the courts might regard as decisions wrong in law, these are to stand. The Foreign Compensation Commission is certainly within this category; its functions are predominantly judicial; it is a permanent body, composed of lawyers, with a learned chairman, and there is every ground, having regard to the number and the complexity of the cases with which it must deal, for giving a wide measure of finality to its decisions. There is no reason for giving a restrictive interpretation to section 4(4) which provides that its 'determinations' are not to be 'called in question' in courts of law.[16]

Anisminic made no change to the traditional approach to preclusive provisions.[17] But over the intervening years, judges at various times opined that the presumption against ousting judicial review of inferior tribunals was weaker in relation to judicial bodies than administrative ones, or to bodies exercising judicial functions than other functions, or to courts than tribunals, or to a tribunal administering a special, local system of law than one administering the ordinary law of the land. *In re Racal Communications Ltd*[18] concerned an appeal against a High Court judge's refusal to grant a warrant to search the premises of the company under the Companies Act 1948. Section 441(3) provided that the judge's decision was not appealable, but the Court of Appeal nevertheless allowed the Director of Public Prosecutions' 'appeal'. The House of Lords

[14] [1960] 2 AC 147, 208.
[15] [2019] UKSC 22 [160].
[16] [1969] 2 AC 147, 207. This was not necessarily the view of the Civil Service, at any rate in the Foreign Office: see text n 78 below.
[17] See text at nn 8 and 9 above.
[18] [1981] AC 374 (HL).

reversed this, holding that section 441(3) meant what it said and was not affected by *Anisminic* which related only to the original supervisory jurisdiction of the High Court, and that a High Court judge was not subject to judicial review. But Lord Diplock (with whom Lord Keith agreed), obiter, thought that *Anisminic* was 'concerned only with decisions of administrative tribunals', and (unlike Lord Wilberforce in *Anisminic* itself) classified the FCC as such. Legislation could confer on such tribunals power to decide questions of law,

> but this requires clear words, for the presumption is that where a decision-making power is conferred on a tribunal or authority that is not a court of law, Parliament did not intend to do so … But there is no similar presumption that where a decision-making power is conferred by statute upon a court of law, Parliament did not intend to confer upon it power to decide questions of law as well as questions of fact. Whether it did nor not and, in the case of inferior courts, what limits are imposed on the kinds of questions of law they are empowered to decide, depends upon the construction of the statute unencumbered by any such presumption.[19]

Lord Salmon thought that *Anisminic* applied also to inferior courts; his distinction was between the High Court and other courts and tribunals, not between courts and administrative tribunals.[20]

This did not mean that the jurisdiction did not extend to all or most decision-makers,[21] but the applicability of the presumption against allowing bodies other than courts to make final decisions about questions of law affected the willingness of the High Court to hold that a preclusive provision was effective. Even when there was no preclusive provision, a court might legitimately decline to exercise the supervisory jurisdiction. It was well established before *Anisminic* that the High Court had a structured discretion to refuse leave to apply for *certiorari*, and the requirement to apply for permission for an application for judicial review was continued under the Senior Courts Act 1981 and now Part 54 of the Civil Procedure Rules 1999. In *R (Cart) v Upper Tribunal (Public Law Project and another intervening)* the Court of Appeal and Supreme Court, while asserting once more that the supervisory jurisdiction was always available (unless effectively excluded by statute), held that it should not always be exercised.[22] As Lady Hale wrote:

> [T]he scope of judicial review is an artefact of the common law whose object is to maintain the rule of law – that is to ensure that, within the bounds of practical possibility, decisions are taken in accordance with the law, and in particular the law

[19] ibid 382–83.

[20] ibid 386.

[21] But there are some special jurisdictions in which judicial review does not run. This may include Visitors adjudicating on University Statutes, and similar jurisdictions: *R v Hull University Visitor, ex parte Page* [1993] AC 682 (HL), a 3:2 majority decision.

[22] [2011] EWCA Civ 859, [2011] QB 120 (CA) at [20]: 'In our judgment, as in that of the Divisional Court, the supervisory jurisdiction of the High Court, well known to Parliament as one of the great historic artefacts of the common law, runs to statutory tribunals both in their old and in their new incarnation unless ousted by the plainest possible statutory language.' This was not disputed on appeal to the Supreme Court, [2011] UKSC 28, [2012] 1 AC 663.

> which Parliament has enacted, and not otherwise … The question is, what machinery is necessary and proportionate to keep such mistakes to a minimum? In particular, should there be any jurisdiction in which mistakes of law are, either in theory or in practice, immune from scrutiny in the higher courts?

The Upper Tribunal's special expertise and functions and the need to make optimal use of scarce judicial resources led the Supreme Court to hold that, while within the supervisory jurisdiction, permission to apply for judicial review of the Upper Tribunal's decision to refuse permission to appeal from the First-tier Tribunal should be granted only where an important issue of law or practice was at stake or there was some other compelling reason for allowing it. The rule of law did not normally require a further layer of judicial scrutiny, so judicial review should normally be denied in those circumstances. This shows that the rule of law is a double-edged sword: it mandates some judicial review, but also limits the range of cases in which it is mandated. If the tribunal is sufficiently judicial and trustworthy, suspected legal error will not necessarily suffice to require that judicial review be available.

Using the rule of law in this way helps to legitimate judges' supervisory jurisdiction, especially as it has been identified in section 1 of the Constitutional Reform Act 2005 as the direct concern of judges and politicians alike. That does not make the task of articulating its normative elements easier, or less controversial. Despite its importance, it is only one principle among several. We enjoy the rule of law in the United Kingdom because members of institutions agree that they should carry out their activities in accordance with legal principles and rules, and submit to independent judgement if someone claims that they have acted unlawfully. Acceptance of this is not guaranteed. There may be powerful political or social pressures which make it difficult or even inappropriate to give effect to rule-of-law principles in particular circumstances. As Professor Joseph Raz has pointed out, law can do a great deal of good but also gives rise to a risk that it will also do harm. The rule of law goes some way to protect people against the evil which law can do or authorise.[23] It was in this spirit that the Marxist historian EP Thompson described 'the notion of the regulation and reconciliation of conflicts through the rule of law' as 'a cultural achievement of universal significance', adding that 'the rule of law itself, the imposing of effective inhibitions upon power and the defence of the citizen from power's all-intrusive claims, seems to me to be an unqualified human good'.[24] But as Raz has also reminded us, the rule of law is but one, albeit an important one, of many moral principles, and may be outweighed by others or by pressing need. 'Sometimes, violation of the rule of law is the only way in which important interests of the people can be protected. The rule of law is an important moral

[23] J Raz, 'The Law's Own Virtue' (2019) 39 *OJLS* 1, 13.

[24] E Thompson, *Whigs and Hunters: The Origin of the Black Act* (Harmondsworth, Penguin, 1977) 265, 266; see also D Hay, 'Property, Authority and the Criminal Law' in D Hay, P Linebaugh, J Rule, E Thomson and C Winslow, *Albion's Fatal Tree: Crime and Society in Eighteenth-Century England* (Harmondsworth, Penguin, 1977) ch 1.

doctrine. But on occasion its violation may be morally justified'.[25] The rule of law can help to combat the risks arising from abuse of law, but is not in itself a complete answer to questions about the proper scope of judges' supervisory authority in the face of a statutory preclusive provision. Nevertheless, in *Privacy International* the Supreme Court employed reasoning similarly founded on the rule of law when deciding whether, and how strongly, the presumption against excluding review applied to the Investigatory Powers Tribunal. This contrasts with the House of Lords in *Anisminic*, where the restriction on the scope of a preclusive provision was achieved by way of the theory of jurisdictional error.

Unlike the plaintiff company in *Anisminic*, the claimant in *Privacy International* went a stage beyond relying on the interpretation of the relevant legislation, arguing in addition that preclusive provisions of the type in question were constitutionally outside the legislative competence of the Queen in Parliament. Having decided the case in the claimant's favour on the interpretation point, Lord Lloyd-Jones found it unnecessary to address Parliament's constitutional competence. Lord Carnwath for the same reason need not have done so, but decided to express some views as the matter had been fully argued. Lord Sumption and Lord Wilson, dissenting, decided the interpretation point against the claimant, and so considered the constitutional argument, without their conclusion influencing the overall result. Nevertheless, some fairly startling statements were made.

Lord Carnwath thought that it had been clearly established by the time of *Anisminic* that

> there are certain fundamental requirements of the rule of law which no form of ouster clause (however 'clear and explicit') could exclude from the jurisdiction of the courts. The first relates to what I would call 'excess of jurisdiction': that is, a decision arrived at by a tribunal of limited jurisdiction through a process which goes outside those limits whether at the inception or at any stage of the proceedings.

There had been total agreement about this in *Anisminic*; the disagreement had concerned whether the FCC had done something which led it to exceed its jurisdiction. 'The same approach can in my view be applied to what I would term "abuse of jurisdiction": that is, a decision made within the limits prescribed by Parliament but in breach of basic principles governing the making of such decisions', including natural justice and good faith.

> It can be seen as a short step from excess of jurisdiction to abuse in this sense. To deny the effectiveness of an ouster clause is again a straightforward application of existing principles of the rule of law. Consistently with those principles, Parliament cannot entrust a statutory decision-making process to a particular body, but them leave it free to disregard the essential requirements laid down by the rule of law for such a process to be effective.[26]

[25] Raz, 'The Law's Own Virtue' (2019) 14.
[26] *Privacy International* (n 4) [122], [123].

He drew once again on the judgment of Laws LJ in *Cart*, distinguishing between a case where a judge 'simply gets it wrong' and one 'where the judicial process itself has been "frustrated or corrupted", including "substantial denial of the right to a fair hearing" or in other words "a wholly exceptional collapse of fair procedure: something as gross as actual bias on the part of the tribunal"'.[27]

In developing this line of argument, Lord Carnwath accepted that he was moving beyond both *Anisminic*, which had left in place a distinction between errors of law which took a tribunal beyond its jurisdiction and those which did not, and cases following it, which had continued to use the concept of 'jurisdiction' but had recognised that, outside the context of the courts' supervisory jurisdiction, it had different meanings.[28] He cited *In re McC (a minor)* as such a case, where justices had ordered a juvenile to be detained without telling him of his right to legal aid. The question had been whether the justices' order had been 'without jurisdiction or in excess of jurisdiction' so as to deprive them of their immunity from suit. Lord Bridge had referred to the 'many different shades of meaning in different contexts' that jurisdiction had acquired, that adopted by the majority in *Anisminic* being 'at one end of the spectrum'.[29] This showed, said Lord Carnwath, that the courts had not made consistent use of the idea of 'nullity', which was artificial, but had

> felt free to adapt or limit the scope and form of judicial review, so as to ensure respect on the one hand for the particular statutory context and the inferred intention of the legislature, and on the other for the fundamental principles of the rule of law, and to find an appropriate balance between the two. Even if this was not always the way in which the decisions were justified at the time, it may be seen as providing a sounder conceptual basis.

This was 'wholly consistent with the modern constitutional settlement, as confirmed by the 2005 Act, and recognised by this court in *Miller*'.[30] In this light, the judgments in the Supreme Court in *Cart*

> point the way to an approach which ... is both pragmatic and principled. The critical step ... was to confirm, what was perhaps implicit in some of the earlier cases, that it is ultimately for the courts, not the legislature, to determine the limits set by the rule of law to the power to exclude review.[31]
>
> This proposition should be seen as based, not on such elusive concepts as jurisdiction (wide or narrow), ultra vires, or nullity, but rather as a natural application of the constitutional principle of the rule of law (as affirmed by section 1 of the 2005 Act), and as an essential counterpart to the power of Parliament to make law.[32]

[27] ibid [125] per Lord Carnwath quoting Laws LJ in *Cart* [2011] QB 120 (DC) at [96] ff.

[28] *Privacy International* (n 4) [128], [129].

[29] *In re McC (a minor)* [1985] AC 528 (HL) at 536, 546; *Privacy International* (n 4) [129] per Lord Carnwath.

[30] *R (Miller) v Secretary of State for Exiting the European Union (Birnie intervening)* [2017] UKSC 5, [2018] AC 61 (SC).

[31] *Privacy International* (n 4) [130], [131].

[32] ibid [132].

Although presented as a rationalisation of earlier case law, these comments foreshadow a constitutional revolution. Dinah Rose QC, for the claimant in *Privacy International*, did not merely argue that, in interpreting preclusive provisions, it should be assumed that it was not the purpose of the legislation to create such an inconsistency (an interpretative argument). She went further, and argued that preclusive provisions preventing courts from policing those limits would be outside Parliament's competence. Lord Carnwath took this to its logical conclusion:

> [A]lthough it is not necessary to decide the point, I see a strong case for holding that, consistently with the rule of law, binding effect cannot be given to a clause which purports wholly to exclude the supervisory jurisdiction of the High Court to review a decision of an inferior court or tribunal, whether for excess or abuse of jurisdiction, or error of law. In all cases, regardless of the words used, it should remain ultimately a matter for the court to determine the extent to which such a clause should be upheld, having regard to its purpose and statutory context, and the nature and importance of the legal issue in question; and to determine the level of scrutiny required by the rule of law.[33]

As a matter of constitutional law, this represents a significant incursion into the area of legislative omnicompetence of the Queen in Parliament. It signals a willingness among at least some Supreme Court Justices to give some teeth to the striking but more abstract suggestions in *R (Jackson) v Attorney General* that judges might in certain circumstances feel constrained to refuse to give effect to an Act of Parliament. Lord Steyn, for example, wrote of parliamentary sovereignty:

> The judges created this principle. If that is so, it is not unthinkable that circumstances could arise where the courts may have to qualify a principle established on a different hypothesis of constitutionalism. In exceptional circumstances involving an attempt to abolish judicial review or the ordinary role of the courts, the Appellate Committee of the House of Lords or a new Supreme Court may have to consider whether this is [a] constitutional fundamental which even a sovereign Parliament acting at the behest of a complaisant House of Commons cannot abolish.[34]

Lord Carnwath's speculations, albeit obiter, are more concrete and even more threatening to Diceyan notions of parliamentary sovereignty. In terms of *stare decisis*, too, Lord Carnwath's comments are noteworthy. They mark the rehabilitation of what had previously been regarded as an heretical view of Lord Denning concerning judges' proper approach to preclusive provisions. In *Pearlman v Keepers and Governors of Harrow School*,[35] the statutory question was whether installing central heating was a 'structural alteration … or addition' to a rental property. Paragraph 2(2) of Schedule 8 to the Leasehold

[33] ibid [144].

[34] *R (Jackson) v Attorney General* [2005] UKHL 56, [2006] 1 AC 262 (HL) [102] per Lord Steyn. See further Lord Hope at [107] and Lady Hale at [159]: 'The courts will treat with particular suspicion (and might even reject) any attempt to subvert the rule of law by removing governmental action affecting the rights of the individual from all judicial scrutiny.'

[35] [1979] QB 56 (CA).

Reform Act 1974 provided that a determination by a county court judge was to be 'final and conclusive', and section 107 of the County Courts Act 1959 provided that *certiorari* did not lie to bring up a decision of a county court judge into the High Court. Different county court judges had given different meanings to 'structural alteration … or addition'. Some regarded installing central heating as a 'structural alteration … or addition'; others did not. The Divisional Court refused leave to the tenant to apply for *certiorari*. The Court of Appeal allowed his appeal and, by a majority (Geoffrey Lane LJ dissenting) granted *certiorari*. Lord Denning MR saw value in being able to use the supervisory jurisdiction to secure consistency in matters affecting citizens' rights, and said that the distinction between jurisdictional and non-jurisdictional error for deciding whether a preclusive provision applied should be discarded.

> So fine is the distinction that in truth the High Court has a choice before it whether to interfere with an inferior court on a point of law. If it chooses to interfere, it can formulate its decision in the words: 'The court below had no jurisdiction to decide this point wrongly as it did.' If it does not choose to interfere, it can say, 'The court has jurisdiction to decide it wrongly, and did so.' Softly be it stated, but that is the reason for the difference between the decision of the Court of Appeal in *Anisminic* and the House of Lords.[36]

When an inferior court or tribunal went wrong, the High Court should be able to put them right, both to do justice to individual litigants and

> to secure that all courts and tribunals, when faced with the same point of law, should decide it in the same way. It is intolerable that a citizen's rights in point of law should depend on which judge tries his case, or in what court it is heard.[37]

This view was disapproved not long afterwards,[38] but Lord Carnwath has now revivified Lord Denning's flexible approach to preclusive provisions, and has made explicit what was implicit in *Pearlman*: instead of 'interpreting' preclusive provisions in any normal sense, his Lordship contemplates a firm rule that, in this area, Parliament proposes and the judiciary disposes, according to criteria set by the judiciary themselves. He looked beyond the institutional characteristics which ensured that the IPT was a competent and independent reviewer. Its role in deciding questions of law which could also arise elsewhere in the legal system made it important to ensure that it does not develop the law in isolation, but 'conforms to the general law of the land'. The point before the IPT had been of general public importance and the judgment had provided guidance of general importance to ministers, the Security and Intelligence Services, and ordinary people affected by their work. 'Consistent application of the rule of

[36] ibid 70 (fn omitted).

[37] ibid.

[38] See *South East Asia Fire Bricks Sdn Bhd v Non-Metallic Mineral Products Manufacturing Employees Union* [1981] AC 363 (PC) at 370; *In re Racal Communications Ltd* [1981] AC 374 (HL) at 384 per Lord Diplock and 390 per Lord Edmund-Davies.

law requires such an issue to be susceptible in appropriate cases to review by ordinary courts.'[39]

Had there been another way of getting issues of law before an ordinary court, it might not have been necessary to insist on judicial review being available.[40] This raises the interesting possibility that, while the original version of section 67(8) in issue in *Privacy International* might not have been effective to exclude review, the version currently in force, as amended by the Investigatory Powers Act 2016, might be effective, as there is now a right of appeal on a point of law from the IPT, with leave of the IPT, to the Court of Appeal in England and Wales or the Court of Session in Scotland if the Tribunal considers that it raises an important point of principle or practice or there is another compelling reason to grant leave to appeal.[41] There might, however, still be an issue as to whether section 67(8) as amended is effective to exclude judicial review of a decision by the IPT to refuse leave to appeal. In view of *Cart*, judicial review of refusal of leave might still be available where the Divisional Court considers that the matter raises an important point of principle or practice or there is another compelling reason to grant permission to apply.

Other Justices in *Privacy International* were less categorical than Lord Carnwath in contemplating a restriction on the capacity of an Act of Parliament to exclude access to courts and subject it to judges' assessments of the requirements of the rule of law. Lord Lloyd-Jones showed discretion in declining to express a view on a matter not necessary for his decision.[42] Lord Wilson thought that at first sight there was 'much to be said for' Lord Carnwath's negative answer to the question whether Parliament, when it sets a limit to a decision-maker's jurisdiction, can 'deprive it of an essential element of a law, namely that observance of its limits will be enforced in the courts'.[43] He distinguished, however, between that and a statute excluding only review of an 'ordinary error of law'. He criticised Lord Carnwath's failure to identify robust criteria for foretelling the decision in a particular case, and observed that finality of decisions at some point was essential and there was no constitutional requirement for an appeal. After drawing attention to the IPT's status, the qualifications and standing of its members, the requirement that it must apply standards applicable on an application for judicial review, its investigative procedure and its separation from the ordinary courts and tribunals system, Lord Wilson concluded that the IPT was different from the Upper Tribunal and that Parliament had power to exclude judicial review of 'ordinary errors of law'.[44] This would resurrect the distinction between ordinary errors of law and those which deprive a decision-maker

[39] *Privacy International* (n 4) [138]–[139].

[40] ibid [142], citing *Farley v Secretary of state for Work and Pensions (No 2)* [2006] UKHL 31, [2006] 1 WLR 1817, HL.

[41] Regulation of Investigatory Powers Act 2000, s 67A, inserted by Investigatory Powers Act 2016, s 242 (in force from 31 December 2018).

[42] *Privacy International* (n 4) [168].

[43] ibid [236].

[44] ibid [237]–[239], [244]–253].

of jurisdiction. Many would consider that this would reintroduce undesirable technicality to the law, but it would be a way (if not the simplest way) of reflecting the obvious fact that not all errors are equally significant or should be equally destructive of the foundations of a decision-making power. It has been argued elsewhere that trying to treat all errors as being of the same quality and having the same effects obscures real differences and makes it difficult to fashion sensible, principled results in cases where public-interest considerations pull in different directions, although pragmatic considerations must often give way to people's basic rights.[45] A possible implication of moving away from reasoning on the basis of *Anisminic* is that a distinction between 'outright' or 'true' jurisdictional error in the pre-*Anisminic* sense and the extended notion of jurisdictional error flowing from *Anisminic* and cases interpreting it: that distinction may be relevant when deciding whether the rule of law requires judicial review of particular decisions by specific tribunals, especially if the tribunal is judicial in nature.[46]

Lord Sumption, unlike Lord Carnwath, thought that legislation might create a tribunal with unlimited power to determine its own jurisdiction and combine it with a clear and all-embracing preclusive provision. Such legislation would escape the conceptual inconsistency between limiting power and excluding any independent policing mechanism, and Lord Sumption seems to have considered that the courts would have to give effect to it, if it could not be interpreted in a more restricted way; he saw the argument from inconsistency as a guide to Parliament's intention, rather than a frontal assault on Parliament's unlimited legislative competence. But section 67(8) of the 2000 Act did nothing of that sort. Lord Sumption interpreted it as only excluding review of decisions made by a tribunal which (like the High Court in normal judicial review cases) was itself reviewing the conduct of officials and making decisions going to the merits of that conduct. There was nothing unconstitutional in excluding judicial review of such decisions. By contrast, he thought that courts should not interpret a provision like section 67(8) as excluding courts' power to review for procedural failure.[47]

It is possible to offer the following tentative conclusions about the current state of the law. First, four members of our Supreme Court (Lady Hale and Lords Carnwath, Kerr and Lloyd-Jones) were prepared to adopt an interpretative approach to preclusive provisions which would make it even more difficult, though not impossible, for legislative drafters to exclude the courts' supervisory jurisdiction than it was after *Anisminic* and its progeny. This approach

[45] D Feldman, 'Error of law and flawed administrative acts' [2014] *CLJ* 275–314; cf *R (DN (Rwanda) v Secretary of State for the Home Department* [2020] UKSC 7.

[46] *Privacy International* (n 4) [99] per Lord Carnwath, distinguishing between the High Court and other bodies, [161] per Lord Lloyd-Jones, distinguishing between judicial and other bodies, and [205] per Lord Sumption, distinguishing between judicial and other bodies.

[47] ibid [210]–[211].

was based, not on *Anisminic*'s view of the nullity of decisions taken without jurisdiction, but on the ideas that judicial resources should be directed towards cases in which the rule of law requires them, and that this turns on the character of the decision-maker and the nature of the decision as well as the scope of the decision-making power and the terms of any preclusive provision. This is the ratio of the majority. Secondly, it seems that the same principles operate in relation to exclusion of judicial review as in respect of exclusion of appeals, as demonstrated by reliance by the majority on *Cart*. This also has the support of Lords Sumption and Reed, dissenting: they considered that preclusive provisions might be interpreted as excluding review on 'merits' while allowing review for 'procedural' failures, calling in aid the judgment of the Supreme Court in *Lee v Ashers Baking Co Ltd*.[48] Thirdly, there is at least a possibility, embraced or contemplated in different circumstances by Lord Carnwath (with the agreement of Lady Hale and Lord Kerr) and Lord Wilson, with Lord Lloyd-Jones declining to express a view, that a court might refuse to give effect to a preclusive provision if it had the effect of undermining the requirements of the rule of law. If such a power exists, a further question arises: does the power of courts to deny effect to a preclusive provision relate to exclusion of judicial review of any kinds of error, or only to errors of law going to the merits of a case (whatever those may be), or only to errors of law which would take a decision-maker beyond the outer limits of its power? The fact that we can ask such questions shows that we are now in a conceptual and methodological world far distant from that in which *Anisminic* was decided.

III. DRAFTING AND INTERPRETATION

If there is still scope for interpretation, how should it be done, and how should preclusive provisions be drafted in the light of it? *Anisminic* reinforced the interpretative presumption that preclusive provisions did not deprive the ordinary courts of their supervisory function over inferior courts and tribunals where it was claimed that they had acted outside their jurisdictions. The presumption applied to non-judicial tribunals, and to exclusion of potentially jurisdictional errors. As already noted, Lord Wilberforce considered that the FCC exercised judicial functions, and so considered that the presumption that it had no power to decide questions of law authoritatively did not apply when interpreting section 4(4) of the Foreign Compensation Act 1950,[49] but this did not save the FCC from review if it made a decision which took it beyond its jurisdiction. *Anisminic* did not abolish the distinction between errors within jurisdiction and those that took a decision-maker outside its jurisdiction. The FCC's decision was

[48] [2018] UKSC 49, [2018] 3 WLR 1294, SC. See *Privacy International* (n 4) [205] per Lord Sumption.

[49] Above, text at n 16.

reviewable not because it committed an error of law but because that error, erroneously interpreting its empowering instrument (Article 4 of the Egypt Order), caused the FCC to embark on an inquiry (as to whether the company's 'successor in title' was a British national) with which 'they had no right to deal' (Lord Reid), so that they 'exceeded or departed from their mandate' (Lord Pearce), or transgressed 'architectural directions binding the commission'.[50]

Construing the power-conferring and power-limiting legislation, to see whether the challenged decision was or might be of that kind, was therefore crucial to determining whether the preclusive provision would bite. At the time, this was understood to be the ratio of the majority's speeches. The history of immediate moves to amend section 4(4) of the Foreign Compensation Act 1950 demonstrates this.[51] On 31 December 1968 Terence Skemp, parliamentary counsel, instructed to draft a 'safe but unprovocative' clause to add to the Foreign Compensation Bill then before Parliament, suggested reversing the effect of *Anisminic* by enabling an Order in Council to confer power on the FCC 'to determine any question as to the construction or interpretation of any provision with respect to claims falling to be determined by them', while adding that it would be more likely to be 'unprovocative' if this move to reinstate the prior understanding of section 4(4) were accompanied with provision for an appeal to the Court of Appeal.[52] In due course section 3(1) of the Foreign Compensation Act 1969 conferred the extended interpretative power on the FCC, and (despite opposition from the Government) also included a right of appeal to the Court of Appeal, as Skemp had suggested.

But subsequent discussion of *Anisminic* failed to focus on the scope of the decision-making power, becoming fixed instead on the types of errors which might take a decision-maker beyond jurisdiction. Commentators and judges argued that the logic of the reasoning in *Anisminic* (rather than the Law Lords' express words) undermined the distinction between jurisdictional and non-jurisdictional errors, because (i) it was hard to envisage a situation in which misinterpreting relevant legislation could not be regarded as causing the decision-maker to embark on an unauthorised inquiry, or to provide clear criteria for distinguishing between those errors of law which it was within the power of a decision-maker to make and those which were not,[53] (ii) there were some procedural errors which had been held, expressly or impliedly, to deprive a decision-maker of jurisdiction such as breach of natural justice or lack of good faith,[54] and (iii) dicta in the speeches of Lord Reid and Lord Pearce in *Anisminic* had indicated that other flaws in decision-making might go to jurisdiction,

[50] *Anisminic* (n 2) 174, 201 and 211 respectively.

[51] Feldman, '*Anisminic* in perspective' (n 2) 83–90.

[52] TNA FCO 64/131 f 8.

[53] See eg Lord Denning MR in *Pearlman* [1976] QB 56, 70; J Beatson, 'The scope of judicial review for error of law' (1984) 4 *OJLS* 22.

[54] See eg *Ridge v Baldwin* [1964] AC 40 (HL).

such as taking account of an irrelevant consideration or acting for an improper purpose.[55] It came to be said that the effect, though not the ratio, of *Anisminic* was that 'error of law' was a single category, and any such error would automatically render a decision outside jurisdiction and void. What was more, a steadily growing range of matters came to be characterised as errors of law.[56] As a result, it was said that any error of law would make a decision into a nullity.[57]

Approaching jurisdiction and nullity in an abstract way, without careful attention to the empowering legislation read in its institutional and constitutional context, understandably encouraged parliamentary counsel, drafting later legislative attempts to protect decision-makers from review, to focus on finding a form of words in preclusive provisions which would improve on section 4(4) of the 1950 Act, instead of following Skemp's 1968 approach of expanding the power conferred. It has been used in relation to deciding disputes in charities and cathedrals,[58] but it is likely that it has not appeared in any Act of Parliament since the 1969 Act.[59] The result can be seen in legislation concerning tribunals established to deal with complaints about use by officials of powers to intercept or interfere with communications or property and to conduct surveillance of other sorts, which provided the context for *Privacy International*. First, section 7 of the Interception of Communications Act 1985 established a tribunal to entertain applications from anyone who believed that communication had been interfered with. The tribunal was to establish whether a warrant was in place for the interference and, if one was in place, whether there had been a breach of the requirements of the Act in relation to it. Section 7(8) provided: 'The decisions of the Tribunal (including any decisions as to their jurisdiction) shall not be subject to appeal or liable to be questioned in any court'.

In *Privacy International*, it was suggested that the drafter had intended the phrase to include a decision as to any matter on which, as the case law stood immediately prior to the enactment of the 1985 Act (25 July 1985, although it did not come into force until later), an erroneous decision would have been regarded as being outside the tribunal's jurisdiction. If that was the drafter's intention, it would have been far simpler to say so: 'including any matter as to which a decision might deprive them of jurisdiction', for example. A more natural reading of the phrase 'decision as to their jurisdiction' would be that

[55] Feldman (n 2) 92–93.

[56] See eg *O'Reilly v Mackman* [1983] 2 AC 237, 278 per Lord Diplock; *R v Hull University Visitor, ex parte Page* [1993] AC 682, 701–02 per Lord Browne-Wilkinson; *Boddington v British Transport Police* [1999] 2 AC 143, 158 per Lord Irvine LC; *R (Lumba) v Secretary of State for the Home Department (JUSTICE intervening)* [2011] UKSC 12, [2012] 1 AC 245 (SC) [66], though cf Lord Walker at [193].

[57] *Boddington* (n 56) 158 per Lord Irvine LC. Cf D Feldman, 'Error of law and flawed administrative acts' (2014) 73 *CLJ* 275.

[58] See eg Charities (Alexandra Park and Palace) Order 2004 No 160; Charities (Cheadle Royal Hospital, Manchester) Order 2006 No 921; Cathedrals Measure 1999 No 1, s 6).

[59] Westlaw searches for 'any question as to the construction' and 'any question as to the interpretation', 16 February 2020.

it concerned a decision as to whether or not the tribunal had jurisdiction when there had been a challenge to its jurisdiction in a case before it. Such a challenge would normally have related to the scope of its powers and whether any preconditions to its jurisdiction had been met.[60]

Next came the Security Service Act 1989, which put the Security Service (MI5) on a statutory footing and allowed the Secretary of State to grant warrants to authorise entry on or interference with property, subject to certain conditions. MI5's function was described in section 1 of the Act as being 'the protection of national security and, in particular, its protection against threats from espionage, terrorism and sabotage, from the activities of agents of foreign powers and from actions intended to overthrow or undermine parliamentary democracy by political, industrial or violent means', and 'to safeguard the economic well-being of the United Kingdom against threats posed by the actions of persons outside the British Islands'.[61] Section 5 of, and Schedule 1 to, the Act established a tribunal to investigate complaints that the power had been misused. If the tribunal found that there had been unlawful action it could grant a remedy to the complainant.[62] By its very nature, the matters investigated by the Tribunal would be likely to be highly sensitive and confidential, so a complainant would be entitled to be notified of the Tribunal's conclusion but not to receive any reasons.[63] Section 5(4) used a similar formula to that in section 7(8) of the 1985 Act: 'The decisions of the Tribunal and the Commissioner under that Schedule (including decisions as to their jurisdiction) shall not be subject to appeal or liable to be questioned in any court'.

Five years later, the Intelligence Services Act 1994 put the Secret Intelligence Service (MI6) and Government Communications Headquarters (GCHQ) on a statutory footing and conferred statutory power on the Secretary of State to issue warrants to them authorising entry on or interference with property or with wireless telegraphy.[64] Like MI5, the functions of MI6 and GCHQ made it likely that any investigation would touch on highly sensitive matters and information. MI6's functions were 'to obtain and provide information relating to the actions or intentions of persons outside the British Islands' and 'to perform other tasks relating to the actions or intentions of such persons', in the interests of national security (especially defence and foreign policies) of HM Government in the United Kingdom or of the economic well-being of the United Kingdom, or in support of the prevention or detection of serious crime.[65] To those same ends, GCHQ was 'to monitor or interfere with electromagnetic, acoustic and other emissions and any equipment producing such emissions and

[60] In *Privacy International*, this point was made by Lord Carnwath (with the agreement of Lady Hale and Lord Kerr) and by Lord Lloyd-Jones at [111], [165] respectively.

[61] Security Service Act 1989, s 1(2), (3).

[62] Security Service Act 1989, s 5 and Sch 1, paras 2–7.

[63] ibid Sch 1, para 5; Sch 2, para 4(2).

[64] Intelligence Services Act 1994, ss 1–5.

[65] ibid s 1.

to obtain and provide information derived from or related to such emissions or equipment and from encrypted material', and to provide advice and assistance relating to languages, cryptography and the protection of information and other material to the armed forces, the Government, or any other organisation which is determined in a manner specified by the Prime Minister.[66] There was to be a Tribunal to investigate complaints about the services.[67] In view of the secrecy of the matters under investigation, the Tribunal was not to give reasons for its decisions,[68] and section 9(4), using what was by then the normal form of words provided: 'The decisions of the Tribunal and the Commissioner under Schedule 1 to this Act (including decisions as to their jurisdiction) shall not be subject to appeal or liable to be questioned in any court'.

In 1997 the police, too, were given power to enter on or interfere with property. Part III of the Police Act 1997 allowed a Chief Constable or officer of equivalent rank to authorise, in specified circumstances, 'the taking of any such action, in respect of such property in the relevant area, as he may specify' or 'the taking of such action in the relevant area as he may specify, in respect of wireless telegraphy'.[69] Certain authorisations required the approval of a Commissioner, a judicial officer. Complaints could be made to a Commissioner, who would investigate and might quash an authorisation.[70] The Commissioner was to give notice to the complainant of the conclusion reached on the complaint, but the complainant was not to receive reasons.[71] An appeal lay from a Commissioner's conclusion to the Chief Commissioner, but otherwise decisions of a Commissioner or Chief Commissioner '(including decisions as to his jurisdiction) shall not be subject to appeal or liable to be questioned in any court'.[72]

The various intrusion powers under those Acts were put on a consolidated footing in the Regulation of Investigatory Powers Act 2000 ('the 2000 Act'). A single tribunal, the Investigatory Powers Tribunal, become responsible for investigating all complaints made relating to the use of the newly consolidated powers. Section 67(8) provided, 'Except to such extent as the Secretary of State may by order otherwise provide, determinations, awards, orders and other decisions of the Tribunal (including decisions as to whether they have jurisdiction) shall not be subject to appeal or be liable to be questioned in any court'. The words in parentheses were preferred to 'including decisions as to their jurisdiction'. This new wording seems, on a natural reading, to make it even clearer that the preclusive provision was specifically to protect decisions on direct challenges to the tribunal's jurisdiction, rather than to prevent challenges to other decisions

[66] ibid s 3.
[67] ibid s 9(1) and Schs 1 and 2.
[68] ibid Sch 2, para 4(2). There were very limited exceptions.
[69] Police Act 1997, s 93(1).
[70] ibid s 103.
[71] ibid Sch 7, para 3.
[72] ibid s 91(10).

which, if erroneous, might have deprived the tribunal of jurisdiction. The key point is that, unlike the Foreign Compensation Act 1969, section 3, the 2000 Act did not expressly confer on the tribunal power to determine questions relating to the interpretation of its own enabling legislation.

In view of that, it is not surprising that a majority of Justices in *Privacy International* thought that the addition of 'including decisions as to their jurisdiction' to the formula in section 4(4) of the 1950 Act did not sufficiently distinguish it from the decision in *Anisminic*. Willingness to follow *Anisminic* in its interpretative approach was bolstered first by the general presumption against displacing the High Court's supervisory jurisdiction, to which Lord Carnwath attributed constitutional significance which could, and in that case did, override the normal process of statutory interpretation, which (as Sir James Eadie QC for the Government had submitted) would have involved 'careful examination of the language of the provision, having regard to all aspects of the statutory scheme, and the status or [*sic*] the body in question, in order to "discern the policy Parliament intended in the legislation"'.[73] That, thought Lord Carnwath, 'treats the exercise as one of ordinary statutory interpretation, designed simply to discern "the policy intention" of Parliament, so downgrading the critical importance of the common law presumption against ouster'. One had to look beyond the plain words; ordinary meaning 'had to yield to the principle that such a clause will not protect a "nullity" and that there are "no degrees of nullity"'.[74]

This metaphysical approach was not related to the theory of jurisdiction, which Lord Carnwath discarded in favour of a different question: how important does a reviewing court think it is, in order to give effect to the rule of law, that there should be judicial review of the decision? Nevertheless, it made preclusive provisions constitutionally special to the point at which principles of statutory interpretation did not apply to them. Lord Lloyd-Jones did not think that the presumption against excluding review was applicable to a judicial body exercising judicial functions, but even without it he, like other members of the majority, was very demanding. He speculated that a preclusive provision along the lines of the one proposed in, but deleted from, the Asylum and Immigration (Treatment of Claimants etc) Bill in 2003, might be sufficiently clear and explicit to have the effect of excluding review of even 'ordinary' errors of law. The clause would have prohibited invocation of the courts' supervisory jurisdiction over a tribunal and any questioning of the tribunal's decisions, and gone on to specify that this prevented courts from

> entertaining proceedings to determine whether a purported determination, decision or action of the Tribunal was a nullity by reason of – (i) lack of jurisdiction, (ii) irregularity, (iii) error of law, (iv) breach of natural justice, or (v) any other matter …

[73] *Privacy International* (n 4) [106] per Lord Carnwath, quoting Thomas LJ in *R (Woolas) v Parliamentary Election Court* [2010] EWHC 3169 (Admin), [2012] QB 1, DC, at [54].

[74] *Privacy International* (n 4) [107].

(This clause showed real antipathy to the supervisory jurisdiction; even section 3 of the Foreign Compensation Act 1969 had preserved judicial review for breach of natural justice by the FCC.)

But if an Act were to contain such a provision, there is a risk that it would call forth an even more drastic response from courts than that which the majority adopted in *Privacy International*, drawing on dicta in *R (Jackson) v Attorney General* concerning parliamentary sovereignty, particularly if they follow Lord Carnwath's view about the limits of Parliament's competence to exclude judicial review.[75]

Lord Sumption in *Privacy International* took a less absolute constitutional position. He, like Lord Carnwath and Lord Lloyd-Jones, moved away from the ordinary meaning of the legislation in the light of what he thought were requirements of the rule of law, but he interpreted section 67(8) of the 2000 Act as precluding review of 'errors in the treatment of the merits notwithstanding that they were treated in *Anisminic* as an excess of jurisdiction'.[76] By 'merits' he did not mean questions about unreasonableness or proportionality, but the core issue remitted to a tribunal. In *Privacy International*, it was the scope of the power to issue warrants; in *Anisminic* it had been whether the company was eligible to claim compensation. He thought that the words 'including decisions as to whether they have jurisdiction' referred to review of decisions of that kind, effectively removing the Tribunal from the ratio of *Anisminic*, while leaving open the possibility of review if it stands accused of '"outright" excesses of jurisdiction' (in the sense in which Laws LJ in *Cart* had used the term) or acting outside its 'permitted field'.[77] As Lord Wilson pointed out, however:

> Lord Sumption interprets the word "jurisdiction" in the words in parenthesis so as to relate only to ordinary errors of law and so no longer to include errors of jurisdiction in the proper sense [i.e. undertaking an inquiry or making an order entirely outside its jurisdiction] ... Had Parliament's intention been to allow judicial review of the IPT's errors of jurisdiction in the proper sense, it would not have borrowed from the 1985 Act words which, on any conventional construction of them, so obviously appear to exclude it.[78]

Lord Wilson's dissenting judgment started from a different standpoint from those of the other six Justices. Instead of accepting the *Anisminic* decision as widening the scope of jurisdictional error and either replacing the whole idea of jurisdictional error with something different (Lord Carnwath and Lord Lloyd-Jones) or applying it but allowing section 67(8) to limit its scope (Lord Sumption), Lord Wilson deprecated *Anisminic*'s extension of jurisdictional error and all the subsequent extensions of the idea. He would have re-established the distinction between errors of law which deny a decision-maker jurisdiction, in

[75] See text at nn 31–34 above.
[76] *Privacy International* (n 4) [201].
[77] ibid [198] (referring to *Cart* [2011] QB 120, DC, at [94] per Laws LJ) and [204].
[78] *Privacy International* (n 4) [231].

the narrow, pre-*Anisminic* sense, and those which do not.[79] He was therefore willing, unlike all the other Justices, to follow the ordinary meaning of the provision as a whole, accept that a preclusive provision in the form of section 4(4) of the Foreign Compensation Act 1950 would not protect a tribunal from review for errors which take it outside its jurisdiction in the sense of the four corners of its power, and treat the addition of the words in parenthesis in the 2000 Act as sufficient to make the subsection 'totally clear in excluding judicial review of all the IPT's decisions'.[80] This was loyal to the idea that statutory provisions are there to be interpreted, and would have left *Anisminic* as an extreme example of a case where judges held that a tribunal had exceeded the four corners of its remit. In effect, it would have been disapproved as a significant precedent.

The other judgments leave in place *Anisminic* as explained in later cases, and further expand its scope in relation to decisions by administrative decision-makers, in respect of whom the constitutional presumption against excluding judicial supervision is strongest. Would the FCC be regarded as administrative for this purpose? Perhaps: at the time, although it acted in a judicial manner and Lord Wilberforce thought that it had judicial functions, it was regarded within the Foreign Office as not determining the rights or liberties of subjects; some civil servants doubted whether it was even an administrative tribunal 'in the ordinary sense'.[81] It was certainly very different from the IPT, which has the task of reviewing, with judicial personnel and applying judicial review principles, decisions and acts of officials. Dr Robert Craig has suggested that the constitutional difference between officials exercising executive power and tribunals exercising judicial functions, including review of executive behaviour, calls for different treatment of preclusive provisions protecting the exercise of judicial functions from those protecting administrative or executive functions, and Lord Carnwath referred to his article approvingly.[82] This is one of the factors which influenced the majority in deciding on the applicability and weight of the presumption against excluding judicial review. Its effect is to reinvigorate debates about the hallmarks of administrative or executive, as compared with judicial, bodies and functions.

With regard to judicial tribunals, *Privacy International* departs significantly from *Anisminic*. The majority rejected the distinction between jurisdictional and non-jurisdictional errors, whether of fact or law, and the idea of nullity as guides to the availability of judicial review in the face of preclusive provisions.

[79] ibid [219], [220] and [231].

[80] ibid [229]. A number of people had formed the same view, albeit on the basis of less exhaustive analysis. See eg D Foulkes's annotation on s 7(8) of the Interception of Communications Act 1985 for the *Current Law Statutes* edition of that Act; D Feldman, *Civil Liberties and Human Rights in England and Wales* 2nd edn (Oxford, Oxford University Press, 2002) 681–82; *R (A) v Director of Establishments of the Security Service* [2009] UKSC 12, [2010] 2 AC 1 [23] per Lord Brown.

[81] Sir Alexander Morley to Franklin Berman, TNA FCO 64/133 f 4, 23 December 1968.

[82] R Craig, 'Ouster clauses, separation of powers and the intention of Parliament' [2018] *PL* 570; *Privacy International* (n 4) [39].

Lord Carnwath for the majority substituted for it a form of principled pragmatism based on the requirements of the rule of law. Lord Sumption, dissenting, invented a new distinction, perhaps applicable only to the IPT (since it was based on an interpretation of section 67(8) of the 2000 Act), between review of 'merits' and other forms of review. Only Lord Wilson would have kept the distinction between jurisdictional and non-jurisdictional error, but without approving *Anisminic*; he regarded *Anisminic* as having stretched the idea of a jurisdictional error too far and was unimpressed by subsequent further extensions of it, whether in earlier cases or by other Justices in *Privacy International* itself. He would have returned to the narrow idea of jurisdictional error used in nineteenth- and early twentieth-century cases.[83]

IV. EPILOGUE

Anisminic was by any standards one of the most significant decisions of the House of Lords on a public law matter. It is often forgotten how controversial was the structure of the compensation scheme which the FCC had to interpret, for losses suffered by people who had to bear 'the burden of our collective insanity' in invading Egypt in 1956.[84] We forget how important it was for the FCC to keep the range of eligible claimants and compensable losses within bounds in order to make possible the fullest permissible compensation for those claims which were held to be established, and to be free to make distributions when any challenge to any determination might necessitate delaying all distributions to all claimants until the litigation was finished. (This was ultimately avoided, in the case of the Egypt Fund, only because the Government and Parliament finally agreed to top up the Fund from the Consolidated Fund.) It is also easy to forget how long it took for any consensus to emerge as to the implications of the decision, and how many oddities that consensus, based on a greatly enlarged conception of jurisdictional error and the idea that decisions without jurisdiction are nullities, threw up.

Privacy International has reignited debates about the concept of jurisdiction, the idea of nullity, and the proper approach of courts to preclusive provisions. The judgments have moved the focus away from the ideas that there is only one category of error of law and that all errors of law go to jurisdiction. We now have a fluid, pragmatically shaped boundary between law and fact,[85] a new focus on the extent to which courts need to exercise their supervisory jurisdiction in

[83] See P Murray, 'Escaping the wilderness: *R v Bolton* and judicial review for error of law' (2016) 75 *CLJ* 333.

[84] *Hansard* HC (series 5) Vol 672, col 373 (5 February 1963), Geoffrey Hirst MP quoting from *The Daily Telegraph* during a debate on the draft Foreign Compensation (Egypt) (Final Distribution) Order SI 1963 No 365.

[85] *Privacy International* (n 4) [134] per Lord Carnwath.

order to protect the rule of law, and the emergence of the rule of law as a legal instrument. The elevation of a constitutional principle into a legally enforceable standard is a process that has gathered speed in recent years, and *Privacy International* is a prime example of it. That is not to say that the Law Lords in *Anisminic* were blind to the rule of law. Far from it: the spirit of the rule of law pervades every page of their speeches. What is new is the idea that we can find clear guidance in a more granular articulation of rule-of-law principles for more concrete decisions in hard cases.

Finally, it is important to remember how contested the legal outcome was in *Anisminic*. The case raised fundamental, and fundamentally difficult, constitutional, legal and conceptual problems, including issues of statutory interpretation in the shadow of constitutional principles. *Privacy International*, and especially but not solely the dissenting judgment of Lord Wilson, reminds us that those disagreements are still with us, and must be confronted or as elegantly as possible by-passed. Where there are tensions between different judicial and constitutional philosophies, judgments come and go, but problems do not disappear. Four of the seven Justices who decided *Privacy International* retired from the Supreme Court within a year of the judgment: Lady Hale and Lord Carnwath from the majority; Lords Wilson and Sumption from the dissenting minority. New appointees are unlikely to be less divided in their views, if the opinions of Leggatt J (now Lord Leggatt) in the Divisional Court and Sales LJ (now Lord Sales) in the Court of Appeal in *Anisminic* are any guide.[86] It is quite possible that, after another 50 years, lawyers will still be arguing about the same issues, and perhaps coming up with yet more ways of trying to resolve them.

[86] [2017] EWHC 114 (Admin), [2017] 3 All ER 1127, DC; [2017] EWCA Civ 1868, [2018] 1 WLR 2572, CA.

Part III

The Legacy of the Quartet

7

Plus ça Change? *An Empirical Analysis of Judicial Review in Modern Administrative Law*

SARAH NASON*

I. INTRODUCTION

IN THIS CHAPTER I argue that '*plus ça change, plus ça reste pareil*' – 'the more things change, the more they stay the same' – is a fitting epithet for judicial review in the modern administrative law of England and Wales. Drawing on previous research alongside new empirical data, I consider what has changed most about judicial review and what may have stayed the same. This chapter is organised around two key tensions. The first tension is that while individual grievance claims make up the larger share of judicial review caseload, as a 'form of action', the application for judicial review is generally ill-suited to the resolution of individual disputes. The second tension is between a generalist approach to administrative law – one that seeks to articulate general grounds of review applicable across areas of administrative activity – and a more specialist, context specific approach.

The Application for Judicial Review (AJR) was introduced in order to simplify and harmonise public law procedures and remedies, rationalising routes to challenging administrative action. Channeling this diet of cases into the High Court via the AJR procedure is said to have supported the development and consolidation of modern general principles of administrative law. However, this funneling may have contributed to reduced access to justice, especially when coupled with a judicially imposed principle of 'procedural exclusivity' closing off alternative, often more subject matter specific, redress routes.[1] Although later civil justice reforms restored flexibility, recently the process of applying for judicial review in

* With thanks to the organisers and participants of the SLS Annual Seminar 2018, especially to Professor Maurice Sunkin and Richard Kirkham for comments on this chapter.

[1] *O'Reilly v Mackman* [1983] 2 AC 237.

the High Court (Administrative Court) has involved more technicalities. Some of these technicalities reflect the judiciary's approach to using procedural discretion, especially the permission stage, to manage their own resources. Another factor is a government desire to insulate itself from challenges especially when these are perceived to be delaying economic progress. However, in this chapter I argue that the development of newer procedural technicalities also suggests a preference towards accommodating the variable policy issues arising within particular (subject-specialist) areas of administration that is reflective of a more contextual approach to administrative law.

The regular conflation of 'general administrative law' and 'grounds of judicial review' obscures the importance of statutory, often subject-specific administrative law. This may also have contributed to the comparative under-theorising of administrative law (as compared to the many theories on the constitutional justification for judicial review).[2]

Yet despite judicial review's constitutional significance, its expanding remit in terms of bodies subject to review, remains to be contrasted against the practical reality of people being excluded from accessing the process.[3] Despite admitted growth in the number of AJRs per annum since the procedure was established, little may have changed in terms of practical access for individuals, particularly when comparing caseloads to population statistics and the scale of public administration.

The AJR itself is perhaps most significantly a procedure of last resort, when no other route is available to challenge government or those who work on its behalf. This also means that judicial review functions as a barometer of people's comparative access to, and satisfaction with, available routes to redress across the administrative justice system. As such, the AJR process highlights where other mechanisms are lacking, by identifying the absence, ineffectiveness or inaccessibility of rights to appeal or administrative remedies. It can also provide a means to redress systemic failings where no other route to do so is available. However, in light of recent government reforms restricting access, the AJR procedure is becoming less relevant to a range of areas of administration where it once played a significant oversight role, such as social security and prisons.

Whilst there are limitations to the conclusions that can be drawn from litigation data, the account developed here shows that outside specific areas of public decision-making, there has been no explosion in judicial review. I demonstrate

[2] As Thomas Adams, Hasan Dindjer and Adam Perry argue 'Administrative law theory traditionally takes a back seat to constitutional law theory'. However, in a showcase of eight new theoretical approaches they also note that: 'In the past several years, administrative law theory has become a more active area, with new scholars taking the subject in new directions. The best of this recent work is rigorous, analytical, interdisciplinary, and deeply engaged with legal doctrine'. T Adams, H Dindjer and A Perry, 'Showcase: New Directions in Administrative Law Theory', *International Journal of Constitutional Law Blog* (8 September 2019), available at www.iconnectblog.com/2019/09/showcase-new-directions-in-administrative-law-theory.

[3] C Harlow and R Rawlings, *Law and Administration*, 3rd edn (Cambridge, Cambridge University Press, 2009) 669.

that there has been a significant decline in non-immigration judicial review, coinciding with government reforms initiated in 2013. These reforms have been highly effective in their objective to restrict access to the AJR procedure. This means that whilst judicial review may be experiencing one of its most constitutionally important, and contentious, eras (note the wide range of Brexit-related litigation)[4] it is conversely experiencing a low point in providing resolution for individual grievances against the state.

For some, establishing an 'exclusive' AJR procedure in the High Court was never really about increasing access to justice for individuals, but rather it helped accelerate and rationalise the development of general administrative law (which either began with or was significantly catalysed by the Quartet cases). Nevertheless, the seemingly broadened and rationalised remit of general administrative law has been seen as both a partial cause and effect of the expanding judicial review caseload in the twentieth century.

In this chapter I argue that more recent divergences in AJR procedures have developed as a means to address the subject matter specificity of particular areas of administration (ie, planning, the environment, prisons) partially in recognition of the limitations of general administrative law at the substantive stage of review. However, some of these procedural devices have also disproportionately impeded access to justice. I consider whether they should be replaced with a more contextualised approach to substantive administrative law doctrine that may better be developed by various tribunals, in conjunction with the High Court (Administrative Court). This necessitates giving more thought to the availability of tribunal appeal processes and reconsidering the AJRs appropriateness as a mechanism to resolve particular types of individual grievance claim.

II. JUDICIAL REVIEW AND GENERAL ADMINISTRATIVE LAW

The standard story of an expanding caseload is demonstrated by Figure 7.1, which shows judicial review-type claims issued per annum from 1968 to 2019 inclusive. The data from 1968 to 2011 was collated by Ruth Dixon and Christopher Hood.[5] The data on 'judicial review' prior to the Order 53 procedure (now Senior Courts Act 1981 and CPR Procedure) only includes claims for prerogative orders in the Queen's Bench Division and is under-inclusive of the different types of applications then available to challenge administrative action. Thanks to research from 1987 onwards, and more detailed recording of Ministry

[4] See eg, *R (Miller) v Prime Minister* [2019] UKSC 41, [2019] 3 WLR 589, which began as a judicial review application: *R (Gina Miller) v The Prime Minister* [2019] EWHC 2381, [2019] EWHC 2381 (QB).

[5] Available at docs.google.com/spreadsheets/d/1Kcm2Buf8ykb9otUleY5gQCW1DKaaYSpWoNzabR7AmAs. Later data is taken from Ministry of Justice Civil Justice Statistics, available at www.gov.uk/government/collections/civil-justice-statistics-quarterly.

of Justice statistics in recent years, the latter data is split between asylum and immigration claims, other civil claims, and criminal claims.

Figure 7.1 Prerogative order and judicial review applications over time

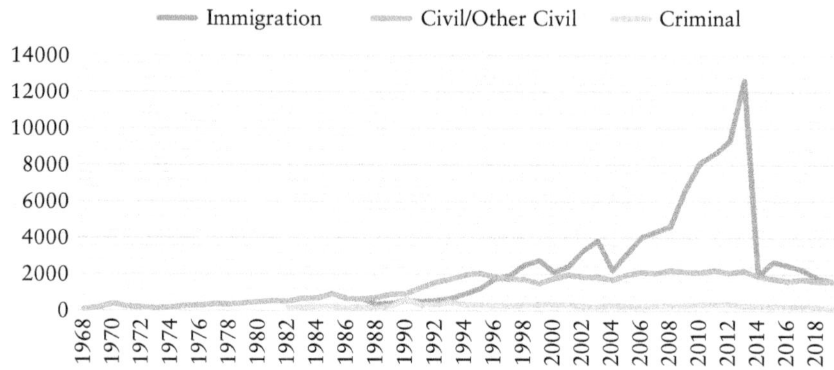

Dixon and Hood's data (which is taken from the Lord Chancellor's Official Statistics) shows that applications for the prerogative orders rose significantly in the late 1960s: from 87 in 1968 to 396 in 1970. The figures are then more variable up until the mid-1980s, after which there was a period of sustained increase in other civil (non-immigration) judicial review (up until the mid-1990s). The immigration caseload has risen more dramatically. However, before concluding that the 1960s marked the beginning of period of rapid expansion in judicial control of administration, it is worth considering some historical data. After interrogating the record of prerogative writs, Paul Craig found that between 1220 and 1867 there were 6,637 mentions of *certiorari*, 5,563 to prohibition, and 7,111 to mandamus.[6] Of course these mentions do not each constitute individual cases, and the figures also do not include other historic actions where administrative decisions could be challenged either directly or collaterally such as in cases of trespass or trover against administrative officials. Craig concludes that whilst these figures may be crude estimates, they are 'a corrective to the view that we never had any administrative law before the 1960s, since "we" clearly were doing quite a lot of this activity that supposedly barely existed'.[7]

Why then did Lord Diplock describe judge-led development of a 'comprehensive system of administrative law' from the 1950s to the 1980s as 'the greatest achievement of the English courts' in his judicial lifetime?[8] The key is likely in

[6] P Craig, *UK, EU and Global Administrative Law* (Cambridge, Cambridge University Press, 2015) 25–29.

[7] ibid 29.

[8] *R v Inland Revenue Commissioners, ex p National Federation of Self-Employed and Small Business Ltd* [1982] AC 617 (HL) 641.

his reference to an administrative law that is both comprehensive and systematic, in other words a general administrative law.

To understand this better it is worth considering what Arvind and Stirton refer to as the 'the curious origins of judicial review'.[9] They point out that around the Quartet period, and prior to it in many submissions to the 1957 Franks Committee on Tribunals, there was an appetite for reform wider than the procedure eventually consulted on by the Law Commission. This reforming attitude expressed interest in subjecting administration to the rule of law, but not purely in a restrictive sense, reformers were also concerned with the articulation of good governance and substantive administrative law principles that could mediate between public and private interests, seeking to guide and improve administration. Arguably, an administrative law conceived on this basis, of mediating between public and private (individual interests), would have shown more recognition of the position of the individual subject to administration and their centrality to judicial review litigation. But, somewhat to the contrary, from the late 1960s onwards judicial review tended to proceed based on a central aim of legal accountability, controlling and regulating administrative action, it did not develop as a means of securing individual redress.

As such the problem of the individual could be seen primarily as a 'trigger' to propel a case into the system, which would then allow a small set of judges to progressively develop a comprehensive and systematic administrative law. Under this account, the ability of judicial review to determine the limits of public power, and the place of law and the judiciary in that system, appears more important than providing redress to particular claimants, or indeed to actively articulating broader principles of good administration. This has, to an extent, set judicial review on a particular trajectory, one based on legal significance over and above access to remedies for individuals. I argue that such a pathway also tends to emphasise general, rather than more subject matter contextualised administrative law, posing less risk of interference with the substantive expertise of administrators. By general administrative law, I mean administrative law doctrines that are said to apply to all subject matters of administrative decision-making such as planning, housing and professional discipline. This represents a break with earlier accounts, particularly those of the so-called 'functionalists' whose positions on the nature of good administration might have led to more contextualised or subject-matter-specific administrative laws (based on the characteristics of particular public bodies and the context of their decision-making). Harlow and Rawlings suggest, however, that the seminal 1951 functionalist textbook written by Griffith and Street, rowed back from these implications by focusing instead on describing types of central government powers and their respective limitations.[10] However, the main distinction comes with the later

[9] TT Arvind and L Stirton, 'The Curious Origins of Judicial Review' (2017) 133 *LQR* 91.

[10] C Harlow and R Rawlings, 'Administrative Law in Context: Restoring a Lost Connection' (2014) *PL* 28, 35.

works of de Smith (in 1959)[11] and Wade (in 1961)[12] which are both organised around general principles and techniques designed to impose legal control and accountability on administrative power across a range of subject matters.

The trend towards a generalist account of administrative law was evident, at least by implication, in the Law Commission's proposals recommending a specific application for judicial review. Arvind and Stirton lay responsibility for the narrowness of the Law Commission's terms of reference on the shoulders of Lord Diplock,[13] for persuading the then Lord Chancellor not to take a more substantive look at administrative law. Lord Diplock's own later case law development of 'procedural exclusivity', under which claims against public bodies should only be brought via judicial review in the High Court, went against the Law Commission's rejection of exclusivity and the traditional flexibility of common law procedures and remedies.[14] Maurice Sunkin asserts that the development of 'exclusivity' represented an important step towards consolidating litigation against public authorities in a distinctive High Court administrative law jurisdiction based on judicial review.[15] Sunkin further notes that a prime function of this consolidation was 'to maximise judicial control over public law litigation and thereby enable the judiciary to regulate its and the law's role within government'.[16] In consequence, limiting access to justice for individuals might have been seen as a fair price to pay for allowing judges to develop a systematic and comprehensive body of general administrative law, which they saw to be in the public interest.

III. JUDICIAL REVIEW AND INDIVIDUAL GRIEVANCES

Whatever the implications of establishing a specific AJR to the development of modern administrative law, it is clear that the procedure has remained only minimally relevant as a means to provide redress to individuals. Looking back to the 1940s to 1960s (the so-called 'dark ages' of pre-systematised administrative law), Susan Sterett cites the Lord Chancellor's statistics, showing that the number of applications for prerogative orders averaged approximately 100 per annum; subsequently increasing from 1968 to 1970.[17] It may be that high-profile judgments against the administration, including the Quartet cases, played some part in emboldening lawyers to bring claims.[18] Nevertheless, whilst the Quartet cases

[11] S de Smith, *Judicial Review of Administrative Action* (London, Stevens and Sons, 1959).

[12] W Wade, *Administrative Law* (Oxford, Oxford University Press, 1961).

[13] Arvind and Stirton, 'Curious Origins of Judicial Review' (2017).

[14] In the case of *O'Reilly v Mackman* [1983] 2 AC 237 (HL).

[15] M Sunkin, 'What is Happening to Applications for Judicial Review?' (1987) 50 *MLR* 432, 463–64.

[16] M Sunkin, 'Judicial Review: Rights and Discretion in Public Law' (1983) 46 *MLR* 645, 653.

[17] S Sterett, *Creating Constitutionalism? The Politics of Legal Expertise and Administrative Law in England and Wales* (Michigan, University of Michigan Press, 2000).

[18] L Blom-Cooper, 'The New Face of Judicial Review: Administrative Changes in Order 53' [1982] *PL* 250.

are important to the qualitative story of general administrative law and its perceived influence on administration, there is no real evidence of their quantitative impact.[19]

During its consultative process in the 1960s and 1970s, the Law Commission had access to unpublished research into the Queen's Bench caseload. This research (conducted by Blom-Cooper and Drewry for Bedford College, London) showed that the prerogative caseload was increasing, and that just over one-third of applicants were refused leave. However, from 1971 the caseload fell up to and including 1973. It is from 1974 onwards that there is a sustained period of growth. Some of this mid-1970s growth is likely attributable to litigation driven by the Immigration Act 1971 and the parallel expansion of relevant legal services apt to support subject-specialist claims. The 1971 Act provided a specific appellate regime through the Immigration Appeal Tribunal (IAT). The number of immigration-related AJRs was not separately identified until 1987, but Sunkin notes that at least by the early 1980s applications to review decisions of the IAT (which could not be appealed) were rising. Sunkin's empirical studies in the 1980s found that immigration claims made up 46 per cent of the overall civil caseload in 1981, increasing to 59 per cent by 1985.

As one would expect, following introduction of the specific AJR procedure, the caseload quickly expanded much beyond the previous number of prerogative applications. This was because the AJR was specifically designed to subsume a wide range of other methods for bringing claims against administration. However, as both Sunkin and Sterett's analyses suggest, immigration claims became central to the AJR caseload, constituting much of the increase in litigation. For example, by the mid-1980s Sunkin's research recorded a drop in other civil (non-immigration) cases; a reduction of nearly 32 per cent at a time when, as he put it 'most of us would have assumed a continued general and uninterrupted increase'.[20]

It is near impossible to say whether introducing the AJR led to an overall increase in litigation against public bodies. This is because there is no prior baseline data on use of the range of other mechanisms, such as applications for declaratory relief or what were then perceived as 'tort' claims against public bodies, subsumed into the AJR. There was also no estimate of the combined total number of statutory appeal applications through various mechanisms in various jurisdictions.

Paul Craig attempts some historical comparison by situating his statistics about references to prerogative remedies, and other actions (such as trespass and trover), in the context of population data. The comparisons suggest at least that modern administrative law makes much less use of prerogative remedies than might have been expected given population growth.[21] Whilst this could be in

[19] M Sunkin, 'The Use of Empirically Based Information when Reforming and Evaluating Judicial Review' in A Higgins (ed), *The Civil Procedure Rules at 20* (Oxford, Oxford University Press, 2020).

[20] Sunkin, 'What is Happening?' (1987) 444.

[21] Craig, *UK, EU and Global Administrative Law* (2015) 28–29.

part due to the development of other remedies such as declarations and injunctions, the data gives some weight to the view that introducing the AJR has not had significant ramifications in terms of the number of people being awarded a prerogative remedy. Indeed, over the lifetime of the AJR procedure the number of people awarded a remedy each year through the process (whether prerogative or otherwise) has changed little.[22]

Data cited by Harlow and Rawlings in *Law and Administration*, first published in 1984, states that 20 prerogative remedies were awarded in 1967, and 31 were awarded in 1978 (higher numbers were awarded in some of the intervening years).[23] Harlow and Rawlings report that in 1981, after the AJR procedure was introduced, there were 560 applications (165 of which related to criminal proceedings). In that same year 108 orders were granted (and 44 of these were in criminal proceedings); this includes both prerogative and other remedies. From 1987 to 1989 inclusive Sunkin's more specific 'cohort' data tracked particular cases and demonstrated that claimants were successful at final hearing in on average 214 claims per annum (and that much of the increase from the early to late 1980s was due to immigration AJRs).[24]

For cases issued in 2002, after the Human Rights Act 1998 had come into effect, the number of other civil non-immigration substantive claimant wins stood at 175, and has remained between 150 to 200 ever since, with notable lows of 154 (in 2017) and 158 (in 2018) (for closed cases – a small proportion had yet to be determined at the time of writing). Adding successful immigration and criminal AJRs, the total figures for claimant success were 201 for claims issued in 2017 and 203 for claims issued in 2018; very much in line with the late 1980s when claimants were successful at final hearing in on average 214 claims per annum.[25] Crudely, this striking consistency in the number of remedies awarded may be evidence supporting the view that public law is not at base about providing individual rights to redress.

IV. GENERAL ADMINISTRATIVE LAW AND PUBLIC INTEREST JUDICIAL REVIEW

From the above, it could then be argued that the lack of any increase in substantive claimant success over the years shows the AJR procedure working as

[22] Nason and Sunkin use population data in their analysis of regionalisation showing the London and south-east of England centricity of the claims issued, but the ongoing research also shows an overall decrease in claims per head of population including in London especially following the Legal Aid, Sentencing and Punishment of Offenders Act (LASPO) 2012. S Nason and M Sunkin, 'The Regionalisation of Judicial Review: Constitutional Authority, Access to Justice and Specialisation of Legal Services in Public Law' (2013) 76 *MLR* 223.

[23] C Harlow and R Rawlings, *Law and Administration* (London, Weidenfeld and Nicolson, 1984) 256–63.

[24] L Bridges, G Mesaros and M Sunkin, *Judicial Review in Perspective* (London, Cavendish Publishing Ltd, 1995).

[25] Success should, however, be understood more broadly than being awarded a remedy at final substantive hearing. Eg, there is evidence that many claims settling before a final hearing do so in

prominent Quartet era judges, most notably Lord Diplock, perhaps thought it should do. That is, being limited mainly to cases raising 'higher level policy' issues,[26] important matters of legal principle or practice, and cases most likely to succeed in the public interest. However, this narrative neglects the extent to which AJRs are primarily used *in fact*, rather than perhaps by design, as a procedure to resolve individual grievances. A factor that has changed little over the years is that the overwhelming majority of AJRs issued and heard relate to individuals and turn on their own facts.

In Sunkin's sample of 1,106 applications made from 1983 to 1985 inclusive, 85 per cent of claims were issued by individuals.[27] Research into the *Value and Effects of Judicial Review*[28] found that 77 per cent of a sample of 502 cases from July 2010 to February 2012 inclusive were issued by individuals. Of these challenges, 75 per cent could be classified as own fact cases; these are individual grievances where the claimant seeks to challenge how law, policy or procedure has been applied to their specific circumstances.

In practice then, it can be argued that most claims are really about individual interests, reflecting neither the generalised administrative law narrative of controlling government and policing accountability, nor a more 'functionalised' account of judicial review as a means to develop subject-matter-specific principles of good administration based on analysis of relevant law and overarching policy.

In the *Value and Effects* research only 18 per cent of sample cases were categorised as involving broader impacts on legal principle and policy beyond the facts of the individual claim. This does show that judicial review can work to articulate legal standards. Though it is worth pointing out that the research was not specifically tasked to consider whether these impacts on legal development and clarity were generally applicable across administration, or if they were subject-specific to particular areas of administrative activity (eg, planning or education).

The *Value and Effects* research also investigated the narrative of judicial review as directed towards the public interest. The researchers classified 'wider public interest' cases as: AJRs 'brought by claimants for broader public interest reasons without seeking a remedy for themselves' and found that only eight per cent of the sample claims fell into this category. Research from the 1980s to the present day has consistently shown that only a small proportion, around three per cent, of AJRs are issued by non-individual 'others' (including pressure groups and interest organisations).[29]

favour of the claimant. See V Bondy and M Sunkin, 'The Dynamics of Judicial Review Litigation: The Resolution of Public Law Challenges Before Final Hearing' (Public Law Project, 2009).

[26] A phrase explained by Peter Cane in P Cane, 'Understanding Judicial Review and its Impact' in M Hertogh and S Halliday (eds), *Judicial Review and Bureaucratic Impact: International and Interdisciplinary Perspectives* (Cambridge, Cambridge University Press, 2004) 15.

[27] Sunkin (n 15) 437.

[28] V Bondy, L Platt and M Sunkin, 'The Value and Effects of Judicial Review: The Nature of Claims, their Outcomes and Consequences' (PLP, LSE, University of Essex 2016).

[29] Sunkin (n 15) 462–63, and Bondy, Platt and Sunkin, 'Value and Effects' (2016).

In this regard, Arvind and Stirton argue that a sub-set of judges and common law scholars have encouraged the view that the claimant seeking judicial review represents the public interest. This perception has caused particular problems around understanding the distinction between the public interest in a particular policy outcome (not the preserve of the AJR procedure), and the public interest in upholding the rule of law.[30] Arvind and Stirton suggest commentators have tended to lose sight of the fact that it is often the public body which seeks to represent the public interest in administrative efficiency.

Whilst true public interest cases, under the *Value and Effects* classification, are comparatively rare, they tend to attract publicity to issues of local and national importance. AJRs also clearly play an important role in facilitating litigation aimed at settling wider constitutional questions. However, there is no evidence that using AJRs in this way is the central focus of the procedure, or that such use has increased exponentially in recent years. One can appreciate that controversial issues ultimately resolved in the highest appellate courts may not be reflective of everyday practice. However, there is a concern that academic focus on these cases has led to somewhat distorted accounts of administrative law doctrine, and that political responses to high-profile claims have led to the enactment of procedural reforms with devastating impacts on access to justice to resolve individual grievances. Sunkin notes that the government case in favour of reforms, particularly from 2012 onward, was itself backed up by a reading of statistical data that ignored the nuances between subject areas of judicial review, and which failed to place the judicial review caseload in the context of the scale of public decision-making.[31]

In terms of administrative law doctrine, modern public interest theorist, Jason Varuhas, bases his account of generalist administrative law on distinctions between interests and rights.[32] Under his taxonomy, the doctrines of judicial review are to be divided between ordinary administrative law that is concerned with the public interest, and human rights law AJRs which are about individual private interests. He argues that the content of doctrines should be attuned accordingly such that administrative law retains something like a *Wednesbury* reasonableness test, with proportionality used only in AJRs involving human rights. Whilst others have argued that normative concerns do not necessitate Varuhas's proposed doctrinal divide,[33] this theory also rests on tenuous empirical foundations. It requires the function of claims to be restated in quite a

[30] See eg, C Harlow, 'Public Law and Popular Justice' (2002) 65 *MLR* 1 and the famous dictum of Sedley J in *R v Somerset CC ex parte Dixon* [1997] COD 323 (QB): 'Public law is not at base about rights, even though abuses of power may and often do invade private rights; it is about wrongs – that is to say misuses of public power.'

[31] Sunkin 'Empirically Based Information' (2020).

[32] J Varus, 'The Public Interest Conception of Public Law: Its Procedural Origins and Substantive Implications' in J Bell, M Elliott, JNE Varuhas and P Murray (eds), *Public Law Adjudication in Common Law Systems: Process and Substance* (Oxford, Hart Publishing, 2016).

[33] P Craig, 'Taxonomy and Public Law: A Response' [2019] *PL* 281.

different way to how those actually issuing cases would frame their intentions. This isn't fatal to the coherence of the theory, but as I have argued elsewhere, such a disconnect from empirical reality weakens a theory's value as an interpretation of the social practice of judicial review, it also prevents Varuhas's taxonomy from functioning as the practical map of the subject matter which he intends it to provide.

The crux of Varuhas's normative account is that the fields of administrative, human rights, and constitutional law, have different normative foundations. The AJR in the Administrative Court is particularly problematic here, as in the absence of a specific form of action to protect human rights and constitutional values, it has evolved into a constitutional review procedure. For many this constitutionalisation of administrative law has been the most significant development of the late 1990s and early twenty-first century.[34] Constitutionalisation has influenced (though not necessarily been the sole cause of) an increased focus on more substantively flavoured legal principles; eg substantive legitimate expectations, expanded *Wednesbury* and proportionality, and consultation (particularly examining the scope and value of consultation, not just whether it was attempted). In this context, Lord Diplock's tripartite account of illegality, procedural impropriety and irrationality no longer fits.

However, whilst the grounds of judicial review may have expanded, newly constitutionalised general administrative law has had little empirical impact in terms of caseloads and remedies for individuals. For example, the cornerstone of these developments, the Human Rights Act 1998, has had little lasting impact on caseloads. In the first six months of 2002, research by the Public Law Project found that at the permission stage 53 per cent of asylum and immigration AJRs and 46 per cent of other AJRs included a human rights claim. However, the researchers concluded:

> When taken together with the *evidence that the HRA has not led to a major increase in case numbers*,[35] it would appear that the HRA is most often being used to supplement established grounds for judicial review in cases that would have been pursued in any event on such grounds prior to the introduction of the HRA.[36]

From my own analysis of a sample of 482 reported substantive AJRs in 2013 and 2015, I found that only 14 per cent of cases across the sample involved a human-rights-based ground;[37] this is compared to a PLP research sample in 2002

[34] T Poole, 'The Reformation of English Administrative Law' (2009) 68 *CLJ* 142; Lord Steyn, 'The Constitutionalisation of Public Law' (University College London, Constitution Unit, 1999), available at www.ucl.ac.uk/constitution-unit/sites/constitution-unit/files/38_0.pdf; J Jowell, 'Beyond the Rule of Law: Towards Constitutional Judicial Review' [2000] *PL* 671, 674–80; Lord Lester, 'Developing Constitutional Principles of Public Law' [2001] *PL* 684.

[35] Emphasis added.

[36] V Bondy, *Impact of the Human Rights Act on Judicial Review – An Empirical Research Study* (London, Public Law Project, 2003).

[37] S Nason, *Reconstructing Judicial Review* (Oxford, Hart Publishing, 2016).

which found that 43 per cent of post-permission cases raised the Human Rights Act 1998. It may be that specific references to the HRA 1998 are reducing with increased focus on so-called common law constitutional rights.[38] Whilst scholarly analysis tends to conclude that the impact of the HRA 1998 across many areas of public law doctrine has been extensive, this has not been matched by a subsequent increase in use of the AJR procedure. In contrast, the workload of the UK Supreme Court is dominated by human rights, and it is self-confessedly rarely tasked to determine administrative law cases.[39] This provides some evidence that it is in fact human rights issues, rather than administrative law matters, which most engage the public interest.

V. TOPICS OF CLAIM AND LEGAL EXPERTISE: SPECIALIST OR GENERALIST?

More important to judicial review in practice than doctrinal divides between administrative, human rights and constitutional law, is the prominence of particular subject matters (topics) of claim, some of which have dominated cases against the administration for centuries.

Sterett argues that during the apparent slumber of administrative law in the early twentieth century, both the High Court and various tribunals were regularly engaged in determining statutory appeals, in addition to the High Court's prerogative jurisdiction, particularly in the areas of tax, rates, rents and land use. She notes too that these are areas of litigation which: i. concern the propertied classes; ii. were (and remain) heavily structured by statutes; and iii. where there is a well-established tradition of legal professional specialism and other interest group activity.[40] Sterett's view is that, at least in these areas of litigation (land and tax), judges regularly found in favour of individuals as against the administration. Although noting that it should be interpreted cautiously, her sample of reported judgments against administrative officials (including statutory appeals and prerogative cases) in law reports from 1946 through to 1970 shows taxes, rates, rents and land use to be the most prominent categories, followed by public housing, benefits and licensing.

In 2018, 15 per cent of civil non-immigration AJRs issued in the Administrative Court (237 claims) concerned town and country planning, and a further four per cent (61 claims) involved taxation. The Administrative Court also determines

[38] See eg, M Elliott and K Hughes (eds), *Common Law Constitutional Rights* (Oxford, Hart Publishing, 2020).

[39] R Reed, 'Comparative Public Law in the UK Supreme Court' in M Elliott, JNE Varuhas and S Wilson-Stark (eds), *The Unity of Public Law? Doctrinal, Theoretical and Comparative Perspectives* (Oxford, Hart Publishing, 2018) 253, noting that 'it has become relatively uncommon' (for the Supreme Court to be asked to determine appeals on the basis of domestic constitutional and administrative law).

[40] Sterett (n 17) 61–67.

approximately 190 statutory town and country planning appeals per annum. The relatively high proportion of land and tax claims exposes a seam of judicial activity where comparative ease of access stems from a combination of claimants with financial resources; accessibility of lawyers with specialist property law expertise; and a legal cultural sense that bringing and defending claims is a normal part of law and administration. Professional discipline may be an area with similar characteristics; it has been a prevalent topic of AJRs since Sunkin's analyses in the 1980s and 1990s. In the twenty-first century it has consistently made up around six to seven per cent of the non-immigration AJR caseload, and as much as 80 per cent of the Administrative Court's statutory appeal jurisdiction.

However, alongside property and professional discipline litigation that can often, though not always, concern the propertied and professional classes, other prominent areas of judicial review relate to issues affecting the most vulnerable and disadvantaged in society, including asylum and immigration, social housing and homelessness, prisoners and mental health. Although this observation might suggest that generalised individual redress can be accessed in the Administrative Court by people from a range of different (and sometimes disadvantaged) groups, the more detailed picture indicates that patterns in the use of judicial review are heavily subject-matter-specific and linked to the activities of other professionals such as private lawyers, independent advice providers and public administrators.

Outside the immigration context, eight topics have consistently accounted for close to half the AJR caseload. In Sunkin's analysis between 1987 and 1989 inclusive, on average 58 per cent of the total civil non-immigration caseload concerned disciplinary bodies, education, family, children and young persons, housing (including homelessness), local government, prisons, social security, and town and country planning.[41] In research by Nason and Sunkin these same categories accounted for on average 52 per cent of the civil non-immigration caseload from 2007 to 2015 inclusive.[42] In 2018, these eight classes of claim made up 46 per cent of the total civil non-immigration caseload.

There has been variation in the overall proportion of claims made up by each of these topics over time; for example, prisons claims accounted for a quarter of the non-immigration civil caseload in 2010, up from two per cent in 1989, having reduced since to eight per cent in 2018. This reduction is just one example where legal aid policy has impacted access to judicial review. Following the Legal Aid, Sentencing and Punishment of Offenders Act 2012 (LASPO), legal aid remains available for judicial review, but in an attenuated form. In the case of prisoners, legal aid has been removed from a range of other types of claim affecting the

[41] Bridges, Mesaros and Sunkin, 'Judicial Review in Perspective' (1995).

[42] This research was based on an analysis of data extracted from the Administrative Court IT system, the Crown Office Information Network (COINS) from 1 May 2007 to 30 April 2015 inclusive. Nason and Sunkin, 'The Regionalisation of Judicial Review' (2013).

prison population, with the consequence that law firms which used to handle this work, alongside AJRs, have closed down, with knock-on effects. Whilst legal aid remains available in principle, the general presumption that lawyers will not be paid for significant amounts of work done if a permission application is unsuccessful has also had an effect on the number of AJRs issued.

In terms of the overall number of solicitors' firms issuing claims in the Administrative Court, this peaked in 2009 and has reduced since, notably following implementation of LASPO 2012. At least from this evidence, it is difficult to see judicial review as the 'lucrative industry' some politicians have made it out to be.[43]

Sunkin's research from a sample of cases in the early 1980s found that across the total AJR caseload (including immigration) on average 75 per cent of solicitors who represented claimants acted in only one issued case per annum,[44] rising to 77 per cent in the late 1980s.[45] From 1 May 2007 to 30 April 2018, 65 per cent of solicitors who represented claimants in civil non-immigration judicial review acted in only one claim in any given year (the figure barely fluctuated from 65 per cent across the 11 years). In immigration judicial review the figures are more variable, but still on average around 55–60 per cent of solicitors representing claimants in immigration AJRs are involved in one application per annum.

That said, a significant proportion of the caseload is concentrated within a smaller number of firms. For example, from 2007/08 to 2017/18 on average in civil non-immigration AJRs, claimants in half of all the claims issued were represented by 11 per cent of the total number of firms involved. The firms handling the highest proportion of cases have tended to be those specialising in a particular area of law, such as planning, not generalist public law practices. For immigration judicial reviews work is more concentrated with on average seven per cent of solicitors' firms acting for claimants issuing half of all Administrative Court AJRs in any given year. Sunkin's 1980s and 1990s research similarly exposed a high concentration of work among particular firms.[46] The data shows that representation is concentrated among firms with subject matter expertise, such as immigration, town and country planning, land and the environment, tax, and education, family, children and young persons.

The picture created, then, seems to be of a set of solicitors (often in larger specialist firms) who are experts in a particular area of administrative law, most notably planning and tax, fairly regularly involved in AJRs within their specialism. On the other hand, there is a second set of smaller high street or regional firms whose lawyers have a particular subject area of administrative law (such as education, community care or housing) as one of their specialisms, and who

[43] C Grayling, 'The Judicial Review System is not a Promotional Tool for Countless Left-Wing Campaigners' *The Daily Mail* (11 September 2013).

[44] Sunkin (n 15) 462–63.

[45] Bridges, Mesaros and Sunkin (n 24).

[46] Sunkin (n 15) 462 and Bridges, Mesaros and Sunkin (n 24).

might regularly be engaged in giving advice relating to these issues, and acting in tribunal and county court claims, but for whom an AJR is a rare occurrence.

Work at the Bar is more concentrated, with just five per cent of counsel instructed in half of all civil non-immigration claims in some years. Despite this, the majority of barristers instructed will only act for claimants in one application per annum, and those dealing with a higher concentration of work are active in particular subject matters such as planning and tax. In short, legal practice is not organised around general administrative law (whether constitutionalised or otherwise) or around a specific law of judicial review as the primary locus of general administrative law doctrines. Practice is instead organised around contextualised (subject-matter-specific) administrative activity. That practice is arranged around the needs of particular subject areas is not a reason in and of itself to conclude that administrative law doctrine should be equally so arranged. However, there is an increasingly prevalent view that existing taxonomies of administrative law, based on general principles said to have developed, or been consolidated, through the vehicle of the AJR procedure, are not satisfactory.[47] In particular, that doctrine is too far removed from legal and administrative practice, and from judicial methods.

Peter Cane argues that some of this dissatisfaction, and with it the turn to empirical research, is more to do with the methods and limitations of doctrinal scholarship as an occupation than with its results. He argues that common law scholars aim 'to place individual decisions into wider doctrinal and social contexts and in so doing to develop "principles" that make the whole body of relevant law as internally consistent and coherent as reasonably possible'.[48] Since the higher appellate courts are at the apex of this body of relevant law it is not then surprising that most doctrinal scholars are concerned with analysing appellate decisions, using these as a basis from which to construct a coherent theory of administrative law doctrine, composed of particular classifications such as jurisdiction, rationality, legitimate expectations and so on. Administrative law per se remains (in many textbooks) structured around concepts of jurisdiction, ultra vires, distinctions between questions of fact, questions of law and matters of application, attempting to ascribe specific 'standards' of review to each 'ground'.[49]

As I have argued elsewhere,[50] and as Joanna Bell explains, these grounds as 'general analytical tools, which play such a central structuring role in much textbook analysis, seem to do little in the way of ex ante "legal work" in identifying concrete solutions to difficult questions concerning the proper approach to

[47] J Bell, 'Rethinking the Story of Cart v Upper Tribunal and Its Implications for Administrative Law' (2019) 39 *OJLS* 74.

[48] P Cane, 'Review of Dean R Knight, Vigilance and Restraint in the Common Law of Judicial Review, (Cambridge, CUP, 2018)' (2019) 82 *MLR* 200.

[49] A 'grounds' approach perhaps under Dean Knight's four schemata in D Knight, *Vigilance and Restraint in the Common Law of Judicial Review* (Cambridge, CUP, 2018).

[50] Nason, *Reconstructing Judicial Review* (2016).

review, even in the most well-known case law'.[51] Even Supreme Court judges have begun to reject these 'parades of learning'[52] in favour of what some academics have subsequently termed a blasphemous retreat to pragmatism over principle.[53]

Doctrinal theorists have reached an impasse between those who wish to stick with traditional categorisations of general administrative law, defending their analytical rigour, and those for whom the wide variation in administrative contexts necessitates a deeper assessment of the principles justifying judicial involvement in every single case. For some the disconnect between general administrative law scholarship and the reality of legal practice and public administration, means that the whole project of generalist administrative lawyers might have been fundamentally misconceived, appealing more to sentiment than reality.[54]

In my view, the data about the structure of legal practice in the context of AJRs helps provide a way out from between the rigid (arguably outdated) doctrines and the so-called 'wilderness of single instances'.[55] Administrative law in England and Wales, and with it judicial review, should now focus more on the subject matter specificity of substantive grounds, but this first requires people to be able to access court procedures.

VI. CONTROLLING ACCESS TO JUDICIAL REVIEW

An aspect of judicial review that *has* changed over the years has been the proportion of claimants being refused leave (now permission). Sunkin's research shows that from 1981 to 1985, approximately 27 per cent of AJRs were refused leave,[56] by 1986 this had increased to 38 per cent (including immigration claims). More recent data distinguishes between immigration claims and other civil claims and shows a significant drop since the mid-1990s. See Figure 7.2 (other civil judicial review) and Figure 7.3 (immigration judicial review).

Some of the more recent decline in permission success is attributable to procedural reforms, including the Law Commission recommendations in 1994[57]

[51] Bell, 'Cart v Upper Tribunal' (2019) 96 and see also R Williams, 'When is an Error not an Error? Reform of Jurisdictional Review of Error of Law and Fact' [2007] *PL* 793.

[52] Lord Carnwath, 'From Judicial Outrage to Sliding Scales – Where Next for Wednesbury?' (Constitutional and Administrative Law Bar Association Annual Lecture, London, UK Supreme Court, 2013).

[53] C Forsyth, '"Blasphemy Against Basics": Doctrine, Conceptual Reasoning and Certain Decisions of the UK Supreme Court' in Bell, Elliott, Varuhas and Murray (eds), *Public Law Adjudication* (2016) 161.

[54] MG Heyman, 'Judicial Review of Discretionary Immigration Decision making (1994) 31 *San Diego Law Review* 861, 871.

[55] D Feldman, 'Comparison, Realism and Theory in Public Law' in Bell, Elliott, Varuhas and Murray (n 32) 379.

[56] Sunkin (n 15).

[57] Law Commission, Administrative Law: Judicial Review and Statutory Appeals (Law Com 226, 1994).

and the Review of the Crown Office List (Bowman Review) in 2000.[58] Bondy and Sunkin attribute the declining permission success rate post-2000 largely to the Bowman reforms, which they suggest may have increased access to justice despite fewer claims making it to a substantive hearing. They concluded that whilst the reforms 'heightened the de facto barrier facing claimants', a larger number of claims were subsequently being resolved in the claimant's favour prior to permission.[59] They attribute the steeper decline in permission success between 1998 and 2000 to various 'deck clearing exercises' executed in anticipation of a large increase in cases post-HRA (an increase that did not in fact materialise).

Figure 7.2 Permission grant rate ordinary civil (non-immigration) judicial review

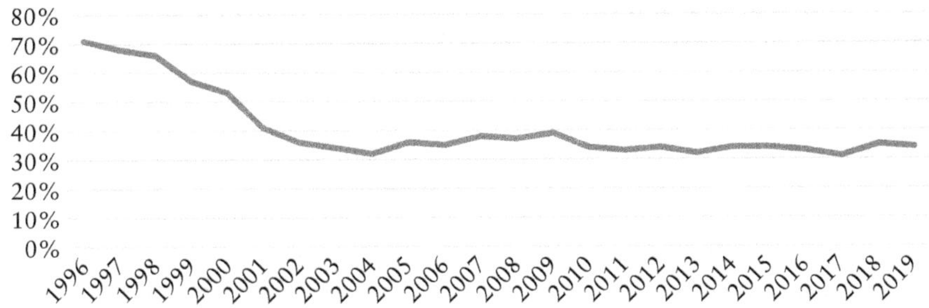

Figure 7.3 Permission grant rate immigration and asylum judicial review

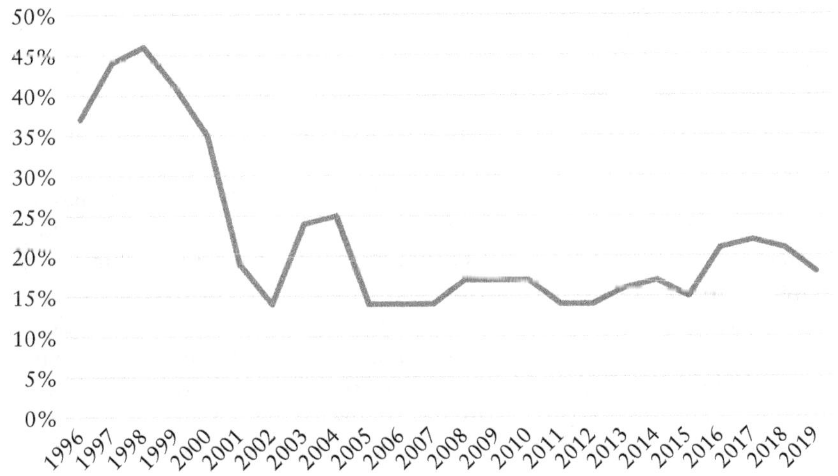

[58] J Bowman, *Review of the Crown Office List* (London, Lord Chancellor's Department, 2000).
[59] V Bondy and M Sunkin, 'Accessing Judicial Review' [2008] *PL* 647.

As Bondy and Sunkin show, however, a significant decline in permission success rates occurred prior to these procedural and deck-clearing reforms and can be attributed to changes in judicial approaches to the discretion to grant permission, in particular increased emphasis on the need to proceed speedily, and concerns about judicial resources.[60] Limiting permission success was achieved by refashioning arguability from a test of whether a case was not truly 'hopeless', to whether it was 'potentially arguable'; done in part to stem the tide of individual grievance applications relating to immigration and homelessness. This suggests judicial adherence to the narrative that judicial review is not at base about individual interests and remedies.

Whilst the caseload did fall for a time, it then picks up again and the bigger change becomes evident: the permission grant rate reversed. Whereas approximately two-thirds of applicants in civil non-immigration cases were granted permission before the mid-1990s, after this time just one-third were granted permission. Permission success rates also fell in immigration AJRs, though from a lower starting point.

Alongside judicial case management and less controversial civil procedure reforms, successive governments have attempted to restrict judicial review. However, a perceptible modern trend is the severity of contemporary reforms designed to exclude or condition access to judicial review, beyond traditional ouster clauses and towards a broader set of exclusionary practices requiring further academic attention.[61] It seems that emphasising the 'modern' role for judicial review as a procedure for vindicating constitutional principles and human rights, alongside misunderstandings about judicial control of policy in the so-called 'public interest' has met with striking back and clamping down by government. Harlow and Rawlings define 'striking back' as 'official responses to court rulings that are deliberately negative in the sense that government or administration sets out to rid itself of a judicial decision that it finds inconvenient or otherwise dislikes'.[62] Tactics include ouster clauses, delaying tactics and retaking annulled decisions. A sub-set of 'striking-back' is 'clamping-down', which occurs where government attempts to 'protect itself against future judicial "interference" by changing the rules of the game in a restrictive fashion' such as through procedural and costs reforms.

One example of clamping down is section 84 of the Criminal Justice and Courts Act 2015, under which permission must be declined if 'it appears to the court to be highly likely that the outcome for the applicant would not have been substantially different if the conduct complained of had not occurred'. This restriction appears to fit with resolution of individual grievances as a central aim of judicial review. However, it takes a narrow view of resolution, since for

[60] See in particular the changing approach of Lord Donaldson between *Parr v Wyre BC* (1981–82) 2 HLR 71 and *R v Panel on Take-Overs and Mergers, ex p Guiness Plc* [1990] 1 QB 146 (CA) 177–78.

[61] See ch 8 in this volume (Tomlinson).

[62] C Harlow and R Rawlings, '"Striking Back" and "Clamping Down": An Alternative Perspective on Judicial Review' in Bell, Elliott, Varuhas and Murray (n 32) ch13.

many people confirmation that the public body acted unlawfully, even if this has not practically impacted on the outcome of its processes, is a form of resolution. The narrowness of section 84 also goes against the role for AJRs (about one-quarter of cases in the *Values & Effects* research) as having broader implications for legal practice and/or the public interest in cases where the individual is not necessarily seeking a remedy for themselves.

More specifically, however, instructing the court to consider how particular forms of 'conduct' could have impacted on the outcomes of public body decision-making processes may take judges closer to the substantive merits of administrative decision-making than might be thought acceptable under a generalist administrative law paradigm. On the contrary, this might not be so problematic for subject-matter-contextualised administrative law, which could more realistically allow judges to consider the practical impact of administrative conduct in the field of law and policy at issue. But this should be as part of analysing the substantive merits of the claim, and the longer-term implications of any precedent it lays down, not at the permission stage when only limited evidence can be presented.

A second restriction is the introduction of a 'totally without merit' certification. If a judge certifies a claim as 'totally without merit' at paper permission the applicant will not be able to request an oral renewal. This is significant as the data shows that success rates in oral permission hearings are much higher than at paper permission.[63] The restriction is at the discretion of the judiciary (even if provided for in statute). According to the case of *Wasif*,[64] a claim is 'totally without merit' if it is 'bound to fail', and there is no 'rational basis' for it. This is apparently to be compared with a normal refusal of permission where the case is classed as 'in-arguable', because there is a rational basis to it, but the judge finds that basis to be wrong.

Controlling access to judicial review also varies depending on the subject matter of the claim, and the nature of the defendant. A current growth area is 'Cart' claims challenging Upper Tribunal decisions. In *Cart v The Upper Tribunal*,[65] the Supreme Court held that certain unappealable decisions of the Upper Tribunal (a superior court of record that can determine statutory judicial reviews) can be subject to judicial review in the Administrative Court, but only in circumstances raising an important matter of legal principle or practice, or that are otherwise compelling.

In 2018 there were 617 Cart-immigration AJRs (34 per cent of the Administrative Court's immigration caseload), and 63 Cart-other applications (four per cent of the non-immigration civil caseload). These cases are more likely to be issued by unrepresented litigants, less likely to be granted permission

[63] Nason and Sunkin (n 22).

[64] *Wasif and Others v Secretary of State for the Home Department* [2016] EWCA Civ 82.

[65] *R (Cart) v The Upper Tribunal* and *R (MR (Pakistan)) (FC) v The Upper Tribunal (Immigration & Asylum Chamber) and Secretary of State for the Home Department* [2011] UKSC 28; [2012] 1 AC 663.

(as low as two per cent success rate) and more likely to be classed as totally without merit.

Unlike totally without merit and no substantial difference, the Cart criteria are a judicially imposed restriction. Yet having analysed case law on the application of this test, Joanna Bell concludes there is little consistency in how it has been applied, with some judges treating the criteria as an additional permission filter, and others (who have applied the standard 'arguability' permission test) using the criteria to restrict the grounds of review (a contextualised approach to administrative law, but also a new use for the second-tier appeals criteria and something they were not designed for).[66] This latter approach is similar to another discrete practice where applications to review the decisions of county court judges attract normal permission criteria, but grounds are restricted to jurisdictional error and fundamental denial of justice (in effect severe procedural irregularity).[67]

In other subject matter contexts, the needs of the specialist field are accommodated by different court procedures (whilst the permission test and grounds are ostensibly the same as with generalised administrative law). For example, the establishment of a specialist Planning Court (within the Administrative Court) adopting its own procedures including shorter skeleton arguments and expedited hearings for 'significant' planning cases.[68]

According to Lady Justice Cockerill in her address to the Public Law Project's 2019 Trends and Forecasts Conference, there are over 100 flow charts in use in the Administrative Court, showing the range of different procedures for seeking judicial review and the other actions determined by the Court, such as statutory appeals and appeals by way of case stated.

My concern here is that contextuality (the needs of different subject areas of administration) is being accommodated, by government and the judiciary, through procedural reforms rather than explicit developments in substantive law doctrine. Yet as the examples above (Cart among others) show, sharp demarcations between procedures and grounds have long proven unworkable. Adjusting procedure, rather than doctrine, however, has serious implications for the accessibility of judicial review. The current level of transference of context from being a matter of substantive doctrine to one of procedural (and to an extent, remedial) limitations is a significant problem for modern administrative law, and one that may have parallels with the procedural and remedial fine distinctions that led to the need for a harmonised AJR in the first place.

There is already evidence of significant inconsistency in the procedural (permission) stage of judicial review; further fine distinctions are likely to exacerbate existing problems. Research in the late 1990s and early 2000s found high degrees of inconsistency in permission grant rates between individual judges,

[66] Bell (n 47).
[67] *R (Sivasubramaniam) v Wandsworth County Court* [2002] EWCA Civ 1738, [2003] 1 WLR 475.
[68] Practice Direction 54E Planning Court Claims.

and serious concerns from litigants and practitioners.[69] Regional Administrative Court outcomes (both at permission and substantive stage) have also proven less consistent than in London. To an extent this is to be expected given the lower caseloads in the Regional Centres, but it could also be a factor of less specialist subject matter expertise (and legal jurisdictional expertise in the case of Wales) among judges agreeing to regularly travel outside London. Permission and substantive success rates vary massively across the different Administrative Court locations, as does the proportion of claims classified as 'totally without merit'.

VII. FUNDING JUDICIAL REVIEW AND UNREPRESENTED LITIGANTS

Other data also shows just how much the current climate is set against allowing a wide range of individuals to access AJRs to resolve their grievances. For example, a recent increase in litigants in person (LiPs) is a significant change from the earlier days of the procedure. In Sunkin's six-month samples in 1983, 1984 and 1985, on average nine per cent of applicants were unrepresented across all subject matters of claim.[70] The proportion of claims issued by LiPs increased to 36 per cent of civil non-immigration applicants in 2017/18,[71] and also to 36 per cent of immigration applicants between 2014 and 2017 (though this figure has reduced to 27 per cent of immigration applicants issuing as LiPs in 2017/18). The proportion of claims issued by LiP applicants has been growing in London as well as in all the regions.[72]

Regionalisation itself was designed to increase access to justice, against a backdrop that the vast majority of claims were being issued by applicants from London and the south-east of England. However, the expressed aim of the relevant Practice Direction is to ensure that cases are issued and determined at the most appropriate location, not specifically to rebalance or increase the caseload.[73] Whilst there was some initial increase in the overall proportion of cases involving claimants and lawyers from outside London and southern England, this has subsequently fallen back (following LASPO 2012). In 2017/18 there were fewer claims issued by regional applicants than in 2007/08 (two years before the regional courts were opened).

Access to affordable advice is often central to claims against local authorities.[74] Research in the early to mid-2000s found that advice providers tended to concentrate in areas of deprivation, leading to more legal challenges.

[69] Bondy and Sunkin, 'Accessing Judicial Review' [2008].

[70] Sunkin (n 15) 463.

[71] Taken from Administrative Court Office data 1 May 2017 to 30 Aril 2018.

[72] S Nason, 'Justice Outside London? An Update on 'Regional' Judicial Review', *UK Constitutional Law Blog* (16 November 2016), available at ukconstitutionallaw.org.

[73] Practice Direction 54D Administrative Court (Venue).

[74] L Platt, M Sunkin and K Calvo, 'Judicial Review Litigation as an Incentive to Change in Local Authority Public Services in England and Wales' (2010) 20 (supp 2) *Journal of Public Administration Research and Theory* 243.

The *Value & Effects* research found that restrictions on legal aid funding to support AJRs have likely had a disproportionately adverse effect on those forced to resort to litigation to obtain services to which they are legally entitled.[75] That is particularly true for those relying on legal aid in own fact cases. Judicial review litigation against local authorities has been falling, tied to the dearth of advice provision. Opening local Administrative Courts has not done much to reverse the centralised and generalised nature of administrative law, or the legacy of procedural exclusivity. That a small number of local authorities continue to attract a larger number of challenges reinforces the image of specific administrative cultures, and the accessibility of specialist legal services, as central to the incidence of litigation.

Joe Tomlinson has revealed that the total number of applications for legal aid in judicial review reduced from 6,589 applications made in 2009/10 down to 3,131 in 2016/17.[76] Crown Office Information Network (COINs) data shows that whilst in 2001, 36.7 per cent of AJRs were supported by legal aid, in 2015 just 4.4 per cent were; this reduction coincides with the increase in unrepresented litigation. After LASPO 2012, legal aid remains available for judicial review, but Tomlinson describes the process of application as having 'byzantine complexity'.[77] Despite some modifications, the general principle is that legal aid funded work done on a permission application will only be paid for if the claimant is successful at the permission stage, likely leading to a 'chilling effect' where legal aid lawyers will take on only the least complex cases, or those well within specialist subject matter expertise. One subject matter example may be in social security, where Ahluwalia and Tomlinson note that despite the grave risks of unfairness in various stages of the decision to impose benefit sanctions, 'judicial review has largely been an irrelevance'.[78] Another is community care, where some lawyers say they are reframing cases that might previously be run as AJRs, as claims to the Court of Protection. A regional example may be Manchester, where judicial review practice has declined significantly following LASPO 2012; listed hearings have fallen from one or two per day to one per fortnight. Some Manchester-based lawyers have also anecdotally reported that they are increasingly being asked to prepare submissions for ombudsman complaints as an alternative to judicial review.

VIII. CONCLUDING REMARKS

A generalist administrative law paradigm, anchored in the Quartet era cases, can be seen as prioritising a single route to judicial review in the High Court as

[75] Bondy, Platt and Sunkin (n 28).

[76] J Tomlinson, 'Crowdfunding public interest judicial reviews: a risky new resource and the case for a practical ethics' [2019] *PL* 166.

[77] ibid 169.

[78] M Ahluwalia and J Tomlinson, 'Benefit Sanctions, Illegality and Administrative Justice: After Judicial Review?' (2018) 23 *Judicial Review* 225.

the exclusive, or at least the dominant, means through which public law disputes should be resolved. Such would arguably maintain the integrity of general administrative law, but access for individuals is highly limited. When the integrity of general administrative law itself is revealed as a façade, significantly due to the pluralistic nature of public administration, the exclusion of people and weakness of judicial review as a means to resolve individual grievances becomes even more problematic.

The picture I have painted suggests that more subject-matter-specific redress mechanisms, as alternatives to judicial review or complementary to it, are needed to ensure access to justice for individuals and to promote the development of bodies of contextualised administrative law.

One example of an alternative route is the statutory appeal process under the Housing Act 1996 for England (Housing (Wales) Act 2014 for Wales) in which county courts are authorised to apply the same judicial review principles as the Administrative Court. The initial introduction of this route (in England and Wales) precipitated close to a 300 per cent reduction in the number of housing and homelessness AJRs. This route was purposefully developed, and the design process took into account empirical evidence. On the other hand, increasing resort to the Court of Protection, or even to the ombudsman, to resolve matters that might previously have been the subject of an AJR, is a grassroots evolution that could have significant, and unpredictable, consequences elsewhere in the administrative justice system.

A better approach may be to create specific new routes to appeal within tribunal systems. The Commission on Justice in Wales has recommended this way forward for the Welsh system. It noted that substantive administrative law is the area where Welsh law has the greatest potential to diverge from English law, and that access to judicial review in Wales may be even more problematic than in England. Recognising the specialist expertise of the devolved Welsh tribunals, the Commission recommended that 'Welsh tribunals should be used for dispute resolution relating to future Welsh legislation'.[79]

In their recent analysis of immigration judicial review, Robert Thomas and Joe Tomlinson make many recommendations around improving initial decision-making, quality and consistency of legal representation, and the judicial review process itself, but they also recommend that 'Parliament and the Government ought to consider whether to re-introduce appeal rights in certain categories of case, such as: human trafficking; statelessness; and domestic violence cases'.[80]

Whilst judicial review is an exercise of the common law supervisory jurisdiction, legal appeals are grounded in specific legislation, and in some instances the

[79] Report of the Commission on Justice in Wales, 'Justice in Wales for the People of Wales' (October 2019) Recommendation 27, available at gov.wales/sites/default/files/publications/2019-10/Justice%20Commission%20ENG%20DIGITAL_2.pdf.

[80] R Thomas and J Tomlinson, 'Immigration Judicial Reviews: An Empirical Study' (Nuffield Foundation, 2019) Recommendation 9, available at drive.google.com/file/d/1IsTGQJgs4W8ERvmtWBFYrdexPQd9cXqr/view.

procedures around evidence, representation and processes will be different. But, as has been noted of the similar New Zealand context, judicial review on the one hand, and appeals on points of law and against exercises of administrative discretion on the other, can often be seen as functionally equivalent.[81] Where a statute is key to the subject matter of the case, the ground of legality coupled with various standards of judicial review function as principles of statutory interpretation. One main distinction between appeal and judicial review is in the foundation of the power rather than the conditions of its exercise; statutory appeal routes could be completely withdrawn, whereas more protracted measures are needed to restrict judicial review. The other main distinction is that remedies available on appeal are often more appropriate to the resolution of individual disputes.

The *Value and Effects* of judicial review research proposed that some current subject matter types of own fact grievance disputes 'could be more proportionately dealt with by courts and tribunals other than by way of JR in the Administrative Court … Such developments may be applauded if they allow cheaper, quicker and more local methods of resolving legal disputes'. This recognition that there are, and should perhaps increasingly continue to be, more proportionate means to resolve individual grievance claims, could also be seen as weakening the grip of generalist administrative law. New routes to appeal could both improve access to justice, and contribute to the potential flourishing of subject-matter-specific, or contextualised administrative law. Recognising the need for a more contextualised approach to doctrinal administrative law, could also be coupled with an appreciation that judicial review's centrality to administrative law has been waning. This provides a counter narrative that the Quartet era, and its immediate aftermath, represents a high-water mark followed by a decline in the significance of judicial review and with it generalist administrative law, rather than a staging post on the route to 'exponential' growth.

A focus for the future should be on subject-matter-specific administrative law, developed perhaps as 'not quite lawyers' law', within the post-Leggatt Tribunal system. Here we might see an expanding system of contextualised 'administrative law',[82] where individual grievances, and the concerns of particular areas of administrative activity, can both be well addressed.

An alternative vision of an Administrative Court with 100 different procedural flow charts (many of which relate to particular subject areas of judicial review) and where access for most people 'is simply not available', is not an attractive prospect. It is not then entirely clear what should be the remaining role for the Administrative Court. The notion that it should provide generalised

[81] MB Rodriguez Ferrere, 'The Functional Convergence of Appeal and Judicial Review' [2016] *New Zealand Law Review* 157.

[82] Sedley LJ referring to the Upper Tribunal's 'potential to develop a legal culture which is not in all respects one of lawyers' law – a system, in other words, of administrative law': *R (Cart) v Upper Tribunal* [2010] EWCA Civ 859, [2011] 2 WLR 36 [42].

administrative law oversight of the specialist tribunal system has been raised, but also questioned, not least due to the difficulties of demarcating specialist administrative laws from any residual categories of generalist administrative law.[83] Perhaps, the Administrative Court could focus on its more recently prominent function, and one it arguably performs well, acting as a constitutional court of first instance. A significant challenge for the next 50 years of judicial review in the Administrative Court may then continue to be controlling a species of litigation, and consolidating developing principles, but this time of more overtly constitutional rather than administrative law. *Plus ça change, plus ça reste pareil*!

[83] E Laurie, 'Assessing the Upper Tribunal's Potential to Deliver Administrative Justice' [2012] *PL* 288.

8

The Reawakening of Common Law Rights: Are they Still 'Suitable for the Winning of Freedom in the New Age'?

PAUL BOWEN QC

I. INTRODUCTION

THE LATE SIR Henry Brooke, as a young barrister in the 1960s, experienced first-hand the judge-made changes in public law that took place in that tumultuous decade. He later described[1] the parlous state of public law at the beginning of that period with a quote from Lord Denning's 1951 Hamlyn Lectures, *Freedom under the Law*:

> Our procedure for securing personal freedom is efficient, but our procedure for preventing the abuse of power is not. Just as the pick and shovel is no longer suitable for the winning of coal, so also the procedure of mandamus, certiorari, and actions on the case *are not suitable for the winning of freedom in the new age*.[2]

Sir Henry spoke of the 'breakthrough' of *Ridge v Baldwin* followed by the other cases in the Quartet,[3] although he would have made it a quintet by including *Wiseman v Borneman*,[4] in which he appeared as junior counsel. In case after case the House of Lords, led by Lord Reid, swept away arid distinctions, rules and procedures and set in train the development of a comprehensive system of public law that came to be described by Lord Diplock in 1982 as 'the greatest achievement of the English courts in my judicial lifetime'.[5]

[1] H Brooke, 'Law and practice in the 1960s: (2) Public law' (1 December 2005), available at www.sirhenrybrooke.me/2015/12/01/law-and-practice-in-the-1960s-2-public-law.

[2] AT Denning, *Freedom under the Law* (London, Stevens, 1949) 126.

[3] *Ridge v Baldwin* [1964] AC 40; *Padfield v Ministry of Agriculture, Fisheries and Food* [1968] AC 997; *Conway v Rimmer* [1968] AC 910; *Anisminic v. Foreign Compensation Commission* [1969] 2 AC 147.

[4] *Wiseman v Borneman* [1971] AC 297.

[5] *R v Inland Revenue Commissioners, ex p* National Federation of Self-Employed and Small Businesses Ltd [1982] AC 617, 641.

Sir Stephen Sedley, who also spent his early years in practice at this time, has written extensively of the common law developments of this period. In *Lions under the Throne*[6] he described the 'long sleep' of public law from the end of the nineteenth century – briefly interrupted by the 'loud snore' of *Wednesbury* in 1948 – and how the 'princess' of public law was finally awoken by the senior judges of the 1960s. 'Few of the senior judges,' he wrote, 'least of all Lord Diplock, were candidates for the role of Prince Charming, but it was their jurisprudence which woke English public law from its long sleep and set it on the path it remains today'.[7]

That jurisprudence is exemplified by the cases in the Quartet. The extension of the common law principles of natural justice to administrative bodies (*Ridge*), the rejection of 'class' based claims of Crown (now 'public interest') immunity (*Conway*), the recognition that executive action is ultra vires the statutory powers conferred by Parliament if it is inconsistent with the underlying objects of the legislation (*Padfield*) and the restrictive interpretation of statutory provisions purporting to oust the public law jurisdiction of the courts (*Anisminic*) represented, and in turn led to further, significant developments in the ensuing decades and the cases remain landmarks in the common law protection of rights and of the rule of law. It is in public law principles such as these that 'common law rights and obligations … are to be found'.[8] Despite Lord Denning's scepticism, then, through these landmark cases public law became more 'suitable for the winning of freedom in the new age'.

The judges of the 1960s (and the decades that followed) achieved their advances in rights protection without the benefit of a written constitutional document like the Human Rights Act 1998 (HRA), which came into force in October 2000. The introduction of the HRA accelerated the development of human rights jurisprudence, but at the expense of common law rights as practitioners and judges focused on the HRA and the rights to which it gave effect under the European Convention on Human Rights (the Convention). In recent years, however, there has been a renaissance of 'common law constitutionalism',[9] with common law rights 'on the march',[10] and the judges of the Supreme Court in particular have made it very clear that, where a right is protected both under common law and the HRA, it is to the common law that the courts will wish

[6] S Sedley, *Lions under the Throne: Essays on the History of English Public Law* (Cambridge, CUP, 2015).

[7] ibid 39.

[8] *R (Elgizouli) v Home Secretary* (SC(E)) [2020] 2 WLR 857 [174].

[9] See also Lady Hale, 'UK Constitutionalism on the March?' (Constitutional and Administrative Law Bar Association Conference, 12 July 2014); Lord Neuberger, '"Judge not, that ye be not judged": Judging judicial decision-making' (FA Mann Lecture, London, 29 January 2015); R Masterman and S Wheatle 'A Common Law Resurgence In Rights Protection?' [2015] *European Human Rights Law Review* 57.

[10] Lady Hale, 'UK Constitutionalism on the March?' (2014).

to look first.[11] As the late Lord Toulson memorably put it in *Kennedy*, 'It needs to be emphasised that it was not the purpose of the Human Rights Act that the common law should become an ossuary'.

The anniversary of the Quartet offers an opportunity for reflection, and this chapter considers whether these recent common law developments represent a reawakening to rival that of the 1960s and whether the common law is (to use Lord Denning's phrase, quoted above) still 'suitable for the winning of freedom in the new age' of the 2020s. This question is particularly apt given government proposals to 'update' the HRA[12] or, as some would have it, repeal it, and the fact the EU Charter of Fundamental Rights will no longer be a source of human rights law after the date of EU exit on 31 December 2020. This could leave the common law as the sole source of human rights protection, at least in some areas currently embraced by the HRA. It seems appropriate to address this question by asking two questions: do common law rights now provide the same level of human rights protection as is available under the HRA? If not, are they capable of doing so in future?

II. DO COMMON LAW RIGHTS NOW PROVIDE THE SAME LEVEL OF PROTECTION AS THE HRA?

In this section, it will be contended that the Convention and HRA together create rights that are wider in their *normative reach*, more potent in their *protective rigour* and enjoy greater *constitutional resilience* than those under the common law.[13] There is inevitably an overlap between these tests, but by 'normative reach' is meant the scope of the rights created by the law, both substantive and procedural; by 'protective rigour', the mechanisms available in law for the enforcement of those rights; and by 'constitutional resilience', the degree to which those rights are constitutionally entrenched and so protected from amendment or repeal.

A. Normative Reach

As to normative reach, the HRA together with the Convention and its Protocols go significantly further than the common law in the substantive and procedural rights that they confer, in six ways.

[11] *Osborn v Parole Board* [2013] UKSC 61, [2014] AC 1115 [54]–[62]; *Kennedy v Charity Commission* [2014] UKSC 20, [2015] 2 AC 455 [133]; *A v BBC* [2014] UKSC 25, [2015] AC 558 [56]–[57]; *R (Sturnham) v Parole Board* [2013] 2 AC 254 [28]–[29]; *R (Guardian News and Media) v City of Westminster Magistrates Court* [2013] QB 618 [88]–[89]; *S v L* [2012] UKSC 30 [15]–[17], [76].

[12] Conservative Party Manifesto 2019, 48.

[13] The three-fold test applied by, and borrowed from, Professor M Elliott, 'Beyond the European Convention: Human Rights and the Common Law' (2015) 68 *Current Legal Problems* 1.

First, the rights expressly guaranteed by the Convention[14] and its protocols,[15] which the UK has signed and ratified[16] and which, with one exception (Article 13), are given effect by s 1 and Sch 1 HRA, ('the Convention rights') are wider in ambit than those protected by the common law. Many, but not all, of the Convention rights are protected at common law. In his *Commentaries on the Laws of England*, William Blackstone identified three common law rights 'founded on nature and reason', namely the right to personal security, the right to personal liberty and the right to private property.[17] Foundational examples of each of these are *Bushell's case*[18] in 1670 (which emphasised the primacy of the writ of *habeas corpus* to secure release from unlawful detention[19]), *Entick v Carrington* in 1765[20] (establishing the right to privacy of the home, and the need for lawful authority for a public authority to enter in the form of a warrant) and *Somersett's* case,[21] 1772 (in which Lord Mansfield ruled that slavery was not authorised by either statute or the common law, so an escaped slave was not to be returned to his owner, but was to be released). Other common law rights to have been recognised include the right to be heard (*audi alteram partem)*, access to justice,[22] access to a lawyer,[23] non-retroactivity of criminal penalties,[24] open justice,[25] freedom of expression,[26] the privilege against self-incrimination and

[14] The right to life (Art 2); the right not to be subject to torture or inhuman or degrading treatment or punishment (Art 3); the right not to be held in slavery or servitude or required to perform forced or compulsory labour (Art 4); the right to liberty (Art 5); the right to a fair trial (Art 6); the right not to be subject to retroactive punishment (Art 7); the right to respect for private and family life (Art 8); the right to freedom of thought, conscience and religion (Art 9); the right to freedom of expression (Art 10); the right to freedom of assembly and association (Art 11); the right to marry (Art 12); the right to an effective remedy (Art 13); the right not to be discriminated against in the enjoyment of the Convention rights (Art 14); the right of peaceful enjoyment of possessions (Art 1 Protocol 1); the right to education (Art 2 Protocol 1); and the right to free elections (Art 3 Protocol 1).

[15] The UK has signed and ratified Protocol 1, Protocols 6 and 13. Protocol 6 restricts the death penalty to times of war and Protocol 13 requires Member States to outlaw the practice altogether. The UK has signed, but not ratified, Protocol 4 (which prohibits (Art 1 Protocol 4) the imprisonment of people for inability to fulfil a contract (Art 2 Protocol 4) the right to free movement within a country once lawfully there and for a right to leave any country, (Art 3 Protocol 4) the expulsion of nationals and provides for the right of an individual to enter a country of his or her nationality and (Art 4 Protocol 4) prohibits the collective expulsion of foreigners).

[16] The UK was one of the first to sign the Convention in 1951.

[17] W Blackstone, *Commentaries on the Laws of England*, 4th edn (London, John Murray, 1876), vol 1, 100–10.

[18] And also the right of a jury to return the verdict they chose, following the jury's acquittal of Penn and Meade: *Bushell's case* (1670) 89 ER 2.

[19] See *A v Secretary of State for the Home Department* [2004] UKHL 56, [2005] 2 AC 68 [36].

[20] *Entick v Carrington* (1765) 95 ER 807.

[21] *Somerset v Stewart* (1772) 98 ER 499.

[22] *R (UNISON) v Lord Chancellor* [2017] UKSC 51, [2017] 3 WLR 409; *R v Lord Chancellor ex p Witham* [1998] QB 575.

[23] *R v Secretary of State for the Home Department ex p Leech (no 2)* [1994] QB 198, 210 (Steyn LJ).

[24] *Pierson v Secretary of State for the Home Department* [1998] AC 539.

[25] *Scott v Scott* [1913] AC 417, 477.

[26] *R v Secretary of State for the Home Department, ex p Brind* [1991] 1 AC 696, 757; *Redmond-Bate v Director of Public Prosecutions* [2000] HRLR 249.

(closely related) the right to silence,[27] freedom of association,[28] the right to jury trial,[29] access to information,[30] the right of autonomy,[31] the right to life,[32] the right to vote,[33] the prohibition on torture and 'cruel and unusual punishment',[34] the right to subsistence[35] and property rights.[36]

But not all of the express or implied Convention rights have a common law analogue. For example, the common law confers no substantive right to privacy and so was powerless to prevent unregulated interception of private telephone conversations by the police (*Malone v Metropolitan Police Commissioner*[37]) or to provide a remedy for an unlawful strip search (*Wainwright v Home Office*[38]). In each case the claimants had to go to Strasbourg to obtain a remedy for breach of Article 8 (*Malone v United Kingdom*;[39] *Wainwright v United Kingdom*[40]).

Second, even where a common law right may be identified it may lack the normative reach of its Convention counterpart. In the *Bournewood* case[41] a mentally incapacitated man, L, was removed from his home, sedated and placed in a secure psychiatric hospital and deprived access to his foster family. The House of Lords held that he had not been 'detained' at common law because he was not objecting to his placement and was free to leave. Lord Steyn, dissenting on this issue, observed that the idea L was free to leave was a 'fairy tale',[42] deprived as he was of the means of effecting his release. The European Court of Human Rights agreed, finding that L had been unlawfully deprived of his liberty applying a more flexible notion of detention under Article 5 than the common law provides.[43]

[27] *R v Director of SFO ex p Smith* [1993] AC 1, 30–44.

[28] *McEldowney v Forde* [1971] AC 632, 657 (banned Republican organisations).

[29] *R (Misick) v SSFCA* [2009] EWCA Civ 1549 [20]; *R v Islington North Juvenile Court ex p Daley* [1983] 1 AC 347, 364 (Lord Diplock).

[30] *R v Mid-Glamorgan Family Health Services Authority ex p Martin* [1995] 1 WLR 110.

[31] *R v Secretary of State for the Home Department ex p Robb* [1995] Fam 127 (right of competent hunger striking prisoner to refuse nutrition and hydration).

[32] *R (Amin) v Secretary of State for the Home Department* [2004] 1 AC 653 [30] (Lord Bingham): 'A profound respect for the sanctity of life underpins the common law'; *R v Cambridge AHA ex p B* [1995] 1 FLR 1055 (overturned on appeal [1995] 1 WLR 898).

[33] *Moohan v Lord Advocate* [2015] 2 WLR 141.

[34] *A v Secretary of State for the Home Department* [2006] 2 AC 221 [11]–[12]; the prohibition on 'cruel and unusual punishment' was enshrined in the Bill of Rights 1689.

[35] *R. v Secretary of State for Social Security ex p Joint Council for the Welfare of Immigrants* [1997] 1 WLR 275 (CA) (Simon Brown LJ, citing Lord Ellenborough, CJ in *R v Inhabitants of Eastbourne* (1803) 4 East 103: 'the law of humanity, which is anterior to all positive laws, obliges us to afford them relief, to save them from starving'.

[36] *Sainsbury's Supermarkets v Wolverhampton City Council* [2011] 1 AC 437 [9]; *AG v Blake* [2001] 1 AC 268, 297, 289G.

[37] *Malone v Metropolitan Police Commissioner* [1979] Ch 344; see also *Kaye v Robertson* [1991] FSR 62.

[38] *Wainwright v Home Office* [2004] 2 AC 406.

[39] *Malone v United Kingdom* (1984) 7 EHRR 14.

[40] *Wainwright v United Kingdom* (2007) 44 EHRR 40.

[41] *R v Bournewood Community Mental Health NHS Hospital ex p L* [1999] AC 458.

[42] ibid 495E.

[43] *HL v United Kingdom* (2005) 40 EHRR 32.

Third, common law 'rights' are often not rights so much as 'principles', 'privileges', 'values' or 'liberties'. A right – including a Convention right – has as its correlative a duty:[44] someone is required to do, or not to do, something in order to give the right effect and that duty is enforceable in law. The correlative of a liberty or a privilege, on the other hand, is 'no right': the possessor of a privilege is free to enjoy that privilege but if he is prevented from doing so he has no right to enforce it. Take, for example, the common law right to vote. In *Moohan*[45] the Supreme Court held that, while the common law recognised a right to vote, it had not developed to a point 'from which any derogation must be provided for by law and must be proportionate' and could not be used as a basis for challenging a statutory ban on prisoner voting. Analysed in Hohfeldian terms, the common law right to vote is a 'privilege': a citizen is free to enjoy that privilege unless and until it is taken away, but has no right that he can enforce through the courts.[46] That proposition should be qualified by Lord Reed's recent statement in *Elgizouli*[47] in which he noted that the authorities did not support the existence of a common law 'right' to life, but 'support the recognition of what might more aptly be described as a value to which the courts attach great significance when exercising their supervisory jurisdiction'. This 'value' may not be ignored, then, but it lacks the hard edge of a right properly so-called.

Fourth, common law lacks some of the dynamic interpretative tools of the Convention and, by extension, the HRA. These tools allow judges to give greater content to Convention rights and to imply additional rights giving the express rights a far greater normative reach. Three interpretative tools have been adopted by the Strasbourg Court. First, the Convention is interpreted as a 'living instrument' in accordance with developing standards among Council of Europe Member States. Those developing standards are best evidenced by other international treaties which may be given indirect effect by a process of interpretation and development of the normative content of Convention rights,[48] including international treaties which the contracting state appearing before the Court has not ratified.[49] Second, Convention rights are interpreted so as to be 'practical and effective' rather than 'theoretical and illusory', so additional rights may be

[44] See WN Hohfeld, *Fundamental Legal Conceptions as Applied in Judicial Reasoning and other Legal Essays* (New Haven, Yale University Press, 1919).

[45] *Moohan* (n 33).

[46] Although not many judges would place as low a value on the right to vote as Lord Sumption in *R (Chester) v Secretary of State for Justice; McGeoch v Lord President of the Council* [2013] UKSC 63, [2014] AC 271 [115]: 'But I decline to regard it as any more significant than the fact that it may coincide with a special anniversary, a long anticipated holiday or the only period of fine weather all summer'.

[47] *Elgizouli* (n 8) [175].

[48] Tyrer *v United Kingdom* (1979–80) 2 EHRR 1; *Blokhin v Russia* [GC] App No 47152/06 (ECtHR, 22 March 2016) [203]–[210].

[49] For example, in *NTS v Georgia* App no 71776/12 (ECtHR, 2 February 2016) [76], the Court referred to the Council of Europe Convention on the Exercise of Children's Rights 1996 (ECECR) as a 'useful tool for the interpretation of relevant principles' notwithstanding that Georgia had not ratified it.

implied, in particular procedural rights.[50] Third, the overarching obligation on contracting states in Article 1 of the Convention to 'secure to everyone within its jurisdiction the rights and freedoms defined in the Convention'[51] has led the Strasbourg court to develop so-called positive rights and obligations, considered below. These principles have been adopted by the domestic courts when interpreting and developing the Convention rights under the HRA and have led to a rich stream of case law, considered below.

The common law also develops, sometimes radically,[52] as the cases in the Quartet demonstrate. But this process can hardly be called 'dynamic': as Lord Neuberger has said, extra-judicially, common law rights have developed in a 'haphazard and leisurely fashion'.[53] That development is restricted by the institutional and constitutional limitations embodied in the UK's dualist approach to international law, by which international treaties do not give rise to enforceable rights unless they are incorporated by primary legislation.[54] That is because the executive is responsible for signing and ratifying international treaties which bind the UK on the international plane but only Parliament can make laws having binding effect domestically.[55] The courts will develop the common law in accordance with international law obligations, but 'only so far as they are free to do so',[56] which is an 'important limitation'.[57] So the courts will not interpret statutes consistently with international treaties if it runs counter to the ordinary words of a statute.[58] Moreover, the courts will not develop common law rights so as to give effect to international human rights treaties in an area where Parliament has legislated, or is considered the more appropriate decision-maker.[59] For example, the House of Lords in *Brind* refused to develop the common law to give direct effect to the Convention right to free speech[60] and the Supreme Court in *SG*[61] declined to apply the UN Convention on the Rights of the Child so as to give it direct effect. Lord Kerr dissented on this issue, stating that the time had come 'for an exception to the dualist theory' to

[50] *Airey v Ireland* (1979–80) 2 EHRR 305; *Őneryildiz v Turkey* (2004) 39 EHRR 12 [69].

[51] eg *Z v United Kingdom* (2002) 34 EHRR 3 [73].

[52] In *Kleinwort Benson Ltd v Lincoln City Council* [1999] 2 AC 249, Lord Woolf said at 378: 'Occasionally, a judicial development of the law will be of a more radical nature, constituting a departure, *even a major departure*, from what has previously been considered to be established principle, and leading to a realignment of subsidiary principles within that branch of the law'. See also *Re Spectrum Plus Ltd (In liquidation)* [2005] 2 AC 680 [32]–[34].

[53] Per Lord Neuberger in 'The role of judges in human rights jurisprudence: A comparison of the Australian and UK experience' (Supreme Court of Victoria, 8 August 2014).

[54] *J H Rayner (Mincing Lane) Ltd v Department of Trade and Industry* [1990] 2 AC 418, 500B–C (Lord Oliver); *Moohan* (n 33) [29]–[31].

[55] *R (Miller) v Secretary of State for Exiting the EU* [2017] UKSC 5, [2017] 2 WLR 583.

[56] *Chester* (n 46) [121].

[57] *Moohan* (n 33) [33].

[58] *R v Lyons* [2003] 1 AC 976 [13] (Lord Bingham) [27]–[28] (Lord Hoffmann); *Osborn* (n 11) [62] (Lord Reed JSC); *Chester* (n 46) [121]; *Moohan* (n 33) [33].

[59] *Moohan* (n 33) [34].

[60] *Brind* (n 26) [1991] 1 AC 696, 747G–748F (Lord Bridge of Harwich).

[61] *R (SG) v Secretary of State for Work and Pensions* [2015] UKSC 16.

be recognised in relation to human rights conventions (at [254]). However, the dualist nature of the constitution is an aspect of the doctrine of Parliamentary sovereignty which, for reasons considered in the second part of this chapter, is unlikely to be varied without legislation.

The common law does assimilate automatically those international human rights that have become established norms of customary international law,[62] breach of which is automatically unlawful in international law: for example, the prohibition of slavery, torture,[63] genocide, wars of aggression and crimes against humanity. However, the process by which such norms are established is positively glacial and their assimilation is hardly an example of the 'dynamic' development of the common law. It is certainly no more dynamic in this respect than the Convention which also assimilates such principles automatically.[64] In any event, if assimilation of a norm of customary international law into common law is inconsistent with the clear words of primary legislation, Parliamentary sovereignty dictates that the latter will prevail.

Fifth, the common law lacks many of the implied rights that exist under the Convention and HRA. The Strasbourg Court has implied a number of positive rights under the Convention, with correlative obligations on the state to have in place laws (a 'law-making duty'[65]) and systems ('a systems duty'), to provide relevant information ('an information duty'[66]) and to take operational measures (an 'operational duty'[67]) to protect individuals against human rights violations, including by third parties. The Strasbourg organs have also implied procedural duties requiring states to assist individuals whose rights may have been breached, including by carrying out criminal and other investigations (an 'investigative duty'[68]), prosecuting those responsible ('a prosecuting duty'[69]) and making available judicial remedies to vindicate their rights (a 'judicial remedy duty'). These positive obligations are a particular feature of the Convention and have led to significant developments in rights protection under the HRA. For example, in *Savage*[70] and *Rabone*[71] the 'systems duty' and 'operational duty' of Article 2 were applied and extended to require public authorities to take steps to protect detained and informal psychiatric patients from acts of self-harm. These cases also established that where there is a breach of these duties leading to a

[62] *Trendtex Trading Corporation v Central Bank of Nigeria* [1977] QB 529, approved by the House of Lords in *I Congreso del Partido* [1983] AC 244.

[63] See *Jones v Ministry of Interior for Saudi Arabia* [2007] 1 AC 270 for discussion of the prohibition under international law.

[64] *Cudak v Lithuania* [GC] (2010) 51 EHRR 15 [66].

[65] See eg *A v United Kingdom* (1999) 27 EHRR 611; *R (Collins) v SSJ* [2016] EWHC 33.

[66] *Brincat v Malta*, App No 60908/11 (2014) [113]; *Vilnes v Norway*, App No 52806/09 (2013) [235]–[236], [244].

[67] See eg *Osman v United Kingdom* (2000) 29 EHRR 245.

[68] This investigative duty was first implied under Art 2 in the context of state killings in the 'Death on the Rock' case of *McCann v United Kingdom* (1996) 21 EHRR 97.

[69] *R (B) v DPP* [2009] 1 WLR 2072.

[70] *Savage v S Essex Partnership NHS Trust* [2009] 1 AC 681.

[71] *Rabone and another v Pennine Care NHS Trust (Inquest and others intervening)* [2012] 2 AC 72.

patient's death their family members have a cause of action in damages under the HRA, notwithstanding no cause of action arose at common law or under the Fatal Accidents Act.[72] In *Middleton*[73] the 'investigative duty' under Article 2 was applied by the House of Lords to transform the inquest process, requiring (among other things) a jury to be able to make findings relevant to the wider circumstances leading to the death, greater involvement of the relatives in the inquest (including a right to legal aid) and a more extensive duty of disclosure by public authorities in whose care the death occurs than obtained pre-HRA. And in *R (B) v DPP*[74] the 'prosecuting duty' under Article 3 was found to have been violated by an unjustified decision of the CPS to discontinue a criminal prosecution and an award of compensation made to the victim.

None of these claims would have succeeded at common law which has not developed a concept of 'positive obligations' of the kind recognised under the Convention and, by extension, the HRA. There is no analogue at all to the 'law-making duty' at common law. A failure to have in place laws that afford adequate protection to common law rights would be simply non-justiciable. As to the systems, information and operational duties, the closest common law equivalent is the private law tort of negligence. Although negligence (unlike the HRA) is not limited to the acts and omissions of state actors but applies equally to private individuals, the protection afforded by the Convention duties is more extensive. For example, the police do not owe a duty of care to a victim of crime at common law.[75] By contrast, under Article 2 of the Convention the police owe a positive obligation to protect a person who is at a real and immediate risk of death at the hands of a third party (an *Osman* duty).[76] In *Smith v Chief Constable of Sussex*[77] the House of Lords refused to extend the common law tort of negligence in circumstances where an *Osman* claim under the HRA would have otherwise been available. As to the 'investigative duty', again this has no counterpart at common law. The House of Lords rejected the argument that there was such a common law obligation in *Re McKerr*,[78] a decision endorsed by the Supreme Court in *R (Keyu) v Foreign and Commonwealth Office*.[79] Although the Supreme Court left open the question of whether such a common law obligation may be developed from principles of customary international law it is striking that no such duty could be identified in the common law itself.

[72] *Savage* (n 70); *Rabone* (n 71).

[73] *R (Middleton) v West Somerset Coroner* [2004] 2 AC 182.

[74] n 69.

[75] *Hill v Chief Constable of West Yorkshire* [1989] AC 53; *Brooks v Comr of Police of the Metropolis* [2005] 1 WLR 1495.

[76] *Osman v United Kingdom* (n 67).

[77] *Van Colle v Chief Constable of Herts Police; Smith v Chief Constable of Sussex* [2009] 1 AC 225; see, more recently, *Michael v Chief Constable of South Wales Police (Refuge intervening)* [2015] AC 1732, [124]–[127].

[78] *Re McKerr* [2004] UKHL 12, [2004] 1 WLR 807 [30].

[79] *R (Keyu) v Foreign and Commonwealth Office* [2015] 3 WLR 1665 [118]–[119].

B. Protective Rigour

Turning, then, to the benchmark of protective rigour, the HRA and common law provide similar mechanisms for the protection of rights, but common law falls short of the protection provided by the Convention and HRA in at least five domains.

First, the Convention doctrine of 'lawfulness' is harder edged than its common law counterpart, the principle of legality. The various Convention Articles use different formulations imposing this 'lawfulness' requirement ('in accordance with a procedure prescribed by law' (Article 5), 'in accordance with the law' (Article 8), 'prescribed by law' (Articles 9, 10 and 11), 'subject to the conditions provided for by law' (Article 1, Protocol 1)) but these have been interpreted by the Strasbourg Court as having the same meaning. The interference must, first, have some basis in and be in accordance with domestic law (the common law analogue of which is the doctrine of ultra vires). Second, the law must meet the *minimum quality standards* required by the rule of law in a democratic society (the 'quality of law' requirement): it must be adequately accessible and foreseeable, that is, formulated with sufficient precision to enable the individual – if need be with appropriate advice – to regulate his or her conduct. Where the law confers a discretion upon a public authority it must indicate with sufficient clarity the scope of the discretion and the manner of its exercise and confer adequate legal safeguards to protect against its arbitrary exercise.[80] If the 'quality of law' criterion is not met the interference will be *ipso facto* unlawful, even if otherwise justifiable.[81]

The closest common law analogue of the 'quality of law' requirement is the 'principle of legality'. A provision of primary legislation will be interpreted narrowly so as to authorise the least restriction possible to common law rights consistent with the ordinary meaning of the words and the purpose of the statute, whether indicated by express words or by necessary implication from the surrounding context.[82] In addition, provisions of secondary legislation such as statutory instruments and Orders in Council made under prerogative powers that cannot be read compatibly with fundamental common law rights may be struck down in so far as they conflict with fundamental common law rights.[83] A provision of secondary legislation may also be struck down if it lacks sufficient

[80] eg *MM v United Kingdom* App no 24029/07 (ECtHR, 13 November 2012) [191]–[193] (Art 8); *Beyeler v Italy* [GC] (2001) 33 EHRR 52 [109] (Art 1 Protocol 1).

[81] *R (T) v Manchester Police* [2015] AC 49 [113]–[15].

[82] *R v Secretary of State for the Home Department ex parte Simms* [2000] 2 AC 115; *Ahmed v HM Treasury* [2010] 2 AC 534, *Black Clawson International Ltd v Papierwerke AG* [1975] AC 591, 638; *Sorby v Commonwealth* (1983) 152 CLR 281, 289, 309, 311; *Baker v Campbell* (1983) 153 CLR 52, 96–97, 104, 116, 123; *Corporate Affairs Commission (NSW) v Yuill* (1991) 172 CLR 319, 348.

[83] See eg *R (UNISON) v Lord Chancellor* (n 22); *Ahmed v HM Treasury* (n 82); *Witham* (n 22). A statutory instrument may be struck down even though it has been debated and approved by Parliament under the positive resolution procedure. However, this does not undermine parliamentary sovereignty because a statutory instrument involves the exercise of a statutory power by a minister under the terms of primary legislation. The courts therefore treat such measures as being the act of

certainty or precision for its meaning to be ascertained.[84] The courts may also read in rules of natural justice to supplement an unfair procedure, provided that it is not excluded expressly or by necessary implication by the statute.[85]

The common law principle of legality is therefore capable of being deployed with great effect to protect common law rights and is capable of further development to bring it closer in effect to the Strasbourg 'quality of law' concept.[86] However, it has not gone as far as the Convention in imposing minimum quality of law standards, breach of which render a provision of unambiguous primary legislation *ipso facto* unlawful.

Second, the Convention and HRA test for assessing the substantive lawfulness of governmental action, proportionality, allows for a more intensive review than the common law test of *Wednesbury*[87] unreasonableness. *Wednesbury*, in its orthodox conception, imposes an extremely high threshold to establish unlawfulness, allowing a discretionary area of judgment to the decision-maker that is so wide that only a decision that is so unreasonable as to be irrational or perverse will fall outside it.[88] Moreover, it does not permit considerations of weight and balance to be taken into account by the court on judicial review. Such considerations are at the heart of the proportionality test, which requires the state to establish convincingly that any interference with a Convention right has an objective which is sufficiently important to justify the limitation of a fundamental right; is rationally connected to that objective; cannot be achieved by a less intrusive means; and that, having regard to these matters and to the severity of the consequences, a fair balance has been struck between the rights of the individual and the interests of the community.[89] While courts will still afford the decision-maker a discretionary area of judgment within which they will not intervene, that area narrows the more important the right in issue and the more direct the interference with the right.[90]

The distinction between proportionality and *Wednesbury* unreasonableness is potentially critical to the outcome of a challenge to an administrative decision.[91] Lord Sumption pointed out in 2014 that proportionality is a 'much

the relevant Minister, rather than of Parliament: *Bank Mellat v HM Treasury* [2014] AC 700 [43] (Lord Sumption).

[84] *McEldowney v Forde* (n 28) 665.

[85] *Cooper v Wandsworth Board of Works* 14 CBNS 180, 194; *Bank Mellat* (n 83) [35] (Lord Sumption); *Osborn* (n 11) [54]–[62].

[86] Recent examples of which include *R (Evans) v AG* [2015] AC 1787 and *R (Privacy International) v Investigatory Powers Tribunal* [2019] UKSC 22, [2019] 2 WLR 1219.

[87] *Associated Provincial Picture Houses Ltd v Wednesbury Corporation* [1948] 1 KB 223.

[88] *Council of Civil Service Unions v Minister for the Civil Service* (GCHQ) [1985] AC 374, 410G (Lord Diplock): an irrational decision is one which is 'so outrageous in its defiance of logic or of accepted moral standards that no sensible person who had applied his mind to the question to be decided could have arrived at it'.

[89] *Bank Mellat* (n 83) [20] (Lord Sumption); [74] (Lord Reed).

[90] P Sales, 'Legalism in Constitutional Law – Judging in a Democracy' [2018] *PL* 687, 697.

[91] 'The differences in approach between traditional grounds of review and the proportionality approach may … sometimes yield different results': Lord Steyn in *R v Home Secretary ex p Daly* [2001] 2 AC 532 [28].

more exacting test' than unreasonableness.[92] Lord Neuberger in *Keyu* observed that a move from unreasonableness to proportionality would have 'potentially profound and far reaching consequences, because it would involve the court considering the merits of the decision at issue'.[93]

The courts have tried repeatedly to resolve the apparent dichotomy between proportionality and orthodox *Wednesbury* review. Over 30 years ago Lord Diplock suggested that proportionality might be adopted as a separate ground of public law review,[94] but that invitation was never taken up. By 2003 the Court of Appeal considered the distinction between the two tests to have shrunk and considered reading the 'burial rites' for *Wednesbury*, but recognised that it still had a part to play.[95] Instead, the courts have adapted the *Wednesbury* test in cases engaging fundamental rights. In 1987 the courts first introduced the concept of 'anxious scrutiny' in human rights cases,[96] the effect of which was that the greater the interference with human rights the narrower the range of responses open to a rational decision-maker and the more the court requires by way of justification before it can be satisfied that the decision was rational.[97] However, in 2001 the 'anxious scrutiny' version of *Wednesbury* was held to be inadequate to ensure the proper protection of Convention rights by the Strasbourg Court in *Smith v United Kingdom*.[98] In response, the courts have continued to adapt *Wednesbury* so that there is, now, little *practical* distinction between the two tests, at least in cases where the lawfulness of interferences with fundamental common law rights is concerned.[99] *Wednesbury* 'is in reality a sliding scale, in which the cogency of the justification required for interfering with a right will be proportionate to its perceived importance and the extent of the interference',[100] although the stage has not yet been reached that proportionality can be taken to have entirely suffused or supplanted *Wednesbury* unreasonableness. Until an expanded bench of the Supreme Court has unconditionally adopted a proportionality test for common law rights, as the justices have proposed on more than one occasion,[101] the advances the courts have so far taken in that direction remain vulnerable to a retreat beaten by a more conservative Supreme Court, if one should emerge.

[92] Lord Sumption, 'Anxious Scrutiny' (speech to the ALBA Conference, 14 October 2014).

[93] *Keyu* (n 79) [133].

[94] In *GCHQ* (n 88) 410E.

[95] *R (ABCIFER) v Defence Secretary* (CA) [2003] QB 1398.

[96] In *Bugdaycay v Secretary of State for the Home Department* [1987] 1 AC 514.

[97] *R v Ministry of Defence ex parte Smith* [1996] QB 517.

[98] *Smith & Grady v United Kingdom* (2001) 31 EHRR 24.

[99] *R (Lord Carlile of Berriew) v Secretary of State for the Home Department* [2014] 3 WLR 1404; *Kennedy v Charity Commission* (n 11); *Pham v Home Secretary* [2015] UKSC 19, [2015] 1 WLR 1591 [60], [95]–[96], [103]–[108], [114]–[116].

[100] *Pham* (n 99) [106] (Lord Sumption).

[101] In both *R (Keyu) v Foreign and Commonwealth Office* (n 79) [132] and *R (Youssef) v Foreign Secretary* [2016] UKSC 3, [2016] AC 1457 the Supreme Court called for an 'authoritative' review of this question by the full Court.

Third, the interpretative obligation under s 3 HRA is stronger than its common law analogue – again, the principle of legality – which requires the courts to interpret legislation compatibly with common law rights *unless* that is inconsistent with the clear and unambiguous words of the statute.[102] Section 3, on the other hand, allows the Court to interpret legislation compatibly with the Convention right even when that is contrary to the unambiguous meaning of a provision of primary legislation. Section 3 provides that 'so far as it is possible to do so primary legislation and subordinate legislation must be read and given effect in a way which is compatible with the Convention rights'. It has been described as the 'key section' in the HRA and 'one of the primary means by which Convention rights are brought into the law of this country'.[103] So as to ensure a Convention compatible meaning, s 3 requires courts to 'depart from the unambiguous meaning the legislation would otherwise bear',[104] if necessary to 'adopt an interpretation which linguistically may appear strained', which may include the 'implication of provisions',[105] ie reading words into the statute that are not there. The only limitation on this obligation is that the interpretation is 'possible' in that it is 'compatible with the underlying thrust of the legislation'.[106] This is nevertheless a more powerful tool of judicial interpretation than is available at common law, as Lord Phillips recognised in *Ahmed*.[107]

Fourth, if a Convention compatible interpretation is not possible using s 3 HRA that is not the end of the matter. Although Parliament has not given the Courts the power to strike down incompatible legislation – by s 6(2)(b) HRA the courts must still apply a provision of incompatible primary legislation and the claimant will not be entitled to any substantive remedy for the breach of his Convention rights under the HRA – the courts may still make a declaration of incompatibility under s 4 HRA. This triggers the 'fast track' process for legislation to remedy the incompatibility under s 10 HRA, establishing a dialogue between the courts and Parliament and creating a political environment in which the law may be changed without undermining the principle of Parliamentary sovereignty.[108] There is no equivalent mechanism at common law to obtain a declaration that primary legislation is incompatible with fundamental common law rights, although the point has yet to be tested. Even if such a declaration could be made there is no equivalent to the fast-track process for remedial legislation under s 10 HRA.

[102] *Ahmed v HM Treasury* (n 82) [117] (Lord Phillips): 'I do not consider that the principle of legality permits a court to disregard an unambiguous expression of Parliament's intention. To this extent its reach is less than that of section 3 of the HRA.'

[103] *Ghaidan v Godin-Mendoza* [2004] 2 AC 557 [26] (Lord Nicholls); *R v Lambert* [2002] 2 AC 545 [78]–[81] (Lord Hope); *Re S (Minors)* [2002] UKHL 10 [39]–[40] (Lord Nicholls).

[104] *Re S* (n 103) [30].

[105] *R v A (no 2)* [2002] 1 AC 45 [44].

[106] *Ahmed* (n 82) [115].

[107] n 102.

[108] *R (Nicklinson) v Ministry of Justice* [2015] AC 657 [117], [204].

Fifth, the Convention creates a cause of action for a 'victim' of a breach of Convention rights[109] sounding in damages by way of 'just satisfaction'[110] in a wider range of circumstances than the common law. This remedy may be pursued before the domestic courts under s 7 HRA or before the European Court of Human Rights by way of individual petition. By contrast, the common law does not provide a remedy in damages for breaches of fundamental rights per se. Executive action or secondary legislation that breaches fundamental common law rights may be challenged by way of judicial review and public law remedies may be granted to quash the relevant act or to require a public authority to take steps to comply with those rights. But there is no tort of 'maladministration' so no cause of action in damages is available for breach of common law rights if there is not also some breach of a recognised private law duty.[111] A private law cause of action in tort may be available for breach of a common law right, such as false imprisonment. However, where there is no private law cause of action sounding in damages no remedy in damages is available for a violation of common law rights beyond bringing the violation to an end, if it is still continuing. The courts have, moreover, proved reluctant to fashion free-standing causes of action sounding in damages for breaches of common law rights. In 2003 the House of Lords in *Cullen* refused to make an award of damages for breach of a 'constitutional right' where the appellant had been unlawfully refused access to a solicitor while detained for police questioning.[112] In 2012 in *Lumba*[113] the Supreme Court declined the opportunity to develop a head of 'vindicatory damages' for breach of the fundamental common law right to liberty. This may be contrasted with the approach of the Privy Council which has awarded such vindicatory damages where they have found breaches of fundamental constitutional rights under the written Constitutions of former colonial states even though no explicit power to award damages existed: see, for example, *Attorney-General of Trinidad and Tobago v Ramanoop*.[114] Where the domestic courts have been presented with a similar opportunity to develop common law remedies so as to match those available under the HRA they have usually declined to take it up, as in *Wainwright v Home Office*, *Smith v Chief Constable of Sussex*, *Re McKerr*, *Moohan* and *Watkins v Home Office*.[115]

In all of these cases the courts' reluctance stemmed from their concern that a development of the common law would overstep the constitutional limits of the courts' function. In *Smith*, *Wainwright* and *Watkins* the concern (at least of the

[109] Article 34 of the Convention.

[110] Article 41 of the Convention.

[111] *R (Quark Fishing) v SS FCA* [2006] 1 AC 529 [96]; see the discussion in M Fordham, *Judicial Review Handbook*, 6th edn (Oxford, Hart, 2012) [25.3].

[112] *Cullen v Chief Constable of the Royal Ulster Constabulary (Northern Ireland)* (HL) [2003] UKHL 39, [2003] 1 WLR 1763.

[113] *R (L) v Secretary of State for the Home Department* [2012] 1 AC 245.

[114] *Attorney General of Trinidad and Tobago v Ramanoop* [2006] 1 AC 328.

[115] *Watkins v Home Office* [2006] 2 AC 395.

majority) was that Parliament had provided a remedy under the HRA so that it was inappropriate and unnecessary to develop the common law to provide an equivalent remedy. In *McKerr* and *Moohan* the objection was that to develop a common law right in a field regulated by statute risked 'shaping powers and duties and provisions inconsistent with those prescribed by Parliament'.[116] In each case the opportunity to develop a common law right to give it the substance of an analogous Convention right was declined on constitutional grounds.

There have been exceptions. In *Campbell v MGN Ltd*[117] the House of Lords was prepared to develop the common law right of confidentiality in line with rights arising under Article 8 to fashion a new tort of misuse of private information from the old tort of breach of confidentiality. That development, however, did not involve extending common law rights as against the state but against private individuals; was a relatively limited extension of the existing common law right of confidentiality; and was set against a backdrop of pre-HRA case-law in which the courts had bemoaned the fact that common law could not provide a remedy for unjustified media intrusions.[118]

C. Constitutional Resilience

The last measure, constitutional resilience, concerns how easily fundamental common law rights can be dispensed with or overridden compared with those protected by a written constitutional document such as the HRA. On this measure, neither source of rights is immune from being nullified by a sufficiently strong and determined government but, on balance, the HRA and Convention are probably more difficult to override. Although both the HRA and the Convention allow the Government to derogate from some Convention rights, the mechanism for doing so requires an exceptionally high threshold,[119] which is rigorously policed by the courts,[120] to be crossed. And although the HRA is not entrenched and may be repealed by a simple majority in Parliament,[121] the rights under the Convention cannot be entirely repealed unless the United Kingdom also withdraws from the Convention or, at least, withdraws the right of individual petition.

[116] *Moohan* (n 33) [34] (Lord Hodge); *McKerr* (n 78) [30] (Lord Nicholls).

[117] *Campbell v MGN Ltd* [2004] UKHL 22, [2004] 2 AC 457, following the lead of the Court of Appeal in *A v B plc* [2002] EWCA Civ 337, [2003] QB 195, 202. Another possible example is *Barrett v Enfield BC* [2001] 2 AC 550.

[118] See eg *Kaye v Robertson* (n 37).

[119] Article 15 of the Convention (given effect by s 14 HRA) provides: '1. In time of war or other public emergency threatening the life of the nation any high contracting party may take measures derogating from its obligations under this Convention to the extent strictly required by the exigencies of the situation, provided that such measures are not inconsistent with its other obligations under international law'.

[120] *A v Home Secretary* (n 19).

[121] C Gearty, 'States of Denial – What the Search for a UK Bill of Rights Tells Us about Human Rights Protection Today' [2018] *European Human Rights Law Review* 415.

On the other hand, primary legislation can override common law rights. The principle of legality, discussed above, may be employed to prevent repeal of a common law right by anything but the clearest of statutory language. However, if the language is clear enough then even the most fundamental rights may be overridden.[122] There is a contrary view expressed by both senior modern judges[123] and those of greater antiquity[124] that, were Parliament to enact primary legislation that involved a major breach of a fundamental common law right – for example, by removing the right to vote, or the right to a fair trial, or the prohibition on torture – the courts could strike it down as unconstitutional, notwithstanding the principle of Parliamentary sovereignty. However, equally senior judges take the contrary view that the courts could never strike down a provision of primary legislation, however fundamental the right that it has removed.[125] Moreover, the circumstances in which it has been said the courts might exercise that power are truly extreme, so that only the most fundamental rights could be protected against only the most flagrant of breaches.

III. WILL COMMON LAW RIGHTS PROVIDE THE SAME LEVEL OF HUMAN RIGHTS PROTECTION AS THE HRA IN FUTURE?

For the reasons outlined in the previous section, this chapter has argued that the HRA and Convention currently provide more effective human rights protection than the common law by reference to the three measures of normative reach, protective rigour and constitutional resilience. This second part of the chapter considers whether, over time, the common law could provide broadly equivalent protection to the HRA and Convention. Some commentators have suggested that common law rights are capable of developing in this way: Professor Mark Elliott,

[122] In *Boodram v Baptiste* [1999] 1 WLR 1709, 1711G–H, the Privy Council held that the prohibition on 'cruel and unusual punishment' in the Bill of Rights 1689 could be overridden by express statutory wording permitting execution by hanging.

[123] *R (Jackson) v Attorney-General* [2006] 1 AC 262 [102] (Lord Steyn), [104]–[109] (Lord Hope), [159] (Baroness Hale); *AXA General Insurance Co Ltd v HM Advocate* [2012] 1 AC 868 [49]–[51] (Lord Hope of Craighead DPSC); *Moohan* (n 33) [35] (Lord Hodge). See also *Taylor v New Zealand Poultry Board* [1994] 1 NZLR 394, 398, per Justice Cooke (later Lord Cooke of Thorndon) in discussing the common law right to silence: 'I do not think that literal compulsion, by torture for instance, would be within the lawful powers of Parliament. Some common law rights presumably lie so deep that even Parliament could not override them'. (See 'Lord Cooke and Fundamental Rights' Justice Michael Kirby, Justice of the High Court of Australia. President of the International Commission of Jurists.)

[124] In *Dr Bonham's Case* 77 ER 646, (1610) 8 Co Rep 113, Lord Coke stated that 'it appears in our books, that in many cases, the Common Law will control Acts of Parliament and sometimes adjudge them to be utterly void; for when an Act of Parliament is against common right and reason,. the Common Law will control it, and adjudge such act to be void'.

[125] Former Senior Law Lord, Lord Bingham, considers that it would not be possible for the courts to disregard Parliament's will in this way, even in such extreme cases: see T Bingham, *The Rule of Law* (London, Penguin, 2010) ch 12. Lord Neuberger has expressed the same view: see 'Who are the masters now?' (Lord Alexander of Weedon Lecture, 6 April 2011).

for example, has written that 'there is no a priori reason why the body of such rights should not develop in a way that over time yields a degree – perhaps a very high degree – of convergence with the Convention'.[126] He may be right: there remains plenty of scope for the development of common law rights which could, in time, share many features of the Convention rights, particularly if the HRA and Convention remain part of our law so that the two sources grow and develop together. However, there are a number of obstacles to such development under our existing constitutional arrangements which may prove to be insurmountable, particularly if the Government amends or repeals the HRA and withdraws from the Convention.

First, the particular conception of the separation of powers in our unwritten constitution, the doctrine of Parliamentary sovereignty,[127] dictates that Parliament, not a court, is the final arbiter of the law. Judges must defer to Parliament by applying the clear and ordinary meaning of statutes, however 'inexpedient, or even unjust or immoral' the consequences,[128] including the overturning of established common law rights, and will not expand common law rights in those areas considered more suitable for determination by Parliament, for example where an issue is particularly morally or ethically contentious (such as assisted suicide[129]) or involves the expenditure of money (such as legal aid[130]). As former JSC Lord Walker has explained: 'In a representative democracy changes in the law are in general a matter for Parliament, often acting on the advice of an expert law reform commission, and not for unelected judges'.[131] This echoes what Lord Reid said in 1972:[132] 'Parliament is the right place to settle issues which the ordinary man regards as controversial'. In the recent case of *Elgizouli*,[133] Lord Reed reaffirmed this principle:

> Secondly, that constraint on judicial law-making is also compatible with the pre-eminent constitutional role of Parliament in making new law, and with the procedural and institutional limitations which restrict the ability of litigation before the courts to act as an engine of law reform.

[126] Elliott, 'Beyond the European Convention' (2015).

[127] 'Parliament has … the right to make or unmake any law whatever; and, further, … no person or body is recognised by the law of England as having a right to override or set aside the legislation of Parliament': AV Dicey, *Introduction to the Study of the Law of the Constitution*, 8th edn (London, Macmillan, 1915) 37–38; cited in *R (Miller) v Secretary of State for Exiting the EU* [2017] UKSC 5, [2017] 2 WLR 583 [43].

[128] *Duport Steels v Sirs* (HL) [1980] 1 WLR 142, 157.

[129] See the judgments of the Divisional Court (notably that of Toulson LJ, as he then was) and the Court of Appeal in *R (Nicklinson) v Ministry of Justice* (n 108).

[130] *Witham* (n 22).

[131] Lord Walker, 'Developing the common law: how far is too far?' (Banco Court, Supreme Court of Victoria, 4 September 2012); see also Lord Bingham in 'The Judge as Lawmaker: an English Perspective' in P Rishworth (ed), *The Struggle for Simplicity in the Law: Essays for Lord Cooke of Thorndon* (Wellington, Butterworths, 1997); Lord Dyson MR, 'Where the Common Law Fears to Tread' (ALBA Annual Lecture, 6 November 2012).

[132] Lord Reid, 'The Judge as Law Maker' (1972) 12 *Journal of the Society of Public Teachers of Law* 22.

[133] *Elgizouli* (n 8) [170].

The effect of Parliamentary sovereignty, as it is currently applied, is therefore to limit the development of common law rights. It is, of course, possible for a political constitution to strike a slightly different balance between judiciary, legislature and executive. The United States' Constitution, for example, prohibits Congress from legislating in a manner that is incompatible with the Constitution and confers upon the Supreme Court the power to strike down any legislation that purports to do so.[134] The HRA, while not conferring upon the judiciary the same power of striking down incompatible legislation, has modified Parliamentary sovereignty by conferring on the judiciary the powers in ss 3 and 4 to 'read down' legislation that is on its face incompatible and to declare such legislation to be incompatible if it cannot be read down: see above. However, these are legislative changes; it is difficult to conceive of such profound constitutional changes being made by the judges at common law employing the principle of legality. As Lord Sales JSC has explained, by contrast with the task judges are mandated by Parliament to perform under the HRA:[135]

> It is more of a challenge to identify relevant authoritative criteria when the court is asked to employ the principle of legality in novel situations. There is a risk the courts might be perceived to be acting outside the legitimate scope of their authority if they modify what appears to be the clear meaning of a statute on the basis of their own choice of fundamental values or rights.

Second, and connected to this first reason, judges wishing to develop rights at common law are constrained by their relative lack of democratic *legitimacy* compared with the exercise of legislative powers. The HRA is itself an expression of Parliamentary sovereignty and the democratic principle. Judges enjoy greater legitimacy – and, therefore, self-confidence – in developing and enforcing the Convention rights to which it gives effect. It was this democratic legitimacy that Lord Bingham emphasised in the *Belmarsh Detainees* case when rejecting the Home Secretary's argument that it would be 'undemocratic' for the court to overturn his decision to derogate from the Convention right to liberty in order to detain a number of terrorist suspects:

> The Attorney General is fully entitled to insist on the proper limits of judicial authority, but he is wrong to stigmatise judicial decision-making as in some way undemocratic. *It is particularly inappropriate in a case such as the present in which Parliament has expressly legislated in section 6 of the 1998 Act to render unlawful any act of a public authority, including a court, incompatible with a Convention right … The 1998 Act gives the courts a very specific, wholly democratic, mandate.*[136]

Parliament's imprimatur is key, then, to the enhanced legitimacy enjoyed by the domestic courts in developing Convention rights under the HRA, reinforced by the

[134] *Marbury v. Madison*, 5 US 137 (1803), 176.

[135] See Philip (now) Lord Sales JSC: P Sales, 'Legalism in Constitutional Law – Judging in a Democracy' [2018] *PL* 687, 699.

[136] *A v Home Secretary* (n 19) [46]; emphasis added.

fact the Convention itself is signed and ratified by all 47 state parties of the Council of Europe in what Lord Sales has called 'a considered West European expression of liberal democratic values',[137] with principles interpreted and developed by an international court. The judiciary, while able to draw on the Convention, but without the legitimacy of primary legislation and subject to the *grundnorm* of Parliamentary sovereignty,[138] is unlikely to respond to encroachments by the executive using the common law as confidently or effectively as it can under a written bill of rights such as the HRA. By way of example, and as described above, the Privy Council was prepared to imply a power to grant vindicatory damages for breach of a right guaranteed by a written constitution in *Ramanoop*,[139] but the House of Lords and Supreme Court were not prepared to do the same in respect of breaches of common law rights in *Cullen*[140] and *Lumba*.[141]

Third, the principle that judicial decision-making operates retrospectively, rather than prospectively, means that the development of new common law rights offends against the principle of legal certainty.[142] Although the courts have developed a common law exception to the retrospective operation of judicial decisions,[143] this factor (along with the principle of Parliamentary sovereignty) was considered by Lord Reed in *Elgizouli* to be a powerful one that operated against the recognition of a new common law right not to have a trial in a foreign jurisdiction facilitated where there is a prospect that such a trial would lead to the death penalty being carried out.

Fourth, the political tides are presently running strongly against the extension of further powers to the judiciary. In recent years there has been vociferous and sustained criticism of the judge-led development of rights under the Convention, the HRA and the EU, as exemplified by Brexit and the furore following the two *Miller* judgments.[144] This criticism has come from elected politicians, the media, academics[145] and senior judges, notably former Supreme Court Justice Lord Sumption who, in his 2019 Reith Lectures, characterised the judicial development of human rights, at least in some cases, as an undemocratic usurpation of power by an unelected elite.[146]

[137] P Sales, 'Rights and Fundamental Rights in English Law' (2016) 75 *CLJ* 86.

[138] G Winterton, 'The British Grundnorm: Parliamentary sovereignty re-examined' (1976) 92 *LQR* 591.

[139] n 114.

[140] n 112.

[141] n 113.

[142] *Elgizouli* (n 8) [170], per Lord Reed.

[143] *Re Spectrum Plus Ltd (In liqidation)* [2005] 2 AC 680.

[144] *R (Miller) v Secretary of State for Exiting the EU* (SC(E)) [2017] UKSC 5 ('*Miller No 1*'); *R (Miller) v Prime Minister (SC(E))* [2019] UKSC 41 ('*Miller No 2*').

[145] See, for example, Prof John Finnis, 'Judicial Power: Past, Present and Future', lecture given on 21 October 2015 relaunch of Policy Exchange's Judicial Power Project; see also G Webber, P Yowell, R Ekins, M Köpcke, B Miller and F Urbina, *Legislated Rights* (Cambridge, CUP, 2018).

[146] Lord Sumption's arguments were well known. They were first set out in his 2011 FA Mann Lecture, 'Judicial and Political Deicsion-Making: the Uncertain Boundary', then again in the 27th Sultan Azlan Shah Lecture in Kuala Lumpur in 2013. The latter forms the centrepiece of R Ekins, P Yowell and N Barber, *Lord Sumption and the Limits of the Law* (Oxford, Hart, 2016),

These criticisms reflect the sometimes fierce, longstanding debate as to the proper boundary between law and politics. It may be helpful to sketch out the battle lines. One may take as relatively uncontroversial the orthodox judicial function of resolving disputes between parties by applying and interpreting existing common law and legislation. This function includes the determination of the proper limits of executive power by way of judicial review which may, on occasion, require judges to quash government decisions. That is a quintessentially judicial function in a constitutional system based on the separation of powers and is 'universally recognised as a cardinal feature of the modern democratic state, a cornerstone of the rule of law itself".[147] Also relatively uncontroversial – although not entirely so[148] – are judge-made changes to the common law, which may sometimes be 'radical'.[149] Such developments are inherent in a common law system, although they may (within limits) overturn long-settled law upon which many people have settled their affairs.[150] More controversial has been the approach of the judiciary, here and in Strasbourg, in developing the HRA and Convention (and EU law), with two particular developments attracting the most criticism. First, the detractors complain that the development of proportionality rather than *Wednesbury* irrationality as a tool of judicial review has involved judges in substituting their own decisions on the merits on political issues that are more properly for elected government officials. Second, the judicial interpretation of human rights treaties has led to the discovery of 'new' rights, sometimes in very controversial areas, which could not have been contemplated at the time the treaty was drafted or the contracting states ratified it. Critics claim it is for elected representatives, not unelected judges, to make these decisions and the judiciary have overreached themselves and trespassed on the territory of the legislature and executive, in breach of the doctrine of separation of powers.

Those on the other side of the debate argue that there is nothing undemocratic about the judicial protection of human rights. A distinction must be drawn between majoritarianism, which can lead to the tyranny of the majority over the minority, and democracy under the rule of law, which brings with it an obligation on the majority to afford legal protection to the rights of the minority. As Baroness Hale has said, 'Democracy values everyone equally even if the majority does not'.[151] It is the role of judges in a democracy based on

which contains a number of responses to Lord Sumption's argument. For an elegant refutation of Lord Sumption's argument see S Sedley, 'Judicial Politics' *London Review of Books* (23 February 2012) 15–16 and a number of the contributors to *Lord Sumption and the Limits of the Law*.

[147] *A v Secretary of State for the Home Department* (n 19) [42] (Lord Bingham of Cornhill).

[148] See, for example, Prof John Finnis' chapter in *Lord Sumption and the Limits of the Law* (n 146), ch 6.

[149] To use Lord Woolf's term in *Kleinwort Benson* (n 52).

[150] Tempered, to some extent, by the innovation of declarations having only prospective effect introduced in *Re Spectrum Plus* (n 52).

[151] *Ghaidan v Godin-Mendoza* (n 103) [131]–[132].

the rule of law to protect the rights of minorities from breaches of their rights, even when the breach occurs with the vocal support of the majority. If judges overstep the mark it is always open to Parliament to reverse any judicial development by legislation. The development of proportionality as a tool of judicial review represents what was already nascent in the common law, is common to many jurisdictions and part of the jurisprudence of the Convention when the HRA was passed by the (democratically) Parliament in 1998. Furthermore, when conducting their traditional role of interpreting and enforcing rights, it is sometimes necessary for judges to make new law. This is not only inherent in a common law system, but also arises from the process of judicial interpretation of legislation and international treaties in order to reflect changing societal values. Under the Convention and HRA this is known as the 'living instrument' doctrine;[152] domestically, the term 'always speaking' describes the same principle as applied to certain domestic statutes[153] and to the constitutions of other common law jurisdictions;[154] in Canada the phrase 'living tree' is used.[155] These are orthodox, long-standing, common law and international principles of interpretation, the alternative to which is arid originalism whereby judges applying legislation vainly seek to divine the intentions of the original legislators in relation to a problem they cannot, at the time, have conceived of.

This chapter does not seek to resolve the two sides of the debate. Clearly, the source and legitimacy of judicial powers are proper subjects of scrutiny and discussion. But it is instructive to compare the nature of the debate today with that of the 1960s that preceded the changes leading to the Quartet. The developments of the 1960s occurred at a time of consensus that public law needed to be adapted to redress the balance between politics and law, which at that time was seen to be weighted too far in favour of the executive.[156] A rebalancing of power in favour of the judges was anticipated and tacitly accepted. By contrast, the modern renaissance of common law rights has coincided with calls to amend or repeal the HRA and to withdraw from the Convention. The politicians who have called for those changes most loudly are now in government, whose stated policy it is to 'update' the HRA and to restore the 'proper balance between the rights of individuals, our vital national security and effective government'.[157] Tides change, but these are not auspicious times for a sea change in favour of greater judicial power.

It is difficult to avoid the conclusion that the senior judges have retreated to 'home-grown' common law rights in a bid to defuse some of the recent criticisms

[152] *Tyrer v United Kingdom* (n 48) [31].
[153] *R (Quintavalle) v Secretary of State for Health* [2003] 2 AC 687.
[154] *AG for Trinidad & Tobago v Maharaj* [2019] UKPC 6 [22].
[155] First stated by the Privy Council in *Edwards v AG for Canada* [1930] AC 124 and repeatedly reaffirmed since, eg *Reference re Same-Sex Marriage* 2004 SCC 79 [22]–[23].
[156] See TT Arvind and L Stirton, 'The Curious Origins of Judicial Review' (2017) 133 *LQR* 91; and see ch 16 in this volume (Bailey).
[157] Conservative Party Manifesto (n 12).

of the Convention and HRA. If that is the intention, there must be some doubt as to whether it will be achieved. The judicial protection and development of human rights will continue to be condemned by some as undemocratic, whether the purported source of those rights is the common law or the HRA and Convention. For example, the academic Judicial Power Project website identifies 50 'problematic' cases in which, according to its authors, judges have overstepped the proper boundaries of the judicial role. While the majority of the cases involve the Convention or EU law, one of the Quartet – *Anisminic* – is cited as an example of 'judicial adventurism'.[158] This is a sign: repeal the HRA, withdraw from the Convention and the focus of critics will switch from the 'foreign' nature of rights protection to the legitimacy of the judges themselves, leading to further calls to restrict judicial power or for political oversight of judicial appointments and the undermining of judicial independence. Those critics' objections will be particularly loud if, following any amendment or repeal of the HRA, the judges simply replace whatever statutory rights have been removed by newly minted common law rights.

IV. CONCLUSION

Despite the apparent similarities between the judicial activism of the 1960s and the more recent judicial development of common law rights, there are significant differences between the two. The Quartet was decided at a time of consensus that the power balance between law and politics required rebalancing in favour of law after the 'long sleep' of public law in the previous century and presaged a period of radical change in the common law. The more recent cases, on the other hand, have come at the end of a period of significant expansion of human rights jurisprudence and in response to an anti-European backlash and criticism of judicial over-reach. The rights that were developed in the 1960s began a process of sometimes radical development of common law rights without the need for a written constitutional instrument. But those developments have now been overtaken by the introduction of the HRA, giving effect to the rights created by the Convention, to the extent that the common law now falls some way short of the protection provided by the HRA's written constitutional guarantees. This chapter contends that is likely to remain the case, at least for the foreseeable future. While common law rights have developed in recent years, there must be some doubt whether that would have happened without the inspiration of the Convention and HRA.[159] While there may be more scope for innovation in the common law protection of human rights, any developments are likely to remain

[158] For a response see TT Arvind and L Stirton, 'Why the Judicial Power Project Is Wrong about Anisminic', UK Constitutional Law Blog (20th May 2016), available at ukconstitutionallaw.org/2016/05/20/tt-arvind-and-lindsay-stirton-why-the-judicial-power-project-is-wrong-about-anisminic.

[159] *Elgizouli* (n 8) [197] per Lord Carnwath.

within the bounds set by the Convention.[160] There is no sign of any appetite by the senior judiciary to arrogate to itself any additional common law powers or to erode the principle of Parliamentary sovereignty to the extent necessary to make common law rights that are equivalent to, and certainly not to exceed, those under the HRA and Convention.

Judges need the legitimacy of a written constitutional document to keep human rights hard-edged, up to date and effective. Were effect to be given to the threats to repeal the HRA and withdraw from the Convention, the idea that the 'princess' of the common law could be reawoken to restore rights deliberately taken away by Parliament is not so much a fairy tale as a fantasy.[161] The reality is that the best protection for human rights is provided by a written constitutional guarantee operating alongside the common law. The HRA and Convention together provide a well-balanced, well-understood model for the protection of human rights that moderates but respects Parliamentary sovereignty while mitigating the scope for majoritarian abuse of the rights of the minority. We dispense with either of them at our peril, and should not even contemplate doing so without our eyes wide open to the inherent weaknesses of the common law in protecting fundamental rights or a commitment to replace the HRA with an equivalent UK bill of rights. However much we owe the common law, and the judges who made it, we cannot rely on them alone to win the freedom of the new age.

[160] *Elgizouli* (n 8) [193] per Lord Carnwath.

[161] C Gearty 'On fantasy island – British politics, English judges and the ECHR' [2015] *European Human Rights Law Review* 1.

9

Beyond the End of Ouster Clause History?

JOE TOMLINSON*

I. INTRODUCTION

THE RULING OF the House of Lords in *Anisminic*[1] was quickly in 'every administrative lawyer's manual' but was not necessarily in their good books.[2] Analysis of the judgment was produced in a steady stream in the years after it was handed down.[3] In keeping with the dominant style of the times, much of this commentary was in the best traditions of technical, doctrinal administrative law, only obliquely connected to normative concerns about the overarching constitutional order.[4] Fifty years later, styles of public law scholarship have changed significantly, but *Anisminic* remains relevant and the subject of active debate. Also in keeping with the prevailing style of public law, contemporary analysis of ouster clauses typically frames the issue as a perpetual, complex conflict between the rule of law, Parliamentary sovereignty, and the separation of powers – and differing conceptions of the nature, status

* I am grateful to the organisers of and participants at the SLS Quartet seminar, especially for comments which led to a significant reframing of this chapter. I am also grateful to Paul Daly for organising a symposium at the University of Cambridge on the *Privacy International* litigation. Participants there provided much helpful input which assisted in the development of the thesis presented in this chapter, particularly Stephen Daly and Robert Craig. Jake Rylatt also provided extensive comments on various drafts.

[1] *Anisminic v Foreign Compensation Commission* [1969] 2 AC 147. For a contextual analysis of the case, see: D Feldman, '*Anisminic v Foreign Compensation Commission*: In perspective' in S Juss and M Sunkin (eds), *Landmark Cases in Public Law* (Oxford, Hart Publishing, 2017) 63–96.

[2] J Griffith, 'Judicial Review for Jurisdictional Error' (1979) 38 *CLJ* 11, 11.

[3] See eg W Wade, 'Constitutional and Administrative Aspects of the *Anisminic* Case' (1969) 85 *LQR* 198; DM Gordon, 'What did the *Anisminic* case decide?' (1971) 43 *MLR* 1.

[4] P McAuslan, 'Administrative law and administrative theory: the dismal performance of administrative lawyers' (1978) 40 *Cambrian Law Review* 9. See also: T Prosser, 'Towards a Critical Public Law' (1982) 9 *Journal of Law and Society* 1; M Loughlin, 'Procedural fairness: a study of the crisis in administrative law theory' (1978) 28 *University of Toronto Law Journal* 215.

and the relationship of those constitutional principles.[5] For the most part, the debate consists of some scholars critiquing the continued application of the ruling as an affront to Parliamentary sovereignty and others suggesting it recognises and protects the fundamental character of the rule of law. Between these two stances are a spectrum of different views about how these two principles, along with the separation of powers, ought to relate to each other. The contours of the contemporary debate around ouster clauses are very well known, almost to the extent that the debate around the next ouster clauses case (whenever it may arise) is largely predictable.

When this state of affairs is seen in light of the fact that the UK Supreme Court has once again effectively confirmed the *Anisminic* approach in the recent case of *Privacy International*,[6] there is almost a sense that we appear to have reached, to coin a phrase, the 'end of ouster clause history'.[7] It therefore seems a fitting moment to ask one of the most basic questions that can be posed of any legal principle: does it work? If we assume, as most appear to do, that the broad purpose of *Anisminic* was to ensure common law control on minimum access to judicial review, does it achieve that end? The argument here is that, when placed in the wider context of restrictions on access to judicial review, the *Anisminic* approach can only make a minimal substantive contribution to ensuring the accessibility of the judicial review process. Other factors, such as the cost risks of bringing a case, exclude far more people from judicial review than ouster clauses. I therefore suggest that those genuinely concerned with access to judicial review, and how it may be protected through law, must now move beyond traditional *Anisminic*-type arguments and towards considering what the ruling's underlying philosophy, and constitutional law generally, may have to say about other types of restriction.

This argument is made in three main parts. First, the framing of the current debate is discussed through a case study of the recent *Privacy International* litigation and the scholarly responses to it. Second, a discussion of some other key exclusions operating in the context of judicial review, and the nature of them, is presented. Ouster clauses are also located within this wider context. The central suggestion in this part of the chapter is that ouster clauses are a relatively esoteric form of restriction and judicial control of them has a similarly marginal impact on the substantive issue of exclusion. Finally, some implications of this analysis for the advancement of public law thought are suggested. In short, I suggest there is a need to imagine a wider public law jurisprudence on

[5] G Gee and G Webber, 'Rationalism in Public Law' (2013) 76 *MLR* 708; M Loughlin, *Public Law and Political Theory* (Oxford, Clarendon Press, 1992).

[6] *R (Privacy International) v Investigatory Powers Tribunal* [2019] UKSC 22, [2019] 2 WLR 1219.

[7] That is to say that the issue appears to have achieved a degree of lasting stability, with even the disagreement contained within predictable parameters. For one use of the reference, see eg F Fukuyama, *The End of History and the Last Man* (New York, Free Press, 1992) (the phrase is, however, of much older origin).

legal exclusion, while tracing how leading scholars of public law and the courts themselves seem to be gradually making this move.

II. THE END OF HISTORY?

There are two features of the current debate on ouster clauses which provoke the sense we have reached an 'end of history' moment. First, that the core principle of *Anisminic* – that the courts will treat ouster clauses with suspicion and will ultimately be the final judge of them – seems, 50 years on, to be firmly established.[8] For sure, it is controversial. There may also be points of technical differentiation to be elaborated, eg in respect of the specific statutory wording in different cases. But the courts have consistently stated and demonstrated that the broad *Anisminic* approach is the one that is to be adopted. Second, the frame of scholarly analysis of ouster clauses is now so widely shared that the response to ouster clause judgments is, to a large extent, predictable. From this analytical frame, ouster clauses are understood as a complex clash between differing conceptions of three major constitutional principles: the rule of law; Parliamentary sovereignty; and the separation of powers. Both of these features of contemporary debate were neatly demonstrated in the recent *Privacy International* litigation and the response to it.[9]

In *Privacy International*, the complaint related to whether the intelligence services could justify the use of a general warrant to engage in hacking.[10] The Investigatory Powers Tribunal (IPT) made a decision on this point and judicial review against the ruling was sought. The IPT is a creature of statute designed to allow actions taken by the security services to be challenged. The constitutional issues arose because section 67(8) of the Regulation of Investigatory Powers Act 2000 states: 'Determinations, awards, orders and other decisions of the Tribunal (including decisions as to whether they have jurisdiction) shall not be subject to appeal or be liable to be questioned in any court'. This provision thus created an *Anisminic*-type situation, albeit with the added complexity of a statute drafted in such a way that it appeared to be evading the particular type of jurisdictional reasoning in *Anisminic* itself.

After the High Court and the Court of Appeal found section 67(8) to effectively oust judicial review, the Supreme Court handed down 113 pages of ouster clauses analysis. There was a plurality judgment by Lord Carnwath (with whom

[8] See the authorities cited and analysis presented in H Woolf, J Jowell, C Donnelly and I Hare, *De Smith's Judicial Review*, 8th edn (London, Sweet & Maxwell, 2018) [4-032–4-046] (also describing the first instance *Privacy International* ruling as 'highly unusual').

[9] *Privacy International* (n 6). The Supreme Court judgment followed two rulings from the High Court and Court of Appeal which went the other way, see *R (Privacy International) v Investigatory Powers Tribunal* [2017] EWCA Civ 1868; *R (Privacy International) v Investigatory Powers Tribunal* [2017] EWHC 114 (Admin).

[10] This was ostensibly under Intelligence Services Act 1994, s 5.

Lady Hale and Lord Kerr concurred), and a separate but ultimately concurring judgment from Lord Lloyd-Jones, and dissenting judgments by Lord Sumption (with whom Lord Reed concurred) and Lord Wilson. There is clear disagreement within the Supreme Court, ranging from the obvious and subtle. It is important, however, to not lose the forest for the trees: it *was* decided conclusively that the IPT is subject to judicial review for error of law, notwithstanding the apparently clear ouster clause in section 67(8) of the Regulation of Investigatory Powers Act 2000. Lord Carnwath displayed admirable clarity in putting this point:

> This proposition should be seen as based, not on such elusive concepts as jurisdiction (wide or narrow), *ultra vires*, or nullity, but rather as a natural application of the constitutional principle of the rule of law … and as an essential counterpart to the power of Parliament to make law. The constitutional roles both of Parliament, as the maker of the law, and of the High Court, and ultimately of the appellate courts, as the guardians and interpreters of that law, are thus respected.[11]

He later concludes:

> In all cases, regardless of the words used, it should remain ultimately a matter for the court to determine the extent to which such a clause should be upheld, having regard to its purpose and statutory context, and the nature and importance of the legal issue in question; and to determine the level of scrutiny required by the rule of law.[12]

That broad proposition, clearly elaborated by Lord Carnwath, seems to be the core of *Ansiminic* and, 50 years later, the core of *Privacy International*.

As the litigation progressed through the High Court, Court of Appeal, and up to the Supreme Court, there was a flurry of scholarly commentary. All of these contributions adopt much of the same general framework of constitutional principle. Paul Scott, for instance, argues that 'One of the principles most dear to the UK's constitution' is the rule of law and that this commitment 'manifests itself in particular in a deep suspicion of "ouster clauses" by which statutes purport to limit or exclude the exercise of the supervisory jurisdiction'.[13] From this starting point, he argues that the High Court's judgment, which found that section 67(8) prevented judicial review, was 'unusual in recognising that an ouster clause has that effect', 'incorrect', and a 'failure to insist upon the rule of law ideal'.[14] His conclusion was that the High Court ruling represented an error of 'constitutional significance' and that this 'wrong should be put right at the first available opportunity'.[15] Tom Hickman expressed a similar view: 'The issue raised by the *Privacy International* case is … nothing less than compliance with the rule of law as it is understood in this country'.[16] To Hickman,

[11] *Privacy International* (n 6) [132].
[12] ibid [144].
[13] P Scott, 'Ouster clauses and national security: judicial review of the Investigatory Powers Tribunal' [2017] *Public Law* 355, 355.
[14] ibid.
[15] ibid.
[16] T Hickman, 'The Investigatory Powers Tribunal: a law unto itself?' [2018] *Public Law* 584, 586.

'whatever resemblance the tribunal may have to a court, in common with an election court, it is not a court of law. It is not even an inferior court of law'.[17] Invoking *Anisminic*, he concluded that 'once the jurisprudence on jurisdictional fact is taken into account, s.67(8) can be interpreted in a manner consistent with the rule of law'.[18]

Robert Craig took a different view, seeking to 'explore the wider constitutional implications of ouster clauses and, in particular, the relevance of the concept of separation of powers'.[19] For Craig, there can be 'no doubt that Parliament has the power to alter, amend or reallocate the jurisdictional authority of the courts'.[20] Though talking primarily about the separation of powers (and the difference between judicial and administrative functions), it is clear Craig is animated by a strong commitment to Parliamentary sovereignty in the orthodox sense:

> Parliament intended to reallocate judicial supervision usually undertaken by the High Court to a new statutory body operating in a judicial capacity that cannot itself be judicially reviewed by the High Court for error of law. This clear parliamentary intention should be respected.[21]

Displaying a particularly strong commitment to an orthodox understanding of Parliamentary sovereignty, Richard Ekins has also been vocal in the debate. Ekins is a leading part of the Judicial Power Project – a progamme of work undertaken by the think tank Policy Exchange. The aim of this programme is stated in the following terms: 'judicial overreach increasingly threatens the rule of law and effective, democratic government. The project aims to address this problem – restoring balance to the Westminster constitution – by articulating the good sense of separating judicial and political authority'.[22] Unsurprisingly, the *Anisminic* approach to ouster clauses has received less than glowing attention from this outfit. Indeed, *Anisminic* itself found its way onto the Project's list of '50 Problematic Cases'.[23] In response to the Supreme Court's ruling in *Privacy International*, Ekins penned an article for *The Spectator* magazine, asking: 'Do our Supreme Court judges have too much power?'.[24] He cast the approach taken by the Supreme Court as 'dubious', claiming it 'be sophistry – and bad

[17] ibid.

[18] ibid 594.

[19] R Craig, 'Ouster clauses, separation of powers and the intention of Parliament: from *Anisminic* to *Privacy International*' [2018] *Public Law* 570, 570.

[20] ibid 573.

[21] ibid 583.

[22] The Judicial Power Project has been the subject of extensive criticism by public lawyers, see eg P Craig, 'Judicial Power, the Judicial Power Project and the UK' (2017) 36 *University of Queensland Law Journal* 355; T Poole, 'The Executive Power Project', *London Review of Books Blog* (2 April 2019), available at www.lrb.co.uk/blog/2019/april/the-executive-power-project.

[23] For a helpful corrective, see: TT Arvind and L Stirton, 'Why the Judicial Power Project Is Wrong about *Anisminic*', *UK Constitutional Law Blog* (20 May 2016), available at ukconstitutionallaw.org.

[24] R Ekins, 'Do our Supreme Court judges have too much power?' *The Spectator* (15 May 2019), available at blogs.spectator.co.uk/2019/05/do-our-supreme-court-judges-have-too-much-power.

law – to say that the statute only means what the court says it means'. The rule of law, Ekins asserts, 'requires judges, just as much as anyone else, to follow the law, which includes section 67(8)'. As a result, Lord Carnwath's conclusion, stated above, is to be considered simply as 'not the law of our constitution'. For Ekins, this (somewhat astonishingly) ought to potentially have consequences for the judges that subscribe to the view of the Supreme Court:

> Any judge who openly refused to give effect to an Act of Parliament would be liable to be removed from office by way of the procedure set out in the Senior Courts Act 1981 … removal for openly flouting parliamentary sovereignty would be no violation of judicial independence.

These are all clear examples of divergent constitutional law analysis of an ouster clause flowing from *Privacy International*. While there is disagreement, the framing and the nature of disagreements are not new. The originality to be found in the academic discussion around the case arose from the particular factual circumstances and investigatory powers context. From one viewpoint, the presence of a similar framing of the issue could be said to represent the maturing of public law thought – the sign of a discipline establishing a refined grammar.[25] It certainly also shows more sophistication than a field famously condemned for its 'dismal performance' underpinned by a 'mind … shut to theory'.[26] However, as with all frames of analysis, the one dominating the debate around *Privacy International* has its limitations. As Griffith and Street pointed out in their seminal *Principles of Administrative Law*, any analysis based on a limited

> view of law or politics or public administration is obtained if any one of these social sciences is surveyed to the exclusion of the others. It is not so much that the study of one is incomplete without reference to the others, but rather that the landscape is single and entire. There are not different views to be seen, but only different viewers with variously adjusted blinkers.[27]

Given what appears to be the 'end of history' sense around ouster clauses post-*Privacy International*, it seems an appropriate time to adjust the blinkers slightly and ask one of the most basic questions about the courts' approach to ouster clauses and which is given little attention in the current debate: what role does it actually play in ensuring access to, and preventing exclusion from, judicial review?

III. OUSTER CLAUSES AND EXCLUSIONS ON JUDICIAL REVIEW

Though it was hardly transparent in its approach and its method was controversial, it is generally accepted that what the House of Lords in *Anismінic* was

[25] Gee and Webber, 'Rationalism' (2013).
[26] McAuslan, 'Administrative law and administrative theory' (1978) 42–43.
[27] JAG Griffith and H Street, *Principles of Administrative Law* (London, Pitman, 1963).

seeking to achieve was to prohibit restrictions on judicial review and protect access to the process. Behind this approach there is an assumption that judicial review serves valuable functions – for the individual, society and the wider constitutional system – that ought to be guarded.[28] The traditional textbook theory of this 'good' in judicial review is that it gives practical effect to the rule of law and/or Parliamentary sovereignty, as understood by reference to ultra vires and common law theories.[29] Another, less abstract, account of the functions of judicial review can be seen in Harlow and Rawlings' classic text, *Law and Administration*.[30] There, Harlow and Rawlings outline a range of purposes that judicial review may serve. These include: upholding the rule of law; protecting the individual; determining institutional relationships; establishing general principles; being a vehicle for interest representation; structuring deliberative and administrative processes; insisting on core values of good governance; and elaborating and vindicating fundamental rights. While there is a need to question the extent to which these benefits accrue as a matter of empirical reality and whether they are in fact all benefits (in the sense that they are normatively desirable), it is clear judicial review can and does serve such functions.[31] Equally, it is clear that lack of access to judicial review restricts these functions and directs their benefit towards particular parts of the population.

It is plain that ouster clauses pose a threat to the functions of judicial review. In many ways, ouster clauses are the 'nuclear' threat. However, it should not to be forgotten that ouster clauses are both ambiguous and esoteric in their exclusionary function. They are ambiguous in so far as they come in a wide variety of forms and many forms are widely seen as entirely legitimate.[32] One example is time limitation clauses. Such clauses are pervasive in the legal system and their effect can be identical. The courts are reluctant to meddle in their operation.[33] Another way to restrict judicial review is to provide that the fact that a particular decision-maker has done a particular thing will provide 'conclusive evidence' that a statutory requirement has been met.[34] Courts have not been as concerned by such clauses either.[35] The type of provision in *Anisminic*, a finality clause,

[28] Similar could also be said about litigation more generally, see eg A Lahav, *In Praise of Litigation* (Oxford, OUP, 2017); T Farrow, *Civil Justice, Privatization and Democracy* (Toronto, University of Toronto Press, 2014); J Resnik, 'The Democracy in Courts: Jeremy Bentham, "Publicity", and the Privatization of Process in the Twenty-First Century' in B Hess and A Koprivica (eds), *Open Justice: The Role of Courts in a Democratic Society* (Baden-Baden, Nomos, 2019).

[29] CF Forsyth (ed), *Judicial Review and the Constitution* (Oxford, Hart, 2000).

[30] C Harlow and R Rawlings, *Law and Administration*, 3rd edn (London, Sweet & Maxwell, 2009) 668 ff. See also: S Nason, *Reconstructing Judicial Review* (Oxford, Hart, 2016).

[31] S Halliday and M Hertogh, *Judicial Review and Bureaucratic Impact: International and Interdisciplinary Perspectives* (Cambridge, CUP, 2004).

[32] For a recent taxonomy, see: A Eliasson, R Chiarella and S Ahmad, 'Ousting the Ouster Clause?' [2017] *Judicial Review* 263.

[33] See eg *R (IA) v Secretary of State for Communities & Local Government* [2011] EWCA Civ 1253.

[34] Extradition Act 2003, s 193; Poisons Act 1972, s 8.

[35] See eg *R (Sultan of Pahang) v Secretary of State for the Home Department* [2011] EWCA Civ 616.

is thus only one form of ouster clause and presents a particularly vexing form. This type of provision is also relatively esoteric. Though they are not unheard of, the statute book is hardly riddled with them.

Of all the barriers operating in the context of judicial review, perhaps the most important relates to money. Judicial review is expensive for a variety of reasons.[36] A claimant must pay court fees in order to bring a judicial review claim, unless they are exempt or are granted legal aid.[37] Table 9.1 outlines the relevant fees that are charged in judicial review proceedings at present. Fees have risen in recent years. While civil (higher courts) fees overall were achieving 100 per cent recovery as long ago as the 2007 Comprehensive Spending Review, this was not the case for judicial review. In the December 2013 consultation exercise on a proposal to increase court fees,[38] the accompanying impact assessment made reference to judicial review:

> Current fees for the [*sic*] judicial review are below cost. Financial modelling has calculated that these fees do not recover the full cost of these processes. The government therefore proposes to increase fees for judicial review to their full cost prices, involving an increase from £60 to £135 for an application and £215 to £680 for a hearing or an oral renewal, with the hearing fee waived if an oral renewal is successful.[39]

In April 2014, judicial review fees were increased to achieve full costs recovery pursuant to the December 2013 consultation proposal. In August 2015, the Government consulted on further fee increases, including a general ten per cent rise in civil fees.[40] The August 2015 consultation document explained that the Government's longstanding aim 'has been to cover the entire cost of the court service, less the cost of the remissions system (fee waivers), through fee income', and that although the April 2014 fee increase achieved 'near to full cost recovery across the civil court system', the surplus income generated by the proposed further fee increases would 'finance the costs of HMCTS as a whole, and specifically, those parts of HMCTS such as the criminal courts and the tribunals which are otherwise funded through general Government expenditure rather than fee income'.[41] Judicial review fees were stated in the consultation document to have been set, following the April 2014 increase, at full cost.[42] In July 2016, judicial

[36] For an overview, see: J Tomlinson and R Low-Beer, *Financial Barriers to Judicial Review: An Initial Assessment* (London, Public Law Project, 2018).

[37] Courts Act 2003, s 92(1) (which empowers the Lord Chancellor with the consent of the Treasury to, by order, prescribe fees payable in respect of anything dealt with by the Senior Courts, which include the Administrative Court).

[38] Ministry of Justice, 'Court Fees Costs Recovery: Impact Assessment' (2 December 2013), available at consult.justice.gov.uk/digital-communications/court-fees-proposals-for-reform/supporting_documents/costrecoveryia.pdf.

[39] ibid [63].

[40] Ministry of Justice, 'Court and Tribunal Fees: The Government response to consultation on enhanced fees for divorce proceedings, possession claims, and general applications in civil proceedings and Consultation on further fees proposals' (Ministry of Justice, August 2015).

[41] ibid [47]–[53].

[42] ibid [78].

review fees were further increased by ten per cent pursuant to the consultation proposals. These fees may look like small numbers but for many, and particularly the disadvantaged, such fees can create a substantial and growing obstacle to access.

Table 9.1 Court fees for judicial review

Type of fee	Amount
For permission to apply for judicial review	£154
On applying for a request to reconsider at a hearing a decision on permission (Fee A)	£385
Where the court has made an order giving permission to proceed with a claim for judicial review, there is payable by the claimant within seven days of service on the claimant of that order:	
If the proceedings have been started by an application for permission to apply for judicial review (Fee B)	£770
[But where Fee A has been paid and permission has been granted at a hearing, the amount payable under Fee B is £385]	[£385]
Application for urgent consideration (unless made when lodging the claim in which case no fee is payable)	£255
Interim application	£255
Consent order	£100

Another critical barrier is created by the rules on costs liability. A 2007 estimate placed costs of a judicial review in the region of £10,000 to £20,000 for a straightforward case, possibly much higher for a more complex matter.[43] This has likely increased in the decade since the estimate was made. Hickman, writing in 2017, estimates that a 'very simple two hour judicial review against a government department' would cost around £8,000 to £10,000.[44] A 'moderately complex claim lasting a day and not brought against a central government department' would run in excess of £40,000, plus VAT. For a 'substantial two day judicial review', Hickman estimates that costs will run to between £80,000 and £200,000. Claimants who lose their cases are likely to be made liable for the defendant's costs as well as their own. CPR 44.2 sets out the general rule in civil litigation that costs will follow the event (ie the loser pays). Although the court has a discretion to make a different order as to costs (including to make

[43] The Public Law Project, 'How to fund a judicial review claim when public funding is not available' (London, Public Law Project, 2007) (which was informed by discussion with practitioners). Further and similar estimates are available in the government response to a Ministry of Justice consultation, made available via a Freedom of Information Act 2000 request, see: FOIA Request No 171204020.

[44] T Hickman, 'Public Law's Disgrace' *UK Constitutional Law Blog* (9th February 2017), available at ukconstitutionallaw.org/2017/02/09/tom-hickman-public-laws-disgrace.

no order)[45] and although cost caps may be available,[46] the risk is likely to act as a severe deterrent. This was recognised on multiple occasions by Sir Rupert Jackson in his Review of Civil Litigation Costs,[47] although the Government refused to accept his concern about access to judicial review as valid.[48]

Beyond fees and costs liability rules, there is a much wider range of financial issues which affect judicial review proceedings, including the availability of funding.[49] While there is a dense complexity here, unhelpfully accompanied by a lack of detailed data, the ostensible practical reality is that somebody in a typical household is, quite rationally, unlikely to ever want to bring a judicial review. To state, as it often has been said, that there is a 'middle class' access to justice problem would be to severely understate the present situation. The present position effectively amounts to a sweeping economic ouster clause for a large part of the population. This represents a grave risk to the rule of law and Parliamentary sovereignty, whatever conception of those ideas one adopts.

In reality, barriers, whether financial, legal or otherwise, are often messy and do not fit easily into one category. A recent episode concerning the provision of legal aid demonstrates this. An exclusionary effect emerged from the Legal Aid Agency's stance that it would not backdate funding for urgent work undertaken by lawyers prior to the date a decision to fund a case is made.[50] In judicial review litigation, cases are often conducted quickly and heavy preparation work is invested at the start of the litigation process due to the requirements of the permission stage. Given this, it does not take a great deal of imagination to realise that a possible consequence of this seemingly banal bureaucratic rule is that legal professionals may be forced either to carry out urgent judicial review work at risk of going unpaid or to refuse instructions on what they deemed to be meritorious claims.

Empirical research suggested that the operation of the exclusion, which impacted vulnerable claimants, had multiple interrelated elements, of which five were particularly important.[51] First, there was the general government

[45] Senior Courts Act 1981, s 51.

[46] Criminal Justice and Courts Act 2015, ss 88–90. See also: *R (Corner House Research) v Secretary of State for Trade and Industry* [2005] 1 WLR 2600.

[47] Lord Justice Jackson, 'Review of Civil Litigation Costs: Preliminary Report' (2009); Lord Justice Jackson, 'Review of Civil Litigation Costs: Final Report' (2009); Lord Justice Jackson, 'Review of Civil Litigation Costs: Supplemental Report, Fixed Recoverable Costs' (2017). See also: M Fordham QC and J Boyd, 'Rethinking Costs in Judicial Review' [2009] *Judicial Review* 306.

[48] For the latest response, see: Ministry of Justice, Extending Fixed Recoverable Costs in Civil Cases: Implementing Sir Rupert Jackson's proposals' (2019) ch 6 (where it is stated: 'we do not consider there to be an access to justice issue in respect of non-Aarhus JRs').

[49] Tomlinson and Low-Beer, *Financial Barriers to Judicial Review* (2018).

[50] This claim hung on the Agency's interpretation of the relevant empowering regulations; see Civil Legal Aid (Procedure) Regulation 2012 (SI 2012/3098). For a fuller analysis, see: J Tomlinson, 'Foundations for a "secret history" of judicial review: a study of exclusion as bureaucratic routine' (2019) 41 *Journal of Social Welfare and Family Law* 252.

[51] ibid.

policy of restricting access to legal aid.[52] Second, there was the interpretation of the relevant regulations adopted by Legal Aid Agency, which gave rise to its stance on backdating. A third key element of the exclusion was the ruling in *Kigen*, a case which concerned a judicial review in the Upper Tribunal brought out of time.[53] The delay, the claimants argued, was caused by awaiting a decision from the Legal Aid Agency. The Court of Appeal held that, though the appellants could not afford to instruct solicitors to conduct the proceedings, shortage of funds could not provide a good explanation for the delay.[54] Instead, the choice for a 'litigant who has applied for legal aid is in essentially the same position as any litigant who is unable to afford legal representation. As such, he has an unenviable choice between representing himself and abandoning his claim'.[55] This ruling, though conceived and justified as a way of promoting proportionate judicial management of caseload by the judges in the case, transformed into an aggravating factor when located in the context of the Legal Aid Agency's approach to urgent judicial review applications.[56] Fourth, there was straightforwardly poor administration of some urgent applications, which often made the exclusion more complex.[57] Finally, there was the straightforward lack of economic means of claimants. The barrier in operation here was eventually removed by a change in the law, forced by the bringing of a judicial review claim challenging the Legal Aid Agency's approach.[58] What this demonstrates, however, is how barriers to judicial review can crystalise in a variety of complex forms.

Although some exclusions are a perpetual challenge (eg financial barriers), the nature of exclusions may change over time.[59] One prominent example of an emerging risk in the justice system is that of digital exclusion. The important context here is that the UK Government is putting many justice processes online, including key public law mechanisms such as tribunals.[60] The central aim is to improve access to justice and to cut public expenditure. Given how pioneering the reforms are in terms of the use of technology and also given how quickly traditional services (such as courts buildings) are being reduced, these reforms

[52] For critical discussion, see The Bach Commission, *The Right to Justice* (London, Fabian Society, 2017).

[53] *R (Kigen) v Secretary of State for the Home Department* [2015] EWCA Civ 1286.

[54] ibid [16] (Moore-Bick LJ).

[55] ibid [17] (Moore-Bick LJ).

[56] ibid [12]–[13]; [26] (Moore-Bick LJ).

[57] On problems in Legal Aid Agency administration, see eg The Bach Commission, *The Right to Justice*; *Re R (Children: temporary leave to remove from jurisdiction)* [2014] EWHC 643 (Fam) [81]–[97] (HHJ Bellamy); *Kinderis v Kineriene* [2013] EWHC 4139 (Fam) (Holman J).

[58] Civil Legal Aid (Procedure) (Amendment) Regulations 2019, SI 2019/130.

[59] Although many barriers remain similar over time too, for instance see the discussion of judicial review in H Street, *Justice in the Welfare State* (London, Stevens, 1968) 65–69.

[60] Ministry of Justice, 'Transforming Our Justice System' (London, 2016); For an overview and discussion, see: J Rozenberg, *The Online Court: Will IT Work?* (London, Legal Education Foundation, 2017); H Genn, 'Online Courts and the Future of Justice' (The Birkenhead Lecture, Gray's Inn, 2017).

represent nothing less than a significant gamble.[61] One of the main concerns is digital exclusion: that people, particularly vulnerable people, will not be able to bring a claim due to lack of digital capability. One example of a vulnerable population in this regard is elderly citizens. A 2015 study by Age UK found that three out of ten people aged 65 to 74, and two-thirds of those aged 75 and over, are not online.[62] The study concluded that moving public services online without adequate support is making it harder for some who do not use the internet to access services, could deter people from seeking the support they need, and can increase dependency. Age UK recommended that the speed of change requires renewed efforts to help people get online, and stay online, with adequate and sustainable funding. It was also suggested that design needs to start from a strong understanding of older people's attitudes and experiences.

The Government is seeking to alleviate anxieties around digital exclusion by introducing assisted digital services (provided by a contracted-in supplier) and committing to ensuring non-online routes remain available, at least to a proportionate extent required in light of new digital services becoming available. Whether these fallbacks are sustainable and effective in the long term remains an open question. A major review of digital exclusion from justice in the UK was undertaken recently by JUSTICE.[63] It concluded that there is a risk that technology might exacerbate existing barriers to justice as people can be digitally disadvantaged in many ways – including through an inability to access the internet or digital devices, lack of basic digital skills, or problems with confidence and motivation. With more investment in digital inclusion, creative thinking, and inclusive design and technology, it was thought that there is an opportunity to realise the full potential of the 'online court' and to improve access to justice for many people. However, there is no signal that more investment will be forthcoming. JUSTICE, much like Age UK, suggested there was a need for a continuing programme of learning from users' experience and understanding and responding to users' needs. They also suggested that assisted digital services should be tested in regions where internet access is still limited and support services may be difficult to access, while specific attention should be paid to solutions for highly excluded groups, like homeless people and detainees. While there are no public plans to take judicial review fully online (yet), if the application process migrates to an online platform or alternative remedies that need to be exhausted prior to judicial review are online then the risks of digital exclusion from judicial review are not necessarily remote.

[61] J Tomlinson, *Justice in a Digital State: Assessing the Next Revolution in Administrative Justice* (Bristol, Bristol University Press, 2019) ch 4; J Tomlinson and B Karemba, 'Tribunal Justice, Brexit, and Digitalisation: Immigration Appeals in the First-tier Tribunal' (2019) 33 *Journal of Immigration, Asylum & Nationality Law* 47; J Tomlinson and R Thomas, 'Remodelling Social Security Appeals (Again): The Advent of Online Tribunals' (2018) 25 *Journal of Social Security Law* 84.

[62] Age UK, 'Later Life in a Digital World' (London, 2015).

[63] JUSTICE, 'Preventing Digital Exclusion from Justice' (London, 2018).

When placed in the context of the wider range of exclusions operating in the context of judicial review, a new light is cast upon the current constitutional law analysis on ouster clauses, as demonstrated by reference to *Privacy International* above. From one point of view, it can seem like courts have attended primarily to a very particular type of legal exclusion of judicial review much more than to other forms of exclusion, perhaps making their efforts to combat exclusion from judicial review through restricting ouster clauses somewhat marginal, and potentially arbitrary, in effect vis-à-vis the substantive problem of exclusion. From another perspective, perhaps the underlying legal principle which does exist on ouster clauses has been radically underexplored by legal practitioners and under-applied by the courts in respect of other types of exclusion on judicial review.[64] It is to this latter prospect that I turn in the next section of this chapter.

IV. TOWARDS A JURISPRUDENCE OF LEGAL EXCLUSION

Given the arguably distorted level of attention that ouster clauses have received from constitutional lawyers, there is a risk that analysis becomes ossified, effectively stuck in 1969. To be clear, ouster clauses remain significant in both effect and symbolism. So too is how the courts are determining the legality of such clauses. But if our keen interest in them as public lawyers is animated by the concern for the accessibility of judicial review and the enforceability of public law (whatever basis for the jurisdiction is preferred as a matter of constitutional theory),[65] then other sources of exclusion within the contemporary system deserve similar levels of attention. Whether a potential claimant cannot enforce a public law norm due to an ouster clause or being without sufficient funds to bring a claim, the effect is much the same: no access to judicial review and unequal opportunity to enforce public law. Such other sources of exclusion should therefore concern constitutional law scholars such as Ekins, Hickman, Craig and Scott in much the same way as section 67(8) of the Regulation of Investigatory Powers Act 2000.[66] This is a vital question of public law which has received insufficient attention so far: what does constitutional principle have to say about other exclusions from judicial review?

Interestingly, both the courts and constitutional scholars are now starting to explore this issue. Mark Elliott's work provides an interesting case study. In

[64] There are other areas where accessibility jurisprudence has developed, but that is not the concern here. On this, see P Erdunast, 'The multiple legal sources of the common law right of access to the courts' [2018] *PL* 427.

[65] On the constitutional foundations of judicial review, see Forsyth, *Judicial Review* (2000).

[66] Some have indeed expressed such concern, see eg T Hickman, 'Public Law's Disgrace' *UK Constitutional Law Blog* (9 February 2017), available at ukconstitutionallaw.org/2017/02/09/tom-hickman-public-laws-disgrace; C McCorkindale and P Scott, 'Public Interest Judicial Review in Cross-Border Perspective' (2015) 26 *King's Law Journal* 412. On the relevance of issues such as economic equality to constitutional foundations, see: G Sitaraman, *The Crisis of the Middle-Class Constitution: Why Economic Inequality Threatens Our Republic* (New York, Knopf, 2017).

a recent chapter, he provided an authoritative review of the line of authorities concerning ouster clauses.[67] He explains that two 'related phenomena' form the backdrop. First, is the 'increasing willingness of judges explicitly to invoke constitutional principles that … are in tension with the doctrine of parliamentary sovereignty'.[68] Second, that 'divergent conclusions' on ouster clauses 'ultimately turn upon underlying differences of constitutional philosophy'.[69] On Elliott's analysis, any case considering 'ouster, and similar, clauses are thus a theatre in which we see such principles interacting'.[70] This is adopting much the same framework as discussed in the first section of this chapter. However, Elliott goes on to discuss the Supreme Court's ruling in *Unison* as a 'quasi-ouster' case.[71]

Unison concerned a power under section 42 of the Tribunals, Courts and Enforcement Act 2007. The power provides that 'The Lord Chancellor may by order prescribe fees payable in respect of' various tribunals, including the Employment Tribunal and the Employment Appeal Tribunal. In 2013, the Lord Chancellor, relying upon that power, made an order, the effect of which was to require most people who wished to make use of the employment tribunals to pay fees.[72] There were no such fees prior to this. As could have been predicted, the numbers of claimants using the tribunal declined quickly.[73] It was argued before the Supreme Court that the Fees Order made by the Lord Chancellor was unlawful because it imposed restrictions upon access to justice which, properly construed, section 42 of the Act did not authorise. Striking down the fee, Lord Reed, giving a unanimous judgment for the court, emphasised not only the importance of courts and tribunals being practically capable of enforcing legislation, but also the need for such judicial bodies to 'provide authoritative guidance as to its meaning and application'.[74] Without access to the courts, 'laws are liable to become a dead letter, the work done by Parliament may be rendered nugatory, and the democratic election of Members of Parliament may become a meaningless charade'.[75]

From the perspective of the Supreme Court, this was constitutional innovation, justified by reference to the constitutional principles of the rule of law and Parliamentary sovereignty, to protect access to a tribunal in a scenario where

[67] M Elliott, 'Through the Looking-Glass? Ouster Clauses, Statutory Interpretation and the British Constitution' in C Hunt, L Neudorf and M Rankin (eds), 'Legislating Statutory Interpretation: Perspectives from the Common Law World' (Toronto, Carswell, 2018) https://doi.org/10.2139/ssrn.3097074. See also M Elliott, '*Lightfoot*: Tracing the Perimeter of Constitutional Rights' [1998] *Judicial Review* 217.

[68] ibid 7.

[69] ibid 13.

[70] ibid 14.

[71] ibid 5; *R (Unison) v Lord Chancellor* [2017] UKSC 51, [2017] 3 WLR 409.

[72] Employment Tribunals and the Employment Appeal Tribunal Fees Order 2013 (SI 2013/1893).

[73] A Adams and J Prassl, 'Vexatious Claims: Challenging the Case for Employment Tribunal Fees' (2017) 80 *MLR* 412.

[74] *Unison* (n 71) [72].

[75] ibid [68].

economic circumstances barred access. As for Elliott's analysis, he argues that if *Unison* was right,

> it follows that provisions that render judicial processes inaccessible – whether on financial or other grounds – raise concerns that are very similar to those raised by regular ouster clauses. Such provisions prevent the judiciary from performing not only its function of enforcing the law, but also its equally axiomatic, and logically prior, function of determining what the law means.[76]

He goes even further in defining what is the very essence of an ouster clause: 'what renders them common members of a meaningful category, is the way in which they impede the exercise of central judicial, including interpretive, functions'.[77] This appears to be a welcome turn towards introducing the wider issue of exclusion into the constitutional law debate on ouster clauses, raising the question of what constitutional principle has to say about other such exclusions from judicial review.

Similar developments in Elliott's thought can be seen in his analysis of a lecture given by Lord Sumption.[78] In a keynote speech to the 2018 Annual Bar and Young Bar Conference, the issue of legal aid was on the agenda.[79] In addressing this issue, Lord Sumption drew what Elliott saw to be a 'surprising and questionable distinction' between criminal and civil legal aid.[80] Lord Sumption started with the observation that 'legal aid cuts have fundamentally changed the nature of practice in every area where the clients are too poor to do without it'.[81] He continued by stating that there are essentially two categories of government expenditure: those which are discretionary where governments can 'decide how much money is available and cut their suit according to their cloth'; and those which are 'fundamental to the whole purpose of government, and have to be paid for whatever the costs'.[82] Criminal legal aid was placed in the second category of this dubious distinction, in the following terms:

> The maintenance of a functioning system of justice is not discretionary … [T]hat means a functioning system of criminal legal aid; enough judges of the right calibre to do the work without undue delay or haste; an effective police force; and a humane prison service to receive the unusually large number of people whom we sentence to be locked up. A court system which leaves criminal defendants to face the state's prosecutors with no, or no adequate, representation, is not a functioning court system.[83]

[76] Elliott, 'Through the Looking-Glass?' (2018) 6.

[77] ibid 5.

[78] M Elliott, 'Civil legal aid as a constitutional imperative: A response to Lord Sumption' *Public Law for Everyone* (28 November 2018), available at publiclawforeveryone.com/2018/11/28/civil-legal-aid-as-a-constitutional-imperative-a-response-to-lord-sumption.

[79] Lord Sumption, 'Lecture: Annual Bar and Young Bar Conference 2018' (London, 24 November 2018), available at www.supremecourt.uk/docs/speech-181124.pdf.

[80] Elliott, 'Civil legal aid as a constitutional imperative' (2018).

[81] Sumption (n 79) 6.

[82] ibid.

[83] ibid.

Civil legal aid – or 'much of it' at least – was relegated to the first category: 'Supporting the cost of civil litigation *may* be desirable in cases where people are too poor to fund it themselves'.[84] In case there was any lingering ambiguity remaining in his point, Lord Sumption concluded that civil legal aid 'is not fundamental in the way that criminal legal aid is fundamental' and it 'has to compete with all the other calls on public funds: health, education, defence, social security and so on'.[85]

For Elliott, Sumption's analysis was 'disappointing' in that he saw there to be 'powerful normative counterarguments, rooted in considerations of access to justice and the rule of law, with which Lord Sumption simply does not engage' and because 'financial inhibitions upon access to courts and tribunals raises fundamental rule of law concerns'.[86] He goes back again to ouster clauses jurisprudence:

> It is sometimes said that the constitutional right of access to courts is as close as the UK's unwritten constitution comes to a fundamental, in the sense of immovable, right. Certainly the courts' robust jurisprudence on ouster provisions might be taken to suggest that. But, for reasons that *Unison* makes clear, such jurisprudence is largely worthless if access to justice can readily be denied through indirect financial means, even if it cannot easily be denied via the sort of full-frontal assault that ouster clauses constitute.[87]

This all seems to be the welcome signs of a growing recognition in mainstream constitutional law scholarship that the ouster clause jurisprudence from *Anisminic* is at risk of being rendered peripheral if other exclusions on courts (and judicial review) are pervasive.

A similar line of thought also seems to be appearing from developing projects in constitutional theory to elaborate the social dimensions of the rule of law. Conventional accounts of the rule of law have emphasised legal form over substance, ie the procedural aspects of law rather than substantive rights.[88] For instance, Joseph Raz famously stated the rule of law is a political ideal that imposes obligations on states to: (i) make clear law; (ii) do so in a transparent and consistent manner; (ii) apply it consistently to all persons without distinction, and especially to public officials; (iv) adjudicate all legal disputes fairly before independent and impartial courts; and (v) secure access to such courts.[89] As traditionally understood, this type of formal rule of law theory does not require the protection of substantive rights and entitlements. Other accounts

[84] ibid (emphasis added).
[85] ibid.
[86] Elliott (n 78).
[87] Elliott (n 78).
[88] P Craig, 'Formal and Substantive Conceptions of the Rule of Law: An Analytical Framework' [1997] *PL* 467.
[89] J Raz, *The Authority of Law: Essays on Law and Morality* (Oxford, OUP, 2009) ch 11. See also AV Dicey, *Introduction to the Study of the Law of the Constitution* (London, Macmillan, 1885); L Fuller, *The Morality of Law* (New Haven, Yale University Press, 1964).

of the rule of law have directly claimed such substantive rights ought to be included in the formula,[90] but these accounts have routinely been subjected to the critique that they go beyond explaining the intrinsic value of law itself and start expounding a wider political philosophy under the guise of the principle.[91] Scholars are now challenging this orthodoxy from various angles, suggesting there is a need to introduce 'social dimensions' into our accounts of the rule of law in a way that does not encounter traditional objections.[92]

Nick Barber proposes one such route.[93] His thesis is that formal theories of the rule of law, such as that advocated by Raz, are inherently 'drawn towards social issues'.[94] The reason for this is because, assuming the 'guiding function' of law requires generally stable and prospective rules, a 'legal system requires some level of material well-being if the purported laws are to prove effective'.[95] For example, in a context of 'significant poverty', Barber argues, 'people will not be able to get to courts to secure their rights. They will not be able to afford the advice of lawyers, or, perhaps, they will not be able to expend the time necessary to mount a legal case'.[96] From this point, power inequalities will result. Similarly, even formal accounts assume minimal level of education across the population of a political community: 'If folk do not understand their rights then, again, to these people the purported laws are valueless'.[97] Barber's thesis is thus not a case to directly abandon formal conceptions of the rule of law but to suggest that they naturally imply more substance than is generally recognised.

Jeff King is developing a similar but distinct line of critique.[98] His challenge is to the core justification for the rule of law offered by formal theorists, ie that law should guide behaviour and it cannot do that unless it meets certain requirements (such as those elaborated by Raz). King sees no reason for accepting this as the core of the principle and that the risk of conflating 'the rule of law with justice is not only exaggerated but falsified in practice'.[99] Instead, his approach is to construct an account of the principle under which, due to a state's duty to protect through law, anarchy is incompatible with the rule of law. From this starting point, King suggests it follows that the absence of anarchy requires

[90] See eg T Bingham, *The Rule of Law* (London, Penguin, 2011).

[91] Raz, *The Authority of Law* (2009).

[92] It ought to be noted that challenging dominant formal theories of the rule of law is not new, see eg HW Jones, 'The Rule of Law and the Welfare State' (1958) 58 *Columbia Law Review* 143 (offering a critique of Dicey).

[93] NW Barber, 'Must Legalistic Conceptions of the Rule of Law Have a Social Dimension?' (2004) 17 *Ratio Juris* 474.

[94] ibid 483.

[95] ibid.

[96] ibid 483–84.

[97] ibid 484.

[98] J King, 'The Social Dimension of the Rule of Law' *I-CONnect* (27 April 2018), available at www.iconnectblog.com/2018/04/i-connect-symposium-on-constitutional-boundaries-the-social-dimension-of-the-rule-of-law.

[99] In this respect, Raz has also revised his initial theory; see J Raz, 'The Law's Own Virtue' (2019) 39 *Oxford Journal of Legal Studies* 1.

a positive programme of legal regulation to be undertaken by the state. Both Barber's and King's work in this context could potentially assist in articulating a constitutional basis for a more extensive legal response to the range of exclusions operating on judicial review.

This chapter does not seek to comment on the particular form the intellectual project ought to take but, more simply, its purpose is to make the case that it is imperative that concerns about the range of substantive exclusions from judicial review are engaged with alongside the established analysis of ouster clauses. These exclusions have been marginalised for far too long by public lawyers despite their significance to the operation of the constitution. It is a daunting task, given the varied nature of exclusions, but a necessary one. Some recent signs in public law thought are encouraging, but more ought to be done. In basic terms, what is required now is an effort to imagine what a general public law jurisprudence on exclusion from judicial review looks like. This, no doubt, will raise a variety of tricky questions, especially around the role of positive legal duties to facilitate access and the role of the court in enforcing them, but it is in many ways a natural progression of public law thought in a post-*Privacy International* landscape.[100] This is not necessarily a call for further judicialisation to manage exclusion from judicial review, but it is a call for fuller exploration of what is jurisprudentially possible in this respect.

[100] The task would, of course, not start with a blank slate. Aside from jurisprudence in cases such as *Unison* and under Art 6 ECHR, there are also heuristic frameworks, particularly those developed in the field of social rights, which may prove useful, eg J King, *Judging Social Rights* (Cambridge, CUP, 2012).

Part IV

The Quartet Outside England

10

Administrative Law and the Administrative Court for – or in – Wales

DAVID C GARDNER*

I. INTRODUCTION

IN 2016 THE sign outside Cardiff Civil and Family Justice Centre was to be updated. The Administrative Court Office Lawyer based in the building was asked a question. Should the sign read 'The Administrative Court *in* Wales' or 'The Administrative Court *for* Wales'? From this innocuous query arose an important question.

Fifty years on from the significant common law development of administrative law in *Ridge v Baldwin*,[1] *Padfield v Minister of Agriculture, Fisheries and Food*,[2] *Conway v Rimmer*,[3] and *Anisminic v Foreign Compensation Commission*[4] ('the Quartet'), this chapter will discuss the extent to which a different administrative law jurisdiction has developed in Wales, the extent to which separate administrative law has developed in Wales, and whether Wales could develop its own administrative law in a different way from England in the future. Finally, this chapter will seek to answer the important question; what should be on the sign outside Cardiff Civil and Family Justice Centre?

II. ADMINISTRATIVE LAW IN WALES[5]

When considering administrative law in Wales it is important to keep in mind that the law in Wales is, and has been since the sixteenth century, the law of

[1] [1964] AC 40.
[2] [1968] AC 997.
[3] [1968] AC 910.
[4] [1969] 2 AC 147.
[5] For more information on the history and development of the law in Wales see D Gardner, *Administrative Law and the Administrative Court in Wales* (Cardiff, University of Wales Press, 2016) ch 1.

England and Wales, not just Wales. Law made by the UK Parliament that only affects England is part of the law of England and Wales; law made by the Senedd Cymru / Welsh Parliament ('the Senedd'), formerly known as the National Assembly for Wales,[6] is part of the law of England and Wales; even a by-law that only affects a single street is part of the law of England and Wales. Thus, the principles of administrative law, including those established by the Quartet, are as applicable in Wales as they are in England. Administrative law in Wales is a quickly developing area in terms of the effect administrative law is having on the decisions and decision-making processes of public bodies in Wales, but it must not be forgotten that the fundamental principles behind administrative law in Wales and the Administrative Court in Wales do not differ from England.

This is not to say that there is no such thing as 'Welsh law'. The existence of separate Welsh law has been confirmed by the UK Parliament in section A2(1) of the Government of Wales Act 2006, which states 'The law that applies in Wales includes a body of Welsh law made by the Senedd and the Welsh Ministers'. The laws that have been made in Wales have not, to date, affected the principles of administrative law in Wales. However, there have already been a host of Acts made by the Senedd which set out how public bodies are to act and do so in a different manner (in various degrees) from the English counterparts to those public bodies. Examples are the Well-being of Future Generations (Wales) Act 2015, which is discussed in greater detail later in this chapter; the Social Services and Well-being (Wales) Act 2014, which sets out powers and responsibilities with regards to social care in Wales; the Housing (Wales) Act 2014, which sets out duties regarding homelessness and housing in Wales; and the Public Health (Wales) Act 2017, which sets out powers and duties to improve public health in Wales. These Acts and others like them impact upon administrative law in Wales in a way which differs from England in that Welsh public authorities' duties under these acts will be subject to the principles of administrative law and the scrutiny of the Administrative Court by way of judicial review. Thus, the process of applying the principles of administrative law to Wales will inevitably differ in some respects to that adopted when applying those same principles to English law. It follows, then, that whilst principles of administrative law currently remain the same in England and Wales, administrative law will and is diverging in England and Wales to the same extent that the law differs in any given area.

III. THE ADMINISTRATIVE COURT IN ENGLAND AND WALES[7]

The Administrative Court is part of the Queen's Bench Division of the High Court of England and Wales. It hears applications for judicial review and also

[6] Amended on 6 May 2020 by s 2 of the Senedd and Elections (Wales) Act 2020.

[7] For more information on the history of the Administrative Court and the drivers for change see Gardner, *Administrative Law* (2016) 1-32–1-34.

some statutory appeals and applications. It is by way of the judicial review procedure that an individual, company or organisation may challenge the act or omission of a public body and ensure that the public body is meeting its obligations in complying with the law.

After the ground-breaking decisions in the Quartet, the judicial review procedure as we now know it was first recommended by the Law Commission in the Report on Remedies in Administrative Law.[8] The recommendations were implemented by an amendment to the Rules of the Supreme Court[9] and in January 1978 RSC Order 53[10] came into force. Modern judicial review in England and Wales was born, although it was not given statutory force until 1981 under section 31 of the Senior Courts Act 1981.

In 1981 the then Lord Chief Justice, Lord Lane, handed down the Practice Direction (Trials in London),[11] which provided for the allocation of administrative law claims, including judicial, into a new High Court list known as the crown office list. At this time the exercise of this jurisdiction for all England and Wales was confined to London.

In March 2000 in the Review of the Crown Office List (The Bowman Report)[12] it was recommended that the Crown Office list be renamed 'The Administrative Court' with a view to making it clear that administrative law cases were separated from other High Court work. On the 20 July 2000 Lord Woolf, as Lord Chief Justice, handed down Practice Direction (Administrative Court: Establishment).[13] The Practice Direction followed the recommendations of the Bowman Report and ordered the establishment of the new Administrative Court and administrative court office. On 2 October 2000, Part 54 of the Civil Procedure Rules (CPR) was brought into force.[14] Alongside the implementation of CPR Part 54 and the new procedural code for judicial review, the Administrative Court was created, but all cases for England and Wales were still filed and heard in London.

IV. THE ADMINISTRATIVE COURT IN WALES – JURISDICTION[15]

A. History of the Administrative Court in Wales

The creation of the Administrative Court in Wales was a landmark moment in terms of decentralising judicial checks and advancing the principles of

[8] [1976] Cmnd 6407.

[9] RSC (Amendment No 3) 1977.

[10] RSC Order 53 1978.

[11] [1981] 1 WLR 1296.

[12] 'Review of the Crown Office List' (Lord Chancellor's Department, London, 2000).

[13] [2000] 1 WLR 1654.

[14] Civil Procedure (Amendment No 4) Rules 2000 (SI 2000/2092).

[15] For more information on the history of the Administrative Court in Wales and the drivers for change see Gardner (n 5) ch 2.

devolution. After the enactment of the Government of Wales Act 1998, which has since been superseded by the Government of Wales Act 2006, it was soon acknowledged by executive and judiciary alike that it was essential that legal challenges to decisions of the new Welsh institutions and other public bodies in Wales should be brought, heard and decided in Wales.

On the 30 June 1999, the then Lord Chief Justice, Lord Bingham, issued the Practice Direction (Supreme Court: Devolution),[16] which allowed Welsh judicial reviews to be heard in Wales if the relief sought or the grounds of the application involved a devolution issue or an issue concerning any Welsh public body. Further, when CPR Part 54 was enacted and the current judicial review procedure was brought into force, the Practice Direction to Part 54 incorporated Lord Bingham's Practice Direction in CPR PD 54 paragraph 3.1. Judicial review claims could, for the first time, be heard in Wales, but applications could still be lodged in London, if a claimant so preferred.

Despite these changes, the practical arrangements were not indicative of an Administrative Court *in* or *for* Wales. If the claim was lodged in Cardiff it was then immediately sent to the administrative court office in London where the claim file was kept, where all correspondence was forwarded, where the administrative court office staff and lawyers were based and from where the claim was managed. In effect the Cardiff office was nothing more than a postbox. The working practices were, in terms of the autonomy and development of Welsh institutions, a significant advancement, but those practices did not go far enough for many. The judiciary took notice of these concerns and established a working group to address them.

The 2007 working group report 'Justice Outside London' recommended that fully operational offices of the Administrative Court should be established in Cardiff, Birmingham, Manchester and Leeds, and that its judges should regularly sit to hear Administrative Court cases in those centres. The main basis for the recommendation to decentralise the Administrative Court was that 'proper access to justice is not achieved if those in the regions can only bring judicial review and other claims in the Administrative Court in London'.[17]

As well as advancing access to justice, the report gave special attention to the case for devolved justice in Wales based on constitutional considerations, concluding that 'decisions in relation to Wales are made in Wales by the Assembly or by the ministers of the Welsh Assembly Government and a judicial review of such decisions should be heard in Wales'.[18]

The idea of a decentralised Administrative Court was opposed by some judges and staff from within the administrative court office in London[19] and

[16] [1999] 1 WLR 1592.

[17] Judicial Working Group, 'Justice Outside London Report' (10 April 2010) para 51, available at www.judiciary.uk/publications/justice-outside-london-report-of-judicial-working-group.

[18] ibid para 60.

[19] ibid appendix L.

some members of the legal profession.[20] The working group concluded that the arguments in favour of decentralisation outweighed those against it and recommended a new, decentralised Administrative Court and administrative court office in Wales with a strong recommendation that Welsh Administrative Court cases should be heard in Wales.[21]

On the 21 April 2009, in conjunction with the coming into force of CPR PD 54D, the Administrative Court in Wales was created and the administrative court office in Wales, the office that supports the Court, has been handling the administrative aspect of those claims since that date.

B. Jurisdiction of the Administrative Court in Wales

Until 1 October 2020, the provisions which determined where Administrative Court cases were to be filed and heard suffered from the same loopholes and vagueness which they had since the Administrative Court first began sitting outside of London. Under CPR PD 54D the considerations which a party lodging a judicial review were to have in mind when assessing an appropriate venue (and also the considerations for a judge considering transfer) were contained at paragraph 5.2 of that Practice Direction:

> 5.2
>
> The general expectation is that proceedings will be administered and determined in the region with which the claimant has the closest connection, subject to the following considerations as applicable –
>
> (1) any reason expressed by any party for preferring a particular venue;
> (2) the region in which the defendant, or any relevant office or department of the defendant, is based;
> (3) the region in which the claimant's legal representatives are based;
> (4) the ease and cost of travel to a hearing;
> (5) the availability and suitability of alternative means of attending a hearing (for example, by videolink);
> (6) the extent and nature of media interest in the proceedings in any particular locality;
> (7) the time within which it is appropriate for the proceedings to be determined;
> (8) whether it is desirable to administer or determine the claim in another region in the light of the volume of claims issued at, and the capacity, resources and workload of, the court at which it is issued;

[20] See S Nason, 'Regionalisation of the Administrative Court and the Tribunalisation of Judicial Review' (2009) *PL* 440, 442, S Nason, D Hardy and M Sunkin, 'Regionalisation of the Administrative Court and Access to Justice' [2010] *Judicial Review* 220 at paras 3–8, and S Nason and M Sunkin, 'The Regionalisation of Judicial Review: Constitutional Authority, Access to Justice and Specialisation of Legal Services in Public Law' (2013) 76 *MLR* 223, 229. Nason et al's research also goes on to suggest that these concerns have been largely overcome.

[21] 'Justice Outside London Report' (n 17) para 65.

(9) whether the claim raises issues sufficiently similar to those in another outstanding claim to make it desirable that it should be determined together with, or immediately following, that other claim; and
(10) whether the claim raises devolution issues and for that reason whether it should more appropriately be determined in London or Cardiff.

Despite these 10 considerations, including one on devolution, the Practice Direction gives priority to the location of the claimant, thus underpinning the conclusions of 'Justice Outside London' that access to justice should be improved by decentralisation. However, if the point of an Administrative Court in Wales is to increase access to justice and autonomy, and ensure the appropriate application of Welsh law by having Welsh cases administered and heard in Wales, then the above provisions could be criticised on a number of fronts:

(1) The list was only a list of considerations. CPR PD 54D paragraph 2.1 stated that the claimant may lodge a claim in any administrative court office. There was no mandatory requirement to abide by these considerations and no system of mandatory transfer upon issuing by the administrative court office to the most appropriate office (albeit transfer may occur after issuing). This was in contrast to other jurisdictions. For example, in the Court of Protection the efficacy of automatic transfer to 'regional hubs' and automatic listing in the Court closest to the protected party has been recognised and implemented.[22]
(2) The considerations themselves were vague and do not assist with the weight to be given to each consideration.
(3) There is a list of exceptions to the principle that the claimant may choose their venue. If the case is one which falls within the class of cases outlined in the list of exceptions then the case is automatically transferred to the administrative court office in London.[23] The list of exceptions can be found at CPR PD 54D paragraph 3.1 and includes cases that deal with terrorism, extradition, proceeds of crime, discipline of solicitors[24] and cases which require a Divisional Court to sit.[25] Security considerations and logistics may provide practical barriers to the first three in this list, but these practical barriers could be overcome with proper investment. There is no clear reason why disciplinary cases for solicitors and mandatory Divisional

[22] Court of Protection Handbook Update, 'Regional Applications Scheme Launched' (Legal Action Group, 29 April 2018), available at courtofprotectionhandbook.com/2018/04/29/regional-applications-scheme-launched.

[23] CPR PD 54D para 3.2.

[24] But strangely, not barristers. This is presumably because the procedure for appeals to the Administrative Court in these cases post-dates the implementation of CPR PD 54D and the Practice Direction has not been updated.

[25] To clarify, CPR PD 54D para 3.1(6) does not suggest that Divisional Courts cannot be convened by judicial order to hear cases in Wales. In fact, they are often convened to consider some of the more high-profile cases. CPR PD 54D para 3.1(6) requires that those cases where a Divisional Court is required by statute be transferred to London.

Court cases cannot be heard in Wales. Indeed, disciplinary cases against medical professionals[26] are heard in Wales as are Divisional Court cases where statute does not require the case be considered by a Divisional Court.

(4) Urgent applications may be dealt with by the Administrative Court in Wales,[27] but only within the office hours of 10am to 4pm. Outside these hours, if the application cannot wait, the application must be made to the out of hours duty Judge in London.[28]

Whilst the Practice Direction arguably failed to ensure Welsh cases were filed and heard in Wales, save for a presumption that the case will be filed and heard at the location closest to the claimant, case law emerged which sought to close the gap. In 2006 the Court of Appeal gave judgment in the case of R (Condron) *v* The National Assembly for Wales.[29] In that claim all the hearings, in the Administrative Court and Court of Appeal, took place in London. Richards LJ condemned that fact:

> There are procedures in place to enable Welsh judicial review cases and similar statutory challenges to be heard in the Administrative Court in Wales ... In my view the present case cried out to be heard in Wales both at first instance and on appeal, and it is a matter of considerable regret that efforts were not made to have it listed for hearing accordingly. Practitioners and listing officers alike need to be alert to this issue.[30]

Condron was followed by *R (Deepdock)* v *The Welsh Ministers*.[31] This claim was brought after the National Assembly (as it then was) had given planning permission for the building of a marina at Gallows Point, Beaumaris, Anglesey. The point on venue was considered prior to the actual determination of the claim and HHJ Hickinbottom (as a Judge of the High Court), as he then was, went further than the Court in *Condron*:

> The devolution settlement as a matter of principle transfers political accountability to the organs of devolved government in Wales; and, where a decision of such a body is challenged, the devolved administration is directly accountable through the Courts. The location of the relevant arm of government is in any event a factor that must be taken into account in considering the appropriate venue for proceedings ... [W]ith the increased impetus given to devolved government by the Government of Wales Act 2006 and with increasing powers actually being devolved to the National Assembly for Wales, there is in my view a deepening imperative that challenges to any devolved decisions are (like the decisions themselves) dealt with in Wales ... [S]uch cases should be heard in Wales unless there are good reasons for their being heard elsewhere.[32]

[26] See the list of such appeals in the table at CPR PD 52D. They provide for appeal to High Court, which by convention are dealt with in the Administrative Court.

[27] CPR PD 54D para 4.1.

[28] CPR PD 54D para 4.2.

[29] [2007] 2 P & CR 4.

[30] *R (Condron)* v *The National Assembly for Wales* [2007] 2 P & CR 4, 68.

[31] [2007] EWHC 3347 (Admin).

[32] *R (Deepdock)* v *The Welsh Ministers* [2007] EWHC 3347 (Admin) [20].

Deepdock set a precedent that devolved public bodies in Wales will be answerable for their decisions to the Administrative Court in Wales. There have been post-decentralisation decisions which confirm *Deepdock*, for example, *R (Condron) v Merthyr Tydfil County Borough Council*[33] and *Jones* v *The Director of Public Prosecutions*.[34] As such, it appears there is a judicial drive to go beyond the terms of the pre-1 October 2020 version of CPR PD 54D to seek a system closer to that envisaged in 'Justice Outside London' which places the constitutional importance of Welsh cases being heard in Wales on a par, if not above the principle of claimant choice.

Public figures in Wales have spoken frequently on the issue of the decentralised Administrative Court and their support for the principle that cases with a Welsh connection should be heard in Wales. This includes the former First Minister, Carwyn Jones, who, when addressing the Cardiff Law School commented:

> The increasing divergence of the law in relation to England and the law in relation to Wales, and the bilingual character of the legislation produced by both the Welsh Assembly Government and the National Assembly for Wales, has also given impetus to the need for institutions of justice managed locally, which are responsive to the needs of Wales and are familiar with the law as it applies to Wales … [S]ince 2000 there has been a growing expectation that administrative cases relating to Wales should also be heard in Wales. In that respect it has for some time been the practice of the Assembly Government in response to judicial review applications to apply for a direction that the case be heard in Wales.[35]

The executive in Wales supports a decentralised Administrative Court in Wales and this highlights the importance that the Welsh authorities put in a Welsh system of judicial checks.

The final voice to be added to the criticisms of a system in which Welsh Administrative Court cases may be heard outside Wales was that of the Commission on Justice in Wales, chaired by the former Lord Chief Justice, Lord Thomas of Cwmgiedd. The Commission recommended amendment of Practice Direction 54D to make it compulsory that Welsh administrative law cases are issued and heard in the Administrative Court in Wales.[36]

Following the recommendations of the Commission on Justice in Wales, the Civil Procedure Rules Committee acted to implement a new system which may be said to be closer to that envisaged by the 'Justice Outside London' report. On 16 July 2020, the Civil Procedure (Amendment No 3) Rules 2020 were made

[33] [2009] EWHC 1621 (Admin) [61].

[34] [2012] RTR 3, 43.

[35] C Jones, 'Getting the Devolution Dividend: Legal Wales in the next ten years', 7 May 2009, Cardiff Law School Public Lecture Series.

[36] See recommendation 24 of the Commission on Justice in Wales Report, 'Justice in Wales for the People of Wales' (October 2019) 21.

which, as of 1 October 2020, amended Part 7 of the Civil Procedure Rules 1998 by including the following provisions:

> **Claims against Welsh public bodies to be issued and heard in Wales**
>
> **7.1A.** Unless required otherwise by any enactment, rule or practice direction, any claim against Welsh public bodies which challenges the lawfulness of their decisions must be issued and heard in Wales.
>
> **Claims against Welsh public bodies to be forwarded for issue in Wales**
>
> **7.1B.** If a court or centre in England receives a claim which should pursuant to paragraph (1) be issued in Wales a court officer shall forward it for issue in the Administrative Court Office in Wales or other appropriate court office in Wales.

Further, by way of 122nd Update to the Practice Directions supplementing the Civil Procedure Rules 1998, Practice Direction 54D itself was amended to include the following provision:

> **1.3** This Practice Direction is subject to the requirement in rule 7.1A that any claim against Welsh public bodies which challenge the lawfulness of their decisions must be issued and heard in Wales.

As a result, from 1 October 2020, all Administrative Court claims, including judicial reviews, which challenge the decision of a Welsh public body must be issued and heard in Wales. This represents a new era for Welsh administrative law, the constitutional position arising out of devolution, and a newly recognised need for increased autonomy and access to justice in Wales

C. Welsh Language

A further meritorious consideration is the fact that Wales, unlike England, is a dual-language nation. The Welsh language has official status in Wales by virtue of section 1(1) of the Welsh Language (Wales) Measure 2011. Whilst the legislation made by the UK Parliament or UK Government is not produced bilingually, the Senedd and Welsh Ministers produce legislation in Welsh and English. Those bilingual texts are, by virtue of section 156(1) of the Government of Wales Act 2006, to be treated for all purposes as being of equal standing.

A hearing before the Administrative Court in Wales is subject to the provisions of section 22 of the Welsh Language Act 1993 and as such any person addressing the Court may exercise their right to speak in Welsh. Notably, no such statutory right exists in the courts in England, even if the court is determining a Welsh case. Under the Practice Direction Relating to the Use of the Welsh Language in Cases in the Civil Courts in Wales, the court may hear any person in Welsh on an ad hoc basis and without notice of the wish to speak in Welsh, providing all parties and the court consent.[37] There are bilingual judges who can

[37] Paragraph 1.2 of the Practice Direction Relating to the Use of the Welsh Language in Cases in the Civil Courts in Wales.

consider claims conducted in Welsh, but nonetheless, it is likely that an order will be made for simultaneous translation, where a translator appears in court translating as the parties speak.[38] The reason for this is that judicial reviews are public hearings which anyone may attend and watch. For open justice to take place those attending must be able to understand proceedings.

Whilst there are bilingual judges it should be noted that the numbers of judges who are bilingual is relatively small and, the number of bilingual judges who are ticketed to consider Administrative Court claims is in the single digits. Where the claim is in Welsh, but does not relate to Welsh language issues, the lack of bilingual judges can be, on the whole, compensated for with the use of simultaneous translation. However, where the claim involves the analysis and interpretation of Welsh, be that in the form of the interpretation of a bilingual statute or otherwise, then a bilingual judge will be a necessity. There are two key reasons behind this necessity. Firstly, the true meaning of a word may be context dependent or there may be no direct translation at all. A bilingual judge would be best placed to deal with these issues over a translator or expert adviser on languages. Secondly, where a judge is not bilingual, but requires evidence as to the meanings of words or phrases in one language but not the other, it is questionable whether the two versions could properly be said to have been treated as of equal validity for the purposes of their interpretation, thus contravening the intention behind section 1(1) of the Welsh Language (Wales) Measure 2011 and section 156(1) of the Government of Wales Act 2006.[39]

An interlinking example of the distinctive nature of the Administrative Court in Wales arises out of this issue. Under the Welsh Language (Wales) Measure 2011 the Welsh Language Commissioner has certain powers and duties to require compliance with Welsh language standards and to advance the Welsh language.[40] An appeal against a decision of the Welsh Language Commissioner is to the Welsh Language Tribunal.[41] There is a further appeal on a point of law to the High Court.[42] Under CPR PD 52D paragraph 27A.3(1)–(2), that appeal

[38] This was certainly the format ordered in two judicial reviews where the claimant requested the hearing be conducted in Welsh: *R (Welsh Language Commissioner) v National Savings and Investments* [2014] PTSR D8 and *R (Aron Wyn Jones) v Denbighshire County Council* [2016] EWHC 2074 (Admin).

[39] For a discussion of the issues surrounding bilingual legislation in Wales see: T Watkin, 'Bilingual Legislation: Awareness, Ambiguity, and Attitudes' (2016) 37 *SLR* 116; T Watkin, 'Bilingual legislation and the law of England and Wales' (2014) 2 *Theory & Practice of Legislation* 229; K Bush, 'New Approaches to UK Legislative Drafting: the Welsh Perspective' (2004) 25 *Statute Law Review* 144; and the summary by the Law Commission in 'Form and Accessibility of the Law Applicable in Wales', Consultation Paper No 223, Part 3, paras 12.52–12.53.

[40] For a discussion of the powers and duties under the 2011 Measure see C Ffluer-Huws, 'Administrative Justice and the Welsh Language (Wales) Measure 2011' in S Nason (ed), *Administrative Justice in Wales and Comparative Perspectives* (Cardiff, University of Wales Press, 2017) 86–90.

[41] See Welsh Language (Wales) Measure 2011, ss 58(2), 95(2), 103(2).

[42] See ss 59(2), 97(2), 105(2) of the Welsh Language (Wales) Measure 2011.

is to the Administrative Court in Wales (notably, not the Administrative Court generally).[43]

To date, the Administrative Court in Wales has heard only four cases in Welsh, none of which dealt with the interpretation of bilingual legislation. As such, there is no direct precedent outlining how the Court would go about interpreting bilingual legislation.[44] What will happen, then, is yet to be determined,[45] but clearly the Welsh language and the ability to use and analyse it in the Administrative Court in Wales, but not in England, adds substance to the assertion that the Administrative Court in Wales should be the sole arbiter of Welsh administrative law cases, as is now and has only been the case since 1 October 2020.

D. Concluding Comments on Jurisdiction

Following the creation of the National Assembly, now the Senedd, and the Welsh Government, both legislative and executive powers have been transferred to Wales. It was perhaps inevitable that judicial checks were to follow. Cases that directly affect the devolved institutions and/or that involve uniquely Welsh matters are best considered in Wales. For example, *R (Brynmawr Foundation School Governors)* v *The Welsh Ministers*[46] in which the Administrative Court in Wales was required to determine the extent to which the Welsh Government could delegate its powers to Welsh local authorities, was issued, managed and determined in Wales. Equally, the case of *R (Aron Wyn Jones) v Denbighshire County Council*,[47] a case heard in Welsh that determined the lawfulness of the closure of a Welsh medium school and replacement by a bilingual school, was also issued, managed and determined in Wales. If this were not the case then the principle behind devolution – that decisions that directly and only affect Wales and the people of Wales should be taken by Welsh public authorities – would be thwarted by the judicial arm of the state providing for judicial checks from across the border. Further, an Administrative Court in Wales allows greater access to justice as local persons may more easily attend and watch justice in action.

[43] CPR PD 27A is a little-known provision that provides a procedure for Welsh Statutory Appeals to the Administrative Court. There are only, to date, three such statutory appeals. The other two relate to disciplinary proceedings against local counsellors and disciplinary proceedings against teachers. It is, in the author's submission, likely that this number will be added to in time.

[44] Although there is precedent concerning the use of the other language in a bilingual text where the meaning of the English text is ambiguous. See, *James Buchanan & Co Ltd* v *Babco Forwarding & Shipping (UK) Ltd* [1978] AC 141.

[45] To consider a possible scheme see S Nason and D Gardner, 'The Administrative Court and Administrative Law in Wales and Comparative Perspectives' in Nason (ed), *Administrative Justice in Wales* (2017) 280–82.

[46] [2011] EWHC 519 (Admin).

[47] [2016] EWHC 2074 (Admin).

There is a clear constitutional need for Welsh cases to be considered in Wales, which has recently entered a new phase, incorporating a mandatory requirement for these cases to be issued and heard in Wales. To truly reflect the constitutional importance of the Administrative Court in Wales and to increase access to justice, a third phase of the Administrative Court in Wales has begun. The devolution settlement in Wales continues to evolve. Since 1 April 2018,[48] the reserved powers model brought into force by the Wales Act 2017 has been operating in Wales. Whilst the Wales Act 2017 has been criticised for not going far enough in terms of further devolution of powers, the intention of the Act was no doubt to allow for greater autonomy in terms of Welsh law-making powers. If greater autonomy for Wales is the goal then a fully decentralised system of checks and balances will assist in meeting that goal.

It is early days in the third phase of the Administrative Court in Wales and no doubt further consideration of this issue will be forthcoming. For example, the newly implemented provisions do not define a 'Welsh Public Body' within the Civil Procedure Rules 1998. It may be that the definition as set out in section 157A and Schedule 9A of the Government of Wales Act 2006 will be adopted. This remains to be considered. Nonetheless, the newly implemented changes would appear to represent a step in the right directions for an Administrative Court *for* Wales.

V. THE FUTURE OF ADMINISTRATIVE LAW IN WALES

It is important to consider not just the jurisdiction of the Administrative Court in Wales and the desirability of its links with England, but also the future of administrative law itself in Wales. The question, in essence, is whether Wales wishes to retain the English model of common law principles of administrative law, as established by the Quartet and subsequent cases, or whether it would be better for Wales to go a different way. Certainly, there is much support for maintaining the common law system. For example, both Lord Justice Hickinbottom and Mr Justice Dove have stated that the flexibility of the common law system made it more effective and better able to offer its protection to citizens than they would envisage any administrative law act or code could provide.[49] It would be fair to say that this is probably a majority view.

A. The Moving Legislative Landscape in Wales

Wales is about to undergo a radical change to the legislative process. In June 2016 the Law Commission presented the report, 'Form and Accessibility of the Law

[48] Wales Act 2017 (Commencement No 4) Regulations 2017.

[49] Speaking at the No5 Chambers Event celebrating the 70th Anniversary of *Wednesbury*, 24 November 2017 at the Clayton Hotel, Birmingham.

Applicable in Wales'.[50] In that report the Law Commission recommended the Welsh Government and the Senedd should consider codifying the law in certain devolved subject areas. The Welsh Government, in its response to the report agreed 'that a sustained, long term programme of consolidation and codification of Welsh law would deliver societal and economic benefits and is necessary to ensure that the laws of Wales are easily accessible'.[51] Since that date a number of Welsh Government reports have identified the benefits of and desire for codification.[52] Indeed, access to justice is a key concern for the Welsh Government, as evidenced by the fact that section 2(1) of the Legislation (Wales) Act 2019 provides: 'The Welsh Ministers and the Counsel General must prepare a programme setting out what they intend to do to improve the accessibility of Welsh law'.

Further, the Commission on Justice in Wales, in the report 'Justice in Wales for the People of Wales' (October 2019) considered the accessibility of the law, and in particular on the administration of justice, in Wales at length.[53] Perhaps the most controversial matter is recommendation 58, which states:

> There should be legislative devolution of justice. Restrictions and reservations governing the Assembly's power to legislate on all forms of justice … should be removed, so that it corresponds more closely with the position of the Northern Ireland Assembly and the Scottish Parliament.[54]

Were such a recommendation implemented, which would require an act of the UK Parliament, it would allow the Senedd and the Welsh Ministers (see recommendation 59) to take control of how justice is administered in Wales and, indeed, to focus on the accessibility of justice in Wales in line with their aforementioned obligations under the Legislation (Wales) Act 2019.

Notably, whilst accessibility is an issue that troubles Wales and must be a driving principle behind codification, the Welsh Government has stated that it does not intend to undertake wholesale codification of the common law.[55] The remainder of this chapter will seek to provoke discussion and argue that a code bringing together the principles of administrative law, including the common law principles, should fall for consideration as part of the legislative programme.[56]

[50] Law Commission Report No 366, London: Parliamentary Printers, HC 469-I, 29 June 2016.

[51] Welsh Government (Mick Antoniw, then Counsel-General), 'Final Response to the Commission's Report on the Form and Accessibility of the Law Applicable in Wales' (19 July 2017), available at s3-eu-west-2.amazonaws.com/lawcom-prod-storage-11jsxou24uy7q/uploads/2016/06/2017-07-19-Law-Commission-Final-Response.pdf.

[52] See: Justice Stakeholder Group, 'Law and Justice in Wales: Some Issues for the Next Assembly' (March 2016); Welsh Government, 'Report on the implementation of Law Commission proposals' (February 2017); Welsh Government, 'Progress update on the work of the Justice Stakeholder Group' (April 2017).

[53] See Commission on Justice in Wales Report, 'Justice in Wales for the People of Wales' (October 2019) ch 12.

[54] See recommendation 58 of 'Justice in Wales for the People of Wales' (2019) 25.

[55] Welsh Government Consultation on the Draft Legislation (Wales) Bill, 20 March 2018, Document Number WG34368, at para 29.

[56] For a full discussion of the advantages of an administrative law code for Wales see D Gardner, 'An Administrative Law Code for Wales: Benefits to Reap and Obstacles to Overcome' (2019) 40 *Statute Law Review* 273.

B. Advantages of Codification for Wales

There is certainly a wider debate as to the advantages and disadvantages of codification and there has been extensive writing on codification generally.[57] There are a number of advantages to codification in general. A key and recurring criticism of the law as it is in Wales is that it is not easy to understand what the law in Wales is on any given topic.[58] This is a direct result of the diverging nature of the law in England and the law in Wales and it 'is the legacy of an incremental approach to devolution'.[59] A single legal code that details the entire law on a topic in Wales would provide greater clarity and thus it would ensure greater access to justice by allowing the people of Wales to easily access the law. It can be argued that the diverging nature of the law in Wales, moving as it is in a different direction from the law in England in many respects,[60] brings a pressing need for more accessible and clearer law in Wales. As observed by Professor R Gwynedd Parry:

> Although having two legislatures making laws for the same territory is not of itself unusual, it does pose challenges in terms of clarity and accessibility. The people need to know the law that applies to them. A unified body of Welsh law, the law that applies in Wales, regardless of where it is made, must be clear and accessible to the public. The Law Commission has recognised the challenges to accessibility and clarity which the current position poses, and made proposals based on the fundamental tenet, in the context of legislation, that accessibility is central to the rule of law. It made proposals for the codification in new National Assembly legislation of legislation whose subject matter is within the legislative competence of the National Assembly for Wales and which is currently dispersed in pieces of legislation of the United Kingdom Parliament and/or the National Assembly.[61]

A four-pronged approach would be necessary to make sure that any administrative law code for Wales (ALCW) incorporates current principles, draws together disparate principles, advances the principle of good administrative justice, and outlines clear redress mechanisms.

i. The Traditional Principles

An ALCW should start with the traditional common law principles of administrative law and give them the clarity of being outlined in a single place.

[57] For a deconstruction of the potential benefits of codification of judicial review and in particular a potential danger to the principle of the separation of powers see T Jones, 'Judicial review and codification' (2000) 20 *Legal Studies* 517.

[58] Good examples of this in a number of areas of law can be found in ch 5 of Law Commission, 'Form and Accessibility of the Law Applicable in Wales' (2015) Law Commission Consultation Paper No 223. The issue is also discussed in D Hughes and H Davies, 'Accessible Bilingual Legislation for Wales' (2012) 33 *Statute Law Review* 103, 113.

[59] Law Commission Consultation Paper No 223, para 5.2.

[60] As an illustrative example, compare and contrast the Care Act 2014 in England and the Social Services and Well-being (Wales) Act 2014 in Wales.

[61] R Gwynedd Parry, 'Is breaking up hard to do? The case for a separate Welsh jurisdiction' (2017) 57 *Irish Jurist* 61, 74.

The broad principles (lawfulness, reasonableness, procedural propriety and human rights compliance) are longstanding principles, arising out of the Quartet and identified by Lord Diplock in *Council of Civil Service Unions v Minister for the Civil Service*,[62] although human rights principles have been greatly affected by the coming into force of section 6(1) of the Human Rights Act 1998. These broad headings can, in turn, be sub-divided. For example, an act or omission by a public body may be vitiated by procedural impropriety where the public body:[63]

- failed to observe procedural rules;
- has fettered its discretion;
- failed to give adequate reasons where reasons are required; or
- failed to consult properly where a requirement to consult existed.

As can be observed from the duty to act in a procedurally proper manner, the common law principles, whilst summarised above, are disparate and relatively difficult to draw together for a lawyer, let alone a lay person attempting to understand their administrative law rights. The broad categories must form the basis for an ALCW with subdivisions within the code to reflect and give more substance to those sub-divisions. By properly outlining the traditional administrative law principles in a code, administrative law rights would be understandable and access to justice would be greatly improved.

ii. Consolidating and Enhancing Principles

The Senedd would be able to add to the traditional administrative law duties by incorporating and clarifying other duties that have been brought in by way of legislation.

An example of an appropriate area in which this could occur would be the sustainable development and well-being duties that have been brought into the law in Wales under the Well-being of Future Generations (Wales) Act 2015 (the 2015 Act). The 2015 Act is seminal public law legislation. In enacting it the National Assembly (as it then was) became 'the first legislature in the world to enshrine in law a duty, falling on public bodies, to safeguard the well-being of future generations'.[64] Under sections 3 and 5 of the 2015 Act, public bodies in Wales[65] must carry out sustainable development. In fulfilling this duty, they must set and publish well-being objectives.[66] In addition, they must take all reasonable steps, in exercising their functions, to meet their objectives.[67]

[62] [1985] AC 374.

[63] See Gardner (n 5) at ch 3, where the sub-divisions are discussed for all four broad categories. The list sets out common law examples of procedural unfairness. As it is based in common law it cannot be said to be an exhaustive list.

[64] H Davies, 'The Well-being of Future Generations (Wales) Act 2015: duties or aspirations?' (2016) 18 *Environmental Law Review* 41.

[65] Which are defined in s 6 of the Well-being of Future Generations (Wales) Act 2015.

[66] ibid s 3(2)(a).

[67] ibid s (2)(b).

In essence, there is a duty on Welsh public bodies to act in a way that maximises the well-being goals. There has been no reported judgment that confirms whether these duties are aspirational or binding duties, albeit there has been some non-binding guidance from the Administrative Court in Wales. In *R (B) v Neath Port Talbot County Borough Council*,[68] Andrew Baker J refused permission to apply for judicial review in a claim which sought to advance the argument that the 2015 Act creates binding duties. If the 2015 Act duties were incorporated into an ALCW then they would sit with equal standing alongside the common law administrative law principles and, it is submitted, would do much to further the goals. It may even be argued that to truly 'embed sustainable development as the "central organising principle" of public governance in Wales'[69] then the sustainability principle needs to be approached as a binding principle that is equal to the traditional public law principles. Were sections 2–5 of the 2015 Act incorporated into an ALCW, then failure to set objectives, setting objectives that did not comply with the goals, failure to take reasonable steps to meet the objectives, or failure to act in accordance with the objectives, would be clearly identifiable, challengeable decisions (or indeed a failure). Such a failure or decision would be of equal significance to a failure to conduct a lawful consultation or a failure to abide by a legitimate expectation, which under the 2015 Act it is arguably not. This is, of course, just one example of a potential area which could be incorporated into an ALCW.

iii. Further Principles

The aim of an ALCW cannot simply be to clarify and consolidate administrative law in Wales. It must 'promote Wales as a progressive nation in the development of its administrative justice system, and as a nation demonstrating the highest commitment to standards of public decision-making, human rights, and the protection of vulnerable groups within society'.[70]

Codification of the principles of administrative law for Wales can do more than draw together the current principles. An appropriate way to progress administrative justice (which is a broader term than administrative law) in Wales in would be the incorporation in the ALCW of the principles advocated in the Bangor University Report, 'Understanding Administrative Justice in Wales' (2015) ('the Bangor Report').[71] The Bangor Report suggests, in 12 proposed

[68] [2019] (unreported, CO/4740/2018).

[69] Davies, 'Well-being of Future Generations (Wales) Act 2015' (2016) at 44, in turn referring to phrase used by the Welsh Government in *One Wales, One Planet* 9, available at senedd.wales/Laid%20Documents/GEN-LD8219%20-%20One%20Wales%20One%20Planet%20-%20The%20Sustainable%20Development%20Annual%20Report%202009-2010-21092010-196494/gen-ld8219-e-English.pdf.

[70] Nason (n 40) para 2.49.

[71] Nason (n 40). The conclusions of the Bangor Report were supported by the Wales Governance Centre; see H Pritchard, 'Justice in Wales: Principles, Progress and Next Steps' Wales Governance Centre (2016) para 2.1.

principles, that Wales would benefit from adopting broader principles of administrative justice,[72] such as making citizens and their rights and needs central, treating them with fairness and respect at all times.

The alignment of the principles of administrative law with these broad administrative justice principles, would increase access to justice and it would do so in a socially progressive way. If the Bangor Report principles were incorporated into an ALCW, alongside the traditional common law and statutory principles, Wales would not just be clarifying administrative law and providing better access to justice, it would be leading the way in terms of ensuring that public bodies approach administrative justice in the most user friendly fashion and 'shows considerable commitment to social justice and individual rights'.[73]

iv. Redress Mechanisms

A major criticism of the aforementioned Well-being of Future Generations (Wales) Act 2015 is that it does not clearly outline what, if any, redress mechanisms exist if public bodies are failing to comply with their sustainability and well-being duties. The same criticism can be directed at other decisions of public bodies where there are methods of redress in law but those methods of redress are not clear. The exact nature of any redress mechanisms is too large a topic to cover in detail in this chapter. It is sufficient to note that any ALCW must include a procedural section to outline how non-compliance with the code can be enforced. Without clearly defined redress mechanisms and procedures the principles are either not enforceable or difficult to enforce. After all, the law is only as good as it is enforceable.

C. Overcoming the Disadvantages of an Administrative Law Code for Wales

The key argument against an ALCW is that such a code would be less desirable than the common law system of administrative law currently in place. There is a fear that codification of common law principles may 'stultify progressive development' of those principles.[74] The first point to make to counter this is that development of clear and express principles must be favourable. As Paul Bowen QC noted (albeit in reference to human rights principles):

> Even where common law rights have been established for many years, the absence of express words means that these rights are less certain in scope, their underlying justification often unclear or the subject of conflicting judgments and therefore more easily displaced or qualified by statute or other legal norms.[75]

[72] Nason (n 40) para 2.49.

[73] ibid.

[74] Law Com No 366 (n 50) para 2.42, per Sarah Nason.

[75] See P Bowen, 'Does the renaissance of common law rights mean that the Human Rights Act 1998 is now unnecessary?' [2016] *European Human Rights Law Review* 361, 366.

This point was echoed by the Association of London Welsh Lawyers and the Association of Judges in Wales who considered that codification of common law principles would 'improve the accessibility of the law because judge-made law is uncertain and … is not accessible to those not trained in it'.[76]

The second point to make is that common law and statute law (the latter as the code would be) can and do exist side by side. An example comes from human rights law. The Human Rights 1998 Act brought clarity and structure to the human rights regime in the UK and brought human rights values in the UK into line with the human rights values of Europe. When the Conservative Government suggested that the 1998 Act should be repealed[77] many feared that this would mean the removal of human rights protections within the UK. A number of commentators, however, have asserted that the repeal of the Human Rights Act 1998 would not reduce or diminish human rights protections in the UK because those rights are protected in common law.[78]

A statutory ALCW would take precedence over the common law system. Parliamentary sovereignty was the reason why the Court in *R (Nicklinson) v Ministry of Justice*[79] refused to read in a defence of necessity to the criminal offences of murder and assisted suicide in order to give effect to common law rights of autonomy and dignity. See particularly Toulson LJ's statement who said that to do so would 'usurp the role of Parliament'.[80] Further, the courts would be unlikely to rely on common law rights to act in a manner contrary to clearly articulated principles in the ALCW, but the common law principles would remain in place to cover those situations where there is no statutory code covering the point.

For a precedent as to how this would work in practice we can look to the Family Court. Since the creation of the single Family Court on 22 April 2014,[81] the majority of family law matters are dealt with in the Family Court, including the majority of those statutory matters that were previously assigned to the Family Division of the High Court.[82] However, the Family Division of the High Court has not been abolished. It is still needed as it retains an inherent jurisdiction to deal with common law matters.[83] Similarly, were an ALCW

[76] Law Com No 366 (n 50) paras 2.43 and 2.46.

[77] Conservative Party, 'Protecting Human Rights in the United Kingdom: the Conservative Party's Proposals for Changing Britain's Human Rights Laws' (2014), available at adam1cor.files.wordpress.com/2014/10/protecting-human-rights-in-the-uk-copy1.pdf.

[78] See, for example, M Elliott, 'Beyond the European Convention: Human Rights and the Common Law' (2015) 68 *Current Legal Problems* 85 and M Tugendhat, *Liberty Intact: Human Rights in English Law* (Oxford, Oxford University Press, 2016).

[79] [2012] EWHC 2381 (Admin).

[80] ibid [84].

[81] Crime and Courts Act 2013, s 17(3) implemented by Crime and Courts Act 2013 (Commencement No 10 and Transitional Provision) Order 2014 (SI 2014/954) Art 2(a).

[82] See the Matrimonial and Family Proceedings Act 1984, ss 31A, 31C and 31E (1)(a).

[83] Section 61(1) and Sch 1 of the Senior Courts Act 1981.

implemented the code would not entirely oust the common law jurisdiction of the Administrative Court.

Where the Administrative Court determines that a common law administrative law principle exists and it is not sufficiently outlined or it is not outlined at all in the code, then the judge may declare as such in a judgment. The judgment would still have common law force and the Senedd would then consider whether the point would need to be incorporated into or clarified in the code. Common law arguments would be rare and would become increasingly rare as the code developed, but retention of the inherent jurisdiction would act as a back-stop for administrative law rights and would help to finesse the code.

At present, judicial review of administrative law remains a matter reserved to the UK Parliament under Sch 7A, paragraph 8(1)(f) of the Government of Wales Act 2006, inserted by Sch 1 of the Wales Act 2017, which prevents any administrative law code from circumventing the common law judicial review principles. However, as illustrated above, an ALCW in the form argued for by this chapter would not circumvent the common law judicial review principles or prevent access to the Administrative Court by way of judicial review. The judicial review procedure would still exist to challenge the decision of UK wide public bodies acting in Wales (such as the Secretary of State for the Home Department when making immigration decisions) and it would still act as the common law backstop. The ALCW would complement the judicial review procedure in a way that would benefit the people of Wales by establishing clear administrative justice principles for devolved Welsh authorities and it would increase access to justice when seeking to challenge the decisions of those Welsh devolved authorities.

D. Conclusion on an Administrative Law Code for Wales

If there is to be an ALCW it must come sooner rather than later. At the Legal Wales Conference in Cardiff in October 2013, the then Lord Chief Justice Lord Thomas of Cwmgiedd suggested that Wales should look towards a codified form of legislation now:

> In Wales, there is a huge advantage that Welsh legislation has but a short history. There is no reason, therefore, why it cannot develop its own innovative style … Furthermore, Wales can begin its own sensible organisation of Welsh law into a Code with chapters into which new laws can be inserted and old laws amended, much along the lines of what is done in most states. Westminster is burdened by history. It is therefore a model that does not have to be followed.[84]

[84] Justice Stakeholder Group, 'Law and Justice in Wales: Some Issues for the Next Assembly' (March 2016) para 31.

Implementation as soon as possible would mean a code that benefits from avoiding the historical problems that dog the law of England and Wales. Such a code could act as a code for administrative decision making in Wales in the devolved subject areas for Welsh authorities. This would have the advantage of improving access to justice and administrative justice in Wales in those devolved areas. It would also, perhaps even more importantly, allow the Welsh Government and Senedd to iron out any issues with a codified administrative law before (and if) a separate legal jurisdiction for Wales is created. That way a tested system would already exist that could be built on and modified under the new jurisdiction.

VI. CONCLUSION – 'FOR' OR 'IN'?

Back to the sign outside Cardiff Civil and Family Justice Centre. The sign currently reads 'The Administrative Court in Wales' and, importantly, 'Y Llys Gweinyddol Yng Nghymru'. The use of 'in Wales' was chosen as it reflects the constitutional position of the Court. The Administrative Court is a single Court for England and Wales as part of the Queen's Bench Division of the High Court of England and Wales. There being one Administrative Court for all England and Wales, the Court is sitting 'in Wales'. This analysis is supported by the terms of the Practice Direction on venue, CPR PD 54D. Similarly, the common law administrative law principles, as established by the Quartet and built upon thereafter, are equally binding upon the authorities in England and Wales and will be applied by the Administrative Court in England and Wales. Thus, the use of the more traditional nomenclature, the Administrative Court in Wales, is understandable.

However, the changes to the Civil Procedure Rules, and in particular CPR PD 54D, which requires Administrative Court claims against Welsh public bodies to be issued and heard in Wales, and which in turn gives weight to the constitutional principles behind the devolution settlement represents, in the author's view, a step towards an Administrative Court *for* Wales. This position will be strengthened in the event that Wales does decide that it should seize the opportunity that is the codification programme to implement an ALCW and/or when the justice system itself is devolved to Wales.

Now that action has been taken to ensure that Welsh cases are dealt with in Wales it may be time for a name change. If Wales develops its own system of administrative law and/or controls its own justice system, then Wales will truly have an Administrative Court that works *for* Wales, and its name should then properly reflect its status.

11

The Rule of Law against Judicial Review? The Quartet in Scots Administrative Law

PAUL F SCOTT*

I. INTRODUCTION

AT THE HEART of 'the Quartet'[1] – four cases claimed to have broken with older patterns of judicial deference to executive decision-making in the first half of the twentieth century, moving administrative law forward and clearing the ground for further developments over the decades to come[2] – stands the figure of James Scott Cumberland Reid, Baron Reid, of Drem in the county of East Lothian.[3] Lord Reid, elevated to the House of Lords as a Lord of Appeal in Ordinary without prior judicial experience, had previously held the posts of Solicitor General and Advocate General for Scotland, and at the time of his appointment to the bench was the Dean of the Faculty of Advocates.[4] And yet the relation of this figure, so central to the legal profession in Scotland, to Scots law, is an ambiguous one. So successful was he in his contributions to the development of English law that his Scottish origins – personal and legal – have

* My thanks to the editors, and to Richard Kirkham in particular, for the invitation to contribute to this collection and their comments on my chapter.

[1] See TT Arvind and L Stirton, 'The Curious Origins of Judicial Review' (2017) 133 *LQR* 91, fn 6. Sometimes, reference is made instead to a quintet, which includes – alongside the four cases which make up the Quartet – *Burmah Oil v Lord Advocate* [1965] AC 75: L Blom-Cooper and G Drewry, 'Towards a System of Administrative Law: The Reid and Wilberforce Era, 1945–82' in L Blom-Cooper QC, B Dickson and G Drewry (eds), *The Judicial House of Lords: 1876–2009* (Oxford, OUP, 2009).

[2] Arvind and Stirton, 'Curious Origins' (2017) 91: In the orthodox narrative, which the authors challenge, the Quartet is seen as a key aspect of a process in which 'the judiciary abandoned its earlier quiescence and, building on doctrines, approaches and remedies that had been used to control inferior tribunals since Victorian times, fashioned a new body of law capable of subordinating the administrative state to the rule of law'. (91).

[3] Oxford Dictionary of National Biography (ODNB), 'Reid, James Scott Cumberland, Baron Reid' (3 January 2008).

[4] ODNB (n 3).

not been treated as being of any great significance. This is, perhaps, natural in the context of administrative law, the relationship between Scots and English versions of which is paradoxical. In their fundamentals, the two are said to be utterly distinct, based upon different and incompatible conceptual frameworks. In their implementation, however, the two are often indistinguishable, with substantive (sometimes also procedural) developments south of the border incorporated almost automatically into the jurisprudence of the Court of Session.[5]

This chapter argues that Scots administrative law – trapped between a fundamental framework which distinguishes it directly from its English counterpart and the rule of law rhetoric which now structures so much administrative law in England and so also Scotland – has not lived up to its important, perhaps even radical, potential. The rule of law, that is, the idea that stands at the centre of the modern (English) law of judicial review, has been taken to imply a distinction between public and private which Scots administrative law is not supposed to know, and developments based upon which have – perhaps as a result – often been treated with suspicion in the Scottish courts. A more expansive understanding of that concept would allow for Scottish administrative law to meet its full potential.

II. ADMINISTRATIVE LAW IN SCOTLAND

A. The Supervisory Jurisdiction in Scotland

In Scots law the availability of judicial review of some act or decision is not a function of the status of the nature of the act in question or of the nature of the actor or decision-maker: whether, in short, he or she, or it, is relevantly 'public' rather than 'private'.[6] Instead, the possibility of recourse to the supervisory jurisdiction of the Court of Session is said most usually to be a function of the existence of a so-called 'tripartite relationship'.[7] As Lord Hope, then

[5] See *West v Secretary of State for Scotland* 1992 SC 385, 413: 'There is no substantial difference between English law and Scots law as to the grounds on which the process of decision-making may be open to review. So reference may be made to English cases in order to determine whether there has been an excess or abuse of the jurisdiction, power or authority or a failure to do what it requires'; and *Eba v Advocate General for Scotland* [2011] UKSC 29, [34]: 'Once again it must be stressed that there is, in principle, no difference between the law of England and Scots law as to the substantive grounds on which a decision by a tribunal which acts within its jurisdiction may be open to review'.

[6] The jurisdiction which is now exercised by the Court of Session was traced by Kames to the Privy Council of Scotland, which was abolished in 1708: 'Under the cognisance of the privy council in Scotland came many injuries, which, by the abolition of that court, are left without any peculiar remedy; and the court of session have with reluctance been obliged to listen to complaints of various kinds, that belonged properly to the privy council while it had a being.' Kames, *Historical Law Tracts*, 4th edn (Edinburgh, Bell & Bradfute and Creech, 1792), 228–29, cited in A Page, *Constitutional Law of Scotland* (Edinburgh, W Green, 2015) [16-03].

[7] See, most fully, S Thomson, 'The Doctrinal Core of the Supervisory Jurisdiction of the Court of Session' [2016] *Public Law* 670. For a strong critique, see A McHarg, 'Border Disputes: the Scope and Purposes of Judicial Review' in A McHarg and T Mullen (eds), *Public Law in Scotland* (Edinburgh, Avizandum Publishing 2006).

Lord President, put the point, having reviewed a long line of Scottish case law in which the boundaries of the Court of Sessions jurisdiction were considered, the 'essential feature of all these cases is the conferring, whether by statute or private contract, of a decision-making power or duty on a third party to whom the taking of the decision is entrusted but whose manner of decision-making may be controlled by the court'.[8] Where such a relationship exists, the court will have jurisdiction to review the exercise of the authority thus conferred, whether or not the party exercising it (or the act itself) would, in other contexts, be recognised as public or private in character.[9]

The framing of the 'tripartite relationship', though often relied upon, is problematic, and potentially works to limit the significance of the distinction between Scots and English law on this matter. That is, putting the emphasis upon the tripartite relationship (between a party which grants a power, a party which exercises it and a party in relation to which it is exercised) means that though judicial review will be available in the context of private relationships, it will only be available in that minority of such relationships in which there exists, in effect, a delegation of power to the person whose exercise of that power is being reviewed. Interpreted strictly, the standard excludes a merely bipartite relationship between two parties to a contract, and so would not permit one party to a contract to challenge, by way of judicial review, actions taken by another (or the) party to that contract. In such cases, any remedy must be found within the law of contract. Moreover, the tripartite rule would seem to exclude the possibility that there might be limits upon the acts of the 'third party' (to whom the power is delegated) which do not derive from the instrument by which power is delegated or granted – whether that instrument is a statute or a contract – but are instead free-standing. So, for instance, in remarks which he has pointedly reaffirmed in recent years,[10] Lord Reed – like his near namesake, a Scottish judge on the UK's highest court – has observed that the remarks in *West* should not 'be applied in an excessively literal fashion, as if they contained a statutory definition':

> It is not difficult to discern a tripartite relationship of the kind described in most situations falling within the supervisory jurisdiction: the decision-maker usually exercises a power over individuals, conferred by legislation or by contract. Even in such a situation, however, some of the limits upon the powers in question may be imposed by the common law, and cannot realistically be regarded as impliedly imposed by the legislature or by the contracting parties. In some other situations – for example, where prerogative powers are concerned – the powers, and their limits, may derive entirely from the common law. Although, therefore, the concept of a tripartite relationship, broadly understood, is valuable as a paradigm of the situation in which

[8] *West v Secretary of State for Scotland* 1992 SC 385 (IH), 400.

[9] See Lord Hope in *West* referring to the 'unimportance for this purpose of the distinction between public and private law', demonstrated – he says – by *McDonald v Burns* 1940 SC 376 and *St Johnstone Football Club Ltd v Scottish Football Association Ltd* 1965 SLT 171: 1992 SC 385 (IH), 400.

[10] R Reed, 'The Development of Judicial Review in Scotland' (2015) *Juridical Review* 325, 330.

> a body exercises a limited power or authority, it is not ... to be applied inflexibly, as if it were a Procrustean bed which every situation must be forced to fit.[11]

There are, it would seem, two ways to read this passage. On one hand, it might be read narrowly, as a reminder that not every exercise of ('public') judicial review easily fits within the schema Lord Hope has constructed. Either the limits applied by the courts cannot plausibly be traced back to the intention of the legislature in delegating the power or there may never have been a delegation of power at all: no statute which said that some aspect of the executive can do this thing or that other thing. In this sense, it is perhaps a subtle contribution to the debate between ultra vires and common law accounts of the basis of judicial review,[12] which might be read as seeking to ensure that the justification of private judicial review does not rest on a misleading account of the reality of public judicial review.

On the other hand, and noting that the references to contract run right through the passage quoted above, this passage might be read as suggesting something more radical: that judicial review is available in 'public' situations which involve no delegation of power (through legislation) and so could (perhaps even should) be available in private situations which involve no such delegation (by contract). It could be, that is, that 'private' judicial review is available beyond the context of the 'tripartite relationships' on which Lord Hope placed the emphasis in *West*. If so, what is the limit on its availability? The answer – within this reading – is clear, if underdetermined: it is a 'situation in which a body exercises a limited power or authority', of which a tripartite relationship is, it can be admitted, a 'paradigm', but not a sine qua non. And what are the limits in question other than those which – quite apart from the content of the delegating 'instrument' – the courts, in exercise of the common law method, impose? Limitations which if now few, might over time – quite legitimately – multiply. This passage, I suggest, therefore lays the logical foundations for a rethinking of the supervisory jurisdiction, with the potential to involve the imposition of (common law) limits upon the acts and deeds of private parties. That these foundations have not (yet) been built on says nothing of the basic logic of the point.

B. Scots Administrative Law and the Rule of Law

This (long-standing) distinctiveness of the supervisory jurisdiction in Scotland creates an interesting contrast with the situation in England when considered in historic perspective. It is well known that Dicey insisted, as one facet of the rule of law, upon the equality before the law of public and private actors – an equality

[11] *Crocket v Tantallon Golf Club* 2005 SLT 663 [40].

[12] On which see, amongst a voluminous though now aging literature, C Forsyth, 'Of Fig Leaves and Fairy Tales: The Ultra Vires Doctrine, the Sovereignty of Parliament and Judicial Review' (1996) 55 *CLJ* 122; P Craig, 'Ultra Vires and the Foundations of Judicial Review' (1998) 57 *CLJ* 63.

which makes possible what has been called private law constitutionalism[13] – and that he explicitly (indeed forcefully) linked that equality to the absence in England of a system of administrative law.[14] There were, however, two problems with Dicey's account (which he later, somewhat half-heartedly, repudiated).[15] One was that it relied upon a conceptualisation of administrative law as a set of special immunities or procedural exceptions of which public authorities might avail themselves, rather than (as it would now be understood in English law) a series of additional obligations (procedural and substantive) imposed by the courts upon such bodies. Administrative law was a subtraction from, rather than an addition to, the 'ordinary law' which Dicey held so dear, and so – in turn – a threat to the rule of law as he conceived it.

That understanding of administrative law has, it goes almost without saying, long since been supplanted, and in English law principles which effectively hold public bodies (or those exercising public functions) to a higher standard are not now understood as compromising the rule of law – quite the opposite. This reverse, though taken for granted in modern discourse, has important implications for our understanding of Scots administrative law. The second difficulty is that – as has often been pointed out – Dicey neglected in his insistence of legal equality the impact of the law relating to the Crown, and in particular the functional immunity of the Crown in tort which was a feature of English law before the enactment of the Crown Proceedings Act 1947. Here again, there is a Scottish angle: such immunity was never part of the law of Scotland (the application to which of the 1947 Act has therefore been the source of some difficulty).[16] In at least one sense, therefore, Scotland adhered more clearly to the Diceyan ideal – there, the equality of public and private parties could be asserted without one having to overlook a major *in*equality between them.

The problem, however, has come as Dicey's understanding of administrative law has been replaced by the modern one, and so the opposition between that phenomenon and the concept of the rule of law has been transformed. Now the two are more usually considered to be complementary, or even mutually constitutive. The language of the rule of law has been central to the development of judicial review in England, particularly in the period of consolidation and growth which took place under the intellectual leadership of Lord Diplock in the decade after the Quartet was decided.[17] The rule of law demands administrative law;

[13] See TT Arvind, 'Restraining the State through Tort? The Crown Proceedings Act in retrospect' in TT Arvind and J Steele (eds), *Tort Law and the Legislature* (Oxford, Hart Publishing, 2012).

[14] AV Dicey, *Introduction to the Study of the Law of the Constitution*, 8th edn [1885] (Indianapolis, Liberty Fund, 1982) 114–15.

[15] AV Dicey 'The Development of Administrative Law in England' (1915) 31 *LQR* 148.

[16] See *Davidson v Scottish Ministers* [2004] UKHL 34, discussed below, and A Tomkins, 'The Crown in Scots Law' in McHarg and Mullen (n 7). TB Smith (on whom more below) called the Act 'one of Scotland's contributions to British justice': TB Smith, *British Justice: The Scottish Contribution*, London: Stevens and Sons (1961) 198.

[17] In the four cases that make up the Quartet, only *Conway v Rimmer* contains the phrase 'rule of law', where it is used however to refer to a specific rule rather than a more general concept.

demands, that is, the imposition on public actors (or those acting publicly) of a set of standards that do not apply to private actors. In England this shift is unproblematic: that understanding of the rule of law matches the scope of judicial review. In Scotland it creates a tension. The scope of judicial review is not determined by a distinction between public and private, and so the feature of Scots administrative law which made it consonant with the Diceyan understanding of the rule of law risks putting it at odds with the contemporary rule of law. In recent years, therefore, as the House of Lords and then the Supreme Court have pushed a rule of law oriented approach to administrative law, they have found themselves at odds – sometimes subtly, sometimes less so – with the fundamental of Scots administrative law and the Scottish courts which apply it.

Though it is not the only example of this phenomenon, the point is best illustrated by the reform of the law of standing in Scotland in *AXA General Insurance*. Previously, the Scottish approach to standing was narrower than that which had triumphed in England in the late 1980s.[18] There, the language of 'sufficient interest' had been interpreted generously, in large part on the basis that the rule of law prefers the legality of an act by a body exercising a public function be tested by the court than be allowed to stand for want of a person qualified to test it.[19] In *AXA*, a revolution was effected: the old requirement of title and interest was replaced by references to 'standing, based upon a sufficient interest'.[20] Lord Reed justified the point by reference to the public interest in judicial review and the requirements of the rule of law:

> There is thus a public interest involved in judicial review proceedings, whether or not private rights may also be affected. A public authority can violate the rule of law without infringing the rights of any individual: if, for example, the duty which it fails to perform is not owed to any specific person, or the powers which it exceeds do not trespass upon property or other private rights. A rights-based approach to standing is therefore incompatible with the performance of the courts' function of preserving the rule of law, so far as that function requires the court to go beyond the protection of private rights: in particular, so far as it requires the courts to exercise a supervisory jurisdiction.[21]

Though these comments followed immediately a citation to the judgment of Lord Hope in *Eba* (itself making reference to Lord Hope's own judgment in *West*), it seems clear that they were directed only to that subsection of judicial review cases brought against public authorities. Let us leave aside the question of whether or not the liberalisation of public law standing was desirable.

[18] See the discussion in T Mullen, 'Public interest litigation in Scotland' (2015) *Juridical Review* 363 and C McCorkindale and PF Scott 'Public interest judicial review in cross-border perspective' (2015) 26 *King's Law Journal* 412.

[19] Most importantly in the 'Fleet Street Casuals' case: *R v Inland Revenue Commissioners, ex parte National Federation of Self Employed and Small Businesses Ltd* [1982] AC 617.

[20] *AXA General Insurance Ltd v Lord Advocate* [2011] UKSC 46, [171].

[21] [2011] UKSC 46, [169].

What is important for present purposes is that, as has been noted by Aileen McHarg,[22] it effectively draws a distinction between public and private law proceedings, in which the old rules of standing remain in place – a distinction, that is, within the scope of the supervisory jurisdiction, rather than one by which that scope is defined.[23] And it is notable too, that this invocation of the rule of law and associated distinction between public and private actors came from the Scottish judges on the Supreme Court rather than the Court of Session, which was slow – and sometimes reluctant – to adopt the new standard which had been identified for it.[24]

Notwithstanding that it was a period of probably unprecedented growth in the powers of the state, the Scottish administrative case load in the decades leading up to the Quartet was fairly light. The same slumber of the supervisory jurisdiction noted south of the border by Wade and Sedley[25] was – it has been claimed – evident also in Scotland.[26] By the 1970s, it was, says Page, 'essentially moribund'.[27] And, as in England, the modern judicial review procedure post-dates the substantive leap forward of which the Quartet forms such a prominent part. Only in 1985 were the rules of the Court of Session amended to create a distinct procedure.[28] This new procedure made more limited provision for the 'protection' of public authorities from judicial review than was made by the English equivalent (though both a time limit and a requirement for leave were eventually legislated for),[29] and it was uncertainty as to whether or not the new procedure was, as in England, obligatory for cases raising questions of public law that prompted Lord Hope's famous (re)statement of the scope of the supervisory jurisdiction in Scots law and the irrelevance to it of the public/private distinction.[30] When considering, therefore, the fundamental rules of administrative law put in place by the cases which make up the Quartet, and how those rules have developed over time, one – perhaps key – question to bear in mind is the extent to which the Scottish context has managed to balance the

[22] A McHarg, 'Public Law, Private Law and the Distinctiveness of Scots Judicial Review', UK Constitutional Law Association Blog (20 January 2012).

[23] McHarg, 'Public Law' (2012).

[24] See C McCorkindale, 'Public interest litigants in the Court of Session' (2015) 19 *Edinburgh Law Review* 248, discussing amongst other cases *Walton v Scottish Ministers* [2012] CSIH 19 and, on appeal, *Walton v Scottish Ministers* [2012] UKSC 44.

[25] S Sedley, 'The Long Sleep' in M Andenas and D Fairgrieve (eds), *Tom Bingham and the Transformation of the Law: A Liber Amicorum*, (Oxford, OUP, 2009).

[26] Though see Lord Clyde and DJ Edwards, *Judicial Review* (Edinburgh, W Green 2000) [2.36].

[27] Page, *Constitutional Law of Scotland* (2015) [16-04].

[28] Implementing (in large part) the recommendations of the Dunpark report (Working Party on Procedure for Judicial Review of Administrative Action, 'Report to the Rt Hon Lord Emslie, Lord Pesident of the Court of Session', HMSO (1985)) and 'inspired by similar reforms in England' which had taken place in 1977 and were consolidated in the Supreme Court Act (now the Senior Courts Act) 1981: C McCorkindale, A McHarg and T Mullen, 'Judicial Review at Thirty' (2015) *Juridical Review* 317.

[29] Courts Reform (Scotland) Act 2014.

[30] See Reed, 'Judicial Review in Scotland' (2015).

fundamental distinctiveness of the supervisory jurisdiction with an openness to absorbing (English) conceptual doctrinal innovation. Can judicial review in Scotland promote the rule of law when the rule of law requires the drawing of a distinction whose rejection is at the heart of Scottish administrative law? I consider that question now in the context of the Quartet and its legacy in Scots law.

III. THE QUARTET IN SCOTS LAW

Though the extent of the four cases' direct significance to Scots law (and of Scots law to them) varies significantly, they illustrate well the distinctiveness of the Scottish context. But they demonstrate, I argue, something more than that: they highlight what might be seen as the lost promise of Scottish administrative law, which is not and which never has been a type of public law, but which has never managed either to transcend its inherent publicness. Just as the Scottish courts have been resistant to the rule of law-inspired reforms of modern administrative law, so too have they been hesitant to endorse the logic of the Quartet in its entirety.

A. Padfield

The existence of the principle established by *Padfield* – that statutory powers must be exercised compatibly with the policy and object of the statute (or, subtly different, that they must not be exercised incompatibly with such policy and object) – in Scots law is clear, and uncontroversial.[31] The question which arises is – given the fact of legislative rather than merely administrative devolution in Scotland – how far it might stretch beyond the executive. In *Moohan* it was argued at first instance that the *Padfield* principle applies not only to acts of executive bodies, but also to the Scottish Parliament, whose acts (in this case, legislative) were therefore 'subject to review on the ground that they run counter to the policy and objectives of the enabling legislation, which policy and objectives are identified by construing the legislation as a whole'.[32] That claim failed, but it is worth considering its implications. On one hand, the point is clear enough: in *Padfield* the rule is justified (if loosely and inconsistently) with reference to the Parliament's intentions.[33] When Parliament legislates, it does so

[31] See, eg *RM v The Scottish Ministers* [2012] UKSC 58 [42]–[48] (Lord Reed).

[32] *Moohan, Re Judicial Review* [2013] CSOH 199.

[33] [1968] AC 997, 1030: 'Parliament must have conferred the discretion with the intention that it should be used to promote the policy and objects of the Act, the policy and objects of the Act must be determined by construing the Act as a whole and construction is always a matter of law for the court'.

with some (usually implicit) purpose in mind. When it empowers an executive actor, therefore, it does not do so blindly, but rather on the understanding that the power will be used to advance that purpose (or, again, not to obstruct it). A statutory power which appears, on its face, to be subject to no limitation whatsoever, is in fact always and everywhere subject to this overarching restriction: there is no such thing as an unfettered discretion in English (or Scots) law.

That Parliament has a single, perceptible intention as to the policy and object of a statute is – within this framework – taken as read; so too is the idea that the courts might identify that policy (object) via a process of interpretation which involves construing the statute as a whole, rather than as a series of discrete provisions. That the effect of the principle (as developed by the courts, naturally) is to subject the executive to a set of restrictions whose content is identified not by Parliament, in whose name, and by reference to whose intention, they are imposed, but rather by the courts, is of course merely fortuitous. But if the logic of the principle is accepted, there seems to be no reason not to extend it to a body which just so happens to be legislative rather than executive or administrative in nature:[34] the democratic character of the former as compared to the latter does not by itself negate any limitation which a judge might convincingly read into the statutory framework. Indeed, such an argument resembles that of Lord Reed in *AXA General Insurance*, justifying the conclusion that there exist grounds upon which the competence of an Act of the Scottish Parliament might be challenged other than those which are enumerated within it. Though more immediately couched in the language of the principle of legality (in opposition to Lord Hope's invocation of the rule of law), the claim that the Westminster Parliament 'did not legislate in a vacuum: it legislated for a liberal democracy founded on particular constitutional principles and traditions'[35] might fairly be read as a reference to the 'policy and object' of the statute which brought the Scottish Parliament into being.

Might the rule in *Padfield* be applied across the breadth of the supervisory jurisdiction? In most if not all non-public tripartite relationships, there is not one intention, but two – that of the parties to the contract – but the law of contract is well-attuned to issues of intention, primarily in the formation of the contract itself. Might a contract have behind it also a 'policy' or an 'object' which should limit also the discretion of a person who is empowered by it to make some decision or other? If so, then the rule in *Padfield* might not be as distinctive as it is sometimes held to be, and it (or an analogue) might apply wherever there exists a discretion to be exercised – a limit, or set of limits, which are inherent both to the very concept of a discretion, but also to particular discretions, and which can be justified without reference to, for example, the rule of law.

[34] See *Whaley v Watson* 2000 SC 340, 348: the Scottish Parliament is a 'body which – however important its role – has been created by statute and derives its powers from statute' and so, 'like any other statutory body, must work within the scope of those powers'.

[35] *AXA General Insurance Ltd v Lord Advocate* [2011] UKSC 46 [153].

This in turn suggests that references to the intention of Parliament are unnecessary to justify the rule in *Padfield*: all that is needed is a concern for context, and an understanding that context always fetters discretion – the nature of a power or decision-making authority, and the reason for which it exists. More immediately, however, there appear to be no clear examples of this reasoning or any analogue of it being applied in the context of non-public tripartite relationships, and so it is not possible to say whether Scottish administrative law has been either willing or able to give full effect to the logic of *Padfield*.

B. *Anisminic*

What exactly was decided in *Anisminic* remains contested. Let us assume, however, that the case stands for the proposition that there is no distinction between errors of law within jurisdiction and those which go to jurisdiction; that, instead, any error of law made by a body charged with exercising a statutory power will render its decision unlawful. In (or, perhaps better, after) *Anisminic*, the key consequence of that decision has related to the effect of ouster clauses. Pre-*Anisminic*, the distinction between intra and ultra vires errors of law was used to delimit the effect of ouster clauses: the former were protected by such a clause, the latter were not. After it, that approach was no longer tenable, and what – if anything – might be the effect of a statutory ouster clause was (and indeed remains) unclear. In Scotland, however, the distinction lived on. In *Watt v Lord Advocate*, the Lord President (Lord Emslie) declared it 'clear' that 'however much this is to be regretted, the Court of Session has never had power to correct an intra vires error of law made by a statutory tribunal or authority exercising statutory jurisdiction'.[36] This dictum, even if its application in subsequent cases was 'somewhat patchy',[37] was outright incompatible with the principle which *Anisminic* came, over time, to represent.[38] And so, when the Supreme Court was required to determine the availability in Scots law of judicial review of the unappealable decisions of the Upper Tribunal, Lord Hope took the opportunity to disclaim Lord Emslie's remarks:

> Lord Diplock said that the decision in *Anisminic* was a legal landmark which proceeded on the presumption that, where Parliament confers on an administrative tribunal or authority power to decide particular questions defined by the Act, it intends to confine that power to answering the question as it has been so defined and that, if there is any doubt what that question is, this is a matter that the court must resolve. I would hold that the dictum in *Watt* cannot be reconciled with that interpretation of the decision and that it should no longer be followed.[39]

[36] *Watt v Lord Advocate* (1979) SC 120, 131.
[37] *Eba v Advocate General for Scotland* [2011] UKSC 29 [33].
[38] In, most importantly, *Re Racal Communications Ltd* [1981] AC 374.
[39] [2011] UKSC 29 [34] (internal citations omitted).

In doing so, he 'stressed' (again) that 'in principle, no difference between the law of England and Scots law as to the substantive grounds on which a decision by a tribunal which acts within its jurisdiction may be open to review.'[40] And, following the approach that had been taken to the same question in English law, Lord Hope – writing for a unanimous court – held that the second-tier appeal criteria (which limit a second appeal to cases in which there is 'some important point of principle or practice' or 'some other compelling reason') 'provide a benchmark for the court to use in the exercise of its supervisory jurisdiction in relation to decisions that are unappealable that is in harmony with the common law principle of restraint'.[41] The effect of these remarks in *Eba* was that, since *Anisminic* was decided, Scots law had fallen in line with the position considered to have been staked out there. But the reasoning in *Anisminic* – the technicalities of the different types of error of law and their effect – is, from a more broadly constitutional point of view, usually secondary to the immediate practical significance in the case: the ineffectiveness of the ouster clause in the Foreign Compensation Act 1950 and the resulting uncertainty as to where an ouster clause might now be effective. That an ouster clause might still be effective was accepted in *Anisminic* itself, and the (in)famous dicta in *Jackson* as to the possibility that judicial review was a 'constitutional fundamental' which 'even a sovereign Parliament acting at the behest of a complaisant House of Commons cannot abolish'[42] seem to reflect an understanding an ouster clause might be made, as it were, *Anisminic*-proof; that, like the ouster clause originally contained in the Asylum and Immigration (Treatment of Claimants etc) Bill, a provision might be drafted whose effect could not be interpreted away, preventing the review of a decision of an inferior body even of the type that pre-*Anisminic* was treated as going to jurisdiction.[43]

What, then, is the significance of this element of *Anisminic* in modern Scots law? Even if we treat the question of the effect of ouster clauses as one of substance (on which the Scots and English law of judicial review are presumptively aligned), and so say that the effect of an ouster clause is equivalent in each jurisdiction, the Scottish context raises particular issues. One is that such equivalence presumes that the ouster clause whose effect in Scots law is under consideration is contained in an act of the Westminster Parliament, rather than that of the devolved legislature at Holyrood. Though the *Jackson* dicta remain controversial, in that they inevitably imply the qualification of the fundamental rule of Parliamentary sovereignty, it has been held that a broadly equivalent rule of law limitation applies also to acts of the Scottish Parliament.[44] In that

[40] ibid. Chris Himsworth notes that the final sentence of this passage implies the existence of a category of errors of law which are within jurisdiction but nevertheless reviewable: 'Jurisdictional aspects of judicial review in Scots law' (2015) *Juridical Review* 353.

[41] [2011] UKSC 29 [48].

[42] *R (Jackson) v Attorney General* [2005] UKHL 56 [102].

[43] Asylum and Immigration (Treatment of Claimants, etc) Bill HC 5 (2002–03), cl 10(7).

[44] *AXA General Insurance Limited v The Lord Advocate* [2011] UKSC 46 [53]–[64] and [155]–[175].

context, where the legislature is a creature of statute and of explicitly limited competence, the notion that the common law places controls on what might be done by the legislature presents no challenge to the fundamentals of the constitutional order. It follows that an ouster clause which (contra those *Jackson* dicta) would have one effect if found in an Act of Parliament may have a more limited, or even no, effect were it found instead in an Act of the Scottish Parliament.

A second point is that the archetypal ouster clause relates to the decisions or acts of an inferior decision-maker – whether a tribunal or some facet of the executive – which is assumed to be public, and so otherwise subject to the supervisory jurisdiction of the High Court. But the supervisory jurisdiction of the Court of Session is not so limited, and so the effect of *Anisminic* in Scots law must be assessed not only in the context of public bodies, but also in the context of tripartite relationships where the party which has acted, or proposes to act, is in no sense public. Here, the ouster in question may be a general one, found in the law of the land, or it might be found within the contract which, in Lord Hope's words, confers 'a decision-making power or duty on a third party to whom the taking of the decision is entrusted but whose manner of decision-making may be controlled by the court'.[45]

We have seen above that the liberalised approach to standing in Scots judicial review applies only to that which is 'public', a limitation which is implicitly justified by the language of the rule of law – the belief that there is a wider public interest in the enforcement of the law against public authorities which does not exist in the context of private relationships and so 'private' judicial review.[46] Given that the courts' suspicion of ouster clauses is similarly grounded (now, at least) in the rhetoric of the rule of law, it would not be surprising to find that the logic of *Anisminic* is, in Scotland, applied differently as between public and private contexts, creating another such division within the supervisory jurisdiction. Such an approach – to say that statutory ouster clauses implicate the rule of law in a way that a contractual equivalent does not – should be resisted, for essentially the reasons given by Aileen McHarg in the context of a critique of the decision in *AXA* to liberalise public law standing but not its private law equivalent:

> While it may be true in some cases that contractually-based decisions are of no interest to third parties, just as some decisions taken under statutory authorities have no wider implications, it is not necessarily true in all cases, and certainly not in the more important instances of judicial review in the private sphere, such as in relation to self-regulatory bodies or contracted-out service providers.[47]

[45] *West v Secretary of State for Scotland* 1992 SC 385 (IH), 400.

[46] McHarg (n 22): 'The essential problem is that, in *West* and subsequent cases, the Scottish courts have attempted to maintain two mutually inconsistent positions: first, that the Scots law of judicial review is fundamentally different from English law; but, second, that Scotland should follow England's lead in relation to the substantive grounds of review, and now also in relation to procedural matters'.

[47] McHarg (n 22).

To do justice to the question of judicial review in private contexts, therefore, might reasonably be thought to require not only a more generous approach to standing than is left in place by *AXA* but also a limit – perhaps a total one – on the ability of parties to a contract to prevent challenges to the acts of a person to whom a power has been thereby delegated: to say, that is, that parties to a contract should not be permitted to oust the supervisory jurisdiction of the Court of Session in situations where it would otherwise run.

Whether or not the approach of the courts accords with this view – whether, that is, a contractual ouster clause protects also a jurisdictional error of law by a private body – is unclear. One of the best-known modern cases, *St Johnstone Football Club Ltd v Scottish Football Association Ltd*,[48] related to a decision taken under the authority of the defenders' articles of association. Those articles contained a provision whereby 'legal proceedings shall not be taken on any matter except with the previous consent of the Council'.[49] Lord Kilbrandon in the Outer House held that the pursuers, as a point of construction, had not in fact agreed 'to accept as final and binding the decision of the Council in all cases of dispute even between a member and the association itself in which the member was maintaining that the association was in breach of the implied terms of the rules themselves'. He also suggested, however – in necessarily obiter remarks – that such an agreement might be without effect in law:

> Public policy must surely insist upon a rule that when a *quasi*- judicial tribunal is set up, albeit by a contract between private persons voluntarily entered into, with privative jurisdiction, then since that tribunal must accept the obligation of conducting its proceedings in accordance with the rules of natural justice, the privative nature of the jurisdiction cannot be permitted to prevent the Court from stepping in to enforce those rules.[50]

Though the principle is sound, this does not – it would seem – imply an absolute bar upon a 'contractual' ouster clause, for Lord Kilbrandon explicitly left open the question of what might be the result in 'a case in which an association's rules provided expressly a power to depart from natural justice which had been conferred by one party contractually upon the other'.[51] The case law in fact shows that, contrary to Lord Kilbrandon's instincts, contractual ousters will succeed in certain circumstances. In *Stringfellow v The Showmen's Guild of Great Britain*,[52] the petitioner challenged the decision of the respondent's Appeal Committee to dismiss a complaint brought to it under its Rules and By-Laws which, the Committee had held, was out of time. An analogous situation had been considered in *Codona*.[53] There, it had been held that a provision

[48] *St Johnstone Football Club Ltd v Scottish Football Association Ltd* 1965 SLT 171.
[49] ibid 174–75.
[50] ibid 175.
[51] ibid.
[52] *Stringfellow v The Showmen's Guild of Great Britain* [2017] CSOH 62.
[53] *Codona v Showmen's Guild of Great Britain* 2002 SLT 299.

of those rules which declared that decision of the Committee 'shall be final and binding on all members of the Guild' prevented judicial review of a decision where the alleged error of law was not one which went to jurisdiction:

> It appears to me that, perhaps in some contrast to the exercise by a public official or body of an administrative power, where parties have by agreement conferred on a body the power of interpretation of the law and its application to their dispute and have agreed to accept the determination as final, that agreement on finality is a matter to be respected and provides reason for the court's not interfering with an intra-jurisdictional error of law.[54]

This, though, pre-dated the decision in *Eba*, which – it was argued in *Stringfellow* – meant that (almost)[55] any error of law will go to jurisdiction.[56] Lord Armstrong, however, disagreed, holding that the decision of the Appeals Tribunal was not amenable to review. In doing so he drew attention to four contextual features: 'the absence of any element of public law', 'the fact that the issue at large concerned a form of domestic law comprised of internal rules, rather than UK or Scots law', 'the requirement for the application of a particular specialist expertise', and 'the final and binding nature of the process, as set out in the rules which regulate the decision-making process'.[57] He explicitly declined, however, to state whether the basis of his decision was that the petition was outwith the scope of supervisory jurisdiction or because the petition was within that scope but incompetent.[58] Given that this appears to be an example of a tripartite relationship, the better view must be the latter one – the petition was within the scope of the supervisory jurisdiction (and the use of the language of amenability is therefore misleading), but the challenge to it nevertheless failed. That the reasons for it doing so include points relating to both the substance of what was challenged and the contractual 'ouster' clause is concerning, for it leaves open the possibility that such an ouster clause might suffice to prevent judicial review even where clear grounds are evident. The rule of law may have special bite in the context of the relationship between citizen and state, but – we note again – it is not exclusive to such relationships, and if we are genuinely committed to that ideal it would be intolerable to allow a contractual clause of the sort at issue in *Stringfellow* to exclude the right to challenge any violation of the requirements of natural justice. The overall effect is that, though we do not have in the 'private' tripartite context a clear statement of the *Anisminic* principle (as received into Scots law in *Eba*), nor do we have any clear authority that the distinction between intra vires and ultra vires errors of law holds good in

[54] 2002 SLT 299 [17].

[55] What was described here as the 'vanishingly small number of narrow areas which' represent 'exceptions to the general rule' was illustrated by reference to *R v Lord President of the Privy Council, ex parte Page* [1993] AC 682.

[56] *Stringfellow* (n 52) [13].

[57] ibid [36].

[58] ibid [33].

those contexts. The better view is the former one, and attempts to subordinate private contexts to public contexts – especially where justified on the basis of the rule of law – must be resisted.

C. *Ridge v Baldwin*

The significance of *Ridge v Baldwin*[59] derives from the fact that – even more so than *Anisminic* – it marks the clearing of the ground: the effective abolition of a complex distinction, easier to state than to apply, and consequent liberation of those who seek to understand modern administrative law from any obligation to venture back beyond that case. In this case, the distinction was that elaborated in *Arlidge* between judicial and administrative decision-making,[60] the significance of which derived from the fact that – until *Ridge* – the courts insisted on the full requirements of natural justice only in cases of the former type, and not in those which were merely administrative. This distinction was, of course, a division within public decision-makers, and so was more easily applied in that context than outside it. Though it is evident also in some of the 'private' judicial review case law – including in the passage from the *St Johnstone* case quoted above – the abandonment of the distinction makes it is unnecessary to think through its coherence and significance in modern 'private' judicial review. And *Ridge* has had direct significance in Scots law, where the distinction between judicial and administrative acts – which the Scottish courts had previously rejected[61] – seems to have taken hold in the years following *Arlidge*.[62] Indeed, what is more striking with hindsight is not that *Ridge* was needed as much in Scots law as in English law, but rather that it took so long for the basic lesson regarding the generality of the requirements of natural justice to be learned. As late as 1995 the distinction between judicial and administrative decision-making, and the argument that the latter brought with it lesser procedural requirements than did the former, continued to be invoked (though without success) before the Scottish courts.[63]

Moreover, *Ridge* marks the belated acceptance of the existence of a system of administrative law ('We do not have a developed system of administrative law – perhaps because until fairly recently we did not need it'),[64] now understood – as discussed above – not in the Diceyean sense of a set of special immunities of which public authorities might avail themselves in order to avoid the legal consequences which would be felt by a private actor acting similarly, but rather

[59] *Ridge v Baldwin* [1964] AC 40.

[60] *R v Local Government Board, ex parte Arlidge* [1915] AC 120.

[61] Though in the context of asserting the duties of an actor acting judicially as regards natural justice rather than the absence of such duties in the case of those acting in an administrative fashion. See *School Board of Parish of Dalziel v Scotch Education Department* 1913 1 SLT 457, 460.

[62] See, eg, *M'Lean v Paterson* 1939 JC 52.

[63] *Errington v Wilson* 1995 SC 550.

[64] *Ridge v Baldwin* [1964] AC 40, 72.

in a series of additional requirements to which such actors must adhere. Given that many of the most important immunities were not enjoyed by the Crown in Scotland, however, the Diceyan account arguably applied better north of the border than south of it.[65] And though administrative law, in its more modern, more conventional sense, did indeed emerge in England, it is open to question whether it makes sense to speak of it having done so in Scotland.

What, then, are the implications of *Ridge* (and, more generally, the modern law of the natural justice of which it is the standard bearer) for judicial review in Scotland? The first point to be made is that the rules of natural justice apply also in 'private' contexts which are within the scope of the supervisory jurisdiction. In the *St Johnstone* case, mentioned above, a fine had been imposed on the pursuers without notice and without it being given the opportunity to be heard. Lord Kilbrandon accepted that *Drennan v Associated Ironmoulders of Scotland* was binding authority for the proposition that the Court of Session 'will entertain actions arising out of the "judgments" of the governing bodies of private associations, whether or not the civil rights and patrimonial interests of its members have been interfered with by the proceedings complained of, where a gross irregularity, such as a departure from the rules of natural justice, has been demonstrated'.[66] In *Crockett*, arguments as to alleged breaches of natural justice were rejected by the Court:

> It is clear that the petitioner was entitled to a fair hearing, and that an essential element of such a hearing was that he should be informed of the gravamen of the complaint against him. In fact, the petitioner was informed of the terms of the complaint verbatim. Although not drafted with the precision one might expect of an indictment in criminal proceedings, the letter of complaint appears to me to have made tolerably clear the aspects of the petitioner's conduct which had occasioned concern.[67]

These cases accord with the dictum of Lord Hope, whereby 'The principles of natural justice may be invoked in all cases where there is an issue to be decided which affects the rights of the person who is entitled to be heard by the

[65] Though Dicey showed little interest in the existence of a separate Scottish legal system except as an example of the failure of the Treaty of Union to create legal, rather than merely political, limits on the legislative competence of Parliament. In his work with Rait on the Union of 1707, Dicey noted that the (United Kingdom) Parliament had legislated in contravention of Article XVIII of the Treaty of Union only occasionally, and that in both Scotland and England there remained significant objections to the harmonisation of law: 'How much of this feeling has survived in both countries is shown by the practical impossibility of assimilating the Marriage Law of England and of Scotland, whilst the convenience of maintaining the same Marriage Law throughout the whole of Great Britain is obvious'. AV Dicey and RS Rait, *Thoughts on the Union Between England and Scotland*, (London, McMillan and Co, 1920) 284–85.

[66] 1965 SLT 171, 174. And in *Hardie*, it was held that the decision of a local authority to remove a teacher from a list of supply teachers which it maintained was unlawful both because insufficient notice of the allegations against him had been given, and because a report had been relied upon which he had not seen and upon which he had had no opportunity to comment: *Hardie v City of Edinburgh Council* 2000 SLT 130.

[67] *Crocket v Tantallon Golf Club* 2005 SLT 663 [47].

decision maker'.[68] This seems both appropriate and inevitable: the application of the rules of natural justice after *Ridge* is almost infinitely context-dependent, in large part because of the acceptance that they apply equally to what would previously have been characterised as administrative decisions. It is neither necessary nor desirable to draw any sort of formal distinction (even if only implicit) between 'public' and 'private' contexts. For exactly the same reason that it is inevitable, however, it is also not necessarily meaningful: so context-dependent is the application of the rules that to say they extend to private contexts in itself tells us nothing about how natural justice might be protected in such contexts. All that can be said with certainty is that any attempt to apply them which ignores, for example, the asymmetries of power which often characterise 'private' relationships and the fact that the interests at stake in such contexts can be equally and indeed more important than the 'public' rights more commonly associated with judicial review will fail to do justice to their professed status as universal principles.

D. *Conway v Rimmer*

Of the four cases that make up the Quartet, it is in *Conway v Rimmer*[69] that the influence of Scots law and Scottish thinking is perhaps easiest to discern. The case, as discussed in chapter five, represents a step back from the deference to the executive – in the domain of (what we now call) 'public interest immunity' – which had been endorsed in *Duncan v Cammell Laird*.[70] No longer was the balance between public interest in disclosure and public interest in non-disclosure to be determined once and for all by the relevant executive actor. Rather, the balance as thus asserted could be tested by the courts, who therefore possessed the right to disagree with the executive's assertion of the outcome of the balancing process.

But when the House of Lords decided this point in *Conway*, they were not doing so for the first time. They had already done so, more than a decade previously, in *Glasgow Corporation v Central Land Board*.[71] The Corporation was seeking to challenge development charges imposed by the Board under the Town and Country Planning (Scotland) Act 1947, and sought – for the purpose of those proceedings – the disclosure of documentation held by it relating to those decisions. In response, the Secretary of State lodged a certificate noting that some of the documents in question 'belonged to a class which it was necessary for the proper functioning of the public service to withhold from production'.[72]

[68] *Errington v Wilson* 1995 SC 550, 554.
[69] *Conway v Rimmer* [1968] AC 910.
[70] *Duncan v Cammell, Laird and Company Limited* [1942] AC 624.
[71] *Glasgow Corporation v Central Land Board* 1956 SC (HL) 1.
[72] ibid 12.

At first instance, Lord Strachan – with evident reluctance – had held himself bound both by *Duncan* and by the judgment of the Inner House in *Admiralty v Aberdeen Steam Trawling and Fishing Co*,[73] in which it had been held that documents might be withheld from disclosure at the discretion of the public department even where the department itself had instigated the litigation. When the Inner House considered the point in the context of *Glasgow Corporation*, Lord Russell accepted that the practice of the courts was not to demand to see for itself those documents in respect of which privilege was claimed. He asserted, however, that the Scottish courts maintained 'an inherent power to order production of a document in spite of a Minister's objection to its production based on grounds of public policy'.[74] He was unwilling, that was, to accept that what was said in *Duncan* overruled a contrary Scottish position which had been asserted in a number of cases both before and after *Aberdeen Steam Trawling*:

> As regards the position in Scotland, I have found great difficulty in determining whether the reasonable inference from what was laid down in the Lord Chancellor's speech is to treat as overruled what had hitherto been the law and practice in Scotland. But I have ultimately come to the conclusion that it would not be proper to do so. It seems to me that it would be an unprecedented step to hold that a long-established practice in Scotland, affirmed on many occasions, has been impliedly overruled by a decision pronounced in the House of Lords in an English appeal where the Scottish decisions, in which the existence of the inherent power had been affirmed, had not been cited to or considered by the House of Lords.[75]

Taken together the judgments of the Inner House all demonstrate this unhelpful juxtaposition: a willingness to allow claims for privilege almost automatically, and the assertion of a theoretical right, the circumstances of whose exercise are left unstated, to nevertheless insist upon disclosure. In the House of Lords, the distinctiveness of the Scottish position was accepted by Viscount Simonds:

> [D]esirable though it may be that in matters of constitutional importance the law of the two countries should not differ, yet it would be clearly improper for this House to treat the law of Scotland as finally determined by a decision upon an English appeal unless the case arose upon the interpretation of a statute common to both countries.[76]

Moreover, though there were references to Scots case law in the judgment of Lord Simon in *Duncan*, they were for a number of reasons drawn upon in such a way as to 'give an imperfect view of the law of Scotland',[77] a point emphasised by several of the Law Lords. The House of Lords therefore held that – as it was put by Lord Radcliffe – 'the true view of the law of Scotland on this subject is that, however unexceptionable the form of a Minister's certificate to

[73] *Lords Commissioners of the Admiralty v Aberdeen Steam Trawling and Fishing Co, Ltd* [1909] SC 335.

[74] *Glasgow Corporation v Central Land Board* 1955 SC 64, 75–76.

[75] ibid 78.

[76] *Glasgow Corporation* (HL) (n 71) 9–10.

[77] ibid 10.

the effect that production would be against the public interest, the tender of that certificate does not absolutely exclude the Court from making an order for production'.[78] Again, when and where the power to make such an order might be exercised was left unclear.

If *Duncan v Cammell Laird* demonstrates the casualness with which Scots law has occasionally been treated – implicitly assimilated with the English position on the basis of a treatment of the Scottish jurisprudence which was cursory, bordering on negligent – *Conway* represents a more edifying interaction.[79] Lord Reid noted as one of 'several abnormal features' of *Duncan* that the law of England, under discussion in *Conway*, was different from that in Scotland:

> There are many chapters of the law where for historical and other reasons it is quite proper that the law should be different in the two countries. But here we are dealing purely with public policy – with the proper relation between the powers of the executive and the powers of the courts – and I can see no rational justification for the law on this matter being different in the two countries.[80]

Not only was harmony preferable, but the fact that the Scottish position was as it had been declared to be in *Glasgow City Council* demonstrated conclusively that to permit the court to overrule the objection of a minister involved no 'constitutional impropriety'.[81] Lord Morris of Borth-Y-Gest drew attention to the remark of Viscount Simonds that the Scottish rule 'provides an ultimate safeguard of justice in that country which is denied to a litigant in England'[82] noting that it would be 'unfortunate if such a denial must continue for litigants in England'.[83] Scots law, suitably mangled, having been a justification for a retrograde step in the 1940s, it now became, in the late 1960s, a light guiding English law out of the error into which it had fallen.

Similar inconsistency has been shown in later cases, both in the same court and at different levels of the judicial hierarchy. In *Davidson* the Inner House of the Court of Session held that section 21 of the Crown Proceedings Act 1947 prevented the Court of Session making of an order for specific performance against the Scottish Ministers in the exercise of its supervisory jurisdiction, this falling within the statutory formulation 'civil proceedings'.[84] It did so notwithstanding that – as noted above – coercive remedies against the Crown had been available in Scotland before the 1947 Act and that the effect of the legislation

[78] ibid 18.

[79] Smith noted that he could think of 'numerous occasions' on which the Scottish counsel had 'gained support for their contentions by conceding quite unwarrantably that the laws of Scotland and England were identical on the question in issue'. Smith, *British Justice* (1961) 87.

[80] [1968] AC 910, 938. See also Lord Upjohn, 990: 'While the law of England and that of Scotland may differ in many respects it is really essential, in the interests of justice to Her Majesty's subjects in both parts of the United Kingdom, that the rules relating to Crown privilege should be the same'.

[81] ibid 951.

[82] *Glasgow City Council* (HL) (n 71) 11.

[83] *Conway* (n 80) 961.

[84] *Davidson v Scottish Ministers* 2002 SC 205.

in England had been to increase the range of remedies available as against the Crown.[85] Lord Marnoch noted that reference had been made to Lord Reid's remarks in *Conway v Rimmer* as to the absence of 'rational justification' for permitting the relationship between the courts and executive to differ in the two jurisdictions. This he found to be of no assistance:

> If that dictum is read out of context, then it may appear to have some relevance to the present case. The fact is, however, that it was pronounced in a case which was concerned solely with the common law of Crown privilege in relation to the production of documents, being a context far removed from a construction of sec 21 of the Crown Proceedings Act 1947.[86]

When an appeal against this conclusion was allowed by the House of Lords – a decision more in keeping with the Lord Reid's approach to administrative law, and which effectively brought Scots law into harmony with the decision in *M v Home Office*[87] – the reasons offered include both common sense and Parliamentary intention, alongside the predictable references to the desirability of the legal position being the same in both jurisdictions.[88]

Nevertheless, the reasoning in *Davidson* is problematic in the sense noted above. It implicitly distinguishes between public and private judicial review. The House of Lords held that the phrase 'civil proceedings' in section 21 excluded from its scope – by analogy with the exclusion in England of what were known as 'Crown side proceedings' – what Lord Rodger described as 'proceedings invoking the supervisory jurisdiction of the Court of Session in respect of acts or omissions of the Crown or its officers'.[89] Lord Hope, arriving at the same conclusion, drew a distinction between public law and private law proceedings, identifying as 'public law proceedings' those in which 'the supervisory jurisdiction is being invoked against the Crown'.[90] Though this is not equivalent to a direct distinction between public and private judicial review – including as it does only a subset of the former, and not (for example) proceedings against bodies which, though recognisably public, are not emanations of the Crown – it has nevertheless been claimed that the effect is to turn what was intended as a 'reaffirmation' of the decision in *West* into a revision of it,[91] meaning that the bare assertion of the absence of a public/private distinction is now likely to hide as much as it reveals.

This might be contested. Though a distinction between public law proceedings and private law proceedings is here recognised, it is employed in such manner as to ensure that the practical availability of remedies does not vary as

[85] See the discussion in Tomkins, 'The Crown' (2006).
[86] *Davidson* (n 84) 213.
[87] *M v Home Office* [1994] 1 AC 377. See McHarg (n 22).
[88] *Davidson v Scottish Ministers (No 1)* [2005] UKHL 74 [33].
[89] ibid [88].
[90] ibid [53].
[91] McHarg (n 22).

between the different actors against whom a judicial review might be brought. Only within private law proceedings – which may, of course, be brought against the Crown as against any other individual – does the 1947 Act limit the remedies which might be granted.[92] Though it features in the judgment of Lord Roger, the relationship of 'rule of law' reasoning to this outcome is most evident in the judgment of the Inner House, where Lord Marnoch was openly dismissive of the concept and its relevance to the issue before him:

> I note, for the record, that this particular line of argument was heavily embellished by references to the 'rule of law' and the supposed requirement to read the 1947 Act as if it was 'speaking' in light of the 'new constitutional settlement' embodied in the Scotland Act and Human Rights Act ... Speaking for myself, I did not find any of these embellishments to be of much assistance and, indeed, I have to say that at times the extensive references made to them seemed to me, if anything, to obfuscate the true thrust of the argument.[93]

That the House of Lords, in order to vindicate the rule of law, was required to draw a distinction between public law and private law proceedings illustrates once more the tension which this chapter has argued exists between that concept and the scope of the supervisory jurisdiction in Scots law. This is true even if one agrees – as seems obvious – that the overall effect of allowing for the same coercive remedies against the Crown in judicial review proceedings as are available against other parties in such proceedings justifies the recognition of a distinction which is not supposed to exist.

IV. LORD REID, THE QUARTET AND SCOTS ADMINISTRATIVE LAW

A. The Politics of Administrative Law

Two aspects of Lord Reid's background are potentially relevant to his approach to the judicial task, both generally and in the context of administrative law. One is his political experience, which – it has been said – gave him 'an innate sense of the relationship of the legislature and the courts',[94] as well (one might add) the position of the executive in relation to both of these. Though historically such experience was relatively common, Reid's experience was nevertheless exceptional in terms both of quantity (approximately 15 years as a Conservative Member of Parliament, first for Stirling and Falkirk, and later for Glasgow Hillhead) and quality (having been both Solicitor General and Lord Advocate, before an interlude as Dean of the Faculty of Advocates).

[92] *Davidson* (HL) (n 88) [54].
[93] *Davidson* (SC) (n 84) [14]–[15].
[94] R Stevens, *Law and Politics: The House of Lords as a Judicial Body, 1800–1976* (Littlehampton Book Services Ltd, 1979) 468.

It is notable, however, that while many appointments in this category may well have had more than a little political motivation behind them, the offer to Reid came from a Labour Prime Minister, Clement Attlee, and so was – again, it has been claimed – 'almost certainly prompted by an appreciation of Reid's potential contribution to the development of the law'.[95] Certainly, taken as a whole, the Quartet – and Reid's public law jurisprudence more generally – does not suggest an excessive deference to government generally. Does it though reflect a slight partisan dynamic? Recall Stephen Sedley's claim that the 'long sleep' of public law in England came to an end when judges began to act on 'the silent imperative' that 'no government should again be ceded such unchallenged command of public administration as the Attlee government was allowed'.[96]

In this context, it is notable that all but one of the cases which make up the Quartet were decided under a Labour government, and though the facts of *Anisminic* long predate the decision of the House of Lords, the statute at issue – the Foreign Compensation Act 1950 – was passed by Attlee's Government. The case decided under a Conservative government is *Ridge*, which is by far the least obviously political of the four cases, both in the general and partisan senses, while it is possible to construct a (crude) narrative in which the decisions in *Anisminic* and *Padfield*, even if decided in neutral terms, privilege the interests of capital. The same goes for *Burmah Oil*, and several of the cases which bridge the gap between the Quartet and the more famously politicised jurisprudence of the 1980s. In *Laker Airways*, for instance, the judgment of Lord Denning begins in terms which mix his famous narrative style with a paean to the entrepreneurial spirit.[97] And so we might say only that Lord Reid's political background is congruent with some of his most prominent decisions. In response to which it might fairly be noted that many other judges, without the explanation (excuse?) of Reid's background in politics, took similar stances.

B. Lord Reid and the Scottishness of Scots Administrative Law

The second potentially relevant aspect of Lord Reid's background is his Scottishness. A discussion of the Quartet in the context of Scots law must acknowledge immediately that administrative law does not feature prominently – perhaps at all – within 'legal nationalism'.[98] Scottish legal nationalism, however,

[95] Blom-Cooper and Drewry, 'Towards a System of Administrative Law' (2009) 219.

[96] Sedley, 'The Long Sleep' (2009) 191.

[97] *Laker Airways Ltd v Department of Trade* [1977] QB 643.

[98] On which see HL MacQueen, 'Legal Nationalism: Lord Cooper, Legal History and Comparative Law' (2005) 9 *Edinburgh Law Review* 395. An important critique of what is often called the 'Smith-Cooper ideology' is found in ID Willock, 'The Scottish Legal Heritage Revisited' in JP Grant (ed), *Independence and Devolution: The Legal Implications for Scotland* (Edinburgh, W Green & Son Ltd, 1976).

has only infrequently and contingently overlapped with its political counterpart,[99] and so there is no contradiction in considering the possible influence of that phenomenon on a judge whose political allegiances were both unionist and Unionist. Legal nationalism as a school of thought, though varying between thinkers and over time, generally emphasises not so much Scots law's superiority over, or even distinctiveness from, analogous English rules (though there are certainly examples of such claims) as the need to avoid unthinking assimilation of the two legal orders.

The reasons for the exclusion of (what we now call) administrative law from the purview of the legal nationalists – most legal nationalism related to private law; many legal nationalists were, in the first instance, private lawyers – are not difficult to discern. First, the distinctiveness of Scots law and in particular its status as a 'mixed' legal system with Roman-Dutch influences, relates only to its private law aspects, with neither criminal nor public law evidencing its fundamental distinctiveness.[100] And though legal nationalism is largely a twentieth-century phenomenon, this fundamental public/private divide within the study of Scots law is much older. Most tellingly, though, the separateness of Scots law was an imperative reflected in the Treaty of Union, that imperative was selective: where the law concerning 'public Right, Polity, and Civil Government' could be 'made the same throughout the whole united Kingdom', 'no Alteration' – the Treaty provided – was to be made to Scots private law 'except for evident Utility of the Subjects within Scotland.'[101]

Secondly, and more pressingly, legal nationalism was at its most vigorous in the early to mid-twentieth century, and it is unsurprising that a body of law which barely existed as a distinct object at that time (and which as late as the 1970s was not taught in Scottish universities)[102] did not feature strongly in the imagination of those concerned with ensuring that the law of Scotland was not casually superseded, whether by a legislature that seemed at times to struggle with the intricacies of the Scottish legal order, or the judicial House of Lords.[103] The growth of administrative law in Scotland therefore not only post-dates the high-water mark of legal nationalism but takes place in an era in which legal nationalism (by definition, a lawyers' phenomenon) has been obscured by

[99] C Kidd, *Union and Unionisms: Political Thought in Scotland, 1500–2000* (Cambridge, Cambridge University Press, 2008) 198–210. The primary exception is Andrew Dewar Gibb, on whom see L Farmer, 'Under the Shadow over Parliament House. The Strange Case of Legal Nationalism in Scotland' in L Farmer and S Veitch (eds), *The State of Scots Law. Law and Government after the Devolution Settlement* (Edinburgh, Butterworths, 2001).

[100] For a rather sceptical take, see A Rahmatian, 'The political purpose of the 'mixed legal system' conception in the law of Scotland' (2017) 24 *Maastricht Journal of European and Comparative Law* 843.

[101] Treaty of Union 1707, Art XVIII.

[102] Reed (n 10) 325.

[103] See Smith (n 16) 85.

a resurgent political nationalism, of which lawyers, though often prominent contributors,[104] are necessarily a more modest part. Moreover, the culture of specialisation in the modern academy means that those who are perhaps most likely to be minded to argue for the distinctiveness of Scots administrative law are less likely than in the past to have a detailed knowledge of it. But neither of these (somewhat banal) points is incompatible with the inclusion – however partial and secondary – of certain public law issues within the loose legal nationalist project (or, perhaps, worldview). One important legal nationalist – TB Smith – ranks amongst the leading Scottish public lawyers of the twentieth century,[105] and produced a number of important works on Scottish constitutional law, including one considering the notion that the Union of 1707 might act as a form of fundamental law.[106] Another key figure, Lord President Cooper, wrote into the legal record – albeit in obiter – a variant of that same idea in his famous judgment in *MacCormick v Lord Advocate*.[107]

It is against that background that Lord Reid's Scottishness may be considered. Reid was born in East Lothian and schooled in Edinburgh, returning there to enter the Faculty of Advocates following a period at Cambridge, where he graduated BA and LLB.[108] This Scottishness, however, not only of birth but also of legal practice, did not of course prevent Reid from leaving a significant mark on (English) common law, and may indeed have assisted him in doing so. In his biography of Reid, Smith specifically noted Reid's distinctive status, situated as he was between two legal systems:

> What was unique about Reid's contribution in the Lords was that, though a Scots lawyer exclusively by professional training, he was accepted by his English colleagues and by the whole legal profession in England as the 'helmsman of the [English] common law'. Since his conception of the judicial function accorded with the older Scottish tradition, his exercise of it in Scottish appeals, though widely respected, was not considered remarkable.[109]

One might, of course, note that a similar point could be made about Smith, characterised – it has been said – by a number of paradoxes, chief amongst

[104] See, at the dawn of the devolution era, JG Kellas, 'Lawyers in Contemporary Scottish Politics: A New "Dundas Despotism"?' in Farmer and Veitch, *The State of Scots Law* (2001).

[105] See HL MacQueen, 'Two Toms and an Ideology for Scots Law: T B Smith and Lord Cooper of Culross' in E Reid and D Carey Miller (eds), *A Mixed Legal System in Transition: TB Smith and the Progress of Scots Law* (Edinburgh, Edinburgh University Press, 2005).

[106] TB Smith, 'The Union of 1707 as Fundamental Law' [1957] *PL* 99.

[107] *MacCormick v Lord Advocate* 1953 SC 396, 411. See also *Gibson v Lord Advocate* 1975 SC 136 and *Pringle, Petitioner* 1991 SLT 330.

[108] ODNB (n 3).

[109] ODNB (n 3). Smith continues by suggesting that Reid himself contributed to the casual assimilation of Scots and English law: 'Not having been formed in both Scots and English law, he assumed somewhat readily their identity on certain matters where there were latent distinctions. When Reid spoke in House of Lords debates, on matters of Scots law he was accepted as an infallible oracle'. The online edition of the ODNB does not identify Smith as the author of the entry for Lord Reid, but other (older) sources referencing the same version do so identify him: see, eg, A Paterson, *Final Judgment: The Last Law Lords and the Supreme Court* (Oxford, Hart Publishing, 2014).

them that 'the man who came to seem the very embodiment of Scots law having trained, in the first instance, not in that system at all but in English law' and whose 'mother tongue' was therefore English rather than Scots law.[110] The reference to Lord Reid's understanding of the 'judicial function' is significant, however, for it seems to mirror one aspect of the relationship between Lord Reid, the Scottish legal system, and the House of Lords that parallels – perhaps prefigures – the pattern identified in this chapter's first part.

C. Precedent and Principle

The status of the judicial House of Lords – based in London but deciding cases not only from England and Wales but also from Scotland and indeed Northern Ireland – was always a source of considerable (if productive) tension. The Treaty of Union had precluded the hearing of Scottish cases in specified English courts, but said nothing explicit as to the position of the House of Lords.[111] When the upper chamber began to hear Scottish appeals – first in civil cases,[112] but also, for a period, in criminal ones[113] – it therefore acted without express sanction, and despite including no guaranteed representation of the distinct legal system preserved by the Treaty. This was not a marginal element of the House of Lords' work: at certain points in history the bulk of its case load appears to have been Scottish cases.[114] When the Government, having previously failed in its attempt to create a (judicial) life peer by way of the prerogative, occasioned the enactment of the Appellate Jurisdiction Act 1876, one effect was (Robert Stevens has said) that the two traditions of English law – common law and equity – were supplemented by a third: 'representatives of the Scottish judiciary had appeared, bringing with them a broader attitude to the law than had been usual in England'.[115] Such breadth of approach has often gone hand in hand with, or been exemplified by, a generalism that distinguished the Scottish Law Lords (and, indeed, their Supreme Court successors) from their English

[110] KGC Reid, 'While One Hundred Remain TB Smith and the Progress of Scots Law' in Reid and Carey Miller, *A Mixed Legal System in Transition* (2005) 3.

[111] For a discussion see PH Brodie, 'From Scotland and Ireland (a) Scotland after 1707' in Blom-Cooper, Dickson and Drewry (2009), and Lord Hope. 'Taking the Case to London: Is it all Over?' (1998) *Juridical Review* 135.

[112] *Rosebery v Inglis* (lodged on 16 February 1708, but not ultimately proceeded with); *Greenshields v Magistrates of Edinburgh* (1709) 1 Rob 12.

[113] See *Magistrates of Elgin v Ministers of Elgin* (1713). The practice was brought to an end in *Bywater v Lord Advocate* (1781) 2 Paton's Ap 564.

[114] Brodie, 'From Scotland and Ireland' (2009) 282: 'between 1794 and 1807, of 501 appeals presented to the House, 419 came from Scotland'.

[115] Stevens, *Law and Politics* (1979) 130. The first Scottish law lord under the 1876 Act was Lord Gordon, replaced in 1880 by Lord Watson. In 1867, the Lord President of the Court of Session, Duncan McNeill had, on retiring from that post, been elevated to the Peerage as Lord Colonsay: Brodie (n 111) 287. The decision to do so may have reflected the fact that McNeill was unmarried, which meant that the peerage would (and did) become extinct upon his death.

counterparts: 'while Scottish law lords undoubtedly take on some camouflage from their surroundings, their training and style may well be better adapted to a flexible model of the appellate process than is the English barrister's training'.[116] And, of course, Lord Reid only ever adjudicated within that appellate process, having been appointed to the Appellate Committee of the House of Lords without any prior judicial experience.

In his address on 'The Judge as Law Maker', remembered for his assertion (or admission) that 'for better or for worse judges do make law', Lord Reid addressed the operation of the doctrine of precedent in Scotland:

> I must confess my ignorance as regards England but the history is easier to perceive in Scotland where, until early in the last century, every civil case that mattered was decided by the same court-the fifteen judges who sat in the Inner House of the Court of Session. They were not averse from changing their mind but certain leading cases came to be recognized as settling certain points.[117]

An absolute doctrine of precedent, Reid argued, is not only futile but counterproductive, creating confusion rather than clarity. '[J]udges are human', and so, if they do not approve of 'an existing decision or *ratio* because it will produce an unjust or unreasonable result in the case before them they try to distinguish it': 'And that is where the trouble starts, and you begin to get an impenetrable maze of distinctions and qualifications which destroy certainty because no one advising on a new case can predict how it will go'.[118]

These remarks therefore link the realistic approach to the judicial role which now dominates to the fact, emphasised by legal nationalists, that Scots law took a much more equivocal approach to the doctrine of precedent than its English counterpart, and may even have disclaimed it altogether until, belatedly, English influence – via the House of Lords – began to tell.[119] But here, as (almost) everywhere else in the Union, there is no reason to believe that influence has, or could, operate only in one direction: Lord Reid himself was vital in shaping the approach of the House of Lords to the Practice Statement it issued in 1966 – roughly two-thirds of the way through his time on the bench – whereby 'too rigid adherence to precedent may lead to injustice in a particular case and also unduly restrict the proper development of the law', and so the Law Lords would in future depart from the previous decision of the Appellate Committee 'when it

[116] Stevens (n 94) 269.

[117] Lord Reid, 'The Judge as Law Maker' (1972) 2 *Journal of the Society of Public Teachers of Law* 22; republished (1997) *Arbitration* 180.

[118] Reid (n 117) 24. Lord President Cooper had, in 1950, asked whether the common law systems would soon face the question of 'whether a better cement than rigid precedent cannot be found in more codification and methodized reasoning from clear principles in accordance with the civilian tradition': TM Cooper, 'The Common and the Civil Law. A Scot's View' (1950) 63 *Harvard Law Review* 468, 473–74.

[119] TB Smith, *The Doctrines of Judicial Precedent in Scots Law* (Edinburgh, W Green and Son, 1952) and Smith (n 16) 84–87.

appears right to do so'.[120] This approach seems to reflect, in an attenuated form, the same dispositions which are evident in what has been called the Court of Session's 'predilection for principle'.[121] Though care must be taken not to overstate the point, it may be that we can perceive that predilection (or something akin to it) not only in Lord Reid's approach to precedent but also in the (related) terms of his substantive decision-making, where – as in the Quartet – broad principles are put into action; favoured over the overly-subtle distinctions then prevailing.

To return to where we began: the House of Lords has now, of course, been supplanted by the Supreme Court, which in the field of administrative law has continued its predecessor's outwardly principled approach to the development of administrative law – an approach which can be traced back, via Lord Diplock, to Lord Reid and the Quartet. Now, however, the principle in question has a name, and its name is the rule of law. Though the rule of law in the modern vocabulary of the upper courts means many things, it means most frequently (and most urgently) the requirement that the executive act according to law, and – flowing directly from that – the need to ensure that is possible to challenge action before the courts, so that the courts have the opportunity to determine its legality. It was in this guise that the rule of law was identified by Lord Diplock as requiring a generous approach to standing, and was posited as a possible limit upon the competence of Parliament in *Jackson*. But the rule of law must mean something more than that if it is to fulfil its Diceyan promise of excluding arbitrary power. For the threat of arbitrary power does not derive solely from the state and its emanations, but is present too in private relationships, in which ideas of formal legal equality often disguise significant imbalances in the objective bargaining power of those party to, say, some contract. It is for this reason that the supervisory jurisdiction in Scotland is potentially – only potentially – better suited to protecting the rule of law, in fact, than is a supervisory jurisdiction framed by a stark distinction between the public and the private.

As we have seen, however, in the consideration of the way in which the Quartet has been implemented in Scots law, the courts have not generally followed through the logic of the supervisory jurisdiction to its fullest ends. As well as resisting the attempts of the Supreme Court to increase the possibility of challenging the actions of public authorities, the courts in Scotland have at the same time and for their own part continued to draw implicit, sometimes unhelpful, distinctions between public and private contexts in implementing the

[120] Practice Statement [1966] 3 All ER 77. See AA Paterson, 'Lord Reid's Unnoticed Legacy – A Jurisprudence of Overruling' (1981) 1 *OJLS* 375, 376 discussing seven criteria identified by Lord Reid for the exercise of the over-ruling discretion: 'In setting out these criteria Lord Reid showed that … he believed that the discretion asserted in the 1966 Practice Statement ought to be exercised according to set principles or guidelines. It is also clear that in his pronouncements on this matter … he was consciously seeking to influence his colleagues'.

[121] *Stewart v London, Midland and Scottish Railway Co* 1943 SC (HL) 19, 39 (Lord MacMillan).

modern administrative law. In so doing, they appear to implicitly accept that there is a wider public interest in ensuring that public actors obey the law than there is in ensuring that private power is subject to the limits which are intended to exist upon it. That assumption is unjustified, and it is therefore welcome that what will now be the leading statement of the rule of law – that of Lord Reed in *UNISON*[122] – recognises that the rule of law has a broader value, and that it is a constitutional, even public, good to have independent courts decide *private* legal disputes.

That does not, however, go quite as far as we might want to push the ideal of the rule of law, in that – taken at face value – it would seem to perpetuate the distinction between the rules of public law (which the rule of law requires be enforced against those acting publicly) which those of private law (which must be enforced against both public and private actors). That is, though, the vision of the rule of law at work in *UNISON* is not the deracinated rule of law of *Jackson* (in which private power, and private law, play no role) it is still one in which – contrary to Dicey's injunction – the protection which the individual has against arbitrary power varies as between public power and private power. It would hardly be plausible to deny that the situation thus described represents some sort of failure to achieve the rule of law in its more ambitious form.

It is, therefore, legitimate to ask whether this is the best we can do – though, as with many of the points made in the present chapter, one must be careful not to overstate it, we might recall here the words of Lord Reed quoted at p 236 above as to the scope of the supervisory jurisdiction in Scotland. There it was said that there were two interpretations which might be given to his comments as to the need not to overstate the significance of the tripartite jurisdiction. One is narrower. The other is a broader, verging on the radical, interpretation, in accordance with which the supervisory jurisdiction might range more widely and as a result of which we might see the sort of limitations placed upon the exercise of public power expanded, carefully but insistently, to forms of private power which are analogous to them in their potential effect upon the individual, but which are caught neither by contractual rules nor by the supervisory jurisdiction in its current form.

V. CONCLUSION

An alleged preference for principle has been a theme of this chapter: a preference for principle over precedent in the decision-making of the House of Lords in the cases which make up the Quartet, where fine-grained distinctions were overthrown, often in the name of principles which are central to the modern body of administrative law; a preference for principle over precedent specifically in the judgments of Lord Reid, which links him (it is claimed) to a number of his

[122] *R (UNISON) v Lord Chancellor* [2017] UKSC 51.

Scottish brethren; a preference for principle in Scots law, which the adoption of a general adherence stare decisis has not excluded altogether. There is, or course, a degree of mythologising in each of these claims, and yet it is not implausible that the approach of the House of Lords in the Quartet might be traced back, however loosely, to the Scottish origins of its chief author, who though no legal nationalist, was as a result of his professional origins undoubtedly acutely aware, as TB Smith certainly was, of the irrepressible contingency of legal rules and legal practice.

If this is one of this chapter's themes, however, a second must be the contrast which exists between these points as made in the abstract or in the rarefied atmosphere of the House of Lords during the era of the Quartet and the more mundane reality of administrative law in modern Scots law. In part, I have suggested, that is a function of the tension which exists between the scope of judicial review in Scots law – which does not distinguish public from private – and understandings of the rule of law which assume those acting publicly should be held to higher standards than those acting privately; that whether the executive obeys the rules which apply to it is a more important question than whether those acting within or under contract do so. The effect is to risk pitting the rule of law against judicial review. Fortunately, however, a solution is at hand. It is to be found in the recognition that when rules are enforceable in law, the law cannot be neutral on whether they are complied with. Though the supervisory jurisdiction in Scots law does not fulfil this promise, it offers the foundations of an approach which does do so.

12

The Quartet Plus Two: Judicial Review in Northern Ireland

GORDON ANTHONY*

I. INTRODUCTION

THIS CHAPTER PICKS up on a theme that is central to much of this book: that the 'Quartet' of cases not only modernised aspects of administrative procedure in the UK but also foreshadowed a constitutionalising function for judicial review.[1] The particular focus of the chapter is on the role that judicial review has played under the constitution of Northern Ireland – essentially, the Belfast Agreement and the Northern Ireland Act 1998.[2] While the Northern Ireland constitution is of course nested within the wider UK constitution and influenced by decisions taken in that context – Brexit providing an obvious example[3] – the courts in Northern Ireland have had to resolve a range of disputes with uniquely local dynamics. In some instances, this has simply

* I was Junior Counsel for the Applicant in the *Buick* case that is analysed below. All comments in relation to that case are mine alone and are not attributable to the applicant or to William Orbinson QC (who led me in the High Court) or David Scoffield QC (who led me in the Court of Appeal). On the wider themes, I have benefited from very helpful discussions with my colleagues Professor John Morison, Dr Conor McCormick, and Mr Terence McCleave. Again, all comments are mine. My thanks are also due to the editors, both for their invitation to contribute to this book, and for their comments on an earlier draft of this chapter.

[1] See ch 1 in this volume (Arvind, Kirkham, Mac Síthigh and Stirton). On administrative procedure see, eg, JA Garner, 'Administrative Law – A Step Forward' (1968) 31 *MLR* 147 (noting *Padfield*). On the constitutional function see, eg, Sir S Sedley, *Lions Under the Throne* (Cambridge, CUP, 2015).

[2] On the Belfast Agreement in its original terms see C Harvey (ed), *Human Rights, Equality and Democratic Renewal in Northern Ireland* (Oxford, Hart Publishing, 2001). For the text of the Agreement see www.gov.uk/government/publications/the-belfast-agreement. Note that references to the Northern Ireland constitution also include references to the range of political agreements that have been concluded since the time of the Belfast Agreement and which led to amendment of the Northern Ireland Act 1998, primarily the St Andrews Agreement (2006) and the Hillsborough Agreement (2010).

[3] See G Anthony, 'Sovereignty, Consent and Constitutions: The Northern Ireland References' in M Elliott, J Williams and A Young (eds), *The UK Constitution After Miller: Brexit and Beyond* (Oxford, Hart Publishing, 2018) 181; and, eg, *Re McCord's Application* [2019] NICA 49.

reflected the fact that Northern Ireland has its own legal system with distinctive administrative law features, whilst in others it has taken judicial review towards the 'sharp end' of asymmetrical devolution.[4] Northern Ireland's historical divisions are such that political instability is a commonplace, and the courts have sometimes had to hear disputes about government in the absence of local institutions. When doing so, they have perhaps shown what a constitutionalising function for judicial review can entail *in extremis*: courts must reason creatively against political backdrops that can challenge understandings of, among other things, democratic principle and the separation of powers.

The chapter develops the above point by analysing two cases from 2018 and 2019, which was a period of time when Northern Ireland's devolved institutions were not sitting. The cases – *Re Northern Ireland Human Rights Commission (NIHRC)*[5] and *Re Buick*[6] – were heard in a political vacuum that was caused not just by the absence of the Northern Ireland institutions but also of any 'direct rule' from Westminster.[7] In broad terms, this meant that the cases became part of a system of 'government by default', as the rulings identified gaps in the constitution that were subsequently addressed by legislation enacted at Westminster. While the *NIHRC* ruling has since been criticised for pursuing 'judicial supremacy' in the UK, it will be argued here that both it and *Buick* are defensible given that political difficulties had complicated the very idea of government in Northern Ireland.[8] The point that will be made is (the admittedly contestable one) that courts can legitimately rule on matters of wider public interest when there are manifest failings within the other branches of the state. The chapter in that way borrows from Lord Woolf's well-known comments about how judicial review can ensure balance in the constitution whilst protecting the values that underlie it.[9] It also illustrates just how far the law at the time of the Quartet has evolved to involve courts in constitutional adjudication.

The chapter begins with a brief explanation about why the Northern Ireland institutions came under political strain in 2017. It then contains a section which discusses *NIHRC* and *Buick* – the 'plus two' – and how they intersected on important questions of governance. These began with the question of whether the law on abortion in Northern Ireland was incompatible with, among other things, Article 8 ECHR, where the Supreme Court in *NIHRC* gave a clear indication (without formally deciding the point) that it was. In political dispatches,

[4] See, generally, G Anthony, *Judicial Review in Northern Ireland*, 2nd edn (Oxford, Hart Publishing, 2014).

[5] [2018] UKSC 27, [2018] NI 228.

[6] [2018] NIQB 43 and [2018] NICA 26.

[7] On which model of government see D Birrell, *Direct Rule and the Governance of Northern Ireland* (Manchester, Manchester University Press, 2009).

[8] For the supremacy argument see, eg, D Campbell and J Allan, 'Procedural Innovation and the Surreptitious Creation of Judicial Supremacy in the United Kingdom' (2019) 46 *Journal of Law and Society* 347, considered below.

[9] See H Woolf, 'The tensions between the executive and the judiciary' (1998) 114 *LQR* 579.

this prompted debate about how the law might be amended in the absence of the Northern Ireland Assembly, where *Buick* commenced a process that had that inadvertent effect. The central issue in *Buick* was whether the Northern Ireland constitution could accommodate decision-making by civil servants in the absence of 'direction and control' from ministers who would be accountable to the Northern Ireland Assembly.[10] In holding that it could accommodate certain categories of decisions, the Court of Appeal identified an ambiguity in the scheme for devolution that suggested that ministerial direction and control need not always underlie civil service decision-making. This resulted in the enactment of legislation at Westminster that both consolidated the civil service's power of decision and later required the Secretary of State for Northern Ireland to change the law on, among other things, abortion.[11] The final section of the chapter describes how such 'government by default' coincided with the return of the devolved institutions, while the conclusion offers some more general comments about the balance of power under a constitution that often has only a 'staccato' form of government.[12]

II. POLITICS AND THE NORTHERN IRELAND CONSTITUTION

The understanding that the Belfast Agreement and the Northern Ireland Act 1998 are a constitution for Northern Ireland is famously associated with the House of Lords ruling in *Robinson v Secretary of State for Northern Ireland*.[13] The central issue in that case was whether the First and Deputy First Ministers had been lawfully elected by the Northern Ireland Assembly when that had happened outside a six-week time limit specified in section 16(8) of the Northern Ireland Act 1998.[14] Had their election been unlawful, the Secretary of

[10] The words in quotation are found in art 4(1) of the Departments (Northern Ireland) Order 1999 (SI 1999/283).

[11] Northern Ireland (Executive Formation and Exercise of Functions) Act 2018; Northern Ireland (Executive Formation etc) Act 2019; and Abortion (Northern Ireland) Regulations 2020 (SI 2020/345), as revoked and replaced by Abortion (Northern Ireland) (No 2) Regulations 2020 (SI 2020/503).

[12] On the political agreement that facilitated the return of the devolved institutions, see 'New Decade, New Approach', available at assets.publishing.service.gov.uk/government/uploads/system/uploads/attachment_data/file/856998/2020-01-08_a_new_decade__a_new_approach.pdf, discussed below. For the term 'staccato' see *Robinson v Secretary of State for Northern Ireland* [2002] UKHL 32, [2002] NI 390 [7] (Lord Bingham).

[13] [2002] UKHL 32, [2002] NI 390. Note that some earlier schemes for devolution had also been described as constitutional in form: see *Belfast Corporation v OD Cars* [1960] AC 490, 517 (Viscount Simmonds), referencing the Government of Ireland Act 1920 as a 'constitutional Act'. For commentary on *Robinson* see, eg, J Morison and M Lynch, 'Litigating the Agreement: Towards a New Constitutionalism for the UK from Northern Ireland?' in J Morison, K McEvoy and G Anthony (eds), *Judges, Transition and Human Rights: Essays in Memory of Stephen Livingstone* (Oxford, Oxford University Press, 2007) 105.

[14] Section 16 has since been substituted by sections 16A–C.

State for Northern Ireland would have been obliged by section 32(3) of the Act to call fresh Assembly elections at the very moment when there was growing unionist opposition to the Belfast Agreement. In holding that the election of the First and Deputy First Ministers had been lawful, a majority in the House of Lords said that the Northern Ireland Act 1998 should be interpreted 'generously and purposively, bearing in mind the values which the constitutional provisions are intended to embody' and that '[it] is a constitution for Northern Ireland, framed to create a continuing form of government against the background of the history of the territory and the principles agreed in Belfast'.[15] While these comments were to be overtaken by political events that resulted in the imposition of direct rule under the (now repealed) Northern Ireland Act 2000, *Robinson* still elevated the Belfast Agreement and Northern Ireland Act 1998 to a position of very real constitutional importance.[16] In doing so, the case positioned the Act of 1998 alongside a number of other 'constitutional statutes' that had been identified by the courts in England and Wales.[17]

Robinson was, at source, a case about the rules that govern mandatory coalition in Northern Ireland, and these provide the context to Northern Ireland's most recent political difficulties. Although there are many other aspects of the Belfast Agreement that underlie devolution – among them, North–South cooperation, and human rights guarantees – 'consociational' power-sharing between Northern Ireland's two main ethno-national groups is fundamental to its system of government.[18] The basis for such power-sharing begins with the requirement that Members of the Legislative Assembly (MLAs) designate themselves as 'Nationalist', 'Unionist' or 'Other' when signing the roll of membership, where that designation can be key to controlling exercises of power within the Assembly and Executive Committee.[19] While the institutions are (of course) subject to constraints that are paralleled in the other devolved settlements – notably as regards territorial extent, human rights and retained EU law[20] – the designation rules underpin unique blocking mechanisms that are intended to

[15] [2002] UKHL 32, [2002] NI 390 [11] (Lord Bingham), and [25] (Lord Hoffmann).

[16] For subsequent judicial references see, eg, *Re McComb's Application* [2003] NIQB 47 [31]; *Re Coláiste Feirste's Application* [2011] NIQB 98 [22]; *R (Miller) v Secretary of State for Exiting the European* [2017] UKSC 5, [2018] AC 61 [128]; *Re McMahon's Application* [2019] NICA 29 [34]; *De Souza v Secretary of State for the Home Department* [2019] UKUT 355 (IAC) [58]; and *Re JR80* [2019] NICA 58 [5]. For the repeal of the Northern Ireland Act 2000, see Northern Ireland (St Andrews Agreement) Act 2006, Sch 4, para 1, as read with Northern Ireland (St Andrews Agreement) Act 2007, s 1.

[17] *Thoburn v Sunderland CC* [2003] QB 151. For commentary see M Elliott, 'Embracing "Constitutional" Legislation: Towards Fundamental Law?' (2003) 54 *Northern Ireland Legal Quarterly* 25.

[18] On which model see B O'Leary, *A Treatise on Northern Ireland, Volume III: Consociation and Confederation* (Oxford, Oxford University Press, 2019). On North-South Co-operation see Strand Two of the Belfast Agreement, as read with Northern Ireland Act 1998, ss 52A–53 and 55, and Sch 2, para 3(b). On rights see Part 6 of the Belfast Agreement, as read with the Human Rights Act 1998 and Northern Ireland Act 1998, ss 6(2)(c) and 68–70, and Sch 5.

[19] Northern Ireland Act 1998, s 4(5); and Assembly Standing Order 3.

[20] See, eg in relation to legislative competence, Northern Ireland Act 1998, ss 6–6A; Government of Wales Act 2006, ss 108A–109A; and Scotland Act 1998, ss 29–30A.

protect ethno-national interests. The most high-profile such mechanism is the 'petition of concern' under section 42 of the Northern Ireland Act 1998. This mechanism enables 30 MLAs – a minority within an Assembly of 90 members – to petition the Assembly about a measure that is to be voted on and which can thereafter only be passed with 'cross-community support'.[21] Such support is expressly linked to the Act's designation requirements and it means that an impugned measure will be carried only if it has the support of a majority both of Nationalist and Unionist MLAs.[22] While there has recently been political agreement about using the petition less frequently and only when it is triggered by members from two or more political parties,[23] its use to date has often been criticised, partly because it has been used to block matters with no obvious ethno-national association.[24] The law on abortion provides one such example.[25]

Blocking mechanisms also exist in relation to exercises of ministerial power, where departmental portfolios are for the most part allocated on the basis of party political strength, and where ministers have a statutory duty to observe a Ministerial Code.[26] Section 17(3) of the Northern Ireland Act 1998 provides that ministers are to be 'in charge' of their departments, and article 4(1) of the Departments (Northern Ireland) Order 1999 provides that, 'The functions of a department shall at all times be exercised subject to the direction and control of the Minister'.[27] As will be seen below, the meaning of these provisions was central to the *Buick* case on the powers of the civil service and the Court of Appeal's finding that there was an ambiguity in the statutory scheme for devolution. However, the point to be made here concerns the mechanisms that can be used to constrain exercises of ministerial power, where the Executive Committee

[21] The Assembly initially had 108 elected members, but that number was reduced to 90 by the Assembly Members (Reduction of Numbers) Act (Northern Ireland) 2016, s 1.

[22] Northern Ireland Act 1998, s 4(5)–5(A); and Order 3(7) of the Standing Orders of the Assembly. Section 4(5) defines 'cross-community support' as: '(a) the support of a majority of members voting, a majority of the designated Nationalists voting and a majority of the designated Unionists voting; or (b) the support of 60% of the members voting, 40% of the designated Nationalists voting and 40% of the designated Unionists voting'.

[23] See paragraphs 9–13 of, and Annex B to, the 'New Decade, New Approach' agreement (n 12). For earlier agreement on the need to constrain use of the petition, see paras 57–58 of The Stormont House Agreement (2014), available at www.gov.uk/government/publications/the-stormont-house-agreement; and Appendix F3 to the 'Fresh Start Agreement', available at www.gov.uk/government/news/a-fresh-start-for-northern-ireland. For judicial analysis of the role of the petition – here, in the context of a case about same sex-marriage rights – see *Re Close's Application* [2020] NICA 20 [4] and [54].

[24] For commentary see A Schwartz, 'Petitions of Concern', Northern Ireland Assembly Knowledge Exchange Seminar Series, 20 March 2014, available at www.niassembly.gov.uk/globalassets/Documents/RaISe/knowledge_exchange/briefing_papers/series3/schwartz200314.pdf.

[25] See, 'Abortion amendment set to be blocked by petition of concern' BBC News (1 June 2015) available at www.bbc.co.uk/news/uk-northern-ireland-32961428.

[26] Northern Ireland Act 1998, s 18. For the appointment of the First and Deputy First Ministers see s 16A; and for the currently exceptional position in relation to the Minister of Justice see s 21A(3A), as read with the Department of Justice Act (NI) 2010, s 2. On the Ministerial Code, see s 28A; its text is available at www.northernireland.gov.uk/topics/your-executive/ministerial-code.

[27] SI 1999/283.

and the Ministerial Code are of central importance. Taking first the Executive Committee, section 20(3) of the Northern Ireland Act 1998 provides that it is to 'provide a forum for the discussion of, and agreement on, issues which cut across the responsibilities of two or more Ministers'.[28] While this section has since been amended by legislation enacted in the light of *Buick* – the Executive Committee (Functions) Act (Northern Ireland) 2020 – it is still intended to provide the ethno-national groups with a form of control over individual ministers. That position is then embedded by the Ministerial Code, which was placed on a statutory footing after the St Andrews Agreement of 2006. For instance, under section 28B of the Northern Ireland Act 1998, 30 MLAs can again petition the Assembly to express a concern that a ministerial decision would contravene the Ministerial Code or would otherwise relate to a matter of 'public importance'.[29] Moreover, under the Ministerial Code itself, ministers are required to bring to the attention of the Executive Committee decisions that, among other things, cut across departmental interests and/or are significant or controversial.[30] The Code is also required by section 28A(8)(c) of the Northern Ireland Act 1998 to

> provide ... that, if any three members of the Executive Committee require the vote on a particular matter which is to be voted on by the Executive Committee to require cross-community support, any vote on that matter in the Executive Committee shall require cross-community support in the Executive Committee.[31]

The number 'three', in turn, is of particular significance, as the larger parties in the executive typically hold that number of portfolios and are thereby in a position to engage in ethno-national blocking.[32]

The Ministerial Code provides a helpful bridging point to the constitutionalising role of judicial review in Northern Ireland, as there have been a number of cases on its meaning and the obligations of ministers.[33] These have sometimes arisen in the context of inter-departmental/ministerial disputes where the central question has been whether a minister should have brought a particular matter to the attention of the Executive Committee.[34] The details of such cases

[28] This is the effect of section 20(3), as read with para 19 of Strand One of the Belfast Agreement.

[29] Section 28B contains a range of procedural safeguards to prevent abuse of the mechanism: a decision may be referred to the Executive Committee only once; matters of 'public importance' can be referred only after the Presiding Officer has consulted the political parties whose members hold seats in the Assembly; and references must be made within seven days of the decision being taken or, where appropriate, notified to the Assembly.

[30] See para 2.4 of the Code.

[31] And see para 2.12 of the Code.

[32] Para 6 of the 'New Decade, New Approach' agreement (n 12) contains agreement to establish 'a robust, independent enforcement mechanism to deal with breaches of the Ministerial Code'. Details about the precise nature of that mechanism have not, at the time of writing, been published in full.

[33] See, eg, *Re Neeson's Application* [2016] NIQB 58; *Re Central Craigavon's Application* [2011] NICA 17; and *Re Solinas' Application* [2009] NIQB 43.

[34] See, eg, *Re Minister of Enterprise, Trade and Investment's Application* [2017] NICA 28; and *Re Minister for Finance and Personnel's Application* [2013] NIQB 137. *Solinas' Application* (n 33) also raised this issue, but did so in the context of proceedings brought by a private individual.

are perhaps not as important here as the fact that they have been part of a move towards a pronounced form of 'legal constitutionalism' in Northern Ireland.[35] In short, the cases under the Code have been part of a much larger body of litigation on the Belfast Agreement and the Northern Ireland Act 1998 in areas that have included police reform, equal community representation on public bodies, and the legacy of the Northern Ireland conflict.[36] While some of the cases have been deemed 'political' and have resulted in marked judicial restraint, others have raised hard-edged questions of law about the powers and duties of public bodies under the Northern Ireland constitution.[37] The answers that have been given have sometimes had far-reaching implications: not only have the courts held that the political powers have (for instance) failed to discharge some of their duties under the Northern Ireland Act 1998; they have also found breaches of Article 2 ECHR in the context of dealing with Northern Ireland's past.[38]

Of course, this litigation – which has variously been brought by politicians, private individuals, and NGOs – has often reflected political tensions within the institutions and in wider Northern Ireland society. Certainly, the issue of human rights has presented something of a fault line, as the largest political party in the Unionist community has been criticised for opposing measures on, among other things, the legacy of the conflict, Irish language rights, same-sex marriage and abortion reform.[39] While it would be misleading to suggest that opposition to reform has always divided along ethno-national lines – each of the main Christian churches were opposed to same-sex marriage and abortion reform[40] – there have still been very different narratives about the role and relevance of human rights standards. At its height, these have been characterised

[35] On which form of constitutionalism see, eg, P Craig, *UK, EU and Global Administrative Law: Foundations and Challenges* (Cambridge, CUP, 2015) 166–99, and references therein.

[36] For commentary on some earlier case law see G Anthony, 'Public Law Litigation and the Belfast Agreement' (2002) 8 *European Public Law* 401 and G Anthony, 'Judicial Review in Northern Ireland – A Guide to the "Real" Devolution Issues' (2009) 14 *Judicial Review* 230.

[37] For restraint see, eg, *Re Williamson's Application* [2000] NI 281.

[38] On breaches of the Northern Ireland Act 1998 see, eg, *Re CAJ's Application* [2015] NIQB 59 (Executive Committee in breach of s 28E duty to adopt an anti-poverty strategy) and *Re Conradh Na Gaeilge's Application* [2017] NIQB 27 (Executive Committee in breach of s 28D duty to adopt a strategy relating to the enhancement and development of the Irish language). On Art 2 ECHR see, eg, *Re Finucane's Application* [2019] UKSC 7, [2019] NI 292; and B Dickson, *The European Convention on Human Rights and the Conflict in Northern Ireland* (Oxford, OUP, 2010) ch 9.

[39] For commentary on the past in particular see L Mallinder, 'Metaconflict and International Human Rights Law in Dealing with the Past' (2019) 8 *Cambridge International Law Journal* 5. On the dominant party, see J Tonge and others, *The Democratic Unionist Party: From Protest to Power* (Oxford, OUP, 2014).

[40] See, R Hewitt, 'Northern Ireland churches insist same-sex weddings won't be held in places of worship' *Belfast Telegraph* (23 October 2019) available at www.belfasttelegraph.co.uk/news/northern-ireland/northern-ireland-churches-insist-same-sex-weddings-wont-be-held-in-places-of-worship-38621931.html; R Hewitt, 'Figures from across political divide unite to oppose abortion law changes in Northern Ireland' *Belfast Telegraph* (12 December 2019) available at www.belfasttelegraph.co.uk/news/northern-ireland/figures-from-across-political-divide-unite-to-oppose-abortion-law-changes-in-northern-ireland-38776177.html.

by a Nationalist narrative that has sought to elide all matters of rights and to link them to a protean conception of political equality.[41] In the context of a system that allows reforms to be blocked from within the devolved institutions, this inevitably consolidated political differences and came to complicate the very idea of power-sharing.[42] Indeed, while disagreement on rights was not the formal reason for the breakdown in devolved government in 2017 – that was instead caused by a controversial renewable energy scheme[43] – rights were to become central to debates about how power-sharing might be resumed. This was thus the context in which the rulings in *NIHRC* and *Buick* were to be given and in which the development of the post-Quartet judicial role was to be at its most advanced.[44]

III. THE 'PLUS TWO'

A. *NIHRC*

The *NIHRC* case involved a challenge to sections 58 and 59 of the Offences Against the Person Act 1861 and section 25(1) of the Criminal Justice Act (Northern Ireland) 1945, which were impugned as incompatible with Articles 3, 8 and 14 ECHR. The effect of the legislation – which reflected the law as pre-dated the Abortion Act 1967 – was to criminalise abortion in Northern Ireland, save where an abortion was needed to preserve the life of the mother, or where the continuation of a pregnancy would have serious physical or mental implications for the mother.[45] The particular focus in *NIHRC* was on the prohibition of abortion in three categories of cases: (a) serious malformation of the foetus; (b) pregnancy as a result of rape; and (c) pregnancy as a result of incest. Factually, the applicant Commission had relied upon the background point that large numbers of women in these categories were required to travel to England to obtain abortions, in circumstances where opinion polls indicated majority

[41] See Sinn Féin, 'Rights for All', available at www.sinnfein.ie/contents/16428.

[42] On blocking see, eg, G Cross, 'DUP will use veto to block abortion rights in Northern Ireland says Wells' *Belfast Telegraph* (28 May 2018), available at www.belfasttelegraph.co.uk/news/northern-ireland/dup-will-use-veto-to-block-abortion-rights-in-northern-ireland-says-jim-wells-36953043.html; and as regards the past, eg, *Re Hughes' Application* [2018] NIQB 30.

[43] The Renewable Heat Incentive Scheme Regulations (Northern Ireland) 2012 (SR 2012/396); and S McBride, *Burned: The Inside Story of the 'Cash-for-Ash' Scandal and Northern Ireland's Secretive New Elite* (Newbridge, Merrion Press, 2019). An inquiry into the scheme was subsequently was held; see 'The Report of the Independent Public Inquiry into the Non-domestic Renewable Heat Incentive (RHI) Scheme' (13 March 2020), available at www.rhiinquiry.org/sites/rhi/files/media-files/RHI-Inquiry-Report-Volume1-Chapters1-19.pdf.

[44] On the post-Quartet judicial role in relation to rights see further ch 8 in this volume (Bowen).

[45] There had been earlier challenges to aspects of legal regime, notably regarding a lack of guidance for medical professionals: see *Re Family Planning Association of Northern Ireland's Application* [2004] NICA 37–39, [2005] NI 188.

support for reform of the law in Northern Ireland. The applicant had brought the proceedings in its own name acting under sections 69(5)(b) and 71(2B) of the Northern Ireland Act 1998, which provide that it may 'bring proceedings involving law or practice in relation to the protection of human rights' and 'need not be a victim or potential victim of the unlawful act to which the proceedings relate … the Commission may act only if there is or would be one or more victims of the unlawful act'.

The Supreme Court addressed two main issues in its ruling. The first – which might ordinarily have been dispositive of the case – was whether the applicant Commission had standing to bring the proceedings. For a minority of the Court, this was an 'arid question' not just because the Commission could have found and supported women who would have been victims of an unlawful act under the Human Rights Act 1998, but also because section 69(5)(b) could be read as conferring the power to challenge legislation under sections 3 and 4 of the Human Rights Act 1998.[46] However, for a majority, the need for an identifiable victim was key to the legislative scheme, and the Court held that the Commission's case thereby was procedurally compromised. Leading on this point, Lord Mance cross-referred sections 69(5)(b) and 71(2B) to section 7 of the Human Rights Act 1998, which allows a person to bring proceedings under the Act only where they are, or would be, the victim of an unlawful 'act' within the meaning of section 6(1) of the Act.[47] Noting that the term 'act' does not include a failure to introduce or lay before the UK Parliament a proposal for legislation or to make any primary legislation, Lord Mance held that the Commission's powers could not include the power to engage in the abstract review of primary legislation as defined by the Human Rights Act 1998.[48] Nor was its position improved by challenging devolved legislation in the form of the 1945 Act: while a failure on the part of the Northern Ireland Assembly to repeal or amend the 1945 Act might well be an 'act' within the meaning of section 6(1) of the Human Rights Act 1998, the victim requirement remained.[49]

The second issue – which was addressed because it had 'been fully argued' and because it would 'be unrealistic and unhelpful to refuse to express' conclusions[50] – was the compatibility of the legislation. Here, a majority of the Court (which on this point included Lord Mance) considered that the legislation was incompatible with Article 8 ECHR in each of the three categories of cases, with two judges (Lords Kerr and Wilson) also holding that it was incompatible with Article 3 ECHR. The Court's engagement with this issue inevitably took it towards questions about institutional competence and whether value judgements

[46] [2018] UKSC 27, [2018] NI 228 [11]–[18] (Lady Hale) and [2018] NI 228 [168]–[213] (Lord Kerr, with whom Lord Wilson agreed).
[47] ibid [48]–[73].
[48] ibid [61]. For the meaning of 'act' see Human Rights Act 1998, s 6(6).
[49] [2018] UKSC 27, [2018] NI 228 [72].
[50] ibid [42(c)] (Lord Mance).

about abortion would better be left to the devolved institutions in Northern Ireland. On this point, the Court noted that the Assembly had been considering the matter of reform prior to the breakdown of power-sharing and that it had established a working group to prepare a report on the matter.[51] However, the Court also noted that the subsequent political impasse in Northern Ireland meant that no progress had been made on the issue and that it was unclear when the institutions would return.[52] For Lady Hale, this was a point of only secondary importance, as she considered 'that this is not a matter on which the democratic legislature enjoys a unique competence. It is a matter of fundamental human rights on which … the courts are as well qualified to judge as is the legislature'.[53] Lord Kerr likewise was of the view that the Court could legitimately play a role and that the question of 'usurping the function of the decision-maker … simply does not arise'.[54] Noting some of the uncertainties in party-political positions on the issue of abortion reform, he implied that the Court may have had a role to play even if the institutions had been sitting. As he put it: 'The courts should feel no sense of inhibition in relation to the question of whether the current law offends Article 8 of the Convention, in the light of the absence of any firmly expressed view of the democratic institutions of Northern Ireland'.[55]

The Supreme Court's ruling has since been the subject of strident criticism in an article by David Campbell and James Allan.[56] Describing it as 'a procedural innovation which was … extraordinary', they suggest that the ruling 'was the latest of a number of such innovations which … are the means by which judicial supremacy is now being surreptitiously created in the United Kingdom'.[57] Their fundamental objection to the ruling was that it amounted to an exercise in abstract review, even though the majority had ruled that such review was not possible under the relevant provisions of the Northern Ireland Act 1998 and the Human Rights Act 1998. Noting that, 'One cannot really say that [the Court] found the legislation to be incompatible because their descriptions were categorically and deliberately *obiter*', they nevertheless comment that there is 'no point speaking of possible legal limits because the example set … is to ignore legal limits even when acknowledged'.[58] Taking their point to its height, they argue that a procedurally flawed application was still heard by the Supreme Court, which 'told parties *in advance* what is very likely to be the result of future

[51] ibid [109] (Lord Mance).
[52] ibid [117] (Lord Mance).
[53] ibid [38].
[54] ibid [295].
[55] ibid.
[56] Campbell and Allan, 'Procedural Innovation' (2019).
[57] ibid 348. They also analyse, in similar vein, *Simmons v Castle* [2012] EWCA Civ 1039 and [2012] EWCA Civ 1288, [2013] 1 WLR 1239, and *R (Miller) v Secretary of State for Exiting the European Union* [2017] UKSC 5, [2018] AC 61.
[58] ibid 361 and 362.

litigation of matters never properly brought before the court'.[59] The result was that *NIHRC* was 'not adjudication as adjudication has previously been understood in constitutional theory and practice ... It [was] adjudication in advance; that is, it [was] not adjudication at all'.[60]

Campbell and Allan finish their article by stating that their critique is not 'focused on the desirability or otherwise of the courts actively seeking to involve themselves in undeniably "political" cases', though they add that they 'would not wish to dissimulate over [their] intense opposition' to such involvement.[61] For the purposes of this chapter, this is perhaps the most telling of the comments that they make. As was noted in the introduction, this chapter argues that there will be occasions when the courts ought to adopt a more interventionist approach on matters of public interest, notably when there are manifest failings in the other branches of the state. For Campbell and Allan, such an approach could presumably never be justified, particularly if the legitimacy of the legal process is taken to depend upon strict adherence to procedural rules and recognition that law and politics perform separate constitutional functions.[62] However, for other commentators, such a limited role for the law is neither necessary nor justifiable, notably where there is a need to safeguard individual freedom and autonomy.[63] While such arguments are (of course) contestable, they identify judicial review as a central part of the constitution rather than a remedy that merely exists underneath it.[64] Seen in this way, *NIHRC* perhaps did nothing more than signpost how fundamental rights were to be protected in the absence of definitive legislative engagement with the issue.

B. *Buick*

The central issue in the *Buick* case has already been outlined above, viz, whether civil servants could lawfully take decisions in the absence of Northern Ireland ministers (none of whom had taken office after Assembly elections held on 2 March 2017). The case arose when the most senior civil servant in the Department for Infrastructure took a decision, under section 26 of the Planning Act (Northern Ireland) 2011, to grant planning permission for a waste incinerator on the outskirts of Belfast. The planning application in question had been made before the political impasse had started, and two ministers – who had been from different political parties – had taken an active interest in it whilst they had been

[59] ibid 364.

[60] ibid. Campbell and Allan (n 8) reference at (fn 43) subsequent litigation brought in the name of Sarah Ewart: see *Re Ewart's Application* [2019] NIQB 88 and [2020] NIQB 33.

[61] ibid.

[62] For argument to this effect see, eg, C Harlow, 'Public Law and Popular Justice' (2002) 65 *MLR* 1.

[63] See, eg, TRS Allan, *The Sovereignty of Law: Freedom, Constitution and Common Law* (Oxford, OUP, 2013).

[64] Sedley, *Lions* (2015).

in post. However, by the time the decision was made, there had been no ministerial oversight for some eight months, and the senior civil servant considered that it was in the public interest for him to act. He did so after consulting with officials from the Department of Agriculture, Environment and Rural Affairs, and relied on the fact that decisions under section 26 of the Act of 2011 concern 'developments of regional significance' within the 'Department's jurisdiction'.[65]

The application for judicial review came to focus on the meaning of article 4(1) of the Departments (Northern Ireland) Order 1999, as read with, among other provisions, section 17(3) of the Northern Ireland Act 1998. As already noted, article 4(1) provides that, 'The functions of a department shall at all times be exercised subject to the direction and control of the Minister', while section 17(3) refers to ministers being 'in charge' of their departments. The applicant argued that these provisions meant that civil servants could take decisions only when ministers are in place – where 'direction and control' underscores 'democratic accountability' – and also that the inter-departmental consultation meant that the decision was 'cross-cutting' and ought to have been brought to the Executive Committee under the Ministerial Code. The respondent's reply, in turn, rested upon three main points: (i) that departments are bodies corporate that exist at one remove from ministers and have free-standing powers of decision where powers are vested in them (as per the example of section 26 of the Planning Act (Northern Ireland) 2011);[66] (ii) that section 16A of the Northern Ireland Act 1998 includes a 14-day period for filling ministerial posts after Assembly elections and that the process of government continues during that time;[67] and (iii) that the UK Parliament had impliedly authorised decision-making in the absence of ministers because it had recently enacted budgetary legislation that would require decision-making on the part of Northern Ireland departments.[68]

The application for judicial review was granted in the High Court, where Keegan J held that the natural and ordinary meaning of article 4(1) rendered the planning decision unlawful and that the respondent's argument faced the 'formidable obstacle of democratic accountability'.[69] On appeal to the Court of Appeal it was likewise held that the decision was unlawful, though the reasoning of the majority differed from that in the court below.[70] Stating that article 4

[65] The words are used in the heading to s 26.

[66] Article 5(1) of the Departments (NI) Order 1999 reads: 'A department shall be a body corporate'.

[67] Northern Ireland Act 1998, s 16A: '(1) This section applies where an Assembly is elected under section 31 or 32. (2) All Northern Ireland Ministers shall cease to hold office. (3) Within a period of 14 days beginning with the first meeting of the Assembly (a) the offices of First Minister and deputy First Minister shall be filled … (b) the Ministerial offices to be held by the Northern Ireland Ministers shall be filled'.

[68] The Northern Ireland Budget Act 2017 and the Northern Ireland Budget (Anticipation and Adjustments) Act 2018.

[69] [2018] NIQB 43 [40], referencing Sir Paul Girvan's ruling in *Re Hughes' Application* [2018] NIQB 30 [67]–[68].

[70] [2018] NICA 26.

was ambiguous when placed in its wider statutory setting, Morgan LCJ and Stephens LJ held that the illegality lay in the fact that the decision was cross-cutting within the meaning of the Ministerial Code. This left the broader question of whether there were decisions which could lawfully be taken by civil servants, where the majority stated that 'any decision which as a matter of convention or otherwise would normally go before the Minister for approval lies beyond the competence of a senior civil servant in the absence of a Minister'.[71] Treacy LJ dissented on this point and preferred Keegan J's reading of article 4:

> The default position contended for by the Department is profoundly undemocratic. If correct Departments in NI would be empowered, in breach of fundamental constitutional principle, to act without being accountable to Ministers. This would be a striking consequence for [the Belfast Agreement] which was intended to usher in a new era of accountable governance and power sharing … Even if Article 4(1) were ambiguous it ought to be construed consistently with established constitutional principle and the Agreement.[72]

IV. GOVERNMENT BY DEFAULT

It was suggested in the introduction to this chapter that *NIHRC* and *Buick* might best be thought of in terms of a process of 'government by default'; that is, a process whereby the courts identify gaps in the constitution that are later addressed by legislation enacted at Westminster. Certainly, as regards *NIHRC*, the Supreme Court moved to isolate of an area of law in which Northern Ireland was perceived to have fallen behind other national systems and in which it had drawn international censure (the Court referred to, among other things, recent changes in the Irish Constitution and a report from the UN's Committee for the Elimination of Discrimination Against Women (CEDAW)).[73] While it is, of course, possible to analyse the Court's ruling in terms of institutional 'dialogue' under the Human Rights Act 1998, the case also had implications for debates about rights in Northern Ireland and hence the terms for any possible return to devolved government.[74] Moreover, in terms of *Buick*, the approach of the majority in the Court of Appeal was one that recognised the constitutional difficulties in the case whilst accepting (perhaps for reasons of pragmatism) that civil servants needed some degree of decision-making authority. The alternative

[71] ibid [56].

[72] [2018] NICA 26 [64] and [67]. Note that the Attorney-General for Northern Ireland subsequently referred to the Supreme Court a number of questions related to the powers of the civil service in the absence of ministers, but the Court declined to hear them: [2019] UKSC 1.

[73] [2018] UKSC 27, [2018] NI 228 [27] (Lady Hale) and [120] (Lord Mance).

[74] See M Enright, K McNeilly and F de Londras, 'Abortion activism, legal change, and taking feminist law work seriously' (2020) 71 *Northern Ireland Legal Quarterly* OA7. On inter-institutional dialogue under the HRA see A Young, *Democratic Dialogue and the Constitution* (Oxford, OUP, 2017), esp ch 7.

would have been to read Article 4(1) as precluding any such authority in its entirety, in circumstances where historical experience pointed towards 'direct rule' from Westminster as a proxy means for 'direction and control'.[75] However, the political problem with that option was that it would have alienated nationalist opinion in Northern Ireland and potentially complicated any commitment to return to power-sharing.[76] *Buick* was thus a ruling that had the (inadvertent?) effect of allowing some form of governance to continue whilst avoiding a heightened constitutional crisis.

The issues of abortion reform and civil service decision-making were subsequently addressed in the Northern Ireland (Executive Formation and Exercise of Functions) Act 2018. This Act, which was supplemented by a further Executive Formation etc Act 2019, extended the period of time during which ministerial positions could be filled up until 13 January 2020, and also consolidated the powers of the Northern Ireland departments.[77] This was the effect of section 3 of the Act, which provided that senior officers in departments could exercise functions during the extended period 'if satisfied that it is in the public interest' to do so, and notwithstanding that a matter would ordinarily be brought to the Executive Committee.[78] While any such exercise of functions was to have regard for guidance issued by the Secretary of State, the power of decision was otherwise to 'have effect despite anything in the [Northern Ireland Act 1998 or the Order of 1999] that would prevent decisions being taken'.[79] The issue of abortion, in turn, was addressed in section 4, which referenced the need 'to address the matters identified by recent, current and future court proceedings in relation to the human rights of the people of Northern Ireland'. In the absence of ministers, section 4 imposed on the Secretary of State a duty to issue guidance about how departments might exercise their functions in the light of (in effect) *NIHRC* when providing and managing public services. Section 4 also imposed a similar duty in relation to the marriage rights of same-sex couples – another issue that had been in political dispute before and during the impasse.[80]

[75] See, eg, para 4(1)(f) of the Schedule to the (now repealed) Northern Ireland Act 2000.

[76] 'We will not be intimidated by the threat of direct rule: Sinn Féin' *Belfast Telegraph* (14 March 2019), available at www.belfasttelegraph.co.uk/news/northern-ireland/we-will-not-be-intimidated-by-threat-of-direct-rule-sinn-fein-37911651.html.

[77] On the extension of time see Executive Formation Etc Act 2018, ss 1–2, as read with Executive Formation Etc Act 2018, ss 1–2, and Northern Ireland (Extension of Period for Executive Formation) Regulations 2019 (SI 2019/616) and Northern Ireland (Extension of Period for Executive Formation) Regulations 2019 (No 2) (SI 2019/1364).

[78] Note that s 3 also safeguarded decisions that had previously been taken during the impasse, save where legal proceedings in respect of decisions were ongoing. Even then, nothing prevented 'the re-exercise of the function in the same way' under the Act: see s 3(4)–(6).

[79] And see, 'Guidance on decision-making for Northern Ireland Departments during the period for Northern Ireland Executive formation', 5 November 2018, available at assets.publishing.service.gov.uk/government/uploads/system/uploads/attachment_data/file/754029/Cm9725_Guidance_on_decision-making_for_NI_Dpts.pdf.

[80] Guidance was to issue on 'the incompatibility of the human rights of the people of Northern Ireland with the continued enforcement of section 13(e) of the Matrimonial Causes (Northern Ireland) Order 1978': Executive Formation Etc Act 2018, s 4(1)(b). Note that the issue of same sex

The Acts of 2018 and 2019 could never provide a long-term solution for constitutional governance in Northern Ireland, and the Court of Appeal was later to say that: 'the present arrangements do not provide good governance for Northern Ireland, they are not democratic and have led to government by civil servants with only an attenuated degree of accountability'.[81] The Court's comments were made in a case in which the victims of historical institutional abuse sought a remedy that would require either civil servants or the Secretary of State for Northern Ireland to implement recommendations about the payment of compensation for harms suffered.[82] That issue, whilst ultimately addressed in a discrete piece of legislation enacted at Westminster,[83] was one of a number that had shown how the absence of ministers was affecting the performance of public duties, and political talks about re-entering government were occurring against that backdrop. Indeed, the Northern Ireland (Executive Formation etc) Act 2019 came to include a requirement that the Secretary of State should lay reports before the UK Parliament that explained the progress that had been made towards the formation of an Executive in Northern Ireland. The list of matters on which he was to report was lengthy and included not only compensation for institutional abuse, but also matters related to Northern Ireland's troubled past (for instance, the prosecution of army veterans) and its future (for instance, gambling, and libel law). It was, in other words, a constitutional 'to do' list that revealed just how far governance in Northern Ireland had started to drift.

The 2019 Act also contained a much more controversial provision on reform of the law of abortion (as well as a new provision on same-sex marriage).[84] The Act here provided that, in the event that an Executive were not formed by 21 October 2019, sections 58 and 59 of the Offences Against the Person Act 1861 would be repealed and the Secretary of State would come under a duty to make regulations to 'ensure that the recommendations in paragraphs 85 and 86 of the CEDAW report are implemented in respect of Northern Ireland'.[85] The corresponding controversy lay in the fact that Westminster had authorised the Secretary of State to make subordinate legislation in an area of devolved competence and, of course, on a matter that animated very different moral and ethical viewpoints.[86] However, it was also the case that the legislative deadline of 21 October 2019 meant that the Secretary of State's duty need not inevitably come into force and that the matter could thereby revert to the Northern

marriage rights had also been litigated through the courts: *Re Close's Application* [2020] NICA 20. For commentary see C McCormick and T Stewart, 'The Legalisation of Same-Sex Marriage in Northern Ireland' (2020) 71 *Northern Ireland Legal Quarterly* OA21.

[81] *Re JR80's Application* [2019] NICA 58 [109].

[82] Report of the Historical Institutional Abuse Inquiry, available at www.hiainquiry.org.

[83] Historical Institutional Abuse (Northern Ireland) Act 2019.

[84] Executive Formation etc Act 2019, ss 8–9.

[85] Executive Formation etc Act 2019, s 9, as read with s 13(4).

[86] N O'Loan, 'Abortion vote in Westminster was a denial of democracy' *Irish News* (8 August 2019) available at www.irishnews.com/news/northernirelandnews/2019/08/08/news/platform-abortion-vote-in-westminster-was-a-denial-of-democracy-1680031.

Ireland institutions, should they begin sitting before that date. In the event, that did not happen: the necessary agreement on an Executive was not reached until 8 January 2020 and the relevant changes to the law of abortion (and same sex-marriage) had by that time been made.[87]

V. CONCLUSION

This chapter began by noting that judicial review can perform a constitutionalising function and that, in the particular circumstances of Northern Ireland, some rulings have been given *in extremis*. Its central point has been that the courts can legitimately perform that function on matters of public interest, notably where there are failings in the other branches of the state. While arguments of this kind are not specific to Northern Ireland – Lord Woolf has previously written about judicial review more broadly and how it can bring balance to the constitution[88] – it is an argument that assumes an added dimension in that context. Fully representative government under the Northern Ireland constitution has, in short, only ever been a 'staccato' endeavour, and complex constitutional rules mean that Northern Ireland's political institutions can be afflicted by stasis almost by design.[89] It is, thus, a constitutional setting in which only the courts have existed as a constant and in which litigation has sometimes been a proxy means for political engagement.[90]

At the time of writing, the Northern Ireland political institutions continue to function, and legislative and administrative choices are being made within more recognisable democratic parameters. This perhaps raises the question of whether the balance of power under the Northern Ireland constitution should now change, in the sense that a more engaged political branch should lead the courts to exercise an increased level of restraint. In this regard, the Executive Committee (Functions) Act (Northern Ireland) 2020 – which was enacted in the light of the cross-cutting element of the *Buick* case – may reveal something about any future balance. On its face, the 2020 Act seeks to safeguard decision-making powers under the Planning Act (Northern Ireland) 2011 by providing that such decisions need not be brought before the Executive Committee.[91] However, in making this change, the Act has arguably also narrowed the scope for challenging other ministerial decisions that cut across departmental interests

[87] Abortion (Northern Ireland) Regulations 2020 (SI 2020/345), as revoked and replaced by Abortion (Northern Ireland) (No 2) Regulations 2020 (SI 2020/503); and Marriage (Same-sex Couples) and Civil Partnership (Opposite-sex Couples) (Northern Ireland) Regulations 2019 (SI 2019/1514). For the agreement that resulted in the formation of an Executive see, 'New Decade, New Approach' (n 12).

[88] Woolf, 'Tensions' (1998).

[89] For the term 'staccato' see *Robinson v Secretary of State for Northern Ireland* [2002] UKHL 32, [2002] NI 390 [7] (Lord Bingham).

[90] See nn 34–39 above, and text.

[91] Executive Committee (Functions) Act (Northern Ireland) 2020, s 2(7).

by providing that any effects on other ministers must be 'more than incidental' and that this test will not be met simply because 'there is a statutory requirement to consult' another minister.[92] The enactment of this provision met with some unionist opposition as it was thought that it might lessen the scope for ethno-national control within the Executive Committee, even though the unionist leadership emphasised that that would not be the outcome.[93] Given these different understandings of the 2020 Act, it might be expected that the courts will to continue to play a dominant role under the Constitution whether in terms of hearing challenges to planning decisions and/or in terms of giving meaning to phrases such as 'more than incidental'.

Of course, any argument in favour of the courts performing such a task rests upon normative assumptions about the judicial role and the merit of judicial activism and/or legal constitutionalism and/or common law constitutionalism.[94] Such labels have animated debates about the changing judicial role since the time of the Quartet, where the opposite approach would prefer a model of democracy centred much more immediately on political institutions and with only a minimal, residuary role for the courts.[95] This latter approach would undoubtedly be preferred by Campbell and Allan, whose concerns about *NIHRC* focused upon a presumed disregard of procedural rules and established approaches to adjudication. However, given Northern Ireland's political setting, it is unclear if NIHRC should really be seen in those terms, precisely because the democratic model that supports restraint was largely absent in Northern Ireland at the time of the ruling. Indeed, even with the post-*Buick* resumption of power-sharing in early 2020, government in Northern Ireland has simply returned to a model of democracy that seeks to accommodate ethno-national division. If that feature of its constitution continues to require judicial intervention, the courts may be doing nothing more than safeguarding Northern Ireland's complex democratic settlement.

[92] Executive Committee (Functions) Act (Northern Ireland) 2020, s 2(8)–(9).

[93] R Bullick, 'The DUP won key safeguards for unionism at St Andrews, yet now the party seems to be sleepwalking into removing them', Newsletter, 24 July 2020, available at www.newsletter.co.uk/news/opinion/columnists/richard-bullick-dup-won-key-safeguards-unionism-st-andrews-yet-now-party-seems-be-sleepwalking-removing-them-2923348.

[94] On such debates see, eg, B Dickson (eds), *Judicial Activism in Common Law Supreme Courts* (Oxford, OUP, 2007) and Sir J Laws, *The Common Law Constitution* (Cambridge, CUP, 2015).

[95] A leading account remains R Bellamy, *Political Constitutionalism: A Republican Defence of the Constitutionality of Democracy* (Cambridge, CUP, 2007).

Part V

Comparative Perspectives on the Quartet

13

Israeli Administrative Law and the Quartet – One Step Ahead

DAPHNE BARAK-EREZ

I. INTRODUCTION

TRADITIONALLY, THE STUDY of legal relationships between colonial powers and their former territories focused on the influence the 'parent system' has had on the 'offspring' legal systems, which were once subject to colonial control. This method assumes a centre–periphery relationship, with a one-direction inspiration, a notion that is embedded in the concept of 'legal transplants'.[1] Accordingly, jurists engaged in the study of these systems have been interested in researching the parent legal system as well as other 'sibling' systems (that is, other legal systems that have emerged under the auspices of the same colonial power). In contrast to this tradition, I would like to concentrate on the lessons that, sometimes, the parent system can learn from its 'offspring'. In other words, the new systems that developed under the umbrella of the colonial power may also offer an interesting vantage point into the parent system. This insight may show directions of legal development that were not entirely explored by the parent system, especially since the colonies were not burdened by the centuries of legal tradition and *stare decisis* which have shaped the parent system.

I demonstrate this argument by taking a closer look at the development of Israeli administrative law. In general, Israeli administrative law is based on the principles of English law. The process of adopting and transplanting these principles in Mandatory Palestine was primarily accomplished through two important provisions of the Palestine Order in Council, 1922. First, article 46 of this Order in Council stated that courts are called to decide legal questions to

[1] See A Watson, *Legal Transplants: An Approach to Comparative Law*, 2nd edn (Athens, University of Georgia Press, 1993). See also generally H Spamann, 'Contemporary Legal Transplants: Legal Families and the Diffusion of (Corporate) Law' [2009] *Brigham Young University Law Review* 1813.

which there is no answer in local law by using the principles of English common law and equity.[2] Second, article 43 of the same Order in Council established the Supreme Court of the land and authorised it to function as a High Court of Justice, based on the model of the High Court of Justice in the UK (even borrowing its name), with the power to issue prerogative orders against the Government.[3]

During the years of the British Mandate, judicial decisions gradually adopted principles of English administrative law and influenced the local professional community with its precepts. These decisions covered a wide range of doctrines from English administrative law, including questions relating to the authorisation to act (the ultra vires doctrine), as well as to the appropriateness of administrative discretion and administrative process in general.[4] This process of importing English administrative law was enhanced by what is now known as the 'Anglification' of the law of Palestine during that period, which also occurred in other branches of law.[5]

[2] Palestine Order in Council 1922, Art 46: 'The jurisdiction of the Civil Courts shall be exercised in conformity with the Ottoman Law in force in Palestine on November 1st, 1914, and such later Ottoman Laws as have been or may be declared to be in force by Public Notice, and such Orders in Council, Ordinances and regulations as are in force in Palestine at the date of the commencement of this Order, or may hereafter be applied or enacted; and subject thereto and so far as the same shall not extend or apply, shall be exercised in conformity with the substance of the common law, and the doctrines of equity in force in England, and with the powers vested in and according to the procedure and practice observed by or before Courts of Justice and Justices of the Peace in England, according to their respective jurisdictions and authorities at that date, save in so far as the said powers, procedure and practice may have been or may hereafter be modified, amended or replaced by any other provisions. Provided always that the said common law and doctrines of equity shall be in force in Palestine so far only as the circumstances of Palestine and its inhabitants and the limits of His Majesty's jurisdiction permit and subject to such qualification as local circumstances render necessary.'

[3] Palestine Order in Council, Art 43: 'There shall be established a Court to be called the Supreme Court of which the constitution shall be prescribed by Ordinance. The Supreme Court sitting as a Court of Appeal shall have jurisdiction subject to the provisions of any Ordinance to hear appeals from all judgments given by a District Court in first instance or by the Court of Criminal Azzize or by a Land Court. The Supreme Court sitting as a High Court of Justice, shall have jurisdiction to hear and determine such matters as are not causes or trials, but petitions or applications not within the jurisdiction of any other Court and necessary to be decided for the administration of justice.'). On the basis of this provision, the powers of the court were defined also by the Courts Ordinance, enacted in 1924. Section 6 to this ordinance stated: 'The High Court of Justice shall have exclusive jurisdiction in the following matters – (a) applications (in nature of habeas corpus proceedings) for orders of release of persons unlawfully detained in custody; (b) orders directed to public officers or public bodies in regard to the performance of their public duties and requiring them to do or refrain from doing certain acts.'

[4] See eg HC 69/25 *Federman v Sir Ronald Storrs, District Commissioner, Jerusalem – Southern District*, 1 PLR 57 (1920–1933); HC 78/38 *Havkin v Inspector General of Police and Prisons*, 7 PLR 35 (1940); HC 9/38 *Weinberg v District Commissioner, Jerusalem District*, 5 PLR (1938); HC 76/39 *Abir Company Ltd v Inspector-General of Police and Prisons*, 7 PLR 31 (1940); HC 3/42 *Ben-Ami v Local Council Kfar Yona*, 9 PLR 75 (1942).

[5] See generally D Friedman, 'The Effect of Foreign Law on the Law of Israel: Remnant of the Ottoman Period' (1975) 10 *Israel Law Review* 192; D Friedman, 'The Effect of Foreign Law on the Law of Israel: Infusion of the Common Law into the Legal System of Israel' (1975) 10 *Israel*

Against this background I argue that the Israeli Supreme Court's flexibility in applying the principles inherited from England enabled it to develop the potential ingrained in them in a manner that preceded developments in English administrative law.

More specifically, this chapter analyses the so-called 'Quartet' decisions – four monumental English law decisions that are believed to symbolise the revival of English administrative law during the 1960s – *Ridge v Baldwin*,[6] *Padfield v Minister of Agriculture*,[7] *Conway v Rimmer*[8] and *Anisminic v Foreign Compensation Commission*.[9] This chapter illustrates that the Israeli Supreme Court developed similar principles years prior to those adopted by the Quartet. In this way, Israeli administrative law, at the time, portended future developments in English administrative law. This was possible due to the fact that Israeli jurisprudence was based on similar principles, but, at the same point in history, was less burdened by the tendency to respect tradition. In fact, the duty to follow classic English precedents was relaxed by the fact that the Israeli system was an independent system, free to choose its routes of development.

To some extent the perspective offered here fits with scholarship that has already made the argument that legal ideas do not always flow in one direction from the parent to the offspring system. Colonial legal systems sometimes served as 'laboratories' for testing new ideas and reforms which were later imported into the parent system.[10] Here, however, the emphasis is somewhat different. I do not argue that the Israeli system served as an example for the Quartet decisions, but rather that it demonstrated the potential for change embedded in the English system.

II. ENGLISH ADMINISTRATIVE LAW AND THE FOUNDATIONS OF ISRAELI ADMINISTRATIVE LAW

The legacy of English administrative law continued to be influential in Israel after Israel's independence in 1948. Despite the fact that at its founding Israel perceived itself as an independent state that did not function as a continuation of

Law Review 324. For more background on the legal system in Mandatory Palestine, see generally R Shamir, *The Colonies of Law: Colonialism, Zionism and Law in Early Mandate Palestine* (Cambridge, CUP, 2000); R Harris, A Kedar, P Lahav and A Likhovski (eds), *The History of Law in a Multi-Cultural Society: Israel 1917–1967* (Aldershot, Dartmouth, 2002); A Likhovski, *Law and Identity in Mandate Palestine* (Chapel Hill, University of North Carolina Press, 2006).

6 *Ridge v Baldwin* [1964] AC 40 (HL).

7 *Padfield v Minister of Agriculture* [1968] AC 997 (HL).

8 *Conway v Rimmer* [1968] AC 910 (HL).

9 *Anisminic v Foreign Comp Commission* [1969] 2 AC 147 (HL).

10 See eg E Kolsky, 'Codification and the Rule of Colonial Difference: Criminal Procedure in British India' (2003) 23 *Law and History Review* 631.

Mandatory Palestine, for practical purposes Israel made the decision to absorb the former system subject to 'modifications as may result from the establishment of the State and its authorities' (an exception that was supposed to serve as a 'safety valve').[11] The result has been an almost total absorption of the law of Mandatory Palestine.[12]

Despite the fact that English administrative law served as the ultimate point of reference for the Israeli Supreme Court in developing its case law, the establishment of Israel as an independent state qualified its use. As demonstrated by the cases discussed below, the Court made it clear that, Israel, as an independent state, did not regard itself as bound by all the details of the English doctrines.[13] Therefore, the Court allowed itself to be innovative and set new rules when certain English precedents were considered to be too rigid or unjust. This was an especially important policy to adopt since English administrative law found itself at the time in a comparatively gloomy position, saddled with the restrained attitude of the courts during World War II.[14]

III. THE PROPHECY OF THE QUARTET IN ISRAEL

I will now turn to each of the cases included in the famous 'Quartet' of English administrative law decisions and show how each was preceded by Israeli case law.

A. *Ridge v Baldwin*

Ridge v Baldwin, the first modern English case to acknowledge the right to be heard in administrative proceedings, without limiting it to judicial and quasi-judicial ones, was decided in 1963. It was preceded by an Israeli case, *Berman v Minister of Interior*,[15] decided in 1958. In this decision, the Israeli Supreme

[11] Law and Administration Ordinance 1948, s 11 (Israel): 'The law which existed in Palestine on the 5th Iyar, 5708 (14th May 1948) shall remain in force, insofar as there is nothing therein repugnant to this Ordinance or to the other laws which may be enacted by or on behalf of the Provisional Council of State, and subject to such modifications as may result from the establishment of the State and its authorities.'

[12] See generally A Likhovski, 'Between Mandate and State: On the Periodization of Israeli Legal History' (1998) 19 *Journal of Israeli History* 39.

[13] It should be mentioned that even during the time of the British Mandate, the absorption of English law was subject to adaptations. See A Likhovski, 'In Our Image: Colonial Discourse and the Anglicization of the Law of Mandatory Palestine' (1995) 29 *Israel Law Review* 291. The tendency towards legal independence and innovation has, however, greatly intensified since the establishment of the state.

[14] See eg *Liversidge v Anderson* [1942] AC 206 (HL).

[15] HCJ 3/58 *Berman v Minister of Interior*, 12 PD 1493 (1958) (Israel) (translated in 3 Selected Judgments 29 (1958–1960)) (citations are to the translation).

Court introduced the same rule, stating that individuals have the right to be heard irrespective of the definition of the proceedings as either 'administrative', 'judicial' or 'quasi-judicial.' The *Berman* case dealt with a decision of the Israeli Minister of Interior to move the municipal area of a neighbourhood from one city to another. One of the main arguments presented to the Court was that the Minister of Interior had not heard the residents of the neighbourhood who opposed the change. Initially, the Court considered several tests in deciding whether the decision of the minister had been 'quasi-judicial'.[16] However, it later went on to state the following:

> [A]ccording to the rule adhered to by the common law for some hundreds of years, an administrative body – even one that is purely administrative (not quasi-judicial) – will not be permitted to attack the citizen in his person, property, occupation, status and the like, unless he is given a reasonable opportunity to be heard in defence against the contemplated act. The scope of the duty and the form of the opportunity will, of course, depend upon the concrete circumstances of any given matter.[17]

The Court stated that it was fully aware that, 'in very recent years there have been two English decisions which diverge considerably from the above principle' but believed, 'that precisely because of the wide divergence this is only a temporary and passing phase' and English courts would eventually return to the 'traditional line'.[18]

Thus, because the Court did not feel bound by the English decisions that deviated from tradition, it was able to fully realise the essence of English common law and implement it. The result was a clear precedent stating that no administrative body may deprive people of their rights or protected interests without giving them an opportunity to be heard.

B. *Padfield v Minister of Agriculture*

Padfield v Minister of Agriculture, decided in England in 1968, held that administrative discretion is not absolute and is, in principle, subject to judicial review. In contrast, the Israeli Supreme Court rejected the concept of absolute discretion, which shields administrative decisions from judicial review, several years before *Padfield*, in the *Kardosh v Registrar of Companies* decision.[19] In this case, the Court dealt with a petition against a decision made by the Registrar of Companies, who refused to register a company as requested by the

[16] ibid 41–44.
[17] ibid 46.
[18] ibid 47.
[19] HCJ 241/60 *Kardosh v Registrar of Companies*, 15 PD 1151 (1961) (Israel) (translated in 4 Selected Judgments 7 (1961–1962)) (citations are to the translation).

petitioner (with several other individuals). Those who made the request were individuals who belonged to a group that called itself El-Ard and was regarded as hostile to the state of Israel. The Registrar claimed that he was free to make this decision since according to the statutory provision in the relevant legislation (the Companies Ordinance) he had 'absolute discretion' regarding registration requests of companies. The Supreme Court, in a majority decision, accepted the petition and ordered the registration of the company since the Registrar weighed considerations that he was not authorised to take into account. The Court found that the 'absolute discretion' of the Registrar was not immune from effective judicial review. This decision was later approved in a procedure known as a 'further hearing', under which cases that raise novel legal questions are reheard by an enlarged panel.[20]

C. *Conway v Rimmer*

Conway v Rimmer, decided in England in 1968, stated that immunity from disclosing government documents in judicial proceedings is not absolute, but rather, subject to judicial review. It reversed the earlier precedent set in *Duncan v Cammell Laird*,[21] which initially gave the Government the 'last word' on the immunity issue. In contrast, the Israeli Supreme Court had declined to follow the *Duncan* holding 10 years before in its *Haetzni v Ben Gurion* decision.[22] In *Haetzni*, the Israeli Supreme Court rejected the possibility of awarding the Government absolute immunity. This view was adopted in proceedings that were highly sensitive as they involved allegations of corruption directed at Amos Ben Gurion, the son of Prime Minister Ben Gurion, a high-ranking police officer at the time. Amos Ben Gurion sued individuals who accused him of corruption and the defendants, in turn, demanded the disclosure of official government documents they believed would assist them in the proceedings. In fact, the Supreme Court rejected the *Duncan* precedent, finding that it did not suit the Israeli legal system, where there was no room for concepts such as royal prerogative.[23]

[20] FH 16/61 *Registrar of Companies v Kardosh*, 16 PD 1209 (1962) (Israel) (translated in 4 Selected Judgments 32 (1961–1962)) (citations are to the translation). See also R Harris, 'State Identity, Territorial Integrity and Party Banning: The Case of a Pan-Arab Political Party in Israel' (2008) 4 *Socio-Legal Review* 19, 45–53. In fact, the concept of absolute discretion was considered foreign to Israeli administrative law from its very beginning, and thus *Padfield*, in contrast to the other 'members' of the Quartet, was only once mentioned by the Israeli Supreme Court and not for the sake of rejecting the concept of absolute discretion. See HCJ 287/69 *Meron v Minister of Labour*, 24(1) PD 337 (1970) (Israel).

[21] *Duncan v Cammell Laird* [1942] AC 624 (HL).

[22] CA 65/57 *Haetzni v Ben Gurion*, 11 PD 403 (1957).

[23] ibid 411.

Later, Israeli legislation regarding the laws of evidence introduced the concept of qualified immunity and codified the procedures for judicial review of government immunity.[24]

D. *Anisminic v Foreign Compensation Commission*

A similar observation can be made regarding *Anisminic v Foreign Compensation Commission*, decided in England in 1969, which stated that courts are not precluded from judicial review of decisions of administrative tribunals that, due to an error of law, are a nullity, even if these are defined as 'final' by the relevant legislation ('ouster clauses'). The change brought about by this case has two dimensions. The first concerns the idea that 'ouster clauses' cannot function as a total bar to judicial review. The second concerns the extent to which an error of law may serve as satisfactory grounds for judicial review. These two dimensions were recognised in Israeli case law in an incremental manner through several decisions, all of them preceding the *Anisminic* case.

First, in two Israeli cases decided in the first half of the 1950s – *Zerubavel v Appeals Tribunal Under the Families of Fallen Soldiers*[25] and *Yehoshua v Appeals Tribunal Under the Invalids (Pensions and Rehabilitations Law), 1949*[26] – the Court recognised that 'ouster clauses' were not a total bar to judicial review. In these matters, the petitioners applied to the Supreme Court for an order of *certiorari* against statutory appeals tribunals, asking to have the decision of the tribunal set aside. The Court clarified that although 'ouster clauses' should be respected, they could not bar judicial review in cases where petitions are targeted at decisions that are ultra vires and, thus, null and void. Accordingly, Israeli case law made a clear distinction between decisions that are ultra vires and decisions that are merely erroneous (and thus are voidable but not void).[27]

Similarly, in 1963, the Israeli Supreme Court, in the *Trudler v Elections Officer to the Agricultural Committees* decision,[28] stated that judicial review of

[24] In a later court decision, the Supreme Court of Israel noted that the *Haetzni* case was adopted in legislation and that the *Duncan* holding was eventually rejected even in the UK, in the *Conway* decision. See CrA 383/71 *Yehudai v State of Israel*, 26(1) PD 267 (1972).

[25] HCJ 5/53 *Zerubavel v Appeals Tribunal Under the Families of Fallen Soldiers Law*, 7 PD 182 (1953) (Israel).

[26] HCJ 176/54 *Yehoshua v Appeals Tribunal Under the Invalids (Pensions and Rehabilitations) Law, 1949*, 9 PD 617 (1955) (Israel) (translation available at versa.cardozo.yu.edu/opinions/yehoshua-v-appeals-tribunal-under-invalids-law).

[27] In this sense, Israeli case law did not adopt the rhetoric of the *Anisminic* decision, which applied to decisions that were null due to an error in law

[28] HCJ 77/63 *Trudler v Elections Officer to the Agricultural Committees*, 17 PD 2503 (1963) (Israel).

tribunals would no longer be limited to an error that was clear 'on the face of the record'. The *Trudler* case is also important due to its more general statements regarding the 'independence' of Israeli law from English precedents.[29]

IV. BEYOND THE QUARTET: WHY WAS ISRAELI ADMINISTRATIVE LAW ONE STEP AHEAD?

More broadly, one can point to further administrative law developments promoted by the Israeli Supreme Court beyond the doctrines identified with the Quartet – around the same time, as well as beyond – that preceded their English counterparts. For example, in the 1950s, the Israeli Supreme Court began applying a reasonableness review of regulations promulgated by government ministers prior to its recognition by UK courts.[30] An even more significant development in this area has been the emergence of the new reasonableness doctrine in Israeli case law. Indeed, the formal recognition of reasonableness as grounds for judicial review has always been part of Israeli administrative law, which followed English administrative law precedent.[31] However, due to the legacy of the English cases, *Kruse v Johnson*[32] and *Associated Provincial Picture Houses Ltd v Wednesbury Corporation*,[33] this originally was a relatively narrow ground for judicial review that applied only in extreme cases. All this changed in the late 1970s and early 1980s. The decision of Justice Aharon Barak[34] in *Dapei Zahav Ltd v Broadcasting Authority*[35] introduced a new reasonableness test according to which an administrative decision would be declared unreasonable if it severely distorted the proper balance between considerations that were all legal as such. Accordingly, the reasonableness test has become a much broader and effective tool for the review of administrative decisions. In fact, within a few years, it went from being a relatively remote and rare ground for review to a central and influential doctrine in Israeli administrative law. In addition, in the beginning of the 1990s, the Supreme Court started to apply a new standard for judicial review – proportionality.[36] This doctrine had

[29] The Court explained that it was free to depart from English precedents with the aspiration that the law would suit local needs and do justice. See generally I Zamir, *Latent Errors of Law in Decisions of Administrative Tribunals* (1966) 1 *Israel Law Review* 162.

[30] CA 311/57 *Attorney General v M Dizengoff & Co (Navigation) Ltd*, 13 PD 1026 (1959) (Israel). In England, at the time, reasonableness review was applied only to by-laws of municipalities.

[31] See, eg HCJ 21/51 *Binnenboim v Municipality of Tel-Aviv*, 6 PD 375, 386 (1952) (Israel); CrA 40/49 *Nachmias v Attorney General*, 3 PD 127, 137–39 (1950) (Israel).

[32] *Kruse v Johnson* [1898] 2 QB 91

[33] *Associated Provincial Picture Houses Ltd v Wednesbury Corporation* [1948] 1 KB 223 (EWCA).

[34] Barak became later the President of the Court (1995–2006).

[35] HCJ 389/80 *Dapei Zahav Ltd v Broadcasting Authority*, 35(1) PD 421 (1981) (Israel).

[36] See eg HCJ 3477/95 *Ben-Atiyah v Minister of Education, Culture and Sports*, 49(5) PD 1 (1996) (Israel).

not been part of traditional administrative law in the UK. Eventually, however, it was formally adopted by the English courts after the enactment of the Human Rights Act 1998, as a result of the growing influence coming from Europe.[37]

V. CONCLUSION

This chapter argued that the Israeli legal system, although indebted to its English parent, was able to portend developments in administrative law. This was possible because Israeli law, as a new system, was less burdened by tradition. As a result, it was prepared to pave its own way. Indeed, the same tendency to go beyond the traditional case law of the English courts is seen in later case law of the Israeli Supreme Court in an even more pronounced way.

Taking a step back, this case study may stand for additional conclusions. First, it stresses the fact that quoting foreign materials does not necessarily mean that the solutions offered by them were indeed adopted. Therefore, empirical studies which only 'count' references to foreign sources do not adequately illustrate the scope of their influence. They may only show the judges' preferences regarding the systems they look at for comparative purposes. Second, as already noted in the introduction, although we generally tend to think of legal influence from the perspective of the flow from the centre to the periphery, parent systems may also learn from their offspring. The offspring systems not only portend developments in their parental system, but also illustrate paths not taken, thus proving that learning from one another does not always have to be a 'one-way street.' In addition, parallel changes in both the parent and offspring systems may emerge around the same period, reflecting the spirit of the time, without any direct causal link between them.

[37] See generally M Cohn, 'Legal Transplants Chronicles: The Evolution of Unreasonableness and Proportionality Review of the Administration in the United Kingdom' (2010) 58 *American Journal of Comparative Law* 583; M Cohn, 'Pure or Mixed? The Evolution of Three Grounds of Judicial Review of the Administration in British and Israeli Administrative Law' (2012) 6 *Journal of Comparative Law* 86.

14

Importation and Indigeneity: The Quartet in New Zealand Administrative Law

DEAN R KNIGHT*

I. INTRODUCTION

WHAT INFLUENCE DID the famous Quartet of English cases – *Ridge v Baldwin*,[1] *Padfield v Minister of Agriculture, Fisheries and Food*,[2] *Conway v Rimmer*[3] and *Anisminic v Foreign Compensation Commission*[4] – have on judicial review in New Zealand?

As an offspring of the English system of judicial review, it is no surprise that these cases were faithfully followed in the South Pacific, as New Zealand's supervisory jurisdiction echoed developments in the motherland.[5] Each of the key cases found its way into the administrative law jurisprudence in New Zealand, with the English developments generally being mirrored locally. We can point to local landmark cases which echo the different turns, along with lines of authority that still carry the colour of the Quartet. Sometimes with embellishment, sometimes with a little erosion. And the cases that make up the Quartet continue to be cited today, sometimes in their own right and sometimes to fortify the analogical local precedents.

* Thanks, subject to the usual caveat, to Eddie Clark, Sir Ken Keith, Geoff McLay and the editors of this volume for comments and feedback. Thanks also to William Britton, Anna Prestidge and Pita Roycroft for research assistance.

[1] *Ridge v Baldwin* [1964] AC 40 (HL).

[2] *Padfield v Minister of Agriculture, Fisheries and Food* [1968] AC 997 (HL).

[3] *Conway v Rimmer* [1968] AC 910 (HL).

[4] *Anisminic v Foreign Compensation Commission* [1969] 2 AC 147 (HL).

[5] For the purposes of simplicity, I use the terms 'England' and 'English' to capture the system of judicial review in England and Wales; see generally R Ireland, 'Law in Wales' in P Cane and J Conaghan (eds), *The New Oxford Companion to Law* (Oxford, OUP, 2008) 1231; and T Jones and J Williams 'Wales as a Jurisdiction' [2004] *PL* 78.

But there is another side to this story. Parallel to the continuing importation of English developments, we can also detect a fledging fight for indigeneity on the part of the New Zealand courts. A creation story of sorts – the struggle of an offspring judiciary and an inherited common law to blossom in its own right. The last half century or so has seen the maturation and patriation of the local judiciary, as a matter of institutional form. For example, a permanent Court of Appeal was established in 1958 and subsequently the Supreme Court as final appellate court in 2004. But has that institutional development been matched by jurisprudential substance? In the mid-1980s, Lord Cooke said: 'The time has probably come to emphasise that New Zealand administrative law is significantly indigenous'.[6] The Quartet provides a useful starting point to explore the question of indigeneity.

I track these parallel stories by first focusing on the importation point: the reception of the principle represented by the Quartet in New Zealand jurisprudence. I explain the local landmark cases in some detail, while also providing, as necessary, a brief sketch of broader context before and after. I then reflect on the question of indigeneity and whether the treatment of the Quartet provides any signals about a uniquely New Zealand jurisprudence. In the end, we see a fair bit of importation, along with some doses of indigeneity – at least in relation to the lines of jurisprudence flowing from the Quartet. The struggle between importation and indigeneity is an ongoing project for judicial review in New Zealand and is deserving of continued attention.

II. THE QUARTET IN NEW ZEALAND

A. *Ridge v Baldwin*

Daganayasi is usually regarded as being the key New Zealand case on the generous approach adopted toward natural justice.[7] This means it is often identified as the local counterpart to *Ridge v Baldwin*, although *Dagayanasi* was about the content of natural justice rather than its applicability. But numerous cases, before and after *Daganayasi*, nodded to the generalisation of natural justice in *Ridge v Baldwin* and its instrumental impact on the position in New Zealand.

Prior to *Ridge v Baldwin*, the New Zealand courts applied the then traditional English approach when assessing whether natural justice applied, based on whether the decision-maker was obliged to act judicially.[8] The first mention

[6] *Budget Rent A Car Ltd v Auckland Regional Authority* [1985] 2 NZLR 414 (CA) 418.

[7] *Daganayasi v Minister of Immigration* [1980] 2 NZLR 130 (CA).

[8] See eg *New Zealand Dairy Board v Okitu Co-operative Dairy Co Ltd* [1953] NZLR 366; *New Zealand United Licensed Victuallers Association of Employers v Price Tribunal* [1957] NZLR 167 (CA); *Buller Hospital Board v Attorney-General* [1959] NZLR 1259 (CA), drawing on especially *R v Electricity Commissioners, ex parte London Electricity Joint Committee Co (1920) Ltd* [1924] 1 KB 171 (CA), *R v Legislative Committee of the Church Assembly* [1928] 1 KB 411 and

of *Ridge v Baldwin* was oddly in a private law case, *AC Hatrick (NZ) Ltd*, where the case provided assistance on the question of whether natural justice principles should be imported into arbitration provisions in a building contract.[9] *Ridge v Baldwin* was also warmly received and generously cited by the Court of Appeal in *Jeffs*, even though the case itself concerned a different dimension of natural justice (delegation).[10] *Ridge v Baldwin* was, curiously, not referred to by the Privy Council or the local lower courts in *Furnell*.[11] The case was a significant one about whether a teacher was entitled to be heard in relation to a preliminary decision to suspend him pending investigation for misconduct (the Privy Council ruling the legislative scheme meant he did not). Yet, *Furnell* reflects the principle in *Ridge v Baldwin*. Delivering the majority's decision, Lord Morris expressed the principle so tritely there was no need for any citation: 'Natural justice is but fairness writ large and juridically. It has been described as "fair play in action". Nor is it a leaven to be associated only with judicial or quasi-judicial occasions.'[12]

Thus, it fell to the Court of Appeal in *Lower Hutt City Council v Bank* to directly herald the reception of *Ridge v Baldwin*.[13] When ruling a city council was obliged to afford natural justice to affected persons when considering whether to stop a street, McCarthy P acknowledged the death of the 'clear-cut distinction' between administrative and judicial functions and the rise of a generalised approach to natural justice. In doing so, he singled out Lord Reid's speech in *Ridge v Baldwin* as one of the 'directions from highest authority' that had led to these distinctions being 'blurred'.[14] Numerous other cases followed suit.[15]

As mentioned, the spirit of *Ridge v Baldwin* is most vividly seen, though, in *Dagayanasi*, a case in 1980 addressing when the requirements of natural justice require disclosure of adverse material to an affected person.[16] An overstayer

Nakkuda Ali v Jayaratne [1951] AC 66 (PC). See generally, K Keith, '*Ridge v Baldwin* – twenty years on' (1983) 13 *Victoria University of Wellington Law Review* 239; DE Paterson, 'Lord Reid and the Writ of Certiorari' [1966] *NZLJ* 107; GDS Taylor, 'Natural Justice – the Modern Synthesis' (1975) 1 *Monash University Law Review* 258.

[9] *AC Hatrick (NZ) Ltd v Nelson Carlton Construction Co Ltd (In Liquidation)* [1964] NZLR 72 (HC) 85.

[10] *Jeffs v New Zealand Dairy Production and Marketing Board* [1966] NZLR 73 (CA) (subsequently overturned by the Privy Council: *Jeffs v New Zealand Dairy Production Marketing Board* [1967] 1 AC 551, [1967] NZLR 1057 (PC)).

[11] *Furnell v Whangarei High Schools Board* [1973] AC 660, [1973] 2 NZLR 705 (PC); *Whangarei High Schools Board v Furnell* [1971] NZLR 782 (CA); *Furnell v Whangarei High Schools Board* SC Auckland, 22 October 1970.

[12] *Furnell* (PC) (n 11) 718.

[13] *Lower Hutt City Council v Bank* [1974] 1 NZLR 545 (CA).

[14] ibid 593 (citations omitted).

[15] *DG Allan Ltd v Blakely* [1974] 2 NZLR 723 (CA); *Otago Polytechnic Council v Teachers Court of Appeal* [1976] 2 NZLR 91 (SC); *Ronaki Ltd v Number One Town and Country Planning Appeal Board* [1977] 2 NZLR 174 (CA); *Chandra v Minister of Immigration* [1978] 2 NZLR 559 (SC). For a blip along the way, *Meadowvale Stud Farm Ltd v Stratford County Council* [1979] 1 NZLR 342 (SC).

[16] *Daganayasi* (n 7).

sought ministerial intervention to stay her deportation due to her son's medical condition; the controlling legislation provided a ministerial discretion to do so if they were satisfied that, 'because of exceptional circumstances of a humanitarian nature, it would be unduly harsh or unjust to deport the offender from New Zealand'. But the minister refused, relying on a (undisclosed) doctor's assessment that the boy could be adequately treated abroad. When the case came to the Court of Appeal, Cooke J deftly took the opportunity to endorse the trajectory of natural justice following *Ridge v Baldwin*:[17]

> Perhaps it is as well to repeat some points that by 1980 have become fairly elementary. The requirements of natural justice vary with the power which is exercised and the circumstances. In their broadest sense they are not limited to occasions which might be labelled judicial or quasi-judicial. Their applicability and extent depend either on what is to be inferred or presumed in interpreting the particular Act (as is suggested by the speech of Lord Hailsham LC in *Pearlberg v Varty*) or on judicial supplementation of the Act when this is necessary to achieve justice without frustrating the apparent purpose of the legislation (as Lord Reid put it in *Wiseman v Borneman*).

The principle in *Ridge v Baldwin* was perhaps already so elementary that the case itself did not need to be explicitly cited in support, even though the case clearly underpinned the statement of principle!

Cooke J returned to *Ridge v Baldwin* when discussing four specific cases he obtained guidance from. He commended Lord Reid's distinction between 'an exercise of power on a large scale and one relating solely to the treatment of an individual', noting that the former was 'more difficult for the Court to control'.[18] The controlling provision, Cooke J said, 'makes it perfectly clear that the individual circumstances are the crucial consideration' and this was 'a pointer towards a procedure ensuring that the individual circumstances can be fairly assessed'.[19] To this he added the *Durayappah* case and its identification of the types of matters that should be taken in account, beyond the language of the provision, when assessing whether the *audi alteram partem* principle applied.[20] While *Durayappah* invited consideration of the nature of the property, office or status at stake, Cooke J did not think this dimension should be 'dominated by what is now commonly seen as a nineteenth-century concentration on the rights of property'.[21] Instead, he pointed to the hope the mother might have of a favourable decision – or 'something akin to a legitimate expectation'.[22] The mandated circumstances of intervention ('narrowly defined in the Act') and the sanctions ('lift[ing] the drastic sanction of deportation') also required

[17] ibid 141. Both Richmond P and Richardson J endorsed Cooke J's analysis of natural justice but preferred to leave open the separate question addressed by Cooke J about whether mistake of fact should be recognised as a ground of review.

[18] ibid 143 (citations omitted).

[19] ibid 143.

[20] ibid, citing *Durayappah v Fernando* [1967] 2 AC 337 (PC).

[21] ibid 144.

[22] ibid.

consideration. Cooke J also drew on *Jeffs*, which emphasised concern about decision-makers acting in ignorance of the evidence.[23] The risk was the medical report 'was likely to have given a wrong impression of the evidence'.[24] Also providing guidance was *Ryan*: a Privy Council case which itself made 'special reference' to *Ridge v Baldwin* and spoke of the importance of providing a right to be heard when determining a question affecting the rights of individuals.[25]

These factors wove together to highlight the importance of fairness and natural justice being afforded to the mother, such that the medical report or an adequate summary be disclosed 'to allow her a reasonable opportunity of answering them'.[26] And Cooke J concluded by noting that the requirements of fairness should not trouble the administration: fairness is 'not a rigorous or technical test' and 'should not cause any concern that administrative efficiency will be unduly shackled'.[27] Thus, the Court concluded that the mother's application for humanitarian relief was 'not validly dealt with' by the minister.[28] As she had been deported while her appeal was pending, the Court allowed her appeal and made a declaration accordingly.

Since then, *Dagayanasi* has come to represent the orthodoxy in New Zealand: a simplified and generous approach to natural justice and procedural fairness.[29] And *Ridge v Baldwin*, too, continues to be cited on numerous occasions.[30] For example, the Supreme Court in *Wyeth* relied on both *Dagayanasi* and *Ridge v Baldwin* when recounting the 'fairly elementary' position to natural justice in New Zealand, in a case turning on the nature of the natural justice entitlement.[31] The key passage from *Daganayasi* (quoted above) which implicitly recognised the work of *Ridge v Baldwin* was quoted and endorsed; so too was *Ridge v Baldwin* approvingly mentioned.[32]

[23] ibid, citing *Jeffs* (n 10).

[24] ibid.

[25] ibid 144, citing *Attorney-General v Ryan* [1980] AC 718 (PC).

[26] ibid 145.

[27] ibid.

[28] ibid 149.

[29] For example, see *Fraser v State Services Commission* [1984] 1 NZLR 116 (CA) 121 which referred to *Daganayasi*, along with *Ronaki Ltd v Number One Town and Country Planning Appeal Board* [1977] 2 NZLR 174, as a summary of New Zealand's principles and authorities on natural justice. *Daganayasi* continues to be cited in modern cases as such: eg *Graeme Martin Contracting Ltd v Disputes Tribunal* [2018] NZCA 328; *Obiaga v Visiting Justice at Auckland Prison* [2018] NZHC 3095 [14]; *Contact Energy Ltd v Moreau* [2018] NZHC 2884.

[30] *W v Health Practitioners Disciplinary Tribunal* [2019] NZHC 420; *Wilson v R* [2015] NZSC 189, [2016] 1 NZLR 705; *Guy v R* [2014] NZSC 165, [2015] 1 NZLR 315; *Wyeth (NZ) Ltd v Ancare New Zealand Ltd* [2010] NZSC 46, [2010] 3 NZLR 569; *Combined Beneficiaries Union Inc v Auckland City COGS Committee* [2008] NZCA 423, [2009] 2 NZLR 56; *R v Smith* [2003] 3 NZLR 617 (CA); *B v Attorney-General* [1999] 2 NZLR 296 (CA); *Royal Australasian College of Surgeons v Phipps* [1999] 3 NZLR 1 (CA); *Peters v Davison* [1999] 2 NZLR 164 (CA); *Tertiary Institutes Allied Staff Association Inc v Tahana* [1998] 1 NZLR 41 (CA); *Estate Homes Ltd v Waitakere City Council* [2006] 2 NZLR 619 (CA).

[31] *Wyeth* [40], drawing on Cooke J's words in *Daganayasi* (n 7) 141.

[32] *Wyeth* (n 30) [42].

B. *Padfield v Minister of Agriculture, Fisheries and Food*

New Zealand's landmark cases of *Ireland* and *Unison Networks* are usually taken as the analogical expression of the purpose principle in *Padfield*.[33] But, in truth, the purpose principle – the idea that discretion must be exercised for mandated purposes (namely, the policy and objects of the statute or other instrument conferring power), not ulterior or improper purposes – has been deeply ingrained into the common law method in administrative law,[34] along with allied approaches to statutory interpretation.[35]

As a common law ground of review, the improper purpose ground can be seen in a variety of cases.[36] Even before *Padfield*, the courts recognised that decision-makers could not exercise their powers for purposes other than the mandated purpose.[37] *Padfield* received an early incidental mention from Wild CJ in *Shand*, in the course of rejecting an allegation that a minister had exercised his power to close a railway in a bona fide manner.[38] Cooke J subsequently endorsed the principle, albeit in an obiter aside, in the Court of Appeal's decision in *New Zealand Institute of Agricultural Science Inc v Ellesmere County*.[39] Numerous references to the principle followed.[40] *Poananga* was a notable

[33] *Attorney-General v Ireland* [2002] 2 NZLR 220 (CA); *Unison Networks Ltd v Commerce Commission* [2007] NZSC 74, [2008] 1 NZLR 42.

[34] H Wilberg, 'The Ireland Principle on Unauthorised but not Improper Purposes: An Exploration and Defence' [2016] 1 *New Zealand Law Review* 95; and M Smith, *The New Zealand Judicial Review Handbook*, 2nd edn (Wellington, Thomson Reuters, 2016). For its kindred principle, relevancy, see *CREEDNZ Inc v Governor-General* [1981] 1 NZLR 172 (CA).

[35] The legislative direction on statutory interpretation requires the meaning of an enactment to 'be ascertained from its text and *in the light of its purpose*': Interpretation Act 1999, s 5(1) (emphasis added). For background, see Law Commission, 'Legislation and its Interpretation' (NZLC PP8, 1988) 20 citing *Northland Milk Vendors Association Inc v Northern Milk Ltd* [1988] 1 NZLR 530 (CA). The emphasis on text and purpose can be traced back to 1881: C Nijman, 'Ascertaining the Meaning of Legislation – A Question of Context' (2007) 38 *Victoria University of Wellington Law Review* 629, 630. See also J Burrows, 'Approaches to Statutory Interpretation' in Law Commission, *Legislation and its Interpretation* 130 citing Lord Diplock in *Carter v Bradbeer* [1975] 1 WLR 1204 (HL) 1206.

[36] In some cases, *Associated Provincial Picture Houses Ltd v Wednesbury Corporation* [1948] 1 KB 223 was cited as the leading authority for the proposition, rather than *Padfield*; see eg *Buller Hospital Board* (n 8) 1271; *Opua Coastal Preservation Inc v Far North District Council* [2018] NZCA 262, [2018] 3 NZLR 538 (CA) [107]; *Environmental Defence Society Inc v South Pacific Aluminium Ltd (No 2)* [1981] 1 NZLR 153 (CA) 164.

[37] See eg *Quinlan v Mayor, etc of Wellington* [1929] NZLR 491 (SC); *McKenna v Palmerston North City Corporation* [1952] NZLR 767 (SC).

[38] *Shand v Minister of Railways* [1970] NZLR 615 (SC) (although not mentioned in subsequent appeal: *Shand v Minister of Railways* [1970] NZLR 615 (CA)).

[39] *New Zealand Institute of Agricultural Science Inc v Ellesmere County* [1976] 1 NZLR 630 (CA) 637.

[40] See eg *Rowling v Takaro Properties Ltd* [1975] 2 NZLR 62 (CA); *Takaro Properties Ltd v Rowling* [1987] 2 NZLR 700, [1988] AC 473 (PC); *Murdoch v New Zealand Milk Board* [1982] 2 NZLR 108 (HC); *Transport Ministry v Alexander* [1978] 1 NZLR 306 (CA); *Fiordland Venison Ltd v Minister of Agriculture and Fisheries* [1978] 2 NZLR 341 (CA); *Dannevirke Borough Council v Governor-General* [1981] 1 NZLR 129 (HC); *Ashby v Minister of Immigration* [1981] 1 NZLR 222 (CA) 230 (per Richardson J); *Brightwell v Accident Compensation Corporation* [1985]

instance of the force of the principle, where the decision to transfer a government employee to another department – for unauthorised punitive purposes, rather than for mandated administrative reasons – was quashed; while *Padfield* itself was not cited by any of the Court of Appeal judges, it seems clear that *Poananga* followed that tradition.[41]

It is *Ireland* which came to be associated with *Padfield* in the modern era, perhaps oddly.[42] The case concerned the use of a historic purpose reserve – North Head, a former site of Māori occupation and later coastal defence site – by a department to house its regional operations. The controlling legislation permitted the administering department to do 'such things as may be considered necessary or desirable for the proper and beneficial management, administration, and control of the reserve'. At first instance, the High Court ruled that such use was improper and unlawful. While there was some benefit arising from occupation of the buildings for the local reserve itself, there was also material benefit for the wider region; in other words, an ulterior purpose. On appeal, the Court of Appeal took a different approach to addressing questions of lawfulness when there was both a legitimate and ulterior purpose present. Drawing on, amongst other cases, *Padfield*, Keith J said 'purposes not within the statute are not necessarily "invalid" or "improper"; the additional pursuit of such other purposes may not thwart or frustrate the policy of the Act in question'.[43] Mere presence of an ulterior purpose was not enough. Thus, as the statutory purpose was satisfied and the additional purpose did not prejudice that purpose, the department's actions were not unlawful.

The Supreme Court's decision in *Unison Networks* also strongly endorsed *Padfield*'s purpose principle.[44] The point arose in discussion of the Commerce Commission's regulation of the prices charged by electricity line companies; a price threshold was set which, if breached by any line company, would trigger further investigation and, perhaps, the imposition of price controls. Unison was aggrieved by the price threshold, which it thought amounted to an effective price freeze for over two and a half years. It argued that such an approach was not justified under the legislation, which had as its mandated purpose the promotion of the efficient operation of electricity distribution markets for the long-term benefit of consumers, through targeted control of line companies extracting excessive profits. The Supreme Court did not accept that the imposition of a

1 NZLR 132 (CA); *New Zealand Maori Council v Attorney-General* [1987] 1 NZLR 641 (CA) 678 (per Richardson J); *R v Salmond* [1992] 3 NZLR 8 (CA); and *Mackenzie District Council v Electricity Corporation of New Zealand* [1992] 3 NZLR 41 (CA).

[41] *Poananga v State Services Commission* [1985] 2 NZLR 385 (CA); see eg Somers J's reference to the section of W Wade, *Administrative Law*, 5th edn (Oxford, Clarendon Press, 1982) 369 which addresses relevancy and purpose, including discussion of *Padfield*.

[42] *Ireland* (n 33). See also *PF Sugrue Ltd v Attorney-General* [2005] UKPC 44, [2006] 3 NZLR 464 [20] and [23]–[24].

[43] *Ireland* (n 33) [42]. Keith J noted Cooke J in *Poananga* (n 41) used similar language too.

[44] *Unison Networks Ltd v Commerce Commission* [2007] NZSC 74, [2008] 1 NZLR 42.

blanket price threshold trigger was outside the mandated purpose; it was sufficient that the price threshold was 'relevant to that purpose in the sense that [the threshold] will contribute to the administration of the targeted control regime'.[45] In reaching this conclusion, McGrath J directly incorporated the language from *Padfield* into the key statement of principle:[46]

> A statutory power is subject to limits even if it is conferred in unqualified terms. Parliament must have intended that a broadly framed discretion should always be exercised to promote the policy and objects of the Act. These are ascertained from reading the Act as a whole. The exercise of the power will be invalid if the decision maker 'so uses his discretion as to thwart or run counter to the policy and objects of the Act'.

He also went on to endorse the treatment of multiple purposes in the earlier *Ireland* case; pursuit of a collateral improper purpose only invalidates the decision if it compromises the legitimate purpose.[47]

Since *Unison Networks*, the purpose principle has continued to be applied in those terms, sometimes with the citation of *Unison Networks*, sometimes with the citation of *Padfield*, and sometimes with both.[48]

The commitment to *Padfield*'s purpose principle thus seems, at first blush, quite strong in New Zealand. Yet, there is a sense the local sequels have somewhat eroded the force of the principle, despite their approval of *Padfield* itself. First, there is some concern that the approach to multiple purposes adopted in *Ireland* – namely, an action is unlawful only if the ulterior purpose undermines or thwarts the lawful purpose – gives too much potential for unlawful considerations to creep into the motivations of decision-makers.[49] Secondly, the Supreme Court's application of the purpose principle in *Unison Networks* was quite deferential.[50] The combination of a broadly expressed power and a public body with expertise on the subject matter meant 'wide policy considerations' may animate the decision; intervention was unlikely if the body, amongst other

[45] ibid [69].

[46] ibid [53].

[47] ibid [53].

[48] *New Health v New Zealand Inc v South Taranaki District Council* [2018] NZSC 59 [317], [2018] 1 NZLR 948 (per Elias CJ); *Brook Valley Community Group Inc v Brook Waimarama Sanctuary Trust* [2018] NZCA 573; *Attorney-General v Haronga* [2016] NZCA 626, [2017] 2 NZLR 394; *Royal Forest and Bird Protection Society of New Zealand Inc v Minister of Conservation* [2016] NZCA 411, [2016] 3 NZLR 828; *Criminal Bar Association of New Zealand Inc v Attorney-General* [2013] NZCA 176, [2013] NZAR 1409; *Back Country Helicopters Ltd v Minister of Conservation* [2013] NZHC 982, [2013] NZAR 1474; *Exide Technologies Ltd v Attorney-General* [2011] NZCA 651; and *Chief Executive of Department of Labour v Yadegary* [2008] NZCA 295, [2009] 2 NZLR 495.

[49] P Joseph 'Constitutional Law' [2012] *New Zealand Law Review* 515, 533–37. Compare Wilberg, 'The Ireland Principle' [2016]. In *Criminal Bar Association of New Zealand Inc v Attorney-General*, the Court of Appeal indicated that any revisiting of the approach adopted in *Ireland* was for the Supreme Court; while it may have been 'pro forma', the Supreme Court affirmed the *Ireland* case generally: *Criminal Bar Association* (n 43) [55].

[50] H Wilberg, 'Administrative Law' [2010] *New Zealand Law Review* 177, 189.

things, 'exercised the power in a way which cannot rationally be regarded as coming within the statutory purpose'.[51] This implicitly suggests that the circumstances of some decisions may mean the judicial parsing of proper and improper is done with a light touch.

C. *Conway v Rimmer*

Conway v Rimmer made less impression because New Zealand had earlier chosen not to adopt the conclusive approach to Crown privilege that *Conway v Rimmer* sought to cure. Since 1936, the New Zealand courts had retained the right to examine documents to assess whether the public interest would be injuriously affected by production,[52] based on the Privy Council's decision in 1932 in *Robinson v State of South Australia*.[53] It was after the adoption of the discretionary approach in *Robinson* that the House of Lords, in 1942, took a different, more conclusive approach in *Cammell Laird*.[54]

The conflicting approaches were not considered in New Zealand until the Court of Appeal's 1962 decision in *Corbett*.[55] The Court of Appeal approached the conflict as a constitutional question about *stare decisis*, rather than a normative choice about the most appropriate principle.[56] That is, should the New Zealand courts follow a House of Lords decision that was inconsistent with an earlier Privy Council decision? By majority, the Court of Appeal ruled there was no justification for adopting the House of Lords decision in *Cammell Laird* over the controlling Privy Council precedent in *Robinson*.[57] Thus, the Court of Appeal affirmed the discretionary approach to Crown privilege:[58]

> I am of opinion that we should re-affirm that Courts in New Zealand still possess the power to overrule a ministerial objection to the production of documents in respect of which privilege is claimed if they think it right to do so, but it should nevertheless be borne in mind that it is a power to be held in reserve and not to be lightly exercised.

Therefore, it took the House of Lords decision in *Conway v Rimmer* in 1968 to bring harmony between English and New Zealand jurisprudence, but by reframing English law to coincide with New Zealand law. New Zealand's *Corbett* case was not, however, mentioned in the House of Lords decision.

[51] *Unison Networks* (n 44) [55].
[52] *Gisborne Fire Board v Lunken* [1936] NZLR 894 (CA).
[53] *Robinson v State of South Australia* [1931] AC 70 (PC).
[54] *Duncan v Cammell Laird and Co Ltd* [1942] AC 624 (HL).
[55] *Corbett v Social Security Commission* [1962] NZLR 878 (CA).
[56] The Court of Appeal did record some of the criticism of the approach in *Cammell Laird*, but this did not directly affect the decision.
[57] *Corbett v Social Security Commission* [1962] NZLR 878 (CA) (per North and Cleary JJ, Gresson P dissenting).
[58] ibid 911 (per North J). However, in the particular circumstances, the case for such a production order failed.

Following the House of Lords decision in *Conway v Rimmer*, the New Zealand Court of Appeal in *Konia* reaffirmed its commitment to a discretionary approach to Crown privilege, this time nodding to the English developments.[59] McCarthy P explained that *Corbett* and *Conway v Rimmer* were 'very much in parallel'.[60] And, in resolving questions about the production of police [papers] subject to a claim of Crown privilege, the judges drew heavily on *Conway v Rimmer* (as well as the *Lewes Justices* case).[61] After inspection, the Court ordered the production of most of the documents on the basis that the public interest in the proper administration of justice outweighed the basis of the claims for Crown privilege.

Despite *Conway v Rimmer* not being directly instrumental in kicking off the discretionary approach to Crown privilege in New Zealand, it continued to be cited as the 'leading case' in support of this approach. In *Elston*, Richardson J referred to *Konia* and the convergence of New Zealand and English approaches, but then went on to cite heavily from *Conway v Rimmer* (and *Lewes Justices*).[62] Ultimately he rejected most claims for the production of Cabinet papers and similar high-level documents.[63] Ringing endorsement of *Conway v Rimmer* (and *Lewes Justices* too) was also evident in the Court of Appeal's reasoning, delivered by Richardson J, in *Tipene v Apperley*.[64] Subsequently, in *Environmental Defence Society (No 2)*, the Court of Appeal distanced itself from the dicta in *Conway v Rimmer* on the application of Crown privilege to Cabinet papers.[65] Rejecting any suggestion of a firm rule about the non-production of Cabinet papers,[66] the Court of Appeal ruled that, while deference would be shown to a ministerial certificate, the discretionary approach to Crown privilege was equally applicable to Cabinet papers.[67] Thus, the Court inspected the Cabinet papers to determine whether they should be disclosed, but subsequently ruled they did not.[68]

[59] *Konia v Morley; Cullen v Attorney-General* [1976] 1 NZLR 455 (CA).

[60] ibid 460.

[61] *R v Lewes Justices, ex parte Secretary of State for Home Department* [1972] 1 QB 232.

[62] *Elston v State Services Commission* [1979] 1 NZLR 193 (SC) 197.

[63] ibid 201–02.

[64] *Tipene v Apperley* [1978] 1 NZLR 761 (CA). The recent decision in *D v National Society for the Prevention of Cruelty to Children* [1978] AC 171 (HL) was also referred to.

[65] *Environmental Defence Society (No 2)* (n 36).

[66] Both Richardson and McMullin JJ pointed to *Conway v Rimmer* as the 'leading English case' on the point, until the House of Lords and High Court of Australia signalled a different approach in *Burmah Oil Co Ltd v Bank of England* [1980] AC 1090 (HL) and *Sankey v Whitlam* (1978) 142 CLR 1 respectively.

[67] *Environmental Defence Society (No 2)* (n 36) 162. Cooke J, perhaps oddly, did not directly analyse the authorities, suggesting there would be no value embarking on 'a written analysis of the various shades of opinion and modes of expression in the speeches in the House of Lords and the judgments in the High Court of Australia'.

[68] ibid 169.

Subsequent cases also illustrate the discretionary approach and the influence of *Conway v Rimmer*.[69] The discretionary approach was applied in a number of cases in which disclosure was required, including, for example, *Fletcher Timber*,[70] *Brightwell*[71] and *Birss*.[72] *Conway v Rimmer* was directly cited and relied on in two of those three cases. Notably, too, the Court of Appeal in *Brightwell* fortified the discretionary approach with reference to the transparency principles evident in the Official Information Act 1981. Standing apart from the others is *Choudry*, where a minister's certificate about national security risks was ultimately sufficient to resist disclosure.[73] Again, *Conway v Rimmer* was extensively cited, even though the application of the principle weighed against disclosure. The Court expressed concern that the minister's reasons were 'of a character which judicial experience is not competent to weigh' and the judicial process was not able 'responsibly, to go behind a ministerial certificate that to disclose more would itself jeopardise national security'.[74]

It also seems reliance on the Crown privilege waned in recent decades, as the spirit of transparency became stronger.[75] And, following a major reform of the law of evidence, the discretionary approach to Crown privilege was codified in section 70 of the Evidence Act 2006.[76]

D. *Anisminic v Foreign Compensation Commission*

Bulk Gas stands as New Zealand's *Anisminic*, where the protective cloak of non-jurisdictional errors is cast away in favour of more generalised review for

[69] See also *R v Strawbridge (Raymond)* [2003] 1 NZLR 683 (CA).

[70] *Fletcher Timber Ltd v Attorney-General* [1984] 1 NZLR 290 (CA) (applicant did not have any onus to show documents likely to help their case; sufficient that documents were relevant).

[71] *Brightwell v Accident Compensation Corporation* [1985] 1 NZLR 132 (CA) (documents of independent body not immune merely because might be used by minister to formulate government policy).

[72] *Attorney-General v Birss* [1991] 1 NZLR 669 (CA) 671 (fair trial needs outweighed confidentially concerns in relation to disclosure of transcript of evidence given to a commission of inquiry).

[73] *Choudry v Attorney-General* [1999] 2 NZLR 582 (CA) and *Choudry v Attorney-General* [1999] 3 NZLR 399 (CA) (court initially ruled the certificate was inadequate but allowed the Crown to provide another certificate with more specificity).

[74] *Choudry v Attorney-General* [1999] 3 NZLR 399 [31].

[75] M Downs (ed), *Cross on Evidence* (online looseleaf edn, LexisNexis) at [EVA70.3]: 'In recent years the Crown has hardly ever claimed public interest immunity in litigation in New Zealand.'

[76] Under the Evidence Act 2006, s 70, a judge may direct that a communication or information relating to 'matters of State' not be disclosed if 'the public interest in the communication or information being disclosed in the proceeding is outweighed by the public interest in withholding the communication or information'. See Law Commission, 'Evidence Law: Privilege' (NZLC PP23, 1994) 148 and, for a recent example, *Dotcom v Attorney-General* [2019] NZCA 412, [2019] 3 NZLR 387. Also see, however, Crown Proceedings Act 1950, s 27(3) (rules must provide Crown can refuse to confirm existence of certain documents if would prejudice natural security or the prevention, investigation, or detection of offences).

error of law, effectively neutralising the effect of privative clauses.[77] But the realisation of these developments took some time,[78] as the jurisdictional–non-jurisdictional dichotomy was deeply embedded in administrative law jurisprudence as a key mediating device regulating the degree of judicial deference.[79]

It is no surprise that the first New Zealand judge to seize on *Anisminic*'s approach to matters jurisdictional was Robin Cooke; his PhD thesis at Cambridge in the 1950s addressed that very topic.[80] For example, in the first instance decision in *Car Haulaways* – one of his early cases as a judge – Cooke J nodded to the significance of the 'landmark' *Anisminic* case.[81] Facing a privative clause purporting to exclude review 'except on the ground of lack of jurisdiction',[82] Cooke J said the majority opinions in *Anisminic* 'should be accepted as authoritative in New Zealand'.[83] Thus, although it was not strictly necessary for him to decide the point, he described the effect of the privative clause in the following terms:[84]

> If an Act plainly empowers an authority … to decide a question of law conclusively … or if in exercising its true jurisdiction the tribunal decides a purely incidental question of law … a clause [like section 164] makes the decision immune from challenge, even though an error of law may be apparent on the record … Unless the errors of law … go to jurisdiction, they are not redressible; although strictly speaking it is unnecessary for me to decide the point. A fortiori, findings of fact on the very question which the tribunal is set up to decide, and conclusions based on an evaluation of the evidence bearing on such questions, would be immune.

While the decision-maker had acted 'within the ambit of its statutory jurisdiction' in relation to most matters which had been subject to criticism, Cooke J identified three criticisms of the decision-making which went to jurisdiction and quashed the decision on the basis of those errors. On appeal, the Court of Appeal took a different view from Cooke J on whether those criticisms amounted to errors and overturned the first instance decision to intervene.[85]

[77] *Bulk Gas Users Group v Attorney-General* [1983] NZLR 129 (CA) [*Bulk Gas* (CA)].

[78] See also M Taggart, 'The Contribution of Lord Cooke to Scope of Review Doctrine in Administrative Law: A Comparative Common Law Perspective' in P Rishworth (ed), *The Struggle for Simplicity in Law: Essays for Lord Cooke of Thorndon* (Wellington, Butterworths, 1997) 189, where Robin Cooke's contribution on this point is traced in more detail.

[79] See eg *Waterside Workers' Federation Industrial Association of Workers v Frazer* [1924] NZLR 689 (SC). See generally J Pemberton, 'The Judicial Approach to Privative Provisions in New Zealand' [2015] *New Zealand Law Review* 617, 619; and DR Knight, *Vigilance and Restraint in the Common Law of Judicial Review* (Cambridge, CUP, 2018) 48–50.

[80] R Cooke, *Jurisdiction: An Essay in Constitutional, Administrative and Procedural Law* (PhD, University of Cambridge, 1954). See also Taggart, 'Lord Cooke' (1997) 190.

[81] *Car Haulaways (NZ) Ltd v Attorney-General* SC Auckland A8/73 (8 August 1973) 36.

[82] Transport Act 1962, s 164.

[83] *Car Haulaways* (n 81) 36.

[84] *Car Haulaways* (n 81) 36–37, as quoted in *Attorney-General v Car Haulaways (NZ) Ltd* [1974] 2 NZLR 331 (CA) 333.

[85] *Car Haulaways* (n 81).

However, much of Cooke J's imprimatur of *Anisminic* was recorded without dissent from counsel or the Court of Appeal.[86]

Shortly thereafter, the Court of Appeal in the *Engineering Union* case recognised that *Anisminic* suggested a 'widening field of review' but the Court was also mixed about its implications in New Zealand and within the particular legislative framework in which the case arose.[87] On the one hand, both McCarthy P and Richmond J signalled some tentative scepticism towards the *Anisminic* approach to privative clauses and jurisdictional error.[88] On the other hand, Cooke J was quick to show his support for *Anisminic*'s trajectory:[89]

> First, my present opinion is that if *Anisminic* widened the field of jurisdictional review or jurisdictional error, it did so in the sense of preferring one of two long-competing lines of reasoning and authority to the other. Secondly, I think the courts of general jurisdiction should be slow to hold that when establishing a court or tribunal of limited jurisdiction Parliament meant it to have authority to determine conclusively for the purposes of any given case the meaning of provisions in the Act by which it is constituted and under which it operates. Questions of fact or discretion are in a different category.

Strictly speaking, the remarks made about *Anisminic* were only obiter because the Court ruled the Court of Arbitration had not fallen into error in the case under review and were also expressed as tentative thoughts because the point was not subject to direct argument.

Thus, we had to wait 10 years to see the *Anisminic* tradition take hold in New Zealand in the 1983 case, *Bulk Gas*.[90] A dispute arose about the meaning of 'direct interest' in a code setting out consultation rights in relation to the imposition of price controls. The Secretary of Energy was charged with approving applications to increase the price of natural gas but was required to first consult with any persons who had a 'direct interest in the matter'.[91] The Natural Gas Corporation applied to increase the price of gas it supplied to wholesalers. Bulk Gas Group, a collection of customers, sought to make submissions on that application. But Bulk Gas Group did not purchase gas directly from Natural Gas Corporation; they purchased gas from the Auckland Gas Company, the sole wholesaler within the region, who purchased the gas from Natural Gas Corporation. As they were not a direct customer of the Natural Gas Corporation, the best they could argue was that the price increase would inevitably be passed

[86] ibid 333. Sian Elias, later Chief Justice, appeared as junior counsel in her first appearance, arguing the legal point; S Elias, 'Righting Administrative Law' in D Dyzenhaus, M Hunt and G Huscroft (eds), *A Simple Common Lawyer: Essays in Honour of Michael Taggart* (Oxford, Hart Publishing, 2009) 58.

[87] *New Zealand Engineering, Coachbuilding, Aircraft, Motor and Related Trades Industrial Union of Works v Court of Arbitration* [1976] 2 NZLR 283 (CA).

[88] ibid 285 and 295.

[89] ibid 301.

[90] *Bulk Gas* (CA) (n 77).

[91] Natural Gas (Price Restraint) Regulations 1981, reg 10 and Commerce Act 1975, ss 92 and 97.

on to them by Auckland Gas Company. Ultimately, the Secretary ruled that the Bulk Gas Group did not have a direct interest in Natural Gas Corporation's application (but accepted they would have a direct interest in any application by Auckland Gas Company). Bulk Gas Group sought to judicially review the decision of the Secretary refusing its request to make submissions. But a privative clause potentially provided a hurdle to such a challenge; the clause said that a decision of the Secretary could not be 'challenged, reviewed, quashed or called in question' in court, except 'on the ground of lack of jurisdiction'.[92]

The High Court ruled that the Secretary's decision could not be impugned, because no jurisdictional error had been made.[93] The question of whether Bulk Gas Group had a direct interest – a question on which there 'may well be room for judgment' – was a matter within the Secretary's jurisdiction to decide, 'even to decide it wrongly'; the language and scheme of the Act was such that Parliament had intended to leave that judgement to the Secretary.[94] 'Judicial minds on this topic in England at least,' Davison CJ said, 'do not yet appear to be unanimous.'[95] Thus, he felt bound to apply the traditional jurisdictional approach.[96]

Bulk Gas Group appealed to the Court of Appeal, where the appeal was unanimously rejected. The Court of Appeal accepted the Secretary's approach to the question of 'direct interest'. Cooke J, with whom Somers J agreed, issued the lead judgment.[97] *Anisminic* is boldly embraced and privative clauses effectively nullified, perhaps in even more simplified and constitutional terms that the landmark English case.[98]

The concept of jurisdiction is jettisoned (despite its operative role in the statutory privative clause): 'a rather elusive thing' and 'a vague and probably undefinable concept'.[99] Instead, the focus turns to the question of whether the decision-maker has been empowered to decide conclusively. A privative clause does not apply 'if the decision results from an error on a question of law which the authority is not empowered to decide conclusively, even though in carrying

[92] Commerce Act 1975, s 96. The privative clause reflected in statutory form the common law position pre-*Bulk Gas* (CA): Taggart (n 78) 193.

[93] *Bulk Gas Users Group v Attorney-General* [1982] 2 NZLR 306 (HC) 314.

[94] *Bulk Gas* (HC) 312 and 314.

[95] ibid 311.

[96] ibid; that is, Davison CJ wasn't prepared to follow the collapse of the distinction between jurisdictional and non-jurisdictional errors by Lord Denning and Lord Diplock in *Pearlman v Keepers and Governors of Harrow School* [1979] QB 56, [1978] 3 WLR 736 (CA) and *Re Racal Communications Ltd* [1981] AC 374 (HL) respectively.

[97] *Bulk Gas* (CA) (n 77). As Taggart notes, it is 'a difficult judgment to grasp', especially 'because of the intricacy of the reasoning': Taggart (n 78) 194.

[98] This nullification is effected, even though it is acknowledged that such clauses may be legally effective: *Bulk Gas* (CA) (n 77) 133: 'It is generally accepted in New Zealand that an Act may empower an authority to decide a question of law conclusively and that a privative clause of this kind will then protect the authority's decision even though an error of law (in the opinion of the Court) may be apparent on the record: *Attorney-General v Car Haulaways (NZ) Ltd*.'

[99] *Bulk Gas* (CA) (n 77) 135. See also R Cooke, 'The Struggle for Simplicity in Administrative Law' in M Taggart (ed), *Judicial Review of Administrative Action in the 1980s* (Auckland, OUP, 1986).

out its functions it will have to form a working opinion on the question'.[100] *Anisminic* is recorded as the 'modern leading case' on this point.[101] Thus, Cooke J deftly reshapes the question into a more constitutional analysis, building on Lord Diplock's words in *Racal Communications*.[102] 'The Courts of general jurisdiction will be slow to conclude,' Cooke J records, 'that power to decide a question of law conclusively has been conferred on a statutory authority or tribunal.'[103] Matters of legal interpretation are 'for courts of law to resolve in fulfilment of their constitutional role as interpreters of the written law and expounders of the common law and rules of equity'.[104] The corollary of this proposition is that if empowering legislation laid down 'a definite test', a decision will be invalid if the decision-maker has not applied that test.[105]

Thus, the privative clause did not provide any impediment to the Court forming its own view on the meaning of 'direct interest' in the price-setting legislation – albeit the Court agreed with the Secretary's conclusion.[106] The question was 'a pure question of statutory interpretation' (viz a 'definite test') and there was 'no good reason' why the Secretary should be treated as having the power to determine the question conclusively (in modern terms, an absence of relative expertise on the part of the decision-maker).[107] Reaching the conclusion that the decision-maker was 'not exercising [their] true powers' in this matter was simply another way of saying that the privative clause did apply, 'because there [was] a lack of jurisdiction in the sense recognised in *Anisminic*'.[108]

Bulk Gas therefore built on *Anisminic* to mandate the courts' predominant role on questions of law – but through simplified constitutional reasoning rather than contorted linguistic gymnastics. The powerful role of the courts on matters of law is now vested deeply within the administrative and constitutional system in New Zealand. Any hint that a question raises a matter of law mandates close attention from the judiciary; deference on such matters has been strongly frowned on.[109]

The *Bulk Gas* tradition has since had mixed success in the modern era. First, as it relates to review for error of law, the Court of Appeal in *Peters v Davison*

[100] *Bulk Gas* (CA) (n 77) 133.

[101] ibid 133. The Privy Council's decision in *South East Asia Fire Bricks Sdn Bhd v Non-Metallic Mineral Products Manufacturing Employees Union* [1981] AC 363 (PC) is also cited.

[102] *Racal Communications* (n 96).

[103] *Bulk Gas* (CA) (n 77) 133.

[104] *Racal Communications* (n 96) [14] (per Lord Diplock), adopted by Cooke J in *Bulk Gas* (CA) (n 77) 133.

[105] *Bulk Gas* (CA) (n 77) 133. Taggart (n 78) rightly ponders whether this caveat left the door open for deference on some questions of law to develop.

[106] *Bulk Gas* (CA) (n 77) 133.

[107] ibid 135 and 136.

[108] ibid 135.

[109] See Professor Taggart's critique of this approach: Taggart (n 78) and, for a recent update, see Wilberg, 'Administrative Law' [2010] 191.

definitively confirmed the breadth of illegality as a ground of review and reiterated its commitment to *Anisminic*'s direction of travel:[110]

> Error of law is a ground of review in and of itself; it is not necessary to show that the error was one that caused the tribunal or Court to go beyond its jurisdiction. The effect of the House of Lords' decision in *Anisminic Ltd v Foreign Compensation Commission* as interpreted in *O'Reilly v Mackman*, and in *R v Lord President of the Privy Council, ex parte Page*, is in general to render redundant any distinction between jurisdictional and non-jurisdictional error of law.
>
> The availability of error of law as a ground for review of the exercise of public power is also now well established in New Zealand as appears from the decisions of this Court in *Bulk Gas Users Group v Attorney-General* and *Hawkins v Minister of Justice*.

Peters v Davison is now routinely cited in New Zealand on the nature and scope of the illegality ground.[111]

Secondly, as it relates to the effectiveness of privative clauses, the position in the modern era is more mixed, perhaps even inconsistent.[112] On the one hand, received wisdom continues to be that courts generally interpret such clauses narrowly.[113] As one judge observed, such a proposition 'hardly seemed to need authority'.[114] On the other hand, the courts exhibit a degree of willingness to respect privative clauses and exclude review, at least in cases where the privative clauses protect other statutory dispute processes that adequately provide for judicial supervision of errors. In other words, the courts should also be mindful of 'Parliament's intention to prevent duplicative proceedings'.[115]

The narrow interpretation can be seen in a number of cases. For example, in *Zaoui (No 2)*, the Court of Appeal rejected the Crown's argument that a privative clause (drafted in similar form to the one in *Bulk Gas*) protected errors made by the Inspector-General of Intelligence and Security when reviewing a security certificate issued in respect of a refugee.[116] Material errors of law relating to the relevance of human rights instruments and need to provide a summary of allegations were not protected by the clause, especially when the privative clause

[110] *Peters v Davison* [1999] 2 NZLR 164 (CA) 180 (citations omitted). See PA Joseph, 'The Demise of Ultra Vires' [2001] *PL* 354.

[111] See eg *Ye v Minister of Immigration* [2008] NZCA 291, [2009] 2 NZLR 596 (CA) [403] and *Vector Ltd v Utilities Disputes Commissioner* [2018] NZHC 3096 [7].

[112] Pemberton, 'Privative Provisions in New Zealand' [2015].

[113] For example, the Legislative Design Advisory Committee notes ('Legislation Guidelines' (2018) [28.1]) that the courts give privative clause 'a narrow interpretation to preserve their ability to review decisions in at least some circumstances' and 'may not be fully effective even if included'.

[114] *National Hydatids Council v Ward* HC Tauranga M55/88, 7 June 1989, 1, cited in Pemberton (n 79) 626–27.

[115] *H v Refugee and Protection Officer* [2019] NZSC 13, [2019] 1 NZLR 433 [63] (O'Regan J).

[116] *Zaoui v Attorney-General (No 2)* [2005] 1 NZLR 690 (CA) [105] and [181]. See also *O'Regan v Lousich: Proprietors of Mawhera v Maori Land Court* [1995] 2 NZLR 620 (HC).

was read narrowly in accordance with sections 6 and 27(2) of the NZ Bill of Rights Act 1990.

The Supreme Court's decision in *Tannadyce Investments* is as an example of greater willingness to respect privative clauses where doing so prevents unnecessary duplicative proceedings, although the Court was split about how privative clauses should be read in such circumstances.[117] The case was about a privative clause in tax administration legislation which deemed certain decisions correct unless challenged through a statutory dispute process (a merits and legality dispute process involving a specialist tribunal and/or the High Court). Both the majority and minority endorsed *Bulk Gas* as the controlling authority on the interpretation of the privative clause and accepted the courts should be slow to conclude that the judicial review was ousted.[118]

The majority thought the privative clause legitimately protected the statutory review process, a process itself which provided for the prospect of High Court scrutiny of the legality and merits on the assessment (either directly or through an appeal from the specialist tribunal). Notably, there was 'no need to strain' the interpretation of the privative clause the statutory review procedure had 'a built-in right for the taxpayer to take the matter to the High Court, if that is thought necessary or desirable'.[119] And, the majority said, judicial review would still be available if it was 'not practically possible' for a taxpayer to engage the statutory dispute process or there was some flaw in the statutory dispute process itself.[120] In contrast, the minority placed more emphasis on the constitutional importance of 'full supervision by the courts of the conformity of activities of government with the rule of law'.[121] In their view, a statutory right of appeal should not exclude judicial review. The minority favoured a more contextual assessment in the circumstances of particular cases about whether access to judicial review might be preferred over the statutory dispute process for reasons such as adequacy or effectiveness. In any event, though, the Court unanimously agreed that the taxpayer was precluded from challenging its tax assessment by judicial review in this case. It was not able to bring itself within the residual categories of judicial review under the majority's approach or make a general circumstantial argument that judicial review was preferable under the minority's approach.

This willingness to apply privative clauses if adequate legal accountability is otherwise provided through statutory processes has become pretty common. For example, the Court of Appeal has a number of times ruled that an extensively

[117] *Tannadyce Investments Ltd v Commissioner of Inland Revenue* [2011] NZSC 158, [2012] 2 NZLR 153.
[118] ibid [56] (Tipping J for the majority); see also [3] (McGrath J for the minority).
[119] ibid [57] (Tipping J for the majority).
[120] ibid [58].
[121] ibid [4] (McGrath J for the minority).

engineered privative clause protects the Employment Court from judicial review (unusually, a review jurisdiction conferred on the Court of Appeal by statute).[122] The courts have also followed suit in the immigration sphere, where privative clauses protect tribunal decision-making but are teamed with a right of appeal on questions of law.[123] And the Supreme Court in *McGuire* recently enforced a privative clause against a lawyer challenging the loss of his legal aid authorisation; the Court ruled that it was not impracticable for the lawyer to exercise his statutory review rights first and then, if necessary, issue judicial review proceedings later, as the privative clause contemplated and required.[124] One notable exception is *H v Refugee and Protection Officer* where the Supreme Court allowed judicial review proceedings despite a privative clause ostensibly protecting an immigration officer's original assessment in refugee legislation.[125] The Court took a different view from the lower courts on whether a statutory appeal process provided an effective remedy for the unfair cancellation of a refugee claimant's initial interview.[126] While mindful of the concern about duplicative proceedings in *Tannadyce*, the Court was not satisfied the statutory appeal to a tribunal was adequate to address the error, especially because the in-person interview and ability to argue the merits of their case twice (once in an initial interview and secondly before the tribunal on review) were critical aspects of fairness and key features of the statutory regime.

Thus, while *Anisminic* and *Bulk Gas* are still regarded as rarefied landmarks and frequently cited as expressing the controlling principle,[127] there has been some dilution of the previous strong hostility towards privative clauses.

[122] See eg *Parker v Silver Fern Farms* [2011] NZCA 564, [2012] 1 NZLR 256; *Moodie v Employment Court* [2012] NZCA 508, [2012] ERNZ 201; *Huang v Li* [2013] NZCA 135, (2013) 10 NZELR 514; *AFFCO New Zealand Ltd v Employment Court* [2017] NZCA 123, [2017] 3 NZLR 603. The privative clause in Employment Relations Act 2000, s 193 excludes review except 'on the ground of lack of jurisdiction' but explicitly defines lack of jurisdiction in historic and narrow terms (no entitlement to enter upon the inquiry in question; outside the classes of decisions or orders authorised to make; bad faith). Notably, the *AFFCO* case ruled the privative clause did not unjustifiably the right to judicial review in s 27(2) of the NZ Bill of Rights Act 1990.

[123] See eg *Phan v Minister of Immigration* [2010] NZAR 607 (HC); *Ibrahim v Associate Minister of Immigration* [2012] NZCA 229 (observation in course of determining security for costs); *Liu v Minister of Immigration* [2015] NZHC 2048. Compare *Kaur v Ministry of Business, Innovation and Employment* [2016] NZHC 2595.

[124] *McGuire v Secretary for Justice* [2018] NZSC 116, [2019] 1 NZLR 335.

[125] *H v Refugee and Protection Officer* [2019] NZSC 13, [2019] 1 NZLR 433.

[126] *H v Refugee and Protection Officer* [2017] NZHC 2160, [2017] NZAR 1518 and *H (CA580/2017) v Refugee and Protection Officer* [2018] NZCA 188, applying *Tannadyce* (n 117).

[127] *Anisminic* itself continues to be heavily cited in the modern era: *H v Refugee and Protection Officer* [2018] NZCA 188; *Ririnui v Landcorp Farming Ltd* [2016] NZSC 62, [2016] 1 NZLR 1056; *Siemer v Solicitor-General* [2013] NZSC 68, [2013] 3 NZLR 441; *Huang v Li* [2013] NZCA 135, (2013) 10 NZELR 514; *Parker v Silver Fern Farms Ltd* [2011] NZCA 564, [2012] 1 NZLR 256; *Zaoui v Attorney-General (No 2)* [2005] 1 NZLR 690 (CA); *Commissioner of Inland Revenue v Chesterfields Preschools Ltd* [2010] NZCA 400, (2010) 24 NZTC 24,500; *R v Strawbridge* [2003] 1 NZLR 683 (CA). See also regular citation in the High Court: *Carter v Coroner's Court at Wellington* [2015] NZHC 1467, [2016] 2 NZLR 133; *Bain v Minister of Justice (Discovery)* [2013] NZHC 2123, [2014] NZAR 892; and *Attorney-General v Palmer (Informer Privilege)* [2007] NZAR 112 (HC).

Whether this represents repudiation of the spirit of *Anisminic* and *Bulk Gas* or is acknowledgement of the greater sophistication in legislative design and statutory dispute processes is difficult to say. My sense is that it is perhaps the latter, as there seems to be greater attentiveness to the strength (or otherwise) of the accountability and grievance processes provided other than by judicial review. Certainly, it still seems unlikely that the courts would allow privative clauses to protect erroneous decisions from judicial review when judicial review is the only meaningful remedy available.[128]

III. IMPORTATION AND INDIGENEITY

The story so far has been about importation and the way in which key developments in the motherland were echoed in New Zealand. But to what extent does the story of indigeneity also feature? It is beyond the scope of this chapter to provide a full assessment of the success or otherwise of the indigeneity project. However, I offer some reflections on the balance between importation and indigeneity and related tensions, especially through the lens of the Quartet and the principles they represent.

A. Derivative Relationship

The treatment of the Quartet paints a picture about a *derivative relationship* between the two jurisdictions, especially in the time of the Quartet and the decades that followed. The treatment of this Quartet in New Zealand shows the English influence during this era and beyond. These cases have found their way into New Zealand jurisprudence and have helped shape local administrative law principle, to different degrees.[129] *Anisminic* and *Ridge v Baldwin* were strong catalysts for change in New Zealand for the generalisation of intervention for error of law and process. *Padfield* fortified and amplified a purposive tradition. And, although not causative, *Conway v Rimmer* played a role in exposing a greater range of Crown documents to scrutiny. This is consistent with the general assessment at the time. For example, Lord Diplock observed, when sitting on the

[128] For a similar turn to a broader constitutionality assessment, rather than linguistic gymnastics or nullity analysis, see M Elliott, 'Through the Looking-Glass? Ouster Clauses, Statutory Interpretation and the British Constitution' in C Hunt, L Neudorf and M Rankin (eds), *Legislating Statutory Interpretation: Perspectives from the Common Law World* (Toronto, Carswell, 2018).

[129] We could add others. *Wellington City Council v Woolworths New Zealand Ltd (No 2)* [1996] 2 NZLR 537 echoes *Wednesbury*. Standing rules were relaxed in *Environmental Defence (No 2)* (n 36). Local extensions to the supervisory jurisdiction mirror English developments: eg *Burt v Governor-General* [1992] 3 NZLR 672 (prerogative); *Phipps* (n 30), and *Electoral Commission v Cameron* [1997] 2 NZLR 421 (private non- statutory entities). Local rationalisation of the grounds can be pointed to in *NZ Fishing Industry Association v Minister of Agriculture & Fisheries* [1988] 1 NZLR 544.

Privy Council deciding a New Zealand case in 1983, the 'principles underlying the exercise of judicial review in New Zealand and in England, at any rate, are the same'.[130] Looking back, Elias CJ characterised New Zealand's jurisprudence in the latter part of the twentieth century as 'slavish imitation' of English law.[131] Even today, Francis Cooke QC, son of Lord Cooke, then leading silk and now High Court judge, noted 'we still take our lead from the United Kingdom'.[132]

Thus, we can think of most of the Quartet, especially *Ridge v Baldwin* and *Anisminic*, as 'legal transplants', as they are sometimes described.[133] This type of sharing within the 'common law family' has been, Saunders suggests, 'largely uncontentious'.[134] But, extending the familial metaphor, the parental relationship animated the attentiveness of the New Zealand courts to English law. As a child of the English common law,[135] developments in the motherland could not be ignored.

Various institutional and environmental features might go some way to explaining the strength of the derivative relationship. First, *institutional form* and *stare decisis* drove attentiveness to the English courts, especially the final appellate courts. Until the establishment of the New Zealand Supreme Court, the common membership of the Privy Council and House of Lords meant judges within the New Zealand judicial system needed to be mindful of the views of English judges when sitting in the House of Lords, for they would also determine any final appeals within the New Zealand system. Strictly speaking, decisions of the House of Lords were not binding, but highly persuasive. Since the establishment of the Supreme Court, the principles of stare decisis have been relaxed.[136]

Secondly, the challenge of *scarce resources* inevitably conditions the outward-looking eye. As Hammond J observed in the *Lab Tests* case, New Zealand's case law suffers from a scarcity problem. Common law judicial review 'scores its

[130] *Re Erebus Royal Commission; Air New Zealand Ltd v Mahon* [1983] NZLR 662, [1984] AC 808 (PC) 668.

[131] S Elias, 'Address at the Memorial Sitting for the Rt Hon Sir Richardson PCNZM' (2015) 46 *Victoria University of Wellington Law Review* 15, 16.

[132] F Cooke, 'Relief at Last' in *Administrative Law* (New Zealand Law Society Intensive, August 2008) 31, cited in *Lab Tests Auckland Ltd v Auckland District Health Board* [2008] NZCA 385, [2009] 1 NZLR 776 [395] per Hammond J.

[133] A Watson, *Legal Transplants: an approach to comparative law* (Charlottesville, University Press of Virginia, 1974); and A Watson, *Comparative law: law, reality and society*, 2nd edn (Lake Mary, Florida, Vandeplas Publishing, 2008). See also J Allison, 'Transplantation and Cross Fertilisation in European Public Law' in J Beatson and T Tridimas (eds), *New Directions in European Public Law* (Oxford, Hart Publishing, 1998).

[134] C Saunders, 'Apples, Oranges and Comparative Administrative Law' [2006] *Acta Juridica* 423, 426. The Anglo-Commonwealth jurisdictions have been characterised as having 'a significant degree of doctrinal and institutional similarity, overlying a substratum of considerable cultural difference': 427.

[135] English common law applied the New Zealand colony via the English Laws Act 1858 and subsequent statutes.

[136] D White, 'Originality or Obedience? The Doctrine of Precedent in the 21st Century' (2019) 28 *New Zealand Universities Law Review* 653.

runs in singles' and, in a small democracy like New Zealand, there is 'only an irregular supply of cases'; thus, 'the run accumulation technique becomes highly problematic'.[137] Similarly, we might point to the paucity of domestic scholarly works, only recently largely overcome. While New Zealand had a suite of fine administrative law scholars,[138] it lacked a leading textbook of the kind found in England. Paterson's early and short treatise did not survive and his taxonomy was heavily littered with English authority.[139] Joseph's constitutional and administrative law text did not arrive until 1993 and then its strength was probably more in relation to matters constitutional.[140] Taylor's contribution on judicial review came in 1991, but was not next updated until 2010; while grounded in New Zealand jurisprudence, the author also displayed an odd warmth towards Australian administrative law, with lessons from abroad coming as much from New Zealand's nearest neighbour as they did from the motherland.[141] Smith's recent handbook, modelled on Fordham's, is notable for its (almost) exclusive curation of New Zealand cases.[142] In short, local jurisprudential inspiration was hard to come by. It is therefore no surprise to see New Zealand cases replete with references to the likes of de Smith, Wade and Craig and so forth.[143]

Thirdly, university schooling conditioned attentiveness to matters English. Key actors within the judicial system – lawyer advocates, judges and the academy itself – were schooled as technicians in English law as much as New Zealand's. Witness Northey's casebook for administrative law at the University of Auckland in the 1970s: again, English case law dominates.[144] Note Lord Cooke's postgraduate study in Cambridge too.

Fourthly, it seems likely that this derivative relationship was also coloured by broader thoughts about national identity and colonial mentality. New Zealand's 'Englishness' was strong in the early decades being studied. And it was perhaps not until the 1980s that the independence spirit started to gain momentum.[145]

[137] *Lab Tests* (n 132) [396], building on the metaphor seeded by Professor Burrows. The 'small democracy' terminology was also borrowed, from Willis Airey.

[138] For example, Northey, Paterson, Mullan, Keith and Taggart.

[139] DE Paterson, *An Introduction to Administrative Law in New Zealand* (Wellington, Sweet and Maxwell, 1967).

[140] P Joseph, *Constitutional and Administrative Law in New Zealand*, 1st edn (Sydney, Law Book Co, 1993; 4th edn (Wellington, Thomson Reuters, 2014).

[141] On the difficulties of Australia as a comparator jurisdiction, see M Taggart, '"Australian Exceptionalism" in Judicial Review' (2008) 36 *Federal Law Review* 1.

[142] Smith, *Judicial Review Handbook* (2016).

[143] Both older and modern cases cite these authors; see eg *Buller Hospital* (n 8); *Ye v Minister of Immigration* [2009] 2 NZLR 596 (CA); *Hamed v R* [2012] 2 NZLR 305 (SC) citing multiple works by Stanley A de Smith and *Patel v Chief Executive of Department of Labour* [1997] 1 NZLR 102 (HC) and *Progressive Enterprises Ltd v North Shore City Council* [2006] NZRMA 72 citing Paul Craig at [71].

[144] JF Northey (ed), *Administrative law casebook* (Auckland, University of Auckland, Faculty of Law, 1973).

[145] J Belich, *Paradise reforged: a history of the New Zealanders from the 1880s to the year 2000* (Auckland, Penguin, 2001). See also H Wilberg and K Gledhill, 'English Administrative Law in

B. Embellishments and Glosses

The importation of the Quartet was subject to some indigenous embellishments and glosses. *Bulk Gas*, while reflecting *Anisminic*'s hostility to privative clauses, employed a more explicit constitutional lens and cared less about linguistic gymnastics when asserting the judicial authority to determine questions of law. The principle in *Conway v Rimmer* was already embedded in New Zealand jurisprudence and, following convergence, the principle seemed to be applied with considerable vigour, especially as it related to Cabinet papers and documents. Nowadays, the discretionary approach has since been codified. And the transparency culture that has developed in New Zealand (for example, Cabinet papers are nowadays unilaterally disclosed by the Government) means the privilege has almost fallen into abeyance. *Padfield*, too, reflected a spirit already present in New Zealand jurisprudence; *Ireland* and *Unison Networks* are notable for perhaps softening the strength and purity of the *Padfield* principle, by providing some latitude for decision-makers when multiple purposes or actions are in play.

Yet, in the overall scheme of things, these embellishments and glosses seem relatively minor. The dominant impression is that these strong and well-regarded principles have been deeply embedded, at best with a slight New Zealand accent.[146]

C. Durability and Ongoing Gravitas

These transplants imported into New Zealand jurisprudence have proved to be *durable* and continue to have *ongoing gravitas* in the modern era. None of the principles has been repudiated; at worst, a couple have been tempered, but probably only to address circumstances different than the original Quartet. As explained, the generalised approach to natural justice continues, perhaps even flourishing further than *Ridge v Baldwin*. *Padfield*'s purpose principle has been deeply embedded; the only gloss might be the reconciliation of multiple purposes (arguably, this litmus test of not thwarting or undermining the legitimate purpose has its pedigree in *Padfield* itself). Crown privilege has largely waned in New Zealand, such that *Conway v Rimmer* is probably now redundant. *Anisminic* continues to be rarefied in principle, even if its application is somewhat mixed. The potential of *Anisminic* is nowadays carefully anticipated in legislative and regime design; privative clauses must be constitutionally respectable – such as bespoke and robust accountability processes that still enable recourse to superior courts on errors of law – to have any chance of being honoured.

Aotearoa New Zealand' in S Jhaveri and M Ramsden (eds), *Judicial Review of Administrative Action: Origins and Adaptations Across the Common Law World* (Cambridge, CUP, 2020) (pointing to New Zealand's 'pragmatism, anti-intellectualism and lack of dogmatism').

[146] For the accent metaphor, see J McLean, 'The unwritten political constitution and its enemies' (2016) 14 *International Journal of Constitutional Law* 119.

This seems curious. One might expect that the importation and internalisation of the Quartet might allow the English cases to slide into the shadows. Surely the existence, in every case, of equivalent local cases obviates citation and discussion of the original development? That is not the case, though. The Quartet continue to be cited liberally, especially by appellate courts, either in their own right or in tandem with the local landmark cases. Notably, the courts appear to be more ready to cite the older English cases than contemporaneous ones.[147] And the Quartet cases continue to be taught to New Zealand students too. A quick survey finds that *Ridge v Baldwin*, *Padfield* and *Anisminic* regularly feature in the current syllabi of administrative law, judicial review or public law courses in New Zealand (*Conway v Rimmer* features only rarely).[148]

A few factors might inform this durability and ongoing gravitas. First, one possible explanation is the general trajectory of English and New Zealand law from abstract formalism to generalised categories or more circumstantial methods. That is, administrative law doctrine and principle has become more abstracted, such that a singular principle is capable of implicitly providing degrees of nuance not seen before the Quartet. In other words, doctrine itself has become less relevant as it tends to reflect more of a general style or method of analysis. One emblematic example is *Ririnui*, where the majority showed a strong preference for simply curing an obvious error, rather than determining whether it was properly classified as one of law or fact or resolving the uncertainty about the legitimacy of a mistake of fact ground.[149] Thus, we can see little judicial interest in (re)shaping common law principles and doctrine; delivering administrative justice on a case-by-case basis was more important. Top-down principle, rather than bottom-up doctrine.[150] Thus, a focus on principle – rather than application – may obscure the indigenous attitudes of the local courts.

Secondly, the modern-day senior courts in New Zealand may be *reluctant curators of law*.[151] While Lord Cooke was at home with the abundance of legal

[147] For example, *New Health* (n 48), cites *Padfield* [327] for the purpose principle.

[148] Auckland (*Ridge v Baldwin*, *Padfield*, *Anisminic*); AUT (*Ridge v Baldwin*, *Padfield*, *Anisminic*), Canterbury (*Ridge v Baldwin*, *Padfield*, *Anisminic*); Otago (all); Victoria (*Padfield*, *Anisminic*).

[149] *Ririnui* (n 127). Other examples include the surprising refusal of leave in the *Lab Tests* case (n 132) (court's assessment that the case raised no matters of public importance and turned on its own facts); and *Quake Outcasts v Minister for Canterbury Earthquake Recovery* [2015] NZSC 27, [2016] 1 NZLR 1 (court avoided the vexed status of the so-called third source of authority).

[150] For this terminology, see S Gageler, 'The Underpinnings of Judicial Review of Administrative Action' (2000) 28 *Federal Law Review* 303 and RA Posner, 'Legal Reasoning From the Top Down and From the Bottom Up' [1992] *University of Chicago Law Review* 433. See J Bell, 'Rethinking the Story of *Cart v Upper Tribunal* and its Implications for Administrative Law' (2019) 31 *OJLS* 74 for suggestion of a similar turn in English administrative law.

[151] Parsing judicial eras is always difficult. But for this, and other, purposes I have floated the idea of four rough eras: the *early Court of Appeal years* (running from around when the permanent Court of Appeal was established in 1958); the *Cooke era* (opening when Cooke J was promoted to the Court of Appeal until his retirement in 1996); a possible but perhaps overlapping *Richardson* era; and the *Supreme Court pioneers* (capturing the transition of many members from the Court of Appeal as then de facto local apex court to the new Supreme Court after it was established in 2004).

doctrine, both local and English, and was never shy about reshaping doctrine, the recent and current Supreme Court pioneers display a judicial conservatism that seeks to disclaim any normative curation of law and legal principle in the administrative law domain. Elsewhere I have wondered if the legacy of this modern era is the combination of the appearance of legal triteness, on the one hand, and heavily fact-sensitive assessment, on the other.[152] The continuing citation of the Quartet plays right into this narrative. The cases are manifestations of long-standing, deeply embedded and uncontroversial principles. Their citation is almost a signal to say, 'there's nothing to see here'. This frees up the court to wade into the circumstances of the cases under appeal, almost as an error-correction court.

Thirdly, we might point to the rise of contextualism. Unstructured normativism and a strong emphasis on the influence of context are thus commonplace in New Zealand.[153] To the extent that senior courts have reshaped legal principle, the mood is generally in favour of broad and generalised standards which allow for a holistic assessment of the facts.[154] Some developments emblematic of this contextualism include a monolithic but fact-sensitive approach to reasonableness, rejection of doctrinal deference, and occasional deployment of the innominate ground (which mandates intervention *whenever* judicial intervention is justified).

D. Overall Trajectory

If we reflect on the Quartet less in terms of their individual contributions and more as signposts of a jurisprudential trajectory or fashions in judicial philosophy, then the importation/indigeneity picture changes a little bit.

The traditional account of English judicial review tends to start with the 'classic model' – 'highly individualistic and conspicuously marked by judicial restraint'.[155] The Quartet signals the reawakening and the emergence of more

See DR Knight, 'Courts and the Executive: A Story (Some Stories?) About Judicial Review in New Zealand' (paper presented to Institute of Judicial Studies 'Challenge and Change' symposium (Wellington, August 2017)). These comments relate to the latter era.

[152] Knight, 'Courts and the Executive' (2017).

[153] DR Knight, 'Contextual review: the instinctive impulse and unstructured normativism in judicial review' (2020) 40 *Legal Studies* 1; DR Knight, 'Modulating the Depth of Scrutiny in Judicial Review: Scope, Grounds, Intensity, Context' [2016] *New Zealand Law Review* 63.

[154] Wilberg and Gledhill, 'English Administrative Law' (2020), speak of an 'almost complete eschewal of reasoning from general principles or reliance on authority in administrative law, deciding the vast majority of case as matters simply of statutory interpretation'.

[155] C Harlow, 'A Special Relationship? American Influences on Judicial Review in England' in I Loveland (ed), *A Special Relationship? American Influences on Public Law in the UK* (Oxford, Clarendon Press, 1995) 83. See also M Taggart, 'Reinventing Administrative Law' in N Bamforth and P Leyland, *Public Law in a multi-layered constitution* (Hart Publishing, Portland, 2003) 312 and J Steyn, *The Constitutionalisation of Public Law* (London, Constitution Unit, 1999) 2–6.

active judicial supervision.[156] Then followed the systemisation efforts of Lord Diplock, culminating in the *CCSU* re-expression of the tripartite grounds.[157] The so-called rights-revolution then followed, along with Europeanisation.[158]

It is fair to say that the general long-term trajectory is common, especially in the early creation phases, as has been shown with the Quartet. The transition from neglect to reawakening to rationalisation is a shared history: sometimes parallel, sometimes parasitic. We might, though, doubt whether the administrative law rights revolution was as strongly felt in New Zealand. The adoption of a statutory Bill of Rights, some time before the British equivalent, immunised common law judicial review from pressures to recraft doctrine and method to more fully embrace rights. That said, the principle of legality is well embedded in local jurisprudence, without the same fanfare as seen in England.[159] While the Bill of Rights discipline continues to be vigorous, it does not appear to have had the same deep impact on administrative law; in particular, although it is widely assumed that the Bill of Rights mandates proportionality review, there is little evidence of this actually being applied in practice in administrative law cases.[160] And, of course, the New Zealand courts have not had to grapple with the ongoing reach of Continental Europe and its influence – both direct and indirect – on English law.

An alternative way – and one I prefer – to think about the overall trajectory is to think in terms of the meta-structure of judicial method.[161] We can track the trajectory with a different lens, by reference to different methods used to draw the balance between primary issues (the propriety of administrative action in a particular case) and secondary issues (judicial legitimacy in terms of relative expertise and competence to adjudicate on different questions).[162]

[156] Harlow, 'A Special Relationship?' (1995) 84; M Taggart, 'Proportionality, deference, Wednesbury' [2008] *New Zealand Law Review* 423, 429. See R Austin, 'Administrative Law's Reaction to the Changing Concepts of Public Service' in P Leyland and T Woods (eds), *Administrative Law Facing the Future* (London, Blackstone, 1997) 30.

[157] *Council of Civil Service Unions v Minister for the Civil Service* [1985] AC 374. Such work was probably more symbolic than instrumental. As Harlow and Rawlings note, while *CCSU* is '[u]sually cited as the basis of the modern doctrine of judicial review', the grounds 'still conform[ed] largely to the classical grounds as they had evolved over the centuries'; C Harlow and R Rawlings, *Law and Administration* (Cambridge, Cambridge University Press, 2012) 107. See also M Fordham, 'Surveying the Grounds: Key Themes in Judicial Intervention' in Leyland and Woods, *Facing the Future* (1997) 199.

[158] For a recent alternative account, see JNE Varuhas, *Damages and Human Rights* (Oxford, Hart Publishing, 2016).

[159] See eg *Cropp v Judicial Committee* [2008] 3 NZLR 774; *R v Pora* [2001] 2 NZLR 37; *Drew v Attorney-General* [2002] 1 NZLR 58; *Canterbury Regional Council v Independent Fisheries Ltd* [2013] 2 NZLR 57; *Attorney-General v Spencer* [2015] 3 NZLR 449.

[160] C Geiringer, 'Sources of Resistance to Proportionality Review of Administrative Power Under the New Zealand Bill of Rights Act' (2013) 11 *New Zealand Journal of Public and International Law* 123.

[161] Knight, *Vigilance and Restraint* (2018).

[162] ibid.

Four main styles, generalised to a degree of abstraction, are evident over the last half century or so:

(a) *scope of review*, where the effective depth of scrutiny is determined indirectly based on categorical distinctions and formalistic reasoning;[163]
(b) *grounds of review*, where judicial intervention is conditioned by a framework of a few generalised grounds of review, expressed with a degree of abstraction;[164]
(c) *intensity of review*, where the depth of scrutiny is determined explicitly, by reference to a range of constitutional and institutional factors;
(d) *contextual review*, where doctrine is largely abandoned, whether in the form of categories, grounds or factors, in favour of normative reasoning and judgement.[165]

The Quartet fell in the middle of the scope of review period and before the systemisation work of Lord Diplock and Lord Cooke ushered in the grounds of review approach. New Zealand generally tracked the English method during this period and both jurisdictions still employ a grounds of review framework as the general starting point.

Within a 'grounds of review' approach, we might reflect on whether the grounds themselves display any cues of indigeneity. There is symmetry between the traditional grounds of review (illegality, procedural impropriety and irrationality; in accordance with law, fairly and reasonably). Parallel efforts to reshape these grounds and to enlarge the suite of grounds is largely common to both countries, albeit with less cut-through in New Zealand.[166]

[163] The courts' ability to intervene was conditioned according to rigid categories of analysis: jurisdictional-non-jurisdictional, law-fact-policy, process-substance, judicial-administrative-legislative; and was very technical and formalistic, as well as being rigid and circumspect; hence, the style was usually (but not always) teamed with judicial restraint. This echoes Carol Harlow's 'classic model'. On formalism see D Dyzenhaus, 'Constituting the Rule of Law' (2002) 27 *Queen's Law Journal* 445, 450.

[164] The expression of these 'court-recognised rules of good administration' in systemic and simplified form, often in tripartite form (illegality, procedural impropriety and irrationality; in accordance with law, fairly and reasonably), with the grounds themselves expressing different emphases on vigilance and restraint.

[165] In its strong form, doctrine is replaced with the judicial instinct and a discretionary judgment: 'whether something has gone wrong that justifies the intervention of the court?' (eg *R v Panel on Take-overs and Mergers, ex p Guinness plc* [1989] 2 WLR 863); and, in its weaker form, it captures doctrinal frameworks which are so open-textured that their essential feature is an overall evaluative judgement, such as substantive fairness.

[166] Knight (n 151). *Substantive legitimate expectation*: an accepted alternative ground but successful claims are rare, usually failing on the preliminary question of whether a reasonable expectation exists. Free-standing mistake of fact ground of review floated by Lord Cooke in the 1980s (*Dagayanasi*, n 7) but is still not definitely adopted by appellate courts, even though occasionally relied on in High Court decisions. *Proportionality* is not recognised as a generally available ground but provides a basis for intervention in limited situations: arguably human rights adjudication (but less so in practice than received wisdom suggests); disproportionate penalties; and, perhaps, challenges to local authority bylaws. *Inconsistency* of the even-handed kind has only partly been recognised, as a touchstone of unreasonableness. The potential of a ground of *substantive fairness*

And there is a sense that there is greater enthusiasm for, and increasing examples of, contextual review.[167] Perhaps that is the richest site for the development of an indigenous judicial style?

E. Bespoke Procedural Infrastructure

I wonder if the inspiration for Lord Cooke's indigeneity remarks stems largely from the reforming work of the Public and Administrative Law Reform Committee's work to simplify the procedure for judicial review.[168] It is here that the adoption – or, rather, importation from Canada – of the Judicature Amendment Act 1972 as the governing procedure statute for most judicial review applications plotted a different course for New Zealand from the motherland.[169]

Well-known concerns that the prerogative writs and orders were cumbersome for applicants led to procedural reform of the writs in the 1970s and the introduction of the simplified judicial review procedure.[170] The critical provision allows the High Court to grant any relief available under the prerogative writs or other extraordinary remedies 'in relation to the exercise, refusal to exercise, or proposed or purported exercise by any person of a *statutory power*' – a term defined extensively.[171] In general terms, this provision provides a more sympathetic environment in which to engage judicial review. And it avoids the procedural complexities associated with the prerogative writs. Introduced as a 'process' statute, the Judicature Amendment Act 1972 only addressed procedural and remedial matters; it did not purport to codify or modify the common law grounds of judicial review.[172]

One gets the impression that Lord Cooke saw this vehicle as a key means of charting a different course and avoiding the doctrinal morass that had plagued English administrative law, especially in the decades before its enactment.

was promoted in the late 1980s and early 1990s, but has since been overtaken by the variegated forms of unreasonableness. The so-called *innominate ground* (as seeded by the English Court of Appeal in *Guinness*, n 165) has been deployed in New Zealand on a few occasions but recent attempts to revive it have been soundly knocked back.

[167] Knight (n 79) 201–04.

[168] Sir Robin Cooke, 'Public and Administrative Law Reform Committee: The Early Years' (1989) 13 *New Zealand Universities Law Review* 150.

[169] Now re-enacted as the Judicial Review Procedure Act 2016.

[170] New Zealand Law Commission, 'Mandatory Orders Against the Crown and Tidying Judicial Review' (Issues Paper 10, 2001) [49]; New Zealand Law Commission, 'Review of Prerogative Writs' (Issues Paper 9, 2008) [1.10]. In particular, the prerogative writs regime required applicants to correctly specify and rely on a particular writ and provided no sympathy if it was subsequently determined another writ was more apt.

[171] Judicial Amendment Act 1972, s 4 (emphasis added). The one exception is removal from office, which, while an extraordinary remedy under Part 30, is not referred to in s 4 of the Act.

[172] Law Commission, 'Review of the Judicature Act 1908: Towards a New Courts Act' (Report 126, 2012) [2.1] and *Mercury Energy Ltd v Electricity Corporation of New Zealand* [1994] 2 NZLR 385 (PC).

As it relates to procedure, that has generally proved to be the case.[173] But, as the Judicature Amendment Act neither sought to codify or freeze the then existing substantive principles, nor attempted to modify them, the reform was agnostic to the underlying principles of the common law. At best, the reform catalysed a concern for simplicity, something that was a distinctive feature of Lord Cooke's own contribution. Thus, a degree of indigeneity but with little impact on the importation of substantive principles from England.

IV. CONCLUSION

Importation and indigeneity are two stories that can be told about New Zealand administrative law. The Quartet provides useful chapters for these stories. The faithful application of these English cases in New Zealand speaks to a strong tradition of importation. *Ridge v Baldwin*, *Padfield* and *Anisminic* made significant impressions on judicial review doctrine in New Zealand, and *Conway v Rimmer* brought conformity of principle between English and New Zealand law, even if English law was second to move. The indigeneity story is more muted and has failed to realise the full potential presaged by Lord Cooke in the mid-1980s. Local developments hint at indigeneity of administrative law principle. But the reliance on English law – including the Quartet – continues to limit and cloud the development of a distinctive common law of judicial review, even after the establishment of the Supreme Court in New Zealand. Thus, importation and indigeneity continue to be central stories of the historical and contemporary character of judicial review in New Zealand – and are competing stories which suggest an unresolved tension in the legal system's creation story.

[173] See DR Knight, 'Privately Public' (2013) 24 *Public Law Review* 108.

15

The Quartet in the New Commonwealth

PETER CANE

I. INTRODUCTION

EACH OF THE members of the Quartet was a leading case that made important new law. One way of thinking comparatively about these decisions would be to trace their substantive impact on the law of other jurisdictions. This chapter takes a different tack. It treats the four cases together as an episode in the history of English administrative law in which the House of Lords (now the Supreme Court of the United Kingdom) altered the relationship between the courts and the Government by making clear its intention henceforth to engage in more searching review of administrative decision-making on procedural and substantive grounds. Put differently, the Quartet is understood here as an instance of judicialisation and juridification of politics. This approach focuses not on the law made in the Quartet cases, or on their immediate contexts, but on their place in the longer history of administrative law and their relevance to the relationships between law, governance and politics.

This study is comparative. The 'New Commonwealth' provides a particularly suitable topic for comparison partly because the mid-twentieth century witnessed rapid and dramatic change not only in English administrative law (and society) but also in the British Empire. The foundations of the Empire were laid in North America in the seventeenth century; its decline began there in the late-eighteenth century, well before it reached its apotheosis in the late nineteenth century and largely collapsed in the decades following World War II. Decolonialisation involved fundamental changes in political, governmental and legal norms and practices in the newly independent nations. The impact at the periphery of legal change in the metropole at such a time raises important and complex questions about the diffusion and transmission of law in post-colonial contexts.

The New Commonwealth is, of course, a large and complex entity. Leaving aside the US, the UK, Australia, Canada and New Zealand, it is largely coincident with 'the common-law world', which is the legal aftermath of the largest project of conquest and colonialism in human history. Ironically, however, the United Kingdom and the English common law were also both born out of conquest and colonialism. We may distinguish between two different models of the very complex processes of colonial diffusion of law. The first, pluralistic model is exemplified by the Norman Conquest of Anglo-Saxon Britain. The invaders initially made no attempt to displace existing laws and legal institutions. Instead, they competed with local courts in the provision of legal services by gradually establishing a set of central courts to which individuals could gain access by petitioning the monarch. In the space of about 250 years, the royal (common law) courts gained an effective monopoly in all the areas that were of most strategic importance to the monarchy, most notably, land law and criminal law. The other model of legal transfer we may refer to as 'monopolistic'. According to eighteenth-century English law, British settlers took their law with them. The settlers did not always ignore the existing political and legal systems of the local people. For instance, in both North America and New Zealand in the nineteenth century, the settlers made treaties with indigenous populations. In Australia, on the other hand, the British settlers behaved as if the indigenous population lacked political and legal culture and practices. Settler law was unilaterally imposed. By and large, the former colonies that constitute the New Commonwealth were not settled and are best thought of in terms of a pluralistic model of legal diffusion.

Every legal system is unique. For comparative purposes, therefore, it is necessary to disaggregate the New Commonwealth into its component parts. Philip Wood divides common law jurisdictions into 'traditional English' and 'American common law' categories.[1] Counting the UK, the US, Canada and Australia as one jurisdiction each, Wood classifies 66 jurisdictions as traditional English and 11 as American. Of the traditional English, 20 still allow appeals to the UK Privy Council. Even if relevant research were available, it would obviously be impossible in this chapter to consider more than a very few of these jurisdictions. Nevertheless, study of the jurisdictions discussed below reveals a number of important themes that can fruitfully form the basis of further research and which are elaborated later in this chapter.

The chapter is in three main parts. The first locates the Quartet in the story of the development of judicial review law in England. The second section tells stories of the development of public law in a number of New Commonwealth jurisdictions about which I have found significant secondary literature. The third section discusses some general issues and themes that arise out of the analyses in the previous two sections.

[1] PR Wood, *Maps of World Financial Law* (London, Allen & Overy, 1997).

II. THE QUARTET IN HISTORICAL PERSPECTIVE

In broadest outline, the received story about the development of the modern law of judicial review of administrative action in England goes something like this. Judicial review was first developed by the Court of King's Bench in the seventeenth century as a technique for exercising greater and more effective central control over local administration by Justices of the Peace and other administrative entities. From one point of view, this adaptation of the 'prerogative writs' involved a revolutionary power-grab by the common law courts, part of a struggle between the King on the one hand, and Parliament and the common law courts on the other. Originally designed for the protection of royal prerogatives, especially in the administration of justice, the writs were fashioned into mechanisms for protecting citizens against excess and abuse of administrative power exercised at local level in the name of the monarch by royal officials and agents, by Justices of the Peace, and by various boards and commissions. Many of the grounds of judicial review recognised today were established in some form by the middle of the eighteenth century. The nineteenth century witnessed enormous growth in the functions and powers of executive government in England, and most of the administrative functions of the Justices and other local administrative entities were transferred to either elected local authorities or central government departments. The courts gradually reacted by extending judicial control via the prerogative writs to central government instrumentalities and further developing the grounds of judicial review.

The traditional poster child for Victorian judicial activism is *Cooper v Wandsworth Board of Works*,[2] which is generally understood as a strong assertion of judicial power to regulate administrative procedure in the face of Parliamentary silence and inaction. However, around the time of the First World War, judicial review fell into a 'long sleep',[3] characterised by a 'depressing catalogue of abdication',[4] which continued through the Great Depression and the Second World War. An early sign of awakening was the decision in *R v Northumberland Compensation Appeal Tribunal, ex parte Shaw*,[5] which 'revived' the use of *certiorari* to quash for 'error of law on the face of the record' as a substitute for statutory appeals from administrative decision-makers to the courts. The Tribunals and Inquiries Act 1958 (enacted to give effect to recommendations of the Franks Committee on Administrative Tribunals and Inquiries)[6] bolstered the decision in *Shaw* by requiring administrative tribunals, on request, to give reasons, which would form part of the record. At the same time, it created a general right of appeal on points of law from tribunals to a court.

[2] (1863) 14 CBNS 180; 143 ER 14.

[3] S Sedley, 'The Long Sleep' in M Adenas and D Fairgrieve, *Tom Bingham and the Transformation of the Law: A Liber Amicorum* (Oxford, Oxford University Press, 2009).

[4] ibid 190.

[5] [1952] 1 KB 338.

[6] Cmnd 218 (1957).

By the 1960s, memories of the horrors of the first half of the century were beginning to fade, and post-war austerity was giving way to new-found economic prosperity and increasing scepticism towards (government) authority. It is against this background that Lord Reid (in particular) took advantage of the fortuities of litigation to lay the foundations for increasingly active judicial review in *Ridge v Baldwin*,[7] *Anisminic Ltd v Foreign Compensation Commission*,[8] *Padfield v Ministry of Agriculture, Fisheries and Food*,[9] and *Conway v Rimmer*.[10] As a group, the Quartet is significant because it represents a general readjustment of the relationship between the judiciary and the executive, and the beginning of a period of increasing judicial activism in the control of public power.

III. SELECTED NEW COMMONWEALTH JURISDICTIONS

A. South Asia

i. Pakistan

In his PhD thesis, 'Courting Constitutionalism: The Politics of Public Law and Judicial Review in Pakistan', Moeen Cheema[11] traces an historical trajectory from the commercial activities of the East India Company in the seventeenth century to the establishment of the Raj in the nineteenth century, stressing the continuing importance of the colonial legacy in twentieth-century, post-colonial Pakistan. Colonial governance was characterised by extensive executive discretion and penetrating, but strongly controlled, bureaucratisation. In India (including what was to become Pakistan), local bureaucrats exercised both administrative and judicial power, much like Justices of the Peace in England. With the creation of the Raj, High Courts established in Calcutta, Madras and Bombay inherited prerogative writ jurisdiction. The primary function of courts vis-à-vis the administration in the colonial period was to enforce, on the mainly Indian lower bureaucracy, the 'rule of law' established at the discretion of the predominantly British executive class. Higher-level governmental discretion itself was much less amenable to judicial control.

Pakistan achieved independence in 1947. The 1956 Constitution adopted a parliamentary form of government and gave superior courts power to issue writs

[7] [1964] AC 40.
[8] [1969] 2 AC 147.
[9] [1968] AC 997.
[10] [1968] AC 910.
[11] Senior Lecturer, Australian National University College of Law. I had the pleasure of supervising Moeen's research. The thesis is available online via the ANU Library at openresearch-repository-anu-edu-au.virtual.anu.edu.au/bitstream/1885/148428/1/PhD%20Submission%20Draft.pdf. See also M Cheema, 'Two Steps Forward One Step Back: The Non-linear Expansion of Judicial Power in Pakistan' (2018) 16 *International Journal of Constitutional Law* 503.

'in the nature of' the prerogative writs. 'The Lahore High Court,' Cheema writes, 'began to push the boundaries of judicial review [of administrative action] right from the outset.' In a string of cases in 1956, 1957 and 1958, years before the first of the Quartet was decided in 1963, it was held that the courts were 'not bound by the limits on the issuance of writs in English law and … the purview of judicial review [was extended] to purely administrative acts'. However, in the face of bureaucratic reaction, in 1958 the Supreme Court in *Tariq Transport Company Lahore v Sargodha-Bhera Bus Service*[12] effectively imported into Pakistani law the English law of judicial review as it stood at that time, with all its restrictions and limitations on judicial power.

Martial law was declared for the first time in Pakistan in 1958. The transition out of military rule in 1962 was managed with a new Constitution, which (inter alia) conferred judicial review jurisdiction, albeit subject to restrictions and limitations that echoed the Supreme Court's decision in *Tariq*. However, the preservation of the judicial review jurisdiction encouraged courts (in the first half of the 1960s) to spread their wings. 'Within a decade of the establishment of the writ jurisdiction [Cheema writes] it could be stated that the extent of the courts' involvement in scrutinising executive action and laying the parameters of executive power was greater in Pakistan than in any other developing country'. In Cheema's opinion, by the 1960s, 'The sustained erosion in the power and prestige of the bureaucracy was accompanied by a corresponding rise in that of the judiciary'.

Martial law was again imposed in 1969, but was lifted in 1973 following negotiation of a new, parliamentary constitution that entrenched justiciable fundamental rights and used dramatically expansive language in defining the judicial review jurisdictions of the superior courts. However, in 1977 the civilian Government of Zulfiqar Ali Bhutto was toppled by a military coup led by General Zia ul-Haq. '[T]he much greater involvement of the military in executive and judicial functions of the regime under Zia, especially extensive use of Martial Law regulations and military tribunals, rendered even the writ jurisdiction a contested terrain.' Zia attempted further to sideline the secular courts by a process of Islamisation of the law. Islamic Shariat courts

> reviewed and in many cases overturned the actions of the civilian government … a clear beneficiary of this Islamic brand of judicial review were the [secular] courts … which used the dominant narrative of Islamic law and political morality to rebrand … judicial review of executive action as being compliant with fundamental Islamic precepts.[13]
>
> …

[12] PLD 1958 SC 437.

[13] For instance, in the 1980s 'the Shariat courts insisted on the granting of a right of appeal against executive decisions and challenged the ouster of the courts' jurisdiction'.

> [I]n the 1990s … the Courts encountered for the first time in Pakistan's tortuous history a highly contentious and fragmented political landscape, and hence greater space to expand judicial power … The Supreme Court began to use its Original Jurisdiction … and developed the framework of 'Public Interest Litigation' following the model of the Indian judiciary. This rise to unprecedented prominence was not an unqualified good, however … [B]y the end of the 1990s the courts laboured under a perception of politicisation. More significantly, the rhetoric of … Islamic public morality created expectations the courts had no capacity to meet … the courts' aggressive attempts to instil rule-boundedness and meritocracy in [the bureaucracy] had no impact in terms of impeding progressive politicisation of the bureaucracy and the police at all levels.[14]

In 1999 the civilian Government of Nawaz Sharif was overthrown by General Pervez Musharraf. Musharraf announced an agenda of anti-corruption and structural reform, promoted in part by leaving the courts' judicial review jurisdiction more or less untouched. However, increasing tension between the military and the courts reached a climax in 2007, when Musharraf dismissed the Chief Justice of the Supreme Court, Iftikhar Muhammad Chaudhry, 'precipitating a "Lawyers' Movement" that created the conditions precedent for the second wave of judicial assertion of power as Pakistan entered yet another phase of fractious political competition'. The Supreme Court itself reinstated the Chief Justice later in the year, thus encouraging 'the Supreme Court and the Higher Courts … to exhibit a level of activism hitherto unknown in Pakistani jurisprudence'. This resulted in the dismissal of Chaudhry for a second time later in 2007. His second restoration had to wait until 2008, after another wave of the Lawyers' Movement.

The Supreme Court could now 'claim a proto-democratic mandate and popular legitimacy'. The third Chaudhry court 'consistently took up issues of corruption, crony capitalism and abuse of public authority … The Court used the popular support that it garnered through this brand of judicial review of executive action to expand its institutional turf as well as fend off any challenges from the political executive'. The Court's activism predictably led to a backlash, and Chaudhry's immediate successors as Chief Justice promoted a more restrained approach.

Cheema suggests, in conclusion, that 'the judicialization of administrative governance' in Pakistan in which, to a greater or lesser extent, governments have acquiesced, may be explained in terms that 'courts gain relevance and power in weak or fragmented political systems where no one institution or class is able to exert a pre-eminent hold over the state and political processes'. In fragmented systems, even authoritarian governments may be willing to tolerate, and even promote, significant judicial control of administrative activity so long as courts

[14] Cheema, 'Two Steps Forward' (2018).

refrain from undermining the Government itself by interference in high politics in the name of the constitution and constitutional law. Significantly, in the years after independence, the Pakistan Supreme Court generally acquiesced in regime change and focused its efforts to curb government excess on controlling the administration.

ii. Myanmar

Myanmar, colonised by the British under the name of Burma in a process that began after the first Anglo-Burmese War in 1824–26, is commonly identified as a common law system.[15] On the other hand, it has been argued[16] that after 1962, Myanmar ceased to belong to the common law family and joined the socialist family – although without careful definition of terms it is difficult to assess such a claim or its implications. Certainly, since 1974, Burma/Myanmar has operated outside the mainstream common law world, if only because conduct of court proceedings in English was banned and law reporting effectively ceased. At all events, during the colonial period courts were separate from the administration, and were essentially tools of government for maintaining law and order.

Because Burma was administered as part of India, colonial British law as it had developed there was transplanted to the new colony. Burma gained independence in 1948; it did not join the Commonwealth of Nations and appeals to the Privy Council came to an end immediately. The independence constitution (drafted mainly by British-trained lawyers) established a bicameral legislature; an office of President, appointed by Parliament; and an office of Prime Minister, appointed by the President. It also established a separate judiciary and guaranteed its independence. The Supreme Court was given power to issue orders in the nature of prerogative writs, and the High Court had statutory power to issue orders in the nature of *habeas corpus*. In 1948, the Supreme Court declared that the English law of judicial review applied in Burma. Between 1948 and 1962, some 221 writ cases came before the Supreme Court and the High Court. In 1962, there was a military coup. The judicial review jurisdiction survived, in

[15] The following discussion is based mainly on M Zan, 'Judicial Independence in Burma: Constitutional History, Actual Practice and Future Prospects' (2000) 4 *Southern Cross Law Review* 17; M Crouch, 'The Layers of Legal Development in Myanmar' and 'The Common Law and Constitutional Writs: Prospects for Accountability in Myanmar' in M Crouch and T Lindsey (eds), *Law, Society and Transition in Myanmar* (Oxford, Hart Publishing, 2014); M Crouch, 'The Judiciary in Myanmar' in N Farrelly, I Holliday and A Simpson (eds), *Routledge Handbook of Contemporary Myanmar* (New York, Routledge, 2016); M Crouch, *Access to Justice and Administrative Law in Myanmar* (USAID, 2014), available at www.myjusticemyanmar.org/sites/default/files/Access%20to%20Justice%20and%20Administrative%20Law%20in%20Myanmar.pdf; M Crouch, 'Judicial Power in Myanmar and the Challenge of Judicial Independence' in HP Lee and M Pittard (eds), *Asia-Pacific Judiciaries: Independence, Impartiality and Integrity* (Cambridge, CUP, 2018).

[16] A Huxley, 'Case Note: California Refuses to Apply Myanmar Law' (2004) 6 *Asian Law* 88.

attenuated form, for some years after the coup. However, a set of special criminal courts was created 'to disperse and dilute' judicial power at the expense of the ordinary courts.[17] Then, in 1972, the whole court system was deprofessionalised and staffed with members of the Burma Socialist Programme Party (the sole political party), thus effectively ending judicial control of government. A new constitution came into effect in 1974 under which (inter alia) power to interpret the law and the Constitution belonged to the People's Parliament, a unicameral institution selected by non-contested election, which also chose the senior judges from amongst its own number. These developments effectively spelled the end of judicial review of the executive, and blurred the distinctions between legislative, executive and judicial power. The courts played no formal or practical role in controlling the legislature or the executive: the direction of control was the other way.

The year 1988 witnessed a change of regime. The Supreme Court was reinstated, but without a significant increase in power to scrutinise the executive. In 1990, the National League for Democracy, led by Aung San Suu Kyi, won popular elections by a significant margin. Although the regime refused to implement the result, it started a constitution-drafting process that culminated in the adoption of a new document in 2008, which was implemented in 2011. Under the 2011 Constitution, the Union Supreme Court sits alongside a Constitutional Tribunal and Courts Martial. The Supreme Court's writ jurisdiction has been reinstated. However, it appears that writ actions are used predominantly to enable the Supreme Court to control lower courts on behalf of the regime and hardly at all to control the executive to protect citizens. Politically salient cases rarely find their way into the sparse law reports. The Court's position in the system is reflected in the fact that it can be requested by Parliament to draft legislation, and that its judges can be summoned to appear before Parliament.

Finally, one detail of this story deserves to be highlighted. Since independence, the writ jurisdiction of the Supreme Court has been conferred by the Constitution, which appears to be the only source of judicial review jurisdiction in the system – there is no inherent judicial review jurisdiction. In 1948 the Supreme Court of Burma held that the Constitution conferred judicial review power that Parliament could not restrict or exclude. Since 2011, the legislature has begun to use finality clauses in an attempt to exclude judicial review. The Supreme Court has not yet been invited to judge the constitutionality of such clauses. Indeed, there is a question about whether it has power to do so or whether only the Constitutional Tribunal is competent to decide such an issue of constitutional interpretation.

[17] N Cheeseman, 'How an Authoritarian Regime in Burma Used Special Courts to Defeat Judicial Independence' (2011) 45 *Law and Society Review* 801, 808.

B. South-East Asia

In an article reporting the results of a study of citation of foreign cases by courts in Hong Kong, Malaysia and Singapore,[18] Kwai Hang Ng and Brynna Jacobson draw a distinction between 'self-referencing' (or 'sovereigntist') common law systems – exemplified by the UK and the US – and 'pluralistic', 'cosmopolitan' systems, exemplified by Hong Kong, Malaysia, Singapore, and – in the old Commonwealth – Canada.[19] In different terms, the distinction is one between law-exporting and law-importing common law jurisdictions. This suggests another distinction between two modes of diffusion of the common law that we might call 'vertical' and 'horizontal' respectively. The question of the impact of the Quartet on the law of other common law systems is about vertical, 'centrifugal' diffusion. In colonial terms, it concerns the impact of the law of the metropole on the laws of the periphery. The late-nineteenth and early-twentieth centuries were the heyday of Britain's export trade in law. Because metropolitan legal systems tend to be self-referential, the issue of centripetal, vertical influence – from periphery to metropole – springs less readily to mind, but may be significant.

Ng and Jacobson argue that in some sense, a self-referential system tends to view its common law as rooted in its social and cultural soil, an aspect of its zeitgeist and its communal life. By contrast, pluralistic common law systems understand the common law more as 'a globalized system … that operates as a well-tested set of legal know-hows'.[20] In such law-importing jurisdictions, although the concept of 'binding authority' may be understood much as it is in English law, the concept of 'persuasive authority' is given a much wider practical field of operation. The authors find this to be particularly the case in Malaysia. It is unsurprising that systems into which the common law was imported by a colonial power would not associate it with their national identity. On the other hand, given the spread of the common law, smaller jurisdictions and less well-developed legal systems might potentially gain from treating the common law as a global (or, at least, a multilateral) conversation, and a source of wisdom and learning. In this way, the common law may be diffused horizontally rather than vertically. It is, no doubt, true to say that at the time the Quartet was decided, the predominant, if not the only, direction of travel of the common law was vertically between the metropole and the periphery. But much has changed since then, and horizontal diffusion has become more significant.

Kevin Tan argues that the fact that 'developing Asia' as he calls it, 'walked a different developmental and historical path from the West makes a great

[18] KH Ng and B Jacobson, 'How Global is the Common Law? A Comparative Study of Asian Common Law Systems – Hong Kong, Malaysia, and Singapore' (2017) 12 *Asian Journal of Comparative Law* 209.

[19] See HP Glenn, 'Persuasive Authority' (1987) 32 *McGill Law Journal* 261.

[20] Ng and Jacobson, 'How Global is the Common Law?' (2017) 231.

difference to how Asians view power, authority and the rule of law. In Asia, the state has long been a powerful and omnipresent force … Asians … do not have a natural or traditional aversion to power and authority'.[21] Post-colonial governments in developing Asian states have been able 'to accumulate widespread powers and authority to ensure that [they] can intervene sufficiently in the marketplace to ensure that some form of economic development takes place'.[22] The colonial rhetorical legacy of 'the rule of law' and its embodiment in written constitutions drafted by or under the strong influence of British lawyers, such as Sir Ivor Jennings,[23] combined with traditional attitudes to authority, the economic imperatives of development and the continuation of practices of colonial governance, have facilitated and legitimised effective 'rule by law', and stunted the development and operation of independent mechanisms and institutions to control highly concentrated executive power. 'Developmental' (or 'transformational') government may range, at one extreme, from the 'socialist' model found, for instance, in the People's Republic of China (PRC), to what Tan dubs 'soft authoritarianism',[24] a 'benevolent' form found in places such as Singapore. Referring to administrative law, Tan speaks of the tendency of Asian states 'to reduce the role of courts and judicial review of administrative action as much as possible through narrowly framed legislation, ouster clauses and the aggregation of wide executive and bureaucratic discretion in administrative decision-making'.[25]

Against this background, we may look in a little more detail at Hong Kong, Malaysia and Singapore individually.

i. Hong Kong

Of the three jurisdictions, Hong Kong was the last to emerge from the British Empire (in 1997) but the only one to end up, not as an independent nation, but as a colony of a different hegemon. British Hong Kong was not a liberal democracy, and neither is the People's Republic of China (PRC). In the colonial period, the ultimate power over the governance of Hong Kong resided in London, just as the power to interpret Hong Kong's Basic Law now resides in the National People's Congress in Beijing, not in the legislature or the courts of the HKSAR (Hong Kong Special Administrative Region). Nor does China have a common law system[26] or deeply rooted practices of judicial review of government.

[21] KYL Tan, 'The Role of Public Law in Developing Asia' (2004) *Singapore Journal of Legal Studies* 265, 272.

[22] ibid 273.

[23] See, eg H Kumarasingham, *Constitution-Maker: Selected Writings of Sir Ivor Jennings* (London, Cambridge University Press for the Royal Historical Society, 2014).

[24] Tan, 'Developing Asia' (2004) 284.

[25] ibid 283–84.

[26] Given the choice, it might be expected that authoritarian regimes will choose civil law over common law (as China did in the early 20th century). In theory, at least, vis-à-vis the legislature and the executive, civil law courts have less (small-p) 'political' power than common law courts because

There is a significant (though controversial) literature about the incentives of authoritarian regimes (including one-party states, where party and state are inextricably intertwined, as in the PRC)[27] to tolerate and even promote judicial review of administrative action.[28] For whatever reason, China agreed to leave Hong Kong's common law legal system (including judicial review) essentially untouched; and so far, it has honoured that agreement. On the other hand, Hong Kong has a unique, hybrid, 'executive-led'[29] governmental system. The Chief Executive and senior officials constitute the executive; there is a unicameral, part-popularly-elected Legislative Council; and a court system with the Hong Kong Final Court of Appeal (HKFCA) at the apex. Judges from other common law jurisdictions, including Australia and the UK, regularly sit, as Non-Permanent Judges, on the HKFCA. In addition to administrative functions, the Chief Executive, appointed by the PRC, has considerable legislative power.

In the 1960s the Hong Kong legal system was part of the extended English legal system, tied by the umbilical cord of the Privy Council. Under the post-1997 Basic Law (Article 80), laws previously in force continue to apply, and Hong Kong courts are expressly authorised to refer to case law from other common law jurisdictions. The Basic Law (Article 35(2)) confers on Hong Kong residents 'the right to institute legal proceedings in the courts against the acts of the executive authorities and their personnel'. The general rule of British colonial law was that 'reception' of English law into a colony as a result of colonisation (whether or not by settlers) depended on its suitability to local conditions. The status in Hong Kong of decisions of the Privy Council and the House of Lords was considered by the Privy Council as recently as 1979.[30] Decisions of the Privy Council, it was held, were binding; and subject to the locality rule, decisions of the House of Lords were highly persuasive and, in some cases, effectively binding, while decisions of the English Court of Appeal were (merely) persuasive. It may safely be assumed that the Quartet cases were (or would have been, had the issue arisen) treated as directly applicable in Hong Kong when they were decided. According to Johannes Chan, however, 'judicial review of administrative actions

they lack formal power to make law. The irony is that British colonialism, at least in non-settler societies, depended on tight control of the courts. S Thomson, *Administrative Law in Hong Kong* (Cambridge, Cambridge University Press, 2018) 28–31 argues for a strong role for the common law in Hong Kong.

[27] For useful analysis see W-C Chang, L Thio, KYL Tan and J-R Yeh, *Constitutionalism in Asia: Cases and Materials* (Oxford, Hart Publishing, 2014), 173–78.

[28] See, eg T Ginsburg, 'Administrative Law and the Control of Agents in Authoritarian Regimes' in T Ginsburg and T Moustafa, *Rule by Law: The Politics of Courts in Authoritarian Regimes* (Cambridge, CUP, 2008); but contrast W Cui, 'Does Judicial Independence Matter? A Study of the Determinants of Administrative Litigation in an Authoritarian Regime' (2017) 38 *University of Pennsylvania Journal of International Law* 941.

[29] S Jhaveri, M Ramsden and A Scully-Hill, *Administrative Law in Hong Kong*, 2nd edn (Hong Kong, LexisNexis, 2013).

[30] *De Lasala v De Lasala* [1980] AC 546; P Wesley-Smith, 'The Status of English Decisions in Hong Kong' (1979) 9 *Hong Kong Law Journal* 327.

was almost unheard of in Hong Kong before 1950. Even as late as 1988, there were only 29 applications for judicial review. The number of applications then rose exponentially after 1990'.[31]

What appears to have been the first major text, cases and materials book on Hong Kong administrative law, the second edition of which was published in 1993,[32] includes long extracts from *Padfield, Anisminic* and *Conway*, and mentions local decisions only in the notes. Unsurprisingly, more recent scholarship[33] refers to much more, local material. However, as in all small common law jurisdictions, courts often look abroad for guidance. Indeed, Stephen Thomson's recent opinion is that:

> Administrative law in Hong Kong bears remarkable similarity to its counterpart in … England … and though there are questions of divergence, it is clear that … the English common law tradition was exported to Hong Kong and has in large part remained.[34]

That said, contemporary scholars also explore the significance for administrative law of the colonial heritage and the constitutional and institutional changes associated with the 1997 handover.

Chan explains the late flowering of judicial review in Hong Kong in terms, partly, of the inaccessibility of the common law ('scattered in stacks of law reports')[35] and partly that until the late 1980s, English was the only official language of the law in Hong Kong. Other important factors in the increasing role of courts in matters of public law in the last 30 years were the enactment of the Hong Kong Bill of Rights Ordinance in 1991 and the Basic Law in 1997. In constitutional matters, the courts live in the shadow of the National Peoples' Congress's ultimate power of interpretation. More generally, Chan sees Hong Kong as a dysfunctional political system created by excessive diffusion of power between, for instance, popularly elected legislators and those elected by functional constituencies, the legislature and the executive, and the executive and the bureaucracy.[36] In such an environment, those frustrated with politics turn increasingly to courts which, in turn, protect themselves from criticism by drawing a sharp line between law and politics. Jhaveri, Ramsden and Scully-Hill explain increasing recourse to courts as a response to a 'democratic deficit' in the Hong Kong system.[37] At the same time, the discourse of judicial review in Hong Kong is cast in very much the same language – of standing, substantive

[31] J Chan, 'Administrative Law, Politics and Governance: The Hong Long Experience' in T Ginsburg and AHY Chen (eds), *Administrative Law and Governance in Asia: Comparative Perspectives* (London, Routledge, 2009) 143.

[32] D Clark and G McCoy, *Hong Kong Administrative Law*, 2nd edn (Hong Kong, Butterworths, 1993).

[33] See works cited in nn 26 and 29 above.

[34] Thomson, *Hong Kong* (2018) 25.

[35] Chan, 'Administrative Law, Politics and Governance' (2009) 144.

[36] Chan (n 31) 165–7.

[37] Jhaveri, Ramsden and Scully-Hill, *Administrative Law* (2013) (n 29) 24.

legitimate expectations and proportionality, for instance – as administrative law debates across the non-US common law world.

ii. Malaysia

Malaya achieved independence in 1956. In 1963, the Federation of Malaysia was formed by a union between Malaya, North Borneo, Sarawak and Singapore. In 1965, Singapore withdrew from the Federation and became a fully independent republic. English law is the main source of Malaysian law, although Islamic law is also significant in some areas.[38] Section 3 of the Civil Law Act 1956, passed just before independence and still in force, provides for the application in Malaysia of 'English' rules of common law and equity as they were at the date of formal reception, which varies from one part of Malaysia to another. In 1979, Lord Diplock (of the UK House of Lords), after giving an account of the development of English administrative law, stated:

> All I have said about administrative law in England applies also to judicial control of the executive branch of the Government of Malaysia whose constitution so far as concerns the relationship of legislature and executive follows the Westminster model[39]

There are vigorous contemporary debates in Malaysia about whether section 3 should be retained or repealed. Of course, the application of English law is subject to local conditions. Nevertheless, the Malaysian legal system is still formally tied to the English legal system in a way that Hong Kong law, for instance, is not. In terms used earlier, Malaysia provides a contemporary example of the vertical diffusion of English common law, in contrast to horizontal diffusion of a jurisdictionally indeterminate common law around the non-US common law world.

Regarding the Quartet, Malaysia provides an interesting case study of the fate of *Ansiminic* in one post-colonial society. Although the ratio of *Anisminic* was quite narrow,[40] it has subsequently

> been treated as authority for the proposition that any error of law makes a decision a nullity, and the category of "error of law" has been extended to a point where it is hard to find an error which cannot be dressed up as error of law.[41]

In 1974, Lord Diplock stated, extra-judicially, that *Anisminic* had 'rendered obsolete' the distinction between errors of law going to, and errors of law within, jurisdiction;[42] and in 1979, Lord Denning expressed the view, obiter, that the

[38] AH Mohamed and ATrakic, 'The Reception of English Law in Malaysia and the Development of the Malaysian Common Law' (2015) 44 *Common Law World Review* 123, 124.

[39] Lord Diplock, 'Judicial Control of Government' [1979] *Malayan Law Journal* cxl, cxlvi.

[40] D Feldman, '*Animsminic Ltd v Foreign Compensation Commission* [1968] in Perspective' in S Juss and M Sunkin (eds), *Landmark Cases in Public Law* (Oxford, Hart Publishing, 2017) 80.

[41] ibid 93.

[42] ibid 94.

distinction should be 'discarded'.[43] This opinion was, itself, expressly rejected by the Privy Council in the appeal from the Federal Court of Malaysia in *South East Asia Fire Bricks Sdn Bhd v Non-Metallic Mineral Products Manufacturing Employees Union*.[44] On the basis of a review of the Malaysian case law, the Board decided that awards of the Industrial Court could not be reviewed by certiorari on the ground of error of law within jurisdiction. In colonial and post-colonial contexts, ouster clauses have been particularly controversial in relation to detention of suspects on the grounds of national security. Wide, non-justiciable, emergency powers were a feature of British colonial rule in many parts of the Empire, and they are often a feature of post-independence governance arrangements. The distinction between jurisdictional and non-jurisdictional error (like concepts of 'deference')[45] affords courts a sturdy vessel in which to navigate safely through stormy political waters.

According to Jaclyn Neo, writing in 2010,[46] 'until recently, the executive's broad discretionary powers are [*sic*] reinforced by a judicial attitude which was deferential to executive wisdom on national security matters and justified by the valorisation of security concerns.'[47] In this context, at much the same time as the House of Lords in *Padfield* was strengthening the judicial approach to review of executive discretion, a Malaysian court applied a subjective test of satisfaction when reviewing a detention decision.[48] In 1989, the legislature inserted into the relevant legislation an ouster clause purporting to exclude judicial review of detention decisions on any ground except failure to comply with a procedural requirement. In 2008, the Malaysian High Court, departing from earlier local case law, held that the ouster clause was not effective to exclude judicial review for jurisdictional error of law. Neo describes this decision as part of a growing trend, the origins of which she finds in several post-2000 decisions, and which she explains in terms of a new rights culture in Malaysia coupled with the fact that the Malaysian Parliament is not 'sovereign' but subject to the Constitution.[49]

[43] *Pearlman v Keepers and Governors of Harrow School* [1979] QB 56, 70.

[44] [1981] AC 363. Appeals to the Privy Council from Malaysia in civil matters were abolished in 1985.

[45] However, the two techniques are not equivalent. The jurisdictional/non-jurisdictional distinction enables courts to tolerate a degree of illegality for the sake of interests other than the rule of law, while deference doctrines cede to administrative decision-makers a greater or lesser degree of legitimised control over what the law is.

[46] JL-C Neo, 'Parsing Privative Clauses: Rights, Security and Judicial Review in Malaysia' [2010] *PL* 25.

[47] For a general account of Malaysian (and Singaporean) judicial review law in 1985 see CM Chinkin, 'Abuse of Discretion in Malaysia and Singapore' in *The Common Law in Singapore and Malaysia: A Volume of Essays Marking the 25th Anniversary of the Malayan Law Review 1959–1984* (Singapore, Butterworths, 1985). For a stock-taking in 1996 see A Harding, *Law, Government and the Constitution in Malaysia* (Kuala Lumpur, Malayan Law Journal Sdn Bhd, 1996), ch 15.

[48] Neo, 'Parsing Privative Clauses' [2010] 25.

[49] GC Chuan, 'Administrative Law and Judicialized Governance in Malaysia' in Ginsburg and Chen (n 31) exploits a distinction between common law and constitutional review of administrative action in order the strengthen the position and resolve of the courts.

Some commentators also detect a move to more robust, objective standards of review of discretion even in matters of public order and security.[50] Others, however, seem less sure. For instance, Matt Nelson and Diana Shah describe the quite recent decision of the Federal Court of Malaysia in the notorious *Lina Joy* case as 'reinforcing common-law norms of judicial restraint'.[51] As we have noted in relation to Hong Kong, in systems where political power is widely diffused – in the case of Malaysia, between different social, ethnic and religious groups – parties who lose out in the political process may seek aid from courts which, in turn, may adopt a passive, self-defensive stance in order to protect their own 'independence'[52] and protect themselves from direct interference by the dominant political force.[53]

iii. Singapore

As already noted, Singapore was a component of Malaysia between 1963 and 1965, but it broke away and achieved full independence in 1965. Although Singaporean and Malaysian administrative law are often seen as bedfellows they are, in fact, very different systems. Certainly, they share post-colonial Asian developmental imperatives and high concentration of power in the executive, but relations between the executive and the judiciary have been much less tempestuous in Singapore than in Malaysia. The Singaporean judiciary has a reputation for 'independence', integrity and efficiency, despite the fact that the Singaporean governmental system is, by European, liberal-democratic standards, authoritarian and illiberal. This is explicable in terms of Singapore's policies of promoting economic development and creating a financial and commercial hub for Asia, and an acknowledgement of the relationship between success in such goals and

[50] See, eg, SA Shahizam, 'Beyond the 'Objective Test': Towards Stringent Scrutiny of Ministerial Decision-Making' *Administrative Law Blog* (9 February 2018), available at adminlawblog.org/2018/02/09/shukri-ahmad-shahizam-beyond-the-objective-test-towards-stringent-scrutiny-of-ministerial-decision-making.

[51] M Nelson and DAH Shah, 'The Politics of Administrative "Reasonableness in Malaysia"', available at adminlawblog.org/2017/11/14/matt-nelson-and-dian-a-h-shah-operationalizing-and-regulating-religious-freedom.

[52] See A Harding, 'Constitutional Trajectory in Malaysia: Constitutionalism Without Consensus?' in MW Dowdle and MA Wilkinson (eds), *Constitutionalism Beyond Liberalism* (Cambridge, CUP, 2017).

[53] HP Lee and R Foo, 'The Malaysian Judiciary: A Sisyphean Quest for Redemption?' in HP Lee and M Pittard (eds), *Asia-Pacific Judiciaries: Independence, Impartiality and Integrity* (Cambridge, CUP, 2018). For a similarly sad story about Sri Lanka see S Ratnapala, 'Decline and Fall of Sri Lanka's Judiciary and Prospects for Resurrection', in Lee and Pittard (eds), *Asia Pacific Judiciaries*. The apparently tendentious use of Christian imagery in these titles is noteworthy. By contrast, the Indian Supreme Court illustrates a different reaction to ethnic, religious and social divisions in a relatively non-authoritarian, fragmented political system: PB Mehta, 'The Indian Supreme Court and the Art of Democratic Positioning' in M Tushnet and M Khosla (eds), *Unstable Constitutionalism: Law and Politics in South Asia* (Cambridge, CUP, 2015); but for a different, more doctrinal perspective see A Chandrachud, 'Wednesbury Reformulated: Proportionality and the Supreme Court of India' (2013) 13 *Oxford University Commonwealth Law Journal* 191.

a robust, reliable court system.[54] A recent survey of judicial review in Singapore between 1965 and 2012 is consistent with this explanation. The authors find that judicial review claims that involve challenges of high economic but low political salience are much more likely to succeed than ones that raise civil liberties issues.[55] This suggests unspoken judicial acquiescence in the Government's political agenda and administrative style founded, perhaps, on a deeply rooted culture of respect for leadership, bureaucracy and authority.[56]

Jolene Lin observes that although Singapore (in her words) is 'the quintessential administrative' and regulatory state, its administrative law is 'relatively undeveloped'; the judiciary plays 'a relatively small role in regulatory government', and it has 'limited influence on executive decision-making', demonstrating 'significant self-restraint' and 'great reluctance to interfere with executive decisions'.[57] She also points out that Singaporean courts (like Australian courts) have been wary about adopting English, post-Quartet, Europeanising developments in judicial review.[58] Culturally, too, in Singapore (as in the UK, and in contrast to the US) both regulators and regulated prefer regulatory processes that are discretionary and cooperative to those that are highly rule-bound, confrontational and judicialised.[59] Similarly, it is commonly said that Singaporean constitutional arrangements contemplate a collaborative, rather than a confrontational, relationship between the branches of government.

C. Africa

In very crude terms, the typical British post-colonial legacy, in Africa and elsewhere, had four main components: a written constitution with some version

[54] KYL Tan, 'The Singapore Judiciary: Independence, Impartiality and Integrity' in Lee and Pittard (eds), *Asia-Pacific Judiciaries* (2018), 304.

[55] LJ Chua and SL Haynie, 'Judicial Review of Executive Power in the Singaporean Context, 1965–2012' [2016] *Journal of Law and Courts* 43.

[56] For more detailed discussion see SK Chan, 'Judicial Review – From Angst to Empathy' (2010) 22 *Singapore Academy of Law Journal* 469; D Chan, 'An Analysis of Substantive Review in Singaporean Administrative Law' (2013) 25 *Singapore Academy of Law Journal* 296; C Zhida, 'The Nature of Judicial Review in Singapore' (2013) 31 *Singapore Law Review* 79 (esp 96–100 on ouster clauses); C Hong, 'Shaping a Common Law Duty to Give Reasons in Singapore: Of Fairness, Regulatory Paradoxes and Proportionate Remedies' (2016) 28 *Singapore Academy of Law Journal* 24 (on *Padfield* and reason-giving); S Jhaveri, 'The Doctrine of Substantive Legitimate Expectations' [2016] *PL* 1; S Menon, 'The Rule of Law: The Path to Exceptionalism' (2016) 28 *Singapore Academy of Law Journal* 413; EKB Tan, 'Curial Deference in Singapore Public Law: Autochthonous Evolution to Buttress Good Governance and the Rule of Law' (2017) 29 *Singapore Academy of Law Journal* 800; S Jhaveri, 'Localising Administrative Law in Singapore: Embracing Inter-Branch Equality' (2017) *Singapore Academy of Law Journal* 828; K Ching, 'An Uncertain Future for Substantive Legitimate Expectations in Singapore' [2018] *PL* 192.

[57] J Lin, 'The Judicialization of Governance: The Case of Singapore' in Ginsburg and Chen (n 31), 287–88.

[58] ibid 295.

[59] ibid 303.

of separation of powers and judicial independence, a parliamentary system of government, entrenched protections for minority rights, and rule-of-law rhetoric. In modern jargon, decolonialisation involved export from Britain of an ideal form of liberal-democratic constitutionalism that did not actually exist in Britain itself and was very different, indeed, from the forms of more or less undemocratic colonial governance that it replaced. Many of the newly independent states were characterised by long-standing and deeply rooted ethnic and religious divisions (often the result of geo-political haggling amongst the colonial powers), culturally embedded, indigenous forms of authoritarianism, and complex, pluralistic legal regimes. Also, as already observed, the 1960s – the decade of the Quartet – were years of rapid decolonialisation and transition, especially in Africa. For instance, Tanzania and Uganda became independent in 1962, Kenya in 1963 and Malawi in 1964.

i. Malawi, Tanzania and Uganda

In her study of the judiciaries of Malawi, Tanzania and Uganda, Rachel Ellett traces their histories in five phases from the colonial period, through independence, authoritarianism and multi-partyism, to the second multi-party election. In the colonial period:

> Through executive privilege, governors were given broad swathes of power and only under very exceptional circumstances would courts overturn an executive ordinance. Administrative decision-making, from chieftaincy to district commissioner or governor, was largely insulated from legal challenge. Executive fiat was frequently exercised through 'emergency powers' … colonial judges held their office at Her Majesty's pleasure and their employment, like that of any other colonial employee, could be terminated at will[60] … Although colonial courts were critical in terms of social control, the court had no ability to check the political power of the colonial government. Despite the establishment of constitutional organs power remained vested in the executive branch … Rights protection extended only to white citizens and not colonial subjects. Thus the 'accountability role' of courts within the political order was minimal at best. The government was accountable to the colonial office, and to no one within the colony itself … Constitutional law thus defined the relationship between Imperial government and colonial officers, and not between the government and the people.[61]

Independence superimposed 'a liberal constitution onto a despotic colonial order'.[62] In this new environment, judiciaries were seen as obstacles 'to the ambitious development agendas of the new nations' leaders. Subsequently,

[60] RL Ellett, *Pathways to Judicial Power in Transitional States: Perspectives from African Courts* (London, Routledge, 2013) 35–36.

[61] ibid 39–40.

[62] ibid 41. See also HK Prempeh, '*Marbury* in Africa: Judicial Review and the Challenge of Constitutionalism in Contemporary in Africa' (2006) 80 *Tulane Law Review* 1239.

courts were either marginalised or simply attacked and undermined to the point of irrelevance'.[63]

Soon after independence, various of the inherited parliamentary systems were replaced by presidential constitutions that concentrated power in the executive (typically headed by a charismatic leader) in the name of national unity and economic development.[64] 'The promulgation of these constitutions marked the end of a brief period of judicial autonomy'.[65] 'Powers of judicial review were stripped, Africanisation of judicial personnel became highly politicised and the law was used as an instrument of oppression'.[66] '[A] general pattern emerged across the region in which courts were either marginalised (Malawi), ignored or attacked (Uganda), or became an important mechanism of control in the maintenance of the one-party state (Tanzania)'.[67] 'Early signs of independence in the judiciary in Malawi were shut down, first with the wholesale removal of all expatriate judges, then with the removal of powers of judicial review'.[68] In Malawi and Tanzania:

> Powers of judicial review were in effect removed with the passage of wide derogation clauses that protected government policy and behaviour. Presidential decrees in all three countries became the desired method of policy-making, and these decrees were beyond the scope judicial inquiry.[69]

The transition to multi-partyism took place from the mid-1980s to the mid-1990s; and Ellett locates the second multi-party election phase in the decade following that. She treats the second election as a test of the success of multi-partyism in creating genuine democratic political competition, judicial independence and adherence to the 'rule of law'. However, it is often pointed out[70] that there is an important difference between democracy (concerned with the allocation of power) and constitutionalism (concerned with limitation and control of power). Reforms that promote democracy and political pluralism will not necessarily promote constitutionalism. The detailed stories of these two phases in the three jurisdictions are complex and messy. If one general point emerges it is that in periods of political instability and contestation, courts may be presented with opportunities to play assertive and independent roles in controlling the government and protecting individual rights. However, once the political instability has passed, the emergent, dominant political force may take steps to weaken the judiciary. According to Ellett, such cycles of feast and famine characterise

[63] Ellett, *Pathways to Judicial Power* (2013) 41.

[64] YP Ghai, 'Constitutions and the Political Order in East Africa' (1972) 21 *International and Comparative Law Quarterly* 403 (discussing Kenya, Tanzania and Uganda).

[65] Ellett (n 60) 41.

[66] ibid 46.

[67] ibid 61.

[68] ibid 80.

[69] Ellett (n 60) 80.

[70] See, eg HK Prempeh, 'Africa's "Constitutionalism Revival": False Start or New Dawn (2007) 5 *International Journal of Constitutional Law* 469.

the post-independence history of the judiciaries in Malawi and Uganda. By contrast, in Tanzania, opportunities for judicial assertiveness were minimised by the capacity of the dominant political force to maintain tight control over the transition process. Generalising the point even more, the strength of judiciaries (and legislatures)[71] as controllers of government tends to be inversely proportional to the strength of the executive and the concentration of political power in single parties and individuals.

ii. Kenya

Yash Ghai and Patrick McAuslan, writing in 1970, tell us that since 1898 – the date of the first reported case of judicial review of administrative action in Kenya:

> [T]he decisions of administrative tribunals and officials such as immigration officers have been upset on a wide variety of grounds including failure to observe the *audi alteram partem* rule, presence of bias, excess of jurisdiction, insufficient evidence on which to base a decision, wrongful delegation of power, informality, and something akin to abuse of power.[72]

They continue: 'The picture which emerges … is of a constant tussle between the courts and the administration in which both are reasonably circumspect in the exercise of their powers'.[73]

Ghai and McAuslan go on to point out, however, that there was a dual system of colonial administration in Kenya which treated Africans and non-Africans quite differently; and that:

> There was to all intents and purposes no judicial control of native and African administration in practice, other than the somewhat ineffective control of the magisterial powers of administrative officers … The non-African on the other hand has always been accustomed to using the courts … the position has not changed appreciably since the advent of an African Government.[74]

The authors conclude that in Kenya immediately after independence:

> [F]ormally the courts appear as an institution of control performing a function similar to that which they perform in England; effectively, their influence on the

[71] See, eg JD Barkan, 'Legislatures on the Rise?' in L Diamond and MF Plattner (eds), *Democratization in Africa: Progress and Retreat*, 2nd edn (Baltimore, The Johns Hopkins University Press, 2010).

[72] YP Ghai and J McAuslan, *Public Law and Political Change in Kenya: A Study of the Legal Framework of Government from Colonial Times to the Present* (Nairobi, OUP, 1970) 301 (footnotes omitted).

[73] ibid 302.

[74] ibid 302–03, 506–09. For an excellent elaboration of this line of argument in relation to the British colonies of East and West Africa see RB Seidman, 'Administrative Law and Legitimacy in Anglophone Africa: A Problem in the Reception of Foreign Law' (1970) 5 *Law and Society Review* 161.

> administration is small, because there are relatively few people who think of them or use them for this purpose compared to the number of people who could, and the number of occasions when the circumstances warrant it, and because there is little political impediment in the way of administration reducing their control function to a very small ambit.[75]

Moreover, the independence constitution, which established a parliamentary system of government, was very soon replaced by one that installed (semi-) presidentialism. One result was that although the powers of the newly democratic post-independence legislature were significantly larger than those of its colonial predecessors, its control over an increasingly powerful executive was very limited. 'Since independence, the thrust of the Government's constitutional changes, and administrative and political practices has been to whittle down a controlling function of the legislature and curb its political effectiveness'.[76] Regarding administrative law in the post-independence era, Ghai and McAuslan say:

> Few actions could have better demonstrated the sincerity of government's intention to keep within the spirit of the Constitution than a broadening, simplifying and cheapening of the remedies available to challenge administrative action … Far from taking such action, however, the Government has cut down, in several statutes, the possibility of challenge to administrative action in the courts[77] … Parliament and the courts continue to be praised for the performance of their functions, but their power significantly to affect executive action continues to be whittled away.[78]

According to James Gathii:

> [F]or decades after independence, Kenyan Courts did the bidding of the government of the day. They rarely, if ever exercised their power of judicial review of abuses of individual human rights or of the constitutionality of executive conduct. The Courts overwhelmingly used their authority to defend and protect conservative political and economic interests rather than to defend individual rights from state abuse.[79]

In 1978, Daniel arap Moi became President of Kenya, succeeding Jomo Kenyatta. In this period, Kenya was a one-party state, ruled by the Kenya African National Union (KANU). For the 1988 elections, in an attempt to increase its control even further, the Government abolished the secret ballot, precipitating agitation for constitutional change and leading to the introduction of multi-party elections in the 1990s.

Widespread violence following the 2008 elections resulted in further agitation for constitutional change, and the adoption in 2010 of a new, 'transformative'

[75] Ghai and McAuslan, *Public Law and Political Change in Kenya* (1970) 304.
[76] ibid 358.
[77] ibid 515.
[78] Ghai and McAuslan (n 72) 517.
[79] JT Gathii, *The Contested Empowerment of Kenya's Judiciary, 2010–2015: A Historical Institutional Analysis* (Nairobi, Sheria Publishing House, 2016) 23.

Constitution, much influenced by the 1996 South African Constitution.[80] On the surface, at least, the 2010 Constitution greatly strengthens the judiciary and its capacity to control the Government.[81] It also reintroduces the Senate (which was abolished soon after independence) as the upper house of the legislature, and introduces a devolved system of government. In these ways, it is designed to diffuse political power both vertically and horizontally, and to weaken the central executive.

Article 47 of the Constitution (like section 33 of the South African Constitution) confers a right to fair administrative action; and the Fair Administration Act 2015 (like its South African counterpart, the Promotion of Administrative Justice Act 2000) gives effect to that right. Gathii thinks that

> since the coming into force of the 2010 Constitution, an increasing number of Kenya [*sic*] Judges ... have embraced a new judicial philosophy that vigorously defends individual human rights and that puts people rather than the interests of the State and powerful individuals at the center of the decision-making process.[82]

'[T]he post-2010 Judiciary', he says, 'sees itself as a corrective mechanism of both its own previous failures as well as the failure of other governance institutions'.[83] However, this new activism has generated a backlash from the legislature and the executive, both of which have taken steps to curb the judiciary.[84] Migai Akech concludes that in the light of events since 2010, 'it is difficult to assert that Kenyan courts are legitimately exercising the power of judicial review'.[85] Ghai and Ghai are even less optimistic. Comparing Kenya unfavourably with South Africa, they gloomily reflect that since 2010,

> The executive has shown even greater resistance [than the political parties] to the constitution, strengthened the ethnic basis of politics, and frequently disregarded court decisions against it. The prevalence and scale of corruption has greatly increased, as has violence by the police.[86]

Constitutionalisation of judicial review promises significant doctrinal advances in administrative law. For instance, legislative use of wide ouster clauses may

[80] JC Ghai and Y Ghai, 'The Contribution of the South African Constitution to Kenya's Constitution' in R Dixon and T Roux (eds), *Constitutional Triumphs, Constitutional Disappointments: A Critical Assessment of the 1996 South African Constitution's Local and International Significance* (Cambridge, CUP, 2018). The South African Constitution was itself much influenced by the 1994 Constitution of Malawi, as to which see DM Chirwa, 'Liberating Malawi's Administrative Justice Jurisprudence from its Common Law Shackles' (2011) 55 *Journal of African Law* 105.

[81] Gathii, *Kenya's Judiciary* (2016). See also EA O'Loughlin, 'Decolonising Jurisprudence: Public Interest Standing in New Constitutional Orders' in M Elliott, J Varuhas and SW Stark, *The Unity of Public Law? Doctrinal, Theoretical and Comparative Perspectives* (Oxford, Hart Publishing, 2018) 366–71.

[82] Gathii (n 79) 23.

[83] Gathii (n 79) 52.

[84] Gathii (n 79) ch 4.

[85] M Akech, *Administrative Law* (Nairobi, Strathmore University Press, 2016) 452. See also HK Prempeh, 'A New Jurisprudence for Africa' (1999) 10 *Journal of Democracy* 135.

[86] Ghai and Ghai, 'South African Constitution' (2018) 290.

face challenge on constitutional grounds. On the other hand, there are also some technical problems with constitutionalisation. For instance, in Kenya it is not clear whether constitutional judicial review has displaced or runs parallel to common law judicial review inherited from the colonial era. Some fear that this uncertainty may be exploited by opponents of judicial power to distinguish between constitutional and common law judicial review and to restrict the spirit and the word of the new regime to cases that raise constitutional issues.[87] Scholars have regretted the tendency of Kenyan and South African courts to rely on common law precedents in interpreting and applying the constitutional right to fair administration.[88] On the other hand, the South African Constitutional Court has allowed litigants to sidestep constitutional review and the carefully crafted (if not entirely popular) limitations on the constitutional right (in the Promotion of Administrative Justice Act) by appealing to a constitutional principle of 'legality'.[89] The constitutional right applies to 'administrative action', and in South Africa this concept has regrettably become 'the focus of … administrative law'.[90] Cora Hoexter is hopeful that this will not happen in Kenya because there, the definition of administrative action is 'considerably wider and simpler'.[91] Arguably, most of these problems are the result not so much of constitutionalisation as such, but rather of its statutory elaboration. As Hoexter puts it, 'arguably all we really needed (absent the constitutional mandate) was section 33 of the Constitution'.[92]

Ghai and Ghai conclude that South Africa has had much more success than Kenya in shaking off the colonial legacy of authoritarian government and creating a new 'liberal' order of constitutionalism in which political power is subject to meaningful limitations effectively enforced by courts and other unelected institutions.[93] They explain South Africa's relative success in terms of high-quality political leadership 'with a clear vision of the kind of South Africa it wanted';[94] a more developed economy; 'real' political parties with clear policies,

[87] Gathii (n 79) ch 3; Akech, *Administrative Law* (2016) 433.

[88] C Hoexter, 'Administrative Justice in Kenya: Learning from South Africa's Mistakes' (2018) 62 *Journal of African Law* 105, 112–15.

[89] ibid 123–26.

[90] ibid 115.

[91] ibid 116; see also 120–23.

[92] C Hoexter, 'The Constitutionalization and Codification of Judicial Review in South Africa' in C Forsyth, M Elliott, S Jhaveri, M Ramsden and A Scully-Hill (eds), *Effective Judicial Review: A Cornerstone of Good Governance* (Oxford, OUP, 2010) 60.

[93] Concerning the latter see, eg CM Fombad, 'The Role of Emerging Hybrid Institutions of Accountability in the Separation of Powers Scheme in Africa' in CM Fombad (ed), *Separation of Powers in African Constitutionalism* (Oxford, OUP, 2016); C Fombad, 'The Diffusion of South African-Style Institutions? A Study in Comparative Constitutionalism' in Dixon and Roux (eds), *Constitutional Triumphs, Constitutional Disappointments: A Critical Assessment of the 1996 South African Constitution's Local and International Significance* (Cambridge, CUP, 2018); H Klug, 'Corruption, the Rule of Law and the Role of Independent Institutions' in Dixon and Roux (eds), *Constitutional Triumphs, Constitutional Disappointments: A Critical Assessment of the 1996 South African Constitution's Local and International Significance* (Cambridge, CUP, 2018).

[94] Ghai and Ghai (n 80) 292.

neither racially nor ethnically biased; and government willingness to accept adverse court decisions. In these respects, South Africa also seems to stand out from other African jurisdictions such as Malawi, Tanzania and Zambia.[95]

IV. THEMES

This section will pick out for further discussion various themes that run through the previous case studies of specific areas and jurisdictions of the common law world.

A. The Privy Council

For more than 300 years, the Privy Council (PC) and its committees, including the Judicial Committee (JCPC, established in 1833), played an extremely important part in the governance of the British Empire; and on a much-reduced scale, the JCPC continues to do so today.[96] The PC exercised a quasi-judicial jurisdiction of disallowing colonial statutes on the ground of inconsistency with British policy and law. From the end of the nineteenth century, there were vigorous debates about the pros and cons of the abolition of the jurisdiction of the JCPC over various colonies upon their gaining independence.[97] In fact, most colonies retained the jurisdiction for a shorter or longer period after independence. At the end of the nineteenth century, there were so many Indian appeals to the JCPC that there was a series of the Law Reports dedicated to appeals from the sub-continent and some other areas of the Empire. The JCPC was valued partly because of the quality of the judges who staffed it, and also for its role in securing a degree of legal uniformity around the Empire.[98] The calibre of the senior colonial judiciary was variable, and colonial judges held office at will. This practice harked back to the medieval period in England, when there was no clear separation of powers and judges were royal officials who served at the monarch's pleasure.

[95] P Vondoepp, 'The Problem of Judicial Control in Africa's Neopatrimonial Democracies: Malawi and Zambia' (2005) *Political Science Quarterly* 275; S Gloppen, 'The Accountability Function of the Courts in Tanzania and Zambia' (2003) 10 *Democratization* 112.

[96] On the contemporary PCJC see Lord Neuberger, 'The Judicial Committee of the Privy Council in the 21st Century' (2014) 3 *Cambridge Journal of International and Comparative Law* 30; D Clarry, 'Institutional Judicial Independence and the Privy Council' (2014) 3 *Cambridge Journal of International and Comparative Law* 46; T Robinson and A Bulkan, 'Constitutional Comparisons by A Supranational Court in Flux: The Privy Council and Caribbean Bills of Rights' (2017) 80 *MLR* 379.

[97] Concerning Africa see B Ibhawoh, 'Asserting Judicial Sovereignty: The Debate Over the Abolition of Privy Council Jurisdiction in British Africa' in S Dorsett and J McLaren, *Legal Histories of the British Empire: Laws, Engagement and Legacies* (Abingdon, Routledge, 2014) ch 3.

[98] KJ Keith, 'The Unity of the Common Law and the Ending of Appeals to the Privy Council' (2005) 54 *International and Comparative Law Quarterly* 197.

The JCPC did most work in the areas of private law, tax law, commercial law and criminal law. Except in relation to Canada and Australia, there were very few constitutional cases in the colonial period.[99] Most colonies had unitary rather than federal systems of government; and, as AV Dicey observed, federalism breeds legalism.[100] Furthermore, colonial judges in the non-white empire lacked independence; legal limits and controls on the powers of colonial executives and legislatures were sparse; and native populations generally lacked opportunities to challenge decisions of colonial authorities, even if settlers did not. According to Loren Beth, between 1813 and 1865 the Privy Council heard only 16 appeals against decisions in cases challenging non-legislative government action.[101] As we have seen, in parts of the Empire, particularly Africa, the colonial legacy of strong executives but weak legislatures and courts, has had a lasting effect on the governance and politics of independent states.

After independence, probably Malaysia and Sri Lanka sent most public law cases to the JCPC. We have already noted the *South East Asia Fire Bricks* case.[102] Appeals from Ceylon (Sri Lanka) also produced some well-known administrative law decisions including *Nakudda Ali v Jayaratne* (1951),[103] *Durayappah v Fernando* (1966)[104] and *Jayawardane v Silva* (1970).[105] Helena Meng says that between 1957 and 1983, there were eight appeals to the PCJC on matters of 'general administrative law' from Malaysia (out of a total of 140 appeals in civil matters); and that between 1963 and 1983 there were three such appeals from Singapore (out of a total of 49 civil appeals).[106] The Privy Council's work in public law was often criticised not only on the ground of lack of familiarity with local circumstances, but also that judges from a unitary governmental system could not properly understand multi-layered systems with written constitutions.[107] At all events, it seems fair to say that even in its heyday, the Privy Council had, at best, marginal influence on colonial administrative law.

[99] LP Beth, 'The Judicial Committee as Constitutional Court for the British Empire 1833–1971' (1977) 47 *Georgia Journal of International and Comparative Law* 47.

[100] JWF Allison (ed), *AV Dicey, The Law of the Constitution* (Oxford, OUP, 2013) 92.

[101] LP Beth, 'The Judicial Committee of the Privy Council and the Development of Judicial Review' (1976) 24 *American Journal of Comparative Law* 22, 34.

[102] See n 47 above.

[103] *Nakkuda Ali v Jayaratne* [1951] AC 66 (PC); on which see D Clark, 'Natural Justice: A Critical Examination of Re Thomas Cord' (1980) 10 *Hong Kong Law Journal* 136, 155–56.

[104] *Durayappah v Fernando* (1966) 69 NLR 264, [1967] 3 WLR 289 (PC).

[105] *Jayawardane v Silva* [1970] UKPC 20, [1970] 1 WLR 1365 (PC).

[106] HCH Meng, 'The Privy Council as Court of Last Resort in Singapore and Malaysia:1957–1983' in AJ Harding, *The Common Law in Singapore and Malaysia: A Volume of Essays Marking the 25th Anniversary of the Malaya Law Review 1959–1984* (Singapore, Butterworths, 1985) 90.

[107] See, eg, EM Campbell, 'The Decline of the Jurisdiction of the Judicial Committee of the Privy Council' (1959) 33 *Australian Law Journal* 196; M Gleeson, 'The Influence of the Privy Council on Australia' (2007) 29 *Australian Bar Review* 123; P Mitchell, 'The Privy Council and the Difficulty of Distance' (2016) 36 *Oxford Journal of Legal Studies* 26.

B. Regime Type

Elsewhere, I have argued at length that there is a significant relationship between the way public power is allocated and distributed in a system of government and the way public power – particularly administrative power – is controlled.[108] Government structures are often distinguished in terms of categories such as parliamentarism, presidentialism and semi-presidentialism. By contrast, my approach analyses distribution of power in terms of the degree to which power is 'concentrated' or 'diffused'. It also draws a distinction between two paradigmatic modes of controlling power, which I call 'checks and balances' and 'accountability' respectively. The basic argument is that the more power is diffused amongst various components of a governmental system, the more reliance will be placed on inter-institutional checks and balances as a method of controlling power. By contrast, the more power is concentrated in particular components of the system, the more reliance will be placed for control on mechanisms of inter-institutional accountability.

This is not the place to attempt to apply this approach generally to British colonialism and decolonisation. A few random comments must suffice. First, in the period of British imperialism, the English system of government was transformed from a limited (as opposed to an absolute) monarchy to the paradigmatic 'parliamentary democracy'. Under monarchy, public power is typically highly concentrated in the monarch and the monarch's closest advisers and administrators. For a period in the eighteenth and nineteenth centuries, the changes initiated by the Glorious Revolution of 1688 produced a degree of diffusion of power between the (monarchical) executive and Parliament. However, by the mid-twentieth century, as a result of democratisation, and the development of responsible government and strong political parties, power was once again highly concentrated in the (now-non-monarchical) executive to the point where, in the late-1970s, a senior Conservative politician could call the British system an 'elective dictatorship'.

Leaving aside the first polity to escape the imperial orbit (the United States of America) the rest of the Empire can be roughly divided into settled and non-settled colonies. The structure of government in the settled colonies – notably Canada, Australia and New Zealand – developed along roughly the same lines as that in Britain. By contrast, non-settled colonies in Asia, Africa and elsewhere were generally governed, right up until independence, by various forms and degrees of undemocratic, quasi-monarchical, executive dominance. In this respect, colonisation involved a change in the identity of the governors from what it had been in the pre-colonial period, but not in the mode of governance. At independence, colonies were typically bequeathed a parliamentary

[108] P Cane, *Controlling Administrative Power: An Historical Comparison* (Cambridge, CUP, 2016).

system of government in the (self-) image of the British. In some places, the imported Westminster model operated with 'Eastminster' variations that tended to reinforce executive power.[109] In other places, parliamentarism was replaced by some form of presidentialism, once again to strengthen the position of patrimonial elites. In yet others (such as Pakistan), civilian elites lost control of the military, turning elective-executive dominance into unelected dictatorship.

Concentration of power in the executive may, as in Britain in the 1960s, elicit an assertion of judicial power which may, in turn, be met by an executive backlash. Under better circumstances (as in the UK, South Africa and Kenya) government accountability to courts may be supplemented by accountability to other 'independent' institutions, such as ombudsmen and anti-corruption agencies. The general point is that the role of judicial review in controlling administrative power can only be fully understood when account is also taken of the structural features of the governmental system of which courts form a part, and of alternative control mechanisms. This chapter has focused on assertive judicial review as a political phenomenon exemplified in the Quartet. However, the same approach could be applied to micro-analysis of judicial-review doctrine, to understand how specific accountability norms and values are shaped and influenced by the structural features of government and politics.

C. Written Constitutions

A significant difference between the UK legal system and the systems of most of Britain's former colonies is that the UK lacks a codified constitution. The modern, codified constitution is a product of the first case of British decolonialisation, the creation of the USA. The forebears of the US Constitution (and preceding state constitutions) were the royal charters, and instructions to governors, of the North American colonies. The origins of the notion of a constitution as 'higher' or 'fundamental' law and the practice of judicial review of legislation can be found in the 'inconsistency' principle of British imperial law, according to which laws made by colonial lawmakers could be invalidated, typically by the Privy Council, for inconsistency with English law. Just as British colonialism produced the (almost) first codified constitution, so the end of Empire in the mid-twentieth century established codified constitutionalism as the paradigm, leaving the UK and a couple of other modern nations as uncodified constitutional outliers.

For present purposes, perhaps the most important issue arising out of the introduction of a codified Constitution concerns the relationship between the law of the Constitution and the pre-existing, uncodified constitutional

[109] H Kumarasingham, 'Eastminster – Decolonisation and State-Building in British Asia' in H Kumarasingham (ed), *Constitution-making in Asia: Decolonisation and State-Building in the Aftermath of the British Empire* (London, Routledge, 2016).

and administrative law. This topic was touched upon in the earlier discussion of Kenya;[110] and it was noted that the Malaysian Constitution, for instance, explicitly authorises courts to have regard to the English common law. The basic question is: to what extent does the codified Constitution displace and supersede the uncodified 'common law' of the constitution? Or, put differently, to what extent does the Constitution actually codify constitutional law? This is a very complex topic about which only a very little can be said here.

Like the paradigm codified Constitution – that of the US – many Constitutions say relatively little about the executive and the exercise of administrative power compared with provisions dealing with the legislature, the courts, and 'rights'. This feature of the paradigm Constitution reflects the circumstances, preoccupations and concerns of the late eighteenth century. The result is that in many systems, administrative law is mostly subconstitutional and, therefore, subject to invalidation for unconstitutionality. It also means that if the only source of judicial power is the Constitution and if (as in the US) the main function of the courts is to enforce the Constitution, there will be few foundations on which administrative law can be built unless and until the legislature exercises whatever powers it has to regulate the executive. In the classic, English, uncodified model, by contrast, courts have 'inherent' power, by virtue of their very status as courts, to make common law, including administrative law and constitutional law. In Australia, an influential theory (strongly supported, until very recently, by judicial practice) is that not only did the Australian Constitution (which says relatively little about the executive and administrative power) not supersede the pre-existing, inherited common law but, indeed, was founded upon it. In this sense, the Australian Constitution was not treated as a code.

The underlying point concerns the way legal systems and law develop. In the classic English model, law (including constitutional and administrative law) evolves incrementally through the operation of small-scale, problem-solving processes ('litigation'). Its formulation is (in theory, anyway) always provisional and open to development at any and every iteration of the problem-solving process. In this model, statutes in canonical form, however quantitatively significant they may be, operate against the background of, and as interventions in, the ongoing stream of the common law. The introduction of a codified Constitution may revolutionise that situation by substituting a document for inherent lawmaking power as the root source of the legal system, legal power and law. One of the uses of a Constitution is to immunise certain rules and norms from evolutionary change. The balance between evolution and revolution is central to the dynamics of public law and varies from system to system.

[110] For an early (and remarkable) analysis of the potential impact of an independence constitution (in this case, the Nigerian) on inherited English administrative law see RB Seidman, 'Constitutional Standards of Judicial Review of Administrative Action in Nigeria' (1965) 1 *Nigerian Law Journal* 232.

A Constitution is meant to be fundamental and to last. Some, like those of the US and Australia, have lasted a long time with a minimum of amendment; but these are the exceptions, not the rule;[111] and various other techniques have been developed to keep the Constitution up to date with political, social and economic conditions. At the other extreme, listen to what Ghai and McAuslan have to say about the development of 'constitutionalism' (meaning, roughly, entrenched limitation of government power) in Kenya:

> [I]t may be said until very late in the colonial era, Kenya had no constitution … Not until the late [nineteen] fifties did a colonial constitution in Kenya address itself to the problems of the limitation of executive power … Far from being the most fundamental law of the land, the constitutional law of Kenya from 1958 to independence was the least fundamental, undergoing major changes two or three times a year. At independence, however, a complete change of attitude towards the constitution was assumed to have taken place … The new approach … was that the constitution was henceforth to be regarded as permanent … It was deemed to have fixed once and for all the divisions of power between the various governing authorities in Kenya, provided an elaborate set of checks and balances, and topped off the whole thing with a wide ranging Bill of Rights … The Government of Kenya may have regarded the Constitution as the first; it did not regard it as the second … The Constitution is not in practice seen as an umpire above the political struggle, but as a weapon in that struggle which can be used and altered in order to gain temporary and passing advantages over one's political opponents.[112]

The creation of a codified Constitution is often conceptualised as an exercise of a specific form of power – 'constituent power'. Recognition of this species of power, separate from legislative, executive and judicial powers, provides opportunities for its capture. An executive that can control not only the legislature, the bureaucracy (including the police and the military) and the judiciary, but also the 'constituent assembly', defines dictatorship.

In short, the choice between an uncodified and a codified constitution is not one merely of form. It may have fundamental effects on the conduct of government and the practices of politics. On the other hand, as we saw in the case of Pakistan, the distinction between constitutional and subconstitutional public law may provide courts with resources for exercising significant control over government without risking existential retaliation from a powerful executive. There is much work to be done in this area of constitutional theory.

D. National Security and Emergencies

A near-definitional characteristic of British colonial governance was frequent use of extreme security measures and declarations of states of emergency to

[111] Z Elkins, T Ginsburg and J Melton, *The Endurance of National Constitutions* (Cambridge, CUP, 2009).

[112] Ghai and McAuslan (n 72) 510–11.

gain even more control over the governed. It is a sad fact that the history of colonialism and decolonialisation provides ample material for studying the suspension of law as a technique for concentrating power even in systems that formally diffuse it to a greater or lesser extent. The more concentrated legal power becomes, the less effective independent legal controls on that power tend to be. The institutional context in which administrative law doctrine operates is critical to understanding its meaning, force and potential. The doctrine is only as powerful as the institutions that deploy it.

E. Law and Politics, Power and Interests

A fourth theme that emerges from our earlier anecdotal accounts is particularly prominent in the history of decolonisation in Africa, but has more general salience. An important aspect of the development of modern public law was the transition in the eighteenth century from ideas of mixed government to separation of powers as the foundational principle of constitutional design. Montesquieu's account of the English system of government in *The Spirit of the Laws* clearly marks the shift. He attributed the liberty-promoting character of the English Constitution to two features in particular: the division of power ('separation of powers') between the executive monarch, the legislative Houses of Lords and Commons, and the judicial courts; but, equally importantly, the equal ('checking and balancing') participation of the three estates of the realm – monarch, aristocracy and ordinary people – in the most important governmental institution, the legislature. For various reasons, the US Founders, members of a social elite, were suspicious not only of monarchy but also of popular democracy. In the design of the Constitution they attempted not only to create a relatively weak Presidency but also to prevent the only popularly elected element of the system – the House of Representatives – from dominating the legislative process. Many of the Founders envisaged an aristocratic republic in which the few governed, albeit in the name of the many. One effect of increasing democratisation and the development of mass, extra-Congressional political parties in the nineteenth and twentieth centuries was to eliminate from constitutional thinking any idea of a balance between the interests of the aristocracy and the plebs and to substitute the concept of balance between the three institutions of government: legislature, executive and judiciary.

As a result, paradigmatic (predominantly US-derived) constitutional theory understands both division of power and checks and balances in terms of institutions and functions rather than socio-political groups or interests. Of course, this has not led to the demise of socio-political conflict in society; but in theory, anyway, such conflict is now directed, through the operation of the political party system, towards gaining control of functionally defined institutions rather than sharing public powers with competing social interests: separation of powers, not mixed government. Politicians no longer represent groups and interests, but 'people' who vote for parties. To get heard, interests now bypass representative democracy and engage in more direct political activity, such as lobbying.

However well this theory fits Western 'liberal democracies', it does not provide as much help in understanding societies and systems in which socio-political divisions continue to dominate public life. Like medieval England, many pre-colonial societies were 'patrimonial' and interest/status-based. In many colonies, too, the British tolerated the continuation of patrimonial, elitist governance amongst the colonised population, while emulating modern British practice in their dealings with fellow colonialists. After independence, imposed institutionalist/functionalist Constitutions conflicted with resurgent neo-patrimonial politics manifesting, for instance, in single-partyism. It is not difficult to see how the conflicting logics of institutional/functional separation of powers and socio-political mixed government might not only facilitate and aggravate concentration of functions and monopolisation of institutions, but also allow partisan interests to benefit from such concentration.

The wider resonance of this analysis should now be clearer. Representative democracy as it developed in the West has proven incapable of managing socio-political conflict. Populism is a contemporary symptom of the failure of inherited political practices and constitutional theory to recognise and manage socio-political conflict. There is no better illustration of the problem than Brexit. The population of the UK is more or less evenly divided between Brexiteers and Remainers. Internally, the two main political parties are also more or less divided between Brexiteers and Remainers. Despite the dense concentration of power in the executive in the UK system, at the time of writing (but see the Conclusion for an update) the Government lacks sufficient power to govern the situation and has even foreshadowed military intervention to deal with potential social disruption. Recent judicial intervention to force the Government to promote Parliamentary legislation, to give effect to its notice of withdrawal from the EU, elicited loud and widespread political criticism of the judiciary.

The basic point is that a deep understanding, of the role of administrative and constitutional law doctrine and of the courts that are its guardians, in various systems requires a profound appreciation not only of how those systems work but also of human nature. Socio-political disagreement and conflict are facts of human social life. To the extent that our public law theory treats phenomena such 'populism' and 'neo-patrimonialism' merely as aberrations, it has lost sight of this basic fact.

V. CONCLUSION

At one level, this chapter is about four leading cases in the House of Lords in the 1960s. However, it has little to say about the decisions themselves or the legal doctrine they establish. The discussion has, instead, focused on the governmental and political contexts in which courts exercise powers to review administrative decisions and actions and to make decisions such as those in the Quartet. This is partly a reflection of the limits of the author's knowledge and of the relevant literature available in English. However, the chosen method also rests on a conviction that sound analysis of the transmission and spread of legal doctrine between jurisdictions requires careful attention to be paid to much more than the doctrine itself and its expression in law-making and legal decision-making. The chapter has also aimed to contribute to understanding of the process of post-colonial legal change in non-settled former colonies of the British Empire.

In the light of lessons learned in that context, it may be worthwhile to end with a brief consideration of constitutional events in the UK since the last paragraph of the previous section was written. Much has happened in the meantime. A landslide election victory in November 2019 enabled the Prime Minister to neutralise dissenters within the Conservative Party, allowing him to 'get Brexit done'. Along the way, the Supreme Court tightened its control over the use by the Prime Minister of the power to 'prorogue' Parliament (and, presumably, other 'prerogative' powers). It is not only in the post-colonial context that lawyers' understanding of public law can be greatly enriched by casting their gaze beyond the doctrine to the political and governmental contexts in which it operates.

Part VI

The Quartet in Theory, Practice and History

16

The Quartet Cases Compared

STEPHEN BAILEY

I. THE LEGAL CONTEXT

THE REFLECTIONS CONTAINED in this chapter are centred on six bases on which the Quartet cases and their impact can be considered and compared. In order to evaluate the Quartet, it is necessary to understand how what we now know as judicial review[1] in England and Wales was understood in the period up to the mid-1960s. Among the themes that emerge are these. First, at least some of what are recognised as the basic grounds for judicial review had been well established in the common law for centuries. The principle that the Crown, and more generally the Government and other public bodies, could only interfere with private rights where that was authorised by law was very well established.[2] The route by which these matters would be tested tended to be by civil actions, for example for trespass,[3] a petition of right against the Crown or an application for *habeas corpus*. Secondly, it was also well established that the Court of King's or Queen's Bench would exercise control through the writs of certiorari and prohibition over inferior courts, tribunals and other bodies exercising judicial functions.[4] This would include points that jurisdiction should not be exceeded, errors of law should not be made, discretions should be exercised in a 'judicial' manner and natural justice should be observed. There was also a general requirement, enforceable by the writ of mandamus, that public duties be performed. However, the extent to which interests other than private rights and the manner of the exercise of discretionary executive powers were subject

[1] According to Stephen Sedley (S Sedley, *Lions under the Throne* (Cambridge, CUP, 2015) 231), the wording of the 'application for judicial review' in the version of RSC Ord 53 substituted by SI 1977/1958 was based on the title of Stanley de Smith's ground-breaking *Judicial Review of Administrative Action*, 1st edn (London, Stevens, 1959).

[2] Illustrated by the legal struggles over the ambit of the Crown's prerogative powers.

[3] eg *Entick v Carrington* (1765) 19 St Tr 1030.

[4] See S Anderson, 'Judicial Review' in *The Oxford History of the Laws of England, vol XI, 1820–1914: English Legal System, Pt 2* (Oxford, OUP, 2010) ch 6; Sedley, *Lions* (2015).

to any, or any effective, control by judicial review was much more limited. A particular feature was the importance attached to the distinction between judicial and administrative functions.[5]

The significance of this is directly related to the nature and distribution of functions within a decentralised state.[6] In the nineteenth century, it could be said that many of the administrative powers that directly affected the rights of individuals were exercised by local bodies such as justices of the peace and, later, commissioners, tribunals and local authorities, rather than by central bodies. Many of these powers were subject to judicial review.[7] On the other hand, the central departments of state were relatively small, and for a large part focused on the conduct of foreign affairs, defence and the maintenance of national security. Nobody seemed to dream that the manner of exercise of powers at this level might be subject to judicial review.

The twentieth century saw a significant expansion in the role, activities and size of central government departments, with the concomitant growth of administrative law, which included significant statutory powers both to provide public services and to interfere with private rights. There were major preoccupations with the use of delegated legislation and the development of tribunals, many linked to government departments, that discharged judicial functions. Broader concerns about the role of the courts outside these areas took longer to surface, but from the mid-1950s could be seen across the political spectrum:[8]

> Conservative opinion, which in the past showed an unfailing and almost mystical confidence in the ability of the courts to establish and maintain a genuine system of administration according to law, has recently awakened to the fact that the courts are neither able nor willing to control public authorities effectively.[9]

There were also indications of a changed attitude in the Labour Party.[10] The courts, however, remained in the period characterised by Stephen Sedley as that

[5] See n 72; de Smith, *Judicial Review* (1959) ch 2.

[6] For a general survey of developments since the eighteenth century see H Parris, *Constitutional Bureaucracy* (London, George Allen & Unwin, 1969).

[7] See C Stebbings, *Legal Foundations of Tribunals in Nineteenth Century England* (Cambridge, CUP, 2006) ch 7.

[8] See WA Robson, 'Administrative Law' in M Ginsberg (ed), *Law and Opinion in the Twentieth Century* (London, Stevens & Sons, 1959) 198–99.

[9] Robson cited the Inns of Court Conservative and Unionist Society 1955 pamphlet, 'The Rule of Law', which represented a 'mild revolt from the Right at the helplessness of the citizen who seeks redress from arbitrary or unfair action by a department'.

[10] Robson cited RHS Crossman's pamphlet, 'Socialism and the New Despotism' (1956), noting that 'the growth of a vast centralised State bureaucracy constitutes a grave potential threat to social democracy', and G Borrie, 'Justice and the Administration' (Fabian Research Series No 185, 1957). Crossman argued that it was necessary to 'redefine the rights of the citizen' and 'discuss the reforms of the law and the reorganisation of the Judiciary which will be required to defend the individual against oligopolists and oligarchs who threaten his freedom'.

of the 'long sleep'.[11] Here, it should be noted that for this period there was little, if anything, by way of attempts to wake up the courts.[12]

This broad picture is reflected in a series of particular features of both substantive principles of law and the availability of remedies.[13] These included the following:

(1) Many powers of the Crown were derived from the royal prerogative rather than statute. It was generally accepted that the courts could determine whether a prerogative power to interfere with private rights ever existed or had been superseded or modified by statute; the manner of the exercise of a prerogative power was not reviewable.[14]
(2) It was generally accepted that coercive remedies (*certiorari*, prohibition, mandamus, injunctions) were not available against the Crown.[15] The extent to which they lay against servants of the Crown was contested.[16]
(3) The remedy of a declaration first became generally available in 1883 and was recognised to be relevant to exercises of public power in 1911.[17] There were a number of cases where the remedy was sought by the Attorney-General in respect of local authority expenditure claimed to be unlawful,[18] but it was rarely claimed where *certiorari* or prohibition was available.[19] The use of the declaration as major public law remedy only began to gather pace in the 1950s.[20]
(4) The prerogative orders of *certiorari* and prohibition were only available in respect of courts and other judicial bodies, and administrative bodies when 'acting judicially'.[21] There were authorities that gave a narrow interpretation to this concept.[22] There were occasional examples of *certiorari*

[11] S Sedley, 'The sound of silence' (1994) 110 *LQR* 270, 278. cf R Stevens, *The English Judges* (Oxford, Hart Publishing, 2005) 19, referring to the decision of the House of Lords in *Local Government Board v Arlidge* [1915] AC 120, where a panel of Law Lords, 'all of whom had previously been active Liberal politicians', held that Parliament had intended the ordinary procedures of the board rather than the procedures of a court to be followed in determining an appeal against a closing order; accordingly, the report of the inspector after a public inquiry did not have to be disclosed. Stevens comments: 'British administrative law was to sleep for the next fifty years'. Sedley regards *Wednesbury* as a leading illustration of (a 'snore' in) the long sleep (in 'The sound of silence').

[12] A late exception was the revival of the use of *certiorari* to quash for error of law on the face of the record in *R v Northumberland Compensation Appeal Tribunal, ex p Shaw* [1952] 1 KB 338.

[13] For judicial summaries see Lord Denning MR and Lord Diplock in *O'Reilly v Mackman* [1983] 2 AC 237, 250 (CA), 273 (HL).

[14] This position changed with the GCHQ case: *Council of Civil Service Unions v Minister for the Civil Service* [1985] AC 374.

[15] C McCormick, 'Judicial Review of Administrative Action in the United Kingdom: The Status of Standards between 1890 and 1910' (2018) 10 *Italian Journal of Public Law* 49, 65.

[16] See H Street, *Governmental Liability* (Cambridge, CUP, 1953) 137–38 (mandamus), 140–41 (injunction).

[17] *Dyson v Attorney-General* [1911] 1 KB 410, [1912] 1 Ch 158.

[18] I Zamir, *The Declaratory Judgment* (London, Stevens & Sons, 1962) 258–29.

[19] ibid 166. *Wednesbury* was a declaration case.

[20] See eg *Barnard v National Dock Labour Board* [1953] 2 QB 18.

[21] eg *R v Electricity Commissioners* [1924] 1 KB 171, 205 (Atkin LJ).

[22] See nn 85, 86.

lying in respect of a decision of a central government department, but this was unusual.[23] In 1959, de Smith wrote[24] that there was some authority for the proposition that, subject to exceptions, 'certiorari is not generally an appropriate remedy for abuse of discretion'.

(5) There were relatively few cases in which decisions of ministers were challenged at all;[25] it is difficult to think of any that involved a challenge as to *how* a discretionary power (whether under the prerogative or under statute) was exercised.

(6) There was uncertainty as to how far abuses of discretionary power were challengeable. There were authorities that said that the recognised principles applied only where a 'judicial discretion' was involved.[26]

(7) As stated by the Law Commission in a Working Paper published on 24 July 1967, the 'procedural complexities and anomalies which face the litigant who seeks an order of certiorari, prohibition or mandamus have long been the subject of criticism'.[27]

(8) There was no general right of access to official information or to reasons for decisions. More generally, as put by Peter Hennessy, writing in 1989, 'Secrecy is the bonding material which holds the rambling structure of central government together. Secrecy is built into the calcium of a British policy-maker's bones'.[28]

II. SIX BASES FOR COMPARISON

The bases for comparison to be considered here are: (1) What was the case about? (2) What did the case *actually* decide? (3) What did later judges decide it decided? (4) What arguments were rejected? (5) Irrespective of what *doctrine* was applied or developed, what other general messages did they arguably send out? (6) What might the case have got wrong?

A. What was the Case about: Substance or Procedure; Rights or Interests; Judicial or Administrative?

It is generally recognised that intervention by judges on judicial review rests on firmer ground where it holds that the procedure adopted by an administrative

[23] eg *R v Board of Education* [1910] 2 KB 165, *Board of Education v Rice* [1911] AC 179, HL (here, the Board of Education was determining a statutory appeal). Mandamus was also granted.

[24] de Smith (n 1) 209.

[25] They tended to be cases where the Minister was acting in an appellate role.

[26] de Smith (n 1) 168–69: 'today the courts will often characterise a discretion as judicial when they wish to assert powers of review … but as executive or administrative when they wish to explain their inability or unwillingness to measure it by reference to any objective standard'.

[27] Law Commission Published Working Paper No 13, Exploratory Working Paper on Administrative Law (1967) 2.

[28] P Hennessy, *Whitehall* (London, Secker & Warburg, 1989) 346, and see generally ch 9.

decision-maker, as distinct from the substance of the decision, is unlawful. In the case of the former, the administrator commonly has the opportunity to remake the decision;[29] in the case of the latter, legislation may well be needed if the position is to change. That is not of course to deny that substantive review can in many cases easily be justified. Confining a decision-maker to the powers conferred expressly or impliedly by the common law (occasionally) or statute (usually) upholds the rule of law and, in the latter case, the intention of Parliament. However, the position of the judge is more difficult the more open-textured the legal rule or principle to be applied,[30] the broader the wording of a discretionary power conferred upon a decision-maker[31] and the nearer the issue lies to matters of central or local government policy determined by elected politicians. Conversely, the position of judges has been seen to be stronger where the decision challenged interferes with legal rights conferred by the common law[32] or statute as distinct from broader interests.

Bearing those considerations in mind, *Ridge* clearly addressed procedure (should Mr Ridge have been given a fair hearing?) and *Anisminic* substance (what was the correct meaning of the Order in Council?; was judicial review excluded by the ouster clause?). *Conway* and *Padfield* concerned both procedure and substance. *Conway* concerned the conduct of ordinary litigation and the requirements of a fair trial but also a matter of substance (did the Secretary of State have the last word on a claim of Crown privilege?[33]). *Padfield* clearly addressed both substance and procedure. On the one hand, the case involved a challenge to the decision of a central government minister[34] not to exercise a broad discretionary power in the way requested by the applicants and a claim for mandamus to compel him to exercise that power. On the other hand, the power concerned merely involved the appointment of a committee to investigate the applicant's complaint as distinct from a decision as to whether the complaint was valid or otherwise. The remedy actually granted was the claimants' fall-back position, mandamus requiring the Minister to reconsider the matter of whether a committee should be appointed according to law. Overall, the matter seems to pertain more to process than substance.[35]

[29] Not always; the moment for action may have passed.

[30] This is illustrated by the history of political criticism of judicial decisions under the Human Rights Act 1998: on the one hand, the judges are simply exercising powers conferred on them expressly by Parliament; on the other, many of the legal standards set out in the HRA are open-textured. The issues are often politically sensitive, reaching to the heart of government policy.

[31] eg a committee of investigation may be appointed 'if the Minister so directs' (*Padfield*).

[32] eg rights of property, contractual rights and rights protected by the law of tort.

[33] The ultimate answer was no, and the role of the judge in looking at the documents for which Crown privilege was claimed was not merely a review of the decision of the Minister to make a claim.

[34] There is at least a small irony in the fact that both Crichel Down and *Padfield* concerned Ministers of Agriculture, respectively Sir Thomas Dugdale (Conservative) and Mr Fred Peart (Labour), the ultimate decision after *Padfield* on the complaint of the south-east producers being made by Mr Cledwyn Hughes (Labour).

[35] cf M Sunkin, 'Padfield' in S Juss and M Sunkin (eds) *Landmark Cases in Public Law* (Oxford, Hart, 2017) 56–57.

In terms of the dichotomy of rights and interests, *Ridge*, *Conway* and *Anisminic* concern the protection of rights: respectively, the rights inherent in holding a statutory office from which dismissal can only be for cause, the right to a fair trial and the right conferred by the Order in Council to participate in a compensation fund.[36] *Padfield* undoubtedly concerned the protection of the commercial interests of milk producers in the south-east region. One of their arguments was that the practice to which they objected required them to subsidise farmers in other regions. But it was also a central part of their case that the arrangements were contrary to the public interest.

In terms of the judicial-administrative spectrum, *Anisminic* seems most clearly to concern a judicial decision. A Commission comprised of lawyers was determining questions of law and fact in disposing of a claim for compensation in respect of property requisitioned by a foreign power. In *Ridge*, the majority of the House of Lords (Lords Reid, Hodson and Morris) found it relatively straightforward to hold that there was a duty on the part of the Watch Committee to act judicially and to afford prior notice and a fair hearing before a person was dismissed from office not held 'during pleasure'. It would also seem, given the disapproval of the decision in *Nakkuda Ali v Jayaratne*,[37] that this would be required before a statutory licence, needed for a person to pursue their livelihood, was revoked). *Conway* concerned an executive decision (a question of judgment rather than discretion) that affected the fairness of a trial. *Padfield*, by contrast, concerned a challenge in respect of a broadly worded discretionary power by a minister, but its relationship to the substance of government policy on agriculture was only at one remove.

B. What did the Case actually Decide?

One curiosity of the Quartet is that, in each case, a decision of what might be thought to be a strong Court of Appeal was reversed, with powerful dissents by Lord Denning MR in two cases.[38] Nevertheless, it is arguable that, in terms of doctrine *actually applied*, *Ridge* and *Padfield* were relatively cautious; *Anisminic* and *Conway* were not.

The core of *Ridge*[39] can be seen as restoring the application of established principles of natural justice to the dismissal from office of a person dismissible only

[36] On the third of these see Lord Reid in *Anisminic* at 172.

[37] [1951] AC 66 (PC).

[38] In chronological order: *Ridge* [1963] 1 QB 539 (Holroyd Pearce, Harman and (Arthian) Davies LJJ) (30 January 1962); *Padfield* [1968] AC 997 (Diplock and Russell LJJ, Lord Denning MR dissenting) (27 July 1966); *Anisminic* [1968] 2 QB 862 (Sellers, Diplock and Russell LLJ) (22 March 1967); *Conway* [1967] 1 WLR 1031 (Arthian Davies and Russell LJJ, Lord Denning MR dissenting) (8 June 1967). In the event, the House of Lords decided *Conway* (2 May 1968) before *Anisminic* (17 December 1968).

[39] Leaving aside the issues concerning the application of the relevant regulations.

for cause and recognition that a broader range of decisions would be regarded as giving rise to a duty to act judicially, and therefore in accordance with natural justice,[40] than during the period of the long sleep.[41] However, Lord Reid was at pains to say that he did not doubt cases where the principles of natural justice had been held to have a limited effect in respect of 'the wider duties imposed on ministers and other organs of government by modern legislation'.[42] His real objection was that these limitations 'have tended to be reflected in other decisions on matters to which in principle they do not appear to me to apply'.[43] There was no suggestion that the distinction between judicial and administrative decision-making was no longer relevant.[44] Overall, this looks more like the (entirely proper) restoration of the *status quo ante* rather than a giant leap forward.

There are two main elements to the decision in *Padfield*.[45] First, there was the interpretation of the statutory provisions that conferred an apparently unfettered power to appoint a committee of investigation.[46] Secondly, there was the application of general principles applicable in respect of an alleged abuse of that power and, to a limited extent, the fettering of a different discretionary power, the power to decide whether to lay an order before Parliament to implement the recommendations of a committee.[47] As to the first element, the real interest lies in the approach to statutory interpretation. According to Lord Reid, in a sentence frequently cited:

> Parliament must have conferred the discretion with the intention that it should be used to promote the policy and objects of the Act,[48] the policy and objects of the Act

[40] Desmond Ackner QC, counsel for Ridge, accepted in argument ([1964] AC 40, 52), that 'When certiorari is asked for the court cannot act unless the tribunal is judicial or quasi-judicial,' but, here, a declaration was being sought, 'and this is a far wider remedy'.

[41] n 11 above.

[42] [1964] AC 40, 71. Lord Reid did not specify the cases he was thinking of here. Counsel for the Watch Committee, Neville Faulks QC, had relied on, inter alia, *Franklin v Minister of Town and Country Planning* [1948] AC 87, 96, 102. At 102–03, Lord Thankerton said, in respect of the Minister's duties in the proposal and confirmation of an order for a new town under the New Towns Act 1946: 'In my opinion, no judicial, or quasi-judicial, duty was imposed on the respondent, and any reference to judicial duty, or bias, is irrelevant in the present case. The respondent's duties under s 1 of the Act and sch 1 thereto are, in my opinion, purely administrative, but the Act prescribes certain methods of or steps in, discharge of that duty … I am of opinion that no judicial duty is laid on the respondent in discharge of these statutory duties, and that the only question is whether he has complied with the statutory directions to appoint a person to hold the public inquiry, and to consider that person's report.' The only ground of challenge had to be either that the Minister did not in fact consider the report and the objections, of which there was here no evidence, or that his mind was so foreclosed that he gave no genuine consideration to them, which was not established.

[43] ibid. Lord Reid separately doubted the relevance of cases on natural justice determined under war-time legislation: [1964] AC 40, 73–74.

[44] Lord Hodson's approach could be interpreted as broader than Lord Reid's: see 130–03.

[45] *Padfield v Minister of Agriculture, Fisheries and Food* [1968] AC 997.

[46] See n 90.

[47] The fettering point received greater emphasis in the Divisional Court than in the House of Lords: Transcript, 18 (Lord Parker CJ), 23 (Sachs J).

[48] cf Lord Pearce at 1054: 'It was for the Minister to use his discretion to promote Parliament's intention.'

> must be determined by construing the Act as a whole and construction is always a matter of law for the court.[49]

This is important not least as reflective of the general move in the interpretation of statutes away from a literal approach to a more contextual approach, where statutory words are to be read in their context and 'context' is to be construed widely.[50] In the case of the provisions in question, the argument that there was a 'duty to refer every genuine and substantial complaint' was rejected.[51] However, there was in effect[52] a presumption that if a genuine and substantial complaint was raised that the Milk Marketing Board was acting contrary to the public interest then it ought to be investigated unless there were good reasons not to do so.[53] The reasons actually given were legally defective[54] and, had no reasons been given, the court might have been prepared to infer from silence where a decision appeared to frustrate the policy and objects of the Act that the reasons actually adopted were bad.[55]

As to the second element, in terms of doctrine, there seemed to be general agreement between counsel for the applicants and the Solicitor-General, appearing for the Secretary of State, as to the principles that were to be applied, which were drawn from Lord Greene's judgment in *Wednesbury*.[56] The real interest of *Padfield* here can be seen as lying not so much in the content of the doctrine

[49] At 1030.

[50] See J Bell and G Engle, *Cross on Statutory Interpretation*, 3rd edn (Oxford, Clarendon Press, 1995) ch 3.

[51] See Lord Reid at 1029–30; Lord Hodson at 1046–47, Lord Pearce at 1052–53, Lord Upjohn at 1057–58.

[52] The word 'presumption' was not used. There is an echo of the approach of the courts to the duty of a decision maker to follow statutory guidance unless there is a good reason not to: *R v Islington LBC, ex p Rixon* (1998) 1 CCLR 119, 123 per Sedley J.

[53] At 1032, Lord Reid said that if a complaint 'relevantly alleges' that the board has acted contrary to the public interest, 'as this complaint does, then it appears to me that the Act does impose a duty on the Minister to have it investigated. If he does not do that he is rendering nugatory a safeguard provided by the Act and depriving complainers of a remedy which I am satisfied that Parliament intended them to have'. However, his previous remarks (n 51) made it clear that a minister could decide not to appoint a committee if there were good reasons. See also Lord Hodson at 1049; 'As the guardian of the public interest [the Minister] has a duty to protect the interests of those who claim to have been treated contrary to the public interest'; Lord Pearce at 1050, noting that the complaint was 'prima facie suitable to be considered by the committee of investigation'; Lord Upjohn at 1057.

[54] The points that 'wide issues' were raised; that the Minister owes no duty to producers in a particular region; that there was a possibility of political embarrassment should the Minister decide not to act on a view of the committee that arrangements were indeed contrary to the public interest: see Lord Reid at 1031–32, Lord Hodson at 1049, Lord Pearce at 1054–55, Lord Upjohn at 1059–62.

[55] Lord Reid at 1032–33, Lord Hodson at 1049, Lord Pearce at 1053–54, Lord Upjohn at pp 1061–62.

[56] *Associated Provincial Picture Houses v Wednesbury Corporation* [1948] 1 KB 223, 229: 'a person entrusted with a discretion must so to speak direct himself properly in law. He must call his own attention to the matters which he is bound to consider. He must exclude from his consideration matters which are irrelevant to what he has to consider.' *Wednesbury* was cited by Lord Morris (who dissented) at 1041 and Lord Hodson at 1046 and the principles by Lord Reid at 1029 and Lord Upjohn at 1058. *Wednesbury* was also relied on by the Divisional Court: Transcript, 16–17 (Lord Parker CJ).

applied as in to whom it was applied, a minister exercising a broadly worded discretionary power.

The key elements of *Anisminic*[57] were, first, the decision that the FCC had made a jurisdictional error and, secondly, the decision that the privative clause was not effective to preclude judicial review. On the first point, and on the basis that the FCC had made an error in construing the relevant provisions of the Order in Council,[58] the decision can be seen as orthodox on its face but radical in its implications, the seeds that were sown for the future. The key issue was who Parliament intended, leaving aside the privative clause, to have the last word on the correct legal interpretation of the Order in Council, the FCC or the courts. The FCC clearly had to undertake the task of construction, but that, also clearly, does not establish that it was to have the last word.[59] Almost invariably, there is no clear indication from Parliament as to its position on this kind of issue, and the courts have to do their best. In answering this kind of question, there is no path of legal reasoning that can be followed that will provide the answer as a matter of logic.[60] Whichever way the courts jump, critics tend have no stronger basis for their criticism than that they would have chosen to jump the other way. It is understandable that pragmatic considerations may influence the outcome. The majority of the House of Lords came to the conclusion that, here, it was the courts that were to have the last word.

Along the way, there was reliance on what looks like doctrine: the FCC had 'asked the wrong question' or had 'taken legally irrelevant considerations into account'. But this leaves open the issue as to *when* making a legal error amounts to 'asking the wrong question' and *when* taking account of a legally irrelevant consideration amounts to a jurisdictional error. It seemed to be assumed that there was still life and meaning in the jurisdiction of the High Court to quash a judicial decision by *certiorari* where there was an error of law on the face of the record.[61] It is accordingly unlikely that the majority thought that *any* regard to a legally irrelevant consideration or failure to have regard to a legally relevant consideration would amount to a jurisdictional error. That was a can kicked down the road. The problem for defendants in the future was that it would normally be relatively easy for claimants to present an error in respect of the law applicable to the matter to be determined as involving 'asking the wrong question' or 'taking a legally irrelevant consideration into account'.[62]

57 [1969] 2 AC 147.

58 Lord Pearson held that there was no error; Lord Morris left the point open.

59 See Lord Wilberforce at 209.

60 It is submitted that the same can be said about the identification of a 'jurisdictional fact' and application of the distinction between law and fact.

61 *R v Northumberland Compensation Appeal Tribunal, ex p Shaw* [1951] 1 KB 711 (CA) See Lord Morris at 183, Lord Pearce at 196 and Lord Wilberforce at 209.

62 Foreshadowed in 1959 by de Smith (n 1) 210: 'The taking of irrelevant considerations into account and the disregard of relevant considerations are now to be regarded as jurisdictional errors (or as if they were jurisdictional errors) redressible by certiorari'.

The decision on the privative clause point was more radical, given the need to find a proper basis for distinguishing *Smith v East Elloe RDC*,[63] where effect had been given by the House of Lords to a privative clause to protect a decision that was arguably ultra vires where, unlike the position in *Anisminic*, there was provision for challenge by way of an equivalent to judicial review of the decision in question, albeit within a strict time limit.

Conway v Rimmer[64] involved a more substantial change, involving departure from the decision of the House of Lords in *Duncan v Cammell, Laird & Co Ltd*,[65] in holding that it was the courts that in principle had the last word on whether documents claimed by the defendant to be privileged from disclosure by reference to Crown privilege should be disclosed. The outcome was also perhaps the most predictable of the four, given the torrent of judicial and academic criticism of *Duncan* over the years,[66] not least from the Court of Appeal in *Conway* itself.[67] It was not, of course the last word on the topic.[68]

C. What did Later Judges Decide the Case Decided?

The significance of the subsequent treatment of the case is of particular relevance to *Ridge v Baldwin* and *Anisminic* with the respective propositions:

(1) that the view that natural justice did not apply to administrative proceedings was a 'heresy scotched';[69] and
(2) that the distinction between jurisdictional and non-jurisdictional errors of law should be discarded: all errors of law go to jurisdiction.[70]

[63] [1956] AC 736.
[64] [1968] AC 910.
[65] [1942] AC 624.
[66] See HWR Wade, 'Crown Privilege Controlled At Last' (1968) 84 *LQR* 171, 173: '[T]heir achievement can fairly be seen to be the culmination of a widespread movement of legal opinion.'
[67] [1967] 1 WLR 1031.
[68] See A Tomkins, *The Constitution after Scott* (Oxford, Clarendon Press, 1998) ch 5; M Spencer and J Spencer, 'Coping with *Conway v Rimmer* [1968] AC 910' (2010) 37 *Journal of Law and Society* 387.
[69] Lord Denning MR in *R v Gaming Board for Great Britain, ex p Benaim and Khaida* [1970] 2 QB 417, 430: 'At one time it was said that the principles only apply to judicial proceedings and not to administrative proceedings. That heresy was scotched in *Ridge v. Baldwin* [1964] AC 40.'
[70] Lord Denning MR in *Pearlman v Keepers and Governors of Harrow School* [1979] QB 56, 70: 'But the distinction between an error which entails absence of jurisdiction – and an error made within the jurisdiction – is very fine. So fine indeed that it is rapidly being eroded … in truth the High Court has a choice before it whether to interfere with an inferior court on a point of law … Softly be it stated, but that is the reason for the difference between the decision of the Court of Appeal in *Anisminic Ltd v Foreign Compensation Commission* [1968] 2 QB 862 and the House of Lords [1969] 2 AC 147.' This position was not, however, endorsed by Geoffrey Lane and Eveleigh LJJ.

It is no coincidence that Lord Denning had a major role in these developments,[71] as a judge who notably seemed to feel less constrained by precedent than most, if not all, others.

The first development, which clearly goes beyond Lord Reid's approach, can be seen as a reaction against what was seen as arid exercise in classifying functions into compartments (administrative, quasi-judicial, judicial),[72] in the teeth of a reality which was that there was a spectrum of decision-making from purely judicial decisions by regular courts of law to the broadest of administrative discretions conferred on ministers.[73] It was also simply implausible that the detailed content of natural justice would be the same in respect of *any* decision that was analytically 'judicial' or 'quasi-judicial'. An attempt to establish that 'natural justice' applied to judicial or quasi-judicial decisions and 'fairness' to administrative decisions petered out and seems unattractive, for similar reasons.[74] The new approach was to focus on the particular context of the case in question to determine whether the particular procedural safeguard or safeguards sought by the claimant were required as a matter of fairness.[75]

The story of the second development is well known.[76] The distinction between jurisdictional and non-jurisdictional errors has generally been abandoned, with a few exceptions.[77] It has been noted that a key practical contribution to this development was the decision of successive Treasury Devils not to take a point that a particular error of law might not go to jurisdiction.[78] This was 'a recognition that the orderly development of public law required a comprehensive approach to arguable abuses of power in place of the hair-splitting distinctions which had come to disfigure the law in the inter-war years'.[79]

It may be speculated whether a similar sentiment was influential in the development by the courts of the position that significant procedural standards,

[71] Lord Denning MR also dissented in the Court of Appeal in *Padfield* and *Conway* and his positions were essentially endorsed in the House of Lords.

[72] For extended analysis see WA Robson, *Justice and Administrative Law*, 3rd edn (London, Stevens & Sons, 1951) ch 6; de Smith (n 1) ch 2.

[73] *R v Commission for Racial Equality ex p Cottrell & Rothon* [1980] 1 WLR 1580, 1587; *R v Army Board of the Defence Council ex p Anderson* [1992] 1 QB 169, 185–86.

[74] See Lord Pearson in *Pearlburg v Varty* [1972] 1 WLR 534, 547.

[75] See eg Lord Denning's approach in the *Gaming Board* case and in *Schmidt v Secretary of State for Home Affairs* [1969] 2 Ch 149, 170.

[76] See Lord Diplock in *O'Reilly v Mackman* [1983] 2 AC 237, 278; Lord Browne-Wilkinson in *R v Lord President of the Council, ex p Page* [1993] AC 682.

[77] The recognised exceptions cover decisions of county court judges (in this context, the dissent of Geoffrey Lane LJ in *Pearlman* has been preferred to Lord Denning's view: *Re Racal Communications Ltd* [1981] AC 374, 384, 390–91 in this context); a University Visitor (*Page*) and adjudicators of construction contract disputes under s 108 Housing Grants, Construction and Regeneration Act 1996 (*London & Amsterdam Properties Ltd v Waterman Partnerships Ltd* [2003] EWHC 3059 (TCC)). An exception was not created in respect of decisions of the Upper Tribunal: *R (on the application of Cart) v Upper Tribunal* [2011] UKSC 28, [2012] 1 AC 663.

[78] S Sedley, 'Law as History' in S Sedley, *Law and the Whirligig of Time* (Oxford, Hart, 2018) 5–9.

[79] ibid 7.

whether termed requirements of natural justice or fairness, could be applied to administrative decision-making. It is interesting to note here the approach of Nigel Bridge, the Treasury Devil from 1964 to 1968,[80] in arguing *In re HK (An Infant)*.[81] This case concerned the approach to be taken by an immigration officer in determining whether a person was a child under 16; such a person had the right to enter the UK. Counsel for the claimant[82] argued that this was a judicial or quasi-judicial decision and so natural justice had to be observed. According to the argument as reported, Nigel Bridge did not challenge that analysis but focused on an analysis of nature of the immigration officer's duty under the legislation, which included a duty to carry out an examination. He continued:

> It was plain that the interrogations and medical examinations made on November 21, 1966, made it quite clear to HK what it was the immigration officer wanted to know and gave to him and the applicant a fair opportunity to satisfy the immigration officer of the relevant facts. It could not be said that there was any breach of duty, and accordingly the decision to refuse admission could not be questioned.[83]

In his judgment, Lord Parker CJ *did* doubt that the decision was judicial or quasi-judicial but said that in any event the officer was under a duty to act fairly.[84] On the facts, he had done so. The development of the law of natural justice or procedural fairness from this point is again well known.

This kind of issue did not arise after *Padfield* and *Conway*.

D. What Propositions did the Courts Reject?

It is arguable that the real importance of these cases was not so much in the doctrines applied as in the propositions of law rejected. This involves a longer list.

Ridge v Baldwin

- No procedural standards had to be observed unless a person had to determine rights as between two other contending parties – the *lis inter partes*[85] – and

[80] He appeared for the Crown in *Anisminic*. He in due course was a Law Lord as Lord Bridge of Harwich.

[81] [1967] 2 QB 617.

[82] EFN Gratiaen QC and LJ Blom-Cooper at 620.

[83] ibid 621

[84] ibid 630: 'Good administration and an honest or bona fide decision must, as it seems to me, require not merely impartiality, nor merely bringing one's mind to bear on the problem, but acting fairly.'

[85] Central here is Lord Reid's rejection of Lord Hewart's gloss in *R v Legislative Committee of the Church Assembly, ex p Haynes-Smith* [1928] 1 KB 411, 415, on Atkin LJ statement in *R v Electricity Commissioners, ex p London Electricity Joint Committee Co* [1924] 1 KB 171, 205, as to the scope of certiorari: see [1964] AC 40, 76. Counsel for the respondents, Neville Faulks QC, relied on *Haynes-Smith*: 57–58.

that therefore no procedural standards applied to a decision to cancel a licence on which the holder's livelihood depended.[86]

- An unlawful decision might be unchallengeable because no remedy might be available.[87]
- A hearing is not needed if the matter is as 'plain as a pikestaff'.[88]
- If you exercise a right to appeal any right to complain by way of judicial review is forfeited.[89]

Padfield

- The Minister had an 'unfettered discretion'[90] (an argument that seems, at least with hindsight, to be like a red rag to a bull[91]).
- Mandamus did not lie as the applicants' legal rights were not at stake.[92]
- That it was somehow inappropriate – if a minister was courteous enough to provide reasons for a decision – to criticise them.[93]
- If a minister chose to remain silent nothing could be done.[94]

Anisminic

- Jurisdictional matters were limited to: (1) matters determinable at the commencement of proceedings (errors on such matters giving rise to

[86] Note Lord Reid's criticisms of the decision of the Privy Council in *Nakkuda Ali v Jayaratne* [1951] AC 66, which Neville Faulks QC, argued was 'rightly decided' (at 57).

[87] See Lord Reid [1964] AC 40, 77, commenting on *Nakkuda Ali*: '[A]ccording to their judgment certiorari did not lie, and no other means was suggested whereby the appellant or anyone else in his position could obtain redress even if the controller acted without a shred of evidence … [N]othing short of a decision of this House directly in point would induce me to accept the position that, although an enactment expressly requires an official to have reasonable grounds for his decision, our law is so defective that a subject cannot bring up such a decision for review however seriously he may be affected and however obvious it may be that the official acted in breach of his statutory obligation.' In *Ridge*, the claim was for a declaration.

[88] Neville Faulks QC argued at 58 that 'it was inevitable he should be dismissed without pension rights'. See Lord Reid at 68 ('It is at least very doubtful whether that could be accepted as an excuse. But, even if it could, the respondents would … fail on the facts.') and Lord Hodson at 128.

[89] See Lord Reid at 80–81.

[90] See Sir Dingle Foot QC, the Solicitor-General and leading counsel for the Minister, at [1968] AC 997 at 1020: 'The legislature has given the Minister a completely unfettered discretion.' This line had previously been taken in correspondence with the complainants. cf above nn 48–52.

[91] cf Lord Denning MR's comment during argument in *R v Liverpool Corporation, ex p Liverpool Taxi Fleet Operators' Association* [1972] 2 QB 300, 303: 'In *Padfield* …, the court looked into the merits of an exercise of ministerial discretion and decided that the minister was not a law unto himself'.

[92] This point was taken in the Divisional Court by counsel for the Milk Marketing Board, D Kemp, but not by the Solicitor-General, and was rejected by the court (Transcript 20–21 (Lord Parker CJ)).

[93] Sir Dingle Foot QC argued (at 1021): '[The Minister] can refuse to act on a complaint without giving any reasons and in such a case the complainant would have no remedy and his decision cannot be questioned. Accordingly, the reasons which he has given in the present case should not be examined too closely.'

[94] ibid. cf above n 55.

'want of jurisdiction') and (2) the question whether the order ultimately made was a kind of order that could be made (errors giving rise to 'excess of jurisdiction'). This argument was submitted by counsel for the FCC, Nigel Bridge, at first instance before Browne J.[95] However, Browne J held, crucially, that the concept of 'excess of jurisdiction' was broader than that.[96] The first of these propositions derived in particular from the judgment of Lord Denman CJ in *R v Bolton*.[97] Browne J's view was that this statement had to be 'read in relation to question which arose in that particular case', which concerned neither want of jurisdiction nor excess of jurisdiction in the broader sense adopted by him.[98] This led to the proposition that 'a tribunal may have jurisdiction to commence an inquiry but may act without or in excess of jurisdiction at a later stage'.[99] It is submitted that the rejection of this argument by Browne J is of particular importance. It was not raised again before the Court of Appeal[100] or the House of Lords.[101] It accordingly left the way open for errors of law in the course of decision-making to be held to be jurisdictional, being presented as asking the wrong question or giving rise to a considerations challenge.

- Diplock LJ's propositions in the Court of Appeal[102] that 'The jurisdiction of the High Court to give declaratory judgments is limited to declaring the existence of legally enforceable rights or liabilities' and that it is difficult to see 'how the High Court has jurisdiction to make a declaration against a defendant in respect of conduct by him which could never give rise to a cause of action against him by the plaintiff or by him against the defendant'.[103] This approach would have stultified the use of the declaration as a public law remedy (prior to the enactment of s 31 of the Supreme Court (now Senior Courts) Act 1981) and was firmly rejected by the House of Lords.[104]

[95] [1969] 2 AC 147, 235–41.

[96] ibid 238.

[97] (1841) 1 QB 66, 74. For Lord Denning MR, the 'black-out of any development of administrative law' started with *Bolton*: *O'Reilly v Mackman* [1983] 2 AC 250 (CA), 253. *Bolton* has its defenders: P Murray, 'Escaping the wilderness' (2016) 75 *CLJ* 333.

[98] 'The applicant [in *Bolton*] seems to have been asking the court to retry the case on the merits, which can never be done on certiorari' (at 243).

[99] [1969] 2 AC 147, 242.

[100] In the Court of Appeal, Sellers LJ did cite *Bolton* with approval, but also did not question the classification of Browne J, which seems inconsistent: [1968] 2 QB 862, 884.

[101] This position was expressly confirmed by Lord Reid at 171, Lord Pearce at 195 and Lord Wilberforce at 201.

[102] These points were not raised by the FCC and were left open by Russell LJ at 912; they were not mentioned by Sellers LJ. This appeared to be supported before the House of Lords by Sydney Templeman QC, leading counsel for the FCC: [1969] 2 AC 147, 167.

[103] [1968] 2 QB 862, 910, 911.

[104] See Lord Reid at 169, Lord Pearce at 206 and Lord Wilberforce at 214. *O'Reilly v Mackman* [1983] 2 AC 237 can perhaps be seen as Lord Diplock's revenge.

- Publication of their reasons by the FCC[105] had been unnecessary and perhaps undesirable.[106] Lord Reid 'dissented emphatically' from this view.[107]

Conway v Rimmer

- If a minister says that disclosure of a document is against the public interest that is all we need to know.[108]

These propositions seem unattractive and their continued absence not to be mourned. Their rejection forms an important part of the real and lasting contributions of these cases. If that is right, it can be suggested that it is *not* necessarily a good test of the importance of a case how often it is cited. On points of this kind it is to be hoped that it is never necessary for it to be cited again.

E. What Messages did these Cases Send Apart from Doctrine?

It may well be the case, but cannot be proved, that these cases, apart from the doctrines developed and applied, sent important messages to practitioners, members of the public and decision-makers, including that:

(1) You can be successful as what we now call a judicial review claimant even though you are a person whose reputation is, to say the least, under a cloud: *Ridge*.
(2) You can be successful as a judicial review claimant against a minister of the Crown exercising a broad discretionary power: *Padfield*; or exercising a judgment on public interest: *Conway*.
(3) The courts were increasingly willing to require that people be given explanations of decisions made adverse to their interests and have an opportunity to have their say: *Ridge*, *Padfield*[109] and *Conway*.

[105] The Minute of Adjudication had been attached to the defendants' pleadings. It was described by Diplock LJ at [1968] 2 QB 862, 902 as a document in which the FCC had 'recorded for their own use' their reasons.

[106] See Sellers LJ at [1968] 2 QB 862, 886, in declining to express a view on the reasoning in the Minute 'which I think was unnecessarily revealed to the plaintiffs and which alone has given rise to these sustained submissions'. At 882, he had said that he was inclined to think that this had been revealed 'unnecessarily and perhaps undesirably'.

[107] [1969] 2 AC 147, 171. See to similar effect Lord Pearce at 199.

[108] Sir Elwyn Jones QC, the Attorney-General, appearing for the Home Secretary, [1968] AC 910, 925, 926: 'It ought to be enough for the Minister to say that it is contrary to the public interest to produce the document, without more explanation, but the courts have put pressure on Ministers top give reasons … The certificate should be accepted by the court unless it appears that there is mistake or mala fides or unless it is not in due form … In a conflict between the public interest in good government and the public interest in the administration of justice as between private litigants the last word in the resolution of the conflict must lie with the executive and not with the judiciary which is not equipped to ass the effect of the production.'

[109] That is, their say to a formal committee of investigation.

(4) The giving of reasons by the executive for their decisions was a good thing and would be encouraged: *Padfield* and *Anisminic*.
(5) Ministers should avoid in future giving possible political embarrassment as a reason for anything: *Padfield*.
(6) The courts could still be creative in the face of ouster clauses: *Anisminic*.
(7) The courts fully supported the use of the remedy of a declaration, which was seen as providing a more sensible route for applicants than the prerogative orders: *Ridge*, *Anisminic*.

Seeing other people achieving something may encourage many others to have a go. And this includes both lawyers and their clients. One thing that is undeniable is the significant proliferation of case law on procedural fairness and, for a while, jurisdictional error of law that followed these decisions. It is a little more difficult to identify the consequences of *Padfield* and the *Padfield* dicta on inferring bad reasons from silence have rarely been applied.[110] The latter point has perhaps been overtaken by the principle that a duty to give reasons may arise where a decision appears aberrant.[111] A final point that emerges from this analysis is that, on a number of issues, the contribution of Quartet cases was synergistic. For example, the recognition in *Ridge* and *Anisminic* that a declaration might be available where *certiorari* was not,[112] and Lord Reid's comments in *Ridge* on the 'duty to act judicially' probably hastened the day when it was recognised that certiorari was available in respect of unlawful administrative acts.[113]

F. What might the Cases have got Wrong?

There has been little serious criticism of the outcomes in *Ridge* and *Conway*. Given the indeterminacy of the concept of 'jurisdictional error of law' purportedly applied in *Anisminic*, and the 3:2 split among their Lordships, there is of

[110] They were not applied in *Secretary of State for Employment v ASLEF (No 2)* [1972] 2 QB 443, CA, and given a restrictive interpretation in *R v Secretary of State for Trade and Industry, ex p Lonhro plc* [1989] 1 WLR 525 as possibly applicable where 'all other known facts and circumstances appear to point overwhelmingly in favour of a different decision' (see Lord Keith at 539–40).
[111] See Sedley J in *R v Higher Education Funding Council, ex p Institute of Dental Surgery Ltd* [1994] 1 All ER 651, 672–73.
[112] The importance of these cases in the devilment of the declaration as a public law remedy is recognised by Lord Woolf and J Woolf, *Zamir and Woolf, The Declaratory Judgment*, 3rd edn (London, Sweet & Maxwell, 2002) 30–31.
[113] *R v Hillingdon LBC, ex p Royco Homes Ltd* [1974] QB 720 (holding that *certiorari* was available to quash a grant of planning permission to which ultra vires conditions had been attached); Lord Diplock in *O'Reilly v Mackman* [1982] 2 AC 237, 279. Lord Widgery CJ in *Royco* interpreted Lord Reid's speech in *Ridge* as saying that a 'duty to act judicially' was not a requirement at all; Lord Reid's point was that it was not a 'superadded' requirement, which is not the same thing. Counsel for the local authority, Michael Chavasse QC, conceded the point (at 723–24). Bridge J (formerly the Treasury Devil) concurred with Lord Widgery, but thought it a 'strong step' (at 732).

course continuing room for debate as to whether the majority got it right. It is undeniable that aspects of these decisions have caused ongoing difficulty. These include: (1) the proposition that unlawful decisions are *void* (*Ridge*; *Anisminic*); and (2) the further proposition that void decisions cannot be protected by an ouster clause that purport to exclude judicial review completely[114] unless heroic efforts are taken in the drafting.[115] On the first point, David Feldman[116] has demonstrated that the position is much more nuanced than *Ridge* suggested. There are then those who can see value in the application of the old learning on the distinction between jurisdictional and non-jurisdictional errors of law, at least in some contexts.[117] However, there seem to be few who would argue for a wholesale abandonment of what has come to be regarded as the *Anisminic* principle. Any doubters should direct themselves to the exhaustive, and exhausting, series of articles by DM Gordon QC on what he termed the 'pure theory of jurisdiction'[118] before making up their minds on the point.

The most controversial decision has perhaps been *Padfield*, not least in the light of the subsequent history of the complaint. This was referred to and upheld by a committee of investigation, but the (next) Labour Minister of Agriculture (Cledwyn Hughes MP) declined to take steps to implement the report in the light of 'wider questions of agricultural, economic and social policy' which were beyond the scope of the committee's inquiry.[119] (It does not seem, however, that there was any 'political embarrassment'.[120]) It can be argued that the Minister was a better judge of suitability than the judges.[121] At the heart of the complaint was the policy question as to the extent the operation of the free market should be modified to promote the public interest and it was said that acceding to the wishes of the complainants (and the

[114] Time limit clauses are different: *Smith v East Elloe RDC* [1956] AC 736.

[115] As was held to be the case in *R (on the application of Privacy International) v Investigatory Powers Tribunal* [2019] UKSC 22 (the drafter was insufficiently heroic).

[116] D Feldman, 'Error of Law and Flawed Administrative Acts' (2014) 73 *CLJ* 275. See also T Adams, 'The standard theory of administrative unlawfulness' (2017) 76 *CLJ* 289.

[117] See eg Sedley and Laws LJJ in the Court of Appeal in *Cart*: [2011] QB 120; critics of the decision of the Supreme Court in *Cart*: Sir William Wade and CF Forsyth, *Administrative Law*, 11th edn (Oxford, OUP, 2014) 222–23.

[118] See de Smith (n 1) 66–76; DM Gordon, 'The Relation of Facts to Jurisdiction' (1929) 45 *LQR* 459; DM Gordon, 'Observance of Law as a Condition of Jurisdiction' (1931) 47 *LQR* 386; DM Gordon, '*Tithe Redemption Commission v Gwynne*' (1944) 60 *LQR* 250. de Smith noted (at 70) that 'it is not surprising that many of the reported decisions on the jurisdiction of inferior tribunals are manifestly contradictory'.

[119] See SH Bailey, *Bailey, Jones and Mowbray's Cases, Materials and Commentary on Administrative Law*, 5th edn (London, Sweet & Maxwell, 2018) 304–05.

[120] The decision was welcomed by two Welsh Labour MPs, whose constituents would have been badly affected had the Minister's decision gone the other way, in a general debate on the Annual Price Review for Agriculture, but not otherwise mentioned: *Hansard* HC (series 5) Vol 781 cols 40ff (31 March 1969).

[121] See RC Austin, 'Judicial Review of Subjective Discretion' (1975) 28 *CLP* 150, 152–4, C Harlow, 'Administrative Reaction to Judicial Review' [1976] *PL* 116, 117, 120.

recommendations of the committee of investigation) would in effect have meant the end of the milk marketing scheme.[122] However, it must be remembered that the decision itself did not bear directly on government policy for agriculture.[123] The decision merely barred access by the complainants[124] to an inquiry process by a committee (appointed by the Minister himself) which would receive and weigh evidence and argument and make a public report. The report might well remain an authoritative source of information and advice even if its recommendations were not accepted by the Minister (or political party) for the time being in office. In the event, no change was made by the Heath Government and the milk marketing scheme (and other such schemes) was only eventually scrapped, from April 1994, by Mrs Thatcher's free-market-orientated Conservative Government.[125]

III. CONCLUSION

Overall, there is much to celebrate in the Quartet and their 50 years. Their significance is undeniable and both direct and indirect. In terms of the issues identified above,[126] cases in the Quartet made a major contribution to the development of judicial review as a vehicle for challenging the decisions of central government, the use of the declaration bypassing any difficulties arising from the availability of coercive remedies (points (2), (3) in section I above); and, more generally, for challenging errors of law and abuses of discretion (points (4), (5), (6)). They led to the abandonment of the use of a distinction between judicial and administrative action within judicial review doctrine.[127] They illustrated the value of the action for a declaration, thereby, through the contrast it provided, demonstrating the substantive and procedural inadequacies of the prerogative remedies and helping strengthen the case for reform (point (7)). They also formed part of the general move towards more open government (point (8)). Other leading cases were needed to open up the manner of the exercise of prerogative powers to judicial review,[128] to confirm a broad rather than narrow approach to

[122] Economists were divided on the question. For a case for a return to a competitive market see L Whetstone, 'The Marketing of Milk' (IEA Research Monograph 21, 1970).

[123] See Sunkin, 'Padfield' (2017) 57–58. For an analysis critical of the reports of successive committees that the current arrangements were contrary to the public interest, and of Whetstone's position, see AJ Rayner, 'The Regional Pricing Policy of the Milk Marketing Board and the Public Interest' (1977) 28 *Journal of Agricultural Economics* 11.

[124] In respect of what had been a long-standing complaint that was never going to be accepted by majority producer interests on the board.

[125] Agriculture Act 1993.

[126] See text accompanying nn 14–28 above.

[127] There was no longer talk of a distinction between 'judicial discretion' and 'administrative discretion' (cf point (6) above).

[128] *R v Criminal Injuries Compensation Board, ex p Lain* [1967] 2 QB 864; *GCHQ* (n 14).

standing,[129] and to confirm that injunctions were generally available in proceedings against Ministers of the Crown.[130] The reform of remedies was pursued by the Law Commission, in a process initiated before any of the Quartet cases was decided.[131] But all these developments were clearly complementary to the achievements of the Quartet.

[129] *IRC v National Federation of Self Employed and Small Businesses* [1982] AC 617.
[130] *M v Home Office* [1994] 1 AC 377.
[131] Remedies in Administrative Law (Law Com No 73, Cmnd 6407, 1976).

17

'Judicial Power' and Political Power: Reflections in Light of the Quartet

ALEXANDER LATHAM-GAMBI

> It is only after one ceases to reduce public affairs to the business of dominion that the original data in the realm of human affairs will appear, or, rather, reappear, in their authentic diversity.
>
> Arendt, *On Violence*

I. INTRODUCTION

THE QUARTET IS generally thought to have kick-started a dramatic expansion of judicial power in the field of public law,[1] which has since continued to grow through a number of significant events such as the accession of the UK to the European Communities, the decision in the *GCHQ* case,[2] the passing of the Human Rights Act 1998, strong judicial dicta in *Jackson*[3] and perhaps also the decisions in the *Miller* cases.[4] Assuming this to be the case, one might suppose that this new-found judicial power must straightforwardly correspond to a reduction in the power of other political institutions: Parliament, government, administrative decision-makers and so on. In this chapter, I argue that such a supposition would in fact be mistaken. Reflection on the Quartet and its legacy reveals that, appropriately deployed, judicial power may serve to enhance governmental and parliamentary power.

I start off by outlining a basic conception of judicial power that equates the power of the courts with the scope of their decision-making authority (or, in the

[1] See, for example, K Malleson, *The New Judiciary: the effects of expansion and activism* (Aldershot, Dartmouth, 1999) 8–24.

[2] *Council of Civil Service Unions v Minister for the Civil Service* [1985] AC 374 (HL).

[3] *R (Jackson) v Attorney General* [2005] UKHL 56, [2006] 1 AC 262 (HL).

[4] *R (Miller) v Secretary of State for Exiting the European Union* [2017] UKSC 5, [2018] AC 61 (SC); *R (Miller) v Prime Minister* [2019] UKSC 41, [2019] 5 LRC 490.

words of Arendt quoted above, their 'dominion'). The upshot of this conception is that judicial power is in a zero-sum conflict with the power of the political branches of government. Although not explicitly stated, this basic conception is, I believe, implicit in the recent critique of allegedly excessive judicial power by a group of scholars working as the Judicial Power Project.[5] The rest of the first section is then devoted to setting out a number of criticisms of this conception that will go on to inform my analysis of the Quartet. Before getting to that, however, section III highlights a simple but crucial distinction between the personal power enjoyed by particular individuals and the properly political power enjoyed by institutions as such. Without keeping this distinction squarely in mind, we are liable to fall prey to the fallacious supposition that, whenever a court strikes down a decision of a public official, governmental power must have been circumscribed by virtue of the fact that a particular office-holder has been obstructed in the course of what he or she was trying to do. Only if we appreciate the distinction between the personal power of the office-holder and the political power of the office can we begin to understand how exercises of judicial power may serve to enhance rather than impede governmental and parliamentary power.

Sections IV to VII then form the meat of my argument, going through each of the cases of the Quartet in turn. I argue that in *Ridge v Baldwin*,[6] *Padfield*[7] and *Anisminic*,[8] a persuasive argument can be made that the judicial finding against the public decision-maker did not serve to diminish governmental/parliamentary power, all things considered. If this contention is correct, then expansive exercise of judicial authority need not necessarily correspond with a diminution of the power of other political institutions. *Conway v Rimmer*[9] provides a different kind of example: there an ambitious judicial ruling had the counterproductive effect of diminishing the power of the judiciary. We therefore cannot equate judicial power with the scope of the courts' dominion. Section VIII then summarises the conclusions that can be drawn from this analysis.

II. THINKING ABOUT JUDICIAL POWER

The subject of judicial power has recently received academic attention in the form of Policy Exchange's Judicial Power Project, headed by Professors Richard Ekins and Graham Gee.[10] In a relatively short period of time, the Project has given

[5] See judicialpowerproject.org.uk.
[6] *Ridge v Baldwin* [1968] AC 997 (HL).
[7] *Padfield v Minister of Agriculture, Fisheries and Food* [1968] AC 997 (HL).
[8] *Anisminic v Foreign Compensation Commission* [1969] 2 AC 147 (HL).
[9] *Conway v Rimmer* [1968] AC 910 (HL).
[10] See n 5 above.

rise to no little academic controversy,[11] with criticism even reaching the pages of the popular press.[12] But while much of the debate surrounding the Project's goals and strategy has proved instructive, the very notion of judicial power, and its relationship to the political power of Parliament and government, has largely gone unexamined. Certainly, the Project itself has not adopted an explicit working definition of the concept. Nevertheless, I believe that the outlines of a basic conception of judicial power can be inferred from the Project's aims as stated on its website.[13] In this section, I adumbrate and then criticise this conception.[14]

The Judicial Power Project website informs us that 'the project aims to understand and correct the undue rise in judicial power by restating ... the nature and limits of the judicial power within our tradition and the related scope of sound legislative and executive authority'.[15] 'Related' is an ambiguous word, but the implication seems to be that as judicial power augments, legislative and executive authority diminishes correspondingly. Later in the same passage, 'scope of judicial authority' is used as an apparent synonym for 'judicial power', with the wielding of judicial power apparently equated to a 'willingness of some judges to adopt an adventurous understanding of their jurisdiction'.[16] Spatial metaphors abound here. We are presented with a field of possible decisions, over which jurisdiction is contested: here are the issues; who gets to decide them? Any given decision may be made by one or another political authority. The more decisions the courts assume responsibility for – the wider their 'authority' or 'jurisdiction' – the fewer decisions remain for Parliament and the executive. Greater judicial power means less power for the political branches. Power, on this conception, is a zero-sum game.

There are a number of difficulties with this view of judicial power. Firstly, it equates judicial power with the judicial overturning of executive or parliamentary decisions. Courts which frequently find that the political branches have acted unlawfully are *eo ipso* cast as powerful, while those that make such decisions rarely must be in relative terms weak. But why should this be the case? Power, as normally understood, is not a kind of *propensity*, but a kind

[11] See, for example, P Craig, 'Judicial Power, the Judicial Power Project and the UK' (2017) 36 *University of Queensland Law Journal* 355; TT Arvind and L Stirton, 'Why the Judicial Power Project is Wrong about *Anisminic*', UK Constitutional Law Blog (20 May 2016), available at ukconstitutionallaw.org/2016/05/20/tt-arvind-and-lindsay-stirton-why-the-judicial-power-project-is-wrong-about-anisminic; and M Elliott, 'Judicial Power's 50 "Problematic" Cases and the Limits of the Judicial Role' (Public Law for Everyone, 9 May 2016), available at publiclawforeveryone.com/2016/05/09/anisminic-axa-evans-and-nicklinson-judicial-powers-50-problematic-cases-and-the-contestability-of-the-proper-judicial-review.

[12] J Rozenberg, 'A Judge-Shaming List is Bad for Justice' *The Guardian* (12 May 2016).

[13] Judicial Power Project, 'About the Judicial Power Project', available at judicialpowerproject.org.uk/about.

[14] I accept that the conception of power underlying my critique is itself far from uncontroversial, but I cannot set out a full defence of it here. For a useful overview of the debate over the nature of power, see S Lukes (ed), *Power* (Oxford, Basil Blackwell, 1986).

[15] Judicial Power Project, 'About the Judicial Power Project' (n 13).

[16] ibid.

of *capacity*. My capacity to fail my students is a kind of power, but I do not become less powerful just because I decide to pass them instead. I am exercising power whether I give a paper 35 or 75. Similarly, it is difficult to see why a court's endorsement of government action as lawful should not also be considered an exercise of judicial power – assuming, of course, that the court had the capacity to have decided otherwise.

Secondly, power entails the capacity to achieve ends. An appraisal of judicial power therefore cannot be carried out simply by analysing courts' decisions: it requires an understanding of the effects of such decisions. We expect these effects to be wide-ranging: a judiciary whose rulings impacted only upon the immediate parties to disputes would be a very weak judiciary indeed. A powerful judiciary will leave its impact upon the way in which society is governed, on the relationship between individual and state, on the level of citizens' material and psychological well-being, on the operation of the economy, on the functioning of families, on people's sense of what it means to be a citizen, perhaps even their very sense of right and wrong. The extent to which the courts yield such effects will depend upon how other powerful social actors engage with their pronouncements, which in turn depends upon the status of the courts in society. If we focus only on the scope of decision-making authority we will miss this much broader picture.

It follows, thirdly, that any adequate analysis of judicial power must examine not only the instances in which courts have challenged governmental action, but what it is that enables courts successfully to mount such challenges. Two points should be fairly obvious here. One, the courts enjoy a high degree of de facto legitimacy. Despite the fact that ministers frequently find judicial decisions infuriating, they rarely if ever decline to comply with them. Most likely this is because they accept the courts' authority and believe that defying them would be a problematic assault on the rule of law. Alternatively, they may be motivated not by the pull of constitutional propriety but rather out of the fear of criticism from Parliament, the press and the public. Either way, the courts' capacity to change governmental behaviour flows from their de facto legitimacy, whether that be legitimacy in the eyes of the government itself, in the eyes of other powerful political actors, or in the eyes of the general public. Two, the courts enjoy a high degree of independence. Their institutional freedom from sanctions – as well as their relative independence from subtler kinds of political influence – gives them an important form of autonomy. These two factors – legitimacy and independence – are central to judicial power. Crucially, any analysis of judicial power cannot afford to simply assume their existence, as if courts are in their very nature necessarily legitimate and independent actors. Studying judicial power means examining the reasons for the courts' legitimacy and independence, and what factors may cause these attributes to wax or wane.

Fourthly, the focus that the Judicial Power Project places on judicial *decisions* is excessively narrow, restricted as it is to those cases in which a dispute has proceeded to a final judicial resolution.[17] It is important to bear in mind that the vast majority of legal disputes do not make it this far, either because they are settled, or because the claimant simply decides not to bring (or to discontinue) proceedings.[18] A complete analysis of judicial power would have to consider what capacity the judiciary has for influencing the outcomes of these disputes. Out-of-court settlements might be driven by what judges do: for example, if a party chooses to back down because previous judicial decisions have made it clear that he or she is unlikely to win; or if settlement is incentivised by the courts' use of their case management powers. On the other hand, decisions not to litigate might be driven by other factors, such as where a claimant abandons a claim, or a defendant capitulates, out of a fear of being exposed to overwhelming costs, or because the price of legal action is simply unaffordable to him or her.[19]

Finally, it is not the case that any increase in judicial power must be accompanied with a corresponding decrease in the power of the executive and/or legislature. Power is not a zero-sum game. Most obviously, the total power enjoyed by a set of individuals increases when they cooperate and learn from one another. If I have only bricks and you have only mortar, we each gain in power when we decide to work together. Teach someone to fish, wire a plug or play the guitar, and you increase their power without necessarily diminishing anyone else's. Cooperation and learning can lead to a sum increase in power even when it is less than wholly voluntary. When a football manager assigns specific roles to their players, he or she restricts their freedom of action but – assuming they are competent at their job – enhances rather than diminishes their power. A parent's decision to remove the stabilisers from their son's bike, however much the son may object, may have the long-term effect of enhancing the son's power.

More subtly, constraints can serve to shape the field of possible action so as to enhance the power of those subject to them. The rules of grammar are an obvious example: without constraints as to what counts as a grammatical sentence, complex communication would be impossible. Artistic forms are another: to write a novel one must develop a fictional, prose, intimate account of human experiences; to paint a portrait one must make a visual representation of a person; to compose a symphony one must score an extended piece of music for

[17] I am grateful to Richard Kirkham for suggesting this to me.

[18] See, for example, T Hickman and M Sunkin, 'Success in Judicial Review: the current position', UK Constitutional Law Blog (20 March 2015), available at ukconstitutionallaw.org/2015/03/20/tom-hickman-and-maurice-sunkin-success-in-judicial-review-the-current-position; and for a broader discussion, ch 7 in this volume (Nason).

[19] For a critique of the costs regime in civil litigation, see A Zuckerman, 'The Jackson Final Report on Costs: plastering the cracks to shore up a dysfunctional system' (2010) 29 *Civil Justice Quarterly* 263. For an examination of the social consequences of a justice system that is largely unaffordable to most people, see Amnesty International, 'Cuts that Hurt: the impact of legal aid cuts in England on access to justice' (2016).

an orchestra. While these forms do in a sense restrict artists' freedom of action, they nevertheless open up avenues for much more powerful artistic expression than would be possible without them.

Similar arguments have been made in a legal/constitutional context. Holmes has claimed that so-called 'gag rules' – rules removing certain matters from the political agenda – can have the effect of empowering, not disabling government.[20] He argued that a limit on the scope of government's decision-making authority – for example, that it should be prevented from establishing a religion – can serve to prevent it from being paralysed by interminable conflict over deeply divisive issues. Arendt reached a similar conclusion when analysing the use of the doctrine of the separation of powers by the founders of the US Constitution. Far from being a straightforward means of checking governmental power, she argued, the separation of powers was seen as the key to a stable constitutional structure that would prevent the nascent Union from crumbling under the weight of social and political conflict: 'What the founders were afraid of in practice was not power but impotence ... the true objective of the American Constitution was not to limit power but to create more power'.[21]

The power of the judiciary, the executive and the legislature cannot, then, be understood simply as the respective scope of decision-making authority of those institutions. A judiciary that almost always approves executive decisions may be as powerful as one that is more inclined to overturn government decisions. To appreciate the extent of judicial power we need to investigate not just what decisions the courts make on the cases before them but what the wider social effects of those decisions are; the extent of which will depend on the status the courts enjoy in the eyes both of other powerful institutions and of the public as a whole. And rather than judicial power being something that is necessarily pitted against executive/legislative power, the interactions between the different branches of government may operate so as to yield a mutual enhancement (or diminution) of power.

III. POLITICAL POWER: INSTITUTIONAL NOT PERSONAL

Before moving on to my analysis of the Quartet, I would like to highlight a crucial distinction that must be borne in mind when critically analysing judicial power and its relationship with other forms of political power. It is imperative not to conflate the power enjoyed by individual persons and the power held by institutions. When, as public lawyers, we talk about 'the nature and limits of

[20] S Holmes, *Passions and Constraint: on the theory of liberal democracy* (Chicago, University of Chicago Press, 1995) ch 7.

[21] H Arendt, *On Revolution* (London, Faber, 1963) 153–54.

the judicial power ... and the related scope of sound legislative and executive authority',[22] we speak, like Hobbes, 'not of the men, but (in the Abstract) of the Seat of Power'.[23] It has been said about Julius Caesar that he 'had no feeling for the power of institutions ... In Caesar's eyes no one existed but himself and his opponents'.[24] Public lawyers cannot be Caesars: they must appreciate that institutional power is distinctively *public* in nature. Judges, ministers, MPs and so on wield power not in a personal capacity but *ex officio*: as office-holders, they exercise their power on behalf of the public. Institutional power therefore has a teleological nature: it is inherently concerned with the pursuit of the public interest. To use institutional power for private purposes is simply to abuse one's power. We must therefore be on guard not to conflate the public purposes that institutional power exists to serve with the purposes that individual office-holders may intend to pursue.

I emphasise this point because it can otherwise be tempting to fall into the trap of believing that, whenever a court strikes down a decision of a public official, governmental power has necessarily been circumscribed. This may seem like a natural inference to draw, but in fact it is based on a failure to distinguish between public purposes and the subjective intentions of particular office-holders. The distinction can clearly be seen in relation to egregious cases in which public officials have acted with disregard for the proper purposes of their powers in order to pursue entirely personal or partisan objectives. *Porter v Magill* is perhaps the most famous example in English law.[25] The leader of Westminster City Council had sold off council housing in marginal wards for the purposes of attracting more Conservative voters to those areas. The auditor's finding that such conduct was unlawful did not disempower the Council. Far from it: the capacity of councils to fulfil their inherently public ends would be profoundly enervated in the absence of such rulings, since they would be left prey to powerful individuals and groups looking to manipulate them partisan gain. If local authorities are to function successfully, their officers need to be prevented from misusing their resources.

The lesson here – perhaps an obvious lesson in a clear-cut case like *Porter v Magill*, but easy to lose sight of in more difficult cases – is that a judicial finding that a public decision-maker has acted unlawfully does not necessarily constrict, and may well enhance, the institutional power of the body whose decision is overturned. In order to assess the matter one cannot look only at the specific intention of the individual decision-maker in the particular case, one must cast one's gaze more broadly at the public purpose that the institutional power exists to promote.

[22] Judicial Power Project (n 13).
[23] T Hobbes, *Leviathan* (Oxford, Clarendon Press, 1909) 3.
[24] C Meier, *Caesar: a biography* (New York, Basic Books, 1996) 359.
[25] *Porter v Magill* [2001] UKHL 67, [2002] 2 AC 357 (HL).

IV. *RIDGE V BALDWIN*: THE POWER OF PROCEDURE

This last point underscores something central to the approach taken in this volume: the importance of understanding judicial decisions in their broader political context. Thomas's discussion of *Ridge v Baldwin* provides a good example of this.[26] A narrow analysis of the case might conclude that the power of the watch committee to dismiss borough constables was restricted by the judicial imposition of a duty on the part of the committee to observe the principles of natural justice. This statement is certainly not factually incorrect, but nor does it get to grips with the real issues of public power at stake. The power of the watch committee to dismiss borough constables cannot be treated in isolation from their broader supervisory function: the dismissal of constables is not an end in itself, but only one of the possible means of promoting efficiency, effectiveness and integrity in the police force. If we are interested in the committee's political power then we must look at its capacity to effectively carry out its supervisory function. As Thomas reveals, it was broadly accepted at the time of *Ridge v Baldwin* that watch committees were struggling with the task of maintaining policing standards in the face of a complex regulatory scheme and outdated governance structure. In this context, the finding that the Brighton watch committee had failed to adhere to the principles of natural justice served to further highlight the strain that the police governance system was under and thus acted as a catalyst for reform. Far from diminishing governmental power, the House of Lords' decision shone light on a pre-existing power vacuum, encouraging the development of a more powerful system.

A couple of points can be made here specifically in relation to procedural requirements. While administrative lawyers often make reference to the instrumental virtues of procedural requirements,[27] the way in which such requirements may serve to enhance the *power* of the bodies subject to them is not always acknowledged. The instrumental benefits of procedures are often equated with the potential they have to make it more likely that the public body will reach the *correct* decision, suggesting (intentionally or no) that the task of the decision-maker is akin to that of a judge making rulings on the basis of pre-existing legal rights.[28] On this paradigm, procedure performs a kind of disciplining function, prompting decision-makers to consider relevant information and thus encouraging them to base their decisions on the right reasons. Procedural requirements do indeed serve this function in those cases which we

[26] *Ridge* (n 6); see ch 3 in this volume (Thomas).

[27] For an extensive discussion see D Galligan, *Due Process and Fair Procedures: a study of administrative procedures* (Oxford, OUP, 1997).

[28] For example: Galligan, *Due Process and Fair Procedures* (1997) xviii: 'The main object of procedures … is to provide for proper application of the law'; PP Craig, *Administrative Law* (London, Sweet & Maxwell, 2016) 337: 'Procedural rights perform an *instrumental* role, in the sense of helping to attain an accurate decision on the substance of the case'.

may still call (*Ridge* notwithstanding) 'quasi-judicial'. However, the vast majority of public decisions require not merely a determination of pre-existing rights, but the exercise of discretion as to which policy goals ought to be prioritised. In these cases, the instrumental benefit of procedural requirements is not so much that they promote correctness per se, but that they enhance the capacity of the decision-maker to ensure that its decision will promote the goals that it is seeking to achieve.

In addition to providing valuable information, procedures also play a legitimating role which an analysis of power cannot afford to overlook. De facto legitimacy is crucial for the power of public bodies, whose means to secure compliance through brute coercion will always be limited. The willingness of people to accept decisions that they disagree with is likely to be greater if the decision-making process is transparent and those who are affected have had the opportunity to have their voices heard.

These factors need to be borne in mind when considering the effect of *Ridge* on governmental power. At a moment in which reform of police governance was very much on the political agenda, *Ridge* served both as a catalyst for reform and a reminder of the need to incorporate effective procedural safeguards into any new system. If we focus narrowly on the immediate dispute between the parties, we see limits being placed on the scope of a public body's authority, to the benefit of an undeserving plaintiff.[29] But if we look at the broader picture, it is entirely plausible that the decision had the effect of helping to stimulate the development of a form of police governance more effective than the antiquated system of the Municipal Corporation Act 1882 and the Police Act 1919. Furthermore (and even if the direct impact of *Ridge* on police governance cannot be substantiated), the rearticulation of the importance of procedural fairness in public decision-making by the House of Lords clearly had an impact on areas of public life well beyond policing. By making a small incursion into the watch committee's field of discretion, *Ridge* may well have provided a significant boost to governmental power more generally.

V. *PADFIELD V MINISTER OF AGRICULTURE, FISHERIES AND FOOD*: POWER, PROPER PURPOSES AND PARLIAMENTARY SCRUTINY

Reflection on *Ridge* in its political context has suggested that, by forcing public bodies to afford procedural rights to those affected by their decisions, courts may in fact enhance the power of those bodies by ensuring that they are

[29] Ridge had no intention of using his right to a hearing to actually defend himself against charges that he was unfit to serve as the Chief Constable of Brighton. Immediately after the House of Lords handed down their judgment he gave notice of his resignation. By resigning, rather than being dismissed, he was able to retain his pension rights. (See ch 3 in this volume (Thomas)).

furnished with relevant information and by helping to promote their legitimacy. While the decision-makers individually may experience procedural requirements as restricting their capacity to act, such requirements may more broadly serve to augment the capacity of the relevant institution to pursue its public ends. *Padfield v Minister of Agriculture, Fisheries and Food*[30] is in a sense a similar case to *Ridge*, in that it involves a court instructing a public decision-maker to undertake a particular procedure before reaching a decision. In *Ridge* it was ordered that the plaintiff was entitled to a disciplinary hearing before a decision could be made to dismiss him; in *Padfield* the court ruled that a committee of investigation should report on the plaintiff's complaint before the Minister reached a final verdict on it. We can therefore at the outset repeat our point from the previous section: while the individual minister no doubt experienced the House of Lords' ruling as an encumbrance, forcing him to submit to a procedure that he had no desire to follow, it is nevertheless far from obvious that the court's decision had the effect of diminishing the institutional power of the ministerial office.[31] After all, the court did not remove from the Minister his power to have the final say on the matter; it merely ensured that the Minister reached his decision after being provided with further information and argument. It is at least plausible that a report of a committee of investigation would contain relevant information that would assist the Minister in his task of safeguarding the interests of consumers, dairy farmers and the public at large.[32]

In *Padfield* the distinction between the Minister's personal power and the institutional power of the ministerial office is made explicit by the court's ruling that the Minister must exercise his discretion so as to 'promote the policy and objects of the Act'.[33] If we agree that ministerial power is public and institutional not private and personal, then we must accept that an insistence that ministers act for proper purposes need not necessarily restrict such power, so long it goes no further than to ensure that ministers pursue only the public purposes that their offices exist to promote. Certainly, the question of whether a certain purpose is properly public or not requires a sensitive, and often politically controversial, judgment to be made.[34] But to suppose that ministerial power will always be diminished however this judgment is rendered is to succumb to a *non sequitur* borne from a failure to distinguish between a minister's personal

[30] *Padfield* (n 7).

[31] A point made by Maurice Sunkin in this volume (ch 4).

[32] Under s 19(6) of the Agricultural Marketing Act 1958, the Minister's power to amend or revoke the milk marketing scheme was to be exercised if he believed that the way the scheme was operating was 'contrary to the interests of consumers of the regulated products, or … contrary to the interests of any persons affected by the scheme and … not in the public interest'.

[33] *Padfield* (n 7) at 1030 (Lord Reid).

[34] For my part, cases in which the requirement was wrongly used so as to prevent the use of public power for perfectly proper purposes include: *Attorney-General v Fulham Corp* [1921] 1 Ch 440 (Ch); *Roberts v Hopwood* [1925] AC 578 (HL); *Chertsey Urban DC v Mixnam Properties Ltd* [1965] AC 735 (HL); and *Bromley LBC v Greater London Council* [1983] 1 AC 768 (HL). Others will have their own lists.

power and the power of his or her office. In *Padfield* there was a suggestion that the Minister was refusing to refer the plaintiffs' complaint to a committee because he feared that he would find himself in an embarrassing position if the committee were to recommend a change to the scheme. If true then, as Lord Reid said, this 'would plainly be a bad reason'.[35] To allow the ministerial power to be hijacked in order to spare the blushes of an individual minister would be to inhibit the capacity of the ministerial office to promote the public ends that the Milk Marketing Scheme was supposed to realise.

If we take the Minister in *Padfield* to have decided not to refer the matter to a committee of investigation simply so as to avoid political embarrassment, then the case appears similar to *Porter v Magill*: a decision is rightly struck down to protect the integrity of public authority where a power-holder is looking to use their position for purely personal or partisan political ends. But even without such a supposition, it could still be argued the decision of the House of Lords reinforced rather than diminished ministerial power. For if we look at the reasons explicitly given by the Minister, we find him explaining that he 'owes no duty to producers in any particular region' and that for him to intervene would amount to him 'assuming an inappropriate degree of responsibility'.[36] Lord Reid rejected this proposition as an attempt by the minister to place an unwarranted *restriction* on his own remit.[37] *Padfield* therefore cannot be viewed straightforwardly as a judicial intrusion into the minister's sphere of discretionary authority; in fact we see the court arguing that the ministerial power to regulate the Milk Marketing Scheme was more thoroughgoing than the Minister himself had supposed. Had the Minister's interpretation of his own role been accepted, the office of the Minister of Agriculture would have been left with less scope to intervene in the operation of the scheme. This may have suited the Minister, but it is far from clear that it would have empowered his office.

However, if we focus solely on the effect of the *Padfield* decision on *ministerial* power, we omit a crucial aspect of the case. As Sunkin's contribution to this volume shows,[38] the effect of *Padfield* was to wrench the issue out of the corridors of Whitehall and into the chamber of Parliament. By requiring the minister to appoint a committee of investigation, the court ensured that the final decision on the plaintiffs' complaint (which, remember, remained to be made by the minister) met with parliamentary scrutiny. This fact was not lost on their Lordships. Lord Pearce noted that, once the committee have reported, the Minister 'is then answerable only to Parliament, which will have the advantage of being able to understand the pros and cons of the matter from the published

[35] *Padfield* (n 7) at 1032 (Lord Reid).

[36] ibid at 1031 (Lord Reid).

[37] ibid (Lord Reid). Section 19(6) of the Agricultural Marketing Act 1958 charged the Minister with attending to 'the interests of the consumers of the regulated products ... the interests of any persons affected by the scheme and ... the public interest'.

[38] Ch 4 in this volume (Sunkin).

report of an independent committee'.[39] Lord Upjohn was pithier, stating that the Minister 'must be prepared to face the music in Parliament'.[40] This aspect of the case has been sorely overlooked by political constitutionalist critics of the decision. On one hand, *Padfield* has been attacked as a judicial power grab, 'biting into the red meat of statutory powers'.[41] On the other, it has been condemned as futile, since, after the committee report recommended that the Minister uphold the complaint, the Minister declined to follow its advice.[42] Both of these criticisms miss the mark, for precisely the same reason: the Court was not attempting to impose its judgment about how the Milk Marketing Scheme should operate over that of the Minister, but was trying to ensure that the proper constitutional relationship between the executive and Parliament be upheld.

We can thus see a danger with taking as the starting point for administrative law scholarship an assumption that the paradigmatic issue at play is the appropriate limits of judicial power. A blinkered focus on the power of the courts, coupled with an overriding concern about potential judicial overreach, can distort our understanding of the issues, reducing them to a binary paradigm of judicial power *versus* political power. This polarised lens obscures from view the complexity of political power, leading to inadequate attention being paid to the relationships between the various political actors (most obviously Parliament and government, but also local government and the whole array of non-departmental public bodies). The issue of power in public law cannot be reduced to a clash between those who want to see the political branches restricted by strong courts and those who want to see the political system left alone from judicial interference.[43] *Padfield* stands as a reminder – *contra* some commonplace assumptions[44] – that a judicial finding of administrative illegality can lead to an intensification of political debate, and that judicial power, appropriately exercised, can go hand in glove with parliamentary power.

[39] *Padfield* (n 7) at 1054 (Lord Pearce).

[40] ibid at 1061 (Lord Upjohn).

[41] JAG Griffith, *Judicial Politics Since 1920: a chronicle* (Oxford, Blackwell, 1993) 106.

[42] C Harlow, 'Administrative Reaction to Judicial Review' [1976] *PL* 116, 117.

[43] cf P Daly, 'Miller: Legal and political fault lines' [2017] *PL* 73, who describes the case of *R (Miller) v Secretary of State for Exiting the European Union* [2017] UKSC 5, [2018] AC 61 as a clash between two schools of thought, one of which 'emphasises the role of courts in imposing constraints of law and due process on the freedom of action of those in the political branches of government', while the other 'relies on individual interests and the public good being safeguarded by robust debate within the political process' (at 86–87). But how can this be? In holding that the Government lacked the legal power to invoke Art 50 TEU, the Court ensured that the issue was placed before Parliament and thus subjected to 'debate within the political process' (which may or may not have been robust). It is only if we think of public law in the polarised terms of judicial power versus political power that *Miller* can conceivably be viewed as a victory of the former over the latter.

[44] While the judicial power *versus* political power conception of administrative law owes its genesis to those agitating for a more restrained judicial role (the *locus classicus* being JAG Griffith, 'The Political Constitution' (1979) 42 *MLR* 1), its use is not restricted to court-sceptics. Paul Craig, for example, is content to frame his dispute with Adam Tomkins as one 'concerning the balance between the "political" and the "legal" within public law' (P Craig, 'Political Constitutionalism and the Judicial Role: a response' (2011) 9 *International Journal of Constitutional Law* 112, 112).

VI. *ANISMINIC V FOREIGN COMPENSATION COMMISSION*: LEGISLATIVE POWER AND THE RULE OF LAW

Parliament plays a dual role in the UK Constitution: it is both the legislative body and the primary forum in which the Government is held to account. If the analysis in the previous section is correct, *Padfield* served to enhance Parliament's power in carrying out the latter function. *Anisminic v Foreign Compensation Commission*,[45] on the other hand, concerns Parliament's role as legislator.

Anisminic makes the Judicial Power Project's list of '50 problematic cases', with the House of Lords charged with 'judicial adventurism' in 'sidestepping the clear words of the Act'.[46] However, the decision in *Anisminic* was not as revolutionary as this characterisation would suggest; in fact judicial 'sidestepping' of ouster clauses dates back some three centuries.[47] Nevertheless, it is easy to see how this case might be viewed as a judicial usurpation of Parliament's legislative function. Section 4(4) of the Foreign Compensation Act 1950 said that the 'determinations' of the Foreign Compensation Committee 'shall not be called into question in any court of law'. On the face of it, that is exactly what the House of Lords did.

It is common for *Anisminic* to be described as a case in which the court departed from the intention of Parliament in order to protect the rule of law,[48] and thus as an example of the 'balancing' between the Diceyan principles of parliamentary sovereignty and the rule of law that allegedly lies at the heart of our Constitution.[49] On this analysis, the House of Lords' reasoning – that the ouster clause could not prevent the Court from declaring that an apparent decision was a nullity because nullities are not 'determinations' – serves as a 'fig leaf' to 'preserve the decencies' of the Constitution by enabling courts to prevent administrative bodies from being endowed with legally unlimited power without them mounting a direct challenge to the constitutional predominance of Parliament.[50] But this account is hardly likely to assuage concerns about excessive judicial power: if anything, the fact that a judicial 'rebellion against Parliament'[51] is conducted under the cover of a 'fig leaf' is likely to exacerbate fears that *Anisminic* represents a counter-democratic putsch.

[45] *Anisminic* (n 8).

[46] Judicial Power Project, '50 Problematic Cases', available at judicialpowerproject.org.uk/50-problematic-cases.

[47] See, eg *Smith v Commissioners of Sewers* (1669) 1 Mod 44 (KB); *R v Plowright* (1686) 3 Mod 94 (PC); *R v Cheltenham Commissioners* (1841) 1 QB 467 (QB); *R v Wood* (1855) 5 El & Bl 49 (QB).

[48] See, in particular, W Wade and CF Forsyth, *Administrative Law* (Oxford, OUP, 2014) 614.

[49] eg M Elliott, 'The *Ultra Vires* Doctrine in a Constitutional Setting: still the central principle of administrative law' [1999] *CLJ* 129, 151. But note that Dicey himself stated that while these two principles 'may appear to stand in opposition to each other, or to be at best only counterbalancing forces … this appearance is delusive' because 'the sovereignty of Parliament … favours the supremacy of the law' (AV Dicey, *Introduction to the Study of the Law of the Constitution*, 10th edn (Basingstoke, Macmillan Education, 1959) 350).

[50] C Forsyth, 'Of Fig Leaves and Fairy Tales: the *ultra vires* doctrine, the sovereignty of Parliament and judicial review' (1996) 55 *CLJ* 122, 136–37.

[51] Wade and Forsyth, *Administrative Law* (2014) 614.

The Judicial Power Project criticism of *Anisminic* and the 'fig leaf' defence of the decision share a common starting point: the question of what Parliament intended when it enacted section 4(4) of the Foreign Compensation Act 1950. The issue of parliamentary intention is a complex and controversial one, with some denying that such a thing exists, others arguing that it not only exists but determines legal content and yet others accepting its existence but holding that it need not necessarily be followed in all cases.[52] As my topic here is power and not statutory interpretation, I need not stir this particular hornet's nest.[53] The question I want to ask is not whether the House of Lords in *Anisminic* engaged in a sound process of legal reasoning, but whether they diminished Parliament's institutional power. I believe that reflection on the function of Parliament as legislator reveals that they did not; as such, characterisation of the case as a rebellion against Parliament is wide of the mark.

When thinking about the effects of judicial review on parliamentary power it is instructive to consider the original function of the prerogative writs. The writs of *quo warranto*, prohibition and *certiorari*[54] were first developed in the aftermath of the Norman Conquest as a means for effecting a royal policy of centralisation. They were used by or on the behalf of the King as a way of establishing the common law as the law of the land, by limiting the jurisdiction of the ecclesiastical courts and other specialised tribunals and ensuring that the records of petty officials could be examined in the Court of King's Bench.[55] Far from being an instrument for the limitation of royal power, they were a mechanism for bringing a diffuse administrative complex under royal control. The establishment of the rule of law was necessary in order for the King to have reliable means of ensuring that his edicts were enforced across the land. It is also worth recalling here Fuller's fable of King Rex, whose eight attempts to reform the law of his kingdom all met with failure.[56] In his final attempt Rex was frustrated by 'a failure of congruence between the rules as announced and their actual administration'.[57] Without a mechanism to ensure that law as stated would in fact be applied, Rex was impotent to shape the conduct of his subjects in the ways that he had wished.

[52] See, for example, J Laws, 'Statutory Interpretation: the myth of parliamentary intent', Renton Lecture (13 November 2017), available at www.statutelawsociety.co.uk/wp-content/uploads/2017/11/The-Myth-of-Parliamentary-Intent-text.pdf; JH Baker, 'Statutory Interpretation and Parliamentary Intention' (1993) 52 *CLJ* 353; A Kavanagh, 'The Role of Parliamentary Intention in Adjudication under the Human Rights Act 1998' (2006) 26 *OJLS* 179.

[53] Though I cannot resist adding, parenthetically, that I do not quite understand why the focus should be on what Parliament *intended to do* rather than on what Parliament actually *did*. The meaning of a speech act cannot be conflated with the speaker's intention: '*où est la guerre?*' does not mean 'where is the station?' simply because that is what I mean to ask.

[54] Mandamus is of more recent vintage.

[55] E Jenks, 'The Prerogative Writs in English Law' (1923) XXXII *Yale Law Journal* 523; SA de Smith, 'The Prerogative Writs' (1951) 11 *CLJ* 40; J Hanus, 'Certiorari and Policy-Making in English History' (1968) 12 *American Journal of Legal History* 63.

[56] LL Fuller, *The Morality of Law* (New Haven, Yale University Press, 1969) 33–41.

[57] ibid 39.

The parallels with *Anisminic* should not be hard to spot. In marked contrast to the twelfth century, the twentieth century saw a significant diffusion of power to a huge number of administrative bodies carrying out a wide range of tasks. In realistic terms, Parliament lacks the capacity to supervise the operation of these bodies. There is a clear risk that administrative decision-makers become laws unto themselves, free from parliamentary control, the modern version of the medieval ecclesiastical court. To prevent Parliament's power from being thus dissipated, effective checks on administrative action must be maintained. Just as the subjection of inferior tribunals to the rule of law was needed to consolidate the power of the medieval King, so it is necessary to maintain the power of the modern Parliament.

This conclusion can be reinforced if we recall that the power of a political institution is necessarily teleological – that is, tied to a particular purpose. The relevant function of Parliament here is that of *legislator*. Parliamentary power is not the power of parliamentarians, either individually or as a whole, to realise their particular ends. It is the power to further the public interest through the enactment of effective *law*. An ouster clause creates the potential for an administrative body to operate in a manner unconstrained by law. This might, for whatever reason, happen to suit the purposes of parliamentarians. But it does not enhance the legislative power, which persists only insofar as there exist effective mechanisms for upholding the law of the land.

Therefore, even if we assume *arguendo* that the Law Lords in *Anisminic* reached their decision by 'sidestepping the clear words of the Act', we should not conclude that the decision amounted to an expansion of judicial power to the detriment to the power of Parliament. On the contrary, there are reasons to believe that the judicial reading down of ouster clauses in fact preserves parliamentary power by ensuring that administrative bodies are subject to the law and thus within the purview of Parliament's legislative authority.[58] These reasons are not indefeasible. It is, for example, not necessarily the case that administrative bodies will be any less capable of interpreting and implementing the law of the land than would the High Court. We might thus be less concerned about ouster clauses when the bodies they seek to protect from its supervisory jurisdiction can fairly be described as *courts*, that is to say, where we believe that the extent of procedural protection and independence of the decision-makers are adequate to secure adherence to the rule of law.[59] What this shows is that broad claims about judicial power cannot be sustained by a narrow analysis of

[58] cf *R v Hickman, ex p Fox* (1945) 70 CLR 598, 616 (Dixon J): it is 'impossible for the legislature to impose limits upon the quasi-judicial authority of a body which it sets up with the intention that any excess of that authority means invalidity, and yet, at the same time, to deprive this Court of authority to restrain the invalid action'.

[59] This line of reasoning commended itself to the dissenting justices in *R (Privacy International) v Investigatory Powers Tribunal* [2019] UKSC 22, [2019] 4 All ER 1: see [182] (Lord Sumption) and [252] (Lord Wilson).

the courts' interpretation of a particular statutory provision taken in isolation, underscoring, once more, the importance of understanding judicial decisions in their broader political context.

VII. *CONWAY V RIMMER*: AN ASSERTION OF JURISDICTION; A LOSS OF POWER

Conway v Rimmer[60] differs from the rest of the Quartet in that it was not an action for judicial review.[61] It originated as a claim for malicious prosecution, though the appeal concerned an interlocutory application for disclosure of certain documents, which was supported by both plaintiff and defendant but resisted by the Home Secretary on the ground of Crown privilege. This difference between *Conway* and the other cases in the Quartet is reflected in the court taking a different stance in the face of actions of a public decision-maker and, consequently, a different kind of remedy. Rather than making the decision-maker reconsider his decision, in *Conway* the House of Lords assumed responsibility to take the decision itself. The way in which it did so had unfortunate implications for the development of the law on what would come to be known as public interest immunity. With an eye on judicial power and the Quartet, we see an irony in *Conway*: the case in which judicial power appears to have been wielded in the most forceful manner is also the one that had the weakest impact.

To understand *Conway*, one needs to be aware of the case it overturned: the wartime decision of *Duncan v Cammell Laird*.[62] In 1939, a submarine sank during naval tests, with 99 men losing their lives. In an action for negligence, the families of the deceased sought discovery of documents concerned with the construction of the vessel; the First Lord of the Admiralty objected on the ground of Crown privilege. In language redolent of *Liversidge v Anderson*,[63] the House of Lords held that 'an objection validly taken to production on the grounds that this would be injurious to the public interest is conclusive',[64] deciding, effectively, that for the purposes of Crown privilege ministers are the sole judge of what is in the public interest.

[60] *Conway* (n 9).

[61] Or, more accurately, it was not a case which today would need to be brought under the CPR Pt 54 procedure. Of the four, only *Padfield* started life as an application to the Divisional Court for a prerogative writ. *Ridge* and *Anisminic* were both brought as ordinary civil claims seeking declarations: a procedural gambit that would fail after *O'Reilly v Mackman* [1983] 2 AC 237 (HL).

[62] *Duncan v Cammell Laird* [1942] 1 All ER 587 (HL).

[63] *Liversidge v Anderson* [1942] AC 206 (HL). In this well-known case a statement by a minister that he had 'reasonable cause to believe a person to be of hostile origins' was taken as conclusive of the fact that such reasonable cause in fact existed. I agree with the Judicial Power Project that this is a 'problematic case' (judicialpowerproject.org.uk/50-problematic-cases), although, clearly, judicial power is not the problem here.

[64] *Duncan* (n 62) at 595.

By 1968, and in a markedly less deferential era, such an approach was, as Lord Morris put it, 'out of harmony with the spirit which in this country has guided the ordering of our affairs'.[65] The result was a bold *volte-face*, the law on Crown privilege being turned on its head. The House of Lords declared that the responsibility for deciding whether the public interest demanded evidence to be withheld lay with the courts and not the Crown. With one leap the Court took us from complete subservience to the Minister's assessment of the public interest to a position where the assessment was expressly held to be not for the Minister to make.[66]

The approach envisaged in *Conway* was that the Court would weigh the harm that disclosure would potentially cause to the public against the negative impact that suppressing the evidence would have on the court's ability to do justice between the parties. The Minister could not be responsible for striking this balance, as although he would be well-placed to assess the potential harm that would flow from disclosure, he would not be in a position to determine the probative significance of the evidence. Since the latter will vary according to how the evidence in question relates to the matters in dispute, the balancing exercise could only be conducted in light of the full circumstances of the particular case. Thus it could not be the Minister's responsibility, when considering a potential claim of public interest immunity, to attempt to strike the appropriate balance himself.[67]

As Arvind and Stirton's chapter highlights, this attempt by the Court to shine the light of judicial scrutiny into the darker corners of executive practice proved counterproductive.[68] In the cases that followed *Conway*, the courts revealed that they did not generally share Lord Reid's confidence in their ability to weigh up the competing interests in play. The consequence was the antithesis of what *Conway* had set out to achieve: 'large swathes of public administration concealed from the gaze of the courts and immune to the demands of the administration of justice'.[69] While one might be tempted simply to blame persisting judicial timidity for this, in fact, as Arvind and Stirton show, part of the problem lay in the reasoning in *Conway* itself. In making clear that the Minister's role was *not* to make an assessment of the competing interests, the courts deprived themselves of a potentially valuable source of assistance. Administrators responsible for attending to only one side of the balancing exercise were disincentivised from carrying out any thorough assessment of the seriousness of the risk of disclosure in any given case. Ironically, the *Conway* approach encouraged ministers to rely on blanket justifications for excluding certain classes of material, in response to

[65] *Conway* (n 9) at 955.
[66] ibid at 950 (Lord Reid): 'the Minister … has no duty to balance these conflicting public interests'.
[67] See AAS Zuckerman, 'Public Interest Immunity – a matter of prime judicial responsibility' (1994) 57 *MLR* 703, 708.
[68] Ch 5 in this volume (Arvind and Stirton).
[69] Zuckerman (n 67) 709.

which the courts proved themselves incapable of making sensible case-by-case decisions, retreating to a default stance of extreme deference.[70]

The legacy of *Conway* shows that an increased intensity of judicial review does not necessarily translate into an increase in judicial power. We can imagine, as a thought experiment, that *Conway* might have reached the House of Lords not as an interlocutory application for disclosure but on an application for *certiorari* of the Home Secretary's decision to claim privilege. We can imagine the court, with its prerogative writ hat on, holding that claims for Crown privilege are subject to *Wednesbury*[71] reasonableness review with particular attention to be paid to the importance of disclosure of relevant evidence for the common law right to a fair trial. This we would recognise as a weaker intensity of review than that actually exercised by the Court in *Conway*. Nevertheless, in subsequent cases, the Minister would be charged with making a bona fide assessment of the balance of the public interest which the Court would be in a position to scrutinise. There would then be some cases in which the Minister would conclude that, although disclosure would be detrimental to the public interest, on balance this detriment would not outweigh the prejudice to the administration of justice that would follow from the evidence being withheld. In other words, there would be some cases where the Minister would not claim public interest immunity in circumstances in which, under the *Conway* approach, they would have done. Secondly, in cases where public interest immunity were claimed, the Court would be able to assess the reasons why the Minister believed not only that disclosure of documents of the relevant type would be prejudicial to the public interest but that, on the facts of the particular case in hand, on balance the documents ought to be withheld. Armed with fuller reasons the courts may well find themselves emboldened, in appropriate cases, to find that the Minister's case did not hold up to rational scrutiny.[72] So there may well also be cases where, notwithstanding a weaker intensity of review, a minister's decision to seek public interest immunity is denied in circumstances in which, under the *Conway* approach, it would have been allowed.

Reflection on *Conway* and its aftermath gives us yet another reason to avoid equating judicial power with the scope of the court's decision-making authority.

[70] See *Rogers v Secretary of State for the Home Department* [1972] 2 All ER 1057 (HL); *Gaskin v Liverpool CC* [1980] 1 WLR 1549 (CA); *D v NSPCC* [1981] 1 All ER 829 (CA); *Makanjuola v Commissioner of Police for the Metropolis* [1992] 3 All ER 617 (CA); and *Halford v Sharples* [1992] 3 All ER 624 (CA).

[71] *Associated Provincial Picture Houses Ltd v Wednesbury Corp* [1948] 1 KB 223 (CA).

[72] The idea that fuller reasons from a public decision-maker may make it easier for a court to intervene with its decisions will be a familiar one to administrative lawyers. As Sedley LJ said in *R v Higher Education Funding Council, ex p Institute of Dental Surgery* [1994] 1 WLR 242 (DC) at 257: 'The giving of reasons may … alert the recipient to a justiciable flaw in the process'. Indeed, *Anisminic* is an example of a case in which the challenge would likely have failed but for the reasons advanced by the decision-maker in support of its decision: see D Feldman, '*Anisminic Ltd v Foreign Compensation Commission* [1968]: In Perspective' in S Juss and M Sunkin (eds), *Landmark Cases in Public Law* (London, Bloomsbury, 2017) 71.

Of the four cases of the Quartet, it is only in *Conway* that we see the court straightforwardly wrenching decision-making authority from the executive, and yet *Conway* is also the one of the four that is widely accepted as having had the least impact on administrative practice. What we see in *Conway* is the judiciary finding itself in a relative weak position as a consequence of attempting to directly play the role of administrative decision-maker. In the other cases, by contrast, where the House of Lords looked to shape rather than usurp administrative decision-making, it found itself wielding significant influence. In these cases, rather than being pitted against administrative and parliamentary power in a zero-sum struggle, judicial power rowed in synch with the power of the political branches, enhancing the potency of each. *Conway* here serves as the exception that proves the rule.

VIII. CONCLUSION

This analysis of the Quartet has identified some straightforward but important lessons about judicial and political power. Firstly, we cannot simply assume that every judicial invalidation of an administrative decision represents a diminution in governmental power and a corresponding growth in judicial power. Successful challenges to the actions of public bodies may have the consequence of strengthening those bodies in the long run, for example where procedural requirements enhance the capacity of administrators to achieve their desired ends by furnishing them with improved knowledge and buttressing their de facto legitimacy. Furthermore, a judicial venture into a field of administrative decision-making may serve to diminish the capacity of courts to control the behaviour of administrators, as the example of *Conway* shows.

Secondly, when considering the impact of the judiciary on the power of other political institutions, we must not conflate Parliament, government and other public bodies, but instead be attentive to the way in which judicial decisions can affect the relationships between the various institutions. Criticism of *Padfield* as an ultimately futile attempt by the judiciary to usurp executive power overlooked the way in which the decision served to empower Parliament as the primary forum for holding government ministers to account. Today one could say much the same thing about some of the criticism of *Miller*.[73]

Thirdly, far from being a limitation on Parliament's legislative power, the rule of law is a necessary precondition of such power. Those concerned about protecting parliamentary power should therefore view proposals to inhibit access to judicial review with suspicion.[74] The fact that a majority of parliamentarians

[73] See n 43.

[74] The 2019 Conservative Party manifesto stated that: 'We will ensure that judicial review is available to protect the rights of the individuals against an overbearing state, while ensuring that it is not abused to conduct politics by another means or to create needless delays. In our first year we will

may favour such proposals has no bearing on this – assuming, that is, that what we are interested in protecting is the power of Parliament as a democratic legislature rather than the power of persons who happen to be elected as MPs.

In sum, the implicit understanding of the nature of judicial power that appears to underlie the Judicial Power Project's research programme is flawed. Its zero-sum view of power appears attractive only if we 'reduce public affairs to the business of dominion', that is, if we conceive of the relationships between political institutions as a series of competitive struggles for control over particular domains. Such a conception fails to capture the reality of the political sphere. Power is not a zero-sum game: it may be generated – and destroyed – through the interactions between political institutions. If we simply assume that more judicial power means less governmental power, then we surrender the chance to examine the role that the courts might play, alongside Parliament, government and other bodies, in expanding society's collective capacity to pursue public goals.

set up a Constitution, Democracy & Rights Commission that will examine these issues in depth, and come up with proposals to restore trust in our institutions and in how our democracy operates.' (Conservative and Unionist Party, 'Get Brexit Done: Unleash Britain's potential' (2019) 49). At the time of writing, it is by no means clear what the remit of the Commission will be, or what form its proposals are likely to take, but it would seem that the Government's intentions are to make it more difficult for citizens to challenge its actions by way of judicial review.

18

Strategic Judging: Lessons from the Reid Era of Judicial Decision-Making

RICHARD KIRKHAM AND DIMITRIOS TSARAPATSANIS

I. INTRODUCTION

A LIBERAL CONSTITUTION is in part reliant upon an institutional separation of powers between the executive, parliament and the courts, but the exact demarcation of the boundary lines and dynamics of the relationships that result are heavily contested.[1] Using Lord Reid's tenure as a judge in the House of Lords as a case study, this chapter explores one aspect of those dynamics by charting the various moves in decision-making that judges are able to deploy in order to pursue wider strategic inter-institutional goals.

Our main explanatory aims are concentrated on using an institutional approach to add a piece to the puzzle of explaining the nature of the purported *shift* in judicial decision-making practice that began during the Reid era (and which we shall henceforth call 'the Reid shift'). The results of this shift, it is often claimed, has been to expand the reach of the judiciary when reviewing exercises of public power. To comprehend how this shift occurred, we deploy the concept of indeterminacy in the law to explain the room for manoeuvre built into the common law method and the consequent potential for judges to shift the parameters of the law either towards, or away, from enhanced scrutiny of executive action. This indeterminacy grants the judiciary a degree of power to realign institutional relationships between the judiciary and the political branches of the state by developing suitably revised interpretations of the law. The judiciary's power to realign, however, is heavily constrained by factors both internal and external to the law. The strength of such constraints leads us to sketch an

[1] Multiple examples of such contestation could be cited; see eg TA Fairclough, '*Evans v Attorney General*: The Underlying Normativity of Constitutional Disagreement' in S Juss and M Sunkin (eds), *Landmark Cases in Public Law* (Oxford, Hart, 2017); M Loughlin, *The Case of Prorogation* (London, Policy Exchange, 2019).

institutional theory of judicial decision-making, which formulates a number of moves that a rational judiciary can take to intensify judicial challenges to the political branches. Applying this approach to the Reid era, we hypothesise that these moves explain why the House of Lords chose the specific doctrinal forms that it did to engineer a shift in judicial decision-making patterns in the 1960s.

To make this argument, the chapter begins by briefly laying out the context of the Reid era, one in which it is widely accepted that the judiciary were motivated to increase forms and doctrines of review of administrative action. We then apply a relatively novel methodological approach in UK legal scholarship, namely, systematic content analysis,[2] to evidence that the changed pattern in judicial decision-making in the House of Lords cannot easily be attributed to a straightforward shift in doctrinal form – even if this was the eventual outcome. Hence, in the final section we suggest that institutional theory provides a stronger grounding for explaining how the Reid shift occurred.

The analysis in this chapter only supplies the beginnings of the evidence needed to provide a full explanation of the Reid shift. More broadly, however, we claim that this approach offers a more useful tool through which to understand the work that the senior judiciary are involved in than tired debates about judicial activism. Further, we claim that this approach provides clues as to how the judiciary could engineer any future shifts in its relationship with the legislature and the executive, and if extended, focuses our attention on considering the appropriate dialogical responses of the political branch and lower court judges to such shifts.

II. THE REID ERA AS AN INSTANCE OF BEHAVIOURAL CHANGE

A. The Legal Context

The story of the evolving nature of judicial power in the post war-period provides a classic case study in how judges can adjust their decision-making patterns. As we intimated above, most studies of the Reid era concur that a shift in judicial decision-making behaviour occurred, and that this equipped the judiciary with a more extended set of conceptual tools with which to scrutinise the legality of exercises of executive power.[3] This process went well beyond individual cases and eventually led to modern judicial review.

[2] R Kirkham and E O'Loughlin, 'A Content Analysis of Judicial Decision-Making' in N Creutzfeldt, M Mason and K McConnachie (eds), *Routledge Handbook on Socio-Legal Theory and Method* (Abingdon, Routledge, 2019).

[3] eg L Blom-Cooper and G Drewry, 'Towards a System of Administrative Law: The Reid and Wilberforce Era, 1945–82' in L Blom-Cooper, B Dickson and G Drewry (eds), *The Judicial House of Lords: 1876–2009* (Oxford, Oxford University Press, 2009).

The Reid shift challenged the late-nineteenth-century and early-twentieth-century settlement between the judiciary and the political branches. This former settlement had facilitated a specific way of using public power, emanating from a more or less centralised and unchallenged government/parliament nexus. As a consequence of its faith in the abilities of the civil service to deliver public goods efficiently,[4] the judiciary, with a few expressions of concern aside,[5] largely relegated itself to a passive role vis-à-vis the political branches. For defenders of the Reid shift, this so-called period of the 'long sleep' marked a disjunction with the foundations of British public law as laid down in the seventeenth-century battle between Crown and Parliament,[6] and then, later, in its oversight of municipal government.[7] Set against this context, the post-war growth in administrative law was seen, from a normative point of view, as a necessary 'checks and balances' corrective to the centralisation of public power the judiciary had acquiesced in, as well as a reflective response to novel societal demands.[8]

This ex-post narrative, however, makes the Reid shift appear more inevitable than perhaps it was in reality. Not all of the indicators of the day pointed towards the 1960s as a pivotal moment in judicial attitudes. For instance, despite appearances, it is not entirely clear and beyond doubt that the legal process was working systematically against claimants at the time, or that a shift was necessary.[9] Nor was there unanimous approval for increased judicial intervention, particularly from the left who offered the critique that the judiciary pursued a conservative agenda and were selectively destructive of progressive legislation.[10] Above all, Whitehall administration was still in a very strong position to control the agenda of reform in administrative justice[11] and either 'veto'[12] or water down those reforms that did make it through to Parliament.[13]

[4] See S Sterett, *Creating Constitutionalism? The Politics of Legal Expertise and Administrative Law in England and Wales* (Michigan, University of Michigan Press, 1997) 31–42; S Sedley, 'The Sound of Silence: Constitutional Law Without a Constitution' (1994) 110 *LQR* 271.

[5] eg Lord Hewart, *The New Despotism* (London, Ernest Benn, 1929).

[6] For an account of the long history of English administrative law, see P Craig, 'English Administrative Law History: Perception and Reality' in S Jhaveri and M Ramsden (eds), *Judicial Review of Administrative Action: Origins and Adaptations Across the Common Law World* (Cambridge, CUP, 2021, forthcoming).

[7] eg S Sedley, 'The Long Sleep' in M Andenas and D Fairgrieve (eds), *Tom Bingham and the Transformation of the Law: A Liber Amicorum* (Oxford, OUP, 2009).

[8] Blom-Cooper and Drewry), *The Judicial House of Lords* (2009) 230–31.

[9] Sterret's study of the period showed that claimants succeeded in applications granted at rates higher than 50%, a success rate that declined to around 40% only from the mid-1960s onwards: Sterrett, *Creating Constitutionalism?* (1997) 50.

[10] H Laski, *Parliamentary Government in England* (New York, Viking, 1938) 454; I Jennings, 'Courts and Administrative Law: The Experience of English Housing Legislation' (1936) 49 *Harvard Law Review* 426–56.

[11] Sterett (n 4) 79.

[12] K Shepsle and B Weingast, 'The Institutional Foundations of Committee Power' (1987) 81 *American Political Science Review* 85–105.

[13] TT Arvind and L Stirton, 'The curious origins of judicial review' (2017) 133 *LQR* 91.

B. Changing Judicial Culture

Notwithstanding the obstacles to a judiciary seeking to increase its leverage, the period represented an exceptionally favourable moment for a shift to occur. First, there was a growing political and cultural acceptance, one which spread far beyond the judiciary, of the necessity for reimagining the relationships between the state and citizenry and for revising schemes for providing redress for wrongs committed by administration.[14] Indeed, the Reid shift appeared to tap into a wider political and cultural moment, in which deference towards administrative authority declined and attention became more focused on what was understood to be the issue of perceived unaccountability of public administration[15] and the insufficiency of existing options for the redress.[16] This was a trend that the public law community of the day[17] and the Bar[18] picked up on, as fed by ideas transposed from abroad.[19] In this period there were calls for a radical overhaul of the process for considering administrative law disputes and the establishment of a Royal Commission to examine the matter.[20] Above all, not only did the Government-commissioned Franks Report[21] result in the Tribunals and Inquiries Act 1958, but the Parliamentary statements that supported that legislation provided a powerful symbolic message in favour of administrative justice. Set against this background, it can be claimed that the Reid shift followed, rather than led or worked against, public opinion and legislative policy.[22]

Alan Paterson's study of the Law Lords from 1957 to 1973 offers further possible clues as to why the shift occurred when it did. Judges are driven by the need to provide reasoned arguments to justify their decisions, and these must appear convincing to those to whom they are addressed. Importantly, a significant part of the audience of judges is composed by lawyers who form a distinctive kind of epistemic community charged with providing arguments concerned with applying the law in the future. Consequently, the reasons adduced by judges will derive at least in part from the kinds of considerations

[14] ibid 93–102; see also ch 3 section VII in this volume (Thomas).

[15] Sedley, 'The Long Sleep' (2009) 78–80.

[16] See IF Nicholson, *The Mystery of Crichel Down* (Oxford, Clarendon Press, 1986).

[17] eg J Whyatt, *The Citizen and the Administration: The Redress of Grievances* (London, Justice, 1961). For a broader discussion, see Sterret (n 4) 69–89.

[18] A Paterson, *The Law Lords* (London, MacMillan, 1982) ch 3.

[19] Such as the US Administrative Procedure Act 1946, see R Heuston, 'Book Review of Bernard Schwartz, *American Administrative Law*' (1952) 68 *LQR* 250; Paterson *The Law Lords* (1982) chs 2 and 3; JWF Allison, *A Continental Distinction in the Common Law: A Historical and Comparative Perspective on English Public Law* (Oxford, OUP, 1996).

[20] Law Commission, Exploratory Working Paper on Administrative Law, Law Com PWP No 13, 1967.

[21] Franks Committee, Administrative Tribunals and Enquiries, Cm 218 (1957).

[22] Ch 3 in this volume (Thomas). See also W Wade, *Constitutional Fundamentals* (London, Stevens, 1980) 78.

and standards that are deemed acceptable within the wider scholarly community in which the judges operate:

> Such understandings are in no small way the product of a common socialisation pattern, a traditional training with a received body of knowledge and learning. Indeed it has been argued that such traditional practices and ideas, nurtured by a legal caste, are the very essence of the common law.[23]

Here it is significant that in the 1950s and 1960s the communal nature of judging was being fed by a new and much expanded diet of academic writing on administrative law,[24] actively championing the evolution of the law and encouraging judges to enhance their scrutiny of public authority. Moreover, at this moment the workload in the House of Lords gradually increased from a prior period of inactivity.[25] Perhaps most important of all, during the short period between 1959 and 1962 seven of the 12 Law Lords were replaced,[26] joining three other judges who had already shown a propensity to adopt a subtly different perspective on the judicial role than their colleagues.[27] This new body of judges was led by Lord Reid, a man willing to make use of the opportunity.

III. EVIDENCING THE SHIFT IN BEHAVIOURAL DECISION-MAKING DURING THE REID ERA

A. The Underdeterminacy of Law as an Opportunity for Strategic Action

The question we pursue here is how to get from the general contextual parameters just mentioned to a more fine-grained explanation of the forms of intensification of judicial review of administrative action that were operative during the Reid era. One possible answer is to explain the shift by reference to the common law method of resolving disputes.

Our starting point is that shifts in the law, and different decision-making strategies, are possible because there is a certain degree of inherent indeterminacy contained in the legal enterprise. This indeterminacy is allowed for within the common law method, which favours the incremental development of law and provides an arena within which different judicial approaches might productively

[23] Paterson (n 18) 122.

[24] See SA de Smith, *Judicial Review of Administrative Action* (London, Stevens, 1959).

[25] R Stevens, *Law and Politics: The House of Lords as a Judicial Body 1800–1976* (London, Weidenfield and Nicholson, 1978) 415.

[26] Lords Morton, Somervell, Cohen, Keith, Tucker and Simonds retired, and Denning became Master of the Rolls. They were replaced by Lords Jenkins, Morris, Hodson, Guest, Devlin, Evershed and Pearce.

[27] Lords Reid, Radcliffe, Denning and MacDermott. Paterson (n 18) 173 makes this claim on the basis of interviews that he conducted and published lectures, of the 19 Law Lords that served between 1967 and 1973.

manifest themselves. Judicial decision-making, therefore, especially at the level of appellate courts, is seldom fully constrained by the 'law', by which we specifically mean legal materials and the accepted rules of legal interpretation. 'Not fully constrained' here means that the law does not require *a unique acceptable solution* to a given dispute. 'Legal materials' should be understood as a term of art that comprises all the canonical texts that enter as inputs into judicial reasoning (statutes, subordinate legislation, case law and so on) and provide the grounds on which judges base their formulation of the legal norms that should govern the dispute. By 'rules of interpretation' we refer to established legitimate forms of argument about how to attribute meaning to legal materials or make proper inferences from them. These are accepted and diffused by a given scholarly community at a given point in time.

Now, we do not claim, as some radical critical legal scholars have done in the past, that the law is indeterminate in the sense that *any* solution might be inferred from legal materials.[28] All that we contend is that the law, in cases that are argued at the appellate level, frequently *underdetermines* purported outcomes, to wit, that at least two outcomes and perhaps more than two can be rationally justified by reference to applicable legal materials and the established rules of interpretation. We thus fully accept that legal materials and established rules of interpretation can constrain outcomes. Indeed, this is an important reason why the underdeterminacy thesis holds, if at all, mainly at the appellate level where it is often, and perhaps almost always, the case that at least two incompatible and rationally compelling ways of arguing in favour of a given outcome can be formulated.[29] At the senior appellate level there are also fewer binding precedents, particularly in administrative law.

Moreover, the underdeterminacy thesis is general; it applies irrespective of whether given legal actors make claims about how 'formalist' approaches could supposedly resolve the issue at hand without any need to interpret the law, ie by recourse to the 'plain meaning' of the applicable text, at least if by 'law' we understand, as above, applicable legal materials and established rules of interpretation. In fact, whenever the law in the sense defined above underdetermines outcomes, 'formalism' can be understood as just one possible way to resolve an interpretive dispute among others,[30] perhaps by placing emphasis on literal rather than, say, purposive interpretation. Besides, even 'formalism' as an interpretive approach comes in degrees. Thus, insofar as judges at the appellate level typically have a choice between more and less 'formalist' and non-formalist types of solutions to disputes, any explanation of their behaviour which rests on

[28] JW Singer, 'The Player and the Cards: Nihilism and Legal Theory' (1984) 94 *Yale Law Journal* 1. Nor do we claim, as some political scientists do, that judges only care about policy in the strict sense of promotion of political preferences: on such a view, see J Segal and H Spaeth, *The Supreme Court and the Attitudinal Model Revisited* (New York, CUP, 2002) 111.

[29] B Leiter, 'Legal Realism and Legal Positivism Reconsidered' (2001) 111 *Ethics* 278.

[30] JA King, 'Institutional Approaches to Judicial Restraint' (2008) 28 *OJLS* 409–41.

'formalism' understood as the supposed absence of interpretive choice is, from our point of view, question-begging. In particular, when it comes to explaining the evolution of the interpretive methods used by the House of Lords in the area of public law in the 1960s, which is the object of our study, it will not do to try to explain the previous reluctance to intensify the scrutiny of administrative decisions solely by the prevalence of 'formalism': this prevalence itself has to be somehow explained, since other interpretive approaches are almost always typically available to judges.

This brings us to our third point. If the law (in the rather strict and technical sense specified above) underdetermines outcomes in most appellate cases, then outcomes must in part be determined by 'non-legal' factors. Likewise, the justification of the outcomes that were ultimately reached must also rely, at least to the extent that these are unconstrained, on non-legal reasons.[31] As a result, the explanation of judicial behaviour at the appellate level calls for a systematic study of the causal mechanisms that determine decision-making where these mechanisms do not just include the causal impact of legal reasons. Of course, we are well aware that the burgeoning literature on judicial behaviour, especially of US provenance, offers many such approaches.[32] Our ambitions in the present chapter, however, are more limited and focus on one particular explanatory dimension – institutional strategy – as suggested further below.

One final point of clarification is in order. We appreciate that there are deeper jurisprudential debates about the nature of law and that different ways of understanding 'law' would lead to a different classification of legal and non-legal reasons and support a different take on underdeterminacy. We have two responses to such an objection. First, we emphatically do not claim that 'the law' *as such* underdetermines outcomes at the level of appellate courts. In fact, were we to make such a claim, we would have to argue that the very rough definition of what we mean by 'law' outlined above (legal materials and established rules of interpretation) is the best definition of law on offer. Given the current state of play in legal theory, such a claim would not be just wrong but clearly preposterous. Indeed, whether the 'law' underdetermines judicial outcomes or not plainly depends on what one means by 'law'.

Second, and accordingly, in the text we only make a minimal claim about 'law' on the basis of common lawyerly sense, remaining entirely neutral as to the question of the nature of law (and hence the best theory of law). We thus assume that the minimal definition of 'law' our project depends on captures at least the core pre-theoretical commitments of competent lawyers and judges engaging in the law's argumentative practice. From that point of view, and whatever the merits of different comprehensive theories of the deep nature of law, they are

[31] See B Leiter, 'Legal Indeterminacy' (1995) 1 *Legal Theory* 481.

[32] For a UK example, see TT Arvind and L Stirton, 'Legal ideology, legal doctrine and the UK's top judges' [2016] *PL* 418.

orthogonal to our project. In fact, since our aim is merely to lay out the foundations of a description of the decision situation faced by appellate judges in a way best suited to formulate hypotheses about the explanation of their behaviour, we have tried to provide a very rough and pre-theoretical definition of 'law' that stays close to what we take the common sense of legal actors themselves to be. This kind of approach seems particularly well suited for purposes of sociological explanation. We thus make no claim to the effect that what we take the 'law' to be for the purposes of the present research is *indeed* the law from the point of view of the best theory about the nature of law.

B. Evidencing the Received Explanation

The above account suggests that a permanent indeterminacy in decision-making is an inevitable facet of judging. In common law systems, this creates a dynamic tension in which judicial decision-making is confined by the law and established legal doctrine, but the parameters of that confinement are unavoidably adjustable.[33] This makes the judicial role fluid and potentially influenced by the prevalent context within which the judiciary operates, as well as existing law.

Even though law underdetermines outcomes, however, judges can adopt consistent positions in their application of the law. Moreover, there are good reasons for the judiciary to strive for consistency, as embodied in the doctrine of *stare decisis*.[34] In particular, to firm up the constitutional status of the rule of law it is in the interest of the judiciary to legitimate and channel its decision-making through prospective legal doctrine. Legal doctrine, by focusing on some factors and ruling out others, strives for a consistently adhered-to underpinning approach to judicial decision-making.[35] This demand for a consistent underpinning to legal doctrine makes shifts in that underpinning appear even more spectacular once they occur.

In the field of public law, the judicial search for a consistent position is driven by competing judicial goals, in particular of 'restraint' or 'deference' (namely, a reluctance to intervene in the sphere of political decision-making) and 'vigilance' (namely a concern to test the legal accountability of that decision-making and firm up legal principles).[36] In a recent study of judicial review in several commonwealth common law countries, Knight tested for four separate

[33] E Posner and A Vermeule, *The Executive Unbound: After the Madisonian Republic* (New York, OUP, 2011) ch 3.

[34] Even though, we hasten to add, precedent as a constraining or legitimising factor is much less important when it comes to apex courts, such as the House of Lords during the period under study here.

[35] JD Heydon, 'Limits to the powers of ultimate appellate courts' (2006) 122 *LQR* 399, 403–05.

[36] D Knight, *Vigilance and Restraint in the Common Law of Judicial Review* (Cambridge, CUP, 2018) 252, 272–79.

principled approaches towards the management of decision-making, and design of legal doctrine, in judicial review which capture well the possibilities available: scope; grounds; intensity; and context.[37] These approaches are of interest here as they indicate different viable positions on the restraint/vigilance continuum.

'Scope' describes an attempt to build in bright-line boundaries around the judicial role, with a heavy reliance placed on: precedent rather than general principle; ultra vires; the classification of administrative functions as either in or outside of the jurisdiction of the court; and procedurally restricting remedies. Collectively, therefore, 'scope' describes a highly restrained approach towards judicial review. A focus on 'grounds' by contrast describes an approach that channels judicial decision-making through a series of principled doctrinal tests, largely derived from the common law, which delineate the circumstances in which the courts can intervene regardless of the administrative power or function under scrutiny.[38] This approach goes beyond the simple interpretation of statute or prerogative power and allows for a wider range of opportunities for legal accountability to be enforced. Finally, 'intensity' and 'context' are much more fact-specific approaches towards judicial review, and charge the judiciary with providing reasons to rationalise the scale of judicial intervention depending on the institutional and factual context. Cumulatively, these judicial approaches interrogate more the substance of administrative decision-making and thereby anticipates the most vigilant approach towards judicial review.

The relevance of this typology to this study is that a focus on the legitimate 'scope' of judicial-decision making matches the concept of 'substantive formalism', which was the oft-claimed dominant doctrinal approach adopted by the House of Lords in the immediate post-war period.[39] According to the standard narrative, however, by the time that Lord Reid became the senior Law Lord in 1962, alternative approaches to 'substantive formalism'/ 'scope' were being considered and the collective propensity for the House of Lords to innovate had seeped into the judicial mindset.[40] To evidence whether this innovative spirit did indeed lead to a shift in the doctrinal approaches deployed, we conducted a content analysis of the Reid era to test the nature and degree of any changes to decision-making patterns.

Content analysis involves systematically coding a discrete sample of cases according to pre-determined criteria.[41] To gain a more detailed understanding of judicial decision-making during the Lord Reid era, we coded all public law cases heard in the House of Lords across three periods: 13 cases decided during each of the periods 1953–62 (ie before Lord Reid became the senior Law Lord),

[37] ibid ch 1.
[38] ibid 75, and more generally chs 2 and 3.
[39] eg see Paterson (n 18) 132 and Stevens, *Law and Politics* (1978) 320.
[40] ibid.
[41] Kirkham and O'Loughlin, 'Content Analysis' (2019).

1963–69 (the 'Quartet' period), and 1970–74 (post-Quartet until Reid's retirement). Amongst other measures, we recorded for each individual judgment the legal argument(s), broadly conceived, upon which each Law Lord based their decision. The key finding is that over the period there is very little evidence of any profound shift in the legal arguments being considered, at least as practised in the House of Lords. Table 18.1 shows that in all periods most cases were resolved on matters of statutory ultra vires and jurisdiction (ie scope). By contrast, there was a much smaller selection of judgments that considered grounds of law based on the common law (ie grounds), or the substance of the decision itself (ie intensity/context). Further, if only judgments found *against* a public body are considered, throughout the entire period no cases were formally resolved on the substance of the public body's decision[42] and in only two cases was the ratio based on purely common law grounds.[43]

Table 18.1 Legal grounds considered within House of Lords judgments in public law cases (1953–74)

	Scope		Common law grounds	Substance
	Ultra vires	Jurisdiction		
1953–62	25	38	5	5
1963–69	20	49	15	15
1970–74	15	50	10	5

Assuming that the dominant narrative on the Reid shift is correct, therefore, the evidence is weak that change was achieved by systematically introducing different legal grounds in order to alter overtly the underpinning doctrinal approach towards judicial review. Instead, our study suggests that the techniques deployed by the judiciary in the Reid era to achieve change were more subtle.

IV. A SKETCH OF INSTITUTIONAL RELATIONSHIPS

A. Explaining Judicial Behaviour through Strategies not Law

The snapshot of cultural changes at the time of the Reid era outlined earlier provides much evidence that the judiciary *desired* to change the law and its attitudes vis-à-vis the political branches. Such a narrative cannot explain, however, why the House of Lords changed the law to intensify the review of

[42] It might be argued that *R v Minister of Agriculture and Fisheries ex p Padfield* [1968] AC 997 hinged on the court's finding that the 'substantive' decision of the Minister did not match the purposes of the relevant legislation, but here the case is recorded as ultra vires.

[43] *Ridge v Baldwin* [1964] AC 40 (right to be heard); *Malloch v Aberdeen Corporation* [1971] 1 WLR 1578 (right to be heard).

administrative decisions *using the specific doctrinal forms it did*. To address this question, we take here a speculative – but otherwise well-trodden in the relevant literature – explanatory tack. It involves placing the Reid shift within an explanatory framework that seeks to account for judicial choices in terms of strategic institutional relationships between the judiciary and the political branches. More specifically, we formulate the hypothesis that the pattern of case law that we study could perhaps be explained by, among other things, reference to institutional dynamics involving the House of Lords and the government/parliament nexus. These dynamics can be analysed in terms of *strategic interaction*. Such interaction occurs whenever the outcome of a decision that an actor takes partly depends on the action, and thus the decision, of another actor – and both actors know this. At the level of formal theorising, such interactions are part of game theory.[44] The approach has been used to explain the behaviour of judges of the US Supreme Court[45] and is known as the 'strategic model' of judicial behaviour. It can provide interesting insights, since in most developed legal systems the ultimate success of the endeavours of a given actor typically depends on the reaction of some other actor.

Recall at this point that we begin on the assumption that the 'law' (on our definition), insofar as it is underdetermined, does not provide the definitive requisite explanation of the Reid shift. Nor, as demonstrated in the previous section, does the decision-making behaviour of the judges in the period evidence an overt shift in the underpinning legal approach deployed. Accordingly, in order to explain the forms that the Reid shift took, it is crucial to show how the desire of House of Lords judges for change translated itself into specific choices that were constrained by their (perceived) opportunity set. Whilst we do not claim to provide a complete account within the confines of the present chapter, we set out a number of hypotheses for further exploration. Our objective is at the very least to provide an explanatory blueprint from the point of view of a strategic approach.

B. Practical Restrictions on Judicial Power

Our approach assumes that judicial desires for change in the law remained constant during the period, queries the forms of judicial intervention chosen, and proposes explanations of these forms by reference to a specific subset of their Lordships' strategic institutional opportunities. In so doing, we aim to articulate conjectures about whether the legal means used by the House of Lords, and supposing that their Lordships were rational in an ordinary sense,

[44] See, generally, A Dixit, S Skeath and D Reiley Jr, *Games of Strategy*, 4th edn (New York, WW Norton & Co, 2014).

[45] See L Epstein and J Knight, *The Choices Justices Make* (Washington, CQ Press, 1997).

were constrained by such institutional opportunities. Our core assumption is that where judges interpret and apply the law 'to further the accomplishment of [a] broad policy objective',[46] they do so in anticipation of the likely reaction of the actors they are intended to influence. Of course, judges are not always certain that their choices will be resisted and, even if they are, they are not certain about the final outcome of such resistance. Be that as it may, it seems to us that a brief typology of possible abstract judicial moves can be established, which we sketch further below.

Two further points within this approach should be noted. First, insofar as our topic of analysis is a senior court, we assume that judges are able to 'define the limits of [their] own jurisdiction'.[47] Second, however, we also recognise that the senior judiciary operate within a series of powerful technical and institutional constraints to their action. Perhaps the most powerful constraint is that judges can only advance the law through the cases that are brought before them. At the top of the judicial hierarchy this is likely to create thin pickings. This was certainly the situation during the Reid era when there was on average only one or two public law cases per annum, which allowed Lord Reid to sit on almost all of them.[48] This compares to a rate of five per annum by the mid-1980s, whereas during the first five years of the Supreme Court the Human Rights Act 1998 alone accounted for one-third of the caseload.[49]

Another constraint is that the vast bulk of judicial work is carried out in the lower courts. This is significant because when it comes to implementing the full range of judicial innovation developed by senior courts, the lower courts are likely to possess sufficient autonomy to work around precedents. As already noted in this chapter, senior judges are limited in what they can do by the culture of both the judicial and legal community that they work within.[50]

A further constraint on judges is that they are tasked with maintaining the confidence of both the public and the political branches, and this encourages them to self-regulate their decision-making.[51] Whilst active denial of judicial decision-making would be an extreme response, there is a range of other possibilities that are open to the political branches to 'strike back' and 'clamp down' on judicial decision-making.[52] Such responses might come by way of 'correcting'

[46] W Murphy, *Elements of Judicial Strategy* (Chicago, University of Chicago Press 1964) 11.

[47] *In re Spectrum Plus Ltd (in liquidation)* [2005] 2 UKHL 41, [2005] AC 680 [69] (Lord Hope).

[48] According to our selection, Lord Reid sat on 88% of public law cases post-1962.

[49] B Dickson, *Human Rights and the United Kingdom Supreme Court* (Oxford, OUP, 2013) 14, fn 72.

[50] For a discussion of these practical limitations, see JD Heydon, 'Limits to the powers of ultimate appellate courts' (2006) 122 *LQR* 399.

[51] J Ferejohn and L Kramer, 'Judicial Independence in a Democracy: Institutionalizing Judicial Restraint' in J Drobak (ed), *Norms and the Law* (New York, CUP, 2006) 163.

[52] For a discussion, see C Harlow and R Rawlings, '"Striking Back" and "Clamping Down": An Alternative Perspective on Judicial Review' in J Bell, M Elliott, J Varuhas and P Murray (eds), *Public Law Adjudication in Common Law Systems Process and Substance* (Oxford, Hart, 2016).

legislation to address particular decisions, constructing deliberate restrictions on jurisdiction and grounds available, altering the judicial appointments process,[53] or through the imposition of resource restrictions on judicial activity.[54] Typically in Westminster-type systems, because governments and parliaments are ordinarily highly aligned, the possibility of such forms of retaliation acts as a real constraint on the judiciary.[55] This close bond also creates little residual room for the court to play the separate interests of rival veto players against each other.[56]

V. A BRIEF TYPOLOGY OF JUDICIAL MOVES

In the normal case, the practical constraints on the judiciary work to create an in-built dynamic of self-restraint in decision-making, one designed to prevent political backlash. Although these factors may incentivise judicial 'under-activity', they also suggest that a judiciary desiring to adjust the parameters of the law is more likely to pursue certain strategies than others. Adopting this form of logic, we frame our explanatory hypothesis in the following way: *if* a given legal actor (in our case, the House of Lords under Lord Reid) wishes to successfully upset a tradition of acquiescence to the decisions of the political branches *and* that actor is rational in the ordinary sense, *then* the actor, given the possibility of reprisals by the political branches, will probably come to the conclusion that it ought to pick and choose very carefully the cases that upset the general pattern of acquiescence. We propose here a number of options as moves that the judiciary may be tempted to play, and then test for evidence of the deployment of these options both within the Reid shift and the periods immediately either side of it.

A. Ordinary Prudence

i. Short-Term Non-Acquiescence

From an abstract point of view, each individual case might be considered to represent an opportunity. Accordingly, an obvious move that a judge can play to

[53] eg R Ekins, *Protecting the Constitution: Why and how Parliament should limit judicial power* (London, Policy Exchange, 2019).

[54] M Stephenson, '"When the devil turns ..." the Political Foundations of Independent Judicial Review' (2002) 36 *Legal Studies* 59.

[55] For this point see MD McCubbins and DB Rodriguez, 'The Judiciary and the Role of Law' in DA Wittman and BR Weingast (eds), *The Oxford Handbook of Political Economy* (Oxford, OUP, 2008); P Cane, *Controlling Administrative Power: An Historical Comparison* (Cambridge, CUP, 2016).

[56] E Ip, 'The judicial review of legislation in the United Kingdom: a public choice analysis' (2014) 37 *European Journal of Law Economics* 221, 232–33.

shift the boundaries between the courts and the executive is to find more often against public authority in all cases brought before them, and thereby create more space to adjust legal doctrine. It would be surprising, however, if there were any long-term strategic advantage in judges finding against public authorities more frequently than had previously been accepted. Indeed, there is a strong incentive to avoid this outcome, as such an approach would likely attract negative attention from aligned political branches and thus encourage some form of backlash. As a result, one would expect, particularly in Westminster-type systems, that the general pattern will favour judicial deference, with less acquiescent decision-making being a carefully selected and defended residual judicial phenomenon.

However, although a sustained strategy of anti-majoritarian judging may be unwise in the long term, a short-term burst may successfully cash in on previously secured reputational authority and goodwill. The Reid era is interesting in this respect. We broke the era down into three evenly spread periods of 13 public law cases. Between 1953 and 1962 (all cases heard before *Ridge v Baldwin*) 45 per cent of House of Lords judgments found against public bodies, a rate which rose to 67 per cent between 1963 and 1969 (a period which included the Quartet and *Burmah Oil*), before falling to 29 per cent[57] between 1970 and 1974 (see Table 18.2). The relatively accidental manner through which cases travel to the senior court and the low numbers in the sample mean that multiple alternative explanations for this pattern exist. This pattern tantalisingly hints, however, that briefly during the 1960s the judiciary might have chosen to take a more robust approach against public bodies before strategically withdrawing.

ii. Pick your Opponents

Backlash against judicial decisions is more likely to occur where the public body concerned has the power to veto the decision or remove resources from the courts. With this in mind, a move that an 'innovatory' court might take is to develop the law in those cases in which the constitutional status of the impacted body is relatively weak. Thus shifts in the law might occur in cases against public bodies and local authorities rather than central government. The evidence in Table 18.2 suggests that, coincidentally or not, this was the pattern during the entire Reid era, with non-ministerial bodies more likely to be ruled against than central government departments.

[57] This figure excludes the cases of *Ealing LBC v Race Relations Board* (HL) [1972] AC 342 and *Lord Advocate v Glasgow Corporation (No 1)* 1973 SC (HL) 1 as in both cases both parties were public bodies.

Table 18.2 Outcomes of House of Lords judgments in public law cases (1953–74)

	Rate of judgments found against public body		
	All judgments	**Secretary of State**	**Non-central government public bodies**
1953–62	45%	33%	49%
1963–69	67%	54%	67%
1970–74	29%	8%	41%
Total	49%	31%	51%

An example of this move for the period under consideration would be *Ridge v Baldwin*, in which Lord Reid took care to distinguish the Secretary of State's role, and to make it clear that the body against which the House of Lords found was 'merely' the watch committee.[58]

iii. Pick your Moments and Compensatory Judgments

In some instances, opportunities to shift behaviour may only be exercisable against central government and there is a reputational loss to be incurred if the court is too deferential to the state. Alternatively, judges might deem it necessary to rule against the executive because the issue goes to the very heart of the constitutional claim that underpins the value of the rule of law and the court.[59] In other words, not acting would materially weaken the position of the courts in the long term, even if the short-term popular and political backlash may be damaging. Viewed from the perspective of the Law Lord in the 1960s who is culturally minded to reclaim the legal ground conceded by the earlier generations of judges, the underlying issues at stake in *Ridge* (the reach of natural justice), *Anisminic* (jurisdiction), *Conway* (the justiciability of crown privilege) and *Padfield* (that public authorities must not only act within their powers, but for the purpose for which the powers have been conferred) can all be claimed to be of high rule of law import worthy of taking a stance.

To compensate for the frustration caused to the political branch by such moments of judicial radicalism, judges may manifest acquiescence in other kinds of cases. For instance, the relatively timid approach of the majority of Law Lords towards interpreting the Race Relations Act in four cases in the later period of the Reid era may reflect a recognition that Parliament itself had returned to the issue on more than one occasion in recent times.[60] It may also

[58] *Ridge* (n 43).

[59] DS Law, 'A Theory of Judicial Power and Judicial Review' (2009) 97 *Georgetown Law Journal* 723.

[60] In three of the four cases the House of Lords did not uphold the preferred statutory interpretation of the Race Relations Board. The frustration with the Lords' minimalist reading of the Race Relations Act 1968 can be seen in the judgments of Lord Kilbrandon in *Ealing LBC v Race Relations*

represent, however, an unwillingness to push the boundaries of the law so soon after the Quartet, particularly on such a sensitive issue. Similarly, the ruling in *British Oxygen v Minister of Technology*[61] in 1970 could be viewed as a timely pragmatic readjustment of the fettering discretion principle in favour of public administration.[62]

B. Finessing the Moves

The above moves are all opportunistic in nature, insofar as they rely heavily upon the case and the parties being brought to court. In order to secure shifts in the law for the long term, however, judges also need to consider carefully the manner in which decisions are framed so that they can be usefully applied in the future and do not attract an immediate political rebuttal. We suggest here some framing tactics that were adopted to embed the Reid shift.

i. Framing Decisions as Non-Threatening

Ordinarily, following an unfavourable decision, the political branches will have a number of options available to them to retrieve full control of its intended discretionary power, but not every option will nullify the full weight of the judicial authority. Knowing this, judicial politics scholars have long noted that judges often find ways to compensate losses on powerful actors in order to prevent outright rejection of judgments. Such a move lowers the costs of acquiescence for the political branches, but still allows the judicial actor to articulate a holding with far-reaching consequences. For best results, judgments need to be carefully framed so that affected groups can see the compensations made available to them.[63]

This move is one way to explain the holding in *Padfield*, where in quashing the Minister's decision the House of Lords both secured its reputation and confirmed an important principle of law, in the full knowledge that the government Minister ultimately retained the power not to provide redress for the complaint at the heart of the case.[64] Likewise, the principles of law outlined in

Board (HL) [1972] AC 342 and *Dockers Labour Club and Institute v Race Relations Board* (HL) [1976] AC 285. See also *Charter v Race Relations Board* (HL) [1973] AC 868 and *Applin v Race Relations Board* [1975] AC 259.

[61] *British Oxygen v Minister of Technology* [1971] AC 610.

[62] Arguably, *McEldowney v Forde* [1971] AC 632, in which a regulation on Northern Ireland security was upheld, could be placed in the same bracket, but this was a narrow 3:2 decision and could easily have been decided differently had the Panel been different: Blom-Cooper and Drewy (n 3) 267.

[63] E Gonzalez-Ocantos and E Dinas, 'Compensation and Compliance: Sources of Public Acceptance of the UK Supreme Court's Brexit Decision' (2019) 53 *Law & Society* 889, 892.

[64] See ch 4 in this volume (Sunkin).

Burmah Oil v Lord Advocate have subsequently proved influential, even though the decision itself was overridden by the War Damages Act 1965.[65]

ii. Signal a Ruling of Mutual Advantage

It is to the judiciary's advantage if the political branches, in all or in part, can be persuaded that it is in their interests for the court to pursue a certain course of action or role. Examples may include exercising its discretion with the grain of dominant government policy or operating in areas where the legislature only has rare opportunities to legislate. Such a stance is aided where the likelihood of conflict is low.[66] Although ultimately an unsuccessful move for the dispute being litigated,[67] an example may be *Burmah Oil* in which the case centred on whether compensation was payable. Lords Reid and Pearce not only declared on the point of law but provided guidance to the effect that the pursuers' claim was weak, and thereby signalled to the political branches that the costs of the judgment would be minor.

Similarly, there may be cases where judicial actors might exploit the non-alignment of Government and Parliament on a specific issue in order to further their power in ways that avoid subsequent potential retaliation by the political branches. Such potential non-alignment crucially depends on the specific moment chosen to challenge the political branches (or some of them). This, for example, could be one way to interpret *Anisminic*, in the sense that Government and Parliament were much less aligned than normally on the issue of 'ouster clauses',[68] and thus the possibility of statutory override was somewhat less likely. Likewise, Sunkin has made the argument that in *Padfield* the judges were supporting Parliament in its relationship with the executive in order to secure effective political accountability, thus gaining support for its work by signalling to Parliament that the decision was of mutual advantage.[69]

iii. Incrementalism

A key concern for a senior judge wishing to adjust the law is the need to be confident that the lower courts will follow his or her lead. Further, if there are

[65] *Burmah Oil v Lord Advocate* [1965] AC 75. For an account see C Harlow and R Rawlings, *Law and Administration*, 2nd edn (London, Butterworths, 1997) 48–44.

[66] M McCubbins and D Rodriguez, 'The judiciary and the role of law' in B Weingast and D Wittman (eds), *The Oxford Handbook of Political Economy* (New York, OUP, 2006).

[67] Harlow and Rawlings, *Law and Administration* (1997).

[68] In fact, as Arvind and Stirton underline, the Government subsequently failed to pass an amendment in a new Foreign Compensation Bill that would clearly reverse *Anisminic* due mainly to the resistance of the House of Lords and the Bar. See TT Arvind and L Stirton, 'Why the Judicial Power Project Is Wrong about *Anisminic*' *UK Constitutional Law Blog* (20 May 2016), available at www.ukconstitutionallaw.org/2016/05/20/tt-arvind-and-lindsay-stirton-why-the-judicial-power-project-is-wrong-about-anisminic.

[69] See ch 4 section I in this volume (Sunkin).

too many radical adjustments in the law that are not followed up and adopted by the lower courts, then the reputation of the court might be undermined.[70] The senior courts, therefore, are incentivised to work with the prevalent legal culture as far as possible, and avoid controversial shifts in legal thinking too far removed from mainstream thinking. Thus, achieving change whilst simultaneously retaining loyalty to the norms of deeply ingrained legal techniques, is a more attractive option than overturning previous decisions or overt judicial creativity. This in-built push towards incrementalism was very much evident in the Reid era, as illustrated in Table 18.3, which details the approach of the House of Lords towards two key legal techniques, precedent and statutory interpretation.

Table 18.3 Legal techniques deployed in judicial decision-making during the Lord Reid era: House of Lords judgments in all public law cases (1953–74)

	Loyalty to precedent				Mode of statutory intepretation		
	Confirm case law	Distinguish	Reject or reverse		Literal	Textual	Purposive
1953–62	33	15	5[71]		25	21	6
1963–69	46	14	5[72]		17	26	14
1970–74	52	2	0		29	40	3

On the face of it, the results evidence that judges showed no enhanced tendency to veer away from precedent in the later years of the Reid era than in the earlier period. This preliminary analysis, however, conceals the strategic subtlety of judicial decision-making in the common law method, particularly as practised by the House of Lords between 1962 and 1969.[73] In his study of the Law Lords, Paterson claimed that the Reid shift was orchestrated through techniques of 'dissimulation' and, in order to address outdated legal rules, over the same period this pattern occurred simultaneously in private, as well as public, law cases.[74] Potentially radical adaptations of the law were thereby deliberately camouflaged under the façade of a common law evolution of the law as it had always been, rather than the outright confrontation of policy choices. In particular, to achieve reinterpretations of the law, during the 1960s the House of Lords, and most noticeably Lord Reid himself, regularly drew upon older case law to offset the need to feel bound by more recent legal understandings.[75] By

[70] McCubbins and Rodriguez, 'The judiciary' (2016).

[71] *Marshall v Scottish Milk Marketing Board* 1956 SC (HL) 37.

[72] *Conway v Rimmer* [1968] AC 910.

[73] For a discussion of the options open to a judge seeking to evade precedent, see G Dworkin, 'Stare Decisis in the House of Lords' (1962) 25 *MLR* 163.

[74] Paterson (n 18) 140–46 accredits Lord Radcliffe as being the intellectual driver behind this approach: Lord Radcliffe, *The Law and Its Compass* (London, Faber and Faber, 1961) 39.

[75] See for instance, *Attorney General v Nissan* [1970] AC 179; *Anisminic Ltd v Foreign Compensation Commission* [1969] 2 AC 147; *Burmah Oil* (n 65); *Ridge v Baldwin* [1964] AC 40.

contrast, this 'dissimulation' technique is less evident in the earlier period[76] and from 1970 to 1974 largely disappears. The decline of dissimulation techniques Paterson attributed to the adoption of a bolder judicial attitude towards dealing with outdated rules through the 1966 Practice Statement which allowed the overruling of precedent.[77]

Table 18.3 also charts the use of different forms of statutory interpretation, broadly recorded as either literal (clause-specific), textual (attempts to ascertain 'Parliamentary intention' from a broader reading of the text) or purposive (explorations of the purpose of the power concerned).[78] As with the use of precedent, although there is a small shift over time away from overtly literal techniques of statutory interpretation towards more open-ended examinations of the purpose behind legislation, the trail is not as strong as is sometimes claimed.[79] Pre-1962 the judiciary did extrapolate meaning of statute through a broader textual reading on occasion,[80] ordinarily for the underlying need to resolve ambiguity.[81] Otherwise though, the broader interpretative approaches were generally contained in dissenting judgments, with the restrictive majority judgment in *Smith v East Elloe Rural DC*[82] noted as the 'high water mark of judicial timidity'.[83] Likewise, in the 1970s when confronted by the ambiguity of the Race Relations Act 1968, the Law Lords, especially Lord Reid, were highly conservative in their interpretation, with once again it being left to the dissenting judges to explore the potential of broader interpretative approaches.[84] But dig deeper, and the impact of non-literal approaches towards statutory interpretation was particularly powerful in the 1963–69 period. *Anisminic* is the strongest example of this, but there were others,[85] and *Padfield* relied upon placing a significant emphasis on an inferred statutory objective. Here, there is evidence to support interview-based findings in Paterson's Law Lords study of the period that the 1960s judges were willing to 'adapt the law according to social conditions'.[86]

[76] Arguably *Pyx Granite Co Ltd v Ministry of Housing and Local Government* (HL) [1960] AC 260 fits this category.

[77] The small number of House of Lords public law cases where the Practice Statement was considered (*Conway* (applied), *Anisminic* (not applied)) sits alongside a larger body of private law cases where its Practice Statement was much more noticeable, see Paterson (n 18) 146–63.

[78] This threefold typology captures familiar themes in statutory interpretation; see M Favale, M Kretschmer and PC Torremans, 'Is there an EU Copyright Jurisprudence? An Empirical Analysis of the Workings of the European Court of Justice' (2016) 79 *MLR* 31.

[79] A point made by J Beatson. 'The role of statute in the development of common law doctrine' (2001) 117 *LQR* 247, 260.

[80] See *Belfast Corp v OD Cars* (HL) [1960] AC 490, 522–25 (per Lord Radcliffe) and *Marshall* (n 71).

[81] Drewy and Blom-Copper (n 3) suggest that *Preston and Area Rent Tribunal v Pickavance* (HL) [1953] AC 562 is an example where the court subtly used a broader textual approach to avoid the harsh outcome of an excessive faith on literalism.

[82] [1956] AC 736.

[83] Drewry and Blom-Cooper (n 3) 260.

[84] See cases discussed at n 60.

[85] eg *Pfizer Corp v Ministry of Health* (HL) [1965] AC 512.

[86] Paterson (n 18) 143.

Such patterns indicate that the Reid shift did not come about as a uniform change in approach towards judging, but occurred instead through targeted uses of contextual approaches to statutory interpretation, resort to older case law to establish precedential authority, and occasional creativity towards discrete features of the prevalent legal doctrine. In other words, the judiciary in the Reid era were more willing to take selective advantage of the incremental devices which are always open to the court given the loosely defined parameters of the common law method. As Barak-Erez argues in relation to the equivalent development of legal doctrine in Israel, 'the potential for realizing these developments was embedded in the English system' long before Lord Reid became a judge.[87] Further, as separate studies by Paterson and Blom-Cooper and Drewy have demonstrated, this enhanced willingness to adapt the common law was being practised just as much in private law cases as it was in the field of public law.

iv. Create more Opportunities for Judicial Intervention

To maximise the judiciary's impact on public sector decision-making, senior judges are incentivised to facilitate and encourage lower court intervention, as that is where the bulk of judicial activity occurs. Two routes for doing this are most obviously available. First, the senior courts can alter the technical rules of entry into the judicial system, either to facilitate more cases or to provide a broader suite of cases to choose from. Second, the senior courts can 'clear the decks' and/or serve 'to break down' pre-existing barriers to the development of the law.

During the Reid era the latter is the move which is most evident, including, despite its reputation for substantive formalism, the House of Lords in the 1950s. During this earlier Reid period, the power of the court to make declaratory judgments was confirmed,[88] claims to immunity from legal actions treated with scepticism,[89] the rule on unlawful sub-delegation developed in the lower courts was confirmed,[90] and prerogative powers were reviewed.[91] Interestingly, no obvious similar examples exist in the later period of the Reid era, but it is in the Quartet of cases that this move is most evident, all of which to a greater or lesser extent loosened pre-existing orthodoxies that had inhibited the development of the law.

In a similar vein, judgments can free up space for the future by publicly rejecting government lines of argument that restrict judicial review of public

[87] Ch 13 in this volume (Barak-Erez).

[88] *Pyx Granite Co Ltd v Ministry of Housing and Local Government* (HL) [1960] AC 260.

[89] *Marshall v Scottish Milk Marketing Board* 1956 SC (HL) 37; *Glasgow Corp v Central Land Board* 1956 SC (HL) 1.

[90] *Vine v National Dock Labour Board* (HL) [1957] AC 488.

[91] *Smith v East Elloe Rural DC* (HL) [1956] AC 736.

authority decision-making. As Bailey has noted, this may have been one of the strongest legacies of the Quartet.[92]

v. Creating Room for Manoeuvre

Shifts in the relationship do not need to be won or realised immediately. In other words, decisions may be taken that have in the short-term only a minimal impact on public authority, or might even be favourable towards them, but the effect of the decision may be to create the space for lines of reasoning to be pursued that were previously blocked. In the context of the relationship between the judiciary and the political branch, the true import of the shift might not be appreciated or even spotted until multiple cases later.

It is important to note that such development of the law may happen not necessarily as a result of what the chosen doctrines 'really mean', but simply by virtue of the *perception* of what they mean on the part of lower courts. Indeed, senior judges may formulate their opinions in ways that make a number of different interpretations possible, thus arming those lower judges that are willing to choose one rather than the other and treat it as binding precedent. To take again a characteristic example, there has been a decades-long scholarly discussion on whether *Anisminic* should be understood in the sense of recognising a ground for review for any mistake in law. From our point of view, the point is not so much whether that is 'really' the case but, rather, that even the *perception* by lower courts that *Anisminic*, in its ambiguity, had these implications created more opportunities for judicial intervention. Likewise, the reasoning in *Padfield* opened up opportunities for the future around the purposes pursued in administrative decision-making and the need for reasons provided to be sound.

An even more subtle move might be for the court to lay the foundations of new principles of law in obiter statements 'like a squirrel storing nuts to be pulled out at some later time'.[93] This is a harder move to evidence, but by way of example, in *Smith v East Elloe Rural DC*[94] Lord Reid laid down legal logic that looks highly reminiscent of what 40 years later became the legality test:

> So, general words by themselves do not bind the Crown, they are limited so as not to conflict with international law, they are commonly read so as to avoid retrospective infringement of rights, and it appears to me that they can equally well be read so as not to deprive the court of jurisdiction where bad faith is involved.[95]

[92] Ch 16 in this volume (Bailey).

[93] Murphy, *Elements* (1964) 203, citing an undated memorandum by Herbert Wechsler, Law Clerk file, Harlan Fiske Stone Papers, Library of Congress.

[94] *Smith v East Elloe Rural DC* (n 91).

[95] ibid 765.

vi. Building on Pre-Prepared Foundations

Even where shifts are pursued, there may be an advantage to piggy-backing on existing 'advanced parties of knowledge'. The hard work of shifting understandings of the law does not, therefore, rest on the judiciary but on a wider community and pre-existing legal thought. This is, for example, what Lord Reid appears to have done in *Burmah Oil*, citing a range of classical international lawyers (Grotius and Vattel) as well as US case law and John Locke.[96] Likewise, the decision in *Conway v Rimmer*[97] was able to use the separate legal position under Scottish law as a comparator.[98] The overall goal is to attempt to show that the chosen solution is not arbitrary, nor an act of will on the part of the judge, but simply a development from an already existing doctrinal foundation.

Across the Reid era this does not appear a commonly used move, but in a later period when more academic writing exists and international law is more readily available, we hypothesise that this becomes a more regularly used technique to support shifts in the law.

VI. CONCLUSION

Writing in 1993 following a lengthy analysis of judicial decision-making from the 1920s onwards, John Griffith concluded 'that the judicial system has lost much respect and much authority'.[99] Griffith's thesis is a familiar one, founded on the narrative that too much judicial decision-making is based on opaque discretionary activity that facilitates a form of judicial interventionism which thinly disguises political activity. Griffith went on to make a plea for 'the attitudes of the senior judiciary to the powers of public authorities [to] become more principled and more consistent'.[100] Contrary to this vision, the thesis explored in this chapter has been that the inherent indeterminacy in law's design entails that the judiciary will always possess a certain degree of discretion allowing it to shift the parameters of the law according to the context. Further, we hypothesise that because of this indeterminacy, an endemic feature of the judicial mission is periodic shifts between judicial approaches that advance vigilance and those that encourage restraint, as well as shifts that attempt to provide a sounder basis for the judicial function.[101] Such shifts are hard to predict and manage as they

[96] *Burmah Oil* (n 65) 107–12. Ironically, in the same case both Viscount Radcliffe and Lord Hodson adopted a similar approach in their dissenting judgments.

[97] [1968] AC 910.

[98] *Glasgow Corporation v. Central Land Board*, 1956 SC (HL) 1.

[99] JAG Griffith, *The Politics of the Judiciary*, 5th edn (London, HarperCollins, 1997) 20.

[100] ibid.

[101] Which is what Paterson concluded in his study of judicial decision-making in the senior court, A Paterson, *Final Judgment: The Last Law Lords and the Supreme Court* (Oxford, Hart, 2013) 266–74, 320.

will depend upon opportunity and the inputs of numerous judges with different perspectives on the appropriate and stable balance of power between the judiciary and the political branches.

In understanding this dynamic aspect of the law, our focus has been on evidencing and rationalising the manner in which such shifts occur, using the Reid shift as a powerful lesson in how the judiciary can deploy a range of moves to alter patterns of decision-making. We have used the lens of institutional strategy to provide a framework through which to analyse the opportunities and the most efficient moves that the judiciary might focus on to advance that agenda. The overall picture that arises seems a much more mixed and mitigated one than Griffith's narrative would allow. Despite some spectacular cases, especially the famous Quartet on which the present volume focuses, the House of Lords under Lord Reid seems to have displayed a keen sense of the limits that any project of reform of administrative law must respect. As a consequence, the Reid shift was less a fundamental restructuring of the principles of public law and more a subtle loosening of legal norms sufficient to allow future evolution, with judgments selectively deployed to avoid outright rejection by the political branches. All of this work was conducted firmly within the standard, albeit malleable, boundaries of the common law method.

We have recognised that, to a large extent, this sense of limits within the Reid shift is attributable to structural factors, in particular the full knowledge that the political branch is capable of resetting its institutional relationship with the judiciary. Thus, our more specific aim was to propose hypotheses for 'judicial moves' on the basis of the recognition of a dimension of strategic interaction between the House of Lords and the political branches. For instance, we have shown that the Reid court deployed a number of moves aimed at assuring the political branches that the reform sought would not take the form of a radical questioning of those branches' power. Accordingly, our framework sets forth the hypothesis that the judiciary will use strategic moves selectively both to secure an appropriate intellectual coherence to the law, and to retain the long-term legitimacy of their constitutional position. We further suggest that ours is a useful model by which to explain the strategic choices made by judges in other periods of judicial history.

Part VII

Conclusion

19

The Real Argument about Judicial Review

TT ARVIND, RICHARD KIRKHAM, DAITHÍ MAC SÍTHIGH AND LINDSAY STIRTON*

I. INTRODUCTION: THE SIGNIFICANCE OF THE QUARTET

THE CHAPTERS IN this volume have sought to use the Quartet as a lens to subject the modern law of judicial review to critical scrutiny. They have done so in a range of different ways. Some have examined the cases themselves, looking in depth at their background and context, how they were decided and received, and their immediate and longer-term impact. Some have looked at whether and to what extent they form an adequate basis for discussing the challenges that administrative law faces today, and sought to diagnose the causes of their inadequacy. Others have looked at subsequent developments, or at parallel developments elsewhere, and used them as a basis to analyse or evaluate the system of judicial review to which the Quartet gave rise.

These individual contributions are valuable and insightful, and the purpose of this chapter is to use them as a basis to address a broader theme, and point to a final contribution which the study of the Quartet as a formative moment can make to administrative law scholarship. Writing in the middle of 1968, when three of the four cases in the Quartet had been decided, JDB Mitchell set out in a few short pages what he thought was 'the real argument about administrative law'.[1] This, he said, related to the task of 'dealing with the problems of the complex administrative state of the twentieth century',[2] in a manner responsive to 'the real needs of government' as well as 'the value of the individual'.[3] The need was for a mechanism which would not only cope with the problems

* We are grateful to David Feldman for his comments on an earlier draft of this chapter.

[1] JDB Mitchell, 'The Real Argument about Administrative Law' (1968) 46 *Public Administration* 167.

[2] ibid 169.

[3] ibid 167–68.

that had begun to arise in the 1960s, but also be capable of evolving to cope with problems foreseeable in the relationship of individuals and the state in the future, and which could intelligently police 'administrative morality' and realise 'the capacity of the state to do good'.[4]

Mitchell saw little promise in the common law, and was deeply critical about the decisions in cases such as *Conway v Rimmer*[5] and *Burmah Oil*,[6] both of which he thought left important issues unaddressed. The tasks that Mitchell saw as fundamental to administrative law, however, mirror the concerns of this volume. The chapters in this volume, too, have focused on the challenges posed by the task of creating a set of doctrines, procedures and approaches that can accommodate, balance and have due regard to the needs of government, the value and importance of private persons, and the complexity of the processes and functions that characterise the modern administrative state. As the chapters in this volume show, the record of the system to which the Quartet gave rise is mixed. Although the subsequent development of judicial review has helped make things immeasurably better in many areas where it operates, in other areas fundamental problems remain. This chapter argues that, much as in Mitchell's day, these problems relate not just to whether the law adequately recognises the value of the private person, but also whether it facilitates the ability of the state to do good.

This final chapter seeks to shed deeper light on the causes of the continuing weaknesses of judicial review, and point the way towards a research programme for addressing them. Our starting point is a set of three themes and insights that emerge from the chapters in this volume, and which were discussed in more detail in the introduction. The first is the mix of continuity and change that characterised the Quartet. The second is the largely symbolic nature of the impact which the Quartet had – an impact that came at the expense of the Quartet's doctrinal contribution. The third is the legacy of questions which the Quartet seemingly left unresolved.

In section II of this chapter, we turn to the first of these themes. As we show, the system of administrative law which took shape in the 1960s built on existing thinking not just about legal doctrine, but about the judicial role within the constitution, and sought not so much to reshape as to adapt it to the challenges of modern administrative government. The introduction argued that the radicalism of the Quartet is best understood as the radicalism of tradition. The idea of tradition is a useful starting point in helping us advance beyond platitudes about continuity and change in administrative law thinking. Scholars who systematically analyse tradition have pointed out that all traditions contain an element of continuity, that is, the transmissions of beliefs that frame behaviour. More sophisticated traditions (and the common law tradition is nothing if not sophisticated) include one, or in some cases both, of the following: a *canon*

[4] ibid 169.
[5] *Conway v Rimmer* [1968] AC 910 (HL).
[6] *Burmah Oil v Lord Advocate* [1965] AC 75 (HL).

of texts, acknowledged as both belonging to and constitutive of the tradition, although understandings of which texts are included and which are not may be subject to continuous updating or reinterpretation; and a *core* of central truths or teachings that are seen as being the constitutive essence of the tradition.[7] The situation to which administrative law sought to respond during the 1960s, we argue, was one in which the canon of the common law provided no easy answer to the challenges posed by the new administrative state – or, at any rate, none that gave appropriate recognition to the 'value of the individual' or supported the policing of administrative morality. Nor did Diceyan thought, which was then still influential as a way of understanding the core of the constitution, provide any obvious way forward.

Section III of this chapter takes up the second theme, namely, the disjunction between the Quartet's symbolic and doctrinal legacy. As we show, the doctrinal contribution of the Quartet was to reinterpret the core of administrative law and, in doing so, begin a process which involved jettisoning substantial aspects of the canon. This project continued into the 1970s and 1980s and has effects into the present day.[8] Jettisoning elements of a tradition's canon is necessarily a process fraught with danger, particularly in law, where the process of dismantling principles limiting judicial action can easily be taken too far. The Quartet was alive to this danger, and sought to ameliorate it by embedding a clear sense of the ends and purposes of judicial review at the heart of their interpretation of the core. It was a sense of those tasks and their constitutional importance that led the judges to implicitly accept that they were actors who were, in partnership with Parliament, charged by the Constitution with upholding the principles reflected in those tasks. The marginalisation of the Quartet's doctrinal contribution, and the emphasis on their symbolic value, have diverted attention away from those principles and constitutional values, and their role in channelling judicial action.

What, then, are the broader implications of this analysis? Section IV turns to this question, focusing in particular on the unresolved issues discussed in the introduction. As we show, our analysis brings into focus aspects of administrative law that are not just of historical interest but also of continuing importance to the present day, revealing biases, tensions and divisions which are implicit in judicial review doctrine but which are not easily perceived in the everyday functioning of the common law. We focus on three sets of tensions, which map closely on to the three unresolved issues discussed in the introduction: the tension between monism and multifarity in judicial review; the different tasks which judicial review can and should discharge, together with the question of which task or mix of tasks should take priority in different situations; and the role which judges can and should play vis-à-vis the executive and the legislature in the modern state.

[7] J Alexander, 'A Systematic Theory of Tradition' (2016) 10 *Journal of the Philosophy of History* 1.
[8] See the discussion of post-Quartet developments in ch 3 in this volume (Thomas).

II. A FADING CORE: LAW AND ADMINISTRATION BEFORE THE QUARTET

This volume began with the idea of the Quartet as a formative moment, that is, one which saw the emergence of new institutional structures, patterns or configurations which, even if these built on existing institutional structures, nevertheless altered them in ways that go beyond the merely incremental. To study the Quartet as a formative moment is to focus on it, first and foremost, as a response to a particular context and as a moment in time. Formative moments are periods in which choices are made in relation to institutional structures, roles, responsibilities and tasks. These choices reflect the pressures that motivated the formative moment, but they also reflect the implicit assumptions, priorities and predilections of the period in which they were made. Examining the Quartet as a formative moment, therefore, offers an insight into the unspoken assumptions of that period which lay, as Atiyah put it, 'beneath the surface'[9] of those developments. These assumptions concerned the role of the courts vis-à-vis executive decision-making, the need for a system of administrative law, and its tasks within the constitution. Uncovering them helps us, in Richard Stewart's terminology, 'lay bare the inner premises of administrative law'.[10]

An important part of the context of the Quartet is the state of administrative law at the start of the 1960s. Given the inherent disposition towards incrementalism of the common law, formative moments on the scale of the Quartet demand explanation. It has been noted by various scholars that administrative law, which developed vigorously in the latter half of the nineteenth century, fell into a 'period of debility' in the twentieth century, marked by a loss of confidence on the part of judges.[11] To understand the significance of the Quartet as a formative moment, we need to probe more deeply into the reasons for this debility and its subsequent recovery of vigour. A substantial part of the answer, we argue, lies in changes in the scope of administrative government and the manner in which it was carried out. We address this first, before turning to the reasons why this proved problematic to then existing tasks of the law vis-à-vis the executive.

A. From Static to Dynamic Administration

It is commonplace to note the growth of government, and the additional functions it had taken on, over the course of the nineteenth and twentieth centuries.[12]

[9] PS Atiyah, *Pragmatism and Theory in English Law* (London, Stevens and Sons. 1987) 143–84.

[10] RB Stewart, 'The Reformation of American Administrative Law' (1975) 88 *Harvard Law Review* 1667, 1670. Tellingly, Stewart adds that, 'The hazards of expounding so general a theme are all too obvious': ibid.

[11] B Schwartz and HWR Wade, *Legal Control of Government: Administrative Law in Britain and the United States* (Oxford, Clarendon Press, 1972) 13.

[12] As Sir Cecil Carr put it, 'We nod approvingly today when someone tells us that, whereas the State used to be merely policeman, judge and protector, it has now become schoolmaster, doctor,

It is, however, just as important to understand the development of administrative government in qualitative terms, seeing it not just in terms of the acceptance by governments of active responsibility for the management of affairs in many areas of social and economic life, but also in terms of the idea that the powers of management that went with that responsibility were the means by which governments sought to realise the state's capacity to do good.[13]

One way of thinking about the change is in terms of the 'stages' model of the growth of administrative government proposed by Oliver McDonagh.[14] His model was primarily focused on the nineteenth century and has not escaped critical comment,[15] but nonetheless stands up in its essentials as a framework for analysing the progress of administrative government in the twentieth century. McDonagh emphasises the endogenous (or, 'spontaneous', as he puts it) aspect of the development of administration, in that once a cadre of permanent officials has been established for the management of a particular problem, their own perceptions of the problem, and the shape of any solutions, becomes a primary influence in the subsequent development of law and policy. He highlights a distinction between 'static' and 'dynamic' conceptions of administration within administrators' own self-understanding. Earlier stages of administrative development were characterised by, 'a style of thinking in which social problems were seen as … resolvable once for all by some grand piece of legislation or by the multiplication of their own number'.[16] As the transition was made into later stages, MacDonagh describes a subtle transformation in administrative outlook, so that officials 'began to see improvement as a slow, uncertain process of closing loopholes and tightening the screw ring by ring, in the light of continuing experience and experiment'.[17]

In other words, problems which might previously have been seen as resolvable by a specific, one-off measure came to be viewed by the bureaucracy as polymorphous – as a set of changing and evolving targets requiring in turn ever-evolving administrative responses. To govern in the way that the dynamic conception demanded, administrators required broad legal and administrative

house-builder, road-maker, town-planner, public utility supplier and all the rest of it'. CT Carr, *Concerning English Administrative Law* (New York, Columbia University Press, 1941) 10; for a recent expression of this idea see *Meadows v Minister for Justice* [2010] 2 IR 701, 816 (Fennelly J): 'The modern state confers an enormous range of decision making powers on a variety of bodies. Such bodies carry out and supervise vast areas of the work of government and of economic and social life'.

[13] Mitchell, 'The Real Argument' (1968) 169.

[14] O MacDonagh, 'The Nineteenth Century Revolution in Government: A Reappraisal' (1958) 1 *Historical Journal* 52.

[15] For example, H Parris, 'The Nineteenth Century Revolution in Government: A Reappraisal Reappraised' (1960) 3 *Historical Journal* 17; LJ Hume, 'Jeremy Bentham and the Nineteenth-Century Revolution in Government' (1967) 10 *Historical Journal* 361.

[16] MacDonagh, 'Reappraisal' (1958) 60.

[17] ibid 60.

powers to make and to enforce rules, and the ability to adapt their exercise of these powers in light of changing conditions and developing understandings of their task. This was leading, in the words of JAG Griffith, to a constitutional understanding in which, 'Parliament and the executive must be regarded as two interrelated organs of the Constitution, charged with differing functions, neither having any inherent supremacy over the other'.[18]

The pattern of administrative development that began in the nineteenth century continued into the twentieth century, although administrative growth had to accommodate itself to the advent of mass democracy. Moran speaks of the twentieth century as a period in which nineteenth-century administrative and regulatory institutions became 'embedded' within the newly emerging democratic state.[19] This process of embedding was, however, somewhat contradictory. On the one hand, attempts were made to bring the activities of various boards and commissions within the control of ministries, and thereby to allow Parliament to play a full part in making policy. On the other hand, the content of emerging regulatory and administrative doctrines emphasised, in Moran's words 'voluntarism and the tacit knowledge of insiders'.[20] Moran sees the emergence of such understandings as part of a concerted attempt by an oligopolistic elite to limit the impact of democratic politics on the world of 'club government' and 'club regulation' and from an overly rigid system of legal control. The historical record, it might be argued, is at least as compatible with a much less cynical view: the administrators' position was after all not based on a demand for limitless powers. Rather, it was based on an understanding that stressed what Denis Galligan calls the 'internal' component of discretion,[21] supported as necessary through administration-internal hierarchies of command and control, and closely bound up with the phenomenon that we detail below, and elsewhere in this volume, as 'administrative constitutionalism'.[22] The (successful) attempt by the senior civil service to narrow the terms of reference of the Franks Inquiry, for example, appears to have been motivated by a genuine concern on the part of permanent officials about the potential undermining of administrative judgement which, by its very nature, was resistant to control by law.

[18] JAG Griffith, 'The Constitutional Significance of Delegated Legislation in England' (1950) 48 *Michigan Law Review* 1079, 1079. For Griffith, this emerging understanding, though related to the onset of a period of more active administration, was not so much new as a reversion to type, the product of what LS Amery described as the 'inherent tendency, in our system, for Government, as such, to reassert itself whenever the opportunity might arise.' See LS Amery, *Thoughts on the British Constitution* (Oxford, OUP, 1947) 14–15, quoted in Griffith (ibid) 1081.

[19] M Moran, *The British Regulatory State: High Modernism and Hyper-innovation* (Oxford, OUP, 2003) 55–64.

[20] ibid 35.

[21] D Galligan, *Discretionary powers: a legal study of official discretion* (Oxford, Clarendon Press, 1990).

[22] Ch 5 in this volume, section III (Arvind and Stirton).

B. The Limits of Diceyanism

By the middle of the twentieth century, there was a broad consensus that dynamic administration should be subject to some form of external control. Given the breadth of the powers administrators now had over private persons, and the wide discretion statute gave them in the exercise of those powers, self-policing through internal control within administrative systems was seen as constitutionally inadequate and wrong in principle. The effect of leaving dynamic administration to police itself and remedy its own failings was, as the then Parliamentary Counsel William Graham-Harrison put it in an internal memorandum, to leave individuals to 'the tender mercies of the bureaucracy'.[23] The UK's constitutional tradition, in contrast, was widely perceived as requiring the existence of an independent external forum that could exercise scrutiny and control over bureaucratic activity and provide redress to private persons who believed themselves to have been wrongfully affected by administrative action.[24]

At the same time, it was also evident that Parliament did not have the capacity to be that forum, at least when it came to dynamic administration. Parliamentary control, as JAG Griffith pointed out, was more akin to the manner in which the banks of a river control its flow than the manner in which a driver controls a car.[25] As such, it could neither provide effective redress nor deal with even the majority of the systemic issues that dynamic administration might create.[26] But nor was the common law, as it then existed, a more suitable instrument of control over the administrative state. Administrative law's doctrines and conceptual categories, as traditionally understood within the canon of administrative law, were not adapted to dynamic administration. The ultra vires doctrine provided, in WIR Fraser's assessment, 'a most valuable safeguard against unduly autocratic action', but was undermined if Parliament 'does not define the powers reasonably clearly'.[27] But dynamic administration, by its very nature, demanded a style of governing in which powers were conferred in broad enough terms to allow administrators to adapt their responses in line with the lessons of experience and changing circumstances.

The resulting disjunction was an important part of the background to the 'period of debility'[28] to which we have made reference above. Traditionalists

[23] LCO 2/3358, Graham-Harrison to Fisher, 13 October 1927.

[24] See ch 1 in this volume, section II, and the sources cited there (Arvind, Kirkham, Mac Síthigh and Stirton).

[25] JAG Griffith, 'Constitutional and Administrative Law' in G Gardiner and A Martin (eds), *Law Reform Now!* (London, Victor Gollancz, 1963).

[26] See the discussion in TT Arvind and L Stirton, 'The curious origins of judicial review' (2017) 133 *LQR* 91.

[27] WIR Fraser, *An Outline of Constitutional Law* (London, William Hodge, 1948) 184; see also Carr, *English Administrative Law* (1941) 50–51.

[28] Schwartz and Wade, *Legal Control of Government* (1972) 13.

such as Lord Hewart and Sir Carleton Allen inveighed against these changes, but they had no solutions to offer, other than the infeasible one of turning back the clock in terms of the development of the administrative state.[29] As the Report on the Committee of Ministers Powers showed,[30] and the limited changes in practice that were effectuated as a result underscore, the new style of administration depended for its adaptability on powers being conferred in broad terms. Much faith was likewise placed in tort law as a way of holding the state to account, but the failure of the Crown Proceedings Act 1947 to have the revolutionary effect which some scholars had expected showed that tort, too, lacked the ability to deal with the challenge posed by the rise of dynamic administration.[31]

In hindsight, the reason for these failures is not difficult to discover. Existing legal approaches were focused on guiding and directing the courts in policing the outer perimeter of administrative power (as both the ultra vires doctrine and the law of tort, in their different ways, attempted to do). Yet whilst this may have been adequate to maintain the core understandings of the constitutional tradition discussed above in a world of static administration, dynamic administration called out for a different response. This response needed to be one capable of making the administration's own understanding of the nature and extent of that power, and of the ends towards which and manner in which it ought to be exercised, legible to judicial scrutiny. The need was for approaches, concepts and vocabulary which would permit the judiciary to place these administrative self-understandings – the administration's internal 'administrative constitutionalism', to use the language adopted elsewhere in this volume – in a legal frame, and devise and articulate legal and constitutional considerations which drew on both statute and common law and could be used to subject dynamic administration to scrutiny.

The inability to devise such an approach in the years leading to the 1960s is closely connected with the dominance of Diceyan constitutionalism in that period. Dicey was deeply suspicious of the administrative state, and believed that its rise reflected a misjudged idealism on the part of reformers. Reformers, he argued, 'find it in general impossible to acquiesce in the notion – which is often, however, a true one – that no specific cure for a definite evil exists' and thus fell back on the power of the state as 'the only conceivable *deus ex machina* capable of cutting through the knots'.[32] As late as 1915, he continued to argue that the transference of authority to Government departments (or 'servants of the

[29] Lord Hewitt of Bury, *The New Despotism* (London, Ernest Benn, 1929); CK Allen, *Bureaucracy Triumphant*, Oxford, OUP, 1931).

[30] Lord Chancellor, Committee on Ministers Powers Report (Cmd 4060, 1932).

[31] TT Arvind, 'Restraining the State through Tort? The Crown Proceedings Act in Retrospect' in TT Arvind and Jenny Steele (eds) *Tort Law and the Legislature: Common Law, Statute and the Dynamics of Legal Change* (Oxford, Hart Publishing, 2013).

[32] AV Dicey, 'The Social Movement in England – III' *The Nation* (27 March 1884) 272, 273.

Crown', as he continued to call them) 'saps the foundations of that rule of law which has been for generations a leading feature of the English constitution'.[33]

There was little room in this constitutional world for dynamic administration, and Dicey himself continued to maintain that what he conceived of as 'true *droit administratif*' was incompatible with the rule of law.[34] In consequence, the understanding of the nature of administrative order on which it was based had little room to deal with the key challenges posed by the rise of dynamic administration – and, in particular, the ever-increasing need for legal rules and approaches capable of dealing with the task of resolving conflicts between administrative constitutionalism and legal understandings of the power and obligations of the civil service. For Dicey, tort law was a key mode of holding the state to the rule of law. Yet, as the Crown Proceedings Act's failure demonstrated, tort law could only play this role in a world of static administration, where it had to do little more than mediate between competing interests. When it came to the task of mediating, not between competing interests, but between competing visions of the constitution and its implications for the conduct of administration, tort had little to offer.

The challenge of finding a conceptual framework capable of responding to the shift in the bureaucracy's perception of its task was, then, a key factor in the judiciary's weakness and loss of confidence in their own functions, and the consequent changes in the way in which powers were conferred and exercised. It provides crucial context for JDB Mitchell's pessimism about the common law's potential to police 'administrative morality',[35] and it also underpinned Lord Patrick Devlin's remarks to the Bentham Club (quoted by Thomas in his contribution to this volume)[36] that the common law now lacked 'the strength to provide any satisfactory solution to the problem of keeping the executive … under control'.[37] The aggrieved citizen might still get justice through administrative processes but, as Devlin put it, 'he cannot get it by process of law'.[38]

The theory of tradition discussed above lets us restate the position on the eve of the Quartet with more precision. Without confidence that they were in possession of a core of agreed understandings that could guide them effectively as they confronted the challenges of dynamic administration, and hampered by a canon of legal doctrine which limited more than it empowered, the judiciary had become listless and sclerotic. Certainly, they could apply existing doctrines to new situations as they arose, and they continued to do so. And, as Bernard Schwartz has shown, when it came to the use of doctrines like ultra vires the judiciary, far from being asleep as Stephen Sedley has suggested,[39] had

[33] AV Dicey, 'The Development of Administrative Law in England' (1915) 31 *LQR* 148, 150.
[34] ibid 152.
[35] Mitchell (n 1).
[36] Ch 3 in this volume, section IV (Thomas).
[37] P Devlin, 'The Common Law, Public Policy and the Executive' [1956] *Current Legal Problems* 1, 13.
[38] ibid 1.
[39] Stephen Sedley, 'The Sound of Silence' (1994) 110 *LQR* 270.

an acute awareness of the problem.[40] The difficulty was that, as discussed above, the conceptual apparatus of ultra vires was oriented towards a static conception of administration, which gave to the judiciary the task of ensuring administrators' faithfulness to the initial grant of power. This apparatus was insufficient to deal with the challenges posed by dynamic administration. As Devlin rightly saw, the development of modern doctrines capable of controlling the modern style of executive decision-making, 'could not be done by standing pat on existing principles but only by forming new principles'.[41] But in the absence of a conceptualisation of the core of administrative law which was capable of transcending the limits of Diceyanism to make sense of dynamic administration, this was not something judges could easily do. The American administrative lawyer KC Davis later identified the belief that had become prevalent in the English legal profession that:

> [J]udges have no responsibility for reworking previously existing law in order that the needs of society may be better served. The prevailing belief … is that the task of judges is limited to the application of previously existing law and does not extend either to a reexamination of case law with a view to improving it or to the making of policy choices in giving meaning to silent or unclear statutes.[42]

It was thus to Parliament that citizens should now look to for remedies, both in terms of its traditional role of legislative scrutiny, and through the establishment of a new statutory body of administrative law and remedies.[43]

Not everyone shared this pessimism about the loss of dynamism in the common law. Lord Denning struck an upbeat note in his judgments as well as his extra-judicial writings.[44] For example, his judgment in *Shaw* revived the moribund concept of error of law on the face of the record.[45] Nonetheless, these contributions stood apart from the general struggle, before the Quartet, to see how judges and jurists could reimagine the law to cope with the challenges posed by the rise of dynamic administration and the resulting transformation of executive government. The core of the constitutional tradition strongly suggested that some form of legal response to the rise of dynamic administration was necessary but provided no obvious way of framing a consistent response beyond a few isolated areas, while the canon of precedent actively hindered the development of responses.

[40] B Schwartz, *Law and the Executive in Britain: A Comparative Study* (Cambridge, CUP, 1949). An illustrative example is Schwartz's discussion (ibid 174–76) of the case of *Sparks v Edward Ash Ltd*. [1943] KB 223, involving the challenge to two traffic regulations made by a minister.

[41] Devlin, 'The Common Law' [1956] 13.

[42] KC Davis, 'The Future of Judge-Made Public Law in England: A Problem of Practical Jurisprudence' (1961) 61 *Columbia Law Review* 201, 202.

[43] Devlin (n 37) 14–15.

[44] For example, AT Denning, *The Rule of Law in the Welfare State* (London, Birkbeck, 1953), reproduced in AT Denning, *The Changing Law* (London, Stevens and Sons, 1953); see also AT Denning, *Freedom under the Law* (London, Stevens and Sons, 1949).

[45] *R v Northumberland Compensation Appeal Tribunal, ex parte Shaw* (1952) 1 KB 338 (CA). Nonetheless, as Thomas notes in his chapter, administrative tribunals responded defensively by

This tension and the unease to which it gave rise formed an important aspect of the background to the Quartet, and underpinned the peculiar combination of continuity and change which the four cases appear to reflect. The challenge was to restate the core in a way which visibly retained the element of continuity with the past, but which also both enabled and justified departing from the elements of the canon – the accreted body of precedent – which hindered judicial responses to the rise of dynamic administration.[46] It was to meeting this challenge that the Quartet was directed, and in understanding the manner in which it sought to meet it, it is to the Quartet's doctrinal rather than symbolic value to which we must turn.

III. DYNAMIC ADMINISTRATION AND THE COURTS: (RE)DISCOVERING THE DOCTRINAL DIMENSIONS OF THE QUARTET

We distinguished in a previous chapter between the symbolic and the doctrinal contributions of the Quartet, noting that it is in the light of the former that the Quartet is largely read today.[47] In the next section (section IV), we discuss how a focus on the legal doctrine of the Quartet has a lot to offer in terms of how we think about judicial review and – perhaps more importantly – how we could and should be thinking about the tasks of judicial review and the challenges it faces. Before that, however, it is necessary to first explain the nature of the Quartet's doctrinal dimension.

A first aspect of the Quartet's doctrinal dimension relates to the problems which prompted them. As we show in subsection A of this section, all four cases in the Quartet related squarely to challenges that are peculiar to dynamic administration. This shared focus on dynamic administration not only explains the Quartet's departures from the canon, but also how and why the judges deciding the Quartet believed these departures to be justified by what they understood to be the core of the constitutional tradition; and it puts their aims and effects in a very different light from the standard 'timeless' reading of the principles they sought to uphold. We argue, in particular, that the Quartet was rooted in a new understanding of the role of law and the courts vis-à-vis the executive and the legislature, and a new understanding of the ends of doctrine that form the substratum or inner premises of administrative law (to use the language

ceasing to issue a 'speaking record', until the Tribunals and Inquiries Act 1958 obliged them to disclose reasons for their decisions.

[46] Lord Reid himself spoke of the problem of complexity of the canon, but without explicitly connecting this with an inadequately identified core. Instead he described a process by which the canon became incoherent over time leading to 'an impenetrable maze of distinctions and qualifications which destroy certainty because no one advising on the case can predict how it will go'. Lord Reid, 'The Judge as Law Maker' (1972) 12 *Journal of the Society of Public Teachers of Law* 22, 24.

[47] See ch 1 in this volume, section III (Arvind, Kirkham, Mac Síthigh and Stirton).

of Atiyah and Stewart respectively, quoted above). The judges in the Quartet, Lord Reid in particular, approached this new understanding not by developing new principles (as Lord Devlin had thought necessary), but by working out how existing core principles applied in the context of the legal needs of the age. It produced not so much a reworking of the core, as a restatement.

This restatement was characterised by four themes, each of which focuses on a different facet of legal doctrine. These are discussed in subsections B–E, below. The first (subsection B) relates to the problem of ensuring that private persons with grievances against administrative bodies have access to an independent forum in which to air their grievances, and that the category of private persons includes not just individuals but also, as *Anisminic*[48] instantiated, the companies through which individuals conduct commercial affairs. The second (subsection C) concerns the growth of supervisory vacuums – areas where, in practice, there was no body with the practical ability to exercise supervisory powers over dynamic administration. The third (section D) concerns the relationship between the core and the canon, and the manner in which the courts should resolve situations where the rules set out in the canon no longer have a propensity to produce the types of outcomes prioritised by the core. The fourth (section E) relates to the need to articulate a doctrinal basis for a middle ground. This middle ground needed to avoid the extremes of both the oversupervision which would have resulted if the judiciary had adopted the same type of supervision over dynamic administration as they had exercised over static administration, and the undersupervision that would have resulted had they continued withdrawing from the supervisory field altogether as they had done during their period of weakness and loss of confidence.

A. Responding to Dynamic Administration: The Real Significance of the Quartet

A central feature of the cases in the Quartet is that all four concerned grievances that arose out of dynamic administration, and that could not have arisen in the absence of dynamic administration. This feature distinguishes the Quartet from other leading cases decided in the same period. *Burmah Oil*,[49] for example, arose out of fact patterns – the deliberate destruction of friendly property in wartime to prevent it falling into enemy hands – which could have occurred at any time in the past 200 years. This was not true of the cases in the Quartet.

As section II has noted, an important feature of dynamic administration was the creeping transfer of policy-making powers out of the hands of the legislature and into the hands of a new cadre of administrative officials. The

[48] *Anisminic v Foreign Compensation Commission* [1969] 2 AC 147 (HL).
[49] *Burmah Oil* (n 6).

conduct of administrative affairs could no longer proceed on the basis of a one-time declaration by the legislature of a static set of policies and principles. Instead, administrative officials had to be given the power to respond dynamically to changing situations, including by formulating policies themselves. Simultaneously, administrative government also had a growing power to make determinations in the individual case. Such exercises of discretion, even if they did not involve deciding questions of policy of general application, involved deciding questions that concerned, and could affect, a private person's ability to pursue their own ends in a far broader range of areas than was the case under the older, static model of administration.

At the same time, dynamic administration had also changed the relationship with Parliament so that Parliament was no longer 'supreme' in the traditional sense of having a monopoly of power. Parliament's consent might well still be required for new primary legislation, and it still had ultimate authority to unmake any rule of law or aspect of policy through primary legislation. Nevertheless, in an era in which government was expected to do more and did in fact do more, it was practically impossible for Parliament to exercise any real supervision over the executive in matters of detail. The effect was to intensify what LS Amery had called the executive's 'inherent tendency' to assert itself 'whenever the opportunity might arise',[50] and it created the need for a modern understanding of the place of the executive and Parliament in the constitution.

It was to these issues that the Quartet spoke. The cases were wrestling with a new constitutional dispensation in which legislation conferred broad powers on officials to determine policy or otherwise exercise determinative or dispositive power over private persons (in the Hohfeldian sense of the legal ability to alter another's jural position), and in which the sheer volume of administrative work meant that Parliament had little practical ability to exercise supervision over either the extent of the power or the manner in which it was exercised. All four cases in the Quartet arose out of these issues and, as Table 19.1 below demonstrates, the cases represent between them the full range of ways in which the two dimensions of the issue could combine under dynamic administration.

Table 19.1 Dynamic administration in the Quartet

	Extent of power	**Exercise of power**
Policy-making power	*Anisminic*	*Padfield*
Determinative or dispositive power	*Conway*	*Ridge*

[50] Amery, *British Constitution* (1947) 14–15, quoted in Griffith, 'Constitutional Significance' (1950) 1081.

Both *Anisminic* and *Padfield* related to the question of the ability of executive bodies to make general policy determinations. In *Anisminic*, the question was whether the FCC had the power to make a policy decision in relation to who was entitled to the benefit of the compensation scheme. In *Padfield*, the question related not to the scope of the administrative decision-maker's power to make or uphold a policy decision, but to the manner in which an authority exercising that power must behave. *Conway*, in contrast, involved the question of the extent of a department's adjudicatory power: could a department claim the power to balance its interests against the interests of a private person, or could it only claim the power to determine what its own interests required? *Ridge*, similarly to *Padfield*, did not raise issues as to whether the watch committee had the legal ability to dismiss the chief constable, but to the question of how it should behave in exercising that power.

The specificity of these categories is important, and the four facets of the Quartet's doctrinal contribution outlined above, and discussed in more detail below, must be seen against the background of this specificity. The Quartet were not concerned in the abstract with providing broad redress in all cases. In purely doctrinal terms, there is nothing in the Quartet to support the suggestion that the mere fact that an individual disagreed with the outcome of an administrative process or believed that an administrative body had erred would trigger a remedy. Their concern was not with administrative error in a vague or abstract sense. It was, rather, with new issues and concerns created by the rise of dynamic administration and the increased role it implied for the state. Before the Quartet, such decisions would have been dealt through analytical categories which would have attempted either to exclude the intervention of the court in matters of dynamic administration or to confine its role to static interpretations of statutory law.

B. Providing Independent Redress against Administrative Understandings of Power

One of the key themes of the Quartet was to equip judicial review with the tools necessary to get around the shackles of more recent case law, so as to allow the courts to mediate disputes between individuals and the state. All four cases in the Quartet were directly concerned with the question of the right of private persons to seek independent redress against grievances created by the unilateral exercise of powers of dynamic administration. *Conway v Rimmer* provides a particularly clear illustration of this theme and its connection with dynamic administration.

The issue of Crown privilege was, of course, not new to *Conway*. But *Conway* arose at a time when dynamic administration had radically altered the quantity as well as the quality of potentially relevant evidence held by the Government. As Lord Pearce put it in his speech:

> Even since the date of Duncan's case there has been an enormous increase in the extent to which the executive impinges on the private lives of the citizens. New ministries have been created and the old have been enlarged. Inevitably the mass of documentation has proliferated. It now bears little relation to the 'state papers' or other documents of government to which some of the older cases refer.[51]

The demands of dynamic administration for ever more detailed record-keeping had, in other words, banalised the types of papers in relation to which claims of Crown privilege were made and raised serious questions in relation to the implications of extending a privilege originally devised for state papers to these documents. A more fundamental issue, however, was that the rise of dynamic administration also meant that claims of Crown privilege were now being made in cases where the department making the claim, or a person connected with that department, was itself the defendant (and not merely served with a subpoena in an unrelated case, as in *Duncan*[52] itself). Arvind and Stirton in their chapter[53] note the lengths to which the bureaucracy would go to avoid administrative injustice in practice, but the effect was nonetheless to make the position of the individual dependent on the administrative department choosing of its own free will to do justice, and on that department's own self-definition of what constituted justice.

What was missing in this process was a body that could discharge a mediatory role between the conceptions of the purposes and ends of power that were internal to the administrative body, and those that held by persons external to that body. In the absence of such a body, the administrative body had a near-unbridled jurisdiction to determine the scope and extent of its own power. It was to this problem that *Conway* was directed, and the theme is not unique to *Conway*. The similarities of the concerns that underlay *Anisminic* are discussed in more detail below, and they are also visible in both *Ridge*[54] and *Padfield*.[55] In *Ridge*, the issue was the view an administrative body had taken in relation to the manner in which it would exercise its power, and the role the court asserted was a mediatory role which would bring that view into dialogue with broader common law principles in relation to procedural fairness and natural justice. In *Padfield*, it related to the Minister's view of the goals he could prioritise in exercising his statutory discretion, and the court's role was to mediate between the Minister's reading of the statute and other competing and potentially plausible readings of what the statute permitted and prohibited the Minister to prioritise.

[51] *Conway* (n 5), 984F–G.
[52] *Duncan v Cammell Laird & Co Ltd* [1942] AC 624.
[53] Ch 5 in this volume (Arvind and Stirton).
[54] *Ridge v Baldwin* [1964] AC 40 (HL).
[55] *Padfield v Minister of Agriculture* [1968] AC 997 (HL).

Taken together, the cases highlight the courts' understanding of the law's role as mediatory in nature, with the law tasked with bringing into dialogue, and where necessary resolving conflicts between, two potentially contrasting readings of the power and obligations of government: the technocratic readings which dynamic administration is prone to generate, and the demotic readings held by private persons. The operation of any mediatory function, however, depends in turn on the ability of individuals to seek independent redress against an administrative body's interpretations of its power and obligations, the availability of an independent forum, and the existence of independent principles for subjecting to scrutiny the claims of administrative authorities in relation to the nature, scope and extent of their powers. The radicalism of the Quartet came in the court's willingness to question and dismantle doctrinal obstacles to this ability which had been imposed or reiterated by the courts during their 'period of debility'.

C. 'No Alsatia in England': Policing the Assertion of Administrative Power

Scrutinising the assertion of administrative power goes further than performing a mediatory function. In certain circumstances, the function required is the somewhat different one of assessing whether the assertion and exercise of power stayed within the boundaries established by Parliament when vesting a particular administrative authority with administrative power. *Anisminic* instantiates the manner in which the Quartet sought to adapt this function for a world of dynamic administration.

Anisminic on its face related to an ouster clause, or preclusive clause, in a statute creating a tribunal,[56] and the case is today remembered primarily for its ruling that the ouster clause did not preclude the Court's review, since the purported decision of the tribunal – the Foreign Compensation Commission – was outwith its jurisdiction and therefore was a mere nullity. In point of fact, that was the least innovative aspect of the House of Lords decision.[57] What was new was an attempt to work out the respective roles of Parliament and administrative bodies in the making of policy, in the context of dynamic administration where, as section II has discussed, the nature of the relationship of the two had shifted in ways that no longer fit with standard conceptions of 'subordination'. Dynamic administration had vastly increased the power not just of the bureaucratic wing of the administration, but also of the administrative tribunals which were expected to give effect to public policy through their decisions on matters remitted to them.

[56] The clause in question was contained in the Foreign Compensation Act, s 4(4).

[57] As HWR Wade put it in a letter to the *Times* immediately after the Law Lords' ruling, 'The judges … have for 300 years firmly set their faces against such provisions and have, to put it bluntly, refused to apply them'. See HWR Wade, 'Letter to the editor' *Times* (1 February 1969).

The speech of Lord Wilberforce carefully set the work of the Foreign Compensation Commission in this context. The Commission, he explained, was 'one of many tribunals set up to deal with matters of a specialised character, in the interest of economy, speed, and expertise'. These varied in their nature, composition and functions. There were those like the Foreign Compensation Commission 'whose functions are predominantly judicial; it is a permanent body, composed mainly of lawyers with a learned chairman'. Equally, there were those whose task might be better described as fact-finding or even policy-making. The challenge posed by the existence of such bodies was that they might enter into making policy on matters where they were not, in fact, permitted to make policy. *Anisminic* related to a situation where the Court had to decide whether that was what had, in fact, happened.

In *Anisminic*, the Foreign Compensation Commission did not have the authority to devise legal rules on who was or was not eligible for compensation. It did not have the authority to make policy on this point. It had to apply the rules set out in legislation which, in this case, consisted of not just the underlying Act, but also an Order in Council, the Foreign Compensation (Egypt) (Determination and Registration of Claims) Order 1962.[58] The difficulty the Commission faced was that due to poor drafting of the Order, it in effect had to choose between two competing interpretations of eligibility for compensation under the Order – that of the Fund's legal officer, or Anisminic's – both of which produced anomalies and absurdities. Either interpretation had implications as to who was eligible under the scheme.[59] In other words, even if the FCC was in this case simply interpreting the law, the choice between rival interpretations had far-reaching policy implications.

The question this raised was a significant one, and it was not in any way confined to the unique facts of *Anisminic*. Under the welfare state legislation which sought to tackle the social and economic problems of the mid-twentieth century, 'the enforcement of the great majority of the new duties', as Lord Denning had put it in his Hamlyn Lectures, 'is now entrusted to Government Departments or to tribunals whose members are appointed by the Government Departments'.[60] Every one of these would be dealing with issues where the instruments setting out the underlying policy to which they had to give effect might be ambiguous. Did an ouster clause, in effect, operate as an unlimited delegation of policy-making power to these tribunals, empowering them to make policy decisions of their own in any area they chose, even when Parliament had not created them as policy-making bodies in relation to that law?

[58] Foreign Compensation (Egypt) (Determination and Registration of Claims) Order 1962 (SI 1962/2187).

[59] And indeed, as Feldman points out in ch 6 in this volume, the impact of the size of Anisminic's claim on the funds available to other claimants was only avoided after it was agreed to provide an additional amount from the consolidated fund.

[60] Denning, *Freedom under Law* (1949) 76.

This was the question that lay at the heart of *Anisminic*. It was primarily about the question of the limits of the policy-making power of administrative institutions – a question that mattered to dynamic administration in a way it did not in static administration. Whilst it did on its face involve ouster clauses, the issue was not simply about the Court's power to read down ouster clauses, but whether an ouster clause in effect gave an administrative institution the unfettered and unreviewable ability to determine where the limits of its policy-making power lay.

Lord Wilberforce answered the question in clear and non-technical terms. In any grant of decision-making authority to a tribunal, he argued, 'There is always an area, narrow or wide which is the tribunal's area'. He referred to this variously as the tribunal's 'field' or 'area of operation'.[61] Within this field, the tribunal was competent to take any decision, including in relation to matters of law; and whilst the court would ordinarily intervene to correct errors of law if they appeared on the face of the record, as they had in *Shaw*,[62] the existence of a preclusive clause, such as the one in section 4(4) of the Foreign Compensation Act 1950, would oust that jurisdiction. Parliament had intended that authority to enjoy exclusive responsibility for deciding all matters remitted to it, including matters of law.

This did not, however, apply to matters that lay outwith this 'area of operation'. As Feldman's contribution to this collection shows, it had been well established since the seventeenth century that such a privative clause would not save a decision of a statutory body with limited jurisdiction on a matter which was outside that limited area of operation.[63] In *Anisminic*, the House of Lords held that a tribunal's area of operation was subject to two boundaries. The first boundary related to the existence of 'a residual area, wide or narrow, in which the legislature has previously expressed its will and into which the tribunal may not enter'.[64] Sometimes this residual area might be narrow, if 'the legislature, while stating general objectives, is prepared to concede a wide area to the authority it establishes'.[65] The Foreign Compensation Act, however, was a different sort. *Anisminic* was concerned with the sort of situation where 'Parliament is itself directly and closely concerned with the definition and delimitation of certain matters of comparative detail and has marked by its language the intention that these shall accurately be observed'.[66] In such cases, the residual area became a rather hard-edged, substantive category: a set of principles and policies which the legislature required the tribunal to adopt, and from which it was not permitted to depart.

[61] *Anisminic* (n 48) 207.

[62] *Ex parte Shaw* (n 45).

[63] Ch 6 in this volume (Feldman). See also de Smith 'Statutory Restriction of Judicial Review' (1955) 18 *MLR* 575.

[64] *Anisminic* (n 48) 207.

[65] *Anisminic* (n 48) 209.

[66] *Anisminic* (n 48) 209–10.

As is evident from these quotes, the House of Lords in *Anisminic* had in mind something qualitatively different from an ordinary error of law, such as misunderstanding the scope of the *volenti* defence in tort. Its concern was, rather, the problem of unauthorised policymaking by an administrative authority. Underpinning dynamic administration was a broader shift in which the state increasingly made far-reaching policy decisions in matters on which society was divided. The policy at issue in *Anisminic* was less far-reaching than most, but the issue was no less contested for that. Feldman reminds us that in the modern day, 'It is often forgotten how controversial was the structure of the compensation scheme which the FCC had to interpret, for losses suffered by people who had to bear "the burden of our collective insanity" in invading Egypt in 1956'.[67]

In passing the Foreign Compensation Act 1950, Parliament had faced up to the controversial issue and made a policy judgment on the matter of claims for compensation for losses suffered in time of war. It was not for an administrative tribunal to supplant or supplement Parliament's instructions, even where that supplanting or supplementing came not through a deliberate attempt to enlarge its authority but through the misconstrual of a carelessly drafted Order in Council. And although the privative clause was effective in preventing the Court from correcting errors of law on matters within the tribunal's area of operations, it did not prevent the Court from intervening if the tribunal began making decisions on matters of policy – such as the question of the principles that would govern eligibility – that it did not in fact have the power to make. If Parliament did in fact intend to confer unlimited policy-making power on an administrative authority, it would do so expressly rather than tangentially through an ouster clause.

While *Anisminic* itself was concerned only with this first boundary, the case also discusses a second boundary. In addition to being bound by principles and policies laid down by Parliament, the tribunal's field was also bounded by the common law. As Lord Wilberforce put it, 'there are certain fundamental assumptions, which without explicit restatement in every case, necessarily underlie the remission of power to decide'. While these might vary from situation to situation (and it was always within the competence of Parliament to change or in particular instances set aside the common law), Lord Wilberforce mentioned as an example, 'the requirement that a decision must be made in accordance with principles of natural justice and good faith'. In *Ridge*, *Padfield* and, arguably, *Conway*, it was this second boundary that was involved, leading the Court to draw on broader common law values in judicial review.

The function exercised by the courts in *Anisminic*, in contrast, was wholly grounded in Parliamentary policy – a function which section IV below terms the 'executory' function of judicial review. By the House of Lord's own logic, the outcome in *Anisminic* would have been wholly different if Parliament had

[67] Ch 6 in this volume, section IV (Feldman).

in fact conferred the FCC with the power to make policy decisions in relation to who was and who was not eligible for the scheme. The connection of the decision in *Anisminic* with the ability to make policy decisions has been obscured by subsequent case law, in particular the decision in *Racal*[68] and more recently the majority decision in *Privacy International*.[69] Nevertheless, the House of Lords in *Anisminic* carved out a clear role for the courts. In a world of dynamic administration – one in which administrative officials were also liable to move between different roles – it was crucially important for there to be a body which ensured that policy was only made by administrative bodies which were actually authorised to make policy. As with the other doctrinal themes discussed in this section, the Quartet sought to respond to dynamic administration by striking a middle path which avoided the extremes of both 'juristocracy', where judges determine the limits of acceptable policy, and the 'new despotism' which gives carte blanche to the internal decision-making process of the administration subject only to its own internal systems of oversight. Rather, the Quartet sought to render more legible to legal doctrine the task of determining where the limits of the policy-making function of administrative institutions lay in dynamic administration.

D. Rethinking the Canon in Defence of the Core

A common feature in the discussion thus far has been the House of Lords' willingness to move away from trends in the case law that emerged in the decades preceding the Quartet, in order to fashion (or refashion) doctrine to make it more capable of dealing with the issues raised by dynamic administration. This shift was conducted by a variety of means. In *Conway*, the Law Lords invoked their (relatively recent) power to overrule their own past decisions, overturning *Duncan v Cammell Laird*.[70] In other cases they distinguished and narrowly confined precedent, as *Anisminic* did in relation to *Smith v East Elloe Rural District Council*.[71]

Underlying both these approaches was a broader project of rediscovering older approaches, purposes and understandings that could be argued to have at one stage been of importance to the common law, but which were not fully reflected in recent cases. This process of rediscovery necessarily involved reinterpreting the nature of those older approaches, which had not contended with the challenges of dynamic administration. Yet, as the cases also demonstrate, this was motivated by a genuine and sincere attempt to bring back into operative doctrine ideas and approaches that were thought to be of fundamental

[68] *In Re Racal Communications Ltd* [1981] 1 AC 374 (HL).

[69] *R (on the application of Privacy International) v Investigatory Powers Tribunal* [2019] UKSC 22, [2019] 2 WLR 1219.

[70] *Duncan* (n 52).

[71] *Smith v East Elloe Rural District Council* [1956] AC 736.

importance to the core of the constitution. The Quartet sought, in essence, to rethink or reimagine the doctrinal approaches on which the canon of recent precedent was seemingly based because those approaches were seen as having moved too far away from the fundamentals of the core.

The decision in *Ridge v Baldwin*[72] was a clear instance of this approach, one which was adopted in order to deliver what we in section IV below term the 'vindicatory' function of judicial review, in which the law intervenes to upholds the rights of a private person against wrongful administrative action. In re-emphasising this vindicatory element, *Ridge* provides strong evidence for the corrective capacity of the common law. As Thomas's chapter discusses,[73] in a series of decisions starting with *Local Government Board v Arlidge*[74] the House of Lords had restricted the reach of the *audi alteram partem* principle, so that bodies exercising powers that could be characterised as administrative were freed from the requirements of observing the requirements of natural justice. This wrong turning, as Lord Reid saw it, had been followed by the courts.[75] As Thomas also shows, Lord Reid was able to make out a convincing case that this recent line of cases had seriously misunderstood earlier established case law, and could for that reason 'no longer be regarded as authoritative'.[76]

In doctrinal terms, *Ridge* was, as Thomas recognises, rather limited, being concerned to reclaim ground lost since *Arlidge*, rather than to chart a new course. But seen in the context of the challenge posed by dynamic administration and the task it implied of reassessing the canon in light of the core, the importance even of a purely corrective measure should not be underestimated. Hitherto, the canon had suggested that the key to the application of principles of natural justice lay in whether a body or decision was judicial or administrative in character. However, as Lord Reid argued, if one revisited the cases in light of the inner premises of administrative law – and the normative core that lay beneath the surface – the true concern that triggered the application of principles of natural justice was that a body or decision should be concerned with how an individual should be treated. In such a situation, the principles of natural justice apply.[77]

Such decision-making situations were fundamental to the administration of the welfare state, as Lord Denning had pointed out a decade earlier, but were prior to *Ridge* outwith effective judicial supervision.[78] The accomplishment of

[72] *Ridge* (n 54).
[73] Ch 3 in this volume (Thomas).
[74] *Local Government Board v Arlidge* [1915] AC 120.
[75] *Nakkuda Ali v Jayaratne* [1951] AC 66; *R v Metropolitan Police Commissioner* (1953) 1 WLR 1150.
[76] Ch 3 in this volume (Thomas).
[77] *Ridge* (n 54) 72.
[78] As Denning put it, 'The Government Department which requisitions my house, or compulsorily acquires my land, does not exercise a judicial function. It is exercising a statutory power and performing an administrative function. Once the power is exercised the legal position is transformed … New rights and duties are thus brought into being by the exercise of the power: and once it is exercised the courts must enforce them. But over the power itself the courts have little control'. Denning (n 44) 100.

Ridge was to bring such decisions within the ambit of natural justice once more. In highlighting the 'confusion' in the authorities, and in downplaying decisions such as *Nakkuda Ali*[79] and *Parker*[80] as contrary to older, established case law, Lord Reid was able to present his judgment as firmly grounded in precedent, while at the same time re-evaluating the status of decisions that were at variance from what he regarded as the core propositions regarding the applicability of natural justice. Therein lies the real significance of Bailey's observation that the significance of the Quartet was as much due to the way in which it closed off directions that counsel may have sought to persuade the courts to take in future decisions.[81]

E. A Middle Ground of Partnership: Subjecting New Approaches to Administration to Legal Regulation

Central to the decisions in the Quartet was the concern with re-evaluating the canon to see whether, in the light of changed circumstances, it continued to reflect and further the core. Dismantling doctrinal bars to judicial intervention, however, carries dangers. In moving away from judicial quiescence, the courts run the risk of judicial overreach, and creating a culture that is overly legalistic or overly judicialised. The fourth and final facet of doctrine that can be drawn from the Quartet related directly to this point. It sought to avoid the extremes of both judicial quiescence and judicial overreach by creating a middle ground, of judicial partnership so as to enable the court to perform what we describe in section IV below as the 'hortatory' task of judicial review'.[82]

Padfield v Ministry of Agriculture[83] concerns a quintessential example of the role this idea of partnership played in shaping the judicial response to the new style of administration. Between 1931 and 1949, Parliament had passed a series of Agricultural Marketing Acts,[84] which allowed producers of any agricultural product to put forward a 'scheme for its marketing'. Such a scheme, if it received the approval of two-thirds of the producers, as well as the support of Government, would put the marketing of the entire output of the product under control of a co-operative, directed by a board elected by producers. Schemes were established for hops under the 1931 Act and under the 1933 Act for milk, potatoes, pigs and bacon.

[79] *Nakkuda Ali v Jayaratne* (n 75).

[80] *R v Metropolitan Police Commissioner* (n 75).

[81] Ch 16 in this volume (Bailey).

[82] For a prior discussion of the hortatory function of law (albeit in the context of private rather than public law), see PS Atiyah, 'From Principles to Pragmatism: Changes in the Function of the Judicial Process and the Law' (1980) 65 *Iowa Law Review* 1249.

[83] *Padfield v Minister of Agriculture, Fisheries and Food* [1968] AC 997 (HL).

[84] The Act that *Padfield* was concerned with, the Agricultural Marketing Act 1958, was consolidating legislation.

This legislation had been passed in order to 'prepare the way for the social control of agricultural marketing'.[85] Agricultural marketing boards have been credited with addressing problems in the marketing of agricultural produce including the disparity between 'farm gate' and shop prices, and relatedly, the weak bargaining position of farmers.[86] This was, however, accomplished at a price in terms of substantial restrictions on the liberty of farmers to sell their produce on the open market. The schemes were voluntary only in terms of their establishment; once agreed, the boards had very substantial compulsory powers. These varied with each individual scheme, but all boards had punitive powers of enforcement. In the pre-war period, these had been, as Self and Storing point out, 'frequently attacked as wrong in principle and unfairly administered in practice',[87] although this view was rejected by an official inquiry.[88] As with the later development of new institutions constructed in light of developing political and economic theories in the planned economy and the organisation of industry,[89] many of which were well in place by the 1960s,[90] the courts found themselves in unfamiliar territory, navigating a new socio-economic environment grounded in a changing constitutional understanding.

Seen in this context, the issue in *Padfield* was whether these 'domestic executive tribunals' (as they had been characterised by Lord Maugham[91]) were subject to legal standards of administrative justice in their area of operation. As Sunkin shows in his chapter,[92] the south-eastern farmers had a credible case that neither their interests nor the public interest as a whole were served by the scheme. But by the operation of the scheme itself, the south-eastern farmers lacked an effective forum to make their case. Representation on the board itself meant that any suggestion for increasing the price paid to the south-eastern farmers at the expense of other regions would always be blocked. Their only hope lay in a committee of investigation which the Agricultural Marketing Act empowered the Minister to establish.

Everyone who heard the case recognised that the Minister's discretion in deciding whether to establish this committee was constrained by law. Even the

[85] HJ Wadleigh, 'The British Agricultural Marketing Act' (1932) 14 *American Journal of Agricultural Economics* 558.

[86] P Self and HJ Storing, *The State and the Farmer* (Berkeley, University of California Press, 1963) ch 4.

[87] ibid 102.

[88] *Report of the Departmental Committee on the Imposition of Penalties by Marketing Boards and Other Similar Bodies* (Cmd 5980, 1939).

[89] McLean describes 'corporatism, as it was practiced in Britain' as reliant upon intermediaries (e.g. advisory committees), embracing discretion and resisting codification, and facilitated by an absence of US-style formality in rule-making: J McLean, *Searching for the State in British Legal Thought: Competing Conceptions of the Public Sphere* (Cambridge, CUP, 2012) 247–48.

[90] See Ch 3 in this volume, section VII (Thomas) (emphasising the post-war consensus and the debates of the 1950s as of underappreciated significance).

[91] *Rowell v Platt* [1938] AC 101, 113; Schwartz, *Law and the Executive in Britain* (1949) 97–98.

[92] Ch 4 in this volume (Sunkin).

Solicitor General conceded that the Minister could not simply toss the letter of complaint into the bin, unopened.[93] At the same time, the House of Lords also rejected Lord Denning's view in the Court of Appeal, that the Minister had a duty to refer every genuine complaint worthy of investigation to a committee.[94] Instead, they steered a middle ground of institutional partnership. *Padfield* is now remembered for the proposition that a minister's discretion must be exercised in accordance with the object and purposes of the Act. More important, however, was the fact that in so holding, Lord Reid was not rejecting the new approach to administration or the ability of the Minister to adapt statutory policy to the needs of the moment. He was, rather, upholding the power of the courts, even against a minister, to determine and enforce the limits set by Parliament on the extent to which 'policy' could be adapted to the needs of the moment: 'the policy and objects of the Act must be determined by construing the Act as a whole and construction is always a matter of law for the Court'.[95]

As Sunkin recounts,[96] two factors were of particular significance for the majority in understanding the object and purpose of the Act: first, the importance of protecting the interests of producers, over whom the scheme (as noted above) gave far-reaching powers, which might be used to their (or others) detriment; second, the enactment by Parliament of a scheme of 'safeguards' against misuse of power by the board, of which the power to appoint a committee of investigation was a key part. The majority was, in effect, holding, that these safeguards could not be circumvented simply because the Minister's own assessment of *his* interests led him to do so; the interests that must be advanced in all aspects of the scheme had, albeit implicitly and in broad terms, already been laid down by Parliament, and must be followed.

These elements of *Padfield* are similar to *Anisminic*, but as Sunkin also demonstrates in his chapter, *Padfield* goes beyond *Anisminic* in shaping a culture of active institutional partnership. Parliamentary scrutiny of executive action has long been a central pillar of political accountability in the UK's constitution, and one of the reasons the rise of dynamic administration shaped so much anxiety was that it was perceived as having rendered traditional procedures of Parliamentary control much less effective, as section II discussed in more detail. *Padfield* must be read as a response to this anxiety. The judicial process it envisaged provided a measure of supervision, as *Anisminic* would also later do, and a measure of redress, as both *Conway* and *Ridge* later secured.

But *Padfield* also hints at a stronger role for the judiciary in ensuring that institutional accountability is achieved, a role that has become more significant as the task of governance has become more complex. The chapters in this

[93] *Padfield v Minister of Agriculture, Fisheries and Food* [1968] AC 997 (CA) 1006 (Lord Denning MR).

[94] ibid.

[95] *Padfield* (n 83) 1030.

[96] Ch 4 in this volume (Sunkin).

volume by Anthony and Nason demonstrate that where 'gaps' become apparent in the institutional architecture, the task of finding legal solutions has become a feature of modern judicial review. In effect, judicial supervision has become one part of a set of accountability and scrutiny mechanisms, which Prosser, writing about how the management of public finances and the economy developed throughout the twentieth century, described as a 'fragmented rather than networked' set of controls.[97] Within this network, the judicial process can be understood as not just delivering legal accountability, but as also pursuing a broader end of ensuring that statutory tools and institutions should are self-reflective and politically accountable. This is the hortatory task of judicial review, whereby the judiciary outlines to administrative officials the principles which they are expected to uphold, and highlights that if they fail to do so then they 'must be prepared to face the music in Parliament'.[98] This understanding of active institutional partnership between judiciary, Parliament and executive represents perhaps the most distinctive dimension of the Quartet's vision of the core, and of the type of relationship between legal and political accountability that it envisaged judicial review facilitating.

IV. THE QUARTET AND THE REAL ARGUMENT ABOUT JUDICIAL REVIEW

Let us, in conclusion, return to the point with which this concluding chapter – and the volume as a whole – began. What can we learn that is of value to the current challenges facing judicial review from a closer engagement with the four foundational cases on which it is built, and the manner in which they sought to respond to the shifts in the forms, practice and culture of administration in the UK in the course of the twentieth century? In this concluding section, we argue that there are three points, in particular, on which revisiting the origins of judicial review sheds important new light. These points relate to issues that are of fundamental importance to judicial review, but which on the whole receive inadequate consideration in modern judicial review doctrine.

The first of these relates to the tasks of judicial review. In the modern context, it is far from uncommon to see judicial review criticised for overstepping its bounds and occupying areas that are more properly the domain of other branches of the state. As this volume has shown, however, the rise of judicial review was prompted by a context and factors that challenged views very similar to these in relation to institutional roles. The generally accepted core of the constitutional tradition made it hard to accept a situation in which the administrative branch was wholly self-policing and self-supervising. Given this view, the practical hurdles to Parliamentary supervision created by the rise of dynamic

[97] T Prosser, *The Economic Constitution* (Oxford, OUP, 2014) 251–53.
[98] *Padfield* (n 83) 1061F.

administration, and the hurdles that the doctrinal canon had erected to judicial intervention, made some form of change necessary.

Against this background, the changes brought about by the Quartet can be seen as – and, more importantly, were at the time seen as – interventions to defend the core of the constitutional tradition. Section III outlined the themes that ran through the Quartet. Those themes, however, also have implications for how we conceive of the tasks of judicial review in the present day. Section III discussed these tasks and the manner in which the Quartet articulated and sought to discharge them. Table 19.2 below presents a summary of the four key tasks, and the role they envisage for the judiciary.

Table 19.2 The functions of judicial review

Task	Nature of the judicial role
Vindicatory	Policing against wrongs and protecting the private person against wrongful intrusion by dynamic administration
Mediatory	Bringing into dialogue and resolving conflicts between conflicting constitutionalisms and expectations of the power and obligations of government
Hortatory	Engaging in a process of institutional dialogue to develop principles of good governance and the constitutional obligations and expectations of administrative authorities
Executory	Enforcing and implementing decisions of policy taken by the legislature, or by an executive authority with policy-making priority, against other administrative authorities

As the Quartet also illustrates, these tasks should be seen not as alternate goals, but as mutually reinforcing tasks, each of which will assume greater or lesser priority in different contexts. There are individual cases in which they will pull in different directions, but the task of administrative law doctrine – a task the Quartet began but which remains unfinished – is to formulate ways of identifying which task is most salient in a particular situation, and when one takes priority over the other. The Quartet itself was far from perfect in achieving this. *Conway*, for example, has been criticised in this volume for its lack of attention to the hortatory function of administrative law. Rather than guide the administration towards a more sensitive approach to balancing competing aspects of the public interest, its effect was to take the balancing decision out of the hands of administrators entirely.[99] Nor is this volume alone in levying this critique. The shortcomings of such an approach were perceived at the time by commentators such as JDB Mitchell who, comparing the English approach unfavourably with that of the Conseil D'État, criticised 'the lack of response to needs which were

[99] Ch 5 in this volume (Arvind and Stirton).

perceived'.[100] Lacking what he calls a 'coherent philosophy'[101] or 'a firm basis of discipline or principle'[102] the House of Lords was capable only of an inelegant solution which he goes on, 'was rightly rejected out of hand on grounds of clear principle by the Conseil d'Etat, when evolving a satisfactory way of dealing with the problem'.[103]

Other cases, such as *Padfield*, had considerably more success in dealing appropriately with this plurality of tasks, and case law suggests that the judiciary remains aware of the competing demands of the different tasks and of the challenge of identifying factors that accentuate the importance of one or more of them in a particular context. In *Bank Mellat*, for example, Lord Reed in his judgment argued that although applying the common law duty of procedural fairness would contribute to good administration, it was 'apparent that Parliament has given priority to other competing considerations'. The function of the courts was not to 'to rewrite the scheme intended by Parliament'.[104] The fact that this point marked a difference between Lord Reed and Lord Sumption in that case underscores the importance of developing doctrines and approaches to assist the courts in the task of balancing these functions, and it points to an important issue for administrative law scholarship in the coming years.

The challenge of finding a balance between the different tasks of judicial review also points to a second issue, namely, the tension between monistic and multifarious accounts of the principles and goals implicit in judicial review. Public law theory, like legal theory more generally, has a tendency to postulate relatively monistic, monolithic and high-level principles when it discusses the underpinnings of administrative law. These understandings are particularly unpersuasive in some of the contexts discussed in this volume, including consociational Northern Ireland[105] and postcolonial Commonwealth jurisdictions.[106]

As chapter one discussed, the Quartet does not directly set out the understanding of the rule of law on which it relies. The discussion in this volume and in this chapter has, however, suggested that the conception of the rule of law on which it rests is considerably more multifarious than the monistic accounts that dominate legal theory might allow. A vision of judicial review that encompasses as diverse a range of tasks as the Quartet's vision did necessarily requires a greater wealth, and diversity, of principles than a monistic theory of judicial review can support.

[100] Mitchell (n 1) 168.
[101] ibid 168.
[102] ibid 168.
[103] ibid 168.
[104] *Bank Mellat v Her Majesty's Treasury (no 2)* [2013] UKSC 39; [2014] AC 700 [63].
[105] Ch 12 in this volume (Anthony).
[106] Ch 15 in this volume, section IV.E (Cane); See also L Stirton and M Lodge, 'Constitutional Legacies in Politics and Administration: Jamaica's Incomplete Settlement' (2020) 71 *Northern Ireland Legal Quarterly* 233.

Underpinning all of this is the goal, implicit in the Quartet, of creating a set of institutional arrangements through which judicial review underpins an active institutional partnership between judiciary, legislature and executive. It would not be unfair to say that this vision has been at the very most only partially realised in the years since the Quartet. As chapter one discusses in more detail, judges are typically seen either as constitutional actors in their own right or as agents of Parliament. Judges themselves are at pains to emphasise the latter role, especially when dealing with controversial subjects. Yet, arguably, partnership is essential if public law is to play a productive role in creating both an administrative law and an administrative culture which is naturally inclined towards a proper balance between the different tasks and principles outlined above, and towards striking this balance in a manner that respects both the needs of the administration and the values, goals and expectations of private persons. Although the renewed interest in 'good administration' as a value underpinning judicial review might enhance partnership of this nature,[107] the effects of an adverse judicial review on an authority, in terms of improving the quality of administration, remain all too unclear.[108]

It is hard to avoid the conclusion that administrative law's continuing failure to secure a coherent vision of how such a partnership would operate is due in part to the other two failures discussed in this section. In other words, a coherent vision has not been arrived at because of a misguided focus on monistic and dichotomised approaches to the role and functions of the judiciary (which, necessarily, pigeonholes them as either actors or agents), and the continued role of what this volume has described as 'institutional insulation' between the judiciary and the administration. It is perhaps telling that the partially expert composition of the Conseil d'État comprising senior administrators as well as judges, and which was so heavily praised by Mitchell, was designed in such a way as to overcome the problem of institutional insulation. It was designed to provide a broader perspective both on the multifarity of constitutional principles underpinning administrative government and on ways of balancing the range of tasks which any system of judicial review must discharge.

This, in the ultimate analysis, is the real argument about judicial review. The challenge is to devise ways to prioritise and where possible reconcile the different tasks it must accomplish, to create a theoretical and evaluative framework that can accommodate the multifarity of principles and ideas to which it must have regard, and to develop an idea of, and arrangements for, active institutional partnership of the type that can overcome institutional insulation and promote

[107] P Daly, 'Administrative Law: A Values-Based Approach' in J Bell, M Elliott, J Varuhas and P Murray (eds), *Public Law Adjudication in Common Law Systems: Process and Substance* (Oxford, Hart, 2016); on judicial recognition of the point in Ireland, see H Biehler, 'Upholding standards in public decision-making: getting the balance right' (2017) 57 *Irish Jurist (ns)* 94.

[108] See the contributions in M Hertogh and S Halliday (eds), *Judicial Review and Bureaucratic Impact: International and Interdisciplinary Perspectives* (Cambridge, CUP, 2004).

institutional dialogue between the judiciary and the other branches of government. Stressing the need to articulate such a vision has been an important goal of this volume, and the extent to which the movement towards such a vision was central to the early history of modern judicial review is a fitting lesson for public law scholarship to learn from the Quartet 50 years after the origins of modern judicial review.

Index

www.ingramcontent.com/pod-product-compliance
Lightning Source LLC
Chambersburg PA
CBHW071306180926
51613CB00001B/144
9781509930333

THE HISTORY AND THEORY OF INTERNATIONAL LAW

The Battle for International Law

THE HISTORY AND THEORY OF INTERNATIONAL LAW

General Editors

NEHAL BHUTA
Chair in International Law, University of Edinburgh

ANTHONY PAGDEN
Distinguished Professor, University of California Los Angeles

BENJAMIN STRAUMANN
Alberico Gentili Senior Fellow, New York University School of Law

In the past few decades the understanding of the relationship between nations has undergone a radical transformation. The role of the traditional nation-state is diminishing, along with many of the traditional vocabularies which were once used to describe what has been called, ever since Jeremy Bentham coined the phrase in 1780, 'international law'. The older boundaries between states are growing ever more fluid, new conceptions and new languages have emerged which are slowly coming to replace the image of a world of sovereign independent nation states which has dominated the study of international relations since the early nineteenth century. This redefinition of the international arena demands a new understanding of classical and contemporary questions in international and legal theory. It is the editors' conviction that the best way to achieve this is by bridging the traditional divide between international legal theory, intellectual history, and legal and political history. The aim of the series, therefore, is to provide a forum for historical studies, from classical antiquity to the twenty-first century, that are theoretically-informed and for philosophical work that is historically conscious, in the hope that a new vision of the rapidly evolving international world, its past and its possible future, may emerge.

PREVIOUSLY PUBLISHED IN THIS SERIES

The New Histories of International Criminal Law
Retrials
Edited by Immi Tallgren and Thomas Skouteris

Sovereignty
A Contribution to the Theory of Public and International Law
Hermann Heller, edited and introduced by David Dyzenhaus

The Battle for International Law

South-North Perspectives on the Decolonization Era

Edited by

JOCHEN VON BERNSTORFF

PHILIPP DANN

Assistant Editor

MAX H. MAYER

OXFORD
UNIVERSITY PRESS

OXFORD
UNIVERSITY PRESS

Great Clarendon Street, Oxford, OX2 6DP,
United Kingdom

Oxford University Press is a department of the University of Oxford.
It furthers the University's objective of excellence in research, scholarship,
and education by publishing worldwide. Oxford is a registered trade mark of
Oxford University Press in the UK and in certain other countries

First Edition published in 2019

Published in the United States of America by Oxford University Press
198 Madison Avenue, New York, NY 10016, United States of America

British Library Cataloguing in Publication Data
Data available

Library of Congress Control Number: 2019941484

ISBN 978–0–19–884963–6

Series Editor's Preface

In a recent essay, noted intellectual historian Samuel Moyn observes that in the explosion of recent work in the history of international law, the 'historiographical interest in the continuity of [international law's] imperial entanglements' has dwarfed the examination of the period of the 'decolonization of international law' that took place between 1950 and 1970.[1] The eighteenth and nineteenth century transformations of a European public law in to a universal legal order had, as Hegel well-understood, entailed the subordination and incorporation of vast numbers of peoples not-yet-able to conform to the political and social mores of European public law, into empires.[2] But between 1950 and 1970, an epoch-making transformation of international society took place: several intercontinental empires dissolved into dozens of new nation-states, at the outset through violent and often brutal conflicts between colonizer and colonized,[3] and then by a rapid 'delegitimization of any kind of political rule that is experienced as a subjugation' of a population by alien occupants.[4] The result, as Jörg Fisch observes, was that while hitherto trusteeship and colonial domination in international law had been seen as serving the advancement of progress, 'Colonial domination was [made] illegitimate per se and therefore had to be eliminated as quickly as possible . . . now colonialism prevented the development of colonial peoples'.[5] Between 1945 and 1965, sixty-seven new states were admitted as members of the United Nations (UN), transforming its membership from overwhelmingly western and European to Asian, African, and Latin American by a substantial majority. In 1960 alone, seventeen new states joined the UN, sixteen from Africa.

The result of this revolution in the membership of the society of states had immense consequences for the content of international law. Jansen and Osterhammel note that decolonization challenged the 'conceptual underpinnings of the

[1] Samuel Moyn, 'The High Tide of Anti-colonial Legalism,' *Journal of the History of International Law*, forthcoming, at note 14.

[2] Hegel, *Elements of the Philosophy of Right* (Allen W. Wood, ed) (Cambridge University Press, 1991), 367–371.

[3] Famously accounted for in Hegelian and psychoanalytic terms as a negation of a negation, by Frantz Fanon. Fanon, *The Wretched of the Earth*: 'Decolonization is the meeting of two forces, opposed to each other by their very nature, which in fact owe their originality to that sort of substantification which results from and is nourished by the situation in the colonies. . . . Decolonization is the veritable creation of new men. But this creation owes nothing of its legitimacy to any supernatural power; the 'thing' which has been colonized becomes man during the same process by which it frees itself.' (Farrington, trans. Grove Press, New York, 1963) 36–37.

[4] Jan C Jansen and Jürgen Osterhammel, *Decolonization: A Short History* (Princeton, 2017), 1–2.

[5] Jörg Fisch, *The Right of Self-Determination of Peoples: The Domestication of an Illusion* (Anita Mage, trans. Cambridge, 2015) 205.

international order'.[6] It delegitimized colonialism and racism at the level of international society, and also 'contributed greatly to the process that gradually made the principle of national state sovereignty absolute and uncontestable'.[7] But as Getachew has recently argued, it would be a mistake to understand decolonization as limited to state-making and thus simply reproducing the logic of international law as *jus intergentes*. Rather, *through* international law and international institutions, anti-colonial nationalists pursued both state-making *and* 'worldmaking': 'rather than foreclosing internationalism, the effort to achieve national independence propelled a rethinking of state sovereignty, inspired a far-reaching reconstitution of the postwar international order, and grounded the twentieth century's most ambitious vision of global redistribution.'[8]

It is the history of this period of attempted worldmaking in and through a struggle over international law, that this important collection of essays begins to tell. The editors contend that the period from 1950 to 1970 should be seen as a '*Sattelzeit*,' invoking Koselleck's well-known term. Enigmatic in both English ('saddle-time') and German, the concept connoted Koselleck's theory that a certain period of European history was formative for the emergence of modernity because it was in this time that 'a broad series of political concepts acquired their current meanings, and that both defined and reflected the fundamental experiences'[9] of the present. In the story that emerges from the chapters of this volume, decolonization and the rise of the Third World, under the structuring conditions of US-Soviet enmity, resulted in an ambitious attempt to reformulate an international law that had hitherto been a handmaiden of imperial designs, challenging and revising key concepts in international law in ways that registered the imperatives of the post-colonial states. 'The verbal vendetta against the so-called European international law makes sense,' wrote UpendraBaxi in a 1973 essay, 'only as an articulation of the powerful urge felt by emancipated nations for self-assertion as a pre-condition for an international egalitarian order.'[10] But, he noted, 'all emancipated nations are groomed in, and have an interest in the corpus of international law as developed in the preceding three centuries.'[11] The belief in the possibility of international law under transformed global political, economic and legal conditions, is one that deeply shaped the imaginary of international law even in the west after 1960.

The volume proceeds with chapters on key sites, concepts, and individual protagonists, delineating the contours of the battlelines in respect of terms such as the

[6] Jansen and Osterhammel, 153.

[7] Ibid.

[8] AdomGetachew, *Worldmaking after Empire—The Rise and Fall of Self-Determination* (Princeton, 2019) 3.

[9] George S Williamson, 'Retracing the *Sattelzeit*: Thoughts on the Historiography of the French Revolutionary and Napoleonic Eras,' *Central European History* 51 (2018) 66–74, 68.

[10] UpendraBaxi, 'Some Remarks on Eurocentrism and the Law of Nations' in RP Anand, ed, *Asian States and the Development of International Law* (Vikas, Delhi, 1973) 5.

[11] Ibid 7.

common heritage of human kind, acquired rights, *jus ad bellum* and permanent sovereignty over natural resources, and institutions such as the ICJ and the World Bank. The picture which emerges is necessarily incomplete, as this impressive volume of collected essays represents an important starting point for a whole new *oeuvre* of history that begins to pull more determinedly at specific threads of the stories that are gathered together here. One implication is clear, though: the period 1950 to 1970, which was at once the epoch of Cold War and decolonization, was anything but a hiatus of international law making.[12] It was,if anything, a period of surprising anticipation of the potential to forge a new global order of economic and political justice, within and through an international legal order of co-existence *and* cooperation: sovereign equality and non-intervention were to be buttressed, and go hand in hand, with state-led economic development and an internationalized welfarism epitomized in the plan for a New International Economic Order.[13]

Oddly, this quite-recent past seems in many ways stranger to us than earlier epochs—such as the early modern European contexts of the reinvention of the *jus gentium* and the *jus naturale*, the historiography of which is more established. As Moyn suggests in his essay mentioned above, less than seventy years after decolonization began to gather force and speed, it now requires some effort to recover the intelligibility of the hopes and illusions that characterized the 'long transition from imperial to cosmopolitan dreams.'[14] This could be because, as Dann and von Bernstorff as well as Moyn point out, the dreams of an egalitarian post-colonial order in global law and politics steadily retreated, not due to a re-embrace of direct imperial and colonial rule, but through a radical recasting of both former imperial and postcolonial states' relationship to economic governance.[15] But the legal and political concepts of Dann and von Bernstorff's international legal *Sattelzeit* remain very much part of our experience of the international legal order, even as they appear now the subject of a new and more centripetal battle over their content and order-giving possibilities. If we are to have a chance of grasping what is at stake in the present contestation, we need to better understand the battles that went before.

Nehal Bhuta
Edinburgh
July 2019

[12] On the critique of Cold War as hiatus, see: Matt Craven, Sundhya Pahuja, and Gerry Simpson, 'Reading and Unreading: Historiographies of Hiatus', in Craven, Pahuja and Simpson (eds) *International Law and the Cold War* (Cambridge University Press, 2019).

[13] See the special issue of *Humanity* on 'The New International Economic Order,' Volume 6, Issue 1 (2015).

[14] Moyn, 'The High Tide of Anti-colonial legalism', p 7.

[15] See now the new locus classicus, Quinn Slobodan, *The Globalists: The End of Empire and the Birth of Neo-Liberalism* (Harvard, 2018).

Table of Contents

B. Institutions

II. INDIVIDUAL PROTAGONISTS AND REGIONAL PERSPECTIVES

A. Individual Protagonists

B. Regional Perspectives

List of Contributors

Bethania Assy, Professor, Pontifical Catholic University of Rio de Janeiro

Olivier Barsalou, Assistant Professor, Université du Québec à Montréal

Jochen von Bernstorff, Professor, University of Tübingen

Bill Bowring, Professor, Birkbeck College, University of London

Anna Brunner, Judge, Regional Court of Ingolstadt

Matthew Craven, Professor, SOAS University of London

Philipp Dann, Professor, Humboldt-University Berlin

Luis Eslava, Reader, University of Kent

Christopher Gevers, Lecturer, University of KwaZulu-Natal

Rotem Giladi, Lecturer, University of Helsinki

Florian Hoffmann, Professor, Pontifical Catholic University of Rio de Janeiro

Martti Koskenniemi, Professor, University of Helsinki

Carl Landauer, Attorney, Axiom Global Inc.

Umut Özsu, Associate Professor, Carleton University

Sundhya Pahuja, Professor, University of Melbourne

Surabhi Ranganathan, University Lecturer, University of Cambridge

Anna Saunders, MPhil Candidate, University of Melbourne

Guy Fiti Sinclair, Senior Lecturer, Victoria University Wellington

Prabhakar Singh, Associate Professor, Jindal Global Law School

Muthucumaraswamy Sornarajah, Professor, National University of Singapore

Emmanuelle Tourme Jouannet, Professor, Science Po

Ingo Venzke, Professor, University of Amsterdam

List of Abbreviations

AA	Afro-Asian
AD	Anno Domini
AFROSEC	Afro-Asian Organization for Economic Cooperation
AIDS	Acquired Immune Deficiency Syndrome
AJIL	American Journal of International Law
ANC	African National Congress
ARAMCO	Arabian American Oil Company
ASSR	Autonomous Socialist Soviet Republic
BIS	Bank for International Settlements
BIT	Bilateral Investment Treaty
BSAC	British South Africa Company
CDDH	Notification system of the Conférence Diplomatique sur la Réaffirmation et le développement du Droit International Humanitaire Applicable dans les Conflits Armés
CEPAL	Comisión Económica para América Latina y el Caribe
CERD	United Nations Committee for the Elimination of Racial Discrimination
CHM	Common Heritage of Mankind
CIA	Central Intelligence Agency
CSCE	Conference on Security and Cooperation in Europe
CTC	Counter-Terrorism Committee
DoS	Department of State
ECLAC	Economic Commission for Latin America and the Caribbean
ECOSOC	United Nations Economic and Social Council
EEC	European Economic Community
EJIL	European Journal of International Law
EPTA	Expanded Programme for Technical Assistance
ESC	European Social Charter
EU	European Union
FCN treaty	Treaty of Friendship, Commerce and Navigation
FFI	French Forces of the Interior
FLN	Front de Libération Nationale
G77	Group of 77
GA	General Assembly
GATT	General Agreement on Tariffs and Trade
GDP	Gross Domestic Product
GEP	Group of Eminent Persons
GNP	Gross National Product
HIV	Human Immunodeficiency Virus
IBRD	International Bank for Reconstruction and Development

ICAO	International Civial Aviation Organisation
ICC	International Criminal Court
ICCPR	International Covenant on Civil and Political Rights
ICERD	Convention on the Elimination of All Forms of Racial Discrimination
ICESCR	International Covenant on Economic, Social and Cultural Rights
ICJ	International Court of Justice
ICJ Rep	International Court of Justice Reports of Judgements, Advisory Opinions and Orders
ICLQ	International and Comparative Law Quarterly
ICRC	International Committee of the Red Cross
ICSID	International Centre for Settlement of Investment Disputes
IDA	International Development Association
IFAD	International Fund for Agricultural Development
IFC	International Finance Corporation
IFI	International Financial Institutions
IHL	International Humanitarian Law
ILC	International Law Commission
ILCA	International Law and Colonialism in Africa
ILM	International Legal Materials
ILO	International Labour Organization
ILR	International Law Reports
IMF	International Monetary Fund
IO	International Organisation
IPJET	International Platform of Jurists for East Timor
ISA	International Seabed Authority
ISI	Import Substitution Industrialization
ISIs	Import Substitution Industrialization Strategies
ITO	International Trade Organization
LGDJ	Librairie générale de droit et de jurisprudence
LSE	London School of Economics
MNC	Multinational Corporation
NAM	Non-Aligned Movement
NATO	North Atlantic Treaty Organization
NGO	Non-Governmental Organization
NIEO	New International Economic Order
NLR	Nigerian Law Review
NY	New York
OAS	Organization of American States
OAU	Organization of African Unity
OECD	Organisation for Economic Cooperation and Development
ONU	Organisation des Nations Unies
ONUC	Opération des Nations unies au Congo
OPEC	Organization of the Petroleum Exporting Countries
OPIC	Overseas Private Investment Corporation
PAC	Pan African Congress

PCIJ	Permanent Court of International Justice
PLO	Palestine Liberation Organisation
PSNR	Permanent Sovereignty of Natural Resources
RIIA	Royal Institute of International Affairs
RPSNR	Resolution on the Permanent Sovereignty over Natural Resources
RSFSR	Russian Soviet Federated Socialist Republic
SUNFED	Special United Nations Fund for Economic Development
SWAPO	South West African Peoples Organisation
TAB	Technical Assistance Board
TRC	Truth and Reconciliation Commission
TW	Third World
TWAIL	Third World Approaches to International Law
UAS	Union of African States
UDHR	Universal Declaration on Human Rights
UK	United Kingdom
UN	United Nations
UNCIO	United Nations Conference on International Organization
UNCLOS	United Nations Convention on the Law of the Sea
UNCTAD	United Nations Conference on Trade and Development
UNCTC	United Nations Centre on Transnational Corporations
UNDP	United Nations Development Programme
UNEF	United Nations Emergency Force
UNESCO	United Nations Educational, Scientific and Cultural Organization
UNGA	United Nations General Assembly
UNIDO	United Nations Industrial Development Organization
UNITAR	United Nations Institute for Training and Research
UNDP	United Nations Development Programme
UNSC	United Nations Security Council
UNSG	United Nations Secretary General
UNTAET	UN Transitional Administration in East Timor
UNTAG	UN Transition Assistance Group
UNTS	United Nations Treaty Series
UNTSO	United Nations Truce Supervision Organization
US	United States
USAID	United States Agency for International Development
USSR	Union of Soviet Socialist Republics
VCLT	Vienna Convention on the Law of Treaties
VCSSPAD	Vienna Convention on Succession of States in respect of State Property, Archives and Debts
WB	World Bank
WEO	World Economic Outlook
WIPO	World Intellectual Property Organization
WSOY	Werner Söderström Osakeyhtiö
WTO	World Trade Organization
ZANU	Zimbabwe African National Union

The Battle for International Law

An Introduction

Jochen von Bernstorff and Philipp Dann

I. Introduction

On 14 December 1960, five years after the Bandung Conference, the UN General Assembly (UNGA) with an overwhelming majority of 89 votes did 'solemnly proclaim(s) the necessity of bringing to a speedy and unconditional end colonialism in all its forms and manifestations'.[1] No state voted against the resolution, but all of the still-existing colonial powers, including the US, abstained. By the mid-1970s more than two-thirds of the world's population lived in 'newly independent states' having emerged from the former Western and Asian Empires, increasing the absolute number of states dramatically from fifty-one in 1945 to 144 in 1975.[2] This meant not just a numerical change. Instead, the decolonization era came with a fundamental challenge to (legalized) Western hegemony through a new vision of the institutional environment and political economy of the world. It is during this era, which arguably was couched between classic European imperialism and a new form of US-led Western hegemony, that fundamental legal debates took place over a new international legal order for a decolonized world. In fact, this book argues that this era presents, in essence, a battle that was fought out by diplomats, lawyers, and scholars, particularly over the premises and principles of international law. In a moment of relative weakness of European powers, 'newly independent states', and international lawyers from the South fundamentally challenged traditional Western perceptions of international legal structures.

In the words of George Abi-Saab, who himself became a protagonist in this endeavour, the third world rejected

> the traditional view staunchly held in Western quarters, that a new State is born in a legal universe that binds it, newly independent Third World States started

[1] Declaration of the Granting of Independence to Colonial Countries and Peoples, UNGA Res 1514 (XV) (14 December 1960) UN Doc A/RES/1514(XV); for the voting record, see UN Doc A/PV.947, GAOR 15th Session, 1273–74.

[2] See 'Growth in United Nations Membership, 1945–present' <https://www.un.org/en/sections/member-states/growth-united-nations-membership-1945-present/index.html> accessed 6 August 2019.

Jochen von Bernstorff and Philipp Dann, *The Battle for International Law: An Introduction* In: *The Battle for International Law: South-North Perspectives on the Decolonization Era.* Edited by: Jochen von Bernstorff and Philipp Dann, Oxford University Press (2019).
DOI: 10.1093/oso/9780198849636.003.0001

> by contesting the alleged universality and legitimacy of the international legal system: a system developed without their participation and used to justify their subjugation; an unjust system, for whilst formally based on sovereign equality and hence reciprocity, in actuality it works in one direction and in favour of one side only; and finally an antiquated system that does not correspond to contemporary conditions and their specific needs.[3]

International law was at the centre of these decolonization struggles, constituting for third-world international lawyers both an emancipatory promise and manifestation of colonial subjugation, and for Western internationalists a well-known but now threatened order. Up until the early 1950s, international law had been a discursive structure clearly dominated by Western speakers and upheld through communications of diplomats, scholars, and other institutional and individual actors. This language of international law was in itself unstable and highly indeterminate. It was structurally shaped by its nineteenth-century legacy of differentiating between the 'civilized' Europeans (the centre) and the others—the 'non-civilized' at the periphery—even though the standard of civilization as such had increasingly fallen into disrepute in the first half of the twentieth century.[4] That international law was a central battlefield for a new world order was at the same time surprising as well as expected. It was perhaps surprising in that international law in the eyes of many protagonists was somewhat discredited as a mechanism enshrining the old order, to fortify and justify it as a just and necessary structure. Law was hence seen as a powerful tool of subjugation. At the same time, for many of the governments and scholars, international law was also the central medium to achieve a fundamental reform of the old order, to remedy substantive injustices through peaceful cooperation. It nonetheless remained one of the central problems and in a way paradoxical that the third world saw itself compelled to fight the battle within the normative language of the colonizers, that is—within international law.

With greater numbers of new states gaining formal independence during this era international law was fundamentally challenged on various levels: new voices from the third world appeared on the scene and became part of international legal discourse.[5] Formal independence from the metropoles as a political event made some of these voices heard in the centre, provoking counter-reactions and thus opened the 'battle' for international law. Others remained marginalized and continued to be silenced and unheard outside of their local and domestic contexts. Some of these new voices asked for a new international law to be a 'clean slate'

[3] Georges Abi-Saab, 'The Third World Intellectual in Praxis: Confrontation, Participation, or Operation Behind Enemy Lines?' (2016) 37 Third World Quarterly 1957, 1958–59.

[4] Gerrit W Gong, *The Standard of Civilization in International Society* (Clarendon Press 1984); Antony Anghie, *Imperialism, Sovereignty and the Making of International Law* (CUP 2008) ch 2 and 3, especially pp 109–10 and 182–94 (hereafter Anghie, *Imperialism*).

[5] On these voices, see the contributions to this volume in Part II. A.

and to govern the relationship between peoples and human beings on this globe beyond the existing Western order, which they rejected, claiming that the new participants could not be bound by a system created without them—or even with the apparent intention of subjugating them. Other protagonists wanted the third world to 'enter' the existing discursive structures based on the concept of equal state-sovereignty, taking a (sometimes more, sometimes less radical) reformist approach to the concepts, rules, and principles traditionally subsumed under the term international law by the centre.

These voices pulled various sites and fields into the discursive battle that was international law—fields as diverse as were the main protagonists and their strategies: negotiations on new fundamental multilateral treaties[6] were turned into battle-sites. In addition, central concepts of existing international law such as sovereignty, non-intervention, and self-determination, as well as the main tenets of international economic law, were subject to significant controversy within and outside of the United Nations (UN).[7]

These debates and their third-world international legal protagonists, as well as the new embattled concepts, have often been portrayed as a short-lived Southern or socialist (Cold War-) revolt within UNGA with ultimately minor and negligible implications for international law and legal scholarship. As the contributions to this volume show, nothing could be more mistaken. Not only that the outcome of this battle has fundamentally shaped what we presently conceive of as international legal structures. With hindsight, we hold that international legal structures in many areas of international relations have been transformed during this era, albeit with the effect of enabling a transition from classic European imperialism to new forms of US-led Western hegemony. The underlying aspirations, strategies, and failures of this battle thus are of vital importance for any future project aiming to address and alter the relationship between international law and fundamental inequalities in this world.[8] In that sense, this volume attempts to provide an intellectual history of the transformation of international law in the 1950s to 1970s and to offer a better understanding of the contestations to the then-dominant perceptions of order. By doing so it aims to give the reader a better grasp of how the world became what it is today by new historical insights into the conditions, contingencies, and necessities of what led to its current depressing and desolate state. The remainder of this introduction proceeds in three steps. Section II provides a broader context of the 'decolonization era', the aspirations,

[6] For example, the two international human rights covenants, the Vienna Convention on the Law of Treaties, the Vienna Conventions on State Succession, the UN Convention on the Law of the Sea, and the two Additional Protocols to the Geneva Conventions.

[7] On different fields of battle, see the contributions to this volume in Part I.

[8] See Nils Gilman, 'The New International Economic Order: A Re-Introduction' (2015) Humanity 1 (who wonders how it came that an agenda that was seen in its time as necessary and fundamental is today almost forgotten or rejected as unrealistic).

and challenges shaping the battle for international law during this time. Section III introduces the central battle fields. Finally, Section IV looks at the protagonists of battle, that is, authors and scholarly landscapes in which they were set, as well as institutions (III.).

II. The battle period: context and characteristics

1. 1950s–1970s as *Sattelzeit*

The dominant narrative stresses the years of 1945 and 1989 as major turning points in the history of the global order and international law. We want to offer an alternative reading, highlighting the changes that begin to occur in the early 1950s as a transformative phase leading into what is called the 'decolonization era'—a period of time situated between the end of post-1885 European imperialism in the mid-1950s and the beginning of unipolar US hegemony in international relations of the 1980s and 1990s.[9] With this periodization, we argue for an alternative and less Eurocentric perspective on the history of international law.[10]

The third world quest for formal independence first culminated as a conscious and concerted 'trans-civilizational' movement with the Afro-Asian Bandung Conference in 1955[11] and lasted roughly until the mid-1970s with the Declaration on the New International Economic Order. It opened a new chapter in world history. It marked the end of classic European-led imperialism that had crystallized in the Berlin conference of 1885, when only fourteen Western states had carved up Africa without any Asian or African participation, but continued during the negotiations of the UN Charter in 1945, when mere eleven out of fifty-one negotiating states came from Africa or Asia. The post-Bandung era marked the moment in which international law, for the first time, could claim to constitute a universal legal order at least in a formal and geographical sense.[12] Beginning in 1966, sixty-one states from Africa or Asia constituted a majority within the UNGA, in which 'most of the world' (as Partha Chatterjee aptly put it[13]) were at least formally represented.

[9] On periodizations and their implicit authorization and de-authorization of different narratives and perspectives. Oliver Diggelman, 'The Periodization of the History of International Law' in Bardo Fassbender and Anne Peters (eds) *Oxford Handbook on History of International Law* (OUP 2012) 997; see also Pahuja and Saunders, Chapter 6, this volume.

[10] Pahuja and Saunders (this volume) write: 'Periodization is always an argument, never a fact'.

[11] Luis Eslava, Michael Fakhri and Vasuki Nesiah, 'Introduction' in Luis Eslava, Michael Fakhri and Vasuki Nesiah (eds) *Bandung, History and International Law: Critical Pasts and Pending Futures* (CUP 2018) (hereafter Eslava et al., 'Introduction'); Onuma Yasuaki, *A Transcivilizational Perspective on International Law: Questioning Prevalent Cognitive Frameworks in the Emerging Multi-Polar and Multi-Civilizational World of the Twenty-First Century* (Hague Academy of International Law 2010).

[12] Eslava et al., 'Introduction' (n 11).

[13] Partha Chatterjee, *Politics of the Governed: Reflections on Popular Politics in most of the World* (Columbia University Press 2004).

The three decades between the early 1950s and late 1970s connect the end of 'classic' European imperialism with the long rise of US dominance in international relations and a specific model of global capitalism, which was often called 'neo-imperialism' or 'neo-colonialism' by critical contemporary voices.[14] One could understand these years according to Koselleck's *Sattelzeit* concept[15]—the bridging of two different forms of global Western dominance—a transitional phase in which fundamental concepts of international law were re-imagined, politicized, and transformed. These debates were also influenced by the ideological and military rivalry between the US, the USSR, and China, often referred to as the Cold War. The threat of a nuclear stand-off between the US and the Soviet Union especially shaped popular and scholarly perceptions of international politics during this time, masking to an important degree the continuous rise of US economic, political, and cultural dominance in the world. According to Koselleck, such a transitional phase is marked by a change of meaning of 'constitutive' political and legal concepts. Through politicizing, contesting, and defending the content of normative structures, the politico-legal fabric is transformed and then subsists over time in a new historical era.[16] As to international law between the 1950s and 1970s these battles over meaning and new content of rules were the result of the collapse of European imperialism; at the surface, they played out in legal debates around doctrinally recognized 'sources' of international law—in new legislative projects through multilateral conventions, in disputes over changing customary law, and in discursive battles over the meaning of general principles of international law. At the same time, these discursive battles represented deeper challenges and politizations of entrenched post-1885 international legal structures and normative assumptions, such as the pervasive standard of civilization and assumed racial hierarchies. While the third world's battle for a new international law succeeded in abolishing central discursive structures created by European imperialism, it ultimately could not prevent new forms of Western domination from being established, which, in that sense, are a product of the battle for international law. Western governments and international lawyers managed in a classic hegemonic move to translate the discursive rifts created by the Third-World attacks into reforms and processes of restructuration, again portraying *Western* interests in a new world of formally independent states as *universal* interests.[17] International legal discourse and the inherent conservative bias of law as ingrained social practice was used by Western actors to counter requested revolutionary innovations as incompatible with the

[14] Kwame Nkrumah, *Neo-Colonialism: The Last Stage of Imperialism* (International Publishers 1965).

[15] Reinhart Koselleck, 'Einleitung', in Otto Brunner, Werner Conze and Reinhart Koselleck (eds), *Geschichtliche Grundbegriffe*, vol 1 (Klett-Cotta 1994) XV.

[16] ibid.

[17] Ernesto Laclau, 'Identity and Hegemony: The Role of Universality in the Constitution of Political Logics' in Judith Butler, Ernesto Laclau and Slavoj Zizek, *Contingency, Hegemony and Universality: Contemporary Dialogues on the Left* (Verso 2000) 44.

'system' or internal 'coherence' of a specific notion of 'international law'.[18] As this volume shows, this Western process of thwarting the attacks launched by the third world saw the use of further hegemonic discursive moves, including 'boundary drawing'[19] between the political and the legal,[20] international and national,[21] private and public,[22] and legal and economic aspects[23] in order to exclude revolutionary arguments from the legal battle sites. Another frequent tactic was to integrate substantive claims made by the third world in legal and policy projects under Western institutional control in order to eat up their revolutionary potential.[24] And while the standard of civilization became abolished, separate or antagonistic treatment of the new governments in the peripheries of Western powers could be argued because of them being different as 'newly independent', 'non-industrialized', 'developing', 'dysfunctional', or 'debtor' or 'socialist' states. Another hegemonic use of international law was to replace multilateralism by bilateral treaty relations in which the power asymmetry between the superpower or former metropole on the one side, and the newly independent government on the other, could be brought to bear in an unmediated fashion. All these discursive Western countermoves were supported frequently via economic and military coercion emanating from Washington and the old metropoles, rivalled only by Moscow.

2. Precursors, aspirations, and momentum

The contestation of Western colonial domination, the struggle for independent statehood and formal equality of all nations had started long before 1955.[25] However, it was only then that it actually triggered a process of liberation of most Asian and African societies from direct colonial rule. From the perspective of the colonized, neither the League of Nations nor the foundation of the UN had been a major breakthrough in their quest for independence. National self-determination at least as a proto-legal concept was on the international agenda dating at least from Wilson's famous 14 points, although it was originally a principle not conceived as

[18] Bernstorff this volume; on 'conservative or *status quo*-oriented choices' in international legal practice (Martii Koskenniemi, *From Apology to Utopia* (CUP 2006) 610).

[19] Term used by Joscha Wullweber, 'Constructing Hegemony in Global Politics: A Discourse-Theoretical Approach to Policy Analysis' (2018) 40 Administrative Theory and Praxis, relying on Laclau's concept of 'social heterogeneity; Ernesto Laclau, *On Populist Reason* (Verso 2005) 139–56.

[20] Von Bernstorff Chapter 2, this volume.

[21] Pahuja and Saunders Chapter 6, this volume.

[22] Craven Chapter 4, this volume, referring to Carl Schmitt's *Nomos of the Earth*.

[23] Sornarajah Chapter 7, this volume.

[24] Dann Chapter 12, this volume.

[25] Joge Esquirol, 'Latin America', in Bardo Fassbender and Anne Peters (eds), *The Oxford Handbook of International Law* (OUP 2012); Arnulf Becker Lorca, *Mestizo International Law* (CUP 2014) (hereafter Becker Lorca, *Mestizo International Law*).

ripe for universal application.[26] In contrast to Lenin's *The Right of Nations to Self-Determination* (1914), during the Peace Conference Wilson explicitly stated that 'it was not within the privilege of the conference of peace to act upon the right of self-determination of any peoples except those which had been included in the territories of the defeated empires'.[27]

As Mitchell and Massad demonstrate, Wilson`s approach to self-determination before and during the Peace Conference was not only a selective one but also had managed to turn Lenin's anti-colonial understanding of self-determination into an ambivalent concept that could be used for stabilizing and normalizing colonial relationships.[28] Of his famous fourteen points, the fifth promised 'a free, open minded, and absolutely impartial adjustment of all colonial claims, based upon a strict observance of the principle that in determining all such questions of sovereignty the interests of the populations concerned must have equal weight with the equitable government whose tile is to be determined'. The idea to introduce a balancing test between native 'interests' or consent and the interests of the colonizer acting as a trustee of 'civilization' had its roots in the 1885 Berlin Conference, where the US pushed for legitimation of territorial control through formalized agreements with native 'chiefs'.

During the Peace Conference it was the highly influential Jan Smuts, a South African politician and adviser to both the United Kingdom (UK) and the United States (US) government, who managed to convince Wilson to create a mandate system along these lines. Independence was an issue only for fully 'civilized' peoples—for all other populations consent and paternalistic consideration of local interests sufficed. Smuts helped to amalgamate the concept of self-determination with the older quest of white settler colonies for 'self-rule' and independence vis-a-vis the metropole within larger imperial structures.[29] Both for settler colonies and for direct forms of colonialism, the formal consent of local rulers, representing 'communities' usually set up by the colonizers for this very purpose, was supposed to strengthen the legitimacy of the colonial project.[30] When local consent was clearly absent, balancing between the interests of 'civilization' represented by the colonizer (or white settlers) and local resistance would, in the eyes of most Western international lawyers, inevitably tilt towards the colonizer. Additionally, both world organizations institutionalized supervisory structures for mandates

26 Erez Manela, *The Wilsonian Moment: Self-Determination and the International Origins of Anticolonial Nationalism* (OUP 2009); see also Barsalou and Bowring this volume.

27 On the reception of Lenin's and Wilson's diverging concepts: Joseph Massad, 'Against-Self-Determination' (2018) 9 Humanity (hereafter Massad, 'Against Self-Determination').

28 ibid; see also Timothy Mitchell, *Carbon Democracy: Political Power in the Age of Oil* (Verso 2013) (hereafter Mitchell, *Carbon Democracy*).

29 Mitchell, *Carbon Democracy* (n 28) 72; Massad, 'Against Self-Determination' (n 27).

30 Mitchell, *Carbon Democracy* (n 28) 80; see also on the British use of self-determination language in order to legitimize empire, Susan Pedersen, *The Guardians: The Legend of Nations and the Crisis of Empire* (OUP 2017) 109.

(League of Nations) and trust territories (UN) in their founding documents, based on that same balancing logic shying away from a radical break with the colonial era.[31] It found its expression in the mandate or trusteeship concept as such, which presupposes that the colonized still need the colonizer to gradually lead them to a higher Western state of 'civilization', which will then allow for self-rule and independence. In that sense, self-determination as used by European jurists had a different and much more flexible meaning in the colonial context than it had in an intra-European one, where, over the course of the nineteenth century, it had become an 'all or nothing' discursive vehicle of nation building and the quest for immediate and fully independent statehood. As applied in the peripheries of the great powers, the concept thus came with a normalizing internal structure inscribed by the standard of civilization. One of the legacies of the Bandung Conference and GA-Resolution 1514 is bringing into disrepute the normalizing dimension of the concept of self-determination in the colonial context, and in doing so, substantively transforming twentieth-century international legal structures.

Couched between phases of Western dominance, the battle for international law was shaped by a growing momentum and optimism by Third-World protagonists and contemporaries about 'decolonization' and its potential. At the beginning, under the leadership of politicians like Jawaharlal Nehru (India), Gamal Abdel Nasser (Egypt), Kwame Nkrumah (Ghana), Josip Broz Tito (Yugoslavia), and Sukarno (Indonesia), the third world seemed relatively united in its attempt to occupy a space of neutrality in the Cold War's ideological confrontation.[32] The non-aligned movement as it emerged right after the Bandung conference was a self-confident counterproposal to the existing structure of international relations and their legal underpinnings. The widely shared experience of colonial subjugation and liberation was turned into a new ideal of international relations that rejected interventionism, exploitation, and racism—and demanded the respect for equality, non-interference, non-violent solution of conflicts, and material solidarity. The foundation of the UN Conference for Trade and Development (UNCTAD) was meant to further institutionalize this cooperative quest for a joint international agenda beyond the bloc confrontation. With the 1960 UNGA Resolution 1514 on 'the granting of Independence to Colonial Countries and Peoples', the group of newly independent countries had already shown its growing assertiveness in using the UN as platform. There was also an increased willingness to create institutional structures for their demands. Against this background, the soon widely popular notion of third world, as coined by Alfred Sauvy, the French journalist and anthropologist, captured much of this idea. In reference to Abbe Sieyes's notion of

[31] Mark Mazower, *No Enchanted Palace: The End of Empire and the Ideological Origins of the United Nations* (Princeton University Press 2013).

[32] Robert J McMahon, 'Introduction' in Robert J McMahon (ed), *The Cold War in the Third World* (OUP 2013) 1; Khan, Group of 77, MPEPIL (2011) para 5; Vijay Prashad, *The Darker Nations: A People's History of Third World* (The New Press 2008).

the third estate in the context of the French revolution, the notion expressed the self-understanding of the newly independent governments to represent the majority of states and people in the world and the demand that this world's democratic majority should not just be recognized in its position, but also granted its effective rights as democratic majority. It was not a hierarchical notion in the sense of the 'also-ran' third (behind the first and the second) world, but the proud emancipative voice of the democratic majority.

At the same time, the (post-Bandung) decolonization movement in many ways continued earlier struggles of the Latin American states, the Ottoman Empire, China, and other non-Western states for full recognition of the principles of formal equality and non-intervention. Their early twentieth-century struggles for independent statehood and against unequal treaties, gunboat diplomacy, extraterritorial jurisdiction, corporate exploitation, and institutional under-representation in many ways served as blueprints for the third world before and after decolonization.[33] These early twentieth-century struggles for full inclusion into—and modification of—nineteenth century European international law also had made it virtually impossible for the Europeans to infinitely defer formal decolonization in Africa and Asia. Already within the League of Nations, references to civilizational superiority as a justification for colonial rule had increasingly become discredited as an official argument.[34] The gradual demise of the standard of civilization as a widely shared official European doctrine in the 1930s prepared the ground for the non-discrimination clause in the UN Charter and the fight against 'racialism' proclaimed in Bandung in 1955. According to scholars of the third world, racism was not only tolerated by international legal structures, but also by a constitutive element of nineteenth-century international law:

> International law was imbedded with white racism and thus promoted the interests of the whites while rigorously subordinating those of others. White racial discrimination was thus a fundamental element of international law during the period in question.[35]

In general, the third world followed the Latin-American emancipatory project in particular in its attempt to adapt international legal structures to its needs from within the system.[36] As many of the resistance movements in the third world began in the 1920s and 1930s, the first generation of third world resistance fighters

[33] See Eslava this volume.

[34] On this development Becker Lorca, *Mestizo International Law* (n 25); see also: Gary Wilder, *Freedom Time: Negritude, Decolonization and the Future of the World* (Duke University Press Books 2015); Mohamad Shababuddin, *Ethnicity and International Law* (CUP 2016).

[35] Oji Umozurike, *International Law and Colonialism in Africa* (Nwamife Publishers 1979) 36 (hereafter Umozurike, *Colonialism*).

[36] Eslava this volume; Becker Lorca, *Mestizo International Law* (n 25).

was shaped by the legal debates of this era; Ho Chi Min was a delegate at the 1919 Versailles conference. Both the interwar struggles as well as the post-Second World War decolonization movement pressured the governments of the great powers—and their lawyers—to accept that they had a formal right to have the same rights as the great powers granted each other through their diplomatic and legal practice. Statehood, in the European nineteenth-century sense, was regarded as a precondition to receive that status of a sovereign equal.

But the era of the battle for international law was also different than previous moments of decolonization. Regardless of the emancipatory path dependencies, many Third-World politicians and scholars saw independent statehood and UN membership more as a means to the end of radically transforming the international political and economic order, and its law.[37] Within reach was a truly universal law, not only in terms of the subjects of that legal order, but also regarding its substantively reformed content, which for the first time would take into account the interests of all states. In that sense, the Third-World project was more revolutionary than that of their Latin-American, Turkish, and East-Asian predecessors. Projects like the New International Economic Order bear testimony of the substantive transformations of colonial and neo-colonial structures that were at the heart of the Third-World battle for a new international law. The battle for international law in the *Sattelzeit* between the 1950s and the late 1970s thus closely linked two consecutive and interrelated discourses: the initial struggle for formal independence and the one for substantive political and economic independence of the entities now organized in formally recognized states. While international law was eventually being transformed during this era, it was not the change the third world had wanted. In the contemporary view of many Third-World politicians and scholars, it was precisely in this era that colonialism had been replaced by 'neo-colonialism', and where both had been sustained by international legal structures imposed on the third world. In his 1958 address to the first Conference of Independent African Sates in Accra, Kwame Nkrumah declared:

> The imperialists of today endeavour to achieve their ends not merely by military means, but by economic penetration, cultural assimilation, ideological domination, psychological infiltration, and subversive activities even to the point of inspiring and promoting assassination and civil strife.[38]

In the literature on this historical period, the battle for international law is often reduced to the recognition of a formal right to self-determination of the colonized, while the struggle for a substantive reversal of international legal structures associated with 'neo-colonial' domination goes unmentioned. But

[37] On the role of the UN in this process, see Sinclair this volume.
[38] Umozurike, *Colonialism* (n 35) 126.

it is this dimension of the struggle which deserves historical reflection as an unattained quest for a more just world order. Our argument is that this *Sattelzeit* era brought about the international law of today—not as a simple continuation of colonialism, but as a transformed legal and political order that allows for new forms of hegemonic rule.

3. The quest for statehood

Despite the attempt of a number of Third-World leaders via the non-aligned movement to create a space of neutrality in the Cold War, both colonial legacies and new super-power interventionism into the inevitably weak and contested structures of post-independence statehood made it increasingly difficult, disadvantageous, or impossible for the new governments of the third world not to join one of the major ideological blocs. At the same time, statehood and the quest for 'development' were not only largely unquestioned in both ideological blocks, but also came with heavy burdens for the newly independent countries.

The struggle for independence was connected in an ambivalent way to the unquestioned ideal of modern statehood.[39] While the independence movements fought for international conditions that made the common goal of independent statehood possible, at home they faced existing colonial proto-state structures,[40] which were usually based on the colonial policies of racial segregation and the 'divide and rule' strategies of the colonizer, both of which had created and instrumentalized ethnic divisions. Odd Arne Westad describes the experience of local populations with the colonial state, saying:

> As such, the state therefore emerged as something extraneous to indigenous populations, even at the elite level. The 'foreignness' of the state led to a constant need for policing at all levels, even in the most assimilationist of colonies. And the lack of local knowledge, the availability of labour, and the abundance of resources led to the inauguration of grand projects, intended both to deliver raw materials to the empire and to show the indigenous peoples the efficacy and superiority of the colonial state. It is no wonder that the colonized often described their existence as living within a giant prison.[41]

[39] See Eslava this volume; Bertrand Badie, *The Imported State: The Westernization of Political Order* (Stanford University Press 2000).

[40] Crawford Young, *The Colonial State in Comparative Perspective* (Yale University Press 1994). For the post-colonial ramifications of this, see Upendra Baxi, 'Constitutionalism as a Site for State Formative Practices' (2000) 21 Cardozo Law Review 1183.

[41] Odd A Westad, *The Global Cold War: Third World Interventions and the Making of Our Times* (CUP 2005) 75 (hereafter Westad, *The Global Cold War*).

As a consequence, local economies at the moment of decolonization were focused on exporting raw materials and had not been built to generate income, let alone welfare, for an independent society. Worse, these new states, with their old colonial borders and their remaining legal structures, often did not correspond to ethnic and linguistic identities or existing societal and political structures on the ground. And the alleged principle of *uti possidetis* as advanced by the former colonizers made independence dependent on the recognition of these existing colonial borders.

In close connection, the concept of economic growth was equally ambivalent. In many ways the modernization strategy of the new states followed the footpaths of grand scale and often disastrous economic and infrastructural interventions of the late colonial era.[42] More subtle, but also more effective, the notion of 'development' and the 'invention of poverty'[43] created and dynamized a logic of othering and a 'rationality of rule'[44] that set the 'underdeveloped' up for an unwinnable race to catch up with the West, and allowed the North to dictate the standards pursued. Now framed as a universal value and appealing to all, 'development' was also considered beyond the realm of political contention, a matter of technocratic reform rather than political struggle.

It is one of the tragic ironies of the decolonization era that modern European statehood and economic growth through industrialization remained a quasi-unquestioned ideal of the elites ruling the new states.[45] Cooption through education of central parts of the local elites, a key element of colonial control, had prepared the ground for the local appropriation of these concepts. Only very few scholars or elite politicians doubted the necessity to think in these ideals.[46] Of course national liberation movements and intellectuals in the third world had a complex and ambivalent attitude towards late nineteenth-century Western modernity and its nationalist, evolutionary, and social-Darwinist undercurrents, oscillating between hatred and admiration, as can be exemplified by Sutan Sjahrir, one of the founders of the Indonesian nationalist movement:

> For me, the West signifies a forceful, dynamic, and active life. It is a sort of Faust that I admire, and I am convinced that only by utilization of this dynamism of the West can the East be released from slavery and subjugation. The West is now

[42] ibid 79; John Martinussen, *State, Market, Society: A Guide to Competing Theories of Development* (ZED Books Ltd 1997) 56.

[43] Arturo Escobar, *Encountering Development: The Making and Unmaking of the Third World* (Princeton University Press 2011) (hereafter Escobar, *Encountering Development*); see also Balakrishnan Rajagopal, *International Law from Below* (CUP 2003) (hereafter Rajagopal, *International Law from Below*).

[44] Sundhya Pahuja, *Decolonizing International Law: Development, Economic Growth and the Politics of Universality* (CUP 2011) (hereafter Pahuja, *Decolonizing International Law*).

[45] Gilbert Rist, *History of Development: From Western Origins to Global Faith* (ZED Book Ltd 2008) 100 (hereafter Rist, *History of Development*).

[46] Even a radical critique of Northern neo-colonialism, such as Nkrumah, did not.

> teaching the East to regard life as a struggle and a striving, as an active moment to which the concept of tranquillity must be subordinated [. . .] Struggle and striving signify a struggle against nature, and that is the essence of the struggle: man's attempt to subdue nature and to rule it by his will.[47]

Under the emerging development paradigm, economic, technical, and humanitarian assistance by one of the superpowers, or even by the former colonizers, was in high demand. It was accompanied by a Keynesian engagement of the state in economic development and a broadly shared acceptance of modernization theory held to provide a path to development that was shared in West and East.[48] Beginning in the 1950s, Western-dominated financial institutions, such as the World Bank, assumed a central role as lenders for large-scale development projects.[49] The UN declared the 1960s a 'development decade'. Several states and multinational institutions created institutional structure for technical and financial support of these 'development' efforts and hence a system of development cooperation infrastructures emerged in West and East.[50]

This search for outside assistance tragically also required newly independent states to position themselves in the antagonistic Cold War environment. Both the US and the Soviet Union more or less openly attempted to create and preserve ideological, economic, and military 'satellite-states' among the former colonies in Africa and Asia. While direct and open military interventions of the two superpowers and the former colonizers over the course of these three decades became less frequent, so called 'proxy' wars grew in numbers and intensity: the Vietnam War; the US invasions in Guatemala and the Dominican Republic; the Soviet intervention in Hungary and Czechoslovakia; US-sponsored coups against socialist governments in Iran, Jordan, Congo, Brazil, Indonesia, and Ghana; numerous wars of national liberation inter alia in Algeria, Namibia, Angola, and Guinea; and perhaps most importantly, dozens of other post-independence civil wars in Africa, Asia, and the Middle East with covert participation and support to warring factions delivered by neighbouring states, the US, the Soviets, Cuba, China, or the former European colonizers. The physical and economic violence unleashed in these liberation and post-independence wars created new and deepened existing collective traumas, constituting a heavy burden for most of the new societies emerging out of the ruins of the old empires, and now being politically framed in the iron *Gehäuse* of the nation state.

[47] Sutan Sjahir, *Out of Exile* (Greenwood Press 1969), quoted after Westad, *The Global Cold War* (n 41) 77.

[48] Walt W Rostow, 'The Stages of Economic Growth' (1959) 12 The Economic History Review 1; Rist, *History of Development* (n 45).

[49] Rajagopal, *International Law from Below* (n 43); Dann this volume; Devesh Kapur, John P Lewis and Richard C Webb (eds), *The World Bank: Its First Half Century*, Vol 2: Perspectives (Brookings Institutions Press 1997).

[50] Philipp Dann, *The Law of Development Cooperation* (CUP 2013) 37 ff.

III. Sites of battle

At stake was both achieving formal political independence and a substantive reversal of international legal structures. The Western world, for the first time since the early nineteenth century, witnessed a fundamental challenge to the existing order and to its entrenched interests. The conflict over the shape, scope, and the mere possibility of such a reversal was a hard-fought, long, and multifaceted battle. Sites of battle included not only contested re-interpretation of existing concepts, new counter-concepts such as 'permanent sovereignty over natural resources', requested reforms of the institutional landscape, and new multilateral treaty projects, but also the more fundamental issue of whether or not the old rules would continue to apply and bind the newly independent states.

1. Delegitimizing alleged pre-independence rules

Generally, all new states faced the continued application of colonial-era international law. Furthermore, numerous rules of customary international law appeared to enable the continuation of colonial relationships, such as the rules concerning the treatment of foreign nationals.[51] Since its inception in 1949, the UN International Law Commission was concerned with questions over state succession, for example, the extent to which the new states were bound by international law that existed prior to their independence.[52] The 1969 Vienna Convention on the Law of Treaties, the 1978 Vienna Convention on Succession of States in respect of Treaties, and the 1983 Vienna Convention on Succession of States in respect of State Property, Archives and Debts were all results of controversial debates between East and West on the one hand, and between North and South on the other.[53] A number of third-world scholars demanded a *tabula rasa* approach regarding alleged normative ties to pre-independence rules and principles. But even these more radical doctrines remarkably justified their approach within the discursive structures provided by European international law, namely on the basis of consent theories.[54] Their central argument was that the new states had not given their consent to the old law and henceforth these rules for them had no binding force.[55] In this battle over the validity of the old law, Western diplomats and lawyers

[51] See Georges M Abi-Saab, 'The Newly Independent States and the Rules of International Law: An Outline' (1962) 8 Howard Law Journal 95, 101.

[52] United Nations, *Yearbook of the International Law Commission* (United Nations 1949) 39; see also MG Maloney, 'Succession of States in Respect of Treaties: The Vienna Convention of 1978' (1978/1979) 19 Virginia Journal of International Law 885, 900.

[53] For example, the negotiations at the United Nations Conference on the Law of Treaties, Second Session Vienna, 9 April–22 May 1969, Official Records, 90.

[54] A Krueger, *Die Bindung der Dritten Welt an das postkoloniale Völkerrecht* (Springer 2017).

[55] Brunner, Chapter 5, this volume.

resorted to the argument that stability and continuity had to be preserved, insisting that with the creation of a new state this entity inevitably gives its tacit consent to the general legal norms of the society it joins.

Again, the third world's quest for membership in the form of legally normalized European-style statehood came with a heavy price. Accepting the customary rules constructing statehood while rejecting other rules of customary law was a position difficult to defend. Therefore, relatively soon a second line of defence became the argument that if their recognition as new states by this order included acceptance of this order (as Western lawyers argued) then the new states should at least have the ability to reshape this order. Resolutions of the UNGA were seen as a central instrument for such a substantive reform of old Western international law.[56] This triggered a fierce debate over the legal nature of such resolutions. It was fostered by Western scholars, who accused the third world of using what they termed 'an automatic majority' of decolonized states in the UNGA —a derogatory term immediately criticized by Southern writers.[57] While rejecting the arguments about the law-making competence of the UNGA, the North also refused to recognize the validity of other norm-setting initiatives by the decolonized South, not least through the formal ways of non-ratification, reservations, and uncounted interpretative declarations and official statements. Thus, even today, the 1978 Vienna Convention on Succession of States in respect of Treaties merely consists of thirty-seven member states, and the 1983 Vienna Convention on Succession of States in respect of State Property, Archives and Debts has only fourteen.[58]

1. Condemning interventions by the metropole as 'aggression'

In their struggle against colonialism and neo-colonialism, the newly independent states focused especially on the principle of sovereign state equality and the related

[56] On the contemporary debate, see FB Sloan, 'The Binding Force of a Recommendation of the General Assembly of the United Nations' (1948) 25 The British Year Book of International Law 1; M Virally, 'La Valeur juridique des Recommandations des Organisations Internationales' (1956) 2 Annuaire Français de Droit International 66; Rosalyn Higgins, *The Development of International Law Through the Political Organs of the United Nations* (OUP 1963); Obed Y Asamoah, *The Legal Significance of the Declarations of the General Assembly of the United Nations* (Springer 1966); Richard A Falk, 'On the 'Quasi-Legislative' Competence of the General Assembly' (1966) 60 American Journal of International Law 782. On the positions of Elias, see Landauer this volume.

[57] See, for example, Mohammed Bedjaoui, 'A Third World View of International Organizations. Actions Towards a New International Economic Order' in Georges M Abi-Saab (ed), *The Concept of International Organization* (UNESCO 1981); Mohammed Bedjaoui, *Towards a New International Economic Order* (Holmes and Meier Publishers 1979) 144.

[58] United Nations Treaty Collection, Chapter XXIII: Law of Treaties, Vienna Convention on Succession of States in Respect of Treaties; United Nations Treaty Collection, Chapter III: Privileges and Immunities, Diplomatic and Consular Relations, etc., Vienna Convention on Succession of States in Respect of State Property, Archives and Debts.

rule of non-intervention and the prohibition of the use of force.[59] A traumatic common experience of the colonized was becoming objects of violent interventions by colonial powers. Motives and forms of European interventions differed from colonizer to colonizer and over time. A common feature was to bring to bear superior forms of weaponry, transport, and communication directly or through chartered companies in search for new markets and raw materials, or out of religious zeal or national prestige. Resistance by local populations was often crushed with utmost brutality. Up until the 1960s, France and the UK in many instances refused to accept classic limits of military violence imposed by international humanitarian law, let alone human rights obligations when (often using excessive military force) crushing rebellions and resistance in the colonies .[60] The estimated death toll among local populations caused by direct colonial military interventions alone since the mid-nineteenth century according to recent estimates was around five and a half million.[61] Two main third world projects can be discerned: The recognition of liberation movements against colonial rule and the entrenchment of a broad prohibition of the use of force and of a widely conceptualized non-intervention principle.

What was at stake legally with regard to liberation movements against colonial rule was not the question as to whether taking up arms against a colonial regime for one's own self-determination was legitimate under international law.[62] Western scholars traditionally had held international law to be indifferent to internal state violence and had more recently also clearly recognized the political struggle of liberation movements against colonialism. What the third-world authors propagated instead was a full internationalization of such conflicts, with a *jus ad bellum* for liberation movements and the depiction of colonial powers as external 'aggressors', as well as the full recognition of liberation wars under international humanitarian law. By internationalizing the conflict they could claim a status of combatants under international humanitarian law—which was a much more favourable status than being treated as 'criminals' in a purely internal conflict. This points to the larger issue behind the debate. The battle for internationalization of wars of national liberation was also a battle about identity and the recognition of the historical justification for freedom fights and rejection of the colonial project as illegitimate aggression.[63] The full recognition of national liberation movements

[59] Gaetano Arangio-Ruiz, *The United Nations Declaration on Friendly Relations and the System of the Sources of International Law* (Springer Netherlands 1979) 153. For a comparison with current positions, see Antony Anghie and Bhupinder S Chimni, 'Third World Approaches to International Law and Individual Responsibility in Internal Conflicts' (2003) 2 Chinese Journal of International Law 77–103, 81.

[60] Fabian Klose, *Menschenrechte im Schatten kolonialer Gewalt: Die Dekolonialisierungskriege in Kenia und Algerien 1945–1962* (DeGruyter 2009) (hereafter Klose, *Menschenrechte*).

[61] Westad, *The Global Cold War* (n 41) 73.

[62] Bernstorff, Chapter 2, this volume.

[63] ibid.

as actors in an international armed conflict came in 1977 after a third-world battle led by Abi-Saab during the entire span of the negotiations over the two Additional Protocols to the Geneva Conventions.[64]

Newly independent states also desired protection against both intervention by European states as well as by the the two superpowers through a ban on economic and political coercion in international relations. Their aim thus was to expand the scope of the principles of non-intervention and the prohibition of the use of force.[65] Newly independent states pushed for their demands in different fora, with varying success. In the UNGA they were able to adopt a number of resolutions that aimed to solidify the principle of non-intervention in the UN Charter,[66] though the legal effect of these resolutions remained contested and later raised increasing Western opposition.[67] In a different venue, negotiations about the Vienna Convention on the Law of Treaties offered the opportunity to define the notion of 'coercion' in Arts 51 and 52. Newly independent states demanded a broader understanding of the concept beyond military coercion, but met with fierce resistance from Western countries.[68]

At the same time, many of the new governments in the South entered into bilateral military assistance treaties with the former metropole or one of the two superpowers, leading to a worldwide US military presence and to numerous military interventions as former metropoles assisted cooperative governments in the Global South in cases of civil unrest and revolution.

2. Banning racial discrimination and establishing human rights as a discursive 'weapon'

Banning racial discrimination was a crucial element in the process of redirecting international law, for which racial inequality had been an essential discursive structure. During this era, the UNGA adopted the 1965 Convention on the Elimination

[64] On this battle, see Georges M Abi-Saab, 'The Third World Intellectual in Praxis: Confrontation, Participation, or Operation Behind Enemy Lines?' (2016) 37 Third World Quarterly 1957; on the role of Soviet government in these discussions, see Bowring this volume.

[65] See Official Records of the General Assembly, Eighteenth Session, Sixth Committee, 789th Meeting, UN Doc A/C.6/SR.789 para 25.

[66] Declaration on the Inadmissibility of Intervention in the Domestic Affairs of States and the Protection of their Independence and Sovereignty, GA Resolution 2131 (XX) (21 December 1965) (adopted without dissent, with one abstention); Declaration on Principles of International Law Concerning Friendly Relations and Co-operation Among States in Accordance with the Charter of the United Nations A/Res/ 2625 (XXV) (24 October 1970). On these efforts, see Barry Carter, 'Economic Coercion' in Rüdiger Wolfrum (ed), *Max Planck Encyclopedia of Public International Law*, paras 6–9.

[67] GA Res 42/173, entitled Economic Measures as a Means of Political and Economic Coercion against Developing Countries of 11 December 1987, used similar language as the 1965 Declaration, but the recorded vote was 128 States for, 21 against, and 5 abstaining.

[68] Richard D Kearney and Robert E Dalton, 'The Treaty on Treaties' (1970) 64 American Journal of International Law 495, 532–35.

of All Forms of Racial Discrimination (CERD) and the 1973 International Convention on Suppression and Punishment of the Crime of Apartheid. CERD, however, was driven primarily by European and Israeli actors, and hardly constituted a strategically pursued project of third-world governments.[69] Establishing a human rights machinery within the UN as a discursive tool to criticize colonialism in all its forms, in contrast, played a more central role for the third world. Except for India, the legally non-binding Universal Declaration of Human Rights, for obvious reasons, had not received substantial input from the colonized states.[70] Simultaneously, the remaining European colonial powers in the late 1940s and early 1950s launched various initiatives in the UN to define colonial regimes as a form of polity, which had to remain outside the reach of international human rights norms; these culminated in a joint proposal to insert a colonial exception clause into the new human rights covenants.[71] This proposal was defeated in the Third Committee by an early demonstration of third-world governmental solidarity in favour of the colonized. Subsequently, the newly independent states fiercely engaged with the negotiations over what would become the major UN human rights covenants and their adoption in 1966 (ICCPR and ICESCR). It was, in fact, mainly the decolonized South in the 1950s that pushed ahead with the human rights discourse at the UN.[72] In reaction to colonial injustice and racial suppression, for most of the newly independent states the right to self-determination and human rights were two sides of the same coin.[73]

In reaction to colonial rebellions in Africa, in the 1950s and 1960s both the UK and France established systematic practices of torture, summary executions, collective punishment, and arbitrary detention. As a result, independence movements like Algeria's FNL realized that discussing such atrocities in an international forum, using the language of human rights, would strengthen their anticolonial struggles within the UN.[74] During the negotiations over the two UN human rights treaties, many third-world interventions also aimed to legally entrench the right

[69] Add to this that the Anti-Apartheid Convention certainly had an important symbolic dimension, but which was hardly put to use; see Giladi this volume. On the ominous role of the ICJ with regard to apartheid, see Venzke this volume.

[70] Mary A Glendon, *A World Made New: Eleanor Roosevelt and the Universal Declaration of Human Rights* (Random House Inc. 2001); Jochen von Bernstorff, 'The Changing Fortunes of the Universal Declaration of Human Rights: Genesis and Symbolic Dimensions of the Turn to Rights in International Law' (2008) 19 The European Journal of International Law 903 ff.

[71] Roland Burke, *Decolonization and the Evolution of Human Rights* (University of Pennsylvania Press 2013) 41 (hereafter Burke, *Decolonization*).

[72] The role of human rights in the decolonization period has been intensely debated—pitting the view of their centrality (Burke) against a 'revisionist' reading of the history, according to which human rights in this era actually served a fairly limited purpose (Moyn). On this debate, see Hoffmann and Assy this volume, who argue that the historical evidence has been greatly researched, but its interpretation now remains ultimately inconclusive.

[73] Roland Burke, '"The Compelling Dialogue of Freedom": Human Rights at the Bandung Conference' (2006) 28 Human Rights Quarterly 947, 962–64 (hereafter Burke, 'Human Rights').

[74] Klose, *Menschenrechte* (n 60).

to self-determination as the fundamental basis for the realization of human rights. Leading governments of the 'decolonized' states argued that human rights could only be fully realized within an environment free from colonial and post-colonial dominance.[75] This attempt to establish a legal connection between the right to self-determination and human rights was formally rejected by Western states largely due to its collective dimensions, which were allegedly incompatible with a treaty project establishing individual rights and freedoms. However, Western governments sensed early on that the anti-colonial and revolutionary dimension of linking self-determination with human rights also contained a volatile undercurrent of unrest for both the still-existing colonial empires and for contemporary racialized forms of rule in the former white settler colonies in South Africa and Rhodesia. This discord and anger also permeated the Palestinian quest for self-determination and non-discrimination.

Eventually, self-determination was included in the common Art 1 of the two key UN human rights Covenants.[76] After independence, many of the new governments often led by former independence fighters themselves established authoritarian political systems, using the repressive and violent potential of the nation state form inherited by the colonizers. They joined the former colonizers and the USSR in using human rights as a diplomatic 'weapon' within the UN, while many third-world governments more or less systematically ignored human rights obligations in various sectors of their own newly formed governmentss. Such aspects of hypocritical and selective insistence on human rights obligations thus constituted a common feature of the emerging human rights discourse in the UN during the Cold War-era, with the two superpowers all great powers having a problematic human rights record either at home or because of their violent interventions in their peripheries, or both.[77] The fact that many third-world leaders adopted this hypocritical practice in their own foreign policy led to the following polemical remark by the Tanzanian President Julius Nyerere, who criticized his African colleagues: 'we will soon be tolerating fascism in Africa as long as it is practised by African governments against African peoples'.[78] Hence, the predominant use of human rights language by all governments within the UN often came with an instrumental dimension. Nonetheless, formal decolonization and the struggle against Apartheid in South Africa had a major impact on the evolution of human rights as the dominant 'lingua franca' of international morality; all of this began

[75] Burke, 'Human Rights' (n 73) 947, 962–64.

[76] Jörg Fisch, *The Right to Self-Determination* (CUP 2015). On the problematic role of the US government in the conceptualization of this right (and its conception as human right), see Barsalou this volume.

[77] Jan Eckel, *Die Ambivalenz des Guten: Menschenrechte in der internationalen Politik seit den 1940ern* (Vandenhoeck & Ruprecht 2014).

[78] Quoted in Burke, *Decolonization* (n 71) 57.

with the immediate reception and discursive use of the Universal Declaration in the UN during the 1950s.[79]

3. Reconfiguring the world's economic system

As former colonies increasingly secured formal political independence, attention turned steadily to the economic dimension of self-determination; economic sovereignty became a key concern. One characteristic feature of debates was that the notion of 'development', which had been in use only for a fairly short time, had almost immediately become popular also among local elites. Together with the goal of economic growth, the term provided overarching and largely uncontested paradigms of understanding and action.[80] However, within the confines of these paradigms, a battle over how to reconfigure the world's economic system unfolded. In this, as in other areas, a variety of battle sites emerged with similar battle lines which mostly pitted Northern against third-world protagonists, with the Soviet bloc sometimes as an important partner of the third world. One element of the increasingly open rifts between North and South was the shift from a more technical economics-perspective that had informed discussions in the 1950s to a more political economy and political take throughout the 1960s and 1970s. But in all areas, political or economic positions were often recounted in legal debates and legal instruments.

The first important site concerned the question of natural resource extraction. As colonies had been economically structured to serve the centre's quest for raw materials, colonial economies were geared towards natural resource extraction. The pertinent question of who should have the final say over those industries soon emerged. Third-world governments understandably demanded ultimate control, and hence 'permanent sovereignty over natural resources'.[81] During European colonial expansion, it was common for colonial powers to secure the exploitation of natural resources through contracts with private investors from the metropole (concessions) and via the imposition of non-reciprocal, so-called 'unequal' treaties.[82] The independence of former colonies thus subjected the continued

[79] While Burke generally makes this point, he somewhat artificially and ultimately unconvincingly differentiates between the 'good' early Third World embrace of human rights and democratic 'self-determination' language in the 1950s, and its more reprehensible instrumental usages in the 1960s.

[80] On the astonishing success or lure of the development paradigm but also on the few more sceptical voices 'from below', see Rajagopal, *International Law from Below* (n 43); Bret Benjamin, *Invested Interests: Capital. Culture, and the World Bank* (University of Minnesota Press 2007) (hereafter Benjamin, *Invested Interests*); Escobar, *Encountering Development* (n 43) 19.

[81] On the evolution of this concept, see Pahuja, *Decolonizing International Law* (n 44); Nico Shrijver, *Sovereignty over Natural Resources: Balancing Rights and Duties* (CUP 1997).

[82] See in the contemporary literature Ram P Anand, *New States and International Law* (Vikas Publishing House 1972) 23 (hereafter Anand, *New States*; for current accounts, see Anghie, *Imperialism* (n 4) 67 ff; Matthew Craven, 'What Happened to Unequal Treaties? The Continuities of Informal

enforceability and in fact validity of both granted concessions and such treaties to question.[83] The most prominent and contentious legal issue here was the question of the fate of colonial concessions for resource extraction granted by the metropole to Western companies.[84] Western international lawyers claimed that these concessions were ultimately the property of private investors who were protected by the supposedly long-standing 'doctrine of acquired rights'.

The fact that Western investors now operated on the territory of a foreign jurisdiction made necessary a complex re-arrangement of the legal relationships between the investor and the involved governments abroad and at home.[85] Similar to most contentious aspects of international law analysed in this volume, Western international lawyers provided the respective argumentative redundancies in order to secure the interests of the industrialized West; or in more concrete terms, scholarly contributions and expert advice helped to ensure that necessary re-arrangements would either lead to new Western business opportunities, or 'full compensation' of those lost. The strategic transformations in the field of colonial concessions ultimately gave birth to a new system of investment protection.[86] With well-known Western international lawyers in the role of leading arbitrators, early arbitral awards on disputes over nationalization projects helped prevent the application of domestic law of the newly independent states regarding such disputes.[87] During this battle Western scholars advanced not only the theory of 'sanctity of acquired rights' but also of the 'internationalization' of investment contracts. Strategically, this Western move aimed to exclude the domestic law of the new host states, and thus their regulatory frameworks, from the scope of applicable law in disputes over regulatory interventions by the new governments. Third-world international legal scholars criticized the rise of the 'theory of internationalization' as well as the sudden discursive rise of the 'acquired rights' doctrine as an alleged fundamental principle of international law. In the ILC, in the context of deliberations on the codification of the laws of state succession, Bedjaoui fiercely objected to the insertion of the principle of acquired rights.[88] Western ILC members accused Bedjaoui of being too 'political' and lacking the required 'objectivity'—a typical reaction of Western authors to substantive protest voiced by third-world international lawyers.[89]

Empire' (2005) 74 Nordic Journal of International Law 335, 344; Anne Peters, 'Unequal Treaties' in Rüdiger Wolfrum (ed), *Max Planck Encyclopedia of Public International Law* (2007).

[83] See debates in the International Law Commission, for example, in United Nations, *Yearbook of the International Law Commission* (United Nations 1962) 4.
[84] See Craven Chapter 4, and Brunner Chapter 5, this volume.
[85] Craven Chapter 4, this volume.
[86] ibid.
[87] Sornarajah Chapter 7, this volume.
[88] Brunner Chapter 5, this volume.
[89] ibid.

Configuration of the international trading system was another central battle site. While it was uncontested that trade would be central to the economic success of the former colonies, the basic understanding of the systems and terms of trade became increasingly contested. Modernization theory and the idea that the third world should replicate Western history, which had dominated the early thinking, was considered increasingly unconvincing in the third world, considering the experience of Latin American states from the nineteenth century onward. Instead, Latin American authors in particular had formulated a counter-narrative in the form of dependency theory, which rebalanced understanding of responsibilities for the problems facing third-world economies.[90] Institutionally, third-world governments complemented the rise of dependence theory with the founding of UNCTAD in 1964 and the Group of 77. Importantly, this debate was over the understanding of the role of multinational corporations—fought along North–South battle lines.[91] Regularly owned by Western actors and very often with histories reaching back to colonial foundations and heritages of violence and exploitation, the multinationals were increasingly seen by third-world writers as harmful, rather than beneficial, for their economies, as Western economists and governments would claim. Discussions culminated at the 1972 UNCTAD III conference held in Chile, where not just the understanding of corporations, but also the question of their regulation, was discussed.[92] While Western states argued that their role was best dealt with in domestic law of the hosts states, many Southern states favoured an international instrument to regulate their conduct. But even though third-world governments succeeded in placing the topic on the agenda and created a Commission to study the role of multinational corporations, they were not successful in creating a binding instrument to regulate their activities.

Additionally, a debate unfolded over the sources and forms of financial assistance to the South that had an important anchoring in legal questions.[93] As much as the general assumptions were that trade would, over time, allow the newly independent states to become equal partners in the global economic system, in these early years of formal independence, financial support from the North was considered essential by most actors.[94] In fact, the final communiqué of the Bandung conference opened with a call for further economic cooperation and assistance. However, the source of such assistance was a major point of contention and struggle. Third-world governments demanded multilateral institutions of support and, in particular, argued that the UN should provide funds. Western governments

[90] David K Fieldhouse, *The West and the Third World* (Blackwell 1999) ch 6.

[91] Jennifer Bair, 'Corporations at the UN?' (2015) 6 Humanity 159; Pahuja and Saunders Chapter 6, this volume.

[92] ibid.

[93] See Dann Chapter 12, this volume.

[94] On the prescience or apprehension of a few critical voices (such as Fanon or Nkrumah), see Benjamin, *Invested Interests* (n 80).

instead preferred bilateral aid. While the third world was unsuccessful in pushing for UN capital assistance, this conflict led Western states in a counter-move to turn the World Bank into a development agency. Frequently during this era, the West came under pressure from the third world, public opinion, and the Soviet bloc in the UN. After having derailed and ignored new institutional blueprints and creations with equitable representation by the third world, the West then took up the respective topic within an institution under its own control.[95] Insulated against meaningful Southern participation, the issue of poverty in the third world could now be framed by the World Bank under the investment-friendly 'growth' and 'development' paradigms. Many third-world governments, in their quest for Western style modernization and industrialization, quickly became 'debtor' states due to volatile prices for the small number of commodities, upon the export of which their internal economies were geared.[96] They now heavily depended on the World Bank and other Western financial institutions, making them ripe for further Western interventions into their political, economic, and social systems.

4. Drafting a new Law of the Sea and the quest for sharing a 'common heritage of mankind'

A further point of discord was the attempt since the 1950s and 1960s to comprehensively codify the law of the sea. This process was only completed in 1982 by the adoption of the UN Convention on the Law of the Sea (UNCLOS). While initially the negotiations were strongly influenced by the Cold War and military questions of strategic importance, during the decolonization era, UNCLOS became the object of a globally controversial debate over justice and redistribution. The core of the redistribution debate concerned the conflict over who was economically entitled to newly discovered maritime resources, for example, minerals and fisheries in the deep seabed. In 1970, UNGA adopted Resolution 2749 (XXV), which declared the deep-sea floor as the 'common heritage of mankind' and planned the common globally administrated economic use of the deep-sea floor.[97] Resulting benefits were supposed to be used for the 'development' of third-world countries. UNCLOS negotiations included numerous divisive issues that pitted socialist states against capitalist states and big coastal states against maritime have nots, including the breadth of the continental shelf, the scope of a future

[95] See Dann Chapter 12, this volume.

[96] Already in the 1930s, Carl Schmitt had sensed that the fundamental 'non-civilized'/'civilized' distinction of European international law was, under US influence, being gradually replaced by a new dichotomy between 'debtor states' and 'creditor states'; see Carl Schmitt, 'Völkerrechtliche Formen des modernen Imperialismus' in *Positionen und Begriffe* (Duncker & Humblot 1940) 164; cf on public debt and the Third World, Pahuja, *Decolonizing International Law* (n 44).

[97] UNGA, Declaration of Principles Governing the Sea-Bed and the Ocean Floor, and the Subsoil Thereof, Beyond the Limits of National Jurisdiction, UNGA A/RES/2749 (XXV) (12 December 1970).

treaty, and the concrete regime governing the seabed.[98] Large G77 coastal states like India had pushed for an extension of economic zones of exploitation for the coastal states. One of the first effects of the seabed conflict was the broken relationships between land-locked states and smaller coastal states.[99] Another casualty was the idea of redistribution based on a sustainable joint use and administration of a 'Common Heritage of Mankind' being denounced as 'socialism' by Cold War Western leaders.[100] Additionally, the resulting enormous extension of exclusive economic zones and continental shelves was a Pyrrhic victory for the third world. For many newly independent states now opened their extended zones for industrial Organisation for Economic Co-operation and Development (OECD)-based fishing fleets through licences in the quest to generate governmental income, or being unable to fight illegal fishing by and environmental pollution from foreign fishing fleets in these zones.

By limiting international administrative structures to the ecologically and economically less-relevant seabed, capitalist exploitation of the ocean's resources in all its other areas could take its new and more excessive forms.[101] It was a given that Western governments engaging in these battles knew it would be much easier in the future to be granted access to these national zones of exploitation when dealing with individual states from the third world on a bilateral basis, rather than having to cooperate with a centralized international institution administering such resources.[102] The implementation of the thus transformed law of the sea regime, despite various substantive norms in UNCLOS on sustainable fishing and environmental protection, destroyed not only dozens of societies along the coasts of the Global South that depended economically on cultivating traditional fisheries, but it also actually led to the ecological 'death' of the seas, predicted since the late 1970s.[103] Innovative third world strategies from this era to pursue projects of joint moderate exploitation of natural resources both on land and sea under strict scrutiny of equitable international institutions, including mechanisms of redistributing generated incomes, were never actually realized.[104]

[98] On this battle, see Ranganathan Chapter 1, this volume.

[99] Pointing to the lack of solidarity between the third and the 'fourth world' W Vitzthum, 'Materiale Gerechtigkeitsaspekte der Seerechtsentwicklung' in Alexander Proelß (ed), *Kleine Schriften* (first published 1980, Duncker und Humblot 2017) 128; on the position of the Third World see Ram P Anand, *Legal Régime of the Sea-Bed and the Developing Countries* (Sijthoff 1975) ch 5.

[100] See Ranganathan Chapter 1, this volume; on the exploitation bias of the regime, see also I Feichtner, 'Sharing the Riches of the Sea' (2019) 30 European Journal of International Law (forthcoming).

[101] cf Ranganathan Chapter 1, this volume.

[102] Information from an interview conducted with a former Western delegate to the UNCLOS negotiations.

[103] For a contemporary voice Wolfgang Graf Vitzthum (ed), *Die Plünderung der Meere: Ein gemeinsames Erbe wird zerstückelt* (Fischer 1981).

[104] Martii Koskenniemi and Marja Lehto, 'The Privilege of Universality: International Law, Economic Ideology and Seabed Resources' (1996) 65 Nordic Journal of International Law 533.

IV. Protagonists in battle

1. Scholars of the third world

The battle over international law was fought in various places—on open battle fields as much as on hilly, uneven, unclear terrain, with open face or in disguise. It was a battle waged in diplomatic fora, on political podia as much as in academic journals and at conferences. Who were the international legal scholars that participated in the battle for international law and how did they position themselves methodologically? What role did institutional actors, for example, the International Court of Justice (ICJ), the UN, or the World Bank, play?

A broad and diverse range of authors, including inter alia RP Anand (India), TO Elias (Nigeria), Mohamed Bedjaoui (Algeria),[105] Charles Alexandrovicz, Upendra Baxi, Syatauw J, Singh N (all India),[106] U Umozurike (Namibia),[107] George Abi-Saab (Egypt) or Francis Deng (South Sudan) from the third world, but also some Western authors, such as Charles Chaumont,[108] Richard Falk, Bert Röling, and Konrad Ginther among others, as well as Soviet writers such as Morozov and Starushenko,[109] attacked central doctrines of international law as instruments of colonialism or simply as outdated.[110] Most of them belonged to the younger generation, were in their 30s or 40s, and the majority of the Southern scholars that were actually heard had received an education in the West. They were on unfamiliar terrain and had few precursors to look at. The epistemic imbalance of the field was tremendous. While the UN provided third world governments a platform on which to present their political positions, the academic world (universities, journals, conferences) offered a much less inviting area for third world voices to be heard. Nonetheless, a small number of voices did enter the conversation. Criticism of European international law was formulated on different levels and with different strategies in mind. Some fought using a more moderate 'contributionist' strategy, conceiving international law as an important but malleable structure, which the new states could further develop into a truly universal order that served

[105] On these three authors, see the contributions by Singh, Landauer, and Öszu this volume.

[106] J Syatauw, *Some Newly Established Asian States and the Development of International* Law (Martinus Nijhoff 1961); N Singh, *India and International Law* (Publishing Company 1969); Anand, *New States* (n 82); Ram P Anand (ed), *Asian States in the Development of Universal International* Law (Vikas Publications 1972); Prakash Sinha, *New Nations and the Law of Nations* (Sijthoff 1967); Umozurike, *Colonialism* (n 35).

[107] See Gevers Chapter 17, this volume.

[108] On Chaumont, see Tourme-Jouannet Chapter 16, this volume (also with reference to the larger number of French authors, which supported the idea of a 'droit international du developpement').

[109] See Bowring Chapter 18, this volume.

[110] The mostly American-driven and -funded 'law and development' movement was equally as concerned with the role of law in the development process, but was less so with international than with domestic law reform. See David M Trubek, 'Toward a Social Theory of Law: An Essay on the Study of Law and Development' (1972) 82 Faculty Scholarship Series Yale Law School 1; on Western perspectives on the battle see Koskenniemi in the Epilogue.

all. Others were more sceptical and pursued a rather radical, critical strategy, considering the existing order as profoundly unjust and difficult to change.[111] Many of the writers mentioned here became very important advisors to their respective governments or took on highly influential positions.[112] Elias became the first non-Western President at the ICJ, Bedjaoui served several times in the ILC and the ICJ, and Anand and Abi-Saab played important roles as advisors to their governments and in various UN bodies. Their performance and arguments in these roles surely changed over time and were highly dependent on context; Bedjaoui was the most critical author, while Anand or Elias, who were equally clear in their demand for profound changes in the international legal order, took more conciliatory approaches to contemporary international legal structures.

The history of international law played a major role in the work of many third world legal scholars in the 1950s and onwards. It was a process of redescription as much as re-appropriation that served a number of different functions. Many scholars put effort into describing the pre-colonial existence of international law of non-Western origins.[113] Outlining complex normative systems in ancient Indian, African, or Chinese writings demonstrated that the modern, *merely European*, system of international law as it emerged in the eighteenth and nineteenth centuries to the exclusion of others was a doctrinal aberration and usurpation born more of ignorance than normative prominence.[114] It was an attempt to demonstrate the much broader and common universal roots of public international law, thereby connecting Western and non-Western conceptions. At the same time, critical scholars in the field used historical and materialist analysis to redescribe colonialism as a history of exploitation of peoples from the third world. In these works, all standard justifications of colonialism, for example, religious, 'civilizational', racial, and technical superiority, were deconstructed as either well-intended or cynical strategies of domination. For those like Anand, classic European international law, with its implicit civilizational hierarchies, had been constructed by colonial powers in order to exclude and dominate non-European nations. In more concrete

[111] On this distinction, see Gevers Chapter 17, this volume. Also M Mutua, 'What is TWAIL?' (2000) Society of International Law Proceedings 31; Obiora C Okafor, 'Newness, Imperialism, and International Legal Reform in Our Time A Twail Perspective' (2005) 43 Osgoode Hall Law Journal 176; James T Gathii, 'Africa' in Bardo Fassbender, Anne Peters and Daniel Högger (eds), *The Oxford Handbook of the History of International Law* (OUP 2012) 407 (hereafter Gathii, 'Africa').

[112] For reflections on such roles today, see Luis Eslava and Sundhya Pahuja, 'Beyond the (Post-) Colonial' (2012) Verfassung und Recht in Übersee (VRÜ) 195.

[113] On Elias in this regard, see Landauer Chapter 14, this volume; see also Charles H Alexandrowicz, *An Introduction to the Law of Nations in the East Indies* (Clarendon Press 1967); KA Nilakanta Shastri, 'International Law and Relations in Ancient India' (1952) Indian Yearbook of International Affairs 97; Bhupinder S Chimni, 'International Law Scholarship in Post-Colonial India' (2010) Leiden Journal of International Law 27 with further references for India.

[114] As a current argument along these lines, see Onuma Yasuaki, *International Law in a Transcivilizational Perspective* (CUP 2017) 59.

terms, authors analysed the function of various doctrines and principles of international law in the colonial enterprise:

> Thus even a cursory look at the history of international law leaves no doubt about the Eurocentric nature of this law developed by and for the benefit of the rich, industrial, and powerful states of Western Europe and the United States.
>
> The vast majority of peoples had neither any voice nor any right and were meant to be exploited and, if necessary, colonized to serve the interests of their masters.[115]

It is this historically grounded critique of colonial legacies that prepared the ground for a new international law after decolonization, and fifty years later also inspired the *Third World Approaches to International Law*—a movement for a new critique of post-millennium international legal structures. But historical analysis was also used in more pragmatic ways to provide arguments in concrete court cases, for example, Bedjaoui argued the Western Sahara case at the ICJ and delved deeply into the history of the *terra nullius* doctrine. It was used also in more scholarly doctrinal skirmishes, for example, in support of the argument that urgent changes were now needed, including the need for law-making powers of UNGA. Ultimately, this re-appropriation of history also served the broader aim of reclaiming identity, rejecting the colonial idea of peoples without history, and concretely the rehabilitation of Africa.[116]

Another inroad for scholars of the third world was the standard assumption that international law (like any law) had to reflect realities and adapt to global sociological changes.[117] They declared that decolonization was a dramatic change that demanded nothing less than a new international law.[118] Such arguments could tap into a standard anti-formalist narrative of international law lagging behind important societal changes. As this volume shows, however, this type of narrative is much more likely to impact on legal discourse if it is supported by hegemonic powers. Moreover, some references to community values, such as human rights and solidarity among nations, had mushroomed in 1940s and 1950s Western legal scholarship, and could now be recycled for the concrete causes of the third world struggle.[119] But here, too, different varieties of the turn to sociology can be discerned.

Sociological inquiries were particularly popular at the Ivy League schools of the eastern US, even though pragmatic voluntarism might have dominated much of

115 Anand, *New States* (n 82) 45.

116 Gathii, 'Africa' (n 111) 410, 414.

117 Martii Koskenniemi, *The Gentle Civilizer of Nations* (CUP 2009) 474 (hereafter Koskenniemi, *Gentle Civilizer*).

118 Anna Krueger, *Die Bindung der Dritten Welt an das Völkerrecht* (Springer 2017).

119 Umut Özsu, '"In the Interests of Mankind as a Whole": Mohammed Bedjaoui's New International Economic Order' (2015) 6 Humanity 6 (hereafter Öszu, 'Mankind').

the Western practice of international law.[120] At Yale, where (among others) Elias, Anand, and Deng studied, and at other schools, the approach to international law was influenced by legal realism in domestic law and built on a close exchange with the international relations field. Formalism generally had lost its hold on legal doctrine, the change was greatest within the field of US international law, where policy guidance had become more important.

Those who received their legal education in France, most prominently Bedjaoui, took a somewhat different view on how to understand and integrate facts. influenced by the neo-Marxist analysis of international legal structures as it was developed by the Reims school in international law (headed by Charles Chaumont),[121] Bedjaoui like Chaumont did see a need for a new international law and based his analysis on a highly critical politico-economic analysis of both the history and the status quo of the international legal order. Solidarity was a value they endorsed for a new international law, but unlike George Scelle, the famous French interwar scholar, they completely dismissed it as a description of the past and current status quo of international law. Both Bedjaoui and Chaumont replaced Scelle's interwar socio-biological eclecticism with a highly realistic analysis of the relationship between the interests of Western economic elites and prevailing international legal structures, but without giving in to determinist approaches.[122] International law could potentially become a different and less unjust international legal order with new norms re-regulating and constraining both public and private economic, military, and political power. An important difference between these two approaches (Yale or Reims) can be seen in the extent to which they took into account the role of global capitalist structures in producing and stabilizing inequalities. This is exemplified by those authors influenced by the 'New Haven School' who operated squarely within the liberal paradigm, such as Elias, while the more radical materialistic thinking practised in 'Reims' and elsewhere during this time perhaps enabled writers to develop more critical voices like Bedjaoui.

2. Institutions

International institutions, such as the UN or the World Bank, were important protagonists in the battle for international law, too. Existing institutions became

[120] Koskenniemi, *Gentle Civilizer* (n 117) 474.

[121] On Chaumont, see Tourme-Jouannet Chapter 16, this volume and Martti Koskenniemi, 'Regarding "Méthode d'analyse du droit international" by Charles Chaumont (1975-I): Dialectics and International Law' (2015) 1–2 Revue Belge de Droit International 330. On Bedjaoui, however, without emphasizing the Reims school, see Öszu, 'Mankind' (n 119).

[122] On Chaumont's legal theory and respective methodology, see Tourme-Jouannet Chapter 16, this volume.

themselves embattled as states from North and South were fighting to preserve or gain representation and control of them, partly turning institutional law itself, including rules of procedure of plenaries and executive councils, into a weapon. Secretariats of international institutions were also important voices and actors in their own right and in the political and legal debates, lending legal and epistemic authority to the positions they supported. As most international institutions had been founded before the decolonization era, third world countries first had to join and often to eke out rights to equal representation and fair participation, which soon became a central part of the third world agenda. But the newly independent states were facing different challenges in different organizations. In the UN, for example, it was not so much a question of accession and representation for the newly independent states as such, but rather the fact that the UN Charter had established institutional hierarchies that favoured the great powers through their status in the UN Security Council. As the Soviets blocked the work of the Security Council with vetoes, the West for a short while favoured a careful strengthening of the role of the UNGA and its Committees.[123] Ultimately, however, the West sternly blocked all efforts to strengthen the UNGA's legislative role via an exercise of 'boundary drawing', holding that the UNGA was a 'political', not a 'legal', forum.[124] Nonetheless, UNGA resolutions became a powerful policy tool for the newly independent states through their role in discrediting colonialism and racialized white settler rule. Additionally, by engaging with the UN, the third world governments could advance their positions while the institution simultaneously shaped them.[125] In international financial institutions like the World Bank, fair representation was even more difficult—and proved ultimately elusive. Voting powers and other organizational rights in the Bank (as in the IMF and in other development banks created in these years) were insulated from the changes in membership. In all of these institutions, institutional law was itself an important battle ground. The (re-) interpretation of the competences of the UNGA or of the World Bank's executive board was instrumental in advancing the interests of one group of members—or the other.

An important additional strategy of third world countries was to reshape the established landscape by creating new institutions. In particular, they used the UN to 'institutionalize' issue areas. A prime example is UNCTAD, which provided a new arena to advance economic ideas that had no place in the Western dominated General Agreement on Tariffs and Trade (GATT) context. The merger of different programs of technical assistance in the UN Development Programme (UNDP) is another example, although the third world's demand to establish a UN fund for

[123] See the UNGA resolution 'Uniting for Peace' (1950); see also Sinclair Chapter 11, this volume.

[124] On 'boundary drawing' see the first section of this chapter, and on the debate over the status and repercussions of UNGA resolutions in the field of international humanitarian law, see Bernstorff, Chapter 2,this volume.

[125] See Sinclair Chapter 11, this volume.

financial assistance next to or instead of the World Bank failed.[126] Western states not only blocked these institutional activities, but started a smart discursive counter-attack by strategically shifting the responsibility for the contentious issue of 'financial assistance' to newly independent states to an institution under firm Western control. A good example of such a reshifting exercise was the creation of IDA as a soft-lending arm of the Bank that would support the third world. Even though this was portrayed as an accommodating programmatic shift in the interest of newly independent states, it rather cemented the institutional inequality by increasing the power of those states that provided funds.[127] The idea of functional specialization and disaggregation of the third world agenda, including the New International Economic Order (NIEO), into various policy fields and institutions was another Western counter strategy. In particular, the separation of 'political' (UN) and 'economic' (international financial institutions) organizations provided an underlying understanding that matters could be dealt with from a technical expertise perspective without political positioning on the demands of the third world. This provided an institutional basis for argument that would be used to delegitimize demands and ideas from Third Word scholars and politicians that had been adopted in the 'politicized' UN, compared to the allegedly 'rational' and expertise-driven financial institutions or specialized agencies.[128] Gaining representation in the ICJ was also difficult and took time, as limited positions had to be re-allocated. Considered a defender of the old European international law, third world states nonetheless invested much strategizing and political capital into gaining a fair representation at the ICJ and the shock over the 1966 *Liberia v South Africa* judgment only strengthened their resolve.[129] But it took till the 1970s to create an approximation of fair representation—but by then the reputation and authority of the Court had already drastically decreased.

Equally important was the use and stabilization of epistemic authority. International institutions in these years gained a central position in the international system not only as fora where states would meet, but also as increasingly autonomous actors or as indirect and effective multipliers of their principal agent's positions. International institutions took sides in the battle for international law. Third world governments assumed that over time membership would translate into policy orientation and hence that international institutions would eventually support their positions by advancing new law to support their economies, creating helpful

[126] See Olav Stokke, *The UN and Development: From Aid to Cooperation* (Indiana University Press 2009).

[127] See Dann Chapter 12, this volume.

[128] On the current role of 'expertise' in creating an unjust status quo, see D Kennedy, *A World of Struggle* (Princeton University Press 2016).

[129] Ram P Anand, *International Courts and Contemporary Conflicts* (Asia Publishing House 1972) 320; hier fehlt das 1966 Südwestafrika-Urteil!Taslim O Elias, *Africa and the Development of International Law* (Martinus Nijhoff Publishers 1988) 51. On the role of the Court, see Venzke Chapter 10, this volume.

knowledge and understanding. However, institutional control generally translated into the substantive positioning of the respective institution. And so, failure or success in gaining institutional control translated into such support, or not.

V. Conclusion

The battle for international law shaped the era situated between the Bandung Conference and the adoption of the NIEO. This transitional phase connects two long eras of Western imperialism, namely the high time of European colonialism that began in 1885 with the Berlin conference lasting until the 1950s, and the current era of US-led Western hegemony that began in the 1970s. Within roughly three decades, two-thirds of the world's population were led out of direct colonial rule exercised by European metropoles. This process came with a substantial transformation of the international legal order. While third world scholars and politicians succeeded in discrediting and delegitimizing the most apparent structures enabling classic colonial rule, the third world on balance clearly 'lost' the battle for a new substantively reformed international law. Western states secured their victories on the various battle sites by using international legal discourse in a strategic and often highly instrumental way. One of the most effective general strategies to ensure gradual transition to a new form of Western hegemony was to block third world initiatives of a more structural dimension while concurrently accommodating requests for change in a highly controlled and moderate way. Various discursive manoeuvres were instrumental in blocking a substantive reversal of the international legal order into one serving the interests of the colonized. Despite the successful politicization of central concepts during that transitional era, the West managed to adapt existing international legal structures to the new situation in which Western states had to deal with around 100 new formally independent states without losing control over the political economy of the world. It is the sum of these battles, skirmishes, counter moves and adaptations that, despite of various tactical third world victories, ultimately led to defeat in the battle for international law. By succeeding in injecting new meaning into central legal concepts and structures, Western governments could justify new forms of military, economic, and political interventionism in the open-ended language of international law that allowed for transformed and long-lasting North–South structures of dependency and exploitation.

PART I
SITES OF BATTLE
A. Concepts—Kampfbegriffe

1

The Common Heritage of Mankind

Annotations on a Battle

Surabhi Ranganathan

I. The seabed as battlefield

Among the battles for international law that unfolded in the decolonization era was that over the seabed[1] and its mineral resources. Until then, the law of the sea had made few references to the deep seabed. The 1958 Continental Shelf Convention provided for national jurisdiction over the *shallow* seabed—or continental shelf—defined vaguely, by reference to criteria of adjacency and exploitability.[2] The 1958 High Seas Convention mainly clarified rights in the water column, referring to the seabed only in the context of the freedom to lay pipelines and cables.[3] At the time these treaties were adopted, possibilities such as drilling the deep seabed for hard minerals had not come into prominence. Scientists had only commenced systematic mapping of the seabed earlier in that decade, producing the first map—of the North Atlantic sea-floor—in 1957. With most of the seabed remaining unmapped and underexplored, its legal regulation was not a key issue.

However, developments followed at a brisk pace thereafter. The idea of drilling the deep seabed gathered momentum in the United States (US), partly due to improvements in oil and mineral drilling technologies, and partly owing to the rising demand for metals. When the Scripps Institution of Oceanography discovered rich deposits of manganese nodules while dredging and photographing the Pacific floor, their findings attracted attention.[4] Such nodules had been found before: the

[1] The chapter draws on archival research conducted in New York, London, and Nairobi, a variety of UN materials, and first-person accounts of seabed exploration and mining initiatives. Some of this research was conducted in connection with previously published work, including Surabhi Ranganathan, 'Global Commons' (2016) 27 EJIL 693 (hereafter Ranganathan, 'Global Commons'); and 'Manganese Nodules' in Jessie Hohmann and Daniel Joyce (eds), *International Law's Objects* (OUP 2018) (hereafter Ranganathan, 'Manganese Nodules'); the piece thus draws upon these works, though it differs in focus and purpose.

[2] Art 1, 4. Convention on Continental Shelf (adopted 29 April 1958, entered into force 10 June 1964) 499 UNTS 311.

[3] Arts 1, 2, and 26, Convention on High Seas (adopted 29 April 1958, entered into force 30 September 1962) 450 UNTS 11.

[4] Roscoe Fleming and WN Fleming, 'Can We Vacuum-Clean the Sea Floor for Valuable Ore?' (July 1959) Popular Science 102.

Surabhi Ranganathan, *The Common Heritage of Mankind* In: *The Battle for International Law: South-North Perspectives on the Decolonization Era*. Edited by: Jochen von Bernstorff and Philipp Dann, Oxford University Press (2019).
DOI: 10.1093/oso/9780198849636.003.0002

famous nineteenth-century *Challenger* expedition had collected samples and reported on their polymetallic—manganese, copper, cobalt, and nickel—content.[5] However, as large-scale collection of the nodules was (at the time) inconceivable, they were forgotten. Scripps 'rediscovered' them at a propitious time, commissioning a study on the possibility of mining the nodules on a commercial scale. For this purpose, Scripps recruited John Mero, a post-graduate researcher, who went on to publish a book and papers that catalysed the development of a seabed mining industry.[6] Mero's writings delivered attractive estimates: billions of tonnes of ore-grade nodules paired with probable costs of $100 million for mining and processing 5000 tonnes of nodules per day would generate a 30 per cent return on investment.[7]

The publication of Mero's calculations coincided with other factors that made the ocean and ocean floor prominent subjects of study and popular discussion in the 1960s, resulting in an increasing sense of possibility of using the ocean in multiple ways on the one hand and a felt necessity on the other. Population explosion and food scarcity were major concerns, exacerbated—from the Western perspective—by decolonization, which had also destabilized existing arrangements for access to natural resources.[8] The ocean, carrying untapped reserves of both food and minerals, was regarded as the panacea.[9] Alongside ideas of marine farming and nodule mining, there even flourished visions of human habitation in the sea.

Such developments generated discussion on the law that should govern the oceans. Particularly with respect to the deep seabed, enterprises planning to make fixed capital investments into exploring mining sites and building equipment sought clarity on the legal framework applicable to their activities.[10] States began to contemplate how, whose, and on what terms jurisdiction could be established over this part of the ocean. It was in this context that the concept of the common heritage of mankind (CHM) came to be articulated, contested, and given specific meaning. The debate on the seabed also catalysed negotiations on all other aspects of the law of the sea, including those previously regulated by the 1958 Conventions. The Third United Nations (UN) Conference on the Law of the Sea (UNCLOS III), inaugurated in 1973, culminated in the adoption of the 1982 UN Convention on the Law of the Sea (LOSC).[11]

[5] John Murray and Alphonse François Renard, 'Report on Deep-Sea Deposits. Based on the Specimens Collected during the Voyage of the HMS Challenger (1873–76)' (1891) 341ff <https://escholarship.org/uc/item/0403495k>.

[6] John L Mero, *Mineral Resources of the Sea* (Elsevier Publishing Company 1965); and for a broader audience: John L Mero, 'Minerals on the Ocean Floor' (1960) 203 Scientific American 64.

[7] On the excitement generated by Mero's research, see Geoffrey P Glasby, 'Deep Seabed Mining: Past Failures and Future Prospects' (2002) 20 Marine Georesources & Geotechnology 161.

[8] Eg, Paul R Ehrlich, *The Population Bomb* (Sierra Club/Ballantine Books 1968); Garrett Hardin, 'Tragedy of the Commons' (1968) 162 Science 1243; see also Ranganathan, 'Global Commons' (n 1).

[9] See, eg, Tony Loftas, *The Last Resource* (Hamish Hamilton 1969).

[10] Philip E Steinberg, *Social Construction of the Ocean* (CUP 2001) 187ff.

[11] UN Convention on the Law of the Sea (adopted 10 December 1982, entered into force 16 November 1994) 1833 UNTS 3.

UNCLOS III negotiations, and those of the preceding UN Committee on the Seabed (1968–1973), are often recalled in the register of battle waged between developed and developing states to write their preferred politico-economic visions into law. The former were dealing with the loss of empire and eager to prolong their rule over economic affairs; the latter were keen to change the rules of economic exchange and distribution and spur their own industrial development. Indeed, the law of the sea negotiations are narrated as an element of the third world's struggle in the 1970s for a New International Economic Order (NIEO).[12]

In keeping with the theme of this volume, Section II tells this story of battle, focusing on the events until 1975 but going beyond where necessary. It illuminates how the seabed became the subject of a protracted legal tussle that focused upon the content to be given to the CHM principle, but also had broader implications for international law and international relations. It avoids recapping details that may be obtained elsewhere and instead concentrates on showing how the terms of the battle changed over time. Section III then returns to the theme implied in the chapter's subtitle and 'annotates' the battle described in Section II by referring to a few key issues—the precise basis for developing states' interest in seabed resources; the antinomies of the CHM principle; and the lurking shadow of another battle, the Cold War, upon the negotiations.

II. The battle traced

Institutional narratives of the battle for the seabed usually identify 1967 as the year the opening salvo was fired. It was then that Malta requested the UN Secretary General (UNSG) to add the seabed as an item on the agenda for the UN General Assembly's (UNGA) annual meeting.[13] And Arvid Pardo, Malta's chief diplomat, made a major speech outlining possibilities and perils of resource extraction from the seabed and introducing the CHM concept.[14] UN Yearbook indices show a rapid increase in the number of entries relating to the seabed from this year, whereas that subject had received no previous mention.

The Maltese initiative was catalysed by information about the rapid development of resource extraction technologies as well as apprehension of the seabed's appropriation and militarization by industrially advanced states. Giorgio Borg Oliver, the Maltese Prime Minister, argued that, rather than permitting these outcomes, the UN should facilitate the use of seabed resources as a source of development

12 See, eg, Robert L Friedham and William J Durch, 'The International Seabed Resources Agency Negotiations and the New International Economic Order' (1977) 31 International Organization 343.

13 Malta: Request for the Inclusion of a Supplementary Item in the Agenda of the Twenty-Second Session (18 August 1967) UN Doc A/6695 (hereafter 'UN Doc A/6695').

14 UNGA, First Committee Debate (1 November 1967) UN Doc A/C.1/PV.1515–1516, (hereafter 'UNGA, A/C.1/PV.1515–1516').

capital for poorer states.[15] Pardo, spearheading the initiative at the UN, echoed these themes, in a speech that—as I have more fully described elsewhere—was part panegyric to the oceans, part tantalizing description of the seabed's material possibilities, and part warning of its approaching enclosure.[16] He described the near-incomprehensible quantities of mineral resources available in the sea—eg, 358,000,000,000 tonnes of manganese, enough for 400,000 years of human consumption, as compared to 100 years' worth available on land.[17] He asserted that these minerals could be profitably extracted, with their commercial recovery imminent.[18] He placed their extraction in a broader context: a first move towards greater engagement with the oceans, heralding long-term uses such as farming and fish husbandry, and perhaps even human settlement.[19] In the shorter term, seabed mining offered both revenue and, what 'technologically advanced countries' would welcome more, freedom from 'import dependency in peace and war'.[20] The seabed was also a possible terrain for military activity, including the placement of fixed missile systems.[21]

Pardo then noted his fear that economic and strategic interests would cause technologically advanced states to appropriate the seabed, sharply increasing world tensions partly by instigating a naval arms race, and partly because of the 'intolerable injustice' of 'reserving the plurality of the world's resources for the exclusive benefit of [a few] nations'.[22] He claimed that a competitive scramble was already underway, and would surpass 'in magnitude and implication [the] colonial scramble for territory in Asia and Africa'.[23] Contemporary international law, permitting—via definition of the continental shelf—claims to jurisdiction based on the exploitability of the seabed would only support such a scramble.[24]

Therefore, Malta (and Pardo) advocated to the assembled states the need for a new legal framework, founded on the CHM principle, for activities on the seabed. This framework would preclude national appropriation of the seabed area and resources lying beyond designated zones of national jurisdiction. It would permit their exploitation under international licence exclusively for peaceful purposes and for the benefit of mankind as a whole; thus, it would mandate sharing financial revenues obtained from commercial exploitation among states, with preferential consideration given to poorer countries. Pardo supported the speedy conclusion of

15 UN Doc A/6695 (n 13).
16 Ranganathan, 'Global Commons' (n 1) 704–06.
17 UNGA, A/C.1/PV.1515–1516 (n 14) paras 26–27.
18 ibid para 34.
19 ibid paras 33–34, 44.
20 ibid para 45.
21 ibid paras 48–50.
22 ibid para 91.
23 ibid.
24 ibid paras 56ff.

a treaty that would delineate the international seabed and establish an autonomous international agency to administer it.[25]

At the time of Pardo's speech, the seabed had already appeared on the agenda of the UN Secretariat, UNESCO, and other agencies. The UN Economic and Social Council (ECOSOC) and UNGA had adopted resolutions asking the UNSG to study prospects of seabed mining, especially for the benefit of developing states.[26] Non-governmental forums had articulated the CHM principle in relation to the seabed in their proposals.[27] US President Lyndon Johnson had asserted that the seabed should remain 'the legacy of all human beings'.[28] Moreover, preambles of the 1959 Antarctic Treaty[29] and the 1967 Outer Space Treaty had referred to those domains in terms of the common interest of all mankind. The Outer Space Treaty even stated that the:

> . . . exploration and use of outer space, including . . . celestial bodies, shall be carried out for the benefit and in the interests of all countries, irrespective of their degree of economic or scientific development, and shall be the province of all mankind.[30]

Yet, following on the heels of these activities, Pardo's speech represented a flash-point. In contrast with the non-governmental forums, it was the first formal proposal to the UN for a treaty on the seabed. In contrast with the Outer Space and Antarctic treaties, it suggested that revenues derived from commercial exploitation should be shared among states. And, in contrast with the UN Secretariat, it pressed for urgent political action. Indeed, much of the influence of Pardo's speech must be attributed to his framing the seabed as presenting either an immediate threat of global conflict—land grab giving on to actual battle—or an opportunity for constructive post-colonial legal and economic engagement between states.

Developed states, both Western and the USSR, opted to emphasize the opportunity rather than the threat. The United Kingdom (UK) Foreign Office records reveal that they had been surprised by Malta's initial request for discussion of the seabed, and worried that it would push for demilitarization of the seabed—a difficult proposition to openly discuss in the Cold War context.[31] Relieved to find from

[25] UNGA, A/C.1/PV.1516–1516 (n 14) para 8ff.

[26] ECOSOC Res 1112 (XL) (7 March 1966); UNGA Res 2172 (XXI) (6 December 1966).

[27] World Peace through Law Center, 'Resolution 15: Resources of the High Seas' (13 July 1967) S-0442-0027-0003; Commission to Study the Organisation of Peace, 'Draft Resolution and Working Paper' (S-0858-0005-03, 21 August 1967).

[28] Lyndon B Johnson, 'Remarks at the Commissioning of the Research Ship—Oceanographer' (13 July 1966) <https://www.presidency.ucsb.edu/documents/remarks-the-commissioning-the-research-ship-oceanographer> accessed 7 December 2018.

[29] The Antarctic Treaty (adopted 1 December 1959, entered into force 23 June 1961) 402 UNTS 71.

[30] Art 1, Outer Space Treaty (adopted 27 January 1967, entered into force 10 October 1967) 610 UNTS 205. Already in 1952 the proposition was that outer space should be regarded as the property of all mankind: Oscar Schachter, 'Who Owns the Universe' (22 March 1952) Collier's Weekly 36.

[31] UK National Archives, Foreign and Commonwealth Office, 10/232–235.

Pardo's speech that this was not Malta's sole focus, they took steps to minimize discussion on the issue, preferring that the discussion concentrate upon the question of a seabed regime governing economic exploitation. For on that topic, while they considered Malta's proposals for redistribution quixotic, they were not averse to some form of international regulation—for which there was also demand from potential investors.[32]

Mainly, developed states hoped to delegate the issue to a smaller committee (much like the one for outer space) that would work at a deliberate enough pace for them to reconcile their multiple domestic interests in seabed delimitation and use.[33] Such interests included corporate interests favouring wide zones of national jurisdiction over the seabed, defence interests favouring narrow ones, interests of non-governmental bodies, individual Parliamentarians, and groups like the Quakers (who embraced the CHM idea), and many others. Different cocktails of these interests had generated differing national positions, which the developed states also hoped to reconcile, given time: to this end, they held regular meetings among themselves, and bilaterally with the USSR and possibly also Japan.[34]

For their part, developing states, recalled in the literature as the champions of CHM, were indeed favourably disposed to the prospect of seabed riches being used for their benefit, and commended this aspect of Pardo's proposal. However, it is wrong to think developing states equally enthusiastic about all implications of the CHM: in particular, several were concerned at the implication that the largest possible portion of the seabed would fall within international jurisdiction. Rather, with a preference strengthened by Pardo's description of seabed riches, they were keen for expansive zones of national jurisdiction.[35] That said, their overall response, as for developed states, was to support discussion of the various issues by committee.

Thus, the 1967 session of the UNGA concluded with the establishment of a Seabed Committee. This Committee did its work in two phases. Until 1970, it focused on formulating guiding principles expressing the CHM concept, and these were adopted as the Declaration of Principles Governing the Seabed.[36] Thereafter, following the UNGA's decision to convene UNCLOS III in 1973, it undertook preparatory work for this conference, including seeking to specify precise mechanisms to regulate seabed mining.[37]

Unfortunately, as the rifts between their positions became clear, the Committee only succeeded in increasing the opposition between developed and developing states. Among the divisive issues were the criteria for determining the breadth

[32] ibid.
[33] ibid.
[34] ibid.
[35] For states' initial reactions, see UNGA, First Committee Debate (8–16 November 1967) UN Doc A/C.1/PV.1524–1530.
[36] UNGA Res 25/2749 (17 December 1970).
[37] UNGA Res 25/2750 C (17 December 1970).

of the continental shelves; the question whether the future treaty might address all other oceans issues; and, most difficult of all, the precise legal framework for seabed mining.[38]

The first issue—breadth of the continental shelves—was one on which we might have expected states to differ across multiple axes, relating to whether and what type of continental shelf, they had access. While this was indeed the case initially, the positions became resolved along developed and developing lines. It was observed that states such as Tanzania and Sri Lanka (at the time Ceylon) had changed their initial positions, and India had even decided to act against its own interest, all for the sake of solidarity with other developing states.[39] Developing states also rejected a proposal made by US President Richard Nixon for a tripartite division of the seabed, into a narrow national continental shelf, a trusteeship zone, and an international area. Although this proposal carried definite benefits for developing states, they were suspicious of US motives, and mistrustful of the language of 'trusteeship'.[40]

The second issue—the scope of the future treaty—emerged from the first in that one of the questions arising from it was the extent to which possession of the continental shelf may have consequences for jurisdiction over the water column above (and its resources). This resulted in developing states' clamouring for a fresh consideration of this and all other matters concerning the law of the sea. Such matters had been previously addressed by treaties negotiated before most developing states had achieved independence. Developed states resisted the proposal, preferring that the treaty solely focus on the regulation of activities on the deep seabed.[41]

These first two divisive issues eventually found resolution; the former at the UNCLOS III negotiations, the latter in the prior decision that the mandate of this conference would include all oceans issues. But the third issue—the regime governing the seabed—remained contested for a much longer time. At its heart was the question of what precise formulation should be given to the CHM, which had been accepted as the proper designation for the seabed. All states were willing to pay lip service to Pardo's ideas. They agreed that the seabed should be immune from national appropriation, and that its resources should be exploited for the benefit of all mankind. They thus supported the 1970 Declaration of Principles (a text that reconciled their varied expectations by way of abstract statement).[42] However, they disagreed—sharply—on the details.

[38] For a detailed account, see Shigeru Oda, *The UN Seabed Committee 1968–1973* (Sijthoff 1977) (hereafter Oda, *The Seabed Committee*).

[39] Per correspondence in FCO 76/328 UK National Archives.

[40] Per correspondence in FCO 76/145, 76/161, and 76/332, UK National Archives.

[41] See UNGA, Plenary Meeting (15 December 1969) UN Doc A/PV.1833. However, they agreed to comprehensive negotiations the following year.

[42] The vote was 108 states in favour, none against, and fourteen abstentions. However, it needed the Chairman, Hamilton S Amerasinghe, to submit a personal draft of the principles, reconciling the texts prepared by developed and developing states, and his good offices, to achieve this resolution: see Oda, *The Seabed Committee* (n 38) 131–32.

Developed states were keen for a regime modelled on the principle of the freedom of the high seas: the seabed should remain a *res communis*, open to economic activity of all states. They wanted an international body to function mainly as a registry of mining sites, although they were willing to further regard it as a body empowered to issue mining 'licences' (though without discretion in the matter) and distribute the fee revenue to developing states. Such a system would ensure both access to mining sites and security of tenure once their claims were registered. Developing states, however, wanted more: an international body that would itself conduct all mining activity (with necessary financial and technological assistance from developed states) and share the profits generated among all states, with especial reference to their needs as developing states. Such a body would enable them to feel they were active participants in the regime. Moreover, excluding national or private mining activity would ensure that seabed resources were recovered at a sustainable rate, protecting the interests of land-based producers of the relevant minerals (for example, Chile was a major producer of copper).

This difference in position carried on into UNCLOS III. A partial resolution was achieved as late as 1976 on the basis of a proposal by Henry Kissinger for a parallel system under which mining might be carried out either by an international body, the so-called 'Enterprise', or by states.[43] Developing states had some misgivings about such a parallel system; they worried that the Enterprise would not survive open competition with the private or public mining enterprises of developed states, and thus pushed for it to enjoy certain privileges in the use of the seabed.

Thus, the battle shifted focus, consolidating now around five issues:

1. Access to technology.

Developing states expected developed states to provide technology to the Enterprise, including for its joint ventures with developing states, on highly favourable terms. However, developed states were only willing to 'facilitate' access to technology at market prices.

2. Site banking.

One of Kissinger's initial concessions was that certain mining sites could be reserved for use of the Enterprise. This morphed into a claim by developing states that developed states seeking mining licences from the proposed International Seabed Authority (ISA) should in fact identify two sites of equal value: one to be allocated to their use, and the other to be reserved for use by the Enterprise or

[43] Edward L Miles, *Global Ocean Politics* (Martinus Nijhoff 1998) 219 (hereafter Miles, *Global Ocean Politics*).

developing states. Developed states were concerned about the costs this would impose on them.

3. Provision of financial support to the Enterprise and the ISA itself.

Developed states were similarly concerned about costs in relation to the issue of financial support to the Enterprise and the ISA itself—the former by financing entirely its first mining operation, the latter in the form of fees and a share in revenue. While not unwilling to pay, they considered the rates imposed too high and too inflexible.

4. Developing states' demands for production ceilings.

In the years following Pardo's speech, developing states had come to recognize that the resources of the international seabed would not include the most valued—petroleum.[44] Rather, manganese nodules would remain the main resource, containing minerals that were still plentifully available on *their* land. They feared a glut in the market from seabed production, and were not much reassured by reports like that of the UNSG, who foresaw an adverse impact on land-based producers of manganese (and possibly cobalt and nickel, but not copper).[45] They thus sought production quotas—a demand strongly resisted by developed states.

5. The ISA's administrative structure.

Developing states wanted an active say in the ISA's decision making, and favoured the vesting of major powers in an Assembly; obviously, they would enjoy a numerical majority in such a body. Developed states pushed for such powers to be vested in a smaller Council, in which they would have greater proportionate representation.

It is not difficult to see why these five issues were to prove intractable. For developing states, they represented essential elements of the CHM—provisions material to their expectations that, for the first time in their experience, a global resource would be used in a way that included them as equal participants and beneficiaries. Their resolve to achieve these outcomes strengthened with time, as the seabed became joined to the NIEO agenda.[46] In Chimni's words, it came to be seen as 'a microcosm of the possibilities the future held and the inauguration of a new era in

[44] Shigeru Oda, *The Law of the Sea in Our Time: New Developments 1966–1975* (Sijthoff 1977) 125 (hereafter Oda, *New Developments*).

[45] UNSG, 'Report on the Possible Impact of Seabed Mineral Production in the Area beyond National Jurisdiction on World Markets, with Special Reference to the Problems of Developing Countries: A Preliminary Assessment' (28 May 1971) UN Doc A/AC.138/36.

[46] Art 29, UNGA Res 29/3281 (12 December 1974).

international relations'.[47] For developed states, however, the developing states' demands were unnecessary and cumbersome extrapolations from the CHM concept, which would eventually stymie the adoption of a practicable regime.[48]

Two procedural decisions taken in the 1973 and 1974 sessions of UNCLOS III further added to the conditions shaping the battle of attrition between developed and developing states. The first was that, as far as possible, all decisions would be taken by consensus;[49] the second was that the treaty would be negotiated as a package deal, with states asked to accept or reject it as a whole.[50] Underlying these decisions perhaps was the expectation that they would facilitate adoption of a seabed regime acceptable to all states. However, these decisions delayed agreement on various aspects, and later became the basis for rejection of the LOSC by a number of developed states, despite their agreement with its provisions on all other oceans issues.

Accounts of the work of the UN Seabed Committee and (even more so) UNCLOS III recollect a frustrating negotiation process in which formal meetings made little headway: personality conflicts, secret meetings, and suspicions of conspiracy abounded, and information asymmetries made it difficult to distinguish proposals made in good faith from those that were not.[51] From the perspective of the developed states, the final outcome—written into the LOSC—was particularly unfortunate. It had been clear to them for many years that the economic promise of seabed resources had been exaggerated, and they resented the complex bureaucracy that the developing states had managed to secure in realization of their aims. With some refusing to sign the LOSC at all, many Western developed states worked systematically to alter its seabed regime.[52] In 1994 they were able to secure an 'Implementation Agreement' which all but rewrote the LOSC provisions.[53] The new regime foregrounded the commercial aspects of seabed mining, reducing the CHM aspirations simply to a few provisions on revenue sharing. The changes were described by Western scholars as an 'excellent example of adapting international law to new circumstances'.[54] To some

[47] Bhupinder S Chimni, 'International Law Scholarship in Postcolonial India: Coping with Dualism' (2010) 23 Leiden Journal of International Law 23, 38.

[48] This view is neatly captured by the title of an account of the US position at the seabed negotiations: Markus G Schmidt, *Common Heritage or Common Burden* (OUP 1989) (hereafter Schmidt, *Common Heritage or Common Burden).*

[49] This point took up most of the opening session: Oda, *New Developments* (n 44) 153–54.

[50] UNCLOS III, 2nd Session, 19th Plenary Meeting, Caracas (27 June 1974) UN Doc. A/Conf.62/SR.19.

[51] See, eg, Oda, *The Seabed Committee* (n 38); Miles, *Global Ocean Politics* (n 43).

[52] Surabhi Ranganathan, *Strategically Created Treaty Conflicts and the Politics of International Law* (CUP 2014) 149ff (hereafter Ranganathan, *Treaty Conflicts*).

[53] Agreement relating to the implementation of Part XI of the United Nations Convention on the Law of the Sea of 10 December 1982 (adopted 28 July 1994, entered into force 16 November 1994) 1836 UNTS 3. On the changes see Ranganathan, *Treaty Conflicts* (n 52) 174–76 and 376–79.

[54] Louis B Sohn, 'International Law Implications of the 1994 Agreement' (1994) 88 American Journal of International Law 696, 704–05

developing state scholars, however, they represented a 'mutilation' of the CHM ideal.[55]

III. Annotations on the battle

As seen in the earlier account, the grounds of the 'battle for the seabed' shifted over the years: from forestalling enclosure (per Pardo's warnings) to negotiating an appropriate scope for national jurisdiction, to arguments over whether only an international body could undertake mining operations to the terms of the assistance that developed states would provide to developing states. That said, the proper conception of the CHM, as the legal foundation for reconfigured political and economic relations between developed and developing states, remained the central issue.

In fact, it is often noted that, since the initial flush of excitement about the material gains from the manganese nodules had quickly receded, the battle was largely about the law and the creation of a legal precedent by securing a concrete articulation of the CHM.[56] In this view, the nodules were just a pretext; the regime itself was the prize, as the potential exemplar for other regimes on natural resources. Evaluations of the outcome of the battle—its winners and losers—are predicated on this view. And the view is correct to a point. The normative dimension (or, as some noted, the ideological one) did to some extent overtake the material dimension of the battle. This section explores whether this was to any party's benefit. However, it first complicates the assertion that the material dimension had lost its importance by the early years of UNCLOS III and argues that this was not, for good reason, the perception of developing states. Finally, the section briefly comments on the need for further analysis of the shadow cast by the Cold War over the battle for the seabed.

1. Persistence of the material dimension

Doubts about the feasibility of seabed mining rose *prior* to the commencement of UNCLOS III.[57] In private meetings, Western states had acknowledged that the

[55] Ram Prakash Anand, 'Common Heritage of Mankind: Mutilation of an Ideal' in *Studies in International Law and History: An Asian Perspective* (Martinus Nijhoff 2004) 180, 196 (hereafter Anand, 'Common Heritage of Mankind').

[56] See, eg, Martti Koskenniemi and Marja Lehto, 'The Privilege of Universality: International Law, Economic Ideology and Seabed Resources' (1996) 65 Nordic JIL 533, 539ff (hereafter Koskenniemi and Lehto, 'The Privilege of University'), describing the seabed negotiations as 'mainly political' (1974–1979) and 'mainly ideological' (1981–1984), as opposed to the 'mainly economic' initial setting (1967–1970). They note that by 1974–1975, '[t]he illusion of an "ocean bonanza" had been lost': ibid 541.

[57] See Geoffrey P Glasby, 'Lessons Learned from Deep-Sea Mining' (2000) 289 Science 551.

economics did not favour seabed mining on a large scale, and that such mining would generate 'insignificant' revenues for distribution among developing states for the foreseeable future.[58] Although they had hesitated to communicate this to developing states,[59] those states too received advice from their scientists that, without further technological development, seabed mining would not be competitive.[60] Nevertheless, they continued to push for an international regime on the terms described in Section II. Not only did they insist on a share in benefits from seabed mining, they also insisted on production limitations to prevent harm to their land-based mineral production. The literature tends to regard theirs as an obdurate insistence on the economic prospects of seabed mining, as well as a possibly strategic one, in order to push their preferred vision of the CHM.[61]

However, to understand why developing states continued to believe in the material prospects of seabed mining, it is important to note the actions of developed states and their corporations.[62] These must bear some responsibility for confirming developing states in their belief that, even if not an imminent prospect, seabed mining was certainly a near-term one. For example, consider the affair of the *Hughes Glomar Explorer*, a massive ship built and operated by the CIA in the early 1970s in order to raise a sunken Soviet submarine from the Pacific bed. The story circulated as cover for this mission was that the ship belonged to the Howard Hughes Corporation, and was being used to mine for manganese nodules.[63] Many, including the UN Secretariat,[64] and even US officials,[65] appear to have believed the story.

Even after the true nature of the mission was revealed in the late 1970s, other developments occurred to convince developing states of corporations' and developed states' serious interest in seabed mining. For one, representations made by developed states focused upon economic opportunities—for example, Henry Kissinger canvassed for the parallel system on the argument that there were 'more than 100 valuable sites on which operations could be conducted at present'.[66] For another, European (particularly German), American, and Japanese companies, having formed various mining consortia, reported successful testing of nodule mining technologies (explaining their decision to postpone developing commercial

[58] Per records in FCO 76/733, UK National Archives.

[59] ibid.

[60] Eg, Letter from the Chief Geologist, Ministry of Natural Resources, Kenya (10 September 1973) (Kenya National Archives, KP/6/9).

[61] See, eg, Schmidt, *Common Heritage or Common Burden* (n 48) 16.

[62] I also discuss some of these actions in Ranganathan, 'Manganese Nodules' (n 1).

[63] Roy Varner and Wayne R Collier, *A Matter of Risk: The Incredible Inside Story of the CIA's Hughes Glomar Explorer Mission to Raise a Russian Submarine* (Random House 1978) (Collier was part of the CIA mission).

[64] See, eg, UNSG, 'Seabed Resources – Recent Developments' (3 July 1973) UN Doc A/AC.138/90, 10–11.

[65] ibid 188.

[66] 'Meeting with Kenyan officials' (13 August 1976) (Kenya National Archives, KL/14/1).

mining systems on the argument that the regime being negotiated at UNCLOS III imposed conditions that were too onerous).[67] Between 1980 and 1982, a number of Western states (the US, the UK, Germany, France, Japan) also adopted domestic legislation authorizing commercial mining under their unilateral (mutually recognized) licence—making good on a long threatened action, and further convincing developing states that they were in a race to grab all the mineral wealth of the seabed.[68] Meanwhile, research expeditions brought to light other types of mineral deposits—polymetallic sulphides and cobalt-rich crusts—which could be recovered alongside manganese nodules.[69] The US government undertook its own exploration of these, generating talks in Washington DC of a new gold rush.[70]

It is not remarkable that, for developing countries—who had frankly acknowledged that the technology to undertake seabed mining would have to come from the developed states and their corporations—these activities were continuing indications of seabed mining's material possibilities, as well as material threats to their land-based production. The economics of seabed mining thus remained a critical factor in their negotiating posture.

2. An ideological victory?

Most scholarship identifies the ideological dimension of the seabed negotiations as key to understanding the long battle of attrition fought between developed and developing states. For instance, Koskenniemi and Lehto note that:

> No immediate pressure to conclude the negotiations with a practical and workable arrangement to govern deep seabed operations was felt. All parties preferred to dwell in questions of principle—all the more so as they seemed to be important precedents for a whole range of future international institutions governing international commons.[71]

For his part, Pardo, looking back at the negotiations, rued the 'almost theological debate' in which 'the viability of the future international regime for the seabed beyond national jurisdiction and economic realities were largely forgotten by the contending parties'.[72] The ideology in focus was, of course, the NIEO for developing states. Developed states, despising the very phrase—which the British Prime

[67] John L Shaw, 'Nodule Mining—Three Miles Deep!' (1993) 11 Marine Georesources & Geotechnology 181, 197 (Shaw headed the consortium that carried out the first venture).

[68] See, eg, records in Kenya National Archives, KP/6/12, and UK National Archives, FCO 76/1957.

[69] See, eg, Kenneth J Hsü, *Challenger at Sea: A Ship That Revolutionized Earth Science* (Princeton University Press 1992) 314–15 (narrating the discovery of polymetallic sulphides).

[70] William J Broad, *The Universe Below: Discovering the Secrets of the Deep Sea* (Fireside 1998) 259ff.

[71] Koskenniemi and Lehto, 'The Privilege of University' (n 56) 541.

[72] Arvid Pardo, 'Before and After' (1983) 46 Law and Contemporary Problems 95, 102.

Minister Harold Wilson suggested sounded 'a bit Muscovite'[73]—and aware of the challenge that the idea represented, were keen to protect their access to resources and world markets, and worked to put in place the neoliberal arrangements that Mazower calls 'the real new international economic order'.[74] In the context of the seabed, they favoured application of the high-seas freedom, protesting the developing states' conception of the CHM as 'socialist'.[75]

I have noted elsewhere that accounts of developing states' commitment to the seabed and the CHM antedate this commitment to the mid-1960s, and wrongly identify Pardo as one of their voices.[76] Pardo's motivations were multiple, and his proposal introducing the CHM lacked the elements that developing states later associated with that concept—at which time they found him, and Malta, opposed to their stance. Meanwhile, developing states did not immediately take up the seabed: they responded cautiously to Pardo's speech, and their solidarity on the issue was forged gradually, in the course of the Seabed Committee's meetings. That said, there is no doubt that the seabed came to constitute an element of the NIEO agenda.

Looking back, it is easy to characterize the 1982 LOSC regime as a victory for developing states, as its text refers to many of their issues of concern and suggests that these are material to any conception of the CHM. Certainly, these states also remained invested in it through the 1980s, with their championship providing one of a few fulcrums of solidarity within the third world. The impression of a temporary third-world ideological victory is also strengthened by evaluations of the 1994 retrenchments as the mutilation of the CHM ideal.[77] However, it is important to keep in view that, at the time of UNCLOS III and its conclusion, prominent voices in the third world expressed discontent with the shape taken by the CHM in the LOSC regime. The underlying ideal had been swallowed up in the minutiae, and the minutiae were disappointing. These voices at least perceived no ideological victory.

For example, in a pair of articles published in 1982, Chimni argued that the 1982 treaty did not protect many of the interests—access to technology, protection of land-based production, a genuine opportunity to participate in seabed production—that developing states considered essential to the CHM. Describing the law of the sea as 'imperialism all the way', he concluded that 'restructuring or altering of existing international property relations is not possible through legal

[73] UK Foreign Office, Internal correspondence (15 April 1975) (UK National Archives, FCO 61/1295).

[74] Mark Mazower, *Governing the World* (Penguin 2012) 343ff, 346 (hereafter Mazower, *Governing the World*).

[75] James L Malone, 'The United States and the Law of the Sea after UNCLOS III' (1983) 46 Law and Contemporary Problems 29, 31–32. Malone was chairman of the US delegation to UNCLOS III.

[76] Ranganathan, 'Global Commons' (n 1) 706ff.

[77] Anand, 'Common Heritage of Mankind' (n 55).

instruments'.[78] Bedjaoui took a similar view, pointing to the antinomies inherent in the CHM that had been exploited to the disadvantage of developing states. The CHM betokened an idea—limited sovereignty in favour of collective economic security—which had merit, but had only been deployed to gain access to developing states' natural resources in the past. In the present context, too, its invocation seemed designed to counter developing states' claims of permanent sovereignty over natural resources; it did not accommodate their interests, for example, access to technology. With 'ill-controlled appetites', he argued, advanced powers were using the CHM as a cover to co-opt the seabed to their uses.[79] These scholarly assessments are complemented by archival records, for example, with Kenyan officials expressing consternation at the late inclusion of new elements, such as a system for protecting the investments into seabed mining that (mainly) developed states had already made.[80] Coming at the end of a long and costly negotiation, this system amounted to—as noted in the pre-eminent textbook on the law of the sea—a 'complete rewriting of the Convention's rules on the sea-bed mining' in favour of those pioneer investor states.[81]

Even apart from the reactions to it, the LOSC regime did not, on merit, represent an ideological victory. Its provisions were unsatisfactory, and, although placed under rubrics corresponding to demands from the third world, obscured the ideas underlying the CHM, which as a principle also has thereafter retreated from view. Moreover, it is worth critically examining whether the battle over CHM advanced the NIEO in any material respect. That this finds only scant mentions in recent appraisals of the NIEO[82] suggests that the presumption should be that it did not. Yet, this needs careful consideration, including assessing the possibility that, far from advancing it, this battle may have undermined the NIEO movement by sublimating many elements of the NIEO agenda into negotiations over one specific regime, which, as it turned out, was not the most relevant from the perspective of the economic needs of the developing states. Much time, energy, and foreign exchange (precious to developing states) were expended on UNCLOS III. What needs to be further analysed is how *these* negotiations impacted upon negotiations around *other* NIEO issues.

[78] Bhupinder S Chimni, 'Law of the Sea: Imperialism all the Way' (1982) 17(11) Economic & Political Weekly 407; Bhupinder S Chimni, 'Law of the Sea: Winners are Losers' (1982) 17(24) Economic & Political Weekly 987.

[79] Mohammed Bedjaoui, *Towards a New International Economic Order* (UNESCO/Holmes & Meier 1979) 224–27.

[80] See, eg, Kenya National Archives, KL/14/2.

[81] Robin R Churchill and Alan Vaughan Lowe, Law of the Sea (3rd edn, Manchester University Press 1999) 230.

[82] Such a discussion has not so far appeared in recent works on the NIEO, including Mazower, *Governing the World* (n 74); and Symposium on the New International Economic Order (2015) 6 Humanity 1–233.

3. The shadow of the Cold War

Full exploration of the influence of the Cold War upon the legal progression of the seabed negotiations is still needed. It certainly loomed large in perceptions of the NIEO, as mentioned in British Prime Minister Wilson's concerns; the British Foreign Office reached the conclusion that, although the Soviet Union had neither originated the concept nor was willing to acknowledge the demands that the movement placed upon itself, it adopted a supportive posture for strategic reasons.[83] Recent work goes further in reading the NIEO as a socialist globalization effort promoted by the second and third worlds.[84]

The Cold War was also a material factor as regards seabed policy formation. It underlay such points as the initial alarms of developed states that the Maltese initiative was concerned with defence aspects. It was also the basis for the division of views between industrial and military interests in these states: for example, in the US, industrial interests favoured broad zones of national jurisdiction over the seabed such that minerals could be recovered under domestic license, while military interests preferred narrow ones that would allow them to operate at greater proximity to other states (the Nixon proposal emerged from an initiative to reconcile these interests).[85] Presumably, it contributed to the uncertainty regarding access to land-based natural resources, and spurred the technological race for the sea, as well as for space.

There are many respects in which we see Cold War influence upon seabed negotiations. For one, the Soviet Union's alignments: on many issues, such as technology transfer, its interests coincided with developed states; like them, it even adopted its own unilateral mining legislation.[86] Yet, afraid at the same time of internal collusion among Western states it adopted a supportive position towards the LOSC regime. A closer examination of its positions on various issues might allow for a richer appreciation of how the East/West tensions fed into the North/South debates.

Secondly, the Cold War was certainly a factor underpinning the information distortions that characterized seabed negotiations. This included—as mentioned—misleading developing states on the practical prospects of seabed mining.

Thirdly, the Cold War also contributed to differing conceptions of legal doctrine and institutional authority among states—hence, for example, the dismissal by Western states of the proposed ISA as 'socialist'. Again the extent to which such

[83] See UK National Archives, FCO 61/1295 and 58/927.

[84] Johanna Bockmann, 'Socialist Globalization against Capitalist Neocolonialism: The Economic Ideas behind the New International Economic Order' (2015) 6 Humanity 109.

[85] Oda, *New Developments* (n 44) 89–104.

[86] 'Edict on Provisional Measures to Regulate Soviet Enterprises for the Exploration and Exploitation of Mineral Resources', 21 ILM 551 (1982). A Kenyan dispatch noted that this move was interpreted at UNCLOS III as an expression of Soviet dissatisfaction with third-world states leaning in favour of Western states: Kenya National Archives, KL/14/2.

differences shaped seabed negotiations and their outcome could benefit from a closer study.

Indeed, the points made here barely scratch the surface of the intersections of the Cold War with the evolution of the CHM concept and the LOSC seabed regime. However, I hope I have established the importance of looking beyond the prism of a purely developed/developing state battle in order to understand fully the development of this area of the law.

IV. Conclusion

This chapter offered a digested account of the battle for the seabed between developed and developing states. It necessarily simplified the narrative, particularly gliding over many of the differences that existed within these groups. However, it conveyed a sense of the various interests and developments that generated interest in the seabed and the crystallization (and evolution over time) of the contest over different visions of the CHM. The chapter sought to highlight overlooked aspects of this battle, including the extent to which economic considerations remained material to the negotiations; the absence of an ideological victory for developing states; and—more as provocation than answer—the role of the seabed in the NIEO movement as a whole, as well as the influence of the Cold War context. These issues were incapable of a full examination in the course of this chapter, but they are critical to a full understanding of this particular battle of the decolonization era.

2

The Battle for the Recognition of Wars of National Liberation

Jochen von Bernstorff

I. Introduction

The last phase of the struggle for decolonization had looked different in different places, ranging from full-blown war of armed independence movements against the metropole's institutions to cooperative treaty-based transfer of executive power to a new formally independent government. Most independence movements embraced European-style nationalism, even though the experiences with European colonization and racism gave third-world nationalism a distinct character. Supported by famous United Nations (UN) resolutions, the growing number of decolonized states had managed to confer increasing institutional legitimacy to the still-ongoing struggles for independence by incriminating colonialism and racism, as well as by actively promoting support for third-world self-determination. Armed revolts of independence movements against colonial or racist rule between 1945 and 1975, for example in Indonesia, Vietnam, Algeria, Kenya, Namibia, Angola, Guinea, and Western Sahara, figured as 'wars of national liberation' in various UN resolutions.

Led from beginning to the victorious end by Georges Abi-Saab, the G77 battle for the full recognition of wars of national liberation framed these wars as 'defensive' military actions against continuing foreign 'aggression' through colonialism. During the 1960s and early 1970s, this move was strongly opposed by most Western authors, who argued that these conflicts were internal struggles and thus merely 'civil wars' or reactions to 'terrorist' activities. With hindsight, it may seem striking that this international legal debate was fought with such intensity on both sides, given that the practical relevance of the fight for recognition of national liberation movements had almost entirely waned when international lawyers in the 1970s waged their fiercest battles over this issue. The decisive victory of the third world regarding this matter was only secured in 1977 after the protracted (but ultimately successful) negotiations on a treaty-based recognition of national liberation movements as 'international' armed

Jochen von Bernstorff, *The Battle for the Recognition of Wars of National Liberation* In: *The Battle for International Law: South-North Perspectives on the Decolonization Era.* Edited by: Jochen von Bernstorff and Philipp Dann, Oxford University Press (2019).
DOI: 10.1093/oso/9780198849636.003.0003

conflicts under humanitarian law in the Additional Protocols of the Geneva Conventions.[1]

Both contemporary and more recent literature on the debates on wars of national liberation tends to explain the call for recognition as the re-emergence of 'just war' thinking in post-Second World War international relations inspired also by Maoist and Leninist thinking.[2] Yet, as this chapter argues, much more was at stake in this fight for legal recognition of wars of national liberation for third-world international lawyers. In his first article on this issue from 1972, Georges Abi-Saab openly revealed his legal strategy, aiming at a re-interpretation of the existing 1949 Geneva conventions in the light of recent UN practice, or (if politically possible) new treaty law: 'development or adjustment through interpretation does not call for new legal instruments. If new instruments can be adopted, however, it would be all to the better'.

Abi-Saab also associated himself with the more far-reaching aim of the independence movements, which he defined as struggles 'to recover their *freedom* and *identity*'.[3] Hence by re-describing European colonialism as an act of foreign 'oppression' committed by one nation vis-à-vis another nation, two further claims were made by third-world international lawyers—one historical and the other *pro futuro*.

The implied historical claim was that European imperialism and the associated 'civilizing mission' were acts of 'aggression', the exercise of which since the interwar period were increasingly seen as a particularly grave violation of international law. The second claim related to contemporary and future wars of national liberation. Those engaged in a war of national liberation were potentially international legal subjects, empowered and also tamed by the rules of international humanitarian law. As in the classic doctrine of 'belligerency', they became an adversary acting on equal terms with the colonizer, thus receiving an internationalized status. Without this recognition, in the future they could—from an internal perspective of the colonizer—still be regarded as ordinary criminals breaking the internal laws of the colony, or at best as a domestic faction fighting a revolutionary civil war against the metropole. Being classified as 'criminals' barred any automatic acquisition of an internationalized status as well as access to the related rights and duties under the laws regulating international armed conflicts.

However, as the majority of Western international lawyers insisted during this time, this would not have automatically meant that liberation movements had no legal protection under the rules of humanitarian law, but only that the rules on

[1] 'Summary Records of Committee I', *Official Records of the Diplomatic Conference on the Reaffirmation and Development of International Humanitarian Law Applicable in Armed Conflicts, Geneva 1974–1977* (vol VIII, Bern, 1978).

[2] Stephen C Neff, *War and the Law of Nations: A General History* (CUP 2005); John Dugard, 'The Organisation of African Unity and Colonialism: An Inquiry into the Plea of Self-Defence as a Justification for the Use of Force in the Eradication of Colonialism' (1967) 16 International and Comparative Law Quarterly 157.

[3] Georges Abi-Saab, 'Wars of National Liberation and the Laws of War' (1972) 3 Annales d'études internationales 93, 117 (emphasis added).

internal armed conflicts applied,[4] which existed since 1949 and were also supposed to be refined in the second Additional Protocol being simultaneously negotiated in Geneva. It is noteworthy, however, that even the application of Common Article 3, which prohibits torture and inhumane treatment of detained fighters and civilians, in the real world had been far from established practice in wars of liberation against the European metropoles in the 1950s and 1960s. Both the United Kingdom (UK) in Kenya and the French government in Algeria systematically applied interrogation techniques involving torture, performed numerous extrajudicial executions, and carried out mass detentions of civilians, including widespread sexual violence against women.[5] In their confidential communications with the ICRC, both governments had initially denied the applicability of Common Article 3 of the Geneva conventions to the Mau Mau in Kenya or to the FLN in Algeria.[6] In line with early twentieth-century colonial practice, rebellions against the metropole in the 1950s were seemingly still considered by the two governments as being law and order issues unregulated by humanitarian law. The traditional Western argument had been that humanitarian law as a whole was only applicable vis-à-vis 'civilized' fighters and civilians.[7] The concept of 'belligerency' well-known to nineteenth-century European international lawyers came with limitations for the states dealing with insurgencies. However, these rules were not applied in the colonial context. Being an 'unprivileged' fighter in the eyes of Western international lawyers meant that states could punish and execute insurgents at will, denying them any status under international humanitarian law, let alone prisoner-of-war status.[8] Regardless of this Western position, the FLN in Algeria had publicly declared that it would nonetheless abide by the rules of the Geneva conventions in its fight for independence against France, thus putting the French government legally on the defensive.

Equally important, perhaps, both the historical and *pro futuro* battle for legal internationalization of wars of liberation came with an identity dimension that went well beyond subtle differentiations under *ius ad bellum* and *ius in bello* rules; namely, that the 'freedom fighters' or 'guerrilla forces' leading the liberation war represented an antecedent and subsisting national entity that could be clearly distinguished from the colonial structures erected by the metropole. Liberation movements were thus fighting a war of self-defence against the metropole on behalf of a nation that pre-existed colonial rule. Hence, also at stake in this debate

[4] Stefan Oeter, 'Terrorism and "Wars of National Liberation" from a Law of War Perspective: Traditional Patterns and Recent Trends' (1980) 49 Zeitschrift für ausländisches öffentliches Recht und Völkerrecht 445, 465–66, with further references.

[5] Caroline Elkins, *Britain's Gulag: The Brutal End of Empire in Kenya* (The Bodley Head 2014).

[6] Fabian Klose, *Menschenrechte im Schatten kolonialer Gewalt: Die Dekolonisierungskriege in Kenia und Algerien 1945-1962* (De Gruyter 2009) 151–64.

[7] Jochen von Bernstorff, 'The Use of Force in International Law before World War I: On Imperial Ordering and the Ontology of the Nation-State' (2018) 29 European Journal of International Law 233.

[8] Colonial insurgents were often considered irregular fighters and as such without 'privileges' under international law; for this view, cf Richard Baxter, 'So-Called "Unprivileged Belligerency": Spies, Guerrillas and Saboteurs' (1951) 28 British Yearbook of International Law 323.

was the underlying rejection of two axioms of European imperialism: first, that the colonized had no history in the European (Hegelian) sense of the term before colonization, and second the paternalistic argument according to which the colonized populations needed to be further 'civilized' by the metropole in order to be able to live an independent life as a collective entity. For the involved third-world scholars, only through the full legal recognition and internationalization of wars of national liberation did the international sphere symbolically endorse this fundamental rejection of the colonial project. It must be noted that prior to the 1977 adoption of the two Additional Protocols, despite numerous critical UN resolutions, the practice of colonialism had not been banned or outlawed, let alone condemned in any international instrument binding also the former colonizers.

Full legal recognition of wars of national liberation in the idiom of nineteenth-century European nationalism in that sense was an attempt to rewrite the history of the colonized through new and in a way retroactive international law—an attempt to pluck one's own history from the jaws of the colonizer. It constituted a fundamental challenge to European international law albeit formulated by the third world in the language of the colonizer. According to Nandy, a general paradox of the early decolonization struggle was that third-world nationalist resistance to colonialism saw itself forced to operate in the language and discursive structures of the colonizer.[9] The same was true for the legal battle for the recognition of wars of national liberation. Embracing European nationalism came with European international law, and European international law was a discursive structure that had legitimized European imperialism. By endorsing European nationalism and the quest for independent statehood as a counter-hegemonic strategy, it thus became more difficult to deny the validity of prior imperial conquests that had been considered 'legal' in European international legal discourse up until the mid-twentieth century. Yet, by arguing that colonial conquest had for centuries been illegal 'aggression' in a post-1945 sense of the term, third-world scholars did just that by seemingly denying the validity of older contemporary structures of the now-strategically embraced legal discourse. Historical research of third-world authors like Anand were conducive to this line of argumentation in their attempt to describe nineteenth- and early twentieth-century international law with its colonial underpinnings as a temporary aberration or dark era in the long history of international law.[10] The claim that colonialism should be banned with full retroactive effect had always been countered by the West by invoking the principle of 'intertemporal law'[11] and the widespread conviction among Western international

[9] Ashis Nandy, *The Intimate Enemy: Loss and Recovery of Self under Colonialism* (OUP 1983).

[10] Ram P Anand (ed), *Asian States and the Development of Universal International Law* (Vikas Publications 1972).

[11] Rosalyn Higgins, 'Some Observations on the Inter-Temporal Rule in International Law' in Jerzy Makarczyk (ed), *Theory of International Law at the Threshold of the 21st Century: Essays in Honour of Krzysztof Skubiszewski* (Kluwer Law International 1996); Markus Kotzur, 'Intertemporal Law' (last

lawyers that historical acquisitions of title had to be judged legally by the law in force at the time of acquisition.

In an attempt to unfold the battle for full recognition in contemporary legal discourse in its political and symbolic dimensions, this chapter proceeds in three steps. First, it briefly reconstructs the G77 battle for a recognition of wars of national liberation as international conflicts through new binding treaty law at the G77 Diplomatic Conference in Geneva (Section II). It next summarizes the mostly negative Western counter-reactions (Section III), and the related contemporary debates over an alleged revitalization of 'just war' theories (Section IV). It concludes with reflections on the unlikely victory of the battle over full recognition of wars of national liberation (V).

II. The G77 line-up

When 126 national delegations gathered in 1974 in Geneva with the declared aim to bring the four Geneva conventions of 1949 in line with changing realities of warfare, the issue of wars of national liberation threatened to derail the whole project before the substantive deliberations had even started. In the very first plenary session, third-world countries demanded that representatives of national liberation movements be invited to participate in the conference. After protracted negotiations, national liberation movements inter alia from Guinea, Mozambique, South Africa, Palestine, and Vietnam were allowed to join the conference without the United States (US), Portugal, South Africa, and Israel leaving the Diplomatic Conference for good under protest. Yet, this was only the procedural prelude to the contested substantive issue of whether or not wars of national liberation should be classified as international armed conflicts or internal conflicts. The G 77, supported by the socialist states as well as by Norway and Australia, sponsored an amendment to the ICRC draft of Article 1 of the First Additional Protocol, according to which wars of national liberation would qualify as international armed conflicts. This highly controversial amendment in a modified wording eventually became Article 1(4) of the First Additional Protocol:

> The situations referred to in the preceding paragraph include armed conflicts in which peoples are fighting against colonial domination and alien occupation and against racist régimes in the exercise of their right of self-determination . . .

Art 1 as a whole in 1976 was adopted with an overwhelming majority. However, because of para 4, Israel voted against and eleven Western Countries, including

updated April 2008) in Rüdiger Wolfrum (ed), *Max Planck Encyclopedia of Public International Law* <https://opil.ouplaw.com/view/10.1093/law:epil/9780199231690/law-9780199231690-e1433> accessed 24 May 2019.

the US, Canada, France, the UK, Italy, and Western Germany, abstained. The practical relevance of this provision for the decolonization struggle in 1977 was limited also because the Portuguese empire, as the last formal European colonial empire, collapsed in 1974 during the early stages of the deliberations. Moreover, the US intervention in the Vietnam war ended in 1975 during the ongoing controversy in Geneva over the appropriate representation of the Vietnamese people. Given that the inserted clause in Article 1 para 4 also included peoples fighting against 'alien occupation and racist regimes', its practical relevance was (for the time being) reduced to the Palestinian cause and the ANC struggle against the South African apartheid regime. While a lot of the wrangling about recognizing liberation movements had to do with geopolitical differences regarding the Vietnam war and Cold War antagonisms more generally, the motives behind the battle over Article 1 para 4 should not be reduced to these factors. As already indicated previously, for the third world, much more was at stake. For this very reason, the G77 had prepared itself well for this battle. Over the preceding ten years the G77 had in an impressive coordination effort launched and defended a whole range of UN initiatives to internationalize liberation movements through UN recognition of their causes and actions, as well as through injecting new meaning in known principles of international law. It had done this most obviously by invoking the right to self-determination, which had been mentioned in the UN Charter already, although its exact legal content had been contested since the early days of the world organization. It eventually became a universally recognized right of peoples living under colonial domination during the 1960s.

In 1965, Resolution 2105 of the UN General Assembly (UNGA) even declared that 'the continuation of colonial rule and the practice of apartheid . . . threaten international peace and security and constitute a crime against humanity'.[12] The UNGA in this resolution had also recognized 'the legitimacy of the struggle by the peoples under colonial rule to exercise their right to self-determination' and invited 'all States to provide material and moral assistance' to national liberation movements.[13] It had stopped short of granting liberation movements an explicit *jus ad bellum* even though it recognized the legitimacy of the quote 'struggle' and of foreign 'material [. . .] assistance'. A similar consensus formulation can be found in the famous Friendly Relations Declaration adopted in 1970.

Prepared by the Sixth Committee, however, UNGA Resolution 3103, which had been adopted less than one year before the Diplomatic Conference, showed that Western states still objected to the 'internationalization' of wars of national liberation. They were reluctant to support UN documents promoting the struggle against the so called 'oppression triad', which consisted of three condemned

[12] Implementation of the Declaration on the Granting of Independence to Colonial Countries and Peoples, UNGA Res 2105 (XX) (20 December 1965), Preamble.

[13] ibid para 10.

forms of domination, namely 'colonial, alien, and racist domination'. In UNGA-resolution 3103 on the 'legal status of combatants' fighting wars of national liberation, the Assembly, without Western support, solemnly proclaimed that struggles for self-determination of peoples under 'colonial and alien domination and racist regimes' were not only 'legitimate' and in 'full accordance with the principles of international law' but also 'international armed conflicts' in the sense of the 1949 Geneva Conventions.[14]

On this basis Abi-Saab in 1974, during the negotiations on Article 1, could argue that the proposed amendment at least was not new but had already been adopted within the UN at various occasions and reflected a well-established international practice. In the words of the official records:

> Mr. Abi-Saab (Arab Republic of Egypt), introducing amendment CDDH/I/l11 and Add.l of which he was a co-sponsor, said that wars of national liberation had formed a very important category of armed struggle in the post-1945 period and a number of them were still continuing. Contemporary international law recognized such wars as international armed conflicts. United Nations General Assembly resolution 3103 was the latest in a stream of resolutions of important international bodies proclaiming that principle. The General Assembly had, indeed, gone further by recommending sanctions against colonial, alien and racist regimes and the provision of assistance to specific liberation movements, and the Security Council in one case had ordered mandatory sanctions. It would be difficult to explain all such international action if wars of national liberation were to be considered merely as armed conflicts of a non-international character. Existing practice provided abundant proof of the international nature of such conflicts.[15]

As Abi-Saab's line of argument makes clear, the G77 pushed for a formal treaty-based endorsement of a long trajectory of UN documents that, at least in part, were consensus resolutions. Hence, what was also on the table in Geneva was the G77 project to change international law through the UNGA. The majority of the newly independent states and their new ruling elites in the process of decolonization had accepted to endorse the legal idiom of the colonizers—European international law, including the central notion of sovereign statehood. This acceptance was both considered the prize for independence and to be a future safeguard against recolonization. Yet, the contemporary legal debates also show that many third-world representatives supported entering into this potentially Faustian agreement with

[14] Basic Principles of the Legal Status of the Combatants Struggling Against Colonial and Alien Domination and Racist Regimes, UNGA Res 3103 (XXVIII) (12 December 1973), adopted by 83:13:19 votes; Austria, Belgium, Brazil, France, West Germany, Israel, Italy, Luxemburg, Portugal, South Africa, the UK, the US, and Uruguay in opposition.

[15] 'Summary Records' (n 1), CDDH/I/SR.2, para 8.

the hope and prospect that the third world would be able to change the rules of the game once having been formally recognized as a player. Such hopes crystalized in the concept of the UNGA as a 'legislator' of a new, more representative, and solidaristic community of states. If, however, all these resolutions and declarations were considered as having no effect on international law as such, the general G77 reform project had failed. That is why in particular third-world international lawyers like Abi-Saab insisted on the recognition of previous UN practice as legally relevant. Yet, a French delegate to the Diplomatic Conference, speaking for the majority of Western countries, rejected this third-world claim out of hand, holding 'that the United Nations and the [International Committee of the Red Cross] ICRC pursued their activities on entirely different levels. The United Nations was a political body whose role was to find political solutions to specific problems of the moment, whereas humanitarian law must provide protection for all war victims at all times'.[16]

In his 1979 Hague Lectures, Abi-Saab forcefully denied the validity of the attempt to distinguish between the UN as a 'political' institution and emanations of international legality in other settings: 'Nobody can deny that the United Nations has become the principle instrumentality for the development of international law'[17]. Many Western governments and international lawyers from the mid-1960s onwards attempted to delegitimize all those UN organs as 'politicized' that—with the new Asian/African majority—adopted documents that were not in line with their political agenda.[18] Given that the battle for international law in the decolonization era had been launched primarily on these institutional platforms, this strategic move of the West went to the heart of the G77 project for a new international law. Conflicts over substantive issues thus increasingly became conflicts over which institution had the power to decide these questions. As long as the Western bloc had been able to mobilize majorities in the UNGA during the late 1940s and early 1950s, it was portrayed as the most democratic and representative organ and actively used by Western states even to bypass the UN Security Council (UNSC), the most famous example being the legally contested US-led Uniting for Peace campaign during the Korean War. But with the UN Conference for Trade and Development (UNCTAD), the UN Economic and Social Council (ECOSOC), and, ultimately, the entire UNGA becoming sites of third-world reformism, the UN was increasingly sidelined as 'politicized' by Western states and scholars. In that sense, post-colonial international legal hegemony was also based on the power

[16] ibid CDDH/I/SR.2, para 49.

[17] Georges Abi-Saab, 'Wars of National Liberation in the Geneva Conventions and Protocols' in *Collected Courses of the Hague Academy of International Law*, vol 165 (Brill Nijhoff 1979) 353, 378.

[18] Taslim O Elias, *Africa and the Development of International Law* (Sijthoff 1972) 74, arguing in general for a legislative function of the GA; cf Christian Tomuschat, 'Die Charta der wirtschaftlichen Rechte und Pflichten der Staaten: Zur Gestaltungskraft von Deklarationen der UN-Generalversammlung' (1976) 36 Zeitschrift für ausländisches öffentliches Recht und Völkerrecht 444.

to discursively legitimize or delegitimize institutional settings, inter alia, by attributing the label 'legal' versus 'political' to various institutional utterances. That Western dismissive arguments regarding the UN's 'legal' credentials were often highly selective is also proven by the discrepancy between the Western perception of the legal 'irrelevance' of the arguably 'politicized' UNGA and the unabated tendency in other contexts to value UNSC practice as an allegedly clear proof of emerging and generalizable international legal trends.

Abi-Saab's strategy at the Diplomatic Conference was to advance impeccable practice-related lawyerly arguments for a full treaty-based recognition of national liberation movements. By using a classic argumentative pattern, according to which international legal rules had to 'adapt' to changing realities, he sought to present the third-world case as being in line with current international norms. But behind the technical arguments, a deeper symbolic dimension of this battle for recognition became apparent and surfaced in statements of third-world governments and liberation movements. Qualifying these wars of liberation as 'internal' conflicts was seen as an (*ex-post facto*) approval of the colonial project and of the prior incorporation of colonial territories into the metropole's territory and state apparatus. It seemed to deny the historical fact that the metropole and its institutions constituted 'foreign' rule over a distinct entity. Hence, constructing resistance against colonial rule as an 'internal' affair in the eyes of the newly independent states denied the existence of a separate non-colonial identity before and during colonial intervention. As the Ugandan representative to the Diplomatic Conference opined:

> Colonialism was invasion par excellence: the colonial armies came from Europe, they were not local forces. The struggle waged by colonized peoples against the invaders therefore could not be included among the situations envisaged in draft Protocol II. Moreover, the international community, expressing itself through the United Nations, had recognized that colonized peoples had identities of their own, different from that of the metropolitan power which had colonized them, and that it was for the liberation movements of their own region, not for the colonizing Power concerned, to express the aspirations of such peoples.[19]

It was as if, through the negation of the international character of wars of liberation in this formal treaty document, the recent struggles for complete delegitimation of colonialism through the UN were reversed. From this perspective, by classifying these wars as 'internal' conflicts, colonial rule reappeared on the international scene as a prima facie legitimate exercise within and through the formal edifice of the state of the colonizer. Given that most formal colonial empires had

[19] 'Summary Records' (n 1), CDDH/I/SR.5, paras 29–30.

ceased to exist at the time of the negotiations, a considerable, if not the main, thrust of the proposed G77 amendment was an *ex post* formal acknowledgment of the aggressive and interventionist nature of colonialism in its various historical emanations. Those who had been forcibly colonized in the eyes of third-world elites were a subject of international law, a national entity that now rose to its feet and liberated itself from external occupation and repression. In the words of a representative from the Zimbabwean liberation movement (ZANU):

> What those who opposed amendment CDDH/I/41 and Add.l to 7 were trying to do was to give preferential treatment to the colonialist, racist and imperialist regimes. As the representative of Uganda had stated at an earlier meeting, those regimes could not claim members of the liberation movements as their subjects merely because they had occupied their countries for so long. The fact that such regimes had found their harsh laws incapable of subduing the indigenous inhabitants of the countries they occupied revealed the true state of affairs.[20]

This statement demonstrates to what extent the third-world struggle was based on the ontological foundations of European nationalism and that the issue of 'internal' versus 'international' conflict went to the heart of these foundations. Nations were conceived of as ontological entities that had a formal right not to be governed by external forces. Colonialism was likened to a state of (permanent) military occupation, which in humanitarian law conceptually was not considered to entail the demise of the occupied nation. That was also the deeper reason for the success of the external oppression triad of colonial domination, alien occupation, and racist régimes, which made perfect sense for the G77 not only because of Arab solidarity with the Palestinians and African solidarity with the ANC and ZANU, but also conceptually by combining three structural emanations of external oppression of a pre-existing nation or people. This *pro futuro* dimension in the view of the third world attempted to unite past and current 'anti-Western' struggles, including those persisting in the former white settler colonies, in one counter-hegemonic formula.[21] At the same time, the triad was resented by Western experts because it allegedly enmeshed decolonization struggles with two current geopolitically sensitive conflict situations (Palestine and South Africa).

Given that the call for decolonization by the independence fighters was generally being justified in the ontological semantic of European nationalism, the denial of the existence of an international conflict repudiated the existence of individual nation- and statehood in the third world before formal independence. Registering wars of national liberation under the 'internal' conflict category thus at least

20 ibid CDDH/I/SR.6, para 7.
21 On the concept of self-determination, see Introduction this volume.

implicitly refused to acknowledge a central ideological substratum of twentieth-century decolonization movements.

III. The Western line-up

Western governments in the Diplomatic Conference defended the classification of wars of national liberation as purely 'internal' conflicts with equally impeccable legal arguments. They stated that they did not have the intention to negate the legitimacy of specific national liberation movements while concurrently raising systematic arguments for denying these conflicts an international status in the sense of international humanitarian law. These conflicts took place within one recognized subject of international law and therefore could from an 'objective' perspective not be classified as international conflicts:

> Mr. CASSESE (Italy) said that his delegation was unable to support proposed amendment [. . .]. The Italian delegation had always strongly supported the right to self-determination in accordance with the United Nations Charter, but did not believe that struggles to exercise this right constituted international conflicts. Such struggles came within the purview of Protocol II, since they were, if viewed objectively, internal conflicts. Furthermore, to include them in Protocol I would disrupt the whole system of the Geneva Conventions, which were based on the fundamental distinction between internal and international armed conflicts.[22]

The claim to 'objectiveness' constituted an open or indirect rejection of an allegedly 'subjective' approach taken by the G77. According to Western critiques, what the G77 attempted with its proposal was to inject 'subjective' criteria into an 'objective' system of international humanitarian law. The oppressiveness of a regime or its questionable legitimacy could not serve as relevant legal criteria for the distinction between internal and international conflicts. Another argument was that it was neither helpful nor necessary to include liberation movements in the First Additional Protocol. Liberation movements would be overburdened with the obligations set out in the First Additional Protocol, which were designed to apply to states and their standing armies. Behind these systematic and practical arguments against the G77 amendment were broader political and legal concerns. Strategically, the US-led Western bloc in the UN was very reluctant to support both the ANC and the PLO, as Israel and the South Africa Apartheid regime were two Western capitalist 'satellites' in fragile regions of highest geopolitical importance.

[22] 'Summary Records' (n 1), CDDH/I/SR.3, para 36.

Additionally, there was the concern that internationalization validated the third-world claim that colonial conquest had been an 'aggressive' act with significant implications for the *ius ad bellum* legality of colonialism. In particular, former colonial empires had no interest in any legally binding *ius ad bellum* incrimination of colonialism as 'aggression' or a 'crime', which could also have strengthened restitution claims by the colonized. Of course, such broader considerations related to the end of formal empires and the Cold War were not openly addressed by Western states. Governmental experts rather voiced technical, systematic, and formal concerns. At the Diplomatic Conference, the Swiss expert Pictet struck a common Western note, saying that:

> the other proposed amendments tended to establish a particular category of conflicts on the basis of subjective criteria stemming from the causes of those conflicts and the aims of the parties. That entailed a move from the field of *jus in bello* to a zone which held dangers for the Conference, namely, *jus ad bellum*. His delegation believed that it would be very dangerous, and against the spirit of humanitarian law, to classify armed conflicts on the basis of non-objective and non-legal criteria. In adopting that position, his delegation was not expressing an opinion on the legitimacy of national liberation struggles with which many people in Switzerland felt in sympathy.[23]

Cassese's and Pictet's statements are representative of a general attitude of Western scholars regarding wars of national liberation. Scholars would generally not question the legitimacy of specific armed struggles against colonialism and repressive regimes; however, they would insist that these were internal conflicts taking place within one single state subject of international law. The duality required for the existence of an 'international' conflict could only be the result of the successful liberation struggle. That this attitude on a symbolic level was perceived by third-world representatives as an *ex post* validation of the colonial project and a reversal of a significant body of UN practice is either brushed aside by Western experts or considered as not being important enough to rethink the classic Western categorizations of colonial revolts as 'internal' rebellions. Moderately sensitive to the position of third-world representatives and scholars regarding the independence struggles were only a handful of Western scholars, including Charles Chaumont, Bert Röling, Quincy Wright, and Richard Falk. Western scholars advanced three main legal arguments against 'internationalization' of wars of national liberation. First, the right to self-determination under the Charter did not constitute a right to formal decolonization. Second, liberation movements had no right to self-defence under Article 51 of the UN charter against the armed forces of the

[23] ibid CDDH/I/SR.3, para 13.

metropole. Third, the alleged revitalization of 'just war' thinking was a dangerous plot by the socialist bloc against Article 2(4) of the UN Charter and the West.

Regarding the principle of self-determination, during the 1960s it became increasingly difficult to deny the existence of this Charter right and its relevance for decolonization struggles. The content of this right, however, was notoriously unclear, and whether it included a right to break away from an existing state entity has never been fully resolved in international legal discourse. Yet, as third-world scholars could plausibly argue, UN resolution practice had continuously invoked a specific right to self-determination for the colonized, which included a right to form an independent state and an incrimination of violence used by the metropole to prevent this from happening. Western scholars usually rejected far-reaching consequences of an acknowledged legal principle of self-determination, in particular, the right to form an independent state. For example, in 1967 in a widely quoted ICLQ article, CJR Dugard argued that the UN Charter did not stipulate a right to independence for the colonies. As the Charter provisions on the Trusteeships in his view demonstrated, a right to independence of the colonized had not been inserted in the Charter.[24] Moreover, proposals to that effect had been rejected in 1945 in San Francisco. Yes, there was a principle of self-determination of the colonized but no right to independent statehood. According to the young researcher from Cambridge, UNGA resolutions proclaiming such a right could not amend the Charter and therefore had no legal effects.

As to a right to self-defence against the metropole, national liberation movements had in many instances in practice invoked this justification. Most famously, in 1954 the Algerian FLN had argued that it acted in self-defence against the French invasion of 1830.[25] Moreover, in 1963 at an OAU summit Guinean President Sekou Touré held it to be 'essential that this conference lays down a deadline for the end of foreign domination in Africa, after which our armed forces should intervene in the legitimate defence of the African Continent against aggressors'.[26] Given that active military assistance to armed rebels abroad prima facie violated the prohibition of the use of force in Article 2(4) of the UN Charter, and in the absence of UNSC resolutions authorizing military support for the liberation movements, the decisive legal question was whether or not such support for liberation movements could be justified as collective self-defence under Article 51 of the UN Charter. Politically, the G77 here also was united in its claim that self-defence could be invoked against the metropole whenever decolonization movements confronted repression by colonial powers. This claim was regularly also supported in the UN by the Soviet-led Eastern European bloc and Cuba. After its Goa intervention in

[24] Dugard (n 2).

[25] Arnold Fraleigh, 'The Algerian Revolution as a Case Study in International Law' in Richard A Falk (ed), *The International Law of Civil War* (Johns Hopkins Press 1971) 190.

[26] Quoted in Dugard (n 2) 165.

1961, India also argued that it had acted in self-defence liberating the Goans from colonial rule. For, according to Nehru's government, the Goans had always been Indians historically.[27]

Most Western states and scholars were very sceptical as to granting liberation movements a right to self-defence under Article 51 of the UN Charter. As a reaction to external support for liberation movements, both South Africa and Portugal had complained several times to the UNSC that the African Union had violated the Charter by organizing and providing assistance to liberation movements. Louis Henkin, Quincy Wright, and John Dugard all rejected the self-defence claims. In these case constellations no current 'armed attack' by the colonial power had occurred because the main title-conferring colonial invasion had taken place long ago. Moreover, colonial 'discovery', 'conquest', or 'occupation' had provided 'good title' according to international law in force at the time. It could not retrospectively be turned into 'aggression'. Invoking self-defence required existing indigenous statehood—a state of affairs that most liberation movements aspired to as a result of their current armed struggles and thus a status they had not yet attained in the eyes of most Western scholars. The American scholar Ginsburg even held that claiming a right to self-defence for national liberation movements was an archaic and unfair reaction of the third world with the result that the colonial powers were left without any legal protection:

> [. . .] the whole *plaidoyer* simply smacks of an enthusiastic espousal of the tribal rule of an eye for an eye, and a tooth for a tooth. One may counter that by pointing out that even *if* the original methods by which certain countries acquired colonies were very seldom simon pure, two wrongs have never yet made a right. [. . .] Indeed, having thus been branded a past aggressor and virtually placed beyond the pale of the law, a colonial power is expected then meekly to submit to whatever treatment is meted out to it, without reacting, without protecting its interests, without recourse to any remedy except, as it were, to take its medicine without a whimper. It cannot even take defensive measures, for, according to the present point of view, the national-liberation movement is presumed to be acting in self-defense and there can be no self-defense against self-defense.[28]

Yet, despite strong opposition against using the notion of self-defence against permanent colonial 'aggression' in the context of wars of national liberation in the West, some authors were more nuanced in their legal analysis than others. Quincy Wright in his AJIL comment on the Goa incident acknowledged that there was a

[27] See the Indian statements before the Security Council in Quincy Wright, 'The Goa Incident' (1962) 56 American Journal of International Law 617.

[28] George Ginsburgs, '"Wars of National Liberation" and the Modern Law of Nations: The Soviet Thesis' (1964) 29 Law and Contemporary Problems 910, 922–23 (emphasis in original).

difference of opinion between third-world states and Western states on the question of the acquisition of 'good titles' by colonialism and in this respect conceded some ground. The peoples in the colonial territories at the time of colonial occupation had, in his view, not been part of the European international legal system, nor had they in a legally valid fashion agreed to be incorporated into European empires.[29] European international law had been external to their legal cultures and customs. Even if colonialism had created 'good title' from a European perspective, this claim could back then not have produced binding legal effects for the colonized. According to Wright, the only counter-argument against this valid contention was that, by entering into the state system after independence, the new states had tacitly accepted European international law lock, stock, and barrel, and in all its prior historical emanations.[30] That the West regarding 'good' colonial 'titles' was in a relatively week argumentative position is illustrated by the contemporary need of Western authors and governments to invoke the vague doctrinal metaphors of 'tacit consent' and 'intertemporal law' in order to construct lawful colonial conquest and interventions.

IV. 'Just war' and the birth of the concept of the 'terrorist'

The third and perhaps most fundamental Western argument against granting an *ius ad bellum* to liberation movements was the alleged destruction of the Charter prohibition of the use of force by a new 'just war' theory.[31] Here, the alleged or real Cold War dimension of the discourse on wars of national liberation is particularly relevant. It is the link between the quest of the colonized for independence and socialist ideologies that, on a theoretical level, had been famously construed by Lenin and Mao; in its various variants for many Western actors it posed a disturbing challenge to international law and the whole capitalist Western hemisphere. Lenin's theory of the class war against capitalist oppression that had to be fought by irregular forces if necessary was a highly influential interwar approach to the issue of liberation wars. It was based on the Clausewitz dictum that war was a 'continuation of politics', and added a Marxist telos to the Prussian concept of liberating a 'nation' from foreign rule through a great nationalist uprising. Wars for Lenin in 1915 were 'defensive' and 'just' when they were waged against an oppressive regime, be it internal or external:

29 Wright (n 27) 630.

30 ibid.

31 Interestingly, only China officially used 'just war' arguments in the context of the Diplomatic Conference, while third-world governments were very sceptical as to this argument, cf Heather A Wilson, *International Law and the Use of Force by National Liberation Movements* (Clarendon Press 1990) 172.

> When speaking of the legitimacy of 'defensive' war in relation to the wars of *such* an epoch, Socialists always had in mind precisely these objects, which amounted to revolution against medievalism and serfdom. By 'defensive' war Socialists always meant a '*just*' war in this sense (Liebknecht once expressed himself precisely in this way). Only in this sense have Socialists regarded, and now regard, wars 'for the defence of the fatherland,' or 'defensive' wars, as legitimate, progressive and just. For example, if tomorrow, Morocco were to declare war on France, India on England, Persia or China on Russia, and so forth, those would be 'just,' 'defensive' wars, irrespective of who attacked first; and every Socialist would sympathize with the victory of the oppressed, dependent, unequal states against the oppressing, slave-owning, predatory 'great' powers.[32]

After the Second World War, Mao, with his 'long march' to Beijing, became the role model of merging nationalism and Marxism into a powerful ideology supporting an impressive war effort of mainly irregular fighters against two standing governmental armies (Japan and the Chinese Nationalist Party). Inspired by Mao's theory of warfare, during the 1950s Castro and Guevara cultivated a similar ideological blend of nationalism and Marxism to conduct and justify their guerrilla wars to 'liberate' Cuba and other Latin American states. Political links between some decolonization movements and foreign Marxist governments became particularly obvious for the West in the 1975 Guevara-led Cuban intervention in Angola on the side of Agostinho Neto, the head of the socialist faction of the Angolan independence movement against Portuguese rule. Socialism of course during that era meant different things to different governments and intellectuals. During the 1960s and 1970s, socialist states and intellectuals led heated debates on the limits of a globalized class war and the notion of 'peaceful co-existence'.[33]

The more aggressive version of the armed and irregular struggle on a worldwide level had been propagated in Guevara's famous message to the 1966 Havana Tricontinental Third World Conference, in which he pointed to hatred as an essential element of the armed struggle:

> a relentless hatred of the enemy, impelling us over and beyond the natural limitations that man is heir to, and transforming him into an effective, violent, selective, and cold killing machine. Our soldiers must be thus, a people without hatred cannot vanquish a brutal enemy. We must carry the war into every corner,

[32] Vladimir I Lenin and Grigory Y Zinovyev, 'Socialism and War: The Attitude of the Russian Social-Democratic Labour Party Towards the War' in Vladimir I Lenin, *Collected Works*, vol 21 (first published 1915, Progress Publishers 1977) 299–317.

[33] On this notion, see Edvard Kardelj, *Socialism and War: A Survey of Chinese Criticism of the Policy of Coexistence* (Jugoslavija Publishing House 1960).

> the enemy happens to carry it: to his home, to his centres of entertainment; a total war.[34]

Guevara's vision of an irregular and violent transnational class struggle was in stark contrast to the positions of the third world voiced ten years earlier at the Bandung Conference in 1955. Third-world representatives under Nehru's leadership in Bandung still attempted to keep a more neutral stance in the ideological Cold War confrontation between the two superpowers and to uphold and defend central UN Charter principles, including non-intervention in internal conflicts and the prohibition of the use of force. However, in the final declaration adopted at the 1966 'Tricontinental' Third World Conference in Havana , the so-called 'solidarity movement' had gone one or perhaps two steps further:

> The Conference proclaims the right of peoples to their *political, economic and social liberation* by the means they deem necessary, including *armed* struggle, so as to achieve that goal.[35]

Here, a right to use force for the purposes of 'political, economic, and social liberation' from capitalism and 'US imperialism' in Vietnam and elsewhere was explicitly proclaimed—accompanied by a solemn claim to support such wars of liberation. The conference went well beyond the assumption of a right to engage in wars of liberation against colonial powers by using a broad definition of the legitimate purpose of an armed struggle, including the fight against basically any form of 'neo-colonial' or social domination. The conference included leftist guerrilla movements who at home fought against their new third-world governments. After the conference the Organization of American States condemned the decisions taken at the Tricontinental as 'a threat to peace'.[36]

This more radical stream of liberation rhetoric, however, should not be equated with the UN-based G77 efforts to internationalize wars of national liberation laid out in Section III. Abi-Saab's attempt to achieve full recognition of national wars of liberation in the colonial context aimed at integrating these wars into the pre-existing *ius in bello* and *ius ad bellum* 'system'. By doing so, these liberation movements were supposed to take on all humanitarian law obligations usually foreseen for states, hereby also taming and limiting the means of warfare, including restraining violence vis-à-vis civilians and prisoners of war. The envisaged result of these legal battles was the exact opposite of the Schmittian 'total war' cherished

[34] Brian Loveman and Thomas M Davies (eds), *Che Guevara: Guerilla Warfare* (3rd edn, SR Books 1997) 190.

[35] Quoted after Dieter Schröder, *Die Konferenzen der 'Dritten Welt': Solidarität und Kommunikation zwischen nachkolonialen Staaten* (Hamburger Gesellschaft für Völkerrecht und Auswärtige Politik 1968) 194.

[36] Chile, Uruguay, and Mexico abstaining.

by Guevara. The first Additional Protocol also clearly qualified the making of civilians an 'object of an attack' as a war crime in Article 85(3)(a), hereby outlawing this typical form of 'terrorist' attacks. Nonetheless, the more radical and completely deformalized approach championed by Guevara, in particular in the eyes of the US government and many of its NATO allies, could be invoked to discredit the G77 battle as a more or less hidden Leninist coup against all Western-oriented states, and against international law as a whole.

It is in this context that the concept of 'terrorism' has evolved in international law, pre-shadowing various unsuccessful efforts in the 1980s to draft international conventions to suppress and combat 'terrorism'. As the following remark of a high-ranking Pentagon official demonstrates, Guevara's 'brutal enemy' and the Western concept of the 'terrorist' are symmetric notions, both attempting to create an antagonism (the 'other'), through which the limits of intra- and interstate violence can be suspended:

> In my view, the upshot of the Diplomatic Conference was a pro-terrorist treaty, that calls itself humanitarian law. It is a vindication of the rhetoric, the aims, and the practices of terrorist organizations.[37]

Whether or not the US should ratify the Additional Protocols for this very reason was subject of controversial debates among US international legal scholars.[38] The concept of the 'terrorist' as being a person that has (and deserves) no rights and no protection under international law because of his/her evil motivations was a US-led counter-reaction to the attempt by the third world to bring legitimate insurgencies against oppressive regimes under the scope of international humanitarian rules. The position according to which irregular fighters promoting non-Western ideologies had to remain 'unprivileged fighters' without any rights under international law has since then evolved into the ubiquitous concept of the 'terrorist'. To be a 'terrorist' in this understanding is to be a person without any rights under international law—a person that can be killed by everybody everywhere in a limitless global 'war against terrorism'.

V. The unlikely victory

The successful battle for the recognition of wars of national liberation as international armed conflicts at the Diplomatic Conference in Geneva, despite its

[37] Douglas J Feith, 'Protocol I: Moving Humanitarian Law Backwards' (1984) 19 Akron Law Review 531, 534, quoted in Oeter (n 4).

[38] Cf. Abraham D Sofaer, 'Agora: The U.S. Decision not to Ratify Protocol I to the Geneva Conventions on the Protection of War Victims' (1988) 82 American Journal of International Law 784, 910–25.

marginal practical relevance, was a historic moment for international law. Article 1(4) of the First Additional Protocol was nothing less than the first treaty-based proscription of colonialism. By classifying liberation movements as international legal subjects on a par with the colonizer, all prior justifications for colonialism in European international legal discourse were cast into doubt. There was not only a right to strive for decolonization, but also the whole concept of the colonial state was fundamentally challenged with potentially retroactive effects. However, it was an unlikely victory because, in this setting, the third world had to fight using the newly appropriated language of the colonizer, which—as Nandy diagnosed—always comes with inherent limitations for the colonized. At the same time, the claim the G77 made at the conference did transcend the limits of this discourse. Colonialism in its intimate relationship with the idea of European statehood conceptually needed its 'other'—the 'non-civilized'. The difference between the 'civilized' and the 'non-civilized' thus became an essential or even constitutive element of modern international law (Anghie). Hence, the recognition of an international conflict instead of an internal rebellion, and thus the recognition that even *before* formal decolonization colonizers and colonized were sovereign equals challenged a persisting discursive structure of international law. Even though this fundamental issue was presented by both sides using formal arguments about practice, UN resolutions, existing conventions, systemic constraints, and the like, at a deeper level it went to the heart of modern European international law. If this deeper level had been specifically addressed in these debates or in the legal texts under discussion, the Diplomatic Conference would have imploded.

This victory also had a tragic dimension. Not only because the ideology of nationalism endorsed by the third world under many of the post-independence rulers later stabilized despotic rule, employing all the negative endowments of European statehood, such as excessive militarism and the employment of the repressive (proto-) state structures left by the colonizers. Another typical postcolonial syndrome according to Ashis Nandy was that the former common feeling of weakness among colonized elites was being replaced 'with an unending search for masculinity and status'. Colonial violence was thus often perpetuated in the form of governmental oppression in the newly independent states.[39] It was a tragic victory also because of the Cold War environment, in which collusive interventionism by the superpowers in internal conflicts on the side of the new governments or by sponsoring coups became a standard practice in what was called proxy warfare. At the end of the twentieth century, the death toll in these post-decolonization conflicts exceeded that of both World Wars combined.

[39] Ibrahim J Gassama, 'Bandung 1955: The Deceit and the Conceit' in Luis Eslava, Michael Fakhri and Vasuki Nesiah (eds), *Bandung, Global History, and International Law: Critical Pasts and Pending Futures* (CUP 2017).

3

The Developmental State

Independence, Dependency, and the History of the South

*Luis Eslava**

I. Introduction

The battle for international law during the era of decolonization was to a large extent a battle fought over the nature, function and objectives of the state. Already the pre-given endpoint of political emancipation according to the international legal order of the mid-twentieth century, the task facing the first generation of post-colonial leaders was to domesticate, harness, and direct the state towards a new future. Crucially, and also tragically, perhaps, their struggles to this end were radically shaped by the development project—another, this time younger child of the international legal order. The state, development and international law were, in this order of things, three of the main coordinates that came to organize the decolonization of peoples in the South. Today, several decades after the end of formal imperialism, we are still grappling with the very particular political, economic, social and administrative formation that resulted from this battle: the 'developmental state'.

In this chapter, I examine the genesis and importance of the developmental state for our thinking about the period of decolonization and, more generally, the history of the global order. Using Latin America's much earlier experience of colonialism and post-coloniality, I show how some of the core elements that would eventually coalesce into the developmental state emerged first in this context, coming gradually to define the outer limits of what was thinkable and doable in the rest of the decolonizing world .

As we shall see, the developmental state proved, during the second half of the twentieth century, a very difficult beast to harness in the interests of Southern populations, both in Latin America and beyond. Too much a part of the larger project of modernity, too close to the institutional machinery of the old colonial powers, and too dependent to the 'advanced' economies, the developmental state

* I thank Rose Parfitt for her close reading of early versions of this chapter, Eric Loefflad for his invaluable research assistance, and Jenifer Evans for her editorial support. All shortcomings are fully mine.

Luis Eslava, *The Developmental State: Independence, Dependency, and the History of the South* In: *The Battle for International Law: South-North Perspectives on the Decolonization Era*. Edited by: Jochen von Bernstorff and Philipp Dann, Oxford University Press (2019).
DOI: 10.1093/oso/9780198849636.003.0004

promised much yet compromised more at every turn. As Wilder has put it, '[t]he world-historical transformation known as "decolonization" was simultaneously an emancipatory awakening of peoples [and] a heteronomous process of imperial restructuring'.[1] My argument here is that the developmental state was the vehicle through which this imperial restructuring was executed.

The chapter is divided into four sections. Section II explains why the developmental state should be understood as a common feature right across the South, rather than being confined to the description of states in which development is considered to have been successful. Section III shows how Latin America's experience of independence and participation in the formation of the international legal order from the late-nineteenth century established decolonization's enduring coordinates. Section IV analyses the evolution of the developmental state in Latin America from the 1950s to the mid-1970s as expressed through import substitution industrialization strategies (ISIs)—the region's response (and soon the rest of the developing world's) to the broader international turn to development as a key post-war geopolitical discourse. Section V then turns to the contestations starting from the mid-1960s around the modality of development promoted by ISIs. Under the rubric of 'dependency theory', radical proposals began to surface in Latin America and beyond, sketching out resilient connections between colonialism and the international order. These proposals questioned traditional readings of the developmental state and its capacity to foster a different future for the South. The state-centric capitalism of ISIs was thus confronted with a sustained critique that portrayed the 'modern' world as an interlocking system of unequal power relations. The post-war international order was already in motion, however, unfolding in a manner that the *dependentistas* were unable to counteract. This was an order predicated on legalized patterns of unequal trade, debt accumulation, environmental exploitation, and social inequality. The developmental state both enabled these processes and contained the agitations that resulted from them.

In short, this chapter undertakes an unusually long view of the genealogy of the relationship between the institution of the state and the idea of development, and to the disputes it gave rise to concerning independence and dependency. It does so in order to reveal how claims to sovereignty and self-determination came to be caught up, during the decolonization years, in legalized developmental disciplines attached to the wider project of nation-building. By the mid-1970s, when many in the South united around the idea of a New International Economic Order (NIEO), these routines had already shaped the Third World so deeply that it was no longer possible to disentangle the everyday life of its institutions and citizens from neocolonial patterns of economic, political, and social exchange. Meanwhile, radical

[1] Gary Wilder, *Freedom Time: Negritude, Decolonization, and the Future of the World* (Duke University Press 2014) 241 (hereafter Wilder, *Freedom Time*). See also, Adom Getachew, *Worldmaking after Empire: The Rise and Fall of Self-Determination* (Princeton University Press 2019).

attempts to undo these trends—to enact other modernities—were neutralized by organized violence aimed at preserving the state as the preferred unit of capital accumulation and social control. A particular kind of global capitalism, combined with an equally distinctive kind of local disciplining, came to dominate the South, and is today coming increasingly to dominate also those 'Southern' parts of the Global North.

II. Locating the developmental state

The origins of the developmental state are usually traced back and contained, in the scholarly literature, to the plan-driven and economically high-achieving state that emerged in East and South-East Asia after the Second World War. Textbook examples include Japan, Singapore, South Korea, and Thailand.[2] However, the connection between the state and the development project is in fact historically and substantively much broader.

Historically, the form and function of the state have been associated with the larger project of modernity, understood as a European phenomenon that emerged in the fifteenth century and evolved through the sixteenth to the nineteenth centuries.[3] Territorial control, the facilitation of transport and circulation, the establishment of national armies and national bureaucracies, the use of public health discourses, and many others were as much expressions of modernity as they were functions of statehood. Modernity, meanwhile, was itself intertwined with ideas of national evolution and progress from the beginning. The history of the state as a 'developmental' unit is thus a familiar aspect of its genealogy everywhere. Nonetheless, the 'developmental state' as such is a specifically post-colonial and hence Southern phenomenon.

The predecessor of the modern state in Europe was, of course, the 'absolutist state', which possessed (thanks to emerging forms of technocratic rule) 'an entirely new ascendency over society', both internally and abroad.[4] By contrast, the predecessor of the modern state in the South was, more often than not, the 'colonial state'.[5] This, according to Young, was defined, first and foremost, as an alien other by the colonizing power. It was, as a result, the object of differentiated institutions and particular classifications directed towards the subject population, which created and sharpened divisions between metropolitan citizens and colonial

[2] See as representative of this approach and for where the term was coined, Chalmers Johnson, *Miti and the Japanese Miracle: The Growth of Industrial Policy: 1925–1975* (Stanford University Press 1982). See also, Meredith Woo-Cumings (ed), *The Developmental State* (Cornell University Press 1999).

[3] See especially, Quentin Skinner, *The Foundations of Modern Political Thought: The Age of Reformation* (CUP 1979).

[4] Crawford Young, *The Colonial State in Comparative Perspective* (Yale University Press 1994) 15 (hereafter 'Young, *The Colonial State*').

[5] ibid.

subjects.[6] Its construction was underpinned by 'the institutionalization of agencies of domination that at once perpetuated rule and upheld the polity's categorization as other'.[7] Through these mechanisms of control and differentiation, the colonial state enabled an imperial modality of extraction of resources and social administration predicated on European superiority and, later on, by rubrics like the 'civilizing mission' and the 'dual mandate'.[8] This enabled and financed the consolidation of the modern project in Europe and its universalization.[9]

When the first independent Latin American states began to appear in the early nineteenth century, therefore, the form and functions of the modern state were already in the process of being determined and idealized by the transformational character of modernity and by its close association with European culture and institutions.[10] As Giddens describes it, European modernity and its institutions had come to offer a view of the world as in need of transformation via human intervention, industrial production, the harnessing of nature, and the establishment of a market economy—all of which were enabled by the figure of the state.[11] Latin American states emerged, in other words, with a modernizing impetus, yet one that had already been marked by an assumed distance between their own post-colonial realities and those of their counterparts in Europe, with the latter providing the benchmark against which Latin American and Southern states more generally would be assessed (see Figure 3.1 and 3.2).[12]

This nexus between modernity and the state in the South was reinforced during the decolonization years, from the 1950s onwards, by the new post-war international development institutions.[13] Although heavily contested, at this point the developmental state—as a bureaucratic centralized machinery geared towards economic and social 'modernization', now embedded in a fully institutionalized international order—came gradually to be consolidated right across the South.[14]

[6] ibid 44.

[7] ibid.

[8] See on international law and the different justifications for the exercise of colonial rule, Antony Anghie, *Imperialism, Sovereignty and the Making of International Law* (CUP 2004).

[9] See, for example, Walter Mignolo, *The Darker Side of Modernity: Global Futures, Decolonial Options* (Duke University Press 2011).

[10] On modernity and its long-term effects in Latin America, see Jorge A Larrain, *Identity and Modernity in Latin America* (Polity 2000).

[11] Anthony Giddens, *Conversations with Anthony Giddens: Making Sense of Modernity* (Stanford University Press 1998).

[12] Figures 3.1 and 3.2 were included in Alwin Oppel and Arnold Ludwig (eds), *Ferdinand Hirts Geographische Bildertafeln* (Hansebooks 1884), a series of popular late-nineteenth century books, which 'reinforce the image of civilized Germany via-á-vis the rest of the world'. Jennifer Askey, 'A Library for Girls: Publisher Ferdinand Hirt & Sohn and the Novels of Brigitte Augusti' in Lynne Tatlock (ed), *Publishing Culture and the Reading Nation: German Book History in the Long Nineteenth Century* (Camden House 2010) 170.

[13] See especially, Gustavo Esteva, 'Development' in Wolfgang Sachs (ed), *The Development Dictionary: A Guide to Knowledge as Power* (Zed Books 1997).

[14] On this 'Weberian' understanding of the state and its expansion, see especially, Max Weber, 'Politics as Vocation' in David Owen and Tracy B Strong (eds), *The Vocation Lectures* (Rodney Livingstone tr, first published 1919, Hackett 2004); Bertrand Badie, *The Imported State: The Westernization of the Political Order* (Stanford University Press 2000).

d. Brunnen und Hochlandsindianer in Colombia.

Fig. 3.1. Engraving of everyday life in the highlands of Colombia. *Hirt's Geographische Bildertafeln* (1884).

i. Reisezug und Seilbrücke in den Anden.

Fig. 3.2. Transport in the Andes. *Hirt's Geographische Bildertafeln* (1884).

As this alone indicates, in substantive terms the relation between the state and the project of development must be understood more broadly than is usual in traditional accounts of the developmental state. As suggested above, Southern states have functioned from their very inception as modernizing *dispositifs*, programmed to enact international requirements and aspirations by means of their

domestic administrative actions, norms, and ethos.[15] When the development project emerged as such at the end of the Second World War, the state in the South channelled its older modernizing impulse through this new idea, expanding its efforts through an international normative and institutional apparatus now openly committed to the wholesale transformation of domestic realities, from the economic to the political, and from the public to the intimate. The developmental state, then, is not limited to success stories, or to stories about how to achieve 'development'. It should instead be understood as a ubiquitous, perennial form in the history of the Global South and indeed, in recent years, as increasingly common in the Global North.[16] The expansion of the developmental state has never been predicated, however, on the replication of fully able modern figures. Instead, if we extend Echeverría's analysis of the Latin American state to its peers elsewhere, we find that the states that have proliferated and increasingly coordinated collective life in the South are, more often than not, 'theatrical versions, mimetic repetitions'; 'constructions in which . . . the imaginary tends to take the place of the real'.[17] 'Repeatedly blocked off' by the political and economic international order, developmental states in the South have remained dependent on 'other larger states'; 'a situation which has meant a substantial reduction of their real power and, consequently, of their sovereignty'.[18]

III. Latin America and the South

By the time decolonization began in Africa, Asia and the Pacific, Latin American states had already experienced around a century and a half not only of formal independence, but also of state- and nation building. *Las guerras de independencia* of the early nineteenth century gave birth to a new political geography, and with it the challenge of making new states viable entities in an already Eurocentric world. From Haiti (1804) and Mexico (1810) to Guatemala and Costa Rica (1821), and from Perú (1811) to Argentina (1816)—and indeed to Brazil, with its less clear-cut experience of independence starting in 1822—nation-states in the region engaged in a systematic process of self-consolidation after their emergence. When decolonization re-erupted in the mid-twentieth century—first with the early (although incomplete) independence of Egypt (1922), then, for example, of Lebanon (1943),

[15] I have in mind here Foucault's definition of *dispositif*: an 'ensemble consisting of discourses, institutions, architectural forms, regulatory decisions, laws, administrative measures, scientific statements, philosophical, moral and philanthropic propositions—in short, the said as much as the unsaid'. 'The Confession of the Flesh' in Colin Gordon (ed), *Power/Knowledge Selected Interviews and Other Writings 1972–1977* (Pantheon Books 1980) 194.

[16] See especially Christoph Hermann, 'Another "Lost Decade"? Crisis and Structural Adjustment in Europe and Latin America' (2017) 14 Globalizations 519.

[17] Bolívar Echeverría, 'Potemkin Republics' (2011) 70 New Left Review 53, 53–55.

[18] ibid.

Sri Lanka (1948), Indonesia (1949), and Cambodia (1953), before the Gold Coast (now Ghana), in 1957, initiated the decolonization of sub-Saharan Africa—the states of Latin America were already familiar with 'imagining' themselves as such. They were, in other words, conversant in the business of 'looking' and 'seeing' like states.[19]

As the forbears of the decolonization movement and as the 'pioneers' of modern nationalism, to quote Anderson, the experience of the Latin American nation-states prefigured that of the twentieth century's post-colonial states in at least three important ways.[20] The first concerns the very adoption of the 'nation-state' as the form to be taken by collective political emancipation (later formalized as the right of peoples to self-determination). After the Latin American wars of independence, the leaders who fought the Spanish and French empires—like Toussaint L'Ouverture in Haiti, Simón Bolívar in Venezuela, Colombia, Ecuador, Perú, Panamá, and Bolivia, José de San Martín in Argentina, Chile, and Perú, and Miguel Hidalgo y Costilla and José María Morelos in México—adopted the nation-state, and for the most part the republican state, as their template. The task was to bring together 'state' and 'nation' under a single institutional umbrella, giving actual shape to a form of political administration that rearticulated strands of political thinking brewed over the previous two centuries in Europe. 'Individual liberty' and 'popular sovereignty' were fused, on the one hand, with the ideas of sovereignty, equality, and non-intervention that resulted from the mythical Peace of Westphalia (1648) and, on the other, with the advent of new property and political interests and the language of rights resulting from the American and French revolutions.[21] The state in Latin America 'took upon itself', as a result, 'the construction of a nation, one nation where ethnicities were supposed to fuse into a unifying entity'.[22] This combination of nation with state, and of these two with the aim of moving ahead, later became the dominant model when colonial territories in Africa, Asia and the Pacific began to 'struggle to integrate different ethnicities, tribal rivalries, and religious differences into a modern unifying version of the nation and the state'.[23]

The task of creating new 'national' identities out of the dispersed realities left by centuries of colonial rule was no easy matter. The objective of the colonial

[19] See especially Benedict Anderson, *Imagined Communities: Reflections on the Origin and Spread of Nationalism* (2nd ed, Verso 2006) (hereafter Anderson, *Imagined Communities*); James C Scott, *Seeing Like a State: How Certain Schemes to Improve the Human Condition Have Failed* (Yale University Press 1998).

[20] Anderson, *Imagined Communities* (n 19), 47–65.

[21] See especially Benno Teschke, *The Myth of 1648: Class, Geopolitics, and the Making of Modern International Relations* (Verso 2003); Don H Doyle and Eric Van Young, 'Independence and Nationalism in the Americas' in John Breuilly, *The Oxford Handbook of the History of Nationalism* (OUP 2013).

[22] Fernando López-Alves, 'Modernization Theory Revisited: Latin America, Europe, and the U.S. in the Nineteenth and Early Twentieth Century' (2011) 38 Anuario Colombiano de Historia Social y de la Cultura 243, 267 (hereafter López-Alvez, 'Modernization Theory Revisited').

[23] ibid 248.

states had, after all, been to organize 'coercive, violent institutions and relations into power structures capable of implementing a grand design'—one oriented towards economic exploitation and a permanent framework of hegemony.[24] Thus, while the task of throwing off this exploitative past offered the new Latin American states some sense of internal cohesion and identity useful to the business of nation-building, they were building on an inherited national colonial identity at the cost of suppressing—or of managing in particular ways, as we will see—the rich ethnic plurality and multiple cosmologies existing within their territories. In many ways, for Indigenous and black communities and rural mestizo peasants, their countries' independence represented a new chapter in an already long history of colonialism.[25]

In addition to all of these dramas, the colonial past of Latin American countries also meant that the new states surfaced with their natural resources already over-exploited and locked into a productive system geared towards satisfying metropolitan needs, which reduced them basically to primary commodity producers. The independence wars left them, as a result, with decimated populations, factional political and economic systems, and a high level of debt owed to the British Empire, which supported these wars to expand its sphere of influence into the region.[26] This debt soon facilitated the extension of what we now know as 'informal' British imperialism.[27]

A second way in which the challenges faced by Latin American states prefigured the experience of the states that emerge during the mid-twentieth century concerns the principle of *uti possidetis iure*: the juridical formula that colonial borders, including administrative borders, should remain the same after independence.[28] Political and administrative stability, and a neat transfer of sovereignty and economic obligations from colonial to creole elites, gave support to this idea. A long century later, it was deployed again during the decolonization of the rest of the Global South. African states in particular applied it from the beginning of their processes of separation from European powers.[29] The official formulation of *uti possidetis* in Africa came in 1964 with the Organization of African Unity's

[24] Steve Stern, *Peru's Indian Peoples and the Challenges of Spanish Conquest* (University of Wisconsin Press 1982) 80, cited in Young, *The Colonial* (n 4) 57.

[25] See, for example, Nicola Miller, 'Latin America: State-Building and Nationalism' in John Breuilly, *The Oxford Handbook of the History of Nationalism* (OUP 2013). See generally, on the question of ethnicity, Mohammad Shahabuddin, *Ethnicity and International Law: Histories, Politics and Practices* (CUP 2016).

[26] Luis Bértola and José Antonio Ocampo, *The Economic Development of Latin America since Independence* (OUP 2013) 48–80 (hereafter Bértola and Ocampo, *Economic Development*).

[27] John Gallagher and Ronald Robinson, 'The Imperialism of Free Trade' (1953) VI Economic History Review 1.

[28] See especially Guiseppe Nesi, '*Uti Possedetis* Doctrine' in Rüdiger Wolfrum (ed), *The Max Planck Encyclopedia of Public International Law* (OUP 2008).

[29] Jörg Fisch, *The Right to Self-Determination of Peoples: The Domestication of an Illusion* (CUP 2015) 206 (hereafter Fisch, *Self-Determination*).

Resolution 16(I). According to Article 2, 'all Member States pledge themselves to respect the borders existing on their achievement of national independence'.

The effects of the global extrapolation of this aspect of the Latin American experience—today considered part of customary international law—are still widely felt.[30] It ensured that political unities would be created out of violent exercises of partition and aggregation that did not correspond to social expectations or cultural, economic, or environmental realities. Colonial borders came to be regarded 'as given and virtually unalterable', silently ridding the emerging 'right of self-determination' of its association with substantive forms of popular will, and thus foreclosing the possibility of different territorial futures.[31] Once created, nation-states could not be reordered without excessive costs in terms of civil war, debt-acquisition, or accession to often ideologically closed international institutions. South Sudan, formed in 2011, is only the most recent example.

Thirdly, in addition to the nation-state form and *uti possidetis*, the Latin American region had an important role in constructing the international order that eventually set the conditions for decolonizing the rest of the South. From the late nineteenth century legal internationalist tradition generated by some of their key practitioners (via the Calvo (1868) and Drago Doctrines (1902), Alejandro Alvarez's *Americanismo*, etc.) to their founding membership of the League of Nations and the United Nations (UN), the Latin American states were keen participants in the creation of the modern international legal order.[32] In practice still marginal, yet procedurally equal to their European counterparts, they advanced a view of international law based on equality, non-intervention, and self-determination in the form of state independence. By the 1930s this had opened up the possibility for Latin American governments to articulate their modernizing ambitions in terms of 'economic development'.[33]

As Obregón has argued, underlying this new relationship between Latin America and international law was a 'creole consciousness', which assumed that these societies were 'part of the metropolitan center (as descendants of Europeans) while at the same time challenging the center with notions of their own regional uniqueness (as natives of America)'.[34] This operated as an explicit instrument of nation and region building predicated on a productive differentiation that reversed

[30] Makau Mutua, 'Why Redraw the Map of Africa: A Moral and Legal Inquiry' (1994–1995) 16 Michigan Journal of International Law 1113.

[31] Fisch, *Self-Determination* (n 29), 207.

[32] Consider also the Estrada Doctrine (1930) and the Montevideo Convention (1933). See especially Arnulf Becker Lorca, *Mestizo International Law: A Global Intellectual History 1842–1933* (CUP 2015) 141–352.

[33] See especially Eric Helleiner, 'Southern Pioneers of International Development' (2014) 20 Global Governance 375. On how early proposals for an Inter-American Development Bank came to inform the US proposal for creating the World Bank, see also Bértola and Ocampo, *Economic Development* (n 26), 154–55.

[34] Liliana Obregón, 'Between Civilisation and Barbarism: Creole Interventions in International Law' (2006) 27 Third World Quarterly 815.

the differentiation to which European empires had subjected these societies, allowing creole elites to claim formal equality while pushing for an international order responsive to regional customs and needs.[35] Pressure from the United States (US), during the birth of the Monroe Doctrine (1817–1825) and then the Roosevelt era of 'big stick' diplomacy (1901–1909), only heightened that demand.[36] This take on international law—based on Latin America's distinctive qualities vis-à-vis Europe—would have important repercussions for the rest of the Global South in the formation of specific regional organizations and international legal norms.

The emphasis on regional differentiation was, however, part of a local elite project, which used the formal equality conceded to Latin American states as an opportunity to coordinate what creole leaders assumed to be a necessary transformation of their countries and populations. Believing that their region formed part of Europe's 'universal history' yet lagged behind due to its weak economies, uneducated populations, and ethnic divisions, they argued for the opportunity to use their states—equipped formally with European norms and institutions—as engines of political, economic, and social change. It was at this point, both in Latin America and elsewhere in the post-colonial world, that the real 'imagining' of nation and state occurred: in fashioning modern nations and cultures out of non-Western realities.[37] In this context, elements of Indigenous cultures, which had been fractured by the colonial project, were resurrected to advance new creole national historiographies. For example, the Aztec Empire, in the case of Mexico, and the Inca Empire, in the case of Perú, were mobilized as evidence of glorious 'autochthonous' pasts.[38] Homogenizing narratives and new social cartographies also had to be developed; a largely illiterate peasant population educated; agrarian economies 'modernized'; an industrial and urban transition executed; and the region's untapped resources had to be marshalled to benefit its nations.[39]

A clear call for modernization thus came to accompany Latin American nation-states' entry into the international order. Leaders such as Getúlio Vargas in Brazil, Arturo Alessandri in Chile, Alfonso Lopez Pumarejo in Colombia, Augusto Leguía in Perú, and José Maria Velasco Ibarra in Ecuador personified this moment.

[35] See, for example, Sara Castro-Klarén, 'The Nation in Ruins: Archeology and the Rise of the Nation' in Sara Castro-Klarén and John Charles (eds), *Beyond Imagined Communities: Reading and Writing the Nation in Nineteenth-Century Latin American* (Johns Hopkins University Press 2003) (hereafter Castro-Klarén, 'The Nation in Ruins').

[36] See, for example, Stewart Brewer, *Borders and Bridges: A History of U.S.-Latin American Relations* (Praeger Security International 2006).

[37] Partha Chatterjee, 'Whose Imagined Community?' in *Empire and Nation* (Columbia University Press 2010) 23–36.

[38] See, for example, Castro-Klarén, 'The Nation in Ruins' (n 35).

[39] See, for example, Barbara Weinstein, *The Color of Modernity: São Paulo and the Making of Race and Nation in Brazil* (Duke University Press 2015); Nancy Appelbaum, *Mapping the Country of Regions: The Chorographic Commission of Nineteenth-Century Colombia* (University of North Carolina Press 2016); Arturo Almandoz, *Modernization, Urbanization and Development in Latin America, 1900s–2000s* (Routledge 2014).

Underpinning their projects was not a horizontal ethos of community, but rather a hierarchical conception both of 'national' social groups and of their place within the international order. Despite their shared objective of a brighter future for their nations and the region, these ruling elites tended to blame their 'rural' economies, 'backward' classes, 'broken' geographies, and 'weak' institutions when their plans did not deliver, and to justify successive new rounds of modernizing policies on this basis.[40]

Facing widespread colonial resistance in the wake of two world wars and a new non-traditional imperial power in the form of the US, Europe eventually came to accept a new model of global governance centred on the nation-state, as prefigured in Latin America.[41] European colonial powers had slowly begun to reread claims for independence not as a threat but as an opportunity for local elites to discipline their own populations and economies. The idea of indirect rule, a component of British imperial administration since at least the nineteenth century, became the model of this new form of control. Beginning with Article 22 of the Covenant of the League of Nations (1919), indirect rule in the form of the Mandates Commission aimed at governing and educating colonial subjects in the task of self-rule through their own authorities and laws, and according to their own 'stage of development'. By the mid-1930s, it had been adopted, in diverse ways, by the late-imperial administrations of France, Belgium, Portugal, Italy and Japan, among others.[42]

After the Second World War, indirect rule resurfaced in the UN's Trusteeship Council, which was charged with supervising the administration of 'trust territories' (previously 'mandates'). The Council and trustee powers were commanded, by Chapter XIII of the UN Charter, to ensure that colonial governments took adequate steps 'to develop self-government, to take due account of the political aspirations of the peoples, and to assist them in the progressive development of their free political institutions, according to the particular circumstances of each territory and its peoples and their varying stages of advancement'.[43] Trustees were also obliged 'to promote constructive measures of development . . . with a view to the practical achievement of the social, economic, and scientific purposes set forth' by the terms of the Trusteeship System.[44]

Achieving self-government began to be imagined, in this context, as a neat incremental transition, to be executed with the help, and according to the interests, of colonial powers and the international community as a whole. The result was the production of several new states until November 1994, when the Trusteeship

[40] López-Alves, 'Modernization Theory Revisited' (n 22) 269.

[41] Roger Louis and Ronald Robinson, 'The Imperialism of Decolonization' (1994) 22 The Journal of Imperial and Commonwealth History 462, 508 (hereafter Louis and Robinson, 'The Imperialism of Decolonization').

[42] See especially Luis Eslava, 'The Moving Location of Empire: Indirect Rule, International Law, and the *Bantu Educational Kinema Experiment*' (2018) 31 Leiden Journal of International Law 539.

[43] UN Charter art 73.b.

[44] ibid art 73.d.

Council suspended its operations a month after the independence of the last remaining trust territory, Palau. However, this new indirect modality of global governance and decolonization did not always operate in the closely-supervised and orderly fashion imagined by Chapter XIII of the Charter. On the contrary, the majority of the new states that emerged in the 1950s and 1960s did so through the actions of anti-colonial movements, with the acquiescence of imperial powers in some cases (a process that Louis and Robinson have called 'the imperialism of decolonization').[45] The energies of this moment were crystallized in the *Declaration on the Granting of Independence to Colonial Countries and Peoples*, adopted by the General Assembly Resolution 1514 (XV) of 14 December 1960.

The combined outcome of the Trusteeship System and decolonization was the multiplication—or 'reproduction' as Parfitt has called it—of a particular kind of state, one that had become dominant long before in Latin America.[46] This was a territorially bounded state, committed to modernization and embedded in, if no longer directly ruled by, the international order. A testament to the success of this new modality of global governance—never fully hegemonic, but never fully emancipatory either—was the sharp increase in new state members accepted to the UN. Having started with fifty-one members in 1945, by 1980 it had added over 100 more to its ranks.

IV. States as developmental states

The turn to less direct forms of international administration, together with the consolidation of the state as the universal endpoint of political emancipation, set up the coordinates for decolonization in Africa, Asia, and the Pacific. This process was accompanied, as suggested above, by a shift in the central locus of global power from Europe to the US, signalling a move from old imperial logics to the more 'internationalized' post-war legal order. With the Global South increasingly able to dominate the debate thanks to the space opened up for Southern voices through the UN General Assembly (UNGA), the struggle to end colonialism turned rapidly into a struggle over the practical meanings of statehood and development.

Under the Mandates and Trusteeship systems, development had already been presented as an apolitical and technical instrument for ending colonialism. After 1945, the US took the lead in endorsing it as the new organizing discourse for a post-imperial world. In his inaugural speech of January 1949, President Harry Truman famously announced that 'a program of development' had to replace what he portrayed as older practices of imperialist exploitation, which had 'no place' in

45 Louis and Robinson, 'The Imperialism of Decolonization' (n 41).

46 Rose Parfitt, *The Process of International Legal Reproduction: Inequality, Historiography, Resistance* (CUP 2019).

US plans for the world.[47] The challenge ahead, for Truman, was clear: 'More than half the people of the world are living in conditions approaching misery. [. . .] Their poverty is a handicap and a threat both to them and to more prosperous areas.' What was required, therefore, was 'a bold new program for making the benefits of [the West's] scientific advances and industrial progress available for the improvement and growth of underdeveloped areas'. This had to be 'a cooperative enterprise in which all nations work together through the United Nations and its specialized agencies'. All countries, including the US, would 'greatly benefit', at the same time, 'from a constructive program for the better use of the world's human and natural resources'. Ironically, as this suggests, the main difference between Truman's development programme and the nineteenth-century 'civilizing mission' or the early twentieth-century 'dual mandate' was that access to Southern resources would now be formally consented to by 'sovereign' nation-states as a necessary precondition to their 'growth'.

Development was presented, in this way, as a project organized around the economic growth of 'all' nations and 'a wider and more vigorous application of modern scientific and technical knowledge'. This keen attention to technology followed from Truman's commitment to an international order focused on the sovereignty and (formal) independence of poor nations and of those 'new nations' that were now being formed, as he put it, 'in lands now advancing toward self-government'. Development was thus not necessarily envisaged as direct economic support for those identified as living in 'underdeveloped areas'. According to Truman, the US had no funds to share with them, even though he drew attention, in the same speech, to the significant financial resources it was deploying via the Marshall Plan 'to invigorate and strengthen democracy in Europe, so that the free people of that continent [could] resume their rightful place in the forefront of civilization'. What could (and should) be offered to the South, Truman argued, was technology—from fertilizers to expert advice. However, this solution carried with it a very specific understanding of Third World problems and how to solve them. Infamously, it also generated astronomical levels of international debt.

The old project of modernity thus tightened its grip in the South again through 'development', an idea reliant on a specific logic of production and accumulation, and on the view that Southern states were responsible for their economic and social 'underdevelopment'. This understanding was associated, above all, with the US approach, which soon came to dominate the burgeoning institutional apparatus of

[47] Harry S Truman, *Inaugural Address* (20 January 1949). See on an earlier endorsement of development by the UN: Economic Development of Underdeveloped Countries A/Res/198(III), (4 December 1948). For a closer analysis of Truman's speech and its impact on international law see, Jennifer L Beard, *The Political Economy of Desire: Law, International Law, Development, and the Nation State* (Routledge-Cavendish 2007); Sundhya Pahuja, *Decolonizing International Law: Development, Economic Growth and the Politics of Universality* (CUP 2011) (hereafter Pahuja, *Decolonizing International Law*); Luis Eslava, *Local Space, Global Life: The Everyday Operation of International Law and Development* (CUP 2015).

international development, notwithstanding the many other developmental theories on offer during the Cold War period.[48] One of its key articulations came from WW Rostow. An MIT professor of economic history and an influential figure in US foreign policy from the mid-1940s, Rostow presented the most modular and closely applied version of US capitalist development in his 1960 book *The Stages of Economic Growth: A Non-Communist Manifesto.*[49] The objective of development for Rostow was to transform 'traditional societies' into 'high mass consumption' states through specific stages of specialization and industrialization. Rostow's 'modernization theory' was enormously influential on US overseas development and foreign policy under the Eisenhower, Kennedy, and Johnson administrations. He was involved, for example, in the drafting of the Marshall Plan, in the 'development' aspects of the Vietnam war, and in other plans to expand US interests in Asia during this period. The World Bank and then the International Monetary Fund drew equally on Rostow's prescriptions after the mid-1950s as they turned their attention to the programmatic 'development' of Third World countries.[50] In this process, many technologies that would later define a new age of global governance were marshalled in support of Rostow's ideas. One example is Gross Domestic Product (GDP), conceptualized in its modern form by Simon Kuznets in a 1934 US Congress report, which the Bretton Woods institutions eventually began to use to measure 'levels' of economic growth and developmental capacity.[51]

One result of these post-war developments was a revised understanding of supposedly 'underdeveloped' states, as 'developmental' states—as states fully dedicated to transforming their populations and economic systems according to the dictates of Western 'progress'. This process was aided by the elites of many of the new Southern states, who also came to view their countries and co-nationals through the lens of development, in an uncanny echo of their predecessors' actions in Latin America a century before.[52] The association between state building and development was reinforced, in turn, by both the Keynesian interventionist energies ascendant on the Western side of the Cold War and the USSR's planned economic model. The combined result of this concatenation of events and projects was a shared set of ideas oriented around state-centred development and state legitimacy

[48] Richard Peet and Elaine Hartwick, *Theories of Development: Contentions, Arguments, Alternatives* (3rd ed, Guilford Press 2015) 119–59 (hereafter Peet and Hartwick, *Theories of Development*); Gilbert Rist, *The History of Development: From Western Origins to Global Faith* (Zed Books 2004) 25–46 (hereafter Rist, *The History of Development*).

[49] Walt Whitman Rostow, *The Stages of Economic Growth: A Non-Communist Manifesto* (CUP 1960). On Rostow's influence on US foreign policy see, Kimber Charles Pearce, *Rostow, Kennedy, and the Rhetoric of Foreign Aid* (Michigan State University Press 2001).

[50] See, for example, Michele Alacevich, *The Political Economy of the World Bank: The Early Years* (Stanford University Press 2009).

[51] Ehsan Masood, *The Great Invention: The Story of GDP and the Making and Unmaking of the Modern World* (Pegasus Books 2016).

[52] Pahuja, *Decolonizing International Law* (n 47), 44–94. See also Alden Young, *Transforming Sudan: Decolonization, Economic Development and State Formation* (CUP 2017).

Fig. 3.3. Trucks moving slowly along a mountain road outside Bogotá. In 1961, the World Bank and the International Development Association provided $39 million to Colombia for a highway improvement program designed to solve the condition of its roads, as captured in this photograph. Photo: Austin Motor Co. Ltd. Folder ID 1719780, World Bank Group Archives. License: CC BY NC-SA 4.0

based on economic growth and industrialization.[53] According to Chatterjee, development emerged at this point as a powerful frame within which post-colonial rule would appear legitimate, both internally and externally, in the face of broadly felt material needs in the Global South (see Figure 3.3).[54]

It was at this moment that the UN's Economic Commission for Latin America and the Caribbean (ECLAC), though established in 1948, took centre-stage, offering a particular South-oriented articulation of development. Although it remained close to Truman and Rostow's version, ECLAC's developmentalism was geared towards the formation of national capital, or 'national capitalism', understood as the essential first step towards satisfying local needs and future international integration. Under Raúl Prebisch from 1950 to 1963, ECLAC outlined

[53] On the shift of state legitimacy from war and expansion to economic growth, see Peter Evans, 'Development and the State' in Neil Smelser and Paul Baltes (eds), *International Encyclopedia of the Social & Behavioral Sciences* (Elsevier 2001) 3557–60.

[54] Partha Chatterjee, 'Development and Planning' in *Empire and Nation* (Columbia University Press 2010) 241–66.

a series of policies based on a historical structuralist approach.[55] Focusing explicitly on colonialism's institutional and economic legacy, and drawing on the work of other Southern and South-oriented economists (Hans Singer, Celso Furtado, Anibal Pinto, and Ifigenia Martínez, for example), it proposed ISI as the most effective way to secure economic development in Latin America. Instead of advocating economic specialization and concentrating on trade and export, ISI strategies (ISIs) aimed at building internal state capacity by backing infant industries via tariffs, import quotas, exchange-rate controls, preferential licensing for capital goods imports, and subsidized loans. Such policies were widely applied in Latin America from the mid-1950s until the early 1980s. Their popularity was based on the room they gave governments and local elites—the 'national' bourgeoisie—to consolidate their national projects and economic base without challenging traditional forms of capital accumulation or neglecting a commitment to 'modernization' and future parity with centre-countries. ISIs were, consequently, rarely attached to fully centrally planned measures and, instead, tended to promote mixed economies.

ISIs' implementation would not have been possible were it not for the leverage obtained by Latin American states on the heated terrain of the Cold War. A key illustration concerns the Alliance for Progress, Kennedy's plan for the economic development of Latin America, which offered international aid and some level of developmental sovereignty to US allies. Announced at the Inter-American Conference at Punta del Este in 1961, the Alliance required that recipient countries commit to drafting 'comprehensive and well-conceived' national programmes of development in exchange for US resources. For several recipients, ECLAC helped draft these programmes. It was through this that ISIs came to be institutionalized as part of a general mainstreaming of the idea of development, involving the articulation of virtually all national variables under a single developmental logic. Colombia's proper first national development plan, for example, was drafted at the behest of the Alliance in 1961, by the newly created National Department of Planning and with ECLAC's support. The *Plan Decenal de Desarrollo Económico y Social—Plan Decenal* was applied from 1962 to 1971. As Colombia's then-President Alberto Lleras Camargo (1958–1962) put it, the time had arrived to mobilize 'the entire nation, its government, its industry, its agriculture, its rural and urban workers, its small communities, its bankers, its traders, its universities and schools' in the service of development.[56] It would be no exaggeration to say that ISIs transformed Latin America's political economic cartography. Indeed, they enabled

[55] Raúl Prebish, 'The Economic Development of Latin America and its Principal Problems' (27 April 1950) UN Doc E/CN.12/89/Rev.1 (United Nations Economic and Social Council).

[56] Alberto Lleras Camargo, 'Presentación' in *Plan de Desarrollo Económico y Social* (Departamento Nacional de Planeación Colombia 1961) [Translation by the author]. Colombia had been the object of an earlier planning exercise by the World Bank's Currier Mission (1949–1953)—the Bank's first significant development operation in the South. See, Eslava, *Local Space, Global Life*; Arturo Escobar, *Encountering Development: The Making and Unmaking of the Third World* (2nd ed, Princeton University Press 2011).

almost the entire region, especially larger (Brazil and Mexico) and middle-sized states (for example, Argentina, Chile, Colombia, Perú, and Venezuela), to take advantage of the nation-state as a sovereign entity and redistributive unit. According to Bértola and Ocampo, the region experienced during this period 'the fastest economic and productivity growth rates in history', not to mention 'a population explosion and rapid urbanization'.[57]

Newly decolonized nations in Asia and Africa were quick to follow suit,[58] as the preoccupations of the 1955 Bandung Conference, the first large-scale meeting of independent Asian and African states, made clear.[59] Though the attendees and organizers were states aligned on both sides of the Cold War, all were committed to the dual project of sovereignty and nation-building, the latter understood essentially as coterminous with economic development. The conference's Final Communiqué called attention, for example, to 'the urgency of promoting economic development in the Asian-African region'.[60] Just like ECLAC in Latin America, Bandung's participants anchored their search for development in 'mutual interest and respect for national sovereignty'—involving, among other things, the diversification of 'export trade by processing . . . raw material[s], wherever economically feasible, before export'.[61]

This commitment to state-led development reached new heights in General Assembly Resolution 1514 (1960), decolonization's legal apotheosis. According to the Resolution, 'inadequacy of political, economic, social or educational preparedness should never serve as a pretext for delaying independence'.[62] It held that 'the continued existence of colonialism prevents the development of international economic co-operation, impedes the social, cultural and economic development of dependent peoples and militates against the United Nations ideal of universal peace'. Self-determination was repositioned by the UNGA—now filled with newly independent states and their allies—not only as a moral necessity and legal right, but also as the more effective route towards 'development'.[63] This association between development and the state was further underscored in the UNGA's 1962 Resolution on Permanent Sovereignty over Natural Resources, which declared: 'The right of peoples and nations to permanent sovereignty over their natural wealth and resources must be exercised in the interest of their national development and of the

[57] Bértola and Ocampo, *Economic Development* (n 26) 138.

[58] See, for example, Rajesh Chandra, *Industrialization and Development in the Third World* (Routledge 1992) 17–29.

[59] See especially, Luis Eslava, Michael Fakhri and Vasuki Nesiah (eds), *Bandung Global History and International Law: Critical Pasts and Pending Futures* (CUP 2017).

[60] Final Communiqué, Asian-African Conference, Bandung (24 April 1955).

[61] ibid.

[62] GA Res 1514 (XV) (14 December 1960).

[63] On an earlier expression of this connection between self-determination and development, see 'Non-Self-Governing Peoples' GA Res 9 (I) (9 February 1946).

well-being of the people of the State concerned.'[64] Against this background, the UN launched the first 'Development Decade' in 1961.[65]

As the 1960s progressed, however, it became clear that state-led development, in the context of the skewed international trade system—a legacy both of centuries of colonialism and of the incomplete institutional arrangements set up in the wake of the Second World War—could not lift Third World living standards alone. The main features of the post-war international trade order had, after all, been decided without considering the needs of the Global South. The General Agreement on Tariffs and Trade (GATT), the trade framework intended for administration by the future International Trade Organization (ITO), had been drafted in Geneva, during the lead-up to the UN Conference on Trade and Employment in Havana in 1948—the key post-war conference at which questions of trade, labour, and economic relations were to be discussed. During this initial drafting process in Geneva, Southern states had demanded the freedom to use tariffs to promote domestic industrialization but their requests were postponed, and linked to the ITO's approval later on, in Havana. In Geneva, the US, the United Kingdom, Canada, Australia, France, Belgium, the Netherlands, and Luxembourg were prepared to approve only a much narrower, and as it turned out momentous, agreement: the Protocol of Provisional Application of GATT, which expressed only certain basic guarantees, together with a series of measures protecting the interests of the major trading powers.[66] In Cuba, a year later, the South asked, as planned, for a preferential treatment to support their development, but the end result was again far from satisfactory. The Havana Conference did indeed decide to establish the ITO, which had some progressive elements to it, but it never came into existence after the US Congress failed to approve it. This left the GATT as a stand-alone framework for regulating international trade.[67]

From the Havana meeting in 1948, at which Southern hopes were elevated only to be dashed, concerns about the international trade order continued to brew, gathering pace as more new states confronted its internal biases. By the late 1950s, the Third World, as it was now known, was eager to engage in further initiatives for Southern trade cooperation to counter those biases at a regional level. In the wake of Bandung, for example, Asian and African countries established the Afro-Asian Organization for Economic Cooperation (AFROSEC) in 1958, while in 1960, ECLAC helped create the Latin American Free Trade Association, replicated by the African Charter in Casablanca the same year. The Organization of African Unity (today the African Union) and the African Bank for Economic Development were

[64] GA Res 1803 (XVII) (14 December 1962).

[65] GA Res 1710 (XVI) (19 December 1961).

[66] Douglas Irwin, Petros Mavroidis and Alan Sykes, *The Genesis of the GATT* (CUP 2009) 5–97 (hereafter Irwin, Mavroidis, and Sykes, *Genesis*).

[67] Vijay Prashad, *The Darker Nations: A People's History of the Third World* (The New Press 2007) 68–71 (hereafter Prashad, *The Darker Nations*).

formed in 1963, and Francophone Africa established the Afro-Malagasy Union in 1964.

As part of this trajectory of attempts to reformulate the international trade and economic order, but now with growing concerns about the increasing presence of multinational corporations in the South, the Third World came together in 1964 to form a new institution, the United Nations Conference on Trade and Development (UNCTAD). In various renegotiations of the GATT contract since 1947, developing countries had introduced some rules better suited to their preoccupations. However, they now felt that 'a more drastic redraft of the GATT was warranted'.[68] With Prebisch as secretary-general (1964–1969), UNCTAD's work brought together all the energies and experiences of the South, from ECLAC to Bandung to the UNGA, to form a single blueprint for collective existence, operational from Latin America to Africa, Asia and the Pacific. This was the 'developmental state' again, but now more clearly thought from, and in the service of, the South. On this, the Joint Declaration of the 77 'developing countries' supporting UNCTAD as a permanent intergovernmental body is clear: the future 'G77' demanded not only 'constructive international action' to support their development, but also a new international framework 'wholly consistent with the needs of accelerated development' in the South.[69]

Crucially, a particular type of nationalism went hand in hand with this emerging state developmentalism. Prashad defines it as an 'internationalist nationalism' aimed at using the colonial past of Third World states as the launch pad for a new international order, from Colombia to Egypt to Bangladesh.[70] By the mid-1970s, this project had solidified into the Declaration for the Establishment of a New International Economic Order (NIEO), adopted by the UNGA on 1 May 1974, and, later that year, the Charter of Economic Rights and Duties of States.[71] (See Figures 3.4, 3.5, and 3.6.)

The NIEO and the Charter clearly express a desire to reconstitute the terms and conditions of international life. More specifically, their language sought to extend the ideas of sovereign equality and cooperation that had been under discussion in the South for over a century. They showed, in this manner, that a more organized and outspoken South was ready to challenge the biases of international structures more directly, and to anchor the source of their problems in the global maldistribution of resources and the consolidation of corporate power. The NIEO Declaration insisted that 'alien and colonial domination, foreign occupation, racial discrimination, apartheid and neo-colonialism in all its forms continues to be among the greatest obstacles to the full emancipation and progress of the developing

68 Irwin, Mavroidis, and Sykes, *Genesis* (n 66), 124.
69 Joint Declaration of the Seventy-Seven Countries (Geneva, 15 June 1964).
70 Prashad, *The Darker Nations* (n 67), 12.
71 GA Res. 3201 (S-6) (1 May 1974); GA Res. 3281 (XXIX) (12 December 1974).

Fig. 3.4. Students receiving mechanical training at a school in Barranquilla, Colombia in 1971. The school was set up as part of a World Bank project to promote technical education in Colombia. Photo: James Pickerell. Folder ID 1719645, World Bank Group Archives. License: CC BY NC-SA 4.0

Fig. 3.5. Cairo train station in 1975. In 1971, the International Development Association approved a loan of $30 million to Egypt for a railway project. Photo: Ray Witlin. Folder ID 1721056, World Bank Group Archives. License: CC BY NC-SA 4.0

Fig. 3.6. With credit from the Swedish government and the International Development Association and a Canadian grant, this project, approved in 1972, aimed to increase production and employment in Bangladesh by constructing irrigation systems and supporting agriculture. Photo: Tomas Sennett, 1974. Folder ID 1716085, World Bank Group Archives. License: CC BY NC-SA 4.0

countries'.[72] Not only was it the case that 'the benefits of technological progress are not shared equitably by all members of the international community', but developing countries, 'which constitute 70% of the world's population, account for only 30% of the world's income'. Its call for channels securing an 'adequate flow of real resources' to developing states was particularly important given that these states had accumulated, by this point, large international debts to support their 'national' industrialization processes, as well as to purchase foreign consumer goods where colonial economies had been systematically oriented towards the mono-production of commodities.

Yet by the mid-1970s, too, it was becoming apparent that embracing the development project and reshaping it on Southern states' terms was achieving little substantive result. This downbeat assessment marked the Second Development Decade.[73] After years of trying to create more emancipatory paths to development than those articulated by Rostow and Truman, it was clear that Southern states and their citizens were simply being interpellated as subjects worthy of

[72] GA Res. 3201 (S-6) (1 May 1974).
[73] GA Res. 2626 (XXV) (19 November 1970).

a differentiated process of modernization and industrialization—a process for which they were held responsible, yet were not able to control. ISIs had not challenged this dynamic sufficiently and, instead, had set countries off on an even more protracted trajectory of dependency. In Latin America, for example, Grosfoguel has described how from the 1950s countries had not only started to import capital goods to ignite their 'endogenous development', but had also witnessed the emergence of new alliances between their 'national' bourgeoisies and multinational corporations.[74]

Apart from an inconsistent handful of Asian success stories, the results of almost two decades of ISI-led development included capture of the state by native and foreign elites, soaring balance of payment and trade deficits, more marginalized populations, mounting inflation, and unmanageable debt levels. Coinciding, as it did, with the first consistent wave of dictatorships across the South, these failures generated a devastating critique of the very legitimacy, let alone the potential, of the developmental state. This critique also gave the claims of the 1974 NIEO Declaration a unique urgency. At this point, the Latin American *dependentistas* and their fellow travellers come into the picture.

V. Dependency after independence

History continued to be unkind to the Latin American states, in spite of their position at the vanguard of the decolonization movement, and notwithstanding their more recent efforts to enact an alternative modality of development through ECLAC. After a century and a half of republican life, followed by a decade and a half of developmental interventions, the region still suffered from what Frank in 1966 called 'the development of underdevelopment'.[75] According to Frank, the 'metropolis-satellite relations' which characterized, first the imperial, and then the international sphere were no longer limited to the interstate level, but had come to 'penetrate and structure the very economic, political, and social life of the Latin American colonies and countries'.[76] Each satellite—each city and rural town—had been constructed 'as an instrument to suck capital or economic surplus out of its own satellites and to channel part of this surplus to the world metropolis of which all are satellites'.[77] Thus every national and local metropolis in Latin America

[74] Ramón Grosfoguel, 'Developmentalism, Modernity, and Dependency Theory in Latin America' in Mabel Moraña et al. (eds), *Coloniality at Large: Latin America and the Postcolonial Debate* (Duke University Press 2008) 305 (hereafter Grosfoguel, 'Developmentalism).

[75] Andre Gunder Frank, 'The Development of Underdevelopment' (1966) 18 Monthly Review 17, republished in Robert Rhodes, *Imperialism and Underdevelopment: A Reader* (Monthly Review Press 1970).

[76] ibid 7.

[77] ibid.

functioned as a conduit through which to 'impose and maintain' a 'monopolistic structure and exploitive relationship . . . as long as it serves the interests of the metropoles'. For Frank, these were 'the principal and still surviving structural characteristics which were implanted in Latin America by the [Spanish and Portuguese] Conquest'.[78]

At the core of this analysis resided a strong critique of ECLAC's assessment of the economic situation of post-war Latin America. In contrast to its assumption that nations were still trapped in feudal structures and must therefore be brought into the realm of capitalist relations via a state-supported 'national' bourgeoisie, Frank argued that Latin America had been incorporated into the world capitalist system since colonial times. Thus, if the region 'was already capitalist and as capitalism was the cause of its underdevelopment, it was capitalism and not feudalism that needed to be abolished'.[79]

Frank's diagnosis and assessment of the road ahead evolved alongside the work of several other intellectuals which came to be identified under the term 'dependency theory'. The proposals of the *dependentistas*—rooted in Latin American economics and American Marxism, and in some cases linked to ECLAC—varied in degrees of radicality. What they did share, however, was an unease with the standard set of assumptions concerning the nature of economic development, and especially with functionalist structural readings of the reasons for, and solutions to, 'underdevelopment'. Henrique Cardoso, Enzo Faletto, Anibal Pinto, Anibal Quijano, and Theotonio dos Santos, with Frank and many others, all advanced the idea that Latin America and its productive system was 'dependent' on the motions of global capital, and its underdevelopment was therefore a function of the development of the North. Development, or lack thereof, was not then the concern of one state, as mainstream development economics insisted; it was a world relational-historical process. Similarly, they argued that traditional understandings of 'modernization', like Rostow's or narrow readings of ISIs, further entrenched dependency. For example, policies of import substitution, thanks to their reliance on capitalist interests, ended up subsidizing the profits jointly accumulated by a politically connected local elite and an international bourgeoisie, with local consumers paying vastly higher prices for 'subsidized' commodities.[80] According to Grosfoguel, the *dependentistas* were also clear that '[f]oreign penetration, diffusion, and acculturation of modern values, techniques and ideas from the centers to the periphery do not necessarily produce development'.[81] In most cases, they argued, these ideas contributed, instead, to reducing policy, political, and economic

[78] ibid.

[79] Cristóbal Kay, 'Andre Gunder Frank: 'Unity in Diversity' from the Development of Underdevelopment to the World System' (2011) 16 New Political Economy 523, 529.

[80] Peet and Hartwick, *Theories of Development* (n 48), 190.

[81] Grosfoguel, 'Developmentalism' (n 75), 319.

options, exacerbating the subordination of underdeveloped countries to states of the Global North.[82]

The *dependentistas*, unlike previous development economists, were thus sceptical about the possibility of Third World countries breaking away from the persistently biased international order without a profound reconsideration of the state's role in the world economy. As early as 1956, for example, uninhibited by his close affiliation with ECLAC (1949–1958) and later directorships of the Brazilian Development Bank (1959) and the Ministry of Planning in Brazil (1961–1964), Celso Furtado had called attention to Latin American countries' economic dependency. By 1967, Furtado was insisting on the detrimental nature of the relationship between the success of developed nations and the conditions of the underdeveloped Third World, basing his argument on a historical structural analysis far more radical than ECLAC's official position.[83] Similarly, Henrique Cardoso, later president of Brazil (1995–2003), argued in 1972 that countries in the South were trapped in a kind of 'associated-dependent development', which must be managed and counteracted through social action.[84]

The *dependentistas* integrated classical Marxists readings of imperialism by Rosa Luxemburg and Vladimir Lenin into their analyses, together with more recent Marxist thinking on monopoly capitalism and its effects in the South from economists like Paul Baran and Paul Sweezy.[85] They also made use of earlier internal Latin American debates about the nature and origins of the region's relationship with the capitalist system. In their insistence that it had long been embroiled in the capitalist system, they advanced the work of Peruvian journalist, activist, and political philosopher José Carlos Mariátegui, for example, who argued as early as the mid-1920s that colonization had destroyed an existing indigenous socialist economy and replaced it with endless capitalist accumulation, first controlled by creole colonial agents and later by republican and foreign elites. For Mariátegui, a proper critique of Latin America's economic situation required a radical recuperation of pre-existing socialist forms of production.[86] For dependency theorists, accordingly, Euro-American development 'was based on external destruction rather than international innovation—brutal conquest, colonial control, stripping

[82] ibid.

[83] See Celso Furtado, *Uma economia dependente* (Ministério da Educação e Cultura, 1956); Celso Furtado, *Development and Underdevelopment: A Structural View of the Problems of Developed and Underdeveloped Countries* (University of California Press 1967).

[84] Henrique Cardoso, 'Dependency and Development in Latin America' (1972) 74 New Left Review 83.

[85] Vladimir Lenin, *Imperialism, the Highest Stage of Capitalism: A Popular Outline* (first published 1917, International Publishers 1939); Rosa Luxemburg, *The Accumulation of Capital: A Contribution to an Economic Explanation of Imperialism* (first published 1913, Routledge 2003); Paul Baran and Paul Sweezy, *Monopoly Capital: An Essay on the American Economic and Social Order* (Monthly Review Press 1966).

[86] José Carlos Mariátegui, *7 Ensayos de Interpretación de la Realidad Peruana* (3rd ed, Biblioteca Ayacucho 2007) 7–25.

non-Western societies of their people, resources, and surpluses rather than single-mindedly undertaking. . . rational modernization'.[87]

This approach to the question of development in Latin America was again underpinned by a broader dissatisfaction with the poor outcomes of inward development policies across the Global South. A key concern for the *dependentistas* was the region's intense penetration by foreign interests at a time that had been heralded so triumphantly as 'post-colonial'. This dissatisfaction hardened further after the successes of the far more radical Cuban Revolution started to become evident. Led by Fidel Castro, the 26th of July Movement had in 1959 overthrown the right-wing government of Fulgencio Batista, who had been in power since 1952. Importantly, Cuba had followed an overtly state-directed and socially integrated path, which many *dependentistas* saw as a more promising model for rethinking the operation of the developmental state, and for eradicating 'indirect' forms of international rule. In addition to the Cuban Revolution, the larger Soviet experience of planned economic development was, of course, also on their radar, as was the Chinese Communist Revolution under Mao Zedong, particularly in the late 1960s and 1970s. During this period, the Peoples' Republic of China itself began to see the developing world as a primary arena of struggle from which to launch a world revolution. Its aim was to support Third World anti-imperialist efforts, such as the nationalization of foreign businesses and the elimination of foreign military bases. However, in contrast to the Soviet Union, enrolling Southern states into a particular geopolitical faction was only a second-order consideration for the Chinese, which naturally appealed to the *dependentistas*.[88]

Questions of dependency in situations of formal independence came, in this way, to mark the views of these theorists. For them, as Rist came to frame it, the right to self-determination in the South had been 'acquired in exchange for a right to self-definition'.[89] In their efforts to end colonial control over their territories and lives, Southern peoples had entered into an economy characterized by policies and institutions that terminated substantive independence before it began. In Latin America, this was exacerbated by the way in which national projects had already been captured, and came increasingly to be captured, by military dictatorships. The peoples of Argentina, Bolivia, Chile, Dominican Republic, Ecuador, El Salvador, Guatemala, Haiti, Honduras, Nicaragua, Panamá, Paraguay, Perú, and Venezuela all became victims of dictators at some point during these decades. In

[87] Peet and Hartwick, *Theories of Development* (n 48), 188.

[88] This was reflected in China's eight principles of aid, laid out in Accra on 15 January 1964, which emphasized mutuality and equality, respect for sovereignty, interest-free credit, provision of equipment, training of local officials, and living standards for Chinese experts not exceeding their local counterparts. Jeremy Friedman, *Shadow Cold War: The Sino-Soviet Competition for the Third World* (University of North Carolina Press 2015) 73, 85, 117–18 (hereafter Friedmann, *Shadow Cold War*).

[89] Rist, *The History of Development* (n 48), 79.

short, for the *dependentistas*, the nation-state, as a capitalist developmental state, was extremely problematic.

These concerns were echoed in many other parts of the South. In 1965, Kwame Nkrumah, who led the Gold Coast to independence from Britain in 1957, encapsulated his frustrations with this post-colonial order under the rubric of 'neo-colonialism'. As prime minister of colonial Gold Coast (1952–1957) and then of independent Ghana (1957–1960), and finally as president of the new nation (1960–1966), Nkrumah confronted the possibilities and limits of the state form and the development project he had inherited. As head of the first British African colony to gain majority-rule independence, Nkrumah adopted developmental measures designed to solve the country's reliance on cocoa, its colonial primary commodity, and to 'modernize' its cultural makeup. In *Africa Must Unite* (1963), he stated:

> When I sat down with my party colleagues after independence to examine our urgent priorities, we framed a short list. We must abolish poverty, ignorance, illiteracy and improve our health services.[90]

Responding to this challenge, he and his government 'were fighting to *construct*, not to destroy'.[91] For Nkrumah it was clear that '[w]e needed to secure the conditions which would allow us to pursue our policy of reconstruction and development'.[92] Based on a dependency rationale, he favoured a socialist future for the post-colonial world:

> Recently emergent states like Ghana are having to tackle the task of industrialization at the period of its highest development in the old-established democracies, in conditions which have precluded the amassing of large capital reserves in the hands of private citizens. Upon the government, therefore, devolves the task of planning and establishing the main base of economic development and of pushing it through at a speedy rate against the formidable odds.[93]

Nkrumah was clear about the challenging context in which these goals were to be pursued, shaped, perhaps irrevocably, by 'the devices of neo-colonialists', including international institutions like the IMF, the European Common Market, and the North Atlantic Treaty Organization (NATO).[94] To counteract these, a strong reconfiguration of national economies and a full-frontal attack on the imperial policy of breaking Africa up into increasingly smaller units amenable to neo-colonial influence had to be enacted. Nkrumah's vision found an institutional

[90] Kwame Nkrumah, *Africa Must Unite* (Frederick A. Praeger 1963) 118.
[91] ibid [emphasis in original].
[92] ibid.
[93] ibid 78.
[94] ibid, xv.

home at the Union of African States (UAS), known also as the Ghana–Guinea–Mali Union, active between 1958 and 1963. One of its main aims was to pool member-states' legal, diplomatic, military, economic, and cultural resources 'in order to consolidate their independence and safeguard their territorial integrity; to work jointly to achieve the complete liquidation of imperialism, colonialism and neo-colonialism in Africa and the building up of African Unity'.[95]

Like many intellectuals in Latin America and beyond, Nkrumah's concerns with dependency and neo-colonialism became more pressing over time as he came to see traditional developmental policies and conceptualizations of the state as directly undermining the future viability of post-colonial nations. Alluding to Lenin's classic text, Nkrumah argued in *Neo-Colonialism, the Last Stage of Imperialism* (1965), that '[t]he essence of neo-colonialism is that the State which is subject to it is, in theory, independent and has all the outward trappings of international sovereignty', but in reality 'its economic system and thus its political policy is directed from outside'.[96] Julius Nyerere, president of independent Tanzania (1964–1985), expressed similar concerns about patterns of dependency in the post-colonial world and the failure of orthodox developmental policies to challenge neo-colonial exploitation. Nyerere sought to tackle Tanzania's 'underdevelopment', therefore, by collectivizing its agricultural system and urging his new nation to rely upon its own forces. Based on African socialist ideas and with close ties to Mao's China, Nyerere's *Arusha Declaration*, spelling out his 'new way of escaping poverty', was adopted by the Tanganyika African National Union in February 1967.[97]

Like its *uti possidetis*-bound state and ISIs, Latin America's dependency theory came thus to form part of a global post-colonial repertoire through which the South sought to engage with the world order, this time from a more radical position. The ideas of Nkrumah and Nyerere were expanded, for example, by Guyanese political activist and historian Walter Rodney, who presented a fully rounded account of Africa's dependency in *How Europe Underdeveloped Africa* (1972). For Rodney, '[i]n the search for an understanding of what is now called "underdevelopment" in Africa, the limits of inquiry have had to be fixed as far apart as the fifteenth century, on the one hand, and the end of the colonial period, on the other'.[98] By the late 1970s Samir Amin expressed a parallel set of concerns about colonialism's broad impact on the 'underdeveloped' world, bringing in a new focus on the Middle East through his formative text *Imperialism and Unequal Development* (1977).[99]

All these thinkers challenged standard accounts of development and traditional readings of the ability of the developmental state to delink itself from the 'world

[95] Union of African States Charter (1961), art 3. See also art 4.

[96] Kwame Nkrumah, *Neo-Colonialism, the Last Stage of Imperialism* (International Publishers 1965) ix.

[97] Rist, *The History of Development* (n 48), 123–39.

[98] Walter Rodney, *How Europe Underdeveloped Africa* (Pambazuka 2012) Preface.

[99] Samir Amin, *Imperialism and Unequal Development* (Monthly Review Press 1977).

system', as Wallerstein came to call it.[100] Their proposals even attracted the disapproval of several Soviet economists, who felt they risked diminishing 'the role of domestic political and economic transformations in favour of an analysis based on global mechanisms'.[101] In the Soviet view, dependency theory abandoned the 'East and West, socialism and capitalism' division central to its own worldview in favour of a conception of the international order as divided between 'poor South' and 'rich North'. The USSR, of course, fell in the latter group.[102]

Despite their staunchly critical stance, however, dependency theorists continued to view the state as the main vehicle through which to resolve the most central questions of material need in the South. This faith resulted, in part, from the difficulties they foresaw when it came to building alternative transnational territorial formations in a world already so tightly organized around nation-states. For example, Nkrumah's anti-neo-colonial regional project lasted, in the form of the UAS, for only five years, and his own administration in Ghana ended shortly afterwards, after a CIA-sponsored coup deposed him in 1966.[103] Nor were attempts by Martinican writer Aimé Césaire and Senegalese thinker Léopold Sédar Senghor to re-imagine independence from France in a way that moved beyond the figure of state sovereignty successful (or, perhaps, even possible at all).[104]

A similar attempt to move beyond the state motivated the First Solidarity Conference of the Peoples of Africa, Asia and Latin America—the Tricontinental Conference—which in 1966 brought national liberation movements and state representatives to Havana from across these three regions. At the Tricontinental, they were understood, for the first time, as a single South. Advancing the energies that had been present at the Bandung Conference in 1955, but with a much clearer anti-imperial agenda, and this time organized explicitly around strands of communist thought, the delegates attempted to devise a framework for an international order that would not be simply inter-national—about inter-state relations—but would, instead, be predicated on a far wider and deeper understanding of Southern solidarity.[105] But the order they sought to challenge was already too well entrenched. This can be seen in the fate of the initially anti-state national liberation movements attending the Conference. For example, the movement represented by the revolutionary anti-colonial leader Amilcar Cabral in what was then Portuguese Guinea proved unable to withstand the pull of mainstream statehood, with 'independence'

[100] Immanuel Wallerstein, *The Modern World-System I: Capitalist Agriculture and the Origins of the European World-Economy in the Sixteenth Century* (Academic Press 1974).

[101] Friedman, *Shadow Cold War* (n 88), 193.

[102] ibid.

[103] Prashad, *The Darker Nations* (n 67), 110–11.

[104] See especially Wilder, *Freedom Time* (n 1). For the possibilities and limits of thinking beyond the nation state, see also Frederick Cooper, *Citizenship Between Nation and Empire: Remaking France and French Africa, 1945–1960* (Princeton University Press 2014); Richard Drayton, 'Federal Utopias and the Realities of Imperial Power' (2017) 37 Comparative Studies of South Asia, Africa and the Middle East 401

[105] Prashad, *The Darker Nations* (n 67), 105–15.

coming eventually to the new state of Guinea-Bissau in September 1973 (eight months after Cabral's assassination). From this point its road towards ever-more standard forms of international disciplining was paved: acceding first to the UN in 1974, Guinea-Bissau became a member of both the IMF and the World Bank in 1977. Today, after four decades of state independence and intense developmental interventions, it remains one of the world's poorest nations. The NIEO, signed as Guinea-Bissau was gaining independence and entering the international order, did little to prevent this trajectory.

VI. Conclusions

This chapter suggests that the history of decolonization in Latin America enclosed the promises as well as the struggles of what Chatterjee has aptly described as 'most of the world'.[106] It led the way towards colonial emancipation, but also prefigured, at every step, each forthcoming agony for the Third World as a whole.

The post-colonial state, then, as it was born and evolved in Latin America, and travelled to the rest of the South, proved to be a cul-de-sac when it came to thinking about alternative post-colonial futures. The task of separating the state from its early use as a *dispositif* through which to discipline territories and populations caught up in the process of differentiated modernization proved to be impossible. Nor could the state's instrumental nature, particularly as rendered after the Second World War, be disentangled from a narrow set of national and international class interests. Either in the form of ISIs or in the dependency theorists' more radical prescriptions, the state to which the decolonization period gave birth struggled unsuccessfully to distance itself from unequal trade relations, debt accumulation, environmental exploitation, and increasing social inequality.

Decolonization encountered its limits in the NIEO. At that point it became abundantly clear that international institutions and powerful states retained the upper hand when it came to the operation of the world order, even at a time when the 'developing' world was at its most outspoken. In Latin America, this upper hand made itself felt via the increasing resort, on the part of the 'developed' world, to bilateral arrangements to break solidarity pacts; by the gradual monopolization by multinational corporations of the region's meagre industries; by the transformation of state infrastructure into collateral; by the denial, on the part of the international financial institutions, of access to special drawing rights and thus to international liquidity, forcing governments to agree to increasingly draconian conditionality requirements, and beyond.[107] Direct military intervention also

[106] Partha Chatterjee, *The Politics of the Governed: Reflections on Popular Politics in Most of the World* (Columbia University Press 2004).

[107] Jorge Lozoya and Jaime Estevez (eds), *Latin America and the New International Economic Order* (UNITAR, CEESTEM, University of Texas 1980) xvi–xvii.

formed part of this repertoire of arms-length manipulation, with the 1973 coup against Salvador Allende's democratically elected socialist government in Chile perhaps the most representative case in the region. The state apparatus, the development discourse, international interests, and regressive forces embedded into the logic of international institutions all supported these actions, directly or indirectly, favouring an emerging transnational set of interests and elites, while at the same time disciplining local populations through repeated interventions.

I leave the story in the mid-1970s, just as the Third World's call for a New International Economic Order was falling on deaf ears, if not actively crushed. In many ways valuable and energizing, this moment represents the high-point of the non-European world's struggle against colonialism and its legacy. Yet when examined as part of the trajectory of the developmental state's emergence, the fate of the NEIO must also be understood as a red flag, warning of the difficulties involved in realizing a more equitable world. The next chapter of this story has, sadly, been marked by the same paradoxes. The debt crisis at the end of the 1970s, the structural adjustment reforms of the 1980s, and later the arrival of neoliberalism and more intractable forms of path dependency gave rise to a revamped *dispositif* of social disciplining, the so-called 'new developmental state', now a common feature across the South and certain parts of the Global North.[108] However, just like the 'old' developmental state, this new developmental state is strongly contested by grassroots activism, Indigenous organizations, alternative transitional alliances, and new 'post-developmental theories' such as '*buen vivir*', 'post-extractivism', and decolonial thought more generally.[109] These forms of resistance confirm that the battle for a different international law is still alive.

[108] On the ongoing effects of dependency, see Andrew Fischer, 'The End of Peripheries? On the Enduring Relevance of Structuralism for Understanding Contemporary Global Development' (2015) 26 Development and Change 700.

[109] See, for example, Arturo Escobar, 'Degrowth, Postdevelopment, and Transitions: A Preliminary Conversation' (2015) 10 Sustainability Science 451.

4

Colonial Fragments

Decolonization, Concessions, and Acquired Rights

Matthew Craven

> The twentieth century, when the future looks back on it, will not only be remembered as the era of atomic discoveries and interplanetary explorations. The second upheaval of this period, unquestionably, is the conquest by the peoples of the lands that belong to them.[1]

I. Introduction

In one of a series of anonymous articles written in *El Moudjahid* in the years between his two most significant works—*Black Skin White Masks* (1952) and *The Wretched of the Earth* (1961)—Frantz Fanon described what he saw to be an emergent pattern in the process of decolonization. On one side, he saw the parties leading the struggle against colonialist oppression as deciding, at a certain moment, and 'for practical reasons', to accept 'a fragment of independence with the firm intention of arousing the people again within the framework of the fundamental strategy of the total evacuation of the territory and of the effective seizure of all national resources'.[2] On the other side, however, he saw an opposite movement at work: the colonial powers, who had formerly privileged the social, cultural, and religious dimensions of the civilizing mission ('conjuring away', as he put it, the concessions, expropriations, and exploitation that accompanied it) had suddenly turned things on their head. 'In the negotiations on independence', he explains, 'the first matters in issue were the economic interests: banks, monetary areas, research permits, commercial concessions, inviolability of properties stolen from the peasants at the time of the conquest, etc . . . . Of civilizing, religious, or cultural works, there was no longer any question'.[3] The actual 'rights of the occupant' he declared,

[1] Frantz Fanon, 'First Truths on the Colonial Problem', in *Toward the African Revolution: Political Essays* (Haakon Chevalier tr, Monthly Review Press 1967) 120 (hereafter Fanon, 'First Truths'). First published in Frantz Fanon, 'First Truths on the Colonial Problem' *El Moudjahid* (22 July 1958).
[2] Fanon, *First Truths* (n 1) 120.
[3] ibid 121.

Matthew Craven, *Colonial Fragments* In: *The Battle for International Law: South-North Perspectives on the Decolonization Era*. Edited by: Jochen von Bernstorff and Philipp Dann, Oxford University Press (2019).

DOI: 10.1093/oso/9780198849636.003.0005

'were then perfectly identified': '[a]rmed with a revolutionary and spectacular good will, it grants the former colony everything. But in so doing, it wrings from it an economic dependence which becomes an aid and assistance programme'.[4]

Fanon identifies here a pervasive theme that was to run throughout the course of decolonization—picked up in one direction by the likes of Nkrumah[5] and Rodney[6] in their discourses on neo-colonialism and, in another, by the various initiatives to promote economic self-determination (most notably in the form of the Declaration on Permanent Sovereignty over Natural Resources,[7] and the New International Economic Order[8]). The theme was as simple as it was seemingly intractable—that political self-determination had to be seen as simply the first stage of a broader, anti-colonial struggle that had to engage, ultimately, with its economic dimensions, and that in order to do so, it had to confront the grounds of its opposition: '[t]he notorious rights of the occupant, the false appeal to a common past [and] the persistence of a rejuvenated colonial pact'.[9]

If, as Fanon suggests, the battle over the economic dimensions of decolonization was often a post-independence preoccupation—focusing on questions such as the right to nationalize, the necessity and quantum of compensation, the terms of trade and investment, the transfer of technology and aid—it was always to be pre-configured by the prior juridico-political settlement that was to accompany formal independence itself. And Fanon's description of the 'fragment' was to exemplify a particular, but yet very common, way of thinking about that settlement: that it was to be understood, above all else, as a moment in which the political landscape was to be profoundly changed, but in which the general terms of economic relations were to be maintained intact. The first half of this equation, of course, was almost axiomatic—decolonization meant, at the very least, the renunciation of political control by the metropole and the emergence to independence of a host of 'newly independent' states. And the very formalities of instituting, in each case, a new juridical order and constituting it as 'sovereign', seemed to signify something of a revolutionary break. If a transformation of the 'public' sphere, thus, was to be taken as read, what remained to be negotiated were the terms under which putatively 'private' legal relations were to remain in place, and the extent to which they were immune to changes in the 'superstructure' of the public order of the polis. To what extent, it was repeatedly asked, should pre-independence relations of property,

[4] ibid.

[5] Kwame Nkrumah, *Neo-Colonialism: The Last Stage of Imperialism* (International Publishers Co., Inc. 1966) xiii.

[6] Walter Rodney, *How Europe Underdeveloped Africa* (Bogle-L'Ouverture Publications 1972).

[7] UNGA Res 1803 (XVII) Permanent Sovereignty over Natural Resources (adopted 14 December 1962). On the PSNR see Nico J Schrijver, *Sovereignty over Natural Resources: Balancing Rights and Duties* (CUP 1997).

[8] UNGA Declaration on the Establishment of a New International Economic Order (1 May 1974) UNGA Res 3201 (S-VI). On the NIEO see Mohammed Bedjaoui, *Towards a New International Economic Order* (Holmes Meier 1979).

[9] Fanon, *First Truths* (n 1) 122.

contract, or debt be deemed to 'survive' the transition to independence? Did the newly independent states 'succeed' to obligations concluded in name of the former colonial authorities? And was there, as Fanon noted, an obligation to respect the 'acquired' rights of the occupant?

Even though the terms of this analytic of (economic) continuity and (political) change were to be largely influential in shaping the discussion of state succession during decolonization—illustrated most visibly in Bedjaoui's assault on the doctrine of acquired rights in the early 1970s[10]—I want to suggest that it is also largely misleading. Beyond the observation that the rubric of 'economic continuity and political change' seemed merely to internalize a set of contested delineations (between the public and the private, the political and the economic), it was also a description that only barely captured the complex legal transformations that were to be necessitated by decolonization. My suggestion is, in fact, that one might better understand the process of decolonization to be precisely the opposite of that proposed—as being marked, in effect, by political continuity (rather than change) and economic change (rather than continuity). If, on the one side, one may understand the political dimensions of decolonization as being couched in the normalizing language of Western sovereignty—the preservation of colonial boundaries, the acquisition of the legal, political, and cultural markers of 'statehood', the assignment of nationality, and the survival of the administrative structures of the colonial state, etc.[11]—so also, on the other, it is apparent that economic relations (of property, contract, and debt) were only capable of being held stable by means of being substantively transformed. Political change, to put it most starkly, was to be achieved largely by keeping the legal arrangements of rule in place, whereas economic continuity necessitated a profound reorganization of existing relations of property, contract, and debt.

In subverting the received account, I do not intend to argue with Fanon and others as to the limits of political independence or indeed displace the insights of the critics of neo-colonialism. Indeed, my account owes much to Nkrumah's observation that, during decolonization, the former colonial powers had simply exported the contradictions of capitalism so as to turn a local competition between capital and labour into an international competition between the exporters of capital and the producers of raw materials.[12] What I do want to call attention to, however, is how the language of legal continuity (and economic stability) provided cover for a fundamental transformation of the legal landscape of the colony, turning regimes of resource extraction into foreign investments, public works into private undertakings, and political institutions into economic enterprises. At the

[10] Mohammed Bedjaoui, 'Second Report on Succession in Respect of Matters other than Treaties' UN Doc A/CN.4/216/REV.1 (1969-II) *Yearbook of the International Law Commission.*

[11] See Antony Anghie, *Imperialism, Sovereignty, and the Making of International Law* (CUP 2005) 204–07.

[12] Nkrumah (n 5) xii–xiii.

centre of this work of transformation were two institutions/ideas—one being the 'concession agreement', and the other the idea of 'acquired rights'.

II. 'Concessions' and the expansion of empire

One of the main themes of the critics of imperialism in the early twentieth century was the perception that the imperial project—associated for several centuries with the establishment of overseas colonies and battles over mercantile trade—had undergone a transformation in the nineteenth century with the emergence of high finance capitalism, cartels, monopolies, trusts, and combinations, in which capital was seen to be moving out of the European metropole to be invested in speculative initiatives overseas.[13] Associated with this were not only projects for the construction of dams, railways, canals, ports, telegraph systems, and other forms of infrastructure for manufacturing and trade, but investments in the extraction of mineral resources (such as gold, diamonds, copper, bauxite, tin, and petroleum) or for the establishment of large-scale agricultural activities (for the production of sugar, timber, tobacco, rubber, and palm oil). The critics were divided as to what to make of this—for Luxemburg[14] it was a feature of Capital's ongoing search for new sites of primitive accumulation, for Lenin[15] a political dimension of the 'highest stage' of imperialism, for Hilferding[16] an offshoot of the emergence of centralized banking, and for Hobson[17] and Woolf[18] a degradation of Metropolitan politics.

Whatever the cause for the 'export' of capital during this period, the conditions under which such projects were pursued were largely undertaken through the medium of what were to become known as 'concession agreements' (later to acquire a variety of designations[19] such as economic development agreements,[20]

[13] See generally, Anthony Brewer, *Marxist Theories of Imperialism: A Critical Survey* (Routledge & Kegan Paul 1980); David K Fieldhouse, *The Theory of Capitalist Imperialism* (Longmans 1967); Bernard Semmel, *The Rise of Free Trade Imperialism: Classical Political Economy the Empire of Free Tade and Imperialism 1750–1850* (CUP 1970).

[14] Rosa Luxemburg, *The Accumulation of Capital: Translated* (Agnes Schwarzschild tr, first published 1913, Routledge & Kegan Paul 1951).

[15] Vladimir I Lenin, *Imperialism, the highest stage of capitalism* (first published 1916, International Publishing Company 1939).

[16] Rudolf Hilferding, *Das Finanzkapital: Eine Studie über die jüngste Entwicklung des Kapitalismus* (Brand 1910).

[17] John A Hobson, *Imperialism: A Study* (James Nisbet & Co 1902).

[18] Leonard Woolf, *Empire & Commerce in Africa: A Study in Economic Imperialism* (Labour Research Department 1920).

[19] See Christoph Ohler, 'Concessions' in Rüdiger Wolfrum (ed), *Max Planck Encyclopedia of Public International Law* (OUP 2013) para 4.

[20] See James Hyde, 'Permanent Sovereignty Over Natural Wealth and Resources' (1956) 50 American Journal of International Law 862; Duncan McNair, 'The General Principles of International Law Recognized by Civilized Nations' (1957) 33 British Year Book of International Law 11; Kenneth Carlston, 'Concession Agreements and Nationalization' (1958) 52 American Journal of International Law 260; James Hyde, 'Economic Development Agreements' (1962) 105 Recueil des Cours de l'Académie de Droit International de La Haye 271; Tom Farer, 'Economic Development Agreements: A Functional

public-private-partnerships, or more simply as state contracts[21]). The terms of such 'agreements' varied enormously[22] but in the metropolitan context at least they were understood to assume the form of a transaction between a 'host' government and a private individual/corporation in which the latter would commit themselves to certain 'public' undertakings (eg, to extract resources, build pipelines, railways, telegraph systems and canals, or supply water and electricity) in return for the right to sell and profit from the resources extracted or recoup investment by operating the undertaking in question.[23] O'Connell was to describe them, thus, in the following terms:

> An economic concession is usually a licence granted by the state to a private individual or corporation to undertake works of a public character, extending over a considerable period of time, and involving the investment of more or less large sums of capital. It may also consist in the grant of mining or mineral and other rights over state property. To this type of concession there are usually annexed rights of marketing and export, as well as provisions concerning royalties. Thirdly, a concession may be merely a grant of occupation of public land for the carrying on of some public purpose, such concession taking the form of a contract between the state and the concessionaire.[24]

The public character of concession agreements was often marked, furthermore, by the granting of *de jure* or de facto monopolies (eg, in relation to navigation or the operation of port facilities) or by endowing concessionaires with administrative authority or rights of eminent domain (eg, the right to compulsory purchase of land).[25]

In many respects, what delineated the concession, as a distinct juridical instrument, was its contrast to other kinds of transaction. Concessions were clearly not merely 'private contracts' insofar as one party to the agreement would be a public

Analysis' (1971) 10 Columbia Journal of Transnational Law 200; Rainer Geiger, 'The Unilateral Change of Economic Development Agreements' (1974) 23 International and Comparative Law Quarterly 73.

[21] Robert Y Jennings, 'State Contracts in International Law' (1961) 37 British Yearbook of International Law 156; Muthucumaraswamy Sornarajah, *International Commercial Arbitration: The Problem of State Contracts* (Longman 1990) 3.

[22] See *Memorial of Reparations Commission* (*Reparation Commission v German Government*) [1923] Annual Digest 341. Huang notes two different usages of the term: (1) a grant by one state to another of political rights over territory (such as the international settlements in China); and (2) 'in municipal law, a grant of exclusive or non-exclusive rights, privileges or franchise, affecting public interest, to an individual, a public or private corporation . . . '. Thomas TF Huang, 'Some International and Legal Aspects of the Suez Canal Question' (1957) 51 American Journal of International Law 277, 292.

[23] Gauthier Gidel, *Des Effets de Vannexation sur les Concessions* (1904) 123.

[24] David P O'Connell, 'Economic Concessions in the Law of State Succession' (1950) 27 British Yearbook of International Law 93 (hereafter O'Connell, 'Economic Concessions').

[25] McNair (n 20) 3.

agency,[26] and the agreements themselves would be visibly oriented towards the achievement of certain designated public ends. Nor for similar reasons could they be regarded as 'treaties' even if the concessionaire itself was a state-owned foreign corporation.[27] While some involved the 'grant' or 'lease' of territory, there would, in addition, be some continued expectation of public benefit (usually revenue in the form of rent or royalties) from the operations of the undertaking. And while many assumed the form of a public 'license' or 'franchise', substantial variations existed as between, for example, natural resource concessions and those concerned with the operation of public services.[28] For those analysing the legal status or characteristics of 'concessions' in the early twentieth century, therefore, it was their 'hybrid' character that stood out.[29] For Moser, they were contracts that 'touched upon the public interest';[30] for Lauterpacht, they lay 'somewhere between a "contract" . . . and a treaty';[31] and for O'Connell, they stood 'midway between the category of a debt owed by the state and the category of the private ownership of land'.[32] As he was to explain:

> The correct opinion would seem to be that the rights of a concessionaire are of mixed public and private character: the matter being public insofar as it involves a concession of sovereignty . . . So far as the concessionaire is concerned, however, the rights which he acquires under the contract are analogous to those to which any contract of private law gives rise.[33]

If this was (and remains) the received framework for understanding the concession within the metropole, the story was far more complex in the context in

[26] David P O'Connell, 'A Critique of the Iranian Oil Litigation' (1955) 4 International and Comparative Law Quarterly 267, 268–69 (hereafter O'Connell, 'Critique of the Iranian Oil Litigation'). In view of this, Amos S Hershey, 'The Succession of States' (1911) 5 American Journal of International Law 285 and Francis B Sayre, 'Change of Sovereignty and Private Ownership of Land' (1918) 12 American Journal of International Law 475 were to treat concessions as a species of 'State contract'. See also, *German Reparations Case* (Interpretation of London Agreement of 9 August 1924) RIAA 429, 480 (hereafter *German Reparations Case*).

[27] *Anglo-Iranian Oil Co* (Preliminary Objection, Judgment) [1952] ICJ Rep 93. See Leo T Kissam and Edmond K Leach, 'Sovereign Expropriation of Property and Abrogation of Concession Contracts' (1959) 28 Fordham Law Review 177, 194.

[28] *Saudi Arabia v Arabian American Oil Co. (ARAMCO)* [1963] International Law Reports 117, 157. It noted that the economic conditions of concessions differed—a mining concession, for example, 'destroys the very substance of the concession' whereas a public service or public works concession may not (161).

[29] In the *Warsaw Electric Company Case (1932)* RIAA vol III 1687, the arbitrator (Asser) held that '. . . the concession granted by the City to the Company has, as is generally the case with all concessions, a double character: it falls within the scope of both public and private law'.

[30] Hermann Mosler, *Wirtschaftskonzessionen bei Änderungen der Staatshoheit: Eine völkerrechtliche Studie zum Hoheitswechsel und zur Hoheitsausübung auf fremdem Staatsgebiet* (Kohlhammer 1948) 66.

[31] Elihu Lauterpacht, 'Some Aspects of International Concession Agreements' (1959) 1 Bulletin of the Harvard International Law Club 5.

[32] O'Connell, 'Critique of the Iranian Oil Litigation' (n 26) 95.

[33] ibid 270.

the colonial and 'semi-colonial' periphery. In those sites, the concession served not only as a means to establish (private) rights over putatively public land or resources, but also as a vehicle through which colonial rule would be expanded and deepened.

For many of the 'concession hunters' of the late nineteenth century,[34] concessions were a means by which they could establish, through agreement with those who they took to be local owners of land, their right to use and exploit that land. Typically, this was either for purposes of the construction of a commercial infrastructure (eg, railroads, ports) or for purposes of the exploitation of natural resources (eg, gold, diamonds, tin, copper, iron ore, bauxite, and oil) in areas beyond the frontiers of colonial rule. While the agreements were visibly 'local' in the sense that they purported to secure for the concessionaires a basis for their claim of ownership over the land/resources in question, they also served as a critical resource in persuading the (sometimes reluctant) metropolitan authorities to broaden the reach of imperial power.

When Rhodes was to secure, for example, the famous Rudd Concession from Lobengula, the leader of the Ndebele, the agreement purported to provide Rhodes with a 'complete and exclusive charge over all metals and minerals' within Lobengula's several 'kingdoms, principalities and dominions'.[35] This immediately provided Rhodes and Rudd (and the sponsoring Gold Fields of South Africa Company) with something they might both exploit and capitalize through the sale of the rights concerned to the 'Central Search Association' (in which they held shares).[36] In addition, however, it also provided Rhodes with a means of persuading the British Government to grant a Royal Charter to him in the guise of the British South Africa Company (BSAC).[37] The Chartering of the BSAC, in turn, not only endowed the Company with public authority (ultimately assuming responsibility for the administration of Northern and Southern Rhodesia) but also served as a means of confirming the legitimacy of the Rudd Concession itself (which had continued to be widely disputed[38]). Ultimately, as Galbraith noted, the limits which the government sought to establish for the chartered company 'had little to do with the rights of an African chief'.[39] 'The Lobengula who mattered' he observed, 'was largely an artificial creation whose power was assumed to be unquestioned in the gold regions of the Mazoe Valley and other areas south of the Zambezi claimed by

[34] For an early critique of the role of concession hunters in the expansion of empire in the nineteenth century see Henry N Brailsford, *The War of Steel and Gold: A Study of the Armed Peace* (Bell 1914) 52–54, 61–63.

[35] See generally John S Galbraith, *Crown and Charter: The Early Years of the British South Africa Company* (University of California Press 1974) 72–80.

[36] ibid 84–86.

[37] See Woolf (n 18) 35.

[38] See Galbraith (n 35) 72, 120.

[39] ibid.

the Portuguese. This invention was essential to undergird the British claim to a sphere of influence as against Portugal.'[40]

What was put into operation through the institution of the concession agreement in such cases, thus, was not so much a blurring of the (putative) boundaries between public authority and private entitlement, but rather the opposite: an attempt to put those conditions in place. For what they sought to enable was not just the acquisition of rights to exploit resources or acquire land for the purposes of the construction of railroads from native 'owners', but the very possibility of such land being owned or possessed in the first place.[41] If, as Lipson observes, one of the preconditions for the export of capital in the nineteenth century was the parallel export of Western regimes of property rights,[42] the means by which that was to occur was not by erasure of existing regimes of ownership (such as were imagined to exist), but by their subsumption. For in order to create such regimes of entitlement without appearing, at the same time, to undermine the very principles that were to be put in place, those rights had to be visibly 'acquired' from their indigenous 'owners'. In purporting to provide the basis for rights of exploitation or of ownership, then, the concession agreement would have a twofold function—both vesting rights in the concessionaire, but creating also, in the same imaginary, the authority to vest. The sovereign right to dispose of land or resources (from which one may adduce sovereignty *tout court*) was thus produced through the instrument of the concession as being its unexpressed precondition.

Two points emerge from this. The first is that, in the context of late nineteenth-century colonial practice, concession agreements rarely assumed, in any straightforward sense, the character of an agreement between a private party and a sovereign state, nor were they limited to the establishment of private rights or interests. Rather, one finds a complex interweaving of economic and administrative functions, a confluence of public and private initiatives, in which the rights of the concessionaire were intimately connected to the *production* of public power as much as a consequence of it.[43] The second, and more straightforward point, is that

[40] ibid 107. He notes elsewhere (73–74) that '[w]hatever the translation may have been, Lobengula did not have the power, even if he had the inclination, to alienate land. Also, leaving aside the issue of whether the Ndebele actually controlled the areas of Mashonaland where the gold deposits reputedly were, Lobengula could have granted the concessionaries only the usufruct . . . . These men [Rudd and Rhodes] in pursuit of their own ends credited Lobengula with an absolute power over his own people which he did not possess and control over other peoples which he did not exercise. "Matabeleland" was aggrandized on the maps to include the Shona and the other peoples, and this imagined empire was colored pink. The hue was important—pink rather than red—because the object was rule by a British company not by the imperial government.'

[41] See, eg, Concessions Ordinance 1900 (No 14) of the Gold Coast Colony, and Mining Rights Regulation Ordinance (1905) section 2.

[42] Charles Lipson, *Standing Guard: Protecting Foreign Capital in the 19th and 20th Centuries* (University of California Press 1985) 14–15, 20.

[43] Woolf notes, for example, that the concessions granted to the British East Africa Association and the German East Africa Company in 1887–1888 included: 'A monopoly of the right to purchase public lands, of regulating trade, navigation, and fisheries, of making roads, railways and canals; the right to

concession agreements operated as an important technology of imperial expansion in both its 'formal' and 'informal guises'—providing both its rationale and its ethos, connecting the resources of the South to the commercial networks of business and commerce in the North through the medium of the contract, which ultimately created its own grounds of validity.

III. Concessions and acquired rights

By the time in which decolonization was placed upon the international agenda in the aftermath of the Second World War, not only had the economies of colonial territories become organized around the export of primary materials to manufacturing centres in the North, but a large proportion of the major economic assets in the colonial world (mining, agriculture, oil production, transportation, etc.) were owned or controlled by companies either registered in the Colonial metropole or with majority shareholding there.[44]

The prospect of decolonization, thus, immediately put in question the fate that might befall such commercial undertakings: was there a duty on the part of the newly independent states to recognize and honour existing concessionary contracts? Did the former colonial powers enjoy a right to seek protection of such interests after independence? Whether they should have been entitled to any kind of protection under international law was not immediately obvious. Quite apart from the merits of any special protection being afforded to those who had already profited significantly from the extraction of resources from the colony, there was a general presumption, as Garcia Amador noted in his reports on State Responsibility at the time, that questions of property and contract (and hence concessions) were matters that presumptively fell within the 'domestic jurisdiction' of states[45] and that, therefore, newly independent states would be in a position to deal with such matters in the manner of their own choosing. The main qualification here concerned the extent to which certain pre-existent 'rights of aliens' might be implicated and be due protection; and in that respect, two fields of international law appeared to be relevant—first, the law of diplomatic protection so far as it governed the treatment of aliens, and second, the law of state succession.

Formally speaking, the question of state succession appeared to be antecedent to that concerning the treatment of aliens: the responsibility of a new state for a putative violation of the rights of an alien claimant (as might appear, for example, from the non-performance of a contractual obligation or the discriminatory

levy taxes on the inhabitants, to establish customs houses, to levy dues; an exclusive privilege to work mines and to issue notes.' Woolf (n 18) 246.

44 See generally Rodney (n 6) ch 5; Nkrumah (n 5) ch 6.

45 See Francisco García-Amador, 'International Responsibility, Fourth Report' UN Doc A/CN.4/119 (1959-II) *International Law Commission Yearbook* 3, para 6.

expropriation of property) depended upon the hypothesis that the rights in question were duly 'acquired' in the first place. That prior question, however, could not simply be answered by reference to the requisite legal formalities applicable within the colony or protectorate (ie, whether the rights had been acquired according to the law applicable within the colony), but demanded also an answer to the question whether the newly independent state itself was also condemned to respect and acknowledge all pre-existent proprietary entitlements—and that was to be answered, it was clear, by reference to the emergent law of state succession. Despite the formal distinction, however, it became evident that the answer to both sets of questions was to take the same form—whether, that is, there existed an international obligation to respect 'acquired rights'. And it was the doctrine of acquired rights that came to be offered as the principal rationale for the protection of concessionary interests during decolonization—being given particular prominence in the influential work of DP O'Connell on state succession,[46] but finding its way also into the work of Garcia-Amador on state responsibility.[47]

While United States (US) courts in the early part of the nineteenth century had, under the sway of CJ Marshall's influential opinion in *US v Percheman*,[48] recognized the continuity of pre-existent private rights in land in territories acquired by the US, it was not until the early twentieth century that scholars such as Gidel[49] and Descamps[50] began to rationalize that practice as a principle of public international law and seek to articulate it in terms of the doctrine of acquired rights. The doctrine of acquired rights itself was a concept they borrowed from von Savigny's work on private international law[51] and which had become, in the intervening years,[52] a key premise or axiom in the conflict of laws: '[e]very right which has been acquired under the law of a civilized country' as Dicey was to put it, 'is recognized and, in general, enforced by English Courts'.[53]

46 O'Connell, 'Economic Concessions' (n 24).

47 García-Amador (n 45).

48 *US v Perchemann* (No. 95) [1833] Peters. See also *Strother v Lucas* [1838] Peters 410, 435, 438; *Smith v United States* [1836] Peters 326, 330; *United States v Auguisola* [1863] Wallace 352, 358; *US v Soulard* [1830] Peters 511; *Ortega v Lara* [1906] US 399; *Vilas v City of Munila* [1911] US 345. For a rationalization of this practice that forefronts the distinction between public and private legal relations see LS Rowe, 'The Political and Legal Aspects of Change of Sovereignty' (1902) 50 The American Law Register (1898–1907) 466, 474–75; and Herbert A Wilkinson, *The American Doctrine of State Succession* (Johns Hopkins Press 1934).

49 Gidel (n 23).

50 P Descamps, 'La définition des droits acquis: sa portée générale et son application en matière de succession d'Etat à Etat' (1908) 15 Revue Générale de Droit International Privé 385.

51 Friedrich C v Savigny, *System des heutigen Römischen Rechts* (Veit 1849) translated by William Guthrie as Friedrich C v Savigny, *Private International Law: A Treatise on the Conflict of Laws: And the Limits of Their Operation in Respect of Place and Time* (Stevens & Sons 1869) 286, 289.

52 Thomas E Holland, *The Elements of Jurisprudence* (5th edn, Clarendon Press 1890) 359; Albert V Dicey, *A Digest of the Law of England with Reference to the Conflict of Laws* (2nd edn, Stevens and Sons 1908); A Pillet, *La théorie générale des droits acquis* (Martinus Nijhoff 1925) 489; Joseph H Beale, *A Treatise on the Conflict of Laws* (Baker Voorhis & Co 1935). See also *Restatement of the Law of Conflict of Laws: As Adopted and Promulgated by the American Law Institute at Washington, DC, May 11, 1934* (American Law International 1934).

53 Dicey (n 52) xxxi.

While, as a conflicts doctrine, the principle of acquired rights was primarily concerned with the recognition of rights vested in an individual under the terms of a foreign legal order, it was only a small step for an equation to be made between the laws of a spatially distinct state and those of a temporally distinct state (the 'predecessor state'). Indeed, in cases in which a portion of the territory of one state was ceded to another, there really was no distinction—one was dealing, in all instances, with the laws of another state. Once, then, one was able to recognize the existence of a general obligation to recognize and respect pre-existent acquired (vested) rights, it was only one small further step to the conclusion that the infringement of such a right following the cession or annexation of territory might constitute an international tort if the right in question was that of an alien.[54]

What was perhaps most significant here in the merging of the doctrine of acquired rights with the doctrine of state succession was the fact that they appeared to share a common generative rationality—the clue to which being found in von Savigny's idea that they gave expression to the 'natural limits' of legislative authority. What was in contemplation was the desirability of securing the grounds for the recognition of a field of 'extra-territorial' or 'trans-national' legal relations that were to be preserved intact irrespective of the legislative/sovereign prerogatives of individual states. Private rights would enjoy, in that sense, a permanence that exceeded any political authority—they survived not in virtue of being 'recognized' but in virtue of being left 'unaffected'. Political authority, for its part, ended at the point at which it encountered private rights.

If the animus for the doctrine of acquired rights was evidently to have its origin in the precepts of classical political economy and laissez-faire government, it was also an idea that Schmitt was to later bring into prominence in his account of the (declining) European spatial order at the end of the nineteenth century. What the doctrine of state succession signified, for him, was the existence of a 'common economic space' or 'free market' within Europe that was underpinned by 'a certain relation of public and private law, of state and state-free society'.[55] The theory and practice of State succession, in his view, paralleled that within the law of occupation,[56] in the sense that it was premised upon the preservation of the underlying economic order—that of a 'common free market transcending he political borders of sovereign states'.[57] As he was to explain:

> Given that state dominion (*imperium* or *jurisdictio*) based on public law, on the one hand, and private property (*dominium*) based on private law, on the other,

[54] See G Kaeckenbeeck, 'The Protection of Vested Rights in International Law' (1936) 17 British Year Book of International Law 7.

[55] Carl Schmitt, *The Nomos of the Earth in the International Law of the Jus Publicum Europaeum* (Telos Press 2003) 197.

[56] cf Article 43, Regulations Respecting the Laws and Customs of War on Land, annex to the Convention (IV) Respecting the Laws and Customs of War on Land (adopted 18 October 1907) (1907).

[57] Schmitt (n 55) 197.

> were separated sharply, it was possible to isolate from juridical discussions the most difficult question, namely that of a total constitutional change tied to territorial change. Behind the foreground of recognized sovereignty, the private sphere, which in this particular case means the sphere of private economy and private property, largely remained undisturbed by the territorial change. With a territorial change, the international economic order—the liberal market sustained by private entrepreneurs and businessmen, which was free in the same sense as free world trade, and the free movement of capital and labour—retained all the international safeguards that it needed to function. All civilized states subscribed to the distinction between public and private law, as well as to the common standards of liberal constitutionalism; for all, property, and thus trade, economy, and industry belonged to the sphere of constitutionally protected private property. This constitutional standard was recognized as fundamental by all states party to the territorial change.[58]

His conclusion, thus, was that a 'territorial change was no *constitutional change* in the sense of the social order and of property'; rather, it was a change only in the public legal sphere, which left unaffected the 'internal currency of private legal property'.[59]

While the doctrine was to acquire considerable valence within international law in subsequent years, [60] there were considerable doubts, at the moment of its articulation, as to whether it was a principle applicable in case of the annexation of non-European territory.[61] In the latter context, concessionary contracts, in particular, became a point of contention. A good deal of practice at the end of the nineteenth century had seen states claiming the right to cancel, or at least review, existing concessionary contracts—this was the case, for example, following the annexation of Tarapaca by Chile in 1884, the annexation of Madagascar by France in 1896,[62] and the annexation of the Boer Republics by Britain in 1900.[63] Even the US, which as we

[58] ibid.

[59] ibid 198.

[60] See, eg, Kaeckenbeeck (n 54); Charles Rousseau, *Principes généraux du droit international public* (Pedone 1944) 901–06; John B Moore, *A Digest of International Law, as Embodied in Diplomatic Discussions, Treaties: In Eight Volumes* (US Government Printing Office 1906) 98; Green H Hackworth, *Digest of International Law* (US Government Printing Office 1940) 562–67; Alexandre Makarov, *Les changements territoriaux et leurs effets sur les droits des particuliers: Rapport et projet de résolutions* (L'Institut de Droit International 1950) 208; McNair (n 20) 16–18.

[61] Arrigo Cavaglieri, *La dottrina della successione di stato a stato e il suo valore guridico* (Archivio giuridico 1910) 122; Arthur B Keith, *The Theory of State Succession: With Special Reference to English and Colonial Law* (Waterlow and Sons 1907); see also Alphonse Rivier, *Principes du droit des gens* (A Rousseau 1896) 437–38.

[62] Moore (n 60) 387–88.

[63] See Parliamentary Papers (Report of the Transvaal Concessions Commission) (1901) (1901) (Cd. 623) in which it stated that 'a State which has annexed another is not legally bound by any contracts made by the State which has ceased to exist'. Moore (n 60) 411–14. The report was, no doubt, informed

have seen had traditionally sought to preserve all existing private rights following its acquisition of territory by way of cession was far more equivocal when it came to the Spanish concessions in Cuba and the Philippines in 1898.[64] In that context it had devised a general formula by which it was prepared to accept the validity of concessions only so far as they were both related to the territory and granted for its exclusive benefit.[65] Those that appeared to be solely for the benefit of Spain[66] or which concerned the purchase of public positions[67] it refused to recognize.

There are two main explanations for emergence of this practice. The first of these related to the character of the contracts themselves. Since, as mentioned previously, concessions appeared to be 'hybrid' instruments involving a mix of public and private law, the normal 'test' for intangibility was unavailable. What had to be brought into the equation was the question of whether the continuity of such legal relations was consistent with the new political settlement[68]—and that, broadly speaking, explained the articulation of the US 'benefit' test. What needed to be distinguished, at the very least, were contracts that were justifiably open to enforcement as against the successor state from those that were clearly not.[69] Not all contracts, it was reasoned, gave rise to proprietary entitlements,[70] and not all proprietary entitlements were capable of being enforced against the successor.

The second explanation, however, concerns the geographical orientation of the practice in question. Schmitt's contention that the law of state succession was a productive facet of a specifically European territorial order—giving expression to the existence of a common economic space—was to suggest that the operative conditions of the doctrine of acquired rights might be similarly confined. This much, at least, was apparent during the late nineteenth century imperial expansion, in

by the British doctrine of Act of State. See *Cook v Sprigg* (1899) AC 572 and *West Rand Central Gold Mining Company v The King*, King's Bench Division, vol 2 391.

[64] See Moore (n 60) 389–411; Charles E Magoon, *Reports on the Law of Civil Government in Territory Subject to Military Occupation by the Military Forces of the United States* (Government Printing Office 1902) 177.

[65] Sayre (n 26) 712–13 (referring to the *Manila Railway Company* case); Moore (n 60) 399–402; Kaeckenbeeck (n 54) 11; Wilkinson (n 48) 50–51.

[66] Eg, *Manila Railway Company* cases, Attorney General Griggs, 23 OP 187.

[67] See *O'Reilly de Camara v Brooke* [1908], Magoon (n 64) 209; *Alvarez y Sanchez v United States* [1910]. See generally Wilkinson (n 48) 46.

[68] See, eg, John Westlake, 'The Nature and Extent of Title by Conquest' (1901) 17 Law Quarterly Review 392, 395–98; John Westlake, 'The South African Railway Case' in John Westlake and Lassa Oppenheim (eds), *The Collected Papers of John Westlake on Public International Law* (University Press 1914) 490, 493; Max Huber, *Die Staatensuccession: Völkerrechtliche und staatsrechtliche Praxis im XIX. Jahrhundert* (Duncker & Humblot 1898) 18–19.

[69] See Sayre (n 26) 707. He cites, by way of illustration, the advice provided by law officer Magoon to the US government denying its liability for a security deposit of 27,503.06 pesos that had been provided to the Spanish collector of customs. See Magoon (n 64) 494.

[70] See *West* (n 63) 411. See also Ernst Feilchenfeld, *Public Debts and State Succession* (Macmillan 1931) 626.

which the question of succession was marked most by its almost total absence. As Schmitt notes, in that context, that

> [t]he power of indigenous chieftains over completely uncivilised peoples was not considered to be in the public sphere; native use of the soil was not considered to be private property. One could not speak logically of a legal succession in an *imperium*, not even when a European land-appropriator had concluded treaties with indigenous princes or chieftains and, for whatever motives, considered them to be binding. The land-appropriating state did not need to respect any rights to the soil existing within the appropriated land, unless these rights somehow were connected with the private property of a member of a civilised state belonging to the order of interstate, international law. Whether or not the natives' existing relations to the soil—in agriculture, herding, or hunting—were understood by them as *property* was an issue to be decided by the land-appropriating state. International law considerations benefiting the property rights of natives, such as those recognized in questions of state succession in the liberal age favouring property rights to land and acquired wealth, did not exist on colonial soil.[71]

Such ideas were to certainly inform the approach adopted by colonizing powers in relation to their liability for foreign debt,[72] and was to inform also sundry other cases relating to the acquisition of title to property,[73] liability for torts,[74] and led to a momentary distinction being developed between the annexation and the cession of territory[75] (in which 'annexation' was to be associated with the appropriation of non-European soil, and 'cession' associated with that of European soil).[76] The doctrine of acquired rights, in other words, was inflected with the engrained supposition that the only rights to be given protection were the 'rights of occupant', as Fanon was to put it.

If the doctrine of acquired rights found its negation in the annexation of non-European soil, it was nevertheless revivified within Europe the aftermath of the First World war having been incorporated as an operative principle in a number of the treaties of Peace, including the (abortive) Treaty of Sèvres (arts 311–12), the Treaty of Lausanne (Protocol XII, art 9),[77] the Treaty of Versailles (arts 297–98),[78]

[71] Schmitt (n 55) 198.

[72] See Feilchenfeld (n 70) 321.

[73] *In Re Southern Rhodesia* [1918] AC 211.

[74] *Robert E Brown (U.S.) v Great Britain* [1923] ILR 66.

[75] See, eg, Rivier (n 61) 438.

[76] See Keith (n 61); Cecil Hurst, 'State Succession in Matters of Tort' (1924) 5 British Year Book of International Law 163.

[77] |See *Mavrommatis Palestine Concessions (Greece v U.K.)* [1925] PCIJ (hereafter *Mavrommatis Palestine Concessions (Greece v U.K.)*) Series A, No. 2 & 5; *Case of the Readaptation of the Mavrommatis Jerusalem Concessions (Greece v Britain)* [1927] PCIJ Series A No 11; *Lighthouses Case between France and Greece (France v Greece)* [1934] PCIJ (hereafter *Lighthouses Case between France and Greece (France v Greece)*) Series A/B No. 62; *Lighthouses in Crete and Samos Case (Greece v France)* [1937] PCIJ Series A/B, No. 71.

[78] *German Reparations Case* (n 26) 479.

the Geneva Convention of 1922 (art 6), as well as being included in a number of the Mandate agreements. Those provisions led the Permanent Court in both the *German Settlers*[79] and the *Certain German Interests Case*[80] to declare it to be a 'general principle of law'[81] and encouraged it also to uphold, in several other cases, the principle of succession to concessionary contracts.[82] This was quickly picked up more broadly leading McNair to proclaim it to be a general principle of law,[83] and Lauterpacht to endorse it as a central pillar in the emergent law of state succession.[84] By the time, then, at which the International Law Commission (ILC) was to survey the state of existing international law in 1949, the voices of sceptics such as Keith and Cavaglieri were crowded out in the apparent, newly found, consensus.[85]

One notable feature of the doctrine that was to emerge in the interwar years, however, was the way in which it had become increasingly intertwined with the more general question of state responsibility for injury to aliens.[86] The backdrop to this, inevitably, was the emergent practice, originating in Mexico and the Soviet Union, of widespread nationalization (a practice which was to become more generalized in the building of welfare states in Europe) but which posed, in the process, questions both as to the conditions under which a power to expropriate property might be exercised and as to the level of compensation that might be payable. Concession agreements were often at the heart of that practice—agricultural land in Romania, oil in Mexico—and the principle of acquired rights came into prominence as a doctrine that provided the grounds for limiting the ability of states to legislate away rights formerly granted to aliens. At this point, its function was no longer simply one of determining the basis for the recognition of rights acquired under foreign law[87] or of specifying the obligations incumbent upon successor states, but one that was expressive of a more general obligation not to arbitrarily interfere in 'patrimonial rights of alien private individuals'.[88]

[79] *Settlers of German Origin in Poland* (Advisory Opinion) [1923] PCIJ Series B, No. 6, 15–36.

[80] *Case concerning certain German interests in Polish Upper Silesia (Germany v Poland)* [1925] PCIJ Series A, No. 7, 42. See also *Oscar Chinn Case (Britain v Belgium)* [1934] PCIJ Series A/B, No. 63, 65, 88.

[81] See also *Niederstrasser v the Polish State (1932)* (Decisions of Upper Silesian Arbitral Tribunal) AD vol II 156, 667; *Romania v Germany (Goldenberg & Sons v Germany)* [1928] RIAA 909; *Jablonsky v German Reich* [1935-1937] Annual Digest, Case No 42; *Sopron Köszeg Local Railway Company Arbitration* [1929–1930] Annual Digest, Case No 34.

[82] See, eg, *Mavrommatis Palestine Concessions (Greece v U.K.)* (n 77); *Lighthouses Case between France and Greece (France v Greece)* (n 77).

[83] McNair (n 20) 16–18.

[84] Hersch Lauterpacht, *Private Law Sources and Analogies of International Law: With Special Reference to International Arbitration* (Longmans, Green & Company 1927) 129–30.

[85] There were clearly residual voices of opposition. See, eg, Kaeckenbeeck (n 54) 14, 17.

[86] For an account of the emergence of the latter see Edwin M Borchard, 'Theoretical Aspects of the International Responsibility of States' (1929) 1 Zeitschrift für ausländisches öffentliches Recht und Völkerrecht 223.

[87] The doctrine of acquired rights, however, had largely been discarded as a key organizing principle in private international law by the 1950s. See RD Carswell, 'The Doctrine of Vested Rights in Private International Law' (1959) 8 International and Comparative Law Quarterly 268.

[88] See Francisco García-Amador, Louis Sohn and Richard Baxter, *Recent Codification of the Law of State Responsibility for Injuries to Aliens* (Springer 1974) 40.

IV. Acquired rights and decolonization

Whatever the cautions associated with the doctrine of acquired rights when applied in relation to concessionary contracts in the early part of the twentieth century, the doctrine itself was to be enthusiastically embraced by scholars in the West as a doctrine that would have considerable salience in the emergent practice of decolonization.[89] When called upon to advise the ILC as to what topics it should prioritize for purposes of codification, Lauterpacht suggested, in light of India's and Pakistan's newly acquired independence, that one of those should be the question of state succession. He went on to suggest, furthermore, that the centrepiece of that work should be the doctrine of acquired rights[90] given that it had been widely accepted (even if, he admitted, there was work to be done in determining the extent of its application to various categories of private rights such as 'those ground in the public debt, in concessionary contracts, in relations of government service, and the like').[91]

The first person to answer the call was not the ILC (which only turned to the matter in 1962) but Lauterpacht's student, DP O'Connell, who, in the following year, published an article in the *British Yearbook of International Law* where he sought to apply the doctrine of acquired rights to the question of the survival of concession agreements in case of state succession.[92] O'Connell was not entirely candid as to why he regarded the question to be important, but by the time at which he was writing, calls for the termination, re-negotiation, or straightforward expropriation of historic concession agreements were widespread, and had been picked up by various independence movements, such as those in Burma and Indonesia.[93] And one may sense that O'Connell was seeking to develop the intellectual groundwork for those within the Metropole who would be addressing such issues in coming years.

In that article O'Connell developed the argument that, while a concessionary contract does not per se survive a change in sovereignty (and hence a successor state would not be automatically 'subrogated in the rights and duties which it created') the concessionaire would, however, retain 'an equitable interest in the money which he has invested and the labour he has expended'. That interest,

[89] See generally, McNair (n 20) 16–18; Rousseau (n 60) 901–06; Alfred Verdross, 'Règles internationales concernant le traitement des étrangers' (1931) 37 Recueil des Cours de l'Académie de Droit International de La Haye 359; Makarov (n 60).

[90] Secretary General, 'Survey of International Law in Relation to the Work of Codification of the International Law Commission: Preparatory work within the purview of article 18, paragraph 1, of the International Law Commission' (New York 10 February 1949) UN Doc A/CN.4/1/Rev.1, 28–29.

[91] ibid.

[92] O'Connell, 'Economic Concessions' (n 24) 93.

[93] On Indonesian nationalization, see Martin Domke, 'Indonesian Nationalization Measures Before Foreign Courts' (1960) 54 American Journal of International Law 305; Hans W Baade, 'Indonesian Nationalization Measures Before Foreign Courts: A Reply' (1960) 54 American Journal of International Law 801.

furthermore, 'constitutes an acquired right which the successor state is obliged by international law to respect'.[94] The consequence of this was that the successor state would have the option of either subrogating itself into the concessionary contract by novation, or, alternatively, expropriating the concession (in whole or part) with the payment of equitable compensation.[95] While we have seen that O'Connell could rely upon the decisions of various courts and tribunals in the interwar years to underpin this argument for the existence of an obligation to respect acquired rights, most of the article was concerned with a constructive reinterpretation of the somewhat more inconsistent practice of the pre-war years with that conclusion in mind.[96]

It was only later in his book of 1956 that O'Connell came to spell out in more detail the underlying rationale for his thesis. His argument ran as follows: in any case of state succession there must be some 'legal continuity bridging the gap created by change of sovereignty',[97] and that is not because the successor has 'willed' the continuance of law, nor indeed, as a consequence of a rule of international law, but in virtue of a 'principle of philosophy without which human society would fall into anarchy'.[98] If the law survives, so do legal rights (with the exception of those that are 'political in character'). The successor state, however, is competent like any other to abrogate or modify such rights by legislative act, but if it chooses to abrogate the vested rights of foreign nationals, it could only do so subject to the payment of full compensation.[99] As regards state contracts, while the contract itself could not survive, the equitable interest does. He explains:

> A man who invests capital and labour in the construction of works of profit and value to a State acquires an equity in that investment that is not destroyed by change of sovereignty. If there were no security of investment, there would be no investment; and a universal refusal to recognize these equities would be destructive of one of the essential economic bases of modern State and international organization. If international law prescribes an obligation on a State to respect investment of foreign nationals there is no theoretical objection to assuming a similar obligation on the part of its successor.[100]

[94] O'Connell, 'Economic Concessions' (n 24) 124.

[95] The grounds for which were based upon the concept of unjust enrichment, see ibid 121. O'Connell was later to suggest that compensation should include *damnum emergens* and *lucrum cessans*, David P O'Connell, 'Independence and Problems of State Succession' in William V O'Brien (ed), *The New Nations in International Law and Diplomacy* (Stevens 1965) 28.

[96] O'Connell, 'Economic Concessions' (n 24) 109.

[97] David P O'Connell, *The Law of State Succession* (CUP 1956) (hereafter O'Connell, *State Succession*) 267.

[98] David P O'Connell, 'Recent Problems of State Succession in Relation to New States' (1970) 130/II Recueil des Cours de l'Académie de Droit International de La Haye 127.

[99] O'Connell, *State Succession* (n 97) 267–68.

[100] ibid.

It is at this point that O'Connell's scheme becomes transparent. The key to the whole field, as he saw it, was the securing of 'equity' and the prohibition of unjust enrichment. The timeless quality of his principle of philosophy undergirding legal continuity was thus supplemented by a contingent, 'modern', economic rationality that underscored the protection of foreign investments through the medium of a surviving equitable interest.

The clear thrust of O'Connell's argument here was to forge an analogy between the obligations of a newly independent state in respect of concessionary contracts, and those that applied more generally in relation to the treatment of concessions owned by foreign nationals.[101] And it was that analogy that led him to import into the legal regime governing decolonization the corpus of doctrine relating to the protection of foreign investments (and specifically the obligation to compensate foreign investors upon expropriation of their interests). Quite apart from the fact that the underpinnings of O'Connell's analysis was to achieve precisely that which was denied by the ICJ in the *Anglo-Iranian Oil Company Case*[102]—namely the effective 'internationalization' of the concessionary contract[103]—it may be asked, more pertinently, whether the analogy was really an appropriate one? Were colonial concession holders really 'foreign investors' when operating under the umbrella of colonial authority? Was it always to be assumed that their 'investments' were to the benefit of the territory concerned such as to give rise to an equitable interest on the part of the concession holders? Would it really make sense to suggest that a former colonial power should be entitled to assert diplomatic protection in order to protect the legal interests of a concessionaire that it, the colonial power, had granted in the first place? Was it appropriate to conceptualize as equivalent the act of a state in terminating a concession agreement to which it was party with that of a new state in determining the political and economic conditions of its own formation?

V. From concession to foreign investment—the legal re-ordering of economic relations

As much as O'Connell worked with an imaginary that equated colonial concessions with foreign investments, it was clear that in the following years, whether as

[101] This is made apparent in his commentary on the *Anglo-Iranian Oil Company* case. See O'Connell, 'Critique of the *Iranian Oil* Litigation' (n 26) 270–71.

[102] *Anglo-Iranian Oil Co* (Preliminary Objection, Judgment) (n 27).

[103] O'Connell's position, here, was informed by two contested propositions: first, that adequate compensation pre-conditioned any right to expropriate (ie, that it functioned not so much as a remedy as a limitation on the sovereign right to expropriate); secondly, that the right to compensation was enjoyed by the foreign concession holder, rather than by the state of nationality. His position on both scores paralleled that of Sohn and Baxter in their Harvard Draft Convention on the International Responsibility of States for Injuries to Aliens. See Louis B Sohn and RR Baxter, 'Responsibility of States for Injuries to the Economic Interests of Aliens' (1961) 55 American Journal of International Law 545.

a consequence of treaty arrangements prior to independence or by way of constitutional enactment, the vast majority of pre-existent concessions were continued uninterrupted after independence. Many were also subsequently the object of nationalization decrees[104] leading, in some cases, to financial settlements that contributed to the further indebtedness of states emerging from colonial rule. What went unacknowledged, however, was the complex remapping of the architecture of concession agreements that was to accompany their 'continuation'. Far from being 'unaffected' by decolonization (in the manner described by Justice Marshall in the *Percheman case*) concessions had to be conceptually reconfigured from top to bottom in order to remain in place.

In the first place, in order for the concessions in question to come within the purview of international law at all, they would have to be invested with the character of 'foreignness' (in the sense that they would then be entitled to the vaunted 'international minimum standard of treatment'). While it was certainly not unknown for concession agreements to be awarded to companies incorporated in territories other than that of the metropolitan state, in the vast majority of cases, the companies concerned were either registered and had their operations in the colony itself (albeit frequently as subsidiaries of metropolitan corporations), or alternatively were incorporated within the financial heartland of the Metropolitan state itself. In original guise, thus, most would merely have been 'local' investments for purposes of international law prior to independence governed solely by the terms of municipal law. After that moment, their foreign character would be dependent upon the subsequent arrangements governing the nationality of legal persons situated within the former colony—and that would be determined by the respective terms of both the law of the metropole and the former colony itself. [105] While in cases of companies registered, or incorporated, within the metropole it might naturally have been assumed that they would automatically become 'foreign' in relation to their site of operations in virtue of the mere fact of independence—and that the former metropolitan power would retain the right to seek protection of its interests under guise of the law of diplomatic protection. There was, however, no guarantee that such companies would continue to have legal personality within the legal order of the newly independent state. Only by avoidance of a requirement of local registration, then, could such corporations effectively secure their status as foreign investors after independence. Given that, in many cases, the main shareholding interests tended to be located within the metropole, the Colonial powers thus routinely either sought to extract guarantees from the new states prior to

[104] Eg, Indonesia, Burma, Ghana, Nigeria, Democratic Republic of Congo.

[105] For a fairly inconclusive review of the nationality of legal entities in case of succession, see Vaclav Mikulka, 'Second report on State Succession and its impact on the nationality of natural and legal persons, Succession of States with respect to nationality/Nationality in relation to the succession of States' UN Doc A/CN.4/474 and Corr. 1 & 2 (1996-II/1) *Yearbook of the International Law Commission*, 147–48.

independence to protect the interests under concession agreements, or superintended the 'relocation' of the centre of operations of the corporations concerned back to the metropole prior to independence.[106]

In the second place, there had to be a subtle interpretive reconfiguration of the concession agreement itself. Whereas, as we have seen, it was widely conceived that concession agreements assumed a hybrid form—part public, part private; part political, part economic. For them to assume the form of a foreign 'investment' as opposed to part of the apparatus of colonial rule, then, their public/political dimensions had to be imaginatively excised, and part of that process was to construe all grants, privileges, powers, and responsibilities that had previously been enjoyed by concessionaires—which extended, in some cases, to a right to acquire and colonize land, to extract revenues, or to police and enforce the rule of law—as essentially 'commercial' or 'private' interests, irrespective of their content.[107] In the same measure, the concessionaires were to be definitively cast as 'private' agencies—mere corporations—rather than armatures of colonial authority.[108] Through this imaginative reinterpretation then, concession agreements themselves were then given a definitively new form—not as hybrid legal instruments, but simply as 'state contracts'.[109]

In the third place, as O'Connell himself intimated, in order for concession agreements to survive, a necessary first step was for them to be legally extinguished.[110] The importance of this was to both displace any responsibility on the part of the metropolitan state for performance, and to preclude the possibility that the continuation of the concessions would be a matter of choice on the part of the newly decolonized state. The problem, here, was not that one the authors of the original contract had 'disappeared' so much as that the metropolitan state would no longer be in a position to guarantee its performance (bringing into play the doctrine of 'frustration'). An obvious response to this might then have been to suggest that the effective unilateral termination of the contract on the part of the metropolitan

[106] Eg, Belgian Law of 17 June 1960, which purported to move the headquarters of the Compagnie du Katanga to Brussels. See 'Explanatory Statement' to Decree-Law of November 29, 1964 (Democratic Republic of the Congo) (1965) 4 ILM 232, 234–35. More generally, Nkrumah (n 5); Wolf Radmann, 'The Nationalization of Zaire's Copper: From Union Minière to Gecamines' (1978) 25 Africa Today 25.

[107] For example, while concession contracts often 'impose obligations of a semi-political character', they are 'not substantially different from ordinary contracts'. See García-Amador (n 45) 25, para 101. See also McNair (n 20) 10.

[108] See, eg, Schwebel's account of the Watercourses in Katanga case in which, having noted that the rights of the Union Miniere 'were so extensive as to partake of quasi-governmental powers akin to those accorded the great trading companies of an earlier concessions era', he was to go on to assert that 'the Company was clearly a company and the State clearly a State'. Gillis J Wetter and Stephen M Schwebel, 'Some Little-Known Cases on Concessions' (1964) 40 British Year Book of International Law 183, 193.

[109] See, eg, FA Mann, 'State Contracts and State Responsibility' (1960) 54 American Journal of International Law 572; Jennings (n 21) 161.

[110] See JG Starke, *Introduction to International Law* (5th edn, Butterworths 1963) 272; Robert Delson, 'Comments on State Succession' (1966) 60 Proceedings of the American Society of International Law at its Annual Meeting 111, 112.

power (by way of relinquishing its claim to administer the territory concerned) gave rise to an unliquidated debt on its part for which *it* (the metropolitan power) would be primarily responsible (unless, and to the extent that, it was 'localized' and thereby 'passed' to the successor).[111] Perhaps unsurprisingly, this was not an option widely canvassed. The alternative, furthermore, that it remained open for the successor state to step into the shoes of the metropolitan state for purposes of continuing the contract was equally unappealing. To admit as much would be to suggest that the fate of concessionary contracts would depend entirely upon the willingness of the latter to recognize the contracts as remaining in force, and that there would be no obligation to compensate the 'investor' if the undertaking were to be appropriated by the agencies of the new state.

The advantage, then, of pronouncing the contract to have 'lapsed', as O'Connell was to suggest, was that rights and interests in question could be detached from the agreement itself, and presented as independent juridical/factual datum—or, in O'Connell's formulation, as 'equitable interests'—the denial of which would lead to an unjust enrichment on the part of the state. And in his view, it was the threat of unjust enrichment that underpinned the obligation of novation/compensation. This formulation—which appeared to involve the subtle reconceptualization of contractual interests as beneficial interests—was dependent, however, upon a particular way of accounting for that interest. In O'Connell's account, the existence of such an equitable interest would be determined by the overall value of the investment concerned, and, in turn, that value would be determined by reference to the level of compensation putatively required in case of its expropriation.[112] So, as he was to conclude, a refusal to recognize a pre-existent concessionary interest on the part of a successor state would require compensation for 'the amount of capital and the value of the labour expended on the concession' or '. . . the lowest market value of the works immediately anterior to the expropriation'.[113]

Two very subtle analytical moves are put in place here. To begin with, in order to identify the very existence of a beneficial interest, O'Connell has resort to the imagined level of compensation that would be payable as a consequence of an act of expropriation. He draws, in other words, a factual inference as to the existence of a beneficial interest from a normative criterion for compensation, and in the process, his argument becomes almost irreducible circular—a legal interest exists because compensation would be payable if that legal interest were to exist. His conclusion, in other words, is manufactured by being embedded in the chain of reasoning as an imagined predicate.

In the second place, the evaluative framework he employs is one that shares the orientation of the Hull formula (which was incorporated into the doctrine of

[111] See, eg, *Manila Railway Co Claim*, Magoon (n 64) 177.
[112] See Delson (n 110) 112–13.
[113] O'Connell, *State Succession* (n 97) 277.

unjust enrichment by its early proponents[114]). The principal concern, there, being to evaluate the equities on one side alone—by reference to what the concessionaires 'invested', or by way of calculation of the present value of the investment as determined by current assets and future (projected) profits. What this entirely removes from view is the extent to which the concessionaires might themselves have benefitted from the undertaking in question—it focuses on inputs, not profits, dividends or repatriated capital. The point here is not that the concessionaire might have drawn 'excess profits' from its investment at the expense of the host state, but that in order to determine whether or not a newly independent state would be 'unjustly enriched' as a consequence of its refusal to continue a concessionary contract would seem to require as much attention being paid to what had been extracted (oils, minerals, etc.) as to what had been invested. In that respect, O'Connell's apparent assumption that every concessionary contract gave rise to an equitable interest on the part of the investor was somewhat at odds with the historical role of concessionary interests within the colony, particularly given the suggestion that, in some cases, the companies concerned had engaged in massive withdrawals of capital from the colonies prior to independence.[115]

VI. Conclusion

By the time at which the ILC was to come to draft articles on state succession and address, in the process, the question of concessionary contracts, most of the former colonies had already gained their independence. The assault launched by Mohammed Bedjaoui against the doctrine of acquired rights in his second report had, as a consequence, a certain sense of futility. As much as he managed to wrest the ILC away from the temptation to codify the doctrine of acquired rights into the draft Vienna Convention on State Succession in Respect of Property, Archives and Debt, it was all too late to have any real significance in shaping the pattern of decolonization itself. In practice, the vast majority of concession agreements appear to have been continued in force either by way of agreement prior to independence[116] or as a consequence of constitutional provisions guaranteeing respect for existing rights in property. It had, indeed, been rare for any incoming authorities to recognize that there was a moment, prior to independence, in which much more ground could be made in renegotiating the terms of concessionary contracts—that the protections they would later be afforded as 'foreign investments' were not yet available,

[114] See *Lena Goldfields Arbitration* (*Lena Goldfields Ltd. v USSR*) [1930] ILR 3; McNair (n 20).

[115] Nkrumah (n 5) 219.

[116] See, eg, Évian Accords. In return for French recognition of Algerian sovereignty, the new state would recognize the acquired rights of the concessionary companies that had established the infrastructure for oil exploitation. Under the terms, then, of the Évian agreements of 19 March 1962, Algeria was to acquire sovereignty over the territory, including the Sahara. See 'Algeria: France-Algeria Independence Agreements (Évian Agreements)' (1962) 1 ILM 214, ch II, A, I. All acquired rights were

that headway could be made in accounting for resources already extracted, and that the arguments in favour of the sanctity of the acquired rights of concession holders were not beyond effective scrutiny.[117]

All of this, however, stands as testament to the extraordinary effectiveness of the idea that what was to be obtained at the moment of decolonization was 'public power', and that all 'private' relations of property and contract should remain 'unaffected' by the transition to independence. That this was to become the default assumption was itself partly a consequence of the instantiation within the colony of a set of relations of power, authority, and ownership in which concessions themselves would serve as vital sources of income for the new regimes. It was also a consequence of the subtle, imaginative re-configuration of concession agreements into private 'foreign investments' whose sanctity was, prospectively, to be guaranteed by international law. The subsequent 'battles' over permanent sovereignty, the right to nationalize, or the requisite standard of treatment of foreign investments, thus, were all battles that took place on ground that had already been largely conceded, and in terms that barely touched upon the historic role such 'investments' had in advancing and deepening colonial rule.

to be respected, see 'Declaration of Principles Concerning Economic and Financial Cooperation', in 'Agreements relating to Algerian Independence' (n 116) 224, Title IV, article 12 ('Algeria will ensure without discrimination the free and peaceful enjoyment of patrimonial rights acquired on its territory before self-determination. No one will be deprived of these rights without fair compensation previously agreed upon.'). Rights 'attached to mining titles granted by France' in application of the Petroleum Code were to be respected and 'preference' would be given under a cooperation agreement to French companies in respect of the granting of new mining titles ('General Declaration', 'Agreements relating to Algerian Independence' (n 116) ch II, B).

[117] O'Connell observes that '[t]here is very little material collected on the treatment accorded contractors by the new governments, but one may take a fairly accurate guess that the discontinuance thought of has not even crossed the minds of either governmental officials or the contractors themselves in 999 cases out of 1000'; see O'Connell, 'Economic Concessions' (n 24) 27. The one notable exception here concerns the termination of the concession of the British South Africa Company's concession in Northern Rhodesia shortly before Zambian Independence in 1964. See Peter Slinn, 'Commercial Concessions and Politics during the Colonial Period: The Role of the British South Africa Company in Northern Rhodesia 1890–1964' (1971) 70 African Affairs 365, 378–84.

5

Acquired Rights and State Succession

The Rise and Fall of the Third World in the International Law Commission

Anna Brunner

I. Introduction

Already at the climax of decolonization in the early 1960s, the idea of post-colonialism[1] developed and an initial form of post-colonial discourse spread all over the discipline of international law, namely in the branches of human rights, international trade and state succession.

The right of state succession was of crucial importance to international lawyers in the new states as a means to get rid of the established (post-)colonial system and advance their 'global-solidary project'[2] of a New International Economic Order (NIEO). They argued that the new states should have the power to 'pick and choose' which rules of the established international system corresponded to their needs and were accordingly acceptable to them, while other rules were not. In contrast, traditional Western scholars favoured the theory of continuity in the law of state succession. Along these battle lines, the International Law Commission (ILC) was occupied by issues of state succession for years. Against strong, mainly Western opposition in the ILC and at diplomatic conferences, the third world largely pushed through the application of the clean slate principle for former colonies in the two new state succession conventions. The most controversial topic in this regard was the question of so-called 'acquired rights'. Because of its far-reaching economic implications, the fate of rights acquired by foreign companies through colonial concession regimes was vital to scholars in the new states.

[1] See María do Mar Castro Varela and Nikita Dhawan, *Postkoloniale Theorie: Eine kritische Einführung* (Transcript 2005); Robert Young, *White Mythologies: Writing History and the West* (Routledge 1990); Robert Young, *Colonial Desire: Hybridity in Theory Culture and Race* (Routledge 1995); Patrick Williams and Laura Chrisman (eds), *Colonial Discourse and Post Colonial Theory: A Reader* (Columbia University Press 1994) 66, 84; Bill Ashcroft, Gareth Griffiths and Helen Tiffin (eds), *The Post-Colonial Studies Reader* (2nd edn, Routledge Taylor & Francis Group 2006); Patrick Williams and Laura Chrisman, *Colonial Discourse and Post-Colonial Theory: A Reader* (Columbia University Press 1994).

[2] See the author's doctoral thesis published under her maiden name Anna Krueger, *Die Bindung der Dritten Welt an das postkoloniale Völkerrecht: Die Völkerrechtskommission das Recht der Verträge und das Recht der Staatennachfolge in der Dekolonialisierung* (Springer 2018) ch 4.

Anna Brunner, *Acquired Rights and State Succession* In: *The Battle for International Law: South-North Perspectives on the Decolonization Era.* Edited by: Jochen von Bernstorff and Philipp Dann, Oxford University Press (2019).

DOI: 10.1093/oso/9780198849636.003.0006

In this respect, the debate was shaped by recurrence to the principle of permanent sovereignty of natural resources (PSNR). Taking a closer look at ILC debates concerning the question of acquired rights, one might recognize the rise and fall of post-colonial international law discourse in the second half of twentieth century. Even though the third world had mobilized the United Nations General Assembly (UNGA) and the ILC for two decades to gain leeway to better control and regulate foreign investors, in the 1980s, legal developments led to more protection of investors against public regulation.

II. Continuity or clean slate? State succession as post-colonial topic

After decolonization, the number of newly independent states grew remarkably in the 1960s, former colonies soon constituted the majority of member states in the United Nations (UN). Directly linked to battle lines during the Cold War, the third world gained importance as a global actor between East and West, and the world started to focus on the new states' political and economic claims and related topics in international law. The main question was how international law had been shaped by colonialism and how it now had to be changed. After winning the struggle for national independence, many new States were challenged by massive economic problems which, according to dependency theory,[3] resulted from colonialism. On the outside, they were confronted with an international legal order that had developed in times of colonialism without the participation of the former colonies.[4] International lawyers in the former colonies were critical of the established international legal order, which they viewed as a European product.[5] For the Indian international lawyer Ram Prakash Anand, for example, international law was shaped by the social context of colonialism in which it had developed and did not serve the needs of the newly independent states:

> The present body of international law is, therefore, naturally affected by the power interests of the last and the early part of the present century and is to a great extent a legacy of the age of colonialism and imperialism. This law was meant to serve the interests of a limited number of powerful states and was

[3] Giorgio Secondi (ed), *The Development Economics Reader* (Routledge 2008) 58–64.

[4] Taslim O Elias, *Africa and the Development of International Law* (Sijthoff 1972) 21.

[5] Tirthankar Roy, 'Is the Law of Responsibility of States for Injuries to Aliens a Part of Universal International Law?' (1961) 55 American Journal of International Law 863, 865; Georges Abi-Saab, 'The Newly Independent States and the Rules of International Law: An Outline' (1962) 8 Howard Law Journal 95, 99; Francisco García-Amador, 'The Proposed New International Economic Order: A New Approach to the Law Governing Nationalization and Compensation' (1980) 12 Lawyer of The Americas 1, 5 et seq (hereafter García-Amador, 'Economic Order'); Jorge Castañeda, 'The Underdeveloped Nations and the Development of International Law' (1961) 15 International Organization 33.

> supposed to be applicable between themselves in their relations with each other. The vast majority of peoples had neither any voice nor any right and were meant to be exploited and, if necessary, colonized to serve the interests of their masters.[6]

The Algerian international legal activist Mohammed Bedjaoui was even more critical of the established international order, which he viewed as a means for economic and political subjugation:

> The historical and political reasons for the present disorder can be mainly expressed in terms of imperialism, colonialism and neo-colonialism. Dependence, exploitation, the looting of the resources of the Third World, and the introduction of zones of influence, have marked international relations with 'organized' or 'institutionalized' disorder. The cruel, inhuman law of maximum profit has finally succeeded in establishing disorder, with the Faustian power of multinational firms, the gigantism of military-industrial complexes, and the ecological disaster.[7]

International lawyers in the third world considered the established international order to be colonial in nature. In many sectors, for example, international economic law, this order was therefore not acceptable to the new States. However, international lawyers in the third world did not turn their back on international law, which the new States found a useful instrument to protect their newly won independence and to bring their demands to the attention of the industrial states. Instead, they believed in what might be called their global solidary project: They placed their hope in the UN system and tried to change international law from within, aiming for a world order oriented towards justice, solidarity, development, and wealth for all as common goals of the 'international community',[8] resulting in the establishment of a NIEO. From their point of view, international law had to be changed in accordance with the needs of new States.

The logical starting point for such a demand within the traditional framework of international law was the topic of state succession, in which changes in sovereignty had been dealt with. Traditionally, theorists favoured universal succession of a new State in the rights of duties of its predecessor and continuity of international

[6] Ram P Anand, *New States and International Law* (Vikas 1972) 114.

[7] Mohammed Bedjaoui, *Towards a New International Economic Order* (Holmes Meier 1979) 20 (hereafter Bedjaoui, *Towards a New NIEO*).

[8] Anand (n 6) 86, 101; AA Fatouros, 'International Law and the Third World' (1964) 50 Virginia Law Review 783, 786; Francisco García-Amador, 'Current Attempts to Revise International Law: A Comparative Analysis' (1983) 77 American Journal of International Law 286, 294; Bedjaoui, *Towards a New NIEO* (n 7) 196; Daniel P O'Connell, 'Recent Problems of State Succession in Relation to New States' (1970) 130/II Recueil des Cours de l'Académie de Droit International de La Haye 95.

relations.[9] This view was confronted with the new states' claim 'to start with a tabula rasa, a clean slate'.[10]

According to the predominant Western view, if the newly independent states wanted to play the game of international law, they had to accept its rules. Some Western jurists argued that when a new State comes into being and joins the international society, it implicitly consents to the rules of international law in existence at that moment.[11] New states, it was said, could not, on the one hand, claim sovereign equality, a right stipulated by customary international law, and on the other hand, refuse to be bound by international law on that very basis:

> New States can hardly claim the privileges and faculties of States and yet repudiate the system from which these derive; yet this is precisely what the argument involves. It overlooks that a State, when it commences to exist as a State, does so in a structural context which gains its form from law, just as a child when born into a society becomes subjected to it by virtue of the order of being in which it is integrated.[12]

This traditional view seemed ultimately unfair to scholars from the third world because of the colonial legacies of established international law. They argued that the new States should have the power to 'pick and choose' which rules of the established international system corresponded to their needs, and which did not.[13]

Facing this disagreement, as well as the urgency of the question, the ILC decided to put the topic on its agenda, along with other topics that were pertinent in the context of decolonization, for example, subjects and sources of international law, recognition of states and governments, fundamental rights and duties of states, regime of the high seas and territorial waters, treatment of aliens, the law of treaties, and state responsibility.[14]

The new States placed great hope in the work of the ILC since this commission of experts seemed to be a platform for scholars from the third world to change international law from within in accordance with their global solidary project.[15] It was

[9] Matthew Maloney, 'Succession of States in Respect of Treaties: The Vienna Convention of 1978' (1979) 19 Virginia Journal of International Law 885, 886ff; Matthew Craven, *The Decolonization of International Law: State Succession and the Law of Treaties* (OUP 2007) 30ff.

[10] Abi-Saab (n 5) 95, 113; Prakash Sinha, 'Perspective of the Newly Independent States on the Binding Quality of International Law' (1965) 14 International and Comparative Law Quarterly 121, 126; Maloney (n 9) 885, 894.

[11] Walther Schönborn, *Staatensukzession* (Kohlhammer 1913) 71ff; Hersch Lauterpacht, *Oppenheim's International Law: A Treatise*, vol 1 (7th edn, Longmans, Green & Company 1948) 18, 19 (hereafter Lauterpacht, *Oppenheim's International Law*); Hans-Ernst Folz, 'Zur Frage der Bindung Neuer Staaten an das Völkerrecht' (1963) 2 Der Staat 319, 329ff.

[12] Mary E O'Connell, 'The Role of International Law' (1966) 95 Daedalus 627, 636; Craven (n 9) 88.

[13] Prakash Sinha, *New Nations and the Law of Nations* (Sijthoff Leyden 1967) 142.

[14] International Law Commission (ILC), 'Report of the International Law Commission on the Work of its first Session, 12 April 1949', UN Doc A/CN.4/13 and Corr. 1-3 (1974-I), *Yearbook of the International Law Commission* 277, 281; Craven (n 9) 96.

[15] Anand (n 6) 73ff; Elias (n 4) 24, 65.

predictable that the ILC would put great emphasis on the special context of decolonization while discussing the topic of state succession, since the UNGA requested the ILC to adequately take into account the third world's view in this regard.[16] The ILC's work on the topic of state succession finally resulted in two conventions: the Vienna Convention on Succession of States in respect of Treaties of 1978, and the Vienna Convention on Succession of States in respect of State Property, Archives and Debts (VCSSPAD) of 1983. The most controversial question in the context of state succession was the handling of acquired rights.

III. History and concept of acquired rights

While the notion of acquired rights lacks precision and has been interpreted in different ways, the focal question after decolonization was whether rights acquired by foreign investors—because of concessions given by colonial masters with regard to their colonies—should also be binding for the newly independent states.[17] From the sixteenth century onwards, companies with limited jurisdiction from European countries had been an important vehicle of colonization.[18] These companies gained concessions to use natural resources like oil or territorial rights, for example, the Suez canal.[19] The foreign companies made remarkable investments to exploit their concessions, resulting in huge profits.[20] The protection of these rights acquired by foreign companies was no original question of international law, but of the conflict of laws; nevertheless, it was treated in the context of the international law of state responsibility and of state succession.[21]

Until the twentieth century, most international lawyers claimed that acquired rights were not affected by changes of sovereignty.[22] Expropriation of former companies by the host country was thought to be unlawful under the law of aliens, leading to compensation claims under the law of state responsibility.[23] This absolute

[16] See UNGA Res/16/1686 (18 December 1961) UN Doc A/Res/1686(XVI); UNGA Res 1902 (XVIII) (18 November 1963) UN Doc A/Res/1902.

[17] Christoph Ohler, 'Concessions' in Rüdiger Wolfrum (ed), Max Planck Encyclopedia of Public International Law (OUP 2013).

[18] Mohammed Bedjaoui, 'Second Report on Succession in Respect of Matters other than Treaties, Economic and Financial Acquired Rights and State Succession' UN Doc A/CN.4/216/Rev.1 (1969-II) Yearbook of the International Law Commission, 69, 92 para 114 (hereafter Bedjaoui, 'Second Report').

[19] Nico J Schrijver, *Sovereignty over Natural Resources: Balancing Rights and Duties* (CUP 1997) 34.

[20] Anand (n 6) 23.

[21] cf David P O'Connell, 'Recent Problems of State Succession in Relation to New States' (1970) 130/II Recueil des Cours de l'Académie de Droit International de La Haye 95, 135.

[22] Hersch Lauterpacht, *Private Law Sources and Analogies of International Law: With Special Reference to International Arbitration* (Longmans, Green & Company 1927) 125; Ernst Feilchenfeld, *Public Debts and State Succession* (Macmillan 1931) 396; see Antony Anghie, *Imperialism, Sovereignty and the Making of International Law* (CUP 2008) 213.

[23] Franceso Francioni, 'Compensation for Nationalisation of Foreign Property: The Borderline between Law and Equity' (1975) 24 International and Comparative Law Quarterly 255, 259; David P O'Connell, *The Law of State Succession* (CUP 1956) 100 (hereafter O'Connell, *State Succession*).

theory of the protection of acquired rights was later replaced by a more liberal theory allowing for expropriation under certain circumstances.[24] However, there was disagreement about the standards an expropriation had to fulfil according to the law of aliens: Western jurists tended to claim an international minimum standard, according to which the expropriating state had to pay full compensation to the company.[25] This was specified by the so-called Hull formula, via which prompt, adequate, and effective compensation should be granted.[26] On the other hand, Latin American states had taken an opposing view as early as the nineteenth century. According to the so-called Calvo doctrine, nationals and aliens had to be treated equally, and the question of equal compensation was one of the national jurisdiction of the expropriating state, not of international law.[27] After the Russian revolution, nationalization without compensation became a more frequent phenomenon,[28] which also inspired international theory.[29] Francioni wrote:

> Equity is in such doctrine identified with the principles of socialist justice; in that view, the suppression of private property, in so far as it implies a restitution of private wealth to the collectivity from which it had been arbitrarily taken, is an act of justice that does not entail any sort of reparation.[30]

For many third-world countries, expropriation and nationalization became welcome means for a redistribution of wealth in their struggle for economic 'development'. They used the notion of PSNR in order to enforce a right of expropriation without having to pay compensation, which they could not afford. The development of the PSNR illustrates the rise of post-colonial discourse in international law. In the 1950s, PSNR was discussed in the context of human rights as an economic dimension of the right of self-determination, resulting in the Common Article 1 para 2 of the International Covenant on Civil and Political Rights, and the International Covenant on Economic, Social and Cultural Rights.[31]

[24] O'Connell, *State Succession* (n 23) 130.

[25] Francioni (n 23) 255, 262; Maarten Muller, 'Compensation for Nationalization: A North-South Dialogue' (1981) 19 Columbia Journal of Transnational Law 35, 36; Fritz Visser, 'The Principle of Permanent Sovereignty over Natural Resources and the Nationalisation of Foreign Interests' (1988) 21 Comparative and International Law Journal of South Africa 76, 80; Schrijver (n 19) 176ff.

[26] Francioni (n 23) 255, 263.

[27] García-Amador, 'Economic Order' (n 5) 1.

[28] Allan Kelly, 'Nationalization: Effective Compensation and International Law' (1964) 4 Virginia Journal of International Law, 97, 99; Francioni (n 23) 255, 266.

[29] Charles de Visscher, *Théories et Réalités en Droit International Public* (Pedone 1953) 238; Arrigo Cavaglieri, 'La Notion des Droits Acquis et son Application en Droit International Public' (1931) 38 Revue générale de droit international public 206.

[30] Francioni (n 23) 255, 268.

[31] See Francisco García-Amador, *The Emerging International Law of Development: A New Dimension of International Economic Law* (Oceana Publications 1990) 132; Azadon Tiewul, 'The Evolution of the Doctrine of Permanent Sovereignty over Natural Resources' (1978–1981) 15 Ghana Law Journal 55, 63; James Hyde, 'Permanent Sovereignty Over Natural Wealth and Resources' (1956) 50 American Journal of International Law 854, 855; Visser (n 25) 76; García-Amador, 'Economic Order' (n 5) 1, 21.

In parallel, the new states used the UNGA to establish the PSNR as a new principle of international economic law, aiming to establish the right of peoples to freely use and exploit their natural wealth and resources as inherent in their sovereignty, corresponding to a right to expropriation without compensation. In the beginning, third-world States tried to reach agreement with the West, leading to equivocal compromise resolutions in the UNGA that granted at least *limited* protection of acquired rights and established a duty to pay 'appropriate compensation' after expropriation 'in accordance with international law'.[32] In the 1970s, under growing pressure of UNCTAD, the new states pressed for progressive changes in the international law of investment protection against strong Western opposition.[33] At this point in time, the UNGA resolutions only referred to possible, instead of obligatory, compensation in accordance with the national legislation of the expropriating State.[34] The protection of acquired rights became an embattled concept, which, in the eyes of third-world scholars, did not have a place in contemporary international law. The third world aimed to stipulate a right to expropriation without compensation. This development finally resulted in 1974 in the well-known Declaration on the Establishment of a New International Economic Order and the Charter of Economic Rights and Duties of States, probably constituting the climax of post-colonial discourse in international economic law.[35]

IV. Acquired rights in the ILC

The rise of a profound critique of the notion of acquired rights and its subsequent fall may best be understood by taking a closer look at the respective developments in the ILC.

[32] UNGA Res 3171 (XXVIII) (17.12.1973) UN Doc A/Res/3171 (XXVIII).

[33] Mohammed Bedjaoui, 'Sixth Report on Succession of States in Respect of Matters other than Treaties, Draft Articles with Commentaries on Succession to Public Property' UN Doc A/CN.4/267 (1973-II) Yearbook of the International Law Commission, 3, 10, 24 (hereafter Bedjaoui, 'Sixth Report'); Mohammed Bedjaoui, 'Seventh Report on Succession of States in Respect of Matters other than Treaties' UN Doc A/CN.4/282 (1974-II) Yearbook of the International Law Commission.

[34] '[. . .] affirms that the application of the principle of nationalization carried out by States, as an expression of their sovereignty in order to safeguard their natural resources, implies that each State is entitled to determine the amount of possible compensation and the mode of payment, and that any disputes which might arise should be settled in accordance with the national legislation of each State carrying out such measures [. . .]'; UNGA Res 3171 (XXVIII) (17.12.1973) UN Doc A/Res/3171 (XXVIII) para 3.

[35] See Katja Gelinsky, *Der Schutz des Eigentums gemäß Art. 1 des Ersten Zusatzprotokolls zur Europäischen Menschenrechtskonvention: Eine Analyse der Rechtsprechung der Straßburger Organe* (Duncker & Humblot 1996) 157; UNGA Res 3201 (S-VI) (1 May 1974) UN Doc A/Res/3201 (S-VI) principle 5; UNGA Res 29/3281 (12 December 1974) UN Doc A/Res/29/3281.

Originally, the question of acquired rights was considered to belong to the right of state responsibility in a rather material sense.[36] As competent Special Rapporteur on State Responsibility in the ILC, Francisco V. García-Amador propagated an international minimum standard of compensation for expropriation of acquired rights, regardless of the nationality of the affected individual, placing the question in the context of diplomatic protection for injuries to aliens.[37] Already in this context, the ILC's opinion on the topic of acquired rights was divided. Since such investment protection standards were highly disputed,[38] Roberto Ago, García-Amador's predecessor as Special Rapporteur, turned to a different approach to state responsibility, focusing on a secondary law matrix, thereby sidestepping the problem of acquired rights.[39]

Consequently, the Sub-Committee on Succession of States and Governments took up the matter.[40] The Sub-Committee had decided to divide the right of state succession into three parts: in treaties, in sources other than treaties, and in international organizations.[41] Sir Humphrey Waldock became Special Rapporteur for the first part, Mohammed Bedjaoui became Special Rapporteur for the second part, and the third part was postponed.[42] Although the members of the Sub-Committee were well aware of the controversy about acquired rights,[43] they nevertheless decided to put it on their agenda because of the topic's great importance, especially to the newly independent states.[44]

[36] Todd Weiler, 'A Historical Analysis of the Function of the Minimum Standard of Treatment in International Investment Law' in Todd Weiler and Freya Baetens (eds), *New Directions in International Economic Law: In Memoriam Thomas Wälde* (Nijhoff 2011) 357.

[37] Francisco García-Amador 'International Responsibility, First Report' UN Doc A/CN.4/96 (1956-II) Yearbook of the International Law Commission 173; Francisco García-Amador 'International Responsibility, Second Report' UN Doc A/CN.4/106 (1957-II) Yearbook of the International Law Commission 104; Francisco García-Amador 'International Responsibility, Third Report' UN Doc A/CN.4/111 (1958-II) Yearbook of the International Law Commission 47; Francisco García-Amador 'International Responsibility, Fourth Report' UN Doc A/CN.4/119 (1959-II) ILC-Yearbook 1; Francisco García-Amador 'International Responsibility, Fifth Report' UN Doc A/CN.4/125 (1960-II) Yearbook of the International Law Commission 41; Francisco García-Amador 'International Responsibility, Sixth Report' UN Doc A/CN.4/134 & ADD.l (1961-II) Yearbook of the International Law Commission 1; Francisco García-Amador, Louis Sohn and Richard Baxter, *Recent Codification of the Law of State Responsibility for Injuries to Aliens* (Springer 1974).

[38] See, for example, Jimenez de Aréchaga, International Law Commission (ILC) 'Report of the International Law Commission Covering the Work of its fifteenth Session, 6 May–12 July 1963' UN Doc Doc A/5509 (1963-II) *Yearbook of the International Law Commission* 237.

[39] Roberto Ago, 'First Report on State Responsibility', UN Doc A/CN.4/217/Add.2 (1969-II) *Yearbook of the International Law Commission* 125 para 5; James Crawford, 'State Responsibility' in Rüdiger Wolfrum (ed), Max Planck Encyclopedia of Public International Law, para 7 (OUP 2013).

[40] Manfred Lachs, 'Report by Mr. Manfred Lachs, Chairman of the Sub-committee on Succession of States and Governments (Approved by the Sub-Committee)', UN Doc A/CN.4/160 and Corr.1 (1963-II) *Yearbook of the International Law Commission* 266; Shabtai Rosenne, in Lachs (n 41) 285, 288; Erik Castrén, in Lachs (n 41) 290, 292; Milan Bartoš, in Lachs (n 41) 293, 294.

[41] Lachs (n 41) 260, 261 para 13.

[42] International Law Commission (ILC), 'Reports of the Commission to the General Assembly', UN Doc A/6309/Rev. 1 (1966-II) *Yearbook of the International Law Commission* 169, 368 para 39.

[43] TO Elias, in Lachs (n 41) 282 para 3; Milan Bartoš, in Lachs (n 41) 293, 294.

[44] Lachs (n 41) 260, 261 para 15.

In 1968, Bedjaoui already had focused on the question of acquired rights in his first report as Special Rapporteur for the Succession of States in respect of matters other than treaties. In Bedjaoui's view, the question whether new states were bound by concessions given by their predecessor state was of decisive importance to the economic development of the third world.[45] Bedjaoui's goal was to establish a norm of international law according to which states had the right to expropriate acquired rights without paying compensation, at least in the context of decolonization. He attached great value on the specific economic (that is to say, colonial) circumstances in which a concession was granted as well as on the expropriating state's need to establish its own commercial policy while downgrading the question of the rights of foreign investors. Bedjaoui's reasoning was clearly shaped by ideas originating from socialism and dependency theory.[46] Contrary to former Special Rapporteurs, Bedjaoui was less concerned about evaluating different sources of international law concerning this topic, but rather wrote a pamphlet supporting the cause of the former colonies.

Most ILC member reacted positively on Bedjaoui's first report, but also quietly pointed out their surprise concerning the unusual methodology of the Special Rapporteurs.[47] Concerning the substance of his report, Western ILC members especially stressed the importance to satisfy the rights dimension (particular property rights) of concessions.[48] However, members from the third world welcomed Bedjaoui's focus on decolonization.[49] That being said, most members prioritized general economic and financial relations between the predecessor State and the successor State; the question of acquired rights should be deduced from the result of this general inquiry.[50] Bedjaoui initially agreed to preliminary focus on 'Succession of States in Economic and Financial Matters' instead of concentrating on the question of acquired rights at the very beginning.[51]

[45] Mohammed Bedjaoui, 'First Report on Succession of States in Respect of Rights and Duties Resulting from Sources other than Treaties', UN Doc A/CN.4/204 (1968-II) *Yearbook of the International Law Commission* 94, 116 para 144ff.

[46] Sundhya Pahuja, *Decolonising International Law: Development, Economic Growth, and the Politics of Universality* (CUP 2011) 125.

[47] International Law Commission (ILC), 'Summary Record of the 961st Meeting, Succession of States in Respect of Matters other than Treaties', UN Doc A/CN.4/SR.961 (1968-I), *Yearbook of the International Law Commission* 105 para 8 (hereafter ILC, '961st Meeting'); International Law Commission (ILC), 'Summary Record of the 962nd Meeting, Succession of States in Respect of Matters other than Treaties' UN Doc A/CN.4/SR.962 (1968-I), *Yearbook of the International Law Commission* 111, 114 para 35 (hereafter ILC, '962nd Meeting').

[48] ILC, '961st Meeting' (n 48) 105, 107 para 23, 109 para 56.

[49] International Law Commission (ILC), 'Summary Record of the 963rd meeting, Succession of States in Respect of Matters other than Treaties', UN Doc A/CN.4/SR.963 (1968-I), *Yearbook of the International Law Commission* 118, 120 para 19: 'The international community intervened to prevent a de facto and necessarily provisional settlement—usually the outcome of an attempt by the colonial Power to maintain its prerogatives—from taking the place of a permanent solution of the problems of State succession. State succession in the context of decolonization therefore deserved special study.'

[50] ILC, '962nd Meeting' (n 48) 111, 117 para 81.

[51] International Law Commission (ILC), 'Summary Record of the 965th Meeting', UN Doc A/CN.4/SR.965 (1968-I -), *Yearbook of the International Law Commission* 127, 130 para 36, 38.

Despite this commitment, Bedjaoui named his 1969 Second Report 'Economic and Financial Acquired Rights and State Succession', in which he argued that he considered the question of acquired rights to be at the heart of all state succession problems and therefore wanted to reflect on it first.[52] He argued passionately and at length against a duty to compensate in cases of expropriation after decolonization because of sociological, historical, economical, or juristic-logical reasons. According to Bedjaoui, the very controversial views on the question of acquired rights resulted from its sociological underpinnings and the conflicting interests at stake,[53] saying:

> Basically, these conflicts are nothing more than a reflection of the struggle which inevitably occurs, after every upheaval, between the old structures which resist with waning strength and the new structures which assert themselves with increasing vigour. At the end of this necessary transitional phase, which varies in length and is regulated by the intertemporal law and is the sum and the reflection of the contradictions between what is accepted and what is contested, a normalized period begins. This does not mean that 'the fight is over, because there is no one left to fight', but simply that society has assimilated the new norms and harmonized them into a new equilibrium. This situation will last until such time as it is once again disrupted by further normative upheavals, when the same doctrinal conflicts will break out anew. This is a problem as old as the world, constantly occurring and recurring, and it is always solved without the supporters of acquired rights having fully learnt the lesson that change is inevitable, because force of habit engenders a feeling of hostility towards everything new and because it is in the nature of things that novelty should arouse resistance for a time.[54]

Bedjaoui saw the concept of acquired rights as being reactionary per se, putting it in the context of liberalism:

> With the disappearance of the patrimonial State in the seventeenth century, a distinction began to be drawn between *imperium*, which was reserved for the liberal State, and *dominium*, which enabled individuals to exercise the right of property. When there was a change of sovereignty, *imperium* alone changed hands, while *dominium* remained undisturbed. The rights of individuals (*dominium*) constituted acquired rights. Traditional State succession involved only the substitution of one sovereign—who was often a monarch—for another and left the legal relationships between individuals intact. This trend was reinforced during the nineteenth century in Great Britain by the *laissez-faire* doctrine of property

52 Bedjaoui, 'Second Report' (n 18) 71 para 3.
53 ibid, 71 para 7.
54 ibid.

> and in the United States by the provisions of the Constitution relating to property rights. [. . .] Hence, if the doctrine of acquired rights is, as has been seen, inseparable from political liberalism, it may be expected *a priori* to be called in question again in an age and an environment where the liberalism which nurtured it is itself under attack. From a more general standpoint, it may be said that the political regime of a given community is linked to the private property regime in the territory which it controls, and the political upheavals which affect it automatically involve, sooner or later, new property arrangements. It is therefore not surprising that failure to respect acquired rights in cases either of succession or of non-succession constitutes a fairly marked trend in modern times, which are characterized by the growing denial of the absolute nature of private property and by the possibility of creating other forms of ownership. His Holiness Paul VI stated in his encyclical *Populorum Progressio* that 'private property does not constitute an absolute and unconditional right for anyone'.[55]

To Bedjaoui, liberalism was challenged by decolonization, and so was the concept of acquired rights:

> If the colonial system cannot operate without a hierarchical economic order, characterized by the predominance of the interests of the metropolitan country and of its nationals and by the existence of a structural imbalance between the colony and the metropolitan country, conversely decolonization can only be the restoration of egalitarian structures, which implies the rejection of certain economic situations resulting from the colonial regime. *Thus, it is clear that decolonization and the renewal of acquired rights are contradictory.* Either decolonization or acquired rights must be sacrificed. [. . .] The fundamental incompatibility between decolonization and acquired rights derives from the fact that the successor State is confronted with a choice, over which it cannot hesitate, between the possible equity which requires it to respect private rights and the real necessity which forces it to consider the public interest and national development. It was for no other reasons at bottom that the United Nations recognized the right of peoples to dispose of their natural resources and exploit them themselves, and exempted former colonies from any acquired right and from payment of any compensation.[56]

While ILC members from the second and third world applauded his report,[57] Western members were massively affronted and criticized Bedjaoui vehemently,

[55] ibid 73 para 14.
[56] ibid 91 para 108.
[57] International Law Commission (ILC), 'Summary Record of the 1000th Meeting', UN Doc A/CN.4/SR.1000 (1969-I-) *Yearbook of the International Law Commission* 53, 56 para 25.

and even personally.[58] The American ILC member Richard D. Kearney described at length the 'technical imperfections', the 'unsystematic approach', and the 'pure Marxist mythology' from which he found the report to suffer.[59] Kearney was also substantively opposed to Bedjaoui's approach:

> That statement seemed to pay too much deference to legal formalism and too little to the basic principles which law was intended to serve. Law, after all, was not a mere abstraction, but was intended for the achievement of peace and harmony in human society. If the theory of acquired rights was regarded from that point of view, it was difficult to reach the bald conclusion that it was useless, since it undoubtedly did tend to promote stability, especially in the financial and economic spheres, and to encourage capital investment and technical assistance. It also avoided certain possible consequences that might result from a denial of the concept of acquired rights, such as the possibility of a resort to sanctions by a foreign State which had lost what it considered to be acquired rights. Foreign investment, after all, was an important element in the finances of many States, particularly in their balance-of-payments situation, so that any large-scale nationalization without compensation might involve their interests either directly or indirectly.[60]

Quickly it became obvious that the ILC was not able to reach any agreement on the question of acquired rights. Most members favoured setting the topic aside and returning to the original plan to preliminarily focus on 'Succession of States in Economic and Financial Matters'.[61] While Bedjaoui raised concern that the urgent matter of acquired rights might be swept under the carpet,[62] he also had to realize that he would not be able to establish an international right to expropriation without compensation.

Bedjaoui's following reports were much tamer, but he had changed his strategy. In line with the new position of the UNGA, he now aimed to establish that all questions concerning concessions and acquired rights fell within the national jurisdiction of the expropriating state, which would result in a new state's right to expropriation without compensation. But to avoid another open conflict between ILC members, he tried to establish this principle in a less confrontational way:

58 ibid 57 59 para 17ff.

59 ibid.

60 International Law Commission (ILC), 'Summary Record of the 1008th Meeting, Succession of States in Respect of Matters other than Treaties', UN Doc A/CN.4/SR.1008 (1969-I), *Yearbook of the International Law Commission* 90, 93 para 18.

61 See International Law Commission (ILC), 'Summary Record of the 1005th Meeting, Succession of States in Respect of Matters other than Treaties', UN Doc A/CN.4/SR.1005 (1969-I-), *Yearbook of the International Law Commission* 73, 75 para 21, 76 para 31.

62 ILC, '961st Meeting' (n 48); International Law Commission (ILC), 'Summary Record of the 1009th Meeting, Succession of States in Respect of Matters other than Treaties', UN Doc A/CN.4/SR.1009 (1969-I) *Yearbook of the International Law Commission* 95, 96 para 20ff.

In his Sixth Report in 1973, Bedjaoui formulated an article concerning the right to grant concessions instead of a duty to protect concessions:

> Article 10. Rights in respect of the authority to grant concessions
>
> 1. For the purposes of the present article, the term 'concession' means the act whereby the State confers, in the territory within its national jurisdiction, on a private enterprise, a person in private law or another State, the management of a public service or the exploitation of a natural resource.
> 2. Irrespective of the type of succession of States, the successor State shall replace the predecessor State in its rights of ownership of all public property covered by a concession in the territory affected by the change of sovereignty.
> 3. The existence of devolution agreements regulating the treatment to be accorded to concessions shall not affect the right of eminent domain of the State over public property and natural resources in its territory.[63]

Bedjaoui explained that he did not aim to resume the debate on acquired rights, but merely to guarantee the rights of the successor state.[64] In 1975, he put his position as follows:

> United Nations practice showed that for about fifteen years the General Assembly had been referring, in numerous resolutions, to 'permanent sovereignty over natural resources'. That sovereignty might be defined as the use by the State of the sum total of its powers—its 'paramount competence' (*competence majeure*)—to regulate the status of natural resources. Why, then, speak of 'permanent sovereignty over natural resources'? Resources were not an additional attribute of sovereignty, but an object, or subject-matter, over which single and indivisible sovereignty was exercised. And yet the expression 'sovereignty over resources' was used, as though it referred to some particular kind of sovereignty. In fact, the word 'sovereignty' in that instance meant 'ownership' of natural resources, and the words 'permanent sovereignty' meant that such sovereignty was inalienable, although to say so might be thought redundant.
>
> [. . .] The traditional conception of sovereignty, disembodied, formal and based on the rules of classical law, was giving way, together with the problem of natural resources, to a new conception based on the principle of national economic independence. That principle had been given a new and very important

[63] Bedjaoui, 'Sixth Report' (n 34) 3, 10, 24.
[64] ibid 24 para 2ff.

legal function and had thus been erected into a principle of modern public international law.[65]

Other ILC members felt provoked to ask Bedjaoui about the aim of his provision, since every state obviously had the right to grant concessions because of its sovereignty according to national law; therefore, the proposed article would be unnecessary.[66] This was exactly the reaction Bedjaoui had hoped for, because without directly reanimating the question of acquired rights, he had gained consensus at least insofar as the right to grant concessions was generally considered to be a question of national law. In his opinion, the step from this point to a right to expropriation without compensation was comparatively smaller.

However, even though the UN Conference on Succession of States in Respect of State Property, Archives and Debts adopted the VCSSPAD in 1983, it was done regardless of the strong opposition of many industrial states.[67] The VCSSPAD should never come into force, and Bedjaoui's efforts faded. According to Craven, one issue was 'that the idea of decolonization was a radical or constitutive moment: a moment at which international lawyers were faced not only with the task of managing political changes on the "outside", but of managing the decolonization of the legal imagination itself'.[68] Therefore, the whole debate, as well as the resulting VCSSPAD, focused too much on decolonization, ignoring the dimensions state succession could develop in a different context.[69] In accordance with the Western conception, the question of acquired rights became specified by the law of aliens.[70] In the 1980s, the demand for a NIEO and corresponding new international investment law standards (for example, concerning acquired rights) collapsed and were replaced by neoclassic, liberal development theory, which led to a system of bilateral investment treaties (BITs) protected according to the Hull formula and

[65] International Law Commission (ILC), 'Summary Record of the 1320th Meeting, Succession of States in Respect of Matters other than Treaties', UN Doc UN Doc A/CN.4/SR.1320 (1975-I) *Yearbook of the International Law Commission* 82, 87 para 40ff.

[66] ibid para 46ff.

[67] 'In favour: Algeria, Angola, Argentina, Brazil, Bulgaria, Byelorussian SSR, Chile, Costa Rica, Cuba, Czechoslovakia, Democratic Yemen, Ecuador, Egypt, Gabon, German Democratic Republic, Guatemala, Hungary, India, Indonesia, Iran, Islamic Republic of, Iraq, Jordan, Kenya, Kuwait, Lebanon, Libyan Arab Jamahiriya, Mali, Mexico, Morocco, Mozambique, Namibia, Nigeria, Pakistan, Panama, Peru, Philippines, Poland, Republic of Korea, Romania, Senegal, Suriname, Syrian Arab Republic, Thailand, Tunisia, Turkey, Ukrainian SSR, USSR, United Arab Emirates, Uruguay, Venezuela, Viet Nam, Yemen, Yugoslavia, Zaire.
Against: Belgium, Canada, France, Germany, Federal Republic of, Israel, Italy, Luxembourg, Netherlands, Switzerland, United Kingdom of Great Britain and Northern Ireland, United States of America.
Abstaining: Australia, Austria, Denmark, Finland, Greece, Ireland, Japan, Norway, Portugal, Spain, Sweden', 'Meeting Records', *United Nations Conference on Succession of States in Respect of State Property, Archives and Debts: Official Records*, vol I (United Nations 1983) 31, para 62.

[68] Craven (n 9) 5.

[69] David P O'Connell, 'Reflections on the State Succession Convention' (1979) 39 Zeitschrift für ausländisches öffentliches Recht und Völkerrecht 725; Craven (n 9) 16.

[70] cf Visser (n 25) 76, 86ff.

the dominance of liberal institutions as the International Monetary Fund and the World Bank for Reconstruction and Development.[71]

V. Conclusion

A closer look at ILC debates concerning the question of acquired rights exemplifies the rise and fall of the third-world battle for international law in the second half of twentieth century, which not only occurred in the field of state succession, but also in international economic law. While the concept of acquired rights had not been fundamentally challenged before the Second World War, decolonization led to a softening of this notion, to a certain extent even with Western support. The third world tried to lower further the level of protection for foreign investments, aiming to establish an international right of expropriation without compensation. Bedjaoui, who openly addressed this radical claim in the ILC, was confronted with insurmountably resistance. Hence, he tried—as the UNGA did in its early years—to push the question from the international to the national level. Bedjaoui's endeavours and the third-world position on acquired rights per se was even more marginalized by the industrialized nations' refusal to sign the VCSSPAD. Whereas the third world mobilized for decades to gain leeway to deal with foreign investors, in the end the debate led to even rising standards in investment protection law.

Taking a closer look at this debate, a certain pattern of Western argumentative structure and discursive strategy, as well as its logical pitfalls, become as obvious as the third world's attempts to answer these tactics. Established customary international law had developed though state practice and *opinio iuris* of a number of states in the colonial 'state community', to which the colonies themselves did obviously not belong. International lawyers in the West considered the former colonies to be bound by this established international law, particularly by general norms of international customary law concerning acquired rights of aliens. New states, it was said, could not, on the one hand claim sovereign equality, a right stipulated by customary international law, and on the other hand, refuse to be bound by international law on that very basis.[72] The acceptance of international law was viewed to be the price new states had to pay in return for their acceptance as a state by other states.[73] In this theory, a new state had no opportunity to reject international law, or parts of it, at all since it was bound automatically and

[71] Philipp Dann, Stefan Kadelbach and Markus Kaltenborn (eds), *Entwicklung und Recht: Eine systematische Einführung* (Nomos 2014) 71, 88; Pahuja (n 47) 168; Schrijver (n 19) 183.

[72] O'Connell (n 12) 627, 636; on O'Connell's position see also Craven (n 9) 88.

[73] Schönborn (n 11) 71ff; Lauterpacht, *Oppenheim's International Law* (n 11) 18, 19; Folz (n 11) 319, 329ff.

consequently de facto in a non-consensual way. However, international lawyers in the third world wanted to reform international law so that it corresponded to the interests of all members of the new international society, including the former colonies.[74] The West claimed that changing this customary international law by opposite state practice was not sufficient to establish a state practice and *opinio iuris* of the majority of the post-colonial 'state community', which consisted of newly established states; instead, 'representative' consent of nation states from all state groups (first-, second-, and third-world) was required.[75] So while customary international law developed without consent of the former colonies, which were nevertheless bound by these respective rules, new rules required the consent of the Western nations. Since the change of customary international law seemed as a much too slow and inflexible means to change international order, the third world turned towards the making of multilateral treaty law, using the ILC to reach its goals. But the West simply refused its consent to change the rules concerning, for example, acquired rights of aliens. While García-Amador tried to pull the question of acquired rights into the international legal field of state responsibility, Ago pushed it away by redefining the subject. Bedjaoui tried to pull the issue of acquired rights into the subject of state succession but failed against the resistance of mainly Western international lawyers. Many third-world initiatives to change international law from within had already failed,[76] and Bedjaoui's hope in what today might be called 'emancipatory power of international law'[77] was noticeably shaken, notwithstanding his critical attitude to law in general.[78] Bedjaoui's attempt to pull the question away from international law and push it into the sphere of the national jurisdiction of the newly independent states did also not succeed as the VCSSPAD never came in force. This is even more remarkable because the most controversial questions in the field of state succession in respect of state property, archives, and debts had been solved in the convention according to the view of the Western states, who nevertheless refused to sign it. The idea of a minimum standard in accordance with customary international law was finally reinforced by the conclusion of a network of BITs between third-world states acting under economic pressure and Western countries. In this way, third-world attempts to reform international customary law concerning acquired rights became marginalized.

While international lawyers from the first world as well as from the third world pushed and pulled the debate between consent and community, between different

[74] Bernard Röling, *International Law in an Expanded World* (1960) 124 ff; Anand (n 6) 115.

[75] See, for example, *North Sea Continental Shelf* (*W Germany v Denmark, W Germany v Netherlands*) [1969] ICJ Rep 3, 42.

[76] Concerning the law of treaties and state succession in respect of treaties, see Krueger (n 2) 125ff, 279ff.

[77] Bedjaoui, *Towards a New NIEO* (n 7) 97.

[78] ibid 50.

topics of international law as well as between international and national jurisdiction, in the end, the Western view prevailed. International law has therefore become a platform for fundamental challenges to concepts protecting colonial and neo-colonial domination . However, it has also revealed itself to be mostly resistant against these discursive upheavals.[79]

[79] cf Anghie (n 22) 222; Balakrishnan Rajagopal, *International Law from Below: Development Social Movements and Third World Resistance* (CUP 2003) 14; Pahuja (n 47) 95.

6

Rival Worlds and the Place of the Corporation in International Law

Sundhya Pahuja and Anna Saunders

I. Introduction

Struggles in the arena of international law and institutions in the years between 1955 and 1974 should be understood not so much as a battle to control a pre-existing international law in an already-constituted world, but rather as marking a series of encounters between rival practices of world-making,[1] which travelled with rival accounts of international law. The question of the corporation[2]—how it should be understood, its relationship to both law and the state, and how it travels—was a key element of those rival worlds.

This chapter sketches the lineaments of that encounter through an account of the (successful) effort to establish the UN Commission on Transnational Corporations, and the (unsuccessful) attempt to draft a binding treaty.[3] In our critical redescription of this telling institutional moment, we pay particular attention to how legal forms emerge and are stabilized as authoritative, and to what might be at stake in that stabilization.[4] In historically inflecting the legal and institutional

[1] Nelson Goodman, *Ways of Worldmaking* (Hackett Publishing Company 1978).

[2] We are using the terms 'company' and 'corporation' interchangeably in this chapter, but there is a story to be written about the different traditions of thought to which they each belong, and the implications of their respective usages.

[3] For a succinct account of the shift in institutional placement (and framing) of the corporation, from the United Nations Centre on Transnational Corporations (UNCTC) and its task of drafting a binding Code of Conduct, to the Human Rights Council, and its Draft Norms and Guiding Principles, see Jennifer Bair, 'Corporations at the United Nations? Echoes of the New International Economic Order' (2015) 6 Humanity 159. For recent scholarship that doubles as a 'collective memoir' of the work of the Commission and its associated research body, the UNCTC, see Khalil Hamdani and Lorraine Ruffing (eds), *United Nations Centre on Transnational Corporations: Corporate Conduct and the Public Interest* (Routledge 2015); Karl P Sauvant, 'The Negotiations of the United Nations Code of Conduct on Transnational Corporations: Experience and Lessons Learnt' (2015) 16 Journal of World Investment and Trade 11.

[4] Our methodological orientation is engaged, rather than explained, in this short chapter. The idiom in which we are writing may be described as a novel methodological orientation toward an 'historically inflected jurisprudence'. For previous engagements with this, see Sundhya Pahuja, 'Letters from Bandung: Encounters with Another Inter-National Law' in Luis Eslava, Michael Fakhri and Vasuki Nesiah (eds), *Bandung, Global History and International Law: Critical Pasts and Pending Futures* (CUP 2017) (hereafter Pahuja, 'Letters from Bandung'); Sundhya Pahuja and Cait Storr, 'Rethinking Iran and International Law: The *Anglo-Iranian Oil Company Case* Revisited' in James Crawford, Abdul Koroma, Said Mahmoudi and Alain Pellet (eds), *The International Legal Order: Current Needs*

Sundhya Pahuja and Anna Saunders, *Rival Worlds and the Place of the Corporation in International Law* In: *The Battle for International Law: South-North Perspectives on the Decolonization Era*. Edited by: Jochen von Bernstorff and Philipp Dann, Oxford University Press (2019).
DOI: 10.1093/oso/9780198849636.003.0007

story in this way, we discover that the struggle over the proper understanding of the relationship between international law, the state, and the 'multinational' corporation had two distinct layers: one that operated within what has retrospectively become the usual frame of reference, and another more radical layer that contested the frame itself.

Looking back, we tend to see only the more familiar level of the contest which centres on the question of whether or not the presence of foreign corporations, and foreign investment more generally, were 'good for development'. This battle appears as a set of pre-constituted actors (companies, developed states, developing states, and international institutions) disagreeing about the nature and effect of the interactions between them. But if we slow down our reading and take a different imaginative vantage point than the present, the struggle over the corporation reveals itself to engage two a priori issues, both questions of authority and of form. The first was whether a company should be understood as a 'private' or 'political' entity. [5] The second was whether a corporation could 'travel', or —maintain its legal personality across jurisdictional lines, —and if so, under what conditions.[6] Together these questions of form were expressed as the problem of how to control the negative social, economic, and distributive effects generated by highly mobile and economically powerful corporations.

In contrast to these a priori questions of enframing, the redescribed question as to whether or not the presence of foreign corporations was 'good for development' was empirically unresolvable at any level of generality—the devil was always in the detail.[7] Slowing down our reading of the period also reveals that the battle lines around that question were more complex than they now appear. Those lines were drawn in ways which upset a comfortable rehearsal of a North-South divide.[8] The

and Possible Responses: Essays in Honour of Djamchid Momtaz (Brill 2017) 53 (hereafter Pahuja and Storr, 'Rethinking Iran'); Sundhya Pahuja, 'Public Debt, the Peace of Utrecht and the Rivalry between Company and State' in Alfred Soons (ed), *The 1713 Peace of Utrecht and Its Enduring Effects* (Brill 2016). On 'critical redescription', see Sundhya Pahuja, 'Laws of Encounter: A Jurisdictional Account of International Law' (2013) 1 London Review of International Law 63 (hereafter Pahuja, 'Laws of Encounter').

[5] On this question, see David Ciepley, 'Beyond Public and Private: Toward a Political Theory of the Corporation' (2013) 107 American Political Science Review 139. See also Morton J Horwitz, 'History of the Public/Private Distinction' (1982) 130 University of Pennsylvania Law Review 1423 (hereafter Horwitz, 'Public/Private Distinction'). See also Shaunnagh Dorsett and Shaun McVeigh, 'Jurisprudences of Jurisdiction: Matters of Public Authority' (2014) 23 Griffith Law Review 569 (hereafter Dorsett and McVeigh, 'Jurisprudences').

[6] Horwitz discusses the seminal cases exploring this question across state lines within the US, *Western Union Telegraph Co v Kansas* 216 US 1 (1910); *Pullman Co v Kansas* 216 US 56 (1910); *Ludwig v Western Union Telegraph Co* 216 US 146 (1910); *Southern Railway Co v Greene* 216 US 400 (1910); Horwitz, 'Public/Private Distinction' (n 5).

[7] David K Fieldhouse, *The West and the Third World: Trade, Colonialism, Dependence, and Development* (Wiley 1999) (hereafter Fieldhouse, *The West and the Third World).*

[8] Natasa Miskovic, Harald Fischer-Tiné and Nada Boskovska (eds), *The Non-Aligned Movement and the Cold War: Delhi–Bandung–Belgrade* (Routledge 2014).

incipient 'Cold War', Sino-Soviet Rivalry,[9] the invention of 'Development', and the implementation of a (Marshall) plan to (re)construct Europe all played into generating rival imaginaries and competing anxieties and produced both unexpected commonalities across what was to become a North-South 'divide' and instructive alliances of interest between what we now think of as 'public' and 'private' actors.

And yet precisely because of its political valencies and empirical irresolvability, the 'mere' redescription of the issue through a developmentalist lens was key to the stabilization of the juridical outcomes sought by the United States (US) and its allies. These were 'formal' outcomes in the strictest sense of the word. Specifically, the framing of the disagreements as political questions over whether the 'protection' of foreign property belonged in the domestic or international sphere and over whether the regulation of corporate conduct should be internationalized or left to the domestic sphere effected an implicit resolution of crucial questions of legal form.

Thus, in the 'success' of establishing the United Nations Centre on Transnational Corporations (UNCTC) as a forum for disputes over the relationship between companies and states, what was stabilized was an enframing of that dispute that carried with it an account of private property as a universal institution, and the corporation as both 'private' and as able to travel freely with its personality intact. And so, what was experienced as a (minor) victory is perhaps better understood in the genre of tragedy.[10] That juridical (or more properly 'jurisdictional')[11] defeat paved the way not only for political defeat in the failure of the attempt to craft a treaty that addressed the conduct of multinational corporations directly, but also in the subsequent efflorescence of investor-state arbitration, which together produced a series of outcomes precisely opposite to those sought by the third world and its friends.

II. Instituting the battle lines

> The multinational companies are the 'chartered companies' of modern times.
>
> Mohammed Bedjaoui, 1979[12]

[9] Jeremy Friedman, *Shadow Cold War: The Sino-Soviet Competition for the Third World* (UNC Press Books 2015).

[10] See David Scott, *Conscripts of Modernity: The Tragedy of Colonial Enlightenment* (Duke University Press 2004). For an account of the 'narrative arc of tragedy' see Simon Critchley, 'Tragedy's Philosophy and Philosophy's Tragedy' (As part of the series *What is Philosophy?*, Humanities Center Annual Lecture, Brigham Young University, 2014). See also Adil H Khan, 'Inheriting a Tragic Ethos: Learning from Radhabinod Pal' (2 August 2016) 110 AJIL Unbound 25.

[11] See generally Shaunnagh Dorsett and Shaun McVeigh, *Jurisdiction* (Routledge-Cavendish 2012); Pahuja, 'Laws of Encounter' (n 4).

[12] Mohammed Bedjaoui, *Towards a New International Economic Order* (UNESCO 1979) 36–37 (hereafter Bedjaoui, *Towards a New International Economic Order*).

The long backstory to the question of the multinational corporation is colonialism. The jurisdictional and historical story of companies in that context is too complex for our purposes here, but two elements bear mentioning. First, regardless of how they are theorized, the chartered or 'colonial' companies had been experienced in much of the world not simply as agents of empire, but as themselves imperial masters.[13] This mastery was not effected simply through the exercise of 'private' power, but of political, or public, authority.[14] As Bedjaoui was later to put it, the chartered companies enjoyed 'the right to recruit armed forces, levy taxes and make regulations'.[15] They also made laws, adjudicated disputes, and administered territory.[16] Second, by the middle of the nineteenth century, and after several crucial shifts in the quality of the ongoing encounters between the European and non-European worlds,[17] the idea of private property and its ownership by foreigners, was being protected outside Europe through multiple modalities of violence. Colonialism, economic coercion, and the use (or threat) of force in the form of 'gunboat diplomacy'[18] were all elements of that protection. As the twentieth century dawned and the legitimacy of protecting foreign property ownership through force was questioned, both the US and European states tried to assert a legal basis for the protection of private property, including that being claimed by foreign corporations. But this 'legal' basis remained both putative and contested,[19] and as decolonization

[13] See for example, Ngũgĩ wa Thiong'o, *Resisting Metaphysical Empire: Language as War Zone* (New Beacon Books Limited 2014) (John La Rose Memorial Lecture, 2013) (hereafter Ngũgĩ, *War Zone*). See also Philip J Stern, *The Company State: Corporate Sovereignty and the Early Modern Foundations of the British Empire in India* (OUP 2011) (hereafter Stern, *The Company State*).

[14] This is mostly theorized as delegated sovereignty, although Sundhya Pahuja's current research relates to a different theorization of this authority that is beyond the scope of this chapter. On the question of the exercise of public authority, see also Dorsett and McVeigh, 'Jurisprudences' (n 5); Janet McLean, *Searching for the State in British Legal Thought: Competing Conceptions of the Public Sphere* (CUP 2012); Paul G Mahoney, 'Contract or Concession? An Essay on the History of Corporate Law' (2000) 34 Georgia Law Review 873, 874.

[15] Bedjaoui, *Towards a New International Economic Order* (n 12).

[16] Stern, *The Company State* (n 13).

[17] Two tipping points but with complex implications around this time were the Opium Wars between Britain and China (1839–1842), and later, Britain and France and China (1856–1860), and the acquisition of ruling powers over India in August 1858 (after the 1857 Rebellion) by the Government of India Act 1858—pursuant to which the East India Company was formally dissolved and its ruling powers over India were transferred to the British Crown.

[18] Alfred Vagts, *Defense and Diplomacy: The Soldier and the Conduct of Foreign Relations* (King's Crown Press 1956); Charles Lipson, *Standing Guard: Protecting Foreign Capital in the Nineteenth and Twentieth Centuries* (University of California Press 1985) (hereafter Lipson, *Standing Guard*).

[19] Borchard, for instance, in 1915, writes in relation to the question of legal personality, that 'there is more uncertainty as to the extent of the obligation to recognize the legal capacity of foreign corporations': Edwin M Borchard, *The Diplomatic Protection of Citizens Abroad, or, the Law of International Claims* (The Banks Law Publishing Co. 1915) 41. The Drago (debt) and Calvo (investor–state disputes) doctrines were both opposed to the idea that a right of diplomatic protection inhered in states with respect to the treatment of foreign property. See Muthucumaraswamy Sornarajah, *The Pursuit of Nationalized Property* (Martinus Nijhoff Publishers 1986) 11. Contrast this to some extent with the argument made in Lipson, *Standing Guard* (n 20).

proceeded, the foreign ownership of property—particularly by transnational corporations—became a key site of struggle.[20]

The new post-war institutions quickly became sites of that struggle. In the context of the success of the anti-colonial struggles, those institutions (and institutionalization itself) seemed to hold out the glimmer of a promise of an international society organized around nation-states, rather than empires, and in which the fragile principle of formal sovereign equality held at least some meaning. That meaning centred on staving off the 'neo-colonial' international order, which threatened to replicate the political economy of empire in the guise of universal legality.[21] And despite its fragility, such a society seemed to offer the chance to assert a form of legal authority over companies long seen as illegitimate and exploitative.[22]

By the time of the Bandung conference of 1955, the non-European World was using international fora to denounce imperial systems of labour, production, agriculture, extraction, and finance in both the formal colonies and in the wider 'spheres of influence', as having been geared toward the satisfaction of the needs of the 'metropole', and the immiseration of the rightful inhabitants of the colonies.[23] The experience of the Latin American states, nominally independent since the nineteenth century,[24] also provided evidence for many that the colonial mode of 'integrating' places and people into a 'world economy', as well as developing an 'international division of labour',[25] created enduring economic structures and patterns of integration that would continue the impoverishment of the third world into the future and deepen international inequalities.[26] From the perspective of

[20] Indeed, the NIEO was eventually to address this problem head on. See, for example, Anthony Anghie, 'Legal Aspects of the New International Economic Order' (2015) 6 Humanity 145.

[21] On neo-colonialism, see, for example, Frantz Fanon, 'First Truths on the Colonial Problem' in Frantz Fanon, *Toward the African Revolution* (Francois Maspero tr, first published 1964, Grove Press 1967).

[22] A good example of this is the Anglo–Persian oil company in Iran: See Pahuja and Storr, 'Rethinking Iran' (n 4).

[23] If not well before. See Luis Eslava, Michael Fakhri and Vasuki Nesiah (eds), *Bandung, Global History and International Law: Critical Pasts and Pending Futures* (CUP 2017).

[24] For example, Ecuador, 1810; Venezuela, 1810; Paraguay, 1811; Argentina, 1816; Chile, 1818; Colombia, 1819; Mexico, 1821; Peru, 1821; Guatemala, 1821; Nicaragua, 1821; Costa Rica, 1821; Panama, 1821; Brazil, 1822; Bolivia, 1825; Uruguay, 1825. But Cuba and the Dominican Republic did not gain independence from the US until 1902 and 1924, respectively, while Puerto Rico remains a territory.

[25] Fieldhouse, *The West and the Third World* (n 7). See generally ch 6, 'The Concept of a Colonial Economy', which contains a magisterial survey of much of the literature.

[26] The 'dependency theorists' argued that that the way poor states are integrated into the 'world system' creates a resource flow from a 'periphery' of poor and underdeveloped states to a 'core' of wealthy states, further enriching the latter at the expense of the former; on this point, see Hans W Singer, 'The Distribution of Gains between Investing and Borrowing Countries' (1950) 40 American Economic Review 473, 479; Raul Prebisch, *The Economic Development of Latin America and Its Principal Problems* (United Nations Department of Economic Affairs 1950); Andre Gunder Frank, 'The Development of Underdevelopment' (1966) 4 Monthly Review: An Independent Socialist Magazine; Celso Furtado, *Economic Development of Latin America: Historical Background and Contemporary Problems* (CUP 1976); Paul A Baran, *The Political Economy of Growth* (Monthly Review Press 1957). See also Walter Rodney, *How Europe Underdeveloped Africa* (Bogle-L'Ouverture Publications 1972) (on Africa); Samir Amin, 'L'Afrique de l'ouest bloquée: l'économie politique de la colonisation, 1880–1970' (1974)

both the second and third worlds, the 'multinational corporation', as it came to be known after about 1960,[27] was widely understood to be a key moving part in this structural account of the 'world economy,' potentially continuing the role of the chartered companies.

But by the very early 1960s, despite the invention of an international rubric addressed to the question of material need,[28] and a decade inaugurated by international institutions in its name,[29] it had become clear that countries in the third world were not benefitting from these institutional efforts. Indeed for many, relative to the first world, their economic position was declining.[30] At the international institutional level, Latin American economists led the drive to change the structural features of the 'world economy' that were seen to induce the dependency of the 'periphery'.[31] They did this through a range of measures, starting with a series of resolutions in the UN General Assembly (UNGA) asserting the right to nationalize land and resources as part of the doctrine of Permanent Sovereignty over Natural Resources,[32] and later through the initiation of an intergovernmental forum at the United Nations (UN) on trade and development as a way of tackling the unfavourable terms of trade.[33] The realization that the position of the third world was not likely to improve under current rules encouraged those in the South increasingly to assert a radical account of the emergent concept of development understood in terms of political economy rather than through the technical lens (favoured by the first world) of 'development economics'.[34] It also prompted a push for the

29 Annales: Histoire, Sciences Sociales 291 (on West Africa); PJ Marshall, 'Conclusion: Empire in Retrospect' in Peter J Marshall (ed), *The Cambridge Illustrated History of the British Empire* (CUP 1996).

[27] Fieldhouse, *The West and the Third World* (n 7) 260. Fieldhouse (following Mira Wilkins) attributes the neologism to David Lilienthal, one-time head of the Tennessee Valley Authority, who it seems probably coined the term between 1958 and 1960.

[28] This was, of course, 'development'. See Sundhya Pahuja, *Decolonising International Law: Development, Economic Growth and the Politics of Universality* (CUP 2011) (hereafter Pahuja, *Decolonising International Law).* On the continuity between development, the civilizing mission, and before that, Christian tropes of salvation, see Jennifer L Beard, *The Political Economy of Desire: International Law, Development and the Nation State* (Routledge-Cavendish 2007).

[29] United Nations Department of Economic and Social Affairs, *The United Nations Development Decade: Proposals for Action: Report of the Secretary-General* (United Nations Publications 1962).

[30] See Karl P Sauvant, 'From Economic to Socio-Cultural Emancipation: The Historical Context of the new International Economic Order and the New International Socio-Cultural Order' (1981) 3 Third World Quarterly 48, 50 (hereafter Sauvant, 'From Economic to Socio-Cultural Emancipation).

[31] Examples include the establishment of the UN Economic Commission for Latin America and the Caribbean (ECLAC or CEPAL in Spanish). Argentine economist Raúl Prebisch was a key figure in this kind of structuralist economic thought. Prebisch was appointed as the inaugural Secretary-General of UNCTAD: Diego Cordovez, 'The Making of UNCTAD: Institutional Background and Legislative History' (1967) 1 Journal of World Trade Law 243, 272 (hereafter Cordovez, 'The Making of UNCTAD').

[32] Pahuja, *Decolonising International Law* (n 28). See also United Nations General Assembly Res 1803 (XVII) (14 December 1962) 17th Session: 1962.

[33] This started life as an ad hoc conference but became a permanent institution in 1964: GA Res 1995 (XIX) (30 December 1964) 19th Session; see also Cordovez, 'The Making of UNCTAD' (n 31).

[34] Sauvant writes that, prior to the 1970s, economic development had largely been approached as a technical, rather than a political, matter: see Karl P Sauvant, *The Group of 77: Evolution, Structure Organization* (Oceana Publications 1981) 4 (hereafter Sauvant, *The Group of 77)*; see also Sauvant,

establishment and strengthening of institutional arenas in which new policies for 'international development' could be formulated.

The establishment of the UN Conference on Trade and Development (UNCTAD) was one expression of that push. At a meeting in Cairo in 1962, thirty-six states drawn from each of the three regions of the South (Asia, Africa, and the Middle East) came together to call for the creation of a forum in which to discuss 'all vital questions relating to international trade, primary commodity trade, [and] economic relations between developing and developed countries'.[35] Despite opposition from almost all nations of the European Economic Community, many of whom feared such a conference would threaten the prevailing legal–economic order underpinned by the (European) Common Market and the GATT,[36] UNCTAD was eventually convened, although it was inaugurated as a conference, rather than the permanent institution it was later to become.[37]

At the conclusion of the first conference in June of 1964, seventy-five countries issued a joint declaration on a new agenda for trade and development.[38] Along with the promotion of that agenda, in which UNCTAD I was positioned as a 'significant step towards creating a new and just world economic order',[39] the declaration was a forging place of the Group of 77 (G77).[40] In order to achieve the desired transformation, the Group stressed the importance of establishing 'international machinery in the field of trade and development' that was democratically run and which provided equal representation to all states.[41] Maintaining a sense of political solidarity between the Group was to be key to achieving their aims within the fora of the UN, as recognized by the timing of their meetings. At its next meeting in Algiers in 1967, the Group resolved to hold a Ministerial Meeting prior to each session of UNCTAD 'in order to harmonize the positions of developing countries

'From Economic to Socio-Cultural Emancipation' (n 32) 55; GA Res 3202 (S-VI) (1 May 1974) A/Res/S-6/3202 GA Sixth Special session Agenda item 7; For a brief account of the emergence of the discipline of development economics, see Susan N Engel, 'Development Economics: From Classical to Critical Analysis' in Robert A Denemark (ed), *The International Studies Encyclopedia Volume II* (Blackwell Publishing 2010) 874–92.

---

35 Giuliano Garavini, *After Empires: European Integration, Decolonization, and the Challenge from the Global South* (Richard R Nybakken tr, OUP 2012) 35 (hereafter Garavini, *After Empires*). See also Cairo Declaration of Developing Countries (18 July 1962).

36 With the exception of the Netherlands: Garavini, *After Empires* (n 35) 35.

37 ECOSOC Res 917 (XXXIV), (3 August 1962) Agenda Item 27: Arrangements Regarding the Report of the Council to the General Assembly; GA Res 1785 (XVII) (8 December 1962).

38 Joint Declaration of the Seventy-Seven Developing Countries Made at the Conclusion of the United Nations Conference on Trade and Development (UNCTAD) (Geneva, 15 June 1964) (hereafter Joint Declaration of the Seventy-Seven Developing Countries).

39 ibid.

40 Sauvant, 'From Economic to Socio-Cultural Emancipation' (n 30) 50. The two subsequent recruits were the Republic of Korea and the Republic of Vietnam: Sauvant, *The Group of 77* (n 34) 18–19. The name persisted despite the membership numbering 122 countries by 1980.

41 Joint Declaration of the Seventy-Seven Developing Countries (n 38).

and to formulate joint programmes of action in all matters related to trade and development'.[42]

Levels of cooperation of this kind were internationally unprecedented, and although the political orientations of this large group of countries were inevitably disparate,[43] a sense of solidarity operated as a counterweight to the effect of political diversity. This sense arose from the shared burden of history, the experience of the 'racialism' of Europe and the US,[44] the legacies of empire, the either/or choices being produced by the 'Cold War', and to a different extent, between Soviet and Chinese communism,[45] and the explicit attempts to take control of the new international fora by Europe and the US. And so, political solidarity sought its expression in a new institutional, as well as legal, framework—with the first seen from the outset as being critical to the second. This drove several initiatives, including the agenda of what was to be a fateful third conference from the perspective of the corporations question.[46]

III. UNCTAD III: decolonizing political economic imaginaries?

The third session of UNCTAD was held between 13 April and 21 May 1972 in Santiago, Chile. As president of the host country, Salvador Allende gave the opening speech.,[47] Allende's speech must have been electrifying.[48] In a clarion

[42] Charter of Algiers, 25 October 1967. The second such meeting was held in Lima in 1971, producing the *Declaration and Principles of the Action Programme of Lima*. See UNCTAD Group of 77. Ministerial Meeting, *Declaration and Principles of the Action Programme of Lima: Adopted by the Group of 77 at the Second Ministerial Meeting on 7 November 1971* (UNCTAD 1971). For a discussion of the Algiers min isterial conference and the opening statement made by Algerian president Hourari Boumedienne, see Garavini, *After Empires* (n 35) 75–76.

[43] Ranging from more pragmatic (Asia and Africa) to radically progressive (Latin America): ibid 134.

[44] Pahuja, 'Letters from Bandung' (n 4).

[45] See, for example, Nataša Mišković, Harald Fischer-Tiné and Nada Boškovska, *The Non-Aligned Movement and the Cold War: Delhi, Bandung, Belgrade* (Routledge 2014) and Jeremy Friedman, *Shadow Cold War: The Sino-Soviet Competition for the Third World* (University of California Press 2015).

[46] Sauvant, *The Group of 77* (n 34) 2–3, 9–10.

[47] Allende was a democratically elected socialist and accordingly, a troubling figure for the US, which had expended much effort in trying to prevent his election and topple him when he was elected, finally engineering the infamous coup of General Augusto Pinochet. On the investigations by the US Senate of such covert activities, see US Senate, 'Hearings before the Select Committee to Study Governmental Operations with Respect to Intelligence Activities of the United States Senate: Covert Action' (4/5 December 1975) (Ninety Fourth Congress, First Session, Volume 7, US Government Printing Office 1976) <https://www.intelligence.senate.gov/resources/intelligence-related-commissions> accessed 10 June 2017.

[48] The journalist for the *Observer* wrote that 'Western delegates, expecting a platitudinous inauguration, writhed in their seats as the Chilean leader, conscious that he was speaking for virtually the whole of the Third World, tore into the trade and aid practices of rich countries. [. . .] Few orators could successfully have followed that speech [. . .] As Allende left the rostrum . . . covered symbolically in Chile's main export, copper, the atmosphere was electric. One Western European Cabinet Minister looked almost apoplectic. A Scandinavian delegate chuckled quietly that one could have expected nothing less

call to action, he outlined the mission of the third session as continuing the work of replacing the 'outdated and essentially unjust economic and trade order'.[49] Colonialism could not be forgotten while it cast long shadows over both national and international political economies. Even after their formal decolonization, many countries 'exist[ed] under unbearable conditions . . . their economy [still] dominated by foreign powers; outsiders hold[ing] all or part of their territory; they still endure[d] the yoke of colonialism . . . deep social disparities oppress[ed] the masses and benefit[ted] only the privileged few'.[50]

And yet despite these tentacular legacies of empire, Allende was hopeful. World developments since the last session of the Conference had created a moment in which transformative change was possible.[51] 'The financial conceptions of the post-war period are tottering,' he said, and the 'new or strengthened centres of political and economic power [would generate] striking changes of front among the industrialized countries'.[52] Having already seen the beginnings of a new era of 'coexistence and dialogue' between capitalist and socialist countries, Allende speculated that the same might be possible for the colonial powers and formerly colonized 'dependent peoples'.[53] Growing instances of successful resistance, and imperial defeats, as well as the energizing political solidarity between the peoples of the global South led him to be certain that they would reject an international order which perpetuated 'their backward state'. Instead, 'they will seek and they will obtain their economic independence and will conquer underdevelopment'.[54]

But if his rhetoric was impassioned, Allende's analysis offered no illusions.[55] Chile was under immense pressure from multinational corporations resistant to its plans to nationalize key sections of the Chilean economy, and they were openly

from a country which was being squeezed in a vice by the US'. Hugh O'Shaughnessy, 'Poor Nations Warn: Give Us a Better Deal or Else' (16 April 1972) The Observer.

[49] UNCTAD, 'Address Delivered by Mr Salvador Allende Gossens, President of Chile, at the Inaugural Ceremony on 13 April 1972' in 'Proceedings of the United Nations Conference on Trade and Development: Third Session Santiago de Chile, 13 April to 21 May 1972, Vol 1' (1973) UN Doc TD/180 (Vol 1) 9 (hereafter UNCTAD, 'Allende's UNCTAD III Address').

[50] ibid para 12.

[51] ibid paras 49, 96. Here he refers to both China's recent entry into the 'international community' and to the 'invincible heroism' of Vietnam, where communism, as an alternative model of socio-economic ordering, had risen despite resistance from both former imperial powers and local elites.

[52] ibid para 50. He also attributed the potential for change to 'a tide of new technical and scientific discoveries': ibid para 54.

[53] ibid para 97.

[54] Whether peacefully, through 'cooperation, based on solidarity, justice and respect for human rights' or alternatively being forced to take the path of 'conflict, violence and suffering': ibid paras 108–09.

[55] One could also read his hope as threatening from the perspective of those with vested interests in the maintenance of the system he was attacking. As much is plain from the CIA-backed coup d'état led by Augusto Pinochet which, on 11 September 1973, deposed Allende and led to his death. See, for example, William Blum, *Killing Hope: US Military and CIA Interventions since World War II* (first published 1995, Common Courage Press 2004).

interfering in Chilean sovereignty.[56] The concert between the American Central Intelligence Agency and those same corporations to destabilize Allende, as they had others before him, was already notorious. For Allende, not only was a more just Chile under threat, but the unchecked power and further expansion of multinational corporations would be fatal to the new worlds being made through third-world solidarity and would scuttle the possibility of cooperation between the developed and the developing world. The question of the large multinational corporation was thus thrust onto the stage of international institutionalism, and the agenda for the rest of the conference was set.

Allende's critique of the corporation operated at the radical—or 'root'—level alluded to earlier, engaging a priori questions of how the company should be understood, and how the company–state relation should be enframed. Although Allende deployed the term 'development'[57] as a rhetorical proxy for the question of material well-being,[58] he related it neither to an internationalized promise, nor to an instrumentalized programme. Instead, he reminded the assembled conference of the imperial origins of foreign investment, which although 'often presented as an instrument for progress, has almost always proved negative in its effects,'[59] and made it clear that it was through its recent conceptual connection to 'development' that 'self-interest and altruism' seemed suddenly to be compatible.

He understood that the rhetorical merger between self-interest and altruism—a 'dual mandate' for the present day[60]—had long been deployed by foreign corporations who represented their actions as being in the interests of those whose resources they exploited, but even more crucially, that this story provided authority for their actions.[61] Multinational corporations 'which arrogate to themselves the role of agents promoting the progress of the poorer countries [. . .] have become a supranational force that is threatening to get completely out of control'.[62] Acting with authority in his account, rather than simply exercising power, Allende suggested that corporations should be understood as political, rather than private, entities who threatened to compete with states on the international stage. These

[56] Anthony Sampson, *The Sovereign State of ITT* (Stein and Day 1973). See also Paul E Sigmund, *Multinationals in Latin America: The Politics of Nationalization* (University of Wisconsin Press 1980); Laura Randall, *The Political Economy of Latin America in the Postwar Period* (University of Texas Austin 1997); Edgar J Dosman, *The Life and Times of Raúl Prebisch, 1901–1986* (McGill-Queen's University Press 2008).

[57] On the institutionalisation of development, see Pahuja, *Decolonising International Law* (n 28).

[58] By now the term was thoroughly institutionalized as a proxy for this conversation. See generally Gilbert Rist, *The History of Development: From Western Origins to Global Faith* (Patrick Camiller tr, University of Chicago Press 2014).

[59] UNCTAD, 'Allende's UNCTAD III Address' (n 49) para 16.

[60] Frederick JD Lugard, *The Dual Mandate in British Tropical Africa* (W Blackwood and Sons 1922).

[61] One could also say that it provided 'legitimacy'. However, here we place emphasis on the question of authority and practices of authorization rather than legitimacy and legitimization.

[62] UNCTAD, 'Allende's UNCTAD III Address' (n 49) para 58.

companies would not act in conformity with agreements among states, he warned, but would instead adhere to their own interests and policies:

> [t]hey have their objectives, their own policies with regard to trade, shipping, international affairs and economic integration, their own view of things, their own activity, their own world. We spend our time at international meetings discussing the visible features of the third world's structure of dependence, while its underlying determinants slip by us unseen, like the submerged three quarters of an iceberg.[63]

As Allende repeatedly pointed out, this was not an historically new phenomenon. Through the control of key industries such as telecommunications and mining, multinational corporations threatened to capture the current moment of change and to repeat the experience of the Industrial Revolution, which had represented 'a mere transition from colonial to neo-colonial status'.[64] And, by subtle yet pervasive methods of intervention, he warned, they would eventually undermine the norm of non-intervention that, for Allende, was the foundation of the international legal order.[65]

Allende offered the Chilean experience as instructive, both in respect of corporate interventions in the South as well as with respect to the claims of the first world, that multinationals brought beneficial flows of foreign direct investment.[66] In order to counter the influence of multinationals and to capitalize on the possibilities offered by the Conference, continued cooperation and unity among the countries of the developing world was essential.[67] The delegates would need both to 'face the world as it is, defending [themselves] against illusions and mystifications', but also to 'throw[] . . . wide the gates of imagination' to create a replacement for the post-colonial order.[68] Otherwise, in Allende's words, the 'new hopes that promise liberation may lead only to new forms of colonialism'.[69]

For Allende, a key element of the power of the transnational corporation lay in both its mobility vis-à-vis the state, and detachment from the nation in both

[63] ibid 59–61. Another story to be told is the way in which the secrecy shrouding the commercial world, or the world of the corporation, becomes or remains unquestionable—the Chilean example being an exception to this general rule.

[64] ibid para 55.

[65] ibid para 62.

[66] See Fieldhouse, *The West and the Third World* (n 7). Allende had begun the process of nationalizing the copper and minerals industries after his election, but much harm to the Chilean economy had already been done. According to the financial records of the copper companies, the original investment they had made in Chile was $30 million, but they had since extracted over $4,000 million from Chile—almost equalling the Chilean debt—without any further investment: UNCTAD, 'Allende's UNCTAD III Address' (n 51) para 40.

[67] ibid paras 27–28.

[68] ibid para 11.

[69] ibid para 53.

effective and affective terms. His speech to the UNGA on 4 December 1972 puts the point succinctly;

> We are witnessing a pitched battle between the great transnational corporations and sovereign states, for the latter's fundamental political, economic and military decisions are being interfered with by worldwide organisations which are not dependent on any single State, and which, [. . .] activities, are not accountable to or regulated by any parliament or institution representing the collective interest. In a word, the entire political structure of the world is being undermined. 'Merchants have no country of their own. Wherever they may be they have no ties with the soil. All they are interested in is the source of their profits.' Those are not my own words; they were spoken by Jefferson.[70]

The mobility of the large corporations, and the corresponding challenge that posed for the existing political order prompted the delegates at UNCTAD III to argue for new, internationalized forms of regulation. As the Chilean representative stated, it was 'no longer possible to ignore the serious gap in the system of international institutions, namely, the lack of any arrangements for the supervision and regulation of the activities of multinational corporations'.[71] De Seynes, then Under-Secretary General for Economic and Social Affairs, emphasized that, in the absence of such regulation, 'it would be increasingly difficult to rely, for a development policy, on the combined advantages of financial resources, technology, managerial capacity and world-wide distribution networks that international corporations could offer'.[72] Instead, according to Argentinian economist Raul Prebisch, what was needed was for the developed world to abandon its 'geocentric approach' and to take seriously the interests and concerns of the developing countries, acknowledging them as different from its own.[73]

[70] UNGA, 'Address by Mr Salvador Allende, President of the Republic of Chile on 4 December 1972 Summary Records of the 2096th Meeting of the UN General Assembly' (4 December 1972) UN Doc. A/PV.2096, 59 (hereafter UNGA, 'Address by Mr Salvador Allende'). The origin of the quote is found in Thomas Jefferson, *The Writings of Thomas Jefferson* (HW Derby 1861) 334.

[71] UNCTAD, 'Summary of Statement made at the 93rd Plenary Meeting, 20 April 1972, by H. E. Hernan Santa Cruz, Ambassador with Rank of Minister of State Chile', in 'Proceedings of the United Nations Conference on Trade and Development: Third Session, Santiago de Chile, 13 April to 21 May 1972, Vol Ia, part 1 (1973) UN Doc TD/180, 57.

[72] UNCTAD, 'Summary of Statement made at the 89th Plenary Meeting, 18 April 1972, by Mr. P De Seynes Under-Secretary-General for Economic and Social Affairs of the United Nations' in 'Proceedings of the United Nations Conference on Trade and Development: Third Session, Santiago de Chile, 13 April to 21 May 1972, Vol Ia, part 1' (1973) UN Doc TD/180, 57 (hereafter UNCTAD, 'Summary of the Statement by P De Seynes').

[73] Then Under-Secretary General and Director of the Latin American Institute for Economic and Social Planning, as well as former Secretary-General of UNCTAD, 'Summary of Statement Made at the 103rd Plenary Meeting, 26 April 1972, by Raúl Prebisch Under-Secretary-General of the United Nations' in 'Proceedings of the United Nations Conference on Trade and Development: Third Session, Santiago de Chile, 13 April to 21 May 1972, Volume I (1973) UN TD/180, 383.

Ultimately, Allende's critique and the shared concerns of many of the delegates would be taken up at the Conference in two forms. The first was through conceptualizing the problem of corporate behaviour through the lens of 'restrictive business practices'.[74] The second, in response to the mounting evidence that foreign private investment had a detrimental impact on the economies of the countries that received such investment, was to ask how such impact might be remediated and minimized through law—whether domestic or international. Although still much broader than the turn to business and human rights that was to come some thirty years later, what was already being lost in this enframing were the more radical questions about the benefits of private foreign investment per se, as well as an attention to the continuities between older forms of corporate activity and the current international order.

1. Second Committee—restrictive business practices

The question of the effect of 'restrictive business practices on developing countries, and the possibility of their regulation' was taken up by the Second Committee of the 1972 conference.[75] This question had been agreed on during the previous UNCTAD due to a growing perception that the practices of companies from the 'developed' world were inhibiting the ability of states from the global South to create wealth through increasing exports.[76] However, the definition of restrictive business practices' was contested from the outset. Most could agree that cartel practices of companies should be included, but based on their experience, many from the South would also include contractual practices impeding integration with the local economy and intellectual property protections that kneecapped the promised benefits of technology transfer,[77] as well as a number of other practices about

[74] On the future of the code on restrictive business practices, see Joel Davidow, 'The UNCTAD Restrictive Business Practices Code' (1979) 13 The International Lawyer 587; Dale A Oesterle, 'United Nations Conference on Restrictive Business Practices' (1981) 14 Cornell International Law Journal 1.

[75] Following the pattern established by the work of the Preparatory Committee in setting up the first Conference, each Conference creates a number of sessional bodies—both numbered Committees and Working Groups—in order to facilitate the work of the Conference. The Committees are each assigned agenda items and participation in the Committees is ordinarily open to all participating States. The Conference in plenary considers and votes on resolutions either recommended or referred for further consideration by the Committees: see Cordovez, 'The Making of UNCTAD' (n 33) 281. For examples, see UNCTAD, 'Proceedings of the United Nations Conference on Trade and Development Vol I' (1964) E/CONF.46/141, Vol I, 101–106; UNCTAD, 'Proceedings of the United Nations Conference on Trade and Development, Third Session Vol I: 13 April to 21 May 1972' (1973) UN Doc TD/80, 15–17 and annexes (hereafter UNCTAD, 'Proceedings of the UNCTAD Third Session, vol 1').

[76] UNCTAD Res 25(II) (27 March 1968) (hereafter UNCTAD Res 25 (II)); UNCTAD, 'Proceedings of the UNCTAD Third Session, vol 1' (n 77) agenda item 14(d). Before them was a report of the UNCTAD secretariat which had been instructed to consider these practices specifically 'from the standpoint of the trade and development of developing countries': see UNCTAD Res 25(II); 'Second Committee, Summary Records of the Fifth Meeting'(24 April 1972) UN Doc TD/III/C.2/SR.5, 57 (hereafter 'Summary Records of the Fifth Meeting') (Krishnamurti, Director, Manufactures Division).

[77] Krishnamutri, 'Summary Records of the Fifth Meeting' (n 76).

which little was known.[78] As Director of Manufactures, Krishnamurti pointed out '[i]n some cases, the restrictions were not explicit in contractual arrangements but implicit in the nature of control exercised by a foreign enterprise over a firm in a developing country'.[79]

The language of restrictive business practices had been used to capture these problems since at least the Havana Charter of 1948.[80] However, participants at the 1972 Conference agreed that although the Havana Charter could usefully be examined as part of the work of the proposed expert group, the regime on restrictive business practices[81] would need to be revisited in light of the changed role of multinational corporations.[82] Older attempts to regulate restrictive business practices were founded on a benign image both of the corporation as an actor which could easily be subjected to legal control, and of the state as willing and able to assert this control, which could no longer be assumed.[83]

At the meeting of the Second Committee, representatives drew attention to the sizeable and growing power of multinational corporations as compared to most countries of the global South. Viewed through the prism of trade, for instance, de Rivero from Peru highlighted that just 300 multinational companies controlled over 40 per cent of the total volume of trade in manufactured exports from developing countries and approximately 30 per cent of international trade as a whole.[84] And following Allende's evidence of corporate intervention in Chilean elections, in the view of many, this power was clearly spilling over into areas of sovereign authority.[85] Against this background, the broadening of the definition was an attempt

[78] ibid.

[79] ibid.

[80] See Havana Charter for an International Trade Organization, concluded 24 March 1948. The Havana Charter, negotiated at the beginning of the post-war era, sought to create principles for the uniform regulation of international trade, administered by an International Trade Organization: Clair Wilcox, *A Charter for World Trade* (Macmillan Company 1949) vi–ix (hereafter Wilcox, *A Charter for World Trade*). See further Richard Toye, 'Developing Multilateralism: The Havana Charter and the Fight for the International Trade Organization, 1947–1948' (2003) 2 International History Review 282. It was concluded in 1948 but never entered into force after the US withdrew its support: Dale B Furnish, 'A Transnational Approach to Restrictive Business Practices' (1970) 4 International Lawyer 317, 326.

[81] Chapter V of that Charter contained a list of 'restrictive business practices' that could be subject to complaint by aggrieved member states, largely reflecting concerns around corporate cartel practices which might reduce competition: Wilcox, *A Charter for World Trade* (n 82) 110.

[82] The regime in the Havana Charter contemplated only 'the publication of infringements and the pressure of public opinion' as a consequence of breaching its provisions; it relied on proof of harm as a result of any infringement rather than imposing prospective rules against particular behaviours; and enforcement of the Charter was left to individual states: see Second Committee, 'Summary Records of the Seventh Meeting' UN Doc TD/III/C.2/SR.7, 83 (Israel).

[83] The story of the Havana Charter is also relevant to this story, but has been removed for reasons of space.

[84] Second Committee, 'Summary Records of the Seventh Meeting' UN Doc TD/III/C.2/SR.7, 74. See also Second Committee, 'Summary Records of the Sixth Meeting' UN Doc TD/III/C.2/SR.6, 65 (Bulgaria).

[85] Second Committee, 'Summary Records of the Sixth Meeting' UN Doc TD/III/C.2/SR.6, 60 (Mexico).

to capture the increasingly evident power relationship between company and state in political-economic context.

However, the extent to which these restrictive business practices should be understood as harmful to developing countries—and the proper role of law in dealing with such practices—was also contested. On the one hand, countries in which transnational corporations were operating subsidiary companies were experiencing the operations as making few, or even negative, contributions to the 'development project'.[86] Supporting the calls for enhanced regulation were the many damaging practices that had come to light through studies conducted in developing countries and detailed in the secretariat's report.[87] Ethiopia, for example, pointed to the way in which multinational corporations discouraged exports from developing countries because it was against their interests to create competition between their subsidiary companies.[88] The Bolivian representative added that half of the parent companies were based in the US, and around one-quarter in the United Kingdom (UK), and that it was through these extensive subsidiary networks that multinational corporations could and did exert influence over the exports of developing countries.[89] Other states cited their experience of parent firms based in the global North using contractual clauses to restrict exports of firms in the South,[90] and the impact of the emerging international patent and trademark system increasingly used to restrict the export of competing goods manufactured using intellectual property created in the global North.[91]

While states hosting investments tended to characterize these concerns as an unwanted corollary of corporate activity, the socialist countries saw them as intrinsic to Western European practices of investment. The size of these companies, coupled with the control exerted by their parent through the corporate structure, translated into the domination of domestic economies. For Bulgaria, for instance, this both posed 'an obstacle to the development of the economies of the developing countries and . . . [had] a nefarious impact on the exports of those countries'.[92] As the report showed, even where corporations professed a desire to assist in the creation of industry in parts of Asia, Africa, and Latin America, their aim in doing so

[86] For their part, first world countries warned that hasty regulation would prove fatal to the ability to attract corporate activity sufficient to transform 'backward' economies. And on the part of the socialist countries (the third grouping), there was at best an agnosticism toward the idea of potential benefits, and often a wholesale rejection of the idea of foreign investment, echoing Allende's warning that such benefits would always come at the cost of independence. For further exploration of these three approaches to the economic effects of multinational corporations on the host state that prevailed at the time, see Fieldhouse, *The West and the Third World* (n 7) 267–71.

[87] UNCTAD, 'Proceedings of the UNCTAD Third Session, vol 1' (n 75), Annex VI, Report of the Second Committee 182.

[88] Second Committee, 'Summary Records of the Sixth Meeting' UN Doc TD/III/C.2/SR.6, 62.

[89] ibid 62–63 (Bolivia).

[90] ibid 66 (Malaysia)

[91] ibid 62 (Ethiopia);

[92] ibid 65.

was to 'consolidate the dependent status of the developing countries . . . to limit their industrial exports while deriving benefits from them'.[93] Thus, for the socialist countries, the 'supposed advantages [of foreign investment] were more than offset by the outflow of financial resources which they generated'.[94]

In direct contrast to the idea that restrictive business practices might (and should) be addressed through an international agreement of some kind, first world countries took the view that it was the responsibility of developing countries themselves to enact legislation dealing with corporate conduct. This position was based on the promise that such activity could make an 'overriding contribution'.[95] Should tighter controls be put in place around these contributions, they argued, multinational corporations would be deterred from investing and developing countries would lose the benefits of such investment.[96] The 'benefits' promised were conceptually aggregated, tutelary, and amorphous.[97] It was further underpinned by the fiction of the large corporation as a '*multi*national' enterprise, collaboratively conducting a business venture emanating from multiple sites, rather than a '*trans*national' one, which was controlled in one place but operative in others. Ellis from the International Chamber of Commerce told delegates that the 'multinational enterprise' was not a single entity, but a parent company with a web of subsidiaries. As such, 'each of the subsidiaries was subject to the sovereign powers of the State in whose territory it operated . . . [which] had the sovereign authority to enact legislation and to introduce controls to curb any harmful restrictive business practices'.[98] In this respect, some developed countries offered their own national laws as a model for emulation.[99] Insistence that the proper sphere of regulation was domestic was joined by the scepticism of some toward the potential for international law to reduce these practices.[100]

And yet for many, the very fact of both the obvious need for domestic legislation and its proven inadequacy in controlling the activities of multinational corporations pointed to the need for new international legal principles. As Ceylon's representative stated, 'the majority of developing countries had no means of controlling

[93] Second Committee, 'Summary Records of the Seventh Meeting' UN Doc TD/III/C.2/SR.7, 75 (Byelorussian Soviet Socialist Republic).

[94] Second Committee, 'Summary Records of the Eighth Meeting' TD/III/C.2/SR.8, 93 (Cuba).

[95] UNCTAD, 'Proceedings of the UNCTAD Third Session, vol 1' (n 75) Annex VI, Report of the Second Committee 185, 196.

[96] ibid.

[97] See the comments of Japan and the US: Second Committee, 'Summary Records of the Sixth Meeting' UN Doc TD/III/C.2/SR.6, 63.

[98] ibid 79–80 (International Chamber of Commerce).

[99] UNCTAD, 'Proceedings of the UNCTAD Third Session, vol 1' (n 75) Annex VI, Report of the Second Committee 191. See especially Second Committee, 'Summary Records of the Seventh Meeting' UN Doc TD/III/C.2/SR.7, 70 (UK), 84 (Denmark); Second Committee, 'Summary Records of the Eighth Meeting' UN Doc TD/III/C.2/SR.8, 95–96 (Australia).

[100] Second Committee, 'Summary Records of the Seventh Meeting', UN Doc TD/III/C.2/SR.7, 86 (France).

the restrictive business practices of private enterprise . . . The time had therefore come to study the problem and to take measures at the national and international level'.[101] India, despite having taken measures to align foreign investment with national priorities, found it had 'not yet been possible to control entirely the adverse effects of private foreign investments'.[102] And Chile noted that, while the developing countries' introduction of legislation was part of the solution—and the Andean Group's experience was instructive in this respect—neither domestic nor regional laws would be sufficient to assert control unless working in concert with international measures.[103] These sentiments found echoes in those expressed by some European nations—Belgium noted that in many cases domestic legislation rendered public authorities 'powerless' to intervene in corporate activities, and new legal principles were needed to supplant it.[104] In this way, delegates framed both their desire for, and ambivalence toward, a new international regime governing restrictive business practices by reference to not only economic or political, but *legal* (im)possibility.[105]

2. Debate in the Third Committee on private foreign investment

In the Third Committee the following week, a rather more heated debate took place over private foreign investment and the role of multinational corporations in the world economy.[106] The debate centred on the draft resolution of the G77 on Foreign Private Investment in its Relationship to Development.[107] This resolution expressed concern about evidence of financial outflows caused by private foreign investment, its 'excessive' use of local financial resources, and the disruption of

[101] ibid 67. See also at 62–63 (Bolivia), and 65 (Bulgaria); Second Committee, 'Summary Records of the Seventh Meeting', UN Doc TD/III/C.2/SR.7, 69–70 (Philippines).

[102] Second Committee, 'Summary Records of the Seventh Meeting' UN Doc TD/III/C.2/SR.7, 72–73.

[103] Second Committee, 'Summary Records of the Eighth Meeting' UN Doc TD/III/C.2/SR.8, 97 (Chile). Colombia and Tunisia also called for the creation of guidelines or an international code of conduct governing the behaviour of multinationals: Second Committee, 'Summary Records of the Sixth Meeting' UN Doc TD/III/C.2/SR.6, 65 (Colombia); Second Committee, 'Summary Records of the Seventh Meeting' UN Doc TD/III/C.2/SR.7, 89 (Tunisia). It is unclear from the debates whether these were intended to be binding or not. See, further, United Nations Department of Economic and Social Affairs, *The Impact of Multinational Corporations on Development and on International Relations*, UN Doc E/5500/Rev.1, 54–55.

[104] Second Committee, 'Summary Records of the Seventh Meeting' UN Doc TD/III/C.2/SR.7, 83.

[105] Ultimately, the disagreement over substance was deflected through the commissioning of the Ad Hoc Group of Experts on Restrictive Business Practices, which was composed of both governmental experts in the field of international trade and experts from 'competent international organizations' such as WIPO and the International Chamber of Commerce. International trade unions were not named in the resolution: UNCTAD Res 73 (III) (19 May 1972).

[106] UNCTAD, 'Proceedings of the UNCTAD Third sessions, vol 1' (n 75) 233.

[107] Group of Seventy-Seven Developing Countries, 'Foreign Private Investment in Its Relationship to Development', Draft Resolution by G77, UN Doc TD/III/C.3/L/5.

competition by foreign companies operating in the markets of developing countries.[108] In short, the problem was that private foreign investment was not performing what the resolution took to be its proper function, namely to 'facilitate the mobilization of internal ressources [sic], generate inflows and avoid outflows of foreign reserves, incorporate adequate technology, and enhance savings and national investment'.[109] Instead, it was impeding rather than assisting in the project of development. The draft resolution therefore urged developed countries to 'take the necessary steps to reverse the tendency for an outflow of capital'.[110]

During this debate, views on whether foreign private investment was inherently beneficial or not also split between three main positions. One group of developing countries was hopeful that multinational corporations could contribute to development. Zaire, for instance, had 'made sacrifices' to encourage and facilitate foreign private investment 'in the hope that at a second stage investment would help to raise the level of living of the population'.[111] Other countries shared this hope, but were more wary of making concessions, feeling that foreign private investment could further national development only 'so far as the government succeeded in turning it to good account . . . and in so far as the investors played the host country's game, so to speak'.[112] Still others within this grouping were in the process of establishing regional schemes to regulate foreign investment in order to capitalize on its benefits while recognizing its potentially harmful aspects. For example, the Council of the Cartagena Agreement recognized the precariousness of depending on the benevolence of investors, and had adopted a joint regime for foreign investment that 'reserved the right to authorize foreign investment after having evaluated the conditions in which it was offered and its conformity with the development priorities of the country in which the capital was to be invested'.[113] Notwithstanding different approaches to corporate control, what was common was an implicit acceptance of the potentially beneficial link between foreign investment and development.

[108] See, for background, the report before the Committee for consideration: Sanjay Lall, 'Balance-of-Payments Effects of Private Foreign Investment in Developing Countries: Summary of Case Studies in India, Iran, Jamaica and Kenya', UN Doc TD/134/Supp.1.

[109] For the text of the draft resolution, see UNCTAD, 'Proceedings of the UNCTAD Third Session, vol 1' (n 75), Annex VI, 239, UN Doc TD/III/C.3/L/5, 2.

[110] ibid 3. This mirrors exactly the language found in the Lima Declaration: UNCTAD, 'Proceedings of the UNCTAD Third Session, vol 1' (n 77) Annex VIII, 'The Declaration and Principles of the Action Programme of Lima' (7 November 1971) 391.

[111] Third Committee, 'Summary Records of the Fourteenth Meeting' UN Doc TD/III/C.3/SR.14, 136.

[112] Third Committee, 'Summary Records of the Sixteenth Meeting' UN Doc TD/III/C.3/SR.16, 164 (Cameroon).

[113] The Cartagena Agreement, signed in 1969, created the customs union (initially comprising Bolivia, Colombia, Chile, Ecuador, and Peru) then known as the Andean Pact, and now referred to as the Andean Community: Agreement on Andean Subregional Integration (signed 26 May 1969) 8 ILM 190. Foreign purchasing of national enterprises, which was often considered to be of no benefit to the host country, was subject to 'special rules'. See Third Committee, 'Summary Records of the Fourteenth Meeting' UN Doc TD/III/C.3/SR.14, 140–41.

A second group considered that foreign private investment was critical for development and that the potential harms that worried the G77 were overstated. This view was often accompanied by calls for any international regulation to further accommodate the interests of the *investor*. Even where it was accepted that countries might wish to protect their legitimate interests, 'reasonable stability' in conditions within the recipient country was necessary for investment and '[s]udden and arbitrary changes in the conditions under which foreign private investors operated could only be counter-productive'.[114] The US likewise asserted that private investment was critical to development and that certain actions of developing countries—such as 'expropriations in one or another form'—were in danger of reducing the pool of investment available to other developing states.[115] As the question of whether to invest was up to the private investor, the critical role of 'host' governments was to work out a 'mutually beneficial arrangement' which would ensure the security of that investment.[116] Already, moves had been made at the institutional level to facilitate an increase in volume of foreign private investment.[117] The promise of this increase came, then, with strings attached—the implicit replacement of official development assistance with foreign private capital, and the injunction to accommodate the interests of corporations as its carrier.

A third group resolutely opposed the idea that foreign private investment might be considered to perform the role of a catalyst for development—a role more properly performed by official development assistance. The USSR, for instance, asserted that investment 'by its very nature' was incapable of complying with the conditions outlined in the draft resolution of conforming to national priorities and stimulating capital formation.[118] History had shown developing countries that in many cases, investment had led to 'the complete exhaustion of their economies'.[119] Cuba added that the case studies before the committee showed the direct effects of foreign private investment on the balance of payments to be overwhelmingly negative—even if the net effect was judged to be favourable.[120] In addition, companies' demands for guaranteed conditions for their investment 'implied a violation of national sovereignty'.[121] For this group, more research was needed to understand the phenomenon of capital outflows linked to foreign private investment, and how it

[114] Third Committee, 'Summary Records of the Sixteenth Meeting' UN Doc TD/III/C.3/SR.16, 160.

[115] ibid 157–58. The critical and expanding role of private investment in the development process, for the US, eclipsed that of the limited and finite flows of 'official development assistance'.

[116] ibid 158 (United States).

[117] For example, Belgium had established a financing corporation to provide capital for investment in developing countries: Third Committee, 'Summary Records of the Fifteenth Meeting' UN Doc TD/III/C.3/SR.15, 152 (Belgium).

[118] Third Committee, 'Summary Records of the Fourteenth Meeting' UN Doc TD/III/C.3/SR.14, 129.

[119] ibid, 129.

[120] ibid 137. However, given the assumptions underpinning the report, Cuba also questioned the extent to which their findings were reliable. In addition, the report paid no attention to the negative impact of investment on aspects of economic life beyond the prism of balance-of-payments effects: ibid 138.

[121] ibid (Cuba).

impacted the states of the global South and made profit for the companies of the global North.[122] In the meantime, the USSR encouraged developing countries to take advantage of its offer of credit on terms unaccompanied by 'any political or economic tie or condition'.[123]

Against these divided views on how to understand the relationship between development and foreign private investment, states coalesced into two broad stances on the best way to control or otherwise regulate it. This replicated the divide playing out in relation to restrictive business practices in the Second Committee. One grouping—which included France, West Germany, and the UK—insisted that host states were always free to establish rules governing the conditions under which companies could invest. Although it was difficult for countries to exercise 'authoritarian control' over investors, '[c]ontrol of private investment nevertheless remained one of the essential attributes of the sovereignty of the host countries, which were free to fix their own rules'.[124] West Germany explicitly tied the disagreement over the empirical question (whether investment is good for development) to the question of the appropriate regulatory jurisdiction, noting that as it was impossible to determine as a matter of principle whether foreign investment was good or bad for development, 'each case should be separately investigated' by the host state.[125] This move is illustrative of the way in which the argument about the empirical question was being reshaped toward the impossibility of international regulation. Similarly, the UK insisted that 'each investment proposal needed to be looked at on its own merits' and that where foreign investment had deleterious effects, this was generally due to the failure of the host country to properly screen the investment.[126] In other words, it was for that state to make a decision about whether or not it wished to welcome the investment. For this group, locating this decision in the host state meant that the decision and the legal frameworks structuring it were malleable.[127] As 'it was impossible to lay down formal rules on an international basis to regulate foreign investment', for these states the better legal vehicles were bilateral agreements.[128]

Another grouping—that included Algeria, Venezuela and Guyana—resisted this view, each articulating in different ways a common opposition to the idea that

[122] ibid 129 (USSR).

[123] ibid 130. As opposed to the terms of the capitalist countries, which 'often resembled in nature the relations that existed previously between the metropolitan countries and their colonies': ibid 131.

[124] Third Committee, 'Summary Records of the Fifteenth Meeting' UN Doc TD/III/C.3/SR.15, 151.

[125] ibid 148, 149.

[126] Third Committee, 'Summary Records of the Sixteenth Meeting' UN Doc TD/III/C.3/SR.16, 159–60. In other words, they put forward the view that the multinational corporation 'will only be as useful or as dangerous as the host country allows it to be': see Fieldhouse, *The West and the Third World* (n 7) 285.

[127] Hence, the UK warned that it would be undesirable for the Andean regional framework to crystallize into 'rigidity' and to impede foreign private investment from being able to do its work: Third Committee, 'Summary Records of the Sixteenth Meeting' UN Doc TD/III/C.3/SR.16, 160 (UK).

[128] ibid 160–61.

the domestic sphere, on its own, offered a way to regulate the activities of corporations. Algeria, for instance, endorsed a unified system for the supervision and control of multinational corporations.[129] For Venezuela, 'foreign private investment had been the cause of the relationships of colonialism and dependency' that were imbricated in the current international economic order. Its delegate proposed that foreign private investment should be governed in accordance with the 'principle of international social justice' geared to the priorities needs of host countries. However, he considered that decision-making centres about those priorities should be located in the host countries themselves, pushing back against the incipient hierarchization of authority at play in the debate.[130] Guyana, on the other hand, advocated action both 'at the national level and also by pressing for a new strategy for development within the group of 77'.[131] Recognizing that developed countries had a vested interest in existing structures of economic relations within developing countries, the solution lay in maintaining and reinforcing solidarity in the developing world itself.[132] So, although a common theme was that the international was implicated in the relationship of dependency between host states and investor corporations, no common solution or vision was articulated as a means for resolving this dilemma.

In the end, the Third Committee was unable to reach agreement on the draft resolution.[133] The Conference considered the draft resolution in its plenary session and after amendments, adopted the resolution by seventy-three votes to three, with twenty-three abstentions.[134] The final resolution recorded the concerns of developing countries over the outflow of capital as a result of foreign investment and the failure of foreign investment to generate wealth.[135] However, a number of countries emphasized their decision not to take part in the vote,[136] while the UK and the US voted against the resolution on the grounds that it did not give enough weight to the merits of private investment.[137] Ultimately, the resolution affirmed only the right of developing countries to regulate foreign investment within their own legal systems, and urged developed countries to prevent the outflow of capital from the countries in which multinational corporations did

[129] Third Committee, 'Summary Records of the Fifteenth Meeting' UN Doc TD/III/C.3/15, 153.

[130] ibid 157.

[131] Third Committee, 'Summary Records of the Sixteenth Meeting' UN Doc TD/III/C.3/SR.16, 163.

[132] ibid.

[133] UNCTAD, 'Proceedings of the UNCTAD Third Session, vol 1' (n 75) Annex VI, 'Report of the Third Committee' 106.

[134] UNCTAD Res 56 (III) (19 May 1972); UNCTAD, 'Proceedings of the UNCTAD Third Session, vol 1' (n 75) Annex II, 'Action with Respect to Reports' 143.

[135] UNCTAD Res 56 (III) (19 May 1972) operative paragraphs 2 and 3.

[136] UNCTAD, 'Proceedings of the UNCTAD Third Session, vol 1' (n 75) Annex I, 'Observations and Reservations by Delegations on the Decisions of the Conference' 122 (China), 122 (Denmark), 130 (Switzerland).

[137] ibid 132 (UK), 134 (US).

business.[138] It therefore did not envisage any solution based on international, rather than domestic, legal authority.

IV. A culmination of sorts? The Group of Eminent Persons report

Despite the lack of a consensus on international action at UNCTAD III, the question of the international regulation of corporations would resurface in the work of the Group of Eminent Persons (the Group) set up by the UN Economic and Social Council (ECOSOC). The setting up of the Group marked the shift from UNCTAD to ECOSOC as a venue for the realization of the aspirations of the G77 in response to the perceived failures of UNCTAD. The third world had perceived a critical need to establish a comprehensive international trade organization, recognizing that 'world economic problems could not be compartmentalized' and that fragmenting deliberation on key economic issues could prejudice their interests.[139] However, the G77's attempt to make UNCTAD more representative and to transform it into a forum for the negotiation and adoption of multilateral trade treaties had been stymied.[140] Accordingly, following the failure of UNCTAD III to move toward internationalized regulation, Chile had introduced a proposal that a group of persons 'of the highest moral and intellectual character and of international repute in their various fields' be appointed to study the problem of multinational corporations in depth.[141]

As Chile proposed it, the group would be constituted by members 'from developed market-economy countries, developing countries and socialist countries, and [would] include representatives of student movements whose future was at stake'.[142] An aspect of the group's task would be to remedy the gap identified by the Under-Secretary General at the Third Session of UNCTAD: the 'lack of any arrangement for the supervision and regulations of the activities of multinational corporations'.[143] But like the previous deliberations in UNCTAD, the ensuing debate in the Council[144] was tellingly illustrative of 'the two aspects of the

[138] Through measures such as offering tax exemptions for reinvesting profits: UNCTAD Res 56 (III), (19 May 1972) operative paragraphs 1 and 4.

[139] UNCTAD, 'Proceedings of the UNCTAD Third Session, vol 1' (n 75) Annex VI, 'Report of Working Group 1' 301 (Brazil). For the opposing view, see the statement by the GATT representative at UNCTAD III (urging the maintenance of an effective division of responsibility: ibid 301.

[140] ibid 299 (comments by the representative of the G77). For the G77's proposed alterations to the institutional arrangements of UNCTAD, see United Nations Commission on International Trade Law, *Yearbook Volume II* (1976) UN Doc TD/III/WG.l/L.l/Rev.l. For the resolutions ultimately adopted, see UNCTAD Res 80(III) (20 May 1972); UNCTAD Res 81(III) (20 May 1972).

[141] Economic and Social Council, '1831st meeting' (14 July 1972), UN Doc E/SR.1831 9.

[142] ibid 9.

[143] See UNCTAD, 'Summary of the Statement by P De Seynes' (n 72) 57.

[144] ESC, '1831st–1834th meetings' (14–25 July 1972) UN Docs E/SR.1831–4.

problem of multinational corporations: on the one hand, "aberrations" and "distortions" . . . and on the other, the undeniable role played by those corporations in . . . the provision of the capital needed for economic development'.[145]

The strongest supporters of such a study thought that companies should not remain unregulated by international law with regard to activities that did not coincide with the interests of developing countries. Mexico, for instance, supported the implementation of a binding code of conduct on the basis that 'the increasingly complex structure of the world economy had given birth to multinational corporations and the only limit to their expansion was the question of profitability'.[146] Peru was similarly concerned with the increasing power of corporations and their potential to infringe on sovereignty. It felt that there was an 'obvious need for some measure of control over their activities or some international code of conduct for them';[147] the USSR agreed.[148] Its representative argued that recent events had demonstrated that 'economic problems could not be considered in isolation from their political aspects,' referring particularly to the ability of large multinational companies to influence, or even alter the composition of, governments of States.[149] Although the problem was an old one, he said, the difference now was that the countries being affected were 'no longer powerless to defend their interests against the multinational corporations'.[150]

The proposed study also found significant support among a number of Western countries (other than the US), which had begun to witness the pernicious effects of corporate activity on both their own economies and on their foreign relations.[151] As such, they were eager for the study to assess 'the impact of multinational corporations' activities on both developed and developing countries'.[152] Even the UK, which had opposed the resolutions put forward at UNCTAD III, felt the study would be useful for this reason.[153] However, these states wanted the study to 'be of a

[145] Economic and Social Council, '1832nd meeting' (20 July 1972) UN Doc E/SR.1832, 87 (Italy). By 'aberrations', the Italian representative referred to incidents such as the interference in the Chilean election.

[146] Economic and Social Council (n 141) 12.

[147] ibid 43.

[148] ibid 53.

[149] Appearing to refer to the activities of ITT in Chile, but also noting that other companies far exceeded the economic clout of ITT—such as General Motors, whose sales in 1971 were higher than the GNP of 110 of the then-136 UN member-states: Economic and Social Council (n 141) 18–21. The representative of Poland also denounced corporate promotion of 'the interests of neo-colonialism and [interference] openly in national politics': Economic and Social Council (n 145) 33.

[150] Economic and Social Council (n 141) 53.

[151] For example, Denmark, Spain, France, the Netherlands, and especially Poland. The external relations point was emphasized by New Zealand, but by few others: Economic Committee, '586th meeting' (26 July 1972) UN Doc E/AC.6/SR.586, 229 (New Zealand).

[152] ibid 229 (Denmark).

[153] Economic and Social Council (n 141) 41. Although Argentina was careful to point out that the matters meriting inclusion which concerned developed market-economy countries—monopolies and inflation—were very different from those that concerned socialist or developing countries.

technical character and . . . not go into the political implications of the issue'[154] lest it meant 'foregoing the concentration and pooling of means and efforts which had become necessary for economic progress'.[155] This was firmly opposed by Chile, as the examination of the impact of multinational corporations on international relations was 'an essential aspect' of the proposal.[156]

In its final form, the resolution establishing the Group of Eminent Persons contained elements of both the technical, developmentalist approach to company–state–international law relations, as well as Allende's approach, which recognized companies as independent, political, international actors. It proposed that the group would 'formulate conclusions which may possibly be used by Governments in making their sovereign decisions regarding national policy in this respect, and to submit recommendations for appropriate international action', leaving indeterminate any eventual mechanism through which international law might relate to the questions at hand.[157] At the same time, the views that had remained unchallenged about the intrinsic value of 'development', fuelled by private foreign capital, were inscribed into the group's terms of reference.

This orientation was further cemented by the make-up of the Group itself, criticized by Chile for its failure to include trade union leaders or academics from various fields,[158] and for its over-representation of directors of private companies.[159] Such criticisms were dismissed by the Under-Secretary-General for Economic Affairs, who argued that, rather than focusing on the Chilean experience, 'it was necessary to look to the future . . . to ensure that multinational corporations played a positive role in the developing countries'.[160] As the US put it, questions of equitable geographical distribution and corporate representation were of minimal relevance given that all members, regardless of their origins, had a shared 'bias toward development'.[161]

[154] ibid 44 (France), which also contains the comments by the observer for the Netherlands, who 'assumed that the proposed study was intended to be entirely objective'.

[155] Economic and Social Council (n 145) 25 (Spain).

[156] Economic Committee (n 151) 219.

[157] ESC Res 1721 (28 July 1972) 1.

[158] Specifically referring to the fields of political science, international trade, economics, and international affairs: Economic Committee, '630th meeting' (15 May 1973) UN Doc E/AC.6/SR.630, 167.

[159] ibid 167. The Chilean experience had continued to provide evidence that developing countries were 'extremely vulnerable to the activities of imperialist multinational corporations'—since the passing of the resolution, the US Senate Sub-Committee examining the ITT's activities in Chile had uncovered irrefutable evidence of what Allende had described, while at the same time the Kennecott Company had taken steps to embargo the purchase of Chilean copper in Europe: ibid 168–170.

[160] Economic Committee, '632nd meeting' (16 May 1973) UN Doc E/AC.6/SR.632, 214.

[161] ibid 218. Although these states and others, including Algeria, Hungary, and Mongolia, would continue to express their concerns later in that year, no change was made to the candidates thus far selected apart from the addition of Mario Trindade (Brazil), Vice President of the National Bank of Commerce. See UN Secretary General, 'The Impact of Multinational Corporations on the Development Process and on International Relations: Progress Report of the Secretary-General' (11 May 1973) UN Doc E/5334. On the concerns of some states about the composition of the group, see Economic Committee, '651st and 652nd meetings' (27–30 July 1973) UN Docs E/AC.6/SR.651–2

The Group met between September of 1973 and March of 1974 and eventually issued a report on 22 May 1974 entitled the 'Impact of Multinational Corporations', recommending that a Commission on multinational corporations be established to assist the work of the Economic and Social Council.[162] The complexity and breadth of the issue required a 'continuing elucidation and analysis of the problems involved, based on more information, professional studies and consultations with the various parties concerned'.[163] The Commission was to be composed of members serving in an individual capacity, hailing from both developed and developing states and from a variety of professions.[164] It would meet at least once a year and act as a 'focal point' through which the Economic and Social Council could debate, consider, and respond to issues posed by multinational corporations.[165]

The proposed terms of reference for the Commission were, for the most part, open-ended: receiving reports, providing a venue for exchange of views, and building 'technical capacity'.[166] Partly to facilitate this, the Group proposed that an information and research centre on MNCs be established to assist the Commission.[167] The Commission would now also serve to facilitate a process which had been ongoing in other fora—namely, the 'adoption of specific arrangements or agreements in selected areas pertaining to the activities of multinational corporations' (such as restrictive business practices or transfer of technology).[168] In contrast to these piecemeal efforts, however, it should act holistically to 'evolve a set of recommendations which, taken together, would represent a code of conduct for Governments and multinational corporations'.[169] Although there was significant difference of opinion about what such a code should entail, the Group clarified that, in its view, the proposed code of conduct should not be compulsory in character but would 'act as an instrument of moral persuasion' for multinational corporations.[170]

The more controversial aspect of the Commission's task was to 'explore the possibility of a general agreement on multinational corporations, enforceable by appropriate machinery, to which participating countries would adhere by means of an international treaty'.[171] Although this was included in the set of recommendations

[162] Department of Economic and Social Affairs, The Impact of Multinational Corporations on Development and on International Relations (1972) UN Doc E/5500/Rev.1 19, 52 (hereafter Department of Economic and Social Affairs, 'Group of Eminent Persons Report'). This recommendation was fully endorsed by the UNCTAD Secretary-General: ibid 6.

[163] ibid 52.

[164] ibid 57–58. The rationale for this, the Secretary-General's report stated, was that a non-governmental body would 'facilitate the consultation process and encourage greater involvement', including by private parties. In fact, the Secretary-General went so far as to suggest that the achievements of the Group itself would likely not have been possible had it been constituted by states: ibid 7.

[165] ibid 57–58.

[166] ibid 57, recommendations (b) and (c), 36–8, 53–4.

[167] ibid 53–4.

[168] ibid 57 recommendation (d).

[169] ibid 57 recommendation (e).

[170] ibid 55.

[171] ibid 57 recommendation (f).

transmitted to ECOSOC, the Group itself considered that it would be 'premature to propose serious negotiations on such an agreement' as significant preparation was required.[172] In the meantime, the Group reasoned, action on more 'specific issues' could take place, such as taxation or labour arrangements which could be concluded without such delay.[173] In this way their conviction that 'the benefits which can be derived from multinational corporations are fully realised' could be implemented.[174]

As one might have expected given the temperature of the debates leading up to the report, the response was also lively. One immediate response by some within the Group itself related to something understood to have been lost in translation between a background document and the report itself. This document, prepared by the Department of Economic and Social Affairs of the UN Secretariat to assist the work of the Group,[175] had aimed to 'clarify various concepts pertaining to multinational corporation, provide basic data on their size, geographical distribution, industrial structure and ownership patterns, and assess their dimensions in the world economy'.[176] However, in its final form, it went further, assessing the multinational corporations' 'impact on international relations, and on home and host countries, including tensions that may develop between them and these countries'.[177]

Unlike the report of the Group of Eminent Persons, the background document openly stated that the 'political and social dimensions of the problem of multinational corporations [were] only too apparent'. To illustrate these, it meticulously laid out a series of facts, including those concerning the pattern of corporate distribution, and concluded that it closely mirrored the pattern of former colonial ties.[178] The international economic system that had been developed earlier in that century further complicated this picture, as the porousness of national economic boundaries no longer corresponded to political–legal conceptions of national sovereignty.[179] The critical question for the writers of that background report, therefore, was not what benefit could be derived from the company as a carrier of investment, but 'whether a set of institutions and devices can be worked out which will guide the multinational corporations' exercise of power and introduce some form of accountability to the international community into their activities'.[180]

[172] ibid 54.
[173] ibid 54.
[174] ibid 26.
[175] ibid 3. It is unclear at whose request this report came about.
[176] Department of Economic and Social Affairs, *Multinational Corporations in World Development* (1973) UN Doc ST/ECA/190, vi.
[177] ibid vi.
[178] ibid 1, 9.
[179] ibid 3: 'However sacred and inviolable national sovereignty may be from the political point of view, few national boundaries correspond to economic demarcation lines and few states are self-contained economic entities'.
[180] ibid 2. The report was strongly sceptical of the ability of non-binding measures, such as the code of conduct proposed by the Group, to achieve this end: ibid 78–79.

From comments made by members of the Group, it is clear the political–economic orientation of that document sat uneasily with the more technical and developmentalist orientation of the Group's report. One delegate, Juan Somavia,[181] suggested that the analysis contained in the background document should continue to live side by side with the report as a necessary complement to its perceived limitations.[182] He criticized the 'tendency of the report to concentrate on the micro-relationship between a multinational corporation and a given country' and corresponding neglect of the corporation as situated within the history of international political and economic relations.[183] In doing so, it was blind to the multinational corporation as 'the expression of a . . . system whose values, basic orientations and general structure have stimulated their unprecedented expansion'.[184] Another delegate, Ahmed Ghozali,[185] pointed to the absence in the report of any mention of the events which had happened since the initiative had begun.[186] First among these was the 'Chilean tragedy'—the coup in Chile and the death of Salvador Allende—perhaps what Allende had feared when he launched the initiative.[187] For both Ghozali and Somavia, the divorcing of the problem of multinational corporations from both politics and history augured badly for third-world autonomy and fairer international wealth distribution.

When the report eventually came before the Economic and Social Council at its 57th session, the initial response to the recommendations of both the Group and the Secretary-General was strikingly pragmatic.[188] There was a difference in emphasis over the Commission's most urgent programme of work: many states, as well as the representative from the International Chamber of Commerce,[189] emphasized the importance of the (non-binding) code of conduct. Others, such as India, considered that the body 'should take up as a matter of priority the development of a [binding] regulatory framework'.[190] And, although some states were

[181] Later to be appointed Director-General of the ILO.

[182] Department of Economic and Social Affairs, 'Group of Eminent Persons Report' (n 162) 162 (comments by Juan Somavia, the Chilean Former Permanent Representative to the Andean Group, Former President of the Commission of the Cartagena Agreement, and Former Chairman of the Board of the Andean Development Corporation). See also the comments of Ahmed Ghozali on this point: ibid 103.

[183] ibid 162.

[184] ibid.

[185] Then Minister of Energy and Investment of Algeria.

[186] Department of Economic and Social Affairs, 'Group of Eminent Persons Report' (n 162) 103. Ahmed Ghozali was the President Director-General of SONATRACH, an Algerian state-owned company.

[187] Also, developments in relation to energy and raw materials, which would have shed 'essential light both on the role of multinational corporations and the machinery of their operations and on the problems and aspirations of the developing countries': ibid.

[188] ESC, '1901st meeting' (4 July 1974) UN Doc E/SR.1901, 71. See also ESC, '1902nd meeting' (4 July 1974) UN Doc E/SR.1902, 8 (Canada); ESC, '1903rd meeting' (5 July 1974) UN Doc E/SR.1903, 43–44 (Mexico).

[189] ESC, '1906th meeting' (8 July 1974) UN Doc E/SR.1906, 65.

[190] ESC, '1903rd meeting' (5 July 1974) E/SR.1903, 35.

in favour of the commission being constituted by experts, as the Group had suggested,[191] others felt strongly that it should be constituted by states, with experts playing a supplementary role.[192] In short order, the Chairman of the Group presented the report to the Economic Committee. Given the limited time available to debate the report, both the UK and Canada proposed that the Committee confine itself to the 'passages which concerned international machinery and action'.[193] The debate that followed showed that states had by this time become committed to the establishment of the proposed Commission in one or another form.[194] Only China voiced a concern that the report had failed to reflect the 'plundering and exploitation of the developing countries perpetrated by the multinational corporations' and that the recommendations of the report should be viewed with caution.[195]

The Economic Committee reached agreement on 1 August on a resolution deciding in principle to establish a permanent machinery 'to assist the Council in dealing with the issue of transnational corporations'.[196] The resolution convened a Special Intersessional Committee of the Council to more closely examine the report and the views of States on its recommendations.[197] By 5 December 1974 the Intersessional Committee had unanimously recommended Resolution 1913 to the Council.[198]

That resolution would establish a forty-eight-member inter-governmental body to be called the Commission on Transnational Corporations.[199] It was to be composed of state-appointed experts, and supported by an information research centre.[200] Although the programme of work for the Commission remained relatively unchanged from the report of the Group, there was one notable difference: the task of creating an international treaty adequate to the problems that Allende had outlined had been dramatically de-emphasized. Instead, the Commission was now to consider 'possible arrangements or agreements on specific aspects relating to transnational corporations with a view to studying the feasibility of formulating a general agreement and . . . to consolidating them into

[191] ESC, '1905th meeting' (8 July 1974) E/SR.1905, 8 (Pakistan); ESC, '1906th meeting' (8 July 1974) UN Doc E/SR.1906, 11 (United Kingdom).

[192] Economic and Social Council, '1901st meeting' (n 188); see also 1905th meeting of the Economic and Social Council (8 July 1974) E/SR.1905, 58 (Yugoslavia). Except for the Chilean representative, who did not feel it was necessary to establish the commission in order to deliver a 'mandatory code of conduct': 1911th meeting of the Economic and Social Council (11 July 1974) UN Doc E/SR.1911, 12.

[193] Economic Committee, '705th meeting' (18 July 1974) E/AC.5/SR.705, 197 (Canada), 198 (United Kingdom).

[194] Economic Committee, '708th meeting' (19 July 1974) UN Doc E/AC.6/SR.708, 233.

[195] Economic Committee, '707th meeting' (19 July 1974) UN Doc E/AC.6/SR.707, 218.

[196] Which was adopted without a vote the next day: ESC Res 1908 (LVII) (2 August 1974) 6.

[197] ibid 7.

[198] No summary records exist of the Committee's deliberations, and the final consensus was reached through informal consultations: 1931st meeting of the Economic and Social Council (5 December 1974) UN Doc E/SR.1931. See also Special International Committee, 'Report of the Special Intersessional Committee' (8 January 1975) UN Doc E/5599.

[199] ESC Res 1913 (LVII), (5 December 1974) 1.

[200] ibid 4.

a general agreement at a future date'.[201] The possibility of an enforceable agreement that could reimagine the place of the transnational corporation in the international order seemed remote.[202]

V. 'Our common success': The establishment of the UNCTC and the Kissinger response to the 'New International Economic Order'

By the time of the first session in March of 1975, the question of a treaty had fallen off the Commission's programme of work altogether. Instead, efforts refocused on the proposed (and potentially non-binding) 'code of conduct', to be taken up by the Commission as a matter of priority.[203] However, the Commission's preparation for negotiations on a code of conduct could only proceed through putting to one side two unresolvable questions. The first was the question of the enforceability or mandatory nature of the code, and the second was whether, under it, governments would also be subject to obligations.[204]

At around the same time, and as part of the ongoing efforts to establish the principles of a New International Economic Order (NIEO), the UNGA had resolved to hold a Special Session from 1 September 1975, on development and international economic cooperation.[205] The purpose of the session was to consider 'new concepts and options with a view to promoting effectively the solution of world economic problems, especially those of developing countries'.[206] At the very forefront of the session was the US, the second state to speak.[207] Then US Secretary of State Henry Kissinger had intended to be present, but was unable to attend. Instead, he wrote a speech that was read in his absence—'a programme of practical steps' to address the concerns of the developing world.[208] In contrast to the third world's insistence on the continued presence of history, for Kissinger the moment was ruptural, representing a radical break with the past: the 'global order of colonial power that lasted through centuries has now disappeared'.[209] Even 'the cold war

[201] ibid 4, but cf the wording of the recommendations made by the Department of Economic and Social Affairs, 'Group of Eminent Persons Report' (n 162).

[202] For the way in which this was taken up at the first session of the Commission, see Commission on Transnational Corporations, 'Report on the First Session' (17–28 March 1975) UN Doc E/5655.

[203] ibid 2.

[204] ibid 9.

[205] This was in the wake of the Declaration at the UN General Assembly in 1974: 'Declaration on the Establishment of a New International Economic Order'(1 May 1974) GA Res 3201 (S-VI) UN Doc A/RES/3201(S-VI).

[206] UNGA, '2327th meeting' (1 September 1975) UN Doc A/PV.2327, 3 (Brazil), citing GA Res 3172 (XXVIII) (17 December 1963).

[207] After Brazil ibid.

[208] Kissinger served as US Secretary of State from 1973–1977.

[209] UNGA, '2327th meeting' (n 206) 38.

division of the world into two rigid blocs ha[d] now also broken down', and there remained, he said, only states united in the common endeavour of development.[210] And yet third-world solidarity was positioned in opposition to the inauguration of what could be a new era of 'human progress'. The threat lay in the formation of the Non-Aligned Movement, a 'new bloc' which was counter-productive to this endeavour, engaging 'in a kind of solidarity that often clearly sacrifices practical interests'.[211] What was required to address the economic problems faced by all states was not division, said Kissinger, but 'consensus, first and foremost, on the principle that our common development goals can be achieved only by co-operation, not by the politics of confrontation'.[212]

The 'transnational enterprise' was among the most contentious of these lines of 'political division'. The ongoing 'controversy over their role and conduct' that had continued in various forms and fora since Allende's speech was 'itself an obstacle to economic development'.[213] In his view, 'if the world community [was] committed to economic development, it [could] not afford to treat transnational enterprises as objects of economic warfare'.[214] Nevertheless, Kissinger conceded that 'the time [had] come for the international community to articulate standards of conduct' for corporations, and acknowledged that the UNCTC, 'had begun such an effort'. But for Kissinger, 'transnational enterprises ha[d] been powerful instruments of modernization', and 'may well be one of the most effective engines of development'.[215] And given that only 'transnational enterprises' could facilitate the solution to the problem of underdevelopment, standards should be formulated which applied both to the behaviour of corporations and to the governments that hosted them.[216]

The principles that Kissinger laid out underpinning these standards were extensive, but, two elements were key to the question of the transnational corporation. First was an insistence that corporate conduct should be governed by local, not international law. Transnational corporations were of course 'obliged to obey local law', and should 'refrain from unlawful interference in the domestic affairs of the host country', 'respect local customs and employ qualified local personnel'.[217] But second, in return, those corporations must receive a stable, apolitical environment in which to operate, characterized by equitable and non-discriminatory treatment. And unlike corporate conduct governed by local law, 'host states' must accord transnational enterprises protection 'in accordance with *international law*'.[218]

[210] ibid.
[211] ibid 44.
[212] ibid 47.
[213] Ibid, 105.
[214] ibid 119.
[215] ibid 103.
[216] ibid 108.
[217] ibid 110.
[218] ibid 111 (emphasis added).

In Kissinger's account, these protections would be supported by a suite of international endeavours, including the harmonization of tax treatment, the promotion of arbitral procedures for the settlement of investment disputes, the reduction of restrictive business practices, and the multilateralization of the insurance of foreign investment.[219] These would be underpinned by the 'development of agricultural technologies' for food production, 'assistance to improve productivity and competitiveness' in relation to non-agricultural food production, and the assurance of future access to 'borrowing in the [international] capital market', which was already relied upon heavily in the Latin American countries.[220] In essence, what Kissinger was mapping was a different kind of 'new international economic order' that drew for its authority on 'development', and the needs of the poorest 'one billion people',[221] but which precisely contradicted in its every element the other 'New International Economic Order' that the global South was simultaneously proposing . At the centre of this map, stabilized by the failure to operationalize opposition to the investment-as-development shibboleth, was the assertion of the impossibility of international legal control of the company. And as we know now, Kissinger's map was prefigurative of what was to come.

VI. Conclusion

Much is at stake in how we narrate past struggles. Many conflicts between different groups of people may be recounted either as political contestations over the 'proper' meaning of things within a pre-constituted frame, or as more radical struggles over the frame of reference through which meaning is to be determined. The stakes are particularly high when jurists are involved, for when we write about 'law' in the context of struggle, we are also participating in the construction, diffusion, and stabilization of the authority of the 'law' in the name of which we write.[222] The problem is especially acute for international lawyers who sit perennially at the crossroads of difference, or at the point of encounter between, plural traditions and multiple laws.[223] When international lawyers write about struggles over and around 'international law' as though the battle were self-evidently a question of politics, empirical fact, content, legitimacy, or a bid for 'inclusion', rather than (also) a meeting of, and struggle between, different legal traditions or different laws, we join in a project of both authoring 'international law', and authorizing that particular international law. When such struggles are in the past, our retrospective

[219] ibid 112–118.
[220] ibid 84.
[221] ibid 165.
[222] Not for nothing does 'doctrine'/*la doctrine* (as in 'teachings') have an ambiguous etymology and ongoing life, signalling 'the rules' in English, but 'scholarly writings' in French.
[223] Pahuja, 'Laws of Encounter' (n 4); Pahuja, 'Letters from Bandung' (n 4).

acts of authorization take on a teleological cast,[224] and participate in practices of international legal historiography through which encounters—whether diplomatic, developmental, or genocidal—between radically different traditions of law, are ultimately smoothed over into a story of the progressive expansion, if not the 'universalization' of 'one' international law.

In the battles over the relationship between states, corporations and international law, Allende's radical critique of the corporate form, the company's historical exercise of political authority, its capacity to travel, and the power that capacity engendered were taken up in ways which planted the seeds for the adverse effects of corporate activity to be exceptionalized, for foreign investment to be normalized, and for private capital flows to be related axiomatically to 'development.' These discursive shifts both effected and were reinforced by the stabilization of particular legal forms, including the institution of private property and the 'private' corporation whose legal personality could travel across national borders. In turn, these reframings began to legitimize what was later to become an article of faith in many quarters—that the core, 'normal', activity of corporations was unquestionably 'good', and that a sphere of corporate freedom of action was therefore needed. What our story reveals is that as the experiential, historical knowledge being insisted upon by the second and third worlds gave way to the 'expert' knowledge generated in the first world, the effects of corporate activity and private foreign investment came gradually to be redescribed as apolitical questions, and the difficulties came slowly to be understood as questions of technique, rather than as challenges of one political agenda — and it vision for international law — to another. Debates about regulation accordingly became increasingly technical, conducted among gatherings of experts and business leaders, and cloistered from political scrutiny.[225] Questions about the ways in which the activities of powerful corporate actors engaged fundamental questions about international relations, as well as how to live and promote a good life, grew increasingly distant until they seemed to disappear altogether from the horizon of institutional concern. And yet slowing down our study of this moment reveals that much of what was at stake then remains so today, and that as long as they are imaginable, other worlds are still possible.

224 Richard Drayton, 'Where Does the World Historian Write From? Objectivity, Moral Conscience and the Past and Present of Imperialism' (2011) 46 Journal of Contemporary History 671, 671. Drayton was writing of contemporary history as an idea, but the same can be said of contemporary histories of international law.

225 David Kennedy tells a contemporary story of this transformation of politics and government to expertise and governance in *World of Struggle*. The generalization of this transformation is perhaps an example of the way in which 'we are all developing countries now'. We borrow this phrase from Kerry Rittich.

VII. Epilogue

> The corporate phase of the empire remains, though not in its old form; its pre-colonial form has mutated into post-colonial corporate rule, almost as if the colonial period was an interregnum in the continuity of corporate rule.
>
> Ngũgĩ wa Thiong'o[226]

Periodization is always an argument, never a fact. The years between 1955 and 1974 repay a slow rereading but perhaps not for the reasons we might imagine. In the incipient telos implied by the two dates, 1974 stands as the 'culmination' of the initiative launched at Bandung in 1955. And the twin declarations of the New International Economic Order [227] and the Charter of Economic Rights and Duties of States[228] seem like the 'high water mark' of the Bandung spirit. In that story, the high tide of solidarity suddenly retreated before the tsunami of the debt crisis, which broke close to a decade later.

But by contemporaneous accounts, the decades moved slowly. And the demand for a wholesale 'new international economic order' seems to have become necessary in part because the initiatives for self-help and international reorganization taken by the third world were strongly resisted by the first world. The 'spirit of Bandung' is perhaps what kept those initiatives alive, displacing first-world resistance to third-world change through struggles that moved into different fora and morphed into different forms. When we move slowly through the archive of the two decades at hand, we see that these years may perhaps be better read as a time during which the third world was attempting to assert its authority on the international level, and specifically a capacity to decide, but in which the water was rising perilously all the time.

For the battle over transnational corporations, the arc between 1955 and 1974 is both particular and generalizable. The creation of the UNCTC would appear to have been a victory of sorts, but it failed to produce the collective state action sought by the third world to regulate the conduct of multinational corporations. The UNCTC was quietly put to rest in 1993, folded into the UNDP as part of the 'Division on Investment and Enterprise.' Today, that particular attempt to establish a conversation at the UN about multinational corporations is almost invariably forgotten. When it is remembered at all, it is characterized as an ill-fated attempt to assert a third-world sovereign jurisdiction against an international jurisdiction, with

[226] Ngũgĩ, *War Zone* (n 13) 18.

[227] UNGA, 'Declaration on the Establishment of a New International Economic Order' (1 May 1974) GA Res 3201 (S-VI) UN Doc A/RES/3201(S-VI).

[228] UNGA, 'Charter of Economic Rights and Duties of States' (12 December 1974) GA Res 3281 (XXIX) UN Doc A/RES/3281(XXIX).

all the hierarchies of value that characterization implies. The story is now largely retold (for better or worse) as 'sovereignty' versus international 'community'.

But perhaps more accurate than both that story and a narrative of the 'failure' of the initiative is a story of the eventual inversion of what was being attempted. Not a simple 'domestic' versus 'international' story, but an attempt to put different matters into the basket of 'domestic' versus 'international', and with differential consequences. As it emerged from formal empire, the third world sought to assert authority over private property in the national realm, and to internationalize the capacity to regulate corporate conduct as a response to the essential rootlessness of the multinational corporation. But what we have seen during the period from the end of the Cold War to the present is the *internationalization* of the protection of private property through an emerging regime of 'international investment law', and the relegation to the national sphere of the regulation over corporate conduct, along with the vulnerabilities and collective action problems that brings. Tracing the story beyond the year 1974[229] reveals that the narrative arc is not that of an arrow that is shot up and falls to the ground, but the arc of the boomerang, in which we launch something into the world and 'it comes back and hits us in the face.'[230] This is the narrative arc of tragedy.

[229] Sundhya Pahuja, 'The Changing Place of the Corporation in International Law' (*Hersch Lauterpacht Memorial Lectures*, University of Cambridge, March 2018).

[230] Simon Critchley, 'Critchley Explains Tragedy's philosophy' (Brigham Young University Humanities 21 February 2014) <http://humanities.byu.edu/critchley-explains-tragedys-philosophy/> accessed 7 December 2018. We owe this reference to Adil Khan.

7

The Battle Continues

Rebuilding Empire through Internationalization of State Contracts

Muthucumaraswamy Sornarajah

I. Introduction

Even as the triumph of the liberation movements of Africa and Asia were succeeding through the ending of empire, international lawyers of the former centres of imperialism were creating new structures of domination to ensure that their control over the wealth and resources of the developing world continued. Investment and trade were the purposes of empire. The British and Dutch East India Companies and their counterparts in other parts of the colonial world justified their entry and later control of lands through conquest on the basis of investment and trade. As in the earlier period of Spanish expansion, jurists of the period justified these adventures on the basis of a natural right to trade and exchange commodities on the ground that all people did not have access to the same types of resources in their lands. [1] In terms of power, it was easier to conquer lands with plenty of resources than to carry out equal exchanges; the former would ensure unfettered access. When conquest was accomplished, international law was fashioned in such a manner as to retain control over the subject people of the colonies. They were denied personality in international law so that they could not formally articulate any rights on the basis of an artificial standard of civilization that was purportedly enjoyed only by the European states.[2] The standard of civilization was employed as a shifting standard that enabled the imperial powers to decide when a foreign people they had colonized were entitled to be released from imperial control.[3]

[1] As Suarez and Vittoria did in the earlier stage of Spanish expansion in Latin America, Grotius and other writers used trade and investment as the reasons for colonial expansion of the Dutch and the English into Africa and Asia. See Anthony Pagden, *The Burdens of Empire* (CUP 2015). Antony Anghie, *Imperialism, Sovereignty and the Making of International Law* (CUP 2007) 182.

[2] Gerrit W Gong, *The Standard of Civilization in International Society* (OUP 1984).

[3] Religion played a role. The local religions were decried. Colonialism had an evangelizing mission to ensure the spread of Christianity. The collision between local habits and those of the West was an ever-present factor with the British embarking on a policy of 'Westernizing' the colonies. For the important role of Macaulay in achieving this in India, see Zareer Masani, *Macaulay: Britain's Liberal Imperialist* (The Bodley Head 2013).

Muthucumaraswamy Sornarajah, *The Battle Continues* In: *The Battle for International Law: South-North Perspectives on the Decolonization Era*. Edited by: Jochen von Bernstorff and Philipp Dann, Oxford University Press (2019).
DOI: 10.1093/oso/9780198849636.003.0008

It also enabled the construction of a subject people on the basis of a false theory of civilization so that they could be ruled over, evangelized, and plundered. The notion of standards of civilization was a mythical creation. Clearly China and India had older civilizations than any European state. History did not matter as the standard of civilization could be manipulated in order that criteria absent in other civilizations could be added so that the other would not qualify as civilized. It was the creation of a myth that was maintained by power. There are many accounts of myth creation to subjugate people internationally as well as domestically and the use of the law to do so is recounted in the literature.[4]

Lands of aboriginal people were forcibly occupied on the ground that they were *terra nullius* that could be settled by other people as no formal administration existed in these lands. Australia was colonized on this basis and the common law introduced to govern the settlements. It took many years for white Australians to accept that Australia belonged to its aboriginal people before the coming of the white man and that it was conquered from them. It was not empty land that was occupied, as the story of the introduction of the common law implied.[5] The use of force was legitimized to ensure such control. Mutinies were suppressed callously without any accountability for atrocities as the law permitted such suppression.[6] Resources were transported to fuel the industrialization[7] of the European states without hindrance. The finished products were sold in the captive markets of the colonies, with the existing competition for such goods crushed and the emergence of new markets by local entrepreneurs eliminated. The legal systems of the colonies were altered so as to accommodate the interests of the imperial powers and their citizens, enabling the change in existing agricultural production, supplanting it with new crops such as tea, coffee, and rubber, which had global markets. [8] All these good things for the empire would be over with the success of the struggle of the colonial people for self-determination, if it were to take its natural course. That it was not allowed to do so is the contention that is made here.

[4] For example, Lauren A Benton and Lisa Ford, *Rage for Order: The British Empire and the Origins of International Law, 1800-1850* (Harvard University Press 2016). The work unravels the manner in which the law, both international and domestic, was redesigned by the imperial power to suit its interests.

[5] The Australian High Court in *Mabo v Queensland* recognized the prior right of the aboriginals to the land and reversed the view that Australia was planted and not conquered.

[6] Biswamoy Pati (ed), *The Great Rebellion of 1857 in India: Exploring Transgressions Contests and Diversities* (1st edn, Routledge 2010) deals with the atrocities that attended the suppression of the Indian Mutiny of 1857 and non-accountability for the atrocities.

[7] Benton and Ford (n 4).

[8] For colonial enterprise in the cotton trade, see Sven Beckert, *Empire of Cotton: A Global History* (Vintage 2015).

1. The principle of self-determination

The principle of self-determination was a change in international law of major proportions.[9] It dismantled an imperial order involving European dominance, resulting in the freedom of peoples in Africa and Asia. This period of change began with the independence of India in 1947 and moved through the 1950s and the early part of the 1960s, ensuring the dissolution of empire and the creation of new states from the old colonies. Self-determination quickly achieved the status of a *ius cogens* norm making colonialism totally unacceptable and hastening the process of decolonization.[10] Freedom became a valued possession, but the Afro-Asian people could not achieve it in any true sense as their economies were still controlled by the multinational corporations (MNCs) of the former imperial states. The original purpose of colonialism—the tying up the resources and markets of the colonies—continued. As a result, the former colonies sought to assert economic control through the formulation of principles that came to be collectively contained in the New International Economic Order (NIEO). The NIEO contained collectively a body of norms that had been articulated by the former colonies, now formed into a loose group of non-aligned countries.[11] One major facet of the NIEO was the assertion of permanent sovereignty over natural resources, a doctrine that had been independently asserted in the Declaration on Permanent Sovereignty over Natural Resources in 1964. Its aim was to ensure that control over the exploitation of natural resources, vital to the economies of the newly independent countries, were recovered by them. It involved the rearrangement of existing structures of exploitation, mainly based on concession agreements made in the past, so that state entities established for the purpose of controlling the natural resources sectors, could recover control over the exploitation of natural resources. The NIEO also contained propositions affecting trade, such as the payment of just prices for commodities and resources sold by the developing countries and preferential access to the markets of developed countries.

But, these efforts were strenuously resisted by the developed states. Most importantly, the international lawyers of the developed states were in the forefront in opposing the force of the norms that were being proposed by the developing countries. These international lawyers, 'highly qualified publicists', no doubt, acted as agents of MNCs ensuring that the new norms did not displace the control these

[9] On the development of the principles of self-determination in international law, see Antonio Cassese, *Self-Determination of Peoples: A Legal Reappraisal* (CUP 1995). The principle quickly came to be recognized as a *ius cogens* principle of international law and led to the independence of many of the colonial states of Africa and Asia.

[10] Resolution 1514(XV) on the Granting of Independence to Colonial Countries and Peoples was adopted in 1960 by eighty-nine votes to none against, with nine abstentions. The 1966 Covenants on Human Rights contain identical statements on self-determination.

[11] This group, in the context of the United Nations (UN), came to be known as the Group of 77, as it originally consisted of 77 countries. Its number increased as new independent states joined the UN.

corporations exercised over the exploitation of the resources of the former colonial states. They were intent on ensuring that the structure of the economic order was not changed despite the fact that the colonies had achieved independence. What occurred was that the MNCs were always a source of power in international relations. Yet, they were not recognized in international law, where they had no personality as actors with responsibilities.[12] They asserted private power both directly and indirectly through their states. As a result, they were able to construct normative systems to ensure that their power to form laws favourable to their continued dominance in international relations continued. In this sense, empire came to be recreated. Those with power ensured that the system survived albeit in an altered way. Though self-determination ensured a fundamental change in ensuring the equality of all peoples, its promise of economic equality was never achieved. It was replaced by an alternative system that continued the stranglehold that the former imperial powers had prior to decolonization.

2. The battle continues

Although colonialism was ended and new independent states were brought into existence, it did not mean that the power equations within international life changed; rather, the personnel in the battle may have been replaced, and new actors and new institutions may have come onto the scene. But, essentially, the purpose of ensuring dominance, which was the purpose that existed during colonial rule, continues unabated. The lines along which this dominance continued were defined in the immediate post-colonial period, the ten years after the independence of India—the first major state to achieve independence in 1947. This decade and the one succeeding it are crucial in the demarcation of the battle lines that came into being - one seeking new ways of conserving the dominance of colonial times, the other seeking to advance normative structures that would lead to a more just and equal situation among states. The latter are the overtly articulated premise on which the international society is constructed, as justice, equality, and self-determination are fundamental principles and objectives of the United Nations (UN) system. Yet, those who were responsible for the creation of the system—principally the leading states of the world that won the Second World War—also could be credited with supporting the construction of a parallel, iniquitous system designed to profit MNCs. This is due to the obvious nature and extent of the political power that the

[12] A recent British textbook states: 'The question of the international personality of the transnational corporations remains an open one', Malcolm N Shaw, *International Law* (7th edn, CUP 2014) 182. It has been easier for writers on international relations to recognize the extent of the power of MNCs in shaping legal regimes. Claire Cutler, 'Private International Regimes and Interfirm Cooperation' in Rodney Bruce Hall and Thomas J Biersteker (eds), *The Emergence of Private Authority in Global Governance* (CUP 2002).

MNCs wield in the domestic politics of their home states. What they desired was the perversion of the openly stated objectives of the UN Charter so that, under its cover, they could profit through the continuation of rules that perpetuate economic dominance. As such dominance was in the interests of the developed states, they became willing tools, participating in the project for the creation of an alternative system that continued dominance over the newly independent states.

A parallel is provided by what was taking place within American law. The tussle for equality for the Afro-American resulted in the landmark decision of *Brown v Board of Education* (1954).[13] It is touted as the leading case in American Constitutional Law—it shattered the fiction of separate but equal treatment as the formula of black equality, and ensured true equality through the access of black children to schooling and black people to every public facility as equals of the white citizens. It led to an affirmative action programme. However, many black scholars point to the hollowness in the result in that, despite the lip-service that was paid to equality through the vesting of rights, the status quo between the whites and blacks in terms of economic power and the quality of life has largely remained unchanged. Seeming changes in the law do not truly bring about changes to the status quo. The status quo could be preserved through other means. Dominant interests always ensure that, despite apparently monumental changes to the law, the pre-existing system of dominance continues. It was similar in the context of international law. The thrust of this chapter is to show that decolonization in the fifties did bring about the freedom of Africa and Asia, but that freedom did not affect the economic status quo to any significant extent. There were other ways of ensuring dominance that replaced the more direct way of colonialism.

3. Decolonization and its effects on international law

This chapter starts by recalling the colonial period, during which there was no need to institute any rules on the protection of foreign private property. The law of the imperial power applied to the colony. Whatever law on property, contract, or commercial relations that had existed in the colony was replaced with the law of the imperial power.[14] If communal property had existed among the natives, this was displaced by individual ownership, which was so necessary for the carrying out of commercial activities. The purpose of colonialism (ie, the exploitation of resources, the transactions in commodities)—particularly finished products made with the natural resources of the colonies from the imperial state in the colonial market and the provision of services—required that a capitalist market economy

[13] *Brown v Board of Education of Topeka* 347 US 483 (1954)

[14] This is studied in Lauren A Benton, *Law and Colonial Cultures: Legal Regimes in World History, 1400–1900* (CUP 2002).

be instituted in the colonies so that the imperial power could maximize the advantages of the colonial situation.

The transformation of the property structures of the colonial states has been recounted in literature,[15] both old and new. These transformations largely continue in the legal systems of the former colonial states. To this extent, there is already a preservation of a system conducive to the protection of whatever property relationships are created anew by the foreign investors of the metropolitan states. It will extend into the future of these independent states, which will retain the colonial legal structures. No former colony has sought to displace these systems of commercial law. Even where they change them, they will do so in reliance of changes that take place in the systems of the imperial states.[16] There is a near-slavish need among the legal elite to continue the tradition of the imperial law in the belief that stability needs such continuation. It ensures the preservation of the interests of the elite classes. The basic structure of the imperial law has not been changed. This ensures the possibility of a system to protect continuing investment by the former imperial powers.

But, in the sphere of foreign investment laws, changes were made by the newly independent states as it was regarded as an area that needed to be controlled in order to ensure that economic sovereignty was recovered from imperial companies. Imperial companies dominated sectors, particularly the planation and natural resources sectors, which were vital to the economy. The ending of this dominance was necessary to recover control over the economy. The imperial system had ensured that the colonial economies served the needs of the imperial state. They were either plantation economies like Ceylon (now Sri Lanka), producing tea or natural resources economies, like Zambia producing copper. Though many of the colonies did effect changes to existing investments made by companies of the former colonial powers through nationalization, it is the making of fresh investments that were in need of protection. Such fresh investments did flow into the former colonies with which companies had familiarity due to historical and other links. It was the protection of such new investments and other investments seeking natural resources and markets that were in need of protection. The urgency was to create a new system of protection that used new techniques of public international law to serve the interests of private power of MNCs. This is what enables the claim, that in this, as in many other spheres of international law,[17] the interests of colonial

[15] See ibid.

[16] Indian and Asian lawyers exhibit their ready familiarity with legal developments in England and their acquaintance with English judges in the most carping way still. This network ensures the success of the dependency and continuation of the imperial system in independent states.

[17] There were other spheres in which the interests of the former imperial powers were preserved through new formulations of international law rules. For example, the right of minority and tribal groups to secession from the newly independent states were denied in the interest of preserving the illogical borders drawn by the imperial powers so that the states they created could remain intact. This ensured that resource rich regions of these states—like Biafra in Nigeria or Katanga in the Congo—did not break away to form new states.

powers were reflected in the new post-colonial systems that were created. These new systems conserve or create rules that enabled the continuance of power that the imperial powers had lost. The creation of a system to conserve virtually imperial powers over resources and markets is a situation that the former imperial powers and their MNCs sought to achieve. The extent of its success is measured in the following sections.

This paper is not concerned with the modern period where bilateral investment treaties (BITs) protect foreign investments made by MNCs through a compulsory arbitration of investment disputes. This came at a later stage, the first rudimentary investment treaty being made in 1959 and the first arbitration award recognizing compulsory jurisdiction being decided in 1991. The system of investment treaties concretized a system of investment protection that had been made earlier. The period that is studied here is the immediate decolonization period between 1947 and around 1974 when the NIEO norms came to be firmly articulated. The norms that emerged during this period mark the battle lines between the two group of states: the former imperial states and the newly independent states. There could be other descriptions of these states. The former imperial states were rich as a result to a large extent because of the one-way flow of wealth into them from the colonies. Consequently, the newly independent states were poor. The rich group of states were the capital exporting states, keen on having their capital exported to assure supplies of raw materials, and ensure flows of profits under conditions in which such foreign investments enjoy stability and protection. The poor states were the capital importing states, which hoped that flows of foreign investment would lift them out of poverty. The contention here is that within this period of a few years, the former imperial powers, along with the MNCs, had worked out a system that enabled the continuation of imperial control over much-needed natural resources as well as control over markets of their erstwhile colonies, making decolonization a myth so that the battle again erupted, this time pitching the developing states against the emergence of these new structures.[18]

II. Glimpses of past patterns

The crucial first step in the making of an investment in a foreign state is to make a contract with a party in the host state. If that party is a private party, the domestic

[18] The charge is here made that there was concerted action by the former imperial states, MNCs, international law scholars, and arbitrators in the construction of this system. A study of an early dispute like the Anglo-Iranian Oil Company dispute which went before the ICJ and was litigated elsewhere provides an example of such collaboration. The idea that the contract between the oil company and Iran amounted to an instrument akin to a treaty was stated in the arguments in the case. There was litigation before the courts of Aden seizing oil exported from Iran on the ground that it was illegally expropriated. The role of Hersch Lauterpacht in the case is detailed in Elihu Lauterpacht, *The Life of Sir Hersch Lauterpacht* (CUP 2010) 349–53.

law of the host state would usually govern the transaction. The domestic law of the host state has the most dominant ties with the process of the contract. If the contract is with an entity of the state, as contracts in the plantation or natural resources sector usually are, it would be no different, as the link between the state and the contract are stronger.[19] The presence of the state entity in the transaction makes the transaction inherently unstable from the point of view of the risk of the state interfering with the working of the contract, for a variety of reasons involving the public interest as well the need to rescue the state entity from contractual difficulty, should such difficulty arise. There is considerable political and economic risk involved in the foreign investment transaction. Its long duration, the public interest elements involved in it, and possibilities of changes in external circumstances make the foreign investment contract very unstable.[20]

The situation would seldom have arisen in imperial times, because the imperial state would have ensured that the legal conditions were favourable to foreign investment. But while colonialism had ended, the need of the former imperial powers for natural resources continued. A plan was necessary to ensure that supplies were safe and that the original investment had long-term stability. The need now was to ensure that, where the situation of risk does arise, the foreign investor is ensured remedies that would restore him to the position prior to the dispute, usually through access to damages. The fact that damages would have to be paid will also act as a deterrence against government interference with the contract. Domestic courts cannot be expected to provide relief under these circumstances. For one thing, there is the possibility of bias. The other is that if the state interference was through legislation, as it would usually be, there is little that the domestic court could do.[21] Alternatives had to be devised. The effort at upgrading the contract of foreign investment into public international law was a project that was begun early in the decolonization period. Such a scheme would put the foreign investment contract beyond the sovereign reach of the host state. The working out of this scheme is associated with the writings of scholars who had begun thinking about the protection of foreign investment in the 1930s along with the rise of large MNCs taking business out of their states into other lands.[22] The major problem were the positivist theories of international law. These theories ensured that personality in inter national law was confined to states and states alone. International law was thought of as a law between states. The protection of the foreign investor was to be achieved

[19] Upon nationalizations, newly independent states create state corporations in which they vested the task of running the sector. The presence of the state entity makes the transaction materially different from the private transaction.

[20] The risks to foreign investment are discussed in Muthucumaraswamy Sornarajah, *The International Law on Foreign Investment* (4th edn, CUP 2017) 88–98 (hereafter Sornarajah, *Foreign Investment*).

[21] Review of such legislation is illusory in most systems. The legislature being sovereign, there is little that courts could do.

[22] In a sense, the British and Dutch East India Companies were MNCs, but they operated within the colonial context.

only obliquely through the rules of diplomatic protection, with the state mediately protecting the interests of the injured foreign investor through the notion that the unremedied injury caused to him was, in effect, an injury caused to the state. This system of mediate injuries and state responsibility for such injuries provided the system of investment protection in earlier phases of international law.[23] Vattel and other institutional writers had referred to the existence of the system of diplomatic protection, which nicely got over the problem of the absence of personality in the MNC. What was even nicer was that not only did the MNC receive protection in international law through this indirect manner, but also it avoided any responsibility as it had no personality in international law. The British East India Company fought wars, conquered states, killed people, and plundered riches without any responsibility in terms of either domestic law or international law.[24] It was a good position to hold. The MNC could cause injury to the interests of the host state and its people. There was no avenue of redress except at domestic law, which would not be able to provide adequate remedies to redress the extent of the injuries caused.[25] There was no way of pursuing an international remedy against the MNC as no mechanism existed to do so.

Yet, the system was insufficient from the point of view of direct protection of the foreign investment and the investor. The need was to ensure that the MNC was protected without upsetting existing theories of responsibility as the direct conferment of personality would make the MNC a bearer of responsibilities and may also involve responsibility of the home state on the basis of attributability principles based on agency. So, there was a scurrying to find a basis on which the foreign investment contracts made by MNCs could be protected. It can be seen that this was a game of power. The MNC, obviously an agent of power in itself, and its home state were intent on the creation of a new international law under which the corporation could sue the home state, but yet avoid any responsibility for any damage to the home state interests. The strategy should also protect the home state, which could interfere to protect the MNC without incurring any responsibility for the conduct of the corporation within the home state on the basis of agency. The case for such agency was cogent as the MNC repatriated profits home, was taxed by the home state, and general benefits arose for the home state as a result of the outward flow of foreign investments. The avoiding of home state responsibility, despite the need and the existence of good reasons for it, was part of the strategy being created. Simply put, if the MNC did not have personality in international law, it could not

[23] *Panvezys-Saldutiskis Railway Case* (1939) PCIJ Series A/B No 76 at 16, the PCIJ explained the rule of mediate injuries.

[24] For an interesting study of the British East India Company, see Tirthankar Roy, *The East India Company: The World's Most Powerful Corporation* (Penguin 2012).

[25] The Bhopal Catastrophe is an example. The domestic courts could not provide an adequate remedy in the light of the extensive damage caused to thousands of lives. There was no international remedy. Suing the corporation before its home state courts failed.

have responsibility for damages nor inculpate its home state on the basis of any theory of attributability of responsibility like agency. But, a way had to be found in order to enable the corporation to pursue means of protection of its assets and interests.

As early as the 1930s, Verdross, for example, suggested that the lack of personality in the MNC could be dealt with through the supplying of the requisite personality for any specific transaction by the state that deals with the MNC.[26] The situation was analogized to minor's contracts where the deficiency in the minor was supplied or corrected by the major dealing with him. Another technique suggested was that the contract should contain clauses that put the sovereign state and the MNC on the same footing on the ground that this was essential for the contract to function. Such a view would demand that the contract be treated as something akin to a treaty—at least a quasi-treaty—that would implicate international law obligations towards the foreign investor.

In terms of practice, the genesis of the notion of internationalizing an investment contract can be seen in an award made in the *Lena Goldfields Arbitration*.[27] The arbitral tribunal that decided the dispute did not have lawyers on it; nevertheless, it demonstrated the thinking of the times as to the need to consider the host state responsible. The dispute resembles a foreign investment situation where foreigners had invested in a gold mine in Russia. The mining activity ceased after the Russian Revolution, the mine being now taken over by the Communist government. There was a provision for arbitration and the foreigners sought arbitration against the Russian government, who predictably did not turn up. But, the arbitrators, none of whom were lawyers, proceeded to make an award against the Russian state. Later writers have used the case to read in theories the arbitrators may not have intended. The reports of the award are scant, the most authoritative of them a short report in the London Times. Nussbaum and Veeder have written articles on the case,[28] and these later writings seek to rationalize the case in accordance with developments that had taken place after the case. It is thus safer not to draw conclusions from the *Lena Goldfields Arbitration*.

The arguments presented by Hersch Lauterpacht as UK counsel to the International Court of Justice in the *Anglo-Iranian Case*[29] are more relevant.

[26] Alfred Verdross, 'Quasi-International Agreements and International Economic Transactions' (1964) 18 The Yearbook of World Affairs 230. Verdross had written on the theme much earlier in German. He claimed to be the initiator of the theory. But, the theory is associated with other leading names such as Lord McNair and Hersch Lauterpacht. There were 'highly qualified publicists', mercenaries of the law, willingly promoting this project of perfidy.

[27] *Lena Goldfields Limited v USSR* (1930).

[28] Arthur Nussbaum, 'Arbitration Between the Lena Goldfields Ltd. and the Soviet Government' (1950) 36 Cornell Law Review 31; VV Veeder, 'The *Lena Goldfields Arbitration*: The Historical Roots of Three Ideas' (1998) 47 International and Comparative Law Quarterly 747. The *Schufeldt Claim* made in 1930 is in close support in finding a breach of contract an illegality in terms of a possible external law. Though the law of Guatamala was applied, it was stated that that law is the same as in other states. So, what was probably hinted at is a general principle of law.

[29] Anglo-Iranian Oil Co. Case (*United Kingdom v Iran*) [1952] ICJ Rep 93 [23].

Contrary to his standing as an early participant in the human rights discourse in international law, Hersch Lauterpacht, who appeared for the UK, made an argument that is favourable to the interests of the Anglo-Iranian Oil Company, the predecessor of British Petroleum. The argument was that the concession agreement the British company had made with Iran had a status in international law as it was akin to a treaty. The effort at assimilation of the foreign investment contract to a treaty having status in international law was present in the thinking of influential international lawyers of the time. They had set the stage for thinking that was to come later. The strategy that was initiated was to ensure that the contract that was made by the foreign investor had an external base that was protected by external mechanisms such as arbitration conducted in accordance with an external law as the substantive and procedural law of the arbitration. The process of establishing this mechanism is described in Section III. The gathering of opposition to the system is described in the section that follows.

III. The Western battle lines

As indicated in Section II, a rudimentary framework for a strategy of foreign investment was worked out as colonialism was being dismantled. The making of this law was an endeavor in which the minds of the best international lawyers of the time participated. The project was undertaken to benefit the MNCs that operated largely in the vital petroleum industry. The sources employed were the low-order sources of international law—what are described as subsidiary sources of international law in Article 38(2) of the Statute of the International Court of Justice—'the decisions of judicial tribunals and the writings of "highly qualified" publicists'. They were sources that were themselves private in that they depended on the prejudices of individuals and were amenable to the service of the private power of MNCs. No doubt, the home states of these corporations, the former colonial powers, lent vigorous support to the formation of the law but there is no direct participation by them in the endeavor.[30] What is recorded are the hallmarks of the situation brought about and the reasoning behind them. They are largely in the form of a series of arbitrations that arose in the 1950s during the period of decolonization and the writings of 'highly qualified' publicists writing in support of these arbitral awards. The chain of events consists of a succession of such arbitral awards.

[30] This may be argued. The better view may be that governments were hand in glove with MNCs in constructing this law. The arguments made in *Anglo-Iranian Oil Co v Iran* by Lauterpacht were made on behalf of the British Government. The role of Hersch Lauterpacht in the case is to be found in the biography written by his son Elihu Lauterpacht (Lauterpacht (n 18)). The UK memorandum prepared by Lauterpacht is in Hersch Lauterpacht, *International Law Collected Papers Vol. 4: The Law of Peace* (Elihu Lauterpacht ed, CUP 1978) 23.

Three awards, made in fairly quick succession, have dominated subsequent thinking.[31] They accept that the law that would generally apply to disputes arising from petroleum contract would be the law of the host state. Indeed, existing authorities on the point refer such disputes to the host law. The tribunals accepted this view but proceeded to argue that the law of the Middle Eastern states was not sophisticated enough to deal with complex contracts like petroleum contracts. The assumption was that the law of the nomadic tribes of this region may be good enough for dealing with the sale of camels or tents but they lacked the wherewithal to deal with sophisticated contracts of long duration. There is nothing to suggest that European law of the time was any better. The contemporary texts on English law on contracts deal with the buying and selling of simple household goods. The reasoning was simply based on racial superiority. Once this stage was reached, the second stage was to argue that the rules could be culled from the major European systems of law. There is nothing to justify such a procedure. It was chosen simply because the arbitrators were European and were familiar with European law.

These awards are the basis of what has come to be known as the theory of the internationalization of foreign investment contracts. Under the more extreme version of the theory, a foreign investment contract ceases to be subject to the domestic law of the host state *ipso facto*.[32] In the moderate version, the effect of internationalization takes place when the contract contains clauses such as a stabilization clause, a choice of law clause, and an arbitration clause. These clauses are said to indicate the intention of the parties to externalize the base of the contract. This process of internationalization is justified on the policy ground that foreign investors will be reluctant to make investments unless the investments are safeguarded from the legislative and administrative processes that could change the original terms of entry of the investment. Local courts will not be sufficient as they are either biased or will not be able to countermand the wishes of the other branches of government for constitutional reasons. The ultimate rationale is that the theory is needed to ensure the economic development of the poorer host states because of the benefits such investment flows bring them. So, there is a hearkening back to an altruistic reason for the theory, which ensures that a host state through a contract ties its mineral wealth or other sectors to a foreign MNC. As in the case of the standard of civilization, the altruistic motive of achieving the economic development of the people of the former colonies becomes the rationale for the new system. This system enables the continuous flow of resources to the home state of the MNCs, as in the days of colonialism.

[31] The awards were *The Abu Dhabi Arbitration* (1951) 18 ILR 144; *The Qatar Arbitration* (1955) 20 ILR 534; *The Aramco Arbitration* (1958) 27 ILR 117. These awards have been described in Sornarajah, *Foreign Investment* (n 20) 340–45.

[32] *The Sapphire Arbitration* (1953) 35 ILR 136 where the existence of an international arbitration clause was held to exclude the law of the host state.

If this rationale was honest—that the betterment of these people should be achieved—the more just solution would have been to repay what was taken from them in the past. The transportation of the mineral resources at hardly any cost back to the metropolitan states fuelled the industrial progress of the imperial states. There is a duty to transfer some of the wealth to the people who were denied the profits from their own resources. Instead, what we have now is a theory that continues the tying down of these resources in contracts that clearly benefitted the foreign MNC and its home state. The contracts were of long duration; some extended to sixty years.[33] There was no semblance of justice in the situation that emerged.

Of greater importance is the nature of the resistance to the formation of this theory. It is this resistance that has received less attention for the obvious reason that the mainstream writers on international law (among them, the so-called 'highly qualified' publicists) acted as mercenary purveyors of the internationalization theory, which cannot be reconciled with basic concepts of existing international law. That system does not accommodate, at least at the time of the formation of the doctrine, a contract made by a non-state actor to be within the purview of international law. Contortions had to be engaged in to accommodate this result. As indicated earlier, Verdroß argued that the absent personality in the MNC could be supplied by the state, very much as in the making of contracts with minors where deficiency in capacity can be made up by the other party's knowledge and consent to treat the minor as having capacity.[34] It is a far fetched idea. Others tried to assimilate the contract to a treaty or at least a quasi-treaty so that international law could apply to it. These writers at least recognized the theoretical difficulties attending the project. However, with the passage of time, these difficulties were ignored and the theory as stated as fact due to a stream of later awards accepting and applying the theory.

The formation of the internationalization theory has been adequately discussed in the literature.[35] There is unanimity as to the manner of its origins as well as the circumstances that trigger off its application. There may be incidental variations but the original manner in which internationalization has been conceived

[33] The oil concession contract involved in *Aminoil v Kuwait* (1982) 21 ILM 976 was to last for sixty years. The highpoint of the theory was in *Texaco v Libya* (1977) 53 ILR 389. The theory was used in the other two Libyan cases: *BP v Libya* and *Liamco v Libya*. There are later cases: *Revere Copper and Brass Inc v Overseas Private Investment Corp (OPIC)* (Award, 1978) 56 ILR 258; *AGIP SpA v Govt of the Peoples Republic of Congo* (Award, 1979), (1982) 21 ILM 726 [88]; *Elf Aquitaine Iran v National Iranian Oil Company (NIOC)* (1986) 11 *YbCA* 97. Peter Cameron, *International Energy Investment Law: The Pursuit of Stability* (OUP 2010) would have it that the use of the theory is pervasive in the petroleum field.

[34] Verdross (n 26).

[35] Ivar Alvik, *Contracting with Sovereignty: State Contracts and International Arbitration* (Hart 2011); Prosper Weil, 'Problèmes relatifs aux contrats passés entre un État et un particulier' (1969) 128 Recueil des Cours de l'Académie de Droit International de La Haye 98. Jean Ho, 'Internationalisation and State contracts: are State contracts the future or the past?' in CL Lim (ed), *Alternative Visions of the International Law on Foreign Investment: Essays in honour of Muthucumaraswamy Sornarajah* (CUP 2016). Jean Ho, *State Responsibility for Breaches of Investment Contracts* (CUP 2018).

has continued to the present without much change. The only change, perhaps, is with the popularity of treaty-based arbitration, where the ideas contained in internationalization and facets of it have been reinforced.[36] That is a later development not addressed here. The paucity of arbitrations that supported internationalization resulted in a large amount of writing affirming the theory. The belief was that repetition will lead to the emergence of an affirmative rule relating to internationalization. The project was one that the leading lawyers of the times engaged in probably because the making of the law was profitable to them as well as to the MNCs and the states they advised. It was evident that they acted for the companies and states that were bent on creating such law. Thus, the pattern was laid in which scholarship was bent to achieve purely mercenary purposes making law that protected the interests of the MNCs. The great names of academic international law had engaged in this endeavour, thus calling into question the sanctity that attaches to scholarship.[37] There was a duality in their approach. As already pointed out, MNCs were hidden from liability by the veil that colonial international law drew over corporations in that they did not have personality in international law. This fiction was maintained despite the fact that the British and Dutch East India Companies were conquering Asian peoples and fighting wars against them. These two companies were indistinct from the governments of their home states as the leading politicians of the European states were shareholders of these companies. So, they were permitted untrammelled exercise of power without any hindrance through the law by a simple fiction that only states had personality in international law. Yet, now, the argument was that they could acquire rights against states. What is more, a mechanism was created for the enforcement of those rights through international arbitration; the paradox was never explained. It was a tradition that continued in developing the law under investment treaties, a succeeding phase in the development. The developing countries fought vigorously to resist the development of the theory.

Importantly, internationalization theory was developed on the basis of the low order sources of international law. They depend on the subjective choice of rules of European systems of international law by arbitrators who sat to settle oil disputes[38]

[36] The role of umbrella clauses in investment treaties has been to reinforce the internationalization theory.

[37] The leading articles in the area are revealing. Duncan McNair, 'The General Principles of International Law Recognized by Civilized Nations' (1957) 33 British Year Book of International Law 1 [note it seems to me that it would be better to keep the comma, as it frames the bibliographic details together with the comma after 'McNair', distinguishing it from the text, M.M.] linked the external law applied in the three arbitrations involving oil to a source of international law. See also Robert Y Jennings, 'State Contracts in International Law' (1961) 37 British Yearbook of International Law 156; Hans Wehberg, 'Pacta Sunt Servanda' (1959) 53 American Journal of International Law 775 linked the Kelsenian grundnorm to the process of internationalization. See also Weil (n 36).

[38] They were largely distinguished English and European lawyers (eg, Dupuy in *Texaco*, Lagegren in *BP*, Asquith in *Abu Dhabi)* with the exception of Mahmassani, who was sole arbitrator in *Liamco v Libya*.

and the commentaries on those awards, written often by those who were involved in the process of those arbitrations. The proposition that was chosen as a general principle was the sanctity of contracts, despite the fact that major legal systems of the world had begun to move away from sanctity of contracts. Leading lawyers gave the principle respectability in terms of international law by tying it with the international law principle, *pacta sunt servanda*,[39] given even higher status by Kelsen, who identified it as the Grundnorm of international law. There was a definite project here as a conglomeration of European, American, and English international lawyers moved simultaneously to lend their weight to the advancement of an idea that had no theoretical basis within international law. International law had hitherto stressed the primacy and exclusivity of domestic law.[40]

The acme of the development was to come with the award of Professor Dupuy in *Texaco v Libya*.[41] The distinguished French academic lawyer spilt much ink to stabilize the doctrine of internationalization in an uncontested award. There was a wholesale repudiation of the arguments made against internationalization and a concrete affirmation of the doctrine. It was a gratuitous performance. Every argument against internationalization was refuted in the award. Dupuy regarded the doctrine of permanent sovereignty over natural resources as *lex ferenda* couched in UN General Assembly (UNGA) resolutions that did not have law creating effect in terms of the UN Charter. He rejected the view long put forward by developing countries that foreign investment contracts are a species of administrative contracts similar to the *contrat administratif* of French law and hence defeasible in the public interest on the ground that the *contrat administratif* was unique to French law. Interestingly, the Western international lawyers have now seen it to their advantage to treat the foreign investment process as a public law process simply because the change of events favours such an argument.[42] Professor Dupuy did a hatchet job on the arguments that developing countries had put forward against the notion of internationalization of foreign investment contracts. Issuing a unilateral award as the sole arbitrator appointed by the claimant company Texaco, he anticipated all the arguments that a developing country could have made. On the basis of the claims they were then making through the UNGA Resolutions and earlier arbitral awards, he anticipated them, and spent much intellectual energy in rejecting them. In this, he merely reflected attitudes of the larger number of European international lawyers before and after him in being universally adverse to the views of the developing countries. It was a continuation of the project to

[39] Wehberg (n 37).

[40] *Serbian Loans Case* (1929) PCIL Series A no 20.

[41] *Texaco Overseas Petroleum Co. v Libya* (1978) 17 ILM 1.

[42] See Stephan Schill, *International Investment Law and Comparative Public Law* (OUP 2010). It is now not unknown for doctrines of single systems like the proportionality theory of German law to be advanced as relevant to investment disputes.

ensure that the structures of extractive colonialism were maintained in a different way, despite that colonialism itself had ceased to be.

What needs to be stressed is that, as colonialism came to be dismantled and the former colonies that supplied natural resources were able to control the flow of these resources, the former imperial powers were intent on devising methods of ensuring that their control did not diminish despite that they had had to relinquish political power in these newly independent states. They achieved this through several means. One was through elite formation in the developing states so that a class of persons similar to thinking as the former colonial rulers replaced them in the colonies and continued to be favourable to the interests of the former colonial powers. But, more meaningful was the domination through the structures of the law. The construction of the doctrine of internationalization enabled extractive colonialism to continue.

IV. The other battle line

Mainstream international lawyers ignore the principle of self-determination, or look upon it as of little significance. It is also a strategy to turn a Nelsonian eye or to be blind to the existence of opposition in the hope that it would go away. But the principle of self-determination has a staying power of its own and is seen as emerging into significance through persistent resistance to the mainstream of international law that was built through deceit. This alternative set of norms were articulated largely through a series of UNGA Resolutions made at the behest of the newly independent states of the world. They begin along with the anti-colonial movement. The movement in terms of international law is expressed through the principle of self-determination that all people are entitled to be free from domination by others. It is the triumph of that principle that led to the emancipation of the colonial world.

Every major authority regards self-determination as a defining moment that reordered the world from a system that was mired in the exploitation of the peoples of Africa and Asia by those of Europe. Because of the revolutionary change it effected to the existing international legal order, the principle of self-determination is regarded as a *ius cogens* principle of international law.

The principle had a necessary corollary. Recognizing that political independence was meaningless unless the newly independent states had economic independence as well, the leaders of these newly independent states argued for a principle of economic self-determination. That principle came to be articulated as early as 1951 as the Afro-Asian states began to achieve independence.[43] It became

[43] MS Rajan, *The Doctrine of Permanent Sovereignty over Natural Resources* (1982) traces the history of UNGA involvement from a declaration of economic self-determination in 1951.

an annual feature at the meetings of the UNGA. This effort at norm creation was openly made evident.

Coupled with a *ius cogens* principle of self-determination that altered international legal order, the prestige of economic self-determination was immense. It also received support of the large numerical majority of the UNGA. Around the time, fearing that the rule would come to be soon recognized as part of international law, the developed countries fought a rear-guard action. The main emphasis was concentrated on the denial of the capacity of UNGA Resolutions to generate international law. While those supporting this capacity argued that these resolutions indicating the *opinio juris* of a large majority of the states of the world had quasi-legislative authority, others relied on the fact that the UN Charter gave the UNGA only the power to make recommendations. This debate has no traction any longer. The power of the UNGA to generate norms which could lead to hard international law is no longer doubted. Indeed, many areas of international law rely heavily on statements in UNGA resolutions declaring the law on a particular area.[44]

The constant repetition of a norm in an UNGA resolution has a specific significance in the promotion of that norm to the status of international law. Such repetition of economic self-determination is a feature of the period. Added to the fact that the idea has its pedigree in political self-determination, already the organizing principle of the post World War order, the quick promotion of the principle to a legal rule can hardly be doubted.[45] The norm was well on its way to recognition. It became more specific when it took shape as the Resolution on the Permanent Sovereignty over Natural Resources (RPSNR).[46] Colonialism was based on extraction of natural resources from the colonies to fuel the industrial furnaces which produced manufactured goods, again, to be sold in the colonial markets. The control over the extraction of natural resources still remained in the hands of MNCs of the former colonial powers. The RPSNR was intended to end this situation. It was passed overwhelmingly in 1962 and, like the resolutions on economic self-determination, continued to be repeated annually.

The resolution asserted the obvious fact that the natural resources of a state belonged to the state and fell within its sovereignty. The only change was that the resolutions stated that the resources belonged not to the state, but to the people of the state, thus bringing about the idea that the people were sovereign over natural

[44] The law on space clearly commenced with the Resolution on the Peaceful Use of Outer Space, referred to by Bin Cheng as constituting instant customary international law. Many principles of human rights law began life in UNGA resolutions. The prohibition of torture, now regarded as constitution *ius cogens*, was contained in an UNGA resolution.

[45] Sundhya Pahuja, *Decolonising International Law: Development, Economic Growth, and the Politics of Universality* (CUP 2011) 98–120.

[46] Permanent Sovereignty over Natural Resources, UNGA Res 1803 (XVII) (14 December 1962). Georges Abi-Saab, 'Permanent Sovereignty over Natural Resources and Economic Activities' in Mohamed Bedjaoui (ed), *International law: Achievements and Prospects* (Martinus Nijhoff 1991) 600.

resources, with the state acting merely as the trustee of the people when it decided to permit the exploitation of the resources. The implicit theory was that the state could not make decisions as to exploitation in a manner that was not in the interests of the people. There was a notion of trusteeship in the state when it came to the disposal of the natural resources. There was always an inherent public interest element to be satisfied. This was intended to be a constant presence in the consideration of all transactions relating to natural resources. Natural resources could be exploited and transferred so long as the state ensured that it was in the public interest to do so. Where the public interest showed that the exploitation of the resources had ceased to benefit the public, it was incumbent on the state to put an end to the transaction.

The norms relating to permanent sovereignty and the principle in the Article 2(2)(c) of the Charter of Economic Rights and Duties of States and the affirmation of these principles are no different from the basic premise of international law that a territorial sovereign has control over all resources of the state and that the disposal of these resources are always subject to sovereign control. The only difference they sought to make was that sovereignty of the resources vested not in the state, but in the people of the state, so that when the state makes arrangements as to the disposal of these resources they must always be in the public interest. The clear implication of this principle is that any contract that involves natural resources becomes defeasible when the public interest element in the contract changes or becomes extinct. This is the thrust of the developments that took place through the declarations and resolutions associated with the NIEO. The concept of a trusteeship notion in the state was buttressed by the idea of justice that the state, which has natural resources as the primary source of its economic progress, must always act in the public interest. The idea of a people's sovereignty over natural resources is to be widely found in the constitutions of developing states. Compared with this justice interest that concerns the rights of a poverty stricken people emerging from centuries of colonial exploitation, any justice-related argument in favour of the survival of contracts of foreign MNCs will not stand much examination. This will be particularly so if the foreign corporation had been exploiting the resources for a substantial period of time.

The immediate purpose of the articulation of these doctrines is to bring an end to extractive colonialism, which had sought to tie down the exploitation of resources for long periods of time through contracts made with foreign MNCs. Developed countries strenuously opposed these measures. The arguments used traversed a well-worn track. The fact that these norms were couched in an UNGA resolution was said to attest to their weakness as the UNGA under the Charter had only recommendatory powers. These norms were only aspirational and did not have any binding quality, according to this argument. This was an argument that was repeated in the *Texaco Case* by Professor Dupuy. He argued that the norms, contained in the UNGA Resolutions were *de lege ferenda*, and not *lex lata*. At the

time, this view was resisted by the developing country lawyers and those who supported them. They pointed out that there was a quasi-legislative competence in the UNGA as a body consisting of all the member states of the United Nations. Clearly, in many areas of the law, UNGA resolutions were becoming the founding norms of important branches of international law. This particular argument must be considered lost.

Another argument is that the UNGA resolutions were not passed unanimously. The developed states, which were the more powerful states, voted against the resolutions or abstained. The argument was a non-democratic one. It did not matter how many states representing how many people had supported the norms. What mattered was the nature of the states that opposed it. This was an argument that bolstered up colonial international law: power was what counted. But international law had begun veering away from such considerations towards an orientation that was more consistent with justice.

V. Analysing the two competing battle lines

In any event, the merits of the two opposing positions need to be analysed. International lawyers have not been dispassionate in their analysis. They have divided on the basis of the camps to which they belong; this writer is no exception. But, because the writings of the international lawyers of developed states are more plentiful for the simple reason that there are so many different points of access for the publication of their views, there is a need for a forceful statement of the position from the point of view of the developing countries.

Most developed country international lawyers assume that the battles over the NIEO are now passé. One wrote a requiem for the NIEO, and another pronounced it dead. This has been the general tenor if the NIEO is discussed in the literature generated within developed countries. So, while the NIEO was in progress it was derided as not based on proper sources of international law. Now that events have bypassed it, discussion has become futile. This is the mainstream view among developed country lawyers. Obviously, as in the time of the NIEO itself, there continue to be supporters of the norms of the NIEO, although there is a definite project to dismantle the effect it had on international law. There is sometimes not even an acknowledgment that there could have been a slight impact as a result of the collective endeavours of so many states of the world. It is for this reason that the continuing impact of the NIEO needs to be assessed so that the views of the other front could be conserved. This front maintains that the NIEO continues to be significant and may even be making a comeback.

First, it is necessary to state what impact the NIEO had on the competing stance relating to the internationalization of foreign investment contracts. As indicated, the internationalization theory was based on two weak sources of international

law—the string of arbitral awards, some of which were uncontested and the writings of 'highly qualified' publicists, often hired hands rewriting briefs or legal opinions as learned articles in journals that they edited or to which they had ready access. As opposed to these sources, the norms of the NIEO are based on the UNGA resolutions, derided as having only recommendatory value. In terms of modern international law, the comparison in the strength of the sources of law generation are weighted in favour of the norms of the NIEO, for no amount of awards that are subsidiary sources of international law or writings of 'highly qualified' publicists can stand against the solemn and collective pronouncement at the highest international forum of what the law on a particular subject is, by the majority of the states of the international community. In this context, whatever sophistry that can be mustered to favour the theory of internationalization must be regarded as highly suspect.

The fact that favours this analysis is that the developed states themselves acknowledged the weakness of the notion of internationalization by shifting the focus onto an entirely different base of investment protection—BITs. These treaties are almost contemporaneous with the formulation of the theory of internationalization of foreign investment contracts. The first of these treaties was the one concluded between Pakistan and Germany in 1959.[47] Thereafter, the Abs-Shawcross Convention which was adopted by the OECD in 1961 gave a model to these treaties and led to their general proliferation.[48] Though the genesis of the US treaties may have been their earlier FCN treaties, the model of BITs take forms that are similar to the European treaties, except with the rule that American investment should be provided a right of entry and establishment in the host state partner. This wholesale adoption of a new strategy through which the colonial structure could be continued became almost universal.[49] The vigour with which colonial structures continued under this structure is a story that needs to be told. The aim of the treaties, until its failure, was to tie up the extractive sectors to multinational exploitation and ensure that other sectors were brought within the same framework so that everything could continue as if colonialism still existed. The backlash to the system was soon to appear. Once the developed states, including the United States (US), became targets of arbitration under these treaties, they began to take refuge in sovereignty-centred arguments very much along the lines made by the developing world.[50]

[47] Treaty between the Federal Republic of Germany and Pakistan for the Promotion and Protection of Investments (adopted 25 November 1959, in force 28 April 1962) 457 UNTS 23.

[48] Hartley Shawcross, 'The Problems of Foreign Investment in International Law: Speech' (1961) 102 Recueil des Cours de l'Académie de Droit International de La Haye 335 contains an explanation of the Abs-Shawcross Convention.

[49] For constitutional reasons, Brazil kept out of this treaty practice. North Korea was a unique exception.

[50] The briefs of the US and the arguments made for the revival of regulatory expropriation carrying no compensation in *Methanex v United States* (2005) 44 ILM 1345 are very reminiscent of the arguments of the developing world. Canada, Australia, Germany, the US, and the European Union are in

The next few paragraphs recount briefly the story of the battle to its present situation and focus on the revivification of the NIEO, which did not die; rather, it was eclipsed by events. Now that the clouds have cleared, its principles remain as vivid as when formulated. One may even announce its triumph. International law needs this story to be recorded as told by one from the non-Western front.

The NIEO could not have become defunct simply because its investment principles had already been transferred into constitutions of states and their investment laws. Every major resource-producing state believes that the natural resources of the state belongs to its people; this reflects the principle of permanent sovereignty over natural resources. In this sense, there had been an interaction between the norms stated at the international level and those at the domestic level. The domestic law reinforced the norms that developing states espoused as international law. It can well be said that the uniformity in these *constitutional* principles contributed to a *general* principle that natural resources of a state belong to its people. This is a more credible general principle than the principle of sanctity of contracts, on which the internationalization theory relies. This is even more so because it restates essentially a principle of Roman law received into international law and into domestic legal systems that a state has control and jurisdiction over the land up to the skies and underneath.[51] Leading international lawyers have argued that the principle constitutes a peremptory norm.[52]

The states also established mechanisms for the working out of the principle by establishing state corporations and vesting management of the resources in them. They were the ones that became responsible for contracts of foreign investment. In the petroleum area, the Indonesian state corporation Pertamina devised a new type of contract—the production sharing agreement—that ensured control over the exploitation of petroleum resources in the state oil company. The form of contract became universally used, thereby dispelling any notion of internationalization of foreign investment contracts, an idea that arose largely in the context of petroleum disputes involving the old type of concession agreements. The existence of such types of contracts internalizes control over natural resources including disputes that arise from it. While ultimately the contract itself is the result of power balances reflected in the negotiation of its terms, the fact is that new forms of contracts negating any notion of internationalization were coming *en vogue*, emphasizing principles in the NIEO. So, in domestic law, the principles of the NIEO had become firmly entrenched and continue to this day to be the dominant feature.

favour of doing away with investment arbitration which formed the cornerstone of internationalization. The new 'balanced' investment treaties that are made come with many sovereignty centred defences protecting the public interest.

[51] *Cuius est solum, eius est usque ad coelom et ad inferos.*

[52] Ian Brownlie, 'Legal Status of Natural Resources in International Law' (1979) 162 Recueil des Cours de l'Académie de Droit International de La Haye 245, 255.

The principles of the NIEO underwent an eclipse as the contextual circumstances for its advancement changed.[53] The third-world cohesion began to dissipate with the onset of financial crises, the dissolution of the Soviet Union, and the triumph within the US, now the sole hegemon of a neoliberal philosophy, driven by the 'Washington Consensus'. It was in this context that a virulent form of investment protection came about, driven by strong investment treaties administered through a system of arbitration under the institutional systems, for example, the International Convention for the Settlement of Investment Disputes. The number of investment treaties catapulted. On their basis, the investment tribunals decided over 465 cases, many of them involving lavish interpretations of the treaty provisions so as to expand the extent of the protection that the treaties were intended by the parties to give to foreign investment protection against expropriation and wrongful treatment.

There has been a reaction against investor–state arbitration due to the expansion of the scope of protection of foreign investment brought about through investment arbitration. This has led to the formulation of restrictions through the reaction of states to these excesses. There are obvious examples of this in recent times. The revival of the notion that regulatory expropriations are non-compensable is an idea that owes much to the notion of state control over foreign investment contained in the NIEO.[54] The ouster of jurisdiction as well as liability on the ground that state regulations on entry, as well as subsequent conduct of the foreign investment, did not comply with domestic laws again asserts control of the host state over foreign investment.[55] The new forms of foreign investment create what are referred to as balances against exclusive investment protection by ensuring that a state acting to protect certain interests, for example, labour standards, environmental rules, and the health and welfare of its citizens, are provided defences against liability.[56] A renewed interest in the police powers doctrine that enables a state to act in the public interest reinforces notions that are inherent in the NIEO. It would appear that the tenets of the NIEO are revived in these trends. At the least, what can be said is that there is a movement away from the notion that foreign property is sacrosanct and must be protected at all cost. There may be practical reasons for the renewal of this wisdom. As the developed states of Europe and the US are massive recipients of

[53] Further see John Linarelli, Margot E Salomon and Muthucumaraswamy Sornarajah, *The Misery of International Law: Confrontations with Injustice in the Global Economy* (OUP 2018).

[54] The notion is sovereignty-centred in that it seeks to prioritize the public interest over that of the foreign investor.

[55] *Fraport v Philippines* ICSID Case No ARB/03/25 (16 August 2005).

[56] Increasing numbers of defences to liability are created in the so-called balanced treaties, which seek to recover control over a state's right to act in the public interest. In addition to the rediscovery of regulatory, non-compensable expropriation, the new treaties provide defences to liability on the ground that the measure complained of was justified by the need for the protection of labour standards, the environment, human rights, the welfare, health, preservation of cultural property, and other interests of the public. In addition, the new model treaties like that of India require the foreign investor to follow rules of corporate responsibility, thus opening the way to the responsibility of MNCs, albeit indirectly.

investments from China, India, and other industrializing states, they increasingly become targets of the international law they had created. Pragmatism, not justice, requires withdrawal from a stance of strict protection. It is not necessary to expand on these new developments as they are covered in the literature.[57] What this portends is that the NIEO principles are being revived. The recovery of state control over foreign investment was very much an objective of the NIEO. The reaction of states to investment arbitration indicates a revival of that objective. We can observe that the battle for control has been ongoing. Colonial structures are revived but soon meet with resistance. This power game continues in a cyclical fashion with inconsistent victories. The ideological formations remain. The lines of advances and retreats of these formations keep shifting. The battle will go on. Personnel in the formations shift, and thus, China and India, once champions of the third world, are now capital exporters, showing a willingness to change camps. But, despite these changes of personnel, the essential ideological formations remain relatively constant. It would be an error to state that neither ideological disposition suffers total defeat. It may go into eclipse, but circumstances change, enabling revival.

[57] Muthucumaraswamy Sornarajah, *Resistance and Change in the International Law on Foreign Investment* (CUP 2015).

8

(De)colonizing Human Rights

Florian Hoffmann and Bethania Assy

I. Battling human rights from decolonization to colonization (and back)

The story of human rights in the decolonization era is a story about a story about a story. It starts with a story about the crucial role the (then) incipient discourse of human rights is deemed to have played in and for the decolonization process. Its crucial plot elements feature the reception of the Universal Declaration of Human Rights (UDHR) by the still-colonized militants of decolonization, and their subsequent adoption of the language of human rights to articulate their core demands of self-government, self-determination, and racial equality. It also showcases an ultimately successful march through the institutions—in particular of the United Nations (UN), where rights-based arguments put the colonizing powers against a wall of adverse international public opinion and which led, first, to their withdrawal, and then to the gradual formation of the newly independent states into the 'third world'.[1] It also recounts defining events (the Bandung and Teheran conferences), movements (the Non-Aligned Movement and the Pan-African Movement), and concepts (the right to non-discrimination and the right to development) in order to show the positive and potentially crucial impact human rights have had on the decolonization process and that decolonization has had on the incipient international human rights system. It is the most familiar and, to an extent, still predominant story of human rights and decolonization, widely referenced in human rights textbooks and in UN documents, and, thus, a crucial plotline of the

[1] See, for instance, Roland Burke, *Decolonization and the Evolution of International Human Rights* (University of Pennsylvania Press 2010); Steven LB Jensen, *The Making of International Human Rights: The 1960s Decolonization and the Reconstruction of Global Values* (CUP 2016); Fabian Klose, *Human Rights in the Shadow of Colonial Violence: The Wars of Independence in Kenya and Algeria* (1st edn, University of Pennsylvania Press 2013); Jenny S Martinez, *The Slave Trade and the Origins of International Human Rights Law* (OUP 2012); Daniel Maul, *Human Rights, Development and Decolonization: The International Labour Organization, 1940–70* (Palgrave Macmillan 2012); Meredith Terretta, '"We Had Been Fooled into Thinking that the UN Watches over the Entire World": Human Rights, UN Trust Territories, and Africa's Decolonization' (2012) 34 Human Rights Quarterly 329; see also, generally, Philip Alston, 'Does the Past Matter? On the Origins of Human Rights' (2013) 126 Harvard Law Review 2043.

Florian Hoffmann and Bethania Assy, *(De)colonizing Human Rights* In: *The Battle for International Law: South-North Perspectives on the Decolonization Era*. Edited by: Jochen von Bernstorff and Philipp Dann, Oxford University Press (2019).
DOI: 10.1093/oso/9780198849636.003.0009

(post-1990) grand narrative about the ascendancy of human rights 'as a fact of the world'.[2]

Yet, this story has itself of late become the object of storytelling in the wake of a revisionist turn in the historiography of human rights. This second story seeks to deconstruct the earlier one by recounting it as an exercise in anachronistic mythmaking that obscures the 'real' role, or rather, lack thereof, human rights allegedly had in the decolonization process. In this re-telling, human rights have played a less important but more ambivalent role for decolonization, with the clichéd outer layer of the plot being portrayed as no more than the anachronistic back-projection of contemporary views held by the self-professed human rights movement.[3] It pits that projection against a historically reconstructed 'reality' in which the use of human rights by decolonization activists (and then by governments of newly independent states in Africa and Asia) is shown to have been deeply strategic, with rights language frequently serving merely as a cipher, or indeed, as an empty signifier to articulate much broader political demands. It also purports to show how the (former) colonial powers were either unreceptive to rights-based critique or how they learned quickly to direct it back to their former colonies as a way of political 'monitoring'. This story, then, is a classical demythologization exercise, where a re-reading of the historical record is used to contrast a newly revealed 'reality' to an established myth.[4]

[2] Eduardo Rabossi, 'La Teoria de los Derechos Humanos Naturalizada' (1990) 5 Revista del Centro de Estudios Constitucionales 159; see also Florian F Hoffmann, 'Shooting in the Dark: Reflections Towards a Pragmatic Theory of Human Rights (Activism)' (2006) 41 Texas International Law Journal 403.

[3] See, for instance Samuel Moyn, *The Last Utopia: Human Rights in History* (Belknap Press of Harvard University Press 2010) (hereafter Moyn, *Last Utopia*); Samuel Moyn, 'The Embarrassment of Human Rights' (2015) Texas International Law Journal: The Forum 1; Jan Eckel, 'Human Rights and Decolonization: New Perspectives and Open Questions' (2010) 1 Humanity 111–35 (hereafter Eckel, 'Human Rights and Decolonization'); as well as Jan Eckel, *Die Ambivalenz des Guten: Menschenrechte in der internationalen Politik seit den 1940ern* (2nd edn, Vandenhoeck & Ruprecht 2015); and essays in Stefan-Ludwig Hoffmann (ed), *Human Rights in the Twentieth Century* (CUP 2010); although the revisionist literature on decolonization does not squarely map onto the post- and decolonial approaches in the ambit of the Third World Approaches to International Law (TWAIL), the latter has, in the present context, nonetheless to be considered as both a precursor and companion to the former; see, hence, and now classically, Antony Anghie, *Imperialism, Sovereignty and the Making of International Law* (CUP 2007); as well as, inter alia, Balakrishnan Rajagopal, *International Law from Below: Development Social Movements and Third World Resistance* (CUP 2003); James T Gathii, 'International Law and Eurocentricity' (1998) 9 European Journal of International Law 184; Luis Eslava and Sundhya Pahuja, 'Beyond the (Post) Colonial: TWAIL and the Everyday Life of International Law' (2012) 45 Journal of Law and Politics in Africa, Asia and Latin America-Verfassung und Recht in Übersee (VRÜ) 195; Luis Eslava, *Local Space, Global Life: The Everyday Operation of International Law and Development* (CUP 2015); and the contributions in Antony Anghie and others (eds), *The Third World and International Order: Law, Politics and Globalization* (Nijhoff 2003).

[4] For a take on this form of ideology critique, see Susan Marks, 'Big Brother Is Bleeping Us—With the Message That Ideology Doesn't Matter' (2001) 12 European Journal of International Law 109; for the classic (Frankfurtian) account, see Max Horkheimer and Theodor W Adorno, *Dialectic of Enlightenment: Philosophical Fragments* (Gunzelin Schmid Noerr ed, Edmund Jephcott tr, Stanford University Press 2002).

However, history by itself, or rather, historiographical militancy, will not resolve the debate on the significance, or lack thereof, of human rights in and for decolonization. While human rights discourses are necessarily historically constituted, the use of rights language in a particular (historical) context is bound to transcend historiographical determination on account of its inherent power of (re-)signification at moments of (intellectual) crisis. As the inconclusive debate on their role in the decolonization process illustrates, human rights were invoked because decolonization resulted in an epistemic crisis occasioned by the very 'otherness' of a world after colonialism.[5] For this reason, the historiographical 'battle' over human rights in the decolonization era provides an important but incomplete part of the picture about the role and significance of human rights. A complementary aspect comes from contextualizing the use of human rights in *decolonization* by revisiting its use in *colonization*; it was during the historical colonial encounter that rights language was first used to grapple with the experience of radical alterity.

This chapter briefly reviews the contemporary battle over the role of human rights in the decolonization period of the mid-twentieth century, and examines the way in which Iberian scholars during the sixteenth century colonization period used (natural) rights discourse to (re-)signify the (Amerindian) other. Hopefully, it then provides a glimpse both of where human rights 'stand' in relation to decolonization and of the limits of history in telling this story.

II. The battle over the historiography of human rights during decolonization

The historiographical battle over the role human rights played in the decolonization process can only be understood through the broader discussion that has unfolded over the past decade or so regarding the way the history of human rights ought to be constructed. This discussion involved a debate about the origins and periodization of human rights, which has followed the usual dramaturgy of an established orthodoxy being challenged by a revisionist counter-narrative.[6] On the face of it, it has been a contest over historical facts, that is, over the particular moments on a linear timeline at which the concept of human rights can be said to have emerged and how the concept is then thought to have evolved on that timeline. On a deeper level, however, this *querelle* is about the semantic unity of the concept of human rights and about whether what is referred to as human rights on different

[5] Florian F Hoffmann, 'International Legalism and International Politics' in Anne Orford and Florian F Hoffmann (eds), *The Oxford Handbook of the Theory of International Law* (OUP 2016) 946; and William E Scheuerman, 'International Law as Historical Myth' (2004) 11 Constellations 537.

[6] Devin O Pendas, 'Toward a New Politics? On the Recent Historiography of Human Rights' (2012) 21 Contemporary European History 95, 96; see also Christopher McCrudden, 'Human Rights Histories' (2014) 35 Oxford Journal of Legal Studies 1.

points of the timeline can (or cannot) be plausibly connected to form a continuum and, thus, a progress narrative.

The spectrum of this exchange has been demarcated by, on one side, an orthodoxy that has assumed both the semantic continuity of (the idea of) human rights over time as well as general progress in their recognition and realization; and, on the other side, a revisionist critique that has denied both semantic unity and (therefore) progress.[7] There are nuances within the orthodox reading, with classical 'linear progress narratives' attributing cross-temporal (and cross-cultural) self-evidence to the idea of human rights and adopting a teleological account of history as a gradual progression towards their ever greater realization. There are also more recent 'precise-timeframe theories' that focus on different historically significant moments and their impact on the contemporary semantics of human rights.[8] However, as revisionist critics of the historiographical orthodoxy point out, it generally remains wedded to a contrived progress narrative and is, therefore, necessarily prone to the eclecticism and overinterpretation of all Whig history.[9]

Indeed, it is as a reaction to this presumption of continuity and coherence in the history of human rights that a strongly revisionist historiography has positioned itself as a polar opposite to the orthodox narrative. In the words of Samuel Moyn, its grand-apostle, this anti-anachronistic 'new revisionism' sees as 'the most troubling shortcoming of the contemporary attempt to give human rights a history [. . . the distortion of] the past to suit the present'.[10] As an antidote, the revisionists have contested the semantic unity of human rights and have preached a 'discontinuist' reading of the various events around which the human rights narrative has been constructed.[11] While these histories have tended to present themselves as more accurate and 'realist' interpretations of the facts, their main argument actually rests on a fundamentally different historiographical approach; where orthodox historiography seeks to inductively (re)construct causal connections between different event contexts (or periods) in order to establish the cross-temporal meaning of human rights, the revisionist approach starts from a particular premise about that meaning, and then proceeds to find its articulation in a specific event context.

[7] Alston (n 1) 2063.

[8] Michael J Lacey and Knud Haakonssen, *A Culture of Rights: The Bill of Rights in Philosophy, Politics and Law–1791 and 1991* (CUP 1992); Mary A Glendon, *A World Made New: Eleanor Roosevelt and the Universal Declaration of Human Rights* (Random House 2002); Johannes Morsink, *The Universal Declaration of Human Rights: Origins, Drafting, and Intent* (University of Pennsylvania Press 1999); Jay Winter and Antoine Prost, *René Cassin and Human Rights: From the Great War to the Universal Declaration* (CUP 2013) and Lynn Hunt, *Inventing Human Rights: A History* (1st edn, W.W. Norton & Company 2008).

[9] Pendas (n 6) 95; see also Justin Zaremby, 'On the Uses and Disadvantages of History for Human Rights Law: Reading Samuel Moyn's *The Last Utopia: Human Rights in History*' (2012) 15 Yale Human Rights and Development Law Journal 155.

[10] Samuel Moyn, *Human Rights and the Uses of History* (Verso 2014) 13.

[11] Moyn, *Last Utopia* (n 3) 20.

In other words, the former approach seeks to establish meaning from presumed facts, and the latter the facts from presumed meaning.

Moyn is a case in point: for him, human rights in their contemporary usage have to be understood (only) as expressions of an anti-sovereigntist cosmopolitan utopia that springs from the liberal internationalist tradition and that has emerged as a partial replacement of socialism as the primary ideal of emancipatory politics. According to Moyn, this particular understanding of human rights stems from the 1970s and it is, therefore, (only) the period from then onwards that is historically significant for the contemporary meaning of human rights.[12] Furthermore, Moyn suggests that what was denoted by the term 'rights' in previous periods—and most particularly, as will be seen, during decolonization—carries the opposite connotation, notably of appeals to the protection afforded by sovereign statehood and, by implication, to the ideal of sovereign statehood itself. Thus, despite their linguistic similitude, domestic and international (human) rights are entirely different ideas and, in fact, spring not only from different, but from conflicting, utopias. To forcefully read a unified idea of human rights into what to Moyn are disparate historical episodes is not just anachronistic, but rather misses the intrinsic meaning of 'human rights'.

To underscore his point, Moyn particularly has focused on debunking the event clusters that orthodox histories tend to highlight as crucial stepping stones in the evolution of the idea of human rights, starting with the founding of the UN and the drafting of the UDHR, as well as and crucially, the role played by human rights during the decolonization process. Indeed, the latter context is especially important to Moyn's narrative, as it allows him to contrast the (post-1970s) internationalist concept of human rights with the sovereigntist use of rights language during decolonization, notably as a mere cipher for claims to self-determination, to co-equal development, and against racial discrimination. Yet, to Moyn, more important is the contention that this use of human rights during the decolonization process cannot be seen as a direct legacy of earlier foundational moments, most notably the founding of the UN and the drafting of the UDHR. For Moyn, these earlier foundational moments simply did not exist: thereis neither sufficient evidence to claim that the international community really endorsed human rights at the end of the Second World War, nor were human rights a tangible driving force of international legal discourse as of that moment.[13]

Indeed, in Moyn's (history) book, the very term 'human rights' only slipped into the UN Charter as a gesture to a liberal (Anglo-American) public and was never intended to qualify the document's predominantly realist outlook on the incipient post-war world.[14] While shock over the Holocaust and a brief social-democratic

[12] ibid 210.
[13] ibid 44, 176.
[14] ibid 47.

consensus enabled the drafting of the UDHR in 1948, this did not mark the universalization of those rights previously linked to national citizenship and, therefore, to state sovereignty. Rather, it was a toothless diversion that ultimately only reaffirmed the precedence of the latter over an internationalism oriented towards human dignity.[15] By this account, even most liberal international lawyers initially rejected the idea of human rights as legal norms binding sovereign states—influential minority voices arguing just that, such as Hersh Lauterpacht's, notwithstanding.[16] The early Cold War quarrels over the drafting of the Covenants and the consequent tardiness of their adoption (1966) and entry into force (1976) is taken as further evidence of the lack of commitment by the international community to take human rights seriously.[17]

Moyn's revisionist narrative is, of course, just one among a host of attempts in recent years to draw a historically more precise picture of human rights and to, on that basis, either re-affirm or reject the classical story of conceptual continuity. The decolonization process tends to feature prominently in this *querelle*, as it is seen, not least by Moyn himself, as a test case for the ideology critique of human rights—for, if it can be shown that the actual reference to human rights by many actors across the spectrum during that period were but superstructural reverberations of different causal bases (such as, in Moyn's case, the quest for self-determination within a sovereigntist ideological framework) then a strong point can be made that this might be so with regard to other periods and uses of human rights as well. Decolonization, thus, occupies an epistemically privileged position in most revisionist histories.

According to Jan Eckel, a fellow revisionist traveller of Moyn, whether the revisionist account of human rights in the decolonization period is deemed plausible or not depends on three distinct areas of inquiry: notably, firstly, on the significance of human rights language for and within anticolonial movements; secondly, on the use of human rights by newly independent states within the UN system; and thirdly, on the reception and appropriation of human rights by the (former) colonial powers during and after decolonization.[18] On each of these issues, the recent literature divides into a continuist/anti-revisionist and a discontinuist/revisionist camp, both premised on a critique of the earlier continuous progress narratives, but each applying a different historiographical gaze to draw opposite conclusions. The continuists generally argue that human rights are neither semantically closed nor is their evolution monocausal. They tend to see all uses of the language as pieces of a continually growing human rights jigsaw that evolves in a non-linear yet interconnected way; thus, they concentrate on filling in blank spaces with what

15 ibid 176.

16 See Hersch Lauterpacht, *International Law and Human Rights* (Stevens 1950).

17 Moyn, *Last Utopia* (n 3) 176.

18 Eckel, 'Human Rights and Decolonization' (n 3) 113.

they deem to be forgotten or underappreciated pieces. Recent works in this vein include, inter alia, Roland Burke's *Decolonization and the Evolution of International Human Rights* (2011),[19] Meredith Terretta's 'We Had Been Fooled into Thinking that the UN Watches over the Entire World": Human Rights, UN Trust Territories, and Africa's Decolonization' (2012),[20] Fabian Klose's *Human Rights in the Shadow of Colonial Violence* (2013),[21] or Steven Jensen's *The Making of International Human Rights—The 1960s, Decolonization and the Reconstruction of Global Values* (2016).[22] For the most part, these pieces build their case on the basis of (re-)readings of specific episodes, such as Terretta on the role of anticolonial activists both in the third world itself—here the British and French Cameroons—and in the West in relation to the UN's Trusteeship system. Klose on colonial power conduct during the colonial wars in Kenya and Algeria, Jensen on the role two specific Third World states, Jamaica and Liberia, played in the construction of the UN human rights system, as well as on the role the issue areas of race and religion played in this context. Burke, by contrast, takes a longer-term view and focuses on what he sees as four moments that symbolize the trajectory of human rights in relation to decolonization: the Bandung conference in 1955; the 'turn to self-determination' in the early 1960s; the descent to hypocrisy during the First World Conference on Human Rights in 1968; and the emergence of the cultural relativist critique of human rights from with the third world itself in the 1980s. Burke stresses, among others, the initial importance that the presumed universality of the international protection of human rights had for newly independent states, although he also highlights that much of the third world's early support for international petitioning came from autocratic regimes.[23] Although partly critical of each other for overlooking either of Eckel's three dimensions, these contemporary continuist readings share the conviction that repeated invocation of the language of human rights during the decolonization period was not merely coincidental and strategic, neither on part of anticolonial activists in the third world and the West, nor on part of new third-world governments acting within the UN machinery, or even on part of the (former) colonial powers. And there is also a consensus (albeit subtle) among authors in this line that the term 'human rights' forms a bracket around the period between the 1940s and the 1970s that cannot be argued away.

This has, of course, been the contention of the discontinuist/revisionist fold in Moyn's wake. With regard to decolonization, it preceded Moyn's account, inter alia, with Brian Simpson's seminal *Human Rights and the End of Empire* (2001)[24]

[19] Burke (n 1).
[20] Terretta (n 1).
[21] Klose (n 1).
[22] Jensen (n 1).
[23] Burke (n 1) 91.
[24] Alfred WB Simpson, *Human Rights and the End of Empire: Britain and the Genesis of the European Convention* (OUP 2004).

and Mark Mazover's *No Enchanted Palace: The End of Empire and the Ideological Origins of the United Nations* (2009),[25] both of which seek to relativize the anti-revisionist argument about the crucial and positive role played by the UN in the formation of the international human rights regime of today. Following closely in Moyn's trail are then Jan Eckel's *Die Ambivalenz des Guten: Menschenrechte in der Internationalen Politik seit den 1940ern* (2014),[26] which represents perhaps the most thorough revisionist reading of the same period covered by Burke. While he actually agrees with much of Burke's and Klose's work, from the picture that emerges Eckel draws different conclusions, notably, that despite the seemingly ubiquitous reference to human rights in all three of his issue areas, 'anticolonialism, anti-neocolonialism, anti-imperialism, anti-racism, anti-discrimination, and anti-apartheid [remained] the foremost catchwords' of the anticolonial imagination, and not human rights.[27] Indeed, he goes as far as calling that imagination an 'ideology *ex negativo*' driven, on both sides of the colonial divide, by stylized antagonisms for which human rights became modes of articulation, rather than expressions of a positive and concrete vision.[28] Other longer-*duré* analyses, such as Roger Normand and Sarah Zaidi's *Human Rights at the UN: The Political History of Universal Justice* (2008) add to this cautious scepticism.[29]

Nor is the decolonization process that spans, roughly, the late 1950s and the 1960s a human rights game changer in Moyn's book. If others have seen decolonization not only as an important event cluster of its own, but also as one of the main drivers behind the global phenomenon that the 1960s would become—and which, in turn, produced the 'conditions of possibility' for those '1970s' about which Moyn is concerned—[30] it is not so in his historiography of human rights. For anti-colonialism, as he terms the ideological framework of decolonization, and the reactions against it are here interpreted to have used the language of human rights not only 'merely' strategically but also in a mindset that starkly differs from the internationalism he identifies with (post-1970) human rights. In essence, the anti-colonial quest for self-determination, that is, for co-equal state sovereignty, is here first strategically framed as both a right in and of itself, and as a movement for the realization of (human) rights in the context of (colonial) racial discrimination.[31] If, to Moyn, the UDHR was at most a reference to the 'rights of man' enjoyed under the auspices of national citizenship, at worst the mere attempt by (European) Christian-democratic conservatives to (re-)appropriate rights-language to counter

[25] Mark Mazower, *No Enchanted Palace: The End of Empire and the Ideological Origins of the United Nations* (Princeton University Press 2009).

[26] Burke (n 1).

[27] Eckel, 'Human Rights and Decolonization' (n 3) 115.

[28] ibid.

[29] Roger Normand and Sarah Zaidi, *Human Rights at the UN: The Political History of Universal Justice* (Indiana University Press 2008).

[30] See Fredric Jameson, 'Periodizing the 60s' (1984) 9 Social Text 158.

[31] Moyn, *Last Utopia* (n 3) 84.

the socialist/communist utopia, it provided only the stage props for the great decolonization play that was to unfold shortly thereafter.[32]

Human rights only properly entered the anti-colonial frame afterwards, and then only in at once haphazard and paradoxical ways, for, as Moyn seeks to show, outside of the *sui generis* claim for a 'right to self-determination', general rights language played not only a merely ancillary role in anti-colonial discourse, but also was used in parallel by opponents of decolonization to diffuse claims for self-determination.[33] If anything, human rights gained some anti-colonial currency on account of the disappearance of a concrete commitment to self-determination, originally enshrined, as it was, in the Atlantic Charter, in the later Dumbarton Oaks documents, and the UDHR itself, which led some anti-colonial activists to invest into the post-UDHR debates around the drafting of the Covenants.[34] Yet, Moyn insists that insofar as both the anti- and the pro-colonial use of human rights in this period was unavoidably bound up with advocacy for or opposition against self-determination, the vision behind that use was fundamentally different from the internationalist vision that emerged in the late 1970s.

The 1955 Bandung conference, all-important for the formation of an (anti-colonial) third-world consciousness, is taken as a case in point: it at once endorsed the UDHR, yet surrounded it with co-equal commitments to national sovereignty and non-interference; whereas the latter represented a broad consensus at the conference, the former only emerged after considerable debate, not least on account of the evident lack of (post-colonial) universality of the (still-colonial) UDHR.[35] Likewise, Moyn largely dismisses two further developments in the decolonization context that have often been held up as (pre-1970s) stepping stones towards the contemporary (internationalist) understanding of human rights. One concerns the use of human rights in ad hoc petitioning both to the Trusteeship Council and to the Commission on Human Rights, the other, the widespread introduction of bills of rights in post-independence constitutions. As to the former, Moyn acknowledges the importance of rights-oriented petitioning for the way the trusteeship system evolved in the wake of decolonization, but claims that this did not establish an independent standing for the rhetoric of human rights apart from or on top of claims for self-determination.[36] Ultimately, the redemptive horizon at this stage remained independence, and human rights mere instruments thereto. Likewise, the widespread adoption of constitutional bills of rights in newly independent states is seen by Moyn as more of a gesture to the (status) symbols of the aspired Westphalian statehood than as earnest expressions of interest to subordinate the incipient nation-building projects to individual rights claims.[37] In fact, some of the

[32] ibid 44; see also Pendas (n 6) 44.
[33] Moyn, *Last Utopia* (n 3) 118.
[34] ibid 100.
[35] ibid 94; see also Burke (n 1) 13.
[36] Moyn, *Last Utopia* (n 3) 109; Terretta (n 1).
[37] Moyn, *Last Utopia* (n 3) 111.

former colonial powers, after initial scepticism, came to see bills of rights as a way both to protect (White) minority interests and to 'condition' the new governments in their conduct, not least through the incipient UN (human rights) machinery.[38]

Lastly, Moyn points to the persistent ambivalence within the anti-colonial movement as to the means of revolution, notably violence or non-violence. While even voices arguing for armed resistance would occasionally frame their vision in terms of the unfulfilled promise of human rights, the inherent contradiction this implied effectively sidelined the moral force of such arguments. And even those favouring non-violent means rarely used human rights as expressions of their utopia.[39] It is, hence, according to Moyn, only once Western imperialism is transformed from direct colonial rule to indirect forms of (economic) control, and once, therefore, conditions within the new third world move into focus, that human rights start to take off—conditions that begin to be met only in the 1970s.[40]

Hence, the historiographical divide over the role of human rights in decolonization is no longer one between an (over)generalizing anachronism and a differentiating historicism. Instead, the debate takes place within a (broadly) historicist horizon and is driven by disparate interpretations of an ever-more finely-grained picture of the historical facts. Where, for instance, the continuist position musters the well-documented reference to human rights in anti-colonial thought to underscore its argument, the discontinuist position draws attention to the overall (smaller) proportion that human rights references represent in comparison to all documentary evidence of anti-colonial thought. Likewise, where the continuists tend to focus on the UN to showcase rights-oriented anti-colonial activism, the discontinuists point out that the UN itself was less relevant to the decolonization process than the UN-centric reading suggests. Indeed, to an extent, the debate between continuists and discontinuists appears to have yielded to minute quarrels over the method by which particular narratives are constructed, which actors and institutions are deemed important, and what type of documentary evidence is deemed as more or less expressive of their attitudes and positions. Are official pronouncements sufficient to fathom either side's thinking, or do behind-the-scenes records and *travaux-préparatoirs* need to be considered? Are elite or grassroots attitudes more relevant for any claim about the salience of human rights during decolonization, and how, if at all, can—or should—authentic commitments to human rights be distinguished from 'shrewd political calculations'?[41]

Ultimately, the debate is about a number of underlying assumptions and their historical plausibility, notably, whether the particular use of rights language during the decolonization period (1950s and 1960s) forms—or doesn't form—a semantic

[38] ibid 114.
[39] ibid 115.
[40] ibid 117.
[41] Eckel, 'Human Rights and Decolonization' (n 3) 115.

connecting link between their earlier (1940s) and later (1970s onwards) connotations; whether rights language played—or didn't play—a privileged role in articulating the decolonization agenda on part of anti-colonial activists and/or the response to the latter by colonial powers (and their publics); whether—or not—the decolonization context was relevant for the emergence of the international human rights (protection) regime within the UN; and, inversely, whether—or not—the incipient UN human rights machinery impacted the decolonization process. In essence, the continuists affirm all four hypotheses, whereas the discontinuists are sceptical.

However, if this debate has produced a highly differentiated picture of the archival evidence, it has, if anything, underlined the openness of the question of the role of human rights during decolonization. For while rights human rights can clearly be found in the discourses of virtually all actors, their precise meaning to each actor, as well as their aggregate impact, remain indeterminate. And no amount of additional evidence is likely to change this, as both positions are affected by what could be termed a hermeneutic 'problem of induction', namely, that within a certain set of premises, no amount of additional evidence will corroborate the correctness of the premises vis-à-vis their opposite, but will tend to merely reinforce them.[42] History alone is not going to answer the question. What lacks is a complementary inquiry about why human rights appear in the discourses of virtually all actors as one way to signify their particular aspirations. One direction to look for clues is backwards, notably, to the colonization period and the way human rights came then to be used to accommodate the experience of radical alterity within a given set of premises.

III. Looking back to see ahead: human rights during the colonization period

In the sixteenth-century context of the colonization of the Americas, the concept of (natural) rights was introduced by Iberian counter-reformation scholastics in and around the 'School of Salamanca'. It was an intellectual move that sought to respond to the experience of radical alterity in the encounter with Amerindian civilizations that seemed, to contemporary Europeans, at once highly sophisticated and entirely alien.[43] The latter posed a challenge to a European narrative that, at

[42] See Aviezer Tucker (ed), *A Companion to the Philosophy of History and Historiography* (Wiley-Blackwell 2011).

[43] As nomenclature varies across different regions in the Americas, the common (anthropological) denomination *Amerindian* shall be used here; and in relation to the School of Salamanca, we shall, despite the significant differences between the authors commonly counted as belonging to the School, refer to them collectively as the 'Salamancans' on the basis of the assumption that there is a broad core of shared ideas that unite all of its exponents; see, inter alia, Martti Koskenniemi, 'Colonization of the 'Indies': The Origin of International Law' (2009) talk at the University of Zaragoza, published in Yolanda Gamarra Chopo (ed), *La idea de América en el pensamiento ius internacionalista del*

that moment, was itself being challenged, inter alia, by the ongoing reformation. The Salamancans' response to this crisis has, of course, become one of the most referenced moments in (post/de-)colonial historiography for the role it played in the formation of international law, not least because of its reappropriation of the language of natural rights as a means to articulate the relationship between human beings and the incipient state system. Like with the moment of decolonization, its historiography has also been deeply contested, with a conventional position that has seen the use of natural rights as mitigating the colonizing universality of the incipient *ius gentium*, and a strongly revisionist position that has viewed these same natural rights as instruments of colonial domination.[44] Yet—and arguably—this debate has mostly focused on the impact of Salamancan thought on the European history of ideas and it has tended to leave the latter's significance as a response to the experience of radical alterity vis-à-vis the Amerindian encounter (relatively) underexplored. While this focus on European reception history remains crucial for understanding the deep coloniality of the international legal project, it is bound to underestimate the extent to which the Salamancans' resort to rights language was *also* their particular way of coming to grips with the experience of radical alterity—in the form of Amerindian—from within their existing (scholastic) framework of reference.

As (very) briefly outlined below, if seen in this light, certain aspects of Salamancan natural rights theory come to the fore that highlight the power of (re-) signification that the language of human rights has had at this foundational moment. On the face of it, this is, of course, a counterfactual contention. As Giuliano Gliozzi argues in a seminal piece on the birth of anthropology as colonial ideology, the sixteenth-century literature on the 'conquest' has tended to be simplified to a reading in which the West constructs itself and its others through stylized colonial binaries, such us 'good versus bad savage', 'civility versus barbarism', and 'rationality versus bestiality'.[45]

Instead, what marks out the Salamancan literature is a deep ambivalence flowing from their quest to render the experience of radical alterity consistent with their

siglo XX: Estudios a propósito de la conmemoración de los bicentenarios de las independencias de las repúblicas latinoamericanas (Institución Fernando el Católico 2010); Martti Koskenniemi, 'Vitoria and Us: Thoughts on Critical Histories of International Law' (2014) 22 Rechtsgeschichte-Legal History 119.

[44] For the first position, see Pablo Zapatero, 'Legal Imagination in Vitoria: The Power of Ideas' (2009) 11 Journal of the History of International Law 221; Georg Cavallar, 'Vitoria, Grotius, Pufendorf, Wolff and Vattel: Accomplices of European Colonialism and Exploitation or True Cosmopolitans' (2008) 10 Journal of the History of International Law 181; for the latter position, see Anghie (n 3) 13; and José-Manuel Barreto, *Human Rights from a Third World Perspective: Critique, History and International Law* (Cambridge Scholars Publishing 2013); see generally Koskenniemi (n 43).

[45] See Giuliano Gliozzi and Frank Lestringat, *Adam et le Nouveau Monde: La naissance de l'anthropologie comme idéologie coloniale; des généalogies bibliques aux théories raciales; 1500–1700* (Théétète Éd 2000); see also Tzvetan Todorov, *The Conquest of America: The Question of the Other* (University of Oklahoma Press 1999).

scholastic mindset, while preserving the latter's original premise of (European) epistemic supremacy and its corollaries for the formation of international law.[46] The deep otherness of Amerindian populations and the concomitant need to engage with a radically diverse symbolic universe posed an enormous intellectual challenge to those attempting to translate indigenous categories into the scholastic rationality of contemporary Catholic Christianity.[47] The Salamancans' objective was, thus, to make sense of the Amerindian universe from within the Catholic missionary setting, which formed the horizon of their practical experience, but stood in an ambivalent relationship with the secular colonial project.[48] It is in this specific context that the concept of natural rights presented itself as one line of attack against the legitimation of conquest sovereignty. In this struggle to square the static Aristotelian category of humanity with the historical facticity of cultural difference, the Salamanca School notoriously resorted to the earlier concepts of *ius naturale, ius gentium*, and *ius civile* and grafted them onto the scholastic dichotomy between divine law and human law.[49]

Divine law, which was deemed to govern the whole universe and which only existed in the divine mind, was, in turn, divided into natural divine law and positive divine law. The former connoted the participation of all humans in the divine law by virtue of the social and rational capacity to spontaneously comprehend common principles. The latter consisted of human law, which, even though derived from natural law, was created by humans and reflected the singularity of each community. It was, in turn, sub-divided into an *ius gentium* and an *ius civile*, with the former also deemed to derive from natural law and concerning the laws governing the peaceful co-existence of sociable subjects, and the latter incorporating the precepts of civil law. With the *ius gentium*, thus, set between divine natural law and human positive law, it became, for the Salamancans, a conceptual staging

[46] See, inter alia, Anghie (n 3) 23; Koskenniemi (n 43) 121; and Peter Fitzpatrick, 'The Revolutionary Past: Decolonizing Law and Human Rights' (2014) 2 Metodo International Studies in Phenomenology and Philosophy 117, 118; Monica Garcia-Salmones Rovira and Luis Eslava, 'Jurisdictional Colonization in the Spanish and British Empires: Some Reflections on a Global Public Order and the Sacred' in Hélène Ruiz Fabri, Jana Gogolin and Rüdiger Wolfrum (eds), *Select Proceedings of the European Society of International Law* (Hart 2010).

[47] Giuseppe Tosi, 'Sins Against Nature as Reasons for a 'Just War': Sepúlveda, Vitoria and Las Casas' in Alfredo S Culleton and Roberto H Pich (eds), *Right and Nature in the First and Second Scholasticism* (Brepols 2014).

[48] For early accounts of this see, for instance, Robert W Carlyle, *A History of Medieval Political Theory in the West* (W. Blackwood and Sons 1903); Otto V Gierke, *Natural Law and the Theory of Society: 1500 to 1800* (The Lawbook Exchange 2003); see also Knud Haakonssen, *Natural Law and Moral Philosophy: From Grotius to the Scottish Enlightenment* (CUP 1996) and Richard Tuck, *The Rights of War and Peace: Political Thought and the International Order from Grotius to Kant* (OUP 1999).

[49] See, inter alia, Kaius Tuori, 'The Reception of Ancient Legal Thought in Early Modern International Law' in Bardo Fassbender, Anne Peters and Simone Peter (eds), *The Oxford Handbook of the History of International Law* (OUP 2012) 1016; and Randall Lesaffer, *Peace Treaties and International Law in European History: From the Late Middle Ages to World War One* (CUP 2004) 225.

ground for the encounter between nature and culture in and through the contact with Amerindia.[50]

To understand the specific take the Salamancans had on natural law and the *ius gentium*, we must consider an originally patristic distinction, later taken up by Thomas Aquinas, between paganism and Christianity.[51] It presumed the pre-existence of two epochs in world history: an age of innocence (the golden age before the Fall), which the Salamancans identified with the Amerindian universe and which was deemed to be governed by natural law; and an age of sin (the iron age after the Fall) governed by the law of nations (*ius gentium*). This distinction implied, of course, that the law of Amerindian populations had to be considered as originary, received prior to the law of nations, and, thus, necessarily a form of (Amerindian) *ius naturale*. As Sílvia Loureiro showed, several conclusions derived from this premise became important conceptual tools for dealing with the Amerindian 'problem'.[52] Firstly, the original sovereigns of the people of the New World had to be considered as legitimate—they had both ownership of the land and authority over its people (*dominium jurisdictionis vel auctoritatis*); secondly, the enslavement of gentile peoples was incompatible with the contemporary legitimation of slavery, as it was forbidden to subject a previously free and peaceful people without just cause and without any (purported) benefit to those enslaved; it must, of course, here be noted that the Salamancans notoriously did *not* apply this logic to the enslavement of Africans, which represents an evident aporia in their naturalism and underlines the ambivalence of their Amerindian approach.[53]

Thirdly, based on Thomas Aquinas, the doctrine of property ensured that in the state of nature all things were deemed to have been common and the possession of property (*dominium proprietatis*) was a natural right.[54] Hence, for the Salamancans, both Amerindian *dominium jurisdictionis vel auctoritatis* and *dominium proprietatis* were rooted in natural law and natural right(s). As such, the correlation between *ius gentium* and *ius naturale* was more ambiguous than is commonly assumed and it led to a more complex and paradoxical conception of the relationship between nature and culture, for the postulate of the existence of an Amerindian *ius gentium* required the assumption that the *ius naturale* was

[50] See: Camilo B Trelles, 'Francisco Suarez (1548-1617)' (1933) 43 Recueil des Cours de l'Académie de Droit International de La Haye 386, 426.

[51] Gliozzi and Lestringat (n 45); and Silveira Loureiro, 'By What Right? The Contributions of the Peninsular School of Peace for the Basis of International Law of Indigenous Peoples' (2013) 5 Goettingen Journal of International Law 9; see also Pedro Calafate and Silvia M Loureiro, 'A Escola Peninsular da Paz: a contribuição da vertente portuguesa em prol da construção de um novo direito das gentes para o século XXI' (2013) 13 Revista do Instituto Brasileiro de Direitos Humanos 262.

[52] Loureiro (n 51) 17.

[53] See Walter D Mignolo, 'The Many Faces of Cosmo-polis: Border Thinking and Critical Cosmopolitanism' (2000) 12 Public Culture 721; and Ashley J Bohrer, 'Just Wars of Accumulation: The Salamanca School, Race and Colonial Capitalism' (2018) 59 Race & Class 20.

[54] Pedro Calafate, *Da origem popular do poder ao direito de resistência: Doutrinas políticas no século XVII em Portugal* (Esfera do Caos 2012).

mediated by the *ius gentium*—that is, by the natural common sense of each people and of each culture. On the basis of this construct it then became possible to see Amerindian title as an original right and, thus, as prior to the law of nations—a notion that amounts to a recognition (of sorts) of an Amerindian jusnaturalism.[55]

The attribution of rights to Amerindian populations, including in relation to their (own) political and social organization, derives from the fact that they were deemed to have inhabited the new world before the arrival of the *ius gentium*. For that reason, Amerindian original rights had necessarily to be grounded in natural law, which, in turn, means both that natural law is capable of accommodating cultural diversity, and that the subsequent *ius gentium*, as a derivative of natural law, must also be premised on this diversity.

Pedro Calafate, among others, has drawn attention to this entanglement of universal principles with a conception of radical plurality. For Calafate, it represents the essence of a baroque form of thinking that is symbolized by the labyrinth that transgresses, compromises, and dispenses with abstract rationality.[56] Indeed, the discussion around natural law did not take place around a set of purely speculative and abstract principles, but instead focused on a realist conception of natural rights founded on the consonance with 'reason', but also on the backdrop of a radical openness to historical otherness.[57] Hence, the very complexity of the Salamancan argument on natural rights is due to their attempt to situate it within historical time as opposed to within a (mere) abstract universality. As such, the *ius gentium* becomes effectively the historical expression of natural law, with the latter's conception of rationality being tied to the concreteness of the Amerindian experience. Within the shell of late scholastic universalist realism, that experience then opened up the space to think its opposite—notably, a realist universalism based on the factual plurality of humans and justified not by abstract principle, but rather by cultural particularity.

Thus, the Salamancans' conception of natural law, to use Ambrosio Gomez' expression, can be read to amount to a non-relativist *multicultural jusnaturalism*. It expresses the shared access to a universal, which ties together the *ius naturale* and the *ius gentium*. At the heart of this reading lies the contention that the universalization of the *ius naturale* on account of reason can only be thought historically and empirically, notably, through the concreteness of the factual experiences of the other, which, in the case of the Salamancans, came in form of the Amerindian world. If Francisco de Vitoria recognized this only tentatively and reluctantly, Bartolomé de las Casas went all the way when he directly engaged with what at the

[55] For this notion, see Ambrosio Velasco Gómez, 'Las ideas republicanas para una nación multicultural de Alonso de la Veracruz' in Carolina Ponce Hernández (ed), *Innovación y tradición en fray Alonso de la Veracruz* (Facultad de Filosofía y Letras, UNAM 2007).

[56] Calafate and Loureiro (n 51).

[57] Carolina Ponce Hernández (ed), *Innovación y tradición en fray Alonso de la Veracruz* (Facultad de Filosofía y Letras, UNAM 2007).

time was considered to be a primary sign of the radical otherness of Amerindians—cannibalism. In fact, not only did he mount a culturalist defence of the practice, but he sought to invert its connotation, showing it to be culturally superior to the Spanish *conquistadors* and thereby rendering the latter as the true 'barbarians'.[58]

With this move, as Enrique Dussel recently argued, Las Casas makes a highly innovative contribution to at least two of the core themes of his times—namely, how to deal with radical otherness and whether that otherness could, by right, be conquered.[59] Unlike some of the more influential Salamancans, such as Vitoria, las Casas was immersed in the Amerindian world and felt compelled to think about the epistemological consequences of the encounter with radical alterity from within this context, even if still in an essentially European cognitive frame. Although most subsequent interpretations of the Salamancan literature have centred on either the well-known defence of natural bondage by Juan Ginés de Sepúlveda or on its contention that rationality was a (mere) prerequisite for conversion, the figure of the 'natural-cultural' Amerindian that emerged from this debate contradicts either position.[60] In this vein, Anthony Pagden has argued that the Salamancans, in order to avoid at once the 'secular' relativism of their contemporary Michel de Montaigne and of Sepulveda's denial of the humanity of Amerindians, ended up concocting a new doctrine of universal natural rights.[61]

To modern (Eurocentric) eyes, this paradoxical effort to decode and defend indigenous culture without giving up the notion of natural law has a bearing on the deadlocked contemporary dispute between abstract universalism and pure cultural relativism. Seen from this perspective, and despite their irreducible entanglement with colonial violence, the Salamancans can be read as developing a new 'multi-naturalistic' vocabulary that not only challenges the particular rationality of (European) modernity, but also incorporates an archaic perspectivism based on the historically contingent experience of Amerindia.[62]

[58] See Alfredo S Culleton and Roberto H Pich (eds), *Right and Nature in the First and Second Scholasticism* (Brepols 2014) and Quentin Skinner, *Foundations of Western Political Thought* (CUP 2004) 170; and Bartolomé de las Casas, Paulino Castañeda Delgado and Angel Losada, *Obras Completas* (Alianza Editorial 1988).

[59] *Actas del Primer Simposio Internacional del Pensamiento Iberoamericano* (Enrique D. Dussel, 2002).

[60] For the former debates, see classically Lewis Hanke, *All Mankind is One: A Study of the Disputation between Bartolomé de Las Casas and Juan Ginés de Sepúlveda in 1550 on the Intellectual and Religious Capacity of the American Indians* (Northern Illinois University Press 1994).

[61] See Casas, Castañeda Delgado, and Losada (n 58); and Anthony Pagden, *The Fall of Natural Man: The American Indian and the Origins of Comparative Ethnology* (CUP 1986).

[62] Represented, in contemporary anthropological theory, by, amongst others, Eduardo Viveiros de Castro; see, for instance, Eduardo B de Castro and Gregory D Morton, *The Inconstancy of the Indian Soul: The Encounter of Catholics and Cannibals in 16th-Century Brazil* (Prickly Paradigm Press 2011); and Eduardo Viveiros de Castro and Peter Skafish, *Cannibal Metaphysics* (University of Minnesota Press 2014); for a broader reflection of some of the repercussions of this logic on the conception of subjectivity, see Bethania Assy, 'Insurgent Subjectivities and the Political Empowerment of the Streets' (2014) 7 Revista di Pratica Filosofica e Scienza Umane 118; and Bethania Assy, 'Injusticia Social, Empoderamiento Político e Subjetivación' in Roseni Pinheiro and others (eds), *Cultura do cuidado e o cuidado na cultura: dilemas, desafios e avanços para efetivação da integralidade em saúde no Mercosul* (Cepesc Editora 2015).

IV. Beyond the battle: human rights as signifiers of the (de)colonial other

Zooming out again, the scenario that emerges shows both the colonization and the decolonization experiences as marked by the encounter with something outside of the established epistemic horizon—something genuinely 'other' that challenges the integrity of these horizons and therefore provokes a new type of response. In both cases, the established epistemic horizon is the European mode of governmentality as it emerged between the periods of colonization and decolonization—a mode inherently premised on colonialism as a form not just of control over people and territory but also (and primarily) of epistemic domination. It involves a particular rationality that constitutes the specific techniques of power that the ordering of people and space in what would become the Westphalian world requires—a rationality that would come to be epitomized in sovereign statehood and which is articulated by what would eventually be called international law.[63]

The latter is much more than a set of rules devised by states to regulate relations among each other with a view to (thereby) control access to sovereignty as the key to their hegemony. It is, in the Foucauldian sense, a discourse—that is, a specific configuration of power/knowledge that constitutes an epistemic horizon, or a mental map by which people know and act in the world.[64] This map of uniform states and nationalities divided by clear-cut borders did not, of course, emerge as a representation of the world 'out there' which, in the sixteenth century as much as during the 1950s and 1960s, consisted of much more than what is represented on the map. It was always merely a simulacrum of the world, superimposed over its raw plurality to produce a stratified order privileging those purporting to be at its top. Over time—notably in the period during which the parochial and contingent European map was forcibly imposed on everyone and everything across the globe—it merged with established truth and became one of the mythological foundations of the modern world.

International law would, hence, at once draw in what lay yet outside of it and reaffirm itself through the antagonistic differentiation against that outside. The other was, hence, transcribed into the language and categories of the inside, yet it simultaneously served as the indicator for an exterior that was framed as the inside's opposite. It is, arguably, this paradoxical move that characterizes the specific imperiality of international law and, indeed, of modernity itself, a continuous

[63] Florian F Hoffmann, 'Discourse' in Jean D'Aspremont and Sahib Singh (eds), *Fundamental Concepts for International Law* (Edward Elgar Publishing forthcoming).

[64] See, inter alia, Thomas Lemke, 'Foucault, Governmentality, and Critique' (2002) 14 Rethinking Marxism 49; Nikolas M Rajkovic, '"Global Law" and Governmentality: Reconceptualizing the "Rule of Law" as Rule "through" Law' (2012) 18 European Journal of International Law 29; Ben Golder, 'Foucault and the Incompletion of Law' (2008) 21 Leiden Journal of International Law 747.

oscillation between inclusion and exclusion, recognition and rejection, universalization and particularization.

This ambivalence and in-betweenness has come to be embodied in certain (legal) concepts such as human rights, for they at once express an abstraction from individual humans in the name of a (Eurocentrically defined) humanity and a recognition of individual dignity on account of that humanity. The Salamancan resort to human rights in their effort to recognize Amerindians as (other) humans, while at the same time allowing for the incorporation of their world into the European map, is a case in point. For human rights are here rendered polyvalent by the application of their universalist logic to a scenario outside of it, the result being both contradictory and coherent, hegemonizing and self-relativizing. Hence, while Salamancan thought is clearly woven into the colonialist fabric of what would become international law, it cannot be reduced to it, in the same vein as the idea of human rights applied to Amerindians cannot be reduced to epistemic imperialism. The complex repercussions that the Salamancan position generated beyond the European debate, notably in the Americas itself, and the ways in which human rights ended up being semantically re-appropriated by different interlocutors across the (colonial) board, shows that, as a discourse, they are fundamentally marked by semantic indeterminacy and openness.

It is arguably this aspect that bestows on human rights their particular power of (re-)signification in moments of intellectual crisis—for example, the period of decolonization. For it is at moments of transition during which established vocabularies are challenged by radically new experiences and cognitive horizons, that the language of human rights has, time and again, been resorted to in order to (re-)signify what cannot yet be signified. This power is not grounded in concrete universalities or absolute semantic identities, but in the diverse discursive practices of people here, and elsewhere.

9

Picking Battles

Race, Decolonization, and Apartheid

*Rotem Giladi**

I. Introduction

If race had been an analytical category in international law,[1] when did that category lose its relevance? What role, if any, did decolonization have in the 'de-racialization' of international law—to echo Theodor Meron's claim of the 'humanization' of international law in the post-war era?[2]

These are weighty questions. This chapter, however, is more limited in scope. It focuses on the *effect* that decolonization had on the question of race in international law. After all, decolonization sought to achieve concrete political aims. These may well have involved reversing the consequences of the operation of racial inequality and exclusion underwriting international law in the nineteenth century.[3] But, if making race irrelevant had been among the goals of agents and movements of decolonization, it was at most a tactical, not a strategic, goal.

What follows are preliminary reflections and observations on the effects of decolonization on the race category in international law. These are drawn, in particular, from the vantage point of the battle against apartheid that culminated, in 1973, in the adoption of the United Nations Apartheid Convention.[4] Rather than engaging with the construction of norms or offering a systematic account of the

* This research received funding from the European Research Council under the European Union's Seventh Framework Programme (FP/2007–2013)/ERC Grant Agreement No. 615564. I thank Professor Louise Bethlehem for the research fellowship in her project 'Apartheid—The Global Itinerary: South African Cultural Formations in Transnational Circulation, 1948–1990' and for her invaluable support, advice, and comments.

[1] Ediberto Roman, 'A Race Approach to International Law (RAIL): Is There a Need for Yet Another Critique of International Law?' (2000) 33 University of California Davis Law Review 1519.

[2] Theodor Meron, 'The Humanization of Humanitarian Law' (2000) 94 American Journal of International Law 239; recently, I explored this continuity in the laws of war in respect of an episode at the conclusion of the First World War: Rotem Giladi, 'The Phoenix of Colonial War: Race, the Laws of War, and the "Horror on the Rhine"' (2017) 30 Leiden Journal of International Law 847 (hereafter Giladi, 'The Phoenix').

[3] *E.g.* Martti Koskenniemi, *The Gentle Civilizer of Nations: The Rise and Fall of International Law 1870–1960* (CUP 2001).

[4] International Convention on the Suppression and Punishment of the Crime of Apartheid (adopted 30 November 1973, entered into force 18 July 1976) 1015 UNTS 243.

Rotem Giladi, *Picking Battles* In: *The Battle for International Law: South-North Perspectives on the Decolonization Era.* Edited by: Jochen von Bernstorff and Philipp Dann, Oxford University Press (2019). © The Several Contributors.
DOI: 10.1093/oso/9780198849636.003.0010

travaux préparatoires of the Apartheid Convention, this chapter delves into a number of episodes forming its broader historical, political, and legislative context. These give rise to exploratory claims on the effects of decolonization on the race category.

Much-neglected by the international law (and diplomatic) history literature, in the Apartheid Convention decolonization produced the most focused, perhaps even radical, reading of race and international law. Earlier legal texts framing decolonization, such as the 1960 UNGA Resolution 1514 or the 1970 Friendly Relations Declaration, had referenced race only fleetingly.[5] The 1966 Covenants did enunciate the right to self-determination in their Common Article 1, and prohibited distinction or discrimination on grounds of race.[6] Yet they neither linked the two, nor framed self-determination in terms of overcoming the race category. Even the 1965 International Convention on the Elimination of All Forms of Racial Discrimination (ICERD), though its preamble recalled United Nations' (UN) condemnation of 'colonialism and all practices of segregation and discrimination associated therewith',[7] offered no reading of self-determination as the undoing of the legal category of race. ICERD, besides, was not quite the product of decolonization; it originated in East-West divisions and Middle East recriminations; North-South divisions were factored into its text only at a late stage.

By contrast, the Apartheid Convention dealt with 'inhuman acts committed for the purpose of establishing and maintaining domination by one racial group of persons over any other racial group of persons and systematically oppressing them'; it declared apartheid itself a crime against humanity and dubbed resulting 'inhumane acts' as crimes violating the principles of international law. It offered, in other words, a reading of racial domination and oppression, not merely as discrete displays of racism, but as an organized form of governance. For this and other reasons, the battle against apartheid furnishes useful vantage points from which to gauge and assesses whatever footprints decolonization had left on post-colonial international law.

This chapter first looks at multiple projects that had placed race on the legislative and judicial agenda of the international community. It traces why some, but not others, culminated in the adoption of the Apartheid Convention (Section II).

[5] Declaration on the Granting of Independence to Colonial Countries and Peoples, UNGA Res 1514 (XV) (14 December 1960); Declaration on Principles of International Law concerning Friendly Relations and Co-operation among States in accordance with the Charter of the United Nations, UNGA Res 2625 (XXV) (24 October 1970).

[6] International Covenant on Civil and Political Rights (adopted 16 December 1966, entered into force 23 March 1976) 999 UNTS 171 arts 2, 4, 24, 26; Article 20 provided for the prohibition of 'advocacy of . . . racial . . . hatred' reaching the threshold of 'incitement'. International Covenant on Economic, Social and Cultural Rights (16 December 1966) 993 UNTS 3 (entered into force 3 January 1976) arts 2, 13.

[7] International Convention on the Elimination of All Forms of Racial Discrimination (adopted 21 December 1965, entered into force 4 January 1969) 660 UNTS 195; Article 15 did involve the Committee on Elimination of Racial Discrimination in petitions from territories governed by Resolution 1514.

It then considers the relationship between apartheid and decolonization—and a common view according to which the anti-apartheid cause, including with regard to banning racial discrimination, had served as a banner of decolonization (Section III). Section IV proposes that, in effect, apartheid came to be treated as an aberration—rather than the extreme iteration—of colonialism and notes some of the consequences of that framing: raising the apartheid banner did not serve well the cause of de-racializing international law; and making apartheid the banner of the battle against (colonial) racism may not have been all propitious for the cause of the battle against apartheid itself. Section V considers the Convention's *acquis* and effect. It suggests that the Apartheid Convention, in treating apartheid as an aberration, vindicated colonialism, and that criminalizing apartheid signified the end of a conversation on race in the era of decolonization more than its beginning. Section VI considers the fate of other anti-racial causes, while Section VII raises the possibility that the Apartheid Convention in fact confirmed the continued relevance of race in international law. Finally, Section VIII offers a critical reading of the lasting footprints decolonization has left, in the matter of race, on the normative landscape of international law.

II. The causes of race

One insight about the effect of decolonization on the issue of race in international law is that that deracializing international law was not quite a linear progression of a single trajectory.[8] It took place at multiple sites, and sprung out of several agenda. It was driven by different political forces headed in different, sometimes opposing, directions and acting on a variety of motives. And it was fraught with unintended consequences that produced surprising but important marks on the race category in international law.

Neither was decolonization the only (or, for that matter, the first) launching pad for the *legislative* battle on race at the UN. The protagonists in the UN debate that followed India's 1946 complaint against the Union of South Africa's discriminatory treatment of persons of Indian origins at times framed their contentions in terms of racial discrimination.[9] But this started (alongside the Union's recalcitrance over South-West Africa) as a single-issue campaign that sought to put pressure on South Africa and carve a world role for India, rather than set or elaborate a general standard.[10] This was true also in 1952, when India realized it could not demand

[8] Giladi, 'The Phoenix' (n 2) 847–48, 860, 874–75.

[9] Evoking 'a striking resemblance to the Nazi principle and practice of race superiority and concentration of power in the superior race': quoted in Lorna Lloyd, '"A Family Quarrel": The Development of the Dispute over Indians in South Africa' (1991) 34 The Historical Journal 703, 722–23 (hereafter Lloyd, 'Family Quarrel').

[10] ibid.

equality for a small, somewhat newly disenfranchised Indian minority but remain silent on the systemic disenfranchisement of the majority in South Africa.[11] That year saw, accordingly, the inclusion of 'The question of race conflict in South Africa resulting from the policies of apartheid . . . ' in the UN General Assembly (UNGA) agenda.[12] And while the Union was repeatedly singled out in successive UNGA sessions,[13] such debates saw no attempt to revise old or generate novel norms. Besides, a close reading suggests that India's original grievance itself was couched in terms confirming that race was as relevant as ever: after commenting that under South African legislation, Jesus Christ would have been considered a prohibited immigrant, Vijaya Lakshmi Pandit—India's representative and Jawaharlal Nehru's sister—proceeded to say that 'if the country belonged to anyone, it was the "barbaric indigenous population" ' from which it was taken.[14] Her own memoire notes how, in the midst of the 'Asian victory' celebrations, she approached Smuts on the Assembly floor—as if to ask for the patriarch's pardon and regain his goodwill.[15] Race was largely still framing the debate even when its concrete manifestations came under challenge.

Legislative efforts originated elsewhere. Jewish lawyers and organizations were contemplating international legislation on anti-Semitism already during the Holocaust.[16] Such initiatives, seemingly, were lost in the plurality of post-war legislative (and political) projects touching on Jewish questions. On Christmas Eve 1959, however, anti-Jewish slogans were painted on a rededicated synagogue in Cologne; slogans and swastikas soon spread across West Germany, and in the next two weeks, more than 500 episodes were recorded in thirty-four countries.[17] The alarm caused by the 'Swastika Epidemic'[18] soon appeared on the UN agenda.

[11] Rotem Giladi, 'Negotiating Identity: Israel, Apartheid, and the United Nations, 1949–1952' (2017) 132 The English Historical Review 1440 (hereafter Giladi, 'Negotiating Identity').

[12] Letter dated 12 September 1952 addressed to the Secretary-General by the permanent representatives of Afghanistan, Burma, Egypt, India, Indonesia, Iraq, Iran, Lebanon, Pakistan, the Philippines, Saudi Arabia, Syria and Yemen (12 September 1952) UN Doc A/2183.

[13] ES Reddy, *Apartheid, the United Nations and the International Community: A Collection of Speeches and Papers* (Vikas 1986); Özdemir A Özgür, *Apartheid: The United Nations & Peaceful Change in South Africa* (Transnational Publ 1982).

[14] Lorna Lloyd, '"A Most Auspicious Beginning": The 1946 United Nations General Assembly and the Question of the Treatment of Indians in South Africa' (1990) 16 Review of International Studies 131, 141 (hereafter Lloyd, 'Auspicious Beginning').

[15] Mark Mazower, *No Enchanted Palace: The End of Empire and the Ideological Origins of the United Nations* (Princeton University Press 2009) 179 (hereafter Mazower, *No Enchanted Palace*); Vijaya Lakshmi Pandit, *The Scope of Happiness: A Personal Memoir* (Weidenfels and Nicolson 1979) 211.

[16] Mark Vishniak, *An International Convention against Anti-Semitism* (Research Institute of the Jewish Labor Committee 1946); Oscar I Janowsky and Melvin M Fagen, *International Aspects of German Racial Policies* (OUP 1937).

[17] James Loeffler, *How Zionism Became Racism: International Law, Anti-Semitism, and Jewish Lawyering at the United Nations, 1945–1975* (hereafter Loeffler, *Zionism*) (unpublished manuscript; I thank James Loeffler for permission to quote this paper): 'the total for 1960 rose to 2500 incidents in 41 countries'; Michael Brecher, *The Foreign Policy System of Israel: Setting Images Process* (OUP 1972) 237–38, 550.

[18] Nemiah Robinson, 'The Swastica Epidemic' (June 1960) (World Jewish Congress Records, American Jewish Archives, C130/18).

In early 1960, the UN's Sub-Commission on the Prevention of Discrimination and the Protection of Minorities condemned the incidents.[19] Jewish non-governmental organizations (NGOs) with UN consultative status were heavily involved. The question of 'Manifestations of anti-Semitism and other forms of racial prejudice and religious intolerance of a similar nature' was discussed by the Commission on Human Rights, then the Assembly. NGOs were invited to submit materials. At the end of 1960, at the invitation of the UN Economic and Social Council (ECOSOC), the Assembly adopted a resolution on 'Manifestations of Racial and National Hatred'.[20] Notwithstanding early consensus in the sub-Commission, Cold War issues touched the final text;[21] and the Israeli–Arab conflict now caused the deletion of any reference to anti-Semitism; colonialism or apartheid were not mentioned.

Soon after, early proposals on an international convention on racial discrimination foresaw a 'far narrower scope' for such an instrument than ICERD would eventually encompass.[22] Although the deliberations at the Sub-Commission occasionally referenced colonialism, its consensus first was a focus on 'racial, national and religious hatred'—that is, discrimination within states, not among nations.[23] The issue was still largely conceived as addressing a European problem, to be discussed within the setting of a largely European international system. It was in 1962 at the UNGA Third Committee, during the consideration of such proposals, that a change of direction and emphasis was recorded. Although the path for drafting a declaration, then a convention, on racial discrimination by the Assembly was now largely determined, this came at a cost. Arab and Eastern bloc opposition bifurcated the cause through a distinction between 'racial discrimination' and 'religious intolerance'.[24] Of the two tracks, the former was to gain priority. So it did: in late 1963, the Assembly adopted a 'Declaration on the Elimination of All Forms of Racial Discrimination';[25] two years later, the Assembly adopted ICERD.[26] The Convention contained a brief condemnation of 'segregation and apartheid' and an undertaking 'to prevent, prohibit and eradicate all practices of this nature in

[19] UN Commission on Human Rights (UNCHR), 'Report of the Twelfth Session of the Sub-Commission on Prevention of Discrimination and Protection of Minorities to the Commission on Human Rights' (8 February 1960) UN Doc E/CN.4/800, paras 163–94.

[20] Manifestations of Racial and National Hatred, UNGA Res 1510 (XV) (12 December 1960). For background, Nātān Lerner, *The U.N. Convention on the Elimination of all Forms of Racial Discrimination* (Sijthoff & Noordhoff 1980) 1.

[21] Lerner (n 20) 22 (early draft work by representatives of the US, USSR, UK, and Poland).

[22] Egon Schwelb, 'The International Convention on the Elimination of All Forms of Racial Discrimination' (1966) 15 International and Comparative Law Quarterly 996, 998.

[23] UN Commission on Human Rights (UNCHR), 'Report of the Thirteenth Session of the Sub-Commission on Prevention of Discrimination and Protection of Minorities to the Commission on Human Rights' (9 February 1961) UN Doc E/CN.4/815, para 176.

[24] Schwelb (n 22) 998–99. See UNGA Res 1780, 1781 (XVII) (7 December 1962); neither referenced colonialism. How to classify anti-Semitism was debated, the crux being whether Judaism was a religion or Jews a race or a nation.

[25] UNGA Res 1904 (XVIII) (20 November 1963).

[26] UNGA Res 2106 (XX) (21 December 1965).

territories' of state parties (art 3); but colonialism itself remained a minor concern, notwithstanding the marginalization of anti-Semitism, which ICERD did not mention.[27] The involvement of African and Asian countries in the legislative process was undoubtedly on the rise, and colonialism was deployed by the Soviet bloc as a rhetorical weapon against Western countries during the drafting process;[28] yet, if ICERD attested to the persistence of a race problem, this was at best only marginally the problem of the racial structuring of authority in international relations. As marginal were the solutions it prescribed for that problem. 'Religious intolerance'—for some, the appropriate framework to deal with anti-Semitism—remains to this day the subject of UN declarations with no treaty emerging to combat it.

III. The banner of apartheid

One may consider, next, the relationship between apartheid and decolonization; specifically, the role of apartheid in UN legislative initiatives on race in the context of decolonization. Specific apartheid practices in the Union of South Africa, then 'the policies of apartheid' themselves, were debated at the UN at India's initiative since 1946 and 1952, respectively.[29] As decolonization came to occupy the agenda of the world organization, apartheid came to take centre stage in the battle to produce new norms on racial discrimination. ICERD, to the disappointment of its Jewish promoters, failed to include the draft article on anti-Semitism;[30] that 'apartheid is the only form of racial discrimination to which a specific article is devoted in addition to mentioning it in the Preamble' did not assuage their disaffection with the fruit of their labour.[31] One dismissed the 'not convincing explanation' that, unlike Nazism or anti-Semitism, 'apartheid is *today* the only instance of racial discrimination as an official policy'; 'what decided the final text', he repeatedly observed, 'were political considerations'.[32] 'In law,' another commented, 'Article 3 (on apartheid) hardly adds anything to either the general . . . or the more specific . . . provisions and prohibitions of the Convention.[33]

[27] Owing to Arab opposition ('could be interpreted as support' for Israel) and Soviet sensitivity to criticism of treatment of its Jewry: Lerner (n 20) 73; R Cohen, 'International Convention . . . ' (10 January 1966) (World Jewish Congress Records, American Jewish Archives, B91/4) 5; I thank Jim Loeffler for drawing my attention to this source.

[28] Ofra Friesel, 'Race Versus Religion in the Making of the International Convention Against Racial Discrimination, 1965' (2014) 32 Law and History Review 351.

[29] Text accompanying (n 9); Lloyd, 'Family Quarrel' (n 9); Lloyd, 'Auspicious Beginning' (n 14); Mazower, *No Enchanted Palace* (n 15).

[30] Cohen (n 27).

[31] Lerner (n 20) 11, 68 et seq. The preamble recorded alarm caused by 'manifestations of racial discrimination still in evidence in some areas of the world and by governmental policies based on racial superiority or hatred, such as policies of apartheid, segregation or separation'; Article 3 reported: 'States Parties particularly condemn racial segregation and apartheid and undertake to prevent, prohibit and eradicate all practices of this nature in territories under their jurisdiction'.

[32] ibid, 22–23, 42–43, 72–73.

[33] Schwelb (n 22) 1021.

The decision not to reference any specific form of 'ism', *after* the article on apartheid was secured, was 'led by the Afro-Asians'.[34] This was part of a trend. One World Jewish Congress officer lamented in early 1966 that 'for a large number of Member States, particularly the African-Asian states of the United Nations, [anti-Semitism] is of peripheral importance'. He also recorded that, 'accelerated no doubt by the . . . admission of the newly independent African states, especially since 1960, there is a powerful tendency to narrow all references to racial discrimination down to color relations or, more specifically, apartheid'.[35] Jewish advocacy was losing not only individual battles, but also the impetus and initiative.[36]

By contrast, during the 1960s apartheid in Southern (not merely South) Africa became a unifying force. As Saul Dubow notes:

> the iniquity of apartheid was one moral and political issue that countries, large and small, aligned and non-aligned, could mostly agree on—albeit not always from the purest of motives. Whereas pre-war segregation was not so different from practices elsewhere in British colonial Africa and Asia, statutory racial discrimination was becoming indefensible in a world where decolonization and rights were gaining ground.[37]

In the years that followed the Sharpeville Massacre (21 March 1960), apartheid became a cause that Asian, African, Eastern Bloc and, increasingly, certain socialist Western European countries—as well as some liberal and labour constituencies in the West—could rally around.[38] Unity could be forged by such events as Nelson Mandela's 'I Am Prepared to Die' speech from the dock during the Rivonia trial (20 Aprril 1964),[39] or fostered by the presence of ANC leadership in exile. Different factors combined to ensure the apartheid regime would largely enjoy Western political cover and economic advantages (especially by the United States (US) and the United Kingdom (UK)) well into the 1970s and 1980s.[40] Yet these

[34] Cohen (n 27) 6.

[35] 'M. Melamet to World Governing Council' (11 January 1966) (World Jewish Congress Records, American Jewish Archives, B91/4) 4.

[36] These trends were exacerbated by Israel's Cold War positioning, the Middle East conflict, and, soon, its estrangement from Africa and its relations with South Africa: Giladi, 'Negotiating Identity' (n 11).

[37] Saul Dubow, *Apartheid, 1948–1994* (OUP 2014) 47.

[38] Ryan M Irwin, *Gordian Knot: Apartheid and the Unmaking of the Liberal World Order* (OUP 2012) 5 ('lodestar'); Rob Skinner, *The Foundations of Anti-Apartheid: Liberal Humanitarians and Transnational Activists in Britain and the United States, c.1919–64* (Palgrave Macmillan 2010).

[39] Dubow (n 37) 96–97; Owen Collins (ed), *Speeches that Changed the World* (Westminster John Knox Press 1999) 404.

[40] Dubow (n 37) 190 ('Up until 1976, countries sympathetic to South Africa, the United States and Britain most notably, had been able to use diplomatic pressure in order to avert international diplomatic and economic sanctions. South Africa remained a loyal ally of the West and its firm anti-communism received considerable international support, backed by conservative media commentary. But Western support of—or association with—South Africa was becoming more costly').

very same factors—including strategic and economic import and its portrayal as the last bastion of the white man in Africa *and* a bulwark against spreading communism—often rendered South Africa's apartheid such an effective symbol of racial discrimination, whether in domestic arenas, at the UN, or at the Peace Palace. To address race, the agents of decolonization treated apartheid as an essential representation of the racial underpinnings of colonialism in legislative, institutional,[41] and judicial arenas. The Court was asked first to comment on the Union's position in South West Africa,[42] then rule on applications by Liberia and Ethiopia that alleged violations of the mandate instrument and the Covenant, including that

> The Union, by law and in practice, distinguishes as to race, color, national and tribal origin in establishing the rights and duties of the peoples of South West Africa. This official practice is referred to as apartheid.[43]

In general, and in particular with regard to banning racial discrimination, apartheid became a banner.

IV. The aberration of apartheid

Raising the banner of apartheid did not serve well the cause of de-racializing international law. Whatever its effect on other causes espoused by various advocates of ICERD, or on ICERD's own perception and reception, making apartheid the banner of the battle against (colonial) racism may not have been all propitious for the cause of the battle against apartheid itself. Following the crush of ANC domestic resistance in the 1960s, it hoped to receive material assistance from liberated African countries. While, after Bandung, the cause of the anti-apartheid struggle offered to consolidate African nationalism domestically and cement its block politics,[44] it also allowed newly independent states to offer the ANC no more than robust rhetoric denouncing the racism of the apartheid regime.[45] African nationalism, at any rate, was often suspicious of both the ANC inclusive racial composition and its communist membership/affiliations; it was more attuned to the ANC's competitor, the Pan-African Congress.[46] Here, international organizations provided both podium and opportunity to talk against the evil of settler colonialism

[41] For example, the UN Special Committee on apartheid, established by UNGA Res 1761 (6 November 1962); in 1971, the UN Centre Against Apartheid was established.

[42] See Ingo Venzke, Chapter 10 this volume.

[43] *South West Africa Cases (Ethiopia v South Africa; Liberia v South Africa)* (Application Instituting Proceedings) ICJ Pleadings vol I 4, 6.

[44] Steven LB Jensen, *The Making of International Human Rights: The 1960s Decolonization and the Reconstruction of Global Values* (CUP 2016).

[45] For background, Dubow (n 37) 132.

[46] ibid 133.

and apartheid in lieu of furnishing those resisting these forms of oppression with the means to succeed.

Another effect of making apartheid the banner of the struggle against racism (colonial or otherwise) may have been to deflect attention away from the structural racial underpinning of international law. In and outside the UN, treating apartheid as a banner implied that the struggle against apartheid would serve as a panacea. Rallying against the scandal of race in South Africa portrayed apartheid as an aberration, rather than what it really had been: among many other things,[47] the entrenchment (and only later the reification) of segregation laws and practices that long preceded the 1948 electoral victory by the National Party. These were often rooted in British colonial policies and comparable to other colonial regimes in Africa and elsewhere.[48] Enshrining the right to self-determination signified that peoples, not races, were now the political unit of reference in international law without, however, considering (let alone undoing) the lingering products of the operation of old units of reference. This levelled the playing field, but on the formal level alone.

Treating apartheid as an exception, rather than an extreme iteration of the (old) rule, likely made such outcomes even more resilient to reverse or reform. As an aberration, apartheid vindicated colonialism, or in the very least obviated the need to reflect on racialized structural formations of international law and obfuscated how these conditioned post-colonial independence. At a time when decolonization politics inevitably emphasized 'sovereign' more than 'racial' equality as a new organizing principle of international relations, marking apartheid as an aberration pronounced that race had become irrelevant without, however, either reflecting on the need to undo its systemic relevance or in fact addressing the myriad ways in which race had underwritten legal norms and institutions, categories and distinctions, or the structures and decision-making processes of international bodies. It was as if, in Grovogui's words, 'the only requirement for decolonisation is the elimination of the legal instruments that provided for direct foreign rule'.[49] This left newly independent states to individually negotiate their entrance into the international community based on formations that placed them at a disadvantage[50] or, collectively, through 'looking back in anger',[51] make prospective law predestined to matter little in practice.[52]

[47] I do not discount here the role of ideology or theology, economic, or other structural explanations of apartheid; the conclusion to Dubow provides a very useful survey.

[48] Siba N'Zatioula Grovogui, *Sovereigns, Quasi Sovereigns, and Africans: Race and Self-Determination in International Law* (University of Minnesota Press 1996) 160, observes: 'That South Africa always looked outward to Australia, New Zealand, and the United States for ideas concerning apartness was confirmed during the court proceedings' of the South West Africa case.

[49] ibid 1.

[50] Antony Anghie, *Imperialism, Sovereignty and the Making of International Law* (CUP 2007) 111; Matthew Craven, *The Decolonization of International Law: State Succession and the Law of Treaties* (OUP 2007).

[51] Jan Klabbers, *International Law* (CUP 2013) 83, attributing the phrase to Bruno Simma.

[52] The controversial internationalization of armed conflict by national liberation movements in Article 1(4) of the 1977 Additional Protocol I comes to mind. While it did refer to 'peoples . . . fighting

V. Apartheid as scapegoat

Apartheid 'was a symbol, a lightning-rod, even a scapegoat that took away the sins of the world'.[53] In the historical framework of decolonization, this has taken place through treating apartheid as an outmoded exception, rather than an outlier of the rule. This reached its apex in 1973, when apartheid was made into a crime against humanity.[54] Making apartheid a crime under international law confirmed that it was, in fact, but an aberration. This also confirmed, effectively if implicitly, that less sweeping or blatant forms of colonial rule drawing on similar racial ideologies or implementing similar racial policies were not. The Convention, in short, vindicated colonialism; criminalizing the aberration offered to wash away the sins of colonialism.

This point was not lost on Hercules Booysen, a Professor in the Department of Constitutional and International Law at Pretoria's University of South Africa, in a journal article he published upon the Convention's entry into force. Other than considering the Convention a Soviet plot that 'runs counter to the basic principles of the Charter of the United Nations', he also dubbed it 'a masterpiece of hypocrisy'.[55] This targeted the record of the Convention's supporters as well as the fact that South Africa was being singled out among the Convention's opponents. If the crime comprised of '[a]ny measures . . . designed to divide the population along racial lines by the creation of separate reserves', as Article 2(d) provided, that must surely mean that 'America, Canada and perhaps even Australia are also committing the "crime of apartheid" as a result of the existence of Indian and other reserves in these countries'.[56] Booysen warned: 'It is not only South Africa which has been branded as a criminal in this convention, but other western states as well.'[57]

against colonial domination and alien occupation . . . in the exercise of their right of self-determination', subsequent interpretation and understanding placed emphasis on peoples fighting 'against racist régimes'. This has rendered the provision not only uninvoked since 1977 but, rather, uninvokable: Protocol Additional to the Geneva Conventions of 12 August 1949, and relating to the Protection of Victims of International Armed Conflicts (Protocol I) (adopted 8 June 1977, entered into force 7 December 1978) 1125 UNTS 3.

---

53 Dubow (n 37) 277–78, referencing 'an image borrowed from a poem by van Wyk Louw [by] veteran Afrikaans journalist Piet Cillié'. See JV Crewe and NP van Wyk Louw, 'Two Poems by N. P. van Wyk Louw' (1970) 35 Theoria: A Journal of Social and Political Theory 59.

54 Preceded by GA Res 2202 (XXI) (16 December 1966), and Convention on the Non-Applicability of Statutory Limitations to War Crimes and Crimes Against Humanity (adopted 26 November 1968, entered into force 11 November 1970) 754 UNTS 73, art 1. See Ronald C Slye, 'Apartheid as a Crime against Humanity: A Submission to the South African Truth and Reconciliation Commission' (1999) 20 Michigan Journal of International Law 267.

55 H Booysen, 'Convention on the Crime of Apartheid' (1976) 2 South African Yearbook of International Law 56 (Convention brought about by states 'either dominated by or are under the influence of the USSR'). The draft was sponsored by Guinea and the USSR: Guinea and USSR, 'Draft Convention on the Suppression and Punishment of the Crime of Apartheid' (28 October 1971) UN Doc A/C.3/L.1871.

56 Booysen (n 55) 61.

57 ibid 95.

While slightly more than half of UN members are today parties to the Apartheid Convention, membership extends to none of the former colonial powers. Of the P5, only Russia and China have ratified or acceded it.[58]

If the expressive value of the Apartheid Convention should therefore be called into question, so can its practical utility. First, marking apartheid as an aberration and focusing on its racial underpinning in fact facilitated the construction of apartheid in narrow terms. Thus, in 1971, when the ICJ was given finally a chance to extricate itself from the 'disaster of 1966' (by the Security Council, not the Assembly), it announced in the South-West Africa Advisory Opinion that

> To establish . . . and to enforce, distinctions, exclusions, restrictions and limitations *exclusively based on grounds of race*, colour, descent or national or ethnic origin which constitute a denial of fundamental human rights is a flagrant violation of the purposes and principles of the Charter.[59]

This left unaffected 'distinctions, exclusions, restrictions and limitations' not 'exclusively based on grounds of race', whether or not they amounted to a denial of fundamental human rights. While apartheid may have been the conduit for denouncing colonialism at large, singling it out affected precisely the opposite outcomes.

Second, no single person has ever been charged, let alone convicted, for committing the crime of apartheid.[60] Ambiguity was built into the Convention's definitions and scope of application; on the one hand, apartheid was portrayed as bounded by a historical specificity of country-specific practices and policies; on the other it was, simultaneously, phrased as universal, and universally applicable. This, undoubtedly, had contributed to the Convention's limited utility. It is instructive, however, that the Convention's uselessness was revealed most poignantly precisely at the moment the apartheid regime in South Africa came to its end. The delicate balances represented by the Truth and Reconciliation Commission of South Africa (TRC) precluded resorting to the criminal justice model on which the Convention was predicated.[61] The TRC affirmed in an annex to its report that 'its judgement that apartheid, as a system of enforced racial discrimination and separation, was a crime against humanity'; it also noted that 'the recognition of apartheid as a crime against humanity remains a fundamental starting point for reconciliation

[58] Multilateral treaties deposited with the Secretary-General, <https://treaties.un.org/Pages/ViewDetails.aspx?src=TREATY&mtdsg_no=IV-7&chapter=4&clang=_en> accessed 12 September 2016.

[59] *Legal Consequences for States of the Continued Presence of South Africa in Namibia (South West Africa) notwithstanding Security Council Resolution 276* (Advisory Opinion) [1971] ICJ Rep 4 [131] (emphasis added).

[60] Carola Lingaas, 'The Crime Against Humanity of Apartheid in a Post-Apartheid World' (2015) 3 Oslo Law Review 86.

[61] The TRC did discuss crimes against humanity both with regard to 'apartheid as a system' and to 'specific acts': Truth and Reconciliation Commission of South Africa (TRC), 'Report' (2008), vol 1, ch 4 and vol 5, para 101.

in South Africa'.[62] But the report itself considered that the 'vexed issue of apartheid as a crime against humanity impinges perhaps more directly on moral than on legal culpability'.[63] The TRC also took care to distance itself from the operational implications of such conceptualization: 'sharing of the international community's basic moral and legal position on apartheid should not be understood as a call for international criminal prosecution of those who formulated and implemented apartheid policies. Indeed, such a course would militate against the very principles on which this Commission was established.'[64] The minority position submitted by Commissioner Malan was more explicit in casting doubt 'whether an investigation of apartheid under international law would have any present or future legal or political value'.[65] This, apparently, is the reason why South Africa, the template and impetus for the treaty definition of apartheid (as a particular yardstick demonstrating the universality of the norm[66]) has, to date, neither signed or ratified the Apartheid Convention.[67]

The Apartheid Convention signified more the end of a conversation on race in the era of decolonization than its beginning. To the best of my knowledge, no legal or diplomatic history of the Apartheid Convention has ever been written.[68] Rather than panacea, apartheid proved a dead end. It remains a largely a forgotten and quite understudied instrument by lawyers, diplomatic historians, or historians of apartheid.[69] What little familiarity it commands owes much to its inclusion in the Rome Statute of the International Criminal Court.[70] The international criminal law literature following that inclusion tends, nonetheless, to treat the crime of apartheid briefly and focus, naturally, more on technical aspects of the criminality of apartheid, rather than what it signifies for the role of race in international law.

62 ibid vol 1, ch 4, Appendix: 'Apartheid as a Crime against Humanity'.

63 ibid vol 1, ch 5, para 103 (adding: 'A simple focus on the criminal culpability of isolated individuals responsible for apartheid can ignore the broader responsibilities presently under discussion. It is not enough merely to identify a few high-profile 'criminals' as those responsible for the atrocities of the past—and thus give insufficient attention to a deeper analysis of the underlying nature, cause and extent of apartheid').

64 ibid vol 5, para 64. Malan's submission revealed the discord on this question within the Commission.

65 ibid vol 1, ch 4, Appendix: 'Apartheid as a Crime against Humanity'.

66 Apartheid Convention (n 4) art 2 ('similar policies and practices of racial segregation and discrimination as practised in southern Africa').

67 John Reynolds, 'Third World Approaches to International Law and the Ghosts of Apartheid' in David Keane and Yvonne McDermott (eds), *The Challenge of Human Rights* (Edward Elgar Publishing 2012) 210. South Africa did ratify the Rome Statute on 27 November 2000.

68 For example, only cursory mentions of apartheid in the otherwise thorough Paul Gordon Lauren, *Power and Prejudice: The Politics and Diplomacy of Racial Discrimination* (Westview Press 1988) 228;

69 Reynolds (n 67) 209 ('a largely forgotten and neglected concept in international law'); Lingaas (n 60) 87 ('legal scholarship has largely turned a blind eye onto this crime'); John Dugard and John Reynolds, 'Apartheid, International Law, and the Occupied Palestinian Territory' (2013) 24 European Journal of International Law 867 (the concept of apartheid 'never given enormous attention by international lawyers').

70 Rome Statute of the International Criminal Court (adopted 17 July 1998, entered into force 1 July 2002) 2187 UNTS 90, art 7(1)(j).

Scholars of international criminal law debate the customary status of the crime, whether it survived the transition to democracy in South Africa, or try to use it to denounce contemporary policies in other parts of the globe.[71] Yet, such debates obfuscate the effects of criminalization of apartheid: it posits apartheid as a scandal, dramatizes a spectacle of its denunciation, generates reforms—which all, in the end, serve to regularize, entrench, even legitimize the system that produced the scandal in the first place.[72]

VI. Law of unintended consequences

There were other unintended consequences of engaging with the race category. The anti-Semitism initiative of Jewish NGOs at the UN had led to codification of general non-discrimination norms; but the contingencies of the Cold War, the Middle-East conflict, and the sea change in the composition of the international community all combined to divert and pervert such agenda items. This begun, in the course of negotiations of the ICERD draft, as a device for the Union of Soviet Socialist Republics (USSR) to mute criticism of Soviet treatment of Jews behind the Iron Curtain:

> the Soviet Union introduced a sub-amendment to the United States–Brazilian amendment declaring that 'States Parties condemn anti-Semitism, Zionism, Nazism, neo-Nazism and other forms of the policy and ideology of colonialism'. The Soviet delegate declared that Zionism was as 'dangerous' a form of racial discrimination as Nazism, fascism and anti-Semitism'.[73]

In 1975, two years after the adoption of the Apartheid Convention, that device would devolve into a condemnation of Zionism—the political movement of Jewish nationalism, and Israel's foundational ideology—as 'a form of racism'.[74] That Assembly Resolution was titled 'Elimination of all Forms of Racial Discrimination'. One paragraph recalled a 1973 resolution where the Assembly 'condemned, inter alia, the unholy alliance between South African racism and Zionism'.[75] It also recited an Organization of African Unity (OAU) resolution noting the 'common imperialist origin' and 'racist structure' of apartheid and Zionism. My first political

[71] For example, Lingaas (n 60); Reynolds (n 67); Dugard and Reynolds (n 69).

[72] I owe a debt here to Nicholas B Dirks, *The Scandal of Empire: India and the Creation of Imperial Britain* (Belknap 2006).

[73] Cohen (n 27) 5; Ofra Friesel, 'Equating Zionism with Racism: The 1965 Precedent' (2013) 97 American Jewish History 283.

[74] UNGA Res 3379 (XXX) (10 November 1975).

[75] UNGA Res 3151 (XXVIII) (14 December 1973). On Israel's relations with South Africa, see Sasha Polakow-Suransky, *The Unspoken Alliance: Israel's Secret Relationship with Apartheid South Africa* (Vintage Books 2010).

engagement consisted of being dragged by my mother, not a model of political activism, to a protest rally denouncing the UN. At seven, I could not know that the 1975 Resolution, 'revoked' by the Assembly in 1991,[76] had its roots in the 1960 Jewish UN initiative against anti-Semitism.

Another fallout of the same process concerned agents. A month after ICERD was adopted, the USSR representative to the 18th Session of the Sub-Commission on Prevention of Discrimination and Protection of Minorities decried NGOs with UN consultative status—some routinely critical of the Soviet Union for how its treated its Jews—as unrepresentative, and tools of Western states in the Cold War.[77] Driven by the USSR and the Arab bloc, such charges had seen the presence and influence of consultative-status Jewish advocacy at UN severely diminished.[78]

VII. Apartheid and genocide

The appendix to the TRC report dealing with apartheid as a crime against humanity recorded the 'almost total unanimity within the international community that apartheid as a form of systematic racial discrimination constituted a crime against humanity'. At the same time, it took care to dispel the 'confusion in public debates in South Africa' and 'state that a finding of a crime against humanity does not necessarily or automatically involve a finding of genocide',[79] implying that the 'intent to destroy, in whole or in part, an ethnic or racial group' in Article 1 of the Genocide Convention[80] was lacking.

This draws into attention a curious choice made by the drafters of the Apartheid Convention. In rough terms, they elected to follow the overall structure and the general technique of the 1948 Genocide Convention, rather than developing a criminal law model out of the terms and forms of racial discrimination elaborated by ICERD or developing a unique framework for elaborating the criminality of apartheid and putting it into operation. The reasons for following a familiar structural criminal law template, or signifying the intellectual and moral proximity of genocide and apartheid, appear obvious. The rivalry of the 1960s between the different causes of combating racial discrimination—specifically, anti-Semitism and apartheid—may well also explain this choice. Still, with this choice the drafters, inadvertently and indirectly, lent some authority to the proposition that race was still a relevant category.

[76] UNGA Res 46/86 (16 December 1991).
[77] M. Melamet to World Governing Council (n 35) 281.
[78] Loeffler, *Zionism* (n 17).
[79] TRC (n 61) vol 1, ch 4, Appendix.
[80] Convention on the Prevention and Punishment of the Crime of Genocide (adopted 9 December 1948, entered into force 12 January 1951) 78 UNTS 277.

The Genocide Convention gave effect to Raphael Lemkin's project to extend the protection of international law not to individuals as such, but rather to the separate existence and identity of the group[81]—including the racial group.[82] At a time when the protection of minority rights became almost entirely discredited,[83] and the rights of the individual were coming into vogue, this swansong of the interwar minority system stamped the most extreme abuses of racial (and other) groups with criminality. For Lemkin, whatever made the group worthy of protection, it was the *group* that had merited such protection. And the group was, among other criteria, racially defined. US Judge Joseph Proskauer, President of the American Jewish Committee and one of the promoters of the Universal Declaration, wrote in March 1944 that the idea of minority rights was an 'exaggeration of the race concept'.[84] So was, then, the crime of genocide. The Genocide Convention, perhaps paradoxically, reasserted the relevance of race.

Did the Apartheid Convention, other than by following the Genocide Convention's design, unwittingly confirm the continued relevance of the race category? To some extent, the answer seems positive. Criminalizing 'policies and practices of racial segregation and discrimination' perhaps entails the rejection of the analytical relevance of race. And yet defining apartheid as comprising of 'inhuman acts committed for the purpose of establishing and maintaining domination by one racial group of persons over any other racial group of persons and systematically oppressing them' and requiring that such acts be directed against 'member or members of a racial group or groups' does require decision makers to subscribe, in order to impose liability, to the value system of perpetrators of apartheid by assuming it has objective meaning that the decision maker can share, if only in order to denounce it. That, perhaps, is another reason why the TRC confirmed the criminality of apartheid, but refused to engage it.[85]

[81] His 1933 proposal were directed at 'attacks carried out against an individual as a member of collectivity': Raphael Lemkin, 'Acts Constituting a General (Transnational) Danger Considered as Offences Against the Law of Nations' (Additional explications to the Special Report presented to the 5th Conference for the Unification of Penal Law in Madrid (14–20 October 1933), Jim Fusell tr, first published 1933) <http://www.preventgenocide.org/lemkin/madrid1933-english.htm> accessed 16 August 2018. See also Mira L Siegelberg, 'Unofficial Men, Efficient Civil Servants: Raphael Lemkin in the History of International Law' (2013) 15 Journal of Genocide Research 297, 309; Anthony D Moses, 'Raphael Lemkin, Culture, and the Concept of Genocide' in Donald Bloxham and Anthony D Moses (eds), *The Oxford Handbook of Genocide Studies* (OUP 2010) 23–24.

[82] Raphael Lemkin, *Axis Rule in Occupied Europe: Laws of Occupation Analysis of Government Proposals for Redress* (Carnegie Endowment for International Peace 1944); Raphael Lemkin, 'Genocide as a Crime under International Law' (1947) 41 American Journal of International Law 145.

[83] Mark Mazower, 'The Strange Triumph of Human Rights, 1933–1950' (1999) 47 The Historical Journal 379, 387.

[84] Quoted in James Loeffler, 'The Particularist Pursuit of American Universalism: The American Jewish Committee's 1944 'Declaration on Human Rights'' (2015) 50 Journal of Contemporary History 274, 281.

[85] See Section V.

VIII. In the aftermath of battle

Are these episodes representative? They may be, but if so, they are admittedly too few. Yet, they are certainly instructive. They suggest that race had been, whatever its rhetorical deployment in the battle for international law waged in the decolonization era, neither a strategic goal nor a major battlefield. They demonstrate how, notwithstanding early opportunities for coalitions, contingencies made the cause of decolonization—increasingly considering apartheid the embodiment of colonial racism—eventually come to compete with, divert, obstruct, or supplant other causes in the battle to overcome the race category in international law. These episodes also highlight the costs and unintended consequences of making apartheid a banner in the battle for international law. One involved portraying apartheid as an aberration; this, while seeking to denounce colonialism, in effect validated it and its lasting consequences. The more strenuously one decried apartheid, the more were the sins of colonialism washed away. Another was the paradox, in transitioning South Africa, of the crime of apartheid: while validating the work of the TRC, at the same time that crime threatened to undermine its very foundations.

When it came to race, decolonization has left lasting footprints on the normative landscape of international law. Only some of these were mentioned here. Still, these footprints are sketchy, disjointed, borrowed, or sporadic, and often the product of accident and convenience, not design. They do not address racialized structuring of international authority, but rather concern national governance and treatment. And these footprints tend to obfuscate rather than reveal: they cover the imprints of older and other causes of combatting racism; they mark the cause of formal sovereign equality, but conceal how it abandoned substantive racial equality; and they draw attention away from the myriad ways in which race remains imprinted in the genetic material of many international norms and institutions, obscuring the lingering consequences of an explicitly racialized international law predating decolonization but, alas, not quite de-racialized by it.

B. Institutions

10

The International Court of Justice During the Battle for International Law (1955–1975)

Colonial Imprints and Possibilities for Change

*Ingo Venzke**

I. Introduction

When newly independent states challenged the international legal order in whose formation they had no voice, especially from the 1950s onward, they turned to international law's key concepts, to more specific legal obligations, and to some of its established institutions. Given that great powers benefited from international law and international institutions that had taken shape under their influence, those powers were sure to oppose nearly all changes that independent states sought to introduce. The result was a veritable battle for international law with many well-known standoffs and sites of engagement.[1] This chapter explores the role of the International Court of Justice (ICJ)—the United Nations' (UN) 'principal judicial organ'[2]—during this battle for international law, roughly between the years of 1955–1975. It examines the sceptical attitudes that prevailed with regard to the ICJ among newly independent states and how predominantly they saw the ICJ as an institution that reinforces international law's colonial imprints. The ICJ seemed to stand in the way of rectifying past wrongs (Section II).

There was still a moment of hope that the ICJ could be useful in combatting one of the most troubling remnants of colonialism: the apartheid regime in South Africa and in the mandate territory of South West Africa.[3] The chapter explores the

* I am indebted to Jochen von Bernstorff and Philipp Dann for their comments, to Wiebe Hommes and Marta Lozano Sanchez for their research assistance, and to Katherine Skinner for her assistance in finalizing the text.

[1] See the Introduction to this volume.

[2] UN Charter art 92; ICJ Statute art 1.

[3] On the context of the Mandate system see Antony Anghie, *Imperialism, Sovereignty and the Making of International Law* (CUP 2007) 147–60; Ralph Wilde, *International Territorial Administration: How Trusteeship and the Civilizing Mission Never Went Away* (OUP 2008) 306–45; Nele Matz-Lück, 'Civilization and the Mandate System Under the League of Nations as Origin of Trusteeship' (2005) 9 Max Planck Yearbook of United Nations Law 47.

Ingo Venzke, *The International Court of Justice During the Battle for International Law (1955–1975)* In: *The Battle for International Law: South-North Perspectives on the Decolonization Era*. Edited by: Jochen von Bernstorff and Philipp Dann, Oxford University Press (2019).
DOI: 10.1093/oso/9780198849636.003.0011

ICJ's momentous decisions in the *South West Africa Cases* because they centred on two focal points for demands of non-white liberation: apartheid and the mandate system.[4] What is more, for the ICJ, the decisions in the *South West Africa Cases* proved to be the single most important moments during the battle for international law, even during its entire history.[5] Famously, in 1962 the ICJ affirmed its jurisdiction by a narrow majority. But whatever hope remained that the ICJ would assist in the struggle against remnants of colonialism, it was dashed in 1966, when the ICJ unexpectedly rejected the applicants' standing by the tie-breaking vote of its President.[6] The *South West Africa Cases* are the ICJ's captivating highpoint during the battle for international law. After its 1966 Judgment, the ICJ was largely sidelined as a discredited actor on this terrain of struggle (Section III.).

According to newly independent states, the ICJ had to change. Even before *South West Africa*, the composition of the ICJ's bench had come into view. But the dynamics of the debates changed with the 1966 Judgment. Through archival material, this chapter draws particular attention to the effects of that decision in the judicial elections. While Judge Badawi from Egypt was the only member at the ICJ from the African continent prior to 1964, four African judges were on the bench in 1970. And within three years from the 1966 Judgment, only two of the judges who were then in the controversial majority were still on the bench (Section IV.).

The chapter then argues that changes in the ICJ's composition made a positive difference in later practice, especially in the 1971 *Namibia* Advisory Opinion. The game seems to have been worth the candle. But the ICJ continued to show considerable ambivalence between either entrenching colonial imprints in the international legal order or working towards international law's progressive change (Section V.).

This account of the battle for international law—of the ICJ's role, the composition of its bench, and its practice—serves as a vivid reminder of how legal and institutional developments are the product of a veritable struggle, and not the simple expression of a timeless, unsituated rationality. Such a production of international law and its institutions may pass as one of the few constants across history. It calls out from the 1966 Judgment in *South West Africa*, just as well as from the most recent 2016 Judgment in *Nuclear Arms Race (Marshall Islands)* (Section VI.).

[4] On the importance of the anti-apartheid struggle for newly independent and non-aligned states and other political actors, see Ryan M Irwin, 'Apartheid on Trial: South West Africa and the International Court of Justice, 1960-66' (2010) 32 The International History Review 619, 620–21.

[5] See Waldemar Nielsen, *African Battleline: American policy choices in southern Africa* (Harper & Row 1965) 110, quoted in Anthony A D'Amato, 'Legal and Political Strategies of the South West Africa Litigation' (1967) IV Law in Transition Quarterly 8, 8 (noting that '[t]he *South West Africa Case* may be, as some have said, the Achilles' heel of apartheid. It could also be the Achilles' heel of the International Court, of the United Nations').

[6] *South West Africa Cases* (*Ethiopia v South Africa; Liberia v South Africa*) (Second Phase, Judgment) [1966] ICJ Rep 6 (hereafter *South West Africa Cases* (Second Phase, Judgment)).

II. Colonial imprints and prospects for change

Many voices from newly independent and non-aligned states held that the ICJ above all gave effect to the colonial imprints that continued to mark international law.[7] From their perspective, the ICJ entrenches an international legal order that was, both in its core concepts and in its concrete manifestations, shaped during the times of great power domination. Specifically, the ICJ was seen to enforce unequal treaties and to prevent newly independent states from rectifying what they believed to be historic wrongs. A series of cases in the ICJ's early years seemed to support such a view.

For example, when France brought proceedings against Egypt in 1949 after the Egyptian government had placed approximately forty French nationals in camps and sequestered their property during the Arab–Israeli War, France did so on the basis of a convention signed in Montreux in 1937 while Egypt was still a British protectorate.[8] In principle, the 1937 convention ended the special protection of foreigners through consular and mixed courts, but only after a transitional period of twelve years that was possibly subject to extension.[9] Egypt withdrew the challenged measures shortly after France brought the proceedings, and after it was defeated in the war with Israel. Even if the case was thus swiftly removed from the ICJ's docket, it presented the ICJ as enforcing great power privileges of the past.

Other early cases were read in a similar fashion. The United Kingdom (UK) instituted proceedings against Iran in response to the nationalization of the Anglo–Persian Oil Company (now British Petroleum, BP).[10] Although the ICJ ultimately declined jurisdiction, it first issued provisional measures that would have undone the effects of nationalization.[11] In yet another case, Portugal brought proceedings against India to claim the right of passage of its aircraft over Indian territory to reach Portuguese territories within India and on the

[7] Sure enough, other views existed. There was also hope, if not too simple expectation, that the Court would work to support weaker states; see Bhupinder S Chimni, 'International Law Scholarship in Post-Colonial India: Coping with Dualism' (2010) 23 Leiden Journal of International Law 23, 36–37. On the European imprint on the structures of international law, see Upendra Baxi, 'Some Remarks on Eurocentrism and the Law of Nations' in Ram P Anand (ed), *Asian States and the Development of Universal International Law* (Vikas Publications 1972) 3.

[8] *Protection of French Nationals and Protected Persons in Egypt* (*France v Egypt*) (Institution of Proceedings) [1949] ICJ Pleadings 8. Convention Regarding the Abolition of the Capitulations in Egypt, which had been signed in Montreux in 1937.

[9] It also contained a compromissory clause that provided the Permanent Court of International Justice with jurisdiction Article 13, Convention Regarding the Abolition of the Capitulations in Egypt 1937. According to Article 37 ICJ Statute, references to the PCIJ in compromissory clauses vest the ICJ with jurisdiction.

[10] *Anglo-Iranian Oil Co* (*United Kingdom v Iran*) (Application Instituting Proceedings) [1951] ICJ Pleadings 8.

[11] *Anglo-Iranian Oil Co* (*Iran v United Kingdom*) (Preliminary Measures, Order) [1952] ICJ Rep 81 (hereafter *Anglo-Iranian Oil Co* (Preliminary Measures, Order)); *Anglo-Iranian Oil Co* (Preliminary Objection, Judgment) [1952] ICJ Rep 93.

Indian coast. Portugal relied on a series of historical treaties, starting with a 1779 treaty that it had concluded with the sovereign of Punem.[12] Even if a narrow majority actually denied any Indian wrongdoing, the ICJ in principle affirmed Portugal's rights.[13]

Ram Prakash Anand summarized the broader sentiment that this set of early cases evoked among many governments of newly independent states:

> All these so-called legal rights had been created and forced upon these states in a former age—the age of colonialism and imperialism—under such conditions of lawlessness, aggression, and plunder of their territories . . . that these countries could hardly be expected to honour them so far as lay in their power, and they came to be recognized merely on the basis of the superior power of the European countries. As the International Court is only expected to enforce these legal rights, the 'new' countries refuse to go before the Court.[14]

Looking back at the first decades of the ICJ, Georges Abi-Saab observes the dissatisfaction of the new states with large parts of classical international law which legitimized their subjugation and reflected the outlook and interests of the limited community from which it ensued and of which they did not partake except as objects of appropriation. Whence their refusal to submit to a procedure of settlement of disputes that is congenitally constrained to the strict application of precisely the contested law until its rules were updated and developed with their participation to make them more universal in their approach and in the values and interests they are called upon to further and protect.[15]

The ICJ was bound to be conservative and bound to preserve the law that newly independent states wished to change.[16] According to Mohammed Bedjaoui, '[e]ven when a weak country would naturally seek the protection of the law, it avoids submitting its case to the Court for fear of having to submit to the application of

[12] *Right of Passage over Indian Territory* (*Portugal v India*) (Application Instituting Proceedings) [1955/I] ICJ Pleadings. Also see Jan HW Verzijl, *International Law in Historical Perspective* (Sijthoff 1973) 370.

[13] *Right of Passage over Indian Territory* (*Portugal v India*) (Preliminary Objections, Judgment) [1967] ICJ Rep 125; *Right of Passage over Indian Territory* (*Portugal v India*) (Merits) [1960] ICJ Rep 6. Also see Georges Abi-Saab, 'The Newly Independent States and the Rules of International Law: An Outline' (1962) 8 Howard Law Journal 111 (hereafter Abi-Saab, 'Newly Independent States') (noting newly independent states' resistance to accepting the territorial burdens from the colonial era).

[14] Ram P Anand, *International Courts and Contemporary Conflicts* (Asia Publication House 1974) 320.

[15] Georges Abi-Saab, 'The International Court as a World Court' in Alan V Lowe and Malgosia Fitzmaurice (eds), *Fifty Years of the International Court of Justice: Essays in Honour of Sir Robert Jennings* (CUP 1996) 5 (hereafter Abi-Saab, 'World Court'); also see Abi-Saab, 'Newly Independent States' (n 13).

[16] Also see JJG Syatauw, *Some Newly Established Asian States and the Development of International Law* (Springer Netherlands 1961) 221, critiquing that newly independent states are treated like a child who, 'finally grown up . . . should behave. The child may want to do so, but will not necessarily wish to accept all rules of conduct set by the once-stronger adult'. Quoted in Anand (n 14) 320.

customary norms which operate to its disadvantage and in the establishment of which it played no part'.[17]

The rights of French citizens, of British companies, and of Portuguese aircraft all stemmed from treaties of bygone times. It could not be expected that the judicial process would introduce change in this regard. Using Iceland as an example, Anand argued that political, diplomatic channels were needed to push for change. When Iceland wished to change the extent of its fishing zones it could only have lost in proceedings before the ICJ. The ICJ would have rejected the straight baselines from which Iceland wanted to count the twelve miles of exclusive fisheries jurisdiction. Iceland therefore reached a compromise according to which Great Britain tolerated the Icelandic practice and Iceland, on its part, initially allowed British vessels to enter its newly defined fishing zones.[18] Anand points out that such a dynamic development of international law would have been stifled had Iceland accepted Great Britain's offer to adjudicate the matter.[19]

When compared to the process of negotiation, third-world international lawyers saw even greater possibilities for change—less cumbersome and more certain—in plenary bodies such as the UN General Assembly (UNGA) where they held a growing majority.[20] Resolutions of international organizations should be the modern sources of a progressive international law.[21] Resolutions should free international law from its colonial imprints, not difficult treaty negotiations nor conservative adjudication.

But the path via resolutions had its own limits, especially when it came to their enforcement. In particular, a growing pile of condemning UNGA Resolutions could not irritate South Africa in its blatantly racist apartheid policies.[22] Security Council action was held back by the United States (US) and the UK, who each

[17] Anand (n 14) 102. It does not readily follow from this sentiment that newly independent states were less willing to submit to the jurisdiction of the court when compared to other states; see Ibrahim FI Shihata, 'The Attitude of New States Toward the International Court of Justice' (1965) 19 International Organization 203.

[18] Anand (n 14) 321–22.

[19] This is precisely what happened in 1972, see *Fisheries Jurisdiction* (*United Kingdom of Great Britain and Northern Ireland v Iceland*) (Merits) [1974] ICJ Rep 3. Anand further notes that pushing for change in international law may well start with a violation, which can then lead to a new compromise. Anand (n 14) 324.

[20] Anand (n 14) 330; Mohammed Bedjaoui, *Towards a New International Economic Order* (Holmes Meier 1979) 142.

[21] Bedjaoui (n 20) 138–40; Bin Cheng, 'United Nations Resolutions on Outer Space: "Instant" International Customary Law?' 1965 The Indian Journal of International Law 23, 23; Taslim O Elias, 'Modern Sources of International Law' in Wolfgang Friedmann, Louis Henkin and Oliver Lissitzyn (eds), *Transnational Law in a Changing Society: Essays in Honor of Philip C. Jessup* (Columbia University Press 1972) 51.

[22] On the importance of these resolutions all the same see Richard A Falk, 'On the Quasi-Legislative Competence of the General Assembly' (1966) 60 American Journal of International Law 782, 790. The Security Council only placed apartheid politics on its agenda in 1960 after the so-called Sharpeville massacre, when police forces shot sixty-nine unarmed demonstrators—men, women, and children—and wounded about 200 more.

catered to their strong business interest in South Africa.[23] According to Ernest Gross, former US representative at the UN and then lead agent for Ethiopia and Liberia in *South West Africa*:

> 'If any realistic prospect had existed that members of the United Nations would repress, rather than merely condemn, South Africa's violations of its clear and present duties under the Mandate, the hazards, burdens and, above all, the time involved in litigation would have been avoided.'[24]

Acting through the UNGA, newly independent and non-aligned states thus asked the Committee on South West Africa (which became Namibia) to explore the possibilities of instituting proceedings against South Africa.[25] In May 1960 the Liberian Ambassador—in consultation with other African States—also requested an opinion on the matter from Ernest Gross. Gross's suggestions were promptly discussed at the Second Conference of Independent African States held in Addis Ababa in June.[26] Ethiopia and Liberia instituted proceedings in the same year.[27] While South Africa had so far shrugged off even sharp criticism of its apartheid regime, it showed genuine apprehension in view of the judicial proceedings.[28]

III. 'The disaster of 1966'

A. South Africa's mandate and the struggle against apartheid

The former German colony of South West Africa was a mandate territory within the system of the League of Nations. In the words of Article 22 of the Covenant, the territory was 'inhabited by peoples not yet able to stand by themselves under the strenuous conditions of the modern world'. For those peoples 'there should be applied the principle that the well-being and development of such peoples form a sacred trust of civilisation'.[29] The Council of the League of Nations put South Africa

[23] Ernest A Gross, 'The *South West Africa Case*: What Happened?' (1966) 45 Foreign Affairs 36, 41–42; Irwin (n 4) 624. On the US American and British business interests in South Africa also see Department of State, 'National Policy Paper—South Africa, Part One' (National Archive, S/P Files: Lot 72 D).

[24] Gross (n 23) 41.

[25] See in further detail Edward McWhinney, *The World Court and the Contemporary International Law-Making Process* (Sijthoff Noordhoff 1979) 93 (hereafter McWhinney, *World Court*); D'Amato (n 5) 16–17.

[26] It had to be Ethiopia and Liberia because they were already members of the League of Nations and thus deemed in the best legal position to challenge South Africa it the performance of duties that continued to stem from the League's mandate system.

[27] D'Amato (n 5) 17; Gross (n 23) 40.

[28] For a discussion of the assessments of a binding judgment from the perspective of South African politics, see Irwin (n 4) 621.

[29] Covenant of the League of Nations (1919) art 22.

in charge as the mandate power.[30] After the Second World War, South West Africa was the only territory for which no formal transition could be arranged so as to place the mandate within the framework of the UN Trusteeship Council. South African Prime Minister Jan Smuts resisted any agreement with the UN on the issue. He defied any UN oversight and instead annexed the territory.[31] Domestic South African law and apartheid policies applied equally in the mandate territory of South West Africa after 1949.[32]

The struggle against apartheid became the cause célèbre for newly independent and non-aligned states. It allowed them to indict colonialism in its contemporary manifestation. While they focused their struggle within the UNGA, on three occasions in the 1950s they brought in the ICJ via requests to deliver advisory opinions.[33] In 1950 the ICJ unanimously affirmed the international status of the mandate territory in spite of South Africa's decision to annex it.[34] In 1955 the ICJ held, again unanimously, that the UNGA could take decisions on the mandate by majority,[35] and a year later it affirmed that the UNGA could hold hearings with petitioners from the mandate territory.[36] Even though five judges dissented on the last question, these advisory opinions did not draw the ICJ out into rough waters, nor did they pit great powers against newly independent and non-aligned states. The stakes were not yet high enough.

That changed radically when Ethiopia and Liberia brought contentious proceedings against South Africa.[37] Even if the precise focus of the case shifted with developments in the claimants' litigation strategy, South Africa's apartheid regime was always on the line. Was apartheid compatible with international law? Did

[30] The Council of the League of Nations decided on 17 December 1920 that South West Africa would be a so-called 'C' mandate, to be administered by South Africa.

[31] The Future of South West Africa, UNGA Res 65 (I) (14 December 1946). Also see Mark Mazower, *No Enchanted Palace: The End of Empire and the Ideological Origins of the United Nations* (Princeton University Press 2009) 50–61.

[32] South West Africa Affairs Amendment Act, No 23 of 1949.

[33] For an overview see *Anglo-Iranian Oil Co* (Preliminary Measures, Order) (n 11); Soloman Slonim, *South West Africa and the United Nations: An International Mandate in Dispute* (Johns Hopkins University Press 1972).

[34] *International Status of South West Africa* (Advisory Opinion) [1950] ICJ Rep 128, 143–44 (hereafter *International Status of South West Africa* (Advisory Opinion)). After 1949 domestic law made no further reference to South West Africa as mandate or trusteeship territory and applied equally on that territory. See South West Africa Affairs Amendment Act, No 23 of 1949. For the political vision of Jan Smuts, see Mazower (n 32) 46–61.

[35] *Voting Procedure on Questions relating to Reports and Petitions concerning the Territory of South West Africa* (Advisory Opinion) [1955] ICJ Rep 67.

[36] *Admissibility of Hearings of Petitioners by the Committee on South West Africa* (Advisory Opinion) [1956] ICJ Rep 23 (hereafter *Admissibility of Hearings of Petitioners by the Committee on South West Africa* (Advisory Opinion)). The League Council already provided for petitions in 1923 to make the supervisory system more effective. It did not include hearings, but the mandate power would comment on any such petitions. South Africa did not do that and the UNGA thus claimed that hearings could better establish the factual situation. See Christof Heyns and Magnus Killander, 'South West Africa/Namibia (Advisory Opinions and Judgments)' (2007), in Rüdiger Wolfrum (ed), *Max Planck Encyclopedia of Public International Law* (OUP 2013) para 28–30. Context: Anghie (n 3) 147ff.

[37] Abi-Saab, 'World Court' (n 15) 5.

the introduction of the apartheid regime within South West Africa violate South Africa's obligations as a mandate power? These questions drew the front line in the battle for international law, among state representatives at the UN, and among judges at the Court.

B. Contentious proceedings: the Court's jurisdiction (first phase)

The proceedings were an orchestrated affair with a leading role for the Group of African States at the UNGA.[38] The litigators were a small team around Ernest Gross.[39] They worked on a small budget and their arms were no match to those of South Africa, whose fifty lawyers worked on the case around the clock.[40] Of the 3,756 pages of written pleadings, 3,105 (83 per cent) came from the respondent's side.[41] South Africa invested significant efforts into establishing its readings of the facts and into supporting the necessity of the apartheid regime in the context of 'African realities'.[42] The applicants did not want to be drawn on that terrain as they argued on more principled grounds. They also feared lengthy proceedings. Their first main argument was that apartheid led to a despicable standard of treatment for the black population and therefore breaches South Africa's obligation to work towards that population's 'well-being and development'. The second main argument was more radical: Apartheid was per se illegal because it separated people according to their membership in a group, that is to say, race.[43] Since the first argument was of course difficult to make without engaging with the facts on the ground, the emphasis gradually shifted towards the latter more principled, but also more difficult, argument.[44]

Two key issues stood out during the first phase of the proceedings on the ICJ's jurisdiction. First, according to Article 7 of the Mandate for South West Africa, the Mandatory 'agree[d] that, if any dispute whatever should arise between the Mandatory and another Member of the League of Nations relating to the interpretation or the application of the provisions of the Mandate, such dispute, if it cannot be settled by negotiation, shall be submitted to the Permanent Court of International Justice'. The narrow majority of eight votes to seven held that Article 7 did not require the claimants to show an individual material interest to bring a

[38] See UNGA Res 1565 (XV) (18 December 1960), '[c]*ommends* the Governments of Ethiopia and Liberia upon their initiative in submitting such a dispute to the International Court of Justice'.
[39] International lawyer Anthony D'Amato was also part of the team.
[40] D'Amato (n 5) 22–23.
[41] ibid.
[42] ibid 22.
[43] ibid 24–25.
[44] ibid.

case.[45] Paraphrasing the language of the League's Covenant, the majority argued that the well-being and development of the peoples of underdeveloped territories form a sacred trust. It held that, as part of this system, Article 7 implements one of the 'securities for the performance of this trust'.[46] According to the majority, the mandate 'vest[s] the right of invoking the compulsory jurisdiction against the Mandatory . . . in each of the other Members of the League. Protection of the material interests of the Members or their nationals is of course included within its compass, but the well-being and development of the inhabitants of the Mandated territory are not less important.'[47]

Second, would it stand in the way of the ICJ's jurisdiction that the League had dissolved? In its advisory opinions the ICJ had already stated that 'the effective performance of the sacred trust of civilization by the Mandatory Powers required that the administration of mandated territories should be subject to international supervision' and that '[t]he necessity for supervision continues to exist despite the disappearance of the supervisory organ under the Mandates System'.[48] The majority in 1962 reasoned similarly that the method of looking at

> the natural and ordinary meaning of the words . . . is not an absolute one. Where such a method of interpretation results in a meaning incompatible with the spirit, purpose and context of the clause or instrument in which the words are contained, no reliance can be validly placed on it.'[49]

The applicants had standing to challenge South Africa's conduct as a mandate power. The majority understood the institution of proceedings as part of the structure of effective supervision—as part of the sacred trust 'laid upon the League as an organized international community *and* upon its Member States'.[50] The 'system is dedicated to the avowed object of promoting the well-being and development of the peoples concerned and is fortified by setting up safeguards for the protection of their rights'.[51]

Flanking the majority, Judges Bustamente (Peru) and Jessup (US) each stressed in their separate opinions the responsibility of the mandate power towards all

45 *South West Africa Cases* (*Ethiopia v South Africa; Liberia v South Africa*) (Preliminary Objections, Judgment) [1962] ICJ Rep 319, 343 (hereafter *South West Africa Cases* (Preliminary Objections, Judgment)).

46 ibid 344.

47 ibid.

48 *International Status of South West Africa* (Advisory Opinion) (n 35) 136; *Admissibility of Hearings of Petitioners by the Committee on South West Africa* (Advisory Opinion) (n 37) 27.

49 *South West Africa Cases* (Preliminary Objections, Judgment) (n 46) 336. On the principle of effectiveness in the advisory opinions, see Hersch Lauterpacht, *The Development of International Law by the International Court* (Stevens 1958) 291.

50 *South West Africa Cases* (Preliminary Objections, Judgment) (n 46) 329 (italics added).

51 ibid.

states.[52] In Jessup's words, the mandate's compromissory clause 'protect[s] the general interest of Members of the international community'.[53] Judge ad hoc Mbanefo (Nigeria) agreed in his separate opinion and further expanded on the need for a wide understanding of what constitutes a dispute.[54] Six of the seven judges in the minority wrote dissenting opinions: President Winiarski (Poland), Judge Basdevant (France), jointly Judges Sir Percy Spender (Australia) and Sir Gerald Fitzmaurice (UK), Judge Morelli (Italy), and Judge ad hoc van Wyk (South Africa). Judge Spiropoulos (Greece) only attached a very short declaration in which he simply stated that the Court's jurisdiction cannot be established with sufficient certainty.[55] It is the joint opinion of Judges Spender and Fitzmaurice that stands out for its strong contrast with the majority—for its length (it was three times longer than the Judgment) and for the way in which it foreshadows the proceedings' second phase. Judges Spender and Fitzmaurice rejected Ethiopia's and Liberia's standing due to the applicants' lack of an individual interest in the subject matter of the case. They argued that the mandate system only contained substantive provisions 'for the benefit of the people of the territory', or 'for the national benefit of the Members of the League and their nationals (commercial rights, open door, freedom for missionary activities, etc.)'.[56] Spender and Fitzmaurice stressed how the mandate system was understood at the time when South Africa became the mandate power and, on that basis, they concluded that Article 7 only extends to 'a dispute between the actual parties before the Court about their own interests'.[57]

The ICJ had sustained the hopes of newly independent and non-aligned states that apartheid would be internationally scrutinized and criticized through judicial proceedings, hopefully driving the US and UK to change their protective stance towards South Africa. But when the ICJ's Judgment on jurisdiction was announced, a loud cheer went up among the group South African officials just as well.[58] The judgment was incredibly close, and emboldened by the narrow outcome, South Africa grew bolder in the second phase of the proceedings.

[52] *South West Africa Cases* (*Ethiopia v South Africa; Liberia v South Africa*) (Preliminary Objections, Separate Opinion of Judge Bustamente) [1962] ICJ Rep 346, 359.

[53] *South West Africa Cases* (*Ethiopia v South Africa; Liberia v South Africa*) (Preliminary Objections, Separate Opinion of Judge Jessup) [1962] ICJ Rep 387, 432.

[54] *South West Africa Cases* (*Ethiopia v South Africa; Liberia v South Africa*) (Preliminary Objections, Separate Opinion of Judge Mbanefo) [1962] ICJ Rep 437.

[55] *South West Africa Cases* (Preliminary Objections, Judgment) (n 46) 347–48.

[56] *South West Africa Cases* (*Ethiopia v South Africa; Liberia v South Africa*) (Preliminary Objections, Joint Dissenting Opinion of Judges Spender and Fitzmaurice) [1962] ICJ Rep 465, 549–50 (hereafter *South West Africa Cases* (Preliminary Objections, Joint Dissenting Opinion of Judges Spender and Fitzmaurice)).

[57] ibid 558–59.

[58] As reported in D'Amato (n 5) 21–22.

C. The Court's turnaround on the merits (second phase)

South Africa was sure of the necessity of apartheid rule, of the righteousness of its politics and, increasingly so, of its legal argument before the ICJ. It responded to the applicant's initially vague arguments with an emphasis on clear definitions and, above all, with a focus on the facts. South Africa pointed to Sudan and Rwanda as disastrous examples for what would happen if it did not enact apartheid.[59] Judges Spender and Fitzmaurice could relate to that, as the latter had been the British Foreign Office's Senior Legal Advisor during the uprising of the Mau Mau in Kenya,[60] and the former was Australia's Minister for External Territories before coming to the ICJ; as such he was in charge of the administration of Australia's former mandate territories (including Nauru and Papua New Guinea).[61] South Africa furthermore asserted that the black population in South West Africa was better off than in many other parts of Africa.[62] The South African legal team wished to bring in thirty-eight witnesses to support its claims on the facts. The applicants, conversely, deliberately maintained distance from arguments about facts and did not intend to call on witnesses at all. At the pre-trial conference in 1965, South Africa's agents even invited the judges to come to South West Africa to visit other neighbouring territories and to see 'African reality' for themselves.[63]

The applicants concentrated on principle to the point of abstraction. They were partially constrained by limited resources and, more generally, they wanted to strike a more general blow at apartheid per se, not to criticize some technicalities of administering the mandate. Lead agent Gross's opening of the second phase was thus marked by an emphasis on the systemic, collective importance of this case:

> [T]he Applicants have not sought judicial recourse in order to secure a narrow material or selfish interest peculiar to themselves. [. . .] Their legal interest encompasses nothing less than observance by the Respondent of the totality of its legal obligations under the 'sacred trust' of the Mandate.[64]

By all means, Gross wanted to avoid that the judges accepted the respondent's invitation for a visit. He therefore let go of the first, more moderate argument about the effect of apartheid on the well-being and development of the black population

[59] *South West Africa Cases* (*Ethiopia v South Africa; Liberia v South Africa*) (Verbatim Records) [1956/II] ICJ Pleadings, 100 (hereafter *South West Africa Cases* (Verbatim Records II)).

[60] Victor Kattan, 'Decolonizing the International Court of Justice: The Experience of Judge Sir Muhammad Zafrulla Khan in the South West Africa Cases' (2015) 5 Asian Journal of International Law 310, 332.

[61] With further reference to support what was arguably on Spender's mind, see ibid 331.

[62] *South West Africa Cases* (Verbatim Records II) (n 60) 100.

[63] D'Amato (n 5) 32.

[64] *South West Africa Cases* (*Ethiopia v South Africa; Liberia v South Africa*) (Verbatim Records) [1956/I] ICJ Pleadings, 107.

in South West Africa. Instead, he fully embraced the more radical and more demanding argument that apartheid per se violates international law because it separates people on the basis of their belonging to a racial group.[65]

The composition of the Court in the proceedings' second phase had slightly changed with the judicial elections of 1963.[66] What is more, Judge Badawi (Egypt) had died in 1965 and Judge Bustamante (Peru) was absent due to illness.[67] In this constellation, Sir Percy Spender, now the Court's President, and Judge Fitzmaurice saw the opportunity to reverse the Court's 1962 decision.[68] Together they urged Judge Sir Muhammad Zafrulla Khan (Pakistan) to recuse himself. Their standoff led to the remarkable fact that Judge Zafrulla did ultimately not sit on the case, even though he neither recused himself, nor did the ICJ ever take a formal decision on this issue.[69] Only twelve of the fifteen permanent judges thus ended up deciding on the case. They were now evenly split down the middle and President Spender could cast his tie-breaking vote so as to deny the claimants' standing after all.[70] According to the new majority—the new majority of Judges Spender and Fitzmaurice,

> in order to determine what the rights and obligations of the Parties relative to the Mandate were and are . . . the Court must place itself at the point in time when the mandates system was being instituted, and when the instruments of mandate were being framed. The Court must have regard to the situation as it was at that time, which was the critical one, and to the intentions of those concerned as they appear to have existed, or are reasonably inferred, in the light of that situation.[71]

In 1966 the ICJ thus held that the mandate system did not provide members with any right 'to require the due performance of the Mandate in discharge of the "sacred trust" '.[72] It rather held that '[t]his right was vested exclusively in the League, and was exercised through its competent organs'.[73] The new majority did not try very hard to gloss over the fact that it had effectively overturned its 1962 Judgment. Half-heartedly, it suggested that the two Judgments could be reconciled

[65] ibid 84.
[66] See (n 96) for further information on the judicial elections and accompanying text.
[67] Judge Ammoun (Lebanon) replaced Judge Badawi but as is common practice he did not join in the ongoing proceedings. Kattan (n 61) 345.
[68] The elements of intrigue and bickering indeed provide the material for a seductive thriller. For a thrilling but academic exposition of those elements, see ibid.
[69] ibid 344.
[70] According to Article 55 of the ICJ Statute, 'in the event of an equality of votes, the President . . . shall have a casting vote'.
[71] *South West Africa Cases* (Second Phase, Judgment) (n 6) 23, para 16. This corresponds exactly to *South West Africa Cases* (Preliminary Objections, Joint Dissenting Opinion of Judges Spender and Fitzmaurice) (n 57), 549–50, also see at 558–59.
[72] *South West Africa Cases* (Second Phase, Judgment) (n 6) 29.
[73] ibid.

in the sense that in 1966 the ICJ still dealt with issues of jurisdiction that were not of an 'antecedent character'.[74]

Apart from President Spender (Australia) and Judge Fitzmaurice (UK), the majority was comprised of Judges Gros (France), Morelli (Italy), Spiropoulos (Greece), Winiarski (Poland), and Judge ad hoc van Wyk (South Africa). Not only did President Spender cast the tie-breaking vote, but he also attached a declaration directly to the Judgment that was clearly supposed to undermine the authority of any dissenting votes. His message was that the ICJ's job was done and that dissenting judges should not take the matter further in their individual opinions, so as not to pronounce on the ultimate merits of the applicants' case.[75] According to Spender that would simply not be 'permissible or proper'.[76]

However, each of the seven dissenting judges wrote a dissenting opinion: Vice-President Wellington Koo (China), Judges Koretsky (USSR), Tanaka (Japan), Jessup (US), Padilla Nervo (Mexico), Forster (Senegal), and Judge ad hoc Mbanefo (Nigeria). Their criticism was thundering, certainly in its combination.

All dissenting judges criticized the new majority for its treatment of the 1962 decision.[77] According to Judge Nervo, the new majority simply 'reproduce[s] on the present occasion the arguments adduced in dissenting opinions against the Judgment of 1962'. All dissenting judges also emphasized once more the multilateral, collective set-up of the League's mandate system. Judges Jessup and Tanaka wrote the longest dissenting opinions by far. Jessup strongly opposed the majority's decision and its methodological stance, saying that the 'Court now in effect sweeps away this record of 16 years on the ground that the Applicants have no legal right or interest'.[78] But even if he argued that South Africa's conduct must be measured by the present state of international law, he did not accept that there is an international legal norm that per se prohibited the separation of individuals on account of their membership in a racial group.[79] Judge Tanaka did accept such a norm. He tied his reasoning closely to human rights law and to an underlying principle of equality.[80] He echoed most closely the applicants' line of reasoning, holding that 'the practice of apartheid is fundamentally unreasonable and unjust'.[81]

[74] ibid 18, para 5; Yuval Shany, 'Jurisdiction and Admissibility' in Cesare Romano, Karen Alter and Yuval Shany (eds), *The Oxford Handbook of International Adjudication* (OUP 2014) 788–89.

[75] *South West Africa Cases* (*Ethiopia v South Africa; Liberia v South Africa*) (Second Phase, Declaration of Judge Spender) [1966] ICJ Rep 49 [30–33].

[76] ibid para 36.

[77] For a summary overview also see John Dugard, *The South West Africa–Namibia Dispute: Documents and Scholarly Writings on the Controversy between South Africa and the United Nations* (University of California Press 1973) 326–27.

[78] *South West Africa Cases* (*Ethiopia v South Africa; Liberia v South Africa*) (Second Phase, Dissenting Opinion of Judge Jessup) [1966] ICJ Rep 325, 328.

[79] ibid 432–433, 441.

[80] *South West Africa Cases* (*Ethiopia v South Africa; Liberia v South Africa*) (Second Phase, Dissenting Opinion of Judge Tanaka) [1966] ICJ Rep 250, 287.

[81] ibid 314.

IV. Crisis and change in the ICJ and on its bench

A. The Court in crisis

The criticism from outside the ICJ was still stronger. The President of Senegal termed the 1966 decision 'un vrai scandale'.[82] He asserted that

> ce n'est pas la peine d'être un grand professeur de droit pour maintenir le racisme or le formalisme juridique [. . .]. Quel que soit le problème qu'on leur soumet, ces juristes sont pour la ségrégation et pour le racisme. Nous, Africains, nous n'acceptons pas cela'.[83]

The Liberian government newspaper spoke of the judgment as a 'travesty of human rights. . . . [T]he Court by its infamous decision spits in the face of its applicant by saying "you had no right to come here". What an insult!'[84] The Sidney Morning Herald opined that the judgment is 'unsatisfactory from all points of view . . . This judgment will convince many that the ICJ is indeed a "white man's court" '.[85]

Many scholars, like Taslim O Elias, who eventually became the Court's first African President in 1981, critiqued the ruling as 'legalistic, restrictive and narrow'.[86] Rosalyn Higgins called it an 'aberration'.[87] But for many actors at the time it was much more than that. For them, it was symptomatic of their quest and symptomatic of the world as it presented itself to them—as a white man's world with a white man's court.

Directly after the 1966 Judgment, the UN African Group gave a press conference to declare its 'dismay and indignation at the incredible decision'.[88] It noted that some of the ICJ's members had shown themselves to be 'not very responsible judges' and it would 'never be able to vote for the re-election of these judges'.[89] Disenchanted with the ICJ, African states again acted through the UNGA. Still

[82] 'Letter from Dutch Embassy in Dakar to The Hague' (22 July 1966) (Dutch National Archive, Ministry of Foreign Affairs, Inv No 24849).

[83] ibid.

[84] 'Letter from Dutch Embassy in Monrovia to The Hague' (Dutch National Archive, Ministry of Foreign Affairs, Inv No 24849).

[85] Sidney Morning Herald (20 July 1966) (Dutch National Archive, Ministry of Foreign Affairs, Inv No 24849).

[86] Taslim O Elias, *Africa and the Development of International Law* (Taslim O Elias and Richard Akinjide eds, 2nd edn, Nijhoff 1988) 75 (hereafter Elias, *Africa*).

[87] Rosalyn Higgins, 'The International Court of Justice and Africa' in *Themes and Theories: Selected Essays, Speeches, and Writings in International Law* (OUP 2009) 1071.

[88] Reactions in Western countries were more nuanced. The Dutch advisor to the government, stated it was 'legally understandable, yet very conservative' and was sure to 'affect the prestige of the Court' (16 August 1966) (Ministry of Foreign Affairs, Dutch National Archive, Ministry of Foreign Affairs, Inv No 24847).

[89] 'Letter from Dutch Delegation at UN to The Hague' (19 July 1966) (Dutch National Archive, Ministry of Foreign Affairs, Inv No 24849).

in 1966, the UNGA passed a resolution declaring that South Africa's mandate for South West Africa was terminated.[90] In the immediate aftermath of the 1966 decision a majority of states also refused to adopt supplementary estimates to the ICJ in the Fifth Committee—something that would otherwise have been a routine matter. A look at the ICJ's docket and at its bench reveals the full impact of the 1966 Judgment. Whereas twenty-seven cases were brought to the Court in the 1950s, only eight were brought in the 1960s, and nine in the 1970s. With the exception of the joint proceedings in *North Sea Continental Shelf* in 1967, no single case was filed from 1962 until 1971.[91]

The Court was in such a crisis that the UN Secretary General, upon request by the UNGA, distributed a questionnaire in 1970 to 'Review of the Role of the International Court of Justice'.[92] In a debate on the issue in the UNGA, the representative of Ghana replied in a strong, but far from unique, fashion that the ICJ would be in a much better position 'if international law were more progressive and did not reflect outmoded conservative thought reminiscent of imperialism'.[93] The criticism here as elsewhere was imbued by the ICJ's decision in *South West Africa* and its backward-looking and deeply conservative interpretative stance.[94]

B. The quest for representation

Bargaining and compromise have always characterized the process of electing the fifteen permanent judges—five of them every three years.[95] When Ethiopia and Liberia brought the contentious proceedings against South Africa in 1960, African States already worked towards their better representation on the ICJ's bench.[96]

[90] UNGA Res 2145 (XXI) (27 October 19). See further Edward McWhinney, '"Internationalizing" the International Court: The Quest for Ethno-Cultural and Legal-Systemic Representativeness' in Emmanuel G Bello and Prince B A Ajibola (eds), *Essays in Honour of Judge Taslim Olawale Elias* (vol 1, Contemporary International Law and Human Rights, Nijhoff 1992) 287 (hereafter McWhinney, '"Internationalizing" the International Court'); Taslim O Elias, *The International Court of Justice and some Contemporary Problems: Essays on International Law* (Nijhoff 1983).

[91] The last one was Belgium's application to institute proceedings against Spain on 19 June 1962 in *Barcelona Traction, Light and Power Company, Limited.* India broke the pattern with its application to institute proceedings against Pakistan on 30 August 1971 in *Appeal Relating to the Jurisdiction of the ICAO Council.*

[92] The initiative to review the role of the Court was launched by the Sixth Committee and approved by the UNGA in UNGA Res 2723 (XXV) (11 December 1970).

[93] Quoted in Helmut Steinberger, 'The International Court of Justice' in Max Planck Institute for Comparative Public Law and International Law (ed), *Judicial Settlements of International Disputes: An International Symposium* (Springer 1974) 226–27.

[94] ibid 227; Heribert Golsong, 'Role and Functioning of the International Court of Justice: Proposals Recently Made on the Subject' (1971) 31 Zeitschrift für ausländisches öffentliches Recht und Völkerrecht 673.

[95] See Ruth Mackenzie and others, *Selecting International Judges: Principle, Process, and Politics* (OUP 2010); for concise overviews of the elections see Shabtai Rosenne, *The Law and Practice of the International Court, 1920–1996* (3rd edn, Nijhoff 1985).

[96] See Elias, *Africa* (n 87) 51.

At the outset of the 1963 elections, the Afro-Asian group presented three candidates, even though the group held none of the five seats that opened.[97] According to the Dutch head diplomat in New York: 'The candidatures of Ghana, Lebanon and Pakistan for the seats of the ICJ, which become vacant on the fifth of February 1964, can indeed be seen as nothing else than an intentional attempt to alter the existing division of seats of the Court'.[98] The Afro-Asian group even proposed a fourth candidate, Sir Adetokunbo Ademola of Nigeria. When the Dutch delegation received a letter asking for support for Ademola, a diplomat just scribbled 'Another AA!' onto the letter in apparent surprise.[99]

How did the Western group react to the African demand for at least one extra seat, if not more? According to a firm unwritten rule, each permanent member of the Security Council presents one judge.[100] The seats of the UK and France were thus not at issue. The Dutch representation in New York set out the situation and strategy:

> [t]he three Latino seats remain open to be filled. The Latinos presently have four seats, Europe four plus the U.S. and Australia, the Soviets two, Asia two. There is therefore a large pressure from Africa to receive one or more seats and from Asia to expand its number of seats. This can only go at the expense of Europe or Latin America.
>
> It is therefore in the interest of Europe that this time the wishes of Asia and Africa are met at the expense of Latin America, or else the Greek seat will surely be attacked by the Africans when it becomes vacant in 1969. It is therefore desirable that this year not more than one Latino is chosen and both other Latino seats would go to Asia and Africa, for example Zafrulla Khan and Sir Asafu Adjaye (Ghana).[101]

Western diplomats tried to thwart, or at least redirect, the African quest for a greater share of the seats by closing their ranks and, if necessary, by sacrificing one or even two Latin American seats rather than a European one. The UK signed on to this strategy: 'What concerns the three Latino vacancies in the Court, the British would vote for Nervo (Mexico), Zafrullah Khan (Pakistan) and probably,

[97] See 'Letter from Service International Organizations to New York' (22 November 1962) (Dutch National Archive, PR NY, Inv No 1888).

[98] 'Letter from New York to Ministry of Foreign Affairs' (12 December 1962) (Dutch National Archive, PR NY, Inv No 1888).

[99] 'Letter from the Permanent Mission of Nigeria to the Dutch Delegation' (20 March 1963) (Dutch National Archive, PR NY, Inv No 1888). AA means in this context 'Afro-Asian'.

[100] Chittharanjan F Amerasinghe, 'Judges of the International Court of Justice: Election and Qualifications' (2001) 14 Leiden Journal of International Law 335, 346; Heyns and Killander (n 37) para 20, with further references.

[101] 'Letter from Schumann to Ministry of Foreign Affairs' (26 May 1963) (Dutch National Archive, PR NY, Inv No 1888).

although with very little enthusiasm, for Adaye (Ghana).'[102] In the end, apart from Gros (France) and Fitzmaurice (UK, re-elected), Nervo (Mexico), Zafrullah Khan (Pakistan), and Forster (Senegal) were elected. The European number of judges remained the same but Latin America's representation decreased by two (remaining with two). Asia's as well as Africa's representation each increased by one (now totalling three and two, respectively).

C. The effects of *South West Africa*

The 1966 elections were held just three months after the ICJ's second judgment in *South West Africa*. The judgment's effects were clearly felt. The Dutch representation in New York wrote to The Hague that '[t]he Africans see the judgment as a political, not as a judicial decision and they will connect consequences to it. The upcoming elections for the Court will surely be influenced by this development.'[103] The British representation expected the same: 'Foreign Affairs was of the opinion that, when the election of five new judges for the Court is at issue, intense Afro-Asian activity to be more heavily represented in the Court is to be expected.'[104]

Two seats of the Western group were contested—none other than the one of Judge Spender (Australia), who occupied the so-called commonwealth seat, and that of Judge Spiropoulos (Greece), who had also been in the ICJ's 1966 majority.[105] A Dutch diplomat reports that 'in order to acquire the commonwealth seat, the AA group spares no trouble, partially due to the judgment in the South West Africa case, to elect Onyeama (Nigeria)'.[106] To defend both seats of the Western group, the UK proposed once more to close the ranks by reducing the number of European candidates so that the votes on European candidates would not be scattered.[107] The French delegation agreed: 'Il a été reconnu que l' Europe Occidentale courait le risque de perdre ce siège si les membres du groupe ne se mettaient pas d'accord pour soutenir un candidat unique'.[108]

[102] 'Letter from Joseph Luns (minister of Foreign Affairs) to New York' (5 September 1963) (Dutch National Archive, PR NY, Inv No 1888).

[103] 'Letter from Dutch Delegation at UN to the Hague' (20 July 1966) (Dutch National Archive, Ministry of Foreign Affairs, Inv No 24849).

[104] 'Letter from Dutch Embassy in London to The Hague' (21 July 1966) (Dutch National Archive, Ministry of Foreign Affairs, Inv No 24849).

[105] The other three seats that would become vacant were those of Judges Wellington Koo (China), Winiarski (Poland), and Ammoun (Lebanon). See 'Election of Five Members of the International Court of Justice' Note by the Secretary General (28 September 1966) A/6420, S/7490.

[106] 'Letter from Dutch Delegation in New York to The Hague' (24 August 1966) (Dutch National Archive, PR NY, Inv No 1889).

[107] 'Letter from Dutch Delegation in New York to The Hague' (1 October 1966) (Dutch National Archive, PR NY, Inv No 1889.).

[108] 'Deliberation in Western European Group' (10 October 1966) (Dutch National Archive, PR NY, Inv No 1889).

Concentrating European efforts on one candidate to replace Judge Spiropoulos was easier said than done. None of the states in the Western group was willing to revoke its own candidate. In these circumstances the Afro-Asian group even proposed a deal: African support for the European seat in return for European support for the Nigerian candidate to take the commonwealth seat.[109] The Western group was not amused and did not to respond.[110]

The election was then 'full of surprises'.[111] The European seat could ultimately be defended and went to Sture Petrén from Sweden. But the commonwealth seat was lost to an African candidate. Under the spell of *South West Africa*, Judge Spender's compatriot Sir Kenneth Bailey could not gain sufficient votes in the UNGA and Charles D Onyeama (Nigeria) was elected instead.[112] Despite this loss, the main impression was one of relief: at least the European seat remained in European hands.

The repercussions of *South West Africa* continued to shape delegation's sensibilities and strategies. When the seat of Judge Gaetano Morelli from Italy opened up in 1969, the Italians did not actively support Morelli for re-election. Nor did they seek to 'replace Morelli with another Italian, not just because of the implicitly accepted principle of rotation of legal systems, but also because A-A countries remember all too well how Morelli positioned himself in the *South West Africa* case'.[113] The battle for the seat took features similar to the previous elections. The Europeans were again trying to focus their efforts on a single candidate. Virginia Hartley, an official at the US State Department, argues: 'If this was not the case the danger is that the African countries . . . shall succeed in getting Ignacio-Pinto elected as replacement for Ago Morelli.'[114]

African governments even formally inquired whether the Western group was willing to give Morelli's seat to the African candidate Ignacio-Pinto (Benin).[115] The Western group called an emergency meeting and replied about two weeks later:

> The Western European and others group attached primordial importance to the gentlemen's agreements, which in the past have been applied with regard to

[109] 'Letter from Dutch Delegation in New York to The Hague' (24 October 1966) (Dutch National Archive, PR NY, Inv No 1889).

[110] ibid.

[111] 'Letter from Dutch Delegation in New York to The Hague' (4 November 1966) (Dutch National Archive, PR NY, Inv No 1889).

[112] Sir Kenneth Bailey was notably the likely candidate to have been nominated by Australia instead of Percy Spender back in 1958. See Kenneth J Keith, 'International Court of Justice: Reflections on the Electoral Process' (2010) 9 Chinese Journal of International Law 49, 54–55. Their backgrounds are quite different and Bailey would arguably have made a different decision in *South West Africa*.

[113] 'Letter from Dutch Delegation in New York to The Hague' (20 August 1969) (Dutch National Archive, Ministry of Foreign Affairs, Inv No 24947).

[114] 'Letter from Dutch Embassy in Washington to The Hague' (22 August 1969) (Dutch National Archive, Ministry of Foreign Affairs, Inv No 24947).

[115] 27 August 1969, Letter of the Dutch delegation in New York to The Hague, NL-HaNa, PR NY, Inv No 1889.

> elections to UN bodies to provide the geographical distribution of seats. . . . Thus the Western European group has made it a firm policy to respect the nominations made by other geographical groups as recognized by the above-mentioned resolution and to elect the candidates nominated by them. In return, the group has trusted, and continues to trust, that reciprocal respect will be shown by other groups with regard to its nominations. . . . [T]he forthcoming elections to the Court should result in the seat to be vacated by Mr. Morelli being filled by a nominee from within the WEO group.[116]

Once again, the Western group was divided between too many candidates of its own. Joseph Luns, Dutch Minister of Foreign Affairs, noted in a memo to all embassies in the Western group that

> the African group in the U.N., which desires an expansion of the number of African seats in the Court from two to three, will want to profit from a European fragmentation at the favor of the candidature of Ignacio-Pinto, despite the fact that none of the vacant seats belongs to Africa. In order to prevent the probably permanent loss of a WEO seat, it is desirable to agree on a drastic reduction of the number of WEO candidates.[117]

The Canadian government stated that 'with all due respect for the developing countries, the Court should not become some sort of private hunting ground of this group'.[118] It should at least not hunt Western seats. Ultimately, the Spanish candidate De Castro was elected to replace Judge Morelli. But the Asian seat of Judge Tanaka (Japan) went to place Judge Ignacio-Pinto (Benin).[119] It was not decisive in this regard that Judge Tanaka had elaborately supported the applicants' arguments in his 1966 dissenting opinion.

V. The ICJ's continued ambivalence

Was the game worth the candle? South Africa's actions in South West Africa/Namibia once more came before the ICJ when, in July 1970, the Security Council requested an advisory opinion on the legal consequences of South Africa's continued

[116] 'Letter of West European group to A-A Group' (15 September 1969) (Dutch National Archive, PR NY, Inv No 1889).

[117] 'Circulaire Joseph Luns' (1 September 1969) (Dutch National Archive, Ministry of Foreign Affairs, Inv No 24947).

[118] 'Letter from the Dutch embassy in Ottawa to The Hague' (10 September 1969) (Dutch National Archive, Ministry of Foreign Affairs, Inv No 24947).

[119] Also see Manfred Lachs, 'Some Reflections on the Nationality of Judges of the International Court of Justice' (1992) 4 Pace International Law Review 49, 54–55.

presence in Namibia notwithstanding that the Council had declared that presence illegal about six months earlier.[120] The majority of the judges accepted the invitation to make good on the mistakes that they saw in the law and politics of the 1966 Judgment. The firmness with which the majority asserts its authority to deliver the opinion and the eagerness with which it turns to issues of substance flips around the exuberant formalism of the 1966 Judgment.[121] The 1971 Opinion thus confronts the 1966 judgment head-on, reasserting that

> an international instrument has to be interpreted and applied within the framework of the entire legal system prevailing at the time of the interpretation. In the domain to which the present proceedings relate, the last fifty years . . . have brought important developments. These developments leave little doubt that the ultimate objective of the sacred trust was the self-determination and independence of the peoples concerned.[122]

For the first time the ICJ mentioned all peoples' right to self-determination.[123] Judges Fitzmaurice and Gros certainly disagreed with the ICJ's acceptance to deliver the opinion, its findings and its interpretative stance.[124] But their camp had lost the battle by the beginning of the 1970s.

Many judges at the ICJ then saw the Court less as an instrument in the resolution of individual disputes alone, as Spender and Fitzmaurice had done, and more as an organ that should contribute to the progressive development of the law in the service of the international community—a community enlarged by newly independent states and their legitimate interests.[125] Many judges developed such a community-oriented conception of the functions of the ICJ in contrast to the views espoused

[120] UN Security Council Res 276 (30 January 1970), declaring that 'the continued presence of the South African authorities in Namibia is illegal and that consequently all acts taken by the Government of South Africa on behalf of or concerning Namibia after the termination of the Mandate are illegal and invalid'. UNSC Res 284 (20 July 1970), requesting the advisory opinion.

[121] *Legal Consequences for States of the Continued Presence of South Africa in Namibia (South West Africa) notwithstanding Security Council Resolution 276* (Advisory Opinion) [1971] ICJ Rep 4, 22–27 (hereafter *Legal Consequences for States of the Continued Presence of South Africa in Namibia (South West Africa) notwithstanding Security Council Resolution 276* (Advisory Opinion)). See McWhinney, *World Court* (n 25) 23, arguing the 1971 opinion is as legally (un)persuasive as the 1966 decision because the reasoning is equally driven, just in opposite directions.

[122] *Legal Consequences for States of the Continued Presence of South Africa in Namibia (South West Africa) notwithstanding Security Council Resolution 276* (Advisory Opinion) (n 122) 31, para 53.

[123] ibid para 52. See in further detail Shabtai Rosenne, 'Decolonisation in the International Court of Justice' (1996) 8 African Journal of International and Comparative Law 564.

[124] *Legal Consequences for States of the Continued Presence of South Africa in Namibia (South West Africa) notwithstanding Security Council Resolution 276* (Advisory Opinion, Dissenting Opinion of Judge Fitzmaurice) [1971] ICJ Rep 220; *Legal Consequences for States of the Continued Presence of South Africa in Namibia (South West Africa) notwithstanding Security Council Resolution 276* (Advisory Opinion, Dissenting Opinion of Judge Gros) [1971] ICJ Rep 323.

[125] On these basic conceptions see Armin von Bogdandy and Ingo Venzke, 'On the Functions of International Courts: An Appraisal in Light of their Burgeoning Public Authority' (2013) 26 Leiden Journal of International Law 49.

by Spender and Fitzmaurice. They did so in the 1971 opinion just as well as in the *Barcelona Traction* judgment a year earlier, when the ICJ famously introduced the

> essential distinction . . . between the obligations of a State towards the international community as a whole, and those arising vis-à-vis another State in the field of diplomatic protection. By their very nature the former are the concern of all States. In view of the importance of the rights involved, all States can be held to have a legal interest in their protection; they are obligations *erga omnes*.[126]

This reasoning can hardly be understood were it not in response to the disaster of 1966.

The Court had changed. The game was worth the candle. But neither change in international law nor in the ICJ comes overnight or without setbacks and ambivalence. The ICJ's 1975 Advisory Opinion in *West Sahara* notably coupled the recognition of peoples' right to self-determination with legal concepts such as *terra nullius* that deeply reflect European conceptions of political organization.[127] Judges Ammoun (Lebanon) and Forster (Senegal) critiqued the majority for assessing patterns of African socio-political organization by European standards.[128] The doctrinal position according to which questions of legality should be determined in light of the law as it stands at the time is seemingly straightforward.[129] How to read the law of the past is less straightforward. In particular, choices about the categories with which to make sense of the past tend to contain implicit, European biases.[130] Now, as then, the battle for the Court extends to the way in which it approaches the past.

VI. Conclusions

The political arenas of the UN were the preferred venues for newly independent states' battle towards a different international law. When they turned to the ICJ as

[126] *Barcelona Traction, Light and Power Company, Limited (Belgium v Spain)* (Judgment) [1970] ICJ Rep 3, 32.

[127] *Western Sahara* (Advisory Opinion) [1975] ICJ Rep 12. For critiques see McWhinney, '"Internationalizing" the International Court' (n 90) 72–75 and 83–85; Anghie (n 3) 111–12.

[128] *Western Sahara* (Advisory Opinion, Separate Opinion of Judge Ammoun) [1975] ICJ Rep 83, 86–87, drawing on the pleadings of Algerian Ambassador Mohammed Badjaoui; *Western Sahara* (Advisory Opinion, Separate Opinion of Judge Forster) [1975] ICJ Rep 103.

[129] See Rosalyn Higgins, 'Some Observations on the Inter-Temporal Rule in International Law' in Jerzy Makarczyk (ed), *Theory of International Law at the Threshold of the 21st Century: Essays in Honour of Krzysztof Skubiszewski* (Kluwer Law International 1996) 501; Markus Kotzur, 'Intertemporal Law' (2008), in Rüdiger Wolfrum (ed), Max Planck Encyclopedia of Public International Law (OUP 2013).

[130] That is a question of legal practice as much of scholarly treatment, see Arnulf Becker Lorca, 'Eurocentrism in the History of International Law' in Bardo Fassbender, Anne Peters and Simone Peter (eds), *The Oxford Handbook of the History of International Law* (OUP 2012); Martti Koskenniemi, 'Histories of International Law: Significance and Problems for a Critical View' (2013) 27 Temple International and Comparative Law Journal 215, 221–26.

part of the struggle against South Africa's apartheid regime, the ICJ let them down. The ICJ was seen to protect great power, privilege, and prerogative. It seemed to have permitted South Africa's unabashedly racist policies, even within the mandate territory of South West Africa.

When the dust settled around the ICJ in 1966, the old regime still stood. But the ICJ's authority in the world had taken a heavy toll. Unlike arms or weapons, authority cannot be stored.[131] As a discredited actor, the ICJ mostly remained on the sidelines of the battle for international law. For newly independent and non-aligned states the case was loud and clear: It was a white man's court for a white man's international legal order.[132]

The ICJ's composition continued to change through electoral battles at the UN. African states gained seats, mostly at the expense of the Latin American group. But changes on the bench did not turn the ICJ into a vehicle for progressive politics. With its *Namibia* Advisory Opinion, the ICJ tried to rectify some wrongs. But its practice has remained ambivalent—an ambivalence that it has regained together with gradual increases in its authority.

As time passed, the ICJ wished to think of *South West Africa* as an aberration.[133] But its 1966 Judgment can hardly be understood as a slip of the pen. Albeit narrow, a majority of judges supported it. Half a century later, the ICJ again evoked vivid memories of the 1966 Judgment when, in 2016, it declined its jurisdiction in the *Nuclear Arms Race (Marshall Islands)* cases, once more by the President's tie-breaking vote.[134] More than anything else, an inquiry into the battle for the ICJ, with *South West Africa* as its captivating highpoint, presents legal and institutional developments as a product of struggle. This changes the understanding of its ICJ's practice and of the distribution of its seats, which appear much less as expressions of a timeless rationality, but as temporary victories of different formations of interested actors. Such an inquiry also serves as a reminder that the terrain of struggle is uneven *and* that different outcomes were still possible, in 1966 as in 2016.

[131] Hannah Arendt, 'What is Authority', in *Between Past and Future* (Penguin 2006), especially at 121.

[132] See (n 86).

[133] Higgins (n 88) 1071.

[134] *Obligations Concerning Negotiations Relating to Cessation of the Nuclear Arms Race and to Nuclear Disarmament (Marshall Islands v United Kingdom)*, Preliminary Objections, Judgment, 5 October 2016, ICJ Reports (2016) 833. See Anghie, 'Politic, Cautious, and Meticulous: An Introduction to the Symposium on the Marshall Islands Case' 111 AJIL Unbound (2017) 62.

11

A Battlefield Transformed

The United Nations and the Struggle over Postcolonial Statehood

Guy Fiti Sinclair

I. Introduction

The battle over international law extended to the institutional context within which that law was increasingly formed. As much as the United Nations (UN) provided an arena for the promotion and contestation of decolonization, decolonization itself effected a profound transformation in the legal structures and powers of the UN. This chapter traces a series of interconnected battles or struggles in the early UN, each of which resulted in innovations in the institutional framework and powers of the UN that had immediate implications for decolonization. In particular, the chapter focuses on three axes of struggle, in relation to the meaning of self-government, the values and practices of modern government, and the import of sovereign equality.[1]

The battle over the UN began even before its creation. Planning for the UN was dominated by 'great power' interests, and its Charter strongly reflected those interests, most notoriously in the structure of the Security Council and the veto wielded by its five permanent members. Nevertheless, contestation by smaller states during the negotiation process resulted in the introduction of a number of tensions, ambiguities, and antinomies into the text of the Charter, which were subsequently exploited by countries seeking to promote decolonization. Moreover, even before the Charter had been ratified by a majority of its signatories, a succession of world events—most notably the deepening Cold War conflict between West and East—made it unlikely that many of its key provisions would be implemented as originally foreseen.

Almost immediately after the UN's creation, then, the institutional framework of the organization began to change under the influence—and in service—of decolonization. The first axis of struggle, examined in Section II of this chapter,

[1] This chapter draws on research conducted for Guy Fiti Sinclair, *To Reform the World: International Organizations and the Making of Modern States* (OUP 2017). Thanks to the organizers and participants in the authors' workshop, 'The Battle for International Law in the Decolonization Era'.

Guy Fiti Sinclair, *A Battlefield Transformed* In: *The Battle for International Law: South-North Perspectives on the Decolonization Era*. Edited by: Jochen von Bernstorff and Philipp Dann, Oxford University Press (2019).

DOI: 10.1093/oso/9780198849636.003.0012

concerned the meaning of sovereign equality in relation to the makeup and procedures of the Security Council.[2] Section III analyses the struggles that led to an elaboration of the machinery for promoting self-government in colonized territories. The third axis of struggle, considered in Section IV, arose out of efforts to universalize a model of government that was defined by a core set of social welfare values and techniques of economic intervention. In each case, the UN itself provided the institutional setting (the battlefield) and the normative resources (the weapons) for the struggle for decolonization.[3]

The image of a battle, around which this book is organized, might be understood as necessarily implying an outcome of destruction and negation. This chapter contends, however, that the battle over international law in the UN during the period of decolonization was profoundly creative and generative. Section V argues that the three axes of struggle noted above came together in the invention of a new institutional form, which has become the most visible 'face' of the UN today: the peacekeeping operation. Beginning with the UN Emergency Force in 1956, peacekeeping emerged as a complex technology for managing the end of European imperialism in an orderly fashion, for giving small states a more significant role in the peace and security functions of the UN and protecting their position vis-à-vis the 'great powers', and for the construction of modern states on a broadly Western model in the decolonized world. The tensions inherent between these diverse purposes became visible in the Congo operation of 1960–1964, which at once marked a point of consolidation of earlier institutional innovations, revealed the limits of each of the struggles underlying them, and established a new field of battle that remains in contestation today.

II. The battle over sovereign equality

Despite affirming 'the principle of the sovereign equality of all its Members',[4] the UN Charter granted extraordinary rights to the leading Allied powers—the United States (US), the United Kingdom (UK), the Union of Soviet Socialist Republics (USSR), France, and China—who were designated permanent members of the Security Council, with primary responsibility for achieving the UN's main purpose of 'maintain[ing] international peace and security'.[5] Much of the debate over the terms of the Charter had centred on the extent of the great powers'

[2] General Assembly (GA) Res 377 (V) (3 November 1950).

[3] This chapter focuses on the contributions of the UN's political and administrative organs during the period of decolonization. For consideration of the activities of the UN's principal judicial organ in the same period, see chapter [X].

[4] UN Charter, art 2(1).

[5] UN Charter, art 1(1).

voting privileges, in particular, the veto power of these permanent members of the Security Council.[6] Most controversial was the extension of that power to the process of amendment, which would hinder efforts to remove or attenuate the veto itself.[7] Nevertheless, the final version of the Charter affirmed that any amendment to the Charter had to be passed by a two-thirds vote of the UN General Assembly (UNGA) and ratified by the same proportion of UN members, including all the permanent members of the Security Council.[8]

An initial axis of struggle in the UN during the period of decolonization thus concerned the veto and its relationship to the sovereign equality of states. Proposals to amend the Council's voting procedures and abolish the veto, introduced by the Philippines and Cuba at the Assembly's first session, were defeated.[9] Outnumbered in both the Council and the UNGA,[10] the USSR first exercised its veto power under Article 27(3) in February 1946; it did so again on more than twenty occasions in the UN's first two years alone.[11] Among other things, the veto was often used in the UN's first decade to block the applications for membership by states that held opposing ideological views.[12] In conditions of profound mutual suspicion between the US and USSR, moreover, every region of the globe seemed to be of crucial geopolitical interest to one or the other of the two superpowers. Accordingly, there was little chance of the Council intervening in a series of crises that erupted in the immediate aftermath of the Second World War.[13]

The USSR's prolific use of the veto, and the failure of efforts to eliminate that power, prompted a number of innovations in the Security Council's practice that appeared to contradict the express terms of the Charter. Article 27(3) required any decision on a non-procedural matter to be made by 'an affirmative vote of seven members including the concurring votes of the permanent members'. On its face, this seemed to require all permanent members to be present and voting in favour of the decision. However, a practice quickly developed where a permanent member's abstention was not treated as a veto. By 1947, the sitting president of the Council was able to affirm that it was 'now jurisprudence in the Security Council—and the interpretation accepted for a long time—that an abstention is not considered a

[6] Evan Luard, *A History of the United Nations, vol 1* (Macmillan 1982) 44–51 (hereafter Luard, *History of the UN*); Townsend Hoopes and Douglas Brinkley, *FDR and the Creation of the U.N.* (Yale University Press 1997) 198–200.

[7] Shirley V Scott, 'The Question of UN Charter Amendment, 1945–1965: Appeasing "the Peoples"' (2007) 9 Journal of the History of International Law 83, 85–86 (hereafter Scott, 'The Question').

[8] UN Charter, art 108.

[9] Scott, 'The Question' (n 7) 90.

[10] In 1946, only five out fifty-one member states represented in the UNGA were Soviet allies. Luard, *History of the UN* (n 6) 94.

[11] In the same period, France used the veto twice: once on its own and once jointly with the USSR. Scott, 'The Question' (n 7) 90.

[12] Luard, *History of the UN* (n 6) 364–72.

[13] ibid 87–88, 106–59, 218–21.

veto, and the concurrent votes of the permanent members mean the votes of the permanent members who participate in the voting'.[14]

This interpretation was soon extended to cover occasions when a member—even a permanent member—was absent from the Security Council.[15] From January to August 1950, the USSR boycotted the Council in protest against the presence of a representative from non-communist China. During this period, without the threat of the Soviet veto, the Council was able to pass resolutions condemning the North Korean invasion of South Korea and recommending that member states provide military assistance to the latter, thus authorizing the most dramatic action taken by the UN during its first decade: armed intervention by a UN force under the command of the US Army General Douglas MacArthur.[16]

The Korean action aside, the Security Council's relative inactivity encouraged other UN organs to take more responsibility for the maintenance of international peace and security. The first Secretary-General, Trygve Lie (1896–1968), made repeated efforts to expand that office's political role, among other things attempting to defuse the Berlin blockade crisis, condemning North Korean aggression, proposing a standing UN guard force, and suggesting a twenty-year program to achieve world peace.[17] Whereas Lie's efforts are generally deemed to have failed, his replacement, Dag Hammarskjöld (1905–1961), was more successful, including in negotiating the release of US airmen who had been shot down during the Korean War and were being held in China on charges of espionage. As an early commentator noted, the 'expanding nature' of the Secretary-General's political activities and the growth of influence he exercised was one of the more significant developments within the UN since its inception.[18]

The UNGA similarly assumed authority to take action directly where the Security Council was prevented from doing so.[19] In October 1950, the Assembly passed a resolution that authorized the UN forces under MacArthur's command to follow South Korean forces into the North.[20] Encouraged by this success, the US Secretary of State, Dean Acheson, pursued a plan to enable the UNGA to circumvent the Security Council on a more regular basis. The 'Acheson Plan', later known as 'Uniting for Peace', addressed conditions where the Council was 'unable

[14] Ralph Zacklin, *The Amendment of the Constitutive Instruments of the United Nations and Specialized Agencies* (Sijthoff 1968) 183.

[15] ibid 184–85. This was later confirmed in *Legal Consequences for States of the Continued Presence of South Africa in Namibia (South West Africa) Notwithstanding Security Council Resolution 276 (1970)* (Advisory Opinion) [1971] ICJ Rep 16, para 22.

[16] UN Security Council (UNSC) Res 82 (25 June 1950) UN Doc S/RES/82; UNSC Res 83 (27 June 1950) UN Doc S/RES/83.

[17] Bertrand G Ramcharan, *Preventive Diplomacy at the UN* (Indiana University Press 2008) 29–31; Salo Engel, 'The Changing Charter of the United Nations' (1953) Yearbook of World Affairs 71, 83.

[18] Francis O Wilcox, *How the United Nations Charter Has Developed* (US Government Print Office 1954) 1, 7.

[19] Thomas M Franck, *Nation against Nation* (OUP 1985) 38–40 (hereafter Franck, *Nation against Nation*).

[20] UNGA Res 376 (V) (7 October 1950) UN Doc A/RES/376(V).

to exercise its primary responsibility for the maintenance of peace and security because of lack of unanimity of the permanent members'. In these circumstances, the resolution provided that the UNGA would have power to consider 'any case where there appears to be a threat to the peace, breach of the peace, or act of aggression'. Most significantly, it allowed the Assembly to organize coercive action by 'making appropriate recommendations to Members for collective measures . . . to maintain or restore international peace and security'. Moreover, it could do so in an emergency special session convened on twenty-four hours' notice by a vote of any seven members of the Security Council or a majority of the members of the UN—in other words, over the objections of the Council's permanent members.[21]

'Uniting for Peace' was carefully drafted to reflect the language of the Charter, giving the UNGA authority only to 'recommend' measures, not to 'decide' what measures shall be taken. Nevertheless, as Thomas Franck has argued, it was 'certainly not the intent of the drafters at San Francisco' that the Assembly would exercise even such limited authority in the face of a permanent member's veto in the Council.[22] Soviet bloc diplomats at the UN criticized the resolution as 'an attempt to by-pass the Security Council, to usurp its constitutional powers and relegate it to a secondary position in the United Nations structure, in other words, a back-door way of amending the Charter'.[23] Indeed, much of the UNGA debate on the draft resolution comprised efforts to attack or defend its 'constitutionality', interspersed with plainer statements of ideological and even personal antagonism by representatives of the Western and Soviet blocs.[24]

The innovation of 'Uniting for Peace' was directly relevant to the process of decolonization that was ongoing at the time. To many UN members, the expansion of the UNGA's powers under the 'Uniting for Peace' resolution was justified, in both legal and moral terms, by the principle of sovereign equality among states. Emphasizing those members' concern with the impasse created by conflict between the permanent members, the resolution's Preamble referred to the Charter's aim of developing 'friendly relations among nations based on respect for the principle of equal rights and self-determination of peoples'.[25] In the Assembly debate, several representatives situated the resolution within a longer sequence of struggle in the UN between great and small powers. The Peruvian delegation affirmed that

[21] Uniting for Peace, UNGA Res 377 A (V) (3 November 1950) UN Doc A/RES/377(V)A, para 1 (hereafter 'Uniting for Peace'). The ICJ has more recently confirmed that the practice of the UNGA has evolved so it may make a recommendation in respect of a question concerning the maintenance of international peace and security while the matter remains on the Security Council's agenda; and that this practice is consistent with Article 12(1) of the Charter. *Legal Consequences of the Construction of a Wall in the Occupied Palestinian Territory* (Advisory Opinion) [2004] ICJ Rep 136, 149–50.

[22] Franck, *Nation against Nation* (n 19) 39.

[23] Lester H Woolsey, 'The "Uniting for Peace" Resolution of the United Nations' (1951) 45 American Journal of International Law 129, 133.

[24] GAOR 5th Session Plenary Meeting 299 UN Doc A/PV.299 (1959); GAOR 5th Session Plenary Meeting 301, UN Doc A/PV.301 (1950, 1951) 324.

[25] 'Uniting for Peace' (n 21) Preamble.

its 'position in this matter was settled at the discussions at San Francisco', where '[t]he small nations' had demanded the ability to take action through the UNGA whenever the Security Council might be 'paralysed' through the veto.[26] In a similar vein, the Cuban representative stated: 'We have never shared—neither before San Francisco, nor at San Francisco, nor since San Francisco—the opinion that only the great Powers have the right to act in questions involving international peace and security.' Interpreting Article 27 as imposing a duty on the great powers to maintain international peace and security through agreement among the permanent members, rather than an unfettered right to veto the decisions of the Council,[27] he further asserted: '[W]e must bear in mind that the [UN] is founded on the principle of the sovereign equality of all its Members. This is a world organization of States with equal rights'.[28] Uruguay's representative underscored the resolution's significance in redressing the problem of inequality between states:[29]

> Hitherto the maintenance of collective security has been the affair of the great Powers, which arrogated to themselves the function of preserving peace in the Holy Alliance, in the Concert of Europe, in the Council of the League of Nations—as permanent members, in the Security Council . . . Now, however, the smaller Powers are called upon to contribute, at the international level, to the maintenance of collective security.

Despite its origins in US Cold War strategy, then, the 'Uniting for Peace' resolution provided an opening for small and newly-independent states to assert a greater role for themselves in international affairs. One of the principle aims of these new states was the further promotion of decolonization.

III. The battle over self-government

A second axis of struggle in the early UN concerned the question of self-government by colonized peoples, central to the process of decolonization. The Charter affirmed the 'equal rights and self-determination of peoples', and provided mechanisms to realize that principle.[30] Chapters XII and XIII established an international trusteeship system, largely as a successor to the League of Nations' mandate system, to be administered and supervised by a Trusteeship Council under

[26] Statement of Mr Belaunde (Peru), GAOR 5th Session Plenary Meeting 302, UN Doc A/PV.302 (1950) 343.

[27] Statement of Mr Gutierrez (Cuba), GAOR 5th Session Plenary Meeting 301, UN Doc A/PV.302 (1950) 324.

[28] Statement of Mr Vittone (Argentina), GAOR 5th Session Plenary Meeting 301, UN Doc A/PV.301 (1950) 336.

[29] GAOR 5th Session Plenary Meeting 299, UN Doc A/PV.299 (1950).

[30] UN Charter, arts 2(1), 1(2).

the authority of the UNGA, with the explicit objective of promoting the 'progressive advancement' of the inhabitants of trust territories 'towards self-government or independence'.[31] In addition, Chapter XI comprised a 'Declaration Regarding Non-Self-Governing Territories' concerning those UN members that had responsibility for 'the administration of territories whose peoples have not yet attained a full measure of self-government'. Falling short of referring to the possibility of independence for the peoples concerned, Chapter XI committed administering powers to ensuring their just treatment, to developing 'self-government', and assisting them in the 'progressive development of their free political institutions, according to the particular circumstances of each territory and its peoples and their varying stages of advancement', and to promoting 'constructive measures of development' in trust territories.[32]

These Charter provisions took on greater significance as the worldwide movement toward decolonization, which had gained impetus during the war, accelerated thereafter. Formerly colonized states already comprised a sizable majority of the UN's founding members in 1945, and a steady trickle of Asian colonies achieved political independence in the immediate post-war years. Not all of these new states joined the UN immediately, but by the end of 1955 the organization's membership had grown from fifty-one at its founding to seventy-six. Moreover, the eagerness of these new states to promote decolonization elsewhere was supported, in rhetoric if not always in action, by the two great superpowers of the day.[33]

Chapter XI of the Charter turned out to be crucial in promoting decolonization. The result of strenuous efforts by African and Asian states at San Francisco to create a 'strong system of international supervision over colonial administrations',[34] Chapter XI required administering powers to collect statistical and other technical information regarding the territories for which they were responsible, and to transmit that information to the Secretary-General on a regular basis.[35] A plain reading of the Charter might have suggested that the principal organs for dealing with decolonization were to be the Trusteeship Council and the Security Council.[36] Yet, many more people lived in non-self-governing territories than in trust territories, and the preponderance of smaller, non-colonial powers and previously colonized states in the UNGA made that organ a more natural site for assembling support for anti-colonial resolutions.[37]

[31] UN Charter, arts 75, 76(b).

[32] UN Charter, art 73.

[33] Raymond F Betts, *Decolonization* (Psychology Press 1998) 24.

[34] Yassin El-Ayouty, *The United Nations and Decolonization* (Martinus Nijhoff 1971) xxiii (hereafter El-Ayouty, *UN and Decolonization*).

[35] UN Charter, art 73(e).

[36] UN Charter, chs XII and XIII; Ernst B Haas, 'The Attempt to Terminate Colonialism: Acceptance of the United Nations Trusteeship System' (1953) 7 International Organization 1.

[37] In the interests of brevity, this chapter does not examine the well-known disputes over the Trusteeship system—in particular, its application to South West Africa/Namibia—which became an important focal

Indeed, the practice that built up on the basis of Chapter XI proved far more innovative than any comparable practice under Chapters XII and XIII. In December 1946, the Assembly set a date by which each of the colonial powers were to meet their obligations to transmit information to the Secretary-General, and recommended that the latter summarize, analyse, and classify that information, share it with the UN's specialized agencies, and convene an ad hoc Information Committee to advise the Assembly on steps to be taken.[38] Several administering powers disputed the Information Committee's constitutionality, and strongly resisted its creation.[39] The Belgian government, in particular, developed a forceful argument (the so-called 'salt-water thesis') that the application of Chapter XI solely to overseas colonies and protectorates was discriminatory and erroneous; rather, its provisions properly applied to 'backward ethnic groups' everywhere, including 'primitive' racial, linguistic, and religious minorities located within African, Asian, and Latin American states.[40] Nevertheless, the committee gradually acquired 'new powers of examination of both the functioning and the basis of the colonial system'.[41]

These developments at once drew upon and reinforced the UN Secretariat's expert authority. In practice, the Secretariat took responsibility for the day-to-day administration of issues raised by the Information Committee, and became a regular source of technical advice to many delegates.[42] As the Committee's work advanced, it frequently requested the Secretariat to prepare specialized papers on problems under consideration. Forming technical sub-committees to prepare reports on a variety of matters, the Committee invited representatives of several specialized agencies to participate in its meetings and submit special studies on topics in their areas of expertise.[43] These expansions of powers exercised by UN organs and agencies were understood to be justified by the goal of promoting self-government in colonial territories. Moreover, self-government increasingly meant political independence. To countries in the Asian-African bloc, it seemed obvious that the purpose of Chapter XI was to transform colonies into independent states. But for European metropolitan powers, the question of when a territory became self-governing—whether at the point of independence or earlier—was a matter of

point for decolonization struggles. See generally John Dugard, *The South West Africa/Namibia Dispute* (University of California Press 1973); Solomon Slonim, *South West Africa and the United Nations: An International Mandate in Dispute* (Johns Hopkins University Press 1973). On the role of the International Court of Justice in the South West Africa/Namibia dispute, see Chapter 10 this volume.

38 UNGA Res 66 (I) (14 December 1946) UN Doc A/RES/66(I) paras 1–6.

39 El-Ayouty, *UN and Decolonization* (n 34) 70–76.

40 Josef L Kunz, 'Chapter XI of the United Nations Charter in Action' (1954) 48 American Journal of International Law 103, 108–09 (hereafter Kunz, 'Chapter XI').

41 El-Ayouty, *UN and Decolonization* (n 34) 101.

42 Harold K Jacobson, 'The United Nations and Colonialism: A Tentative Appraisal' (1962) 16 International Organization 37.

43 El-Ayouty, *UN and Decolonization* (n 34) 101–05.

domestic jurisdiction shielded from intervention by any UN organ under Article 2(7) of the Charter.[44]

Consequently, the Information Committee became a site of ongoing struggle over how to determine whether a territory was non-self-governing, and therefore subject to the reporting obligations prescribed in Chapter XI.[45] Indeed, the exercise of defining the qualifications for self-government proved awkward. On the one hand, setting the bar too low meant that many territories would escape the Committee's scrutiny. On the other hand, standards such as 'complete freedom of the people of the territory to choose the form of government which they desire', freedom from interference by other governments in a territory's internal affairs, and 'complete autonomy in respect of economic, social and cultural affairs' seemed to set the bar too high even for many recognized sovereign states, and might result in colonies never meeting the conditions for independence.[46] That struggle continued in a series of debates and landmark resolutions by the UNGA, including the landmark 'Declaration on the Granting of Independence to Colonial Countries and Peoples',[47] and thereafter through the work of the 'Committee of 24' (Special Committee on Decolonization), which remains active today.

IV. The battle over development

The third axis of struggle in the UN system during the period of decolonization emerged from efforts to universalize a model of government shaped by the lessons of Keynesian economic theory and New Deal experimentalism.[48] The UN Charter's Preamble affirmed 'faith in fundamental human rights', the goal of 'social progress and better standards of life in larger freedom', and 'the promotion of the economic and social advancement of all peoples'. More specifically, Chapter IX committed the UN to promote human rights and social and economic development, and provided for a range of specialized agencies to be brought into relationship with the organization to meet those ends.[49] In addition, Chapter X created an Economic and Social Council (ECOSOC) with powers to coordinate the work of the specialized agencies;[50] to study issues relating to 'international economic, social, cultural,

44 Kunz, 'Chapter XI' (n 40) 107.
45 El-Ayouty, *UN and Decolonization* (n 34) ch 5.
46 Clyde Eagleton, 'Excesses of Self-Determination' (1953) 31 Foreign Affairs 592, 599–600 (quoting from a report produced by a 'Committee on Factors', appointed by the UNGA).
47 UNGA Res A/1514 (XV) (14 December 1960).
48 Anne-Marie Burley, 'Regulating the World: Multilateralism, International Law, and the Projection of the New Deal Regulatory State' in John Gerard Ruggie (ed), *Multilateralism Matters* (Columbia University Press 1993) 126; Elizabeth Borgwardt, *A New Deal for the World* (Belknap Press of Harvard University Press 2005).
49 UN Charter, art 55.
50 UN Charter, art 55.

educational, health, and related matters'; and to make recommendations concerning any such matters to the UNGA and relevant specialized agencies.[51]

These values informed the emerging science of development economics, which took decolonized states as its primary objects. As a leading UN economist of the time put it, there was a strong assumption that 'the same principles of planning, macroeconomic management of the economy by governments and mobilization of latent resources based on Keynesian principles, were also applicable to the problems of developing countries'.[52] Moreover, concern for universal, state-guaranteed social welfare took on an increasingly tangible institutional form during the UN's first decade. In December 1948, the UNGA passed two landmark resolutions that prepared the ground for a much-expanded approach to international technical assistance for economic development. The first called upon ECOSOC and the specialized agencies to 'give further and urgent consideration to the whole problem of the economic development of under-developed countries in *all* its aspects', while the second appropriated funds to enable the Secretary-General to provide technical assistance to governments in connection with their economic development programs.[53] That same month saw the enactment of two foundational human rights instruments, the Genocide Convention and the Universal Declaration of Human Rights.[54]

Within the next couple of years, the UNGA had established an Expanded Program of Technical Assistance (EPTA), comprising the UN and seven specialized agencies, and a Technical Assistance Board (TAB) to coordinate their work.[55] That program extended to 'non-self-governing territories' also: the competence of the Information Committee that had been formed to ensure compliance with Chapter XI was extended to deal with issues of equal treatment in education, eradication of illiteracy, and technical assistance, and the Committee demanded increasingly detailed reports from administering powers on a growing list of topics, including questions of social policy, labour legislation, social security, housing, education, public health, human rights, and racial discrimination.[56]

The new states' drive to achieve economic decolonization inspired the UNGA's designation of the 1960s as the UN Development Decade,[57] as well as a proliferation

[51] UN Charter, arts 63, 64, 62(1), 62(2).

[52] Cited in Olav Stokke, *The UN and Development* (Indiana University Press 2009) 594 (hereafter Stokke, *UN and Development*).

[53] UNGA Res 198 (III) (4 December 1948) UN Doc A/RES/198(III) para 3; UNGA Res 200 (III) (4 December 1948) UN Doc A/RES/200(III).

[54] Convention on the Prevention and Punishment of the Crime of Genocide (adopted 9 December 1948, entered into force 12 January 1951) 78 UNTS 277; UNGA Res 217 A (III) (10 December 1948) UN Doc A/RES/3/217(III).

[55] Stokke, *UN and Development* (n 52) 46–50.

[56] United Nations, 'Information on Non-Self-Governing Territories Transmitted under Article 73e of United Nations Charter' in *United Nations Year Book* (United Nations Department of Public Information 1960) 502, 515.

[57] UNGA Res 1715 (XVI) (19 December 1961) UN Doc A/RES/1715(XVI).

of new development-oriented organizations, agencies, programmes, and funds. Some of these were independent of the UN, such as the African Development Bank (established in 1964) and the Asian Development Bank (1966). Others were more or less autonomous specialized agencies, such as the International Bank for Reconstruction and Development and International Development Association (together, the World Bank). But many were part of the UN family, including the UN Special Fund (1958), the World Food Program (1963), UN Conference on Trade and Development (1964), the UN Institute for Training and Research (1965), the UN Development Program (1965, merging the EPTA with the Special Fund), the UN Industrial Development Organization (1966), the UN Capital Development Fund (1966), and the UN Fund for Population Activities (1969).[58]

To many in the West, technical assistance was deeply connected to the UN's primary purpose of maintaining international peace and security. In the first of its 1948 resolutions on economic development, the UNGA noted that 'the low standards of living existing in Member States' had 'bad economic and social effects in the countries directly concerned and on the world as a whole', and created 'conditions of instability' that were 'prejudicial to the maintenance of peaceful and friendly relations among nations and to the development of conditions of economic and social progress'.[59] In his inauguration speech in January 1949, US President Harry Truman proposed a worldwide programme of development through technical assistance, and invited other countries to 'pool their technological resources' in 'a cooperative enterprise in which all nations work together through the [UN] and its specialized agencies wherever practicable'.[60] Here, too, Truman connected the goals of 'peace, plenty, and freedom', offering to make his country's 'imponderable resources in technical knowledge' available to achieve '[g]reater production' for the 'peace-loving' and 'free peoples of the world'.[61]

For the UN, however, the principle of non-intervention in the domestic jurisdiction of states was crucially important.[62] UN technical assistance took four main forms: advice on both general and specific economic development issues; training fellowships for experts from 'under-developed' countries; visits by outside experts to instruct technicians and help organize technical institutions in such countries; and assistance in obtaining technical personnel, equipment, supplies, and other services appropriate for the promotion of economic development, including information exchanges on particular technical problems.[63] Technical assistance

58 On the first UN Development Decade, see Stokke, *UN and Development* (n 52) 137–56.
59 UNGA Res 198 (III) para 1.
60 Cited in Stokke, *UN and Development* (n 52) 49.
61 ibid.
62 UN Charter, art 2(7).
63 UN Department of Economic Affairs, *Technical Assistance for Economic Development Available through the United Nations and the Specialized Agencies* (UN Publications 1948).

was only to be provided to a government at its request, was to be of a kind determined by that government and designed to meet its needs, and was to be neither 'a means of foreign economic and political interference in the internal affairs of the country concerned' nor 'accompanied by any considerations of a political nature'.[64] Balancing the competing concerns for international security and non-intervention in domestic jurisdictions would prove very difficult, however, as became clear in the UN's experience with peacekeeping.

V. A new field of battle? Peacekeeping and decolonization

This chapter has examined the intimate connections between institutional innovations in the early UN—sovereign equality, self-government, and welfare provision—and decolonization, including determination of the forms to be taken and roles to be played in the international system by decolonized states. This part of the chapter argues these innovations were merged in a new institutional form which aimed simultaneously at facilitating the process of decolonization, enhancing the role of small states in the UN's peace and security functions, and constructing modern states on a broadly Western model. That new form—the peacekeeping operation—was the most significant innovation in the UN during its first two decades, with perhaps the most far-reaching implications for the process of decolonization at that time and since.[65]

The remainder of this chapter focuses on the two most important early peacekeeping operations. The organization had already accumulated some limited experience in the deployment of unarmed truce supervisors after the establishment of the UN Truce Supervision Organization (UNTSO) in 1948, and the formation of a UN Military Observer Group in India and Pakistan the following year. But the first armed UN peacekeeping operations were created in 1956 and 1960, in response to the Suez and Congo crises, respectively. It is highly significant that all of these operations involved situations arising out of decolonization at the end of European empires. Yet the invention of peacekeeping did not resolve the battle over international law within the UN. To the contrary, peacekeeping itself became a new terrain of battle for international, as the form, functions, and purposes of peacekeeping themselves became objects of contention and struggle.

64 UNGA Res 200 (III) (4 December 1948) paras 4(a), (b), (d).

65 Though beyond the timeframe covered by this volume, it is significant to consider, for example, the role of peacekeeping operations such as the UN Transition Assistance Group (UNTAG, 1989–1990) and the UN Transitional Administration in East Timor (UNTAET, 1999–2002) in facilitating the transitions to independence of Namibia and East Timor, respectively.

A. United Nations Emergency Force

The Suez crisis directly implicated two permanent members of the Security Council. It arose against the backdrop of a long history of European interventions in Egypt, public opinion that was increasingly hostile to the presence of British troops in the area of the Canal, growing antagonism between Egypt and Israel, and deteriorating relations between Egypt and the West. Following Egypt's declaration as a republic after the 'Free Officers' military coup of July 1952, the new government signed heads of agreement under which all British troops would leave Egypt by June 1956. On 26 July 1956, the Egyptian leader, Gamal Abdel Nasser, announced that he would nationalize the Suez Canal Company. The situation was referred to the Secretary-General and Security Council, but before any settlement could be negotiated, Israel, France, and the UK secretly agreed to launch a concerted attack on Egypt. Israeli forces took offensive action against Egypt on 29 October. The next day France and the UK demanded that both Israel and Egypt cease hostilities and withdraw from the Canal. When Egypt failed to meet that ultimatum, British and French forces launched airstrikes against Egypt on 31 October.[66]

Against the opposition of the US government, France and the UK both used their veto power to block draft Council resolutions that called upon Israel to withdraw its armed forces. The matter was then transferred to an emergency special session of the UNGA —the first ever called under the 'Uniting for Peace' resolution[67]—which requested the Secretary-General to negotiate the implementation of the ceasefire and 'obtain compliance of the withdrawal of forces behind the armistice lines'.[68] While the Assembly was still in emergency session, Hammarskjöld produced two reports, prepared with the assistance of the Canadian representative to the UN Lester Pearson, which set out plans to establish an emergency force.[69] Those plans were quickly approved,[70] and, with a relatively small force, the UN Emergency Force (UNEF) remained in place along the border between Israel and Egypt until just prior to the Six-Day War in June 1967.

Debates in the UNGA regarding the crisis reflected concerns about both decolonization and the sovereign equality of UN members. In his opening statement, the Egyptian representative said that his country had been 'subjected to bloody

[66] Anthony Gorst and Lewis Johnman, *The Suez Crisis* (Routledge 1997); David Carlton, *Britain and the Suez Crisis* (Blackwell 1988); Keith Kyle, *Suez* (Tauris & Company 2003).

[67] Statement of Mr Dulles (USA), GAOR 1st Emergency Session Plenary Meeting 561, UN Doc A/PV.561 (1956) 10.

[68] UNGA Res 999 (ES-I) (4 November 1956) UN Doc A/RES/999(ES-I).

[69] Dag Hammarskjöld, 'First Report on the Plan for an Emergency International United Nations Force' (4 November 1956) in Andrew W Cordier and Wilder Foote (eds), *Public Papers*, vol III, 334, 334–335; Dag Hammarskjöld, 'Second and Final Report on the Plan for an Emergency International United Nations Force' (6 November 1956) in Cordier and Foote, *Public Papers of the Secretaries-General of the United Nations*, vol III (Columbia University Press 1973) 344.

[70] UNGA Res 1000 (ES-I) (5 November 1956) UN Doc A/RES/1000(ES-I); UNGA Res 1001 (ES-I) (7 November 1956) UN Doc A/RES/1001(ES-I).

aggression', and that Israel, the UK, and France had 'conspired together to commit this act of war'.[71] Describing their actions as violations of the Constantinople Convention of 1888, which governed the use of the Suez Canal and gave Egypt the sole right to defend it,[72] he complained: 'We thought the Charter had put an end to the reign of force and that the era of the ultimatum and the *diktat*, of bitter memory, had vanished with the signing of the Charter at San Francisco.'[73] In statements invoking their shared history of colonization, several other representatives likewise condemned the actions of the UK and France.[74] Ceylon's representative explicitly linked the argument against colonialism with the UN's role in protecting the sovereignty of the new states:[75]

> In the view of many responsible nations, the action of the United Kingdom and France is a continuation of the tradition of colonialism. . . . The nations of resurgent Asia and Africa are determined to exercise their sovereign rights in conformity with the principles of the United Nation Charter. It is naïve to assume that this process of change can be arrested by the crushing of a leader or of leaders. The spirit of Asia and Africa can never be crushed.

Speakers on both sides of the debate pointedly criticized the abuse by great powers of their responsibilities as permanent members of the Security Council. The UK representative claimed that his government had acted only because the USSR's persistent 'cynical misuse' of its veto power, an 'irresponsible exploitation of the privileges of a great Power', had meant that 'the world has not been able to rely on the [UN] for the collective security which the Organization was designed to provide'.[76] However, several smaller states expressed outrage that, by taking military action against Egypt, two permanent members of the Council had seriously failed to meet their responsibilities to preserve international peace and security. Ecuador's representative lamented that 'two great nations . . . who gave us our civilization, and who have a moral obligation to continue that great tradition, should have been the ones to violate a sacred undertaking'. The actions of France and the UK were 'doubly immoral', he said, not only because the Charter had been violated, but also because 'the violation has been committed by two great Powers, two Powers in which we have placed all our confidence as guarantors of world peace and security and which, for that very reason, enjoy the right of veto'.[77]

71 GAOR 1st Emergency Session Plenary Meeting 561, UN Doc A/PV.561 (1956) 2, 3.

72 Jose A Obieta, *The International Status of the Suez Canal* (Martinus Nijhoff 1960) ch 4.

73 Statement of Mr Loutfi (Egypt), GAOR 1st Emergency Session Plenary Meeting 561, UN Doc A/PV.561 (1956) 2, 3.

74 See GAOR 1st Emergency Session Plenary Meeting 562, UN Doc A/PV.562 (1956).

75 GAOR 1st Emergency Session Plenary Meeting 561, UN Doc A/PV.561 (1956) 4.

76 ibid 6, 90.

77 GAOR 1st Emergency Session Plenary Meeting 562, UN Doc A/PV.562 (1956) 26.

UNEF thus provided an opportunity to advance both the goal of decolonization and the role of new states in the organization. The plans for UNEF reflected a desire to accommodate small states' concerns about the direct involvement of European great powers in the crisis. Officers for the force were recruited from countries other than the permanent members of the Security Council.[78] An advisory committee established by the UNGA to plan for the force was composed of representatives from small and medium-sized states: Brazil, Canada, Ceylon, Colombia, India, Norway, and Pakistan.[79] Above all, the gathering of UN-led forces in the Sinai was powerfully symbolic of the organization's commitment to protect its smaller and more vulnerable members against domination by would-be imperialist powers.[80]

B. Opération des Nations unies au Congo

The exceptionally brutal colonial history of the Congo—first as the 'Congo Free State' under the personal control of King Léopold and then later as a formal colonial territory of Belgium—is well known.[81] After doing next to nothing to prepare the country for self-government, a series of riots in the capital in January 1959 and further disturbances throughout the year led the Belgian government to fast-track independence to 30 June 1960.[82] Soon after that event, however, a series of mutinies broke out in the Congolese army, reports of violence prompted a mass flight of Belgians from the country, and the Belgian government deployed some 10,000 troops to the Congo to protect European residents and property. On 11 July, the province of Katanga declared independence with the support of Belgian troops stationed there. The following day, the Congo's new President and Prime Minister, Joseph Kasavubu and Patrice Lumumba, cabled Dag Hammarskjöld to make a formal request for military assistance.[83] The Secretary-General brought the situation to the Security Council's attention and recommended the establishment of a force along similar lines to UNEF. On 14 July 1960, the Security Council authorized Hammarskjöld to provide the Congo with military assistance, and called on Belgium to withdraw its troops from the country.[84] The first UN troops began to arrive the next day. By the end of July, the UN military force in the Congo had peaked at almost 20,000 troops.

78 UNGA Res 1000 (ES-I) (5 November 1956).

79 ibid.

80 Richard I Miller, *Dag Hammarskjold and Crisis Diplomacy* (Oceana 1961) 116–19.

81 Martti Koskenniemi, *The Gentle Civilizer of Nations* (CUP 2001) 155–70; Adam Hochschild, *King Leopold's Ghost* (Houghton Mifflin Harcourt 1999); Georges Nzongola-Ntalaja, *The Congo from Leopold to Kabila* (Zed Books 2002) ch 1 (hereafter Nzongola-Ntalaja, *Congo from Leopold to Kabila*).

82 Crawford Young, *Politics in the Congo* (Princeton University Press 1965) 281–90; Nzongola-Ntalaja, *Congo from Leopold to Kabila* (n 81) ch 2.

83 UN Secretary General, 'Cable to the Secretary-General' (13 July 1960) UN Doc S/4382.

84 UNSC Res 143 (14 July 1960) UN Doc S/4387.

The mission of the Opération des Nations unies au Congo (ONUC) quickly became to support the process of decolonization and enforce the territorial integrity of the new state. Manoeuvring between several opposing political forces, and seeking to avert escalation of the Cold War in Africa, Hammarskjöld carefully avoided characterizing the situation in the Congo as illegal aggression, Belgian colonialism, or purely internal disorder. Instead, he reported to the Security Council that the difficulties that had developed in the Congo were 'connected with the maintenance of order in the country and the protection of life', and had 'an important international bearing' as they were 'of a nature that cannot be disregarded by other countries'.[85] Without quoting from the Kasavubu–Lumumba cables or citing the grounds upon which they requested assistance, he focused on the specific actions the UN would take, basing his proposals on the UNEF model in terms that would not raise the objections of either the Soviet or the African and Asian members of the Security Council. As a result, the Council's resolution of 14 July 1960 simply called upon the government of Belgium 'to withdraw its troops from the territory of the Republic of the Congo' and authorized the Secretary-General:[86]

> . . . to take the necessary steps, in consultation with the Government of the Congo, to provide the Government with such military assistance, as may be necessary, until, through the efforts of the Congolese Government with the technical assistance of the United Nations, the national security forces may be able, in the opinion of the Government, to meet fully their tasks . . .

The secessions declared in Katanga and elsewhere in the Congo provided opportunities for the UN political organs to affirm the unity and territorial integrity of the Congolese state. In a resolution passed early in the operation, the Security Council noted it had 'recommended the admission of the Republic of the Congo to membership in the United Nations *as a unit*', while authorizing the Secretary-General to 'take all necessary action' to effect the speedy withdrawal of Belgian troops. The resolution further requested all states 'to refrain from any action . . . which might undermine the territorial integrity and the political independence of the Congo'.[87] Finally, when it came to authorize the use of force against foreign military personnel and mercenaries in Katanga, the Council explicitly rejected the claim that Katanga was 'a sovereign independent nation', affirming its 'full and firm support for the Central Government of the Congo', and its 'determination to assist that Government . . . to maintain . . . national integrity'.[88] In enforcing these edicts, ONUC clearly demonstrated its support for a united Congo, maintained within

[85] SCOR 15th Session Meeting 873 A/4383 (1960), 3 (para 19).
[86] UNSC Res 143 (1960) UN S/4387 paras 1–2.
[87] UNSC Res 145 (22 July 1960) UN Doc S/4405 (emphasis added).
[88] UNSC Res 169 (24 November 1961) UN Doc S/5002, Preamble, paras 8–9.

the same territorial boundaries as its colonial predecessor, under the authority of a single, central government.

In other material and symbolic ways, Hammarskjöld indicated his support for decolonization to the growing 'Afro-Asian' contingent in the UN. Expecting difficulties in the transition to independence, Hammarskjöld had asked Ralph Bunche (1904–71) to represent the UN at the Congo's independence ceremonies, and to remain for some time afterwards to offer any assistance that might be required.[89] An African-American who had served in the Roosevelt administration and who had worked to strengthen the UN machinery for decolonization in its earliest years, Bunche had mediated the armistice between Israel and the Arab states in 1947–1949, for which he had been awarded the Nobel Peace Prize in 1950, and was one of the most respected international figures of the time.[90] After ONUC was established, Bunche became Hammarskjöld's first Special Representative and Commander of the UN Force in the Congo; his presence alone would have clearly signalled the Secretary-General's sympathy for an independent Congo. The appointment of an Indian diplomat, Rajeshwar Dayal (1909–1999), as Bunche's successor, and of several Asian and African officials to Hammarskjöld's closest circle of advisors, conveyed a similar message.[91]

Moreover, in determining the composition of the ONUC Force, Hammarskjöld arranged for assistance to come in the first instance from a 'hard core' of the Congo's 'sister African nations, as an act of African solidarity'.[92] For the Secretary-General, this was primarily a means of framing the operation so as to exclude the big powers and keep the Cold War out of Africa. But he also knew that it would be agreeable to pan-Africanist leaders such as Ghana's President Nkrumah, who wished to bolster the forces of nationalism in other African countries.[93] The vast majority of troops for the Force were drawn from newly-independent states such as Ghana, Tunisia, Morocco, and Guinea.[94]

The Asian and African member states also played a crucial role at the height of the Congo crisis, after Lumumba and Kasavubu each announced the dismissal of the other. With the Security Council deadlocked, another emergency session of the

[89] Ralph J Bunche, 'The United Nations Operation in the Congo' in Andrew W Cordier and Wilder Foote (eds), *The Quest for Peace* (Columbia University Press 1965) 119, 123.

[90] Robert A Hill and Edmond J Keller (eds), *Trustee for the Human Community* (Ohio University Press 2010).

[91] Rajeshwar Dayal, *Mission for Hammarskjold* (OUP 1976); Conor Cruise O'Brien, *To Katanga and Back* (Hutchinson 1962) 51, 53, 56–57.

[92] Dag Hammarskjöld, 'First Report by the Secretary-General on the Implementation of Security Council Resolution S/4387 of 14 July 1960' (18 July 1960) UN Doc S/4389.

[93] Jitendra Mohan, 'Ghana, the Congo, and the United Nations' (1969) 7 The Journal of Modern African Studies 369, 375–76 (hereafter Mohan, 'Ghana, the Congo, and the United Nations').

[94] 'SG's First Report'. See also Rajeshwar Dayal, 'First Progress Report to the Secretary-General from His Special Representative in the Congo, Ambassador Rajeshwar Dayal' (21 September 1960) UN Doc S/4531 (Dayal, 'First Report') Annex 1: 6–7.

UNGA was convened under the 'Uniting for Peace' resolution.[95] The Assembly's resolution, sponsored by nine African and eight Asian members, appealed to all Congolese to seek resolution of their conflicts 'with the assistance, as appropriate, of Asian and African representatives appointed by the Advisory Committee on the Congo, in consultation with the Secretary-General, for the purpose of conciliation'.[96] Two weeks later in the UNGA, responding to Soviet criticism that he had taken sides against Lumumba, Hammarskjöld appealed directly to '[l]et the countries who have liberated themselves in the last fifteen years speak for themselves':[97]

> It is not the Soviet Union or, indeed, any other big Powers who need the United Nations for their protection; it is all the others. In this sense, the Organization is first of all *their* Organization, and I deeply believe in the wisdom with which they will be able to use it and guide it. I shall remain in my post during the term of my office as a servant of the Organization in the interests of all those other nations, as long as *they* wish me to do so.

To the African and Asian states in the UN, whose representatives enthusiastically applauded Hammarskjöld's speech, his ability and willingness to stand up to powerful state interests alone provided sufficient justification for the exercise of UN peacekeeping powers.

Finally, ONUC differed from UNEF in the extent to which it incorporated civilian state-building efforts, particularly concerned with the provision of social welfare. The specialized agencies had had very limited involvement in the Congo before independence, but Lumumba's and Kasavubu's request for assistance provided the best opportunity yet for the UN to offer a comprehensive program of technical assistance to a single country.[98] Under ONUC's organizational umbrella, a corps of some 2,000 experts and technicians, together with funds, training programmes, and equipment provided assistance in myriad fields of administration and government: law- and constitution-making, civil administration, civilian policing, communications, education, finance, foreign trade, medical and public health services, agriculture, food distribution, civil engineering, and civil aviation.[99] By the end of 1960, the International Telecommunications Union's and World Health Organization's programmes in the Congo were the most substantial administered

[95] Georges Abi-Saab, *The United Nations Operation in the Congo, 1960–1964* (OUP 1978) 72–73 (hereafter Abi-Saab, *UN Operation in the Congo*).

[96] UNGA Res 1474 (ES-IV) (20 September 1960) UN Doc A/RES/1474(ES-UV) para 3.

[97] Statement of Secretary-General, GAOR 15th Session Plenary Meeting 883, UN Doc A/PV.883 (1960) 331 (para 8), 332 (para 11).

[98] 'United Nations Technical Assistance in the Congo' (undated, pre-1960) UNA S-0752-0040-06.

[99] Arthur H House, *The U.N. in the Congo* (University Press of America 1978) (hereafter House, *UN in the Congo*); Harold K Jacobson, 'ONUC's Civilian Operations: State-Preserving and State-Building' (1964) 17 World Politics 75; Carsten Stahn, *The Law and Practice of International Territorial Administration* (CUP 2008) 236–46.

by either in any country, and remained so until 1966.[100] Even in 1963, ONUC's civilian operation was still 'the largest programme of technical assistance for any one country in the history of the World Organization',[101] employing 1,431 full-time specialists at the end of the year.[102]

Hammarskjöld designed ONUC's civilian operation as a single, coherent command structure, ultimately reporting to himself. In order to achieve the desired level of integration, he appointed a group of experts who would serve 'on a level of higher administrative responsibility' within government ministries. The group included consultants that could cover the fields of agriculture, communications, education, finance, foreign trade, health, instruction (national security forces), labour market, judiciary, natural resources and industry, and public administration.[103] Each expert was appointed first as a 'local representative' of the relevant specialized agency, thereby remaining in 'the proper relationship to his agency and under its authority', and then as a member of the Consultative Group. Despite never receiving formal approval, the scheme effectively placed much of the Congo under UN administration and subordinated the activities of all specialized agencies to the overall authority of the Secretary-General.[104] Placed in these senior roles, UN-appointed experts were able to act as 'effectively heads of departments with immediate access to their Ministers and authorized to act in their absence'.[105]

It was perhaps unavoidable that many of the reform programmes conducted by the specialized agencies in the Congo would be burdened with assumptions, attitudes, and practices inherited from the colonial past. The immediate post-colonial circumstances of the operation also contributed to the deterioration of relations between Hammarskjöld and Lumumba, who disagreed over the interpretation of Security Council resolutions and actions taken by the Congolese Army to suppress secessionists.[106] And there is considerable evidence that Hammarskjöld and other UN officials secretly sided with Kasavubu against Lumumba, whom they regarded as unstable and susceptible to Soviet influence, and were not above using their connections to US government officials to achieve ends that they believed were for the best for the people of the Congo.[107] Under pressure of emergency conditions, those

[100] Harold K Jacobson, 'New States and Functional International Organisations: A Preliminary Report' in Robert W Cox (ed), *The Politics of International Organizations* (Praeger 1969) 74 (ch 3), 87 (hereafter Jacobson, 'New States').

[101] United Nations Operation in the Congo, 'United Nations Operation in the Congo: Report on Civilian Operations in 1963' (30 April 1964) UNA LEO/PROG/3, I.

[102] House, *UN in the Congo* (n 99) 189.

[103] Dag Hammarskjöld, 'Second Report by the Secretary-General on the Implementation of Security Council Resolutions' (11 August 1960) UN Doc S/4417/Add.5.

[104] United Nations Association, 'Cable B336 from SecGen to Cordier' (date illegible) UNA S-0845-0006-06-00001.

[105] United Nations Association, 'A Tentative Approach to Civilian Affairs–Draft' (23 July 1960) UNA S-0845-0006-06-00001.

[106] Abi-Saab, *UN Operation in the Congo* (n 95) 37–44.

[107] Alan James, *Britain and the Congo Crisis: 1960 - 1963* (Palgrave Macmillan 1996) 66–67, 71; David N Gibbs, 'The United Nations, International Peacekeeping and the Question of "Impartiality": Revisiting the Congo Operation of 1960' (2000) 38 The Journal of Modern African Studies 359, 369–73.

ends also required taking decisions in the place of democratically elected leaders and Congolese officials.

VI. Conclusion

This chapter has argued that decolonization transformed the UN during its first two decades, as that organization focused its attention on facilitating the passage to independence by a growing number of previously colonised states. It has shown how that transformation occurred as the result of a series of struggles, played out in and through the instrumentalities of the UN, and drawing upon its institutional and normative resources, resulted ultimately in the invention of the peacekeeping operation as a new institutional form.

Those struggles led to a set of ambiguous outcomes, especially as a consequence of the peacekeeping operation in the Congo. On the one hand, ONUC galvanized the efforts of the 'Afro-Asian' states to promote decolonization through the UN, provided opportunities for those states to play a more prominent role in the UN's decision-making processes, and stimulated a further series of activities, particularly in the area of development. As Harold Jacobson observed, the Congo experience 'brought the problems of that state, and by extension those of Africa . . . dramatically to the attention' of international organizations, which were then forced to reconsider their activities on that continent.[108] In December 1961, the UNGA launched the first Development Decade, and subsequent years saw the creation of an array of new agencies, funds, and programmes focused on development, as we have seen.

On the other hand, ONUC highlighted the possibility of decolonization being subverted, exposed fissures in the non-aligned movement, and revealed the limits of the modernizing, welfare-oriented project of state building in the global South. In the course of the Congo crisis, a split emerged between those states that favoured a moderate approach and supported the work of the UN (the 'Brazzaville group') and those that advocated a more radical stance (the 'Casablanca group'), with an overall 'deflationary effect' on efforts toward African unity.[109] The Congo crisis also marked a pivot in the Soviet Union's policy towards Africa, a loss of confidence in the utility of the 'socialist model of development' in promoting Soviet influence in the decolonized world, and a turn towards more militarized modes of engagement in the Cold War.[110] And it coincided with a shift in Western development thinking

[108] Jacobson, 'New States' (n 100) 87.

[109] Mohan, 'Ghana, the Congo, and the UN' (n 93) 370. See also Alanna O'Malley, 'Ghana, India, and the Transnational Dynamics of the Congo Crisis at the United Nations, 1960–1961' (2015) 37 International History Review 970, 982–84.

[110] Alessandro Iandolo, 'The Rise and Fall of the "Soviet Model of Development" in West Africa, 1957–1964' (2012) 12 Cold War History 683.

towards greater concern with the maintenance of political order and tolerance toward counter-revolutionary, authoritarian forms of government in the decolonized world.[111]

Since the period of decolonization, peacekeeping and the symbolism of the 'blue helmets' have become intimately inseparable from the public image of the UN. Moreover, UN peace operations have expanded dramatically both in number and in scope, particularly in Africa, since the late 1980s. Peace operations today are engaged in a wide range of complex tasks, including state-building, judicial reform, social and economic development, human rights monitoring, security sector reform, and disarmament. After being considered for years a mere 'artefact of African and global circumstances that belonged essentially to the early 1960s', ONUC is now regarded as 'in many respects a prototype for future UN interventions in sub-Saharan Africa'.[112] In this sense, the battles within the UN which gave birth to peacekeeping during the period of decolonization remain at the conflicted heart of that endeavour.

[111] Colin Leys, *The Rise & Fall of Development Theory* (Indian University Press 1996) ch 3 (on 'Samuel Huntington & the End of Classical Modernization Theory').

[112] Norrie MacQueen, *United Nations Peacekeeping in Africa since 1960* (Longman 2002) 59.

12
The World Bank in the Battles of the 'Decolonization Era'

Philipp Dann

I. Introduction

Today, it seems both easy and difficult to write the history of the World Bank in the 1950s and 1960s. On one hand, major works on this history have been published in the past twenty years; the Bank is the object of various critical and comprehensive accounts.[1] On the other hand, however, the picture that has emerged seems somewhat fixed, showing the Bank as the perfect villain, a posterchild of managerialism, liberal legal expansionism, Western-centric neo-liberalism. The Bank features almost like a magician exemplifying, if not driving, all these trends. But this picture is in parts shaped by the Bank of the 1980s, 1990s, and 2000s, by the neo-liberal era, and by its effects on the global order.

The story of the World Bank, the development system and the battle over financial support for the 'newly independent states' in the 1950s and 1960s is more ambivalent—and full of tragic turns. It is less black and white, less like the story of concessions, corporations or investment law, where Northern governments more brazenly blocked Southern demands or refused interaction.[2] With regard to the history of the Bank, much of what might have been perceived as victories of the third world (TW) governments at the time, turned into ambivalence and problems: With the International Development Association (IDA) a new branch of the Bank was created and the Bank turned into a development agency initially against strong Western resistance—but power in the Bank was not shared and the financial engagement became increasingly linked to substantive influence, foreshadowing

[1] Devesh Kapur, John P Lewis and Richard Webb, *The World Bank: Its First Half Century, Vol 1: History* (The Brookings Institution 1997) (hereafter Kapur, *World Bank*); Sundhya Pahuja, *Decolonising International Law* (CUP 2013) (hereafter Pahuja, *Decolonising International Law*); Balakrishnan Rajagopal, *International Law from Below* (CUP 2003) (hereafter Rajagopal, *International Law);* Gilbert Rist, The History of Development (Zed Books 2014); Bret Benjamin, *Invested Interests: Capital, Culture and the World Bank* (University of Minnesota Press 2007) (hereafter Benjamin, *Invested Interests*); Philipp Dann, *The Law of Development Cooperation* (CUP 2013) (hereafter Dann, *Law of Development Cooperation*); Eric Helleiner, *Forgotten Foundations of Bretton Woods* (Cornell University Press 2014); Guy F Sinclair, *To Reform the World: International Organizations and the Making of Modern States* (OUP 2017).

[2] See Craven, Brunner, Sornaraja, Pahuja/Saunders, all in this volume.

Philipp Dann, *The World Bank in the Battles of the 'Decolonization Era'* In: *The Battle for International Law: South-North Perspectives on the Decolonization Era*. Edited by: Jochen von Bernstorff and Philipp Dann, Oxford University Press (2019).
DOI: 10.1093/oso/9780198849636.003.0013

conditionality. An entire institutional ecosystem was built around the demands of TW governments—but it was also fragmented, over time impeded synergies, and lacked funding. The concept of 'development' was planted at the centre of thinking, which was partly a recognition of Southern concerns in law and institutions—but also initiated the othering mechanism of the 'development' paradigm, which keeps TW peoples in Chakrabarty's 'waiting room of history'.

Ultimately, a certain dynamic and strategy of the Bank and Northern governments comes to the fore when looking at those years that is reminiscent of classic hegemonic moves. Southern demands here were not simply rejected or blocked, but rather redirected, diverted, and ultimately subverted. Almost like in the far-Eastern fighting technique of Aikido, where the energy and dynamic of an attack is not absorbed but returned and redirected against the attacker, the demands of the TW here were responded to by creating the IDA, thereby transforming the World Bank and turning it into the agency that later became 'the symbolic antagonist for a vast array of social movements'.[3] The creation of the IDA in 1960 was a central turning point in the larger battle about financial support for the 'newly independent states'—and ultimately appears like a tactical move of Northern governments in the Bank to integrate certain claims of Southern governments just to cap further, more disruptive demands.

This chapter looks at this Aikido-move of Northern governments and the larger battle from three perspectives. First, Section II describes the political battle to institutionalize more development financing, placing the evolution of the Bank and in particular the creation of the IDA in the broader context of the battle between North and South over institutional structures of redistribution and financial support. Section III then looks at the discursive turn and rhetorical recognition but also placation and pacification of the South undertaken by the Bank mainly in the 1960s. Finally, Section IV investigates the role of institutional law in this battle and argue that law played an important role in deflecting Southern demands and actually shielding the Bank even more.

II. The battle for concessional funding and the creation of the IDA

In most new states, the question of economic independence arose at the moment of formal political independence. Most were in dire straits and in urgent need of economic progress. Hence, as greater numbers of colonies gained independence in the late 1940s and early 1950s, the need for financial support was discussed. In fact, it has been observed that 'from 1950 until at least 1960, 'financing of economic

[3] Benjamin, *Invested Interests* (n 1) 112.

development' was the 'most passionately debated economic issue at UN'.[4] It was consensus that trade would be the most important way for the new states to earn money.[5] But it was also clear that in order to reach sustainable trading relations and produce more than raw materials, a process of industrialization was necessary, for which investments and funds were needed. At the same time, it was understood that TW countries were not able to receive loans on normal market conditions; instead, concessional funding (in particular, loans with lower interest rates and longer payback times) was needed.

The main issue was from whom such concessional funding should come.[6] Economic experts and TW countries (led in particular by Chile, India, and Yugoslavia) in the United Nations (UN) argued for the creation of an international multilateral agency that would provide concessional funding. The concrete idea was that a Special UN Fund for Economic Development (SUNFED) should be created.[7] However, Western countries (led by the United States (US) and the United Kingdom (UK)) strenuously blocked these efforts. They argued that the UN should provide only technical assistance and hence supported the EPTA, but saw no role for the UN in providing capital support. They especially voted against all proposals for SUNFED.

Soon after, the International Bank for Reconstruction and Development (IBRD) (also known as the World Bank, or Bank) became an inflammatory topic in the discussion, as many in the TW demanded it should take on a broader role.[8] The Bank and its Western allies, however, thought nothing of this demand. Created in the context of the Anglo-American attempt to create an international institutional system that would further their interests in the world after the Second World War, its mandate and geopolitical role in the eyes of its main shareholders (ie, Western founding member states) was to provide funding for the reconstruction of war-torn countries of the North, not the South. Neither was 'development' conceptually on the horizon of most Northern negotiators, nor was actual decolonization considered an imminent reality.[9] Early on and in line with these expectations, this created a specific institutional culture that oriented the Bank towards private financial markets, in particular Wall Street. Because even though the IBRD had a base capital, it was supposed to finance its ongoing operations through issuing bonds and selling them at the private financial markets (ie, Wall Street). Therefore,

[4] Edward S Mason and Robert Asher, *The World Bank since Bretton Woods* (The Brookings Institution 1973) 38.

[5] On these discussions, Olav Stokke, *The UN and Development: From Aid to Cooperation* (Indiana University Press 2009) 84 (hereafter Stokke, *The UN and Development*); Kapur, *World Bank* (n 1) 1121.

[6] See Stokke, *The UN and Development* (n 3) 93–98.

[7] ibid 95.

[8] Kapur, *World Bank* (n 1) 1127; Jonas Haralz, 'The International Finance Corporation', in Kapur, *World Bank* (n 1) 811 (on the annual meeting of the bank in 1954); Helleiner, *Forgotten Foundations* (n 1) 268.

[9] On the creation and the slipping of 'development' into the mandate, Pahuja, *Decolonising International Law* (n 1); on planning for decolonization, see Barsalou Chapter 19 this volume.

establishing credibility with financial centre was a necessary strategy. The IBRD aimed to be more of a Bank than an international organization. Loans were awarded only according to strict Wall Street conservative, risk-averse style. There was no interest or sensibility for TW needs and TW countries were unable to fulfil the stringent lending conditions.

In the course of the 1950s, however, the Bank's business model and its original geopolitical role became increasingly questioned. Formal decolonization accelerated and the context changed dramatically. The emerging and intensifying Cold War locked the West in a direct competition with the Soviet Union and created an indirect global contest for geopolitical influence.[10] Any unrest and dissatisfaction in the TW bore the risk of tipping countries into the communist camp. To contain communism it soon became clear that economic support (development aid) and security could form an important link, extending concepts of colonial administration since the 1920s that 'caring for the welfare of the natives was a technique of colonial domination' and that developmental intervention could be used to quell unrest and create loyalties. The IBRD was viewed by many actors in the North as an important instrument to push back Soviets wherever possible, and not acquiescing with the poor had political risk.[11]

At the same time, an ideological paradigm shift took place that Arturo Escobar called the 'discovery of poverty'.[12] While colonial exploitation had always been covered up and justified by motives of salvation (based on Christian or other humanitarian causes), only in the first half of the twentieth century did the economic well-being of the colonial subjects became a topic, and those subjects an object of intervention.[13] By declaring them 'poor' or 'under-developed' (and hence establishing a distinction between developed and under-developed) not only were two-thirds of the world's population defined as lacking something—but also as needing help. [14] This shift became a central tenet of Western foreign policy and its global aspirations, most overtly with the inaugural address of Truman 1949. As the US tried to distance itself from the increasingly untenable imperial justification of foreign interventions, the rhetoric of development provided a welcome rationale for global intervention beyond market interests and the security concerns vis-à-vis the Eastern bloc.

[10] Odd A Westad, *The Global Cold War: Third World Interventions and the Making of Our Times* (CUP 2007) (hereafter Westad, *The Global Cold War*); Rajagopal, *International Law*, (n 1) 99–101.

[11] Rajagopal, *International Law* (n 1) 106.

[12] Arturo Escobar, *Encountering Development The Making and Unmaking of the Third World* (Princeton University Press 2012) 21; Rajagopal, *International Law* (n 1) 105–08; Pahuja, *Decolonising International Law* (n 1) 61–66.

[13] Jennifer L Beard, *The Political Economy of Desire: International Law, Development and the Nation State* (University of Melbourne Research Paper 2009).

[14] Guy Sinclair, *To Reform the Word* (n 1) frames this point a bit differently, namely as 'dynamic of liberal reform, which by seeking to maximize liberty, requires incessant fine-tuning of institutions, individuals and society' (283).

In these circumstances, the battle for a 'development bank' continued and pressure grew on Western states (the US especially) to react. There were many calls for a (multilateral) institution that could provide financial support to poorer nations, which could not fulfil the strict lending criteria of IBRD.[15] This demand was voiced in the UN but also prominently at the Asian–African Conference in Bandung in 1955. The topic of economic cooperation actually topped the final communique, declaring that 'assistance being received [. . .] from outside the region, through international or bilateral arrangements made a valuable contribution'. TW leaders demanded more financial and technological support from the West and clearly preferred multilateral lending over bilateral assistance.[16]

The Bank was a highly ambivalent object in this debate. On one hand it was indeed the only multilateral Bank at the time and well-funded. It had also projected an image of a somewhat objective and ultimately non-aligned institution with special expertise that could be used by TW countries. At the same time, the Bank was also highly suspect because of its discriminatory voting structure. As much as funding was called for, so was equal participation in the economic governance a central demand, and the structures in the Bank a constant reason for critique.[17] The preference for many TW countries therefore was still the establishment of a capital fund at the UN.

Throughout the 1950s, the US government made various moves to diffuse the demands. The Eisenhower administration first tried to influence the debate by suggesting that funds for concessional lending should come from those who agreed to disarmament.[18] In the climate of an intensifying Cold War, this was simply a distraction. The US then signalled openness to another idea. Already in 1952, the UN Economic and Social Council (ECOSOC) had called for the creation of an agency that should provide funding for private corporations investing in the TW. Even though there was clear resistance to this in the Bank, this idea gained momentum, and the US pushed the World Bank to create a second branch to provide such funding, resulting in 1956 in the creation of the International Finance Corporation (IFC).[19]

This did not solve the question of concessional lending to TW states. In this regard, majorities shifted in the second half of the 1950s and sympathy grew also in US (especially in the state department and from Democrats) to redesign the

[15] James H Weaver, *The International Development Association* (Preager 1965) 11–17; 'Report on a Special United Nations Fund for Economic Development', prepared by a committee appointed by the Secretary General and presented to the 16th ECOSOC session 1953.

[16] Though the Bank itself was not present at the conference, its influence at the conference is deemed considerable. On Bank and Bandung, Benjamin, *Invested Interests* (n 1) 117–24 (esp. 121–23).

[17] See Ram P Anand, *Sovereign Equality of States in International Law* (Collected Courses of the Hague Academy of International Law, Vol 197 (The Hague Academy of International Law 1987).

[18] Stokke, *The UN and Development* (n 5) 96.

[19] Stokke, *The UN and Development* (n 5) 100–02; Jonas Haralz, 'The International Finance Corporation' in Kapur, *World Bank* (n 1) 807–12; Bronislaw Matecki, *Establishment of the International Finance Corporation and US Policy* (Praeger 1957).

system. Anti-communists viewed the Bank as an under-utilized instrument to contain communism. Internationalists and those driven by more humanitarian or liberal causes advocated for expanding the IBRD's reach.[20] But there was equally strong resistance from isolationists and conservatives in the State Department, from within the Bank (particularly from its President, Eugene Black) and from other IBRD member states such as Germany.[21] The management of the Bank in particular was very reluctant to endanger its hard fought for reputation as 'neutral' and independent institution.[22]

The battle was decided when the UN, with Soviet bloc support, moved to create a special fund; this move scared the US into action, and the US Senate also pushed for the creation of the IDA.[23] When the US government insured the Bank leadership that control over a new, soft lending institution was not to be relinquished, the Bank management agreed. In July 1959, the US ordered its executive director to draft articles for the IDA. It took up work in 1960 as a soft-lending window of the Bank.[24]

Political control of the new organization was structured the same way as the IBRD and hence it remained in the hands of the US and its allies.[25] Although legally a separate organization, the IBRD's governors, president, and executive director held *ex officio* the same position in the IDA. Also, the outward safeguards 'against politicization' remained.[26] Two aspects of its institutional and legal framework, however, mark the considerable shift away from the IBRD model—and the profound transformation of the Bank that took place: First, the new organization received a mandate 'to promote economic development, increase productivity and thus raise standards of living in the developed areas of the world'.[27] This would allow the support of projects 'for purposes which are of developmental priority'[28] and allowed the IDA to offer financial support to new group of poorer states but also to be thematically open to social issues (eg, education, health, agriculture).

Secondly, the funding of the new organization followed a completely different model than the one used in the IBRD. Instead of financing the institution through

[20] Mark Mazower, *No Enchanted Palace: The End of Empire and the Ideological Origins of the United Nations* (Princeton University Press 2013) Kapur, *World Bank* (n 1).

[21] Benjamin, *Invested Interests* (n 1); on Black's ambivalent/complex position also Sinclair, *To Reform the World* (n 1) 222; Kapur, *World Bank* (n 1) pp. 136, 1124–29; Stokke, *The UN and Development* (n 5) 93–102.

[22] Sinclair, *To Reform the World* (n 1) 222.

[23] Stokke, *The UN and Development* (n 5) 101; Kapur, *World Bank* (n 1) 1127–29.

[24] Sinclair, *To Reform the World* (n 1) 225.

[25] That is to say, voting rights were weighted according to the level of subscriptions; IDA Articles of Agreement art VI s 3.

[26] Non-political mandate (IDA Articles of Agreement art V s 6) and requirement to support only 'specific projects' (IDA Articles of Agreement art V s 1(b)).

[27] IDA Articles of Agreement art I.

[28] IDA Articles of Agreement art V s 1(a–c).

interests from borrowers and bonds placed at private markets, the IDA was to be funded solely by its members states. Every three years, member states who could afford it would be asked to provide new money in so-called 'replenishments'. This severed the dependence of the Bank from its reputation at Wall Street—and allowed the member states (and the IDA) to put its political and developmental interests at the centre of its agenda. It ultimately created the chance to transform the institutional culture and understanding of the institution and create the development agency that the Bank then became—but it also deepened the inequality between the member states.

At the same time, the creation of the IDA was only one element of a wider institutional reconfiguration and institutionalization of the development paradigm. Around the year 1960, a plethora of institutions was created to administer the process of development, including the provision of concessional funding.[29] In this broad move to institutionalization of the development paradigm, two different types of lending institutions emerged: one replicated the power structures at the UN, the other rather the power structures in the World Bank. The first type was advanced by a coalition of TW and the Soviet bloc governments. They created a fund to provide technical assistance, first the UN Special Fund for Development in 1959, which in 1964 was merged with the Expanded Programme for Technical Assistance (EPTA) to become the UNDP.[30] In 1961, the World Food Program was created, the UN Conference on Trade and Development (UNCTAD) in 1964, the UN Industrial Development Organization (UNIDO) in 1966, and the International Fund for Agricultural Development (IFAD) (a latecomer) in 1977. In all of these institutions, the principle of equality and one state–one vote applied.

The other type were regional development banks.[31] All of these copied the institutional model of the World Bank, in which institutional power is reserved to its main shareholder (ie, often the donating Northern countries), the façade of a non-political neutral banks is erected and a separation between soft/concessional lending and hard/non-concessional funding is ensured through a combination of contributions by member countries (IDA model) or independently earned money through interests from loans or bonds issued at the financial markets (IBRD model).[32] These institutions became intensely courted and followed by the US and

[29] Marc Frey, Sönke Kunkel, and Corinna R Unger (eds), *International Organizations and Development 1945–1990* (Palgrave 2014); see also Stokke, *The UN and Development* (n 5).

[30] On these debates, see Stokke, *The UN and Development* (n 5) 98; see also Helleiner, *Forgotten Foundations* (n 1) 268.

[31] Inter-American Development Bank (1959), African Development Bank (1964), Asian Development Bank (1966).

[32] Dann, *Law of Development Cooperation* (n 1) 161; Suzuki Eisuke, 'Regional Development Banks' in Rüdiger Wolfrum (ed), *Max Planck Encyclopedia of Public International Law* (OUP 2013) (here after Suzuki, 'Regional Development Banks'); Stephen D Krasner, Power Structure and Regional Development Banks (1981) 32 International Organisation 32 303; Ruth Ben-Artzi, *Regional Development Banks in Comparison* (CUP 2016) 64; Kapur, *World Bank* (n 1) 137–38.

other Northern governments to ensure that they became like-minded partners and collaborators.[33]

In sum, Southern demands to create more institutions that would provide concessional funding, which were initially focused on a greater role of (egalitarian) UN participation, were diverted into a restructuring of the Bank by creating the IDA. A move that had been intended to bolster not just financial support but also political autonomy in using such finances turned the Bank into an even more hierarchical and oligarchic institution and strengthened the Northern dominance in the 'engine room' of development finance.

III. Changing discourse and red lines

Institutional battles were accompanied by discursive battles, which, as the 1960s unfolded, took place amid a more general atmospheric shift. The Cold War was intensifying, and many observers perceived the Soviets as gaining an upper hand, which put pressure on the West. In the US, Germany, and the UK, new liberal governments came to power and liberalization and emancipation became major themes of societal discussions. These developments also gave North–South relations an increasingly central place in many Western debates. But while there was a growing number of people in the North who advocated fair relations between North and South, many in the North also seemed to consider these times as a global crisis, almost creating the impression of hysteria over the dangers posed by the gulf between poor and rich.[34]

Debates in the TW and attitudes towards the institutionalized development system (including the Bank) became increasingly diverse and critical,[35] and connected to the rise of neo-Marxist dependency theory, which turned the political and ideological focus to a fight for fair trade (and hence rather towards GATT and UNCTAD).[36] However, there were also a number of fundamental critiques from the TW of the development aid system as it had emerged, one of which was Frantz Fanon. In his 1963 book *The Wretched of the Earth*, while not naming the Bank, he lucidly analyses the encounter between national liberation movements and international finance—and formulates political imperatives for those interested in contesting the Bank's (and other financier's) demands.[37] He argues that TW peoples

[33] Allies of the Bank also emerged in the form of bilateral funding agencies in Western countries, for example, in Germany (the Ministry for Development Cooperation was created in 1962), in the US (creation of USAID), and the collective forum of these bilateral agents in the OECD; see Dann, *Law of Development Cooperation* (n 1) 53, 209.

[34] On McNamara in this regard, Benjamin, *Invested Interests* (n 1) 87-89.

[35] On the different camps already at Bandung, see Vijay Prashad, *The Darker Nations: A Peoples History of the Third World* (The New Press 2008) 33.

[36] Dann, *Law of Development Cooperation* (n 1) 65.

[37] Frantz Fanon, *The Wretched of the Earth* (Grove Press 1963) 66 (hereafter Fanon, *The Wretched of the Earth*).

should demand a decisive redistribution of wealth, not the token pieces of aid, insisting that capitalist powers simply 'must pay' and that such a payment is unrelated to charity.[38]

Even more direct was the Ghanaian leader Kwame Nkrumah, who in his 1966 book *Neocolonialism: The Last Stage of Imperialism* took direct aim at the Bank. In the book he argues that the Bank's role was mostly in furthering Northern banking and financial interests by opening up Africa, making investments there profitable for Northern capital without regard for local needs. As he sees it, Northern banking interests (which the Bank serves) are replacing colonial arrangements, while the Bank helps to erect 'neo-colonial trap of "multilateral aid" through international institutions'.[39] At the same time, a Pearson report showed a growing frustration in the North and within the aid system about the slower than expected pace of creating change.[40]

Such voices and the shifts in public mood didn't go unnoticed. The Bank acknowledged the dissent, and tried to divert anger; again, using Aikido-style methods (turning hostile energy against the opponent), it redirected feelings of discord to themes of the TW, announced that it had learned lessons from the past, and tried to diffuse pressures. With the creation of the IDA, it started to provide concessional lending and became active in a number of new policy fields, especially education, health, and agriculture.[41] Its new president George Woods vocally praised this new engagement and was celebrated for it by many representatives from the TW.[42] One reason for this substantive but also rhetorical shift was the new funding structure. The need to raise contributions (replenishments) from its main shareholders forced the Bank to turn (at least in parts) away from Wall Street as its main audience, and to new broader audiences, such as parliaments in Northern states and the general public there, especially in the US (resulting in awarding outsized power to US NGOs and Congress).[43]

At the same time, the Bank aimed to address broader audiences in the South and engage with themes dominant there, for example, colonialism. The Bank in its early years had seen rather through the eyes of its Northern (if not British) shareholders. Now it started to acknowledge at least the colonial trauma and the broad justifications for anti-colonial hostilities, though it framed these more as problems

[38] Ibid 102-3.

[39] Kwame Nkrumah, *Neo-Colonialism: The Last Stage of Imperialism* (Panaf Books Ltd 1971) 242 (hereafter Nkrumah, *Neo-Colonialism*); on Nkrumah's role generally /in the liberation of Ghana, see Martin Meredith, *The State of Africa: A History of the Continent Since Independence* (Simon & Schuster UK 2013) 18 (hereafter Meredith, *The State of Africa*).

[40] Lester Pearson, *Partners in Development: Report of the Commission on International Development* (Praeger 1969); Dann, *Law of Development Cooperation* (n 1) #.

[41] Kapur, *World Bank* (n 1) 140; (Benjamin, *Invested Interests* (n 1) 83–88; Rajagopal, *International Law* (n 1); Pahuja, *Decolonising International Law* (n 1)).

[42] Sinclair, *To Reform the World* (n 1) 233.

[43] Benjamin, *Invested Interests* (n 1) 65–66.

of a dramatic cultural encounters of economic exploitation and political violence.[44] Nationalism was another central and even trickier theme,[45] which had become the central TW sentiment in the age of national independence. But it could also trigger dynamics deeply problematic for the Bank, namely, the tendency towards isolationism and towards economic nationalization, both of which endangered the Bank's mode of operation and ideology (based on international cooperation and open markets). Addressing nationalism, the Bank tried to turn it into a productive instrument of development interventions (state as central economic actor) and to dispel regional solidarity (or opposition; it was easier to negotiate with one than with many). It hence tried to put forward-looking spins on these themes—again, from its Western, liberal perspective.

The difficult nature of the interactions with the South and the ultimate red lines and policy of the Bank, however, resulted in an intense dispute between the Bank and the UN over the Bank lending to both the apartheid regime in South Africa and the still-colonial power in Portugal.[46] In 1961, the UN General Assembly implemented the UN's Declaration on the Granting of Independence to Colonial Countries and Peoples (Resolution 1514(XV)) by establishing a special committee 'to examine the application of the Declaration' and requested 'the specialized agencies concerned to assist the Special Committee in its work within their respective fields'.[47] This was squarely directed at the World Bank and its lending policies, and a copy of this resolution was forwarded to the president of the World Bank. There, however, it lingered for some time without any response. In mid-1964, the UN Secretariat wrote to the Bank, again seeking information about bank loans to Portugal and asking about 'the possibility of representatives of the Bank appearing before the Committee in order to provide clarification'. The Bank again was cool, sending the information but ignoring the invitation. In June 1965, while the Bank continued to ignore the demands, the Committee passed a resolution containing stronger language appealing 'to all the specialized agencies of the United Nations, and in particular the IBRD [. . .] and request[ing] them to refrain from granting Portugal any financial, economic or technical assistance so long as the Portuguese Government fails to renounce its colonial policy, which constitutes a flagrant violation of the provisions of the Charter of the United Nations'. The Bank, however, continued its silence. Instead, it granted two loans to Portugal and South Africa in 1966 and left it to its General Counsel to respond to the UN. What followed were intense and at times heated exchanges between the legal departments of the

[44] ibid 83–86 (arguing that the Bank cast itself as new, uncompromised, and responsible forward-looking actor).

[45] ibid 73–79.

[46] Samuel A Bleicher, '*UN vs IBRD*: A Dilemma of Functionalism', (1970) 24 International Organization 31.

[47] UNGA Resolution 1654 (XVI).

UN secretariat and the Bank, in which the UN demanded that the Bank stop its lending; the Bank rather used these demands to test and fortify its version of institutional autonomy, using in particular its non-political mandate.

Ultimately, next to some critical voices and anger over the symbolism of funding racist and colonial regimes, much of the TW political leadership retained a largely constructive and reformist attitude. The conceptual companionship between elites in South and North was still broad, as modernization theory and Keynesian economic thinking provided a common understanding for the needs of 'development' and respective interventions.[48] The Bank also invested considerable resources to cultivate links to nationalist leaders and diffuse rhetorical and political antagonism.[49] That the Bank portrayed itself as neutral, non-aligned, economic actor might also have resonated with some in the South, for example in non-aligned India, a major client of the Bank.[50]

IV. Institutional law as weapon

In these institutional and discursive battles over the position and course of the Bank, and in the larger questions of development finance, institutional law played a central role. It was not just a major weapon in locking up the institutional 'engine room', preserving Northern power against TW influence, but it also provided argumentative planks to counter demands. In fact, institutional law became the central instrument to deflect and divert Southern demands and launch counter-strikes that further insulated the Bank against the egalitarian dynamic of decolonization, and which thereby strengthened the North's position. Three aspects demonstrate how and under which conditions institutional law was used in this regard: first, the normative basis of the Bank's positioning, second, a strategy of instrumentality and legal acumen to use this normative basis, and finally, functionalism that allowed for the Bank's self-positioning.[51]

[48] Rajagopal, *International Law* (n 1) 31 ff; Dann, *Law of Development Cooperation* (n 1) 58.

[49] Benjamin, *Invested Interests* (n 1) 115.

[50] On the close connection between the Bank and India, see Bruce Muirhead, 'Differing Perspectives: India, the World Bank and the 1963 Aid-India Negotiations' (2005) 4 India Review 1; Kapur, *World Bank* (n 1) 140.

[51] My focus here is on the role of law within the institution. Others have focused on the interaction of the Bank and the process of state formation (especially Guy Sinclair) or on the larger narrative of international law (especially Sundhya Pahuja and Balakrishnan Rajagopal). I think, however, that there is also a distinct and under-researched role that institutional law played in these years with regard to positioning the Bank vis-à-vis the TW. Thinking in a similar vein, see Dimitris Van den Meerssche, 'International Law as Insulation: The Case of the World Bank in the Decolonization Era', Paper presented at the ESIL Interest Group on International Institutional Law, ESIL Annual Conference, Manchester, UK, 13 September 2018 <https://igioesil.files.wordpress.com/2018/10/dimitri-van-den-meerssche_io-ig-conference-draft1.pdf> accessed 31 May 2019.

1. Normative basis

The use of law was based on several legal cornerstones that had been set down in the IBRD Articles of Agreement in 1945 and were preserved or even strengthened in the IDA Articles in 1960. One was the system of weighted votes, linking funding prowess and voting power and hence tying political influence in the Bank to financial investment. Introduced in the IBRD agreement (IBRD Articles of Agreement art V s 3) it was in fact cemented, if not radicalized, with the cyclical funding scheme introduced for the IDA (replenishments, IDA Articles of Agreement art III s 1). This scheme gave those member states, which had and wanted to invest the money, direct political and thematic influence. This scheme aggravated the institutionalized inequality and flew in the face of all demands for fair (if not equal) participation in running the institution. It ensured that accountability in the World Bank was only to first world shareholders, not to Southern member states or those affected in the South. It relegated the South even more to being mere 'borrowers' or 'recipients'. It was the rejection of solidarity[52] and the installation of oligarchic charity.[53]

The other clauses shielding the Bank and providing both legal and political support for its actions were those that created its façade of political neutrality and technicality: the non-political mandate (IBRD Articles of Agreement art IV s 10, and IDA Articles of Agreement art V s 6) and the 'specific project'-clause (IBRD Articles of Agreement art III s 4(vii), and IDA Articles of Agreement art V s 1(b)). These created an aura of objective expertise, which was widely believed—despite the fact they were politically instrumentalized from early on.[54] These aspects were

52 On the fragile concept of solidarity in development law, see Philipp Dann, 'Solidarity and the Law of Development Cooperation' in Rüdiger Wolfrum and Chie Kojima (eds), *Solidarity: A Structural Principle of International Law* (Springer 2009), 55–77.

53 It is a separate but telling story that the EU (at the time the European Economic Community, EEC) took a different path in their dealing with the TW. Here, the shift to soft lending was accompanied by a considerable reconfiguration of the terms of cooperation and a scheme of equal participation (on these developments, see Dann, *Law of Development Cooperation* (n 1) 43, 75; see also Marjorie Lister, *The European Community and the Developing World: The Role of the Lomé Convention* (Gower Publishing Company Ltd. 1988) 14; Enzo R Grilli, *The European Community and the Developing Countries* (CUP 1993) 27. When the EEC was founded in 1957, French and Dutch empires still existed and the new community was immediately used to organize funds for (very different) projects there. However, during the ensuing years of decolonization, two interesting shifts occurred. To accommodate the fact that the partners now had gained independence, the cooperation was based on a multilateral agreement, the Yaoundé Convention, which took effect in 1964. Here, new countries faced Europe not as single countries, but as a collective. This distinguished their negotiation position vis-à-vis the EEC. But second, and more importantly, demands grew over the terms of cooperation for a fair division of labour and Southern influence. This resulted in a widely hailed new treaty, the 1975 Lomé Agreement, which contained a truly cooperative approach and was hailed as a broad success of TW-governments.

54 For example, through the introduction of programming loans, technical assistance, or diplomacy; see Sinclair, *To Reform the World* (n 1); Helleiner, *Forgotten Foundations* (n 1). But see also Michele Alacevitch, *The World Bank's Early Reflections on Development, Review of Political Economy* (Stanford University Press 2009) 227 (who argues that, in its early years, the Bank refrained consciously from more social lending policies).

strengthened by the mandate for 'development and growth', again supported in the IDA (IDA Articles of Agreement Preamble, art I, art V s 1(a)–(b)), which provided a legal basis to give shape to the Bank's take on the emerging ideology of development.

Incidentally, these clauses were young innovations in international institutional law of the time with European roots. The idea of an organization created by states (and an international agreement) but with the power and knowledge structure of a private bank, run not by governments directly but by experts, was invented at the creation of the Bank for International Settlements (BIS) in 1930, considered the first 'international financial institution'.[55] The BIS was created by European governments (Belgium, France, Germany, UK, and Italy) plus Japan to deal with (settle) reparation payments of Germany after the First World War, which proved to be contentious and difficult between the involved governments. The idea at the time was to have an institution that was shielded from direct government interference and run by central banks in order to generate expertise-based trust among partners.[56] It was then picked up at Bretton Woods and introduced into the IBRD articles.

2. Institutional structure and legal acumen

Again, these were only contractual clauses—'law in the books' that could be ignored, and that became a reality only through those applying and using it. It is in this regard that the practice of the Bank, particularly its use of the law, is especially characteristic. It is the masterful deployment and selective use of these clauses and institutional law generally that mark the Bank's strategy in the 1950s and 1960s here. Law (back then as today) had no intrinsic value at the Bank, but rather was seen as strictly instrumentalist. It was put to strategic use to advance the interests of the Bank and its main shareholders.[57] Law was not a value in itself, but rather a weapon used in the battles.

The instrumental use of law was enabled by the institutional structure in the Bank, concretely, the interplay between Executive Board and General Counsel.[58] According to the founding treaties, the executive directors have the power to

[55] Mark Jacobs, 'Bank for International Settlements' in Rüdiger Wolfrum, *Max Planck Encyclopedia of Public International Law* (OUP 2013).

[56] Helleiner, *Forgotten Foundations* (n 1) 55. The plan to create a similar structure in the Americas, that is, an Inter-American Bank, actually faltered because Latin American countries objected both to the dominant position of the US as well as to US policy-makers (Helleiner, *Forgotten Foundations* (n 1) 71).

[57] It is interesting to note how much this is in contrast to the Bank's later use of 'rule of law' vis-à-vis its borrowers. The Law and Development movement, which came to life in these years, had no support from the Bank. On the evolution of the Bank's use of law, see Philipp Dann, *Many Faces of the World Bank as a Legal Actor*, Manuscript on file with the author (hereafter Dann, *Many Faces*).

[58] On the institutional structure generally, Dann, *Law of Development Cooperation* (n 1) 180.

interpret and further develop the Bank's founding treaty (a telling decision, considering that the weighed voting structure thereby applied also to the presumably 'technical' matters of legal interpretation).[59] In practice, however, this power was soon linked, if not outsourced, to the legal advice given by the leading legal minds in the Bank. The executive directors were mostly *not* lawyers, but were happy to get creative advice on how to reach desired outcomes on legally safe ground. Aron Broches in particular gave such advice in those years, and became the Assistant General Counsel of the Bank in 1951, and General Counsel in 1959, in the latter of which he played a formidable and formative role.[60] Broches earned this trust through his astute legal acumen, which contributed majorly to the positioning of the Bank in the battles of the 1950s and 1960s.

A central element of Broche's legal insight was his strategic mix of flexibility and rigidity in using the Bank's law, examples of the former are manifold, the best known being the loose interpretation of the term 'specific project'.[61] Much less known but equally significant was the very unorthodox (to put it mildly) practice of the executive directors to decide about the creation of new branches of the Bank. As described earlier, the decisions to create the IDA (and the IFC) came after long political battles and were therefore politically highly sensitive. Considering this, it is stunning to learn that the IFC and the IDA were both created by a decision of the Executive Board (and hence with all the weighed voting applying) —and not by a separate conference of state parties using the principle of one state–one vote, as per the usual procedure.[62] This approach to the creation of two entirely new international organizations was not based on any formal decision, but simply informal interpretative practice.

But there were also examples where Broches and the Bank used the law with utter rigidity. A prime example is the already mentioned dispute about apartheid and racism in cases of South Africa and Portugal. Despite urgent and direct appeals by the UN to the Bank to refrain from supporting the racist regimes in South Africa and Portugal, the Bank insisted on its inability to take into account the racism of both regimes—in stark contrast to its ability to take into account the (socialist) domestic regimes of other potential borrowers (eg, Cuba or Chile). Here, Broches insisted that the Bank's articles would simply leave no room for manoeuvre.

[59] Art IX IBRD, art X IDA; see Henry G Schermers and Niels M Blokker, *International Institutional Law: Unity within Diversity* (Brill 2011) § 1356.

[60] Aron Broches was a Dutch citizen who had studied law in the US, was a legal officer for Netherland's delegation at the Bretton Woods conference, and joined the Bank in 1946. See Aron Broches, *Selected Essays: World Bank, ICSID, and Other Subjects of Public and Private International Law* (Kluwer Academic Publishers/Martinus Nijhoff Publishers 1995).

[61] Pahuja, *Decolonising International Law* (n 1); Sinclair, *To Reform the World* (n 1), Kapur, *World Bank* (n 1) 168–69.

[62] Aron Broches, 'International Legal Aspects of the Operations of the World Bank' Aron Broches (ed), *Selected Essays: World Bank, ICSID, and Other Subjects of Public and Private International Law* (Kluwer Academic Publishers/Martinus Nijhoff Publishers 1995) 28–29 (hereafter Broches, 'International Legal Aspects').

This strategic mix of flexibility and rigidity can be reformulated as a mix of constitutionalism and formalism in the interpretation of institutional law. Broches often reverted to the language of constitutionalism to understand the founding treaties.[63] Constitutionalist language allowed for a dynamic and expansionist reading of World Bank competences and cast the expansion of the Bank's power as normal organic growth of an international organization. At the same time, he could tap into a still-strong culture of and belief in legal formalism, insisting on the literal reading of legal clauses and drawing legitimacy from such a formalist approach. As in other cases, Northern lawyers were very clever (and shameless) in mixing styles of argumentation, while hypocritically accusing others of doing so.[64]

The strategic use of law by the Bank to position itself and fight in the political, economic, and legal battles of the time went further than this. For example, early on the Bank pursued a strategy of diffusion. The Bank worked to export its institutional model and thereby shape the institutional environment and create partners, for example, in the founding of other development banks.[65] Another strategy was that of proceduralization, where the Bank created procedural structures to help diffuse interests and create institutional hegemony for the Bank's interests, such as done in the ICSID.[66]

3. Functionalism as enabling factor

The instrumentalist and strategic use of institutional law was aided not only by institutional structure and legal acumen, but also by functionalism as the dominant background theory of international organizations and international cooperation of the time. Functionalism complemented the institutional culture of the Bank in particular ways. Its central tenet is the assumption of an apolitical, technocratic nature of most international organizations.[67] This aspect corresponded to the institutional culture and self-understanding of Bank as a non-political and economic institution, but might have also corresponded to the hope and rhetoric of non-alignment that was popular in many administrations of the TW. In fact, where Jan Klabbers distinguishes three broad narratives about international organizations (as grease to global capitalism, as instruments of governmentality, or as forces of progress) the World Bank could be an example of each of them.[68]

[63] Sinclair, *To Reform the World* (n 1) 226–28.

[64] See the Introduction chapter of this volume).

[65] See Suzuki, *Regional Development Banks* (n 32); Dann, *Many Faces* (n 57).

[66] See Antonio R Parra, *The History of ICSID* (OUP 2012); Broches, 'International Legal Aspects' (n 62).

[67] Jan Klabbers, 'The EJIL Foreword: 'The Transformation of International Organizations Law'' (2015) 26 European Journal of International Law 12 (hereafter Klabbers, 'The EJIL Foreword').

[68] ibid 16–17.

But functionalism also played into the hands of the Bank in another, perhaps more surprising, way because it has no sensibility for equality and hence for the politically most obvious development of the time: multiplication of states (and growth in membership of the Bank). International organizations generally were based on the assumption of equal participation of all states in their decision making and operation. In this way, they also had a special 'post-colonial' appeal for the newly independent states at the time.[69] In the case of the Bank, however, this logic was suspended and was replaced by the logic of weighted power; in fact, it insulated the Bank against the rise in the number of new states as well as new *member* states. As mentioned, however, a central pillar of functionalism is its principal-agent conception and dominant role of member states,[70] and functionalism as a theory cannot comprehend the hierarchical and oligarchic character of an international organization. How the principal is composed is irrelevant for functionalist thinking. It does not imply anything in case of changing membership (here, the dramatic growth of development country group). Thus, decolonization according to functionalism did not change the principal.

V. Conclusion

The battle for financial support in the 1950s and 1960s and role of World Bank therein show specific a dynamic: in response to demands for more support and fair participation from Southern governments, the Northern member states of the Bank and Bank management reacted with a move that is reminiscent of the Aikido fighting technique, which uses the opponents attacking energy to defeat the opponent. The demands for financial support were not blocked but taken up and used to fortify the dominance of the North even more. They were also used to place the World Bank as Northern agency at the centre of development thinking, which emerged at the dominant paradigm structuring North–South relations at the time. To that end, different instruments were used: one was rhetoric—to engage and placate opponents; the other was law—instrumental in turning Southern demands into even more dominant techniques. In effect, the Southern contestation of the original institutional basis of the Bank did not lead to a reversal or humbling of the Bank, but rather to a counter-strike. This is particularly interesting from today's perspective, as the Bank is again confronted and under immense pressure, this time from new competition by private markets or Asian-led rivals.

[69] Guy F Sinclair, 'Towards a Postcolonial Genealogy of International Organizations Law' (2018) 31 Leiden Journal of International Law 841–69.

[70] Klabbers, 'The EJIL Foreword' (n 67) 11.

PART II

INDIVIDUAL PROTAGONISTS AND REGIONAL PERSPECTIVES

A. Individual Protagonists

13

Reading RP Anand in the Post-Colony

Between Resistance and Appropriation

*Prabhakar Singh**

I. Introduction

> History teaches us clearly that the battle against colonialism does not run straight away along the lines of nationalism . . . the oppression of mankind will slowly leave the confusion of neo-liberal universalism to emerge, sometimes laboriously as a claim to nationhood.[1]
>
> [The] suggestions for radical, structural legal changes have come from Western scholars.[2]

Frantz Fanon did not advocate nationalism as the cure to colonialism. In the post-colony, the gradual rise of post-war imperialism, for Fanon, gave way to 'the confusion of neo-liberal universalism'. The 'confusion of neo-liberal universalism' also captures professor RP Anand's approach to international law.[3]

In fact, Anand was of the opinion that the calls for 'radical' and 'structural legal changes' came from 'Western scholars'.[4] As such, the third-world lawyers in the initial years after decolonization in India, as Chimni suggests, faced the dilemma of 'decid[ing] the extent to which post-colonial states should remain within the established boundaries of international law'.[5]

* I thank professor Upendra Baxi and Dr. PS Rao for giving multiple readings to my drafts.

[1] Frantz Fanon, *The Wretched of the Earth* (Penguin Books 1967) 119.

[2] RP Anand, *New States and International Law* (Vikas Publishing 1972) 65 (hereafter Anand, *New States*).

[3] See UNGA Resolution A/RES/176(II), Teaching of international law, 123rd Plenary Meeting (21 November 1947) 110-11.

[4] Anand, *New States* (n 2) 65. Becker Lorca, as such, battles a straw-man in saying 'Resistance, therefore, is not exclusive patrimony of third worldist international lawyers'. Arnulf Becker Lorca, 'Universal International Law: Nineteenth-Century Histories of Imposition and Appropriation' (2010) 51 Harvard International Law Journal 476 at 502 (hereafter Becker Lorca, 'Universal International Law').

[5] Bhupinder S Chimni, 'International Law Scholarship in Post-Colonial India: Coping with Dualism' (2010) 23 Leiden Journal of International Law 23 (hereafter Chimni, 'International Law Scholarship'). Luis Eslava and Sundhya Pahuja, 'Between Resistance and Reform: TWAIL and the Universality of International Law' (2011) 3 Trade, Law & Development 103, 116. Diane A Desierto, 'Postcolonial International Law Discourses on Regional Developments in South and Southeast Asia' (2008) 36 International Journal of Legal Information 387, 395.

Prabhakar Singh, *Reading RP Anand in the Post-Colony* In: *The Battle for International Law: South-North Perspectives on the Decolonization Era*. Edited by: Jochen von Bernstorff and Philipp Dann, Oxford University Press (2019). © The Several Contributors.
DOI: 10.1093/oso/9780198849636.003.0014

To be sure, the 1960s in India was a generation that 'had its political vision shaped by the astonishing cosmopolitan sweep' of 'Nehru', as well as from the 'ecumenical thought of Gandhi and Tagore as much as by Marx and Lenin'.[6] Anand was, naturally, inheriting the post-war neo-liberal universalism with its inherent confusions that Fanon had pointed at. A Nehruvian idealist, Anand, like Lauterpacht, believed in the doctrine of legal disputes.[7] In Anand's battlefield, India, discourses on new states and the New International Economic Order (NIEO) were to effectively shape three generations of international legal imagination.[8]

First, Anand's battle was primarily one for recovering the lost histories of the new post-colonial states without rejecting international law.[9] In so doing, Anand was pushing the envelope on the earlier works of Professor CH Alexandrowicz, who was then teaching at the Madras University.[10] Along with the likes of Wright, Syatauw, Abi-Saab, and Sinha, Anand ploughed the discipline of new states, thirdworldism, and Asian contributions to international law.[11] Insofar as this intellectual

[6] Sunil Amrith, *Crossing the Bay of Bengal: The Furies of Nature and the Fortunes of Migrants* (Harvard University Press 2013) 241.

[7] As a foot-soldier in the battle in 1950s, Anand was well instructed by the great generals of the time—Quincy Wright, Julius Stone, PE Corbett, and Elihu Lauterpacht. See Ram P Anand, *Studies in International Law and History: An Asian Perspective* (Martinus Nijhoff 2004) 167.

[8] Anand, *New States* (n 2); Ram P Anand, 'Towards a New International Economic Order' (1976) 15 International Studies 467; Rahmatullah Khan, 'The New International Economic Order: This Side of the Hedge' (1977) 16 International Studies 483–99; KB Lall, 'India and the New International Economic Order' (1978) 17 International Studies 435–61; Upendra Baxi, 'New International Economic Order, Basic Needs and Rights: Notes Towards Development of a Right to Economic Development,' (1983) 23 Indian Journal of International Law 225. SK Agrawala, 'The Emerging International Economic Order' in Frederick E Snyder and Surakiart Sathirathai (eds), *Third World Attitudes Toward International Law: An Introduction* (Martinus Nijhoff 1987).

[9] Ram P Anand, *Development of Modern International Law and India* (Nomos 2005). RP Anand, 'The Formation of International Organizations and India: A Historical Study' (2010) 23 Leiden Journal of International Law 5–21 was Anand's swan song. Prabhakar Singh, 'Indian International Law: From a Colonized Apologist to a Subaltern Protagonist' (2010) 23 Leiden Journal of International Law 79–103 'picks up from where Professor Anand has left off'.

[10] Charles H Alexandrowicz, *An Introduction to the Law of Nations in the East Indies:16th, 17th and 18th Centuries* (OUP 1967) 9. Ram P Anand, *Confrontation or Cooperation? International Law and the Developing Countries* (Banyan Publications 1984). From the very start, Anand had the privilege of operating in a circle of scholars that included names such as Judge Radhabinod Pal, CH Alexandrowicz, Quincy Wright, Julius Stone, PE Corbett, and Elihu Lauterpacht in New Delhi, and Myres McDougal while studying at the Yale Law School for SJD.

[11] SN Guha Roy, 'Is the Law of Responsibility of States for Injuries to Aliens a part of universal International Law?' (1961) 55 American Journal of International Law 863–79 (hereafter Guha Roy, 'Law of Responsibility') ; JJG Syatauw, *Some Newly Established Asian States and the Development of International Law* (Martinus Nijhoff 1961); Georges Abi-Saab, 'The Newly Independent States And the Rules of International Law: An Outline' (1962) 8 Howard Law Journal 95 and S Prakash Sinha, 'Perspective of the Newly Independent States on the Binding Quality of International Law'(1965) 14 International & Comparative Law Quarterly 121 could have over the years influenced Anand's *New States*. Also, Anand's two important papers, RP Anand, 'Role of the "New" Asian-African Countries in the Present International Legal Order' (1962) 56 American Journal for International Law 383–406 (hereafter Anand, 'Role') and RP Anand, 'Attitude of the Asian-African States Toward Certain Problems of International Law' (1966) 15 International & Comparative Law Quarterly 55–75 (hereafter Anand, 'Certain Problems') predated his *New States* (n 2).

movement focuses on the early African and Asian post-colonial authors, Anand finds a pride of place.

Second, Anand made a conscious decision to remain within the established the inherited boundaries of international law and to offer a critique, as it were, from the belly of the beast. This allows Anghie to argue that Anand 'adopted, on the whole, a conciliatory position: the aim was to reform international law rather than dispense with it'.[12] Obviously, Anand's approach was emblematic of the cleavage of opinion among new states where, while there was a recognition of the colonial baggage in the inherited boundaries of such states, for international peace and tranquillity, India, among other states, was ready to accept *uti possidetis*.[13]

Post-colonial lawyers regard Anand as one of the founders of a third-world approach to International law. At the same time, Western scholars cited Anand to argue that an Asian attitude to international law, if any, was only a wishful thinking. How did Anand then nurture a third-world approach in India and beyond? While attempting to address a co-optive reading of Anand's work by Western scholars, post-colonial scholars paid tribute to Anand, but also distinguished themselves from him.

In 2002, Chimni wrote of the two traditions of third-world international law (TWAIL) scholarship—TWAIL I and TWAIL II. Anand belonged to TWAIL I, of which Chimni identified nine weaknesses.[14] At the same time, Anghie brought colonialism to the centre of international legal theory.[15] In fact Anand and Anghie differ on the precise issue of the value or not of 'cultural differences' as a useful analytic for studying international law.[16] As a soldier in the battle for international law, Anand was fully alive to the dangers of legal nihilism and lawlessness after decolonization.[17]

This chapter studies Professor Anand's battle for international law. To that story, Anand's impact on and appropriation by legal scholarship from the South and the North, respectively, are crucial episodes. Anand's strategic silence, as well as his battle cry, are both equally crucial to fully understand his international legal imagination.

[12] Anthony Anghie, *Imperialism, Sovereignty and the Making of International Law* (CUP 2005) 202 (hereafter Anghie, *Imperialism*); Anthony Anghie, 'Imperialism and International Legal Theory' in Anne Orford and Florian Hoffmann with Martin Clark (eds) *The Oxford Handbook of the Theory of International Law* (OUP 2016) 151, 161.

[13] Matthew Craven, *The Decolonization of International Law: State Succession and the Law of Treaties* (OUP 2007) 186.

[14] Chimni found Mohammed Bedjaoui more critical of international law than Anand. Bhupinder S Chimni, 'Towards a Radical Third World Approach to Contemporary International Law' (2002) 5 International Center for Comparative Law and Politics Review 18–21.

[15] Anghie, *Imperialism* (n 12) 2–3.

[16] Antony Anghie, 'Cultural Difference and International Law: The League of Nations and its Two Visions of the Nation-State' (2002) 5 International Centre for Comparative Law and Politics Review 5.

[17] That many of Nehru's allies in the Bandung movement went on to become dictators and authoritarian rulers—Tito in Yugoslavia, Sukarno in Indonesia, and Nasser in Egypt—should not be lost on international lawyers. Curiously, Friedrich Berber, as a scholar and legal adviser in Nazi Germany and later Nehruvian India, was at the forefront of state-led challenges to international law's mainstream. Katharina Rietzler, 'Counter-Imperial Orientalism: Friedrich Berber and the Politics of International Law in Germany and India, 1920s–1960s' (2016) 11 Journal of Global History 113, 115.

Although at the time international law was limited in vocabulary, Anand believed that dispensing with colonial international law would generate only a political explanation of doubtful value. His approach to international law was one of a harmonious construction of the narrative that saw productive, even emancipating, roles for the ex-colonial powers and the post-colonies. Consequently, Anand while critiqued the inheritance of international law for its Eurocentrism in the immediate post-colony, this chapter argues that Anand's optimism allowed his neo-liberal, even patronizing, co-option as 'progressive' by Western scholars.

II. Decolonization and legal post-colonialism

Colonialism, epistemologically speaking, is ever-present in the post-colony as a universal European category. International law in the post-colony thus oscillates between universalism and localism. In 1947 with the end of the British rule in India, the *political* post-colonialism did not engender an immediate *legal* post-colonialism.[18] Arguably, there is a lag of about a decade and a half between political independence and legal post-colonialism in India.

For example, the Constitution of India, 1950, mandated the continuity of colonial laws unless expressly repealed. In the centuries before the Indian decolonization, 'colonialism, capitalism, and Christianity, the three most powerful weapons of the imperial state, severely threatened Indian political selfhood and Indian political sovereignty'.[19] Yet 1947 did not represent the regaining of the 'Indian political selfhood' as political selfhood is hardly the same as political independence. Nehru had a particular faith in the International Court of Justice (ICJ). Speaking to the Chamber of Princes representing some 600 native kingdoms, at the time doubtful about joining the Union of India, Nehru said:

> The present tendency is to go beyond the Supreme Court to the International Court, whether it is the Court of Justice at the Hague or the U.N.O. to which we belong. It is a dynamic conception which is developing and many people think in terms of the International Court or Assembly exercising more and more powers to control national rivalries.[20]

[18] Prabhakar Singh, 'India Before and After the *Right of Passage* Case' (2015) 5 Asian Journal of International Law 176.

[19] Ananya Vajpeyi, *Righteous Republic: The Political Foundations of Modern India* (Harvard University Press 2012) 9 (hereafter Vajpeyi, *Righteous Republic*).

[20] Cited in Manu Bhagavan, 'Princely States and the Making of Modern India: Internationalism, Constitutionalism and the Postcolonial Moment' (2009) 46 Indian Economic & Social History Review 427–56, 446.

In line with this Nehruvian spirit, Anand 'judiciously recognized that, the complete rejection of the rules of international law was not a feasible option for newly independent states'.[21] For Anand, the end of the Second World War signalled the battle to save the universalist project of international law in Asia and Africa. Naturally, Koskenniemi finds that Anand and others who sought to argue that Asians 'too, had an international law' inevitably 'ended up once again projecting European categories as universal'. [22] Nevertheless, as Chimni says, it was the 'absence of an alternative language and requisite authority' that scuttled 'the option of stepping outside the precincts of colonial international law and walking away'.[23]

A. Indian publicists and the role of international courts

Portugal was not ready to let go of its colonial territories on the Indian subcontinent. At its very birth, in 1947, the Indian Government opposed Portugal's inclusion in the United Nations (UN) on those grounds.[24] About a decade and a half after the Indian independence, the *Right of Passage* case presented Indian jurists with an opportunity to defend India's territorial sovereignty before the ICJ against Portugal.[25] After the ICJ's verdict, India assimilated Goa into the Union of India. Consequetly, the Indian jurists began to develop post-colonial doctrinal accounts for India to take back territories from unapologetic colonial powers.[26]

It is in that respect that Justice Hidayatullah argued that the UN Charter Article 2(4) couldn't be read as 'giving priority to peace over justice'.[27] At the Supreme Court of India, Hidayatullah's ruling in *Monteiro v State of Goa* case came two years after his book *The South-West Africa Case* in which he attacked colonialism.[28]

[21] Bhupinder S Chimni, 'The World of TWAIL: Introduction to the Special Issue' (2011) 3 Trade Law & Development 14, 18 (hereafter Chimni, 'TWAIL').

[22] Martti Koskenniemi, 'Histories of International Law: Dealing with Eurocentrism' (2011) 19 Rechtsgeschichte 152, 168.

[23] Chimni, 'International Law Scholarship' (n 5) 23. See, Bhupinder S Chimni, *International Law and World Order: A Critique of Contemporary Approaches* (2nd edn, CUP 2017) 15 (hereafter Chimni, *International Law and World Order*).

[24] See, 'Opposition by India to Portugal being a member of the UN due to the imperialist administration in the possession in India' (1947) External Affairs ID: 25323 (National Archives of India).

[25] *Case Concerning Right of Passage over Indian Territory* (Merits) [1960] ICJ Reports 6 (hereafter *Right of Passage* case).

[26] MK Nawaz, 'Intervention by Invitation and the United Nations Charter' (1959) 1 International Studies 203–09.

[27] Hidayatullah said: 'Thus, although the United Nations Charter includes the obligation that force would not be used against the territorial integrity of other States (article 2 para 4), events after the Second World War have shown that transfer of title to territory by conquest is still recognized . . . If cession after defeat can create title, occupation combined with absence of opposition must lead to the same kind of title.' See *Monteiro v State of Goa* [1969] MANU/SC/0140/1969, para 25. cf. Ram P Anand, 'Legality of the Threatened Soviet Intervention in West Germany' (1968) 8 Indian Journal of International Law 409.

[28] Mohammad Hidayatullah, *The South-West Africa Case* (Asia Publishing House 1967). See the review of the book by RP Anand, 'Review: M. Hidayatullah, *The South-West Africa Case*' (1968) 10 International Studies 627–29.

In the *Goa* case, Hidayatullah J—while dealing with the issue of an ex-Portuguese national—produced, if you will, a *Kadi* moment.[29] At the time, Wright, Anand's mentor, interpreted India's takeover of Goa as an example of 'a major difference between the East and the West in the interpretation' of the UN law.[30] Arguably, while appreciating Anand's optimism, at least some Western scholars displayed the possibility of a two-way cross-fertilization of views.

Notably, both *Monteiro* and *Kadi* cases reject the primacy of the UN Charter in certain situations. The European Court of Justice's alignment with the position taken by the Indian Supreme Court on the UN Charter some forty years ago signals that both India and Europe have had an estranged relationship with international law in the wake of decolonization and regional integration.

B. Scholarly publications: from Madras to Delhi

In 1954, the Indian Council of World Affairs, New Delhi, began publishing the *India Quarterly*, a 'journal of international affairs' with a focus on 'India and Asia'. Africa was still mostly colonized.[31] In 1959, the Indian Society of International Law and its flagship journal began under the direct patronage of Prime Minister Nehru.[32] In early 1950s, the *Indian Yearbook of International Affairs* published by the Madras University's Grotius Society for international law under the editorship of CH Alexandrowicz was India's flagship journal of international law.[33] The Indian Society of International Law represented the geographical displacement of the centre of the production of international legal scholarship from colonial Madras to post-colonial New Delhi. With the editorship of the *Indian Journal of International Law* in the hands of Judge Pal of the Tokyo Tribunal fame—and the slow death of the *Yearbook*—the seat of international law in India began to effectively shift from colonial Madras to post-colonial Delhi.[34]

[29] Case C-402/05 P and C-415/05, *Kadi and Al Barakaat International Foundation v Council and Commission* [2008] ECR I-6351. Opinion of Advocate General Maduro.

[30] Quincy Wright, 'The Goa Incident' (1962) 56 The American Journal of International Law 617.

[31] Quincy Wright, 'The Psychological Approach to War and Peace' (1954) 1 India Quarterly 23–31.

[32] Jawaharlal Nehru, 'Inaugural Address: The Hon'ble Prime Minister of India Shri Jawaharlai Nehru, Patron' (1960) 1 Indian Journal of International Law 4. The Indian Society of International Law 'for teaching, research and promotion of international law, was established in 1959, primarily due to the efforts of the late V.K. Krishna Menon' who from 1952 to 1960 represented India in the UN General Assembly. Indian Society of International Law, <http://www.isil-aca.org/about_ISIL.htm> accessed 11 November 2016.

[33] See the reference to Alexandrowicz in Upendra Baxi, 'New Approaches to the History of International Law' (2006) 19 Leiden Journal of International Law 555–66.

[34] Radhabinod Pal, 'Message from the Honorary Editor-in-Chief: Dr. Radha Binod Pal' (1960) 1 Indian Journal of International Law x. Ram P Anand, 'Reservations to Multilateral Conventions' (1960) 1 Indian Journal of International Law 84. In this shift to Delhi, Anand and his colleague Rahmatullah Khan were inheriting the tradition of international law from, among others, Sir Benegal Rau, even as

No less significant was the start of *International Studies*, a Delhi-based journal of international relations published since 1959 and committed explicitly to exploring 'the theory and practice of non-alignment and the developmental and security problems of Third World countries'. Both Wright and Lauterpacht wrote in *International Studies*—Wright on 'the Asian experience' and Lauterpacht on teaching and researching international law in India.[35]

Post-colonial India thus woke up to a discourse on whether lawyers or diplomats should lead foreign policy.[36] The two journals published from New Delhi had Lord McNair, Jenks, Verdross, Morgenthau, Schwarzenberger, Castrén, Cheng, Lachs, Oda, Tunkin, and D'Amato, among others, gracing the pages.[37] Anand occupies the space between political independence (1947), legal post-colonialism (1960) and Hidayatullah's reinterpretation of the UN Charter (1968). Optimism and doctrinal rigour remain. Anand's hallmark.[38]

Anand's *New States* exudes with his characteristic optimism: 'Despite the horizontal extension of the international society and the multipolar world, our

he was passing it on to scholar-judges like PS Rao, judge ad hoc ICJ and PC Rao at the International Tribunal of the Law of the Sea.

[35] Quincy Wright, 'Asian Experience and International Law' (1959) 1 International Studies 71–87; Elihu Lauterpacht, 'International Law in India: Some Notes On Teaching and Research' (1961) 3 International Studies 318–25.'[T]he same books are prescribed for a degree in political science as well as in law'. RP Dhokalia, 'The Teaching of International Law and International Institutions in the Indian Universities' (1971) 13 Journal of the Indian Law Institute 305, 307.

[36] The jury is still out on whether international law was born from 'colonial conflicts and bureaucratic dispatches rather than legal treatises and case law'. Lauren Benton and Lisa Ford, *Rage for Order: The British Empire and the Origins of International Law, 1800–1850* (Harvard University Press 2016) 11.

[37] Given the ICJ Statute Article 38(1)(d) recognizes the 'teachings of the most highly qualified publicists' as 'subsidiary means' of international law, the above-mentioned two journals from India became a site for the creation of the sources. Lord McNair, 'The Practitioners' Contribution to International Law' (1963) 3 Indian Journal of International Law 271; C W Jenks, 'Law and the Pursuit of Peace' (1965) 5 Indian Journal of International Law 1; Bin Cheng, 'United Nations Resolutions on Outer Space: "Instant" International Customary Law?' (1965) 5 Indian Journal of International Law 23. Eric Castrén, 'Recognition of Insurgency' (1965) 5 Indian Journal of International Law 443; Alfred Verdross, 'The Status of the European Convention for the Protection of Human Rights and Fundamental Freedoms in the Hierarchy of Rules of Law' (1965) 5 Indian Journal of International Law 455. Anthony A D'Amato, 'The Inductive Approach Revisited' (1966) 6 Indian Journal of International Law 509. Georg Schwarzenberger, 'Peace Treaties before International Courts and Tribunals' (1968) 8 Indian Journal of International Law 1. Hans Morgenthau, 'The United States and China' (1968) 10 International Studies 23–34; Hans Morgenthau, 'The United States as a World Power: A Balance-Sheet' (1969) 11 International Studies 111–48. Manfred Lachs, 'The Twenty-Fifth Anniversary of the International Law' (1974) 14 Indian Journal of International 1;. Shigeru Oda, 'The Role of the International Court of Justice' (1979) 19 Indian Journal of International Law 157. Grigory I Tunkin, 'General Theory of Sources of International Law' (1979) 19 Indian Journal of International Law 474.

[38] Among the twentieth-century publicists, Alexandrowicz, Brierly, Borchard, Der Molen, Nussbaum, Friedmann, Fatouros, Holland, Jessup, Jenks, Jennings, Kunz, O'Connell, Starke, Stone, Schwarzenberger, Mushkat, Lissitzyn, Verzijl, and Röling, among others, were Anand's staple.

new world is one world.[39] And therefore—in agreement with Lissitzyn and in disagreement with Northrop—Anand argued that 'cultural differences and their influence on policies of states must not be exaggerated'.[40] Anand further maintains: 'In fact, new states have been and are more interested in participating in the making of new rule than in questioning the validity of the established rules.'[41]

Naturally, Anand was critical of sovereignty since the very beginning. In *Compulsory Jurisdiction of the International Court of Justice*, he declares that the 'greatest obstacle' in the preservation of world peace 'were the false notion of sovereignty and the complete independence of states'. The 'notion of state sovereignty or of the fullest independence power,' for Anand, 'was the source of theories which sanctioned the anarchy in international life.'[42] Anand's optimism, particularly his stress on the importance of the ICJ, appeared unmatched at the time. Penning the foreword to Anand's *Compulsory Jurisdiction*, Corbett noted that Anand 'is an enthusiast for judicial settlement' and he 'deplores the appointment of ad hoc judges as non-juridical substitute' at the ICJ.[43]

In opposition to Anand, in the *Right of Passage* case, the Indian judge ad hoc Chagla argued for India's 'absolute sovereign rights', rejecting the ICJ's jurisdiction in the case.[44] Similarly, a decade later, Hidayatullah also did not agree with Anand on the compulsory jurisdiction of the ICJ. Nevertheless, in 1974, the year the NIEO was passed, and in line with Anand's wishes, the Government of India accepted as compulsory *ipso facto* the jurisdiction of the ICJ over all disputes, with certain exceptions.[45]

As is evident, Anand had always believed in the worth and potential of international law as a discipline. In 1972 Anand wrote: 'The new demands of the new countries did not mean or amount to any wholesale rejection of the traditional

39 Anand, *New States* (n 2) 2.

40 ibid 50; Manohar Sarin, 'The Asian-African States and the Development of International Law' in Snyder and Sathirathai (n 8) 33, 42.

41 Anand, *New States* (n 2) 85.

42 Ram P Anand, *Compulsory Jurisdiction of the International Court of Justice* (2nd edn, Hope India Publications 2008 [1961]) 9 (hereafter Anand, *Compulsory Jurisdiction*); Ram P Anand, *International Courts and Contemporary Conflicts* (Asia Publishing House 1974).

43 PE Corbett, 'Foreword' in Anand, *Compulsory Jurisdiction* (n 42) vii–viii; Ram P Anand, 'The Role of Individual and Dissenting Opinions in International Adjudication' (1965) 14 International & Comparative Law Quarterly 788. In *Compulsory Jurisdiction* Anand acknowledges MC Setalvad, the then Attorney-General of India, for having 'gone through' his book manuscript even as Setalvad recommended Chagla to Nehru for the ICJ ad hoc role.

44 *Right of Passage* case (n 25) 25, Dissenting Opinion of Judge Chagla, 116, 119.

45 Swaran Singh, Minister of External Affairs, 'Declarations Recognizing the Jurisdiction of the Court as Compulsory: India' (18 September 1974) <http://www.icj-cij.org/jurisdiction/?p1=5&p2=1&p3=3&code=IN> accessed 16 November 2016. For an overview of India's approach to international adjudication, see, VG Hegde, 'India and International Settlement of Disputes' (2016) 56 Indian Journal of International Law 1-40.

legal system but merely readjustment of the old law to the new conditions.'[46] In international law Anand saw the potential of a truly universal justice. It is Anand's optimism and eagerness to prove the law-abiding nature of the new States—an attitude that the Western scholars saw as 'progressive'—that led to his co-option for extending an argument that alternative approaches to international law did not exist at all.

III. Anand's rational choice: inheriting Nehru, disinheriting Pal

Indian lawyers were left to choose between two parallel approaches to international law advanced by Prime Minister Nehru and Judge Pal after decolonization. In his non-alignment spirit, Nehru offered a political proposition of the unity of the nations that had experienced colonialism. While it was obvious that post-colonialism politically meant moving to self-government, Nehru did not tease out the translation of the Non-Aligned Movement spirit in international law. Contrarily, in his Tokyo dissent, only Judge Pal, if at all, was able to translate the essence of political post-colonialism into international law.

I do not debate who between Nehru and Pal practiced and knew international law better. At any rate, the Nehru–Pal debate presented a co-optive duality to early post-colonial lawyers. Albeit politically distancing himself from the West, Nehru believed in the role of international law, even as Judge Pal was particularly against international adjudication given his characterization of the Tokyo Trials as victor's justice.

Justice Pal was also Anand's evaluator for his LLM thesis written at the Delhi University; the topic of the thesis being compulsory jurisdiction of the ICJ.[47] Anand's support for India's compulsory jurisdiction of the ICJ was not at all to Pal's liking. Anand owed to Quincy Wright not only his first LLM at the Delhi University but also his publication in the *American Journal of International Law* much the same way 'Morgenthau owed to Hans Kelsen the award of his *habilitation*'.[48] Anand's was a case of a carefully cultivated scholar—supported in no small measure by his Western teachers—ensuring that his 'progressive' attitude to international law and courts represents the voice of the developing countries.

[46] Ram P Anand, 'Editor's Introduction' in Ram P Anand (ed) *Asian States and the Development of Universal International Law* (Vikas Publications 1972) xxxi.

[47] Anand's LLM thesis at Delhi University examined the compulsory jurisdiction of the ICJ and was published in 1961 as Ram P Anand, *Compulsory Jurisdiction* (n 42).

[48] Chimni, 'TWAIL' (n 21) 43; fn 33.

A. Inheriting Nehru

As with other leaders in Asia, India's founders too had a particular sense of the past, and of their political inheritance.[49] By invoking that past, they bolstered the authority and legitimacy of the political claims they made in the present.[50] The early post-colonial Indian lawyers followed the footsteps of modern India's cosmopolitan founders. Accordingly, Nehru, an internationalist, took the Kashmir issue to the UN Security Council for resolution.[51] Nehru stood for both the UN and international adjudication for which the nationalists continued to criticize him in India.[52] Anand had inherited that Nehruvian optimism about international law and international adjudication of disputes.[53] Anand dedicated perhaps his the most thought-provoking book, *New States and International Law*, to the memory of Quincy Wright. After its publication, an overwhelmed Röling wrote to Anand:

> When I was in India, years ago, I had the opportunity to talk to the then Prime Minister Nehru. I asked him to mention to me Indian legal scholars who might be considered as the voice of Asia in the matters of international law. Nehru answered, after having been in deep thought for some time: 'they do not exist yet, the Indian international lawyers are educated in England, and have not yet developed an Asian viewpoint. We have to wait for young scholars, who will express the attitude of the newly independent peoples'.[54]

It is notable that Röling, himself a partial-dissenter, was one of the eleven judges at the Tokyo Tribunal where Indian judge Pal wrote his famous dissent. Unfortunately, Nehru's aspirations of finding homegrown voices to 'express the attitude of the newly independent peoples' remained unfulfilled. With the exception of Chimni, quite literally almost all the leading voices concurring or dissenting to international law's universalism since the 1960s are partially products of the Western legal system. As such, Anand represented 'the particularistic universalism of non-European international lawyers'.[55] While seeking to universalize

[49] Jawaharlal Nehru, *The Discovery of India* (first published 1946 OUP 1985) 87.

[50] Jawaharlal Nehru, *Glimpses of World History: Being Further Letters to His Daughter, Written in Prison, and Containing a Rambling Account of History for Young People* (Drummond 1942). Vajpeyi, *Righteous Republic* (n 19) 11.

[51] The Security Council, '*Having considered* the Complaint of the Government of India concerning the state of Jammu and Kashmir'. See, UNSC Res 47 (1 April 1948) 'The India-Pakistan Question' UN Doc S/RES/47.

[52] 'Notice Under Rule 197 from AB Vajpayee for Lok Sabha Regarding talks held with Dr. Graham on the Kashmir issue, statement made by PM Nehru' (3 March 1958) External Affairs ID: 53103 (National Archives of India).

[53] Ram P Anand, 'Jawaharlal Nehru and International Law' (2002) 42 Indian Journal of International Law 5, 14 (hereafter Anand, 'Jawaharlal Nehru').

[54] 'BVA Röling's letter to RP Anand, 7 January 1973', reproduced on the front jacket of Anand, *New States* (n 2).

[55] Becker Lorca, 'Universal International Law' (n 4) 475.

international law, Anand exhibited, as it were, the symptoms of the older jurists of the semi-periphery. Becker Lorca says 'international law became universal only when non-Western jurists internalized European legal thought'.[56]

Much earlier, in *New States*, Anand too had made this point about the process of the universalization of international law.[57] Reviewing *New States*, Philip Jessup added: Anand 'appears to agree that the sense of the inadequacy of international law was developed by the dissidents when they were students in Western universities.'[58] Having noted Nehru's aspirations for an 'Asian viewpoint' on international law, Röling assessed Anand in warm words: 'I think you have fulfilled Nehru's expectations . . . You have written a fine book, which will play a role in the development of many scholars in the development of international law itself.'[59]

Unlike Nehru's, Röling's prophecy would not go unfulfilled. Baxi suggests that, in the years that followed, Anand nurtured a tradition of 'postcolonial reconstruction of international law' with his teaching and writings,[60] gradually cultivating a crop of Asian scholars with his efforts. Omuma Yasuaki wrote that during the 1960s–1970s Anand was 'almost the only Asian international lawyer whom we could regard as competitive with leading Western international lawyers, publishing actively attractive works in English':[61]

> [W]e are all students of Professor Anand, by learning his great works for years. How have we been proud of him, who was a visible figure in the international lawyers' circle already in the early 1960s, when the term 'international lawyers' virtually meant Western international lawyers. He has truly been a hero to us Asian international lawyers.[62]

Given the overall references to his works, Western lawyers read more of Anand in comparison to almost any other Asian scholar of his generation. In his Hague Academy lectures, Anand chose to speak on the sovereign equality of states.[63]

56 ibid 478.

57 See Anand, *New States* (n 2).

58 Jessup's review reprinted on the cover of Anand, *New States* (n 2).

59 See Röling (n 54).

60 Upendra Baxi, 'A Tribute to Ram Anand' (10 February 2011) *Law and Other Things* <https://lawandotherthings.blogspot.in/2011/02/tribute-to-ram-anand-upendra-baxi.html> accessed 30 October 2016.

61 'Tribute from Prof Onuma Yasuaki' (2011) <http://profrpanand.blogspot.in/2011/04/tribute-from-prof-onuma-yasuaki.html> 30 October 2016.

62 Onuma Yasuaki, 'Tribute from Japanese Society of International Law' (2011) <http://profrpanand.blogspot.in/2011/04/tribute-from-japanese-society-of.html> accessed 30 October 2016. Anand's focus on the history and a post-colonial vision of Indian/Asian international allowed him more visibility over contributions of Nagendra Singh, BS Murty, MK Nawaz, TS Ramarao, Narayana Rao, Surya P Sharma, and Rahmatullah Khan, to mention only a few.

63 Ram P Anand, 'Sovereign Equality of States in International Law' (1986) 197 Recueil des cours reprinted as Ram P Anand, *Sovereign Equality of States in International Law* (2nd edn, Hope India Publications 2008) (hereafter Anand, *Sovereign Equality*).

Among other things, Anand recognized that a 'class criterion in assessing legal standards would be tantamount to measuring events with the yardstick of *bourgeois* law, which is entirely wrong'.[64] Anand critiqued the 'present cruel economic order'[65] saying not only is 'all law . . . a law of inequality', but in some cases 'the inequality is very apparent and conspicuous'.[66] Anand's lecture at The Hague displayed his subtle but sure movement away from his earlier position, towards appreciating injustices embedded in international law.

B. Disinheriting Pal

Since 1948, Nehru had expressed his reservations to Pal's Tokyo dissent, distancing India from the legal position Pal took. Nehru's biographer Noorani flatly states that 'Nehru did not think highly of Pal'.[67] On 6 December 1948 Nehru wrote:

> In Japan the sentence of death passed on Japanese war leaders has met with a great deal of adverse criticism in India. The Indian Judge on that Commission, Justice Pal, wrote a strong dissentient judgment. That judgment gave expression to *many opinions and theories with which the Government of India could not associate itself.* Justice Pal was, of course, not functioning in the [Tokyo Tribunal] as a representative of the Government of India but as an eminent Judge in his individual capacity.[68]

Nevertheless, India unsuccessfully nominated Judge Pal for the ICJ following the demise of Sir Benegal Rau, and later Pal went to represent India to the International Law Commission.

During his LLM evaluation, as mentioned before, Anand had the opportunity to interact, even cross swords, with Judge Pal on the issue of compulsory jurisdiction of the ICJ. Later, Anand found a formidable opposition in Justice Hidayatullah who, in 1969, suggested 'that there should be compulsory submission of the question of international Court of Justice cannot avail in India where Supreme Court will be moved to examine the legality of the consent'.[69] However, Anand's support for the compulsory jurisdiction for the ICJ remained unflinching.[70] In fact, in the

[64] ibid 39.
[65] ibid 118.
[66] ibid 47.
[67] Abdul G Noorani, 'The Yasukuni "Hero"' (2002) 24 Frontline para 10.
[68] Jawaharlal Nehru, quoted in ibid para 11 (emphasis added).
[69] Mohammad Hidayatullah, 'Foreword' in SK Agrawala (ed), *Essays on the Law of Treaties: With Special Reference to India* (Orient Longman 1969) vi (hereafter Hidayatullah, 'Foreword in Agrawala').
[70] Ram P Anand, 'India and the World Court' (1960) 2 International Studies 80–92; Ram P Anand, 'The Acceptability of Compulsory Procedures of International Dispute Settlement' (2001) 5 Max Planck Yearbook of United Nations Law 1–20.

Arial Incident case, the Pakistani judge ad hoc extensively quoted Anand's position on the ICJ to argue that the ICJ should have found jurisdiction in this case.[71]

Anand—and probably Quincy Wright, too—did not celebrate Justice Pal's Tokyo dissent.[72] This silence was perhaps a result of Anand chosing Nehru over Pal. While in Delhi, Corbett and Wright had the opportunity to appreciate Anand's optimism about the role of the ICJ in the developing countries. Anand stood in direct opposition to Pal's views on international adjudication. Anand's obvious rejection of Pal's alighment with the Japanese ensured his alignment with the American policy on international law under the tutelage of Wright and McDougal as well as his co-option as a progressive developing country scholar.

C. Confronting contemporaries

A year before the publication of Anand's paper, Judge Guha Roy had published a scathing criticism of colonialism in international law while critiquing, among others, Vattel, Brierly, and Borchard for 'slipping into the fallacy of arguing in a circle'.[73] Later, McDougal and Laswell characterized it as 'Guha Roy's mystical assumptions,'[74] while Lillich accused scholars of 'playing into the hands of Guha Roy'.[75] A year later, Lillich went even further to say that Guha Roy's was a 'superficially reasoned piece that did not need an answer'.[76] Lillich's attack on Guha Roy could well be compared with that on McNair and Lauterpacht by Justice Hidayatullah. Hidayatuallh had suggested that, in relations to the question of the compulsory submission to the ICJ, 'the suggestions of Brierly, Hersch Lauterpacht and Gerald Fitzmaurice do not serve to remove our difficulties but make them greater'.[77]

71 *Arial Incident of 10 August 1999 (Pakistan* v *India)* Jurisdiction of the Court, Judgment (2000) ICJ Reports 12, Dissenting opinion of Judge ad hoc Pirzada, 60, 82, 95-96, 99, 104.

72 Radhabinod Pal, *The International Tribunal of the Far East: Dissentient Judgment of Justice Pal* (Kokusho-Kankokai 1999). For example, in his article on Japan, Anand does not mention Pal's dissent. Ram P Anand, 'Family of Civilized States and Japan: A Story of Humiliation, Assimilation, Defiance and Confrontation,' in Ram P Anand (ed), *Studies in International law and History: An Asian Perspective* (Martinus Nijhoff 2004) 24. Much of Anand's reference to Pal relates to Pal's works published after his dissent. In *New States* Anand refers to Pal's works published in the *All India Reporter* and the *UN Review* on international organizations. See Anand, *New States* (n 2) 68.

73 Guha Roy, 'Law of Responsibility' (n 11) 876.

74 Myres S McDougal, Lung-Chu Chen and Harold D Lasswell, 'The Protection of Aliens from Discrimination and World Public Order: Responsibility of States Conjoined with Human Rights' (1976) 70 American Journal of International Law 432, 453.

75 Richard B Lillich, 'Duties of Sates Regarding the Civil Rights of Aliens' (1978) 161 Recueil Des Cours 329, 422.

76 A pejorative evaluation of the works of non-Western jurists might not have been a general trend in Western academia. However, some are expected to have been found wanting in the academic protocol in reading and reflecting non-Western scholarship. See, the Guha Roy–Lillich debate in Muthucumaraswamy Sornarajah, *The Pursuit of Nationalized Property* (Martinus Nijhoff 1986) 65.

77 Hidayatullah, 'Foreword in Agrawala' (n 69) vi..

While pursuing higher studies in various foreign universities, academic researchers did not have the kind of freedom of expression enjoyed by the Indian judges. One can therefore see that Pal, Guha Roy, and Hidayatullah, who had full juridical autonomy to express their views, represented the case of the tail wagging the dog.

At the time, Anand's reconciliatory approach in the *American Journal of International Law* (AJIL) must have presented a welcome change for Western lawyers like Lillich and Jessup, allowing, later, a co-optive reading of Anand's works by Keith. Nevertheless, Anand was an idealist who sought a proactive role for universal international law, as opposed to power and power blocs, to shape the world order.

One of the best barometers of Anand's internationalism is to compare him with his contemporaries—Judges Guha Roy and Hidayatullah, and former President of the ICJ Judge Nagendra Singh.[78] Like Anand, all the three judges were jurists and publicists of the highest calibre. While Justice Hidayatullah wrote a monograph on the *West Sahara* case, Judge Singh was the President of the ICJ during the *Nicaragua* case.[79]

Judge Singh and Anand were both united in their belief that ancient Indian law and modern international law had similarities.[80] Notably, both Judge Guha Roy and Justice Pal came from the colonial Calcutta High Court, while Hidayatullah, educated at Cambridge, was a judge of the post-colonial Indian Supreme Court in New Delhi. Between Judges Pal, Guha Roy, and Hidayatullah, on one side, and Anand on the other, India after 1947 had witnessed a range of international legal perspective emerging from the post-colony.

The Nehruvian tradition of international law to stay non-aligned was already a radical one, however.[81] Anand had inherited that Nehruvian tradition.[82] Contrarily, Justice Pal was read as inheriting the tradition of the Bengali nationalist Subhas Chandra Bose; an ally of the Japanese in the Second World War who, before his alliance, had a love–hate relationship with Gandhi.[83] Hence, in the Tokyo dissent some saw Judge Pal repaying the Japanese warlords for their support of

[78] Guha Roy, 'Law of Responsibility' (n 11); Nagendra Singh, *India and International Law* (S Chand 1969).

[79] *Concerning Military and Paramilitary Activities in and against Nicaragua (Nicaragua v United States of America)* (Merits) [1986] ICJ Report 14. In Daniel O Saavedra, 'Condolence Message from the President of the Republic of Nicaragua' (1989) 28 Indian Journal of International Law vii after Judge Singh's death, the Nicaraguan president acknowledged the role Judge Singh played in admitting the matter in the ICJ against the superpower.

[80] Carl Landauer, 'Regionalism, Geography and the International Legal Imagination' (2011) 11 Chicago Journal of International Law 557, 567.

[81] See former Indian Prime Minister PV Narasimha Rao, 'Nehru and Non-Alignment' (30 May 2009) Mainstream Weekly para 3.

[82] Anand, 'Jawaharlal Nehru' (n 53) 6.

[83] Constituent Assembly, Professor SS Saksena, 'Formation of Azad Hind Bank in Burma by Azad Hind Govt., of Netaji Subhas Chandra Bose' (1947) OVERSEAS—II, ID 25280 (National Archive of India).

the Indian National Army created by the nationalist Bose in Singapore.[84] Indeed, Harvard historian Sugata Bose thinks Subhas Chandra Bose may have indirectly influenced Judge Pal's views at Tokyo.[85]

In any case, as noted earlier, it was Nehru's non-alignment internationalism that inspired India's early lawyers.[86] Moreover, Anand, like Alexandrowicz, was critical of the Chinese invasion of Tibet.[87] Perhaps it was Anand's idealism and his 'particularistic universalism' for international law that struck a chord with the legal minds in the post-colonial world. In the year Hidayatullah offered a legal justification for India's annexation of Goa, in rejecting the invasion of Tibet, Anand rejected both blue-water colonialism as well as the new Asian territorial occupation.

IV. Generating resistance, getting co-opted

It would be worthwhile to unpack the resistance to nineteenth-century positivist international law that Anand was generating in his writings. In order to cure international law of its European bias, Anand spoke of a history of international law in pre-colonial India. In such ways he demanded the inclusion of the Afro-Asian countries as civilized states. In effect, Anand was not rejecting international law, but he was attempting to open the province of international law to non-Western states.

A. Resistance

Evidently, Anand and other notable publicists of his generation had to 'deal with the double life of international law'. In 1962, Anand wrote his most influential paper on Afro-Asian concerns in international law where he sought to highlight international law's Eurocentrism.[88] He wrote extensively, inter alia, on the UN System, the ICJ, the NIEO, and the Law of the Sea. He tried to stitch together, within the confines of the doctrine, a productive narrative of international law for Afro-Asian countries:

[84] Aashis Nandy, 'The Other within: The Strange Case of Radhabinod Pal's Judgment on Culpability' (1992) 23 New Literary History 45, 47.

[85] Quoted in Norimitsu Onishi, 'Long After War Trials, Japan Still Honors a Judge' (31 August 2007) New York Times A4.

[86] Judge Pal demonstrated a 'tragic ethos' in assertions of a universal international law. Adil Khan, 'Inheriting A Tragic Ethos: Learning from Radhabinod Pal' (2016) 110 American Journal of International Law Unbound 26, 27.

[87] Ram P Anand, 'The Status of Tibet in International Law' (1968) 10 International Studies 401–45.

[88] The *Indian Journal of International Law* and *International Studies* effectively became the pivot for international law/relations scholarship in India. These were also the two most frequent repositories of Anand's work. Ram P Anand, 'Survey of Recent Research: International Law: Attitude of the "New" Asian-African Countries Toward the International Court of Justice' (1962) 4 International Studies 119–32; Ram P Anand, 'Tyranny of the Freedom of the Seas Doctrine' (1973) 12 International Studies 416–29. Yogesh K Tyagi, 'The System of Settlement of Disputes under the Law of the Sea Convention: An Overview' (1985) 25 Indian Journal of International Law 191.

> Thus, while the fathers of modern international law, Vitoria, Suarez, Gentili, Grotius, Pufendorf, Bynkershoek, Wolff and Vattel, conceived of it as a universal system, leading writers of the last century and the early years of the present century, such as Wheaton, Phillimore, Hall, Oppenheim, Fauchille, Westlake and others, declared it to be applicable only between the European Powers. In order to bring other countries under its sway, they were required to be formally admitted to this closed group.[89]

In other words, from a universal law, the later jurists turned international law into a law of the club; the European club. Ironically, soon after the Asian and African decolonization Western scholars called for the universal potential of international law. India gained its independence in 1947, a decade before most of the African nations. This gave Anand the opportunity to reflect upon both colonialism and post-colonialism. Besides, when speaking of the new states in international law, Anand brought to bear the Yale Law School's policy analysis on the doctrinal approach. The 'uncommitted' new states, Anand wrote,

> have become objects of strong competition and wooing among the big Powers, with the result that they have come to acquire an unusual and disproportionate weight in influencing the course of history.[90] [Anand's assessment of the developing countries came from his prior assessment of the role of peripheral European countries in the making of international law] But even in Europe the small countries existing at that time did not participate very actively in this process. It is only natural that the participation of the smaller and less developed countries in international affairs should be less active.[91]

Anand remained concerned about rivalries among Asian States to achieve their narrowly conceived national goals instead of fighting for common aspirations to achieve an equitable and just world order. As the primary subjects of international law, states were, particularly in the post-colonies, celebrated even as sovereignty as a conceptual category was gradually taking Asian-ness away from Asia.

B. Co-option

While Anand saw *New States* as an exercise in international legal theory, ironically, James Fawcett called it a 'passionate political pamphlet' that 'demolishes the picture of Europe as the home and creator of international law'.[92] Anand was very

[89] Anand, 'Role' (n 11) 383–406, 383.
[90] Anand, 'Certain Problems' (n 11) 55–75.
[91] Anand, 'Role' (n 11) 385; Anand, 'Certain Problems' (n 11) 59.
[92] JES Fawcett, back cover quote on Anand, *New States* (n 2).

widely read in both Asia and the West and his objective and rigorous approach from a newly decolonized world was not lost on Western lawyers. In 1967, Keith—later Judge of the ICJ—wrote 'In a field where inaccurate generalizations abound, one generalization can with confidence be made: there is *no* Asian attitude to international law. Rather there are a series of attitudes—attitudes, moreover, towards particular areas of international law and not towards the system as a whole.'[93]

And in order to bolster this proposition Keith copiously cited Anand—right from the first footnote of his article—as challenging the contention that 'Asian States and peoples are said to be less legalistic, less in favour of codes, and more prone to settlement according to more flexible criteria'.[94] Indeed, in *New States* Anand rejected the overemphasis on the cultural differences in making international law universal.[95] To that end, he noted a vast majority of the new states being non-Christian and therefore 'cultural differences and their influences on policies of states must not be exaggerated'.[96] When Anand referred to culture in international law context, he spoke of culture as history and law.[97] And here Anand politely disagreed with both Wright and Northrop who thought otherwise.[98] And while presenting a 'contrary view' Anand cited his two germinal articles published in the AJIL and the *International and Comparative Law Quarterly* (ICLQ).[99] As argued before, Keith too had previously cited Anand's ICLQ paper to make a claim that '*no* Asian attitude to international law' existed.

Arguably, Keith had misread Anand's *optimism* for the caveated acceptance of international law as Anand's *rejection* of a particular Asian approach to international law. Anand was trying to achieve a fine balance between the colonial history and a decolonial future of international law. When Anand moved on to study a new area of law emerging in 1970s—the Law of the Sea, Anand yet again attempted to prove that a kind of international Law of the Sea existed in Asia prior to colonization.

> In propounding his thesis about the 'Freedom of the Seas or the Right which belongs to the Dutch to take part in the East Indian trade', it is significant that, not only was Grotius well aware of the long tradition of freedom of navigation in the Indian Ocean, but . . . got his helpful cue from the Asian State practice of freedom of commerce and trade between various countries and peoples without any let or

93 KJ Keith, 'Asian Attitudes to International Law' (1967) 3 Australian Yearbook of International Law 1.

94 ibid 2, 27, 33.

95 Anand, *New States* (n 2) 48.

96 ibid 50.

97 Ram P Anand, 'Editor's Introduction' in Ram P Anand (ed) *Cultural Factors in International Relations* (Abhinav Publication 1981) 16; Ram P Anand, 'International Law in a Multi-Cultural World' (1985) 22 International Studies 95–104.

98 Anand, *New States* (n 2) 49–50.

99 ibid 49; see also (n 16).

hindrance. This fact of history has been generally ignored by historians of international law.[100]

Chimni explains Anand's preoccupation with the Law of the Sea: 'First, it was an area where the law was evolving and far from settled . . . Second, it was a test case for what was seen as the transformation of international law from being a law of co-existence to a law of co-operation.'[101] Anand said that, despite the setbacks around the Law of the Sea Convention, the international community was 'better off with a universally recognized, comprehensive treaty on law of the sea with a new agreed law for the twenty-first century, which in itself is no mean achievement'.[102] Chimni suggests that, for Anand and others of his generation, Law of the Sea negotiations 'were seen as offering the possibility of transcending the duality of international law through a Hegelian moment of ascending synthesis'.[103]

C. Anand's critique

If the modern international law is imperial, by analogy, the ancient Indian international law, if any, for which Anand and Judge Nagendra Singh argued must also have been imperial and exploitative. Indeed, Indian publicists primarily cited the *Arthashastra* and scores of Sanskrit texts—not all the Sanskrit texts were Hindu—to prove the presence of international law in India.[104] As argued elsewhere, 'the nature of governments might have been same in the ancient East and the medieval West', even as their conceptualization as nations was not the same.[105] Therefore, the Indian Chanakya, *Arthashastra*'s author, and Chinese Confucius, are both ancient Asian intellectual cousins of Machiavelli and Hobbes.[106]

[100] Ram P Anand, 'Maritime Practice in South-East Asia until 1600 AD and the Modern Law of the Sea' (1981) 30 International & Comparative Law Quarterly 440, 442. Ram P Anand, *Origin and Development of the Law of the Sea: History of International Law Revisited* (Martinus Nijhoff 1982). Ram P Anand, 'International Machinery for Seabed: Issues and Prospects' (1973) 13 Indian Journal of International Law 351. Ram P Anand, 'Freedom of Navigation Through Territorial Waters and International Straits' (1974) 14 Indian Journal of International Law 169. Ram P Anand, 'Winds of Change in the Law of the Sea' (1977) 16 International Studies 207–26. Ram P Anand, 'Peace-time International Cooperation for the Security of the Sea Lanes of Communication in the Indian Ocean' (1988) 25 International Studies 25–44. Ram P Anand, 'Recent Developments in the Law of the Sea' (1989) 26 International Studies 247–55. P S Rao, *Public Order of the Ocean Resources* (MIT Press 1975).

[101] Chimni, *International Law and World Order* (n 23) 38.

[102] Ram P Anand, 'The UNCLOS: Compromise or Mutilation?' (September 1994) 177 World Focus 3, cited in Chimni, *International Law and World Order* (n 23) 39.

[103] Chimni, *International Law and World Order* (n 23) 38.

[104] See, Carl Landauer, 'Passage from India: Nagendra Singh's India and International Law' (2017) 56 Indian Journal of International Law 265–305.

[105] Prabhakar Singh, 'Vernacular Nations: Westphalia and the Many Lives of States in Asia' (2016) 51 Economic & Political Weekly 22.

[106] ibid.

In a book edited by Anand in 1972, Baxi attacked the new wave of nationalism in Indian international law in no uncertain terms, branding the nationalist efforts to invoke Indian history as 'scholarly failings' while condemning the taking of intellectual decolonization too far: 'the tendency to discover the genesis of anything significant in the doctrine or development of the law of nations to Indian traditions cannot always be treated with a gentle bemusement'.[107] The authoritarian working of the Indian state in the 1970s, and later the 1980s, would become the subject of the literature of protest starting to recognize new subjects such as tribal population, women and Dalits vis-à-vis the Indian state.[108]

Baxi would soon stand in opposition to Anand in matters of method, approach and subject. Anand focused on state-sovereignty while Baxi took to people-centricity. Having been a student of the New Haven school, Anand knew international law to be the arena of power, politics, and policy, but this did not deter Anand's belief in the relative autonomy of the discipline.

Nevertheless, Anand, Nagendra Singh, and Alexandrowicz all rejected international law as a purely Western construct. Indian academia, therefore, was not receiving international law uncritically. In fact, much in line with the New Haven spirit, Indian scholars saw national interest as the touchstone on which to measure the worth of international law. And in that pursuit, Anand was one of India's leading academic voices even as jurists like Guha Roy and Hidayatullah took a more radical position in the battle. In times to come, Anand and Judge Nagendra Singh would find a convergence in their approach to fight on a common front.

Yet the decoupling of international law and the West at the hands of Anand on one hand and Baxi on the other is totemic of a varied origin. While the former saw international law from the top, Baxi found international law to be a construct from below; a construct by 'not only states but also peoples'.[109] In effect, Anand and Baxi represented the full spectrum of opinion on internationalism that Nehru and Judges Pal, Guha Roy, and Hidayatullah had represented around the Second World War and the decades that followed. Two ends of the spectrum, Anand and Baxi, pay tribute to the plurality of opinion that is Indian internationalism. While Anand was surgical in his approach to studying the state, Baxi remained pathological.

[107] Upendra Baxi, 'Some Remarks on Eurocentrism and the Law of Nations' in Anand (ed), (n 46) 6.

[108] Anti-colonial nationalism was deep-rooted in the need to distinguish the idea of India from the West—and Indian women from Western women. Ratna Kapur, 'Gender, Sovereignty and the Rise of a Sexual Security Regime in International Law and Postcolonial India' (2013) 14 Melbourne Journal of International Law fn 6.

[109] Upendra Baxi, 'What May the "Third World" Expect from International Law?' (2006) 27 Third World Quarterly 713. Balakrishnan Rajagopal, *International Law from Below: Development, Social Movements and Third World Resistance* (CUP 2003) 173.

V. Conclusion

The silence of the European World War narrative on the role of Indian soldiers aptly iterates the fate of Anand in the battle for international law. The Indian soldiers in the World Wars were a divided soul; fighting for their British masters against fellow Indians. Likewise, Anand had to overcome the duality of nationalism and internationalism in his academic battles. In these big–small battles for international law—as against a never-ending war—Anand moved up the ladder as a commander from his humble start as a foot soldier. From his earlier concerns about the attitude to international law of the Afro-Asia countries, Anand saw the Law of the Sea negotiations as a potential for the inclusion of the voices of Afro-Asian states.

While Anand might have won certain battles in his lifetime, the war of international law is far from over.[110] Yet, while the early Western scholars thought Anand's international law was aligned with the uncritical acceptance of the world legal order, today Anand is cited as part of introduction to international law's leading texts.[111] What has changed between then and now? Today the mainstream view of the discipline has moved towards appreciating the role a third-world approach has played in exposing the doctrinal and theoretical biases of international law. Celebratory and co-optive attitudes aside, Western international lawyers have begun to approximate the nuance of Anand's temporality only now.

In India, where the attitude of the government on international law has been more British than Asian, Anand's importance is increasingly recognized. The Indian Ministry of External Affairs notes that Anand is one of the 'several lawyers, jurists and intellectuals who have played an important role in the fight against colonialism, apartheid and global economic inequality as also in providing a developing world perspective to the discourse of International Law and Human Rights'.[112]

This is a rare feat, as seldom do purely academic publicists receive governmental recognition in India. Governmental appointments in India sit between the Scylla

[110] Sundhya Pahuja, 'The Postcoloniality of International Law' (2005) 46 Harvard International Law Journal 459. S G Sreejith, 'An Auto-Critique of TWAIL's Historical Fallacy: Sketching an Alternative Manifesto' (2016) 38 Third World Quarterly 1511–30.

[111] Anand, 'Role' (n 11) is Anand's most cited paper. Peter Malanczuk, *Akehurst's Modern Introduction to International Law* (7th edn, Routledge 1997) 9; See also Anne Orford and Florian Hoffmann, 'Introduction: Theorizing International Law' in Orford & Hoffmann, (n 12) 4; Anghie, *Imperialism* (n 12) 7; Jeffrey Dunoff, Steven Ratner and David Wippman, *International Law: Norms, Actors, Process: A Problem-Oriented Approach* (4th edn, Aspen Publishers 2015) 3.

[112] The Indian Ministry of External Affairs lists BS Murty, Judge PC Rao, PS Rao, K Krishna Rao, MK Nawaz, SP Jagota, TS Rama Rao, BR Chauhan, and Surya P Sharma, who have contributed to various aspects of International Law. See Government of India Ministry of External Affairs, 'Indian Contribution to International Law', <http://www.mea.gov.in/photo-features.htm?934/Indian+Contribution+to+International+Law> accessed 12 November 2016 (hereafter 'Indian Contribution to International Law'). Other notables in the Anand school of thought include VS Mani, who represented Nauru in *Certain Phosphate Lands in Nauru (Nauru v Australia)*, Preliminary Objections, Judgment [1992] ICJ Reports 240, 243..

of bureaucratic capture and the Charybdis of political affiliation. Unsurprisingly, Anand's reputation as the leading scholar of international law of his time notwithstanding, he never won government nominations for international courts or other appointments for the UN. The closest he came to the international bureaucracy was working as a legal consultant to the UN Secretary General on the matter of the Law of the Sea. Moreover, Anand did not publish most of his books with any major academic presses unlike his contemporary social scientists in India. While his articles appeared in the world's leading journals, he mostly self-published his books.

A product of his time, Anand, nevertheless, tried to reconcile the historical reality of colonialism with post-war imperialism. And in his extensive publications—covering areas such as international law in Afro-Asian countries, functioning of the ICJ, the NIEO, environmental law,[113] and the Law of the Sea—Anand always saw the glass half full—an attitude that was truly remarkable. But for Anand, international law would have remained a much more peripheral discipline in India than it is today. A feature of Anand's works was also a conscious effort to amalgamate and engage with scholarship from South Asia. While doctrinal rigour and conceptual appetite for testing the universality of international law through the prism of the Asian states were the early Anand's hallmark, the latter Anand found the Law of the Sea as the most important area for his doctrinal navigation. For post-colonial lawyers, Anand was not just a publicist and a teacher, but an institution.

[113] Ram P Anand, 'Development and Environment: The Case of the Developing Countries' (1980) 20 Indian Journal of International Law 1.

14

Taslim Olawale Elias

From British Colonial Law to Modern International Law

Carl Landauer

I. Introduction

In 1962, two years after Nigeria's independence, the eminent Nigerian lawyer, Taslim Olawale Elias, published *British Colonial Law: A Comparative Study of the Interaction between English and Local Laws in British Dependencies*.[1] Admittedly, as Mark Toufayan pointed out, it was 'partly written during the previous era'.[2] Although Elias is identified on the title page as Nigeria's Federal Attorney-General and Minister for Justice, the book is almost entirely stuck in the colonial past. The sharpest reference to independence is in the jacket copy: 'The advent of self-government, if anything, enhances the importance of this work[,] for the legal systems of the former colonies are being developed on the firm basis of British colonial law'. Because it is deeply engaged in British colonial law as it stood after the advent of Nigerian independence, Elias's book poses a mystery that can be solved via a foundational perspective for Elias. This chapter works through his book and tries to explicate British colonial law's twin elements of English law and customary law, and the importance that Elias places on traditional customary law. It works through Elias's dedication to the social sciences in the study of law and explores his essential scientism and his view as to how law functions, its role in social ordering, and its relation to social progress.

Based on Elias's position and his vision of international law, particularly in his 1972 volume, *Africa and the Development of International Law*, with its chapter on 'Modern International Law', in 1998, James Thuo Gathii identified Elias with the 'weak tradition' of third-world international legal scholarship.[3] And, indeed, Elias's writing does not carry Bedjaoui's radicalism expressed in *Towards a New*

[1] Taslim O Elias, *British Colonial Law: A Comparative Study of the Interaction between English and Local Laws in British Dependencies* (Stevens 1962) (hereafter Elias, *British Colonial Law*).

[2] Mark Toufayan, 'When British Justice (in African Colonies) Points Two Ways: On Dualism, Hybridity, and the Genealogy of Juridical Negritude in Taslim Olawale Elias' (2008) 21 Leiden Journal of International Law 377, 395.

[3] James T Gathii, 'International Law and Eurocentricity' (1998) 9 European Journal of International Law 184.

Carl Landauer, *Taslim Olawale Elias* In: *The Battle for International Law: South-North Perspectives on the Decolonization Era*. Edited by: Jochen von Bernstorff and Philipp Dann, Oxford University Press (2019).

DOI: 10.1093/oso/9780198849636.003.0015

International Economic Order.[4] Even if Bedjaoui's book was published by UNESCO and Bedjaoui, like Elias, would serve on the International Court of Justice (ICJ), Elias was truly the insider's insider. In fact, in the preface to his book on the Vienna Convention on the Law of Treaties, Elias describes the centrality of his personal effort in managing a compromise between the West and the rest that saved the entire convention at the very end of the conference.[5] And yet, he saw himself as doing more than pushing for newly independent nations having a seat at the table. He was after a 'modern international law'—a vision of law that he drew primarily from British and American scholars like Wolfgang Friedmann, Philip C Jessup, C Wilfred Jenks, and Richard Falk. Ultimately, however, what looks like an anachronistic argument in *British Colonial Law* assists in understanding his way not only of calling for a 'modern international law' that clearly bears the imprint of Jenks's 'common law of mankind',[6] but also infuses international law with the 'customary' or 'traditional' law of former colonies.

II. *British Colonial Law* and the shelf-life of colonial law

As mentioned, Elias's *British Colonial Law* seemingly poses a bit of a mystery as it was published two years after his nation's independence and joining the United Nations (UN). Regarding the advent of independence, Robert July suggests that '[i]n Nigeria, as airliners left bulging with former rulers, it was less their departure than an empty craft standing to one side, almost unnoticed, that embodied the moment's true significance—the plane that was to carry Prime Minister Abubakar Tafawa Balewa to New York, where Nigeria would take its place as the ninety-ninth member state in the United Nations Organization.'[7] If Elias was not on that particular plane, he would have been deeply involved. So the question remains why Elias published *British Colonial Law* in 1962. Admittedly, several of the chapters had appeared as earlier articles and the footnotes seem to run up to 1960, and not beyond. Still, independence had been imminent in the period prior to 1960, so

4 Mohammed Bedjaoui, *Towards a New International Economic Order* (Holmes Meier 1979).

5 Taslim O Elias, *The Modern Law of Treaties* (Oceana Publications 1974) 7 (hereafter Elias, *Modern Law of Treaties*). I thank Matt Craven for mentioning this case of self-congratulation by the understated Elias of the earlier books. In *Modern Law of Treaties*, Elias even calls his book the 'first systematic and the most detailed study of the subject by an "insider"', 8. It was with Elias's status as an insider's insider in mind that I entitled a section of my earlier article on Elias 'Pan-Africanism and the Pan Am Flight Bag'. Carl Landauer, 'Things Fall Together: The Past and Future Africas of T.O. Elias's *Africa and the Development of International Law*' (2008) 21 Leiden Journal of International Law 351, 369–73. The biography provided in the book of essays in his honour shows an astounding number of important professional and international legal activities before his induction into the ICJ in 1976. Emmanuel G Bello and Bola A Ajibola (eds), *Essays in Honour of Judge Taslim Olawale Elias* (Martinus Nijhoff 1992) xv–xx.

6 Clarence W Jenks, *The Common Law of Mankind* (Stevens 1958) (hereafter Jenks, *Common Law*).

7 Robert W July, *An African Voice: The Role of the Humanities in African Independence* (Duke University Press 1987) 14–15.

it is not as if the book's proofs lay on his desk as he attended to state business and flew around the world. Indeed, *British Colonial Law* is a comparative study of the international application of colonial law—stretching from the West Indies through Sub-Saharan Africa to Southeast Asia—and, as it turns out, Elias seems to reflect colonial law as a current status even for nations that achieved independence earlier than Nigeria. Significantly, Elias asserts in one of his rare references to independence that 'Political independence may predispose some nationalist leaders to want to wipe the legal slate as clean as possible, in an attempt to assert new-found freedoms and to disown the "colonial" past'.[8] Clearly, Elias has an agenda in focusing as he does on colonial law.

After clarifying that the law of a colony is not colonial law, Elias declares, 'We venture to suggest that colonial law is the body of principles consisting partly of Imperial legislation and colonial enactments and partly of all applicable English law and local customary law throughout the British colonies.'[9] Elias's true subject is the complex relationship between English law as applied in the colonies and indigenous customary law. Indeed, this twinned legal system of colonial law, although seemingly tied to the British practice of Indirect Rule—the co-opting of traditional governing units under the umbrella of colonial authorities—is not the same. While Indirect Rule is a layering of governing authorities, colonial law rather reflects two legal systems working side by side on two different legal realms, with courts having differing areas of competence.

Throughout the 1950s, Elias published numerous books on Nigerian customary law, including *Nigerian Land Law and Custom* in 1951 and *Groundwork of Nigerian Law* in 1954.[10] In those studies, he sought to establish—simultaneously for British and African audiences—both the vitality and importance of Nigerian customary law that had its own realm separate from English law as applied in Nigeria. As Elias explains at the beginning of his first chapter of *Groundwork*, when English law was first introduced into Nigeria in the nineteenth century, 'it did not at the same time abolish such local laws and customs as were found to be good'.[11] There are specific areas, such as land law and marriage, where customary law is most important. Nevertheless, there are many areas of overlap. Elias wrote that 'our law of contract' with its focus on commercial activity, means that 'contracts of agency, suretyship, carriage and personal service abound to the almost total exclusion of other types normally found in English law'.[12] But he starts his chapter on contracts in *Groundwork* by stating that although English law is 'predominant', there is a place also for customary law, which because of its lesser role would follow his explication

[8] Elias, *British Colonial Law* (n 1) 134.
[9] ibid 6.
[10] Taslim O Elias, *Nigerian Land Law and Custom* (Routledge & Kegan Paul 1951); Taslim O Elias, *Groundwork of Nigerian Law* (Routledge & Kegan Paul 1954) (hereafter Elias, *Groundwork*).
[11] ibid 3.
[12] ibid 206.

of English law.[13] In *British Colonial Law*, where Elias transits from his Nigerian analysis to a comparative analysis of the entire law of British dependencies, he explains that the supreme court or court ordinances basically read almost identically, citing typical language: 'Nothing in this Ordinance shall deprive the courts of the right to observe and enforce the observance, or shall deprive any person of the benefit of any native law or custom not being repugnant to natural justice, equity or good conscience'.[14]

For Elias, customary law is law with its own courts. Regarding its status as law, Elias defends customary law against the Austinian definition of law as enforceable. In *Groundwork*, he explains that there may be a difference between customary law, which is deemed binding, and 'mere custom', which only has moral binding effect. And, rather than refute Austin directly in 1954, he suggests that customary law's inclusion in Nigerian law has 'greater plausibility than is the inclusion of custom in the sources of the law of a much more developed system like the English which, according to the Austinian analysis, sets no store by custom as law'.[15] In addressing the validity of customary law as law in *British Colonial Law*, he asks, 'Is customary law then *law* in the strict sense?' For him, it hinges on the question as to whether judges can make law, and he answers that '[t]here can be little doubt nowadays that most jurists will agree to ascribe to judges a more creative role [than] would have been conceded to them a generation ago'.[16] For Elias, it is clear that customary law—as he will argue regarding customary international law—easily faces the Austinian challenge. And he tells us that the 'investigator must remember from the outset that there is a clear *distinction* to be made between *law* and *custom*' and should look to determine 'whether the particular practice is recognised by the majority of the local community as binding on all and sundry, or whether it is merely conventional or permissive'.[17]

The standard Elias cites repeatedly is that 'the British State practice has invariably been to respect the indigenous system of observed customary rules or, at least, as many of these as are not "repugnant to equity, justice and good conscience"'.[18] Furthermore, regarding the application of natural justice, he declares that '[i]n the sphere of legislation, it has been used to abolish such obnoxious practices as witchcraft, slave-dealing and slavery, trial by ordeal, destruction of twins, and the like'.[19] But he then explains that definitions are not always easy. In fact, it is 'easier by legislation to abolish witchcraft than to define it'.[20] The question is whether Elias

[13] ibid.
[14] Elias, *British Colonial Law* (n 1) 102.
[15] Elias, *Groundwork* (n 10) 12.
[16] Elias, *British Colonial Law* (n 1) 119.
[17] ibid 276.
[18] Elias, *Groundwork* (n 10) 5.
[19] Taslim O Elias, *Government and Politics in Africa* (first published 1961, 2nd edn, Asia Publishing House 1963) 129–30 (hereafter Elias, *Government and Politics*).
[20] ibid 130.

is replicating an essentializing of the African as having 'repugnant' traditions. In *British Colonial Law*, Elias repeats the litany: 'Another common feature is that nearly all colonial criminal codes provide for the abolition of certain barbarous or obnoxious practices like witchcraft, killing of twins at birth, trial by ordeal'.[21] Basically, Elias has broadened the coverage of the rule from Africa to the entire British colonized world. So rather than essentializing the African, the question becomes whether he is reflecting a broader image of the 'primitive'.

Elias does not merely dwell on 'repugnant' traditions. In *British Colonial Law*, he criticizes a court in its denying justice to an accused for mistakenly killing an individual with a hatchet whom he believed to be 'a dangerous evil spirit which was widely assumed among members of his community to take the shape of a small-footed dwarf'—in his deft language, Elias writes that 'the occasions must be infrequent when this species of reasoning is adopted as a criterion in the trial of illiterate and simple persons like the accused in this case'.[22] He is quick to add, however, that 'patently obnoxious superstitions like the practice of ritual murder cannot reasonably be expected to be condoned by any worthwhile body of criminal law'.[23] In the first instance, Elias is sympathetic with a benighted soul, but bringing up such examples is rare for him—and magical thinking is simply not prominent in his writing, as it was for some social anthropologists. Rather, Elias was trying to press the importance of customary law as law and bestow it proper dignity. True, there are differences between the traditions of colonized peoples and Europe. He tells us that 'British colonial courts are enjoined to recognise polygamy, which is the usual form of customary marriage in practically all the colonies',[24] which does not mean he condoned it, referring to the 'growing awareness of the evils of polygamy among the rising generation of educated youth'.[25] Despite his invocation of the great empires of the African past with their treaties and trading, Elias sees the Europeanization of the colonial world as bringing 'increasingly complex economic and industrial activities' and requiring 'an up-to-date and internationally valid body of law capable of meeting the new needs'—namely English law.[26] Still, in *Groundwork*, Elias bemoans the attitude of English-trained Nigerian lawyers who were suffering from 'what the psychologists call "inferiority complex"' and 'say, though not explicitly, that since customary law is not what one goes to England to study, it has neither the dignity of "civilised" law nor the prestige of authority'.[27] Elias's use of scare quotes is telling.

[21] Elias, *British Colonial Law* (n 1) 150.
[22] ibid 194–95.
[23] ibid 196.
[24] ibid 110.
[25] Elias, *Groundwork* (n 10) 286.
[26] Elias, *British Colonial Law* (n 1) 142.
[27] Elias, *Groundwork* (n 10) 365.

Eric Hobsbawm and Terence Ranger's *Invention of Tradition* has generated much use of that term,[28] although they did not invent the 'invention of tradition'. For example, in 1965 Pierre L van den Berge asserted, 'Only recently are we experiencing the explosion of the myths of Africa as a primitive, unchanging, ahistorical, isolated continent, fragmented into a multiplicity of self contained, mutually antagonistic, but internally stable and harmonious "tribes".'[29] Elias talks about the complexity of customary law and its dynamism and change. In addition, he tends to avoid references to the freighted term 'tribal', in part because he seeks a more complicated picture of customary law. A rare example is his observation in *British Colonial Law* that 'in the British African territories, Malay, Fiji and other Pacific Islands, the systems of landholding are still largely customary; while, in such cosmopolitan or detribalised territories as Singapore city, Hong Kong, and most of the British West Indies, land rights and usages approximate to those of individual ownership'.[30] Putting aside the topos of the 'primitive mind' of Lucien Lévy-Bruhl[31] as well as the holistic depiction of indigenous cultures of the early Bronislaw Malinowski and early functionalists, such as Alfred Radcliffe-Brown, many specialists of importance to Elias, as well as Elias himself, did not envision a static anterior society prior to the advent of colonization. And he says quite forcefully in *Government and Politics* that 'African life should be taken seriously, and no longer regarded as a museum object to delight European fancies'.[32]

In *Government and Politics*, Elias does explain that 'the African mechanism for the assurance of orderly social existence has been firmly based upon the concept of the *maintenance of the social equilibrium*', and that 'this concept is synonymous with the British constitutional principle of the Rule of Law'.[33] For Elias, customary law—like English law—is about social ordering. Indeed, he asserts that 'Roscoe Pound, an American, who is probably the leading jurist in the world today, has linked the administration of justice to "social engineering".'[34] Only a couple of pages after introducing Pound, he asserts that '[w]hat we now popularly refer to as the Rule of Law is the same as what European sociologists have described as the African principle of maintenance of the social equilibrium'.[35]

[28] Eric Hobsbawm and Terence Ranger (eds), *The Invention of Tradition* (CUP 1983).

[29] Pierre L van den Berghe, 'Introduction' in Pierre L van den Berghe (ed), *Africa: Social Problems of Change and Conflict* (Chandler Publishing Company 1965) 1.

[30] Elias, *British Colonial Law* (n 1) 224.

[31] Interestingly, Messay Kebede in his *Africa's Quest for a Philosophy of Decolonization* (Rodopi 2004) uses Lévy-Bruhl as his principal foil, showing little interest in subsequent developments in anthropology.

[32] Elias, *Government and Politics* (n 19) 228.

[33] ibid 212 (emphasis in original).

[34] ibid 178.

[35] ibid 181. On the importance of social engineering, see Toufayan (n 2) 394 ('Of all extent theories considered, Elias must have been most seduced by Pound's suggestive metaphor of law's "social engineering" function'.)

Despite the corollaries to the principles of European law, Elias is quite clear that English law—as applied to Nigeria and the other colonies—alongside customary law is not identical with English law applied in England. So, for example, Elias maintains that 'it would seem that the specifically local character of the Act [of Settlement of 1700] and its particular historical antecedents render it unlikely that the Act of Settlement of 1700 contemplates any extension of its provisions beyond the immediate frontiers of England'.[36] Similarly, he suggests that 'there does not appear to be sufficient justification for the practice of invoking the English doctrine of Consideration or the Statute of Frauds 1677 in the courts of Asian or African colonies, if only because the underlying concepts are as alien to the peoples there as they are to nearly all continental Europeans'.[37] And Elias quotes Lord Denning to the effect that 'the common law cannot be applied in a foreign land without considerable qualification'.[38] In *British Colonial Law*, Elias's recognition of the variety of customary law, as well as the changes required for English common law, bring an important assertion—that English colonial law achieves its purpose 'by the simple recognition that there are many roads that lead to justice'.[39]

One of the most important elements of customary law for Elias is that it is flexible and changing, essentially transforming in the manner of common law. He makes clear that it is not following an evolutionary pattern set by Western law. In general, he refutes specific parallels between Western and customary law, for example, efforts to attribute 'usufructuary' interests to Nigerian land law: 'The interest of each member of a family in the family land is neither strictly usufructuary in the Roman sense, nor is it a tenancy in common or a joint tenancy according to English land law'.[40] And he criticizes those who follow Henry Sumner Maine's notion of 'village communities': 'To speak, therefore, of *tribal* ownership or *tribal* tenure is to indulge in the popular fallacy of those writers like Sir Henry Maine who see in early as in modern agricultural communities only rudimentary social organisation in which the conception of family property in land is a late arrival in history'.[41] Ultimately, Elias asserted: 'The problems of Africa are in many ways *sui generis*'.[42]

Elias recognized the 'transition' involved in the colonial encounter and the swift economic changes of the postwar situation. In *Government and Politics in Africa*, he observes, 'Traditional societies are fast disappearing, and new and exciting societies are emerging everywhere',[43] and refers there to 'transitional culture'.[44]

[36] Elias, *British Colonial Law* (n 1) 69.
[37] ibid 140–41.
[38] ibid 288.
[39] ibid 17.
[40] Taslim O Elias, *Nigerian Land Law* (first published 1951, 4th edn, Sweet and Maxwell 1971) 131 (hereafter Elias, *Nigerian Land Law*).
[41] ibid 74 (emphasis in the original).
[42] Elias, *Government and Politics* (n 19) 228.
[43] ibid 200–01.
[44] ibid 200.

Although Elias is quite attuned to the rapid changes of the time 'when society is virtually in a state of flux',[45] he is primarily interested in demonstrating just how flexible customary law is. Rather than following Malinowski's lead in *Dynamics of Culture Change*, which focuses on change driven by racial interaction, Elias instead wants his readers to understand the core flexibility of customary law itself. He approvingly quotes Chief Justice William A Osborne that 'one of the most striking features of West African native custom, to my mind, is its flexibility'.[46] Customary law, for Elias, suits the needs of the developing community by changing along with it, with the exception of Islamic law because, in his view, 'Muslims find it easier to set aside than to modify inconvenient rules of the Shari'a'.[47]

Significantly, in *Groundwork* and *British Colonial Law* Elias addresses whether customary law should be codified or remain subject to the development of case law. In the former, he asserts that 'in the present state of our knowledge, then, codification must be eschewed. If rashly undertaken, it could result in a hotch-pot of rules neatly arranged in numbered paragraphs . . . '.[48] Rather, 'the method of case-law is most conducive to the healthy and flexible growth of Nigerian law'.[49] And taking the broader, international perspective of *British Colonial Law*, Elias argues that 'codification, even if successfully accomplished, would render customary law less customary and more artificial, far removed from the experience and comprehension of the people'.[50] Elias gives as an admonitory example the Natal Code of Native Law promulgated initially in 1878 and passed into law in 1891 as 'sufficient warning to advocates of total codification of customary law' because it 'ossified' customary law.[51] Elias does ponder whether the English common law and customary law in a nation should be unified or remain dual. It is posed as a question in *Groundwork*, but in the final paragraph of *British Colonial Law*, Elias argues for 'the attainment of a fully integrated "common law" for all its citizens', which 'should gradually break down barriers of race and language within a colony even more quickly than through political action'.[52]

Elias's project regarding customary law required, first and foremost, significant study. In *Groundwork* he wrote that most of the problems facing the integration of English and customary law 'should disappear as comparative studies of local law and custom become available'.[53] He devotes a subsection of

[45] ibid 201.
[46] ibid 206, quoting *Lewis v Bankole* [1909] 1 NLR 82, 101–02.
[47] Elias, *British Colonial Law* (n 1) 126. Additionally, he talks of indigenous law where Islamic law has been introduced from the outside; 116.
[48] Elias, *Groundwork* (n 10) 364.
[49] ibid.
[50] Elias, *British Colonial Law* (n 1) 280.
[51] ibid 280–81.
[52] ibid 299.
[53] Elias, *Groundwork* (n 10) 7.

a chapter to list a number of vital textbooks and monographs, including one by prominent anthropologist CK Meek.[54] In *Government and Politics in Africa*, he argues:

> The most urgent aspect of reform is for the curriculum of the legal education of future African lawyers to be reorganised in such a way as to include a scientific study of the various bodies of customary law, their interaction with English law in different aspects, and the undoubtedly large areas where reconciliation or supersession is demanded in the interest of social and economic advance.[55]

Indeed, '[o]nly a systematic course of training in the intricacies of legal science and in comparative jurisprudence, over and above the usual run of subject courses, would equip the African lawyer for the novel task confronting him in his society'.[56] And Elias devotes an entire chapter to 'The Participation of the Institutes of Social, Cultural and Legal Studies in the Development of Africa',[57] in which he points particularly to the International African Institute (of which he was a member starting in 1949) and the Rhodes-Livingstone Institute for Social Research. In this context, it is interesting not only that Elias became a member of the International African Institute in 1949[58] but also that Malinowski wrote on the role of the institute in his article on 'Practical Anthropology', which was published in institute's journal *Africa* in 1929.[59] In *British Colonial Law*, Elias argues for the need for colonial courts 'to adopt the comparative approach to their legal problems'.[60] Regarding customary law itself, Elias writes, 'Many errors and prejudices about customary law, it would seem, have first to be got rid of by patient study and research as well as careful analysis and exposition of its real nature'.[61] Full of calls for study and research, its final chapter 'Codification, Legal Education and Legal Research' recommends anthropological fieldwork, the distribution of questionnaires, and the analysis of the case records of native courts.[62] Customary law, he believes, must be prominent in legal education, and he bemoans the fact that '[a]part from those colonial students and others who are able to offer Roman-Dutch Law or Hindu and Mohammedan Law either at a British University or at the Council of Legal Education, practically all the other colonial students have to pass through exactly the same process and

[54] ibid 30.
[55] Elias, *Government and Politics* (n 19) 209.
[56] ibid.
[57] ibid 226–37.
[58] Bello and Ajibola (n 5) xvii.
[59] Wendy James, 'The Anthropologist as Reluctant Imperialist' in Talal Asad (ed), *Anthropology & the Colonial Encounter* (Ithaka Press 1973) 51.
[60] Elias, *British Colonial Law* (n 1) 8.
[61] ibid 121.
[62] ibid 271–92.

cover precisely the same syllabus as would English students, for whom the courses and general training have been ideally designed'.[63]

The decades-long internal self-critique of social anthropology has framed it as a tool in the toolbox of the colonial as well the neo-imperialist enterprise.[64] A fair amount of the critique involves an attack on the functionalist mode of social anthropology, so that Gutorm Gjessing's essay among among the critical essays published in *Current Anthropology*[65] in 1968, attacked the ahistorical approach of the likes of Radcliffe-Brown as well as the anti-historical approach epitomized by Malinowski. The case against various iterations of functionalism was that it envisioned cultures as holistic organisms. If Malinowski in *Methods of Cultural Contacts in Africa* in 1938 viewed Africa from the perspective of a contemporary changing society, he believed, as Georges Balandier noted, that he was able to gauge social change 'from a "zero point" which would define the conditions of social equilibrium before the intervention of Europeans'.[66]

Interestingly, Balandier was writing roughly contemporaneously with Elias's *British Colonial Law* and turns to Max Gluckman's devastating critique of Malinowski for the mixing of objective and subjective history in his postulation of an anterior culture.[67] Elias had been a Simon Research Fellow (dedicated to studies in social science) at Manchester University from 1951 to 1953, Manchester being the home of Max Gluckman's Manchester School of Anthropology. And although Gluckman would part ways from Fortes and Evans-Pritchard, he wrote one of the chapters of their famous 1940 tome *African Political Systems*, which was published by Oxford University Press for the International African Institute. Significantly, the book makes multiple appearances in Elias's effort to study customary law—and he sticks with them. Even in his 1972 *Africa and the Development of International Law*, he began sentences with 'As Fortes and Evans-Pritchard have observed . . . ',[68] and 'As Fortes and Evans-Pritchard have put it . . . '.[69] If anything, he regrets the fact that '[u]nfortunately, *African Political Systems* has little to say, apart from the chapter on the Tallensi by Fortes, about the political organisations of West African societies'.[70] There is much in *African Political Systems* that is dynamic and diachronic—and not

[63] ibid 290. Elias does insert a footnote—and provide a hint regarding the timing of his text or at least of that chapter—that 'in 1960, the Council of Legal Education in England introduced African Law as a subject at the Bar Examinations. It has already been instituted as a subject for the London University LL.M. degree examination since 1957'; ibid. 291.

[64] See, for a series of essays on the critique, Talal Asad (ed), *Anthropology & the Colonial Encounter* (Ithaka Press 1973).

[65] Gutorm Gjessing, 'The Social Responsibility of the Social Scientist' (1968) 9 Current Anthropology 397, as described by Peter Forster, 'Empricism and Imperialism: A Review of the New Left Critique of Social Anthropology' in Asad, *Anthropology & the Colonial Encounter* (n 59) 25.

[66] Georges Balandier, 'The Colonial Situation' in Berghe, *Africa* (n 29) 36, 43–44.

[67] ibid 44.

[68] Taslim O Elias, *Africa and the Development of International Law* (Sijthoff 1972) 37 (hereafter Elias, *Africa and the Development of International Law*).

[69] ibid 39.

[70] Elias, *Government and Politics* (n 19) 118–119.

merely as a result of the colonial encounter. In his chapter on the Tallensi, Fortes sees a constant cycle upsetting equilibrium: 'This does not mean that Tale society was ever stagnant. Tension is implicit in the equilibrium'.[71] Perhaps more significantly, some of the African societies under study were just not that old. Audrey Richards, for example, asserts that 'In South, Central, and to a lesser extent East Africa most of the ethnic groups now known as tribes have a surprisingly short history of occupation of their present habitat—rarely more than 200 years and sometimes as little as 50 to 100', and she describes small lineage groups 'either split off from a parent stem in search of independence and new territory, or scattered by the onslaught of an enemy'.[72] Evans-Pritchard is particularly good at placing politics within economy and geography, describing the seasonal cycle in which '[a]t the end of the rains, the people burn the grasses to provide new pasture and leave their villages to reside in small camps'; essentially, distinct units coalesce for part of each year.[73] It is unsurprising that Elias was drawn to Fortes and Evans-Pritchard's book, and to books by its contributors Gluckman and Schapera.[74]

With Elias's commitment to the flexibility and dynamism of customary law and its interaction with society as a whole, it is understandable that Fortes and Evans-Pritchard represented such a powerful presence in his writing. Yet, it is interesting that Radcliffe-Brown—from whose work Fortes and Evans-Pritchard represented the next step—wrote the preface. Even more so, Lord Hailey—who after his career in India wrote his massive study of Sub-Saharan Africa under the auspices of the Royal Institute of International Affairs—provided the preface for Meek's comparative study of colonial land law. Of note here is that, despite common calls to separate the government anthropologists from the purely academic,[75] Hailey's 1956 revision of his massive volume is cited repeatedly not only in writings on Africa, but also in Elias's books. Elias hardly distances himself from such a central figure in the colonial framing of Africa.

Adam Kuper, in his book on British anthropology, uses an epigraph to begin the chapter 'Anthropology and Colonialism'. The epigraph describes a painting in the anteroom of the founding leader of Ghana, Kwame Nkrumah, depicting Nkrumah struggling against the chains of colonialism and dispersing three fleeing men, one of whom is carrying a copy of *African Political Systems*.[76] Installed by a

[71] Meyer Fortes, 'The Political System of the Tallensi of the Northern Territories of the Gold Coast' in Meyer Fortes and Edward E Evans-Pritchard (eds), *African Political Systems* (OUP 1940) 239, 271.

[72] Audrey I Richards, 'The Political System of the Bemba Tribe: North-Eastern Rhodesia' in Fortes and Evans-Pritchard, *African Political Systems* (n 71) 83.

[73] Edward E Evans-Pritchard, 'The Nuer of the Southern Sudan' in Fortes and Evans-Pritchard, *African Political Systems* (n 71) 272, 73.

[74] Interestingly, Elias, in comparing Schapera's work to others, states that his 'appears the more valuable in supplying the sociological background to the customary law'; Elias, *British Colonial Law* (n 1) 282.

[75] See, for example, Adam Kuper, *Anthropologists and Anthropology: The British School 1922–1972* (Pica Press 1973) 123–49.

[76] Kuper (n 75) 123, citing Johan Galtung, 'Scientific Colonialism' (1967) Transition 10, 30.

man who did doctoral work in anthropology at LSE, the painting clearly identifies the British anthropologist (placed alongside symbolic figures of the capitalist and the missionary) as a key antagonist to the new Africa. But that was hardly the case for Elias, who was deeply embedded in social science in the British tradition applied to law. His work generally elides the magical thinking that appears in some of *African Political Systems*, but his modernist legal thinking is deeply committed to a social science framing of law and to infusing the special African customary legal tradition characterized by its flexibility and its closeness to African life into the progress of African law. He brings all of the social anthropological study into his Poundian progressive social ordering.

III. The modernization of international law

How, then, does Elias's *British Colonial Law*—with its present-tense setting of the law of (mostly past) British dependencies and with little reference to their independence or emerging independence—bring us to his international law? How should we follow him from his vision of the colonial world to his views of international law, as expressed most poignantly in the essays of *Africa and the Development of International Law*? The emphasis here is that, in Elias's inaugural lecture as Dean of the University of Lagos's Faculty of Law in 1969, Elias spoke very much in line with his earlier views of English-based common law and customary law, and it is important to note its title, 'Law in a Developing Society'.[77] In that lecture, Roscoe Pound assumes a prominent role. If mentioned alongside Hohfeld and various American legal realists in the footnotes of the published version, Pound is particularly important for his 'school of sociological jurisprudence which prescribes for law the task of "social engineering" '.[78] But Elias also wants to underscore the place of morality. In a section of the lecture devoted to 'The Elevation of Man's Moral Nature', Elias turns to HLA Hart and quotes him to the effect that '[t]he law of every modern state shows at a thousand points the influence of both the accepted social morality and wider moral ideals'.[79] But Elias is careful even in over-characterizing Hart's position, so he adds in his footnote: 'Hart's analysis is, of course, more subtle than this, but we cannot enter into that here.'[80] Drawing from WH Twining's 1967 *Law Quarterly Review* article 'Pericles and the Plumber', which he mentions alongside Pound, Elias asserts at the end of his lecture that the

[77] Taslim O Elias, *Law in a Developing Society: Inaugural Lecture Delivered at the University of Lagos on 17 January 1969* (University of Lagos 1969) (hereafter Elias, *Law in a Developing Society*).

[78] ibid 5.

[79] HLA Hart, *The Concept of Law* (Clarendon Press 1961) 199, quoted in Elias, *Law in a Developing Society* (n 77) 21.

[80] Elias, *Law in a Developing Society* (n 77) 21, fn 6. Hart, of course, took the positivist side of a prolonged positivist-natural law struggle with Lon Fuller highlighted by their debate in the *Harvard Law Review* in 1958.

> prevailing social and economic forces call for a type of lawyer who is at once a social engineer and an analyst, a Pericles and a plumber, capable of appreciating the values of existing institutions and mores and yet ever ready to make a dynamic contribution to the maintenance of proper balance between the need for stability and the need for change, between the claims of the State and those of the individual'.[81]

In turning to international law, Elias is also a social engineer and analyst.

James Thuo Gathii, who had identified Elias within the 'weak' tradition of third-world international legal scholars, describes him 'as one of the first among African scholars of international law in exposing the Eurocentricity of international law and in advancing corrective measures', and Elias 'uses the anthropological research and work of Meyer Fortes and E. E. Evans-Pritchard to show that African states and kingdoms had sovereigns just like European states'.[82] For Gathii, Elias has made a 'brilliant move' in being able to transition from African law to international law: 'Fully aware of the anthropological literature on African customary law showing how there was order without law, Elias juxtaposes this insight with similar insights about international law, such as Louis Henkin's observation that most states obey international law most of the time'.[83] Gathii is correct in his assessment of Elias's move from African to international law, but it was not because neither was law. Indeed, Elias was very clear about customary law being law. When Evans-Pritchard talked about the 'ordered anarchy' of the Nuer,[84] he clearly viewed them essentially as an outlier or at least at one extreme in the African spectrum, and clearly separate from the other forms of political organization in the various chapters of *African Political Systems*. What Elias carries over from *British Colonial Law* is his scientism and his notion of law's role in social ordering—at once reflecting and advancing the social order. It was with that background that Elias wrote so forcefully about the move in international law from consent to consensus and places the new states at the helm of international legal development. And, similarly, it was behind his seeing international law in Jenks's terms as 'the common law of mankind',[85] which, for Elias, signified common law both as the shared law of humanity and the progressive evolution associated with the common law tradition, even if Elias was a good deal more committed to the codification of international law than he was in the case of Nigerian customary law.

In the opening chapter of *Africa and the Development of International Law*, Elias makes his case for the glories of medieval African states and their commercial and

[81] ibid 26–27.
[82] James T Gathii, 'A Critical Appraisal of the International Legal Tradition of Taslim Olawale Elias' (2008) 21 Leiden Journal of International Law, 319, 326 (hereafter Gathii, 'A Critical Appraisal').
[83] ibid 328–29.
[84] Evans-Pritchard (n 73) 296.
[85] Jenks, *Common Law* (n 6).

diplomatic stage of development. After referencing a 'random selection of the medieval African empires and kingdoms,' Elias asserts 'the high degree of knowledge and practice of diplomatic law as then known in Europe and Asia'.[86] Elias jumps from that past to the late nineteenth century, mentioning only one seventeenth-century treaty, so he does not adopt the position of CH Alexandrowicz, a proponent of the importance of Asia and Africa in the development of international law. Nor does he align with Alexandrowicz's view that the parties to a treaty up until the late nineteenth century of legal positivism were formally recognized to be on an equal footing, asserting that 'the principle of equality observed in European-African treaty relations under the regime of the classic law of nations'.[87]

For Elias, the colonial period—although his frame also mostly begins in the late nineteenth century—was marked by 'unequal treaties' between European states and indigenous kings 'regarded or treated for all practical purposes thereafter as "chiefs" only, thus implying that they had full sovereign powers to sign treaties which *ipso facto* turned them into subordinates of the new sovereigns deemed to be recognized by the treaties in question',[88]—the same unequal treaties that assume a central role in Antony Anghie's narrative of the colonial core of the making of international law.[89] It is significant that in his overview of the creation of the Vienna Law of Treaties, Elias spends several pages on the Nigerian–French dispute of 1961, in which France was claiming Nigeria to be bound by a treaty that Great Britain had signed in 1922 to allow the French detonation of atomic bombs in the Sahara. Here, Elias marshals his legal advocacy skills regarding the various ways in which Britain's treaty should not apply, including that the subject matter of the treaty would not have been relevant to Western Africa in 1922, and, alternatively, '[e]ven assuming that Nigeria could be presumed to be a party to the treaty in virtue of Great Britain's conclusion of it with France in 1922, Nigeria is entitled to abrogate it as an act [of] reprisal under customary international law'.[90] Matthew Craven describes Elias as taking a middle position in the 1963 International Law Commission's debate over whether universal succession or tabula rasa applied to the large numbers of recently independent states, asserting that what was needed was careful study of the policies of the relevant states and depositaries.[91] Certainly, Elias was quite comfortable in making his case for Nigeria in the dispute with France and was able to use various tools in the international legal toolbox. The new state could make a strong case without resorting to a strong tabula rasa position.

[86] Elias, *Africa and the Development of International Law* (n 68) 15.

[87] Charles H Alexandrowicz, 'The Partition of Africa by Treaty' in Charles H Alexandrowicz, *The Law of Nations in Global History* (David Armitage and Jennifer Pitts eds, OUP 2017) 239.

[88] Elias, *Africa and the Development of International Law* (n 68) 19.

[89] Antony Anghie, *Imperialism, Sovereignty and the Making of International Law* (CUP 2007).

[90] Elias, *Modern Law of Treaties* (n 5) 64.

[91] Matthew Craven, *The Decolonization of International Law: State Succession and the Law of Treaties* (OUP 2007) 99.

During the colonial period, Elias describes the 'metropolitan Powers [as] the exclusive or active parties' in the realm of customary international law while 'the African dependencies were mere spectators at the game'.[92] But Elias is concerned with much more than merely setting a place at the table for the newly independent states. Rather, he makes a case for the move from a consent model law to a consensus model of international law, and in the move to consensus, the sheer number of states from Asia, Africa, and Latin America means that the traditional European powers along with the United States (US) could not easily have their way in the development of international law. Thus, the opening chapter of *Africa and the Development of International Law* ends by asserting that '[i]ndependence has led to membership of the United Nations and its organs and the consequent widening of the international horizon of all member nations, resulting in the establishment of new institutions and processes and in the enlargement of participation in the making and development of contemporary international law'.[93] After arguing that 'modern international law must be based on a wider consensus', Elias ends by asserting that vision of modern international law as fact, stating that '[t] here is already emerging an "international law in a changing world". The contribution which the third world in general and Africa in particular, is making to contemporary international law will in time increase both in quality and in quantity especially within the framework of the United Nations'.[94]

As argued elsewhere, Elias was not really establishing the African, as opposed to the more general third-world, imprint on international law.[95] Although Elias in that same paragraph asserts that the modern international law 'must be a reflection of the principal legal systems and cultures of the world', his international law does not appear ultimately to encompass various cultural inputs. Elias was certainly engaged in emphasizing the role of African states in the future development of international law, but it is never clear what specific African content went into that development. As pivotal a position as Elias had in the launching of the Organization for African Unity (OAU),[96] he does not clearly identify the

92 Elias, *Africa and the Development of International Law* (n 68) 21.
93 ibid 33.
94 ibid. It is important here to note that although Elias broadly adopted the appellation of 'new states', he did not shy away from referencing the third world. In this context, it is also interesting to see that Fatouros, in his essay in Richard Falk and Cyril Black's *The Future of the International Legal Order*, in turn drawing on Pierre Hassner, lists the various uses of the 'new nations', often defined by discipline: 'One may refer to: (1) Newly independent countries (historical and, it may be added, legal, approach); (2) Underdeveloped countries (economic approach—at least in its origins); (3) Nonaligned (or neutralist) countries (political approach); (4) Afro-Asian countries (geographical approach); and Third World countries (politico-geographical approach, according to M Hassner, but perhaps economic and even cultural approach as well).' AA Fatouros, 'Participation of the "New" States in the International Legal Order' in Richard A Falk and Cyril E Black (eds), *The Future of the International Legal Order: Vol 1: Trends and Patterns* (Princeton University Press 1969) 319.
95 See Landauer (n 5).
96 See, in particular, Elias's presenting the importance of the OAU for the *American Journal of International Law* in the role of one of its architects, reprinted in Elias, *Africa and the Development of International Law* (n 68) 121–47.

specifically African element. In an early chapter of *Africa and the Development of International Law*, Elias writes that

> in large areas of Africa there had emerged broadly similar political and economic conditions and, therefore, similar rules of customary law, which makes it possible to speak of the existence of a universal body of principles of African customary law that is not essentially dissimilar to the broad principles of European law. Even today, English law and French law have merely substituted two major juridical regimes in their respective areas of provenance.[97]

If that particular assertion is in tension with Elias's more general framing of the relation between indigenous customary law and English common law, it is important here to recognize that Elias's international law with the emerging role of the new states does not mirror the basic dichotomy of indigenous customary/English common law combination so important to his earlier work. In *The Changing Structure of International Law*, Wolfgang Friedmann sets out two parallel concepts where international law is 'divided between an international law of coexistence and an international law of co-operation' in which there is simultaneously a 'horizontal extension of international law to non-Western civilisations' and 'political and ideological splits that divide the family of nations, a division that does not correspond to that between the Western and the non-Western nations'.[98] At the start of a chapter with its sections 'Latin American Attitudes', 'Islamic Legal Values and International Law', 'Hindu Philosophy and International Law', 'Chinese Civilisation and International Law', and 'The Modern State Practice of Asian States'—note the absence of absence of a section on African, or at least Sub-Saharan African states—Friedmann asserts that '[a]s long as we fail to make this distinction, as long as we regard the whole field of international law without differentiation, as a general problem of universal order, or international anarchy, it is not possible to view the problem of universality in proper perspective'.[99] But he is positive about the pull of coexistence because the 'conditions of coexistence, in a world dominated by the national state and national sovereignty, have proved a far stronger factor than the historical diversities of culture, religion, and political ideology'.[100] Elias, despite his deep knowledge of African society and politics as well as the very title of *Africa and the Development of International Law*, does not truly set out an African international law that differs much from the perspective of the other new states around the world as part of a broader international society.

[97] ibid 43.
[98] Wolfgang Gaston Friedmann, *The Changing Structure of International Law* (Stevens 1964) 297.
[99] ibid.
[100] ibid.

Elias's chapter on 'Modern International Law' begins by attacking the 'cult of political sovereignty', and sets out what he sees as the 'three-dimensional character' of modern international law, that is, 'its encompassing the whole range of relations between states and states, between states and individuals (including institutions) and between two or more international institutions'.[101] This was a set piece of progressive international lawyers throughout the twentieth century. Significantly, Elias's next move is to cite the four sources of international law referenced in Article 38 of the Statute of the ICJ—which have born so much of the brunt of third-world criticism over the years for their clear Eurocentrism. He turns them almost on their head by moving directly into the discussion of international institutions, starting with the International Law Commission, asserting that '[p]robably the most significant developments in public international law have been due to the work of the International Law Commission'.[102] And he gives most prominence to the 'General Assembly and Security Council Resolutions as Sources of Law', in which the Security Council strikingly receives a single paragraph in the six-page section. Essentially, the UN General Assembly (UNGA) is where the action is.

In the first paragraph of his section on the UNGA and Security Council resolutions as sources of law, Elias identifies Article 10 of the Charter as providing the UNGA's power to make recommendations regarding 'any questions or any matters within the scope of the present Charter', and he summons Hans Kelsen's observation from his massive 1950 *The Law of the United Nations* to the effect that 'there is hardly any international matter which the General Assembly is not competent to discuss and on which it is not competent to make recommendations'.[103] Elias goes from there, with a diversion into the 'tangled web of Soviet theories' and a discussion of Czech author Vratislav Pechota and Polish jurist Manfred Lachs, who sat on the ICJ,[104] to turn to some of the most progressive voices among Western international legal theorists, including Richard Falk, Wilfred Jenks, and Wolfgang Friedmann. Elias turns to Falk, who argues in 'On the Quasi-Legislative Competence of the General Assembly' that 'the formal limitations of status, often stressed by international lawyers, may not prevent resolutions of the General Assembly, or certain of them, from acquiring a normative status in international life'.[105]

Philip Jessup observed in 1947 the 'slow but steady development of majority rule in international organizations'.[106] If Jessup's point, made so early in the life of the

[101] Elias, *Africa and the Development of International Law* (n 68) 63–64.

[102] ibid 66.

[103] ibid 71, citing Hans Kelsen, *The Law of the United Nations: A Critical Analysis of its Fundamental Problems* (Stevens 1950) 198–99.

[104] Elias, *Africa and the Development of International Law* (n 68) 72.

[105] ibid 73, citing Richard A Falk, 'On the Quasi-Legislative Competence of the General Assembly' (1966) 60 American Journal of International Law 782, 784.

[106] Philip C Jessup, *A Modern Law of Nations: An Introduction* (Macmillan 1959) 41 (from a chapter published in 1947), citing Cromwell A Riches, *Majority Rule in International Organization: A Study of the Trend from Unanimity to Majority Decision* (Hopkins Press 1940).

UN, was not yet focused on the role of the UNGA, but rather on the shift from state sovereignty with specific reference to the Security Council, the directional move was still towards majority rule. The reference to majority rule would lead to the way to the interpretation of UNGA 'recommendations' under Article 18(2) of the UN Charter as being more than mere recommendations. And that was exactly where Elias was headed, knowing that the large number of newly independent states would hold sway in the UNGA, so that he could assert that the 'recommendations' under Article 18(2) 'are binding upon all concerned once they have been adopted by a two-thirds majority'.[107] Elias was not likely to make much noise about the Bandung conference held before Nigeria's independence, but with the competence he saw in the UNGA, he was confident that power was shifting to the third world.

To make his point about the UNGA, Elias draws heavily on Falk, Jenks, and Schachter, interestingly tucking *The Legal Significance of the Declarations of the United Nations* by Ghanaian author OY Asamoah into a footnote after Falk's article about the 'quasi-legislative competence' of the UNGA. Indeed, when Elias continues through the four sources of international law under the ICJ's Charter with a section on the 'publicists', he gives particular prominence to Jessup, Jenks, Friedmann, and Falk, 'whose contribution lies in re-shaping and remoulding customary law as well as in recognizing the need for wider horizons in our approach to both customary and conventional international law'.[108] Elias points to various publications, including Friedmann's *Modern Law of Nations* (1948), Jenks's *Common Law of Mankind* (1956), and Falk's *Law, Morality, and War in the Contemporary World* (1963). If, according to Elias, Falk 'sounded a liberal note at a time when men were once more tending to lose their heads over internecine strife', it was 'by his "New Approaches to the Study of International Law" that he has made his contribution to the subject'.[109] Interestingly, Falk's article seemingly ends with an overview of four clusters of scholars: 'Policy Science' headed by Myres McDougal; 'Functionalism' represented by Percy Corbett, Jenks, Friedmann, and Julius Stone; 'Systems Theory' led by Morton Kaplan and Nicolas deB. Katzenbach; and 'Phenomenological Perspectives' exemplified by Brainerd Currie, so that instead of picking sides, Falk identifies all of them with an effort to 'move beyond the impressionism of earlier approaches' to studies with 'a scientific character'.[110] For Elias, there may be certain 'traditionalists' fighting a 'rear-guard action',[111] but they were clearly on the losing side of history. For Elias, 'modern international law' was clearly taking root.

[107] Elias, *Africa and the Development of International Law* (n 68) 71.

[108] ibid 83. Directly before his discussion of Jessup, Jenks, Friedmann, and Falk, Elias discusses the positivists, including 'Oppenheim-Lauterpacht, Guggenheim and Schwarzenberger, although it must be said that the last-named has also been a pioneer in the opening up of new frontiers of the subject'.

[109] ibid 84. Richard A Falk, 'New Approaches to the Study of International Law' (1967) 61 American Journal of International Law 477 (hereafter Falk, 'New Approaches').

[110] ibid 487.

[111] Elias, *Africa and the Development of International Law* (n 68) 86.

Elias was totally in sync with the wide range of progressive, and many relatively mainstream, twentieth-century international legal thinkers who criticized the state-as-subject underpinnings of 'traditional' international law, even if states' voting rights in the UNGA emboldened his vision of emerging 'modern international law'. With his book on the Vienna Convention on the Law of Treaties, Elias could state flatly: 'This practice has been based on an obsolete notion of the sovereign rights of States'.[112] His use of the word 'obsolete' mirrors Richard Falk's assertion that '[s]overeignty is as morally obsolete as it is factually inaccurate'.[113] If, as mentioned earlier, Gathii saw Elias as drawing on the likes of Fortes and Evans-Pritchard to establish that 'African states and kingdoms had sovereigns just like European states', Elias was more deeply engrained in the complexities of social thought regarding rights and sovereignty. Among other things, he had to deal with the federal realities of Nigeria, which were being put in place well before independence—the tension remains in the background, with the exception of the chapter 'The Legality of Illegal Regimes in Africa', where he includes a rare discussion of 'the secessionist clique in the former Eastern Region of Nigeria which called itself "Biafra"'.[114]

Although Elias presses the place of individuals in international law, following others from Lauterpacht and Brierly through Friedmann and Falk, Elias particularly urges the growing interdependence of states internationally. Jessup entitled one of the subsections of his *Modern Law of Nations*, 'Independence and Interdependence', declaring that 'each state is *dependent* on all other states'.[115] As Falk refers to the 'interdependence of the modern world',[116] so on the very first page of his preface to *Law, Freedom and Welfare* does Jenks assert 'the emergence of interdependence rather than the independence of states as the basic concept of contemporary international law'.[117] In that mode, Elias ends his chapter on 'modern international law' by asserting the 'constantly changing needs of the world of today and of tomorrow, a world of growing interdependence and indivisibility that is also committed to the achievement of peace and happiness for all mankind'.[118]

Jenks argued that '[t]he law on these matters has given us the elements of a structure of the society of states on the basis of which we can consolidate achievements of the past and go forward to evolve a common law of mankind for a world community.'[119] For him, 'In the last analysis we are left with the moral and social

[112] Elias, *Modern Law of Treaties* (n 5) 33.

[113] Richard A Falk, *Law, Morality, and War in the Contemporary World* (Praeger 1963) 29 (hereafter Falk, *Law, Morality, and War*).

[114] Elias, *Africa and the Development of International Law* (n 68) 107; and Elias unamibuously concludes that '[t]he attempted secession was unconstitional and invalid'; ibid. 113.

[115] Jessup (n 106) 37.

[116] Falk, *Law, Morality, and War* (n 113) 28.

[117] Clarence W Jenks, *Law, Freedom and Welfare* (Stevens 1963) ix (hereafter Jenks, *Law, Freedom and Welfare*).

[118] Elias, *Africa and the Development of International Law* (n 68) 87.

[119] Jenks, *Law, Freedom and Welfare* (n 117) 28.

nature of man as the foundation of his obligations to his fellows.'[120] Despite the emphasis on the moral, this is not pure naturalism, although the push in a naturalist direction was clearly important in twentieth-century international legal thought as a critique of positivism. Jenks asserts that the 'will of the world community is binding because it expresses the fundamental law of our being, the brotherhood of man'.[121] Later he stresses:

> Two areas call for specially urgent attention, the comparative study of the part in a universal legal order of the general principles of law recognised by civilised nations, with special emphasis on the importance which has now been assumed by non-Western legal systems, and the potential contribution of internal law to the solution of the problems posed by new scientific and technological developments.[122]

In essence, we have the 'civilised'—always a freighted phrase for third-world international lawyers[123]—paired immediately with the growing importance of non-Western legal systems. Elias spoke of the importance of the 'increasing participation on the part of African and allied Groups' in international organizations to arrive at 'a progressive development and codification of international law'.[124]

This brings us back to Elias's model of British colonial law, particularly of the role of customary law within it, as well as questions regarding its progressive development, its codification, and its potential fusing with English-based common law. Elias saw customary law as law, making claims similar to Louis Henkin's in *How Nations Behave* with regard to international law. Elias worried about a rush to codify customary law in Nigeria and other British dependencies because not enough knowledge about customary law had been obtained—the social science, questionnaires, and significant case reporting still needed to be accomplished. Nevertheless, Elias was much more comfortable with the codification of international law, principally if it were flexible and progressive; essentially, the common law of humanity should retain some of the flexibility of the common law tradition. Moreover, it should reflect international society. If he turned to Pound's concept of 'social ordering' in his discussion of customary law, we should remember that Friedmann asserted, 'As the purpose of law is the ordering of social relations, every legal system must reflect the principles of the social order that it seeks to regulate.'[125]

[120] ibid 100.
[121] ibid.
[122] ibid 147.
[123] Elias identifies the antagonism for the term 'civilized nations' among the new states. Elias, *Africa and the Development of International Law* (n 68) 52.
[124] ibid 32.
[125] Friedmann (n 98) 3.

When Elias came to write *The Modern Law of Treaties*, he did so having worked on its development as a member of the International Law Commission, having acted as General Rapporteur for the two sessions on the subject in 1965 and 1966, and, as he states, being 'unanimously elected to be the Chairman of the Committee of the Whole Conference not only for the first session but also for the second session'.[126] Elias takes explicit credit for preventing the conference from falling apart due to a dispute between the 'Big Powers' and the 'New States': 'It was at this juncture on the last day but one of the Conference that a compromise solution to be found as Article 66 of the Convention and its Annex was supplied by a thirteen-nation-sponsored text under my leadership'.[127] Elias here played the significant role of go-between, pushing compromise between the two. Although Elias's book proceeds through the Vienna Convention on the Law of Treaties section by section, he is explicit about some of the key political differences, such as whether the 'threat or use of force' would be restricted to 'armed force' as the Western states urged, or be open to the broader interpretation of including 'economic and political pressure'.[128]

Elias clearly understood the stakes as he tried to navigate the Convention to a successful conclusion. Nevertheless, it is clear that he was a moderate in international affairs, representing a state—Nigeria—that assumed a non-aligned posture while nevertheless remaining close to the West. He argued, perhaps in a lawyerly fashion, that when the OAU Council of Ministers made a decision that its member states sever relations with the United Kingdom as a response to events in Rhodesia, it simply did not have the competence to make that determination.[129] Elias was a moderate and a moderator. He did not write as Bedjaoui did of 'predatory economy' and 'froth and veneers of decolonization'.[130] With so many current scholars, for example, Anghie and Puhuja,[131] pointing to the very structural bias of international law, how do we assess Elias?

As an epigraph to *British Colonial Law*, Elias quoted Sir Frederick Pollock: 'Those who make no mistakes, it has been said, will never make anything; and the judge who is afraid of committing himself may be called sound and safe in his own generation, but will leave no mark on the law'. It is, perhaps, revealing that Elias saw his project as bold, and that he expressed that boldness through the voice of the eminent English jurist. But it is also revealing that he quotes Pollock, who, along with Maitland, wrote the classic two-volume *History of English Law*. His choice of Pollock reflects the broad audience of his comparative study, but that Pollock is

[126] Elias, *Modern Law of Treaties* (n 5) 5–6.
[127] ibid 7.
[128] ibid 172.
[129] Elias, *Africa and the Development of International Law* (n 68) 156.
[130] Bedjaoui (n 4).
[131] Anghie (n 89); Sundhya Pahuja, *Decolonising International Law: Development, Economic Growth, and the Politics of Universality* (CUP 2011).

an historian of great eminence. The epigraph is *explicitly* about the courage Elias hoped his project exemplified, but *implicitly* about the 'careful study' that was one of his central refrains. And with that, he was confident in the progress of 'social ordering' that could be achieved both within the blended legal system of nations like Nigeria and within international law.

This brings us back to Elias's use of William Twining's Pericles and the plumber in his address at the University of Lagos. Both are highly Western tropes, with Pericles' 'Funeral Oration' serving literally as the centrepiece of *The Greek Commonwealth* by Alfred Zimmern, the eminent classicist who was also a liberal foil for EH Carr in his *Twenty Years' Crisis*, and plumbing in a developing nation with limited plumbing. Falk asserts, 'World order literature is often flawed by its sentimental naiveté,'[132] and emphasizes the importance of new approaches that 'bring the study of international law into ever closer association with the outlook, method, and concerns of the social scientist'.[133] However, Falk also shows a strong belief in the importance of morality to international law, writing that 'it is correct to identify this essay as being in the natural-law tradition'.[134] We see Falk, then, trying to navigate between moralism and scientism, or, rather, trying to fuse them. It is significant, then, that Koskenniemi saw Falk as the exemplar of the 'late modern mainstream,' which, he tells us,

> often situates itself between the rule and the policy approaches. In Richard Falk's words, the task of an adequate doctrine today is to establish '[a]n intermediate position, one that maintains the distinctiveness of the legal order while managing to be responsive to the extralegal setting of politics, history and morality'.[135]

And Gerry Simpson has recently tried to grapple with an international law that had, for him, developed language that 'just closes off a bit of our humanity'.[136]

In this context, Elias was a writer who, both in his study of colonial law and international law, embodied the scientist, repeatedly pushing for evidence and detailed study. Yet, without question, and despite his typically understated rhetoric, Elias was certainly pressing a deeply moral case. The plumber was also Pericles—in the framework of a developing society. If Fatouros tells us that '[t]he responsible officials of the new states may not be experienced or well-informed enough to realize

[132] Richard A Falk, 'The Interplay of Westphalia and Charter Conceptions of the International Legal Order' in Falk and Black, *The Future of the International Legal Order* (n 94) 40.

[133] Falk, 'New Approaches' (n 109) 479.

[134] Falk, *Law, Morality, and War* (n 113) 38.

[135] Martti Koskenniemi, 'Between Apology to Utopia: The Politics of International Law' in *The Politics of International Law* (Hart 2011) 43.

[136] Gerry Simpson, 'The Sentimental Life of International Law' (2015) 3 London Review of International Law 3.

that the legal principles "in-the-books" were never intended to apply in practice, at least not to all states at all times',[137] Elias was no naïf. Rather, he was interested in using the rules in the books with the realities on the ground, both deeply analysed and contextualized, in developing what he perceived to be a 'modern' international law.

[137] Fatouros (n 94) 343.

15

Determining New Selves

Mohammed Bedjaoui on Algeria, Western Sahara, and Post-Classical International Law

Umut Özsu

I. Introduction

As one of the most significant jurists to emerge from what during the Cold War was widely characterized as the 'third world', Mohammed Bedjaoui is a towering figure in the field of international law—prolific as a scholar, active as a diplomat,and influential as a judge, advocate, and arbitrator. From the thorny issue of state succession to treaties during the 1960s and early 1970s to the New International Economic Order (NIEO) project of the 1970s and 1980s, from debates about the scope and content of collective self-determination to the question of whether the threat or use of nuclear weapons is expressly prohibited by international law, Bedjaoui was positioned at the forefront of a wide range of legal controversies for the better part of the past fifty years. Alongside Georges Abi-Saab, Bedjaoui continues to enjoy significant power as a key representative of the 'global South', not least because he retrospectively has been canonized as a core member of a 'generation' of non-European jurists who sought to reorient and transform international law in accordance with the political and economic imperatives of decolonization.

Given the range of his influence as a scholar, arbitrator, ambassador, and diplomatic representative for Algeria, and judge of the International Court of Justice (ICJ), the expectation could be that Bedjaoui has received a significant degree of scholarly attention over the years. Interestingly, though, Bedjaoui's intellectual and professional trajectory—and the way in which this trajectory tracked the unfolding of the post-1945 wave of decolonization—has not been subject to serious and sustained examination.[1] To a significant degree, this deficiency stems from the fact that there is still nothing approximating a comprehensive account of the way in which socialist and non-aligned jurists have engaged with and attempted

[1] A notable, if predictably prosaic, exception is Emile Yakpo and Tahar Boumedra (eds), *Liber Amicorum Judge Mohammed Bedjaoui* (Kluwer Law International 1999) pt 1. I have situated Bedjaoui's drive to craft a new, post-classical international law in the context of the NIEO project in Umut Özsu, '"In the Interests of Mankind as a Whole": Mohammed Bedjaoui's New International Economic Order' (2015) 6 Humanity 129.

Umut Özsu, *Determining New Selves* In: *The Battle for International Law: South-North Perspectives on the Decolonization Era*. Edited by: Jochen von Bernstorff and Philipp Dann, Oxford University Press (2019).

DOI: 10.1093/oso/9780198849636.003.0016

to reconfigure the basic rules, principles, and institutional apparatuses of international law. Recent years have witnessed a surge of interest in the way in which Euro-American models of international law have been appropriated, modified, and occasionally transformed in the extra-European world.[2] Yet no genuine history of what has come to be known as 'Third World Approaches to International Law' (or 'TWAIL') has ever been written; the movement's intellectual history, historical sociology, and economic history exist only in fragments, limited to particular substantive issues and institutional contexts, not as a sizeable and persuasive corpus of work.[3]

At root, Bedjaoui belongs to a small but ambitious group of mid- to latetwentieth-century jurists who hailed from Asia, Africa, and Latin America, received elite training in Europe and the United States (US) (in law but sometimes also in a second discipline, typically political science or economics), subsequently succeeded in establishing themselves as leading figures in the worlds of international legal scholarship and international dispute-settlement, and generally maintained a somewhat uneasy relationship with the growing corpus of international human rights law that enveloped discussions in and about the United Nations (UN).[4]

[2] From a large and rapidly expanding body of scholarship see, for example, Liliana Obregón, 'Completing Civilization: Creole Consciousness and International Law in Nineteenth-Century Latin America' in Anne Orford (ed), *International Law and Its Others* (CUP 2006); Turan Kayaoğlu, *Legal Imperialism: Sovereignty and Extraterritoriality in Japan, the Ottoman Empire, and China* (CUP 2010); Arnulf Becker Lorca, *Mestizo International Law: A Global Intellectual History 1842–1933* (CUP 2014); Lauri Mälksoo, *Russian Approaches to International Law* (OUP 2015); Umut Özsu, *Formalizing Displacement: International Law and Population Transfers* (OUP 2015).

[3] A sweep of the terrain is offered in James T Gathii, 'TWAIL: A Brief History of Its Origins, Its Decentralized Network, and a Tentative Bibliography' (2011) 3 Trade, Law and Development 26. For a brief but helpful first-hand account of personal experience, see Georges Abi-Saab, 'The Third World Intellectual in Praxis: Confrontation, Participation, or Operation Behind Enemy Lines?' (2016) 37 Third World Quarterly 1957 (hereafter Abi-Saab, 'Praxis'). Muthucumaraswamy Sornarajah, whose work offers the most prominent TWAIL critique of international investment law, has done the same in Muthucumaraswamy Sornarajah, 'On Fighting for Global Justice: The Role of a Third World International Lawyer' (2016) 37 Third World Quarterly 1972. For a similarly informative interview with Kamal Hossain, a key figure in debates about resource sovereignty, see Sharif Bhuiyan, Philippe Sands and Nico J Schrijver, '"I Believe in the Power of Human Beings to be Agents of Change": An Interview with Kamal Hossain' in Sharif Bhuiyan, Philippe Sands and Nico J Schrijver (eds), *International Law and Developing Countries: Essays in Honour of Kamal Hossain* (Brill Nijhoff 2014).

[4] The last point is particularly crucial—and also particularly thorny. A central feature of the growing literature on the history of human rights is the question of the role that such rights played in the self-determination struggles of the post-1945 era. Some argue that human rights were integral to this struggle. For different variants of this type of argument, see Roland Burke, *Decolonization and the Evolution of International Human Rights* (University of Pennsylvania Press 2010); Meredith Terretta, '"We Had Been Fooled into Thinking that the UN Watches over the Entire World": Human Rights, UN Trust Territories, and Africa's Decolonization' (2012) 34 Human Rights Quarterly 329; Steven LB Jensen, *The Making of International Human Rights: The 1960s, Decolonization, and the Reconstruction of Global Values* (CUP 2016). Others contend that human rights never comprised an essential element of the drive for self-determination, or that they rose to prominence only during the 1970s, by which time the politics of national liberation had largely run its course. In this vein see especially Samuel Moyn, *The Last Utopia: Human Rights in History* (Belknap Press of Harvard University Press 2010); Jan Eckel, 'Human Rights and Decolonization: New Perspectives and Open Questions' (2010) 1 Humanity 111. For a recent contextualization of this and related debates, see Stefan-Ludwig Hoffmann, 'Human Rights and History' (2016) 232 Past & Present 279.

Aside from Bedjaoui and Abi-Saab, international lawyers who have followed this path include RP Anand, Taslim Elias, Kamal Hossain, and Muthucumaraswamy Sornarajah. While this trans-continental mobilization of legal talent was not, of course, formidable enough to cut across entrenched race and class divisions or subvert the dominance of Euro-American jurists in every instance, it did have a significant effect on certain aspects of international law, including international development law, international environmental law, international human rights law, and the international law of armed conflict.

This chapter aims to further our understanding of the historical dynamics behind Bedjaoui's development from an advocate of Algerian independence to a champion of self-determination in other states and territories. It first provides a close reading of Bedjaoui's 1961 monograph *Law and the Algerian Revolution*, a detailed and characteristically vigorous defence of the Front de libération nationale (FLN) and its claims to sovereignty on behalf of the people of Algeria.[5] Although it was arguably the most trenchant legal analysis of the war from a specifically Algerian perspective, *Law and the Algerian Revolution* has never received significant attention. It then analyses the arguments that Bedjaoui advanced in 1975 as a representative of Algeria in advisory proceedings relating to the international legal status of Western Sahara.[6] Partly because Algeria was an 'interested party' and not a principal participant in the Western Sahara dispute, Bedjaoui's submissions have generally been neglected, with the unfortunate result that the capacious vision of self-determination he articulated has been side-lined in favour of more general discussion of the case.[7]The chapter's central claim is that Bedjaoui's transformation from legal militant and colonial subject to experienced counsel and post-colonial policymaker reflected an amplification of his earlier commitment to political and economic self-determination—a commitment that underwrote the broader push for decolonization that reconfigured the international legal and economic order in the decades following the Second World War. Specifically, it argues that Bedjaoui's views on self-determination in 1961 and 1975 are indicative of a certain refinement of his thinking—in the sense not of marking a rupture or radical departure, especially since Bedjaoui was always committed to reforming international law from within the discipline's centres of intellectual and professional power,[8] but

[5] Mohammed Bedjaoui, *Law and the Algerian Revolution* (International Association of Democratic Lawyers 1961) (hereafter Bedjaoui, *Algerian Revolution*).

[6] *Western Sahara* (Advisory Opinion) [1975] ICJ Rep 12 (hereafter *Western Sahara* (Advisory Opinion)).

[7] The most notable exception to this rule is the detailed analysis offered in Karen Knop, *Diversity and Self-Determination in International Law* (CUP 2002) 110–67. Subjecting both the case and the various sets of pleadings and ancillary documents to close examination, Knop argues that each of the states involved in the *Western Sahara* proceedings elaborated a distinct understanding of legal identity and allegiance. I have benefitted from Knop's illuminating discussion. However, my concern here is different, having to do with Bedjaoui's struggle to develop a radical critique of classical international law as part of a broader attempt to realize a fully non-Eurocentric international legal order.

[8] This was the case even for his support for and conceptualization of the NIEO project, which he embedded firmly in the work of the UNGA and other UN organs. See Mohammed Bedjaoui, *Towards a*

of demonstrating an expansion and augmentation of his existing beliefs into a broader account of the historical and conceptual relations between colonialism and international law. The Sahara and the concept of collective self-determination figured prominently in both cases, supplying Bedjaoui with an opportunity not only to advance his critique of classical international law, the formalistic pretensions of which he deemed to be theoretically untenable and undermined by the vagaries of imperialist policy, but also to press for the progressive realization of the 'social' and 'solidaristic' international law that he regarded as the necessary culmination of decolonization.[9]

II. Bedjaoui's Algeria

One of his first major works of scholarship, *Law and the Algerian Revolution* was an outgrowth of Bedjaoui's personal and professional involvement in the Algerian liberation movement. No less significantly, it was also a product of his training in law and political science at the University of Grenoble during the 1950s. An attempt to analyse the legal dimensions of the Algerian struggle for independence from France, *Law and the Algerian Revolution* aims to be as exhaustive, even taxonomic, as possible, reading less as a polemic than as a treatise. It defends the claim that Algeria's statehood predated the French invasion of 1830 and was never formally extinguished, its territory having been occupied but not subject to a successful, thoroughgoing, and legally valid process of annexation. It anchors the legal authority of the FLN in the constituent power of the Algerian people, which Bedjaoui regards as having furnished both the organization and the revolution it served with an overarching (and usefully imprecise) mandate. And it demonstrates that the FLN's provisional government managed to secure recognition for itself and an independent Algeria from a large number of foreign states and governments, an exercise partly intended to bolster Bedjaoui's contention that the 1949 Geneva

New International Economic Order (Holmes Meier 1979) (hereafter Bedjaoui, *NIEO*). On the reformatory (rather than revolutionary) character of the NIEO, see especially Samir Amin, 'After the New International Economic Order: The Future of International Economic Relations' in Pradip K Ghosh (ed), *New International Economic Order: A Third World Perspective* (Greenwood 1984); Herb Addo, 'The New International Economic Order and Imperialism: A Context for Evaluation' in Luis Herrera and Raimo Väyrynen (eds), *Peace, Development, and New International Economic Order*. Proceedings of the International Peace Research Association—Seventh General Conference (1979); Herb Addo (ed), *Transforming the World Economy? Nine Critical Essays on the New International Economic Order* (Hodder and Stoughton 1984). See further Umut Özsu, 'Neoliberalism and the New International Economic Order: A History of "Contemporary Legal Thought"' in Christopher L Tomlins and Justin Desautels-Stein (eds), *Searching for Contemporary Legal Thought* (CUP 2017).

[9] Needless to say, Bedjaoui has written extensively about the international law of self-determination throughout his career. I focus upon *Law and the Algerian Revolution* and his interventions in the *Western Sahara* proceedings on account of the centrality of the concept of self-determination to his arguments in both contexts.

Conventions were directly applicable to the armed conflict. Most salient for present purposes, though, is Bedjaoui's strong articulation of the right of collective self-determination and his closely related insistence upon the territorial integrity and indivisibility of Algeria, with all that these naturally entailed for the country's resource-rich Saharan possessions.

For Bedjaoui, colonialism had never generated a rationally integrated system of international law. Rivalries between various European powers had prevented the crystallization of a 'universal system of colonial law', and no 'international standard of colonial law recognised in all periods and places' had ever emerged.[10] In the place of a colonial system that had failed to find 'definite universal legal expression', the world was now witnessing the birth of an anti-colonialism that was to embody a 'substantive international law' reminiscent in some respects of the 'social' breadth of the natural law tradition.[11] Algeria was destined—indeed, duty-bound—to play an important role here, given that the war with France enjoyed a 'leading place' in 'the great movement of disintegration of the colonial system' and that it had already generated innovations in regard to prevailing legal conceptions of intervention on behalf of peoples waging self-determination struggles.[12] Bedjaoui was remarkably lucid here: the FLN's combatants, he wrote, 'do not represent the people because they carry arms', but are instead 'able to continue bearing arms because they represent the people', anticipating an analytical inversion in favour of 'the people' that would later gain fame in the *Western Sahara* case.[13] Further, if it was from the 'will' of the Algerian people that the FLN derived its representative authority, it was also from this 'will' that the FLN laid claim to the Algerian people's right to self-determination, this having been established as a 'legal principle' that 'the colonial powers do not dare to oppose . . . openly on international platforms'.[14] It bears noting here that Bedjaoui's book appears to have gone to press in May 1961, roughly five months after the UN General Assembly (UNGA) adopted the landmark Declaration on the Granting of Independence to Colonial Countries and Peoples, a central point of reference for nearly all those agitating for forthright recognition of self-determination as a legally enforceable right and not simply as an ill-defined if appealing 'principle'.[15]

Intriguingly, Bedjaoui's preferred technique for gauging popular will and securing legitimacy for its expression was the plebiscite—a mechanism that had come into its own during the interwar period but that had been applied nearly exclusively in Europe (and even then only under highly limited circumstances, such

[10] Bedjaoui, *Algerian Revolution* (n 5) 10.
[11] ibid 10.
[12] ibid 11–12.
[13] ibid 57–58.
[14] ibid 66.
[15] See UNGA Res 1514 (XV) (14 December 1960). See also UNGA Res 1541 (XV) (15 December 1960).

as Upper Silesia and the Saar Territory).[16] So long as a referendum procedure could be designed carefully and implemented impartially by an international commission,[17] France's desire to 'dissolve the Algerian people into a multitude of tiny so-called ethnic, religious or linguistic groups, non-viable and highly explosive in character', was bound to fail.[18] This would ensure that France would not be able to 'make another Palestine or Congo out of Algeria, diabolically setting centrifugal forces into motion which will create a permanent state of insecurity in North Africa and the Mediterranean'.[19] For Bedjaoui, the referendum—a signature, if somewhat unreliable, manifestation of modern law's putative commitment to self-determination and democratic decision-making—would play a key role in paving the way for Algerian sovereignty.

Bedjaoui's position with respect to the status of the Algerian Sahara followed directly from his general stance on self-determination. French authorities claimed that Algerian Sahara was 'unowned property'—a 'no man's land'.[20] The claim was factually groundless, of course, as no fewer than one million people inhabited the region. But it was also decidedly Eurocentric, particularly as it presupposed the universal validity of a form of sovereign authority that was (or was deemed to be) unique to modern Europe.[21] Such insistence on the utility and applicability of the doctrine of *terra nullius* was, Bedjaoui argued pointedly, 'one of the most characteristic forms of imperialist argument, based on a system of references which are set up as absolute when in fact they are only relative'.[22] The French also argued that 'northern' and 'southern' Algeria were legally distinguishable, and that fully fledged self-determination, should it be granted to the 'north', need not necessarily for that reason be awarded to the 'south'. Unsurprisingly, the FLN and its supporters threw their weight behind the directly antithetical proposition. Arguing that Algeria's Saharan territory belonged to Algeria alone, they insisted that the territorial unity and indivisibility of the state was unquestionable. Yet Algerians who sought emancipation from French rule were by no means alone in this regard. On the contrary, some of the most vociferous exponents of the thesis that Algerian Sahara was indeed Algerian were to be found within the settler population. The French had seized Algerian Sahara during the late nineteenth and early twentieth centuries, mainly for the purpose of integrating their possessions in western

[16] The classic study is Sarah Wambaugh, *Plebiscites Since the World War (With a Collection of Official Documents)* (Carnegie Endowment for International Peace 1933). This reluctance to organize plebiscites continued long after the Second World War, fed by broader doubts about the scope and content of self-determination at a time when many anti-imperialist and anti-colonialist movements were heavily invested in its legal and political force. See Jörg Fisch, *The Right of Self-Determination of Peoples: The Domestication of an Illusion* (Anita Mage tr, CUP 2015) 185–86.

[17] On this see Bedjaoui, *Algerian Revolution* (n 5) 251–55.

[18] ibid 245.

[19] ibid 246.

[20] ibid 221.

[21] ibid.

[22] ibid 221–22.

Africa and strengthening their strategic and economic presence in the region. Some metropolitan officials had subsequently attempted to restructure Algerian Sahara's administrative order, partly with a view to furthering the exploitation of its sizeable hydrocarbon resources. But the Algerian national assembly, composed disproportionately of settlers and other supporters of the *départements*'s administrative regime, had repeatedly rejected such efforts, resolving on numerous occasions to repudiate any 'amputation of part of Algerian territory with a view to its integration into an independent territory which would come directly under the French metropolitan Government'.[23] In Bedjaoui's view, the issue was therefore clear: Algerian Sahara had always been part and parcel of Algeria, 'the legal history of the Saharan part of the country ha[ving] served as a constant safeguard of this unity',[24] and the Algerian people could not be stripped of its (permanent) sovereignty over the territory's wealth and resources.[25]

It has long been commonplace in many international legal circles to view national liberation movements as preponderantly 'political' rather than 'legal', the default assumption being that they warrant full recognition as international legal persons only once they achieve statehood (and thereby cease to be liberation movements). While not entirely without value, such a stance is ultimately unilluminating. Insisting unconvincingly upon a hard-and-fast distinction between 'law' and 'politics', it elides the crucial importance of law, both domestic and international, in the reconstitution of territories that are subject to foreign rule, whether formal or informal, into *de jure* sovereign and independent states. Matthew Connolly and Jeffrey Byrne have emphasized the fact that Algeria's emancipation and reconfiguration was achieved through 'legal' as much as 'political' means—that sovereignty was at least as much a result of transnational legal activism and argument as it was a product of armed conflict and concrete struggle.[26] Bedjaoui's *Law and the Algerian Revolution* illuminates the extent of this reliance upon law in full force.

III. Bedjaoui's Western Sahara

If the *South West Africa* cases have rightly been denounced as the ICJ's low watermark, doing significant damage throughout the third world to the reputation of international dispute-settlement institutions,[27] arguably no judgment or advisory

[23] This language is from a 1952 resolution of the national assembly. Quoted ibid 235.

[24] ibid 239.

[25] ibid 239–40.

[26] See Matthew Connelly, *A Diplomatic Revolution: Algeria's Fight for Independence and the Origins of the Post-Cold War Era* (OUP 2002); Jeffrey J Byrne, *Mecca of Revolution: Algeria, Decolonization, and the Third World Order* (OUP 2016).

[27] To take a particularly noteworthy example, Abi-Saab has argued that the 1966 decision, 'the most controversial in the history of the two Courts', gave rise to 'multiple repercussions', above all 'a very critical debate on the role of the Court in the General Assembly, which resulted in a rebalancing in the composition of the Court to make it more representative of the international community's diverse

opinion issued by the World Court spoke as directly to legal difficulties arising from 'troubled' cases of decolonization as *Western Sahara*. As has so often been the case with proceedings stemming from colonial and post-colonial disputes, the *Western Sahara* opinion was first and foremost an exercise in international legal history, providing a crucial forum for debates about the doctrine of intertemporal law, the 'effective control' test for state sovereignty, the relation between self-determination and *uti possidetis juris*, and countless other questions arising from or pertaining to decolonization. The UNGA had requested an opinion in respect of two issues—that of the territory's legal status at the time of its formal colonization by Spain in the two final decades of the nineteenth century, in particular the question whether it could justifiably be characterized as having been *terra nullius* at that point, and that of any 'legal ties' which may then have existed between the territory on the one hand and Morocco and Mauritania (or, more accurately, the Bilad Shinguitti or what the Court terms 'the Mauritanian entity') on the other.[28] Strictly speaking, the World Court was consulted not in regard to the validity of Spain's ongoing administrative power in Western Sahara, but in connection with the territory's legal personality (or lack thereof) at a crucial point in its historical development. That said, the legal implications for Spain's authority over the territory and its Saharawi inhabitants were naturally significant.[29]

As already mentioned, Algeria was not a principal participant in the proceedings but simply an 'interested party', one concerned about the matter for reasons that Bedjaoui—heavily involved in Algerian politics and serving as ambassador to France at the time—glossed as its 'common destiny with Morocco and Mauritania, thanks to geography, history, civilization, and language'.[30] Unlike these two neighbouring states, Algeria had no direct claims to the territory. It participated in the proceedings mainly to uphold the extension of the right of self-determination to the Saharawi inhabitants of the territory. In addition to stifling Morocco's regional ambitions (the two countries had become embroiled in a border war shortly after Algeria's independence in 1962), this would facilitate the continuation of the formal decolonization of north-western Africa for which the UNGA had called repeatedly during the 1960s and early 1970s.[31] Algeria was hardly alone in defending the aspirations of the Saharawi people. To take but one example, Marxist revolutionary

components'. See Georges Abi-Saab, 'De l'évolution de la Cour internationale: Réflexions sur quelques tendances récentes' in Marcelo G Kohen (ed), *Le développement du droit international: Réflexions d'un demi-siècle*, vol 1 (Graduate Institute Publications 2013) 248.

[28] *Western Sahara* (Advisory Opinion) (n 6) 14.

[29] ibid 28.

[30] *Western Sahara* (Exposé oral de M. Bedjaoui, représentant du Gouvernement algérien) ICJ Pleadings vol 4 60 (hereafter *Western Sahara* (Exposé oral de M. Bedjaoui vol 4)).

[31] For the most significant resolution in this vein, see UNGA Res 2229 (XXI) (20 December 1966). It bears noting that Western Sahara has long been presented as marking the 'final stage' in the decolonization of western Africa.

Thomas Sankara made a point of voicing his support for the Saharawi during the course of his attempt to transform Upper Volta (which he renamed Burkina Faso) in the mid-1980s.[32] But the fact that Algeria shared a border with Western Sahara, and that the status of its own Saharan territory had been a bone of contention with France, made it a particularly urgent issue for Bedjaoui and other representatives of Algiers.[33]

Giving voice to Algeria's official position, Bedjaoui argued that self-determination, understood both politically and economically, was 'the cardinal principle of contemporary international law', a 'superior norm' that qualified as *jus cogens*.[34] For peoples subject to foreign rule, it had a 'sacred character'.[35] It was neither a 'favour' nor an act of 'charity', but 'the price of the blood shed for their liberation'.[36] That this was the case had been demonstrated by the Algerian struggle for independence, an experience that had confirmed the political value and logistical feasibility of plebiscites as a means of assessing and registering popular support, not to mention post-independence Algeria's fidelity to self-determination in its pivotal role within the Non-Aligned Movement, Group of 77, Organization of African Unity (OAU), and numerous other organizations.[37] Crucially, Bedjaoui saw this prioritization of self-determination as stemming from a broader and even more far-reaching commitment to eliminating the 'traditional' international law that had been cultivated by the 'successive imperialisms' of European colonial expansion.[38] The larger context within which the case unfolded was an essentially 'transitional' or even 'emergent' one,[39] distinguished by a ceaseless, borderline desperate search for 'a law adapted to the new society', a law that would culminate in the entrenchment of norms of non-intervention and sovereign equality.[40] Self-determination was the centrepiece of this effort, the rock upon which the new, post-colonial international law was to be built—by persuasion whenever possible, by compulsion wherever necessary. This was in keeping with Algeria's long-standing dedication to state sovereignty, as exemplified by President Houari Boumedienne's denunciation of foreign intervention in the Nigerian Civil War at the OAU meeting in Algiers in

[32] So much so that he would repudiate the very possibility of an OAU meeting that did not involve recognized representatives of the Saharawi people. See, for example, Thomas Sankara, 'There is Only One Color–That of African Unity' in Michel Prairie (ed), *Thomas Sankara Speaks: The Burkina Faso Revolution, 1983–1987* (Pathfinder Press 2007) 125.

[33] *Western Sahara* (Exposé oral de M. Bedjaoui vol 4) (n 30) 450.

[34] *Western Sahara* (Exposé oral de M. Bedjaoui, reprèsentant du Gouvernement algérien) ICJ Pleadings vol 5 303, 320 (hereafter *Western Sahara* (Exposé oral de M. Bedjaoui vol 5)).

[35] ibid 304.

[36] ibid 303.

[37] ibid.

[38] *Western Sahara* (Exposé oral de M. Bedjaoui vol 4) (n 30) 451.

[39] ibid 451, 493.

[40] ibid 451.

1968 as a series of 'plots from all sides directed against Nigeria, aiming to disintegrate and shake to its foundations this great African state'.[41]

Significantly, it is in Bedjaoui's oral statement that one encounters the claim that '[i]t is the people who decide the fate of the territory and not the territory who decides the fate of the people'[42]—language which, in slightly different form, is conventionally ascribed to Judge Dillard, who in his separate opinion in *Western Sahara* maintained famously that '[i]t is for the people to determine the destiny of the territory and not the territory the destiny of the people'.[43] This is particularly interesting, given that the Court's opinion makes only passing mention of Algeria's position. Indeed, only Judge Ammoun's separate opinion expressed explicit support for Bedjaoui's central argument.[44] No less tellingly, Bedjaoui was clear that he did not regard self-determination as conflicting with the principle of *uti possidetis* or related ideas about the need to respect 'established' borders, whether in Africa or elsewhere. Rather than undermining territorial integrity and independence, self-determination—conceived as the popular basis for national sovereignty—was fully compatible with *uti possidetis*, a 'criterion of general order' whose basic objective was to reinforce the normative inviolability of non-intervention, facilitate the consolidation of newly established states, ensure the stability of the still delicate post-colonial distribution of territory, and prevent the outbreak of what Bedjaoui, like so many others, dubbed 'fratricidal struggles'.[45]

Of special significance in this regard was *terra nullius*, a nebulous concept whose pedigree is usually traced back to Roman law, the School of Salamanca, and early modern political theories of property but whose popularity among late-nineteenth and early twentieth-century international lawyers owed largely to debates about colonial expansion in Africa and the question of sovereign authority in the polar regions.[46] Advocates of *terra nullius* generally aimed to effect what Bedjaoui termed a 'thingification' (he himself spoke of *réification* and *chosification*) of the world's peoples, normalizing an ostensibly homogeneous world order anchored in European models of national statehood and neutralizing other forms of juridico-political organization.[47] To be sure, Bedjaoui did not deny that 'the evolution of

[41] Quoted in Brad Simpson, 'The Biafran Secession and the Limits of Self-Determination' (2014) 16 Journal of Genocide Research 337, 344.

[42] *Western Sahara* (Exposé oral de M. Bedjaoui vol 5) (n 34) 309.

[43] *Western Sahara* (Advisory Opinion, Separate Opinion of Judge Dillard) [1975] ICJ Rep 116, 122. Rosalyn Higgins has suggested that the dictum, while attractive and oft-quoted, is hampered by a crucial ambiguity: it is unclear, she observes, whether the statement grants such weight to self-determination that no 'legal ties', even those rising to the level of 'complete' sovereignty, would have been enough for Morocco or Mauritania to make out its case. Rosalyn Higgins, 'Judge Dillard and the Right to Self Determination' (1983) 23 Virginia Journal of International Law 387, 390 ff.

[44] *Western Sahara* (Advisory Opinion, Separate Opinion of Judge Ammoun) [1975] ICJ Rep 83, 86.

[45] *Western Sahara* (Exposé oral de M. Bedjaoui vol 5) (n 34) 315–18.

[46] See Andrew Fitzmaurice, 'The Genealogy of *Terra Nullius*' (2007) 38 Australian Historical Studies 1. cf. Lauren Benton and Benjamin Straumann, 'Acquiring Empire by Law: From Roman Doctrine to Early Modern European Practice' (2010) 28 Law and History Review 1.

[47] *Western Sahara* (Exposé oral de M. Bedjaoui vol 4) (n 30) 452. Interestingly, Aimé Césaire had already proposed a similar formula for colonialism: 'My turn to state an equation: colonization = "thingification".'

contemporary society' had brought with it the triumph of 'the state form'.[48] To do so would be to retreat into the romanticism of a pointless 'traditionalism'. In fact, he unwittingly echoed the views of modernization theorists like Walt Rostow when he maintained that '[f]or African society, for African peoples, the passage from forms of social organization characterized as tribal to the state form utilized today is a painful fact of decolonization'.[49] What he openly and resolutely opposed, though, was the claim that *terra nullius* constituted a legally sound, morally justifiable, and conceptually coherent means of resolving territorial disputes of the sort that had generated the *Western Sahara* proceedings. Conventional taxonomies of different modes of acquiring territory were belied by 'permanent ambiguity'.[50] Nineteenth-century distinctions between colonies, condominia, protectorates, and 'barbarous' or 'semi-civilized' states that were subject to capitulatory or unequal treaty regimes had been marked by exceptionally high levels of imprecision, distinctions between such categories being notoriously fluid and porous. Similarly, in the state practice of colonial powers, cession, conquest, prescription, and related techniques of acquisition had never been distinguished uncontroversially from the kind of 'discovery' and occupation that underwrote classical invocations of the right to acquire territory on the grounds that it was 'without master'.[51] As a result, European powers had long characterized some territories as *terra nullius* and others as inhabited and governed by a sovereign power exercising effective control on the basis of little more than expediency, self-interest, and arbitrary appeals to discretionary power. Bedjaoui swept widely with this claim: for the Romans, all non-Roman territory had been *nullius*; during the fifteenth and sixteenth centuries, any territory that could not be attributed to a Christian power had been under constant threat of characterization as such; in the late nineteenth century, Hobsbawm's 'age of empire',[52] much the same could be said for territories deemed 'savage' or 'uncivilized'. 'This observation alone', Bedjaoui quipped sardonically, was sufficient to 'ruin all scientific application of the theory of *terra nullius*'.[53] Insofar as it had any meaning at all, the idea of *terra nullius* was best understood not as a distinct mode of territorial acquisition, one that purported to regulate relations between imperial powers and territories subject to colonialism, but simply as a device for mediating

Aimé Césaire, *Discourse on Colonialism* (Joan Pinkham tr, Monthly Review Press 1972) 21. The elective affinity with Marx's analysis of 'fetishistic' attachment to the commodity form barely needs mentioning. See Karl Marx, *Capital*, vol. 1 (Ben Fowkes tr, Pelican 1976) 163–77.

[48] *Western Sahara* (Exposé oral de M. Bedjaoui vol 4) (n 30) 454.

[49] ibid 451. Note that Bedjaoui took pains in other work to distinguish himself from Rostow and other modernization theorists. See, for example, Bedjaoui, *NIEO* (n 8) 66–68.

[50] *Western Sahara* (Exposé oral de M. Bedjaoui vol 4) (n 30) 454.

[51] ibid; *Western Sahara* (Exposé oral de M. Bedjaoui vol 5) (n 34) 308.

[52] See, famously, Eric J Hobsbawm, *The Age of Empire: 1875–1914* (Pantheon 1987).

[53] *Western Sahara* (Exposé oral de M. Bedjaoui vol 5) (n 34) 308 (de-emphasized from original).

or delimiting competing claims to extra-European territory so as to preclude conflict between European powers.[54]

Far from being an analytically precise and rigorously applied criterion for settling the status of different territories, *terra nullius* was 'an *uncontrollable* weapon',[55] a 'theory . . . *for* colonial powers and *between* colonial powers',[56] useful only to the extent that it was able to limit interimperial conflict, at least under special circumstances. To elevate it to the status of an objectively applicable rule of international law would be to blind oneself to the orientalism in which it was evidently grounded. After all, *terra nullius* made sense only if one believed that international law permitted European states to determine unilaterally whether a specific territory could be said to possess a 'master'.[57] *Terra nullius* 'condemned all differentiation and destined every territory organized in a manner different from the canons of dominant states to that which I term "occupation-conquest"'.[58] As such, it was destined to disappear as part of the process of decolonization that would inaugurate a modern and properly inclusive international law.

As with many other World Court cases, the *Western Sahara* opinion—in which the Court determined that Western Sahara was not *terra nullius* at the time of colonization and that neither Morocco nor Mauritania had enjoyed sufficiently robust 'legal ties' to the territory—came to establish itself as a significant object of scholarly analysis shortly after its release. Commentators sided with different parties, articulated different visions of self-determination, and developed different accounts of the UN's role in the resolution of the dispute, in some cases by suggesting that the case could mark the beginning of increased reliance upon the ICJ by the UNGA and Security Council.[59] The opinion was followed within weeks by the 'Green March', during which hundreds of thousands of Moroccan civilians entered Western Sahara with military support, and the Madrid Accords, which paved the way for Spain's withdrawal, its retention of significant powers over Western Sahara's fisheries and phosphate enterprises, the territory's subsequent occupation by Moroccan (and, until 1979, also Mauritanian) forces, the systematic implantation in the territory of a significant number of Moroccan settlers, and the concomitant marginalization of the Saharawi people's right of self-determination during years of armed struggle.[60] Unsurprisingly, all this complicated matters

[54] This claim is not far removed from Carl Schmitt's infamous assertion that a key 'benefit' of European imperial competition in the extra-European world was the minimization of large-scale conflict on the European continent itself. See Carl Schmitt, *The Nomos of the Earth in the International Law of the* Jus Publicum Europaeum (G. L. Ulmen tr, Telos Press 2003).

[55] *Western Sahara* (Exposé oral de M. Bedjaoui vol 5) (n 34) 308 (original emphasis).

[56] *Western Sahara* (Exposé oral de M. Bedjaoui vol 4) (n 30) 455 (original emphases).

[57] ibid 454.

[58] ibid.

[59] For a concise articulation of this last point, see Mark W Janis, 'International Court of Justice: Advisory Opinion on the Western Sahara' (1976) 17 Harvard International Law Journal 609, 620.

[60] Declaration of Principles (Tripartite (Madrid) Accords (Mauritania/Spain/Morocco)) 1975, (1975) 14 ILM 1512.

considerably, generating a range of opinion. In what was arguably the most influential anglophone legal analysis at the time, Thomas Franck even suggested that the political success of Morocco's historic claim would strengthen Palestinian claims against Israel. 'In due course', he wrote, 'an Arab Palestine will almost certainly advance territorial claims against Israel', adding that the willingness of many states 'to tolerate the use of force to effect a restoration of historic title even in disregard of the wishes of the inhabitants' had already 'undermined Israel's legitimacy'.[61] Rather than likening Morocco to Israel and the Saharawis to the Palestinians, as would have been more logical,[62] this argument inverted the relation by pointing to the use of arguments about historic title (as though Israeli and Saharawi representatives did not also deploy such arguments).[63] Of doubtful merit, such analyses nevertheless spoke to the widespread confusion that was brought about by the Western Sahara dispute.

These confusions continue today. The Polisario Front, other Saharawi organizations, and non-Saharawi advocates of the territory's decolonization maintain that the continued denial of a referendum on the question of independence that would be restricted to 'authentic' Saharawis alone (and would thereby exclude Moroccan settlers) violates the principles of self-determination and permanent sovereignty over natural resources, as well as other segments of international human rights law and international humanitarian law.[64] The political economy of self-determination disputes has always come to the fore with special clarity in the context of decolonization,[65] and the availability of significant oil and gas resources in Western Sahara—resources for which both the occupying Moroccan authorities and the representatives of the Polisario Front have concluded exploratory agreements

[61] Thomas M Franck, 'The Stealing of the Sahara' (1976) 70 American Journal of International Law 694, 720.

[62] Not least because of recent moves in both contexts to elaborate notions of 'earned' or 'conditional' sovereignty, indexing the right to independence of the relevant group (Saharawi and Palestinian) to its demonstrated capacity to govern itself in accordance with pre-specified standards and benchmarks. See Catriona Drew, 'The Meaning of Self-Determination: "The Stealing of the Sahara" Redux' in Karin Arts and Pedro P Leite (eds), *International Law and the Question of Western Sahara* (International Platform of Jurists for East Timor (IPJET) 2007) 96–100.

[63] One can only imagine what Bedjaoui would have made of this argument. For his own opinion on Israel–Palestine, replete with charged (and arguably racist) claims of various kinds, see 'Allocution d'ouverture du Colloque prononcée le 22 juillet 1967 par M. Mohammed Bedjaoui, ministre de la justice, garde des Sceaux' and 'Allocution de clôture du Colloque prononcée le 27 juillet 1967 par M. Mohammed Bedjaoui, ministre de la justice, garde des Sceaux' in *La question palestinienne: Colloque de juristes arabes sur la Palestine, Alger, 22–27 juillet 1967* (Alger: Societé nationale d'édition et de diffusion, 1968) 9, 220.

[64] On issues of resource use and exploitation, generally marginalized but in actuality central to the question of Western Sahara's status, see Jeffrey J Smith, 'The Taking of the Sahara: The Role of Natural Resources in the Continuing Occupation of Western Sahara' (2015) 27 Global Change, Peace & Security 263, 273–78, 283; Ben Saul, 'The Status of Western Sahara as Occupied Territory under International Humanitarian Law and the Exploitation of Natural Resources' (2015) 27 Global Change, Peace & Security 301; and a number of contributions in Arts and Leite (n 62).

[65] Think, for instance, of the extent to which conflicts over resources fed the Congo Crisis and Nigerian Civil War.

with transnational corporations[66]—renders the current status of the territory and its population even more complex than would otherwise be the case. That Rabat has insisted on pressing ahead with the construction of large-scale wind farms throughout the territory adds yet another wrinkle to the story, amplifying concerns that its inhabitants have not been consulted about development initiatives that lend additional power and legitimacy to Morocco's ongoing occupation.[67] In light of these later developments, not to mention Western Sahara's well-earned reputation as one of the last 'unique cases' of failed self-determination,[68] Bedjaoui's attempt to articulate a robust vision of self-determination in The Hague is well worth revisiting, particularly because it may profitably be read as a (dated and insufficient, but nevertheless intriguing) contribution to the effort to bolster the international legal personality of indigenous peoples.[69]

IV. Conclusion

Like many other jurists affiliated with the third world, Bedjaoui has always been a historical jurist, one whose interventions in current legal controversies are informed by and articulated with an eye to context and precedent. It is no surprise, then, that he should have devoted much of his defence of the FLN and his oral statement in *Western Sahara* to detailed exposition of the legal histories of sovereignty, self-determination, *terra nullius*, and a host of related concepts. Bedjaoui drew heavily upon his extensive knowledge of international legal history in both cases, circling back time and again to the Monroe Doctrine, the 1884–85 Conference of Berlin, the various partitions of Poland, the exportation of ideas about *uti possidetis* from Latin America to Africa and Asia, and so on. The international law of decolonization was to a very significant degree the product of far-reaching engagement

[66] See, for example, Alicia Campos, 'Oil, Sovereignty & Self-Determination: Equatorial Guinea & Western Sahara' (2008) 35 Review of African Political Economy 435, 436–37.

[67] Western Sahara Research Watch, 'Powering the Plunder: What Morocco and Siemens are hiding at COP22, Marrakech' (Berlin 2016), <www.wsrw.org/a105x3614 accessed 15 October 2017>. See also Arthur Neslen, 'Africa's Biggest Windfarm Sparks Controversy in the Desert' The Guardian (22 November 2016) <www.theguardian.com/environment/2016/nov/22/morocco-saharan-windfarms-tarfaya-fan-accusations-of-green-plunder?CMP=share_btn_tw accessed 15 October 2017>.

[68] And this notwithstanding the fact that the *Western Sahara* opinion has long been cited in support of self-determination struggles elsewhere, both within and beyond Africa. For Eritrean arguments to this effect, for instance, see Bereket H Selassie, 'The Law of Self-Determination and the Eritrean Case' in *Eritrea and the United Nations and Other Essays* (Red Sea Press 1989) 90. Cf. Dirdeiry M Ahmed, *Boundaries and Secession in Africa and International Law: Challenging* Uti Possidetis (CUP 2015) 176–77.

[69] The rights that international law vested in indigenous peoples at the time of the *Western Sahara* proceedings were, of course, even more limited than those that are currently available. See SJ Anaya, *Indigenous Peoples in International Law* (2nd edn, OUP 2004) 49–57; Luis Rodríguez-Piñero, *Indigenous Peoples, Postcolonialism, and International Law: The ILO Regime (1919–1989)* (OUP 2005).

with the history (and theory) of international law. Bedjaoui recognized this fact and skilfully exploited it.

Even more important, though, is what Bedjaoui's development tells us about decolonization as an international legal project. In 1961, the year of the Evian and Lugrin conferences that paved the way for Algerian independence, a young and ambitious Bedjaoui positioned self-determination at the centre of the 'social', broadly anti-formalistic international law that decolonization was widely regarded as being in the process of generating. In 1975, with the 1966 human rights covenants, the 1970 Friendly Relations Declaration, and the formal inauguration of the NIEO project in 1974 behind him, an older, more mature Bedjaoui sought to follow through on the promise of this position. Bedjaoui ultimately failed to convince the World Court to support his radical denunciation of the very idea of *terra nullius*. Although it was of the view that Western Sahara had not constituted *terra nullius* in the 1880s and 1890s, it was unpersuaded by Bedjaoui's suggestion that the legal consequences of a past situation should be assessed in light of contemporary international law, particularly the modern, post-1945 law of self-determination, rather than on the basis of the law applicable at the time of the situation, including the doctrine of *terra nullius*.[70] Nor, for that matter, did it regard *terra nullius* as a hopelessly imprecise notion, as Bedjaoui clearly did.[71] Nevertheless, what is interesting about *Western Sahara* is the way that Bedjaoui sought to deepen and expand his claim—made as early as *Law and the Algerian Revolution*—that the classical international law of colonialism was incoherent and internally fractured, and therefore had to give way to a fully decolonized international law in which self-determination would enjoy pride of place. For Bedjaoui, the intervening years had confirmed that self-determination was a central front—quite possibly *the* central front—in the struggle for a new international law, a struggle in which he generally

[70] *Western Sahara* (Exposé oral de M. Bedjaoui vol 4) (n 30) 492–93. In effect, Bedjaoui had attempted to revise, if not repudiate, Max Huber's twofold theory of intertemporal law in *Island of Palmas*. On this see Knop (n 7) 158–67; Martti Koskenniemi, *From Apology to Utopia: The Structure of International Legal Argument* (CUP 2005) 456–57; Michelle L. Burgis, *Boundaries of Discourse in the International Court of Justice: Mapping Arguments in Arab Territorial Disputes* (Martinus Nijhoff 2009) 223–24. Acting as arbitrator in *Island of Palmas*, Huber wrote: 'As regards the question which of different legal systems prevailing at successive periods is to be applied in a particular case (the so-called intertemporal law), a distinction must be made between the creation of rights and the existence of rights. The same principle which subjects the act creative of a right to the law in force at the time the right arises, demands that the existence of the right, in other words its continued manifestation, shall follow the conditions required by the evolution of law.' *Island of Palmas* (*Netherlands v United States*) [1928] 2 RIAA 829, 845. The World Court made similar points on a number of occasions; see, for example, *Legal Status of Eastern Greenland* (*Denmark v Norway*) (Judgment) [1933] PCIJ Rep Series A/B No 53; *Case Concerning Right of Passage over Indian Territory* (*Portugal v India*) (Judgment) [1960] ICJ Rep 6, 37. Note that regardless of Bedjaoui's doubts in the *Western Sahara* case, the usefulness of the doctrine of intertemporal law was regularly defended by other third-world legal scholars; see, for example, Ram P Anand, *New States and International Law* (Vikas 1972) 17–18, 20; Taslim O Elias, 'The Doctrine of Intertemporal Law' (1980) 74 American Journal of International Law 285, 305–06.

[71] *Western Sahara* (Advisory Opinion) (n 6) 39–40.

understood himself (rightly or wrongly) to be playing the role of a reform-minded insider 'operating behind enemy lines'.[72]

Martti Koskenniemi has famously suggested that international law effectively met its demise sometime around 1960, thanks in no small part to the ascendance of US-based 'realism' in the new, managerialist, and preponderantly 'post-legal' field of 'international relations'. If it continues to exist at all, Koskenniemi has sometimes hinted, it does so mainly as a kind of ghost-like residuum, a hackneyed reproduction of its formerly vital and relevant self, with even putatively foundational concepts like *jus cogens* and obligations *erga omnes* functioning as little more than kitsch.[73] When all is said and done, this stance is both correct and incorrect. It is justified in the sense that faith in international law's capacity to contribute meaningfully to human progress and prosperity fell sharply after the flush of enthusiasm for supranational institution-building in the 1940s and 1950s, particularly after the normalization (and legalization) of programmatic neoliberalism in the 1970s and 1980s. Among other things, many students of decolonization, particularly those working within the Marxist tradition, have voiced suspicions about the relevance of formal legal sovereignty—or 'what is known as independence', as CLR James once put it[74]—for the concrete struggle to do away with the capitalist mode of production, above all in colonial contexts. However, the argument over-reaches by obscuring the central importance of socialist and non-aligned jurists, who invested heavily in projects to transform and decolonize international law from the 1940s through the 1980s. While it is true that these jurists nearly always prioritized the achievement and consolidation of sovereignty, they frequently sought to revamp or even subvert conventional models of statehood in an effort to universalize decolonization once and for all: from the canonization of social and economic rights to the recognition of international *jus cogens* as a central element of the law of treaties, socialist and third-world jurists were responsible for much of international law's evolution in the latter half of the twentieth century.[75] To be sure, such efforts met with very limited success, and depression—even outright self-loathing—set in fairly quickly in some quarters. Nor, of course, were the enacted changes capable

[72] I borrow this expression from Abi-Saab, 'Praxis' (n 3) 1967.

[73] See especially Martti Koskenniemi, *The Gentle Civilizer of Nations: The Rise and Fall of International Law 1870–1960* (CUP 2001) ch 6. For different facets of this argument see further Martti Koskenniemi, 'International Law in Europe: Between Tradition and Renewal' (2005) 16 European Journal of International Law 113; Martti Koskenniemi, 'Miserable Comforters: International Relations as New Natural Law' (2009) 15 European Journal of International Relations 395; Martti Koskenniemi, 'Law, Teleology and International Relations: An Essay in Counterdisciplinarity' (2012) 26 International Relations 3. See also Dana Schmalz, 'On Kitsch, Zombies and True Love—An Interview with Martti Koskenniemi' *Völkerrechtsblog* (21 May 2014) <http://voelkerrechtsblog.org/on-kitsch-zombies-and-true-love-an-interview-with-martti-koskenniemi/> accessed 15 October 2017.

[74] CLR James, *A History of Pan-African Revolt* (PM Press 2012) 123.

[75] On the (modern) history of international *jus cogens*, see Umut Özsu, 'An Anti-Imperialist Universalism? *Jus Cogens* and the Politics of International Law' in Martti Koskenniemi, Walter Rech and Manuel J Fonseca (eds), *International Law and Empire: Historical Explorations* (OUP 2017).

of impeding the growth of new relations of economic and political domination in recently decolonized states, where national liberation frequently revealed itself to be little more than a placeholder for one or another project of comprador collaboration and bourgeois self-empowerment. After all, even a significantly revamped form of Euro-American international law could in many circumstances facilitate the new state's 'exploitative metropolis-satellite *integration* into the structure and development of the capitalist system which produces underdevelopment'.[76] Even so, they did augment entitlements of resource sovereignty, generate specific rights to development and self-determination under international law, complicate received understandings of compensation in the event of expropriation and nationalization, and contest efforts by Western governments to enforce substantively dubious treaties and other legal instruments that had been concluded with dependent administrations throughout the 'global South'.[77] Revisiting Bedjaoui's shifting engagement with international law invites us to develop a more nuanced appreciation of the tangled struggle to realize the promise of self-determination that was (and *is*) the international law of decolonization.

[76] Andre G Frank, *Capitalism and Underdevelopment in Latin America: Historical Studies of Chile and Brazil* (Monthly Review Press 1967) 142 (original emphasis).

[77] From a growing literature see especially Matthew Craven, *The Decolonization of International Law: State Succession and the Law of Treaties* (OUP 2007); Sundhya Pahuja, *Decolonising International Law: Development, Economic Growth, and the Politics of Universality* (CUP 2011). For the socialist contribution to this process see especially John B Quigley, *Soviet Legal Innovation and the Law of the Western World* (CUP 2007) 133–71; Bill Bowring, 'Positivism Versus Self-Determination: The Contradictions of Soviet International Law' in Susan Marks (ed), *International Law on the Left: Re-Examining Marxist Legacies* (CUP 2008); Bill Bowring, *Law, Rights and Ideology in Russia: Landmarks in the Destiny of a Great Power* (Routledge 2013); Scott Newton, *Law and the Making of the Soviet world: The Red Demiurge* (Routledge 2015).

16

Charles Chaumont's Third-World International Legal Theory

Emmanuelle Tourme Jouannet

I. Introduction

Over the course of the 1950s up until the 1970s, Charles Chaumont introduced a critical approach to international law into the French internationalist doctrine.[1] Often qualified as a third-world approach, it locates itself decisively apart from traditional academic doctrines. Against the background of the disintegration of the old French colonial empire, Chaumont deeply influenced a whole generation of internationalists in France and abroad, especially in the then recently decolonized, francophone part of Africa. In an era characterized by a predominance of conservative thinking in France, he opened up the possibility of envisioning international law in a radically new way by constructing an argumentation that provided a framework for defending the rights of colonized or recently decolonized peoples. He argued in favour of a realistic 'new law' to substitute the abstract 'classical international law', which he deemed a historical product of legal formalism practised by a community of lawyers and politicians of past centuries. However, Chaumont was hardly a maverick in defending the rights of decolonized peoples in the context of decolonization in the 1950s and 60s—a time that was marked by high tensions in France:[2] a whole group of eminent French internationalists have not only supported peoples' right to self-determination, but also theorized a new law *of* development to compensate for the enormous economic and social

[1] This is a completely overhauled version of the text. It is inspired by a report presented during the 'Journée en hommage à Charles Chaumont', which was organized by the University of Nancy II, under the direction of Professor JD Mouton and Professor J Charpentier, March 11, 2003. A first version was published in Emmanuelle T Jouannet, 'La Pensee Juridique de Charles Chaumont' (2004) 37 Belgian Review of International Law 259, as well as later in Emmanuelle T Jouannet and Iulia Motoc (eds), *Les doctrines internationalistes durant les années du communisme réel en Europe: Internationalist doctrines during the years of real communism in Europe* (Société de Législation Comparée 2012).

[2] The very strong controversies that took place can be retraced in two symposiums which were organized by the Société française de droit international: Le droit international économique, Orléans, 1971, Paris, Pedone, 1972 and Pays en voie de développement et transformations du droit, Aix, 1973, Paris, Pedone, 1974.

Emmanuelle Tourme Jouannet, *Charles Chaumont's Third-World International Legal Theory* In: *The Battle for International Law: South-North Perspectives on the Decolonization Era*. Edited by: Jochen von Bernstorff and Philipp Dann, Oxford University Press (2019).
DOI: 10.1093/oso/9780198849636.003.0017

inequalities between the North and the South.[3] However, the first particularity that distinguishes Chaumont lies in the fact that he developed a method of dialectical materialism close to Marxism, which is at the heart of what has long contributed, and still contributes, to dividing internationalists in their way of thinking about the relations between the law and facts as well as the law and hegemonic political and economic power relations[4]. Since it conveyed an intellectual structure close to Marxism, or even Maoism, Chaumont's legal theory has hence been particularly ostracized. It triggered strong hostility in the era of decolonization, which took place in the middle of the Cold War. Another particularity of his position is linked to his personality, his well-known charisma, and the fact that he always acted upon his convictions, which earned him respect even among his opponents.

At this point, it is important to revisit elements of Chaumont's life story, since it was the position he held that gave him the means to spread his ideas beyond France, thus giving them a real international impact.[5] He was an outstanding member of the French Résistance during the Second World War and committed to the French Forces of the Interior (FFI). After the war, he resumed his studies and became a Professor of Public International Law, Faculty of Law at Nancy in 1944, later at the Paris Institute of Political Studies, and finally Faculty of Law at the Free University of Brussels in 1961. His academic activities notably led to the organization of the very famous Reims symposiums (1973-1989)[6] with Monique Chemillier Gendreau, Jean Salmon, Jean Pierre Colin, and others, as

[3] On this analysis I refer to my work Emmanuelle T Jouannet, *What is a Fair International Society? International Law Between Development and Recognition* (Hart 2013) (hereafter Jouannet, *Fair International Society*). It seems that the principle of a law of development has first been introduced in France by André Philip at a conference in Nice, May 27-29, 1965: Association pour le développement du droit mondial (ed), 'L'Adaptation de l'O.N.U. au monde d'aujourd'hui: Colloque international de Nice, 27-29 mai 1965' (1965) 129. It was adapted by Michel Virally, 'Vers un droit international du développement' (1965) 11 Annuaire Français de Droit International 3. A whole group of French-speaking internationalist writers have largely developed this so-called 'third-world' approach at the time: Mohamed Bennouna, *Droit international du développement: Tiers monde et interpellation du droit internat* (Berger-Levrault 1983); Mario Bettati, *Le nouvel ordre économique international* (PUF 1983); Maurice Flory, *Droit international du développement* (Presses Universitaires de France 1977); Edmond Jouve, *Le Tiers Monde dans la vie internationale* (2nd edn, Berger-Levrault 1986); Alain Pellet, *Le droit international du développement* (2nd edn, Presses Universitaires de France 1987); Guy Feuer and Hervé Cassan, *Droit international du développement* (Dalloz 1991); Guy d Lacharrière, *Commerce extérieur et sous-développement* (Presses Universitaires de France 1964).

[4] See Charles Chaumont, 'La relation du droit international avec la structure économique et sociale' in Centre d'Études des Relations Internationales, Faculté de Droit de Reims (ed), *La relation du droit international avec la struture économique et sociale.* Actes de la quatrième rencontre de Reims (1978) (hereafter Chaumont, 'La relation du droit international') < https://www.univ-reims.fr/catalogue/themes/rencontres-de-reims-en-droit-international/gallery_files/site/1/1697/4644/40906.pdf> accessed 20 September 2018.

[5] For a complete biography, see the contribution by Charalambos Apostolidis on the website of the Société française pour le droit international: http://www.sfdi.org/internationalistes/chaumont-charles.

[6] The complete results of the 'Rencontres de Reims' are now available online on the website of the Faculty of Law in Reims: http://www.univ-reims.fr/site/editions-et-presses-universitaires-de-reims/catalogue/themes/rencontres-de-reims,15443.html>.

well as numerous publications, including two courses at The Hague Academy of International Law[7]. Notwithstanding this very prolific academic career, Chaumont also was a great legal practitioner. To briefly summarize the essential points: he was a member of the French delegation to the committee of lawyers in Washington that was charged with preparing the statute of the International Court of Justice in 1945, as well as a member of the French delegation to the conference in San Francisco in 1945. He became a legal counsel for the Ministry of Foreign Affairs from 1949 onwards and the French representative to the Sixth Committee of the United Nations General Assembly (UNGA) from 1946 to 1958, the Special Committee of the United Nations (UN) on the Question of Defining Aggression in 1953, 1956, 1969, and 1970, as well as multiple Committees of the Council of Europe in 1950 and 1951, among others the Committee of Experts that was charged with elaborating the European Convention of Human Rights. At the request of Georges Scelle, he lastly took up the position of Secretary General at The Hague Academy of International Law from 1959 to 1965. During these different posts, he was not only respected for the quality of his expertise, but also for his strong political engagements. For example, at several conferences he strongly denounced the American intervention in Vietnam, which he deemed to be a true aggression, even though this contradicted the official position of the French government.[8] However, his most famous act of resistance was his resignation as legal counsel for the Quai d'Orsay during the Suez crisis, affirming that he fundamentally disagreed with the French intervention. He denounced a 'threefold aggression' (French, English, Israeli) against Egypt and slammed the door behind him.

From a doctrinal point of view, the line of thought he introduced developed into a genuine critical school of thought, today named 'École de Reims' in France—after the place where he organized his symposia, which rallied numerous French academics and students to debate the rights of peoples and the contradictions in international society, as well as his method of critical dialectical analysis. Yet, over a course of history which saw the fall of the Berlin Wall, this intellectual movement seems to have gradually vanished. Chaumont's thinking has since become marginalized in France and his type of approach, closer to Marxism than to liberalism, was demeaned as being a typical aberration of a leftist, third-world-oriented period during the years of decolonization. The last thirty years have effectively seen the complete side-lining of his work and his positions in France, as

[7] Charles Chaumont, 'Nations Unies et neutralité' (1956) 89 Recueil des Cours de l'Académie de Droit International de La Haye 1 and Charles Chaumont, 'Cours général de droit international public' (1970) 129 Recueil des Cours de l'Académie de Droit International de La Haye 335 (hereafter Chaumont, 'Cours général').

[8] Charles Chaumont, 'Analyse critique de l'intervention américaine au Vietnam' (1968) 4 Belgian Review of International Law 61 (hereafter Chaumont, 'Analyse critique').

well as a fundamental shift towards a trend in international law that is informed by pragmatism, the preservation of positivist formalism, and liberal or even conservative thinking.

Despite its relegation in favour of this general trend, Chaumont's legal theory nonetheless constitutes a crucial part of our contemporary history. As such, it makes for an interesting object of study that helps to understand a very peculiar period in France, marked by legal battles fought in favour of decolonization and newly decolonized countries. In a contemporary context, the burden attached to Marxism in international law—due to its historic version of a 'real socialism'—furthermore seems to have been lifted by the very fact of its collapse. The distance of several years allows us to reflect today, in a dispassionate way, on the merits as well as the shortcomings of the doctrines it inspired. It is exactly this most disputed aspect of Chaumont's work, which he used for his actions in favour of decolonized peoples and which, at the same time, explains a great deal of its singularity within the French academia and consequently seems particularly interesting to look at. However, it is vital not to reduce the Chaumont's doctrinal contribution to a simplified application of Marxism or Maoism to international law, aimed at supporting peoples' right to decolonization and at helping them fight all the injustices they have suffered. This would improperly summarize a much more subtle and nuanced reflection, in which Marxism and notably Maoism, at least in 1970, certainly played an important role, but was distinguished in certain ways by Chaumont on the basis of his personal philosophy. Chaumont's individual approach, the apparent freedom of thought that emerges from his writings, and the constant concern for intellectual honesty that characterizes many of his ideas suggest to primarily evaluate his thoughts on international law in their profoundly unique nature. At the same time, it is true that they maintain close links to Marxism, which creates numerous burdensome ambiguities. In this regard they share typical strength and weaknesses of other committed intellectual movements that emerged in France during decolonization

This chapter presents Chaumont's strongest proposals, notably those made with regard to decolonization and peoples' right to self-determination in his 1970 general course at The Hague Academy of International Law, and a brief overview over its most important theoretical underpinnings (Section II). It is his personal analysis of international law that constitutes the most important legacy of his reflections during and in support of the battles fought in favour of decolonization. In this regard, Chaumont took the position of a complete epistemological break from the traditional theory by transposing the use of dialectical analysis to international law. In doing so, he formulated a major twofold critique of international law and the legal theory behind it (Section III). These two criticisms have the common effect of inducing a complete and radical demystification of the legal field, furthering a 'new law' that would serve peoples, states, and human beings.

II. Chaumont's third-world-related objective and adoption of legal positions in favour of the third world

This section breaks down Chaumont's analysis, which is based on one decisive assumption. It then shows how he illustrates this by notably using the question of colonized or recently decolonized peoples' rights. Finally, it explains his search for alternative approaches that might be proposed.

1. The assumption

In his famous course at The Hague Academy of International Law in 1970—a crucial year for drawing lessons from some very recent decolonization processes—Chaumont exposed the extent to which the legal formalism of classical international law did not meet the aspirations of the young third world and the newly decolonized states.

To do so, he first of all had to define what he meant by 'classical' international law in order to subsequently juxtapose it with a 'new' international law. From the outset, he defines the former as the 'entire set of rules and legal concepts in international relations prior to the end of the war of 1914'.[9] He suggested that this classical international law possesses two characteristics that must be taken into account, both of which are just as much intellectual errors as moral failures.

To start with, it is a law of an Eurocentric origin that has only later been extended to the rest of the world—that is America, Africa, Asia, and Oceania—by colonization. Drawing from third-world movements, this feature of imposing itself on entities that could otherwise have developed other systems of external legal relations is being presented as the original sin. Its main flaw lies above all in the fact that it restricted the possible participation of colonized peoples or subjugated states in the creation of the rules of international law, and which are supposed to be applied to them once they have been decolonized. Hence, the second feature of this classical international law, which is just as reprehensible and resides in the fact that between states of the same civilizational culture and with more or less similar economic standards, the rules of classical international law have been adopted and applied formally. Possible social and economic inequalities between states have at no time been taken into account. By showing that classical international law is simply indifferent to these inequalities, Chaumont demonstrates the difference between law and facts, between a *legal equality* among states as proclaimed by international law, and an *enormous inequality of wealth* that can exist between rich and poor countries. He specifies this for every source of law, that

> [. . .] once accepted unanimously, customs apply to all, even if they are contrary to the fundamental interests of some; treaties may be the result of inequality,

[9] Chaumont, 'Cours général' (n 7) 344.

pressure, coercion or violence, but their value still remains untouched due to the formalities they entail; the general principles which are in force are those resulting from the internal law of Western states.[10]

As a consequence, classical international law is seen as an abstract system, indifferent towards, and with no impact on, reality. It is completely detached from the sociological underpinnings of international society and the disparities in wealth and power that exist between the old Western and the young decolonized states[11]. As important as they may seem, notions such as equality, solidarity, and cooperation, even international society, are therefore hollow and disembodied. Worse, they serve as a respected vehicle to further acceptance of and even justify forms of voluntary submission to an utterly unjust classical order and intolerable situations of inequality, non-cooperation, injustice, and suffering to which the young nations of the third world are subjected.[12] Furthermore, Chaumont explains how this formalist law, detached from concrete realities, leads to a general loss of 'credibility' in international law, particularly in the vital areas of the law of war and peace, but also of decolonization and the new law of development. This is because even though the law's appearance might be formal, it only conceals the rule of the strongest over the weak. It is for this reason that the classical law may well seem to aim at agreement and cooperation; in reality however, it is devoted to the rule of the strongest and does not at all take into account existing unequal relations. Chaumont thus expressed his unequivocal opinion on classical international law, saying 'It is a mix of cynicism and illusionism'.[13]

2. The example of colonized or decolonized peoples' rights

In his general course of 1970, Chaumont developed multiple concrete examples to show this illusory and abstract nature of classical international law. The same goes for several articles published before and after that. To support his argument, he examined the distance between the formalism of the law and the factual reality. He did so in a manner where it was always the supremacy of the strongest that prevailed: the rich state, the Western colonizer or former colonizer, or simply a state that became dominant after 1945, that is, the United States and the USSR.[14] By using these examples, Chaumont above all aimed to illustrate how the abstract formalism of classical law continued to haunt contemporary law. He notably cited the burning question of that time about 'acquired rights', a concept that enabled

[10] ibid.
[11] ibid.
[12] ibid 345.
[13] ibid 346.
[14] ibid 345.

the old colonizers through foreign exploitations to preserve their profits from natural resources, which should have been returned to the young decolonized nations by virtue of their sovereignty over these resources. He referred to Mohammed Bedjaoui (in his second report on state succession to the International Law Commission, A/CN.4/216 of May 2nd, 1969, para 12) to address this issue, which was intrinsically linked to the newly decolonized states' right to nationalize and the amount of compensation to be given to foreign companies. Here he attempted to show in a concrete way how legal fiction and the formalism of a theory of acquired right, as well as the idea of a nationalization that calls for integral reparation, would be utterly unjust with regard to the power relations camouflaged by the legal rule, which expose a poor state to particularly powerful private economic interests that are nothing but post-colonial extensions of the old hegemony.[15] Integral reparation would in any case be impossible because if the state nationalizes, it does so precisely because it is poor and wants to recover control over its own sources of wealth. Chaumont subsequently insisted on the notions that would, according to him, become cardinal to a new post-colonial international law and which would necessarily replace old formalist legal fictions. In this vein he strongly argued that 'the protection of private interests does not coincide with the protection of human rights'[16] and that from now on, it will be essential to settle this question using four elements adding up to the equation: 'individuals, states, nations, peoples'. The transition from the old to the new law will require a 'synthesis' of these elements and a balance between them, in a manner that the compensation sought for the nationalization of foreign goods will not constitute an obstacle to the sovereignty of the young state, the rights of its people, and of every individual human being of which it is composed.[17]

Chaumont provided many other concrete examples but the limited framework of this chapter prevents their discussion here. Moreover, as Charalambos Apostolidis aptly puts it: 'On a conceptual level, it is probably the original reflection on the people as being the "creative force" in the dynamics of international law', which represents the most personal element of his thinking and places him at the heart of the debates on decolonization as well as the legal battles that go with it.[18] It is no coincidence that the *Mélanges* which were offered to him also focus precisely on 'The right of people to self-determination'.[19] This chapter thus only elucidates his decisive statements concerning the notion of the 'people', especially

[15] ibid 492.
[16] ibid.
[17] ibid.
[18] Review by Apostolidis (n 5).
[19] Jean Charpentier (ed), *Le droit des peuples à disposer d'eux-mêmes: Méthodes d'analyse du droit international. Mélanges offerts à Charles Chaumont* (Pedone 1984). From Charles Chaumont himself, see also the very important article Charles Chaumont, 'Le droit des peuples à témoigner d'eux-mêmes' (1976) II Annuaire du tiers monde 15 (hereafter Chaumont, 'Le droit des peuples à témoigner d'eux-mêmes'). Also in the Mélanges dedicated to Charles Chaumont you will find a whole series of very interesting articles by French third-world-oriented scolars of the time, including Jean Charpentier,

in the context of the 1950s–1970s. For Chaumont, there was an essential difference between a classical international law that only reflects the will of governments and a contemporary international law in which the 'people' are emerging as a historical reality on the international scene during the era of decolonization. To be precise, he principally aimed at peoples being dominated, colonized, or exploited. To Chaumont, the fact that these peoples suddenly burst onto the international scene brings about a whole series of consequences. First of all, in the field of legal battles, to put the emergence of the colonized peoples at the outset of one's thinking necessarily comes down to favouring 'norms of action' (*normes d'action*) over 'norms of language' (*normes de langage*).[20] Thus, in Chaumont's words, struggles for national liberation are first of all the expression of a *right of peoples to bear witness to themselves*,[21] but in a way that eventually overturns the existing politico-legal categories. If the colonized peoples' struggles for national liberation intensify, they can effectively lead to a change of roles from witness to actor, transform the existing power games and change our conception of the state. This constitutes the basis of the norms of action. That being said, Chaumont was a typical third-world-oriented internationalist of his time because his thinking about groups of peoples being a new actor in international relations does not incite him to propose a dismantling of the state as such, but simply to modify our understanding of it. Like other third-world-oriented scholars following the aspirations of the new decolonized states, he vigorously defended the concept of sovereign nation-states. He went even further by inferring from it that the sovereign state is only 'the expression of a national existence', which (strictly speaking) elevates the nation to the status of a precondition for the state.[22] In doing so, he demonstrated his opposition to any construction that would be genuinely supranational, as the contemporary international law he wanted to consolidate rests entirely on the state and thus on a system of sovereign nation-states. This is what today, in the eyes of new generations, makes him appear as very 'classical'. But in light of the decolonization processes that were taking place at the time, the constitution of the decolonized peoples in sovereign states appeared to him to be the only politico-legal framework that allowed for an expression of the liberty of people. The sovereignty of the state thus represented the most reliable legal translation of the independence that was hard-won by the people under

'Autodétermination et décolonisation'; Françoise Batailler-Demichel, 'Droits de l'homme et droits des peuples dans l'ordre international'; Adrian N'Kolombua, 'L'ambivalence des relations entre le droit des peuples à disposer d'eux-mêmes et l'intégrité territoriale des Etats en droit international contemporain' and finally Monique Chemillier-Gendreau, 'Droit des peuples à disposer d'eux-mêmes et réfugiés'.

[20] Apostolidis (n 5).

[21] Chaumont, 'Le droit des peuples à témoigner d'eux-mêmes' (n 19).

[22] Already developed in an article prior to his course in 1970 and considered to be one of his most important ones: Charles Chaumont, 'Recherche du contenu irréductible du concept de souveraineté internationale de l'Etat', in *Hommage d'une génération de juristes au Basdevant* (Pedone 1960) (hereafter Chaumont, 'Recherche du contenu irréductible'). This was pointed out by Monique Chemillier-Gendreau, 'Introduction' in Charpentier, 'Le droit des peuples à disposer d'eux-mêmes' (n 19) X.

the old colonial occupation, as well as the strongest claim of national liberation movements. Thus, Chaumont is not simply holding on to the legal definition of the sovereign state with regard to its independence, since he very firmly insists on its sociological base—in other words, he argues for the people that constitute the nation. In a very important article, he hence called into question what he calls the 'irreducible content of sovereignty' and concluded that this irreducibility is the vitality of the people.[23] This explains why every state is unique and irreducible, since it is itself based on its unique and singular people. Another subtle, but essential, point is that he associates the rights of the human being with a peoples' right to self-determination.[24] He does so by legally linking individual rights to the existence of a nation, without however clearing up a certain ambiguity that can be traced in many debates and post-colonial texts; even though human rights are recognized, they are still intrinsically linked to the nation-state. Contemporally speaking, this is where the seed of possible human rights oppression is sown in the name of national sovereignty and the interests of the people.

Nevertheless, it is still necessary to identify what constitutes a 'people' and how to prove their existence in order to acknowledge the right to self-determination and to form a sovereign state; this question has constantly preoccupied and opposed the actors of that time and which the UNGA has tried to resolve in a very questionable way by identifying what might be called 'good' national liberation movements, which it then recognized as such, as well as 'bad' ones that were not recognized. Chaumont does not prescribe to this approach. He rather looks for criteria rooted in historical realities, such as the one he lived through during the Nazi occupation of France or the one he was experiencing during the time of anticolonial struggles.[25] That is where he puts his realistic method to work. The criterion he ultimately retains from this is not surprising, given the experiences that he refers to and which, even though they are subject to multiple interpretations, are personal. As a result, he effectively considers that a people are 'identifiable' as soon as the individuals of which it is composed are ready to sacrifice their life for the group. In other words, the very fact that death is possible and even foreseen in order to defend the group makes this group a genuine people, hereby bearing witness to its own existence. It is in this mysticism of sacrifice in the service of the group's cause that he saw as the ultimate and highest proof. However, even if he effectively relies on a concrete and factual element by considering the ultimate sacrifice to defend one's people (and even if this element is deeply rooted in historical battles that have been fought) it still remains eminently debatable if it really an apt criterion to confirm the existence of a people. His approach to determine the existence of a people—and

[23] Charles Chaumont, 'Recherche du contenu irréductible du concept de souveraineté internationale de l'Etat', *Hommage d'une génération de juristes au Basdevant* (Pedone 1960) 149 (hereafter Chaumont, 'Recherche du contenu irréductible').

[24] ibid.

[25] Chaumont, 'Le droit des peuples à témoigner d'eux-mêmes' (n 19) 27.

consequently its right to self-determination—was solely based on the observation of a historical social phenomenon examined from the vantage point of his personal contemporary reality. The people, composed of members that are ready to sacrifice themselves in its name, in a sense *bears witness* to its own existence and to the freedom it must be granted to choose its own way by risking death, or even the extermination of the group as such. He did not want to reduce this criterion to a set of abstract rules that are then to be used to assess reality, which would be characteristic of classical international law. Thus, he attempted to establish a practical description of reality that corresponds to a people in struggle. For Chaumont, a specific historical context containing the criterion of individual or collective sacrifice represents a *contingent* criterion applied on a case-by-case basis to every single movement; it is only then that this ultimate proof for the existence of a people has been furnished.

According to Chaumont, the existence of a people-nation being thus proved, the group is consequently also entitled to the fundamental right to self-determination, if necessary by armed force, and to build a sovereign and independent state. It also automatically follows from it that two main principles of classical international law, which are crucial for decolonized peoples to maintain themselves as states, are applicable to them: the principle of territorial integrity, and the principle of non-interference in the internal affairs of another state. From this comes Chaumont's extremely virulent condemnation of external interventions, notably by former colonizers or great hegemonic powers, which he legally qualified as armed aggressions. The following excerpt from his 1968 article on the American intervention in Vietnam declares:

> The first steps of demystification, in Vietnam as well as in other places where a rich state assumes power over a poor nation, are to understand that no political system has, a priori, an absolute or universal value, but that liberal capitalism, just like authoritarian capitalism or socialism in its various forms, can at the same time be abhorred by some and preferred by others; that peoples' right to self-determination is not linked to a predetermined system; that freedom can have many meanings, and that it is for every people to decide exclusively on its own what meaning it wants to prescribe to it, and that, if it chooses suffering and the risk of extermination over the 'freedom' that it gets offered by foreign soldiers and bombers, it is because this meaning of freedom corresponds better to its right to self-determination than the meaning others want to impose on it from the outside, and consequently also to its testimonial value; and that finally the vocation to intervene which is being claimed by the United States is nothing but an avatar of the 'reason of the strongest' as it has been immortalized by La Fontaine.[26]

[26] Chaumont, 'Analyse critique' (n 8) 85.

3. Solutions for a new international law

By denouncing the formalism and conservatism of classical international law, Chaumont advocated for the emergence of a new post-colonial international law as a result of national liberation struggles and the new perception of the law that they involve, as well as for his own method of dialectical analysis being applied to international law. This chapter simply explains what, according to Chaumont, is part of this new international law.

According to his general course of 1970, it is best to first determine what is *not* part of it. He specified that the term 'new international law' is often associated with Alejandro Alvarez, who had chosen it as a title for his series of books.[27] But Alvarez' new international law was in fact the opposite of Chaumont's. Where the former used an idealist and normative description of a law of solidarity, cooperation, and harmony between states and peoples (and which does not exist yet but is called for in the aftermath of two world wars), the latter linked his new international law to a realist, not idealist, method (mainly based on agreements as a temporary means to resolve, most notably in favour of decolonized peoples, the contradictions that run through international society). It starts from the contradictions that mark international relations and undermine the international society in order to formulate a compromise through an international agreement.[28] The new agreements or customs (which to him simply are tacit agreements) express new legal rules as soon as their underlying power relations change with decolonization and the new contradictions generated by it. Two remarks are necessary here.

Firstly, Chaumont gave a central role to the international agreement as a means to transform classical international law. By attributing this kind of value to the international agreement, Chaumont simultaneously substantiated the sovereignty of the state, as an agreement ultimately is an expression of its will. Since agreements and customs are seen as a decisive means to introduce new legal principles and norms, Chaumont attributed a privileged status to them, to the detriment of general principles of law as well as of *jus cogens*.[29] He obviously argued in favour of abandoning certain customary rules and agreements to which the decolonized states had not given their consent. But he simultaneously mocked those who, at the time, feared a complete abandonment of classic legal principles, since in a certain number of cases the decolonized states had already accepted established norms or had already been integrated into all existing international institutions.

The second remark follows directly from the first one. Since for Charmont the agreement in its express or tacit form (customs) allows for the temporary over-ride

[27] See Alejandro Alvarez, *Le Droit International de l'avenir* (Institut américain de droit international 1916) and Alejandro Alvarez, *Le droit international nouveau dans ses rapports avec la vie actuelle des peuples* (Pédone 1959).

[28] Chaumont, 'Cours général' (n 7) 347.

[29] ibid 462.

of existing contradictions in a new and positive sense, he, like Alvarez, remained an advocate of progress. Like many of his contemporaries, and like all Marxists or Maoists, he believed in social progress—in this case in the progress of international society. But, like them, he saw the 'comprehension of the foundations of international relations, which are foremost shaped by contradictions', and their overcoming by national liberation struggles as well as norms of action that were transposed into customary rules or new agreements, as the root of this progress. This corresponds to a Hegelian dialectical method, but as revisited by Marx and Mao and applied in a materialist and concrete way. During his course in 1970, Chaumont even repeatedly cited Mao Zedong while brandishing his 'little red book'. In one of these citations, he picked up Mao's idea of progress through a successive overcoming of contradictions: 'struggle, failure, new struggle, new failure, new struggle again, and so forth until victory, this is the Marxist law' and 'the world is progressing, no one can change this general trend of history' (citating President Mao Zedong, French edition, ch V).[30] In other words, the dialectical method of analysing the contradictions in international law showed that solidarity can emerge from agreements, hence creating hope for a new law that they bring about. The old, classical international law did so, to a much lesser extent, since it rather concealed contradictions, thus generating grave distortions with reality, which ultimately led to a 'distrust in the law'.[31] With his concrete way of rethinking international law, which offered new epistemological and legal tools both to Western internationalists who, like him, were no longer satisfied with a classic law that proved to be contrary to their most profound convictions, as well as internationalists from decolonized peoples and national liberation movements, Chaumont and others like him raised hopes. As outlined elsewhere, the *whole* period of decolonization raised immense hope in millions of people living in these young nations, who finally saw the light of the day[32]. At this point, it is important to remember that, at the time, the third world created a great movement for a reform of classic international law, even within UN bodies[33].

III. A critical analysis of the theories of international law

As mentioned, Chaumont based his analyses on a detailed materialist dialectical examination of international law. Instead of elaborating on the details of theoretical foundations of his work, the remaining part of this contribution focuses on

[30] ibid 348.
[31] ibid.
[32] Jouannet, *Fair International Society* (n 3) 19–23.
[33] ibid.

two concrete and interrelated aspects of his work and which are of particular relevance in this context. First, it looks at how one major strand of Chaumont's work elaborates in detail on how doctrinal discourses on international law can entail an aggravation of the phenomenon of mystification. To oppose the ideology that is being transported by these doctrinal currents, it is necessary to reconstruct a scientific discourse that does not itself become a prisoner of the very same ideology it denounces. The next section then addresses the question of the distinct nature of Chaumont's discourse as well as the role he assigns to himself as an academic lawyer committed to the cause of dominated peoples. At this point, the great third-world thinker finds himself prisoner of the weaknesses of his thinking.

1. Challenging traditional currents

The general principle of his challenge was quite simple, because it built on the same theoretical foundations like the one developed for international law. It is not only the law that amounts to an ideology—there are also all the so-called sciences of law and doctrinal currents that aided the diffusion of a formalist international law and thus directly contributed to the dissimulation of power relations and socio-economic structures that work to the detriment of oppressed peoples and are the ultimate explanation for their condition. Doctrine is therefore not neutral, as positivists claim, but is itself an ideological instrument serving individual interests. For Chaumont, revealing the ideological nature of doctrine did not as such amount to a critique; rather, it was the dissimulation of this ideological nature that represented the major fault. Hence, the twofold consideration found in his work.

First, in some way, certain doctrinal currents continued to maintain a vision of international law which did not entirely correspond to the positivist reality of contemporary international law any longer. As a result, they worked with two successive mystifications: first, throughout the period of classical international law, they contributed to shaping a law that was formalist, unjust, and profoundly unequal; then, once classical international law began to evolve positively into a contemporary international law, more representative of the interests of all and especially of the colonized peoples, they continued to develop a classical vision of the law that masked this contemporary progress. Particularly enlightening of his critical analysis, in 1970 Chaumont declared in his course: 'Even if classical law is disappearing as a historical phase, it is not vanquished as a method or a vision'.[34]

Secondly, this is also the reason why Chaumont seemed much more severe with respect to doctrines that, according to him, profoundly concealed their ideological nature under the guise of science, justice, and morality, namely, the idealist and

[34] Chaumont, 'Cours général' (n 7) 356.

naturalist doctrine. On the other hand, he hence gave credit to a realist positivism that did not consistently try to hide his true nature and which, above all, became less contemptuous in the analysis of its object. It becomes evident upon a more detailed examination of Chaumont's critique vis-à-vis different doctrinal currents that he effectively treated them in an unequal manner.

The most severe critique is without doubt directed at the sociological objectivism of Georges Scelle.[35] It demonstrates that this objectivist sociologism stands exactly for what Chaumont condemned: a formalist theory of international law. It uses an idealist and non-realist conception of international law, but refuses to be categorized as such. In doing so, Scelle becomes totally lost in his allegedly realist analysis of the law by denouncing one of the most fundamental realities of international law—the sovereign will of the states—as a useless fiction. He is therefore not only guilty of defending an idealist law that does not exist, by presenting it as positive law, but mainly of having completely misunderstood the reality of contemporary international law. Chaumont's allegation against Scelle was thus not based on the principle of a sociological analysis as such, meaning the principle of an analysis of the law as a social fact, but on having developed an idealist argumentation under the guise of an ostensibly sociological approach. Simply put: he rejected Scelle's sociologism to a lesser extent than his dogmatic objectivism and the dualist presentation of a positive and an objective law, as *jus gentium* and not as a law of states. This allowed him to oust naturalism and thus the part of idealism, which was underlying such a fundamental dualism. In a similar vein, Chaumont moreover denounced the not only ideological, but also deeply erroneous character of other doctrines that misconceived the major factor that is the state's will. This is how authors like Quadri or Jenks, who attempted to transfer the will into social structures, also fell into the twofold trap of idealism and formalism, as there is no evidence of an international society having the capacity to foster a collective will as a source of law[36]. At the same time there are nonetheless links between Scelle's sociologism and Chaumont's realist sociological analyses that deserve a closer look. That is also why Chaumont gave credit to classical state voluntarists for exposing (at a certain point in time in a straightforward manner) the law in its unequal form, as well as for the general cognisance of the fact of an insurmountable sovereign will. He

[35] ibid 345 and the complementary observations on the official doctrine: see Robert Chavin, 'Le droit international tel qu'il a été enseigné: Notes critiques de lecture des traités et manuels (1850-1950)' in Charpentier, 'Le droit des peuples à disposer d'eux-mêmes' (n 19). This is despite the fact that he pays tribute to Scelle in an article published as part of his Melanges: Charles Chaumont, 'Perspectives d'une théorie du Service public à l'usage du Droit international contemporain', in *La technique et les principes du droit public: Etudes en l'honneur de Georges Scelle*, vol 1 (LGDJ 1950) 115–16. Sociologism brings them closer together but objectivism and voluntarism is what divides them. In any case, Chaumont remains much closer to Jules Basdevant than to Georges Scelle or Louis Le Fur. See Chaumont, 'Cours général' (n 7) 360.

[36] Chaumont, 'Cours général' (n 7) 361.

even fiercely defended voluntarism and positivism against a so-called objectivism; it was this that finally introduced elements of irrationality.

Incidentally, the approximation to these three contemporary currents of positivism, voluntarism, and realism is not devious. While not subscribing to the philosophical current as such, from positivism Chaumont retains the methodological objective of exclusively holding on to observable, positive facts. With voluntarism he shared the conception of legal norms being essentially thought of as international agreements. This vision was reflected by Chaumont, the same as by voluntarists, in a support of realism in its French version.[37]

Since the emergence of international law, the French realist current has continuously attempted to refocus the debate on concrete realities and to assert the acceptance of sovereign acts, notably of the will as primary and fundamental expression of this sovereign liberty. Consequentially, Chaumont subscribed to this realist-voluntarist tradition.[38] More precisely, he shared with voluntarists this primacy of the states' will in the genesis of a norm, but he deducted a conflicting vision of international relations from it, which moved him closer to realism in the proper sense. To Chaumont, this nuance is fundamental: *the law does not only stem from a congruence of wills, but from the power relation of which this congruence is the expression.*

The approximation to these currents is nevertheless only partial, since it does not superpose the intrinsically dialectical scope of Chaumont's analysis. For Chaumont, the main shortcoming of positivist voluntarism was its misjudgment of the fundamental fact that international law follows a constant dialectical development. As a result, this current only offers a static version of international law in which the international realities are depicted in a rigid manner without taking into account the phenomenon of contradictions. As a result, voluntarist positivism is also formalist because it confines itself to the 'observation of legal frameworks without considering the need to acknowledge that contradictions exist'[39]. In other words, the limitation of classical voluntarism lies with the fact that it analyses the states' will in an abstract, not a concrete, manner, without taking into account neither the infrastructures which determine them nor their heterogeneity. This also explains why an international agreement is not, as put forward by classical doctrine, a simple congruence of wills, but a compromise between concrete and heterogeneous wills. It is also to be recognized that the wills that make for an agreement are conditioned by infrastructure. By virtue

[37] On the difference between French and American realism see Emmanuelle T Jouannet, 'French and American Perspectives on International Law: Legal Cultures and International Law' (2006) 58 Maine Law Review 291.

[38] It becomes evident here that Chaumont has without doubt been influenced by his mentor in international law, Jules Basdevant, whom he cites on multiple occasions; see, for example, Chaumont, 'Cours général' (n 7) 365. See also Chaumont, 'Recherche du contenu irréductible' (n 23) 114–15.

[39] Chaumont, 'Cours général' (n 7) 344–45.

of revealing its shortcomings and demonstrating what really is 'behind' international law, the dialectical method thus ultimately replaces the method of logical analysis which is common to these voluntarist authors. Chaumont finally reduced positivist voluntarism to its dimension as an ideological apparatus which, as a superstructure, was conditioned by the dominant economic and social system. He denounced its theoretical inadequacy of not getting to the heart of the reality of international law due to its ideological blindness. This conclusion is not surprising, and provides an insight into how and why even in this regard, Chaumont placed himself in a radically different and not simply complementary position to positive analyses. But even though the epistemological and methodological break that has been unfolded earlier for 'international law' as an object of analysis produces the same effects with regard to the analysis of the 'international doctrine', it does nonetheless not solve the difficulties which come along with such a perspective. This leaves the age-old question of how Chaumont evaluated the status of his own discourse on the law and in what role (as a researching and practising lawyer and as a scholar) committed to the defence of peoples' right to self-determination he sees himself.

2. The problem of the subject and status of Chaumont's discourse

Again, the essential aspect of his contribution can be characterized as a doctrinal engagement with autonomous scientific and practical objectives. In the critique Chaumont formulated with regard to the law and the discourse on the law, there is an earnest attempt of emancipation from the law in its established form, from the analyses that have been made, as well as a rejection of the formalism of international law and the conservatism of doctrines. This desire for emancipation even led Chaumont to constantly claim a total doctrinal independence. It is striking how often he insisted on recalling his refusal both of Marxist orthodoxy as well as of being labelled in any other way. In noting this persistent aspiration not to see his thinking entrapped in specific doctrinal currents, the effort he has made in order to think independently of international law is clear. He also claimed to be doing scientific work by contrasting the idealism and formalism of other currents with his dialectical analysis of international law. Lastly, he not only positioned himself as a theoretical subject or thinker, but also as a practical subject obliged to defend a certain idea of international law, a committed actor who supports struggles, notably of peoples that are currently or have recently been decolonized. For Chaumont, whose whole life mirrored his commitment in favour of a certain idea of the law and his role in society, taking committed action to defend a specific idea of international law is a *fait acquis*. The idea of organizing a series of meetings with JP Colin and M Chemillier-Gendreau to discuss this new way of conceptualizing

international law was a striking example because it bears witness to the fact that, beyond the purely theoretical concern of carefully undertaking this decoding of the existing law, there also is an underlying desire to form a group that is committed to this cause; a group that is certainly open to external personalities, but which nonetheless serves as an necessary tool of collective action.

However, even if these reflections of Chaumont concerning his own status can be clearly defined in this way, they immediately create a difficulty. It does not become clear from the scheme he described how an ideology could effectively emerge from it that is dedicated to the rights of peoples and not instrumentalized by the dominating states of the international society. Further, how can one initiate a scientific discourse on suppressed or colonized peoples that is not totally ideological like the other doctrinal discourses, and how can one take sides with a particular evolution of international law that favours exactly those peoples? These are recurrent objections to any argumentation of the kind that Chaumont developed and applied to international law. But this chapter sticks to an easy and well-known critique; Chaumont's positions concerning his work are rather explored here in order to determine their own logic and the entirety of their implications.

As for the nature of his work, it has already been emphasized that, from the beginning, Chaumont chose a perspective of demystification of international law for his analyses. This affirmation must however be understood and substantiated against the backdrop of his particular epistemology. Let us recall that, starting from the moment in which the norm as the 'ought' is established, it also becomes part of the 'is', since it is part of the psycho-sociological reality of the moment and thus also integral part of reality. In addition, the legal norm also recreates the 'is' in form of a consecutive contradiction. The 'ought' can thus also be read through the lens of it being part of the 'is' as a positive fact and of recreating it. Chaumont stuck exactly and exclusively to a study of the material reality of the modes of production, disappearance, and impact of legal norms, as well as to a study of the norms themselves in their dimension as social facts. Let us also not forget that he rejected any attempt to search for a definition and a specific criterion of legality in order to not debate anything but its manifestation as a positive fact and the dialectical process of contradictions which explained the life of a legal norm. He deliberately avoided any study on what precisely could specify legality without reducing it to its material reality, not as a natural, but as a social, positive fact. By insisting on such a study of the material reality of legal norms, there would however be no place to distinguish between a science of the 'is' and of the 'ought'. Consequently, studying an object that is as essentially normative as international law, characterized by 'ought' dimensions, becomes a sociological enterprise. This ultimate absorption of the study of international law by the study of sociological facts at this point conveys a radical sociologism from which Chaumont did not seem to shy away, but rather which he implicitly claimed to be the only possible way to understand the momentary and transitory truth of

international law.[40] He certainly did not use the term sociologism, except in a negative sense aimed at criticizing his objectivist excesses. As mentioned, he developed a realist theory of international law, which distances itself from what can be called the sociological current in law at that time in France, the most characteristic trait of which is its anti-state orientation. But terminology is not important here, because it is in any case about demonstrating the manner in which he reduced the study of international law to one of its external and material factors of comprehension within a particular, given, socio-economic system. As others have pointed out it is also worth noting that his theory of law was actually a *sociology* of law. This conclusion is by no means pejorative and does not a priori compromise the scientific nature of his approach. It is a sociology of international law which can, with familiar reservations, be qualified as a Marxist sociology of law. It also is a historical sociology of international law in the sense that it does not study law in its purely sociological dimension, but from a socio-historical perspective, which blends the synchronic angle of sociologists with the diachronic angle of historians. Chaumont was a renowned lawyer who undertook several strictly legal analyses, notably in his function as a legal counsel. That is why only his approach to international law as an overarching project, in which he resorts to dialectical analysis, and studies directly linked to it, are part of his sociology of law. With this in mind it might also be possible to resolve a certain misunderstanding. Taking up one of the oldest criticisms of Marxism, some of the members of the École de Reims reproached Chaumont for not having reconstructed a real doctrine of law. However, even though it is perfectly true that he did not accomplish such a reconstruction, there is no reproach as he never really pretended to do so. The criticism brought forward against him hence is partially inadequate, as it does not take into account the self-sufficiency of Chaumont's analyses and the coherence of his overall scientific project. Since Chaumont's project consisted in unearthing a truth that is hidden behind the world of law and which explains the purpose and the life of legal norms, this disclosure is in itself enough. It does not lead to the reconstruction of another theory, because it was not essential to this project to develop a new system of thought, but only to describe an evolving process. One should also refrain from characterizing his work only in light of its methodological aspect, since his dialectical method was rooted in certain foundations of Marxist theory: the ultimate primacy of the economic and social as infrastructure and the retention of a non-hyper-rationalist historicism. His scientific project thus essentially remains an epistemological project of understanding the international legal reality through a dialectical reduction of law and internationalist doctrines to their status of simple ideological instruments.

[40] This is the exact same kind of reduction that is being undertaken by Evgeniĭ B Pashukanis, *La théorie générale du droit et le marxisme* (Jean-Marie Brohm tr, Etudes et documentation internationales 1970) 83 et seq, even though he, like Chaumont, criticizes sociological theories. This seems inevitable and at the same time logical with this type of approach.

These few considerations allow us to conclude on the nature of Chaumont's work, but they do not help us in dealing with the issue concerning his definitive status as a committed scholar. Two questions come up here. It is first of all an unresolved question how Chaumont could justify his own doctrinal positions, even those of sociological nature, if his own discourse on the law inevitably seemed entangled in an ideological process. Secondly, how was Chaumont able to reconcile his doctrinal project with the role he saw himself in as a lawyer? As mentioned, the quintessence of his analyses shows that no legal discourse can be neutral, meaning that the position of ideological neutrality adopted by classical positivism and normativism constitutes a theoretical and practical error. It amounts to a stabilization and consolidation of international law in its current form, which is unjust and unequal. A lawyer can thus not adopt the position of a positivist lawyer-technician who is content applying the law as it presents itself to him: he needs to discover what is 'behind the law' and reveal the process of ideological camouflage that legal norms imply. Consequently, he also must denounce a law that continues to serve the interests of the most powerful. Of course, this does not mean resorting to revolutionary action, but it nonetheless conveys the necessity to be a somehow committed, maybe even militant, lawyer, ready to act upon reality with the help of legal analyses and knowledge. In order to better respond to the questions that are formulated here, it is necessary to return to Chaumont's discussion on the notion of ideology and its relation to the scientific discourse, which has been at the heart of many discussions at the Reims symposiums, and is in effect at the same time central and problematic as it constitutes the starting point from which the status of the theoretical and practical subject has to be conceived. Chaumont believed that there are two possible functions of ideology: ideology as the dominant's instrument of oppression and as a prospective means of action for the dominated; ideology as a 'justification of class domination' and ideology as 'justification of class struggle'.[41] This classical dichotomy of ideology is absolutely essential for Chaumont's thinking. He even specified that this functional duality of ideology must be replaced by a dynamic dialectical perspective that enables the contrasting of a classical international law of conservative and alienating ideology, with a new international law built upon a subversive and liberating ideology. Both cases certainly concern ideologies which conceal special interests, but it is undeniable that there is a 'bad' ideology, meaning the conservative one, and a 'good' ideology, that is, the liberating one. It is easily understandable to what extent this dichotomy was fundamental for Chaumont, because it allowed him to justify the positive value given to certain contested claims in international law, in particular, those concerning peoples' right to self-determination. By furthering the understanding of dialectical phenomena and making new proposals via the famous 'norms of action'

[41] Chaumont, 'La relation du droit international' (n 4) 8.

of colonized or decolonized peoples, it also allowed him to justify why it is necessary that it prevails over the conservative power of the existing law and official doctrine. To put it differently: it justifies the theoretical and practical choices that a lawyer has to make.

As interesting as it may be, this effort also entails two difficulties to which there is still no solution. First of all, it is ultimately not clear how Chaumont was able to establish the distinction between the two ideologies. If it is the deployment of economic power relations that explain the ideologies, how is it possible to criticize one and not the other without reintroducing a value judgement for which there seems to be no foundation? Reintroducing the problem of what is just and what is not cannot be done without reference to an ideal—a certain idea of what is better—which again seems to contradict his understanding of reality. To avoid this difficulty, one could in fact, like Chaumont, suggest that it is the evolution of history and of the economic and social forces that necessarily makes it possible to disseminate a good ideology, hence leading to this result. But even if that is the case, Chaumont's philosophy cannot escape the pitfall of such a historicization of his standpoint, which makes the distinction between the two ideologies particularly delicate and simply doubles the difficulty. If one is effectively to take into account the emergence of a liberating ideology, that of a right of the peoples, as an observable fact, does this also mean that every ideology that resists the positivist conservative ideology must be considered desirable, even if it is not based on the right of the peoples? As an example, take Chaumont's criterion of individual sacrifice as proof of the existence of a 'people' entitled to a right to self-determination. What would he think about today's acts of terrorism to which certain groups resort in a sacrificial manner, placing them entirely outside the law and international society? Moreover, it also follows from this that the status and position of a lawyer are not more certain than those of a practical subject, because if every discourse is ideology, than it makes no difference if it is good or bad ideology: if one is doing science, it still remains nothing but ideology. There is no established demarcation between science and ideology.

This impasse seems insurmountable to a point that even in Chaumont's works, at least to our knowledge, there is nothing to be found in support of an answer to this twofold question. We thus have to leave it open here, only remarking that it cannot be understood without taking into consideration his rejection of hyper-rationalist visions of history as well as his project of furnishing a dialectical explanation of legal phenomena. However, it is impossible not to highlight the courageous, but also contradictory (and in the end tragic) character of this attitude. Its courageous aspect lies in the fact that by committing himself in such a manner, Chaumont was inevitably marginalizing himself and was consequently banned from a certain scientific community. At that time, he exposed himself to extremely violent criticism—the echoes of the last convulsions of the French colonial empire. Its contradictory character followed from his fundamental hesitation between two

positions: the position of the legal scientist and the committed or militant lawyer. As an observer of the dialectical reality at work, he basically accepted limiting his work to the unveiling of this process, renouncing any desire to also transform it, since it is from this process that the solution and the inversion of power games in favour of the rights of the peoples and the oppressed has to emerge. On the other hand, awareness of the relations of inequality through his work of scientific analysis contributed to his work for a more just society. This poses an insurmountable contradiction, which Chaumont also directly acknowledged in consecutive remarks. This might be the proof that the epistemologies of the 'north' have run out of air, notwithstanding their emancipatory self-concept, since they continue to imply a standardizing view of reality, based on a dialectical historical evolution taking place before our eyes. There is a scientism inherent in Chaumont's thought here, even though he would have wanted to distance himself from it, and which besides gives his thinking a strongly Eurocentric character.[42] The tragic character of this attitude finally stems from a fact that could only have affected a man as lucid and sincerely engaged as Chaumont: it concerns the complete and utter failure of historical communism.

* * *

In conclusion, it has to be emphasized to what extent Chaumont's work during the period of decolonization was fundamental. Concerning his contribution to the history of international theory in general, his work can be read as an important moment in it, since it represents not only one of the most sophisticated transpositions of the method of dialectical analysis to international law, but also the bedrock of a school of thought which is still extant, even if marginalized. It is a doctrinal current that, in any case, feels more comfortable, or is being listened to more intensely, rather in historical moments of great confrontation than in a more stable era. Without doubt, it is precisely through this school of thought that Chaumont's work has indirectly helped to influence part of the French doctrine: by comforting its contemporary orientation towards realism, but also by making the old French colonial empire and all of its conservative representatives apprehend the necessity of accepting the liberation of its old colonies. That is also why it is equally interesting to delve into Chaumont's relation to Marxism. With the collapse of real communism and the emergence of the unacceptable ethical and political consequences of doctrinal Marxism, part of his thinking effectively became obsolete and was doomed to fail. Even though this finding is undeniable, the intellectual journey Chaumont undertook nevertheless retains a manifest utility. It was a journey that

[42] See the famous critique of these 'epistemologies of the North' in favor of a 'sociology of the emerging countries' by Boaventura de Sousa Santos, *Epistémologies du Sud: Mouvements citoyens et polémique sur la science* (Desclée de Brouwer 2016).

effectively seemed to be motivated by a twofold intention. First, the strong desire to break with formalism of any type, which is based on Marxist analyses and dedicated to first and foremost serve the peoples and not the states. However, it is tempered by an equal will of permanent comprehension, of contestation of the concepts and methods being used, as well as of the difficulties that his own combat in favour of anticolonial struggles called forth. At a time marked by anxieties caused by globalization, Chaumont is already beginning to regain a certain critical audience,[43] It is thus most certainly not for the assumptions of his thinking, the validity of which is strongly questionable today, but for his battles in favour of the peoples and the contestation and doubts that marked him, and which must continue to nourish our view of contemporary international law, that this great lawyer will continue to be treasured.

[43] See, for example, Monique Chemillier-Gendreau and Yann Moulier-Boutang (eds), *Le droit dans la mondialisation: Une perspective critique* (Actes du Congrès Marx international II, Presses Universitaires de France 2001) 109 and Emmanuelle T Jouannet, 'Regards sur un siècle de doctrine française du droit international' (2001) 46 Annuaire Français de Droit International 1, 22 et seq.

B. Regional Perspectives

17

Literal 'Decolonization'

Re-reading African International Legal Scholarship through the African novel

Christopher Gevers

> Each generation must discover its mission, fulfill it or betray it, in relative opacity . . . .[W]e must shed the habit of decrying the efforts of our forefathers or feigning incomprehension at their silence or passiveness. They fought as best they could with the weapons they possessed at the time, and if their struggle did not reverberate throughout the international arena, the reason should be attributed not so much to a lack of heroism but to a fundamentally different international situation.
>
> Fanon, 'On National Culture', *The Wretched of the Earth (1959).*

I. Introduction

For a number of reasons, the opening lines of Fanon's 1959 essay are an instructive place to begin this chapter on decolonization and African international legal scholarship. First, they suggest an ethics of reading the 'efforts of . . . forefathers'—that is, sympathetically but not uncritically (as Fanon himself proceeded to demonstrate)—one that this chapter takes up in respect of the scholarly efforts of African international lawyers during 'decolonization' (ie, 1955–1975). Second, Fanon calls attention to the need contextualize these efforts—including their apparent 'silence or passiveness'—in order to take into account both the 'weapons . . . possessed at the time' and the prevailing 'international situation'; an attentiveness to context that similarly informs this chapter. Third, central to Fanon's sympathetic critique of 'colonized intellectuals' (ie, writers, artists, poets) was their problematic use of 'techniques and a language borrowed from the occupier'[1]—or *colonial forms*—a critique taken up by Ngugi's wa Thiongo and extended here to the relationship between African international lawyers and their own *colonial form* (ie, international

[1] Frantz Fanon, *The Wretched of the Earth* (Grove Weidenfeld Press 1963) 160 (hereafter Fanon, *The Wretched of the Earth*).

Christopher Gevers, *Literal 'Decolonization'* In: *The Battle for International Law: South-North Perspectives on the Decolonization Era.* Edited by: Jochen von Bernstorff and Philipp Dann, Oxford University Press (2019).

DOI: 10.1093/oso/9780198849636.003.0018

law). Finally, Fanon's essay was provoked by the 1959 Second Congress of Black Writers and Artists in Rome, which in turn inspired the 1962 Conference of African Writers of English Expression in Makarere—an event that is central to the rereading of African international legal scholarship proposed here.

The chapter will proceed as follows: Section II briefly sets out the reading of African international legal scholarship, which divides it into two 'streams'—'weak' and 'strong'[2] (or 'contributionist' and 'critical')—focusing in particular on the work of TO Elias and Umo Umozurike as archetypes of these two 'streams'. The chapter seeks to problematize this characterization of African international legal scholarship by re-reading it *through* African literature.[3] In order to do so, Section III returns to founding moments of these two disciplines, which took place in the midst of 'decolonization': the 1961 World Peace Through Law conference in Lagos and the 1962 Conference of African Writers of English Expression in Makarere. Reading the work of African international lawyers through their literary counterparts reveals how *initially* both adopted a 'literal' account of decolonization; one that did not consider the ways in which their respective *colonial forms* might need decolonizing themselves, instead focusing on 'Africanizing' the content of their craft and confident of their ability to do so. In the years that followed, African writers returned—literally and figuratively—to Makarere to reconsider the colonial 'content of the form' and re-define 'decolonization' in the process; Ngugi wa Thiongo concluding in the late 1970s that true decolonization required nothing less than abandoning the English novel altogether. The chapter argues that reading the work of Elias and Umozurike through these debates among African writers renders a more nuanced account of African international legal scholarship and decolonization.

Section IV extends this analogy by placing the contemporaneous works of these international lawyers and writers in their broader political and intellectual contexts. A close reading of Elias' *Africa and the Development of International Law* (1972) (hereafter *Africa and International Law*) and Umozurike's *International Law and Colonialism in Africa* (1979) (hereafter *International Law and Colonialism*) reveals how these texts were structured by both their changing post-colonial 'presents' (Fanon's 'different international situation[s]'), and their prevailing intellectual contexts (Fanon's 'weapons . . . possessed at the time'). In particular, reading Elias's and Umozurike's radically different histories of international law with an eye

[2] James Thuo Gathii, 'International Law and Eurocentricity' (1998) 9 European Journal of International Law 184 (hereafter Gathii, 'International Law and Eurocentricity').

[3] While international law has not been a focus of the turn to 'law and literature' generally, in recent times scholars from both side of the disciplinary divide have made attempts to remedy this oversight. Although the scholarship remains in its infancy. See Joseph R Slaughter, *Human Rights Inc.: The World Novel, Narrative Form, and International Law* (Fordham University 2007); Ed Morgan, *The Aesthetic of International Law* (University of Toronto Press 2007) and Christopher N Warren, *Literature and the Law of Nations, 1580–1680* (OUP 2015).

to their literary and historian contemporaries goes some way towards explaining the comparative 'weakness' and 'strength' of their scholarship.

The analogy between African international lawyers and writers, however, cuts both ways. While context might dampen the critique of Elias' scholarship in the 1960s, it heightens that critique in the 1970s, when Africa writers responded critically to changing political and intellectual contexts, and international lawyers for the most part did not. The final section of the paper discusses how the vastly different influences of the 'Biafra War' on Elias and Achebe, and Umozurike's conservative turn in the 1980s, call attention to the limits of 'contextualization', and the importance of biography and perhaps discipline.

II. Introduction: the two streams of African international legal scholarship

According to James Thuo Gathii, the body of international legal scholarship by African scholars can be divided into two 'streams'. On the one hand, there is the 'weak' stream of African international legal scholarship, which 'is largely complimentary of the liberatory claims of principles such as self-determination as uncompromising tenets of world peace and indicators of the rejection of the colonial experience', and 'uncritically endorses the United Nations agenda in areas such as human rights and the right to development as having potential and being of continuing benefit to the formerly colonized countries'.[4] Central to this scholarship is a 'contributionist' historiography, which '[re-writes] international legal history to assail Eurocentricity and accommodate African participation', while backgrounding 'the imperial and mercantilist character of international law'.[5]

The scholarship of Taslim O Elias—Africa's most successful professional international lawyer and who became the first President of the International Court of Justice from the continent—is emblematic of this 'weak' anti-colonial stream. In an immense body of work spanning four decades, decolonization generally, and the specific anti-colonial projects of his third-world counterparts received little attention. When considered, they were placed within the story of 'universal' international law generally, and the rise of the United Nations (UN) in particular.[6] In his seminal *Africa and International Law*, Elias proclaims the UN 'the best forum for the airing of grievances about decolonization, apartheid, racial discrimination and colonialism';[7] then, having highlighted its founding principles and commitment to

[4] Gathii, 'International Law and Eurocentricity' (n 2) 184, 189.

[5] James Thuo Gathii, 'Africa' in Bardo Fassbender and Anne Peters (eds), *The Oxford Handbook of the History of International Law* (OUP 2012) (hereafter Gathii, 'Africa').

[6] See, for example, 'Preface' in Taslim O Elias, *Africa and the Development of International Law*, V (Oceana Publications Inc. 1972) (hereafter Elias, *Africa and International Law*).

[7] ibid 24.

sovereign equality among states, says that 'there is little else that the new African states, jealous of their newly won independence, could wish or hope for'.[8] Similarly, the issues of apartheid, racial discrimination, and colonialism are understood through the lens of the UN, when they are discussed at all. For example, Elias discussed the *South West Africa* cases—the attempts by African states to legally challenge South Africa's presence in that territory, a colonial vestige—as part of the development of the International Court of Justice (ICJ), and not the project of decolonization,[9] while the project to create a New International Economic Order (NIEO)—the centrepiece of third-world international lawyers during the 1970s—was notably absent in his scholarship until the 1980s.[10]

To a large extent, Elias's scholarship is both a cause and effect of the particular history Elias tells of international law, which emphasizes Africa's contribution to 'universal' international law and downplays colonialism as a negligible part of this larger story. This 'contributionist' history is set out in detail in *Africa and International Law*,[11] but its traces are visible in his very first article on international law, written in 1963 in the midst of decolonization, where he discussed the 1885 Treaty of Berlin without referring to its role in colonialism.[12] It is set out in detail in *Africa and International Law* which, in its opening chapter on 'The Contribution of Africa to International Law', makes a historical case for the universality of international law by setting out 'the role which different parts of the so-called Dark Continent played [in international affairs] since recorded history'[13] (from 'Ancient and Pre-Medieval Africa' and 'Indigenous African States (300–1500 A.D)' until colonization and colonial rule). [14] He concludes that in pre-colonial times

[8] ibid.

[9] Elias wrote about *South West Africa* on a number of occasions, focusing on the legal aspects of the ICJ decisions and their importance for international law. In *Africa and International Law* he concludes that 1971 Advisory Opinion, in which he had a special interest, 'is on the whole a worthwhile contribution to international law and . . . the United Nations whose prestige, and that of the International Court of Justice itself, has thereby been enhanced'. See further Taslim O Elias, *The International Court of Justice and Some Contemporary Problems* (Springer Netherlands 1983) 350.

[10] Elias made no mention of it in his 1979 book *New Horizons in International Law* (2nd edn, Springer 1992) (hereafter Elias, *New Horizons*), which considered the 'more significant aspects' of international law's development since 1945. His first lengthy treatment of NIEO came in his 1982 book on *The International Court of Justice and some contemporary problems,* but its supporters might have preferred it if he hadn't.

[11] A version of which was presented the previous year at a UNITAR conference. The volume is divided into four sections: 'Ancient and Pre-Medieval Africa', 'The Indigenous African States (300–1500 AD), 'Beginnings of European Trade and Colonization', and 'The Period of Colonial Rule'.

[12] Focusing instead on the technical aspects of the new treaty establishing the River Niger Commission. Taslim O Elias, 'The Berlin Treaty and the River Niger Commission' (1963) 57 American Journal of International Law 873–82.

[13] ibid 3.

[14] He makes the case again in Chapter 2 ('Government under Law') through (colonial) anthropology and political science. Discussing 'Government under Law' in 'African societies', Elias concludes that '[i]n African law . . . the indigenous ideas of government are not essentially dissimilar to that of Locke and Rousseau and . . . that of Grotius as well'. Elias, *Africa and International Law* (n 6) 36. In respect of 'Africa and the International Rule of Law', Elias argues that 'African customary law shares with customary international law the acceptance of the fundamental principle of *pacta servanda sunt* as the basis for the assurance of valid world order'; ibid 43–44.

these African polities—including Carthage, Tripoli, Cyrenaica, Ghana, Songhai, Mali, and Monomotapa—'exchanged diplomatists and envoys, formed alliances and carried on their external relations in much the same way as their European counterparts'.[15]

Notably, Elias' discussion of colonialism in this history is both brief and superficial. For Elias, colonialism itself was brief, while he places the beginnings of sustained European trade in the sixteenth century (when the 'rough and tumble of commercial activities' which resulted in 'occasional inter-State frictions'[16]), the 'Period of Colonial Rule' is limited to 1885–1955 (or there about).[17] Moreover, his discussion of colonialism glosses over its violence, and the role of international law in it (and vice versa). For Elias, colonialism involved the 'constriction' of African sovereignty, or 'the substituted sovereignties of the European states', as a result of which 'the historic modes of international intercourse were closed to these indigenous States and kingdoms'.[18] The problem of colonialism, for Elias, was the brief interruption it occasioned in Africa's participation in international law.

On this basis of this history, Elias later concludes: 'The way is this clear for the emergent States of Africa today to be willing and ready to enter into new international relationships with other States, without feeling too much like strangers in the international community.'[19]

Against this, Gathii sets the *strong* stream of anti-colonial international legal scholarship which focuses on 'the claims and role of economic, political, social and cultural superiority/inferiority in the historical relationship of colonized and colonizing countries in the past and present', and 'expresses [its] desire for self-determination and autonomy from all forms of external or neo-colonial controls'.[20] This stream scholarship is underpinned by a critical historiography that focuses on 'the imperial and mercantilist character of international law',[21] and 'examines Africa's [present] subordination in its international relations as a legacy that is traceable to international law, and the other'.[22]

The scholarship of Umo Umozurike during the 1970s, and in particular his *International Law and Colonialism*, is emblematic of this 'critical' stream. In 1970 Umozurike published an article on 'International Law and Colonialism in Africa: A Critique' that told a very different story of international law, past and present, to that of Elias (the article would later form the basis of this book by the same

[15] ibid 32.
[16] ibid 12.
[17] This is confirmed later when he refers to the 'constriction imposed by colonial rule [on African sovereignty] in the preceding seventy years or so'; Elias, *Africa and International Law* (n 6) 23.
[18] ibid 19.
[19] ibid 45.
[20] Gathii, 'International Law and Eurocentricity' (n 2) 184, 187
[21] Gathii, 'Africa' (n 5) 6.
[22] ibid 1.

name).[23] Umozurike's scholarship—which included a book *Self-determination and International Law* and articles on slavery, economic self-determination, and International Humanitarian Law (IHL)—was centrally concerned with the anti-colonial struggles of the time, adopting a critical disposition towards the present international order and arguing that colonialism, racism, and political economy (or 'neo-colonialism') continue to shape its contours. For example, in *International Law and Colonialism*, Umozurike notes that although '[u]nder the U.N., international law has changed from supporting or acquiescing in colonialism to opposing it', the human and material resources of South West Africa continued to be 'ruthlessly exploited for the benefit of the white minority and the Western combines'.[24]

In contrast to Elias' scholarship during the same period, Umozurike took an active interest in the critical projects of other 'third-world' international lawyers, including the South West Africa occupation and NIEO. The former was a focus of his 1972 book *Self-Determination in International Law*, and in an article published in the same year he argued (in contrast to Elias) that the 'Namibia cases [at the ICJ] demonstrate the close relations between international law and international politics' and the 'crudity and inequality that still persists in aspects of the international relations of black and white states'.[25] Umozurike took an early interest in the NIEO project, and in an 1970 article he argued for the right of newly independent states to nationalize foreign owned property under the principle of economic self-determination (without compensation in certain circumstances),[26] and ended it by noting: 'Political self-determination is . . . incomplete without economic self-determination'.[27] Later, in *International Law and Colonialism*, he noted that '[t]he call for a New International Economic Order is directed towards negating neo-colonialism'.[28]

As with Elias, although to very different effect, Umozurike's scholarship is a function in many respects of his critical history of international law—set out in detail in *International Law and Colonialism*—which begins by centring the slave trade and colonialism as '[t]wo of the foremost experiences the Africans had from contact with the Europeans',[29] and proceeds to discuss

23 Umo O Umozurike, 'International Law and Colonialism in Africa: A Critique' (1970) 3 *East African Law Review* 46–83 (hereafter Umozurike, 'Colonialism in Africa'). It was also published in the *Zambia Law Journal*. The book also draws on other articles, including one published in 1971 on the African slave trade. ('The African Slave Trade and the Attitudes of International Law Towards It').

24 ibid 3.4.

25 Umo O Umozurike, *Self-Determination in International Law* (Archon Books 1972) 220 (hereafter Umozurike, *Self-Determination in International Law*).

26 Umo O Umozurike, 'Nationalization of Foreign-Owned Property and Economic Self-Determination' (1970) 6 East African Law Journal 90–91.

27 ibid 99.

28 Umozurike, 'Colonialism in Africa' (n 23) 128.

29 ibid 1. The slave trade, Umozurike points out, resulted in 'misery, death, destruction and impoverishment' in Africa and 'negated [its] political, economic, cultural and social development', while contributing to the present-day 'prosperity of Western Europe and [the] USA'.

international law's role in both. For example, he locates international law's origins in sixteenth-century Europe 'when the African slave trade was growing roots',[30] noting that international law not only facilitated, it but encouraged it. In respect of colonialism, like Elias he argues that 'African peoples . . . were sovereign' before colonialism, although he does not suggest their sovereignty was 'substituted' for that of European powers. Rather, he sets out in detail how African sovereignty was ignored or denied through various means (settlement, annexation, Treaties of Cession, Prescription and Inter-European bilateral treaties).[31] Furthermore, not only was international law a 'handy instrument in the hands of the colonialists' up until 1918,[32] but also colonialism was intensified and consolidated during the 'League period' through the Mandates system and the unchallenged annexation of Abyssinia by Italy.[33] Throughout the remainder of the text Umozurike refers back to the role of slavery and colonialism—and its underlying racism and imperialism—and its persistence in the present.[34]

On a first reading of Elias' *Africa and International Law* and Umozurike's *International Law and Colonialism*, and their scholarship more broadly, there is much to support Gathii's classification of these two traditions as 'contributionist' and 'critical', 'weak' and 'strong', respectively. However, this classification it is limiting in some respects. It is necessarily broad-brush in its approach—implicating both the history and theory of international law, from 1960 until the present—but as a result, it pays less attention to the context, political or intellectual, of both authors and texts.[35] As a result, it overlooks the complex and changing relationship of their scholarship to 'decolonization', which was itself being contested at the time. One way to overcome these limitations is to reread it through African literature and its own engagement with 'decolonization'.

[30] Umozurike, 'Colonialism in Africa' (n 23) 7.

[31] ibid 22–24. There is a separate chapter on 'Treaties Concluded by Europeans with African Kings before the 20th Century' (and their legal effects thereof).

[32] ibid 34.

[33] ibid 51.

[34] Umozurike's history also differs from Elias in that it includes efforts of by Africans, and those of African descent as well, to resist colonialism. He discusses the early twentieth-century history includes a section on 'Pan-Africanism and Colonialism', and at various points he refers to these efforts (such as WEB Du Bois' efforts at Versailles and the 1945 Pan-African Congress in Manchester). While acknowledging that these efforts lay outside of international law, Umozurike nevertheless suggests that 'the resolutions of the unofficial conferences had some influence, however small'. Umozurike, 'Colonialism in Africa' (n 23) 56.

[35] It must be noted that Gathii himself acknowledged these risks when he first introduced his 'weak' and 'strong' heuristic in 1998, and called for more work to be done on the 'contextual backdrop' of African international lawyers. Gathii, 'International Law and Eurocentricity', 205. A call which this chapter, belatedly, attempts to answer.

III. The battle over 'decolonization'

1. 'Literal' decolonization at Makarere and Lagos

In June 1962, the present and future African *literati*—including Chinua Achebe, Wole Soyinka, Es'kia Mphahlele, and Ngugi wa Thiong'o—met at Makarere College in Kampala for the 'first get-together of African authors writing in English anywhere in the world'.[36] Aside from its historic significance, the gathering would be remembered for the debate that emerged among participants regarding whether 'African literature' could and should be written in colonial languages, a debate that would be revisited time and again over the following decades. The conclusion reached at Makarere, despite continued resistance from some, was that it was both possible and desirable to continue writing in English (albeit with irreverence).[37] The position was summed up in a 1964 essay by Chinua Achebe, the 'Father of African literature', in which he called on his fellow writers to accept the universal status of English brought about by colonialism.[38]

African international lawyers had their own 'Makarere' meeting, of sorts, at the 1961 World Peace Through Law conference, which took place in Lagos six months prior.[39] The meeting, arranged by the American Bar Association as part of a global project on World Peace Through Law, was called to 'consider ways in which lawyers could work together globally to strengthen international law and legal institutions'.[40] Elias was a prominent participant, and gave one of the keynote speeches in which 'support for the international rule of law was strongly advocated'.[41] In the end, the delegates unanimously endorsed the universality of international law—as '[embodying] fundamental concepts of justice and morality common to civilized societies'—and committed themselves to 'working toward world-wide acceptance and application of the rule of law in all international relations'.[42]

Had these discussions among writers and international lawyers assembled in Makarere and Lagos taken place today, they most likely would have been articulated

[36] The Conference was organized by the 'Mbari Writers' and Artists' Club of Ibadan', and attended by forty-five participants (writers, editors, literary critics, and publishers).

[37] See Mphahlele, 'Press Report' (on file with author).

[38] Chinua Achebe, 'The African Writer and the English Language', reprinted in Chinua Achebe, *Morning Yet on Creation Day* (Anchor Press 1975) (hereafter Achebe, *Creation Day).*

[39] Earlier in 1961 lawyers from across the African continent had also met in Lagos for the African Conference on the Rule of Law, organized by the International Commission of Jurists and under the steerage of Elias as Conference Chair. See Laurence M Lombard, 'African Conference on the Rule of Law Held at Lagos, Nigeria, in January' (1961) 47 American Bar Association Journal 563.

[40] Charles S Rhyne, 'World Peace Through Law Conferences' (1962) 56 American Journal of International Law 1001 (hereafter Rhyne, 'World Peace').

[41] Thornburn Reid and James F Sams, 'Conference on World Peace Through Law: Held at Tokyo, Japan and Lagos, Nigeria' (1962) 48 American Bar Association Journal 649, 650.

[42] These were contained in the Consensus of San Jose (adopted at the first World Peace Through Law Conference in San Jose in June 1961) which was unanimously endorsed at Lagos. Rhyne, 'World Peace' (n 40) 1004–05.

using the language of 'decolonization'. However, much like 'post-colonialism',[43] 'decolonization' came to mean different things over time. It began as a quite literal *de*-colonization, based on a 'stubborn etymological literalness' in which 'colonies are what get decolonized' and 'decolonization is fundamentally a matter of politics (in the most conventional sense), state sovereignty, and the transformation of colonies into independent nation-states'.[44] In this 'thin' account of 'decolonization', colonial *forms*—be they the English language (or the novel itself) or international law—were neutral, *if not natural;* they were to be embraced, either pragmatically or even emphatically in order to be turned against the centre. This account of decolonization underpinned the confidence with which both African writers and international lawyers embraced their respective colonial forms in the 1960s, confident that they could make the English language and international law 'their own' without residual colonial influences.

It is this literal construction of 'decolonization' that Elias adopts in *Africa*, where decolonization is equated with formal independence. He refers to 'the process of decolonisation [which] . . . goes on apace until all [dependent and non-self-governing territories] become free and equal independent States'.[45] To the extent that it is discussed at all in,[46] 'decolonization' is figured as 'a linear, diplomatic transfer of power from colonial to postcolonial status'.[47] There is no discussion of the broader impacts of colonialism, and their 'post-colonial' political, economic, and cultural afterlives; in fact, he even dismisses the claims of the Organization of African Unity (OAU) as economic 'neocolonialism'.[48] As the 'event'[49] of 'decolonization' took place, so too was international law decolonized. On this basis, Elias was confident that African international lawyers could appropriate the *colonial form* of international law and make it their own without residual influence.[50]

In his 1964 essay Chinua Achebe set out his reasoning as to why African writers should accept the 'inevitability' of the use of English as a 'world language', albeit

[43] See Neil Lazarus, 'Introducing Postcolonial Studies' in Neil Lazarus (ed), *The Cambridge Companion to Postcolonial Literary Studies* (CUP 2006).

[44] Jennifer Wenzel, 'Decolonization' in Imre Szeman, Sarah Blacker and Justin Sully (eds), *A Companion to Critical and Cultural Theory* (Wiley Blackwell 2017) 3 (hereafter Wenzel, 'Decolonization').

[45] Elias, *Africa and International Law* (n 6) 47, 32 (noting: 'Decolonization has been one of the main preoccupations of the African and the Afro-Asian Groups at the United Nations . . . [which] have served to quicken the pace of independence and self-government . . . ').

[46] Neither 'colonialism' nor 'decolonization' made it into the index.

[47] Christopher J Lee (ed), *Making a World after Empire: The Bandung Moment and Its Political Afterlives* (Ohio University Press 2010) 8.

[48] Recalling the OAU Charter's pledge 'to fight against neo-colonialism in all its forms', he notes that 'Member States, *paradoxical though it may seem*, pledge themselves to eradicate all forms of colonialism from the continent of Africa even if, in achieving this, they should go against the principle of non-interferences in the internal affairs of states'. Elias, *Africa and International Law* (n 6) 128.

[49] See Sundhya Pahuja, 'Decolonization and the Eventness of International Law' in Fleur Johns, Richard Joyce and Sundhya Pahuja (eds), *Events: The Force of International Law* (Routledge 2010).

[50] In fact, Elias goes further, arguing that before the brief interlude of colonialism international law was in fact universal.

it one 'which history has forced down [Africa's] throat'.[51] Achebe's arguments were largely pragmatic,[52] suggesting that while colonialism 'failed to give them a song, it at least gave them a tongue, for sighing'.[53] Notably, Achebe specifically dismissed the argument that the *form* of English might be bound up in the project of colonialism—that 'it came as part of a package deal which included many other items of doubtful value and the positive atrocity of racial arrogance and prejudice which may yet set the world on fire'—arguing that it would be 'in rejecting the evil throw[ing] out the good with it'.[54] On this basis, Achebe was confident about both African writers' ability to use English effectively,[55] and English's capacity to be 'Africanized' to 'carry the weight of . . . African experience' in the process.[56] African writers, he argued, should 'aim to use English which is at once universal and able to carry out [their] peculiar experience'.[57]

Reading the scholarship of Elias through Achebe's essay reveals a number of similar assumptions regarding international law. First, like Achebe's *communicative* understanding of colonial languages, Elias's understanding of international law was pragmatic and instrumental; both argued that these 'colonial forms' were potentially, if not already, universal. Second, and related to this, neither Achebe nor Elias considered whether their form inherited from colonialism might contain structural biases, and might require 'decolonizing' themselves. The supposition that decolonization was an event that had taken place, or would shortly, underlies both Elias and Achebe's confidence that these *colonial forms* could be repurposed, and that colonial history was in the past.

2. From formal 'decolonization' to *decolonizing* form

The general agreeability among African writers in the 'morning of creation day'—to paraphrase Achebe[58]—would soon fade, and over the two decades that followed

[51] Achebe, *Creation Day* (n 38) 59. He went a step further, arguing that one of the benefits of colonialism was to give Africans common colonial language, while 'it failed to give them a song, it at least gave them a tongue, for sighing'. ibid 57.

[52] Noting: '[F]or me there is no other choice', he concluded, 'I have been given this language and I intend to use it'; that as a result of colonialism 'the reality of present-day Africa' was that 'the national literature of Nigeria and of many other countries of Africa is, or will be, written in English' (ibid 57) and that given the continent's size and diversity, communication would only be possible through common languages, adding that as it is 'that language is English . . . [t]omorrow it may be something else, although I very much doubt it' (ibid 58).

[53] ibid 57.

[54] ibid 58.

[55] ibid 59–60. In any event, it was not desirable for African writers to use English as a 'native speaker' (ibid 61).

[56] Achebe was confident that he and his fellow writers would be able to convey 'African experience[s] in a world-wide language', through a 'new English, still in full communion with its ancestral home but altered to suit its new African surroundings'; ibid 61–62.

[57] ibid 61. A strange 'universality', in which African will always occupy the position of 'Other'.

[58] See ibid.

writers returned critically to the questions that animated their inaugural gathering in Makarere. This shift among African writers was dramatically captured by the 'about-turn' by Kenyan novelist and playwright Ngugi wa Thiongo (formerly James Ngugi), the heir-apparent to Achebe. As part of the younger generation of writers present at Makarere in 1962, Ngugi was among the majority who accepted the necessity of writing in English.[59] However, in 1979, the same year that Umozurike's *International Law and Colonialism* was published, Ngugi gave a speech at the Kenya Press club in which he called for the abandoning of colonial languages by African writers, labelling their continued use 'neocolonialism'.[60]

These arguments were elaborated on in *Decolonising the Mind* (1986), in which Ngugi 'returned' to Makarere to ask: 'What was the route from the Berlin of 1884 via the Makerere of 1962 to what is still the prevailing and dominant logic a hundred years later?'[61] The answer, for Ngugi, lay partly in language's 'dual character'—as '*both* a means of communication and a carrier of culture'[62]—and the failure at Makarere to consider the ongoing effects of the imposition of colonial languages as a form of cultural imperialism that led to their acceptance of 'fatalistic logic of the unassailable position of English in [African] literature'; a logic, he added, 'embodied deep in imperialism'.[63] For this and other reasons, Ngugi argued, the continued use of colonial languages was simply neocolonialism—there was essentially no 'difference between a politician who says Africa cannot do without imperialism and the writer who says Africa cannot do without European languages'.[64] The colonial form could not, as Achebe would have it, be redeemed through 'Africanization', nor their effect downplayed on pragmatic grounds.

The title of Ngugi's *Decolonising the Mind* usefully records a shift from the 'literal' construction of decolonization *as an event*, towards a thicker account in which there are 'objects that are to be *decolonized*'[65] (or abandoned), including African literature and, perhaps, international law. This understanding of decolonization as *action* (rather than event), something that gets done *to* colonial forms (colonial languages, statutes, curricula, and so on) is what prevails today. The beginnings of this shift can be seen in Umozurike's *International Law and Colonialism*. To start, Umozurike explicitly abandons Elias's 'literal' conception of *de*-colonization; one which does not conflate decolonization with formal independence.[66] Umozurike's aim, declared at the outset, was to 'show . . . the proper

[59] Ngugi wa Thiong'o, *Decolonising the Mind: The Politics of Language in African Literature (Studies in African Literature)* (East African Educational Publishers 1986) 20 (hereafter Ngugi, *Decolonising the Mind*).

[60] Ngugi wa Thiong'o, *Writers in Politics: Essays* (East African Educational Publishers 1981) 65

[61] Ngugi, *Decolonising the Mind* (n 59) 9.

[62] ibid 13.

[63] ibid 20.

[64] ibid 26.

[65] Wenzel, 'Decolonization' (n 44) 18.

[66] He explicitly rejects the binary understanding of independence (adopted by Elias), in which former colony is 'either dependent . . . or independent'. Umozurike, 'Colonialism in Africa' (n 23) 126.

role of the international community in decolonisation',[67] based on a capacious definition of colonialism (centred primarily on economic, rather than political, exploitation)[68] and understanding that 'neo-colonialism' was ongoing (despite formal independence).[69]

However, Umozurike did not follow Ngugi in calling for the abandoning of the colonial form (ie, international law) altogether; while he acknowledged that '[i]nternational law in its present *form*' has its roots in slavery and colonialism,[70] he asserted (at least at the outset) that international law had and could overcome both (and redeem itself in the process). [71] As such, Ngugi's *Decolonising the Mind*, and in particular his arguments regarding the relationship between colonial *forms* and their content, anticipate later critical 'TWAIL' scholarship—of which Umozurike was a precursor—where scholars like Anghie and Pahuja have specifically addressed international law's persistent colonial form.

A more appropriate Ngugi text through which to read Umozurike's *International Law and Colonialism* is his 1977 novel *Petals of Blood*—his final novel in English—as Ngugi claimed that it was 'in the course of writing the novel that [he] came to be more and more disillusioned with the use of foreign languages'.[72] When *Petals of Blood* was published, many critics suggested that Ngugi's battle with his *colonial* form and its limitations was evident in the text itself.[73] With echoes of Fanon, Chileshe placed Ngugi's 'struggle to come to terms, *within* the novel form, with his authorial ideology' squarely in the post-colonial context:[74]

[67] ibid x.

[68] Noting: 'The main characteristics of colonialism are the differences in race, colour and power between colonialists and the colonized, and the subjugation of the interests of the latter to those of the former'; ibid ix.

[69] Arguing that 'neo-colonialism' is a stage that 'every new African state invariably passes through', but that international law can potentially 'minimize neo-colonialism and make sovereignty a reality'. ibid 126.

[70] ibid 7.

[71] ibid 1.

[72] Reinhard Sander, Bernth Lindfors and Lynette Cintrón (eds), *Ngugi wa Thiong'o Speaks: Interviews with the Kenyan Writer* (James Currey Publishers 2006) 87–88. Notably, it was not only the English language that was implicated, but the novel itself. Gikandi argues that for Ngugi at the time the novel form itself was 'bound up with the culture of colonialism' (ibid 143), and harboured 'serious doubts about both the possibility of change and the ability of the novel to represent spaces of recuperation and resistance' (ibid 129). Simon Gikandi, *Ngugi wa Thiong'o* (CUP 2010).

[73] For a summary of the critical responses see Joseph McLaren, 'Ideology and Form: the Critical Reception of *Petals of Blood*' in Peter Nazareth (ed), *Critical Essays on Ngugi wa Thiong'O* (Twayne Publishers 2000). See also John Updike, 'Books: Mixed Reports from the Interior' (2 July 1079) *New Yorker* 89–94; Charles R Larson, 'Anglophone Writing from Africa and Asia' (1978) 52 World Literature Today 245–47; Homi K Bhabha, '"African Praxis" Review of *Petals of Blood*' (12 August 1977) *Times Literary Supplement* 989; Bernth Lindfors, *Popular Literature in Africa* (Africa World Press 1991), 81; and Peter Nazareth, 'The Second Homecoming: Multiple Ngugis in *Petals of Blood*' in Georg M Gugelberger, *Marxism and African Literature* (African World Press 1986) (hereafter Nazareth 'Homecoming').

[74] John Chileshe, '*Petals of Blood*: Ideology and Imaginative Expression' (1980) 15 Journal of Commonwealth Literature 133, 134.

> [O]ften the contradictions in a work of art have to do with its historical determinants. This the African creative artist who conceived of himself as being engaged in a nationalistic struggle against imperialist hegemony may well find that his struggle is being waged from *within* imperialist hegemonic structures. Not only might the formulation of the struggle be for within the imperialist problematic . . . , but even the weapons used may be largely inherited from the culture at which the struggle is directed.

In his 1959 essay Fanon too had warned of the dangers of using a 'borrowed aesthetic', of using 'techniques and a language borrowed from the occupier';[75] his own battle with, or perhaps against, form found its way into *The Wretched of the Earth* where, Wenzel notes, 'the poetry of utopian possibility . . . jostles with the prose of postcolonial disillusion'.[76]

Through *Petals of Blood, International Law and Colonialism* can also be read as a struggle against imperialism (or 'neo-colonialism') being waged 'from *within* imperialist hegemonic structures', using a weapon (ie, international law) 'inherited from the culture at which the struggle is directed', and one that takes place in part at the level of the text. Reading *International Law and Colonialism* in this way reveals the ambivalences, if not contradictions, that lie surface-deep throughout. It opens with a paradox—namely that '[i]nternational law was used to facilitate . . . both [the slave trade and colonialism]' *but* 'was also . . . used to eradicate the first and, presently, the second'[77]—and then proceeds to undermine international law's claims and ability to do both of the latter. The slave trade, we are told, was ended as a result of economic factors, with '[i]nternational law . . . following the trend of European interests'[78] (and, in any event, is not over).[79] Moreover, its belated abolition in the Treaty of Berlin *then* laid the foundation for colonization: '[t]he legality of the trade was, as it were, substituted by the legitimacy of, and encouragement for, [colonialism]'. [80] Finally, the eradication of both lies, it seems, not international law as it stands but in a combination of Hegelian dialectics and the 'use of force' by African states (including nuclear force).[81] Nevertheless, he concludes 'on an optimistic note' that '[i]nternational law, faithfully applied, holds out hope for a world, ruled by law, in which the rights of all peoples will be protected'.[82] Such contradictions are present throughout the text.[83]

75 Fanon, *The Wretched of the Earth* (n 1) 159–60.
76 Wenzel, 'Decolonization' (n 44) 18.
77 Umozurike, 'Colonialism in Africa' (n 23) 1.
78 ibid, 139.
79 ibid 15–16.
80 ibid 139.
81 ibid 143–44.
82 ibid 143–44.
83 On more than one occasion Umozurike cites a norm of international law (such as the succession of treaty obligations), and then makes a radical counter-claim ('[s]ince neo-colonialism is a detraction

Ngugi's *Petals of Blood* offers a reading of *International Law and Colonialism* in which these and other contradictions, unevenness, and lapses in genre in are symptomatic of Umozurike's battle with the form of international law *itself.* While this reading is somewhat unsatisfying, it is to be preferred to both those that would simply dismiss these features of *International Law and Colonialism* as faults, as well as sympathetic readings that overlook them.[84]

Reading these African international legal scholars alongside their literary interlocutors draws attention not only to the relationships among and between these texts, but also to the role that context—both intellectual and political—played in their construction.

IV. '[A] fundamentally different international situation': context, 'decolonization' and African international legal scholarship

In 1972 South African writer and critic Es'kia Mphahlele—who was present alongside Achebe and Ngugi at Makarere—wrote of the 'new mood in African Literature', as writers began to 'reckon with [their] present'; a present he described as:[85]

> Independence, opposition politics, coups d'état, military government, one-party government; acres of poverty sprinkled with a few castles of wealth and a few blinking neon lights that say Elite Club; the shrinking boundaries of defensive nationalism, the dream that the pan-African center will hold; the insolence of power, the "benevolence" of power, the abdication of power, power vegetating: whether or not neo-colonialism frustrates possible solutions, our continent is the black man's burden this time around.

It was also the year the Elias's *Africa and International Law* was published; however, much of it was written in a quite different 'present', consisting largely of works published in the 1960s.[86] In contrast, Umozurike's *International Law and Colonialism* was published in 1979, and drew on works he published during the 1970s. These changing 'presents'—the political contexts of the 1960s and 1970s—necessarily impacted the work of Elias and Umozurike generally, and their

from sovereignty, a state has a right to prevent or reverse it'), without trying to reconcile the two; ibid 130–31.

[84] *See* Susan Marks (ed), *International Law of the Left: Re-Examining Marxist Legacies* (CUP 2008) 124–25 (suggesting that Umozurike 'sharply counterposes . . . "neocolonialism" from international law itself').

[85] Ezekiel Mphahlele, 'The New Mood in Africa Literature' (1972) 19 Africa Today 54.

[86] See Preface, Elias, *Africa and International Law* (n 6).

constructions of 'decolonization' in particular. As Lazurus notes in relation to the term 'post-colonial', which underwent a similar transformation—from a simple 'periodizing term' (ie, *after* colonialism) to the complex, political, and ideological concept it signifies today—' "postcolonial criticism" could not possibly have existed before the 1980s, not because it would have lacked an adequate audience then, but because it would have made no sense at all in the historico-ideological context of the 1970s'.[87] (Notably, the 'post-colonial malaise' set in among African writers slightly earlier than it did some of their interlocutors in Western academies).

Elias and Umozurike wrote in different intellectual contexts as well, under different 'epistemological conditions' that made their scholarship 'both thinkable and feasible',[88] returning to Fanon, with the *intellectual* weapons they possessed at the time. For example, Elias wrote *Africa and International Law* two years prior to the publication of Diop's landmark *The African Origins of Civilization: Myth or Reality?*[89] In contrast, the influence of Walter Rodney's *How Europe Underdeveloped Africa* (1972) on Umozurike's scholarship is hard to miss, and is acknowledged in the Preface (although Umozurike cites an earlier unpublished version of Rodney's thesis in *International Law and Colonialism*).[90] In fact, all of Rodney's *How Europe Underdeveloped Africa* and much of Umozurike's 'International Law and Colonialism in Africa' was written while they were both at the University of Dar-es-Salaam.[91]

Beyond individual texts, changes in the broader intellectual contexts between the 1960s and 1970s, in both international law and African scholarship, inflect the work of Elias and Umozurike. The 1970s saw the emergence of critical scholarship from the 'first generation' of TWAIL scholars, some of which appears in Umozurike's *International Law and Colonialism*. However, the changes in the broader African intellectual context during this period—under the influence of scholars like Fanon and Rodney—are perhaps the most significant difference between Elias' and Umozurike's texts. This difference, and its origins in broader intellectual shifts, is most obvious in their respective histories of international law.

[87] Lazarus (n 43) 7.

[88] Valentin-Yves Mudimbe, *The Invention of Africa: Gnosis, Philosophy, and the Order of Knowledge* (Indiana University Press 1988) 195.

[89] Which Gathii overlooks when he criticizes Elias's failure to cite the latter. Gathii, 'International Law and Eurocentricity' (n 2) (noting Elias's failure to cite the work of Cheikh Anta Diop's text in support of his claims regarding 'the existence of ancient African Kingdoms or political units equivalent to, if not superior to . . . those found in Western Europe').

[90] Umozurike, 'Colonialism in Africa' (n 23) 3. In addition, Rodney's influence can also be seen in Umozurike's reading; Walter Rodney's 'Brief Guides to Reading' in *How Europe Underdeveloped Africa* (Bogle–L'Ouverture Publications 1972) include the works of WEB Du Bois, George Padmore, Eric Williams, Basil Davidson, and Phillip Curtin, which feature prominently in Umozurike's 'Colonialism in Africa' (n 23).

[91] See Walter Rodney, *How Europe Underdeveloped Africa* (Pambazuka Press 2012), vii (hereafter Rodney, *How Europe Underdeveloped Africa*) (noting: 'the text as a whole has been written within Tanzania'); and Umozurike, 'Colonialism in Africa' (n 23) x (noting: '[w]riting was virtually completed while I was on secondment . . . to the University of Dar-es-Salaam').

Seen from today, Elias's 'contributionist' history appears amateurish and polemical; yet, it resonated strongly with the work of both his historian and novelist contemporaries. At the time, during what Curtin calls the 'first stage of decolonizing African history', African historians 'were mainly concerned to beat back the assertion that Africa had no history . . . [by pointing] to kingdoms and large empires that did indeed have a political history that read like early aspects of European history'.[92] Similarly, shortly after his 1964 essay on Makarere, Achebe declared that he 'would be quite satisfied if [his] novels . . . did no more than teach his readers that their past—with all its imperfections—was not one long night of savagery from which the first Europeans acting on God's behalf delivered them'.[93] For Achebe, the task of the African novelist was to write 'enabling stories' that countered the 'tyrannical discourse of colonialism'[94] reflected in novels such as Joseph Conrad's *The Heart of Darkness* (1899) and Joyce Cary's *Mister Johnson* (1939), where Africans were depicted as lacking both subjectivity ('an Africa without Africans') and history (Hegel's 'land of childhood . . . lying beyond the day of self-conscious history'[95]). For Achebe, this required decentring colonialism in favour of telling the story of a pre-colonial past, a task he undertakes with unrivalled genius in *Things Fall Apart* (1959).

Just as Achebe wrote *Things Fall Apart* in order to restore these elements absent in colonial discourse—subjectivity and history—'to the African character and his or her community', so too might Elias be read as restoring sovereignty and pre-colonial history to Africa—both of which were missing in the standard accounts of international legal history. Even if, as in *Things Fall Apart*, such 'gentle re-creations of the past'[96] meant glossing over 'the darker, more violent, and tragic aspects of the African experience'.[97] Similarly, just as failing to read Achebe's *Things Fall Apart* (and the texts of early African historians) contextually—as part of the struggle by African intellectuals in the 1960s to 'to contest, and wrestle with, the silent shadows and forms of colonialist discourse'—'misses the revolutionary nature of Achebe's text';[98] so too does reading Elias' history of international law *acontextually* do it a disservice.

By the 1970s the intellectual context had changed considerably, in no small measure due to the changing political context, as reflected in the work of historians

[92] PD Curtin, 'Recent Trends in African Historiography and their Contribution to History in General' in Joseph Ki-Zerbo (ed) *General History of Africa I: Methodology and African Prehistory* (UNESCO 1989) 64. See further JD Phage, 'The Development of African Historiography' in ibid 58–59; and Bethwell A Ogot, 'Three Decades of Historical Studies in East Africa, 1949–1977' (1978) 6 Kenya Historical Review 29–33 (hereafter Ogot, 'Three Decades').

[93] Achebe, *Creation Day* (n 38) 45.

[94] Simon Gikandi, *Reading Chinua Achebe: Language & Ideology in Fiction* (East African Publishers 1991) (hereafter Gikandi, *Reading Chinua Achebe*).

[95] Georg Wilhelm Friedrich Hegel, *The Philosophy of History* (James Sibree tr, OUP 1956).

[96] Chinua Achebe, *There Was a Country: A Memoir* (Viking Penguin 2012) 115.

[97] Ogot, 'Three Decades' (n 92)30.

[98] Gikandi, *Reading Chinua Achebe* (n 94) 26.

and novelists once more. For historians, the 'honeymoon period' that 'dwelt rather nostalgically upon what was appealing or virtuous in the African past' was over.[99] For Ogot, writing specifically about East African historiography, the year of significance was again 1972. What followed was a turn towards 'economic history' (underpinned by Marxism) in order to address 'the present economic and political malaise in Africa';[100] a 'usable history', in Ranger's words (notably, Ogot cites Walter Rodney's work as emblematic of this turn). For their part, novelists turned their attention to the present, and 'usable histories' that addressed its problems. In 1972 Ngugi, drawing on Fanon,[101] warned his fellow writers against 'becoming too fascinated by the yesterday of his people and forgetting the present',[102] a critique echoed by his leading character in *Petals of Blood*, Karega (an avatar for Ngugi himself). In *Petals of Blood* Karega criticizes his professors for taking him 'to pre-colonial times . . . [to] wander purposelessly from Egypt, or Ethiopia, or Sudan, only to be checked in his pastoral wanderings by the arrival of Europeans'.[103] He demands a history that uses the past as 'a living lesson to the present', warning that 'we must study it critically, without illusions, and see what lessons we can draw from it in today's battlefield of the future and the present'.[104]

The influence of this context can also be seen in Umozurike's history of international law, which forgoes Elias's (and *Things Falls Apart*'s) extensive discussion of pre-colonial Africa to focus on the depredations of slavery and colonialism, as well as the resistance to it (through Pan-Africanism, for example). Moreover, like Ngugi's *Petals and Blood,* Umozurike history of international law is directed at the 'battlefield of the future and the present', with consistent parallels being drawn between the racial and imperial aspects of 'colonial international law' and apartheid and neo-colonialism.

In light of these similarities, to read Elias and Umozurike's histories of international law, and their scholarship more generally, wholly outside of these intellectual contexts is to misread them. Equally so, contextualizing requires nuance. It is not simply a chronological mapping of influential works. For example, while Diop's *The African Origins of Civilization: Myth or Reality?* (1974) was published two years *after* Rodney's *How Europe Underdeveloped Africa* (1972), the former belongs to the first 'Afro-centric' stage of African historiography; being made up of works published (in French) in the 1960s (much as Elias's text was). It also requires paying

[99] Ogot, 'Three Decades' (n 92) 30.
[100] ibid 30.
[101] In his essay 'On National Culture' Fanon wrote that '[w]hen the colonized intellectual writing for his people uses the past he must do so with the intention of opening up the future, of spurring them into action and fostering hope'; Fanon, *The Wretched of the Earth* (n 1) 167.
[102] Nazareth, *Homecoming* (n 73) 44. See further Carol M Sicherman, 'Ngugi wa Thiong'o and the Writing of Kenyan History' (1989) 20 Research in African Literatures, 349–50.
[103] Ngugi wa Thiong'o, *Petals of Blood* (William Heinemann Ltd 1977) 199 (hereafter Ngugi, *Petals of Blood*).
[104] ibid 323.

attention to place. It is difficult to overemphasize the influence on Umozurike of the intellectual context of Dar-es-Salaam during his time there; where he not only came under the influence of Walter Rodney, but he also was much more likely to have been exposed to Fanon than in his native Nigeria[105]—more so at the Law School where Fanon was compulsory reading.[106]

It is these broader shifts in the intellectual terrain, as much as the particular 'presents', that account to some degree for the strength and weakness of the scholarship of Elias and Umozurike. Fanon, who as much as anyone was responsible for these shifts,[107] had already anticipated them in his 1959 essay on 'National Culture', where he set out the various 'phases of development in the works of colonized writers'. First, the 'colonized intellectual proves he has assimilated the colonizer's culture' (the 'phase of full assimilation').[108] Second, colonized intellectuals 'place themselves in the context of history',[109] in search of 'some magnificent and shining era' that will show that Africa's 'past was not branded with shame, but dignity, glory, and sobriety'.[110] Third, the colonized intellectual 'turns into a galvanizer of the people' and '[c]ombat literature, revolutionary literature, national literature emerges'.[111]

However, even this 'combat stage' is bound to fail, according to Fanon, both because the writer must continue to rely on 'borrowed aesthetic' and remains 'out of step' with the people, and because 'the existence of a nation is not proved by culture, but in the people's struggle against the forces of occupation'.[112] For Fanon, the proper role of the 'colonized intellectual' was to 'take part in the action and commit himself body and soul to the national struggle', as '[o]ne cannot expect African culture to advance unless on contributes realistically to the creation of the conditions necessary for this culture, i.e., the liberation of the continent'.[113]

By the 1970s both Achebe and Ngugi had taken up Fanon's challenges to the 'colonized writer' to varying degrees: Achebe took up the Biafran 'peoples' struggle for self-determination,[114] while Ngugi's 'combat literature' aimed at the 'neo-colonial'

[105] See Alamin Mazrui, 'Fanon in the East African Experience: Between English and Swahili Translations' in Kathryn Batchelor and Sue-Ann Harding (eds), *Translating Frantz Fanon Across Continents and Languages* (Routledge 2017) (hereafter Mazuri, 'Fanon'), noting that by the mid-1970s 'Fanon's ideas were already circulating widely in East Africa'. In contrast, little is known about the 'West African Anglophone reception of Fanon; see Kathryn Batchelor, 'The Translation of *Les Damnes de la terre* into English: Exploring Irish Connections' in Kathryn Batchelor and Sue-Ann Harding (eds), *Translating Frantz Fanon Across Continents and Languages* (Routledge 2017).

[106] Mazrui, 'Fanon' (n 105).

[107] Rodney notes: 'Fanon does not have any equal in analysing the last stages of African colonialism and the advent of neo-colonialism'; see Rodney, *How Europe Underdeveloped Africa* (n 91).

[108] Fanon, *The Wretched of the Earth* (n 1) 158–59.

[109] ibid 147.

[110] ibid 148.

[111] ibid 159.

[112] Fanon, *The Wretched of the Earth* (n 1) 160.

[113] ibid 167, 70.

[114] He wrote extensively about this period in his late memoir Chinua Achebe, *There was a Country: A Personal History of Biafra* (Penguin Books 2012).

Kenyan state resulted in his detention and exile.[115] In fact, despite their generational differences, Ngugi and Achebe ended up in similar places. Achebe came to question the literal understanding of 'decolonisation as independence' and, although he did not give up on the *colonial form* altogether, his experiences in Biafra shook his faith in it (while he had been prolific before the war, he didn't write another novel for almost two decades).[116]

The interests of international lawyers faired quite differently in during the same period. Unlike Achebe, Elias remained seemingly impervious to the changing political and intellectual context in the decades following independence, while Umozurike's critical disposition appeared to weaken over time. This chapter concludes by considering this dissimilitude between African international lawyers and writers in the 'late' decolonization period, which is equally remarkable and brings to the fore the limits of 'context' and the influence of biography and, perhaps, discipline.

V. Concluding remarks

In 1968 Chinua Achebe *actually* returned to Makarere. At the time, he was an envoy for the newly declared Republic of Biafra, and the ongoing conflict in Nigeria formed the substance of his address, titled 'The African Writer and the Biafran Cause'. It began with a history of Africa that was quite different to the 'gentle re-creations of the past' that typified his earlier works. [117] Rather, just like Umozurike's *International Law and Colonialism*, Achebe's history centred on the slave trade and colonialism, to which he added a third: decolonization. According to Achebe, Biafra had demonstrated was that 'decolonization' was a farce: 'independence . . . was totally without content' and '[t]he old white master was still in charge'.[118] As such, Achebe declared that 'Biafra stands for *true* independence in Africa, for an end to the 400 years of shame and humiliation which we have suffered in our association with Europe'.[119] Moreover, taking up Fanon's demands of 'colonized intellectuals', Achebe argued that the role of African writers was to be part of 'the revolutionary struggle of their people for justice and *true* independence'.[120] The

[115] See Ngugi wa Thiong'o, *Detained: A Writer's Prison Diary* (William Heinemann Ltd 1981).

[116] When he did return to the novel in 1987 (Chinua Achebe, *Anthills of the Savannah* (William Heinemann Ltd 1987), he did so in the register of Ngugi, '[turning] his attention to the challenge of envisioning a radically new society out of the elements of a *useable* African past'. Leonard A Podis and Yakubu Saaka, '*Anthills of the Savannah* and *Petals of Blood*: The Creation of a Usable Past' (1991) 22 African Aesthetics in Nigeria and the Diaspora 105.

[117] Reprinted in Achebe, *Creation Day* (n 38) 78–84. After the success of Chinua Achebe, *Things Fall Apart* (William Heinemann Ltd 1958), *No Longer at Ease* (Heinemann Educational Publishers Ltd 1960), and *Arrow of God* (William Heinemann Ltd 1964), the post-colonial anxiety had already begun to set in for Achebe in *A Man of the People* (East African Educational Publishers Ltd 1966).

[118] Achebe, *Creation Day* (n 38) 82.

[119] ibid 84.

[120] ibid 84.

following year he invoked Fanon's critique explicitly, noting that 'while the African intellectual was busy displaying the past culture of Africa, the troubled peoples of Africa were already creating new revolutionary cultures which took into account their present conditions', and as a result African writers had been 'left behind'.[121] The new task of the African writer was therefore 'to hurry and catch up with [the peoples]—to borrow the beautiful expression of Fanon—in that zone of occult instability where the people dwell'. [122]

The Biafran War did not have a corresponding effect on Elias's scholarship. In March 1970 he delivered a speech to the Nigerian Society of International Law—later published in the *Nigerian Law Journal*—addressing the significant international legal aspects what he called the 'recent Nigerian Civil War'.[123] Unsurprisingly, given his position Nigeria's Attorney-General during the war, Elias exonerated Nigeria of all allegations of violating international law. However, it was the issues he selected for discussion that dramatically demonstrated the distance between Elias and the emerging post-colonial critiques of Achebe (and the 'neo-colonial' critiques of Umozurike); he was concerned with, among other issues, the effect of the conflict on the proper payment of oil royalties and the legality of 'mineral and other' concessions made by the 'so-called Republic of Biafra' to foreign companies.[124] There was to be no 'post-colonial awakening' for Elias. Ultimately, and not incidentally, Biafra turned out to also be significant professionally for Elias. His path to the International Court of Justice—the head of the 'Club of International Lawyers' from which he was excluded from in 1963—was cleared when his compatriot Louis Mbanefo sided with the fledgling Biafran Republic. In fact, in a symbolic act worthy of the poetic order, at the end of the conflict Nigeria's first ICJ judge was part of the delegation that surrendered to, among others, its most illustrious.[125]

Umozurike also wrote about the Biafra at the time, and his treatment was somewhat more even-handed than Elias's, although he did not view it in the same 'neo-colonial' terms as Achebe.[126] So while the distance between Elias and Achebe on

[121] Bernth Lindfors, *Palaver: Interviews with Five African Writers* (University of Texas at Austin 1972) (hereafter Lindfors, *Palaver*), 5. Fanon had written in 1959: 'It is not enough to reunite with the people in a past where they no longer exist. We must rather reunite with them in their recent counter move which will suddenly call everything into question . . . '. Fanon, *The Wretched of the Earth* (n 1) 163.

[122] Lindfors, *Palaver* (n 121) 6.

[123] Taslim O Elias, 'The Nigerian Crisis in International Law' (1971) 5 Nigerian Law Journal 1–18.

[124] Elias ended by dismissing 'propaganda about genocide', and noting that '[n]ever . . . has there been any precedent for the generous permission granted to humanitarian and not so humanitarian organisations from all parts of the world to fly in "relief" (both genuine and fake) to rebel-held areas . . . '; ibid 16–17.

[125] Mbanefo served as Judge ad hoc in *South West Africa* (*Ethiopia & Liberia v South Africa*) 1960–1966.

[126] Umozurike included a discussion of the conflict in his book *Self-Determination in International Law* (n 25) 260–68 (concluding, at 267, that Biafrans were entitled to self-determination at the time of their declaration but, having lost the war, that 'they must reconcile themselves to an exercise of self-determination' *within* Nigeria (ie, through the full enjoyment of human rights). See also Umo O Umozurike, 'Geneva Conventions and Africa' (1971) 8 East African Journal 284–85; and Umo O

Biafra might be explained with respect to their individual politics, what is more difficult to explain is the conservative shift in Umozurike's scholarship from the 1980s onwards, such that it ended up being indistinguishable from Elias. In his final book, *Introduction to International Law* (1993) Umozurike recants his critical approach in *International Law and Colonialism* altogether.[127] The history of international law he tells makes no mention of the slave trade and spends less than a paragraph on colonialism—the centrepieces of his previous critical history of international law.[128] Rather, like Elias's 'contributionist' history of twenty years prior, Umozurike sets out the how pre-colonial African kingdoms and empires 'contributed their quota in the development of international intercourse', as well as the exchange of ambassadors with European powers.[129] The first text on his 'Suggestions for Further Reading' list is, in fact, Elias' *Africa and International Law*.[130]

Reading the work of Elias and Umozurike through their literary counterparts, then, is a somewhat frustrating exercise, raising more questions than answers. While it opens up these texts to more complex readings, and highlights the influence of political and intellectual contexts, the ultimate divergence between them undermines the promise of resolution: substituting a reading that it too blunt and acontextual for one that seems too granular and context-dependent. And yet, in this refusal of closure there is potential: just as there is 'a lot to be gained in understanding decolonization . . . as an unfinished project',[131] so too is there much to be gained from reading African international legal scholarship's relationship *with* decolonization as 'unfinished'.

Umozurike, 'The Application of International Humanitarian Law to Civil Conflicts' (1992) 4 African Journal of International and Comparative Law 497.

---

[127] Far from the Marxist bent of Umozurike, 'Colonialism in Africa' (n 23) international law is now about facilitating '[c]ommerce and the exchange of goods and services' which is 'to the mutual benefit of all states'; ibid 7.

[128] Umozurike, 'Colonialism in Africa' (n 23) 1. The book also draws on other articles, including one published in 1971 on the African slave trade. ('The African Slave Trade and the Attitudes of International Law Towards It').

[129] Umo O Umozurike, *Introduction to International Law* (Spectrum Law Publishing 1993) 7–8. His list includes the Kingdom of Ghana (300–1087 AD), Mali (1235–1410 AD), Timbuctoo, the 'Empires of Songhai and Benin', the Buganda, the Shona, Zulu, Swazi, Ethiopia, and others.

[130] It is followed by Elias' *New Horizons in International Law* (n 10). Umozurike's own 'Colonialism in Africa' (n 23) is number ten on the list (of seventeen titles). Needless to say, Rodney and Fanon do not make the list.

[131] Wenzel, 'Decolonization' (n 44) 2.

18

The Soviets and the Right to Self-Determination of the Colonized

Contradictions of Soviet Diplomacy and Foreign Policy in the Era of Decolonization

Bill Bowring

I. Introduction

This chapter suggests that the right of peoples to self-determination is the 'revolutionary kernel'[1] of post-Second World War international law, which both reflected and energized the struggles of national liberation movements for independence from colonial empires. From reference to a 'principle' in the Preamble to the United Nations (UN) Charter, a legal right of peoples to self-determination became common Article 1 to the two UN Covenants on Human Rights in 1966, and an unassailable legal right when the Covenants came into force in 1976. The Union of Soviet Socialist Republics (USSR) played a leading role in bringing about this extraordinary success, in the teeth of fierce resistance from the great colonial powers. In particular, the USSR led the newly independent states, and via a sustained diplomatic effort, contributed materially to the national liberation movements of the time.

The role of the USSR could of course be seen as sheer hypocrisy, given that the USSR, together with the territories occupied by it as a result of the Yalta and Potsdam agreements, constituted the greatest extent of Russian imperial power. This was at the very least a stark contradiction.[2]

Why did the USSR advocate a programme which appeared to be so much against its own interests? The answer is to be found in the period from 1900 to the present, although the main focus is on the twenty-year period from 1955 to 1975. The chapter explores some recent scholarly texts that focus on self-determination,

[1] For an earlier account, see Bill Bowring, *Degradation of the International Legal Order: The Rehabilitation of Law and the Possibility of Politics* (Routledge-Cavendish 2008), ch 1.

[2] Bill Bowring, 'Positivism Versus Self-Determination: The Contradictions of Soviet International Law' in Susan R Marks (ed), *International Law on the Left: Re-Examining Marxist Legacies* (CUP 2008) 133–68.

Bill Bowring, *The Soviets and the Right to Self-Determination of the Colonized* In: *The Battle for International Law: South-North Perspectives on the Decolonization Era.* Edited by: Jochen von Bernstorff and Philipp Dann, Oxford University Press (2019).
DOI: 10.1093/oso/9780198849636.003.0019

and argues that, for whatever reason, these fail or refuse to recognize the role of the USSR after the Second World War.

To begin to answer the question why Soviet diplomats adhered so doggedly to this programme, this chapter traces the policy of self-determination back to its originator, Vladimir Lenin (Ulyanov) in the period immediately before and after the First World War. Third, it examines the *travaux préparatoires* to the Covenants in the period between the Second World War and 1955, starting with the work on the Universal Declaration on Human Rights (UDHR). The senior Soviet diplomat Platon Dmitrievich Morozov (1906–1986), who became a judge of the International Court of Justice (ICJ) from 1970 to 1985, was the leading Soviet representative in the drafting meetings. Next, it traces the crucial events of 1960, with the Colonial Declaration of the UN General Assembly[3] (UNGA) against the background of revolutionary struggle in Algeria and elsewhere. Then it shows how, with Soviet encouragement, the right to self-determination became a norm not only of treaty law as in the Covenants, but of customary international law.

The focus throughout is on the process—the struggles—whereby the right of peoples to self-determination became enshrined in the two UN Covenants on Human Rights, as Article 1 of each of the International Covenant on Civil and Political Rights (ICCPR) and the International Covenant on Economic, Social and Cultural Rights (ICESCR).

II. Depoliticizing the past?—some recent texts

Interest in the topic has not abated. In 2015 Cambridge University Press published an English translation of Jörg Fisch's 2010 *The Right of Self-Determination of Peoples: The Domestication of an Illusion*.[4] In 2016 it also published *The Theory of Self-Determination*, a collection edited by Fernando R Tesón.[5] Both of these significant texts seek to avoid any recognition of the implication of the (contradictory) role played by the USSR in decolonization.

Fisch, in any event, starts by recognizing the role played by Lenin. He writes that ' . . . Lenin's position on the right to self-determination was already clear in 1914, while Wilson probably did not even know of the expression "right of self-determination of peoples" in 1914'.[6] Fisch devotes his chapter 12 to 'The Cold War and the Second Decolonization, 1945–1989'.[7] He suggests that because the Second

[3] Declaration on the Granting of Independence to Colonial Countries and Peoples, UNGA Res 1514 (XV) (14 December 1960).

[4] Jörg Fisch, *The Right of Self-Determination of Peoples: The Domestication of an Illusion* (Anita Mage tr, CUP 2015).

[5] Fernando R Tesón (ed), *The Theory of Self-Determination* (CUP 2016).

[6] Fisch (n 4) 121.

[7] ibid 190–217.

World War was a 'traditional power struggle', the right to self-determination might have disappeared 'definitively'.[8] However, the victorious powers were unable to keep their colonies in check, and in the summer of 1945, when the USSR introduced the 'principle of self-determination' into the UN Charter,[9] '[t]his secured the Soviet Union the approval of the colonial regions'.[10] Fisch adds that the 'Soviet bloc and the Third World took over the substance of the concept that had been created in the Americas between 1776 and 1865, but had not yet been designated as self-determination'.

Fisch also notes that during the drafting of the UDHR in 1948, the USSR did propose the inclusion of the right of self-determination, but this was rejected.[11] The UN decided to draft both a non-binding Declaration and a legally binding Covenant on human rights, and in 1952 it was decided to have two Covenants. Article 1, on the right of peoples to self-determination, was already formulated by the end of 1955, and in an endnote[12] he gives the vote on 29 November 1955 in the UNGA Third Committee: thirty-three in favour, twelve against,[13] and thirteen abstentions.[14] Fisch also recognizes that UNGA Res 1514 (XV) (14 December 1960) was a 'decisive victory'.[15] As he points out, not one single state dared to oppose it. Eighty-nine voted for, and only nine abstained: Australia, Belgium, the Dominican Republic, France, the United Kingdom (UK), Portugal, Spain, South Africa, and the United States (US).

According to Fisch, after 1945 the third world, supported by the USSR and its allies, succeeded in 'monopolising the discourse of self-determination and the right to self-determination for itself'.[16] He concludes that 'Lenin's venture in 1917–18 was a resounding success', and that 'Wilson became a prophet of the right to self-determination, but not of his own concept of it, but rather Lenin's'.[17] Lenin, it appears, is seen as a thoroughly malign influence.

But Fisch's argument, and the reason for the appearance of the word 'illusion' in his title, is that the 'central difficulty' in the 'formula of self-determination' is that it 'contains a promise that cannot be redeemed . . . The idea that such a right could be realised to its full extent is illusory . . . '. It seems an odd way to dismiss, in effect, the bloody and tempestuous history of decolonization.

[8] ibid 190.

[9] UN Charter, art 1, para 2, and art 55.

[10] Fisch (n 4) 191.

[11] ibid 195.

[12] ibid 268, fn 8.

[13] France, Luxembourg, The Netherlands, New Zealand, Norway, Sweden, Turkey, the UK, the USA, Australia, Belgium, Canada. See Antonio Cassese, *Self-Determination of Peoples: A Legal Reappraisal* (CUP 1995) 50.

[14] UN Doc A/C.3/SR.676, para 27.

[15] Fisch (n 4) 197.

[16] ibid 218.

[17] ibid 240.

The collection edited by Tesón, on the other hand, has very little to say about the period of interest here, save in Patrick Macklem's chapter 'Self-Determination in Three Movements'[18]. Unlike Fisch, Macklem seems determined to ensure that the USSR should entirely disappear from the history of Article 1 of the ICCPR and ICESCR. Thus, he starts by informing his reader that it was Arab, Asian, and Latin American delegations which began to press the UN in the early 1950s to recognize a human right of self-determination, to the alarm of 'European officials', who saw this as a pretext for attacks on colonial powers.[19] Lenin and the USSR make no appearance in Macklem's account of the emergence of the concept, as a discourse justifying the liberation of Eastern European nations.[20] He asserts that 'After a decade of efforts by the African, Arab, Asian and Latin American delegations to attempt to persuade numerous UN bodies to recognise self-determination as a human right . . . ', the UNGA 'enacted' Res 1514 (XV).[21] And further: 'The elevation of self-determination to the status of a human right was a spectacular political achievement by the Arab, Asian and Latin American delegations' at the UN.

Macklem refers several times to an even more politicized work—Roland Burke's 2010 '*Decolonization and the Evolution of International Human Rights*'.[22] Burke's message is that the campaign for the recognition of self-determination was the initiative of the Asian-African conference held in Bandung, Indonesia, in 1955, with which his book starts.[23] He adds that 'a right to self-determination formed one of the central articles in the Final Communiqué'.[24] The role of the USSR and its diplomacy (and material assistance to national liberation movements) are nowhere to be found.

Another more recent work in this genre is Steven Jensen's *The Making of International Human Rights: The 1960s, Decolonization, and the Reconstruction of Global Values*.[25] According to Jensen, also referring to Burke, it was Bandung in 1955 that was responsible for the presence of the right to self-determination in the Covenants.[26] Jensen does mention the Soviet Union as wanting to 'gain political advantage' by presenting itself as the leading proponent of decolonization at the UN, and adds: 'The Soviets hailed themselves as champions of anti-colonialism.'[27]

[18] Patrick Macklem, 'Self-Determination in Three Movements' in Fernando R Tesón (ed), *The Theory of Self-Determination* (CUP 2016) 94–119.

[19] ibid 94.

[20] ibid 97.

[21] ibid 99.

[22] Roland Burke, *Decolonization and the Evolution of International Human Rights* (University of Pennsylvania Press 2010).

[23] ibid 13.

[24] ibid 35.

[25] Steven LB Jensen, *The Making of International Human Rights: The 1960s Decolonization and the Reconstruction of Global Values* (CUP 2016).

[26] ibid 43.

[27] ibid 53.

From this starting point Jensen is able to assert that the USSR faced strong opposition from the Afro-Asian group and 'had to agree' despite defeat to Res 1514 (XV).[28]

In Sundhya Pahuja's 2011 *Decolonising International Law: Development, Economic Growth and the Politics of Universality*,[29] self-determination makes two brief appearances: on pages 57–59, where it is presented as part of the 'logic of nationalism'[30], and on pages 119–20, where it is referred to in the context of the Permanent Sovereignty over Natural Resources (PSNR). There is no mention of the 1960 Decolonization Resolution or the 1966 Covenants, much less the roles of Lenin in promoting the concept or the USSR in relentlessly pursuing its realization.

It is worth comparing these recent additions to the literature on decolonization with Antonio Cassese's magisterial 1995 *Self-Determination of Peoples: A Legal Reappraisal*.[31] Cassese was clear: 'Lenin was the first to insist, to the international community, that the right of self-determination be established as a general criterion for the liberation of peoples.'[32] He engages in detail with the positions of Lenin and Wilson, Lenin's call for the immediate liberation of those living under colonial rule, and Wilson's championing of 'orderly liberal reformism'.[33] Cassese's claim that it was the USSR that insisted on the proclamation of the right to self-determination in the UN Charter is supported by several sources and developed in detail.[34] He gives Bandung its proper place, but maintains that the socialist countries were the most active advocates of anti-colonial self-determination, and 'adopted and developed Lenin's thesis that self-determination should first and foremost be a postulate of anti-colonialism'.[35] Furthermore, it was the USSR that 'strongly advocated the need for both Covenants formally to enshrine the right of peoples to self-determination, which, in the Soviet view, was a precondition for the respect of individual rights'.[36]

For Cassese, decolonization took place in a quite different legal world than that depicted by Macklem, Burke, Jensen, and Pahuja. Cassese insisted that self-determination was an 'international political postulate' with a revolutionary content[37]. The latter scholars examine a world from which politics is strangely absent.

[28] ibid 54.
[29] Sundhya Pahuja, *Decolonising International Law: Development, Economic Growth, and the Politics of Universality* (CUP 2011) 59.
[30] ibid 59.
[31] Cassese (n 13).
[32] ibid 14.
[33] ibid 14–23, Wilson's words at 21, fn 30.
[34] ibid 38.
[35] ibid 44.
[36] ibid 47.
[37] The title of Cassese's chapter 2.

III. Lenin and self-determination

In December 1913 Lenin began to write on the question of the 'right of nations to self-determination'. In a short polemic[38] on the question of independence for Ukraine, he insisted on 'freedom to secede, for the right to secede', while allowing that 'the right to self-determination is one thing, of course, and the expediency of self-determination, the secession of a given nation under given circumstances, is another'. Later in December 1913,[39] he again declared that a 'democrat could not remain a democrat (let alone a proletarian democrat) without systematically advocating, precisely among the Great-Russian masses and in the Russian language, the "self-determination" of nations in the political and not in the "cultural" sense'. The latter, he said, meant only freedom of languages.

Between April and June 1914, Lenin published his own substantial work on the question—'The Right of Nations to Self-Determination'—a polemic against Rosa Luxemburg, who opposed the breakup of the Tsarist Empire.[40] In the first chapter, he insisted that '. . . it would be wrong to interpret the right to self-determination as meaning anything but the right to existence as a separate state'.[41] Furthermore, '. . . the national state is the rule and the "norm" of capitalism: the multi-national state represents backwardness . . . from the standpoint of national relations, the best conditions for the development of capitalism are undoubtedly provided by the national state'.[42]

His understanding of the historical significance of the demand is highly significant here, for he says that:

> The epoch of bourgeois-democratic revolutions in Western, continental Europe embraces a fairly definite period, approximately between 1789 and 1871. This was precisely the period of national movements and the creation of national states. When this period drew to a close, Western Europe had been transformed into a settled system of bourgeois states, which, as a general rule, were nationally uniform states. Therefore, to seek the right to self-determination in the programmes of West-European socialists at this time of day is to betray one's ignorance of the ABC of Marxism.
>
> In Eastern Europe and Asia the period of bourgeois-democratic revolutions did not begin until 1905. The revolutions in Russia, Persia, Turkey and China, the Balkan wars—such is the chain of world events of *our* period in our 'Orient'.

[38] Vladimir I Lenin, 'The Cadets and "The Right of Nations to Self-Determination"' in *Collected Works*, vol 19 (Progress Publishers 1977) 525–27.

[39] Vladimir I Lenin, 'National-Liberalism and the Right of Nations to Self-Determination' in *Collected Works*, vol 20 (Progress Publishers 1977) 56–58.

[40] Vladimir I Lenin, 'The Right of Nations to Self-Determination' in *Collected Works*, vol 20 (Progress Publishers 1977) 393–454 (hereafter Lenin, 'Right of Nations').

[41] ibid 397.

[42] ibid 400.

> And only a blind man could fail to see in this chain of events the awakening of a *whole series* of bourgeois-democratic national movements which strive to create nationally independent and nationally uniform states. It is precisely and solely because Russia and the neighbouring countries are passing through this period that we must have a clause in our programme on the right of nations to self-determination.[43]

Thus, Lenin's conception of self-determination in 1914 was wholly and necessarily relevant, not only to the Tsarist Empire but also to the European colonial empires.

Lenin returned to this question in 1916, in the midst of the First World War and before the October Revolution, summing up issues of self-determination, when he wrote that it was autonomy that could enable a nation, hitherto forcibly retained within an existing state (such as Russia) to 'crystallise into a nation'. He had in mind Norway's declaration of sovereignty from Denmark in 1814, and envisaged a declaration by the Polish nation that they would no longer be ruled by the Russian Tsar.[44]

In May 1917 the issue of independence for Poland and Finland was again at the top of the agenda, and Lenin drafted a Resolution on the National Question. His starting point was clear, namely, recognition of the right of all nations forming part of Russia freely to secede and form independent states. To deny them such a right, or to fail as a Russian government to take the necessary measures to guarantee the realization of the right to secede in practice, would be in effect to support a policy of forcible seizure or annexation. [45]

For Lenin at least, self-determination was not a mere slogan, but a principle he put into practice with immediate effect within the former Russian Empire following the Bolshevik Revolution.

According to Igor Blishchenko (1930–2000), in his time one of the most authoritative Soviet scholars of international law,[46] in a text published, ironically, in 1968, the year that the USSR crushed the 'Czech Spring', it was Lenin's Decree on Peace of 26 October 1917,[47] which, for the first time, extended the principle of the right to self-determination to all peoples, thereby discarding the imperialist distinction between 'civilized' and 'uncivilized' nations.[48]

[43] ibid 405–06.

[44] Vladimir I Lenin, 'The Discussion on Self-Determination Summed Up' in *Collected Works*, vol 22 (Progress Publishers 1977) 320–60.

[45] Vladimir I Lenin, 'Resolution on the National Question' in *Collected Works*, vol 24 (Progress Publishers 1977) 302–03.

[46] I worked with Blishchenko for a number of years, in particular on the draft of the Rome Statute of the International Criminal Court; for a touching obituary by the International Committee of the Red Cross, see <www.icrc.org/en/doc/resources/documents/article/other/57jrev.htm> accessed 3 June 2019.

[47] See <www.firstworldwar.com/source/decreeonpeace.htm> accessed 14 August 2018.

[48] IP Blishchenko, *Antisovetizm i mezhdunarodnoe pravo [Antisovietism and international law]* (Mezhdunarodnye otnosheniia 1968) (hereafter Blishchenko, *[Antisovietism]*) 69.

In his article, Blishchenko moved next to answer a series of Western scholars who argued that the Decree was entirely hypocritical, first having no application to peoples within the USSR, and second, having been applied only to Finland in the former Tsarist Empire. He pointed to the substantial autonomy, if short of secession, enjoyed by Union and Autonomous Republics in the USSR in accordance with Article 17 of its Constitution.

More importantly, he underlined the extent to which the principle was indeed put into practice by Lenin in the early years of the USSR. What he failed to point out, not surprisingly in 1968, is the fact that one of Lenin's most bitter struggles with Stalin concerned independence for Georgia.[49]

Blishchenko celebrated the break-up of the colonial system of imperialism, and the broad national liberation movements in Asia, Africa, and Latin America after the Second World War, which had posited the right of peoples to self-determination with new force. He asserted, with reason, that the USSR had done everything to ensure that the right became one of the fundamental principles of contemporary international law. This was due in part the work of the Soviet Delegation at the 1945 San Francisco Conference,[50] which drafted the UN Charter, as a result of which Article 2(1) of the Charter refers to 'respect for the principle of equal rights and self-determination of peoples . . . '.[51]

Writing after the collapse of the USSR, in 1997,[52] Blishchenko showed that the early Soviet government was remarkably consistent in implementing self-determination. He related that on 4 (17) December 1917 the Soviet government recognized the right to self-determination of Ukraine. In response to the request of the Finnish government, the Soviet of Peoples' Commissars on 18 (31) December 1917 resolved to go to the Central Executive Committee with a proposal to recognize Finland's independence. In fact, it was the Whites, seeking to restore the Empire, who opposed Finnish independence. By a Decree of 29 December 1917 (11 January 1918) the right of the people of 'Turkish Armenia' to self-determination was recognized. In answer to a request from the government of Soviet Estonia, on

[49] Moshe Lewin, *Lenin's Last Struggle* (Alan M Sheridan-Smith tr, University of Michigan Press 2005).

[50] *Documents of the United Nation's Conference on International Organization: Vol III* (United Nations Information Organizations 1945) 622; and see Grigorii I Tunkin, *Teoriia mezhdunarodnogo prava [The Theory of International Law]* (2nd edn, Mezhdunarodnye otnosheniia 1970) 67 (hereafter Tunkin, *[Theory of International Law]*). The Conference brought together delegates from fifty Allied nations and took place from 25 April 1945 to 26 June 1945 in San Francisco, USA. The delegates reviewed and rewrote the Dumbarton Oaks agreements. The convention resulted in the creation of the UN Charter, which was opened for signature on 26 June 1945.

[51] Blishchenko, *[Antisovietism]* (n 48) 75.

[52] IP Blishchenko, 'Soderzhaniye prava narodov na samoopredeleniye [The Content of the Right of Peoples to Self-Determination]' in AG Osipov (ed), *Pravo narodov na samoopredeleniye: ideya i voploshcheniye.* [Right of Peoples to Self-Determination: Idea and Realization] (Memorial 1997) 71; see also, on national liberation movements, DI Baratashvili, 'Natsionalno-osvoboditel'noye dvizheniye i razvitiye mezhdunarodnogo prava [The National Liberation Movement and the Development of International Law]' (1967) 9 Sovyetskoye gosudarstvo i pravo [Soviet State and Law] 69–75.

7 December 1918 Lenin signed a Decree on recognition of the independence of Estonia, Latvia, and Lithuania.

Thus, it was clear that before the October Revolution Lenin and the Bolsheviks were in favour not only of a right of secession from Russia by nations, but also of territorial autonomy for minorities. These policies were key components of Bolshevik policy from the moment of Bolshevik success in October 1917. In 'The Tasks of the Revolution', published in October 1917, Lenin declared that a democratic peace would be impossible without an explicit renunciation of annexation or seizure. He emphasized that every nationality without exception in Europe and in the colonies should have the right to decide for itself whether it should form a separate state.[53] This right was enshrined in the 1918 Constitution of the Russian Soviet Federated Socialist Republic (RSFSR). Every people should decide whether they wished to participate in the RSFSR and on what basis. This was the only basis for creating a free and voluntary state.

In his letter of 26 September 1922, at the time of increasing conflict with Stalin as to the right of Georgia to gain independence outside the USSR—to secede—he wrote '... we consider ourselves, the Ukrainian S.S.R. and others, equal, and enter with them, on an equal basis, into a new union, a new federation, the Union of the Soviet Republics of Europe and Asia'.[54]

On the basis of the 1918 Constitution, and Lenin's principles, the Labouring Commune of Germans of the Volga was organized at the end of 1918, which in 1924 became an Autonomous Republic. The Bashkir ASSR was organized within the RSFSR in 1919, followed in 1920–1921 by the Kirgiz (Kazakh) ASSR, and the Tatar, Dagestan, and Gorskiy autonomous republics, the Karelian Labouring Commune, and the Chuvash, Kalmyk, Marii, Botskaya (Udmurtskaya) autonomous oblasts (regions). In 1921–1922 the Yakutsk ASSR, and the Karachaev-Cherkess, Kabardino-Balkar, Komi, Mongol-Buryat, and a series of other autonomous oblasts were created.[55] All of these were descendants of forms of autonomy already existing in Tsarist Russia.

Finally, on 31 December 1922, shortly before his death, in 'The Question of Nationalities or "Autonomisation"', Lenin wrote, warning against Stalin: 'It is quite natural that in such circumstances the "freedom to secede from the union" by which we justify ourselves will be a mere scrap of paper, unable to defend the non-Russians from the onslaught of that really Russian man, the Great-Russian chauvinist, in substance a rascal and a tyrant, such as the typical Russian bureaucrat is'.[56]

[53] Vladimir I Lenin, 'The Tasks of the Revolution' in *Collected Works*, vol 26 (Progress Publishers 1977) 59–68.

[54] Vladimir I Lenin, 'On the Establishment of the U.S.S.R.: Letter to L. B. Kamenev for Members of the Politburo' in *Collected Works*, vol 42 (Progress Publishers 1977) 421–23.

[55] OE Kutafin, *Rossiyskaya avtonomiya [Russian Autonomy]* (Prospekt 2006) 133–34.

[56] Vladimir I Lenin, 'The Question of Nationalities or "Autonomisation"' in *Collected Works*, vol 36 (Progress Publishers 1977) 606.

Lenin by then regarded Stalin as just such a Great-Russian chauvinist. Stalin was utterly opposed to self-determination for Georgia. Lenin was for secession by Georgia, even if under Menshevik rule.[57]

This policy, at least, survived Lenin's death. The 1924 Constitution of the USSR[58] contained a chapter on 'Sovereign Rights of the Member Republics', including the right to freely withdraw from the Union. Article 13 of the Constitution of the RSFSR adopted in 1925, and intended to implement the 1924 USSR Constitution, recognized the right of certain nationalities (ethnicities), by decision of their own congresses of soviets, and with the approval of the highest bodies of the RSFSR, to the formation of autonomous soviet socialist republics and oblasts.

IV. Soviet diplomacy and decolonization

This section traces the continuation of Lenin's principles, or at least their associated discourse, in the post-First World War period. It focuses on two main Soviet protagonists: Platon Dmitrievich Morozov and Gleb Borisovich Starushenko.

Platon Morozov (1906–1986)[59] was born in Leningrad, studied in Moscow, and was for more than twenty years a senior government legal adviser. In 1946 he was a member of the Soviet delegation at the Tokyo war crimes trials, and from 1951 to 1968 was the Soviet representative at the UN Human Rights Commission. He was also the head of the legal department of the Soviet Foreign Ministry. From 1960 to 1968 he was the Soviet representative in the UN Security Council. In 1969 he was elected a Judge of the ICJ and served from 1970 until August 1985, when he was obliged to retire for reasons of ill-health. He died the following year.

Gleb Starushenko (1922–2007) was born in present-day Ukraine.[60] He was educated at the State Institute of Foreign Languages and Moscow State University. Specializing in international law, he was awarded a higher doctorate in legal science (*Doktor Nauk*). He was the author of many books and articles, including *The Principle of National Self-Determination in Soviet Foreign Policy* written in 1960, translated into English in 1961, and referred to by Cassese and others.[61] The Russian

[57] Lewin (n 49) 61.

[58] In Russian at <http://constitution.garant.ru/history/ussr-rsfsr/1924/> accessed 19 September 2018, abridged in English at <https://faculty.unlv.edu/pwerth/Const-USSR-1924%28abridge%29.pdf> accessed 19 September 2018.

[59] Arthur Eyffinger, 'Platon Dmitrievich Morozov' in *The International Court of Justice, 1946–1996* (Kluwer Law International 1996)

[60] Biography at <http://viperson.ru/people/starushenko-gleb-borisovich> accessed 11 December 2016.

[61] Gleb B Starushenko, *The Principle of National Self-Determination in Soviet Foreign Policy* (Ivanov-Mumjiev tr, Foreign Languages Publishing House 1964) (hereafter Starushenko, *Self-Determination*); first published in Russian in 1960 as *Printsip samoopredeleniya narodov i natsii vo vneshnei politike Sovetskovo gosudarstvo.*

original published in 1960 is cited, along with Dmitriy Grushkin's[62] work,[63] in all subsequent Russian texts on self-determination. From 1982 to 1988 he was elected a member of the UN Committee for the Elimination of Racial Discrimination (CERD), and was its Vice-Chairman in the 25th to 28th sessions, in 1982 and 1983. In 1997, at the age of 75, he participated in the seminar on The Right of Peoples to Self-Determination, organized by Memorial.[64]

As Starushenko relates,[65] on 8 December 1948, the Soviet delegation to the Third Session of the UN General Assembly, led by Andrei Vyshinsky, proposed including in the UDHR a clause saying 'Every people and every nation have the right to self-determination . . . '.[66] Mr Vyshinsky said:

> The USSR delegation wished to stress that the draft declaration contained no reference to the highly important question of the right of all nations to self-determination. The establishment of that right was one of the major achievements of the internal policy of the USSR. While the USSR delegation did not expect that right to be proclaimed in the declaration of human rights with the same forcefulness as in the Soviet Constitution, it believed that the example of the Soviet achievement should not be left out of account.

This was rejected in a roll call vote:[67] eight in favour,[68] thirty-four against,[69] and thirteen abstentions.[70]

John P Humphrey, the first Director of the UN Division of Human Rights, wrote in his memoirs:[71]

[62] Dmitriy Valerievich Grushkin, ethnologist, in the middle of the 1990s worked with Memorial publishers, and participated in many missions to the zone of armed conflict in the North Caucasus. See <http://memohrc.org/sites/all/themes/memo/templates/pdf.php?pdf=/sites/default/files/old/files/731.pdf> accessed 5 January 2016).

[63] DV Grushkin, 'Pravo narodov na samoopredeleniye: istoriya razvitiya i voploshcheniye ideyi' in AG Osipov (ed), *Pravo narodov na samoopredeleniye: ideya i voploshcheniye.* [Right of Peoples to Self-Determination: Idea and Realisation] (Memorial 1997) 6–32 and at <www.memo.ru/hr/referats/selfdet/CHAPTER2.HTM> accessed 11 December 2016.

[64] Gleb B Starushenko, 'Samoopredeleniye kak pravovaya osnova predotvrashcheniya konfliktov i zashchity prav cheloveka [Self-Determination as the Legal Foundation for the Prevention of Conflict and Protection of Human Rights]' in Osipov (n 63) 52–64.

[65] Starushenko, *Self-Determination* (n 61) 149–50.

[66] UN Doc A/784 (8 December 1948).

[67] UN Doc A/PV.183.

[68] Ukrainian Soviet Socialist Republic, Union of Soviet Socialist Republics, Yugoslavia, Byelorussian Soviet Socialist Republic, Colombia, Czechoslovakia, Pakistan, Poland.

[69] United Kingdom, United States of America, Uruguay, Venezuela, Australia, Belgium, Bolivia, Brazil, Canada, Chile, China, Costa Rica, Denmark, Dominican Republic, France, Greece, Iceland, India, Iran, Lebanon, Luxembourg, Mexico, Netherlands, New Zealand, Nicaragua, Norway, Panama, Paraguay, Peru, Philippines, Siam, Sweden, Syria, Turkey.

[70] Union of South Africa, Afghanistan, Argentina, Burma, Cuba, Ecuador, Egypt, El Salvador, Ethiopia, Guatemala, Haiti, Iraq, Liberia, Saudi Arabia.

[71] John P Humphrey, 'The Memoirs of John P. Humphrey, the First Director of the United Nations Division of Human Rights' (1983) 5 Human Rights Quarterly 387, chs III, IV, V, VI, VII, and XI.

> The political atmosphere in which the Committee had to work was charged to the point of explosion by the Cold War with irrelevant recriminations coming from both sides. But in one respect the historical context was still favorable, for the debates on human rights had not yet become occasions for political duelling in the growing conflict over colonialism. The Soviet Union did attempt to introduce a reference to the 'right' of peoples to self-determination, but it failed. Had the Declaration been adopted at any time after 1949 a more serious attempt would have been made and would probably have succeeded, with results easy to imagine in the light of what happened to the Covenants.[72]

The Soviet delegation (the representative was Mr AP Pavlov) made a similar proposal in 1949 at the Fifth Session, 9 May to 20 June, of the Commission on Human Rights,[73] this time as a clause of International Covenants on Human Rights, to precede the present Article 20 of the draft Covenant:

> Every people and every nation shall have the right to national self-determination. States which have responsibilities for the administration of non-self-governing territories shall promote the fulfilment of this right, guided by the aims and principles of the United Nations in relation to the peoples of such territories. The State shall ensure to national minorities the right to use their native tongue and to possess their national schools, libraries, museums, and other cultural and educational institutions.

Following the USSR's intervention, the Fifth Session of the UN General Assembly, in Res 421 (V) (4 December 1950), 317th Plenary Session, at letter D, para 6, called upon the ECOSOC 'to request the Commission on Human Rights to study ways and means which would ensure the right of people and nations to self-determination, and to prepare recommendations for consideration by the General Assembly at its sixth session'.

The Commission did not fulfil the task assigned to it, and so the question was again raised at the Sixth General Assembly. It adopted two resolutions. The first, UNGA Res 545 (VI) (5 February 1952), recalled the resolution of 1950, decided to include in the International Covenant or Covenants on Human Rights to be drafted in the following terms 'All peoples shall have the right of self-determination', and requested the Commission on Human Rights to prepare recommendations for the seventh session of the General Assembly.

72 ibid 426.

73 See Economic and Social Council (ECOSOC), 'Report of the Fifth Session of the Commission on Human Rights to the Economic and Social Council' (Lake Success, New York 23 June 1949) UN Doc E/CN.4/350 <http://uvallsc.s3.amazonaws.com/travaux/s3fs-public/E-1371__E-CN_4-350.pdf> accessed 19 September 2018.

The second resolution, UNGA Res 549 (VI) (5 February 1952) requested the ECOSOC to instruct the Commission on Human Rights to '... give priority to the question of the right of people to self-determination which the Commission was forced to defer at its seventh session owing to lack of time'.

On 15 April 1952, the 254th meeting (afternoon) of the eighth session of the Commission on Human Rights[74] discussed a draft clause submitted by Mr Morozov.[75] He wished to explain:

> ... his country's position on self-determination. The national problem had been successfully solved in the USSR, where all races, nationalities, peoples and tribes enjoyed full equality of all rights, including the right to self-determination, and had been developing their own economy and culture in entire freedom and with the generous and disinterested assistance of the USSR.
>
> The right to self-determination was guaranteed by the USSR Constitution, Article 123 of which not only accorded full equality of rights to USSR citizens, irrespective of their nationality or race ... while Article 17 reserved to every Union Republic the right freely to secede from the USSR.
>
> Having eliminated the problem in their own midst, the peoples of the USSR had always viewed with great sympathy all attempts to solve it elsewhere. The USSR had steadfastly supported all peoples fighting for their national independence and sovereignty.

He gave the examples of support to Syria and Lebanon demanding the evacuation of foreign troops from their territory, a similar request in 1947 by Egypt, and most recently in Tunisia. The 'problem' had been far from 'solved' in the USSR.

Mr Morozov also responded to the long intervention at the previous meeting that day of Samuel Hoare, the UK representative.[76] Mr Hoare had argued for a highly restrictive interpretation of the UN Charter's reference to self-determination:

> The Charter established a distinction between the two concepts. On the one hand, in Article 1, paragraph 2 and in Article 55, it proclaimed the principle of equal rights and self-determination of peoples, which it considered as forming a whole. The references to 'peoples' in the Preamble of the Charter were to the peoples of the sovereign states represented at San Francisco. The references to self-determination in those provisions of the Charter would therefore seem to be

[74] UN Doc E/CN.4/SR.254.

[75] Starushenko, *Self-Determination* (n 61) 151; Economic and Social Council (ECOSOC), 'Draft Resolution by the Union of Soviet Socialist Republics' (15 April 1952) UN Doc E/CN.4/L.21.

[76] Samuel Hoare was an Under-Secretary of State in the Foreign and Commonwealth Office and served as UK representative at the UN Commission for Human Rights for many years. See Samuel Hoare, 'The UN Commission on Human Rights' in Evan Luard (ed), *The International Protection of Human Rights* (Thames & Hudson 1967) 79–87. He was knighted in 1957; see <http://media.bufvc.ac.uk/newsonscreen2/Pathe/107587/NoS_107587_other.pdf> accessed 11 December 2016.

to the recognition of the sovereignty of sovereign States and the obligation of such States to respect the sovereignty of other States. That was, at any rate one, and an important aspect of self-determination.[77]

Mr Morozov's reply was:

> The United Kingdom representative had been somewhat less cautious; he had indicated that the formula adopted by the General Assembly only applied an obligation already undertaken by the States signatories to the Charter. This restrictive interpretation was plainly the position of a colonial power and required no comment. The General Assembly, in adopting that formula, had most certainly given it an altogether different meaning. It was worthy of note that, in the conception of the United Kingdom representative, there was a great difference between recognition of the right to self-determination and the assumption by a State of the obligation to implement that right.
>
> The Commission adopted the proposal to include the clause on nations' right to self-determination in the International Covenants on Human Rights, and this was approved by the Third Committee of the Tenth General Assembly.[78]

At the end of 1952, the countries that were former colonies, actively supported by the Soviet Union, succeeded in securing the adoption by the Seventh General Assembly of three very significant resolutions aimed at compelling the colonial powers to respect the principle of self-determination (UNGA Res 637 (VII) (16 December 1952)).[79] Resolution 637A (VII) recommended that states administering trust and non-self-governing territories should not only recognize the principle of self-determination but should encourage and facilitate its implementation. Resolution 637B (VII) asked administering powers to inform the UN about the extent to which the populations of non-self-governing territories enjoy this right. And Resolution 637C (VII) recommended the Commission on Human Rights to continue to draw up recommendations on the observance of the right.

As the Ninth Session of the Commission (1953) had no time to pursue these issues, the Eighth General Assembly asked it to give priority to this question at its next session.[80] The Tenth Session (23 February to 16 April 1954) drew up a draft resolution to establish a Commission that should

> . . . examine any situation resulting from alleged denial or inadequate realization of the right of self-determination, which falls within the scope of Article 14 of the

[77] Commission on Human Rights, 'Eighth Session, Summary Records of the 250th Meeting' (30 April 1952) <https://uvallsc.s3.amazonaws.com/travaux/s3fs-public/E-CN_4-SR_253_0.pdf> accessed 19 September 2018.

[78] Starushenko, *Self-Determination* (n 61) 152.

[79] ibid 153.

[80] UNGA Res 738 (VIII) (28 November 1953).

> Charter and to which the Commission's attention is drawn by any ten Members of the United Nations.[81]

Starushenko reports[82] that the struggle around the content of self-determination was especially heated in the debate on the draft Covenants in the Third Committee of the Tenth General Assembly. The discussion of the proposed common Article 1, on self-determination, took some thirty sittings.

The US inspired the Secretary General Dag Hammarskjöld to address the Committee on 11 October 1955. This is Starushenko's appreciation of what happened.

' Alleging that the confused question of self-determination threatened to prevent the Committee from doing the job efficiently, [he] urged it to remove the article . . . from the covenants. His recommendation was sharply rejected by the delegations of the Soviet Union, Afghanistan, Iran, Saudi Arabia and other countries, and that compelled him to with draw his proposal. Having smashed the resistance to the colonialists, the Committee voted (33 to 12 with 13 abstentions) to include the article on self-determination in the [covenants]'.

But as King and Hobbins point out, Hammarskjöld in fact had achieved his purpose, and the adoption of the Covenants was delayed for a further decade.

" In the event, following Hammarskjöld's decision, just such a debate took place and the Covenants were not opened for signature for another full decade. Had Humphrey's advice been followed, the UN may have side-stepped the political battles by delegating the tough issues to a conference of experts. Such a group, sufficiently far removed from the ordinary politics of the Third Committee, would have a much greater chance for consensus, not to mention flexibility of working methods and greater dedication to the issues involved. Ironically, this was the exact approach the Secretary-General would soon take on the issue of self-determination.

> In thinking of the problem it has occurred to me, therefore, that one possible solution might be for the United Nations to provide a forum where the question [of self determination] can be discussed in an atmosphere of calm. And for this purpose I do see some justification in setting up a new committee of a purely temporary character. For what is needed, in the first instance in any event, is agreement on basic principles -an agreement that can undoubtedly best be reached if the discussion is divorced from burning political controversies. The time of the General Assembly and of the Councils is taken up by specific problems and these problems are, most of them, highly controversial" .[83]

[81] Commission on Human Rights, 'Report of the 10th Session, 23 February-16 April 1954' (1954) UN Doc E/CN.4/705, 78.

[82] Starushenko, *Self-Determination* (n 61) 155–56.

[83] 'Statement by the Secretary-General before the Third Committee at its 633rd Meeting, Tenth Session, Third Committee of the General Assembly, Agenda Item 28' (11 October 1959) UN Doc

The intense conflict between the USSR, the newly independent states and their allies, and the colonial powers continued through the Eighteenth, Nineteenth and Twentieth Sessions of the ECOSOC, and the Eleventh, Twelfth and Thirteenth General Assemblies. Finally, on 12 December 1958 the UNGA adopted the draft submitted by the Commission on Human Rights by fifty-two votes against fifteen (including the US and UK), with eight abstentions. The resolution noted that the right of peoples and nations to self-determination in the two draft Covenants included 'permanent sovereignty over their natural wealth and resources', decided to establish a Commission, 'to conduct a full survey of the status of this basic constituent of the right of self-determination, with recommendations, as necessary, for its strengthening'.

However, King and Hobbins note that the 'Secretary-General was not alone in his concern regarding the problem posed by the issue of self-determination. Cassin and Humphrey felt that the proposal to place the right of peoples to self-determination as Article 1 in both draft Covenants was a mistake.[84]

Indeed, Humphrey worked tirelessly to get it removed from the Covenants. Ultimately, Article 1 was adopted by the UNGA, while consideration of the commissions was deferred and eventually abandoned.[85]

V. Who was responsible for the 1960 Declaration?

The question of a declaration on the granting of independence to colonial countries and peoples was initially proposed for inclusion in the agenda of the UNGA by Nikita Khrushchev, the Chairman of the Council of Ministers of the USSR, during his address to the Assembly on 23 September 1960. [86]

This proposal was formalized in a letter to the President of the UNGA of the same day,[87] which was submitted together with a draft Declaration on the granting of independence to colonial countries and peoples.[88] On 28 September 1960, the General Committee recommended that the item proposed by the USSR be included in the UNGA's agenda at its fifteenth session of the same year and that it be allocated to the First (Political and Security) Committee. On 10 October, the

A/C.3/L.466, 2. In Jeff King and AJ Hobbins, 'Hammarskjöld and Human Rights: The Deflation of the UN Human Rights Programme 1953–1961' (2003) 5 Journal of the History of International Law 337, 351–52.

---

[84] King and Hobbins (n 83) 363.

[85] No mention of the proposed commissions is found in the Secretary-General's annual reports for 1957–1961.

[86] (1960) *United Nations Yearbook* 44. The next paragraphs draw from this sober and authoritative account, which contrasts strongly with the more tendentious arguments of Macklem (n 18) and Burke (n 22).

[87] UN Doc A/4501 (23 September 1960).

[88] UN Doc A/4502 (23 September 1960).

UNGA decided to place the item on its agenda and, on 13 October, a proposal by the USSR to discuss the item in plenary meetings was unanimously adopted. It cannot therefore be denied that this was the initiative of the USSR.

The topic was discussed in the UNGA from 28 November to 7 December 1960 and from 13 December to 14 December 1960.[89] The UNGA had before it, in addition to the draft Declaration submitted by the USSR,[90] another draft submitted by Cambodia on 28 November on behalf of twenty-six Asian and African countries, and which was eventually sponsored by forty-three delegations.[91] This is the draft to which Macklem and Burke, among others, wish to attribute the credit for bringing the issue before the UNGA.

The UN account records that representatives of several of the sponsoring countries of the forty-three-power draft welcomed the initiative taken by the USSR in bringing the question of colonialism before the UNGA; the Asian-African states, they said, had long been concerned with that problem.

Many representatives of Asian-African Members referred to the Bandung Conference in 1955, where countries of Asia and Africa had initiated a number of fundamental principles which had become the cornerstone of their policy towards the colonial countries and peoples and which had been re-emphasized at the conferences of African states at Accra in 1958, at Monrovia in 1959, and at Addis Ababa in 1960. They stressed that the draft declaration they were now submitting was the culmination of those principles.[92] Indeed, Victor Kattan has shown in detail that the USSR's support for self-determination in the third world was attractive to many of the emerging third-world leaders in the inter-war years. Castro, Che Guevara, Nehru, Nasser, and Sukarno were all influenced by the ideas and principles of the French, Russian, and Chinese Revolutions, and by the Leninist ideologies of the communist parties in their own countries.[93]

Australia and New Zealand agreed with the UK's contention that colonialism was a necessary transitional phase and that non-self-governing and trust territories had made remarkable progress towards independence, in accordance with the provisions of the UN Charter. Each case was governed by its own circumstances, and the test was always that of determining what would best suit the interests of the peoples whose destiny was at stake. In some cases, progress had been slow because of the special circumstances of a particular territory.[94]

The US representative also took the opportunity to attack the USSR, and spoke of 'a new colonial system' that had been imposed by force on many peoples of many

[89] UN Doc A/PV.925-939 and A/PV.944-947.

[90] UN Doc A/4502.

[91] UN Doc A/L.323 (23 September 1960) and Adds. 1 to 6.

[92] (1961) *United Nations Yearbook* 46.

[93] See Victor Kattan, 'Self-Determination as Ideology: The Cold War, the End of Empire, and the Making of UN General Assembly Resolution 1514 (14 December 1960)' in Luca Pasquet and Klara van der Ploeg (eds), *International Law and Time: Narratives and Techniques* (Springer forthcoming).

[94] (1961) *United Nations Yearbook* 47.

races, many of whom had been free for centuries. The entire system was disguised by censorship, by ruthless thought control, and by an elaborate misuse of words like 'democratic' and 'autonomous'. However, its tragic reality had been attested to by the millions who had escaped it and by the tens of thousands who had died trying to shake it off. The US representative referred to the USSR at the 'arch-practitioner' of this 'new and lethal colonialism'.[95] He said that the forty-three-nation draft declaration quite rightly spoke out against colonialism 'in all its manifestations'.[96]

For his part, Starushenko did not deny that the Soviet draft had not been adopted, and noted that '. . . the Declaration reflects some of the main Soviet proposals on the issue . . . The final text . . . bears an imprint of compromise. It does not include for instance the proposal in the Soviet draft on the abolition of colonial military bases and leased territories.'[97]

In her recent analysis, Mary Heiss paints a more complete picture:

> The Afro-Asian bloc at the UN was anxious to take the lead itself in drafting an anti-colonial resolution that avoided outright Cold War divisions and set about this task with enthusiasm and dedication even as Soviet diplomats tried to claim that 'this [was] their item'. Borrowing heavily from the Bandung final communiqué of 1955, the draft resolution ultimately co-sponsored by 43 Asian and African states was an effort to eliminate explicit Cold War considerations from the issue of declaring an end to colonialism and to focus instead on the broad goal of seeing the fulfilment of the UN Charter's pledge that all peoples deserved the chance to govern themselves. Condemning 'colonialism in all its forms and manifestations,' the draft resolution avoided the shrill tone of the Soviet declaration, made no mention of dismantling foreign bases, and did not call for specific timetables or target dates.[98]

The forty-three-nation draft was adopted without change by the UNGA, by a vote of eighty-nine to zero, with nine abstentions,[99] in UNGA Res 1514 (XV) entitled 'Declaration on the Granting of Independence to Colonial Countries and Peoples'.

Heiss refers to the US abstention as a 'public relations fiasco', and shows in detail how Eisenhower succumbed in the end to direct pressure from the British Prime Minister Harold Macmillan, who dismissed the resolution as having 'no connection with reality' and issued a plaintive plea that Britain and the United States

[95] See Mary A Heiss, 'Exposing "Red Colonialism": U.S. Propaganda at the United Nations, 1953–1963' (2015) *17* Journal of Cold War Studies 82.

[96] (1961) UN Yearbook 48.

[97] Starushenko, *Self-Determination* (n 61) 156.

[98] Heiss (n 95) 96–97.

[99] The colonial states and their allies: Australia, Belgium, Dominican Republic, France, Portugal, Spain, Union of South Africa, United Kingdom, United States.

'stand together'. Reluctant to go against the country's 'strongest ally', particularly when US officials had themselves noted so many shortcomings in the draft resolution, Eisenhower instructed the US mission to abstain.[100]

Following on the heels of Res 1514 (XV) came a whole series of documents of a similar type: UNGA Res 1803 (XVII) (14 December 1962) on 'Inalienable sovereignty in relation to natural resources'; UNGA Res 2105 (XX) (20 December 1965) 'On the realisation of the Declaration on the granting of independence to colonial countries and peoples'—the UNGA recognized the legitimacy of the struggle of colonial peoples against colonial domination in the exercise of their right to self-determination and independence, and it invited all States to provide material and moral support to national liberation movements in colonial territories.

VI. Self-determination and national liberation

The right of peoples to self-determination became a legal right in the ICCPR and ICESCR and achieved the status of customary law in the 1970 Declaration on Principles of International Law Concerning Friendly Relations and Co-operation among States in accordance with the UN Charter (UNGA Res 2625).

In the 1966 UN Covenants on human rights (ICCPR and ICESCR), which to begin with were developed as a single document, it was decided that the provision on self-determination be included on the basis that:

a) it '. . . is the source or essential foundation for other human rights, since there cannot be authentic realisation of individual rights without realisation of the right to self-determination'
b) in drafting the Covenants the realisation and protection of the principles and goals of the UN Charter must be taken into account, including the principles of equal rights and self-determination of peoples
c) a series of provisions of the Universal Declaration of Human Rights are directly connected to the right to self-determination
d) if the right was not included in the Covenants, they would be incomplete and ineffective.[101]

The success of the USSR and its allies in the 1960s had momentous consequences for the legal and political process of decolonization. Later resolutions of the UNGA

[100] Heiss (n 95) 99.

[101] Grushkin (n 63) 12 citing Aureliu Cristescu, 'The Right to Self-Determination: Historical and Current Development on the Basis of United Nations Instruments' (New York 1981) UN Doc E/CN.4/Sub.2/404/Rev.1.

ensured that the so-called 'national liberation movements'[102] were recognized as the 'sole legitimate representatives' of the relevant peoples. In other words, ex-territorial social and political organizations were in fact made equal to sovereign subjects of international law. Examples were the Palestine Liberation Organization (PLO), the South West African Peoples Organisation (SWAPO), the ANC (African National Congress), and the PAC (Pan African Congress). In 1973 the UN declared that it recognized SWAPO as the 'sole authentic representative of the people of Namibia'. And in 1974 the PLO was recognized by the majority of member states of the UN as the lawful representative of the Palestinians, with corresponding status at the UN.

There are writers like Christopher Quaye who ignore the Soviet role in promoting the legal right to self-determination or supporting the national liberation movements.[103] However, Galia Golan, although seemingly unaware of the international law dimension, wrote in the context of national liberation movements that: 'The term preferred by the Soviets [to "independence"] as an overall, all-inclusive type of objective was self-determination.'[104] Her book demonstrates the huge resources devoted by the USSR to support of all kinds for a very wide range of national liberation movements in the third world. Tables she prepared list forty-three movements in twenty-six countries, with thirteen instruments of 'Soviet behaviour'.[105] Roger Kanet noted that 'Soviet trade with the developing nations increased more than eleven times from 1955 to 1970.' In 1970 it increased an additional 15.7 per cent.[106] Furthermore, Bhabani Sen Gupta pointed out that

> in cultivating friendly, viable forces, the Soviet Union has persistently tried to satisfy some of the *felt* needs of the power elites of Third World societies. In South Asia, they have come forward to provide aid for industrialisation programs in India, for which the Indians could not secure resources either domestically of from Western nations . . . .[107]

I would contend, contrary to these authors, that it was not as a result of Soviet propaganda, but through the logic of the new international law, developed through the efforts of the USSR and its allies, that a people with the right to self-determination faced with aggressive attempts to deny that right enjoyed the right of self-defence under Article 51 of the UN Charter, and was in all respects be considered a subject of international law. I should add that this was not the opinion of the majority of Western jurists. On the contrary, the role of the USSR,

[102] See Galia Golan, *The Soviet Union and National Liberation Movements in the Third World* (Unwin Hyman 1988).

[103] Christopher O Quaye, *Liberation Struggles in International Law* (Temple University Press 1991).

[104] Golan (n 102) 136.

[105] ibid 262–67.

[106] Roger E Kanet, 'The Soviet Union and the Colonial Question 1917–1953' in Roger E Kanet (ed), *The Soviet Union and the Developing Nations* (Johns Hopkins University Press 1974).

[107] B Gupta, 'The Soviet Union in South Asia' in ibid.

as noted earlier, was for the most part ignored. Thus, Portugal was at that time waging war against the peoples of Angola and Mozambique; those peoples were therefore victims of aggression and enjoyed the right of self-defence, and third party states had the right and duty to come to their assistance.[108] A year earlier, in a more formal article defending the dubious concept of 'proletarian internationalism', GI Tunkin also linked the 'struggle for international peace and security' with the 'struggle for the freedom and independence of peoples', with reference especially to Res 1514 (XV).[109]

1968 was not only the year of the Soviet invasion of Czechoslovakia, but also a crucial moment in the American war in Vietnam. The invasion of Czechoslovakia took place against the background of the emergence of a new 'socialist international law', with a new approach to traditional concepts of sovereignty. In 1970, Tunkin published a revised second edition of his textbook *International Law*.[110] Dealing with the Prague events, Tunkin argued that these were a logical extension of the concept already well developed and applied in Hungary in 1956. This was the legal prevention of inroads by capitalist influences into a socialist state.[111] The international law framework is provided through an analysis of the concept of sovereignty.

Tunkin noted that both general and socialist international law respected the concept of 'sovereignty', but concluded that respect is not the same thing in the two systems.[112] Socialist states would continue to insist on respect for the principle as developed in general international law when speaking of the relationships between themselves and capitalist states so as to prevent capitalist states from intervening in the internal affairs of Socialist states, but the concept of sovereignty had evolved within the conceptual framework of 'proletarian internationalism' as regards the mutual relationships of socialist states. His translator, William Butler, commented: 'The Soviet invasion of Czechoslovakia plainly was a difficult moment for his approach to international law, and his treatment of a "socialist international law" impressed, rightly or wrongly, as something less than enthusiastic.'[113]

Writing in 1976,[114] Boris Meissner emphasized that from 1968 the opposition of non-Russian ethnic groups in the USSR to Brezhnev's policies of centralization and Russification had also been growing. The Soviet dissidents, in particular Andrei

[108] Blishchenko, *[Antisovietism]* (n 48) 76–77.

[109] Grigorii I Tunkin, 'Bor'ba dvukh kontseptsiy v mezhdunarodnom prave' (1967) *11* Sovyetskoye gosudarstvo i pravo [Soviet State and Law] 140, 144–46.

[110] Tunkin, *[Theory of International Law]* (n 50) and Grigorii I Tunkin, *Theory of International Law* (Harvard University Press 1974).

[111] Tunkin, *[Theory of International Law]* (n 50) 493, cited in John N Hazard, 'Renewed Emphasis Upon a Socialist International Law' (1971) *65* American Journal of International Law 142, 145.

[112] Tunkin, *[Theory of International Law]* (n 50) 459.

[113] W Butler, 'The Learned Writings of Professor G. I. Tunkin' (2002) *4* Journal of the History of International Law 394.

[114] Boris Meissner, 'The Soviet Concept of Nation and the Right of National Self-Determination' (1977) *32* International Journal 56.

Sakharov, took up the injustice suffered by the Crimean Tatars, deported from their homeland to Central Asia in 1944, and by the Meskhetians, who had been expelled from Georgia. Sakharov first mentioned the Crimean Tatars in a memorandum of June 1968. On 19 March 1970, Sakharov, together with VF Turchin and RA Medvedev, sent a letter to the Soviet leadership demanding that all the rights of nations which had been forcibly resettled under Stalin be restored, and that national autonomy and the right to return to their ancestral homeland be granted to all the peoples who had been forcibly deported. These demands were reiterated in Sakharov's memorandum to Brezhnev of 5 March 1971.

Then, in *My Country and the World*, his English-language book published in October 1975,[115] Sakharov again expressed his opposition to the oppression of the non-Russian nationalities. He drew attention to the fact that many political prisoners were so-called 'nationalists' from Ukraine, the Baltic republics, and Armenia. These individuals had originally been brought to trial principally because of their concern for the preservation of their national culture in the face of Russification, and had been given particularly heavy sentences. As well as the Crimean Tatars, the fate of the Volga Germans and the Jews were the subject of Sakharov's attention.[116]

Thus, the seeds were sown for the collapse of the USSR in 1991, the 'parade of sovereignties' which threatened the continuing existence of the Russian Federation itself, and the continuing relevance of self-determination to Russia's recent actions in Crimea, eastern Ukraine, and to the gathering storms relating to the future of Russia's precarious regionalism and federalism.[117]

It is clear to the present rulers of Russia that Lenin's whole-hearted advocacy for and implementation of the right of nations to self-determination played a crucial role in the destruction of the Tsarist Empire and in the collapse of the USSR, and continues to pose an existential threat to contemporary Russia. My account and analysis in this chapter has shown that although the USSR's diplomacy was instrumental in securing the enshrinement of the rights of peoples to self-determination as a legal right in international law, and that the USSR diplomatically and materially made an enormous contribution to the process of decolonization, the contradictions of the position of the USSR, in particular Mr Morozov's blithe assertion that there was no longer any problem in the USSR to which I have referred, in the end helped to bring about the collapse of the USSR itself.

[115] Andrei Sakharov, *My Country and the World* (Harvill Press 1975).

[116] Meissner (n 114) 76–77.

[117] See the web portal *After Empire: Regionalism and Federalism in Russia* at <http://afterempire.info/2016/11/02/why-after-emp/> accessed 5 January 2016.

19

The Failed Battle for Self-Determination

The United States and the Post-War Illusion of Enlightened Colonialism, 1945–1975

Olivier Barsalou

I. Introduction

Building on United States (US) Department of State (DoS) records and archives, this chapter develops two central arguments: one historical and the other conceptual. Firstly, from a historical perspective, this chapter argues that the US government contributed to transforming, between 1945 and 1975, the right to self-determination—implying a right to decolonization—into a right to internal self-determination—implying a right to democratic participation, a shift embodied by Common Article 1 of the 1966 Human Rights Covenants. But why did the American government defend such a conception of the right to self-determination? While the US opposed colonialism because of the legacy of the American War of Independence, it had strong economic self-interest in seeking the end of the European empires. It was also worried about the spread of communism, which was often confused with the rise of radical nationalist movements in Asia, Africa, and Latin America. Washington DC saw these transformations through Cold War lenses: should it support European allies or follow the decolonial wake to prevent a possible communist takeover?[1] Unsurprisingly, the US government was thus highly sceptical of the non-aligned movement when it emerged in 1954–1955,[2] as it was also of the decolonization movement as a whole[3] (and of its domestic ramifications).[4] The right to internal self-determination arose to accommodate and reconcile US commitment to anti-colonialism with the desire of

[1] For a counter-narrative, see Vijay Prashad, *The Darker Nations: A People's History of the Third World* (New Press 2007).

[2] On the non-aligned movement, the Bandung conference, and its aftermath, see Luis Eslava, Michael Fakhri and Vasuki Nesiah (eds), *Bandung, Global History, and International Law: Critical Pasts and Pending Futures* (CUP 2017); Frank Gerits, 'Bandung as the Call for a Better Development Project: US, British, French and Gold Coast Perceptions of the Afro-Asian Conference (1955)' (2016) 16 Cold War History 255–72.

[3] Odd Arne Westad, *The Cold War: A World History* (Basic Books 2017).

[4] Thomas Borstelmann, *The Cold War and the Color Line: American Race Relations in the Global Arena* (Harvard University Press 2001); Mary L Dudziak, *Cold War Civil Rights: Race and the Image of American Democracy* (Princeton University Press 2000).

Olivier Barsalou, *The Failed Battle for Self-Determination* In: *The Battle for International Law: South-North Perspectives on the Decolonization Era*. Edited by: Jochen von Bernstorff and Philipp Dann, Oxford University Press (2019).

DOI: 10.1093/oso/9780198849636.003.0020

succeeding American administrations to preserve the global order that emerged in 1945 in San Francisco.

Secondly, this understanding of the right to self-determination rested on an intellectual tradition, a jurisprudence, and an argumentative structure that had a long history connecting three distinct periods of European and American (sixteenth-century Spain, eighteenth- and nineteenth-century Great Britain, and twentieth-century US) practices of imperial rule over weaker peoples without their consent, each structured around a specific ethical system promising to bring benefits to the ruled.[5] In each historical setting, the idea (as opposed to the right, which was legally formalized in the twentieth century) of self-determination emerged as a corollary, yet necessary, product of imperial trusteeship designed to govern, improve, and ultimately, emancipate dominated peoples.[6] Post-1945 American administrations became the heirs and the guardians of this connection between imperial trusteeship and the self-determination. For the American government, the right to self-determination in international law arose as a justification and a rationalization of imperial trusteeship practices over subjugated peoples. Self-determination was considered as a conditional right enabling post-colonial self-rule only when colonial powers decided a requisite level of political maturity had been achieved.

This understanding departs from traditional scholarly accounts of the emergence of the right to self-determination in international law.[7] Many international legal scholars (and historians) associate the rise of the right to self-determination with the emergence of an enlightened conception of republicanism in the eighteenth century[8] or a teleological history spanning the early twentieth century from Woodrow Wilson[9] and the interwar period[10] to the Balkan Wars.[11] While this chapter doesn't dispute the idea that the rise of both nationalism and republicanism were historically connected in many corners of the world, it rejects the

[5] Ramendra Nath Chowdhuri, *International Mandates and Trusteeship Systems: A Comparative Study* (Springer Netherlands 1955) 12.

[6] Olivier Barsalou, *International Law and the Path to Liberty: The Imperial Origins of the Right to Self-Determination, 1500–1945*, unpublished article manuscript, on file with the author.

[7] Steven L Jensen, *The Making of International Human Rights: The 1960s, Decolonization, and the Reconstruction of Global Values* (CUP 2016); Roland Burke, *Decolonization and the Evolution of International Human Rights* (University of Pennsylvania Press 2010).

[8] Daniel Thürer and Thomas Burri, 'Self-Determination' in Rüdiger Wolfrum (ed), *The Max Planck Encyclopedia of Public International Law* (OUP 2009) para 1 (hereafter Thürer and Burri, 'Self-Determination'); James D Summers, *Peoples and International Law: How Nationalism and Self Determination Shape a Contemporary Law of Nations* (Martinus Nijhoff 2007); David Raĭc, *Statehood and the Law of Self-Determination* (Kluwer Law International 2002) ch 5; Antonio Cassese, *Self-Determination of Peoples: A Legal Reappraisal* (CUP 1995) ch 2 (hereafter Cassese, *Self-Determination of Peoples*).

[9] Erez Manela, *The Wilsonian Moment: Self-Determination and the International Origins of Anticolonial Nationalism* (OUP 2007) (hereafter Manela, *The Wilsonian Moment*).

[10] Arnulf Becker Lorca, 'Petitioning the International: A 'Pre-History' of Self-Determination' (2014) 25 European Journal of International Law 497–523.

[11] Oded Haklai, 'From Independent Statehood to Minority Rights: The Evolution of National Self-Determination as an International Order Principle in the Post-State Formation Era' (2015) 14 Ethnopolitics 461–69.

argument according to which the right to self-determination *in international law* has republican roots. Furthermore, while self-determination claims admittedly accelerated the break-up of European empires between 1945 and 1975, the parallel construction of the right to self-determination within the United Nations (UN) provided a new template for institutionalizing foreign control over territories and peoples.[12] Post-World War Two imperial trusteeship aimed not only at civilizing subjugated populations but at preparing them for self-government.[13] Following Mark Beissinger's argument, promises of self-determination came to be construed as a 'script and technology for imposing control through hollowing out its substance and embracing its form'.[14]

Ultimately, the right to self-determination failed the battle for decolonization. The UN Charter incorporated a legal justification for the maintenance and renovation of colonial and trusteeship practices which, ultimately, transcended the decolonization era. Such a conception of the right to self-determination still governs contemporary legal claims about international trusteeship and self-determination. As such, 1945 is the 'year zero'[15] of the story of the right to self-determination this chapter tries to tell: a moment where not only ideas about self-determination in global politics coalesced and crystallized in legal form but also (and more importantly) a moment which shaped and defined the strange triumph of sovereignty and the proliferation of the nation-state form in the 1950s, 1960s, and after.[16]

The chapter first analyses the evolution of the US government's attitude on the colonial question between the adoption of the Atlantic Charter in August 1941 and the opening of the UN Conference on International Organization (UNCIO) in April 1945. It shows how the American government slowly departed from a position favouring the outright dismantling of European colonial empires to a more circumspect attitude emphasising the necessity to renovate colonialism and to extend the tutelage of colonial peoples. Next it explains how the US delegation at the UNCIO succeeded in embedding in the Charter the idea of a gradual, managed, and orderly dismantling of European empires. The Charter promised self-determination but only after a transitional period of tutelage. The chapter then shows how that political and legal compromise reached at San Francisco in June 1945 allowed the US and other imperial powers to turn those colonial territories

[12] Guy Fiti Sinclair, *To Reform the World: International Organizations and the Making of Modern States* (OUP 2017); Mark Beissinger, 'Self-Determination as a Technology of Imperialism: The Soviet and Russian Experiences' (2015) 14 Ethnopolitics 479, 480 (hereafter Beissinger, 'Self-Determination').

[13] Ronald Robinson, 'The Moral Disarmament of African Empire 1919–1947' (1979) 8 The Journal of Imperial and Commonwealth History 86–104.

[14] Beissinger, 'Self-Determination' (n 12) 479, 482; Neta C Crawford, 'Decolonization through Trusteeship: The Legacy of Ralph Bunche' in Robert A Hill and Edmond J Keller (eds), *Trustee for the Human Community: Ralph J. Bunche, the United Nations, and the Decolonization of Africa* (Ohio University Press 2010) 94.

[15] Ian Buruma, *Year Zero: A History of 1945* (Penguin 2013).

[16] Eva-Maria Muschik, 'Managing the World: The United Nations, Decolonization, and the Strange Triumph of State Sovereignty in the 1950s and 1960s' (2018) 13 Journal of Global History 121–44.

into Western assets in the global Cold War. In doing so, they turned the revolutionary nature of the right to self-determination into a justification for renovated trusteeship relations.

II. From self-determination to tutelage: the US and the creation of the UN trusteeship regime

Before the Second World War, the principle of self-determination didn't have any formal legal status in international law even if it nonetheless played a significant political role.[17] The Paris Peace Treaties ratified in the aftermath of the First World War incorporated some prototypes of what the right to self-determination might look like in the future. Mandates, minority rights protection regimes, and plebiscites were among the first legal devices developed during the interwar era to protect 'minorities', 'backward peoples', and other stateless peoples.

For the American government, the 1941 Atlantic Charter was a qualified international commitment to dismantling European empires in an orderly and gradual manner, whereas for the British, it was rather a reaffirmation of the 'Victorian idea that Europeans were fit for sovereignty and others not'. Roosevelt (FDR) aimed at stabilizing, not undermining, colonialism.[18] Moreover, both Churchill and FDR wilfully weakened the scope of document by accepting that the Soviet Union retains the 1939 Nazi–Soviet pact boundaries.[19] The document thus highlighted the ambiguity of the US administration's anti-colonial commitment.[20] Moreover, many American officials believed in the idea of racial and cultural hierarchy and therefore never envisioned an early end to colonialism.[21]

Between the conclusion of the Atlantic Charter and the opening of the UNCIO, the US administration's perspective on the right to self-determination grew increasingly conservative.[22] It bowed to pragmatic arguments about the wisdom of preserving empires.[23] These considerations contributed to the 'gradual bastardization'

[17] Erez Manela, *The Wilsonian Moment* (n 9); Cassese, *Self-Determination of Peoples* (n 8) 33.

[18] William Roger Louis, *Imperialism at Bay: The United States and the Decolonization of the British Empire 1941–1945* (OUP 1978) 4, 9.

[19] Warren F Kimball, 'Churchill, the Americans, and Self-Determination' in Arnold A Offner and Theodore A Wilson (eds), *Victory in Europe 1945: From World War to Cold War* (University Press of Kansas 2000) 213, 216.

[20] David Ryan, 'By Way of Introduction: The United States, Decolonization and the World System' in David Ryan and Victor Pungong (eds), *The United States and Decolonization: Power and Freedom* (Palgrave-MacMillan 2000), 3 (hereafter Ryan, 'World System'); Richard H Immerman, *Empire for Liberty: A History of American Imperialism from Benjamin Franklin to Paul Wolfowitz* (Princeton University Press 2010).

[21] Marc Frey, 'Visions of the Future: The United States and Colonialism in Southeast Asia, 1940–1945' (2003) 48 Amerikastudien 365, 367.

[22] This movement grew stronger after FDR's death. See Philip W Bell, 'Colonialism as a Problem in American Foreign Policy' (1952) 5 World Politics 86, 101 (hereafter Bell, 'Colonialism as a Problem').

[23] John J Sbrega, 'Determination versus Drift: The Anglo-American Debate over the Trusteeship Issue, 1941–1945' (1986) 55 Pacific Historical Review 256, 258.

of the original concept of a comprehensive system of international trusteeship to promote independence.[24]

While the US government favoured a planned dissolution of European empires,[25] the United Kingdom (UK) defended the idea of a self-liquidating empire. However, this proposal masked the realities of an unequal empire. The picture of a unified, self-liquidating empire had to be contrasted with the fact that in some parts of the British empire, notably Australia, Canada, and New Zealand, loyalists were making considerable efforts to strengthen the imperial link, as was the case with the dominion status. 'Dominion was a characteristically ambiguous imperial invention that recognized various states of self-government while managing to convey overtones of continuing subordination.'[26] In some other parts of the empire, notably in Asia and Africa, relationships of domination between the empire and the local populations endured. The British Empire was unequally divided between civilized areas ripe for self-government and immature and backward territories not deemed worthy of being granted any political concessions.

Above all, the American government dreaded violent upheavals and revolutionary movements.[27] Following John Stuart Mill,[28] FDR believed in 'positive nationalism' as the best guarantee against the rise of authoritarian ideologies in colonies. Anti-colonial nationalism had thus to be managed and stabilized in order to prevent Western European powers from crumbling alongside their empires. The control and management of the future post-colonial peoples could be achieved through the implementation of a modernized conception of trusteeship, which would allow for the gradual integration of dependent peoples into the world system of sovereign states.[29] With the support of the UN institutions, the US was fulfilling its responsibility as a post-war power by helping colonial peoples in reforming their future countries and putting the final touches to the content of their independence and nationalisms.[30]

Soon after the conclusion of the Atlantic Conference, under the umbrella of the Advisory Committee on Postwar Foreign Policy the DoS created the Subcommittee

[24] Neil Smith, *American Empire: Roosevelt's Geographer and the Prelude to Globalization* (University of California Press 2003) (hereafter Smith, *American Empire)*; John J Sbrega, 'The Anticolonial Policies of Franklin D Roosevelt: A Reappraisal' (1986) 101 Political Science Quarterly 65, 82.

[25] Francis B Sayre, 'Legal Problems Arising from the United Nations Trusteeship System' (1948) 42 American Journal of International Law 263, 280.

[26] AG Hopkins, 'Rethinking Decolonization' (2008) 200 Past & Present 211, 212 (hereafter Hopkins, 'Rethinking Decolonization').

[27] Patrick J Hearden, *Architects of Globalism: Building a New World Order during World War II* (University of Arkansas Press 2002), 93; Michael H Hunt, *Ideology and U.S. Foreign Policy (with a new afterword)* (Yale University Press 2009) ch 4 (hereafter Hunt, *Ideology and U.S. Foreign Policy*).

[28] John Stuart Mill, 'A Few Words on Non-Intervention (1859)' in John Stuart Mill, *The Collected Works of John Stuart Mill, Volume XXI–Essays on Equality, Law, and Education* (University of Toronto Press 1984) 109–24.

[29] Ryan, 'World System' (n 21) 18.

[30] Odd Arne Westad, *The Global Cold War: Third World Interventions and the Making of Our Times* (CUP 2005) 20.

on Political and Territorial Reconstruction.[31] Among its tasks,[32] the Subcommittee had to develop trusteeship proposals. For the first time, the US government discovered the potential magnitude of the colonial problems around the world and how poorly equipped it was to deal with these new issues. The first proposal that emerged from the DoS suggested that trusteeship could be framed as a promise of independence following a transitional period of tutelage. An International Trusteeship Agency was to be set up with important administrative and supervisory powers. However, DoS officials were already profoundly divided over the definition principles that were to guide US policies. For instance, Isaiah Bowman, the DoS chief geographer and close friend of FDR, suggested that the trusteeship proposal could be interpreted not only as a defence of 'natural' inequality 'but as a nature-authorized rationale for intensified exploitation of "backward" peoples for their own good'.[33]

In the summer of 1943, the Secretary of State Cordell Hull suggested in a radio address that it was the responsibility and purpose of the US to support the attainment of freedom by all peoples 'worthy' and 'ready' for it.[34] It was the duty of his government to support dependent peoples who aspire to liberty.[35] Hull nonetheless recognized that his statement begged the question of 'how backward must the people be to be excluded from the discussion of their own rights; and how advanced must they be to become participants on some declared level?'.[36] When Sumner Welles, then Under-Secretary of State and close advisor of FDR, was asked by a puzzled Congressman how long it would take before trusteeship territories achieve independence, he replied more than a hundred years in the case of Congo and certainly more than a thousand years before Portuguese Timor became fit to govern itself.[37]

Hull was more concerned with maintaining Allied unity in the midst of the Second World War than in pursuing a vigorous anti-colonial policy or defending any concept of self-determination. In the fall of 1942, the Secretary of State sent

31 Subcommittees of the Advisory Committee on Post-War Foreign Policy (no date, after the adoption of the Atlantic Charter) (Department of State, F.D. Roosevelt Library, Adolf A Berle Papers, Box 54).

32 Among the nine fields of discussion identified by the Subcommittee, four were directly related to the issue of sovereignty and/or national independence: the restoration of independent nations and re-establishment of stable governments; boundary problems of independent nations; problems of dependent areas; and problems involved in the limitation of national sovereignty.

33 Smith, *American Empire* (n 25) 355.

34 'Radio Address of Secretary Hull (23 July 1942)—Recent Official Statements of American Policy Regarding Dependent Territories' (29 February 1944) (Records of the U.S. Delegation to the United Nations Conference on International Organization, 1944 – 1945, Harley Notter Files, Box 212, Record Group (RG) – 59).

35 'Radio Address of Secretary Hull, (12 September 1943)—Recent Official Statements of American Policy Regarding Dependent Territories' (29 February 1944) (Records of the U.S. Delegation to the United Nations Conference on International Organization, 1944-1945, Harley Notter Files, Box 212, RG – 59).

36 Smith, *American Empire* (n 25) 359.

37 ibid 356.

to FDR a proposal in which he recommended the creation of a trusteeship system covering only the territories held under the League of Nations mandates system and those to be detached from the enemies' territories. Upon the President's approval of these recommendations, in 1944 a group of DoS officials drew up a 'Draft Declaration by the United Nations on National Independence'.[38] It represented the first concrete international proposal discussing the post-war colonial question.[39] It stated 'that the independence of those nations which have been forcibly deprived of independence shall be restored, that opportunity to achieve independence for those peoples who aspire to independence shall be preserved, respected and made more effective'.[40] Unsurprisingly, the declaration granted the US and the UK the power to preside over the advancement of these dependent peoples. They had 'become charged with responsibilities for the future of colonial areas to cooperate fully with the peoples of such areas toward their becoming qualified for independent national status'. According to the draft declaration, it was incumbent upon all dependent peoples who genuinely aspired to autonomy 'to exert themselves in every feasible way to prepare and equip themselves for independence—to the end that they may, as soon as possible, be able to create, conduct and maintain, for, by and of themselves, efficient structures of stable self-government based on sound principles of social and political morality'.[41]

It was the business of the 'parent' states to train and equip the colonial peoples for the responsibilities of self-government. Therefore, according to Col Oliver Stanley, the British Secretary of State for the colonies, there ought to be a twofold test to evaluate the success of the 'parent' state's policy. First, one has to evaluate the essential preliminary work accomplished by the trustee power. Second, and more importantly, there has to be a test of the success and efficiency of self-government when it has been given.[42] Several British officials even suggested replacing trusteeship by partnership because it was better suited to describe what the British envisioned for their colonies: a hierarchy of partnership—from junior and senior to equal partnership—within the Empire.[43]

[38] 'Proposed Declaration by the United Nations on National Independence (9 March 1943)' (29 February 1944) (Records of the U.S. Delegation to the United Nations Conference on International Organization 1944 - 1945, Harley Notter Files, Box 212, RG–59).

[39] George Thullen, *Problems of the Trusteeship System: A Study of Political Behavior in the United Nations* (Droz 1964) 23–24.

[40] 'Proposed Declaration by the United Nations on National Independence (9 March 1943)' (n 38).

[41] ibid.

[42] 'Col Stanley Talks on Colonies, by our Political Correspondent' (undated, probably fall 1943) (Records of Various Inter- and Intra-Departmental Committees (1942–1952), Inter-Divisional Committee on Colonial Problems, Box 1, RG–353).

[43] 'Proposal by W.W. Astor, M.P. for a United Nations Council and for Regional Councils to Assist Dependent Territories' (12 February 1944) (Records of Various Inter- and Intra-Departmental Committees (1942–1952), Inter-Divisional Committee on Colonial Problems, Committee on Colonial and Trusteeship Problems, Box 3, RG–353).

At the Dumbarton Oaks Conference held in the fall of 1944, the new US Secretary of State Edward Stettinius, his assistant Cordell Hull, and FDR met to establish and formalize the US trusteeship policy that would serve as guidelines for future diplomatic discussions on the subject.[44] The 'parent' or 'trustee' state would be obligated to 'guide' and 'develop' colonial peoples 'until they would be able, without danger to themselves and others, to discharge the responsibilities of government'.[45] The document included a reference to the 'political advancement of dependent peoples' as a goal of trusteeship without referring to political independence.[46]

It also reaffirmed the UN's intention 'to assist in the development of the capacities of dependent peoples with a view to realization by them of *reasonable aspirations*'.[47] These wartime discussions played a crucial role because they laid the foundations for the emerging right to self-determination soon to be formalized in the UN Charter and served as a template in Washington for thinking about the decolonization.

III. The San Francisco conference and the colonial question

The UNCIO took place in San Francisco between 21 April and 26 June 1945. The US delegation succeeded in embedding in the Charter the idea of a gradual, managed, and orderly dismantling of European empires. The Charter admittedly promises self-determination but only after a transitional period of tutelage and development during which dependent peoples would learn the propriety of self-government as well as the responsibilities and duties attached to their orderly enjoyment. The Soviets criticized the US overemphasis on the idea of maintaining law and order.[48] US government officials wanted to show, above all, that it was not the intention of the colonial powers to provoke or encourage revolt or revolution.[49] In this regard, the UN Charter Articles 1(2), 2(1), and 4(1), which refer to self-determination, remain extremely ambiguous.

However, what did really matter for the US government were Chapter XI (Declaration regarding non-self-governing territories) and Chapter XII, which

[44] Samuel I Rosenman and Edward Stettinius, 'Development Policy toward Dependent Areas (Top Secret) (Edward Stettinius to Samuel I Rosenman)' (12 September 1944) (Samuel I Rosenman Papers, F.D. Roosevelt Library, Box 7).

[45] ibid.

[46] Rosenman and Stettinius (n 44).

[47] ibid (emphasis added).

[48] Joseph John Sisco, *The Soviet Attitude toward the Trusteeship System* (University of Chicago 1950) 20–21.

[49] Charles W Taussig, 'Arrangements for International Trusteeship: A Commentary' (30 April 1945) (Charles W Taussig Papers, F.D. Roosevelt Library, Box 77) (hereafter Taussig, 'Arrangements for International Trusteeship').

set up the international trusteeship system. Above all, these chapters aimed at modernizing imperial practices by integrating the idea that empires should aim at transforming and furthering the betterment of those peoples deemed incapable of exercising the responsibilities attached to the enjoyment of the right to self-determination. Described by a contemporary commentator as an 'outgrowth of innumerable liberal ideas on colonial administration and native welfare',[50] the Declaration was a restatement and extension of the 'sacred trust' or civilizing mission stated in Article 22(1) of the League of Nations Covenant. US officials analogized the idea of international trusteeship with that found in municipal law or contemporary fiduciary theory of human rights, 'just as a government or private institution acts as trustee for certain types of property or for legally incompetent persons'. According to John Foster Dulles, then a DoS legal advisor, 'Chapter XI offered [dependent peoples] hope and encouragement that they could advance toward autonomy, self-government, or independence in appropriate cases through ordinary processes and not through revolution'.[51] Dulles and his colleagues feared political turmoil, instability, and, above all, the perils of revolution.[52] Dependent people's needs and demands were thus subjected to the imperatives of international peace and security at the UNCIO.[53] The word 'independence' was finally excluded in the final draft of the Declaration. Self-determination could then only be achieved with the help of an external benevolent authority.[54] President Truman's and subsequent administrations until the late 1960s pursued FDR's policy of an orderly and gradual decolonization.[55]

British, French, and Dutch governments feared that the new UN trusteeship system would start meddling in internal affairs and policies of colonial powers.[56] However, American representatives felt that a 'proper and restricted' right to petition was an essential contribution of the new trusteeship system to the

[50] Huntington Gilchrist, 'Colonial Questions at the San Francisco Conference' (1945) 39 American Political Science Review 982, 985 (hereafter Gilchrist, 'Colonial Questions').

[51] Alger Hiss, 'Report of the First Meeting' (8 January 1946) (Alger Hiss Files, US Group on Trusteeship. Box 25, RG–59).

[52] On the fear of revolution in US foreign policy thinking, see Hunt, *Ideology and US Foreign Policy* (n 28) ch 6.

[53] Gilchrist, 'Colonial Questions' (n 51) 982, 987.

[54] William Bain, *Between Anarchy and Society: Trusteeship and the Obligations of Power* (OUP 2003).

[55] Ebere Nwaubani, 'The United States and the Liquidation of European Colonial Rule in Tropical Africa, 1941–1963' (2007) 43 Cahiers d'études africaines 505.

[56] Charles W Taussig, 'Summary of the Statement Made by Lord Cranborne before Committee 4, Commission II' (14 May 1945) (Charles W Taussig Papers, F.D. Roosevelt Library, Box 66); Charles W Taussig, '3rd Meeting of Commission II, Technical Committee 4 (summary of the debate prepared by the U.S. delegation' (11 May 1945) (Charles W Taussig Papers, F.D. Roosevelt Library) Box 66, US II/4 Doc. 3); Records of the U.S. Delegation to the United Nations Conference on International Organization, 1944–1945, Harley Notter Files, '2nd Meeting of Commission II, Technical Committee 4: summary of the debate prepared by the US delegation' (11 May 1945) Box 203, US II/4 Doc. 3, RG–59). The Dutch doubted the usefulness of such a procedure with respect to advanced dependent territories. They thought that the superimposition of international control would be resented by the native peoples.

improvement of the dependent territories. 'Properly safeguarded and conducted' inquiries by responsible agencies could make a real contribution to world order and the 'orderly progress' of colonial peoples.[57] 'This was the only means by which the voice of the inhabitants of the trust territories may be heard,'[58] and yet, they were deemed to be highly disruptive as well. Such procedures 'would have the effect of quieting trouble' while maintaining existing power structures. This idea, albeit summary, was in a way the precursor of how the US government came to conceive of the right to internal self-determination two decades later.

An orderly and rational decolonization process was also aimed at protecting dependent peoples against themselves.[59] European empires and the American government had 'to safeguard the dependent peoples against local nationalist oligarchies which may interfere with a rational and democratic exercise of self-government'. Dependent peoples had to earn their right to self-government. The requirements for self-government had a disciplinary tone. 'There is a reciprocal and equally important duty of dependent peoples to fit themselves for self-government and to justify by their exertion the efforts that will be made on their behalf. Until and unless they show themselves worthy of self-government or independence they are not entitled to demand or attain it'.[60] This could take different forms according 'to the varying circumstances of each territory'.[61]

Any right-based conception of self-determination had to be avoided for 'the principle of self-determination' in any form would be to invite trouble.[62] Harley Notter, an influent US legal advisor, rejected as well any reference to the right to self-determination as a goal of the trusteeship system. He feared that self-determination could be used by the Soviets as an attempt to drive out a definition of the right. This would have direct effects on the legal nature and the legal obligations deriving from the trusteeship system. Leo Pasvolsky an American legal advisor and, according to some, 'the foremost author of the U.N. charter',[63] argued that the main difficulty caused by a right-based conception of self-determination resided precisely in the usage of the word 'right' to qualify the nature of self-determination.

57 Charles W Taussig, 'Minutes of the Preliminary Consultations on Trusteeship by Representatives of the Five Powers, 3rd meeting' (5 May 1945) (Charles W Taussig Papers, F.D. Roosevelt Library).

58 ibid.

59 Jessica Lynne Pearson, 'Defending Empire at the United Nations: The Politics of International Colonial Oversight in the Era of Decolonisation' (2017) 45 Journal of Imperial and Commonwealth History 525–49.

60 Taussig, 'Arrangements for International Trusteeship: A Commentary' (n 50).

61 'Proposed Working Paper for Chapter on Dependent Territories and Arrangements for International Trusteeship' (11 May 1945) (Records of the U.S. Delegation to the United Nations Conference on International Organization, 1944–1945, Harley Notter Files Box 198, RG-59).

62 'UNCIO—Meeting of the United States Delegation' (1 June 1945, morning) (Records of the U.S. Delegation to the United Nations Conference on International Organization, 1944–1945, Harley Notter Files, Box 192, RG-59).

63 'Interview with Stephen Schlesinger' (transcript) (CNN, Diplomatic License, aired 24 December 2004) http://transcripts.cnn.com/TRANSCRIPTS/0412/24/i_dl.01.html accessed 7 December 2018.

For this reason, the American delegation chose to resolve the issue by using the word 'principle'.[64]

The Soviet Union was also a reluctant anti-imperialist. In San Francisco, Soviet delegates often appeared surprisingly willing to compromise on the phraseology itself. For example, the phrase 'wishes of the people' appeared to be an acceptable alternative to 'self-determination' for the Russian delegate. Also, the Soviet representative, Novikov, recognized that the application of the principle (!) depended on the local conditions and that it could be expressed in a variety of forms, such as through the parliament. In response to Lord Cranborne's question of who would have the authority to make such a decision, Novikov pointed out 'that the qualifying phrase "as may be provided in the trusteeship arrangements" remained in the paragraph, and that this would obviously mean the administering power'.[65] In other words, the Soviet Union agreed, alongside the US and the colonial powers, to grant administering states powers to determine whether a dependent people was fit or not for self-government. In addition, during the 7th Five Power meeting, the Soviet delegate Sobolev concurred with Commander Stassen, the American representative, who had suggested that there were some territories that would never achieve independence because they were 'small and weak and incapable of it'.[66] This raised serious doubts as to the reality of the Soviet commitment to liberating colonial peoples. And, as Taussig astutely pointed out in May 1945 (two weeks earlier) in a conversation with his British counterpart, AH Poynton, the representative of the Colonial Office at the UN Conference, 'the Russians would like to have a battle, and would even like to lose the battle in order that they could be in the position of putting before the world the idea of independence and having the United States and the United Kingdom throw it out'.[67]

The Committee II/4 ended its work on 19 June 1945, six days before the closing of the UNCIO.[68] Despite several diplomatic successes, the members of the American delegation knew that, from the liberal point of view, the trusteeship section of the Charter was one of its weakest parts and that it would be carefully scrutinized and caustically criticized. In fact, like the Secretary of Interior Ickes, several DoS

[64] 'UNCIO—Meeting of the United States Delegation' (29 May 1945) (Records of the U.S. Delegation to the United Nations Conference on International Organization, 1944–1945, Harley Notter Files, Box 194, RG-59).

[65] Charles W Taussig, 'Minutes of the Preliminary Consultations on Trusteeship by Representatives of the Five Powers, 8th meeting' (1 June 1945) (Charles W Taussig Papers, F.D. Roosevelt Library, Box 66).

[66] Charles W Taussig, 'Minutes of the Preliminary Consultations on Trusteeship by Representatives of the Five Powers, 7th meeting' (29 May 1945) (Charles W Taussig Papers, F.D. Roosevelt Library, Box 66).

[67] Charles W Taussig, 'Memorandum of Conversation with A.H. Poynton, Colonial Office, London, and representative of the Colonial Office at the United Nations Conference' (13 May 1945) (Charles W Taussig Papers, F.D. Roosevelt Library, Box 77).

[68] 'UNCIO – Meeting of the United States Delegation' (19 June 1945) (Records of the U.S. Delegation to the United Nations Conference on International Organization, 1944–1945, Harley Notter Files, Box 192, RG-59).

officials quietly thought that the trusteeship system was simply window dressing for dependent peoples and anti-colonial movements. The Assistant to the Secretary of State felt that the concluding paragraphs should face squarely up to the fact that the Chapter was a compromise between 'annexationist and imperialist influences on the one hand, and humanitarian impulses on the other, and that one can only hope that the establishment of the system will, in and of itself, permit the development of something closer to the historical aspirations of the nation'.[69] Since colonies would come under the trusteeship system following the voluntary offer of the colonial powers, it was safe to assume that 'the proposed trusteeship system will have little, if any, significance to the colonial world'.[70] This is more or less the conclusion that can be deciphered from the intervention of the Iraqi representative on the Second Commission, Fadhil Al-Jamali. During the plenary session of the Commission on 21 June 1945, he asked Commander Stassen and Peter Fraser, the Prime Minister of New Zealand (1940–1949) and Chair of Committee II/4, four questions. The first had to do with the fact that the new trusteeship system didn't confer the same rights and guarantees to the territories now held under mandate that they had under the League of Nations. Al-Jamali also wondered why the new system contained no assurance that the wishes of the people of the areas to be included in the trusteeship system will be taken into account. He also interrogated the American and New Zealand representatives on the reasons why there was no specific regulation (sunset clause) regarding the termination of trusteeship agreements. Finally, he asked why the peoples of future trusteeship areas were not given a better chance to have their grievances heard by the future Trusteeship Council. Although Stassen and Fraser didn't answer back, these questions implicitly suggested that the new trusteeship system would replicate past imperial trusteeship practices.[71]

The colonial system was thus improved without disturbing existing colonial relationships.[72] Indeed, US legal advisors had anticipated the colonial powers' reluctance to place their colonial holdings under international control 'unless the moral pressure of world public opinion becomes so strong as to induce it. In reality, therefore, the proposed trusteeship system had little, if any, significance to the colonial world'.[73] That was also the opinion of Field Marshall Jan Smuts of South Africa. Smuts stated that the advent of trusteeship didn't signal the abolition of the colonial system. To the contrary, he believed that the new system was designed to help lift up the standards of colonial administration and improve the relationship between

69 Charles W Taussig, 'Archibald MacLeish, Assistant Secretary of State for Public and Cultural Relations, to Isiah Bowman' (19 June 1945) (Charles W Taussig Papers, F.D. Roosevelt Library, Box 66).

70 Taussig, 'Arrangements for International Trusteeship: A Commentary' (n 50).

71 Charles W Taussig, 'Third Meeting of Commission II: summary of debates prepared by the U.S. Delegation', (21 June 1945) (Charles W Taussig Papers, F.D. Roosevelt Library, Box 67, US II/Doc 4).

72 Charles W Taussig, 'Summary Analysis of the Draft Proposal on Trusteeship', (no date, probably spring 1945) (Charles W Taussig Papers, F.D. Roosevelt Library, Box 67).

73 ibid.

metropolitan power and dependent territories.[74] Above all, the renovation of the institutions' trusteeship and colonialism at San Francisco reinforced the idea that the US had succeeded in embedding in the text of the Charter the idea of earned self-determination, which involved the gradual, managed, and orderly acquisition of self-government, even independence, after a transitional period of tutelage.

These early discussions and debates are crucial for our story. They cast the legal framework and vocabularies upon which legal claims to self-determination were made in the following years and decades. As positive international law, the right to self-determination ironically embodied a justification for maintaining existing imperial structures. In a sense, self-determination as a 'right' could not hardly be considered as the engine of the decolonization. However, as a political and moral claim, it grew to become a powerful force and justification for dismantling empires, an idea to be tamed.

IV. Accommodating empires: the domestication of the right to self-determination

The problem then for the faltering empires and the US was to channel anti-colonial forces and to domesticate the right to self-determination by subjecting it to higher principles or considerations such as the stability of the sovereign states system or the defence of human rights. They sought to transform the right to self-determination—which originally implied a right to decolonization in the minds of colonial and American officials—into an anti-revolutionary right to internal self-determination—implying a right to democratic participation within pre-determined sovereign boundaries.

The road to a tamed or domesticated version of self-determination had yet to be achieved by imperial powers and the US. With the emergence of Afro-Asian and third-world solidarities in the background of the Indian (1947) and Cuban (1959) independences and the Algerian and Vietnamese wars for independence, anti-colonial claims for independence and self-determination gained traction and coalesced in the UN 1960 Declaration on the Granting of Independence to Colonial Countries and Peoples.[75] Adopted by the UNGA without dissenting votes,[76] the document repudiated imperial pretences to dominate colonial peoples by virtue of the benefits they claimed to bring, their promises of emancipation by teaching, for example, subjugated peoples how to responsibly enjoy their right to

[74] Charles W Taussig, 'Third Meeting of Commission II: summary of debates prepared by the U.S. Delegation' (n 71).

[75] 'Declaration on the Granting of Independence to Colonial Countries and Peoples', United Nations General Assembly Resolution 1514 (XV) (14 December 1960).

[76] Nine countries abstained: Australia, Belgium, Dominican Republic, France, Portugal, Spain, Union of South Africa, the UK, and the US.

self-determination in a way that promotes the greater good of the international community.[77] The Declaration stated that the 'inadequacy of political, economic, social or educational preparedness should never serve as a pretext for delaying independence'. It further required that 'immediate steps' be taken 'to transfer all powers to the peoples of those [Trust and Non-Self-Governing], without any condition or reservations' in accordance with the 'freely expressed will and desire' of the peoples. The resolution repudiated the inter-imperial consensus reached in 1945 in San Francisco.

The radicalism of Resolution 1514 was, however, soon tempered by Resolution 1541 adopted the following day on 15 December 1960. Formally, Resolution 1541, titled 'Principles which should guide Members in determining whether or not an obligation exists to transmit the information called for under Article 73e of the Charter' developed a list of standards and benchmarks to assess whether a particular territory fell within the ambit of the 'Declaration regarding non-self-governing territories' (UN Charter, ch XI). While the authors of the Resolution most certainly wished to pressurize colonial powers into divulging more information on how they governed their colonies, the text of the Resolution more or less reactivated problems, principles, and ideas that had been discussed at length in San Francisco in 1945 without adding much. More importantly for the current chapter, the Resolution identified potential situations in which 'a Non-Self-Governing Territory can be said to have reached a full measure of self-government'. There were three situations: i) the emergence of sovereign independent State; ii) a free association with an independent State; iii) or the integration with an independent state. It is easy to infer from these options that the right to self-determination could be achieved within the pre-existing imperial boundaries, albeit under a different qualification.

Both resolutions more or less explicitly hinted at the importance of maintaining (or, at least, trying to maintain) the integrity of boundaries—imperial or post-colonial. For both the post-colonial states and the crumbling empires, the right to self-determination harboured the potential for further political fragmentations that could threaten, on the one hand, the newly acquired fragile post-colonial sovereignty, and on the other hand, the stability of a UN Charter-based international system premised on the renovation of imperial powers.[78] In other words, the legitimacy of both the post-colonial states and the faltering empires rested on a commitment to the right to self-determination as an imperial promise and as the

[77] Report of the Commission of Rapporteurs (Aaland Islands Case) presented to the League of Nations Council, League of Nations Doc. B.7.21/68/106 (1921) ['To concede to minorities, either of language or religion, or to any fractions of a population the right of withdrawing from the community to which they belong, because it is their wish or their good pleasure, would be to destroy order and stability within States and to inaugurate anarchy in international life; it would be to uphold a theory incompatible with the very idea of the State as a territorial and political unity'].

[78] Jörg Fish, *The Right of Self-Determination of Peoples: The Domestication of an Illusion* (CUP 2015).

normative foundation of the post-colonial states. And in both cases, the integrity of their respective political structures rested on their ability to tame and domesticate the disruptive aspects of the right to self-determination without denying their prior commitments to the idea.

Common Article 1 to the 1966 International Covenant to Civil and Political Rights and International Covenant on Economic, Social, and Cultural Rights somehow neutralized the revolutionary nature of the right to self-determination by turning it into a human right. This was a crucial turn of events and, yet, an unsurprising one. From a legal standpoint, the UN human rights regime that had been developing over the previous two decades and over which the American government had had a major influence.[79] The regime emphasized a conception of human rights that identifies the state as both the main source of human rights violations and as the main guarantor of those same rights.[80] As such, human rights and, in the present case, the right to self-determination, became a social justification of the state.[81] Principle Five (The principle of equal rights and self-determination of peoples) of the 1970 Declaration on Principles of International Law concerning Friendly Relations and Co-operation among States in accordance with the Charter of the United Nations further reinforces that idea when it declares that 'the establishment of a sovereign and independent State, the free association or integration with an independent State or the emergence into any other political status freely determined by a people constitute modes of implementing the right of self-determination by that people'. The wording of the Principle Five emphasizes, 'as the critical issue, the methods of reaching the decision and not the result'.[82]

The idea here is not to ignore the vast and complex debates over the definition and meaning the right to self-determination that took place both within and outside the UN system between 1945 and 1975 and which involved a multitude of actors operating at various levels—local, regional, national, continental, universal—in a wide array of contexts, and embodying a variety of political projects. This chapter rather suggests that the argumentative structure developed by the American government in San Francisco in 1945 survived the decolonization era. The right to self-determination, construed in 1945 as a conditional right to be achieved when a requisite level of political development had been attained, was revamped into a conditional right authorizing self-government only when the sovereign states had violated its human rights obligations. However, in both

[79] Olivier Barsalou, 'The Cold War and the Rise of an American Conception of Human Rights, 1945–1948' in Pamela Slotte and Miia Halme-Tuomisaari (eds), *Revisiting the Origins of Human Rights* (CUP 2015) 362–80.

[80] Hannah Arendt, *Imperialism: Part Two of the Origins of Totalitarianism* (New York 1968) ch 5; Frédéric Mégret, 'L'étatisme spécifique du droit international' (2011) 24 Revue québécoise de droit international 105, 125–27.

[81] Samuel Moyn, 'The Universal Declaration of Human Rights of 1948 in the History of Cosmopolitanism' (2014) 40 Critical Inquiry 377–78.

[82] Thürer and Burri, 'Self-Determination' (n 8) para 11.

contexts—1945 or 1975—the right to self-determination remained subjected to the vagaries and arbitrariness of a pre-existing sovereignties whose authority and legitimacy rested essentially on their capacities to fulfil their trusteeship and fiduciary duties towards the peoples roaming their realms. In other words, the right to self-determination was an apology for empires in 1945 and became one for states in 1975. The battle for decolonization saw 'the tacit submersion of self-determination in state-determination'[83] and the slow withering away of the human rights ideas that it carried with it.[84]

V. Conclusion

Between 1945 and 1975, self-determination emerged as a right compatible with the transformation, not the elimination, of non-self-governing peoples, whether in imperial or post-colonial contexts. Often equated with a right to secession and, ultimately, to independent statehood,[85] US and European colonial officials after 1945 slowly started emphasizing the internal aspects of the right to self-determination. As this chapter argues, turning the right to self-determination into an apology for empire or into a democratic and individual right was a strategic divide-and-rule choice[86] aimed at limiting its exercise to specific contexts and interpretations.[87]

This was clearly visible in Europe where many 'imperialists' started repudiating the idea of colonialism because of the atrocious European record in Africa and Asia.[88] For these critics of European (and American) imperialism, the colonial project became an unambiguously pejorative term. It was an unmasked and immoral form of domination devoid of any humanitarian character. As a result, European and American officials began to embrace the novel, but imprecise, vocabulary of 'association', 'interdependence', 'partnership', 'union', 'integration', and 'federation'[89]

83 Uriel Abulof, 'The Confused Compass: From Self-Determination to State-Determination' (2015) 14 Ethnopolitics 488–97.

84 Meredith Terretta, '"We Had Been Fooled into Thinking that the UN Watches over the Entire World": Human Rights, UN Trust Territories, and Africa's Decolonization' (2012) 34 Human Rights Quarterly 329–60.

85 Alexandra Xanthaki, 'The right to self-determination: meaning and scope' in Nazila Ghanea and Alexandra Xanthaki (eds), *Minorities, Peoples and Self-Determination: Essays in Honour of Patrick Thornberry* (Martinus Nijhoff 2005) 22.

86 Bradley R Simpson, 'Self-Determination, Human Rights, and the End of Empire in the 1970s' (2013) 4 Humanity: International Journal of Human Rights, Humanitarianism, & Development 239, 240; Kalana Senaratne, 'Internal Self-Determination in International Law: A Critical Third-World Perspective' (2013) 3 Asian Journal of International Law 305, 331.

87 Jure Vidmar, 'The Right to Self-Determination and Multiparty Democracy: Two Sides of the Same Coin?' (2010) 10 Human Rights Law Review 239.

88 For example, see Fabian Klose, *Human Rights in the Shadow of Colonial Violence: The Wars of Independence in Kenya and Algeria* (University of Pennsylvania Press 2013); Jan Eckel, 'Human Rights and Decolonization: New Perspectives and Open Questions' (2010) 1 Humanity 111.

89 Michael Collins, 'Decolonisation and the "Federal Moment"' (2013) 24 Diplomacy & Statecraft 21–40; Hopkins, 'Rethinking Decolonization' (n 27); Ronald Hyam, 'The Geopolitical Origins of the

to describe the relationship between Europe and its colonial subjects. Many postcolonial thinkers and leaders also contributed to those debates and sought to imagine self-determination without state sovereignty.[90]

However, from the perspective of the right to self-determination, this bland terminology rebranded imperial domination and trusteeship by recasting them as ordinary political links between metropolitan powers and their dependent territories.[91] French, British, and Dutch colonial relationships developed and discussed post-imperial constitutional models that borrowed from American federal empire in which the states enjoy some measures of self-government.[92] The right to internal self-determination transformed a potentially revolutionary idea into one compatible with the survival of empires and the sustainability of the sovereign states from the rubbles of empires.

The idea of self-determination that emerged in 1945 in San Francisco thus rested on this never-fulfilled yet lasting imperial promise to reform and transform dependent peoples into international legal subjects able to exercise their right to self-government responsibly in an ever-increasing interdependent world.[93] More particularly, the American government sought to develop a conception of the right to self-determination that could accommodate the interests of colonial powers (and its own) in their residual empire with that of providing colonial peoples with some political horizon. Not without irony, the decolonization thus saw 'the strange demise of self-determination'.[94]

Central African Federation: Britain, Rhodesia and South Africa, 1948–1953' (1987) 30 Historical Journal 145.

[90] Gary Wilder, *Freedom Time: Negritude, Decolonization, and the Future of the World* (Duke University Press 2015); Frederick Cooper, *Citizenship between Empire and Nation: Remaking France and French Africa, 1945–1960* (Princeton University Press 2014).

[91] Henri Brunschwig, 'Colonisation-décolonisation: Essai sur le vocabulaire usuel de la politique coloniale' (1960) 1 Cahiers d'études africaines 44, 52.

[92] Bell, 'Colonialism as a Problem' (n 23) 93.

[93] I borrowed these ideas from Nikolas Rose, *Powers of Freedom: Reframing Political Thought* (CUP 1999).

[94] Uriel Abulof, 'We the Peoples? The Strange Demise of Self-Determination' (2016) 22 European Journal of International Relations 536–65.

Epilogue

What's Law Got to Do with It? Recollections and Impressions

Martti Koskenniemi

I.

The chapters in this volume give a many-sided, deep, and wide image of the legal aspects of the second decolonization, a time that many of us still carry in living memory. The generation that came to adulthood in the late 1960s through the mid-1970s is approaching the end of professional careers, taking early retirement, others working, especially academics, perhaps still some number of years. That generation, to which I of course belong, grew up as professional men and women surrounded by confrontations about conflicts that mostly took place in what we learned to call the third world over self-determination, wars of liberation, and the New International Economic Order (NIEO), Biafra, Vietnam, the Six-Day War, and the first oil crisis; often, we took sides, sometimes emphatically. Although many of these events took place far away from where we lived and worked, they were of great interest, and wholly absorbed some of us. These were politicized years, even hyper-political years—good training ground for later careers. From that perspective—half-personal, half-professional—I reflect on what the editors of this book have chosen to call the 'battle' (although I resist the military tone of the metaphor).

At the time, *public* international law was a fringe discipline at a European law faculty such as mine. Those who chose to specialize in it often did so to avoid the dry-as-dust practices in civil law, shunning careers in courts, administration, or private business. Many had an inclination towards the humanities; political activism was a must. Our minds were reaching out to matters international, and our bodies found access to foreign offices, development agencies, non-governmental institutions. To the extent that we came to mainstream practice in public international law, typically with a foreign ministry or an intergovernmental organization, we found that the substance of our work had little to do with questions bearing upon development or even the third world in any specific way. There were questions of boundary delimitation, of course, of treaty interpretation and State succession—and some of those are discussed in these chapters. But these questions were treated as being

Martti Koskenniemi, *Epilogue* In: *The Battle for International Law: South-North Perspectives on the Decolonization Era.* Edited by: Jochen von Bernstorff and Philipp Dann, Oxford University Press (2019). © The Several Contributors.
DOI: 10.1093/oso/9780198849636.003.0021

standard in the practice of international law—concerned with access to and consequences of formal statehood and the public law aspects of diplomacy, not by rules designed to incorporate the concerns of the developing world. Indeed, 'development' did not seem to be an international law concern.

Some third-world-related issues were treated via reference to classical doctrines about legal sources. Were new states bound by old customary law? What was the legal value of United Nations (UN) General Assembly resolutions? I will expound on those questions later, but first I note that many of us in the 1970s saw decolonization as something that had already passed (a 1960s issue, the independence process) or belonged rather more to international 'politics' than law. The core curriculum at European and American law schools had to do with what Germans called 'external public law' and the Americans 'foreign relations law'—the legal aspects of the country's foreign relations.[1] I have elsewhere noted that the textbook of my university course in Finland in the mid-1970s was Erik Castrén's *Finland's International Law* (in Finnish), which was published in 1959.[2] The book began with a chapter on general principles and legal subjects, but went rapidly onwards to discuss the treaties delimiting Finnish maritime and land territory and the position of the individual. Then followed sections of foreign policy decision-making and Finland's treaty relations and representation in international institutions, State responsibility (of Finland), dispute settlement, sanctions, and many chapters on the laws of war. Although Castrén was an active internationalist, later a member of the International Law Commission (ILC), words such as 'development' or 'decolonization' made no appearance in the book.

Because that work was a little outdated in the 1970s, it was supplemented by the thick volume *United Nations* by Bengt Broms that discussed the different UN institutions and principal Charter provisions, giving a historical overview of their development (the last edition, in English, 1990).[3] The impression received by students, strengthened later by professional orientations of diplomacy, was that there were two kinds of international law: on the one hand, the network of mostly bilateral relations, governed by sovereignty and treaty law as well as issues of domestic constitutional law bearing upon foreign relations, and on the other, the newer and much more 'political' law of the UN and its specialized agencies that *did* have a lot to do with problems emerging from decolonization and development. The seriously formalist spirit of the former contrasted with the invitation to operate with large ideologically tinged principles and objectives under the latter; conservatism and social-democracy transposed into orientations to international law. Awareness of that duality gave a good introduction to work

[1] A hugely important discussion of the non-international aspect of international law today in Anthea Roberts, *Is International Law International?* (OUP 2017).

[2] Erik Castrén, *Suomen kansainvälinen oikeus* (WSOY 1959).

[3] Bengt Broms, *Yhdistyneet Kansakunnat* (WSOY 1968), updated English version *United Nations* (Suomalainen tiedeakatemia 1990).

undertaken in the legal department of the Ministry for Foreign Affairs when I entered in 1978. I do not remember that the public international law section would have treated any item concerned with 'development'—with the significant exception of the Third UN Conference on the Law of the Sea (1974–1982), which did absorb lion's share of the section's UN-related activities. Already at the time (and thereafter), the department on development cooperation had its own lawyers, specializing in bilateral cooperation agreements and coordination within the Organisation for Economic Cooperation and Development and later the European Union. We rarely met with them and had only the vaguest idea of what they were doing.

This is not, of course, to say that the international law practices of the last quarter of the twentieth century would have been oblivious to the 'battle'. But they tended to channel it onto the relatively innocuous terrain of large principles about self-determination, State succession, the treatment of alien property, highlighted in UN General Assembly's declarations from the Decolonization resolution (UNGA Res 1514 (1960)), the Friendly Relations Declaration of 1970 (UNGA Res 2625 (1970)), and the Charter of Economic Rights and Duties of (UNGA res 3314 (1974)). International lawyers differed in their attitudes to these instruments. Many were concerned to integrate them as closely as possible to the traditional law. The second edition of DP O'Connell's two-volume textbook from 1970, for example, had no specific entry on 'decolonization' or 'development', but it discussed related themes at three points. Under 'international action on foreign investment' O'Connell observed that 'underdeveloped countries' right to fully develop their natural resources' may have become customary law through UN resolutions that were nevertheless 'so deliberately ambiguous as to smother rather than elucidate the legal procedures relating to expropriation'.[4] Another section dealt with 'UN action on colonialism' through close reading of the trusteeship system and the actions of the Special Committee on Colonialism, and a third discussed State succession with an effort to suggest that 'full compensation' might help 'balance'-acquired rights with the independence concerns of new states.[5] The discussion was neutral and technical, concentrating on relevant case-law. In two out of those three themes the focus was on the UN. Nor did Ian Brownlie's widely read *Principles of Public International Law* (in which I, for example, was examined twice in the course of my post-graduate studies at the turn of the 1980s, once by Brownlie himself) take up 'development' or 'decolonization' in those terms, although related items were scattered throughout the chapters (Brownlie was very interested in Africa and already in the 1970s had begun to counsel a number of developing countries). Of self-determination he had this to say:

4 David P O'Connell, *International Law* (2nd edn, Stevens & Sons 1970), vol 2, 792.
5 See Craven, Chapter 4 this volume.

> Until recently the majority of Western jurists assumed or asserted that the principle had no legal content, being an ill-defined concept of policy and morality. Since 1945 developments in the United Nations, and the influence of Afro-Asian and Communist opinion, have changed the position and some Western jurists now admit that self-determination is a legal principle.[6]

Brownlie's readiness to highlight the deeply political character of (at least this part of) international law was striking. But he limited his own treatment strictly to the conventional sources and case-law, joining however that latter group of 'Western jurists' by including self-determination into the corpus of international law, though its 'present ramifications' had yet to be worked out.[7] And he stressed that 'economic aid and technical assistance to under-developed areas [had become] an object of the first importance in creating conditions of justice and stable foundations for peace'. He certainly went beyond most European lawyers when he wrote that '[t]here is probably also a collective duty of [UN] member states to take responsible action to create reasonable living standards both for their own peoples and for those of other states'.[8]

Though expressed in a traditional textbook fashion, Brownlie's views were probably left from centre among Anglophone lawyers. Julius Stone, whose whole career had been about reading international law in its social and political context, took a much more combative attitude from the political right, attacking the third world's use of General Assembly resolutions to advance its economic interests. The 'Western States', he wrote in 1977, cannot

> afford to submit supinely to the edicts of hostile majorities . . . What is in issue is no mere objection to particular resolutions, but the checking and arrest of the strategic design of certain States to use the General Assembly for imposing their arbitrary will on others. [9]

Stone was especially outraged at the OPEC oil boycott of 1973, speculating that the 1974 Definition of Aggression might be read to cover this action and authorize self-defence on the part of the West—a position he shared with hawks in the United States (US) international law establishment, and which eerily resembles the US

[6] Ian Brownlie, *Principles of Public International Law* (3rd edn, Clarendon 1979) 593–94. I have assessed that book in relation to James Crawford's more recent re-edition in Martti Koskenniemi, 'Brownlie's Principles of Public International Law' (2013) 83 British Yearbook of International Law 137.

[7] Brownlie (n 6) 595. Brownlie noted that, together with racial discrimination, self-determination had entered the law the 'considerations of humanity' that were embedded in the Charter, 29. This, of course, did not prevent self-determination from being eventually 'domesticated' into a principle of democratic participation at home as discussed in Barsalou, Chapter 19 this volume.

[8] Brownlie (n 6) 259.

[9] Julius Stone, *Conflict Through Consensus: United Nations Approaches to Aggression* (Hopkins 1977) 172.

position on cyber-activities today. Critics followed Stone in castigating what they believed was inappropriate third-world UN activism. Hence, the lively debate on the theory of the law-making character of General Assembly resolutions. Did they have standing on their own? Or did they perhaps create 'instant customary law' as famously suggested by Bin Cheng?[10] While some lawyers did endorse that proposition, others saw it as fundamentally incompatible with the voluntarist basis of the system. Many made serious efforts to classify UN acts by reference to their content, position in the UN system, or support they received from member states.[11] A particularly strong attack not only on legislation through UN majorities but practically the whole of the third-world legal agenda was Gaetano Arangio-Ruiz's dismissal of the Friendly Relations Declaration. The content of the seven principles, he wrote, purportedly drawn from the Charter was overly general, allowing anybody to read into them what they wish, and inappropriate as a legal statement of anything, 'the most typical instance of the misuse of the "soft law" method' that had 'purely hortatory value'.[12] The drafting process had been a failure from the outset, Arangio-Ruiz argued. No group of experts had been engaged. The matter had not been allocated to the International Law Commission (ILC). Instead, it was produced by that 'diplomacy of the law which is typical of the Sixth [legal] Committee and consists essentially in a search for drafting compromise at any price'. Owing to the 'very intense and extended ideological contrast and confrontation' (he meant both North-South and East-West) it was 'inevitable that the United Nations should conform, as a rule, to the lowest common denominator'.[13] More fundamentally, however, he saw the declaration embody an altogether mistaken view of the nature of international law as 'a kind of constitutional or public law of mankind'.[14] It had been inspired by federalist and constitutionalist imaginings wholly inappropriate in a Cold War world.

Arangio-Ruiz had a conservative view of international law. Regional or political groupings or the agendas of the socialist and third-world countries possessed no legal meaning. This was exactly contrary to the 'functionalism' that had been influentially propounded by Wolfgang Friedmann whose *Changing Structure of International Law* (1964) drew a clear line between Arangio-Ruiz's traditionalism and the more progressive or 'social-democratic' ideas of a new generation ready to move from 'co-existence' to 'cooperation' and saw an increasing amount of

[10] Bin Cheng, 'United Nations Resolutions on Outer Space: "Instant" International Customary Law?' 1965 Indian Journal of International Law 23, 23–48.

[11] One widely cited work was Blaine Sloan, 'The Binding Force of a 'Recommendation' by the General Assembly of the United Nations' (1948) 25 British Yearbook of International Law 1 with the ensuing and its follow-up piece Blaine Sloan, 'General Assembly Resolutions Revisited (Forty Years Later)' (1988) 58 British Yearbook of International Law 39.

[12] Gaetano Arangio-Ruiz, *The United Nations Declaration on Friendly Relations and the System of the Sources of International Law* (Sijthoff & Noordhoff 1979) 179, 93.

[13] ibid 156, 186, 189.

[14] ibid 155.

international legal practice take place within technical and economic institutions, especially under the auspices of the UN. It was not in the least surprising that the first generation of third-world international lawyers—such as PS Anand and TO Elias (Chapter 13 and Chapter 14, respectively)—largely accepted that cooperative, functional, and universalist version of international law. That is understandable. How could they possibly have been granted access to the tables of multilateral diplomacy had they not adopted the form in use there, demonstrating that they were part of the club and knew their Oppenheim as well as anyone—that they subscribed to the awkward dualism of simultaneous endorsement of sovereignty and anti-sovereignty that was the hallmark of Western international law. In the mid-1970s, they believed that they could score important victories by playing the game equally well, and of course eventually better than Western colleagues.[15]

In this respect, a different, even revolutionary legal voice could be heard in Mohammed Bedjaoui's Hague lectures of 1976 on non-alignment and international law, dedicated to Salvador Allende, '*mort dans sa loi*'.[16] Bedjaoui excelled in using strong, politically coloured language of colonialism, neo-colonialism, and imperialism and in attacking 'the little syndicate' of Western States. International law had been thoroughly committed to advancing their interests and ambitions; so far, only crumbs from the tables of the rich had fallen to the world's poor—a majority whose number, as he noted at the outset, had not ceased growing. Sovereignty that did not extend to economic relations was a mere 'phantom sovereignty'.[17] But Bedjaoui, too, cited Friedmann's work to prophesize about a coming transformation and made the ultimately conservative point about the need to fit an anachronistic law to its new social and political environment.[18] That would be the objective for which the third-world countries would unite their powers within the non-aligned movement.

In the international legal academy Bedjaoui played a rather singular role; as an ILC Special Rapporteur on State succession and later a judge and president of the International Court of Justice he remained without significant support from his colleagues, who usually expressed sympathy towards his agenda but did not quite know what to think of his rhetoric or how to translate it into legal reform.[19] In the French legal academy, his ideas were supported from two directions. Socialist lawyers associating themselves with the 'Reims school' under Charles Chaumont

[15] See Chapter 13 and Chapter 14 this volume.

[16] Mohammed Bedjaoui, 'Non-alignement et droit international' (1976) 151 Recueil des Cours de l'Académie de Droit International de La Haye 337.

[17] For a contextualisation of the 'weak' and 'strong', or 'contributionist' and 'critical' streams in the writings of African international lawyers Elias and Umozurike, see the contribution by Gevers in this volume.

[18] For the conservatism of the argument about a transformation already 'on the way' that the law would have to follow and 'reflect', see my *From Apology to Utopia. The Structure of International Legal Argument* (reprint with a new Epilogue, Cambridge University Press 2005), 209–18.

[19] See Brunner Chapter 5 and Özsu Chapter 15, this volume.

subscribed to the third-world legal agenda—support for Palestine was especially important—producing some of the best anti-formalist writings on the role of dialectic and contradictions underlying international law.[20] Chaumont's 1970 Hague lectures that concentrated on method, as well as his other writings, were followed closely by a group of younger French academics who tried to imagine how international law could be turned into an instrument in the struggle for global justice.[21] In and around the confines of the 'Institute of the Law of Peace and Development', set up in Nice in 1968 by the Doyen of the French international law community, René-Jean Dupuy, a group of moderate francophone jurists sought to translate the themes of development into research agendas and technical legal initiatives. The institute also served as a rallying point for contacts with Maghreb where, alongside Bedjaoui, a growing generation of international lawyers were associating themselves with the third-world agenda. As part of French legal culture, the Hague Academy of International Law did much to integrate younger lawyers from Africa and Asia into international law. But although Dupuy himself was keen to highlight the legal importance of development, his approach remained utterly conventional; like Friedmann, he saw around himself a confrontation between two types of law—'relational' and 'institutional'—that embodied the values of positivist étatism and 'sovereignty' on the one hand, and a solidarity-oriented 'international community' on the other.[22] Law was above all doctrine and philosophy and the cause of development was to be advanced through elegant rhetorical performances around the themes of 'universalism', 'community', and, especially, 'humanity'.[23] None of this prevented Dupuy from subscribing to an utterly conventional view on the status of concession contracts in the (in)famous Texaco arbitration.[24]

Alongside Dupuy's speculations, a francophone student at the time of the 'battle' would also have encountered texts such as Maurice Flory's textbook on the international law of development; published by the *Presses universitaires de France*, it was compulsory reading, at least in Aix-en-Provence at the turn of the 1980s.[25] At that time, the 'international law of development' was making themes of the NIEO

[20] See Tourme-Jouannet Chapter 16, this volume. See also Martti Koskenniemi, 'Regarding "Méthode d'analyse du droit international" by Charles Chaumont (1975-I): Dialectics and International law' (2015) Revue Belge de Droit International 270.

[21] For example, Madjid Benchikh, Robert Charvin and Francine Demichel, *Introduction critique au droit international* (Presses Universitaires de Lyon 1986). A much less polemical (and less 'left') recent work from a different, but related, Franco-Belgian tradition is Olivier Corten and others, *Une introduction critique au droit international* (Editions de l'Université de Bruxelles 2017).

[22] René-Jean Dupuy, 'Communauté internationale et disparités de développement: Cours général de droit international public' (1979) 165 Recueil des Cours de l'Académie de Droit International de La Haye 9.

[23] See, for example, Florian Aumond, *L'humanité dans l'oeuvre de René-Jean Dupuy* (Publications du laboratoire Angevin de Recherche sur les Actes Juridiques 2005); Evelyne Lagrange, 'The Thoughts of René-Jean Dupuy: Methodology or Poetry of International Law?' (2011) 22 European Journal of International Law 425.

[24] See *Texaco Overseas Petroleum Co. v Libya* 17 ILM 1 (1978) and Sornarajah Chapter 7, this volume.

[25] Maurice Flory, *Droit international du développement* (Presses Universitaires de France 1977).

a growing part of the curriculum; it operated with a finalist or teleological conception of the law, highlighted the economic aspects of self-determination, insisted on the permanent sovereignty over natural resources, and commented on the management of commodity agreements and regimes for technology transfer. Justifying preferential treatment within the General Agreement on Tariffs and Trade (GATT) regime and elsewhere in economic relations was a major objective. For example, the 1975 issue of the *Annuaire française de droit international* presented the UNGA resolutions leading up to the Declaration on the New International Economic Order expressly as a countermove against what it (already then!) called the 'neo-liberal economic order', highlighting in sympathetic tones the 'interventionist' and 'compensatory' aspects of the '*droit dirigiste*' and making a parallel to late nineteenth century developments in domestic industrial law. This would mean giving up the expectation of equality and accepting positive discrimination in favour of developing states. The authors assumed that while there was large unanimity on the *finalités* of the NIEO, many of the means, such as the preferential treatment in trade, reform of investment law, the establishment of commodity stocks, and cartels, there were still matters of great controversy.[26]

A corresponding 'international law of development' failed to materialize in the anglophone world, perhaps because that energy was taken over by the 'Law and Development' movement in the US. Unlike the European (francophone) version, this did not think much of the diplomatic push in the UN or other international agencies but was more concerned with domestic law reform to buttress the modernization and competitiveness of the industries of developing states, diminish graft, and 'strengthen the rights of property and ensure that contracts would be enforceable'.[27] American law and development experts in the 1970s and 1980s operated with private law, supported international investment, and aimed to diminish state role in the economy. Looking backwards, as someone who spent many autumns in the 1980s sitting at meetings of the Sixth Committee of the UN General Assembly, it is striking to what extent all that, as well as the many development projects by international institutions (eg, the World Bank) was invisible to us. We really had no clue that, while multilateral diplomacy was churning out resolution after resolution, these private law oriented rule of law projects were gradually globalizing the 'developmental state' in most of the third world.[28] Although the vocabulary of interdependence was everywhere, few in the international law world—with

[26] Dominique Carreau and others, 'Chronique de Droit international économique' (1975) 21 Annuaire Français de Droit International 647, 648–50.

[27] David M Trubek and Alvaro Santos, 'Introduction: The Third Moment in Law and Development Theory and the Emergence of a New Critical Practice' in David M Trubek and Alvaro Santos (eds), *The New Law and Economic Development: A Critical Appraisal* (CUP 2006) 6.

[28] See Luis Eslava, *Local Space, Global Life: The Everyday Operation of International Law and Development* (CUP 2015).

the exception of some number of left academics—associated these two series of activities with the creation of a world as dependency theory described it.[29]

II.

Only few international lawyers active today were present in the mid-1970s at the time when it was still uncertain how the 'battle' would turn out. I came to the battle at a late stage within the Preparatory Committee for the UNCLOS in 1983, when the Montego Bay Convention had already been signed and President Reagan had decided that the US would not become a party, despite the concessions it had received during eight years of negotiations. Western countries concluded that Part XI of the Convention—the seabed regime—could not be implemented in its agreed form.[30] Negotiations were initiated by the Secretary-General to amend those newly concluded provisions and to set up the 'pioneer investor system' to guarantee priority to private investors and industries in the economic uses of the seabed. The diplomatic embrace of the neo-liberal turn would affect all UN activities.

One of the changes had to do with a shift in the quantitative and qualitative emphasis on human rights. A lot of ink has recently been poured on the role of human rights in decolonization and as an ideological frame for the neo-liberal turn.[31] From the keyhole of my (mostly UN-related) experience, the introduction in international law of 'human rights' in the late-1970s and 1980s was politically ambivalent. I had come to understand it as primarily as part of the western anti-communist agenda. The reading popular in the US and some parts of Western Europe of the Conference on Security and Cooperation in Europe (CSCE) as a human rights event seemed astonishing: wasn't it supposed to be about the intangibility of European frontiers and only secondarily about economic cooperation and human rights ('baskets 2 and 3')? Although human rights embodied important Western values, their integration in diplomatic talk resonated hypocrisy and propaganda, especially as it was often accompanied by an effort to downgrade economic, social, and cultural rights as merely programmatic and unserious in the way of civil and political rights. The one-sided concentration of the work of the UN Human Rights Commission on apartheid and the Palestine question was problematic, but in no way justified the outrage of the Western attacks on it.[32] Not a decade

[29] On these themes, see the contributions by Dann Chapter 12, Eslava Chapter 3, and Sinclair Chapter 11, this volume.

[30] Together with a colleague from the Foreign Ministry (Marja Lehto, presently a member of the ILC) we have reflected on this development in 'The Privilege of Universality: International Law, Economic Ideology and Seabed Resources' (1996) 65 Nordic Journal of International Law 533. See further Ranganathan Chapter 1, this volume.

[31] See the contribution by Hoffmann and Assy Chapter 8, this volume.

[32] See further Giladi Chapter 9, this volume.

had passed from the end of the Vietnam war and the murder of Salvador Allende, and now the US was teaching morals to others!

Since then, human rights have enjoyed their much commented-upon ascent as the *lingua franca* of internationalism. Although they can clearly be used to support third-world agendas (and have been so used), they do have a bias towards liberal ideas and Western policy goals. To me, Samuel Moyn's controversial dissociation of human rights from decolonization rings true.[33] In case the efforts to bring about a more just economic and political order in the 1970s are discussed through the metaphor of 'battle', it is hard to avoid the impression that on most questions, the G77 'lost'. It is true that apartheid is over (at least in South Africa) and legal opinion today converges on thinking of the 1966 judgment by the ICJ as a 'mistake'.[34] But there has been no advance on the question of occupied territories, for example, and the present terrorism obsession leaves little room to defend the cause of national liberation movements.[35] (An informal division of work sometimes operated with respect to such, hotly political matters. When I was posted in the Finnish UN mission in New York in 1989–1990, issues regarding South Africa and Namibia as well as the occupied territories were wholly allocated to political specialists. Nobody expected that a legal advisor would have anything useful to say about them.) As regards the international economic order, trade, investment, and technology, the developing world has had to content itself with quite little. The debate on generic drugs for AIDS/HIV brought a partial 'victory' and in such other questions as climate change or marine genetic resources, for example, old battles are still being waged.

One thing learned from the break-up of the non-aligned movement and the difficulties of the G77 to follow any consistent policy after the 1970s has to do with the heterogeneity of interests of the countries once joined at Bandung. It was only to be expected that their varying histories would point to different strategies of development—what attitude to take to foreign investors or transnational companies, for example.[36] The fall of real socialism in Europe deprived many of them of a key ally, and led them to seek support from other directions, with differing conditionalities. And they were themselves often split into rival political and ethnic groups, with elites tending to remain distant from the population. In the south no less than in the north, political leaders often have no interest to set themselves in opposition to the hegemonic powers. The most successful global versions of democracy and the rule of law have not supported the domestic or international distribution of resources in the way advocated in the 1970s. This is not to say that there would be no themes on which the views of the Global South would not converge.

[33] By now, the secondary literature reacting on Samuel Moyn, *The Last Utopia: Human Rights in History* (Belknap Press of Harvard University Press 2010) is too wide to be reflected here,

[34] See further the contribution by Venzke above,

[35] See further the contribution by von Bernstorff above.

[36] See Pahuja and Saunders Chapter 6, this volume.

There are many—from preferential treatment in trade and financing to a suspicion about the International Criminal Court. But the alliances are today rarely underwritten by any larger ideological agenda.

I end this set of personal reflections on the 'battle' with two remarks. First, surveying the landscape of public international law in the twenty-first century, a surprisingly stable set of concerns and projects is visible. During the period I sat with the UN International Law Commission (2002–2006), there was little on the agenda that would have had a redistributive orientation or would have otherwise been identified in terms of correcting the world's injustices. The Commission in 2006 dealt with the sources of international law—reservations, effect of armed conflict on treaties, unilateral acts and 'fragmentation of international law'—and the responsibility of international organizations, extradition, and a draft on transboundary aquifers. Whatever one thinks of the significance of the Commission's work (even a priori important items such as 'extradition' or the pollution of groundwaters were treated by recommendatory provisions largely repeating what the law already was in non-committal terms), it was based on no significant recognition of third world concerns or need to correct the world's injustices. The members imagined themselves as impartial "experts" even as many of them steadily represented the positions of the domestic elites from which they were chosen. Reading the report from the 70th session in 2018, the picture is not very different—treaty law is still highlighted, two items concern the protection of the environment, and two deal with the most traditional textbook topics—*jus cogens* and the identification of customary law. State succession in respect of State responsibility does not seem to have raised among Asian-African lawyers any concerns of principle.[37] I have elsewhere discussed the difficulty generalists in international law have in trying operate in the narrow room left between technical governance and politics.[38] Here I want to note the continued absence of ambition with regard to the themes of the 'battle'. Most 'progressive development' has moved to functional, especially economic, organizations, the climate change process, international criminal law, and anti-terrorism to be debated among experts, among whom third-world priorities are poorly represented.

[37] See the latest 'Report on Matters Relating to the Work of the International Law Commission at its Sixty-Ninth Session' by the Asian-African Legal Consultative Organization (AALCO/57/TOKYO/2018/SD/S1) 41-44. The AALCO was established in the aftermath of Bandung in 1956 as a consultative 'Committee'. It participates in the work of the ILC as an observer and provides an annual statement at its meetings. Its coordinating functions are listed in a 'Statutes' from 2004, available on the organization's website at <www.aalco.int/Basicdocuments/STATUTES%20OF%20THE%20ASIAN-AFRICAN%20LEGAL%20CONSULTATIVE%20ORGANIZATION.pdf> (accessed 4 February 2018). In the UN legal context, the Organization makes occasional presentation, usually endorsing in diplomatic terms a general position among its members (if such can be found) and paying regularly attention to the situation in the Palestinian Occupied Territories.

[38] Martti Koskenniemi, 'The Fate of Public International Law: Between Technique and Politics' (2007) 70 Modern Law Review 1.

My second point is that the 1970s does have staying power, however, if only of the unplanned kind. So much of the present world in terms of its culture, political and otherwise, its mores and its instinctive practices, come down from that under-appreciated decade. Granted, the 1960s may have initiated that change. And granted, the 1970s, as they went along, may have transmitted to the terrible 1980s an already-stale version of a global consciousness for which decolonization and development were absolutely imperative political projects. If this global cultural and political (and economic) transformation reached its peak in the 1990s, we are today suffering from its after-effect—a reactionary rejection of the cultural and political forms associated with it. The attacks on the international 'elites' in the global West, the expert systems, and a consciousness articulating itself through 'human rights' are also directed against whatever little victories the developing countries may have been able to secure. Nationalism, racism, xenophobia, and nostalgia for white male supremacy—all current features of Europe and the US—target the multicultural, tolerant, feminist consensus among the elite, however thin or superficial. Development assistance and multilateral cooperation are under attack, as are migrants and refugees from 'shithole countries'. The unstated wish of the reactionaries, overjoyed to be finally able to speak their mind, is to return to the time before the 1970s, a time before decolonization and the cultural and political change of which it was a part, a time when all kinds of aliens and activists, women, minorities and Jewish philanthropists did not tell them what to think or say. The battle may be over, but the war rages on.

Name Index

Note: For the benefit of digital users, indexed terms that span two pages (e.g., 52– 53) may, on occasion, appear on only one of those pages.

Subject Index